"A good idea well done. It includes information on all sorts of music, not just classical. For me, it passes the test of any good dictionary: when you look something up, you find yourself reading all the entries around it as well."
—Peter Schickele, composer, and creator of P. D. Q. Bach

"What a delight it is to find a single-volume book with so much useful information packed into it! A good book to have on one's reference shelf, and use." —Shulamit Ran, composer, and recipient of the 1991 Pulitzer Prize for Music

"A fascinating amalgam concerning all types of information. . . . Provides an affordable one-stop reference for brief identifications of many concepts, compositions, and persons past and present. —ALA Booklist

"An authoritative, compact, yet remarkably comprehensive dictionary-encyclopedia that will be of inestimable value to all music enthusiasts. I recommend it highly."
—Robert P. Morgan, Professor of Music, Yale University

"A very useful reference work, especially because of its unusually broad coverage of Canadian and American musicians."
—Ezra Schabas, Professor Emeritus, University of Toronto

PHILIP D. MOREHEAD is a graduate of Swarthmore College, with an M.A. in musicology from Harvard University and an M.M. in piano from the New England Conservatory. He is Music Administrator of the Lyric Opera of Chicago, as well as the editor of many reference works of distinction, including *The New American Roget's College Thesaurus*. He lives in Chicago.

THE NEW INTERNATIONAL DICTIONARY OF MUSIC

by

Philip D. Morehead
Lyric Opera of Chicago

with

Anne MacNeil
The University of Chicago

Drawings by
Charlotte Rollman
Northern Illinois University

A MERIDIAN BOOK

MERIDIAN
Published by the Penguin Group
Penguin Books USA Inc., 375 Hudson Street,
New York, New York 10014, U.S.A.
Penguin Books Ltd, 27 Wrights Lane,
London W8 5TZ, England
Penguin Books Australia Ltd, Ringwood,
Victoria, Australia
Penguin Books Canada Ltd, 10 Alcorn Avenue,
Toronto, Ontario, Canada M4V 3B2
Penguin Books (N.Z.) Ltd, 182–190 Wairau Road,
Auckland 10, New Zealand

Penguin Books Ltd, Registered Offices:
Harmondsworth, Middlesex, England

Published by Meridian, an imprint of New American Library,
a division of Penguin Books USA Inc. Previously published in a Dutton edition,
under the title *The New American Dictionary of Music*.

First Meridian Printing, November, 1992
10 9 8 7 6 5 4 3 2 1

 REGISTERED TRADEMARK—MARCA REGISTRADA

LIBRARY OF CONGRESS CATALOGING-IN-PUBLICATION DATA
Morehead, Philip D.
  [New American dictionary of music]
  The new international dictionary of music / Philip D. Morehead
with Anne MacNeil ; drawings by Charlotte Rollman.
    p.   cm.
  Originally published: The new American dictionary of music. New
York, N.Y. : Dutton, 1991.
  ISBN 0-452-01100-0
  1. Music—Dictionaries. 2. Music—Bio-bibliography—Dictionaries.
I. MacNeil, Anne. II. Title.
ML100.M857   1992
780′.3—dc20   92-80541
                                                 CIP
                                                 MN

ABOUT THIS DICTIONARY

This dictionary has been designed to be your first stop for quick information on a wide variety of musical topics.

Main entries are listed in **boldface** type in their most commonly employed form. Personal names are listed last names first, then first names. Given names not commonly used are enclosed in parentheses. Alternate spellings, nicknames, maiden names, etc. are given in parentheses in lightface type. In most cases, foreign entries (names, titles, etc.) are given in the form and language most commonly used in American concert programs and in print, even when (as in some Russian names) this results in inconsistencies of transliteration.

Alphabetical arrangement of entries is determined by the letters preceding the first comma, ignoring any spaces. Different senses of the same word are identified by a bold face number followed by a comma (**1, 2,** etc.).

Birth and death dates are given in parentheses following the entry name, separated by a dash. A blank space following the dash indicates that the person was still living at the time of publication. Uncertainty about a birth or death date is indicated either by a question mark preceding an approximate date or by a question mark alone; or by the abbreviation *c.* (Lat. *circa* = about) followed by a date. In cases where birth and death dates are unknown and cannot be acceptably approximated, the abbreviation *fl.* (flourished) is given followed by an indication of a period of time.

Cross references are usually indicated by SMALL CAPITALS, with the letter in upper case indicating the letter under which the entry is alphabetized. Hence, CHARLES IVES would be alphabetized under "Ives." Reference to related entries for the purpose of comparing or contrasting is indicated by the abbreviation "Cf." (Lat. *confer* = compare) before the reference. In order to conserve space, cross references are given only when additional relevant information can be found at the referenced entry. However, all musical terms used in the dictionary are defined herein. Names of persons who are covered in the dictionary are often mentioned in other entries by last name only, such as Bach (for J.S. Bach), Mozart, Haydn (for F.J. Haydn), Schumann, Brahms, etc.

Special thanks are due to my collaborator, Anne MacNeil, for her perfectionism and thorough involvement in all aspects of the work's preparation and for her Schenker graph, which appears at the entry on Schenkerian analysis; to Charlotte Rollman, for her willingness to do that "one extra drawing" any number of times; to Neil Tesser of WBEZ-FM, Chicago, for reading jazz entries and making many pertinent and per- spicacious suggestions; to John Shreffler for work on contem- porary composers and performers and for preparing the ref- erence bibliography; to Ethan Nasreddin-Longo for reading portions of the manuscript and making very useful com- ments; to Deborah Lawrence for her inspired rendering of the hexachord system; to Hugh Rawson of New American Li- brary, who prodded me gently but insistently to finish the work and provided support and encouragement throughout the project; and especially to my long-suffering wife, com- poser and oboist Patricia Morehead, who was helpful in many ways at the various stages of the writing, in addition to being supportive and patient throughout the ordeal. She is also the composer of the musical example given for the entry on serial music.

For the technically-minded reader: The musical illustra- tions in this dictionary were produced using SCORE® Music Typography software by Passport Designs, proofed on an NEC LC-890 Silentwriter printer and printed on a Linotronic L-300 phototypesetter by ProTypography of Chicago. Several of the musical instrument illustrations were produced by the editor using Gem® Artline™ software by CCP Software- Entwicklungs Gmbh and Digital Research Inc.

Pronunciation Guide

Suggested pronunciations are given for some entries, enclosed in square brackets ([]) following the entry word(s) and em- ploying the following symbols:

Vowels

[a]	as in fat
[ā]	as in fate; Fr. blé; Ger. gehen; It. vero
[ä]	as in far

[e]   as in met
[ē]   as in meet
[i]   as in pin
[ī]   as in pine, Ger. mein
[ō]   as in note; Fr. rose; Ger. froh; It. dolce
[o]   as in saw
[oo]   as in spoon
[oi]   as in oil
[ow]   as in owl
[ø]   as in Fr. peu, Ger. schön (place the tongue for [ā] and
        the lips for [ō])
[œ]   as in Fr. cœur, Ger. können (position the tongue for
        [e] and the lips for [o])
[u]   as in tub
[ü]   as in Fr. tu, Ger. müde (place the tongue for [ē] and
        the lips for [oo])
[û]   as in pull
[ə]   as in comma, Fr. fenêtre, Ger. singen

Nasal Vowels
[ā]   as in Fr. flan (nasal form of [o])
[ō]   as in Fr. bon (nasal form of [ō])
[ɛ̄]   as in Fr. vin (nasal form of [e])
[œ̄]   as in Fr. un (nasal form of [œ])

Consonants
[b]   as in but
[ch]   as in chair
[ç]   as in Ger. ich
[d]   as in day
[f]   as in fill
[g]   as in go
[h]   as in hat
[hw]   as in when
[j]   as in joke
[k]   as in keep
[kh]   as in blockhouse, Ger. nach
[l]   as in late
[m]   as in man
[n]   as in nod
[ng]   as in sing
[ngg]   as in finger
[p]   as in pen

[r]   as in rat
[s]   as in sit, this
[sh]   as in she
[t]   as in to
[th]   as in thin
[*th*] as in then
[v]   as in van
[w]   as in win
[y]   as in yet
[z]   as in zone, quiz
[zh]   as in azure, Fr. *je*

Stress Marks (preceding the stressed sylable)

[']   primary stress
["]   secondary stress

Abbreviations

abbr.   abbreviation
ABC   American Broadcasting Company
Amer.   America
assoc.   association, associated
c   circa
c.   century
CBC   Canadian Broadcasting Company
CBS   Columbia Broadcasting System
Cf.   compare
Co.   Company
CPS   cycles per second (frequency)
CUNY   City University of New York
dir.   director
esp.   especially
est.   established
Fr.   French
Ger.   German
i.e.   that is
illus.   illustration
incl.   includes, included, including
instr.   instrument
It.   Italian
Lat.   Latin
Lat.-Amer. Latin-American

mvt.	movement
N.Y.	New York
NBC	National Broadcasting Company
No.	number
No. Amer.	North America
occ.	occasionally
Orch.	orchestra
org.	organization
orig.	originally
pl.	plural
PO	Philharmonic Orchestra
Port.	Portuguese
prob.	probably
publ.	published
S. Amer.	South America
SO	Symphony Orchestra
Sp.	Spanish
stud.	student
SUNY	State University of New York
U.	University
UCLA	University of California at Los Angeles
U.S.	United States
usu.	usually

Abbreviations Found in Titles of Works

BWV	Schmieder's Bach Werke-Verzeichnis (for the works of J.S. Bach)
D.	Deutsch (for Schubert's works)
H.	Hoboeken (for F.J. Haydn's works)
K.	Köchel (for the works of W.A. Mozart)
	R. Kirkpatrick (for the works of D. Scarlatti)
	J. Kirkpatrick (for the works of Ives)
Op.	Opus (Lat., work)
RV.	Ryom Verzeichnis (for the works of Vivaldi)

Reference Bibliography

For help in researching a subject beyond the scope of this book, the following brief (and admittedly incomplete) bibliography is offered.

General Classical Music Reference (biography, terms, history)
New Grove Dictionary of Music and Musicians (London, 1980)

American Music
New Grove Dictionary of American Music (London, 1986)

African-American Music and Musicians
Eileen Southern, *Music of Black Americans: A History* (New York, 1983)

Native American Music and Musicians
Frances Densmore, *The American Indians and Their Music* (New York, 1926, rev. 1937)

General Classical Music Biography
Nicholas Slonimsky, ed., *The Concise Bakers' Biographical Dictionary of Musicians* (New York, 1988)

General Musical Terms (Classical)
Don Randel, ed., *New Harvard Dictionary of Music* (Cambridge, MA, 1986)

General Music Theory
Jonathan Dunsby and Arnold Whittal, *Music Analysis in Theory and Practice* (London, 1985)
Ralph Turek, *The Elements of Music: Concepts and Applications* (New York, 1980)
Alan Forte and Steven Gilbert, *Introduction to Schenkerian Analysis* (New York, 1982)
John Rahn, *Basic Atonal Theory* (New York, 1980)

Musical Instruments

Musical Instruments of the World (New York, 1976)
Robert Donington, *Music and Its Instruments* (New York, 1982)

Historical Periods

Early and Medieval Music
Richard H. Hoppin, *Medieval Music* (New York, 1978)
Gustave Reese, *Music in the Middle Ages* (New York, 1940)
Manfred Bukofzer, *Studies in Medieval and Renaissance Music* (New York, 1978)

Renaissance Music
Howard M. Brown, *Music in the Renaissance* (New York, 1976)
Manfred Bukofzer (see under Early and Medieval Music)

Baroque Period
Claude V. Palisca, *Baroque Music* 2nd ed. (New York, 1981)
Robert Donington, *The Interpretation of Early Music* (London, 1979)
James Anthony, *French Baroque Music* (New York, 1978)
Arnold Dolmetsch, *The Interpretation of the Music of the Seventeenth and Eighteenth Centuries* (Seattle, 1980)

Classical Period
Charles Rosen, *The Classical Style* (New York, 1971)
Giorgio Pestelli, *The Age of Mozart and Beethoven* (Cambridge, 1984)

Romantic Music
Leon Plantinga, *Romantic Music* (New York, 1984)
Arnold Whittall, *Romantic Music: A Concise History from Schubert to Sibelius* (New York, 1987)

Modern Music
Robert P. Morgan, *Twentieth-Century Music* (New York, 1991)
Eric Salzman, *Twentieth-Century Music: An Introduction*, 3rd ed. (Englewood Cliffs, NJ, 1988)

Styles

Jazz
Gunther Schuller, *The History of Jazz*: Vol. 1, *Early Jazz* (New York, 1968). Vol. 2, *The Swing Era* (New York, 1989)
Carr, Fairweather & Priestley, *Jazz, the Essential Companion*
New Grove Dictionary of Jazz (New York, 1988)

Country Music
P. Carr, ed., *The Illustrated History of Country Music* (New York, 1979)

Folk Music
Alan Lomax and others, *Folk Song Style and Culture* (Washington, D.C., 1968)
Bruno Nettl, *Folk and Traditional Music of the Western Continents*, 2nd ed. (Englewood Cliffs, NJ, 1990)
Larry Sandberg and Dick Weissman, *The Folk Music Sourcebook* (New York, 1989)

Western and Cowboy Music
J. White, *Git Along Little Dogies: Songs and Songmakers of the American West* (Urbana, IL, 1975)

Rock
Ed Ward, Geoffrey Stokes and Ken Tucker, *Rock of Ages: The Rolling Stone History of Rock & Roll* (New York, 1986)

Popular Music
Charles Hamm, *Music in the New World* (New York, 1983)
Phil Hardy & Dave Laing, *The Faber Companion to 20th-Century Popular Music* (London, 1990)

Musical Theater
Alec Wilder, *American Popular Song: The Great Innovators* (New York, 1970)
David Ewen, *The Complete Book of the American Musical Theater* (New York, 1970)

Opera and Vocal Music
Donald J. Grout, *A Short History of Opera*, 3rd ed. (New York, 1988)
Charles Osborne, *The Dictionary of the Opera* (New York, 1983)
Denis Stevens, *A History of Song* (New York, 1970)
Percy M. Young, *The Choral Tradition* (New York, 1971)

Symphonic Music
Ethan Mordden, *A Guide to Orchestral Music* (New York, 1980)

Ballet Music
The Simon and Schuster Book of the Ballet (New York, 1980)

Selected List of Illustrations

THE NEW
INTERNATIONAL
DICTIONARY
OF MUSIC

A

A the sixth note of the scale of C major. The pitch of A above middle C (a′) is defined by international agreement as 440 cycles per second. See PITCH.

AACM *abbr.* ASSOCIATION FOR THE ADVANCEMENT OF CREATIVE MUSICIANS.

a battuta (It.) see BATTUTA.

Abba Swedish rock group founded in 1973. Their hit albums incl. the award-winning *Waterloo* (1974).

Abbado, Claudio (1933–) Italian conductor, stud. of Hans Swarowsky in Vienna. He has been musical dir. of La Scala, Milan; principal conductor of the Vienna PO and the London SO; principal guest conductor of the Chicago SO; music dir. of the Vienna Staatsoper; and chief conductor of the Berlin PO.

Abbott, Emma (1850–91) Amer. soprano and impresario, stud. of Marchesi in Paris. She returned to the U.S. in 1877 and toured with her own small opera company across the country, often interpolating her own arias and songs in the operas she performed.

abdämpfen [′äb-demp-fən] (Ger.) to apply a MUTE to an instrument.

Abduction from the Seraglio, The (Ger., *Die Entführung aus dem Serail*) comic SINGSPIEL in 2 acts by Mozart to a libretto by Gottlob Stephanie the Younger, adapted from a libretto by Christoph Friedrich Bretzner. Premiere, Vienna 1772. The Spanish prince Belmonte tries to win the freedom of his beloved Constanza from her captor, the Turk Selim Pasha. Mozart adds Turkish flavor through the use of JANISSARY MUSIC in several numbers, incl. the overture.

Abegg Variations work for piano solo (1830) by Robert Schumann, dedi-

cated to his friend Meta ("Countess") Abegg and based on a theme made up of the notes A-B♭-E-G-G.

Abel, Carl Friedrich (1723–87) German viola da gambist, harpsichordist and composer, stud. of J.S. Bach. After 1758 Abel spent most of his time in London, where in association with J.C. Bach he established the BACH-ABEL CONCERTS.

Abelard, Peter (1079–1142) French philosopher, poet and composer of hymns, love songs (lost) and PLANCTUS.

Abendmusik [′ä-bənt-moo″zēk] (Ger., evening music) concerts held in 17th- and 18th-c. Lübeck. Orig. these were organ recitals, but later other instruments and genres were included.

Abgesang [′äp-ge″zäng] (Ger.) the concluding section of a medieval BAR FORM.

Abrams, Muhal Richard (1930–) Amer. jazz pianist and composer. He studied at the Chicago Musical College, then free-lanced as a pianist and arranger. He was a founder of the AACM and was instrumental in bringing that group's music to New York.

Abravanel, Maurice (de) (1903–) Amer. conductor, stud. of Kurt Weill. His varied career incl. conducting at the Metropolitan Opera and on Broadway (esp. Weill's works). He has been conductor of the Utah Symphony (1947–79), which he raised to national importance, and artistic dir. of the Music Academy of the West (1954–80).

absolute music ABSTRACT MUSIC.

absolute pitch 1, the position of a tone in relation to the whole range of pitch as determined by its rate of vibration in cycles per second. **2,** the ability to identify by name or to sing a certain pitch without reference to

Abbreviations
(see also ORNAMENTS)

any previously heard pitch. Also, *perfect pitch*. Cf. RELATIVE PITCH.

abstraction see FREE JAZZ.

abstract music music that is not intended to represent any specific scene, story, person or location. The term is usu. applied to instrumental music. Also, *absolute music*.

Abzug ['äp-tsook] (Ger.) **1,** a SCORDATURA lute tuning made by lowering the pitch of the lowest string. **2,** various 18th-c. ornaments (see ORNAMENT). **3,** an organ stop.

ACA *abbr.* AMERICAN COMPOSERS ALLIANCE.

Academic Festival Overture (Ger., *Akademische Fest-Ouvertüre*) concert overture (1881) by Brahms, composed in appreciation of a doctorate in philosophy conferred by Breslau University in 1879. The work is made up of several popular German student songs.

Academy of Ancient Music a London orch. founded in 1973 by Christopher Hogwood for the purpose of performing music of the 17th and 18th c. on instruments of the time or modern reproductions.

Academy of Music a concert hall in Philadelphia built in 1857 and modelled after La Scala, Milan. It was orig. built as an opera house and is now the home of the Philadelphia Orch.

Academy of St. Martin-in-the-Fields a chamber orch. founded in London in 1959 by Sir NEVILLE MARRINER, esp. noted for its many recordings of baroque and classical repertory.

a cappella also, **da cappella** (It., in choir or chapel style) **1**, of vocal music, to be performed without vocal soloists or instrumental obbligati (see OBBLIGATO), though not necessarily without accompaniment, in contrast to CONCERTATO (1,). The term orig. referred to sacred music of the 16th c., esp. that of Palestrina. **2**, to be performed unaccompanied by instruments. This current usage is not historically justified.

accademia [äk-kä′dä-mē-ə] (It.) a learned association of the 16th c. and later devoted to the study of literature, science and the arts.

Accardo, Salvatore (1941–) Italian virtuoso violinist and conductor, stud. of Luigi d'Ambrosio and Yvonne Astruc. He is esp. noted for his performance of the works of Paganini.

accelerando [ät-che-le′rän-dō] (It.) becoming faster. Abbr., accel.

accent 1, an emphasis produced by an increase in volume (SFORZANDO, MARCATO), duration (AGOGIC ACCENT), or meter (metric accent). **2**, [äk′sä] (Fr.) a type of NACHSCHLAG (1,).

accentus (Lat.) simple PLAINSONG based on recitation tones. Cf. CONCENTUS.

acciaccatura [at-chäk-kä′too-rä] (It., a crushing) **1**, a GRACE NOTE played simultaneously with its principal note or chord and released immediately while the principal note or chord is sustained. Also, crushed note. **2**, erroneously, a short APPOGGIATURA.

accidental a sign indicating the chromatic alteration of a note from its previously understood pitch (i.e., the raising or lowering of the note while retaining the same pitch name, as in raising A one semitone to A♯). In medieval and Renaissance music, the application of an accidental is referred to as MUSICA FICTA.

Accidentals normally refer to occurrences of the same note in the same octave. However, a composer may sometimes intend an accidental to refer to all notes of the same name no matter what octave, without stating this intention. The musical context is the performer's only guide. In music of the 17th to 19th c. the effect of an accidental usu. is ended by a bar line. In the 20th c. composers sometimes intend an accidental to refer only to the note to which it is attached; such usage is usu. pointed out by a comment. Some composers, notably Berg, have tried to avoid possible confusion by attaching an accidental to every note. See NOTATION.

accolade a line or BRACE used to join two or more musical staffs.

accompagnato [äk-kōm-pä′nyä-tō] (It.) also, **accompanied recitative** see RECITATIVE.

accompanied sonata a late 18th-c. sonata for keyboard, joined by violin or flute, which most often doubles the melody line of the keyboard. The form was relatively short-lived, for it was not long before the accompanying line became an equal partner of the keyboard.

accompaniment an instrumental, vocal or rhythmic part subordinate to the main voice or instrument(s). In some cases where the term is commonly used, as in referring to the piano part of vocal music, the accompaniment is often in fact equal to the solo part in importance.

accordion a portable REED ORGAN, dating in Europe from the early 19th c., which produces sound when air from a hand-operated bellows is forced past metallic reeds. Notes (and sometimes chords) are selected with buttons or studs (button accordion) or with a piano-style keyboard for the right hand and buttons for the left

stops   bellows

studs

Accordion

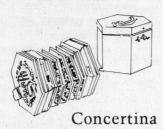

Concertina

hand (*piano accordion*). On a *stradella accordion* the left-hand buttons select chords; on the less common *free-bass accordion* they select single pitches. Cf. CONCERTINA.

Ace, Johnny (1929–54) Amer. rhythm-and-blues singer and songwriter who performed with B.B. King and Bobby Bland. He died by shooting himself while playing Russian roulette.

Achtel ['äkh-təl] (Ger.) EIGHTH NOTE.

acid rock a style of ROCK music prevalent on the West Coast in the 1960s and characterized by music and lyrics designed to evoke a drug-induced state. The principal bands were the GRATEFUL DEAD and JEFFERSON AIRPLANE. Also, *psychedelic rock.*

Acis and Galatea an English masque by Handel, first performed at Cannons (1718). The libretto, written by John Gay and others, is based on Ovid's *Metamorphoses.* Handel later revised the work for unstaged presentation in London (1732), as a macaronic collection of both English and Italian texts. The plot of both the masque and its revision concerns a love triangle among the cyclops Po-

lifemus, the nymph Galatea and the young shepherd Acis.

acoustic 1, of an instrument, not electrically amplified, as an *acoustic guitar;* of a recording, recorded directly by sound waves acting on a diaphragm rather than by electrical impulses. **2,** (often pl.) the sound-reproducing qualities of a space, as the acoustics of a concert hall.

acoustic bass an ORGAN STOP that combines a 16-foot pedal stop with a rank a fifth above to produce a COMBINATION TONE an octave below the 16-foot pitch.

act tune ENTR'ACTE.

action 1, the mechanism connecting the keys of an instrument with the sounding part, as of a piano or organ; also, the response of this mechanism to the player's fingers, as a *heavy action.* **2,** the mechanism by which the pedals of a harp change the pitches of the strings. **3,** the movement of actors in a play, opera, etc.; stage business.

Actus Tragicus (Lat.) J.S. Bach's funeral Cantata No. 106 (c.1707), "Gottes Zeit ist die allerbeste Zeit" (God's time is the very best time).

Acuff, Roy (Claxton) (1903–) Amer. country-music singer, fiddler, composer and publisher, a leading performer of the Grand Ole Opry from 1938 and the first living inductee to the Country Music Hall of Fame (1962).

adagietto (It.) less slowly and seriously than ADAGIO. A famous movement with this marking is found in Mahler's Fifth Symphony (1901–2).

adagio (It., at ease) very slowly, gracefully, slower than ANDANTE and faster than LENTO; also, a movement in an adagio tempo.

Adagio for Strings movement for string orch. Op. 11 (1938), by Barber, an arrangement of the slow movement of his string quartet No. 1 (1936). It is one of his most popular works.

adagissimo (It.) even more slowly than ADAGIO.

Adam, Adolphe (Charles) (1803–56) French critic and prolific composer of over 50 operas, ballet, choral music, etc., stud. of Reicha and Boïeldieu. His best-known works are the opera *Le Postillon de Longjumeau* (1836) and the ballet *Giselle* (1841). He taught at the Paris Conservatoire from 1849.

Adam de la Halle (c1240–c1290) French trouvère poet and composer of monophonic and polyphonic works, esp. the rondeau *Le jeu de Robin et de Marion* (1285).

Adams, John (1947–) Amer. clarinetist and composer, stud. of Kirchner, Sessions and Del Tredici at Harvard. He has been head of composition at the San Francisco Conservatory (1971–81), and composer-in-residence of the San Francisco SO (1982–5) and of the St. Paul Chamber Orch. (1986–8). A winner of a Guggenheim fellowship, he is best known for his opera *Nixon in China* (1988) and his *Grand Pianola Music* (1982).

Adams, Pepper (Park) (1930–86) Amer. jazz baritone saxophonist. He played with Stan Kenton, Maynard Ferguson, Chet Baker, Benny Goodman and Charles Mingus and was an original member of the Thad Jones-Mel Lewis band. He was one of the most innovative baritone saxophonists of the post-bop style.

Adaskin, Murray (1906–) Canadian violinist and composer. He played with the Toronto SO (1926–36) and was composer-in-residence at the U. of Saskatchewan (1952–72).

added sixth chord a major or minor triad, usu. on the subdominant, with a major sixth added above the root. See CHORDS (*illus.*).

Adderley, Cannonball (Julian Edwin) (1928–75) Amer. post-bop alto saxophonist. He worked with Miles Davis and others, and from 1959 led a highly respected quintet with his brother, trumpeter Nat Adderley (1931–).

Addinsell, Richard (Stewart) (1904–77) English composer of theater and film music, best known for his *Warsaw Concerto*, actually a fragment

from a film score for *Suicide Squadron* (1941).

Addison, Adele (1925–) Amer. soprano, stud. of Goldovsky, best known for her work in oratorio and contemporary music. She has taught at the Eastman School and elsewhere.

additional accompaniment instrumental parts added to a work (esp. 17th- and 18th-c. vocal music) which are not part of the original score and are not by the original composer. Handel's *Messiah* in particular has suffered from this type of modification, incl. additions by as illustrious a successor as Mozart.

Adelaïde [ä-de-lä′ē-de] a song, op. 46 (c1796), by Beethoven to words by Friedrich von Matthisson.

Adeste Fideles [a′des-tä fē′dä-les] (Lat., O Come, All Ye Faithful) an 18th-c. hymn now associated with Christmas, prob. composed by J.F. Wade (1710–86).

Adgate, Andrew (1762–93) Amer. voice teacher, conductor and tune-book compiler. His singing schools in Philadelphia, which charged no tuition, were supported by subscribers, who received free tickets to concerts put on by the schools' students.

Adieux, Les [a′dyø] (Fr., farewells) piano sonata in E♭ major, Op. 81a (1809), by Beethoven. The full title is *Les Adieux, l'absence, et le retour* (Farewells, Absence, and Return), the three parts of the title referring to the three movements respectively.

Adler, Kurt Herbert (1905–87) Austrian-born Amer. conductor and opera director. He conducted at the Chicago Opera (1938–43), then was assoc. with the San Francisco Opera (1943–81), first as chorus master, ultimately as general director.

Adler, Larry (Lawrence Cecil) (1914–) Amer. concert harmonica virtuoso and composer, responsible for advances in the technique of the instrument. Milhaud and Vaughan Williams, among other composers, wrote works for him.

Adler, Peter Herman (1899–1990) Czech-born Amer. conductor, stud. of

Zemlinsky and a pioneer of televised opera, both with the NBC Opera Company and with WNET in NY. He conducted at the Metropolitan Opera and was music director of the Baltimore SO and director of the American Opera Center at the Juilliard School.

Adler, Richard (1921–　) Amer. composer and lyricist, best known for his scores for the musicals *The Pajama Game* (1954) and *Damn Yankees* (1955), written with his longtime partner Jerry Ross.

Adler, Samuel (Hans) (1928–　) German-born Amer. conductor and prolific composer of opera, vocal and instrumental music. He studied at Boston U. and Harvard and was awarded the Medal of Honor for his work with the Seventh Army SO. He has been on the faculty of the Eastman School since 1966.

ad libitum (Lat., according to [one's] wishes) at the performer's discretion; used to refer sometimes to choice of instrumentation, sometimes to interpretation. Abbr., *ad lib*. Cf. A PIACERE, SI PLACET.

Adriana Lecouvreur [lø-koo'vrør] romantic opera in 4 acts by Francesco Cilèa on a libretto by Arturo Colautti (from a play by Eugène Scribe). Premiere, Milan 1902. The story is based on the life of Adrienne Lecouvreur, an actress with the Comédie Française.

a due [a'doo-ā] (It., by two) in orchestral music, a score indication that two instruments combined on one staff should play either in UNISON or DIVISI, the context clarifying the ambiguity. Also, *a 2*.

AEC *abbr*. ART ENSEMBLE OF CHICAGO.

Aeolian Chamber Players a quartet consisting of flute, clarinet, cello and piano; founded in 1961.

Aeolian Co. Amer. firm of player piano makers founded in New York in 1878.

aeolian harp 1, a BOARD ZITHER played by the free action of the wind, producing harmonics from metal or gut strings of unequal thickness stretched over a soundbox. **2,** popular name for the Étude in A♭ major, Op. 25 No. 1 (1836), by Chopin.

aeolian mode the authentic MODE with a final on A and confinal on E, identical to the natural minor scale on A.

Aeolian-Skinner Organ Co. Amer. organ-building firm founded in 1901.

aerophone any instrument that produces sound by means of moving air as its vibrating agent. Pitch is altered by lengthening or shortening the air column; tone color is varied by altering the shape of the column. The principle varieties are: instruments with a blow hole (flutes), bagpipes, whistles (recorders, whistles), reed instruments, lip-reed instruments (trumpets, trombones, horns), free reed instruments (mouth organs, accordions, harmoniums), organs and free aerophones (bull roarers). Also, *wind instrument*.

Aerosmith Amer. heavy-metal blues band founded in 1970 in New York.

aevia *also*, **aeuia** *abbr*. an abbreviation of the word *Alleluia* used in medieval liturgical books.

Affections, Doctrine of the an aesthetic concept based on ancient Greek and Latin theories of rhetoric and applied mainly to music of the Baroque era. A composer usu. sought to move the affections (emotions) of the listener through musical means. Expression of a single affect in a composition was seen to provide musical unity, esp. in instrumental works where there were no words to determine musical form. Cf. FIGURES, DOCTRINE OF MUSICAL.

affettuoso (It.) tender, affectionate. Also, *con affetto*.

affrettando *also*, **affrettato** (It.) hastening, becoming faster and more excited.

A flat the PITCH (A♭) a half step below A, the enharmonic equivalent of G sharp.

AFM *abbr*. AMERICAN FEDERATION OF MUSICIANS.

Africaine, L' [ä-frē'ken] (Fr., the African maid) romantic opera in 5 acts by Meyerbeer (his last, first performed after his death) on a libretto by Eugène Scribe. Premiere, Paris 1865. The story of the Port. explorer Vasco da Gama and a native African, Selika, who has fallen tragically in love with him.

African-American music *also,* **Afro-American music** the music of black Americans, resulting from a fusion of African and European traditions. The primary modern forms are JAZZ and its many relatives, incl. BLUES, GOSPEL MUSIC, SPIRITUAL, RHYTHM-AND-BLUES, RAP and SOUL MUSIC.

Afro-American Symphony the Symphony No. 1 (1930) by William Grant Still, premiered by the Rochester SO.

Afro-Cuban jazz a jazz style fusing Lat.-Amer. music with bop, made popular in the late 1940s by Dizzy Gillespie and the Cuban percussionist Chano Pozo. Cf. SALSA.

afterbeat any of the beats of a measure following the downbeat. An accent on the second (and fourth) beats is a characteristic of much jazz and rock music. Also, *backbeat, offbeat.*

Afternoon of a Faun, The PRELUDE TO "THE AFTERNOON OF A FAUN."

afterpiece an 18th-c. English OPERA written to be performed after a play or other theatrical work.

Agazzari, Agostino (1578–1640) Italian organist and composer, mainly of motets and other sacred works with continuo accompaniment. He was the author of one of the earliest treatises on thoroughbass (1607).

Age of Anxiety, The the Symphony No. 2 for piano and orch. (1949) by Bernstein, inspired by a poem by W.H. Auden.

Ager, Milton (1893–1979) Amer. songwriter, whose works incl. "Happy Days are Here Again" (campaign song of Franklin D. Roosevelt) and "Ain't She Sweet?"

aggregate 1, a collection of notes in a composition including only one of each PITCH CLASS. **2,** a collection of sounds produced simultaneously, as a cluster, multiphonic, etc.

agitato [ä-jē′tä-tō] (It.) agitated, excited.

Agnus Dei [′ä-nyoos ′de-ē] (Lat., Lamb of God) one of the acclamations of the Mass Ordinary.

AGO *abbr.* AMERICAN GUILD OF ORGANISTS.

agogic accent an ACCENT produced by lengthening rhythmic duration rather than by dynamic stress or higher pitch. Cf. RUBATO.

agrément [ä-grā′mä] (Fr.) ORNAMENT.

Agricola, Alexander (c1446–1506) Franco-Flemish composer of masses, motets, chansons and instrumental arrangements; active in Italy, France and Spain.

aguinaldo [ä-gwē′näl-dō] (Sp.) a general term for a Venezuelan sacred or secular Christmas song.

Ahlert, Fred (1892–1953) Amer. songwriter, whose hits incl. "I'll get by."

Aida tragic opera in 4 acts by Giuseppi Verdi to a libretto by Antonio Ghislanzoni. It was Verdi's last opera until 16 years later, when, at the age of 74, he produced *Otello*. Premiere, Cairo 1871. The story of the love of the Egyptian commander Radames for the Ethiopian slave girl Aida and the jealousy of her mistress Amneris.

Aida trumpet a long TRUMPET esp. constructed to play the triumphal march in Verdi's opera *Aida*.

Aikin, Jesse B(owman) (1808–1900) Amer. compiler of hymnbooks in SHAPE NOTE notation.

air a vocal or instrumental MELODY. Cf. AYRE and ARIA.

air à boire [bwär] (Fr.) a 17th- and 18th-c. French drinking-song of frivolous nature. Also, *chanson pour boire.*

air column the air inside the tube of a wind instrument (incl. the voice) which, when made to vibrate, produces a sound of a certain pitch and quality depending primarily on the dimensions of the tube. A tube closed at one end produces a pitch an octave lower than one that is open. See AEROPHONE.

air de cour [koor] (Fr.) a French

strophic SONG of the 16th and 17th c. composed to please the monarch. It was either polyphonic and unaccompanied or for solo voice with lute accompaniment.

air de danse [dãs] (Fr.) in Baroque Fr. opera, an instrumental AIR accompanied by dancing.

Air on the G String popular name for the Air from the Suite No. 3 in D major, BWV 1068 (1729–31), by J.S. Bach.

air sérieux [sã-rē'ø] (Fr.) a 17th- and 18th-c. French serious SONG about love, political satire or pastoral life.

Aitken, John (1745–1831) Scottish-born Amer. music publisher in Philadelphia, the first professional publisher of secular music in the U.S.

Aitken, Robert (Morris) (1939–) Canadian flutist and composer, stud. of Marcel Moyse, Nicholas Fiore and others. He has been principal flute of the Vancouver SO and co-principal flute of the Toronto SO and is dir. of New Music Concerts (Toronto). A specialist in contemporary music, he performs regularly in No. America and Europe and has taught at the U. of Toronto, Banff and the U. of Freiburg.

Akhnaten opera in 3 acts by Philip Glass to his own libretto, third part of a historical trilogy with EINSTEIN ON THE BEACH and SATYAGRAHA. Premiere, Stuttgart 1984.

Akimenko, Fyodor (1876–1945) Russian composer, pianist and musicologist, stud. of Balakirev, Lyadov and Rimsky-Korsakov. He was Stravinsky's first composition teacher.

Akiyama, Kazuyoshi (1941–) Japanese conductor, trained at the Toho School in Tokyo with Hideo Saito. He has been conductor of the Tokyo SO, the Osaka PO, the Vancouver SO and the American SO and the Syracuse SO.

Akiyoshi, Toshiko (1929–) Chinese-born Amer. jazz bop pianist, composer and bandleader; trained at the Berklee School in Boston. She worked with Charlie Mariano and Charles Mingus and in 1973 co-founded a band in Los Angeles for which she has written a number of works.

alabado *also,* **alabanza** (Sp., praise) a sacred hymn of praise, introduced to the New World in 1716 by Franciscan monks.

Alain, Marie-Claire (1926–) French organist from a musical family, stud. of Dupré, noted for performances of baroque works and those of her brother **Jehan Alain** (1911–40), who was killed in World War II.

alba (It.) AUBADE.

Albanese, Licia (1913–) Italian-born Amer. lyric soprano, stud. of Emanuel de Rosa and Giuseppina Baldassare-Tedeschi, best known for her performance of Puccini heroines. She sang with the Metropolitan Opera until its move to Lincoln Center in 1966.

Albani (Lajeunesse), Dame **Emma** (1847–1930) Canadian soprano, stud. of L.-G. Duprez and F. Lamperti, a great favorite at Covent Garden from 1872 to 1896 and throughout the world in roles such as Marguerite (*Faust*) and Elsa (*Lohengrin*).

Albéniz, Isaac (1860–1909) Spanish pianist and composer, esp. for the piano, a student of Liszt and a champion of the Spanish "national" style. His best-known work is the piano cycle *Suite Iberia* (1906–9).

Albert, Stephen (Joel) (1941–) Amer. composer, stud. of Rogers, Rochberg, Blomdahl and others. He won the Pulitzer Prize in 1985 for his work *RiverRun*. He has taught at Stanford U. and at Smith College.

Albert Hall see ROYAL ALBERT HALL.

Albert Herring comic opera in 3 acts by Benjamin Britten to a libretto by Eric Crozier adapted from a short story by Guy de Maupassant. Premiere, Glyndebourne 1947. The story of the coming-of-age of the virtuous youth Albert Herring.

Alberti, Domenico (?1710–1740) Italian harpsichordist, singer, and composer, esp. of harpsichord sonatas featuring the broken triad bass which came to be named for him (*Alberti bass*).

Alberti bass

Albinoni, Tomaso Giovanni (1671–1750) Italian violinist and prolific composer of instrumental and vocal works, incl. over 50 operas, most of them produced in Venice.

alboka a Basque HORNPIPE (1,).

Alboni, Marietta (1826–94) celebrated Italian contralto, popular throughout Europe in the operas of Rossini and others.

alborada (Sp., morning song) an instrumental serenade performed at daybreak, usu. for bagpipe or oboe accompanied by a drum. Cf. AUBADE.

Alborada del Gracioso (Sp., The Clown's Morning Song) orchestral work (1918) by Ravel; orig. a piano piece, part of the suite *Miroirs* (1905).

Albrecht, Charles (1759–1848) German-born Amer. piano maker. He produced some of the earliest pianos made in America, four of which are at the Smithsonian Museum.

Albrechtsberger, Johann Georg (1736–1809) Austrian organist; theorist and composer of church, keyboard and other instrumental works; teacher of Beethoven. His organ playing was highly praised by Mozart.

Albright, William (Hugh) (1944–) Amer. organist, pianist and composer, stud. of Finney, Rochberg, Messiaen and others, important in the revival of interest in RAGTIME. He has taught at the U. of Michigan.

Albumblatt (Ger., albumleaf) a short instrumental work, orig. one written in the signature album of a friend; usu. a short, light work for piano.

Alcantara, Theo (1941–) Span. conductor, trained at the Madrid Conservatory. He has been musical dir. of the Grand Rapids SO and the Phoenix SO and has conducted the Metropolitan Opera and other companies in the U.S. and Europe.

Alceste opera in 3 acts by Gluck to a libretto by Ranieri da' Calzabigi, after the play by Euripides. Premiere, Vienna 1767. In a reversal of the Orpheus myth, Alcestis descends to Hades to ensure the return of her husband, Admetus, King of Pherae.

Aldeburgh Festival an annual June festival founded in 1948 at Aldeburgh, England. It is esp. known for performance of works of its founder BENJAMIN BRITTEN.

aleatory determined by chance. The term refers to music (esp. since the late 1940s) in which the composer makes use of chance in the composition of a work, its performance, or both. Methods include varying the order of performance of sections of a work, using GRAPHIC NOTATION (thereby leaving the choice of exact pitches, rhythm, etc., to the performer), even the intentional composition of music so difficult that the performer can only approximate the printed text. Aleatory techniques have been used extensively in works of Cage, Brown, Boulez and others.

Alexander, Alger(non) Texas (1900–54) Amer. blues singer, one of the most successful recording blues artists of the 1920s, often accompanied by guitarist Lonnie Johnson.

Alexander, John (1923–90) Amer. tenor with a remarkably broad repertory, spanning bel canto, Richard Strauss and Wagner. He studied with Robert Weede.

Alexander Nevsky cantata (1939) by Sergei Prokofiev, extracted from his score for a film by Sergei Eisenstein based on the exploits of a 13th-c. Russian prince.

Alexander's Feast ode for St. Cecilia's Day (1736) by Handel, based largely on a poem by John Dryden.

Alexander's Ragtime Band march song by Irving Berlin, publ. in 1911, supposedly named after Jack Alexander, a cornetist and bandleader.

Alfano, Franco (1875–1954) Italian composer of opera, vocal and instrumental music. He completed Puccini's opera *Turandot*.

al fine [äl'fē-nä] (It., to the end) a score indication to play until the point marked FINE, starting either at the beginning of a work or section (DA CAPO) or from a previous sign in the music (DAL SEGNO).

algaita a type of African SHAWM having a brass mouthpiece and usu. played using CIRCULAR BREATHING.

Ali, Rashied (Robert Patterson) (1935–) Amer. jazz drummer and conga player. He has worked with Don Cherry, Earl Hines, Sun Ra, John Coltrane and Sonny Rollins, and has led his own groups. He formed Survival Records and helped organize the New York Jazz Musicians' Festival in 1973.

aliquot scaling a technique for improving the sound of the upper register of the piano by adding a SYMPATHETIC STRING for each pitch.

Alkan (Morhange), **(Charles-Henri) Valentin** (1813–88) misanthropic French virtuoso pianist and composer of music for piano and PEDAL PIANO; a friend of Chopin.

alla breve [brev] (It., by the breve) a metrical mark (¢) indicating duple or quadruple time in which the beat is represented by the half note. Also, *cut time*.

allargando (It.) broadening the tempo, often with increasing volume and rubato.

Alldis, John (1929–) English chorusmaster and conductor, founder of the John Alldis Choir (1962), dir. of the London Philharmonic Choir (1969–) and of the Danish State Radio Chorus (1972–).

Alleghanians, The an Amer. mixed vocal quartet of the mid-19th c., who toured performing sentimental ballads and other repertory.

allegretto [äl-lā'gret-tō] (It.) moderately fast: a tempo between ANDANTINO and ALLEGRO; also, a work or movement in an *allegretto* tempo. Abbr., *All^etto*.

allegro [äl'lä-grō] (It.) orig. an indication of a lively character without suggestion of tempo, the term soon assumed its modern meaning of brisk or fast, between ALLEGRETTO and PRESTO; also, a work or movement in an *allegro* tempo. Abbr., *All^o*.

Allegro musical by Richard Rodgers, lyrics and book by Oscar Hammerstein II. Premiere, New York 1947. Dir. by Agnes de Mille (her first complete production), the story concerns the first 35 years in the life of a Chicago doctor.

alleluia (Heb., praise ye Jehovah) **1**, a chant or hymn of praise. **2**, the third part of the Proper of the Mass, said or sung after the Gradual and before the Gospel and consisting of the refrain *Alleluia* and a verse. The Alleluia is replaced by the TRACT at certain times of the church year (most notably during Lent).

allemande (Fr., from Germany) a 16th- to 18th-c. French court dance of German origin in moderate tempo and duple meter, with a short upbeat; one of the most popular parts of the Baroque suite, usu. paired with the COURANTE. Also, *almain, alman, almand, almayne, almond*.

Allen, Betty (1930–) Amer. mezzo-soprano, stud. of Sarah Peck Moore and Zinka Milanov. She has sung with a number of Amer. opera companies, incl. the New York City Opera, but she is known esp. for her concert and recital appearances. She has taught at the Manhattan School of Music and the North Carolina School of the Arts and since 1979 has been executive director of the Harlem School of the Arts in New York.

Allen, Henry (James) "Red" (1908–67) Amer. jazz trumpeter and singer, soloist with Fletcher Henderson and Louis Armstrong, then leader of his own groups, esp. at the Metropole in New York.

Allen Organ Company Amer. manufacturer of organs and electronic instruments, founded in 1939 in Allentown, PA.

Allen, Steve (Stephen) (1921–) Amer. pianist, composer, singer, writer and comedian. He has performed as pianist and singer and has written songs and a musical, but he is best known for his television appearances, esp. as host of *The Tonight Show* and *Jazz Scene USA.*

all-in the jazz equivalent of TUTTI.

all-interval set a 12-note ROW including all intervals from minor 2nd to major 7th.

Allison, Mose (John Jr.) (1927–) Amer. jazz singer, composer and pianist, combining jazz, country and blues elements. He worked with Gerry Mulligan, Stan Getz and Zoot Sims before concentrating on his wittily philosophical songs with his own trios.

Allman Brothers Band Amer. rock group formed in 1968 in Georgia. The band's music combined elements of blues, country, soul and gospel in a Southern rock style.

all' ottava (It., at the octave) to be played at the octave above or below the written pitch, depending on the placement of the sign. The octave displacement is usu. cancelled by the indication *loco.* Also, *all' 8 va (sopra,* above, or *bassa,* below). See ABBREVIATIONS (*illus.*).

all' unisono [oo-ne′so-no] (It., at the unison) to be played in unison; in figured bass, an indication that no chords are to be added. Cf. TASTO SOLO.

alman *also,* **almain** ALLEMANDE.

Almanac Singers a group of folk singers and writers, active 1941–2, formed in New York by Pete Seeger, Woody Guthrie, Lee Hays and others to use song as a tool for social education.

alma redemptoris mater (Lat., Sweet Mother of the Redeemer) one of the MARIAN ANTIPHONS.

Almeida, Laurindo (1917–) Brazilian classical and jazz guitarist. He has played with Stan Kenton's jazz band as well as with many symphony or-

chestras, has recorded with Stan Getz and is a popular recitalist.

Aloha Oe song (1878) by Lydia Kamekeha Liluokalani, princess regent of Honolulu (1838–1917), written during her imprisonment by the republican government of Hawaii.

Alouette (Fr., lark) a French or French-Canadian folk song, first published in 1879, possibly orig. a work song.

alpenhorn *also,* **alphorn, alpine horn** a straight wooden TRUMPET with an upturned bell ranging from 5 to 15 feet in length, used by Alpine herdsmen for summoning cattle.

Alpert, Herb (1935–) Amer. jazz and popular trumpeter, composer, bandleader and record producer. In the early 1960s he founded A&M Records with Jerry Moss and formed his own band, the Tijuana Brass, which was highly successful until it disbanded in 1970.

Alpine Symphony (Ger., *Eine Alpensinfonie*) the last orchestral tone poem (1915) by Richard Strauss.

al rovescio [rō′ve-shō] (It., back to front) to be played by RETROGRADE motion or by INVERSION.

al segno [′sā-nyō] (It., to the sign) an indication to proceed to the point marked by a sign (usu.(𝄋 *or* 𝄊)).

Also sprach Zarathustra [′äl-zo shpräkh tsä-rä′thoos-trä] (Ger.) THUS SPAKE ZARATHUSTRA.

alt, in IN ALT.

alta danza (Sp.) SALTARELLO.

alta musica [′moo-zē-kä] (It., loud music) *also,* **alta** a 15th-c. term for an instrumental ensemble composed of two or three shawms and a sackbut; distinguished from BASSA MUSICA. Also, *haute musique* (Fr.).

alteration 1, an augmentation of the rhythmic value of the breve, semibreve or minim in pre-17th-c. MENSURAL NOTATION. **2,** *also,* **chromatic alteration** the raising or lowering of a pitch by means of an ACCIDENTAL.

altered scale a type of SCALE used esp. in Jazz.

altered seventh chord a DOMINANT SEVENTH CHORD modified by alteration of the fifth or root or by the addition of other tones, but retaining its cadential function.

alternatim (Lat.) in the Roman liturgy, an alternation of plainsong with polyphony; found in treatment of psalms, magnificats and hymns.

althorn (Ger.) **1**, an upright brass instrument made in various forms with a bugle-like bore and usu. pitched in E♭ a 5th below the cornet. **2**, TENOR HORN.

Althouse, Paul (Shearer) (1889–1954) Amer. tenor, stud. of Oscar Saenger. He sang with the Metropolitan Opera from 1913 to 1940. In his later years he was a prominent voice teacher, whose students incl. Richard Tucker and Eleanor Steber.

Altnikol, Johann Christoph (1719–59) German organist and composer, son-in-law of and a copyist for J.S. Bach.

alto (It., high) **1**, from the 16th to 18th c., the highest adult male voice. Cf. COUNTERTENOR, HAUTE-CONTRE, CASTRATO. **2**, the lowest female voice, having a range from about f to d″. Also, *contralto, contr'alto.* **3**, of an instrument, having a range similar to that of the female alto voice. **4**, (Fr., It.) VIOLA.

alto clef a C CLEF on the third line of the staff, now used primarily for the viola.

alto flute a FLUTE in G, pitched a 4th below the concert flute.

alto horn *also,* **contralto horn** ALTHORN = (1,).

Alto Rhapsody popular name for the Rhapsody for contralto solo, male chorus and orch. (1870) by Johannes Brahms, based on the poem "Harzreise im Winter" by Goethe.

alt voice the highest notes of a singer's range. Cf. IN ALT.

Alva, Luigi (Alva Talledo, Luis Ernesto) (1927–) Peruvian operatic tenor specializing in the music of Mozart and Rossini.

amabile [ä'mä-bē-lä] (It., charming) tender, gentle.

Amacher, Maryanne (1943–) Amer. composer and performer, stud. of

Rochberg and Stockhausen. Her works, which involve electronics and mixed-media presentation, have made use of environmental sounds, as in *City-Links* (1967–79) and *Music for Sound-joined Rooms* (1980–2).

Amadeus Quartet a celebrated English string quartet founded in London in 1947.

Amahl and the Night Visitors miracle opera in 1 act by Gian-Carlo Menotti to his own libretto, inspired by a painting by Hieronymous Bosch. Premiere, NBC-TV 1951. A crippled boy, Amahl, is cured when he gives his crutch to the Three Kings as a gift for the Christ Child.

Amara (Armaganian), **Lucine** (1927–) Amer. soprano, stud. of Stella Eisner-Eyn. She appeared regularly with the Metropolitan Opera from 1950 as well as in Europe.

Amateur Chamber Music Players an Amer. org. of amateurs founded in 1947, headquartered in Washington, D.C., with a membership now exceeding 6000.

Amati an Italian family of violin makers based in Cremona, the best known of whom was **Nicola Amati** (1596–1684), grandson of founder **Andrea Amati** (c1511–c1579), and teacher of ANDREA GUARNERI and ANTONIO STRADIVARI, among others.

Amber, Lenny pseudonym of LEONARD BERNSTEIN.

ambitus (Lat.) the RANGE in scale degrees of a given mode in plainsong or of an instrument, voice or work.

Ambrosian chant a type of PLAINSONG differing from Gregorian chant, associated with St. Ambrose (c340–397), Bishop of Milan, and still used in that city.

Amelia goes to the Ball (It., *Amelia al ballo*) operatic farce in 1 act by Menotti to his own libretto in Italian. Premiere, Philadelphia 1937. Amelia succeeds in going to the ball by framing her lover with the murder of her husband.

Ameling, Elly (Elisabeth) **(Sara)** (1938–) Dutch soprano, stud. of

Pierre Bernac. She is best known as a recitalist and concert singer.

amener [a-mə'nā] (Fr., to lead) a 17th-c. French dance in moderate triple time related to the BRANLE.

America poem (1831) written by Samuel Francis Smith for the Boston Sabbath School Union, set to the music of GOD SAVE THE KING.

American Bandstand influential and immensely popular television rock-and-roll dance program hosted from 1957 by Dick Clark.

American Brass Quintet ensemble founded in 1960 in New York. The group is in residence at Brooklyn College and the Aspen Summer School. It has commissioned many new works for brass quintet.

American Composers Alliance a service org. and music publisher in New York founded in 1938. Abbr., *ACA*.

American Composers Orchestra an ensemble founded by Dennis Russell Davies in the 1970s in New York to perform 20th-c. Amer. music.

American Conservatory of Music a music conservatory est. in Chicago in 1886.

American Federation of Musicians a trade union of Amer. and Canadian professional musicians, founded in 1896 and affiliated with the AFL-CIO. Abbr., *AFM*.

American Festival Overture concert overture (1939) by William Schuman, incorporating American children's shouts and calls.

American Five popular name for a group of American avant-garde composers of the 1930s, including Ives, Ruggles, Cowell, Riegger and Becker.

American Guild of Musical Artists a trade union affiliated with the AFL-CIO representing singers and other trades in the theatrical arts, founded in 1937. Abbr., *AGMA*.

American Guild of Organists org. of organists founded in 1896. Abbr., *AGO*.

American Harp Society org. founded in 1962 as successor to the National Association of Harpists (1920–33).

American in Paris, An 1, orchestral tone poem (1928) by George Gershwin describing an American's day in Paris and incorporating such ubiquitous Parisian sounds as taxi horns. **2,** a film musical starring Gene Kelly (1951) with music by Gershwin, loosely based on the program of Gershwin's tone poem.

American Music Center an org. founded in 1940 to further the cause of Amer. contemporary music.

American Musicological Society org. founded in 1934 in Philadelphia to encourage scholarly research in music. Abbr., *AMS*.

American Opera Center the opera school of the Juilliard School of Music, est. 1970.

American Opera Company short-lived opera company founded in 1885 (dissolved 1888) by Jeannette Thurber to present grand opera in English with American singers. Theodore Thomas was conductor.

American organ a REED ORGAN in which air is drawn past the reeds by a suction bellows.

American Quartet popular name for the String Quartet No. 12 in F major, Op. 96 (1893) by Dvořák.

American Society of Composers an org. founded in 1966 as the Amer. Society of University Composers to represent university composers and to improve teaching standards. Abbr., *ASC*.

American Society of Composers, Authors and Publishers Amer. performing rights org. founded in 1914 to license performance of the works of its members. Abbr., *ASCAP*.

American String Teachers Association org. founded in 1946 to promote student performance on bowed string instruments and to further education and research. Abbr., *ASTA*.

American Symphony Orchestra co-operative orch. founded in 1962 in New York, reorganized in 1973. Its conductors have incl. Stokowski, Akiyama and Mauceri.

American Symphony Orchestra League a service org. founded in 1942 to assist symphony orchestras and conductors. Abbr., *ASOL.*

American Women Composers org. founded in 1976 by Tommie Ewert Carl to promote the music of American women. Abbr., *AWC.*

America the Beautiful poem (1895) by Katharine Lee Bates set to a tune by Samuel A. Ward (1847–1903), an organist, choirmaster and music dealer; first published in 1910. In the 1920s the song was proposed for the national anthem of the U.S. Bates supposedly wrote the poem after being inspired by the view from the top of Pikes Peak in Colorado.

Amériques (Fr., Americas) tone poem for large orch. (1918–22) by Varèse.

Ames Brothers Amer. vocal quartet formed in the 1940s and noted for their highly polished arrangements. They disbanded in the late 1950s.

ametric a term applied to music lacking a perceivable regular metric pulse. Cf. ARHYTHMIC.

am Frosch [äm frosh] (Ger.) in string BOWING, near the frog.

am Griffbrett (Ger.) in string BOWING, above the fingerboard.

Amirkhanian, Charles (Benjamin) (1945–) Amer. composer, educated at Mills College. His works experiment with unusual instruments (esp. percussion), electronic media, nontraditional use of text and new notational systems. He has produced a weekly radio program of avant-garde music for KPFA in Berkeley, CA, and has taught at San Francisco State U.

Ammons, Albert (C.) (1907–49) Amer. jazz boogie-woogie pianist, father of tenor saxophonist **Gene** ("Jug") **Ammons** (1925–74), with whom he performed in his later years.

Amor Brujo, El (Sp., Love, the Sorcerer) ballet by Manuel de Falla to a libretto by Martinez Sierra. Premiere, Madrid 1915. The story concerns a girl haunted by the spectre of a dead lover. The work includes two songs for the lead ballerina.

Amore dei Tre Re, L' (It., Love of the Three Kings) tragic opera in 3 acts by Montemezzi. Premiere, Milan 1913. Set in 10th-c. Italy, the opera is the story of the conflict between Fiora's loyalty to her husband and her old love for Avito, Prince of Altura.

Amphiparnassus, The (It., *L'Amfiparnaso*) a collection of 15 polyphonic vocal pieces (1597) by Orazio Vecchi, grouped into a prologue and three acts.

amplitude a measure of the disturbance in a wave form; LOUDNESS.

Amram, David (Werner) (1930–) Amer. conductor and composer of theater music, opera, songs, choral works, film scores, etc.; stud. of Giannini. He has been musical dir. of the New York Shakespeare Festival and the Lincoln Center Repertory Theater, and was the first composer-in-residence of the New York PO (1966–67).

AMS *abbr.* AMERICAN MUSICOLOGICAL SOCIETY.

am Steg [äm shtäk] (Ger.) in string BOWING, near the bridge.

amusia the inability to produce musical sounds or to understand them, resulting from a brain disorder.

Amy, Gilbert (1936–) French conductor and composer of vocal and instrumental works, stud. of Milhaud, Messiaen and Boulez, whom he succeeded as dir. of DOMAINE MUSICAL in Paris.

anacrusis UPBEAT.

Ančerl, Karel (1908–73) Czech conductor, stud. of Scherchen, a specialist in Czech and modern music; music dir. of the Toronto SO (1969–73).

anche [äsh] (Fr.) **1**, the prepared reed of a wind instrument. Cf. ROSEAU. **2**, *pl.* the reed stops of a pipe organ or the reed-instrument section of an orch.

Anchors Aweigh 1, song by Charles A. Zimmerman (1861–1916) and Alfred H. Miles (1883–1956), apparently written for the Army-Navy football game of 1906. Zimmerman was musical dir. of the U.S. Naval Academy. **2**, film musical (1945) by Jule Styne. A pair of sailors go on leave in Hollywood.

Anda, Géza (1921–76) Hungarian-born Swiss pianist and conductor, stud. of Ernö von Dohnányi, noted for his performances of Bartók and Brahms. His Amer. debut was in 1955.

Andacht, mit ['än-däkht] (Ger.) with devotion.

andamento (It., course) a fugue SUBJECT of extended length. Cf. SOGGETTO.

andante (It., going) at a moderate speed, a tempo between ALLEGRETTO and ADAGIO; also, a work or movement in andante tempo. Abbr., *And^{te}*.
—**più andante**, (It.) usu., slower than andante, although the opposite (faster than andante) is sometimes intended.
—**molto andante**, (It.) usu., much slower than andante, although the opposite (much faster than andante) is sometimes intended.

andante con moto (It.) see MOTO.

andantino (It.) an ambiguous term indicating either somewhat slower or (more often) somewhat faster than andante; also, a work or movement in andantino tempo.

Anderson, Beth (1950–) Amer. composer of text-sound compositions incl. *Torero Piece* (1973) and *Yes Sir Ree* (1978).

Anderson, Cat (William Alonzo) (1916–81) Amer. jazz trumpeter with a remarkably wide range, for many years a featured soloist with the Duke Ellington orch. and then leader of his own band.

Anderson, Laurie (1947–) Amer. composer and performance artist, trained as a violinist. Her works combine the visual and aural arts, often utilizing instruments of her own creation, modified electronically and accompanied by slides and lighting effects.

Anderson, Leroy (1908–75) Amer. conductor, arranger, and composer of lighter orchestral music, sometimes using unconventional instruments. His works incl. *The Typewriter* (1950) and *The Syncopated Clock* (1945).

Anderson, Marian (1902–) Amer. contralto, the first Afr.-Amer. singer

to appear at the Metropolitan Opera (1955). She was esp. known for her performances of spirituals. She retired in 1965.

Anderson, T(homas) J(efferson) (1928–) Amer. composer of vocal and instrumental works, stud. of Milhaud and others. He was the first black composer-in-residence of the Atlanta SO (1969–71) and has been chairman of the Music Dept. at Tufts U. since 1972.

An die ferne Geliebte [ge'lēp-te] (Ger., To the distant beloved) song cycle, Op. 98 (1816), by Beethoven to poems by A. Jeitteles.

André, Maurice (1933–) French virtuoso trumpeter, a specialist on the piccolo trumpet. He teaches at the Paris Conservatoire and has had many works composed for him.

Andrea Chénier [än'drä-ä shä'nyä] romantic *verismo* opera in 4 acts by Giordano to a libretto by Luigi Illica. Premiere, Milan 1896. A fictional story about a historical character, set in Paris at the time of the French Revolution.

Andrews, Julie (Wells, Julia Elizabeth) (1935–) English singer and actress, made famous in the long-running *My Fair Lady* and in many films, including *Mary Poppins, The Sound of Music* and *Victor/Victoria*.

Andrews Sisters a vocal trio (Patti, Maxine and LaVerne) very popular in the 1940s in concert, esp. with the Glenn Miller Orch., and on film.

Anerio, Felice (?1560–1614) Italian composer of sacred and secular vocal music, stud. of Nanino. He succeeded Palestrina as composer to the Papal Chapel in Rome. His younger brother, **Giovanni Francesco Anerio** (?1567–1630), was a stud. of Palestrina and important in the early history of the oratorio.

Angeles, Victoria de los LOS ANGELES, VICTORIA DE.

angel lute *also,* **angelica** (It.), **angelique** (Fr.), **angelot** a fretted two-necked LUTE of the late 17th and 18th c. similar to the theorbo, with two sets of strings situated side-by-side rather than in courses, and tuned diatonically.

anglaise (Fr., from England) continental term for any of several 17th-and 18th-c. English country dances in lively duple or triple meter, sometimes used in a stylized form as part of the Baroque suite. Cf. CONTREDANSE.

angle harp an earlier form of HARP without a pillar.

Anglican chant a type of harmonized chant widely used in the Anglican, Episcopal and some other Protestant churches for singing psalms and canticles. (See *illus.*, below.)

Anhalt, István (1919–) Hungarian-born Canadian pianist, conductor and composer of vocal, instrumental and electronic music. He has taught at McGill U. in Montreal, where he founded an electronic studio, and at Queen's U. in Kingston, Ontario.

animal dances generic term for a number of dances of the 1910s performed to ragtime music, as well as more recent rock-and-roll dances, named for animals whose movements they imitate. Examples incl. the *turkey trot, foxtrot, chicken*, etc.

animando (It.) becoming faster or more lively.

animato (It.), **animé** (Fr.) lively.

animoso *also*, **con animo** (It.) spirited, with spirit.

anklung a Javanese bamboo RATTLE.

Anna Bolena (It., Anne Boleyn) tragic opera in 2 acts by Donizetti to a libretto by Felice Romano. Premiere, Milan 1830. Historical drama based on the last moments of Anne Boleyn's marriage to Henry VIII.

Années de pélérinage [ä'nä də pä-lā-rē' näzh] (Fr., Years of Pilgrimage) a collection of works for piano solo (1836–77) by Liszt.

Anne of Green Gables highly popular musical play with music by Norman Campbell, based on the 1908 novel by Lucy Maud Montgomery. A mainstay of the Charlottetown (PEI) Festival since 1965, the play has been performed throughout Canada and on television.

Annibale Padovano (c1527–75) Italian organist and composer. He was first organist at St. Mark's, Venice (1552–64), then organist and Kapellmeister at the archducal court in Graz. His works incl. organ toccatas and ricercars, church music, madrigals and a battaglia for wind instruments.

Annie Get Your Gun musical by Irving Berlin, book by Herbert and Dorothy Fields. Premiere, New York 1946. The story of the hillbilly Annie Oakley (sung by Ethel Merman), who became the star attraction of Buffalo Bill's Wild West Show.

Annie Laurie setting (1835) by Lady John Scott (c1820–1900) of a poem, allegedly by William Douglas, about the love between members of two rival Scottish clans.

Anschlag ['än-shläk] (Ger.) **1**, a DOUBLE APPOGGIATURA. **2**, TOUCH (in piano playing).

Ansermet, Ernest (1883–1969) Swiss conductor, stud. of Bloch and Nikisch. He conducted the Ballets Russes in Paris (1915–17) and founded L'Orchestre de la Suisse Romande in Geneva, which he conducted until 1966. He was noted for

Anglican chant

Our King and Saviour draw-eth nigh; O come, let us a - dore _ him.
Alleluia. Unto us a child is born; O come, let us adore him. Al-le - lu - ia.

his performances of 20th-c. music, esp. the music of Debussy, Ravel and Stravinsky.

answer in a FUGUE, a transposition of the SUBJECT, usu. at the interval of a fourth below or a fifth above, immediately following its statement by a different voice in the orig. key. The transposition may be exact (*real answer*) or modified to preserve the tonality (*tonal answer*).

Antar a tone poem, the Symphony No. 2, Op. 9 (1868), by Rimsky-Korsakov, the story of an Arabian hermit, Antar, who saves a gazelle (a fairy queen in disguise) from a bird of prey.

antecedent a phrase or section of a musical passage which is answered by a following phrase or section (*consequent*), the two together constituting a PERIOD; in fugue and canon, the same as SUBJECT. The phrases usu. begin with the same material, the antecedent ending on the tonic or mediant, the consequent ending on the tonic.

(Mozart, Piano/Wind Quintet K. 452)

Antes, John (Johann) (1740–1811) Amer. Moravian minister and composer of sacred vocal music. He may have been the first American to compose chamber music.

Antheil, George (Georg Johann Carl) (1900–59) Amer. composer, pianist and journalist, stud. of von Sternberg and Bloch. He lived in Europe from 1922 to 1933. His works are sometimes scored for unusual mechanical "instruments" (his *Ballet mécanique* includes aircraft propellers). After his return to the U.S. in 1933 he concentrated on ballet and film scores until 1942, after which he composed a

number of traditional concert works. His works incl. *Transatlantique, Volpone* and other operas, *Capital of the World* and other ballets, 6 symphonies, concertos and other orchestral works, chamber music, songs, piano solos, and works for TV and films.

anthem 1, an antiphonal or responsorial song or hymn. **2,** a solemn vocal (usu. choral) composition of praise or thanksgiving in English, accompanied or unaccompanied, esp. one performed during the Communion of a Protestant service. See VERSE ANTHEM, FULL ANTHEM, MOTET, NATIONAL ANTHEM.

anticipation an unaccented NONHARMONIC NOTE sounded before the chord of which it forms a part; also, an entire chord so treated. See ORNAMENT.

antiphon 1, a short liturgical prose text chanted before and after a psalm or hymn. Cf. RESPONSORY. **2,** a verse sung by two alternating groups, usu. contrasting, as a men's choir and a boy's choir; in the Mass, the introit, offertory and communion are antiphons. Cf. MARIAN ANTIPHONS.

antiphonal sung or played in alternating groups. Cf. RESPONSORIAL.

antiphonale (Lat.) *also*, **antiphoner, antiphonary** a liturgical book containing the chants for the Office, as opposed to the GRADUAL (1,).

antique cymbal see CYMBALS.

Antoniou, Theodore (1935–) Greek conductor and composer, educated in Athens and Munich. He is a prolific composer of works in all genres and founder of contemporary music groups in Athens, Stanford, Boston and Philadelphia. He has taught at the Berkshire Music Center and since 1979 has been on the faculty of Boston U.

Antony and Cleopatra tragic opera in 3 acts by Samuel Barber to a libretto adapted from Shakespeare by Franco Zeffirelli. Premiere, New York 1966, revised in 1975. The work was written for the opening of the Metropolitan Opera House at Lincoln Center.

anvil a blacksmith's anvil or a steel

bar struck with a hard wooden or metal mallet for use as a percussion instrument in orchestral and operatic music. The most famous examples of its use are in the "Anvil Chorus" in Verdi's *Il Trovatore* and the transition music between the second and third scenes of Wagner's *Das Rheingold.*

Anything Goes musical by Cole Porter, book by Guy Bolton and P.G. Wodehouse, revised by Howard Lindsay and Russell Crouse. Premiere, New York 1934. The story of a night club singer and friends aboard an ocean liner.

apache dance 1, a violent cabaret dance of the 1920's Parisian underworld. **2,** a ballroom dance derived from (1,).

Apaches, Les [ä'päsh] (Fr.) an artistic coterie formed around 1900 in Paris, whose members incl. Ravel, Falla and Schmitt, as well as artists and writers.

aperto (It.) open. See OPEN.

a piacere [pyä'chä-rä] (It., at [one's] pleasure) an indication that the performer should exercise freedom of interpretation, esp. with respect to TEMPO. The term is often used in connection with a CADENZA. In Renaissance music, the altus part is often added after the fact with the designation *a piacere.* Cf. AD LIBITUM, SI PLACET.

Apocalyptic Symphony popular name for the Symphony No. 8 in C minor (1884–90) by Bruckner.

Apollo ancient Greek god assoc. with song and music, a player of the lyre.

Apollo Club name for a number of Amer. singing organizations, incl. a choral society founded in Chicago in 1872 as an all-male ensemble; women were admitted in 1885.

Apollo Theater a popular entertainment center in Harlem, New York, from the mid-1930s until 1975, where many important jazz and blues artists and bands appeared.

apollonicon a large 19th-c. ORCHESTRION.

Apollon musagète [ä-po'lō moo-zä'zhet] (Fr., Apollo, leader of the Muses) ballet by Igor Stravinsky. Premiere, Washington, D.C., 1928. The work is usu. associated with the choreography by Balanchine for the Paris premiere later the same year.

apothéose [ä-po-tä'ōz] (Fr.) an 18th-c. French memorial composition, usu. in honor of a dead musician and imitating the musician's style. A famous example is the *Apothéose de Lully* by François Couperin.

Appalachian dulcimer a fretted, plucked ZITHER used to accompany dance-songs and ballads.

Appalachian Spring ballet by Copland, originally for 13 instruments, with choreography by Martha Graham. Premiere, Washington, D.C., 1944. Copland also orchestrated the work for full orch., and this version is the one most often heard today. The setting is a pioneer wedding at a Pennsylvania farmhouse.

Appassionata (It.) popular title (added by a publisher) for Beethoven's Piano Sonata in F minor, Op. 57 (1807).

appassionato (It.) impassioned.

Applause musical by Charles Strouse, lyrics by Lee Adams, book by Betty Comden and Adolph Green, based on the film *All About Eve.* Premiere, New York 1970. Broadway star Margo Channing takes in, to her sorrow, the young actress Eve Harrington, who scratches her way to the top.

Applebaum, Louis (1918–) Canadian conductor and composer, esp. of music for theater, radio, TV and films; stud. of Willan, MacMillan, Harris and others. He has been dir. of the Stratford Festival (1953–61), exec. dir. of the Ontario Arts Council and an advisor to The Canada Council.

applied dominant SECONDARY DOMINANT.

appoggiatura [äp-pod-jä'too-rä] (It., leaning) **1,** an ornamental note found chiefly in music of the 18th c. It precedes a principal melody note, usually as an upper neighbor tone, and is notated (if it is shown at all) in a smaller size than the principal note or in normal notation. Frequently the ornament is not notated, the performer being expected to insert it according to the conventions of the time, which also determined whether the note should be played before the beat or on the beat. See ORNAMENT. —**double appoggiatura**, a term that can refer to: two appoggiaturas in different voices occurring simultaneously; two conjunct notes approaching the principal note from above or below (slide); or two disjunct notes approaching the principal note from below and above. See ORNAMENT.

Après-midi d'un faune, L' [lä-pre-mē'dē dœ fōn] PRELUDE TO "THE AFTERNOON OF A FAUN."

Après une lecture de Dante [a'pre zün lek'tür də dät] (Fr., After reading from Dante) piano work, subtitled "Fantasia quasi sonata" (1837–9, rev. 1849) by Liszt, evoking the inferno of Dante's La divina commedia.

Arabella romantic opera in 3 acts by Richard Strauss to a libretto by Hugo von Hofmannsthal. Premiere, Dresden 1933. A complex story about Arabella, daughter of a financially strapped Viennese family, and her sister Zdenka, brought up as a boy to save expenses. In the end, Arabella marries Mandryka, a rich country gentleman, and Zdenka lands Matteo, a young officer.

arabesque an ORNAMENT, esp. a passage or work suggestive of arabesque ornamentation, which is based on Arabic art and architecture.

Arányi, Jelly d' (1893–1966) Hungarian-born English violinist, stud. of Grunfeld and Hubay. Her virtuoso technique and Gypsy temperament inspired a number of composers to write for her, incl. Bartók and Ravel. She performed frequently in duo with pianist Myra Hess and in trio with Hess and cellist Felix Salmond.

Arbeau, Thoinot (Tabourot, Jehan) (1520–95) French choreographer, famous for his dance tutor Orchésographie (1588), an important source of information on French dance.

Arbuckle, Matthew (1828–83) Scot-tish-born Amer. cornetist and bandmaster. He played with Gilmore's band (see GILMORE) from 1860 to 1880, then became a bandmaster of the New York Militia.

Arcadelt, Jacob (?1505–1568) Franco-Flemish singer and composer, a member of the Papal Chapel and perhaps court musician in Paris. He was a prolific composer of sacred and secular vocal works, known esp. for his madrigals.

Arcana (Lat., mysteries) orchestral tone poem (1927) by Varèse, inspired by the theories of the German physician Paracelsus.

arcato (It.) coll' arco. See ARCO.

Archduke Trio popular name for Beethoven's Piano Trio in B♭ major, Op. 97 (1811), dedicated to the Archduke Rudolf of Austria.

Archer (née Balestreri), **Violet** (1913–) Canadian pianist and composer, stud. of Claude Champagne, Hindemith and Bartók, professor at the U. of Alberta (1962–78). She is a prolific composer of music in all genres.

archlute a large bass LUTE with two pegboxes and additional unstopped bass strings, often double-strung. Cf. CHITARRONE, THEORBO.

arcicembalo [är-chē'chem-bä-lō] (It.) a harpsichord designed by Nicola Vicentino with divided keys and often a second keyboard tuned to permit playing in the ancient Greek genera (see GENUS).

arco (It.) bow (of a violin, etc.). —**coll' arco** with the bow: opposed to PIZZICATO.

arco saltando (It.) SAUTILLÉ.

Arditti Quartet English string quartet founded in London in 1974, specializing in 20th-c. music.

Arel, Bülent (1919–90) Turkish-born Amer. composer, mainly of electronic music. He has taught at Yale and SUNY, Stony Brook.

Arensky, Anton (1861–1906) Russian conductor, pianist and composer, stud. of Rimsky-Korsakov. He taught at the Moscow Conservatory, where his pupils incl. Rachmaninov, Scriabin and Glière and was dir. of the imperial chapel in St. Petersburg. His works incl. 3 operas, orchestral works, concertos for piano and for violin, chamber music and songs. His *Variations on a theme of Tchaikovsky* for string orch. is frequently performed.

Arezzo, Guido d' GUIDO D'AREZZO.

Argento, Dominick (1927–) Amer. composer, primarily of opera, stud. of Weisgall, Cowell, Dallapiccola, Hanson and Hovhaness. He teaches at the U. of Minnesota and won the Pulitzer Prize in 1975 for his song cycle *From the Diary of Virginia Woolf*. In 1964 he founded the Center Opera in Minnesota, later to become the Minnesota Opera. His works incl. *The Boor, Postcard from Morocco, The Voyage of Edgar Allan Poe* and other operas, orchestral and chamber music, and songs (*Letters from Composers*).

arghul an Egyptian cane double CLARINET having one melody pipe and one drone pipe.

arhythmic a term applied to music lacking any perceivable rhythm or rhythmic change. Sometimes used as a synonym for AMETRIC.

aria (It., air, aria; *pl.* arie *or* arias) a melody or tune for solo voice (or an instrument performing in a vocal manner), usu. relatively extended with a stanzaic structure and with instrumental accompaniment, forming part of a larger work, such as an opera or oratorio. See DA CAPO ARIA, ARIOSO.

aria napolitana (It.) VILLANELLA.

Ariadne auf Naxos (Ger., Ariadne on Naxos) opera in 1 act with prologue by Richard Strauss to a libretto by Hugo von Hofmannsthal. Premiere, Vienna 1916. (The orig. version, without prologue, was written to follow Molière's play *Le bourgeois gentilhomme*. The premiere in this form was in Stuttgart in 1912.) The work is a play within a play: The prologue deals with the conflict between two performing troupes hired to perform for the dinner guests of a Viennese nobleman; the opera presents the result of the collaboration, an *opera seria* about Ariadne and Bacchus with comic intermezzi performed by commedia dell'arte characters.

Arianna, L' (It.) opera with prologue and 8 scenes by Monteverdi to a libretto by Ottavio Rinuccini. Premiere, Mantua 1608. The music is lost, except for the "Lamento d'Arianna," which survives as a monodic song, published separately in 1623, and in madrigal arrangement by Monteverdi in his *Sixth Book of Madrigals* (1614).

arietta (It.) a short ARIA in Italian.

ariette (Fr.) a short ARIA in French, esp. **1**, in 18th-c. French opera, an aria similar to the Italian *da capo aria*. **2**, in the *opéra-comique*, a song usu. preceded and followed by spoken dialogue.

arioso (It.) **1**, in a singing, rather than a declamatory, style; songlike. Also, a short aria or an instrumental movement in such a style. **2**, RECITATIVO ARIOSO. **3**, MADRIGALE ARIOSO.

Arkansas Traveler an Amer. song of unknown authorship that first appeared in 1847 and was used as a tune for square dances.

Arlen, Harold (Arluck, Hyman) (1905–86) Amer. composer who wrote for Broadway, cabarets and films, best known for his scores for the film *The Wizard of Oz* ("Over the Rainbow"), the musical *House of Flowers* (1954) and many hit songs, incl. "Stormy Weather."

Arlésienne, L' (Fr., The Woman from Arles) a play by Alphonse Daudet for which Bizet wrote incidental music. The music is excerpted in two orchestral suites, one arranged by Bizet, the second by E. Guiraud.

Armenian, Raffi (1942–) Egyptian-born Canadian conductor and composer of Armenian extraction, stud. of Swarowsky and others at the Vienna Academy. He has been musical dir. of the Kitchener-Waterloo SO since 1971.

armonica GLASS HARMONICA.

Armstrong, (Daniel) Louis ("Pops," "Satchmo") (1900–71) highly influential Amer. jazz trumpeter, singer and bandleader, orig. from New Orleans, later of Chicago. He played with King Oliver and Fletcher Henderson, then led his own bands. He was often called the "father of jazz" and was famous for his husky voice, scat singing (which he invented) and his bravura style of improvisation.

Arne, Thomas Augustine (1710–78) English violinist and composer of stage works (esp. the masque *Comus*, 1738), organ works, sacred and secular vocal works, etc., most of them lost. His music for the masque *Alfred* (1740) included the song "Rule Britannia," which became a national patriotic song of Great Britain. Arne's son, **Michael Arne** (1741–86), was a successful opera composer.

Arnold, Eddy (1918–) Amer. country and popular singer. During the 1940s he was a highly successful country recording star, also appearing with the Grand Ole Opry. He changed in the 1950s and 1960s to a more popular style. He was elected to the Country Music Hall of Fame in 1966.

Arnold, Malcolm (Henry) (1921–) English composer of vocal, orchestral and chamber music, as well as many film scores (incl. *The Bridge on the River Kwai*), a stud. of Jacob. He trained as a trumpeter and played for some years with the London PO.

arpanetta (It.) an upright 17th- and 18th-c. BOARD ZITHER with two soundboards, one side used for melody, the other for accompaniment. Also, *Spitzharfe* (Ger.).

arpeggio [är'ped-jō] (It., play on the harp) a term for the sounding of the notes of a chord in succession, rather than simultaneously; also, a chord so sounded. See ABBREVIATIONS.

arpeggiando (It.) in arpeggio.

arpeggiato (It.) played in arpeggio.

arpeggione a 19th-c. bowed string instrument similar to the cello, with frets and drone strings. Also, *guitar violoncello*.

arrangement an adaptation of a work for an instrumentation or scoring which was not originally intended,

preserving as much as possible the original character of the piece. See TRANSCRIPTION (1,), ADDITIONAL ACCOMPANIMENT.

Arrau, Claudio (1903–91) Chilean pianist, stud. of Martin Krause in Berlin. He is esp. noted for his interpretations of the Beethoven piano sonatas and concertos.

Array Toronto org. founded in 1971 to promote and present new music.

Arrieu, Claude (1903–) French composer, stud. of Roger-Ducasse and Dukas. She has produced many works for theater and broadcasting, as well as vocal and instrumental chamber and orchestral works.

Arrow Music Press music publisher founded in New York in 1938 and specializing in the support of contemporary Amer. music. It was acquired in 1956 by Boosey & Hawkes.

Arroyo, Martina (1936–) Amer. operatic soprano, stud. of Marinka Gurevich. She specializes in Verdi heroines and is also heard frequently in oratorio and recital. Her Metropolitan Opera debut was in 1959 and she has sung many major roles there from 1965. She has also performed much 20th-c. music.

ars antiqua [ärz än'tē-kwä] (Lat., the old technique) a 14th-c. term for the style of composition prevalent in the 12th and 13th c., exemplified by the NOTRE DAME SCHOOL (Pérotin, Léonin). Also, *ars veterum*. Cf. ARS NOVA.

arsis the unaccented part of a measure; esp., UPBEAT. Cf. THESIS.

ars nova (Lat., the new technique) the music of the 14th c., properly applied only to French music of the first half of the century. Cf. ARS ANTIQUA, ARS SUBTILIOR.

ars subtilior (Lat., subtle art) a term for the mannered, highly complex music of late 14th-c. France.

ars veterum (Lat.) ARS ANTIQUA.

Artaria an Austrian firm of music publishers founded in 1769 in Vienna, whose catalogue incl. first editions of music by Haydn, Mozart, Beethoven, etc.

Art Ensemble of Chicago an innovative free-jazz quintet formed in Paris in 1969 by Roscoe Mitchell. Abbr., *AEC.*

articulation 1, the manner in which a note or phrase is performed, as determined by attack and decay and indicated by terms such as *legato, staccato, pizzicato,* as well as by graphic signs. See NOTATION, BOWING. **2,** the shaping of a musical phrase; PHRASING. **3,** the formation of vowels and consonants in singing.

Art of the Fugue, The (Ger., *Die Kunst der Fuge*) didactic work (1749) by J.S. Bach, consisting of 13 fugues (*contrapuncti*) on a single theme, demonstrating many contrapuntal techniques. The work is usu. published with an unfinished fugue on three subjects, which may (with the addition of the *Art of the Fugue* theme as fourth subject) have been intended to form part of the work.

art rock a type of ROCK music of the 1970s and later that makes claims to a certain aesthetic quality above and beyond regular rock. Groups representative of the movement incl. the Velvet Underground and Frank Zappa's Mothers of Invention.

art song a composed song, usu. with piano accompaniment, having serious artistic aspirations. See LIED, CHANSON. Cf. FOLK SONG.

ASCAP *abbr.* AMERICAN SOCIETY OF COMPOSERS, AUTHORS AND PUBLISHERS.

A sharp the PITCH (A♯) a half-step above A, the enharmonic equivalent of B flat.

Ashkenazy, Vladimir (Davidovich) (1937–) Russian pianist and conductor, stud. of Anaida Sumbatian and Lev Oborin, winner of the Chopin, Queen Elisabeth and Tchaikovsky competitions. He has played and conducted throughout the world and is music dir. of the Royal PO (London).

Ashley, Robert (Reynolds) (1930–) Amer. performer and composer. With Gordon Mumma he founded the Cooperative Studio for Electronic Music

in Ann Arbor and he has also worked at Mills College in CA. His works incl. stage and TV operas, theater pieces, film scores, sonatas, chamber music and electronic works.

ASOL *abbr.* AMERICAN SYMPHONY ORCHESTRA LEAGUE.

Aspen Music Festival an annual summer festival and music school in Aspen, CO, est. in 1950.

assai [äs'sī] (It.) much, very; sometimes used erroneously to mean "moderately."

assieme (It., together) in opera, a stage rehearsal with orch. but without costumes.

Associated Music Publishers firm of music publishers founded in 1927 in New York as representative of leading European houses and a publisher of American music. It was acquired in 1964 by G. Schirmer.

Association for the Advancement of Creative Musicians a non-profit org. founded in 1965 in Chicago by pianist MUHAL RICHARD ABRAMS, devoted to the support of Afr.-Amer. avant-garde jazz.

Astaire, Fred (Austerlitz, Frederick) (1899–1987) Amer. dancer, singer, actor. A giant of the musical theater, first paired with his sister Adele, then with Ginger Rogers and other partners in many hit musicals (*Lady, Be Good; Gay Divorce*) and films (*Top Hat, Easter Parade, Funny Face*).

As Thousands Cheer musical by Irving Berlin, sketches by Moss Hart. Premiere, New York 1933. A highly successful revue in the form of a newspaper, with the various sections represented by sketches.

Aston Magna Foundation for Music a summer music school in the Berkshires founded in 1972 by harpsichordist Albert Fuller for the study and performance of 17th- and 18th-c. music.

ASUC *abbr.* American Society of University Composers (see AMERICAN SOCIETY OF COMPOSERS).

athematic lacking a melodic theme.

Atkins, Chet (Chester Burton) (1924–) Amer. country guitarist, a star of the Grand Ole Opry and largely responsible for the use of electric guitar as a solo instrument in country music. He worked for thirty years as a producer for RCA records and was a significant force in the creation of the NASHVILLE SOUND. He was elected to the Country Music Hall of Fame in 1973.

Atlanta Symphony Orchestra orch. formed in 1947 in Atlanta, GA. It has had only three musical directors, Henry Sopkin (1947–66), Robert Shaw (1967–87) and Yoel Levi.

Atlantic Symphony Orchestra orch. formed in 1968 in Halifax, NS, under conductor Klaro Mizerit.

Atmosphères ['ät-mos-fer] (Fr.) influential orchestral work (1961) by Ligeti, based on the slow changing of a sustained chordal sound.

atonality the absence of TONALITY, i.e., the lack of a tonal center; usually used to refer to music not composed in accordance with the conventions of triadic tonality and not composed using serial techniques. The term is often used erroneously to refer to music with a high degree of dissonance in the traditional sense. Cf. PANTONALITY, SERIALISM, TWELVE-TONE MUSIC.

attacca (It., attack) begin at once; used at the end of a movement or section to indicate that the performer should continue to the following movement or section without pause. Also, *attacca subito, segue.*

attacco (It., attack) a short fugue SUBJECT or motive treated imitatively. Cf. ANDAMENTO, SOGGETTO.

attack 1, the manner in which a sound is begun. **2,** ENSEMBLE (synchronization) among a group of players in attacking a note or phrase.

Attaingnant, Pierre [a-te'nyä] (c1494–1552) French music printer and composer, the first in France to use movable type for music.

Attwood, Thomas (1765–1838) English organist at St. Paul's Cathedral and the Chapel Royal and prolific composer of theatrical and other works; stud. of Mozart.

aubade [ō'bäd] (Fr.) morning music. Also, *alba.* Cf. ALBORADO.

Auber, Daniel-François-Esprit (1782–1871) French composer, stud. of Cherubini and dir. of the Paris Conservatoire (1842–70). As a composer he was best known for his operas (esp. *Fra Diavolo* and *Masaniello*), many written for the Opéra-Comique.

Au Clair de la Lune [ō kler də la lün] (Fr., by the light of the moon) French song, prob. of 18th-c. origin, first publ. in 1843. Composer and author are unknown.

audition 1, the ability to hear. **2,** a critical hearing of a performer, as for the purpose of determining level of ability, accomplishment, etc.

audition piano an early ELECTRIC PIANO invented by Lee de Forest in 1915.

Auer, Leopold (von) (1845–1930) Hungarian violinist, stud. of Joachim. He was professor at the St. Petersburg Conservatory (1868–1917), where he taught Elman, Zimbalist and Heifetz. He came to Amer. in 1918. Auer was a noted interpreter and produced many editions of violin repertory.

Aufderheide, May (Frances) (1888–1972) Amer. composer of piano rags and songs.

Aufstieg und Fall der Stadt Mahagonny, Der ['owf-shtēk ûnt fäll där shtät mä-hä'go-nē] (Ger.) RISE AND FALL OF THE CITY OF MAHAGONNY, THE.

Auftakt ['owf-täkt] (Ger.) UPBEAT.

Augenmusik ['ow-gən-moo"zēk] (Ger.) EYE MUSIC.

augmentation a method of VARIATION by which a theme is restated with the original note values increased by a certain factor, usu. double. See FUGUE, CANON.

augmented of an interval, increased by one half step from a major or perfect interval.

augmented major seventh chord a CHORD composed of an augmented triad and a major 7th.

augmented seventh chord a CHORD composed of an augmented triad and a minor 7th.

augmented sixth chord a first-inversion CHORD having a major third and an augmented sixth. Cf. GERMAN SIXTH, ITALIAN SIXTH, FRENCH SIXTH.

augmented triad a CHORD having a major third and an augmented fifth.

Auld, Georgie (Altwerger, John) (1919–) Canadian jazz saxophonist, clarinetist and bandleader. He played with Benny Goodman and Artie Shaw, then led his own band (1943–6).

Auld Lang Syne song, composer unknown, with a text in part by Scottish poet Robert Burns. The song first appeared in 1799. Its melody is based on a pentatonic scale (C,D,E,G,A,C).

aulos ['ow-lōs] (Gk., *pl., auloi*) a Greek reed woodwind instrument similar to the OBOE (not the flute, as sometimes stated), usu. played in pairs by one player.

Auric, Georges (1899–1983) French composer, stud. of d'Indy and Roussel, a member of LES SIX and dir. of the Paris Opéra and Opéra-Comique (1962–8). He wrote a number of ballet scores for Diaghilev's Ballets Russes and also composed film scores.

ausdrucksvoll ['ows-drŭks-fol] (Ger.) expressive.

Austin, Larry (Don) (1930–) Amer. composer, stud. of Milhaud, Imbrie and Shifrin, and editor of *Source*, an avant-garde journal. A number of his works involve a technique of group improvisation which he calls "open styles." He has been active in electronic composition and mixed-media performance.

Auszug ['ows-tsook] (Ger.) **1**, VOCAL SCORE. **2**, a trombone or trumpet SLIDE (3,).

authentic cadence PERFECT CADENCE.

authentic mode see MODE.

autograph a handwritten manuscript, esp. a manuscript in the hand of its composer (*holograph*). Cf. COPY.

Autoharp (*Trademark*) a ZITHER played by plucking or strumming, in which chords are selected by buttons controlling damper strips which let only certain notes sound when the strings are strummed.

Autry, (Orvon) Gene (1907–) Amer. country singer, songwriter and actor. He began as a popular radio and recording artist in the style of JIMMIE RODGERS, then went to Hollywood to become the first "singing cowboy." He was elected to the Country Music Hall of Fame in 1969.

auxiliary note *or* **tone** a nonharmonic note approached by stepwise motion from above or below and returning to the original note. Cf. NEIGHBOR NOTE.

avant-garde (Fr.) a term describing artists or music whose techniques or aims are markedly different from the accepted conventions of the time or of tradition. In jazz, the term is sometimes used as a synonym for FREE JAZZ.

Ave Maria 1, one of the MARIAN ANTIPHONS. **2**, a song by Schubert, based on a song from Sir Walter Scott's *Lady of the Lake*. **3**, a work by Gounod, orig. for violin and piano, superimposing an original melody on the harmonies of J.S. Bach's C-Major Prelude from Vol. I of *The Well-Tempered Clavier*.

Ave Maris stella (Lat., Hail, star of the ocean) a hymn used frequently during the Middle Ages and Renaissance as the basis for polyphonic vocal and organ works.

Ave Regina Caelorum (Lat., Hail, queen of the heavens) one of the MARIAN ANTIPHONS.

Avery Fisher Hall a concert hall opened in 1962 in New York's Lincoln Center. It was known as Philharmonic Hall until 1973, when it underwent major renovation and was renamed.

Avshalomov, Jacob (1919–) Chinese-born Amer. conductor and composer of works encompassing a broad spectrum of styles, stud. of Toch and Rogers. He was the son of Russian-born composer **Aaron Avshalomov** (1894–1965), who came to the U.S. in 1947.

AWC *abbr.* AMERICAN WOMEN COM-POSERS.

Ax, Emanuel (1949–) Polish-born Amer. pianist, stud. of Mieczyslaw Munz. He is an outstanding interpreter of standard and 20th-c. repertory and has appeared frequently in chamber music groups with cellist Yo-Yo Ma.

ax *also,* **axe** term in popular music and jazz for a musical instrument, esp. an instrument one can carry in one hand.

Ayler, Albert (1936–70) Amer. jazz tenor saxophonist, a major exponent of avant-garde jazz in the 1960s, performing frequently with Cecil Taylor and Don Cherry.

ayre an English song with instrumental accompaniment (usu. lute), made popular by John Dowland's compositions published c1600. Such ayres might also be performed as part-songs for several voices, with or without instrumental accompaniment. Cf. LUTE SONG.

B

B 1, the seventh note of the scale of C major. See PITCH. **2,** (Ger.) B FLAT. Cf. H.

babatoni a one-string bass instrument similar to the WASHTUB BASS, in use in south-central Africa since the 1950s.

Babbitt, Milton (1916–) Amer. composer, teacher and theorist, stud. of Sessions. He has been on the faculty of Princeton and the Juilliard School and dir. of the Columbia-Princeton Electronic Music Center. His compositions, mostly serial, incl. instrumental and vocal works, often with electronic tape. He has also written a musical and several film scores. In 1982 he received a Pulitzer Prize Special Citation.

Babcock, Alpheus (1785–1842) piano maker in Boston credited with the invention in 1825 of a one-piece cast-iron metal frame piano with a hitch-pin plate.

Babin, Victor (1908–72) Russian-born Amer. pianist and composer, stud. of Schnabel and Franz Schreker, and dir. of the Cleveland Institute of Music from 1961. He performed as a duo-pianist with his wife, Vitya Vronsky, and was a member of the Festival Quartet.

Babi Yar popular name for the Symphony No. 13 for bass voice, male chorus, and orch. (1962), by Shostakovich to a text by Yevgeny Yevtushenko. The name refers to the site in the Ukraine of the Nazi massacre of thousands of Jews in 1941.

baby grand a small GRAND PIANO, usu. 4 feet in length.

bacchanale (Fr.) a celebration of the god of wine, Bacchus. Used by various composers as the title for works, esp. ballets in opera. Notable examples appear in Gounod's *Faust*, Wagner's *Tannhäuser* and Saint-Saëns's *Samson and Delilah*.

bacchetta [bäk′kāt-tä] (It.) BAGUETTE.

Bacewicz, Grazyna [bä′tse-vich, grä′zhi-nä] (1909–69) Polish composer and violinist, stud. of Boulanger, Flesch and Touret. She was a successful concert artist and prolific neoclassical composer of 4 symphonies, and ballets, operas, violin concertos and sonatas, chamber and vocal music.

B-A-C-H the Ger. names for the notes B♭-A-C-B♮. J.S. Bach used the notes as a subject in the final, unfinished, fugue of his *Art of the Fugue*, and other composers after him—incl. Schumann, Liszt and Webern—have used it in homage to Bach.

Bach, Anna Magdelena (1701–60) second wife of J.S. Bach, for whom he compiled two books of instructional music by himself and others.

Bach, Carl Philipp Emanuel (1714–88) Ger. keyboard player, theorist and prolific composer; the "German" or "Hamburg" Bach, fifth child of J.S. Bach (with whom he studied) and godson of Telemann. He was harpsichordist for Frederick the Great in Berlin for almost 30 years, then a church musician in Hamburg until his death. He was the chief representative of the EMPFINDSAMER STIL and wrote all types of music except dramatic works, concentrating on works for keyboard. His *Essay on the True Art of Playing Keyboard Instruments* (1753–62) is the standard work on 18th-c. keyboard playing.

Bach, Johann Christian (1735–82) Ger. composer, the "London" or "English" Bach, 18th child of J.S. Bach, stud. of his father and of C.P.E. Bach in Berlin. He went first to Italy in 1754, then to London in 1762, where he remained until his death. In London in 1764 he met Mozart, whose music had an important influence on him. With C.F. Abel, he established the BACH-ABEL CONCERTS in London.

Bach, Johann Christoph (1642–1703) Ger. organist, harpsichordist and composer of vocal and instrumental works, cousin of J.S. Bach, employed for most of his life in Eisenach at St. George's and in the ducal chapel.

Bach, Johann Christoph Friedrich (1732–1795) Ger. keyboard virtuoso and composer, the "Bückeburg" Bach, 17th son of J.S. Bach. He studied with his father and his cousin Johann Elias Bach. He was a chamber musician in the service of Count Wilhelm of Schaumburg-Lippe from 1750 until his death. His compositions progressed in his later years from the contrapuntal style of his father to a Classical style.

Bach, Johann Sebastian (1685–1750) Ger. organist, harpsichordist and composer, a towering figure of the Baroque, who summed up the musical knowledge and techniques that preceded him and developed them further. In composition he appears to have been largely self-taught through copying. He was successively organist at Arnstadt, at Mühlhausen, court organist at Weimar (where most of his organ works were written), court organist in Cöthen, and Kantor at the Thomaskirche and civic dir. of music in Leipzig from 1723 until his death.

During his early years in Leipzig, Bach composed five complete cycles of cantatas for the church year, almost 300 sacred cantatas, as well as the *St. John* and *St. Matthew Passions*. In 1729, Bach took over the Collegium Musicum, founded in 1704 by Telemann, a voluntary association of students and professionals that gave weekly concerts, and many of Bach's instrumental works probably date from this period. He was appointed court composer to Dresden in 1736.

The last decade of Bach's life was marked by a visit in 1747 to the court of Frederick the Great, which resulted in the *The Musical Offering*, based on a theme by the monarch, and by the composition of *Art of the Fugue*.

Bach was influenced by a broad range of styles, encompassing the German, French, and Italian schools; he was esp. interested in the works of Frescobaldi, Buxtehude, Handel and Vivaldi. His work extends into all areas, with the notable exceptions of opera and ballet.

Bach, P.D.Q. pseudo-historical personage invented in 1953, along with a repertory of "newly discovered" works, by composer-humorist PETER SCHICKELE.

Bach, Vincent (1890–1976) German-born Amer. instrument maker, the first to establish a system for the exact duplication of mouthpieces for brass instruments. He is best known for the manufacture of trumpets.

Bach, Wilhelm Friedemann (1710–84) Ger. composer, the "Halle" Bach, first son of J.S. Bach. He studied with his father (who compiled for him the *Clavier-Büchlein*) and with J.G. Graun (violin). He was organist in Dresden and Halle, and spent his last years in Berlin, where he died in poverty.

Bach-Abel Concerts a subscription concert series in London directed jointly by J.C. Bach and C.F. Abel from 1765 to 1781.

Bacharach, Burt (1928–) Amer. composer, stud. of Milhaud and Cowell. His best-known works are film scores (*Alfie, Butch Cassidy and the Sundance Kid*) and Broadway musicals (*Promises, Promises*).

Bach Aria Group an Amer. chamber ensemble formed in 1946 for the performance of J.S. Bach's vocal works.

Bachauer, Gina (1913–76) Greek-born British pianist, stud. of Cortot and Rachmaninov. During World War II she performed for the allied troops, then toured the U.S. and Europe regularly from 1950, playing a varied repertory.

Bach bow popular name for the convex Bow used in the baroque period.

Bach-Gesellschaft a society founded in 1850 to publish a complete critical edition of J.S. Bach's works. It was dissolved in 1900 but was immediately succeeded by the Neue Bach-Gesellschaft, formed to popularize the music and produce a revised complete critical edition.

Bachianas Brasileiras (Port.) set of 9 works (1930–45) by Villa-Lobos for various instrumental groups, some incl. voice, representing the application of the contrapuntal techniques of J.S. Bach to the native music of Brazil.

Bach revival the popular name for the rediscovery of the music of J.S. Bach in Germany and England during the first half of the 19th c.

Bach rock a type of ROCK music of the 1960s featuring baroque music or music in baroque style performed with rock instruments with a rock beat.

Bach trumpet an erroneous term for various high trumpets used in modern performances of baroque music. See TRUMPET.

backbeat AFTERBEAT.

backfall APPOGGIATURA.

background music music designed to be played to provide atmosphere, not to be listened to, as for a party, in an office lobby, etc. Cf. MUZAK.

Backhaus, Wilhelm (1884–1969) Ger. pianist, stud. of d'Albert, esteemed as a Beethoven specialist.

Bacon, Ernst (1898–1990) Amer. composer and conductor, chiefly of works for voice (songs, operas), stud. of Bloch. He has taught at the Eastman School and the San Francisco Conservatory and was a founder of the Carmel (CA) Bach Festival. His Symphony in D major was awarded the Pulitzer Prize in 1932.

Bacon, Frederick J. (1871–1948) Amer. banjo player and maker, designer of the Silver Bell banjo (1923).

badinage [bä-dē′näzh] *also,* **badinerie** [bä-dē-nə′rē] (Fr., joking) a characteristic piece, usu. in a quick 2/4 meter, found esp. in 18th-c. suites.

Badings, Henk (1907–87) prolific Dutch composer of vocal, instrumental, ballet, opera and electronic music; stud. of Willem Pijper. He received the Italia Prize for his electronic radio opera *Orestes.*

Badura-Skoda, Paul (1927–) Austrian pianist, stud. of Edwin Fischer, known for his interpretations of the Viennese classics and 20th-c. works. He has performed and recorded frequently on period instruments from the 18th and 19th c.

Baez, Joan (1941–) Amer. folksinger, guitarist and songwriter, active as a performer in support of various political and humanitarian causes.

bagatelle (Fr., trifle) a short, playful piece, usu. for piano.

bag-hornpipe a primitive type of BAGPIPE without drone.

bagpipe a single- or double-reed instrument for which the sounding wind is stored in a bag, either filled by mouth (Scottish Highland pipes and most other types) or by means of a bellows worked by the player's arm (Irish "Union" pipes or Northumbrian pipes). The bag is usu. of sheepskin, but other animal skins or rubber may be used. The instrument usu. has one or more drone pipes and a pipe with cylindrical or conical bore called the *chanter* with fingerholes for playing the melody. There are

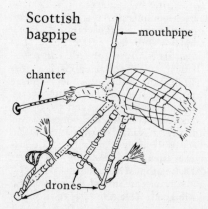

Scottish
bagpipe　　←mouthpipe

chanter

drones

many national variants of the basic instrument, such as the musette, baghornpipe, *piva* and *cornamuse*.

Bags JACKSON, MILT.

baguala [bä'gwä-lä] (Sp.) a S. Amer. lyric song form, performed esp. in Carnival season. It is accompanied by drums.

baguette [bä'get] (Fr.) a stick, as, a drumstick, bow stick or conducting baton.

Bailes Brothers an Amer. country music group popular in the 1940s. They performed regularly on radio on the Grand Ole Opry and on the Louisiana Hayride (which they founded in 1948).

Bailey, Buster (William C.) (1902–67) Amer. jazz clarinetist and saxophonist noted for his virtuoso technique, stud. of Franz Schoepp. He played with Fletcher Henderson, Louis Armstrong's All Stars and in the 1950s with Red Allen at the Metropole in New York.

Bailey, DeFord (1899–1982) Amer. country music harmonica player. He was a regular of the Grand Ole Opry until 1941 and toured with Roy Acuff and Bill Monroe.

Bailey, Mildred (Rinker, Mildred) (1907–51) Amer. jazz singer and pianist, best known for her rendition of Hoagy Carmichael's song, "Rockin' Chair." She sang with the Paul Whiteman band and with Red Norvo (to whom she was married for ten years).

Bailey, Pearl (Mae) (1918–90) Amer. jazz and popular singer. She sang with the Cab Calloway band in the 1940s and appeared in several Broadway musicals, incl. *House of Flowers* (1954) and *Hello, Dolly!* (1967).

Baird, Tadeusz (1928–81) Polish composer of works in a highly individualistic and expressive style. He was a founder of a circle of socialist composers named Group 49 (for the year of its inception).

Baker, Benjamin Franklin (1811–89) Amer. composer, singer and teacher, founder of the Boston Music School in the early 1840s.

Baker, Chet (Chesney H.) (1929–88) Amer. jazz trumpeter and fluegelhorn player. He played with Charlie Parker and Gerry Mulligan. His playing was noted for its cool, lyrical style, heavily influenced by Miles Davis.

Baker, David (Nathaniel, Jr.) (1931–) Amer. jazz cellist, trombonist and composer, stud. of Schuller, George Russell and William Russo. As a trombonist he played with Maynard Ferguson, Lionel Hampton and Quincy Jones, and with the George Russell sextet. He has been chairman of the Jazz Department of Indiana U. since 1966.

Baker, Israel (1921–) Amer. violinist, stud. of Adolph Pick and Bronislaw Huberman, known esp. as a chamber musician, concertmaster and soloist in 20th-c. repertory.

Baker, Kenny (Kenneth) (1926–) prominent Amer. bluegrass and jazz fiddler, a frequent member of Bill Monroe's Blue Grass Boys from the late 1950s into the 1980s.

Baker, Shorty (Harold) (1913–66) jazz trumpeter and fluegelhorn player from St. Louis. He began as a riverboat musician and later played for many years with Duke Ellington's orch.

Baker, Dame **Janet** (1933–) English mezzo-soprano, stud. of Helen Isepp and Meriel St. Clair, equally at home in concert and opera, esp. noted in the works of Benjamin Britten. She retired from opera in 1982.

Baker, Josephine (1906–79) Amer. singer and actress. In 1925 she went to Paris to star in *La revue nègre* and also appeared at the Folies-Bergère, where she made a sensation. After World War II she was active in the civil rights struggle.

Baker, Julius (1915–) eminent Amer. flutist. He was principal flute of the Pittsburgh SO (1941–3), the CBS SO (1943–50), the Chicago SO (1951–53) and the New York PO (1964–83). He has been on the faculty of the Juilliard School since 1954 and the Curtis Institute since 1980.

Bakfark, Bálint (Valentin Greff)

(1507–76) Hungarian virtuoso lutanist and composer of lute works.

bala an African XYLOPHONE with gourd resonators, used for formal concerts and vocal accompaniment.

Balakirev, Mily Alexeyevich [bə'läkē-ref] (1837–1910) Russian railway official and composer of vocal, chamber and orchestral music, stud. of Karl Eisrich and leader of a group of composers sometimes called the MIGHTY HANDFUL (*moguchaya kuchka*). He was an ardent nationalist and an important influence on the composers of his group as well as on the course of Russian music in general.

balalaika a flat-backed plucked LUTE with three strings, a long neck and a triangular body, a popular folk instrument of Russia. See also DÖMBRA.

balancement [bä-läs'mä] (Fr.) the TREMOLO of a clavichord, voice or stringed instrument. Also, *bebung*, *vibrato*.

Balatka, Hans (1826–99) Moravianborn Amer. conductor and composer. He was dir. of the Milwaukee Musical Society (1850–60) and the Chicago Philharmonic Society (1860–69) and conducted throughout the Midwest. In 1879 he founded the Balatka Academy of Musical Art in Chicago.

Baldwin Amer. manufacturer of pianos, organs and electronic instruments, founded in 1865 in Cincinnati.

Baldwin, Dalton (1931–) Amer. pianist and accompanist, stud. of Lipatti and Nadia Boulanger. He is one of the world's leading vocal accompanists and has performed and recorded with Gérard Souzay, Elly Ameling and many others.

Balfe, Michael William (1808–70) Irish baritone and opera composer, best known for his opera THE BOHEMIAN GIRL.

Baline, Israel BERLIN, IRVING.

Ball, Ernest R. (1878–1927) Amer. singer and composer of songs, incl. "When Irish Eyes are Smiling" and "Mother Machree."

ballabile [bäl'lä-bē-lä] (It., danceable) 1, a dance movement in classical ballet or in opera. 2, in a dancing manner; a mark of expression.

ballad 1, orig., a song to accompany dancing or sung while dancing. 2, a strophic song with refrain. 3, a narrative song. 4, a popular song, esp. of a romantic or sentimental character and slow in tempo. 5, erroneously, BALLADE.

ballade (Fr.) 1, a 14th- and 15th-c. French verse form, one of the three FORMES FIXES, usu. having three stanzas sharing the same rhyme and refrain. Cf. BAR FORM. 2, an instrumental composition, usu. for piano solo, reflecting the style of the vocal BALLAD (4,).

ballad horn a valved brass instrument in C similar to the B♭ BARITONE (3,), invented in 1870 for amateurs to play vocal lines without transposition.

Ballad of Baby Doe, The opera in 2 acts by Douglas Moore to a libretto by John Latouche based on a true story. Premiere 1956, Central City, CO. The tragic story of the love between Elizabeth Doe and politician Horace Tabor, who is ruined in the collapse of the silver standard.

ballad opera 1, a type of 18th-c. English MUSIC THEATER alternating traditional or current popular tunes with spoken text. The first example is THE BEGGAR'S OPERA. 2, an opera imitating this style.

Ballard, Louis W(ayne) (Hunka-No-Zhe; Joe Miami) (1931–) Amer. composer and teacher of Native American descent. He has written extensively on Native American music for the classroom and incorporates it into his own compositions.

ballata (It.) an Italian dance-song of the 13th to 15th c. consisting of a refrain (*ripresa*), two strophes (*stanze* or *piedi*), and a third strophe (*volta*), the *volta* and the *ripresa* having the same music.

ballet a theatrical pantomime of dance and music that has inspired many great works of music, esp. in the 19th and 20th c. A high point of ballet composition in the early 20th c. was inspired by the Ballets Russes of DIAGHILEV.

ballet de cour [koor] (Fr.) an elaborate French court ballet of the 16th and 17th c. combining dance, music and poetry.

ballet-héroïque [ā-rō′ēk] (Fr.) a type of French OPÉRA-BALLET of the early 18th c. based on heroic characters and consisting of a prologue and several acts (*entrées*), each with its own plot. Rameau's *Les Indes galantes* (1735) is an example of the form.

Ballet mécanique [mā-kä′nēk] orchestral work (1923–5) by Antheil that created a furor at its premiere because of its use of such unconventional instruments as airplane propellers and a siren.

Ballets Russes see DIAGHILEV.

ballett *also*, **balletto** (It.) a madrigalesque instrumental or vocal composition with fa-la refrain, prominent in late 16th- and early 17th-c. England and Italy.

ballin' the jack an Afr.-Amer. social and theatrical dance. It was introduced in the 1914 stage hit *Darktown Follies*.

ballo (It.) **1**, a social dance. **2**, CHOREOGRAPHY. **3**, a musical work intended to be danced or that is inspired by the dance.

Ballo in maschera, Un [′mä-skā-rä] (It.) MASKED BALL, A.

Ballou, Esther (Williamson) (1915–73) Amer. composer, teacher and pianist, stud. of Luening, Wagenaar and Riegger. She was the first woman composer to have a work premiered at the White House.

Balsam, Artur (1906–) Polish-born Amer. pianist, teacher and composer, known esp. for his work as an ensemble pianist and accompanist. He has taught at the Manhattan School and at Blue Hill, ME.

Baltimore Symphony Orchestra the first Amer. civic orch., founded in 1914. Its conductors have included Gustav Strube, George Siemonn, Reg-

inald Stewart, Massimo Freccia, Peter Herman Adler, Commissiona and Zinman.

bamboula (Afr.) **1**, an African FRAME DRUM. **2**, a West Indian dance popular among black slaves in Louisiana.

bambuco (Sp.) a Colombian pursuit-dance involving elaborate toe-dancing and waving of handkerchiefs, accompanied by guitars.

Bampton, Rose (1909–) Amer. mezzo-soprano (soprano after 1937), a favorite of Stokowski and Toscanini. Her Metropolitan Opera debut was in 1932 and she has taught at the Manhattan and Juilliard Schools. Her roles incl. Kundry (*Parsifal*) and Donna Anna (*Don Giovanni*).

Banchieri, Adriano (Tomaso) (1568–1634) Italian organist, theorist and composer of sacred and secular vocal works. His writings are important for their description of the performance practice of his day.

band a group of musicians playing together; esp. a particular group of related instruments, usu. not including string instruments. Cf. BRASS BAND, MILITARY BAND, JAZZ BAND.

Band, The Amer. rock group formed in 1967 in Woodstock, NY. Their repertory had a distinct folk flavor. The group disbanded in 1976.

banda (It.) a BAND, esp. one playing backstage in an opera.

bandmaster the leader or conductor of a band, esp. a military or brass band.

bandola (Sp.) a flat-backed S. Amer. LUTE related to the bandurria, used to play melody lines to the accompaniment of guitars and *tiples*.

bandoneon *also*, **bandonion** a S. Amer. ACCORDION with single-note buttons for treble and bass notes.

bandora *also*, **bandore** (Fr.), **pandora** (Ger.) a Renaissance plucked bass LUTE, with a distinctive scalloped body. Invented in England in 1562, it is an obligatory instrument of the mixed consort and much used in English baroque theater music.

band organ a portable ORGAN, incl.

built-in bass drum, snare drum and cymbal, used to provide music for circuses, carousels, amusement parks, etc. Also, *fairground organ.*

bandura *also,* **bandoura** one of two Ukrainian instruments: an ARCH-LUTE, or a type of unfretted PSALTERY.

bandurria [bän-doo'ri-ä] *also,* **mandurria** a type of Spanish LUTE played with a plectrum and used currently in S. Amer. and the Caribbean. Cf. BANDOLA.

Bandy, Moe (Marion F., Jr.) (1944–) Amer. honky-tonk singer and guitarist. His period of success began in 1972, with solo recordings and appearances with his group, the Rodeo Clowns, and at the Grand Ole Opry.

Banff Centre School of Fine Arts summer (later, year-round) arts school founded in Banff, Alta., in 1933 under Donald Cameron.

banjo a five-stringed plucked or strummed string instrument of the GUITAR family with a long slender neck and a circular drumlike body covered with stretched parchment, usu. played with the fingers. Cf. TENOR BANJO.

banjolin a type of BANJO with four single strings.

banjorine *also,* **banjeaurine** a small BANJO pitched a 4th higher than the standard instrument.

banjo zither a BANJO-like plucked string instrument invented in 1879. Cf. ZITHER-BANJO.

bar. *abbr.* BARITONE.

bar 1, *also,* **bar line** a vertical line across one or more staffs, orig. used solely for purposes of alignment, but since the later 17th c. as an indication of metric stress (see METER). **2,** (esp. Brit.) MEASURE. **3,** a medieval strophic song similar to the French ballade but lacking a refrain. See BAR FORM. **4,** BASS-BAR.

Barber, Samuel (1910–81) Amer. composer. His First Symphony was the first Amer. work to be performed at the Salzburg Festival. His opera *Vanessa* (winner of the Pulitzer Prize in 1958) and his *Adagio for Strings* have often been performed, and his *Antony*

and Cleopatra was commissioned for the opening of the new Metropolitan Opera House in Lincoln Center (1966). He won a second Pulitzer Prize in 1963 for his Piano Concerto No. 1. His works incl. *Vanessa, A Hand of Bridge, Antony and Cleopatra* (operas), *Medea* (ballet), *The School for Scandal* (overture), 2 symphonies, concertos for piano and violin, 3 orchestral "essays," choral works, sonatas for violin and cello, *Summer Music* (ww quintet), music for piano solo and songs (*Knoxville: Summer of 1915, Hermit Songs, Dover Beach*).

Barber of Seville, The (It., *Il Barbiere di Siviglia*) **1,** comic opera in 2 acts by Rossini, libretto by Cesare Sterbini after the play by Beaumarchais. Premiere, Rome 1816. Rosina, the ward of old Dr. Bartolo, is in love with Count Almaviva; together they outwit the Doctor (who wanted to marry Rosina himself). **2,** comic opera in 3 acts by Paisiello to the same libretto as (1,). Premiere, St. Petersburg 1782.

barbershop a style of ensemble singing originating in the 19th c. and characterized by CLOSE HARMONY sung by solo quartet or chorus, usu. of men. The melody is usu. carried by the second tenor (*lead*). Cf. SWEET ADELINES.

Barbiere di Siviglia, Il [bär'bye-rä dē sē've-lyä] (It.) BARBER OF SEVILLE, THE.

Barbirolli, Evelyn see ROTHWELL, EVELYN.

Barbirolli, Sir **John** (Giovanni Battista) (1899–1970) English cellist and conductor, esp. of late Romantic repertory and English composers (incl. Elgar, Vaughan Williams and Delius). He was conductor of the New York Philharmonic (1938–42), the Hallé Orch. (1943–70) and the Houston SO (1961–67), as well as a frequent conductor of opera. His wife was EVELYN ROTHWELL, the noted oboist.

barbiton an ancient Greek LYRE.

barcarole *also,* **barcarolle** (Fr.) **1,** a boat song of the Venetian gondoliers, characterized by 6/8 or 12/8 rhythm and a rocking alternation of strong and weak beats. **2,** an art song or other work imitating this style; esp., the popular duet for Nicklaus and Giulietta from *The Tales of Hoffmann* by Offenbach.

bard a poet-singer, esp. **1,** a Celtic tribal singer. **2,** a wandering minstrel in early Scotland.

Bardi, Giovanni de' (1534–1612) Italian poet, critic and composer, host of the CAMERATA and patron of Giulio Caccini and Vincenzo Galilei. He was an early proponent of the movement that led to dramatic MONODY and early opera.

Barenboim, Daniel (1942–) Argentinian-born Israeli pianist and conductor, stud. of his father and Nadia Boulanger, conductor of the Orchestre de Paris since 1975 and music dir. of the Chicago SO. As a pianist, he specializes in the works of Mozart and Beethoven. He was married to cellist JACQUELINE DU PRÉ.

Bärenreiter Ger. music publisher founded in 1923 in Augsburg. Initially active esp. in publishing folksongs, Bärenreiter has been a major publisher of musicological works and complete and collected editions.

bar form a three-part A-A-B form related to the BALLADE, consisting of an *Aufgesang* (comprising two *Stollen*) and an *Abgesang*. The names of the form and its parts come from the Ger. Meistersinger tradition. See FORM.

Bar-Illan, David (Jacob) (1930–) Israeli-born Amer. pianist specializing in 19th-c. works, esp. those of Liszt.

bariolage [bä-rē-ō′läzh] (Fr.) **1,** a MEDLEY. **2,** an effect produced on bowed string instruments by playing the same pitch alternately on open and stopped strings.

baritone *also,* **barytone** (*not to be confused with the* BARYTON) **1,** the male voice range between tenor and bass. Cf. BASS-BARITONE, BARYTON MARTIN. **2,** VIOLA bastarda (1,). **3,** a SAXHORN pitched between the althorn and the tuba.

baritone clef an obsolete F CLEF on the third line of the staff, formerly used for vocal music.

baritone oboe *also,* **bass oboe** the lowest orchestral OBOE, often replaced by the HECKELPHONE.

Barker, Sister **(Ruth) Mildred** (1897–) Amer. Shaker singer and songleader. She learned several hundred spirituals and gospel hymns by ear to lead songs in Shaker services. She was spiritual leader of the Shaker Society at Sabbathday Lake from 1972.

Barlow, Howard (1892–1972) Amer. conductor, an ardent supporter of American music. He was conductor of the American National Orch. (1923–5) and the Baltimore SO (1940–3), a staff conductor for CBS (1927–43) and musical dir. of the "Voice of Firestone" radio and TV series on NBC (1943–61).

Barlow, Samuel L(atham) (Mitchell) (1892–1982) Amer. composer and pianist. His opera *Mon ami Pierrot* (1934) was the first Amer. opera to be produced at the Opéra-Comique in Paris.

Barlow, Wayne Brewster (1912–) Amer. composer and teacher, stud. of Edward Royce, Hanson and Schoenberg, on the faculty of the Eastman School (1937–78). His compositions, in a serial idiom, incl. orchestral, vocal and chamber works.

barn dance 1, orig. a rural meeting for dancing, the name was adopted for various country-music radio programs. **2,** an English dance of Amer. origin derived from the SCHOTTISCHE.

Barnet, Charlie (Charles Daly) (1913–91) Amer. jazz saxophonist, singer and leader of a popular swing band in the 1930s and 1940s.

Barnett, Alice Ray (1886–1975) Amer. teacher, patron and composer, mainly of art songs.

Barnum, P(hineas) T(aylor) (1810–91) Amer. impresario. He sponsored a U.S. tour by JENNY LIND in 1850–51 in which she gave 95 concerts. This was the first major tour to be sponsored by a nonperformer, and it established a separate class of agents and promoters.

Baron, Samuel (1925–) Amer. flutist and conductor, stud. of Georges Barrère. He was a founder of the New York Woodwind Quintet and of the New York Brass Ensemble and has been music dir. of the Bach Aria Group since 1980. He has taught since 1966 at SUNY Stony Brook.

Barons of Rhythm COUNT BASIE's first jazz band, formed in 1935.

Baroque a term generally used to refer to the period of European art music from about 1600 to 1750, often further divided roughly into the *early Baroque* (1600–30), *middle* or *high Baroque* (1630–80) and *late Baroque* (1680–1750). The period is characterized by the emergence of tonality, the development of monody, thoroughbass, the vocal forms of opera, oratorio and cantata and the instrumental dance suite, concerto and sonata.

baroque oboe an early form of OBOE with few keys and a light tone.

baroque organ see ORGAN.

baroque pitch a standard pitch level based on a' = 435 cps, widely used for performance of baroque music on original instruments. Also, *old pitch*.

Barraqué, Jean (1928–73) French composer of serial works, stud. of Langlais and Messiaen. His final work, begun in 1955, takes Hermann Broch's controversial *La Mort de Virgile* as a starting point for a "drama having neither actors nor action," a project that remained incomplete at his death.

barre fingering BARRING.

barrel drum a single- or double-headed DRUM having bulging sides.

barrelhouse a style of jazz piano playing related to BOOGIE-WOOGIE and RAGTIME, characterized by a heavy bass vamp (*stomping*) in 4/4 time. Also, *gutbucket*.

barrel organ a portable mechanical ORGAN. The sound is produced by a hand-operated revolving cylinder whose pegs control the valves that allow air to flow from a bellows to a set of pipes. A small form (*street organ*) was used by street musicians, but larger varieties were used in churches during the 18th and 19th c. Also, *Dutch organ, grinder organ*.

barrel piano a mechanical piano with an action similar to the BARREL ORGAN. Also, *street piano, cylinder piano*.

Barrère, Georges (1876–1944) French flutist and a highly influential teacher, stud. of Paul Taffanel. He was founder in 1895 of the Société Moderne des Instruments à Vent in Paris and principal flute of the New York SO from 1905 to 1928. He taught at the Juilliard School from 1931.

Barrier, The opera by Jan Meyerowitz to a libretto by Langston Hughes based on his play *Mulatto*. Premiere, New York 1950. A scathing attack on racial prejudice.

barring a technique for the left hand on plucked and some bowed instruments to facilitate the playing of chords. The first finger stops all or some of the strings, leaving the remaining fingers free to stop other chord tones. Also, *barre fingering*.

Barshai, Rudolf (1924–) Russian violist and conductor, founder of the Moscow Chamber Orch. His conducting posts have included the Israel Chamber Orch., the Bournemouth SO and the Vancouver SO.

Bart, Lionel (1930–) English composer of music for films and theater, his most successful work being the musical *Oliver!* (1960).

Bartered Bride, The (Czech., *Prodaná Nevěsta*) comic opera in 3 acts by Smetana to a libretto by Karel Sabina. Premiere 1866, Prague. Mařenka has been promised to Vašek, but is in love with Jeník, who in the end wins her hand through a clever maneuver. The lively overture is frequently played as a concert work.

Bartholomew, Marshall (1885–1978) Amer. choral conductor, trained in Berlin, founder and conductor of the Yale Glee Club (1921–53).

Bartók, Béla (1881–1945) Hungarian composer, ethnomusicologist and pianist, whose profound interest in Hungarian folk song combined with his involvement in Western art music resulted in an extensive body of works of international importance with a strong national spirit. Bartók's work with Hungarian folksong was carried on in conjunction with Kodály and lasted for most of his life. Bartók also made frequent concert tours as a pianist during the 1920s and 1930s. He moved to America permanently in 1941, where, because of ill health, he produced relatively few works, the most notable being the *Concerto for Orchestra*, commissioned by Serge Koussevitzky for the Boston SO. His works incl. *Bluebeard's Castle* (opera), *The Wooden Prince* (ballet), *The Miraculous Mandarin* (pantomime), 2 violin concertos, 3 piano concertos, *Concerto for Orchestra, Music for Strings, Percussion and Celesta*, viola concerto, choral works and songs, instrumental chamber music, and many piano works, incl. the didactic *Mikrokosmos.*

Bartoletti, Bruno (1926–) Italian conductor, esp. of Italian operatic repertory of the 19th and 20th c. His U.S. debut was in 1956 with the Lyric Opera of Chicago, of which he became artistic dir. in 1975, and he has been artistic dir. of the Teatro Communale in Florence since 1987.

baryton (Ger.) **1,** a bowed string instrument similar to the BASS VIOL having sympathetic strings that can be plucked by the player. Haydn wrote almost 200 works for the instrument, on which his patron, Nikolaus Esterházy, was an enthusiastic performer. **2,** (Fr.) BARITONE (3,). **3,** the tenor TUBA in B♭.

baryton Martin ['bä-rē-tō mär'tē] (Fr.) a high BARITONE voice with a lighter sound and a range bordering on the tenor, particularly well suited for French music. The name comes from French baritone Jean Blaise Martin (1769–1837), a star of the Paris Opéra-Comique.

Barzin, Leon (Eugene) (1900–) Belgian-born Amer. conductor and educator, stud. of Ysaÿe and others. He

played in the New York PO until 1929, then became conductor of the National Orchestral Association, a position he held until 1976.

bas-dessus [bä də'sü] (Fr.) see HAUT-DESSUS.

Basie, Count (William) (1904–84) Amer. jazz pianist and orch. leader. His first band, The Barons of Rhythm, in Kansas City, became the Count Basie Orch., one of the most important and successful bands of the swing era, characterized by a rhythm section of unusual cohesion. He continued to lead the band, which gained sophistication and polish, until his death.

bass 1, the lowest male singing voice. **2,** *also,* **bass line** the lowest part in a polyphonic texture, often having the function of accompaniment compared to the melodic function of the upper voices. **3,** the lowest note of a chord, as distinguished from the ROOT, with which it may or may not coincide. Cf. FUNDAMENTAL BASS. **4,** the lower half of the vocal or tonal range, the upper half being treble. **5,** the lowest instrument in a family, as the bass fiddle or bass viol (contrabass). **6,** referring to the key of a transposing instrument, it indicates a transposition an octave lower than the nearest pitch to C of the given key, as B♭ bass. **7,** a valved brass instrument in E♭ or E♭ bass found in military and brass bands. Cf. TUBA.

bassanello a 16th-c. double-reed instrument similar to the SHAWM, built in various sizes.

bass-bar an oblong piece of wood glued to the underside of the top (belly) of an instrument of the bowed string family, providing support for pressure at the bridge.

bass-baritone a high bass male voice combining the range and qualities of the BASS and BARITONE voices.

bass cittern a large CITTERN with double pegbox and unstopped bass strings like the ARCHLUTE.

bass clarinet a CLARINET, usu. in B♭, pitched an octave below the soprano (standard) clarinet. There are two principal systems of notation: the "French system" uses only the treble clef, sounding a 9th lower than written; and the "German system" uses treble and bass clefs, the notes sounding a whole tone lower than written.

bass clef an F CLEF on the fourth line of the staff, used for bass and baritone voices, the left hand of the piano and lower-pitched instruments.

bass drum 1, a large double-headed FRAME DRUM used in orchestras and bands and played with large padded beaters. **2,** the largest STEEL DRUM, using a full-size barrel.

basse-chantante [shä'tät] (Fr., singing bass) in the Baroque, a vocal bass as opposed to the instrumental bass; in the 19th c., a higher, lighter bass voice. Also, *basso cantante* (It.).

basse danse (Fr., low dance) a dignified court couple-dance of the late Middle Ages and early Renaissance, associated most often with the Burgundian court. Its instr. accompaniment incl. variation sets, improvisations over a ground bass and suites. It was usu. paired with a faster ALTA DANSA. Also, *bassa danza* (It.) Cf. SALTARELLO, GALLIARD, PIVA, PAVAN, PASSAMEZZO.

bassa musica *also,* **bas** [bä] (It., soft music) a medieval term for music produced by softer instruments, incl. viols and fiddles, recorders, harps and zithers; distinguished from ALTA MUSICA. Also, *basse musique.*

basset clarinet a soprano CLARINET with an extended bass range, for which Mozart's Clarinet Concerto, among other works, was written. Cf. BASSET HORN.

basset horn a tenor CLARINET in F, invented around 1770, used by Mozart (esp. in his masonic music) and by R. Strauss. Cf. BASSET CLARINET.

basse-trompette an upright metal SERPENT invented in 1810.

Bassett, Leslie (1923–) Amer. composer and teacher, stud. of Finney and others, since 1952 on the faculty of the U. of Michigan, whose electronic studio he founded. He won the Pulitzer Prize in 1966 for his *Variations for Orchestra.*

bass flute a FLUTE in C pitched an octave below the concert flute. The term is sometimes erroneously used to refer to the alto flute.

bass horn an upright variety of SERPENT invented in the late 18th c., used at that time in wind bands.

bass line see BASS (2,).

bass lute ARCHLUTE.

basso (It.) a BASS singer, esp. an operatic bass.

bass oboe BARITONE OBOE.

basso buffo (It.) an operatic BASS singer specializing in comic roles.

basso cantante (It.) BASSE-CHANTANTE.

basso continuo *also,* **continuo** (It.) **1,** a group of two or more instruments that *realizes* the bass line of a polyphonic composition, usu. of the 17th and 18th c. It usu. comprises a sustained pitch instrument, such as cello or bass viol, which plays the bass line as written, and a chordal instrument, such as organ or theorbo, which fills in the harmonies above the bass. The bass line may have figures to indicate the desired chords (see FIGURED bass). Also, *thoroughbass.* **2,** the bass line played by the basso continuo (1,).

basso da camera (It.) a small CONTRABASS.

bassonore a BASSOON with a large bell, invented c1830 for use in military bands.

bassoon a tenor or bass double-reed WOODWIND instrument with a long, jointed, doubled, conical body and a long, curved bocal. There are two differing key systems, the German or "Heckel" system and the French or "Buffet" system. The bassoon first appeared in the mid-17th c. as a successor to the earlier DULCIAN. Cf. POMMER, HECKEL.

basso ostinato (It.) GROUND (1,).

basso profondo (It.) a deep bass voice.

basso seguente (It.) an early form of BASSO CONTINUO that duplicated on a continuo instr. (such as the organ) the lowest line of a polyphonic vocal composition.

bass viol 1, a 6- or 7-string bowed instrument of the VIOL family, similar to the modern cello. Cf. VIOLA DA GAMBA. **2,** a bass VIOLIN, tuned like a cello. Also, *church bass.*

bata a Cuban two-headed CONICAL DRUM.

Bath Festival an annual series of concerts held since 1948 in Bath, England, orig. devoted to 18th-c. music, but now encompassing a broader repertory.

baton a thin, tapered stick or wand used for conducting a band or orch.

Batson, Flora (1864–1906) Amer. soprano. She sang with James Bergen's Star Concert Company and the South Before the War Company and appeared before Pope Leo XIII and the royal families of Hawaii and England. Her concert repertoire included ballads and 19th-c. opera arias.

battaglia [bät'tä-lyä] (It., battle) a type of work descriptive of battle sounds, popular from the 16th to 18th c. Some famous examples of the genre are Janequin's *La guerre,* Monteverdi's *Il combattimento di Tancredi e Clorinda* and Beethoven's *Wellington's Victory.*

battement ['bät-mä] (Fr., beating) a type of vibrato ORNAMENT.

battery 1, the percussion section of an orch. **2,** the baroque term for playing blocked chords as arpeggios. See ABBREVIATIONS.

Battle, Kathleen (1948–) Amer. soprano, stud. of Franklin Bens. She has sung frequently at the Metropolitan Opera since the early 1970s, appearing in such roles as Despina (*Così fan tutte*) and Sophie (*Der Rosenkavalier*), and has appeared with most major American and European opera companies and orchestras.

Battle Hymn of the Republic the title of a Civil War poem by Julia Ward Howe set to the music of "GLORY, HALLELUJAH." It was first published in 1862. Cf. JOHN BROWN'S BODY, which is set to the same tune.

battle music see BATTAGLIA.

Battle Symphony WELLINGTON'S VICTORY.

battuta (It., beaten) **1,** BEAT. **2,** MEASURE; *ritmo di tre (quattro) battute,* three-(or four-)bar rhythm, i.e., with the main stress falling on the first beat of every third (or fourth) bar. — **a battuta,** (It.) by the beat, i.e., in strict time. —**senza battuta,** (It.) without beat, i.e., freely.

Baudrier, Yves [bō'dryā, ēv] (1906–) French composer, stud. of Messiaen and Daniel-Lesur and joint founder of LA JEUNE FRANCE. His best work was for film, esp. *Le musicien dans la cité* (1937), written for an imaginary film.

Bauer, Harold (1873–1951) English-born Amer. pianist, stud. of Paderewski, a frequent performer in a trio with violinist Thibaud and cellist Casals. He founded the Beethoven Assoc. of New York (1918–41).

Bauer, Marion (Eugenie) (1887–1955) Amer. composer and teacher, stud. of Nadia Boulanger and others. She was co-founder of the American Music Guild (1921) and was on the faculties of New York U. and the Juilliard School.

Baur, Clara (1835–1912) Ger. music teacher, founder of the Cincinnati Conservatory (1867).

Bax, Sir **Arnold** (1883–1953) prolific English composer of tone poems, symphonies and chamber music.

Bay Psalm Book common name for the first book of English metrical psalms printed in America and the first book in the English language printed in No. America. It was published by Stephen Day in Massachusetts in 1640.

Baxter, J(esse) R(andall, Jr.) (1887–1960) Amer. publisher and composer of gospel songs, co-founder in 1926 of the Stamps-Baxter Music Company of Texas.

Bayreuth Festival an annual summer festival in Bayreuth, Ger., founded in 1876. The festival is dedicated to the performance of the works of Wagner, who designed a theater (*Festspielhaus*) specifically for this purpose with an unusual hooded orch. pit.

Bayreuth tuba see TUBA.

BBC British broadcasting corporation.
b.c. *abbr.* Basso continuo.
Beach, Mrs. H.H.A. (Amy Marcy
Cheney) (1867–1944) Amer. concert
pianist and composer. Her *Gaelic
Symphony*, premiered by the Boston
Symphony in 1896, was the first symphonic work by an Amer. woman.
Best known of her many works are
her songs, notable for their melodic
inventiveness.
Beach Boys, The popular male vocal
quintet formed in 1961 in California,
whose songs idealized the pleasures
of California surfing, dating and driving. Their many hits incl. "Surfin'
U.S.A." (1963) and "Surfer Girl"
(1963).
beam a horizontal line connecting
the stems of notes of eighth note or
smaller value. See Note.
Bear, The 1, comic opera in 1 act by
Walton to a libretto by Paul Dehn and
the composer based on the play by
Chekhov. Premiere, Aldeburgh 1967.
Cf. the Boor. **2,** popular name for the
Symphony No. 82 in C major (1786)
by Haydn.
bearcat in jazz, a type of boogie-
woogie piano rolling bass figure.
Beardslee, Bethany (1927–) Amer.
soprano, a specialist in 20th-c., as
well as medieval and Renaissance,
music.
bearing a type of Slide (1,).
beat 1, the basic pulse of measured
music; also, the movement of the
hand or baton of a conductor indicating that pulse. **2,** a name for various
English ornaments; in the 17th c., a
lower Appoggiatura; in the 18th c.,
a Mordent. **3,** a pulsation resulting
from the interference of two sound
waves of slightly differing frequencies, equal to the difference; used in
tuning instruments.
beating reed a Reed covering a hole
in an instrument and caused to vibrate by air passing through the hole.
See also Free reed.
Beatles, The a remarkably popular
English rock group formed in Liverpool in 1956, whose music combined

elements of blues, rhythm and blues,
and rock and roll. In 1967 they pro-
duced *Sergeant Pepper's Lonely
Hearts Club Band*, an influential recording in which all the songs were
designed to produce a unified effect.
The group disbanded in 1970.
Beatrice and Benedict (Fr., *Béatrice et
Bénédict*) opera in 2 acts by Berlioz
to his own libretto, based on Shakespeare's *Much Ado about Nothing*.
Premiere, Baden-Baden, Ger. 1862.
Beaudet, Jean-Marie [bō'dā] (1908–71)
Canadian conductor, pianist and organist. He was program dir. for the
CBC in the 1940s, taught at the Montreal Conservatory and appeared as
conductor of most Canadian orchestras and as accompanist to singers
incl. Ezio Pinza and Raoul Jobin.
Beaux Arts Trio [bō-zärts] an Amer.
piano trio formed in 1955.
bebop see Bop.
bebung ['bā-bûng] (Ger.) a tremolo effect produced on a clavichord by con-
tinually varying the pressure on the
key after a note is struck. It is indicated by a series of staccato dots covered with a slur.
bécarre [bā'kär] (Fr.) Natural.
Bechet, Sidney [be'shā] (?1897–1959)
Amer. jazz clarinettist and soprano
saxophonist from New Orleans, the
first true jazz virtuoso. He played
with King Oliver and other bands in
Amer. and Europe and was the opening act of the Club Basha in New York
in 1926. He lived in France from 1951
until his death.
Bechstein ['beç-shtīn] a Ger. firm of
piano makers founded in Berlin in
1853, acquired by Baldwin in 1963.
The concert hall next to their London
offices became Wigmore hall in
1901.
Becken ['bek-ən] (Ger.) Cymbals.
Becker, John J(oseph) (1886–1961)
Amer. composer, one of the American five, an active advocate of American music. Among his compositions
are large-scale stage works combining
music, dance and visual elements.
Beckwith, John (1927–) Canadian
composer and teacher, stud. of Nadia

Boulanger, on the faculty of the U. of Toronto since 1952 and a founder of the Canadian League of Composers. His works incl. 2 operas, many choral and vocal works, concertos for piano and horn, chamber music and works for radio.

Bedford, David (Vickerman) (1937–) English composer, stud. of Nono and Berkeley, known for his vocal and instrumental works, esp. works for children, often involving improvisation.

Beecham, Sir **Thomas** (1879–1961) English conductor born of a wealthy family. He founded his own orch. in 1909 and opera company in 1915. In 1932 he founded the London Philharmonic and became artistic director of Covent Garden (which had absorbed his own company). During the war years he was conductor of the Seattle SO, then in 1946 he founded the Royal Philharmonic in London. A specialist in the works of Mozart and Haydn, he was a friend and promoter of Delius and noted for his wit.

Beecroft, Norma (Marian) (1934–) Canadian composer, stud. of Weinzweig, Maderna and Copland. She worked from 1954 to 1969 with the CBC as a producer and music consultant and was a co-founder of New Music Concerts in Toronto (1971).

Beeson, Jack (Hamilton) (1921–) Amer. composer, esp. of opera, stud. of Rogers, Hanson and Bartók, on the faculty of Columbia since 1945. His works incl. *Lizzie Borden* and *Captain Jinks of the Horse Marines* (operas), choral music, songs and instrumental music.

Beethoven, Ludwig van (1770–1827) prolific Ger. composer, a towering figure of 19th-c. European music. He studied with Christian Gottlob Neefe in his native Bonn and played in the court orchestras. In 1792 he went to Vienna, where he studied briefly with Haydn, at length with J.G. Albrechtsberger and perhaps with Salieri, and established his reputation as a keyboard virtuoso. He was determined to survive as a free-lance musician, a task that was rendered more difficult by the gradual onset of incurable deafness, which eventually ended his career as a performer. Dedicating himself principally to composition from the early 1800s, he supported himself partly by public concerts, in which he presented his works and his skill as an improviser, and partly through dedication fees, sales of publications and generous gifts from patrons.

His creative life has often been divided into three periods—the first covering his youth in Bonn and his early years in Vienna (1782–1800); the second, or middle period, covering the more heroic and turbulent orchestral works (1800–12); the last spanning his later years of more serious, introspective works, esp. many of the string quartets (1812–27).

Beethoven's large output of works in all genres—theatrical music is the least well represented—includes much occasional music, some of it rather mediocre. In every genre, however, are works of the greatest mastery, and the finest of them are unmatched in originality and expressiveness. His works incl. *Fidelio* (opera), incidental music (*Egmont, The Ruins of Athens*), 2 ballets, 9 symphonies, 2 mass settings (*Mass in C, Missa Solemnis*), *Christ on the Mount of Olives* (oratorio) and other choral works, 5 concertos for piano, a violin concerto, string quartets and quintets, chamber music with winds, sonatas for violin and cello, piano trios, 32 piano sonatas, many variation sets for piano (*Diabelli Variations, Eroica Variations*), works for piano solo and piano duet, dance sets, concert arias and songs, and canons.

befa the note B♭ in the HEXACHORD system.

Beggar's Holiday musical by Duke Ellington, libretto by Jean LaTouche based on *The Beggar's Opera*. Premiere, New York 1946.

Beggar's Opera, The ballad opera in 3 acts by Pepusch, libretto by John Gay, suggested by the writings of Jonathan Swift. Premiere, London 1728,

Later versions by Frederic Austin (1920), Edward J. Dent (1944), Benjamin Britten (1948) and Kurt Weill (1928; see THREEPENNY OPERA). The plot details the exploits of Macheath, dashing captain of a robber band, and his wife Polly Peachum, daughter of the band's leader.

Begleitung [be'glī-tûng] (Ger.) ACCOMPANIMENT.

beguine [be'gēn] a popular dance of Martinique, similar to the RHUMBA.

Beiderbecke, (Leon) **Bix** (1903–31) Amer. jazz cornet player and composer, one of the first great white improvisers, who combined jazz with elements of French impressionism. He played with trombonist Frank Trumbauer in various groups, incl. the Paul Whiteman band. In his last years he worked with the Dorsey brothers and with Benny Goodman.

Beinum, Eduard van VAN BEINUM, EDUARD.

Beissel, (Johann) Conrad (1690–1768) German-born Amer. composer of sacred music for the Ephrata cloister near Philadelphia, for which he devised his own principles of harmony and notation.

bel canto (It., beautiful singing) a style of operatic singing characteristic of the 18th and early 19th c. stressing evenness of tone production, beautiful sound and an agile vocal technique. The term is often used in reference to the works of Bellini, Rossini, Donizetti and others.

Belcher, Supply (1751–1836) Amer. composer and tunebook compiler, heralded as the "Handel of Maine" in 1796.

belebt [be'lāpt] (Ger.) lively.

Belknap, Daniel (1771–1815) Amer. composer, tunebook compiler and singing teacher, publisher of *The Evangelical Harmony* (1800).

bell 1, a hollow metallic IDIOPHONE of open or closed form dating from ancient times and producing a complex sound by vibration when struck by a hammer, clapper, pellet or suspended ball. The pitch of a bell's fundamental tone may be determined by

Bells

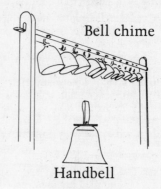

Bell chime

Handbell

Church bell

the size of the bell or by its thickness, greater size or thickness resulting in a lower sound. Iron and bronze are the most common metals for bells. See also CHIME, BELL CHIME, GONG, SLEIGH BELL, HANDBELL, CARILLON, ORCHESTRAL BELLS, JINGLES, CHANGE RINGING. **2,** the part of an open-ended wind instrument opposite the mouthpiece, often flaring open in a bell-like manner.

Bell, Leslie (Richard) (1906–62) Canadian choral conductor and composer, founder and conductor of the Leslie Bell Singers, and music critic for the *Toronto Daily Star* (1946–62).

Bell Anthem popular name for the cantata "Rejoice in the Lord alway" (c.1684) by Purcell.

bell chime a set of tuned BELLS usu. hung on a rack and making a scale, particularly popular in Asia.

bell harp a type of PSALTERY with wire strings that is swung while being

played, producing an undulating tone.
Bellini, Vincenzo (1801–35) Italian composer of opera (*Norma, La Sonnambula*) and other vocal music, stud. of Nicola Zingarelli. He is noted esp. for his flowing melodies, ornamented in the style of Rossini, and for his attention to dramatic values in his works.

bell lyre *also,* **bell-lyra** a portable GLOCKENSPIEL mounted in a lyre-shaped frame, used esp. in marching bands.

Bell Quartet see FIFTHS QUARTET.

bell ringing general term for CHANGE RINGING, carillon playing (stationary bells) and handbell ringing. Handbell ringing, much more than the other two, has taken on a distinctively American style, rather than maintaining the techniques of its European origin.

bells, tubular TUBULAR BELLS.

Bellson, Louis (Paul) (Louis Balassoni) (1924–) Amer. jazz composer and drummer. He has played with the big bands of Benny Goodman, Tommy Dorsey, Harry James and Duke Ellington.

Bell Song the *Légende de la fille du paria* (Fr., The Legend of the Daughter of the Leper), an aria sung by Lakmé in the opera of the same name by Delibes, in which the singer's coloratura imitates the glockenspiel.

Bell Symphony the Symphony No. 2 in A minor (1943) by Khatchaturian.

Bells of Zlonice the Symphony No. 1 in C minor (1865) by Dvořák.

belly the top surface of a stringed instrument, usu. arched in bowed instruments, flat in plucked instruments.

Belmont Music Publishers Los Angeles publishing co. founded in the 1960s by Gertrud and Lawrence Schoenberg, wife and son of composer Arnold Schoenberg.

Belshazzar oratorio (1745) by Handel to a text by Jennens based on Herodotus and Xenophon.

Belshazzar's Feast 1, incidental music (1906) by Sibelius for a play by Hjalmar Procopé. **2,** oratorio for baritone, chorus and orch. (1931) by Walton to a text, mostly Biblical, arranged by Osbert Sitwell.

Belwin-Mills an Amer. music publishing co., founded in 1918.

Belyayef Circle a group of composers which assembled in St. Petersburg on Fridays in the 1880s, incl. Glazunov, Rimsky-Korsakov, Borodin, Scriabin and others.

bemolle [bā′mol-le] (It.) FLAT.

bend see PITCH BEND.

Benecke, Tex (Gordon) (1914–) Amer. jazz singer and tenor saxophonist with the Glenn Miller orch. from 1938 until World War II. His is the voice on "Chattanooga Choo Choo" and other hits. After the war he took over the Miller orch., then formed his own band.

benedicamus Domino a versicle of the CANONICAL HOURS of the Roman Catholic rite, followed by the response *Deo gratias.*

Benedict, Sir Julius (1804–85) Ger.-born English composer, conductor and pianist, stud. of Weber. He was conductor at the Lyceum Theatre and Drury Lane and was Jenny Lind's accompanist on her American tour in 1850. His works incl. the once very popular opera *The Lily of Killarney* (1862).

benedictus (Lat., blessed) **1,** part of the SANCTUS after the first Hosanna. **2,** the first word of four canticles sung at Lauds.

Ben-Haim (Frankenburger), **Paul** (1897–1984) Ger.-born Israeli composer, whose works combine Western with Jewish and Middle Eastern folk traditions.

Benjamin, Arthur (1893–1960) Australian pianist and composer, stud. of Stanford, strongly influenced by the rhythms of Latin American music (*Jamaican Rumba*). He was Britten's piano teacher.

Bennett, Richard Rodney (1936–) English pianist and composer of works for stage, concert hall and film, stud. of Berkeley, Ferguson and Boulez.

Bennett, Robert Russell (1894–1981)

Amer. composer and arranger, stud. of Carl Busch and Boulanger. He wrote many orchestral and chamber works, as well as operas, but he was best known for his orchestrations of Broadway musicals and suites drawn from them.

Benson, Warren (Frank) (1924–) Amer. composer. He has taught at Ithaca College, NY, and at the Eastman School since 1967. He has written works in all genres except dramatic music and has written several books on composition.

Benvenuto Cellini opera in 2 acts by Berlioz to a libretto by Léon de Wailly and Auguste Barbier, based on the life of the famous sculptor. Premiere, Paris 1838.

Benzell, Mimi (1922–70) Amer. soprano, stud. of Olga Eisner. She debuted in 1945 at the Metropolitan Opera, where her roles included Blonde (*Abduction from the Seraglio*) and Gilda (*Rigoletto*). After 1949 she concentrated on popular music in musical theater, concerts, radio and night club appearances.

Berberian, Cathy (Catherine) (1925–83) Amer. mezzo-soprano, specialist in 20th-c. music, esp. that of Luciano Berio (her husband for 6 years), but her repertory also incl. 17th-c. opera and 19th-c. salon music.

berceuse [ber'søz] (Fr., cradlesong) a vocal or instrumental composition of a soothing, rocking nature, usu. in triple or compound meter.

Berg, Alban (1885–1935) Austrian composer, stud. of Schoenberg and an early proponent of atonal and then 12-tone music. His relatively small output belies its extensive influence; his two operas (*Wozzeck, Lulu*) are both masterpieces of the 20th-c. repertory. A special quality of Berg's work is his utilization of classical forms and, at times, diatonic harmonic implications in his 12-tone or atonal works. Cf. SECOND VIENNESE SCHOOL. His works incl. 2 operas, violin concerto, piano sonata, songs, chamber concerto, *Lyric Suite* for string quartet.

bergamasca a 16th- and 17th-c. Italian dance. Its music is usu. in duple time and based on a popular tune on the harmonic pattern I-IV-V-I. This pattern was used by many composers as the basis for variations.

Berganza (Vargas), Teresa (1935–) Spanish mezzo-soprano, stud. of Lola Rodriguez Aragon (a pupil of Elisabeth Schumann). She has appeared internationally in concert and in opera, specializing in roles by Rossini and Mozart.

Berger, Arthur (Victor) (1912–) Amer. critic and composer, stud. of Piston and Milhaud. He was co-founder of the journal *Perspectives of New Music* and music critic for various newspapers, incl. the *New York Herald Tribune* (1946–53). He has taught at Brandeis and the New England Conservatory. His works, mostly for chamber ensembles, combine a diatonic harmonic idiom with serial techniques.

Berger, Jean (1909–) German-born composer and musicologist, resident in France and then the U.S. He became a U.S. citizen in 1943. He is best known for his choral music, and his *Brazilian Psalm* (1941) remains part of the Amer. choral repertory.

bergerette (Fr.) a pastoral song or dance of the 16th c.; also an 18th-c. French air imitating this style. See BRUNETTE.

Bergonzi, Carlo (1924–) Italian tenor, whose extensive repertory includes the operatic roles of Verdi, Donizetti, Massenet and *verismo* works. His U.S. debut was in Chicago, and he sang regularly at the Metropolitan Opera from 1956 to 1974.

Bergreihen ['berk"rī-ən] (Ger.) Ger. popular songs, esp. of the 16th and 17th c., on either sacred or secular themes.

Bergsma, William (Lawrence) (1921–) Amer. composer, stud. of Hanson and Rogers. He has been on the faculty of the Juilliard School (1946–63) and the U. of Washington at Seattle (1963–present). His works incl. operas, ballets, and orchestral and chamber works.

Berigan, Bunny (Roland Bernard) (1908–42) Amer. swing trumpeter and bandleader. He played with several important bands (Paul Whiteman, Benny Goodman) before forming his own in 1937. He was influenced principally by Louis Armstrong and Bix Beiderbecke, whose styles he was the first to fuse successfully.

Berio, Luciano (1925–) Italian composer, stud. of Ghedini and Dallapiccola. A regular participant at Darmstadt (1954–59), he ran a series of concerts with Maderna (*Incontri musicali*) from 1956 to 1960. From 1965 to 1971 he taught at the Juilliard School, where he founded the Juilliard Ensemble. His works span a variety of styles and media, incl. electronic music.

Berkeley, Sir **Lennox (Randall Francis)** (1903–89) prolific English composer of music in all genres, stud. of Nadia Boulanger. He was a close friend of Britten and a teacher at the Royal Academy of Music, where he taught, among others, Tavener, Bedford and Maw. His later works espouse the 12-tone technique, but a tonal center is usu. suggested.

Berklee College of Music an eminent school of jazz in Boston, founded in 1945 as Schillinger House.

Berkshire Music Festival see TANGLEWOOD.

Berlin, Irving (Baline, Israel) (1888–1989) Russian-born Amer. songwriter, son of a Jewish cantor. He began as a street singer and never learned to read music. The name "Berlin" resulted from a printer's error on the cover of his first song. He wrote numerous Broadway revues and film scores, and over 1500 songs, incl. such hits as "Alexander's Ragtime Band," "Easter Parade," "White Christmas" and "There's No Business Like Show Business."

Berlin Philharmonic Orchestra orch. founded by a group of musicians in Berlin in 1882 under conductor Franz Wüllner; its principal conductors have included Joachim, von Bülow, Nikisch, Furtwängler, Celibidache, von Karajan and Abbado.

Berlin School name sometimes given to a group of composers in Berlin during the second half of the 18th c. at the court of Frederick the Great, incl. J.J. Quantz, J.G. Graun and C.P.E. Bach. The name is also sometimes used to refer to a younger group of lieder composers active at the turn of the 19th c., incl. J.F. Reichardt and C.F. Zelter.

Berlioz, (Louis) Hector (1803–69) innovative French composer, conductor and music critic, stud. of Le Sueur and Reicha. He won the Prix de Rome in 1830 after four attempts. His music, because of its originality, was not generally well accepted, and he had to supplement his income by being a critic. He was more successful in winning acceptance of his work on his many concert tours abroad. His use of vast instrumental and vocal resources is legendary. His works incl. *Benvenuto Cellini, Les Troyens, Béatrice et Bénédict* (opera), *Symphonie fantastique, Harold en Italie* (symphonies), *Roman Carnival* and other overtures, *Grande messe des morts* (Requiem) and other choral works, solo scenes and songs. He also wrote a highly influential treatise on orchestration (1843).

Bernac (Bertin), **Pierre** (1899–1979) French baritone and educator, noted for his interpretation of French chanson, esp. the works of FRANCIS POULENC, with whom he often performed. He was the teacher of Gérard Souzay.

Bernal Jiménez, Miguel (1910–56) Mexican composer and choral director. He is credited with the revival of Mexican sacred music.

Bernardi, Mario (1930–) Canadian pianist and conductor. He studied in Venice and at the Royal Conservatory in Toronto. He was musical dir. of Sadler's Wells in London (1966–69) and founding conductor of the National Arts Centre Orch. in Ottawa

(1968) and has conducted frequently for the New York City Opera. Since 1980 he has been music dir. of the Calgary SO.

Bernstein, Elmer (1922–   ) Amer. composer and pianist, stud. of Sessions and Wolpe. He has produced over 70 major film scores, usu. with a distinct jazz flavor, incl. *The Man with the Golden Arm* (1955).

Bernstein, Leonard (1918–90) eminent Amer. conductor, composer and pianist, stud. of Burlingame Hill, Piston and Reiner. He was a protégé of Serge Koussevitzky at Tanglewood. He succeeded Mitropoulos as musical director of the New York Philharmonic (1957–69). As a composer he wrote ballets, operas and concert works, as well as musical theater scores, incl. *West Side Story* (1957) and *On the Town* (1954).

Berry, Chu (1908–41) Amer. jazz tenor saxophone player. He played with Benny Carter, Charlie Johnson, Spike Hughes and Cab Calloway. His playing style was strongly influenced by Coleman Hawkins.

Berry, Chuck (Anderson, Charles Edward) (1926–   ) Amer. rhythm-and-blues and rock-and-roll songwriter, singer and guitarist. His career as a songwriter declined in the 1960s, but he has been enjoying a renaissance as a performer since the 1980s.

Berwald, Franz (Adolf) (1796–1868) eminent Swedish violinist and prolific composer of symphonies, operas, choral works, chamber music and songs.

Bes (Ger.) B double flat.

Besoyan, Rick (Richard) (1924–70) Amer. composer and lyricist, whose best-known score was for the off-Broadway operetta spoof, *Little Mary Sunshine* (1959).

Bethlehem Bach Choir a choral organization founded by J. Fred Wolle in Bethlehem, Pennsylvania. Since 1900 the Choir has presented the annual **Bethlehem Bach Festival**, which in its first season gave the Amer. premiere performance of Bach's *Mass in B minor*.

Bethune, Thomas (Green; "Blind Tom") (1849–1908) Amer. pianist and composer, born a slave and sightless, self-taught in music. He toured Europe and the U.S. as a piano virtuoso and improviser, making a fortune for his master and later guardian, James Bethune.

bewegt [be'vākt] (Ger., agitated; moved) AGITATO.—**mässig bewegt**, (Ger.) MODERATO.

b fa BEFA.

B flat the PITCH (B♭) a half step below B, the enharmonic equivalent of A sharp. The symbol for FLAT comes orig. from the note-letter b, which was the first note to be altered chromatically.

B-flat bass TENOR TUBA.

bhaya a small Indian KETTLEDRUM, part of the TABLA.

Biber, Heinrich Johann Franz von (1644–1704) Austrian violinist and composer, the most celebrated violin virtuoso of the 17th c. He wrote many sonatas for violin, using both normal tuning and SCORDATURA, as well as sacred and secular vocal and instrumental works.

Bible, Frances (L.) (1927–   ) Amer. mezzo-soprano, noted for her interpretation of trouser roles, incl. Hansel, Octavian (*Der Rosenkavalier*) and Cherubino (*The Marriage of Figaro*). She sang with the New York City Opera from 1948 to 1977.

bible regal a small 17th-c. foldable PORTATIVE ORGAN built in the shape of a book.

bicinium a DUO composed for teaching; also, any 2-part composition of the Renaissance or early Baroque.

Biedermeier ['bē-dər-mī-ər] (Ger.) orig., a type of 19th-c. bourgeois furniture; the term has come to be applied to sentimental works of music, literature and painting.

biff on a brass instrument, to miss a high note.

Bigard, Barney (Albany Leon) (1906–80) Amer. jazz clarinetist and tenor saxophonist with the King Oliver (1924–27) and Duke Ellington (1928–42) orchestras.

big band a term for a jazz ensemble consisting of multiple saxophones and brass with percussion, esp. during the SWING era. The bands of the 1920s were usu. comprised of 10–12 players; by the 1940s the big bands had grown to 20 or more players.

Biggs, E(dward George) Power (1906–77) English-born Amer. organist specializing in concert and radio recitals of a broad repertory.

Bikel, Theodore (1924–   ) Viennese-born Amer. actor and singer, known for his performances in *The Sound of Music, Fiddler on the Roof, Zorba* and others.

Billings, William (1746–1800) Amer. composer and singing teacher in Boston, a tanner by trade, largely self-taught in music. He published a number of volumes of vocal compositions for teaching, the best known of which was his last, *The Continental Harmony* (1794).

Billy Budd historical opera in 4 acts by Britten to a libretto by E.M. Forster and Eric Crozier based on a novella by Melville. Premiere, London 1951. The young innocent sailor Billy Budd is provoked by the embittered master-at-arms Claggart into killing, an act for which he must die. The opera is unusual in that it uses only male voices.

Billy the Kid ballet (1938) with music by Copland, incorporating several cowboy tunes. The composer extracted a suite for concert performance.

Bilson, Malcolm (1935–   ) Amer. pianist and fortepianist, on the faculty of Cornell since 1968.

binary form a FORM consisting of two complementary parts, each of which may be repeated (AB or AABB). See BAR FORM, ROUNDED BINARY FORM.

Binchois, Gilles [bē′shwä] (?1400–?1460) Flemish composer of sacred and secular vocal works, esp. rondeaux and ballades, a member of the Burgundian court chapel (?1425–?1455).

bind (Brit.) TIE.

Bing, Sir **Rudolf** (1902–1988) Aus-trian-born English opera impresario, general manager of Glyndebourne Opera (1935–49) and the Metropolitan Opera (1950–72). He was also a founder of the Edinburgh Festival.

Bingham, Seth (1882–1972) Amer. organist and composer of choral, orchestral and chamber works, stud. of Parker, d'Indy, Widor and Guilmant. He was a member of the faculty of Columbia (1919–54) and organist of the Madison Ave. Presbyterian Church in New York for 35 years.

Binkerd, Gordon (Ware) (1916–   ) Amer. composer of instrumental, choral and chamber works, stud. of Rogers and Piston. He was professor at the U. of Illinois from 1947 to 1971. His works are in a highly chromatic tonal idiom.

Binkley, Thomas (Eden) (1931–   ) Amer. musicologist and performer of early music. He founded the Studio für alte Musik in Munich in 1959 (later called the Studio der frühen Musik). He has been dir. of the Early Music Institute at Indiana U. since 1979.

Bird nickname for jazz saxophonist CHARLIE PARKER.

Birdland a cabaret on Broadway in New York famous as a jazz center from its opening in 1948 until the 1970s, immortalized in the song "Lullaby of Birdland" by pianist George Shearing. The cabaret's name is a tribute to saxophonist Charlie "Bird" Parker.

Bird Quartet popular name for the String Quartet in C major, Op. 33 No. 3 (1782), by F.J. Haydn.

Birmingham Festival an annual music festival held in Birmingham, England, from 1768 until World War I. The festival always featured the music of Handel, and in the mid-19th c. Mendelssohn's oratorios (as well as other less familiar choral works) were also made a regular feature.

Birtwistle, Sir **Harrison** (1934–   ) English composer, stud. of Richard Hall. He was a co-founder of the New Music Manchester Group and has been associated with the experimental groups the Pierrot Players (1967) and Matrix. He won the Grawemeier Award in 1987. His works are often ritualistic and deal with the subjects of death and rebirth.

bis [bēs] (Fr., twice) **1**, an indication that a passage is to be repeated. **2**, a call for an ENCORE.

bisbigliando [bēz-bē'lyän-dō] (It., whispering) a tremolando effect on the harp produced by rapidly repeating notes or chords alternately on adjacent strings tuned to the same pitches, usu. *pianissimo* in the upper register.

Bispham, David (Scull) (1857–1921) Amer. baritone, noted for his comic acting and singing (e.g., Beckmesser in Wagner's *Die Meistersinger*). He advocated the use of English language in opera performances and the performance of works by American composers. The Bispham Memorial Medal was established in 1921 by the Opera Society of America for operas in English by Amer. composers.

bitonality see POLYTONALITY.

biwa ('bē-wä) a Japanese, plucked four-stringed LUTE, derived from the Chinese P'I-P'A and dating from the 7th c. There are a variety of tunings and playing styles associated with different uses.

Bizet, Georges [bē'zä, zhorzh] (1838–75) French composer, stud. of Pierre Zimmerman and Halévy. He won the Prix de Rome in 1857. After 1860 he produced mostly operas, songs and piano works, sometimes with success (the opera *Ja jolie fille de Perth*, the "mélodrame" *L'arlésienne*), sometimes with failure (the operas *Djamileh* and *Carmen*).

Björling, Jussi (Johan) **(Jonaton)** ['byør-ling] (1911–60) Swedish tenor, son and father of professional tenors. He was a regular member of the Stockholm Opera until 1938 and an international celebrity from the late 1930s until his death. His repertory emphasized Verdi and Puccini roles.

Bkl. *abbr.* (Ger.) basse-Klarinette (see BASS CLARINET).

Blacher, Boris ['blä-khər] (1903–75) Ger. composer, stud. of Friedrich Koch, after World War II teacher at and then dir. of the Berlin Hochschule für Musik. His students incl. von Einem and Reimann. His many works incl. operas, ballets, orchestral, choral and chamber music, and music for electronic instruments.

Black, Robert (Carlisle) (1950–) Amer. pianist and conductor, stud. of Beveridge Webster and Sessions. He has been conductor for the New York New Music Ensemble (from 1975), Speculum Musicae (from 1978) and Prism (founded by Black in 1983). He is noted for his performances of music by Shapey and others.

Black Artists Group an avant-garde jazz ensemble formed in St. Louis in the late 1960s.

Blackbirds of 1928 musical revue by Jimmy McHugh, lyrics by Dorothy Fields. Premiere, New York 1928. A popular Negro revue, incl. the hit song "I Can't Give You Anything But Love." There were new editions of the revue in 1930, 1933 and 1939.

black bottom *also*, **black shuffle** a ballroom dance performed to ragtime music, with wiggling of the hips and body. Cf. LINDY, SHIMMY.

Black-Key Étude popular name for the Étude for piano Op. 10 No. 5 in G♭ major (1830) by Chopin, in which the right hand plays only on the black keys.

Black Mass Sonata (Fr., *Messe noire*) the piano sonata Op. 68 No. 9 (1912–13) by Scriabin.

Black Maskers incidental music (1923) by Sessions for the play by Andreyev. Sessions later extracted an orchestral suite from the score.

Black Nativity musical version of the Christmas story by Langston Hughes with gospel music by Alex Bradford, Marion Williams and Princess Stewart. Premiere, New York 1961.

blackstick slang name for the CLARINET.

Blackwood, Easley (1933–) Amer. pianist and composer, stud. of Messiaen, Hindemith and Boulanger. He has been on the faculty of the U. of Chicago since 1958. As a composer he has progressed from a highly complex atonal style to a richly chromatic tonal idiom. As a pianist he is noted for his performances of 20th-c. repertory, esp. the works of Ives, Boulez and the Second Viennese School. He is an expert in the theory and use of microtonal and nontempered tunings.

bladder pipe a medieval form of BAGPIPE.

Blake, Blind (Arthur) (?1895–1935) Amer. ragtime and blues singer and guitarist. He was active and influential as a soloist and studio musician in Chicago and Detroit.

Blake, Eubie (James Hubert) (1883–1983) Amer. ragtime pianist and composer of songs and musical comedies, incl. *Shuffle Along* (1921). His piano work was influential in the development of the STRIDE PIANO style.

Blake, George E. (?1775–1871) English-born Amer. music publisher and engraver. He operated a circulating music library out of his publishing house and published the first Amer. edition of Handel's *Messiah* (c. 1830).

Blakey, Art (1919–90) Amer. jazz drummer. He worked with a number of big bands before forming the JAZZ MESSENGERS in 1955, an influential hard-bop group.

Bland, James A(llen) (1854–1911) Amer. minstrel singer and songwriter, best known for his song "Carry Me Back to Old Virginny" (adopted as the state song of Virginia in 1940).

Blanton, Jimmy (James) (1918–42) Amer. jazz bassist with the Duke Ellington band from 1938 until his early death, known esp. for his melodic bass playing and technical facility.

Bledsoe, Jules (Julius) (1898–1943) Amer. baritone. He was the orig. Joe in *Show Boat* (1927), and his other operatic roles incl. Emperor Jones in Gruenberg's opera and Boris Godunov. He also toured widely as a recitalist.

Blegen, Judith (1941–) Amer. soprano, trained at the Curtis Institute. Her Metropolitan Opera debut was in 1970. She is known for her portrayal of lyric and soubrette roles, esp. in the operas of Mozart.

Blessed Damozel, The DAMOISELLE ÉLUE, LA.

Bley (née Borg), **Carla** (1938–) Amer. jazz composer and bandleader, founder of the Jazz Composers Orchestra Assoc. (JCOA) in 1964.

Bley, Paul (1932–) Canadian jazz pianist and composer. In 1957 he formed a quintet with Ornette Coleman that became an influential free-jazz band. In the 1960s he worked with Charles Mingus and Sonny Rollins, thereafter with his own groups, making many recordings.

Bliss, Sir **Arthur (Drummond)** (1891–1975) English composer, stud. of Charles Wood and Stanford. His earlier works exhibit an adventuresome nature, which in the later works is wedded to a more traditional style influenced by Elgar.

Blitzstein, Marc (1905–64) Amer. composer, stud. of Nadia Boulanger and Hanns Eisler. Much of his work was for the stage, radio and film, esp. on subjects dealing with social and political issues (e.g., his operas *The Cradle Will Rock* and *Regina*).

Bloch, Ernest (1880–1959) Swiss-born Amer. composer and conductor, stud. of Jaques-Dalcroze and Knorr. He came to the U.S. in 1916, becoming the first dir. of the Cleveland Institute (1920–25) and then dir. of the San Francisco Conservatory (1925–30). After almost a decade in Switzerland, he joined the faculty of the U. of California at Berkeley (1941–52). His music is noted for its evocation of Jewish folk and ritual music.

block *also*, **wood block** a percussion instrument, usu. a slotted block of wood played with a drumstick. See CHINESE WOOD BLOCK.

block chords see LOCKED HANDS.

Blockflöte ['blok"flø-te] (Ger.) RECORDER.

block harmony HOMOPHONY.

Blockwerk [-"verk] (Ger.) an undivided chest of pipes in a medieval church organ.

Blomstedt, Herbert (1927–) Swedish conductor and teacher, stud. of Markevich, Jean Morel and Bernstein. He has been music dir. of the Oslo PO, the Dresden Staatskapelle and the San Francisco SO.

Blood, Sweat and Tears Amer. jazz-rock band formed in 1968 in New York and performing over the years with varying personnel. The band has toured in Eastern Europe under State Dept. sponsorship.

Bloom, Rube (1902–76) Amer. popular composer and songwriter, best known for the "Song of the Bayou." He worked with dance bands during the 1920s.

Bloomfield, Theodore (Robert) (1923–) Amer. conductor, stud. of George Szell (1946–7). He has been music dir. of the Rochester PO (1959–63) and of the Berlin SO (1975–82).

Blow, John (1649–1708) English organist and prolific composer of vocal and instrumental works, stud. of Henry Cooke and the teacher of Purcell. He was organist at Westminster Abbey from 1668 and joined the Chapel Royal in 1674 as Master of the Children, a post he held until his death. The extensive list of his vocal works includes service music, anthems, odes and songs.

blow 1, to play a wind instrument. **2**, to miss a note.

blue-blowing making music on unconventional wind instruments, such as the kazoo or jug.

Bluebeard's Castle (Hung., *A Kékszakállú Herceg Vára*) fantasy opera in one act by Bartók to a libretto by Béla Balász. Premiere, Budapest 1918. Bluebeard's fourth wife, Judith, seals her own doom when she insists on opening the seventh door in Bluebeard's castle.

Blue Danube, On the Beautiful (Ger., *An der schönen blauen Donau*) waltz for orch. (1867) by Johann Strauss, Jr., with words by Josef Weyl.

Blue Devils a famous jazz band formed in 1925 in Kansas City, MO, led for many years by bassist WALTER PAGE.

bluegrass music a style of COUNTRY MUSIC developed in the 1940s by Bill Monroe and his group the Blue Grass Boys and incorporating elements of traditional folk music, religious spirituals and revival hymns. The music is typically fast-paced, in duple meter, with emphasis on the offbeats.

Blue Jay Singers vocal gospel quartet formed in 1926 by Clarence Parnell. The group helped to develop the midwestern style of gospel music during the 1940s. They disbanded in the 1960s.

blue note a note of the scale, usu. the third or seventh degree (less commonly, the fifth), characteristically lowered by a small amount in jazz and blues.

blues a form of 20th-c. secular Afr.-Amer. folk music related to jazz but much more focused on vocal performance and important in the development of Western popular music, rock and jazz. Largely an improvisational style, its music is frequently based on repetitive harmonic patterns, the most familiar of which is the 12-bar blues, comprising two 4-bar phrases to the same text and a third 4-bar phrase to a different but rhyming text. "The blues" implies a certain state of mind or feeling, which can be best expressed by blues music. The term is also used for pieces that are completely composed, but which use one of the blues harmonic patterns or imitate the blues character.

Blue Sky Boys Amer. country music duo of guitar and mandolin formed by Bill and Earl Bolick, active in the 1930s and 1940s.

blues rock a type of ROCK music combining blues and rock elements, as exemplified in the work of Ike and Tina Turner and the Righteous Brothers.

blues shouting a style of declamatory blues singing of the swing era, a predecessor of rhythm-and-blues, exemplified by singers JIMMY RUSHING and JIMMIE WITHERSPOON.

Blüthner Ger. piano manufacturing firm est. in 1853 by Julius Blüthner, who developed in 1873 an ALIQUOT SCALING for grand pianos.

BMI BROADCAST MUSIC, INC.

b mi the note B natural in the HEXACHORD system.

B-minor Mass MASS IN B MINOR.

board zither a ZITHER whose strings are stretched across a flat or slightly curved board that serves as the top of the box resonator. The most common example is the PSALTERY.

Boatwright, Helen (1916–) Amer. soprano, noted for her performances of 20th-c. music, esp. works of Hindemith and Ives. She is the wife of **Howard Boatwright** (1918–), Amer. composer, violinist and musicologist. He is best known for his sacred choral music.

Boatwright, McHenry (1928–) Amer. bass-baritone, trained at the New England Conservatory. He has sung opera regularly in Hamburg and elsewhere and in concert in Europe and the U.S.

bocal the MOUTHPIECE of a woodwind or brass instrument. Also, *crook.*

Boccherini, (Ridolfo) Luigi (1743–1805) Italian cellist and composer, principally of instrumental music. After a short period with the court theater in Vienna (1757–1766) he embarked on a number of concert tours, spending extended periods in Paris and Madrid. In 1786 he was appointed chamber composer to Prince Friedrich Wilhelm of Prussia, but he remained in Spain until his death.

Bock, Jerry (Jerrold) **(Lewis)** (1928–) Amer. songwriter and composer, frequent collaborator with lyricist Sheldon Harnick. His most successful works have been *Fiorello!* (1959), which won a Pulitzer Prize for drama, and *Fiddler on the Roof* (1964).

Bockstriller (Ger.) TRILLO.

bodhran ['bor-on] an Irish hand DRUM.

Boehm system an improved system of keys and fingering developed by Theobald Boehm (1793–1881) for the flute and later adapted by others to other woodwind instruments. Boehm was also responsible for the adoption of a cylindrical bore and the replacement of the wooden flute by the all-metal flute.

Boelke-Bomart New York music publishing firm founded in 1948. The firm specializes in Amer. composers, incl. Perle, Babbitt and Ives.

Boeuf sur le toit, Le [bœf sür lə twä] (Fr., The Ox on the Roof) ballet (1919) by Milhaud incorporating Brazilian dance music and concerning "events" in an Amer. bar during Prohibition.

Boggs, Dock (1898–1971) Amer. singer and banjoist, an active performer from the late 1920s.

Bohème, La [bō'em] (It., Bohemian life) **1**, lyric opera in 4 acts by Puccini to a libretto by Giuseppe Giacosa and Luigi Illica, based on the novel *Scènes de la Vie de Bohème* by Henri Murger. Premiere, Turin 1896. The story of the stormy love affair between poet Rodolfo and the consumptive seamstress Mimi. **2**, lyric opera in 4 acts by Leoncavallo to a libretto by the composer based on the same Murger novel as (1,). Premiere, Venice 1897.

Bohemian Girl, The opera in 3 acts by Balfe to a libretto by Bunn, after St. Georges. Premiere, London 1843. A highborn heroine is abducted by gypsies. The score incl. the well-known song, "I Dreamt That I Dwelt in Marble Halls."

Böhm, Karl (1894–1981) eminent Austrian. conductor, stud. of Eusebius Mandyczewski and Guido Adler. After six years at the Munich Staatsoper he became musical dir. at Darmstadt in 1927, in Hamburg in 1933, of the Dresden Staatsoper in 1934, and of the Vienna Staatsoper (1943–5, 1954–6), after which he conducted free-lance internationally until his death.

Boïeldieu, (François-)Adrien ['bwäl-dyø] (1775–1834) French composer, a leading figure of the *opéra-comique* tradition, stud. of Charles Broche. Of his many operas, the best known are *La dame blanche* (1825) and *Le petit chaperon rouge* (1818).

Boismortier, Joseph Bodin de ['bwä-mor"tyā] (1689–1755) French composer, esp. of instrumental chamber works. He composed what may have been the first French solo concerto and wrote a large volume of works for flute as well as for bagpipe and hurdy-gurdy.

Boito, Arrigo (Enrico) (1842–1918) Italian composer, critic and librettist, best known for his collaborations with Verdi (the librettos for *Otello* and *Falstaff*) and for his own opera *Mefistofele*. He also wrote the libretto for Ponchielli's *La Gioconda* (under the pseudonym "Tobia Gorrio"). He was equally important as a literary and music critic.

Bojangles ROBINSON, WILLIAM.

Bok (Zimbalist), Mary Louise Curtis (1876–1970) Amer. music patron, founder of the Settlement School of Music (1917) and the Curtis Institute of Music (1924). She was president of Curtis until her death and chairman of the board of directors of the Philadelphia Grand Opera Co. (1929–34). Her first husband was publisher Edward Bok; her second was violinist Efrem Zimbalist.

Bolcom, William (Elden) (1938–) Amer. composer and pianist, stud. of Milhaud, Messiaen and Leland Smith. He has been on the faculty of the U. of Michigan since 1973. His involvement in ragtime and other 19th- and early 20th-c. popular and salon music (in concert with his wife, soprano Joan Morris), is reflected in the flamboyance of his own compositions, which combine serious philosophical and religious subjects with music of all styles. He won the Pulitzer Prize in 1988 for his *12 New Études for Piano*.

Bolden, Buddy (?1868–1931) legendary Amer. jazz cornet player and bandleader in New Orleans until 1907, when he was institutionalized for violent derangement and alcoholism.

bolero 1, a lively 18th- and 19th-c. Spanish DANCE in ¾ time, characterized by twisting body movements and foot-stamping. 2, a Cuban dance in duple time similar to the HABANERA.

Bolero ballet (1928) by Ravel based on a single rhythmic and melodic figure and almost entirely in C major, written for the dancer Ida Rubenstein.

Bolet, Jorge (1914–90) Cuban-born Amer. pianist, stud. of Leopold Godowsky and Moriz Rosenthal. He is noted for his performance of the virtuoso repertory of the 19th c., esp. the works of Liszt.

bolon a large African, arched, three- or four-stringed HARP having a large calabash resonator.

Bolshoi Theater a theater in Moscow built in 1825 and rebuilt (after a fire) in 1856, home of the Bolshoi Opera and Ballet.

Bomarzo opera in 2 acts by Ginastera to a libretto by Manuel Mujica Láinez, after his own novel. Premiere, Washington, D.C. 1967. The story of a 16th-c. Italian hunchback duke and his delusions of persecution.

bomb in jazz, an ornamental loud accent on the bass drum.

bombard see POMMER.

bombarde a reed pipe ORGAN STOP, usu. at 16-foot or 32-foot pitch.

bombardon 1, a bass SHAWM. 2, a bass TUBA; helicon.

bombo ['bōm-bō] (Sp.) 1, string TREMOLO. 2, a S. Amer. double-headed FRAME DRUM similar to the military drum.

bonang a Javanese GONG CHIME used in the gamelan to lead or accompany melody.

Bond (Jacobs-Bond), Carrie (Minetta) (1861–1946) Amer. songwriter and publisher, best known for her song "A Perfect Day" (1910), which sold over 8 million copies in sheet music.

Bond, Victoria (1950–) Amer. conductor and composer, stud. of Sessions, Persichetti and Jean Morel. She was the first woman to receive a doctorate in conducting from the Juilliard School and has been Exxon Arts conductor with the Pittsburgh SO. She has also been conductor of the Bel

Canto Opera in New York and the Roanoke SO.

Bonds (Richardson), **Margaret (Alison)** (1913–72) Amer. composer, pianist and teacher. She was the first black soloist to appear with the Chicago SO (in 1933, performing Florence Price's Piano Concerto at the Chicago World's Fair). Her works include many arrangements of spirituals.

bones a CONCUSSION INSTRUMENT consisting of a pair of rods made of bone, ivory or wood, held between the fingers and struck together to produce a clicking sound. The instrument was frequently used in minstrel shows. Also, *knackers*. Cf. CLAPPERS.

bongo *also*, **bongo drum** a small Cuban tuned (or occ. untuned) drum, played with the fingers, and usu. used in pairs. Bongos are an integral part of Lat.-Amer. dance bands and have also been included in some contemporary scores by Varèse, Boulez, etc.

Bononcini, Giovanni (1670–1747) Italian composer and cellist, stud. of G.P. Colonna. His list of works incl. more than 70 operas, numerous cantatas and other vocal works, instrumental sonatas and concertos.

Bonynge, Richard (Alan) (1930–) Australian conductor and pianist, married to soprano JOAN SUTHERLAND, for whom he has conducted many performances. He has been instrumental in the revival of 18th- and 19th-c. vocal ornamentation. Since 1976 he has been musical dir. of the Australian Opera.

boobams small tunable drums available in a range of two chromatic octaves, played with the fingers or with small drumsticks.

boogie-woogie *also*, **boogie, boog, boogaloo** a style of Amer. blues piano playing originating in the early 20th c., characterized by a forceful, percussive left hand bass figure, a "walking" bass of broken octaves, and a BLUES harmonic progression. In the 1940s the style became a popular hit, and its elements became an important part of rock and roll. Early masters of the style incl. Albert Ammons, Meade Lewis and Pete Johnson.

book the repertory of arrangements of a band or orch.

Boone, Blind (John William) (1864–1927) Amer. ragtime pianist and composer, best known for his work "Marshfield Tornado."

Boone, Charles (1939–) Amer. composer, stud. of Krenek and others. He has been active as a teacher and organizer of new music events in the San Francisco area. His works are mainly for small instrumental ensembles.

Boor, The 1, comic opera in 1 act by Dominick Argento, libretto by John Olon Scrymgeour, based on the Chekhov play. Premiere 1957, Rochester, NY. **2**, comic opera in 1 act by Ulysses Kay, libretto by the composer, based on the Chekhov play. Premiere 1968, Lexington, KY. Cf. THE BEAR.

Boosey & Hawkes English music publisher and instrument manufacturer founded in London in 1930 when Boosey & Co. and Hawkes & Co. merged.

bop *also*, **bebop, rebop** a style of jazz developed in the early 1940s by Dizzy Gillespie, Charlie Parker and others, utilizing standard songs as the basis for elaborate, sophisticated improvisation, often very rapid, accompanied by a small rhythm section. The words bop, rebop, etc., are derived from nonsense syllables used in scat singing. Cf. HARD BOP.

Borden, David (1938–) Amer. composer of works in a minimalist style, incl. *The Continuing Story of Counterpoint* (1976–83). He is founder of the ensemble Mother Mallard's Portable Masterpiece Co.

Bordoni, Faustina (1693–1783) Italian mezzo-soprano, one of the first international prima donnas, performing in London and on the continent works of Handel, Hasse (to whom she was married) and others.

bore the interior of the tube of a wind instrument, the size of which determines the proportions of the air column and consequently the pitch of the lowest note playable.

Boretz, Benjamin (1934–   ) Amer. composer and theorist, stud. of Arthur Berger, Irving Fine, Sessions and Babbitt. He has taught at Bard College and written for *The Nation* and *Perspectives of New Music,* which he cofounded. In his composition he has often utilized group improvisation.

Borge, Victor (Rosenbaum, Borge) (1909–   ) Danish-born Amer. pianist, conductor and comedian. He gave over 800 performances of his Comedy in Music recital and has toured throughout the world with similar shows. He has also conducted in opera and concert.

Borinqueña, La [bō-rēn′kā-nyä] (Sp.) work by F. Astol; the national anthem of Puerto Rico, adopted in 1952.

Boris Godunov historical opera in 4 acts by Mussorgsky to a libretto by the composer based largely on the play by Pushkin. Premiere, St. Petersburg 1874. The music has been rearranged and reorchestrated a number of times, the best-known versions being those by Rimsky-Korsakov (1896), for many years the standard, and by Shostakovich (1960). The tendency in recent years has been to return to the original scoring. The opera deals with the final days of Tsar Boris Godunov of Russia.

Borodin, Alexander Porphyrevich (1833–87) Russian composer, stud. of Balakirev and a member of the MIGHTY HANDFUL. A chemist by profession, he pursued his musical interests as an important sideline, producing a relatively small but significant body of works, the best known of which are his opera *Prince Igor* (1869–87), the tone poem *On the Steppes of Central Asia* (1880) and his three symphonies.

Bösendorfer Austrian manufacturer of pianos, founded in 1828, made famous by Liszt. The firm's "Imperial" grand has an extended bass range, specifically utilized by some composers, incl. Bartók.

Boskovsky, Willi (1909–91) Austrian violinist and conductor, famous as an interpreter of the music of the Johann Strauss family and conductor of the Vienna New Year's Day concert from 1954.

bossa nova a style of Brazilian popular music and DANCE of the early 1960s, an amalgamation of the SAMBA and cool jazz.

Boss Brass Toronto jazz orch. formed in 1968 under trombonist Rob McConnell.

Boston a slow jazzlike WALTZ, dating from the late 19th c. in Amer. and popular in Europe after World War I. Also, *hesitation waltz.*

Boston Academy of Music conservatory founded in 1833 in Boston by Lowell Mason and others to teach children music based on the methods of the Swiss educator Johann Pestalozzi.

Boston Camerata early music vocal and instrumental ensemble founded in Boston in 1954 by Narcissa Williamson.

Boston Conservatory of Music conservatory founded in 1867 by violinist and composer Julius Eichberg.

Boston Festival Orchestra a touring orch. founded in Boston in 1889. For many years under Emil Mollenhauer's direction, the orch. accompanied performances of the HANDEL AND HAYDN SOCIETY.

Boston Ideal Opera Company *also,* **Bostonians** an opera company founded by Effie H. Ober in 1879. The group disbanded in 1905.

Boston Musical Instrument Manufactory manufacturers of band instruments, established c1869. In 1913 the firm reincorporated as the Boston Musical Instrument Co.

Boston Music Company music publishing house, established in 1885 by Gustave Schirmer, Jr. It is now a division of Hammerstein Music and Theater Co., Inc.

Boston Pops Orchestra an orch. formed in 1885 of players from the Boston SO as the Promenade Concerts to play light classics. It was conducted for almost 50 years by Arthur

Fiedler (from 1930), who was succeeded in 1979 by John Williams.

Boston Symphony Orchestra orch. founded in 1881 by banker Henry Lee Higginson, who supported the orch. financially until his retirement in 1918. Its earliest conductors were German and Austro-Hungarian: Wilhelm Gericke, Arthur Nikisch, Emil Paur and Carl Muck (under whose direction it was the first orch. to make phonograph records). Succeeding conductors were Monteux, Koussevitzky, Münch, Leinsdorf, William Steinberg and Ozawa. Cf. BOSTON POPS ORCHESTRA.

Boston Waltz BOSTON.

Bottesini, Giovanni (1821–89) Italian double-bass player, composer and conductor. Nicknamed the "Paganini of the double bass," he contributed significantly to the technique and literature of his instrument. He was also successful as musical dir. for a number of opera theaters in Spain, Portugal and France.

Botticelli Pictures, Three see THREE BOTTICELLI PICTURES.

bottleneck a plastic or metal tube fitted over a finger on the left hand for stopping strings on an ELECTRIC GUITAR.

bouché [boo'shä] (Fr.) STOPPED.

Bouffons, War of the (Fr., *Querelle des Bouffons*) a dispute in the early 1750s in Paris over the relative merits of Italian and French music.

Boulanger, Lili (1893–1918) French composer, stud. of her sister Nadia. She was the first woman to win the Prix de Rome, with her cantata *Faust et Hélène* (1913), and in her short life produced a significant body of vocal and instrumental works.

Boulanger, Nadia (1887–1979) French composer, conductor, and teacher of many important 20th-c. composers, incl. Copland, Berkeley, Françaix, Piston and Legrand. She studied with Vidal, Fauré and Widor at the Paris Conservatoire. As a conductor she was important in the rediscovery of Monteverdi and of Renaissance and Baroque French music,

and she was the first woman to conduct a symphony orch. in London. In Paris she was on the faculties of the École Normale and the Conservatoire, and from 1921 she taught at the American Conservatory at Fontainebleau, of which she later became director. During World War II she taught in Cambridge (MA) and New York.

Boulez, Pierre (1925–) French composer, conductor and theorist, stud. of Messiaen. He has been highly influential and successful as a composer in a complex, serialist style. He was conductor of the Domaine Musicale concerts in Paris and from 1971 to 1978 music dir. of the New York PO. He is director of the Institut de Recherche et de Coordination Acoustique/Musique in Paris and writer of numerous theoretical works about 20th-c. music. His works incl. *Le Marteau sans maître*, *Pli selon pli*, 3 piano sonatas, *Improvisations sur Mallarmé*, *Structures* for piano, works for orch. and chamber ensembles.

Boult, Sir **Adrian (Cedric)** (1889–1983) English conductor. He studied at Oxford and at the Leipzig Conservatory. He was conductor of the City of Birmingham SO (1922–30) and of the BBC SO (1930–50) in addition to making guest appearances throughout the world.

bourdon 1, (Fr.) a drone bass. Cf. BURDEN. 2, a pipe ORGAN STOP of a droning nature, usu. at 16-foot pitch.

Bourgeois, Louis [boor'jwä] (?1510–?1561) French singer and composer, known for his four-part settings of the Psalms in the translations of Clément Marot.

bourrée [boo'rä] (Fr., stuffed) 1, a lively 16th- to 18th-c. French court dance in duple time, usu. beginning with an upbeat; also, a stylized instrumental dance in this character. Cf. RIGAUDON. 2, a CLOG DANCE, possibly originating in the Auvergne.

bout the curved part of the body of a stringed instrument, as a guitar or violin.

boutade [boo'täd] (Fr., fit of temper) an 18th-c. French dance or ballet of a capricious or fanciful nature.

bouteillophone [boo'tā-yə-fōn] (Fr.) an instrument consisting of tuned bottles struck with small mallets, for which Satie and Honegger (among others) have composed. Cf. MUSICAL GLASSES.

bow a device consisting of a flexible, wooden stick with strands of horsehair (or other material) attached to both ends and tightened which, when drawn across the strings of an instrument, cause them to vibrate and produce musical pitches. The amount of arch in the bow stick has changed over the centuries from the usually convex curve of the Renaissance and Baroque (and earlier) to the slightly concave shape of the modern Tourte bow. Similarly, the tension applied to the hair has increased. Early viol bows were usu. held underhand (from the hair side), while the violin family bows are held from above. There are two styles of double bass bows: the "French" bow is similar in size to a cello bow and is held from above; the "German" bow has a wider grip and is held endways, like a saw. Both are in use in the U.S.

bowed lyre CRWTH.

Bowers, Thomas J. (1836–85) Amer. tenor, nicknamed "the black Mario," in comparison with the great tenor GIOVANNI MARIO. He refused to sing before segregated audiences and toured throughout No. America.

bow harp the earliest form of HARP, developed from the MUSICAL BOW.

Bowie, David (David Robert Jones) (1947–) versatile English rock singer, mime and actor, a member of several rock groups, incl. the Spiders, and star of films (*The Man Who Fell to Earth*).

bowing the manner of drawing the BOW across the strings of a string instrument to produce different durations, dynamics and articulations. The bow may be drawn from the frog (*down-bow*) or toward the frog (*up-bow*). Notes may be connected (*legato*) or separated (*staccato* or *slurred staccato*). They may be played in one bowstroke (*legato*) or with separate bowstrokes (*détaché*). They may be accented (*martelé*) or "bounced" (*sautillé, spiccato, ricochet*). In some cases, dyads and even three- and four-note chords are possible, broken or played together.

bowstroke the motion of the bow as it is drawn across the string. See BOW-ING.

box an early slang term for PIANO (2,).

Boyce, William (1711–79) English organist and composer of works for the church and the stage, stud. of Pepusch. He was appointed composer to the Chapel Royal in 1736 and conductor of the Music Meeting of the Society of Apollo in 1737. He became Master of the King's Musick in 1757. In his later years he was active in the publication of early English church music.

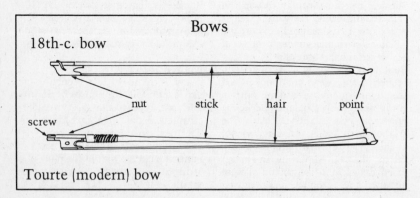

Bows

18th-c. bow

screw

nut   stick   hair   point

Tourte (modern) bow

Bowing

Boyd, Liona (Maria) (1950–) English-born Canadian guitarist and composer, stud. of Alexandre Lagoya. She has appeared in recital and in concert with orchestras across Canada and abroad and has toured with singer Gordon Lightfoot.

boy soprano a young, male singer whose voice has not changed. See SO-PRANO.

Bozza, Eugène (1905–) French composer and conductor, trained at the Paris Conservatoire, known for his large output of chamber music for wind instruments.

brace a mark ({) used to connect two or more staffs, such as those of the piano system or of related instruments in an orchestral score.

Brahms, Johannes (1833–97) Ger. pianist and composer, stud. of Otto Cossel and Eduard Marxsen. As a young pianist, he toured with the Hungarian violinist Reményi, from whom he learned the Hungarian style and the use of rubato which often appears in his music. From 1859 to 1862 he was in Hamburg, where he founded a women's chorus, for which he wrote or arranged many works. He went to Vienna in 1862, where he shortly became the dir. of the Vienna Singakademie and then, in 1872, of the Vienna Gesellschaftskonzerte. He resigned the latter post in 1875 to concentrate on composition and travel. In 1881 Hans von Bülow offered Brahms the Meiningen court orch. as a rehearsal orch., which premiered many of his works.

In 1890, Brahms decided to retire from composition and consolidate his works, destroying some and completing others. His meeting in 1891 with the clarinetist Richard Mühlfeld, however, moved him once more to composition, esp. the Clarinet Quintet and the two clarinet sonatas. His works incl. 4 symphonies, *Academic Festival Overture, Tragic Overture,* sonatas for piano, violin, cello and clarinet, piano trios, quartets and a quintet, string quartets, many works for solo piano, organ preludes, many songs, vocal quartets and duets (*Liebeslieder Waltzes, Zigeunerlieder*), choral works (*German Requiem, Alto Rhapsody*).

Braille notation a system of musical notation for the blind based on a matrix of six dots.

Brain, Dennis (1921–57) English horn player, principal horn of the Royal PO and of the Philharmonia Orch. as well as noted recitalist. Many works were composed for him by Britten, Hindemith and others.

Brand, Max (1896–1980) Polish-Amer. composer, esp. of theatrical

Braille Music Signs

C D E F G A B rest
half notes

quarter notes

eighth notes

sixteenth notes

Accidentals:

♮ ♭ ♯ ♭♭ ×

Intervals:
1 2 3 4 5 6 7 8

music, stud. of Schreker. His opera *Maschinist Hopkins* (1929) includes machines as singing characters. He came to the U.S. in 1940.

Brandenburg Concertos six works for varying instrumental ensembles, BWV 1046–51 (1721) by J.S. Bach, dedicated to the Margrave of Brandenburg.

branle [brãl] (Fr.) *also,* **bransle, brawl (brawnl)** a French popular or rustic couple-dance, possibly dating from the Middle Ages. During the 16th c., rustic dances such as the branle were enjoyed also at court. There are varieties of branle in duple, triple and mixed meters, both lively and sedate. The branle is an important forerunner of the BALLET DE COUR.

Brant, Henry (Dreyfuss) (1913–) Canadian-born Amer. composer, trained in Montreal and New York, where he later taught at the Juilliard School. He has worked as a composer for films, ballet and jazz ensembles. He is esp. concerned with spatial arrangement of his performing forces, indoors and outdoors, and the use of multiple orchestras.

brass band a type of wind band composed of brass instruments, a popular form for both amateur and military bands in the 19th c., but largely replaced in the U.S. in the 20th c. by bands comprised of brass and woodwinds.

brass instruments **1**, wind instruments made of brass or other metal, esp. those which use the lips as a reed. **2**, in rock and jazz, the term usu. encompasses any instrument that is not a string or rhythm instrument.

Bratsche ['brät-she] (Ger.) VIOLA.

brawl BRANLE.

Braxton, Anthony (1945–) Amer. avant-garde jazz composer and woodwind player, active in the AACM and the Creative Construction Company, which he co-founded. He has also worked with the ensemble Musica Elettronica Viva and in the band Circle with Chick Corea, and frequently appears in unaccompanied performance.

break **1**, a cadenza in jazz, with or without rhythm section accompaniment, usu. interpolated in performance between ensemble sections. **2**, a change in REGISTER, as in the voice.

break dancing an Afr.-Amer. competitive street dance of the 1970s and 1980s with acrobatic and jerky, stylized movements; performed to RAP or FUNK music.

breakdown **1**, a folk dance gathering; HOEDOWN. **2**, JUBA. **3**, REEL.

Bream, Julian (Alexander) (1933–) English guitarist and lutanist. He was founder of the Julian Bream Consort, which helped to revive interest in early consort music, and of the Semley Festival in Wiltshire, which specializes in early chamber music. A number of major works for guitar have been written for him.

breathy a term describing a type of vocal sound incorporating released breath that has not activated the vocal cords. Also, *unfocused.*

breeches part see TRAVESTI.

Breitkopf & Härtel ['brĭt-kopf ŭnt 'her-təl] Ger. music publishing firm, est. in 1719 in Leipzig.

Brendel, Alfred (1931–) Czech-born Austrian pianist, stud. of Steuermann and Fischer, whose wide repertory spans the Classical, Romantic and contemporary literature.

breve (Lat., short) a note half as long as a *long* and twice as long as a *semibreve;* double whole note. See NOTE. —**alla breve** (Lat.) ALLA BREVE.

breviary an ecclesiastical book containing the prayers (and sometimes music) necessary to recite the Divine Office. Contents include antiphons, psalms, hymns, lessons, responsories, and specific instructions for the performance of the services. Cf. ANTIPHONER.

Brice, Fanny (Borach, Fannie) (1891–1951) Amer. actress and singer, made famous by her appearances in Ziegfeld's *Follies*. She was known for her performances in Yiddish accent and for her torch songs.

Brice, Carol (Lovette Hawkins) (1918–85) Amer. contralto, stud. of

Francis Rogers. She was the first black Amer. to win the Naumburg Award (1944). Her many roles incl. Maria (*Porgy and Bess*) and Queenie (*Show Boat*) and she has appeared in concert and recital. From 1974 she taught at the U. of Oklahoma.

Brico, Antonia (1902–89) Dutch-born Amer. conductor, stud. of Muck. In 1934 she founded the Women's SO in New York and was the first woman to conduct the New York PO. From 1941 she lived in Colorado, where she founded her own semiprofessional touring orch.

bridge 1, a carved piece of wood separating the strings of a string instrument from the belly and transmitting the vibrations to the body. 2, *also,* **bridge passage** a transitional passage in a composition connecting two important themes or sections. Also, *channel.*

Bridge, Frank (1879–1941) English violist, conductor and composer of orchestral, vocal and chamber works, stud. of Stanford and teacher of Britten.

Bridgetower, George (1780–1860) British virtuoso mulatto violinist. With the composer at the piano he gave the first performance of Beethoven's ''Kreutzer'' Sonata (1803).

brillante [brēl'län-tā] (It.) brilliant, sparkling.

brindisi ('brēn-dē-zē) (It.) a toasting or drinking song, found frequently in 19th-c. Italian opera, the best-known example being in Verdi's *La Traviata.*

brio (It.) vivacity, spirit. See CON BRIO.

brisé [brē'zā] (Fr., broken) 1, a type of TURN. 2, a detached BOWING.

Bristow, George Frederick (1825–98) Amer. composer, conductor and violinist, stud. of George Macfarren and Ole Bull. He played in the New York Philharmonic Society Orch. (1843–79) and was conductor of the New York Harmonic Society (1851–63). His works often dealt with American themes, as in the opera *Rip van Winkle* (1855) and the *Niagara Symphony.*

British Broadcasting Corporation the state-owned radio and television broadcasting system of the United Kingdom, est. in 1922, which operates its own symphony orchestras and choruses. Abbr., *BBC.*

British invasion popular name for a period in the mid 1960s of immense popularity in the U.S. of British rock bands, incl. THE BEATLES and the ROLLING STONES.

Britten, (Edward) Benjamin (1913–76) English composer, conductor and pianist, stud. of Bridge. In the late 1930s he began a lifelong collaboration with tenor Peter Pears, for whom he wrote several song cycles and roles in a number of his operas. In 1947 Britten founded the English Opera Group to produce chamber opera, and shortly thereafter the Aldeburgh Festival, which was the principal outlet for his new works from then on. A collaboration with Russian cellist Rostropovich in 1961 produced a number of cello works, including a sonata, and vocal works dedicated to soprano Galina Vishnevskaya, Rostropovich's wife. His works incl. *Peter Grimes, Albert Herring, The Rape of Lucretia, Billy Budd, The Turn of the Screw, Death in Venice* (operas), concertos for violin and cello and other orchestral works, *A Young Person's Guide to the Orchestra,* many choral works (*A Ceremony of Carols*), songs, chamber music, incidental music, and folk song arrangements.

Broadcast Music, Inc. Amer. performing rights org. founded in 1939. Abbr., *BMI.*

broadside a large sheet of paper printed one side only, a popular means for publishing songs and ballads from the 16th to 18th c.

Broadwood English piano manufacturer founded in 1761 by John Broadwood (1732–1812), now the oldest keyboard instrument makers still in existence. The firm developed a new design for the square piano and greatly improved the design of the grand piano.

broken chord a chord of which the

notes are played consecutively rather than simultaneously. Cf. ARPEGGIO, ALBERTI BASS.

broken consort 1, an instrumental CONSORT combining instruments of different families. **2**, music played by an ensemble of diverse instruments.

broken octaves see SHORT OCTAVE.

Brookmeyer, Bobby (Robert) (1929–) Amer. jazz valve-trombonist, pianist and arranger, collaborator with Stan Getz, Gerry Mulligan, Jimmy Giuffre, Clark Terry and Thad Jones. His cool style incl. elements of early jazz and swing.

Brooks, Shelton (Leroy) (1886–1975) innovative Canadian-born Amer. songwriter, pianist and vaudevillian. He is best remembered for his songs, such as "Darktown Strutters' Ball" (1917) and "Some of These Days" (1910).

Broonzy, Big Bill (William Lee Conley) (1893–1958) Amer. guitarist, folksinger and blues singer, one of the most extensively recorded blues artists.

Brott, Alexander (1915–) Canadian conductor, violinist and composer, stud. at McGill Conservatorium and the Juilliard School. He founded the McGill Chamber Orch. in 1939 and was conductor of the Kingston SO (1963–80), and has been associated with the Montreal SO. As a composer, his works often demonstrate a sense of humor in combining traditional or folk elements in new ways.

Brott, Boris (1945–) Canadian conductor and violinist, son of Alexander Brott, stud. of Monteux, Markevich and Bernstein. He founded the Philharmonic Youth O. of Montreal in 1959, was asst. conductor of the Toronto SO, principal conductor of the Northern Sinfonia in Newcastle, England, and the BBC Welsh Orch. and musical dir. of the Hamilton (Ontario) PO (1969–88).

Broude, Alexander Amer. music publishing firm, founded in 1962 when Alexander left BROUDE BROTHERS.

Broude Brothers Amer. music publishing firm, founded in 1929 by Irving and Alexander Broude.

Brouwer, Leo (1939–) Cuban composer, conductor and guitarist, stud. of Wolpe and Persichetti. His work combines a nationalist style with avant-garde techniques.

Brown, Clifford (1930–56) Amer. jazz trumpeter. He played with Lionel Hampton and Art Blakey, and then formed a quintet with Max Roach (1954). He was particularly noted for his bright tone and lyrically cogent improvisations.

Brown, Earle (1926–) Amer. composer, stud. of McKillop at the Schillinger School (now BERKLEE COLLEGE). He participated in the Project for Music and Magnetic Tape with John Cage and David Tudor and developed the use of GRAPHIC NOTATION.

Brown, James (?1933–) Amer. gospel and blues singer, for many years leader of the Famous Flames and the band the J.B.s.

Brown, Lawrence (1907–88) Amer. jazz trombonist with the Duke Ellington band (1932–51, 1960–70), nicknamed "Deacon" for his mournful demeanor.

Brown, Milton (1903–36) Amer. country-music singer and bandleader, a creator with his band Fort Worth Doughboys (later the Musical Brownies) of the WESTERN SWING style.

Brown, Nacio Herb (1896–1964) Amer. songwriter, frequent collaborator of lyricist-producer Arthur Freed. Among his best-known songs are "Singing in the Rain," "Temptation" and "The Pagan Love Song."

Brown, Ray (Raymond Matthews) (1926–) Amer. jazz bassist and cellist, perhaps the most-recorded jazz bassist. He has worked with Dizzy Gillespie, Oscar Peterson and many others, as well as Ella Fitzgerald, to whom he was married (1948–52).

Browne, Jackson (1949–) Amer. folk-rock singer, guitarist and songwriter, an important figure in the development of West Coast folk-rock.

Browning, John (1933–) Amer. pianist, stud. of Rosina Lhévinne, noted for his technical facility in 19th-c. and a limited 20th-c. repertory.

browning an English 16th-c. popular tune, used as the basis for instrumental variations by William Byrd and others.

Brubeck, Dave (1920–) Amer. cool jazz pianist and composer, stud. of Milhaud and Schoenberg, founder of a quartet in 1951 that was highly successful commercially and known for its use of unusual meters.

Bruch, Max (Karl August) (1838–1920) Ger. conductor and prolific composer, best known for his *Scottish Fantasy* for violin and orch. (1880).

Bruckner, (Joseph) Anton (1824–96) Austrian composer of orchestral and vocal works, stud. of August Dürrnberger and Simon Sechter. He was a teacher at St. Florian (1845–55), then organist at the cathedral in Linz (1855–68), and in 1868 he became professor at the Vienna Conservatory. His symphonic works, strongly influenced by Wagner, were frequently revised as a result of his friends' criticisms, resulting in multiple versions of each. He wrote 9 symphonies, a large body of sacred choral works, incl. a *Requiem*, a *Te Deum*, several Mass settings and many motets.

Brueggen (Brüggen), **Frans** (1934–) Dutch virtuoso recorder and flute player and conductor, member of the avant-garde ensemble Sourcream and conductor of the Orch. of the 18th Century. He has made numerous recordings of early music and 20th-c. repertory and has been responsible for commissioning many new works for recorder.

Brumel, Antoine (?1460–?1525) French composer of sacred and secular vocal and instrumental music. He was Master of the Innocents at St. Peter's in Geneva until 1492 and also worked at Notre Dame in Paris and in Ferrara.

Brün, Herbert (1918–) German composer, stud. of Stefan Wolpe. He worked in electronic music in Munich, Cologne and Paris in the late

1950s, then came to the U.S. in 1963 to teach at the U. of Illinois. His works are mostly instrumental chamber music and sometimes employ computer-generated sounds, alone or combined with live instruments.

brunette (Fr.) a type of 17th- and 18th-c. popular French song, usu. sung without accompaniment and dealing with a pastoral subject that is tender and sentimental. Cf. BERGERETTE.

Bruscantini, Sesto (1919–) Italian bass-baritone, stud. of Luigi Ricci, noted for his wide repertory, esp. the comic roles of Mozart and Rossini.

brush WIRE BRUSH.

Brustwerk ['brûst-verk] (Ger.) see CHAIR ORGAN.

Brusilow, Anshel (1928–) Amer. violinist and conductor, stud. of Zimbalist and Monteux. He was concertmaster of the Cleveland Orch. under Szell and of the Philadelphia Orch. (1959–66). He founded the Chamber Symphony of Philadelphia in 1966 and has conducted it ever since.

Bryn-Julson, Phyllis (Mae) (1945–) Amer. soprano, trained at Tanglewood and with Jan de Gaetani. She is esp. known for her performance of 20th-c. music, and many works have been written for her by such composers as del Tredici and Donald Lybbert.

buccina ['buk-sə-nə] (Lat.) a Roman military TRUMPET shaped like a letter C. Also, *cornu*.

Buchla, Donald (Frederick) (1937–) electronic instrument designer and composer. He developed a line of synthesizers in the 1960s and was co-founder in 1975 of the Electric Weasel Ensemble, a live electronic music group.

Buck, Dudley (1839–1909) Amer. organist and composer, trained in Leipzig. He was organist at various churches in Hartford, Chicago, Boston and Brooklyn, but he was noted for his large-scale choral works.

buck and wing Afr.-Amer. dance of the late 19th and early 20th c.

Buckner, Milt (Milton) (1915–77) Amer. swing jazz pianist who performed with many groups, incl. the bands of Jimmie Lunceford and Lionel Hampton. He was known for his use of block chords and the electric organ, esp. to replace the big band brass section.

buckwheat notation SHAPE NOTE.

Budapest Quartet a string quartet founded in 1917 by members of the Budapest Opera Orch. The quartet was in residence at the Library of Congress, Washington, from 1938 to 1962, after which they were at SUNY Buffalo. They disbanded in 1968.

Buffalo Philharmonic Orchestra orch. formed in Buffalo in 1921 as the Buffalo SO and renamed in 1935. Its conductors have incl. William Steinberg, Josef Krips, Lukas Foss, Michael Tilson Thomas, Julius Rudel and Semyon Bychkov.

buffo (It., comic) a male opera singer, usu. a bass, specializing in comic roles.

buff stop *also*, **harp stop** a device found in some harpsichords that partially dampens the strings by pressing a piece of leather or felt against them.

bugle 1, a brass instrument descended from the POSTHORN, similar to the trumpet in shape but with a shorter and more conical tube, used in military and marching bands. Cf. KEYED BUGLE. 2, a family of brass instruments including the FLUGELHORN and the TUBA used in brass bands.

buisine a medieval herald's straight TRUMPET, forerunner of the SLIDE TRUMPET.

Bull, John (?1562–1628) English composer, virtuoso virginalist and organist, and organ builder, stud. of W. Blitheman and W. Hunnis. He was king's organist at the Chapel Royal, then fled England in 1613 under a charge of adultery to the Netherlands, where he remained in various posts until his death. As a composer he is best remembered for his keyboard works.

Bull, Ole (Bornemann) (1810–80) Norwegian virtuoso violinist and composer. He traveled throughout Europe and the U.S. as a soloist on the violin and the HARDANGER FIDDLE, which he used for some of his own works incorporating Norwegian *slåtter* and folksongs. In 1852 Bull was involved in the establishment of a colony in Pennsylvania and in 1855 he attempted to establish an opera house in New York, neither project ending in success. His last decade he spent partly in the U.S. and partly in Norway, having married in 1870 the daughter of a Wisconsin senator.

bull fiddle DOUBLE BASS.

bull-roarer an ancient AEROPHONE consisting of a slat of wood or metal attached to a thong and whirled to make a roaring sound. It is primarily used in religious rites.

Bülow, Hans (Guido) Freiherr von (1830–94) Ger. pianist and conductor. He was conductor of the Munich Court Opera and court music dir. in Meiningen, whose orch. he elevated to one of the best in Germany. He was a champion of the music of Brahms, whose works he often programmed. His first wife was Liszt's daughter Cosima, who later left him for Wagner.

bumbass an 18th-c. bowed, one-stringed instrument having a heavy gut string stretched over a pig's bladder, usu. used as a DRONE for a folk-song or dance.

Bumbry, Grace (Melzia Ann) (1937–) Amer. mezzo-soprano, stud. of Lotte Lehmann. She was a member of the Basle Opera and was the first Afr.-Amer. to sing at Bayreuth. She has sung both mezzo-soprano and soprano repertory at all major opera houses and is frequently heard in recital.

burden 1, BOURDON. 2, a refrain or chorus of a 15th- or 16th-c. song or hymn. Cf. CAROL.

Burgin, Richard (1892–1981) Polish-born Amer. violinist and conductor, stud. of Auer. He was concertmaster of the Boston SO for 42 years (associate conductor for 19 years) and head of the String Dept. at the New England Conservatory. In 1962 he moved to Florida to teach and conduct.

Burgundian school a school of composition associated with composers of the late 14th and the 15th c., many of whom had served the Dukes of Burgundy. Masters of the period were Dufay and Binchois.

burla *also*, **burlesca** (It.) a piece having a comical or playful character.

Burleigh, Harry (Henry) **T(hacker)** (1866–1949) Amer. composer and singer, stud. of Dvořák. He sang in the choir of St. George's Church in New York and at Temple Emanuel and worked as a music editor for Ricordi. He wrote a large number of songs and arrangements of spirituals, many of which are performed today.

burlesque 1, an instrumental piece in a humorous or satirical style, often for piano solo. **2**, a form of dramatic entertainment, orig. the same as Burletta, later relying more and more on comedy sketches and displays of the female form.

burletta a type of late 18th- and early 19th-c. English comic opera, modeled on the Italian comic Intermezzo, such as Pergolesi's *La serva padrona*.

Burney, Charles (1726–1814) English music historian, organist and composer, primarily of instrumental works. He is best known for his many writings on music, esp. his *General History of Music* (1776–89).

Burning Fiery Furnace, The church opera by Britten to a libretto by William Plomer based on an Old Testament story. Premiere, Suffolk 1966. The second of "three parables for church performance," the others being *Curlew River* and *The Prodigal Son*.

Burton, Gary (1943–) Amer. jazz vibraphone player and bandleader. After several years of work with others, incl. George Shearing and Stan Getz, in 1967 he formed his own quartet, which presaged jazz fusion. He joined the faculty of the Berklee School in 1971.

Busch, Adolf (George Wilhelm) (1891–1952) Ger.-born Swiss violinist and composer, stud. of Willy Hess, brother of Fritz Busch. He formed the Busch Quartet in 1919 and the Busch Chamber Players in 1938, esp. noted for their performances of the Bach Brandenburg Concertos. He moved to the U.S. in 1939 and founded the Marlboro School of Music in Vermont in 1950.

Busch, Fritz (1890–1951) Ger. conductor and pianist, brother of Adolf Busch. He was conductor of the Stuttgart Opera and the Dresden Staatsoper, where he premiered works of Strauss, Busoni, Weill and Hindemith. He was later music dir. of Glyndebourne (1934–39), establishing its reputation for carefully chosen repertory and fine ensemble.

Busnois, Antoine [bü'nwä] (de Busne) (?1430–1492) Franco-Flemish composer of sacred vocal music and chansons in the Burgundian style, possibly stud. of Ockeghem. He was a member of the Dijon ducal chapel from 1467 until his death.

Busoni, Ferruccio (Dante Michelangelo Benvenuto) (1866–1924) Italian-born Ger. composer and pianist, stud. of Wilhelm Mayer. A child prodigy on the piano, he concertized from the age of eight in Italy and in Germany, playing his own works and the classics. From 1886 to 1894 he lived in Leipzig, where he produced his controversial transcriptions and editions of J.S. Bach. In 1894 he moved to Berlin, where he was to remain for the rest of his life. Here he produced his stage works, incl. the monumental opera *Doktor Faustus*, left incomplete at his death.

Bussotti, Sylvano (1931–) Italian composer, stud. of Dallapiccola and Deutsch. He has been active in several areas of the contemporary arts, incl. experimental music, film, theater and graphic art, as composer, director and designer. He was appointed artistic dir. of the Teatro La Fenice in Venice in 1975.

Buswell, James Oliver (1946–) Amer. violinist and conductor, stud.

of Galamian. He has played with the Chamber Music Society of Lincoln Center and pursued an active solo career. He has taught and conducted at the U. of Indiana since 1974.

Butterfield, Billy (Charles William) (1917–88) Amer. jazz swing trumpeter and fluegelhorn player. He played with the bands of Bob Crosby, Artie Shaw and Benny Goodman, before forming his own band after the war. He worked as a studio musician with Eddie Condon, Ray Coniff and others, toured as a soloist in the U.S. and Europe, and was a member of the World's Greatest Jazzband in the late 1960s.

Butterfly Étude popular name for the Étude in G♭ major, Op. 25 No. 9 (1832–4), by Chopin.

Buxtehude, Dietrich (?1637–1707) Danish composer and organist. He was organist of the Marienkirche at Lübeck (marrying his predecessor's daughter, as was sometimes a requirement for such a job at the time). In addition to his church obligations, he revitalized the ABENDMUSIK concerts in the church. He produced a large body of sacred and secular vocal works and organ music as well as chamber music.

BWV *abbr.* Bach-Werke-Verzeichnis. See SCHMIEDER, WOLFGANG.

Byas, Don (Carlos Wesley) (1912–72) Amer. jazz swing tenor saxophonist, strongly influenced by Coleman Hawkins and Art Tatum. He played with a number of groups, most notably Lionel Hampton, Dizzy Gillespie and Count Basie. After 1946 he settled in Paris.

Byrd, Donald (1932–) Amer. jazz trumpeter, fluegelhorn player and composer, stud. of Boulanger. He played with Art Blakey's Jazz Messengers and with many other groups, forming his own quintet in 1958, and was a major force in jazz/soul fusion in the late 1960s and 1970s. He has been active as a teacher at Howard U. in Washington, D.C., and elsewhere.

Byrd, William (?1543–1623) English composer and organist, stud. of Tallis. He was a Gentleman of the Chapel Royal from 1570. Throughout his life he produced highly inventive keyboard works and other instrumental works and songs. Until 1596 he was a music printer, first with his teacher Tallis, later with Thomas East. A Catholic in Protestant England, he produced liturgical music for both the Protestant and the Catholic service, which he courageously published.

Byzantine chant the liturgical music of the eastern Christian Roman Empire, which survives in the Eastern Orthodox rite.

C

C the first note of the scale of C major. See Pitch. **2**, the time signature for 4/4 time, a remnant of Mensural notation, where it signified *imperfect time*, or duple division of the breve, as opposed to the symbol (O), representing *perfect time*, or triple division of the breve. Cf. Alla breve. **3**, see C clef.

cabaça [kä′bä-sä] (Port.) a Latin-American percussion instrument consisting of a gourd attached to a handle and covered with beads (and sometimes filled with rattling pieces). It is used in Latin-American dance bands. Cf. Maracas.

cabaletta [It.] **1**, a song or instrumental piece in a simple, popular style with a stylized rhythmical accompaniment. **2**, the lively concluding section of an extended aria or duet, the first part of which is usu. a Cavatina. The cabaletta is often immediately preceded by an accompanied recitative.

Caballé, Montserrat [kä-bä′yä, mõnt-se′rät] (1933–) Spanish soprano, trained at the Barcelona Liceo. She sang with the Basel Opera and at Bremen before her La Scala debut in 1960. She is best known for her performances of the *bel canto* repertory of Rossini, Donizetti and Bellini, and of the works of Verdi.

cabaret a type of nightclub entertainment dating from the late 19th c. consisting of songs, piano music and other presentations (often politically oriented) for the avant-garde in the arts. Famous cabarets incl. the Chat Noir in Paris (opened 1881), where Satie and others performed, and the Überbrettl in Berlin (opened 1901), for which Schoenberg wrote songs.

Cabaret musical by John Kander, lyrics by Fred Ebb, book by Joe Masteroff, based on Christopher Isherwood's *Berlin Stories*. Premiere, New York 1966. The story of an English girl and an English writer in pre-Nazi Berlin.

Cabezón, Antonio de [kä-bä′thōn] (1510–66) Spanish composer and organist. He became organist to Queen Isabella in 1526 and performed in the chamber consort of Charles V, then joined the chapel of Prince Philip. His many works for keyboard include tientos, canons, hymns and *diferencias*.

cabinet organ a Reed organ with a pedal-operated bellows housed in a cabinet about the size of an upright piano.

Cabin in the Sky musical by Vernon Duke, lyrics by John Latouche, book by Lynn Root. Premiere, New York 1940. A parable of Negro life in the South, the show tells of the battle between the Lawd's General and Lucifer Jr. for the soul of Little Joe Jackson.

Cabrillo Music Festival an international festival of new music, held annually in California. It was founded in 1963 by Lou Harrison, Robert Hughes and Ted Teows.

caccia [′kät-chä] (It.) a 14th-c. canonic part song, often portraying hunt scenes and including animal sounds or town cries. Cf. Catch.

Caccia, La the Violin Concerto in B♭ major, Op. 8 No. 10, by Vivaldi.

caccia motet a Motet containing canonic imitation.

Caccini, Francesca [kät′chē-nē, frän′ches-kä] (Signorini; "La Cecchina") (1587–?1640) Italian singer, instrumentalist and composer, daughter of Giulio Caccini. She served the Florentine court of the Medici and wrote court entertainments in collaboration with Michelangelo the younger. Her opera, *La lib-*

erazione di Ruggiero (1625), was the first Italian opera to be performed outside Italy (Warsaw, 1682).

Caccini, Giulio (Giulio Romano) (?1545–1618) Italian composer, singer and instrumentalist at the Medici court in Florence, stud. of Animuccia. He participated in the discussions of the CAMERATA, from which a new style of song (*stile recitativo*) was developed that may be seen in his innovative collection *Le nuove musiche* (1602) and the two collections that followed it. He wrote some of the music for J. Peri's opera *Euridice* (1600), the first opera, and composed a complete setting of the same libretto two years later.

cachucha (Sp.) an Andalusian solo dance in triple time, usu. accompanied by castanets.

Cäcilienmesse [tsä'tsē-lyən"me-sə] (Ger.) the Mass in C major (1766) by Haydn.

cacophony a subjective term for harsh, dissonant music. See DISSONANCE.

cadence 1, the concluding part of a phrase, movement or work that through resolution of dissonance, or by some other means, affirms the tonality, modality or musical language of the phrase, movement or work.

In modal music, cadential resolu-tion is essentially linear, usu. involving movement by a step to the final of the current mode. As in tonal music, there are several types of cadence, defined by their finality. See MODE.

In tonal music, the *perfect* cadence (also called the *full cadence* or *full close*) consists in the resolution of a dominant chord to its tonic chord (V-I). The *imperfect* or *half* cadence ends on the dominant chord, preceded by any other chord, usu. the tonic, a secondary or applied dominant. In the *deceptive* or *interrupted* cadence, the dominant chord moves to some other chord than the tonic, usu. the submediant (V-VI) or the subdominant (V-IV). The *plagal* cadence consists in the resolution of the subdominant chord to the tonic chord (IV-I). See also SCALES (*illus.*).

In atonal music, where questions of functional harmony do not apply, a cadence (when present) is defined by other means, usu. unique to the particular work in question.

2, (Fr.) a type of TRILL.

cadenza (It., cadence) a virtuoso passage, usu. for solo instrument or voice, coming near the end of a concerto movement or at a cadential location in an aria or other work, intended to be improvised or to have an improvisatory character. It can be

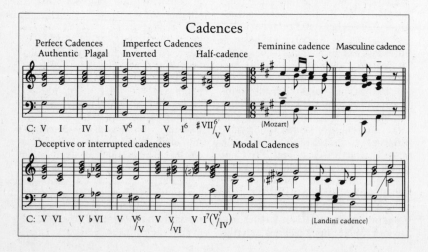

Cadences

short or extended and may have structural importance.

Cadman, Charles (Wakefield) (1881–1946) Amer. composer and pianist, conductor of the Pittsburgh Male Chorus and organist at the United Presbyterian Church in Homestead, PA. He used native American tunes for many songs and an Indian story for his opera *Shanewis, or The Robin Woman*, which was produced at the Metropolitan Opera in 1918.

caesura a brief silence or interruption in a musical phrase, indicated by a comma, apostrophe or other sign (v, "). The break is sometimes indicated for the purpose of taking a breath, but it can also indicate a purely musical interruption. Also, *comma, Luftpause* (Ger.)

café chantant [kä′fä shä′tä] (Fr., singing café) a type of entertainment of mid-19th-c. Paris consisting of popular song and drinking; a predecessor of the British MUSIC HALL.

Caffarelli (Marjorano, Gaetano) (1710–83) Italian mezzo-soprano castrato, one of the most celebrated and sought-after singers of his day, stud. of Porpora. He was a member of the royal chapel in Naples (1734–54) and sang throughout Europe and in England.

Cage, John (Milton, Jr.) (1912–) Amer. composer and writer, stud. of Richard Buhling, Adolph Weiss, Cowell and Schoenberg, and a major figure of avant-garde music since the 1940s. In the late 1930s and early 1940s he worked with percussion, prepared piano and dance and was musical dir. of the Merce Cunningham dance company. In the 1950s he experimented with chance music, deriving pitches from such diverse sources as the tossing of coins and marking imperfections on a sheet of ruled paper. He also explored the idea of events that combined unrelated and uncoordinated elements (see HAPPENING), and works whose specific sound and character would change with every performance. He has written much about music and his ideas concerning

musical composition and performance. His works incl. *Music of Changes, Imaginary Landscape Nos. 1–5, Music for Piano 1–84, Concert for Piano and Orch., 4′33″, HPSCHD, Fontana Mix, The Wonderful Widow of Eighteen Springs, Ryoanji,* etc.

caisse [kes] (Fr.) DRUM. —**grosse caisse**, [grös] (Fr.) BASS DRUM.

caisse claire (Fr.) SIDE DRUM.

caisse roulante [roo′lät] *also,* **caisse sourde** [soord] (Fr.) TENOR DRUM.

Caissons Go Rolling Along, The song (1907) by Edmund L. Gruber (1879–1941), written for the Fifth Artillery in the Philippine Islands. It was later adapted by H.W. Arberg for use as the official song of the U.S. Army artillery. The song was first published in 1918 (credited to JOHN PHILIP SOUSA).

Cajun music folk music of the French-speaking Acadians of southwestern Louisiana. It is characterized by an admixture of French folk music with Amer. southern and Afr.-Amer. styles. The country dance or *fais dodo* (Fr., go to sleep) is the most popular of Cajun musical entertainments. Cf. ZYDECO.

cakewalk a stage dance in minstrel shows employing walking figures, possibly orig. a black Amer. slave competition rewarded with a cake, in which participants parodied the mannered walk and fancy dances of their owners.

calando (It.) becoming slower and softer.

Caldara, Antonio (?1670–1736) prolific Italian composer, probably stud. of Giovanni Legrenzi. He worked in Mantua, Rome and Vienna and wrote a large number of operas, oratorios and cantatas and a lesser number of instrumental works.

Caldwell, Sarah (1924–) Amer. opera impresario and conductor, stud. of Richard Burgin and Boris Goldovsky. In 1958 she founded the Opera Company of Boston, with which she has presented many American premieres, including Roger Sessions's *Monte-*

zuma and Schoenberg's *Moses and Aaron*.

calenda (It.) **1**, a 17th-c. VILLANCICO sung on Christmas Eve. **2**, CALINDA.

Calgary Philharmonic Orchestra symphony orch. formed in 1955 by the amalgamation of the Calgary SO and the Alberta PO. Its conductors have included Haymo Taeuber, José Iturbi, Arpad Joo and Mario Bernardi.

California mission music music developed at the Spanish missions in what is now southern California during the late 17th through early 19th c.

California sound a type of COUNTRY MUSIC created by Buck Owens, who est. a recording complex in Bakersfield, CA, and whose artists incl. Merle Haggard and Wynn Stewart.

calinda *also*, **calenda** (Sp.) an Afr.-Amer. dance dating from the 17th c. in Latin America and the southern U.S. Also, *chica*.

call see SIGNAL.

Callas, Maria (1923–77) Amer.-born Greek soprano, stud. of Elvira de Hidalgo. In her earlier professional years she sang heavy roles, incl. Turandot and Brünnhilde, later relinquishing them for the *bel canto* repertory. She exhibited an exceptional intellectual grasp of style combined with a substantial dramatic talent. Trouble with her voice developed in the early 1960s, and she retired from the stage in 1965.

calliope a wind instrument invented in 1855 by A.S. Denny consisting of steam or air whistles operated from a keyboard; used in circuses, on showboats, etc.

Call Me Madam musical by Irving Berlin, book by Lindsay and Crouse. Premiere, New York 1950. A political satire about a woman ambassador, played memorably by Ethel Merman.

Calloway, Cab (Cabell) (1907–) Amer. singer and bandleader. He led a group called the Missourians (1929–48), which became the house band at the Cotton Club in New York, following Duke Ellington's band. He sang the character Sportin' Life in

Gershwin's *Porgy and Bess* and appeared in musicals and films.

Calvé (Calvet) **(de Roquer)**, **Emma** (1858–1942) French soprano, stud. of Jules Puget, Mathilde Marchesi and Rosina Laborde, famous for her interpretations of Carmen and Santuzza (*Cavalleria rusticana*). She retired from opera performance in 1904 but continued to sing in recitals until the 1920s.

calypso an improvisatory song of the Caribbean (esp. Trinidad), often satirizing current events and often accompanied by a steel band. The rhythm is in duple meter and similar to the SAMBA. The genre was popularized in the 1950s by singer Harry Belafonte. See DANCE (*illus.*).

cambiare (It., to change) an indication in orchestral music for a player to change instruments, crooks, tuning, etc. Also, *muta*.

cambiata (It., changed [note]) **1**, NOTA CAMBIATA. **2**, the voice of an adolescent male after it changes to its deeper, adult register.

camel walk an ANIMAL DANCE of the 1920s.

Camelot musical by Frederick Loewe, lyrics and book by Alan Jay Lerner, based on T.H. White's novel *The Once and Future King*. Premiere, New York 1960. A retelling of the Arthurian legend.

camera (It.) room, chamber. Cf. SONATA DA CAMERA.

Camerata (It.) a circle of intellectuals in Florence that met regularly from 1573 to 1587 to discuss matters of art, music and cultural advancement. Prominent musical members were Bardi, Caccini, Peri and Galilei. Their discussions led to humanist musical experiments with MONODY and to the development of opera.

Cammer-Ton (Ger., chamber pitch) **1**, the 18th-c. standard pitch for chamber and church music, about $a' = 410$ Hz. See PITCH, CHOR-TON. **2**, KAMMERTON.

campana (It.) BELL. —**campane**, (It.) TUBULAR BELLS.

Campanella, La (It., The Bell) the

third movement of the Violin Concerto No. 2 in B minor, Op. 7 (1826), by Paganini, arranged for piano in 1831 by Liszt as *Grand fantasia de bravoure sur La Clochette* (Fr., Grand Bravura Fantasy on The Bell).

campanelli (It.) GLOCKENSPIEL.

campanilla [käm-pä′nēl-yä] (Sp.) HANDBELL.

Campanini, Cleofonte (1860–1919) Italian opera conductor and violinist who conducted throughout Europe, the U.S. and S. Amer. He was musical dir. for the Chicago Grand Opera Company and its successor, the Chicago Opera Assoc., from 1910 until his death.

campanology the art of bell ringing or CHANGE RINGING.

Campbell, Lucie Eddie (1885–1963) Amer. gospel song composer, one of the founders of the National Baptist Training Union. She wrote, for their convention in 1919, 45 songs beginning with the words "Something within me."

Campion, Thomas (1567–1620) English poet, theorist, physician and composer of lute-songs, for which he wrote his own texts. He was a supporter of the experiments in MUSIQUE MESURÉE and of the Florentine monodists.

Camp Meeting the Symphony No. 3 (1904) by Ives. Its three movements are titled "Old Folks Gatherin'," "Children's Day" and "Communion."

camp-meeting spiritual a folk hymn sung at the open-air religious camp meetings during the GREAT REVIVAL in early 19th-c. pioneer America. Cf. SPIRITUAL.

Campra, André (1660–1744) French composer of stage works and sacred choral music. He was choir master at Notre Dame Cathedral in Paris, at the same time writing for the stage (under assumed names, to protect his position) and supplying *divertissements* for the Paris nobility. He was appointed to the royal chapel in 1723.

Canada Council Canadian crown corporation est. in 1957 to encourage and support the arts, humanities and social sciences in Canada.

Canadian Brass a Canadian brass quintet formed in 1970, noted for their combination of virtuoso playing with a lively, tongue-in-cheek presentation.

Canadian Broadcasting Corporation Canadian governmental broadcasting system est. in 1936. For some years the corporation supported orchestras and other performing groups in various parts of the country, most of which have now been disbanded. The corporation also presents frequent broadcasts featuring musical organizations across the country. Abbr., *CBC*.

Canadian Music Centre a central library and information center for Canadian music, founded in 1959.

Canadian Opera Company opera company founded in Toronto in 1950 (as the Opera Festival Association) under director Herman Geiger-Torel and others.

Canal, Marguerite (1890–1978) French composer, winner of the Prix de Rome and the first woman to conduct orchestral concerts in France. She taught solfège for singers at the Paris Conservatoire from 1932 until her retirement. Her works, mainly for voice, incl. the opera *Tlass Atka* (left unfinished at her death), many songs, a violin sonata and other chamber music.

canary 1, *also,* **canarie** (Fr.) a lively 16th- to 18th-c. court dance in triple or compound duple time, an optional part of the Baroque dance SUITE. **2,** a slang term for a female singer in a dance band.

cancan (Fr.) a woman's line dance of French or Algerian origin, characterized by high kicking, splits and a lively tempo in duple meter. The dance first appeared in Offenbach's operetta *Orpheus in the Underworld* (1858), where it is called the "Grand Galop."

Can-Can musical by Cole Porter, book by Abe Burrows. Premiere, New

York 1953. The story of the legitim-
izing of the CANCAN in Paris.

cancel to counteract the effect of a
previous accidental (a sharp or flat) by
use of the NATURAL sign; also, an obsolete term for the natural sign itself.

canción [kän-thē′ōn] (Sp.) a song, esp.
a song of Spain or of Latin Amer.

cancioncilla [-′thē-lyä] (Sp.) a short
17th-c. song similar to the VILLAN-
CICO.

cancionero [kän-thyō′nä-rō] (Sp.) a
collection of Spanish or Portuguese
songs and poems. Until the 19th c.
the term referred to collections of
texts without music.

cancrizans (Lat., crablike) RETRO-
GRADE.

Candide musical by Leonard Bernstein, lyrics by Richard Wilbur, Stephen Sondheim and others; book by
Lillian Hellman, based on Voltaire's
novel. Premiere, New York 1956, revised version, New York 1959. The
adventures of Candide and his beloved Cunegonde in "the best of all
possible worlds."

canon 1, a procedure for deriving a
polyphonic texture from a single melody through exact imitation in successive voices. Also, *chace, round.*
Cf. CACCIA, FUGUE. 2, a plucked
ZITHER derived from the Arabic
QANUN.

canonical hours the daily services of
the Roman Catholic church, also
known as the DIVINE OFFICE.

canso (Provençal) a troubadour love
song.

cantabile [kän′tä-bē-lä] (It., singable)
in a melodious or flowing manner;
also, a work to be performed in a cantabile style.

cantata (It., sung) a sacred or secular
composition for solo voice or voices,
or for chorus and solo voice or voices,
accompanied by several instruments
or orch. A cantata will often be dramatic, but it is not intended to be
staged.

Cantata Singers name for several
choral groups, incl. **1**, a choral group
founded in New York in 1934 by Paul
Boepple. **2**, a professional 40-voice

Canon

Canon at the unison

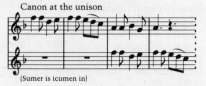

(Sumer is icumen in)

Mensuration canon
orig. notation

realization

(Josquin des Pres, Missa L'Homme armé)

Spiral (modulating) canon

C major

D major

(J.S. Bach, Musical Offering) etc.

mixed choir founded in Vancouver in
1958 by Hugh McLean.

cantatrice (It., Fr.) a female singer.

cante chico (Sp.) all flamenco songs
not of the CANTE HONDO type, esp.
the popular Flamenco of theaters and
night clubs.

cante hondo (Sp., deep song) a type
of flamenco or gypsy song, often
tragic, usu. beginning with a long
melisma.

Cantelli, Guido (1920–56) Italian
conductor. He appeared frequently
with the Philharmonia Orch. in London and the orch. of La Scala. He had
just been named principal conductor
at La Scala when he was tragically
killed in an air accident.

Canteloube (de Calaret), (Marie-)

Joseph (1879–1957) French composer, stud. of d'Indy, best known for his settings of folk songs from the Auvergne region of France.

cantica (Lat.) the sung sections of ancient Roman comedy, esp. those sung by soloists.

canti carnascialeschi [kär-nä-shä'les-kē] (It., carnival songs) polyphonic strophic songs sung in 15th- and 16th-c. Florence during the pre-Lenten and May (*Calendimaggio*) festivals. The songs are usu. lewd and indulge in double meanings. Cf. MASCHERATA, CARRO, TRIONFO.

canticle a song or hymn, esp. one intended for a church service and based on a biblical text.

Canticum Sacrum work for soloists, chorus and orch. (1955) by Stravinsky, his first 12-tone work. The complete title is *Canticum Sacrum ad honorem Sancti Marci nominis* (Lat., Holy Song to the Honor of the Name of St. Mark), written for the basilica of St. Mark's in Venice.

cantiga (Sp., Port.) a Spanish or Portuguese monophonic folk song, usu. treating of love or religion.

cantilena (It., song) **1**, a simple song. The term has been applied to different types of song in different periods of music history, incl. polyphonic works. **2**, LULLABY. **3**, CANTABILE.

cantillation liturgical chanting, esp. in the Hebrew synagogue service; INTONATION.

cantio (Lat.) a Latin strophic, monophonic song of the late Middle Ages, based on a sacred text and usu. having a refrain.

cantional (Lat.) a HYMNAL.

cantique [kän'tēk] (Fr., hymn) a French religious song.

canto (It., Sp.) **1**, melody or song. **2**, the art of singing. See BEL CANTO.

cantor **1**, a singer, esp. a choir leader; precentor. **2**, a synagogue officer who chants the liturgical music and leads the congregation.

Cantor, Eddie (Itzkowitz, Isidore) (1892–1964) Amer. singer and actor. He appeared with the Ziegfeld Follies (1917–27) and later worked in Hollywood films and on radio. Songs associated with him incl. "Dinah" and "If You Knew Susie."

cantorial *also*, **cantoris** (Lat.) relating to or of the cantoris (north) side of a church, the side where the cantor sits; contrasted with DECANAL.

cantus (Lat., melody) a principal melody or voice.

cantus firmus (Lat., fixed melody) a preexisting melody, usu. derived from Gregorian chant, upon which a new composition is based. Cf. CANTUS PRIUS FACTUS.

cantus planus (Lat., plainchant) an unmeasured melody to which liturgical texts are sung during the course of the Roman Catholic liturgy. In a broader sense, any unmeasured melody.

cantus prius factus ['prē-oos] (Lat., preexistent melody) a preexisting melody, not necessarily based on chant, on which a new polyphonic composition is based. Cf. CANTUS FIRMUS.

canzona villanesca *or* **alla Napoletana** VILLANELLA.

canzone *also*, **canzona** [kän'tsō-ne, -nä] (It., song) **1**, a medieval Italian or Provençal lyric poem in stanza form; also, the musical setting of such a poem, usu. polyphonic and related to the FROTTOLA. **2**, an instrumental composition similar in style derived from the French CHANSON.

canzonet [kan-zə'net] *also*, **canzonetta** [kän-tsō'nät-tä] (It.) **1**, a 16th- and 17th-c. part-song similar to a MADRIGAL, but usu. simpler and lighter; also, any light song. **2**, an instrumental work of similar style.

CAPAC COMPOSERS, AUTHORS AND PUBLISHERS ASSOCIATION OF CANADA.

Cape, Safford (1906–73) Amer. conductor, composer and musicologist, founder in 1933 of the early music performing group Pro Musica Antiqua, of Brussels.

Capitan, El comic opera in 3 acts by John Philip Sousa to a libretto by C. Klein and T. Frost. Premiere, Boston 1896. The viceroy of Peru joins a plot against himself in order to foil it.

Caplet, André (1878–1925) French composer and conductor, winner of the Prix de Rome in 1901. A friend of Debussy, he conducted the premiere of *Le Martyre de Saint-Sébastien* and orchestrated a number of the composer's piano works. He was conductor of the Boston Opera (1910–14), then gave up conducting to devote his time to composition.

capo (It., head) see DA CAPO.

Capobianco, Tito (1931–) Argentinian-born Amer. opera dir. and administrator. He has been resident stage dir. of New York City Opera, artistic dir. of the Cincinnati Opera and of the San Diego Opera, and vice president and general dir. of the Pittsburgh Opera. He also founded the American Opera Center at the Juilliard School (1967).

capotasto *also*, **capo** (It.) a device that can be attached to the fingerboard of a guitar and similar instruments to raise the pitch of all the strings for the purpose of transposition.

cappella (It.) CHAPEL.

Cappella Giulia ['joo-lyä] (It.) the choir that sang for the services in St. Peter's in Rome; distinguished from the **Cappella Sistina**, the Papal Choir, which sang for the Pope's private services in the Sistine Chapel.

Cappuccilli, Piero [käp-poo'chěl-lē] (1929–) Italian baritone, stud. of Donaggio, known esp. for his portrayal of Verdi roles.

capriccio [kä'prět-chō] (It.) *also*, **caprice** [kä'prēs] (Fr.) an instrumental composition in a free form and lively tempo usu. exhibiting fanciful imagination. Cf. FANTASIA (1,), CANZONE (2,).

Capriccio opera in one act by Richard Strauss to a libretto by Clemens Krauss. Premiere, Munich, 1942. A dramatization of the eternal question as to which is more important, the words or the music. The question is not answered.

Capriccio espagnol [es-pä'nyōl] (Fr., Spanish Caprice) suite for orch, Op. 34 (1887), by Rimsky-Korsakov, based on original themes with a Spanish flavor.

Capriccio italien [ē-tä'lyē] (Fr., Italian, Caprice) symphonic poem, Op. 45 (1880), by Tchaikovsky, using Italian melodies.

capriccioso [kä-prēt'chō-zō] (It.) free, fanciful.

Captain Beefheart (Vliet, Don Van) (1941–) Amer. rock singer and instrumentalist. He formed the band Captain Beefheart and the Magic Band in 1964 in California, producing a music which combines avant-garde jazz, rock, blues and classical music.

Capricorn Concerto concerto grosso for flute, oboe, trumpet and orch. (1944) by Barber.

caprino (It.) TRILLO (2,).

Capuleti ed i Montecchi, I (It., The Capulets and the Montagues) tragic opera in 2 acts by Bellini to a libretto by Felice Romani, derived from Shakespeare's *Romeo and Juliet*. Premiere, Venice 1830. The role of Romeo was written for mezzo-soprano, but it has also been revised to be sung by a tenor.

caracole (Sp.) an Andalusian gypsy song in flamenco style.

Caramoor Festival an annual summer concert series est. 1946 in Katonah, NY. The festival orch. is largely made up of players from the St. Luke's Chamber Ensemble in New York City. Directors of the festival have incl. Alfred Wallenstein, Julius Rudel and John Nelson.

Cardew, Cornelius (1936–81) English pianist and composer, stud. of Ferguson and Petrassi. In the late 1950s he was an assistant to Stockhausen. He was particularly interested in improvised and indeterminate music and unconventional use of conventional forces, and in 1969 he formed an experimental group in London called the SCRATCH ORCHESTRA to perform such works.

caribo (It.) an instrumental LAI.

Carignan, Jean (Ti-Jean) (1916–) Canadian folk fiddler from Québec. He played with George Wade and Alan Mills and led his own bands, also appearing in various festivals. He retired from performance in 1978.

carillon 1, a set of tuned bells, usu. mounted in a tower, covering as many as 6 octaves and struck by hammers operated from a keyboard. Cf. BELLRINGING. **2,** an electronically generated carillon. **3,** an ORGAN STOP imitating a carillon.

carioca [kä-rē'ō-kä] (Port.) a Brazilian dance similar to the SAMBA in a lively 2/4 meter.

Carissimi, Giacomo (1605–74) important Italian composer of cantatas, oratorios, motets and Mass settings. He was *maestro di cappella* of the Collegio Germanico in Rome in 1629, which position he retained until his death.

Carl, William Crane (1865–1936) Amer. organist and founder of the Guilmant Organ School (1899). The school trained hundreds of church musicians, and Carl introduced a greatly expanded repertory and more virtuosic technique into the standard organ literature and pedagogy.

Carlos, Wendy (Walter) (1939–) Amer. composer, mainly of electronic music. She collaborated with Robert Moog on refining the Moog synthesizer and in 1968 recorded *Switched-on Bach* using that instr. Other compositions incl. the film scores for *A Clockwork Orange, The Shining* and *TRON.* Carlos developed the first digitally synthesized orch. on her album *Digital Moonscapes* (1985).

carmen (Lat., song; pl., *carmina*) a song; also, an instrumental CHANSON.

Carmen tragic opera in 4 acts by Bizet to a libretto by Henri Meilhac and Ludovic Halévy based on the novelette by Prosper Merimée. Orig. written as an opéra-comique with spoken dialogue; the sung recitatives were added later. The gypsy girl Carmen at first attracts then discards the young officer Don José; when he cannot win her back, he stabs her to death.

Carmen Jones adaptation of Bizet's opera CARMEN by Oscar Hammerstein II, making the characters Negro workers in a southern parachute factory during World War II. Premiere, New York 1943.

Carmichael, Hoagy (Hoagland) **(Howard)** (1899–1981) Amer. pianist, singer and composer of popular and jazz songs and Broadway musical scores. His songs incl. "Stardust," "Georgia on My Mind" and "Lazy River."

Carmina Burana scenic cantata (1937) by Carl Orff, based on 13th-c. Latin poems on the subjects of love, drink and the pleasures of life. It is one of a trilogy of works, the other two being *Catulli Carmina* (1952) and *Trionfi dell' Afrodite* (1953).

Carnaval Romain, Le [rō'mɛ̃] (Fr.) ROMAN CARNIVAL, THE.

Carnegie Hall the name given to several concert halls endowed by philanthropist Andrew Carnegie. The most famous, Carnegie Hall in New York, opened in 1891 and is noted for its excellent acoustics.

Carney, Harry (Howell) (1910–74) Amer. jazz baritone saxophonist, one of the first soloists on the instrument. He played with Duke Ellington's band from 1927 until his death and invented the extended technique called CIRCULAR BREATHING.

Carnival 1, a set of twenty piano pieces, Op. 9 (1835), by Schumann, subtitled *Scènes mignonnes sur quatre notes* (Fr., Charming Scenes on Four Notes). The four notes are A-E♭-C-B—representing the letters A-S-C-H, which spell the name of the home town of Schumann's beloved at the time. The scene is a ball attended by Schumann (in his guises as Florestan and as Eusebius), Paganini, Chopin, Clara Wieck and characters from the *commedia dell'arte.* **2,** musical by Bob Merrill, book by Michael Stewart, based on the film *Lili.* Premiere, New York 1961. An orphaned waif, Lili, joins a carnival and falls in love with a magician.

Carnival Joke from Vienna FASCHINGSSCHWANK AUS WIEN.

Carnival of the Animals (Fr. *Le Car-*

naval des animaux) suite (a *fantaisie zoologique*) for two pianos, string quintet, flute, clarinet and xylophone (1886) by Saint-Saëns. The piece depicts a swan, tortoises, fossils, pianists, etc. The composer suppressed the work, except for the swan movement, during his lifetime.

carnyx an ancient Celtic TRUMPET with a bell shaped like an animal head.

carol 1, a ROUND dance, orig. assoc. with May Day celebrations. **2**, a song, esp. a popular song, of rejoicing or praise, orig. commemorating an important occasion, now usu. assoc. with Christmas. It is characterized by a refrain (*burden*) repeated after each stanza.

Carousel musical by Richard Rodgers, lyrics and book by Oscar Hammerstein II, based on Ferenc Molnar's play *Liliom*. Premiere, New York 1945. A fantasy about a carnival barker who marries a local factory girl, is killed in a robbery, and then returns to earth.

Carpenter, John Alden (1876–1951) Amer. composer, stud. of Paine, Elgar (briefly) and Bernhard Ziehn. He was the son of a wealthy industrialist and worked in the family business until 1936. His works show the influence of French impressionism and Amer. jazz; best known are the "jazz pantomime" *Krazy Kat* (1921, rev. 1940) and the ballet *Skyscrapers* (1923–4).

Carr, Benjamin (1768–1831) English-born Amer. publisher, composer and organist, stud. of Samuel Arnold and Samuel Wesley. He founded a publishing business in Baltimore, with outlets in New York and Philadelphia, where he became organist at St. Peter's Episcopal Church. Because of his involvement in all aspects of the city's musical life, he was called the "Father of Philadelphia Music."

Carreras, José (1946–) outstanding Spanish lyric tenor, educated at the Barcelona Conservatory. His U.S. debut was at the New York City Opera in 1972 and he debuted at the Metropolitan Opera two years later.

Carrillo(-Trujillo), Julián (Antonio) (1875–1965) Mexican conductor, violinist and composer. He studied at the National Conservatory in Mexico City, and in Ghent and Leipzig. In 1914 he organized the American SO in New York and was later dir. of the National SO and the National Conservatory in Mexico. Many of his works employ MICROTONES, which he called "sonido 13." In 1930 he formed a full orch. capable of playing in microtones, invented microtonal pianos for the same purpose and developed a new notational system using numbers rather than notes.

carro (It.) a type of Italian festival song performed by costumed singers on floats. Cf. CANTI CARNASCI-ALESCHI.

Carry Me Back to Old Virginny song by JAMES A. BLAND (1854–1911), the state song of Virginia.

Carry Nation opera in 2 acts by Douglas Moore to a libretto by William North Jayme. Premiere, Lawrence, KS, 1966. The story of the early life of the celebrated evangelist.

Cars, The Amer. rock group formed in 1976 in Massachusetts. Its music incorporates minimalism and other avant-garde elements.

Carson, "Fiddlin' " John (1868–1949) Amer. country-music fiddler and singer, seven-time Georgia state champion fiddler. Through his many recordings, he is considered a pioneer of HILLBILLY MUSIC.

Carte, Richard D'Oyly (1844–1901) English impresario, noted for his association with Gilbert and Sullivan operettas. He commissioned their first collaboration, *Trial by Jury*, the success of which led to the formation of the Comedy Opera Company to produce their future works. In 1881 he built the Savoy Theatre, the first theater in London to be fully lit by electricity.

Carter, Benny (Lester, Bennett) (1907–) Amer. swing jazz alto saxophonist, trumpeter, clarinetist and arranger. He played with Duke Ellington, Charlie Johnson and Fletcher

Henderson, later forming his own band in 1932.

Carter, Betty (Jones, Lillie Mae) (1930–) innovative and influential Amer. jazz singer. She toured with Lionel Hampton's band and in Ray Charles's touring show (early 1960s). In 1971 she founded her own recording company, Bet-Car Productions, and in 1975 formed her own trio.

Carter, Elliott (Cook) (1908–) eminent Amer. composer, trained at Harvard and with Boulanger in Paris, winner of many awards, incl. Pulitzer Prizes for his String Quartets Nos. 2 and 3 (1960, 1973). He has held teaching positions at the Peabody Conservatory, Columbia, Queens College (NY), Yale, and the Dartington and Tanglewood summer schools.

His works incl. *Variations for Orchestra, Double Concerto* for harpsichord and piano, *Concerto for Orchestra,* choral works (*Musicians Wrestle Everywhere*), songs, sonatas for cello and piano, 3 string quartets, *Eight Études and a Fantasy* for ww quintet, *Night Fantasies* for piano and other chamber music.

Carter, Ron(ald Levin) (1937–) Amer. jazz double bassist and cellist, educated at the Eastman and Manhattan schools. He played with Chico Hamilton, Cannonball Adderley, Thelonious Monk, Miles Davis (for five years) and the New York Jazz Quartet. He has recorded extensively.

Carter, Shirley VERRETT, SHIRLEY.

Carter, Wilf(red Arthur Charles) (1904–) Canadian country-music singer, songwriter and guitarist, a popular radio host in the 1930s and a successful recording and touring artist.

Carter Family, The influential Amer. country-music trio from Virginia active from the late 1920s to the mid 1940s, during which time they made more than 300 recordings. They were elected to the Country Music Hall of Fame in 1970.

Caruso, Enrico (1873–1921) celebrated Italian tenor, stud. of Guglielmo Vergine and conductor Vincenzo Lombardi. From 1902 until his death he sang frequently at the Metropolitan Opera and in Europe, but seldom in Italy; he also made many recordings. His wide repertory embraced the French and Italian lyric repertory as well as the more dramatic Verdi roles.

Carvalho, Eleazar de (1912–) Brazilian composer and conductor of Dutch and Brazilian Indian extraction, stud. of Koussevitzky at the Berkshire Music Center. He has been conductor of the St. Louis SO, the Hofstra U. Orch. and the orch. of the Yale School of Music in addition to guest engagements in Europe. In 1973 he returned to Brazil to conduct in São Paolo.

Cary, Annie Louise (1841–1921) Amer. contralto. She studied in Boston and with Pauline Viardot in Scandinavia. She specialized in Verdi roles and was the first American to sing a Wagner role in the U.S. (Ortrud in *Lohengrin,* 1877).

Caryll, Ivan (Tillein, Félix) (1861–1921) Belgian-born Amer. composer and conductor, mainly of light operas and musical comedies. He was best known for the waltz from *The Pink Lady* (1911).

Casa Loma Orchestra a cooperative orch. developed in 1929 by saxophonist Glen Gray; a predecessor of the big swing bands. The band continued touring until 1950 and recording until the early 1960s.

Casadesus, Robert (Marcel) (1899–1972) French pianist and composer, educated at the Paris Conservatoire. He toured as a soloist and as part of two duos, one with violinist Zino Francescatti, the other with his wife, pianist **Gaby Casadesus** (1901–). From 1921 he was a professor at the American Conservatory in Fontainebleau, which he later directed. His son, **Jean (Michel) Casadesus** (1927–72), was also a pianist and taught in Fontainebleau and at SUNY Binghamton.

Casals, Pablo (1876–1973) highly esteemed Spanish cellist, pianist, composer and conductor, trained at the Barcelona Municipal Music School, the Madrid Conservatory and in Brussels. Casals left Spain in 1936 and refused to play in any Nazi-dominated country; from 1945 to 1950 he did not play publicly in any country that recognized the Franco regime. Thereafter he recorded, directed an annual festival in Puerto Rico and taught in Siena and Marlboro, VT. He was renowned both as a soloist and as a chamber music player, in trios with violinist Crickboom and composer Granados and later with Thibaud and Cortot. He was associated with the founding of the École Normale de Musique in Paris and served as a dir. of the school.

Casavant Frères Canadian organ manufacturing firm founded in 1845.

cascata (It.) a type of TIRATA.

Casella, Alfredo (1883–1947) influential Ital. composer, pianist and conductor. He was an active figure in several important contemporary Ital. music organizations. As a composer he wrote works in all genres, incl. ballets, operas, symphonies, concertos, songs and chamber music.

Cash, Johnny (John R.) (1932–) Amer. country-music singer and songwriter of Cherokee Indian extraction. His repertory is one of the most eclectic in country music and includes rural, gospel and popular songs as well as rock and roll. He was elected to the Country Music Hall of Fame in 1980.

cassa (It.) DRUM. —**gran cassa**, (It.) BASS DRUM.

cassa rullante (It.) TENOR DRUM.

cassation an 18th-c. instrumental composition similar to a SERENADE, often performed outdoors.

Cassel, (John) Walter (1910–) Amer. baritone, active both in opera and in musical comedy. He created the role of Horace Tabor in Douglas Moore's *The Ballad of Baby Doe* (1956).

Cassilly, Richard (1927–) Amer. dramatic tenor, educated at the Peabody Conservatory. His Amer. debut

was at the Chicago Lyric Opera in 1959 singing Laca in *Jenůfa*. His roles incl. Tannhäuser, Peter Grimes and Siegmund (*Die Walküre*).

Castaldo, Joseph (1927–) Amer. composer and teacher, stud. of Persichetti. He was president of the Philadelphia College of Performing Arts (1976–83).

castanets a CONCUSSION INSTRUMENT of Spanish origin consisting of two small shells (of wood, ivory or other material) held in one hand and struck together to produce a clicking sound.

Castelnuovo-Tedesco, Mario (1895–1968) Italian pianist and prolific composer, stud. of Pizzetti. He came to the USA in 1939 and lived in California from 1940 on, writing film scores (incl. *Gaslight*) and teaching at the Los Angeles Conservatory.

Castiglioni, Niccolò (1932–) Italian composer, pianist and writer on music, stud. of Ghedini. He lived in the U.S. from 1966 to 1969, working at SUNY Buffalo, the U. of Michigan and the U. of Washington (Seattle). His works include stage, vocal, orchestral and chamber music compositions.

Castle Garden a large 19th-c. concert center in New York.

Castleman, Charles (Martin) (1941–) Amer. violinist, stud. of Galamian. He founded the Quartet Program, a training program for chamber ensembles, and was a member of the New String Trio of New York and the Raphael Trio. He has taught at the Philadelphia Musical Academy and the Eastman School and has toured extensively.

castrato (It., pl. *castrati*) a male singer castrated in youth to preserve the soprano or contralto range of his voice. Castrati performed from the 16th c. until the mid-19th c. in church and in opera roles that are now performed primarily by female singers costumed as men or occasionally by falsettists. Also, *musico* (It.).

cat slang for a jazz musician or aficionado.

Catalani, Alfredo (1854–93) Italian composer, trained in Lucca and at the Paris Conservatoire. His best-known work is the opera LA WALLY. His music was frequently conducted by Toscanini.

Catalogue Aria popular name for Leporello's aria "Madamina, il catalogo è questo" in Mozart's opera *Don Giovanni*, which presents a list of Don Giovanni's seductions.

Catalogue d'oiseaux [dwä'zō] (Fr., Bird Catalogue) cycle of 13 piano pieces (1959) by Messiaen, describing French birds in their habitats.

catch a ROUND at the unison for three or more male voices, usu. unaccompanied, on texts that were often racy. The form was popular in England from the 16th to the 18th c. Cf. CACCIA.

cathedral music music composed for use in the liturgical services of the cathedrals of the Church of England, as distinguished from the music of the parish churches.

Catlett, Sid(ney) ("Big Sid") (1910–51) outstanding Amer. swing jazz drummer, noted both for his precision and for his extended solo playing. He played with Louis Armstrong during the late 1930s and the 1940s.

Cat's Fugue a harpsichord sonata in G minor by Domenico Scarlatti, so called because the theme of the sonata was supposedly suggested to the composer by the sounds his cat made walking on the keys.

Caucasian Sketches suite for orch. (1895) by Ippolitov-Ivanov.

cauda ['kow-dä] (Lat., tail) a melismatic phrase often concluding a CONDUCTUS.

Cavalieri, Emilio de' (?1550–1602) Italian organist, teacher, diplomat and composer, known for his *Rappresentatione di Anima, e di Corpo* (1600), the first surviving play set entirely to music and the earliest printed score using figured bass. It has also been called the first oratorio.

Cavalleria rusticana (It., Rustic Chivalry) tragic opera in one act by Mascagni to a libretto by C. Targioni-Tozzetti and G. Menasci after a story by Giovanni Verga. Premiere, Rome, 1890. The "Intermezzo" is often played alone in symphony concerts. The flirting of Alfio's wife Lola with her former sweetheart, Turiddu, leads to a duel and the tragic death of Turiddu.

Cavalli (Bruni), **Pier** (Pietro) **Francesco** (1602–76) Italian singer, organist and composer of operas and sacred and secular vocal music. He sang in the choir at St. Mark's in Venice under Monteverdi's direction and won the post of second organist in 1639. His first opera was composed that same year, and his many works in that genre established him as the principal successor to Monteverdi in Italy.

cavata (It., extraction) an arioso-like passage at the end of a RECITATIVE set in regular meter and tempo.

cavatina (It.) a simple operatic aria of slow tempo often forming the first part of the conventional 18th-c. solo scene, followed by a CABALETTA.

Cavazzoni, Marco Antonio (da Bologna) [kä-vät'tsō-nē] (c1490–1570) Italian organist and composer. He worked at St. Mark's in Venice and in other Italian cities. His ricercars and canzonas are some of the earliest so titled. His son, **Girolamo Cavazzoni** (1510–c1565), was also an organist and composer; he served at the court of Mantua.

Cazden, Norman (1914–80) Amer. composer, pianist and musicologist, stud. of Piston and Copland. He taught at Vassar College, the U. of Michigan, the U. of Illinois and the U. of Maine. His works incl. concertos and orchestral works, many instrumental sonatas and other chamber music, piano works and incidental music.

CBC CANADIAN BROADCASTING CORPORATION.

CBC Symphony orch. of the CBC in Toronto, active from 1952 to 1964.

C clef a sign (𝄡) indicating the position on the staff of middle C (c'). See CLEF.

CD COMPACT DISC.
cebell *also,* **cibell** an old English
dance resembling the GAVOTTE.
Ceccato, Aldo (1934–) Italian conductor trained in Milan and Berlin
and with de Sabata. He is noted in
particular for his opera conducting.
His Amer. debut was at the Chicago
Lyric Opera in 1969, and he was music dir. of the Detroit SO from 1974–
77.
Cecilian movement a 19th-c. movement to reform and modernize the
music of the Roman Catholic
Church.
cédez [sā'dā] (Fr., yield) RALLEN-
TANDO.
cefaut the pitch c in the HEXACHORD
system.
celesta *also,* **céleste** [sā'lest] (Fr.) a
keyboard GLOCKENSPIEL, invented in
1886 by Auguste Mustel. Metal hammers strike steel plates producing a
bell-like sound which is amplified by
a resonator. The instrument sounds
an octave higher than written.
Celestin, Papa (Oscar Phillip) (1884–
1954) Amer. jazz trumpet player and
bandleader. His Tuxedo Jazz Orch.
(a.k.a. Original Tuxedo Orch.) was
popular from 1917 to 1954. In 1953
Celestin gave a command performance for President Eisenhower.
celestina a keyboard instrument, invented in 1772 by Adam Walker,
whose strings were bowed by a continuous band of silk or other material.
The bowing device could also be
added to a harpsichord.
Celibidache, Sergiu (1912–) Rumanian conductor, stud. of Fritz
Stein. He has been principal conductor of the Berlin PO (1945–52) and
more recently musical dir. of the city
of Munich. He is noted for his meticulous attention to detail combined
with an exuberant personality.
cell a small group of pitches, similar
to a MOTIF, used as a compositional
building block, esp. in serial music
(see SERIALISM).
cello 1, *also* **violoncello** the bass
member of the VIOLIN family, tuned
an octave below the viola and played
in a vertical position, usu. supported

by a metal pin between the seated
player's legs. **2**, a deep-toned STEEL
DRUM.
cembalo ['chem-bä-lō] (It.) HARPSI-
CHORD.
cencerro [thän'thä-rō] (Sp.) a type of
Cuban COWBELL used as a percussion
instrument in Lat.-Amer. dance orchestras.
Cenerentola, La [chā-nā'rān-tō-lä]
(It.) CINDERELLA.
cent an INTERVAL equal to 1/100th of
an equal-tempered semitone.
cento (Lat., patchwork) **1**, QUOD-
LIBET. **2**, a melody formed from preexisting chant phrases.
Central City Opera Festival annual
summer opera festival, est. 1932 in
Central City, CO. Most of the performances take place in a restored
Victorian opera house built in 1878.
Central Park Garden Concerts a concert series in New York presented between 1868 and 1875 and conducted
by THEODORE THOMAS.
Central Park in the Dark one of two
"contemplations" (the other is THE
UNANSWERED QUESTION) for small
orch. (1906) by Ives. It describes the
famous park in New York.
Centre for American Music a center
for the study and performance of
Amer. music, est. in 1974 and based
in Staffordshire, England. The center
houses one of the best collections of
Amer. music materials in Europe.
cercar la nota [chär'kär] (It., search for
the note) in singing, the anticipation
of the following syllable, as if searching for the right note.
Ceremony of Carols a work for treble voices and harp (1942) by Britten,
a setting of nine medieval English
carols.
Cerha, Friedrich ['cher-hä] (1926–)
Austrian composer and conductor, a
founder of the Viennese chamber
group Die Reihe, dedicated to the performance of music by young composers. He has been on the faculty of the
Vienna Academy of Music since
1959, where he also directs an electronic studio. He completed the un-

finished Act 3 of Berg's *Lulu* for performance (1979).

Certon, Pierre [ser'tō] (c1510–1572) French composer of sacred vocal works, incl. masses and motets, and of chansons. He was master of the choristers at the Sainte-Chapelle in Paris from 1536 until his death.

cervalat *also,* **cervalas, cervalet** see RACKETT.

cesolfa the pitch c″ in the HEXACHORD system.

cesolfaut the pitch c′ in the HEXACHORD system.

Cesti, Antonio (Pietro) ['ches-tē] (1623–69) Italian singer and composer, prob. stud. of Abbatini. A Franciscan priest, he was at the court of Archduke Ferdinand Karl at Innsbruck for most of his career, except for a brief period at the Papal Court. His surviving works incl. a large number of secular cantatas and 15 operas, the best-known of which are *Orontea* (his first), *La Dori* and *Il pomo d'oro.*

ceterone a bass CITTERN used as a continuo instrument.

Cetra, La ['chä-trä] (It., the zither) the 12 violin concertos of Op. 9 by Vivaldi.

c.f. *abbr.* CANTUS FIRMUS.

C flat the pitch (C♭) one half step below C, the enharmonic equivalent of B natural. See PITCH.

Chabrier,   (Alexis-)Emmanuel [shä'bryä] (1841–94) innovative French pianist and composer of operas, songs, orchestral and piano works. He is best known for his orchestral rhapsody *España* and for his piano works; his operas have not remained in the repertory.

chace [shäs] (Fr.) a 14th-c. French term for CANON.

cha cha cha *also,* **cha cha** couple dance derived from the MAMBO, esp. popular during the late 1950s. See DANCE (*illus.*).

chaconne [shä'kon] (Fr.) *also,* **chacony 1,** an old Spanish dance in slow triple meter resembling the PASSACAGLIA. **2,** a musical composition in triple time with a stress on the second beat, often based on a repeating chord pattern.

Chadabe, Joel (A.) (1938–) Amer. composer, mainly of electronic music, stud. of Elliott Carter. Chadabe founded the electronic music studio at SUNY Albany and later became president of the Composers' Forum in New York.

Chadwick,   George   (Whitefield) (1854–1931) prolific Amer. composer, trained in Europe. In 1897 he became director of the New England Conservatory, where he established an opera workshop and a repertory orch.; he was also director-conductor of the Worcester (1889–99) and Springfield (1897–1901) Festivals. His works—which incl. operas, choral and orchestral works, chamber music and songs—have a distinct American flavor and incorporate elements of Afro-Caribbean dance rhythms and inventive orchestration.

chainsaw a technique of guitar playing used in rock music.

chair organ *also,* **choir organ** a second organ added to the main organ and having its own case, usu. placed behind the organist. It was frequently used for choral accompaniment.

Chaliapin, Fyodor (Ivanovich) (1873–1938) Russian bass, stud. of D.A. Usatov. In Russia he sang with various companies before making his international debut at La Scala in 1901 and the Metropolitan Opera in 1907. He established a reputation as one of the finest singing actors of his time. His roles incl. Boris Godunov, Mefistofele and Philip II (*Don Carlo*), as well as comic roles.

Challis, Bill (William H.) (1904–) Amer. jazz arranger. He played piano and saxophone with Bix Beiderbecke and in Paul Whiteman's band.

Challis, John (1907–74) Amer. harpsichord maker, stud. of Arnold Dolmetsch. He experimented with new styles and materials in an effort to combine the sound of period instruments with the stability of the modern piano. He was the teacher of WILLIAM DOWD.

Chaloff, Serge (1923–57) Amer. jazz baritone saxophonist, a member of George Auld's band and later of Woody Herman's orch. He was strongly influenced by Charlie Parker and was an important figure in the bop movement.

chalumeau [shä-lü'mō] (Fr.) **1,** SHAWM. **2,** an obsolete reed instrument, forerunner of the CLARINET. **3,** the lowest register of the clarinet, having a special dark, musky character. The word is sometimes used as an indication to play a passage an octave lower. **4,** *also,* **schalmei** a clarinetlike ORGAN STOP at 8-foot pitch.

chamade [shä'mäd] (Fr.) **1,** a drum or trumpet SIGNAL. **2,** see EN CHAMADE.

chamber music music for small ensembles of instruments and/or voices, usu. one instrument to a part, intended to be performed in the home or in small concert halls. Cf. SONATA DA CAMERA.

Chamber Music America a corporation of professional chamber music ensembles in the U.S. and Canada, dedicated to the advancement of chamber music.

Chamber Music Society of Lincoln Center a chamber ensemble in residence at Alice Tully Hall at Lincoln Center, New York, since 1969.

chamber opera OPERA of limited length and scope, employing a chamber orch. and reduced vocal forces.

chamber orchestra an orch. smaller than the standard symphony orch., usu. a group of fewer than 40 players.

chamber organ a form of POSITIVE ORGAN having several stops, usu. housed in a single cabinet and designed to be installed in a home.

chamber sonata see SONATA DA CAMERA.

chamber symphony a term coined by Schoenberg for a symphonic work for chamber orch.

Chambonnières, Jacques Champion, Sieur de [shä-bo'nyer] (?1601–72) French composer and virtuoso harpsichordist at the French court and in the salons of Paris. He was the teacher of both Couperins and d'Anglebert,

and an important figure in the development of French harpsichord style.

Chaminade, Cécile(-Louise-Stéphanie) [shä-mĕ'näd] (1857–1944) French pianist and composer, stud. of Godard. Her works include dramatic works, chamber music and many works for piano, incl. the well-known "Scarf Dance."

Champagne, Claude (Adonai) (1891–1965) Canadian composer, strongly influenced by French-Canadian folk music and French impressionism, stud. of Jacques Laliberté. He taught at McGill U. and the École Vincent d'Indy from 1930 and was instrumental in the founding of the Montreal Conservatory in 1942.

Champion, Jacques CHAMBONNIÈRES, JACQUES CHAMPION.

chance music see ALEATORY.

Chandos Anthems 11 anthems and a Te Deum by Handel (1716–18), composed for the Earl of Carnarvon, later Duke of Chandos.

chang a Russian DULCIMER.

change ringing a method for ringing a set of tuned bells in constantly varying sequence arranged so as to avoid the shifting of any bell in the pattern by more than one step and the repeating of any order before the whole series has been completed. Also, *peal ringing, bell ringing.*

changes a jazz term indicating a harmonic chord progression. "Blues changes" is equivalent to "Blues progression."

changing note *or* **tone 1,** an accented passing tone. **2,** NOTA CAMBIATA. **3,** ÉCHAPPÉE.

channel a transitional passage linking two themes. Cf. BRIDGE.

chanson [shä'sō] (Fr.) **1,** a song; esp. a French song or cabaret song. **2,** a 14th- to 16th-c. French song for one or more voices, often with accompaniment, similar to the MADRIGAL or AYRE.

chanson de geste [zhest] (Fr.) an Old French epic poem of the 11th to 13th c. with a simple melodic setting.

chanson de toile [twäl] (Fr.) a spinning or weaving song.

chanson pour boire [poor bwär] (Fr.) a drinking song.

chansonette [shā-so'net] (Fr.) a short song.

chansonnier [shā-so'nyā] (Fr.) **1**, a singer, esp. a French cabaret singer; more generally, a songwriter who sings his or her own songs. **2**, a popular singer-songwriter of Quebec. **3**, a collection of chansons.

chant see PLAINSONG, ANGLICAN CHANT.

Chantels, The the first successful female rock ensemble, formed in New York in 1956.

chanter 1, a CHORISTER or CANTOR. **2**, on a BAGPIPE, the reed pipe having fingerholes, on which the melody is played.

chanterelle (Fr.) the highest string of certain stringed instruments, such as the violin, guitar, lute, banjo, etc.

chanty, chantey see SHANTY.

chanzoneta [chän-thō'nā-tä] (Sp., little song) a sacred Spanish song with refrain, similar to the VILLANCICO.

chapel the orch. or choir of a royal or papal chapel; hence, any musical organization, esp. an orch.

Chapel Royal the part of the English court musical staff employed to perform sacred music, esp. active from the 12th to 18th c.

Chappell & Co. English firm of music publishers and piano makers, established in 1810.

character piece also, **characteristic piece** a work, usu. for piano solo, expressing a particular programmatic idea, usu. specified in the title.

characteristic note the note or notes that distinguish one mode or tonality from another, as the lowered third and sixth degrees of the minor scale.

charivari also, **shivaree** a mock SERENADE of discordant noises, often produced by found instruments (pots, pans, etc.).

Charlebois, Robert ['shärl-bwä] (1945–) Canadian chansonnier and guitarist from Montreal, a major innovating force in pop music and the Quebec chanson.

Charles, Ray (1930–) Amer. blind rhythm-and-blues and soul singer, pianist, composer and arranger, whose works and performance style incorporate elements of gospel, jazz and country music.

Charles, Teddy (1928–) Amer. jazz vibraphonist, composer and leader, trained at the Juilliard School. As a composer and as a performer he has been interested in the interaction of composition and improvisation in jazz.

Charleston a rapid Amer. ballroom dance, perhaps orig. a social dance of Afr.-Americans, assoc. with the 1920s. The dance appeared for the first time as a theatrical dance in the black musical comedy *Liza* (1922). The song of the same name is by Cecil Mack (a.k.a. Richard C. McPherson) and Jimmy Johnson.

Charpentier, Gustave [shär-pä'tyā] (1860–1956) French composer, stud. of Massenet. He won the Prix de Rome in 1887, and most of his important works were begun during his residency in Rome. After 1913, he composed little. He is best known for the aria "Depuis le jour" from his opera *Louise* (1889–96).

Charpentier, Marc-Antoine (?1650–1704) prolific French composer, stud. of Carissimi. He was long associated with Molière's comedy troupe, after the playwright's collaboration with Lully and continuing for more than a decade after Molière's death. His compositions include over 400 sacred vocal works, secular songs and cantatas, intermezzi, and sacred and secular instrumental works.

chart 1, colloquial term for a musical SCORE, esp. an arrangement for band or other ensemble. **2**, the listing and ranking, usu. weekly, of the sales, radio playings, etc., of recordings in a particular genre, as the rock charts.

chase in jazz performance, a sort of musical duel between two players or groups of players, alternating phrases and each trying to excel the other in invention.

Chasins, Abram (1903–87) Amer. broadcaster, writer, pianist and composer, educated at the Juilliard School and at the Curtis Institute. He was music dir. of New York radio station WQXR (1947–65), during which time he produced much innovative music programming.

Chasse, La [shäs] (Fr., the hunt) popular name for various works, incl. **1**, the Piano Sonata in E♭ major, Op. 31 No. 3 (1802) by Beethoven. **2**, the string quartet in B♭ major, Op. 1 No. 1 (c.1757), by Haydn. **3**, the Symphony No. 73 in D major (1781) by Haydn.

Chausson, (Amédée-) Ernest [shō'sō] (1855–99) French composer, stud. of Massenet and Franck. He was independently wealthy, and his salon was the meeting place of many poets, artists, and musicians, incl. Mallarmé and Debussy. His output includes works in all genres, but he is best known for his songs and symphonies.

chastushka (Russ.) a Russian urban song or jingle.

chautauqua a term for a traveling musical tent show, popular in the U.S. and Canada in the early 20th c.

Chautauqua Institution founded in 1874 as an institute in Chatauqua, NY, for Methodist Sunday school teachers, the Institution inaugurated an annual assembly combining religious activities with political and cultural events. Since 1909 the Institution has produced summer programs, incl. orchestral, opera and theater performances, a vocal apprentice program and a school of music. Cf. LYCEUM.

Chauvin, Louis [shō'vē] (1881–1908) Amer. ragtime piano-player and composer, known as the "King of Ragtime Players."

Chávez (y Ramírez), Carlos (Antonio de Padua) (1899–1978) Mexican composer, conductor, and writer on music, self-taught as a composer. He was conductor of the Mexico SO and director of the National Conservatory and the National Institute of Fine Arts. He also held the Norton Chair of Poetics at Harvard (1958–59). As a composer he was strongly influenced by Mexican Indian culture, and many of his works contain elements of Aztec music, sometimes utilizing folk instruments.

Cheap Trick Amer. rock group formed in 1974 in Rockford, IL.

Cheatham, Doc (Adolphus Anthony) (1905–) Amer. jazz trumpeter. He performed with McKinney's Cotton Pickers, Cab Calloway, Teddy Wilson and Eddie Heywood, then appeared in the 1950s with Lat.-Amer. and swing bands.

Checker, Chubby (Evans, Ernest) (1941–) Amer. rock and rhythm-and-blues singer, made famous by his version of Hank Ballard's "The Twist."

cheek music LILTING.

chef [shef] (Fr.) chief, head.

chef d'attaque [dä'täk] (Fr.) a section leader in a choir or orch. Cf. CONCERTMASTER.

chef de musique (Fr.) BANDMASTER.

chef d'orchestre (Fr.) CONDUCTOR.

cheironomy the practice of conducting or teaching music with hand signs indicating melodic motion, rhythm and ornamentation.

Cheney, Amy March BEACH, MRS. H.H.A.

Cheney, Simeon Pease (1818–90) Amer. singer, teacher and composer, the first person to transcribe field recordings of Native American (Indian) music.

cheng SHENG.

Cherepnin TCHEREPNIN.

Cherkassky, Shura (1911–) Russian-born Amer. pianist, stud. of Josef Hofmann, a specialist in the Romantic repertory.

Cherry, Don(ald E.) (1936–) Amer. jazz trumpeter, cornet player, pianist and composer. He was associated with Ornette Coleman and the development of the FREE JAZZ movement in the late 1950s. Since the mid-1960s he has worked primarily in Europe, presaging the movement toward "world music" influences.

Cherubini, Luigi [kā-roo'bē-nē] (1760–1842) Italian composer, trained in Florence and with Giuseppe Sarti. He went to Paris in 1786, where he remained for the rest of his life. He was involved in the formation of the Institut National de Musique (which became the Conservatoire National) in 1793 and in 1822 became director. His large output includes over forty operas, the best known of which are *Médée* (1797) and *Les deux journées* (1800). He also wrote much secular and sacred vocal music, 6 quartets, a symphony and other instrumental music.

Chester, J. & W. English music publishing house, founded at Brighton in 1874.

chest of viols a set (orig. an actual box) of matched viols of different sizes.

chest register or **voice** the lowest REGISTER of the voice.

chest tone a tone sung in CHEST REGISTER.

chevalet [shə-vä′lā] (Fr.) BRIDGE (1,).

chevrotement [she-vro′tmä] (Fr.) a pejorative term for a very fast vocal vibrato, likened to a goat's braying.

chiamata [kyä′mä-tä] (It.) a trumpet FANFARE.

chiavette [kyä′vet] (It., little clefs) *also*, **high key** one of two standardized clef groupings used in the 16th c. for vocal music, the other being *chiavi naturali* (It., natural clefs) or *low key*, probably used to avoid the need for ledger lines in copying. In general, works from the period written in *chiavette* should be performed somewhat lower than written; those in *chiavi naturali*, somewhat higher.

chica (Sp.) CALINDA.

Chicago Amer. rock band formed in 1967 in Chicago. Orig. called Big Thing and then Chicago Transit Authority, arriving at the final, shortened name by 1970.

Chicago Academy of Music CHICAGO MUSICAL COLLEGE.

Chicago Civic Opera successor to the first CHICAGO GRAND OPERA, formed in 1922 by industrialist Samuel Insull. It moved in 1929 to the newly built Civic Opera House but was dissolved in 1932.

Chicago Lyric Opera see LYRIC OPERA OF CHICAGO.

Chicago Grand Opera Company 1, Chicago's first resident opera company, performing at the Auditorium Theater, formed in 1910 with Cleofonte Campanini as musical director. Mary Garden was general manager for the 1921–22 season, after which the company closed. **2**, a company presenting opera in Chicago from 1933 to 1946.

Chicago Musical College conservatory founded as the Chicago Academy of Music in 1867 by Florenz Ziegfeld. It assumed its present name in 1872 and became part of Roosevelt U. in 1954.

Chicago school of jazz a term generally applied to the first generation of white jazz musicians (incl. Jimmy McPartland and Eddie Condon) to adopt the jazz styles of the New Orleans musicians who came to Chicago in the 1910s and 1920s.

Chicago Symphony Orchestra symphony orch. founded in Chicago in 1891 as the Chicago Orch., with Theodore Thomas as its first conductor. It performed in the Auditorium Theater until 1904, when it moved to the new Orchestra Hall. It was called the Theodore Thomas Orch. from 1906 to 1912 and then was renamed the Chicago SO. Its conductors have been, after Thomas, Frederick Stock, Defauw, Rodzinski, Kubelik, Reiner, Martinon, Solti and Barenboim (after 1991).

chicano music music of Mexican-Americans, esp. the music of the Southwest, including such disparate elements as SALSA and folk music.

chicken scratch *also*, **waila** an acculturated form of popular music of the Pima and Papago Indians of S. Arizona, which blends Anglo, Hispanic and Native American traditions. The repertory consists mainly of dance music.

Chickering Boston firm of piano makers founded by Jonas Chickering (1797–1853), noted for the development of the single-piece cast-iron frame in the 1840s, which dominated the world market by the 1870s.

chiesa ['kyä-zä] (It., church) see SONATA DA CHIESA.

Chihara, Paul (Seiko) (1938–) Amer. composer, stud. of Robert Palmer, Boulanger, Pepping and Schuller. He has taught at the U. of California at Los Angeles and the California Institute of the Arts and has been composer-in-residence for the San Francisco Ballet. An oriental influence is evident in his works, which incl. film scores, concertos for guitar, saxophone and string quartet, 2 symphonies, ballets, chamber music and choral works.

Child ballad any of the many ballads contained in the important collection *The English and Scottish Popular Ballads* (1882–98) edited by F.J. Child.

Child of our Time, A oratorio (1939–41) by Michael Tippett that makes extensive use of Afr.-Amer. spirituals.

Childhood of Christ, The ENFANCE DU CHRIST, L'.

Children's Corner suite of piano pieces (1908) by Debussy, written for his daughter. The six movements are "Doctor Gradus ad Parnassum," a mock étude; "Jimbo's lullaby," "Serenade of the doll," "The snow is dancing," "The little shepherd" and "Golliwog's cake walk."

Childs, Barney (1926–) Amer. composer, stud. of Chávez, Copland and Elliott Carter. His works, which experiment with aleatory elements, include orchestral and chamber works and works for chorus.

chime 1, a hollow, open metal tube, which when struck produces a definite pitch. See TUBULAR BELLS. 2, BELL CHIME.

chimney flute an ORGAN STOP.

ch'in a fretless Chinese ZITHER with seven silk strings, played horizontally without a plectrum.

Chinese crescent, Chinese pavilion see TURKISH CRESCENT.

Chinese temple block, *also,* **Chinese wood block** a PERCUSSION INSTRUMENT consisting of a slotted, hollow, wooden block struck with a hard beater to produce a resonant tone. Also, *clog box, temple block*.

chin rest a device attached to the lower part of the violin or viola, separating the chin from direct contact with the body of the instrument.

chironomy CHEIRONOMY.

chitarra [kē'tär-rä] (It.) GUITAR.

chitarrone [kē-tär'rō-nä] (It.) a large Renaissance ARCHLUTE, usu. having six double-strung courses over the fingerboard and eight unstopped bass strings, used to accompany the voice. Cf. THEORBO, ARCHLUTE.

chiuso ['kyoo-zō] (It., closed) see STOPPED.

chocallo [sho'kä-lyo] (Port.) a type of Brazilian wooden or metal tube RATTLE used in Lat.-Amer. dance bands.

Chocolate Dandies, The 1, musical by Eubie Blake, lyrics by Noble Sissle. Premiere, New York 1924. 2, a jazz band of the 1920s to 1940s, a successor to McKinley's COTTON PICKERS.

Chocolate Soldier, The musical by Oscar Straus, lyrics and book by Stanislaus Stange, based on a Viennese operetta derived from Bernard Shaw's play *Arms and the Man*. Premiere, New York 1909. A satirical look at conventional operetta heroics.

choir a group of singers or instruments performing together. Cf. CHORUS.

choirboy a boy member of a choir. Also, *chorister*.

choir organ CHAIR ORGAN.

choke a style of cymbal-playing in dance bands in which the cymbal is stopped by hand after each stroke of the drumstick. A similar effect is produced mechanically by the HI-HAT CYMBAL.

C-hole the round SOUND HOLE in the body of a viol or guitar.

Chopin, Fryderyk (Franciszek) (Frédéric François) [shō'pē] (1810–49) Polish pianist and composer, largely self-taught as a pianist. His fame as a pianist is based on very few public performances, and he gave up concert performance relatively early. His output consists very largely of works for solo piano, with a small number of works for piano and orch., chamber music and songs. He had a major influence on the development of pianistic technique, and his harmonic language was highly innovative and original.

chops (lit., lips) a slang term for a player's instrumental technique.

Chopsticks an anonymous short waltz tune for piano, first publ. in 1877, playable with one finger of each hand. It has been the subject for variations by a number of composers, incl. Liszt.

chorale **1**, a Lutheran hymn tune written for congregational singing in the German Protestant church. **2**, a choral singing group.

chorale cantata a CANTATA in which two or more of the movements are based on the text and often the melody of a German chorale.

chorale concerto a sacred vocal composition based on a German chorale, usu. scored for one or more voices plus continuo, often incl. obbligato instruments.

chorale fantasia any extended organ composition based on a chorale melody.

chorale fugue **1**, a short organ composition in which the first one or two phrases of a chorale melody are used as fugue subjects. **2**, CHORALE RICERCARE.

chorale Mass a Mass setting based on the German chorales derived from sections of the Roman Catholic Mass, prevalent esp. in the 20th c.

chorale monody a sacred composition written in the style of early 17th-c. concertato madrigal and monody, yet based on the text of a German chorale (whose melody is not used).

chorale motet **1**, a polyphonic vocal composition of two or more parts based on a German chorale; a precursor of the CHORALE CONCERTO and the CHORALE CANTATA. **2**, CHORALE RICERCARE.

chorale partita *also*, **chorale varia-**tions a variation set based on a chorale melody.

chorale prelude **1**, an organ setting of a complete chorale melody, intended to introduce the hymn tune to be sung by the congregation. **2**, any chorale setting for organ. Also, *organ chorale*.

chorale ricercare a genre of organ composition, prevalent during the early 17th c., in which each phrase of a German chorale is treated in imitation, with idiomatic embellishment and figuration. Also, *chorale canzona, chorale motet, chorale fantasia*.

chorale variations CHORALE PARTITA.

choral symphony **1**, a work for orch. in symphonic form involving extensive use of chorus. The term is often used to refer to Beethoven's Symphony No. 9 in D minor, whose last movement is a setting of Schiller's "Ode to Joy" for soloists, chorus and orch. Other works in the genre incl. Vaughan Williams *Sea Symphony* and Mahler's Symphony No. 8 (the "Symphony of a Thousand"). **2**, a work of symphonic proportions for chorus alone.

chord the sounding of two or more notes simultaneously. In traditional triadic harmony, the note on which the chord is built is called the ROOT. If the root is also the lowest note, the chord is in root position; if not, the chord is in INVERSION. In works of the Baroque and Classical periods employing BASSO CONTINUO, the intended chords are often indicated by figures (see FIGURED BASS).

chordophone a type of instrument dating from ancient times in which the sound is made by the vibration of strings. The five fundamental types are the MUSICAL BOW, LYRE, HARP, LUTE and ZITHER. Also, *stringed* or *string instrument*.

chord organ an ELECTRONIC ORGAN with a provision for playing chords automatically, esp. to accompany a single-line melody.

chord scale in jazz theory, the SCALE

Chords

or MODE associated with a certain chord, as the dorian mode and the minor seventh chord.

choreography orig., a system for notating dance movements; in recent times the term has been used to refer to the ensemble of dance steps for a dance work as conceived by its creator or *choreographer.*

chorister a choir singer, esp. a choirboy; also, a lead singer in a choir.

chôro ['shō-rō] (Port.) Brazilian music for instrumental ensemble.

Chor-Ton ['kor-tōn] (Ger., choir pitch) the pitch of 18th-c. German church organs used to accompany choirs, usu. higher than modern pitch. Cf. CAMMER-TON.

chorus 1, a group of singers performing together, usu. in parts; also, music written for such a group. **2,** REFRAIN. **3,** in jazz, a complete statement of the tune; also, a solo chorus, or, sometimes, an entire solo. **4,** a combination ORGAN STOP composed of stops from the same tonal family.

Chorus Line, A musical by Marvin Hamlisch, lyrics by Edward Kleban, book by James Kirkwood and Nicholas Dante, with Michael Bennett. Premiere, New York 1975. An innovative musical exploring the lives of dancers auditioning for a show.

Choudens [shoo'dã] French music publisher founded in Paris in 1845.

Chou Wen-Chung (1923–) Chinese-born Amer. composer, stud. of Slonimsky, Luening and Varèse. He has been on the faculty of Columbia U. since 1972. His music combines Western 20th-c. techniques with Chinese music and poetry.

Chowning, John M. (1934–) Amer. composer, chiefly of electronic and computer music, on the faculty of Stanford. He has developed a technique of synthesis involving frequency modulation used for imitating vocal and instrumental sounds and creating new ones.

Christensen, Axel W(aldemar) (1881–1955) Amer. popular piano player and teacher. He simplified ragtime piano playing into three melodic/rhythmic patterns, which form the basis of his teaching method. By 1918 he had piano schools in most major U.S. cities and had become known as the "Czar of Ragtime" and "King of the Jazz Pianists."

Christ on the Mount of Olives (Ger., *Christus am Ölberge*) oratorio, Op. 85 (1802), by Beethoven, to a text by F.X. Huber.

Christian, Charlie (1919–42) Amer. jazz and blues guitarist, a pioneer in the use of the electric guitar. He was a member of the Benny Goodman orch. and small groups and was one of the originators of bop. His recording career only lasted three years, but in that short period he revolutionized the role of the guitar in jazz.

Christiansen, F(rederick) Melius (1871–1955) Norwegian-born Amer. conductor, composer and teacher. In 1903 he became head of the Music Dept. at St. Olaf College in Northfield, MN, and founded the St. olaf choir in 1911. He fostered a distinctive vocal ensemble sound which emphasized a straight tone, uniform color and absolute precision of pitch.

Christie, William (Lincoln) (1944–) Amer. harpsichordist and conductor, founder in 1978 of the early music performing group Les Arts Florissants.

Christmas Concerto the Concerto grosso in G minor, Op. 6 No. 8 (1712), by Corelli.

Christmas Oratorio (Ger., *Weihnachtsoratorium*) 1, a set of six cantatas (1734) by Bach written for Christmas, New Year's and Epiphany. 2, popular name for the *Historia der freuden-und gnadenreichen Geburth* . . . (1604) by Schütz based on the story of Christ's birth.

Christoff, Boris (1918–) Bulgarian bass, educated in Rome and Salzburg, particularly noted for his performance of Boris Godunov, as well as of Verdi bass roles. His Amer. debut was in San Francisco in 1956.

Christy's Minstrels a blackface minstrel group organized in Buffalo, NY, in 1842 by Edwin Pearce Christy (1815–62). A similar very popular group in England was not run by Christy but licensed his name.

chromatic 1, of ancient Greek music, describing a Tetrachord (2,) whose intervals are 1½, ½, and ½ step. 2, of a Scale, including all the semitones comprising an octave; opposed to Diatonic. 3, of harmony, making frequent use of tones not part of the prevailing key.

Chromatic Fantasy and Fugue a work for harpsichord (1720) by J.S. Bach that makes extensive use of chromatic harmonies.

chromatic interval 1, a diatonic scale Interval raised or lowered by a half step while retaining the same pitch name, e.g., E to E♯. 2, an interval resulting from chromatic alteration.

chromatic sign Accidental.

Church a firm of music publishers, active in Boston (1859–1930) and best known for publishing operas and Sousa marches.

church bass Bass viol (2,).

church modes see Mode.

church sonata Sonata da chiesa.

chute [shüt] (Fr.) any of several French baroque ornaments. See Ornament.

Ciamaga, Gustav [chä′mä-gä] (1930–) Canadian composer and teacher, stud. of Beckwith, Weinzweig, Berger, Shapero and Fine. He has taught at the U. of Toronto since 1963 and has been very active in the development of electronic instruments.

Cianchettini, Veronica Rosalia [chänkāt'tē-nē] (1779–1833) Bohemian pianist, harpist, composer and teacher, sister of JAN DUSSEK, stud. of her father. She went to London in 1795. Her works incl. two piano concertos and other solo piano works.

cibell CEBELL.

Ciconia, Johannes [chō'kō-nyā] (c1370–1411) Franco-Flemish composer of masses, motets and secular vocal works, cantor at the Padua Cathedral from 1403 until his death.

Cifra, Antonio ['chē-frä] (1584–1629) Italian composer of sacred and secular vocal music, stud. of Nanino. From 1609 he was *maestro di cappella* of the Santa Casa, Loreto.

Cilea, Francesco ['chē'lä-ä] (1866–1950) Italian composer, stud. of Paolo Serrao. He was dir. of the Palermo Conservatory (1913–16) and the Naples Conservatory (1916–36). His best-known work is the opera *Adriana Lecouvreur* (1902).

Cimarosa, Domenico [chē-mä'rō-zä] (1749–1801) Italian composer, educated in Loreto. By the late 1770s he had become one of Italy's leading composers, esp. of comic opera. He spent most of his life in Naples and Venice. His best-known opera, *Il matrimonio segreto* (1792), is still frequently performed. He also wrote many oratorios and other sacred and secular vocal music, as well as instrumental and keyboard works.

cimbalom *also,* **cymbalom, cymbalon, cembalon** a type of Gypsy DULCIMER, used in the Hungarian café ensembles and written for by some composers, incl. Bartók and Stravinsky.

cimbasso [chēm'bäs-sō] (It.) the lowest brass instrument called for by Verdi, apparently a form of valve contrabass trombone developed by Verdi to replace the ophicleide.

Cincinnati May Festival an orchestral and choral festival, the second oldest in the U.S., established in 1873 by THEODORE THOMAS. Recent musical directors have been Schippers and Conlon.

Cincinnati Symphony Orchestra orch. founded in 1872 by George Brand as the Cincinnati Orch. Its conductors have been van der Stucken, Stokowski, Kunwald, Ysaÿe, Reiner, Eugene Goosens, Thor Johnson, Rudolf, Schippers and Jésus Lopez-Cobos. It was the first U.S. orch. to make a world tour.

Cinderella 1, (It., *La Cenerentola*) comic opera in 2 acts by Rossini to a libretto by Jacopo Ferretti based on an earlier libretto, all derived from the familiar fairy tale by Charles Perrault. Premiere, Rome 1817. Instead of the more familiar glass slipper, Cinderella is identified after the ball by her possession of a bracelet, the twin of which she gave to the Prince's valet (thinking him the Prince) at the ball. **2**, (Fr., *Cendrillon*) opera in 4 acts by Massenet to a libretto in French by Henri Cain based on the same fairy tale as Rossini's opera, but using the traditional glass slipper. Premiere, Paris 1899. **3**, ballet by Prokofiev, based on the fairy tale. Premiere, Moscow 1945.

cinelli [chē'nel-lē] (It.) CYMBALS.

cinema organ THEATER ORGAN.

cipher the unintentional sounding of an organ pipe caused by mechanical failure.

circle of fifths the major or minor keys arranged by order of ascending (for sharps) or descending (for flats) fifths so as to form a closed circle. The arrangement depends on an enharmonic relationship somewhere in the circle, possible only with equal temperament.

circular breathing a technique used in playing a wind instrument, usu. woodwinds, for producing a continuous sound. Air is pushed through the instrument by the cheeks while the player breathes in through the nose.

circular canon a CANON whose sub-

Circle of Fifths

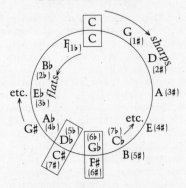

ject leads back to its own beginning, so that it can be repeated indefinitely. Also, *perpetual canon.*

cis [tsis] (Ger.) C SHARP.

cisis ['tsi-sis] (Ger.) C double sharp.

Cisneros, Eleonora de (Broadfoot, Eleanor) (1878–1934) Amer. mezzo-soprano. She claimed to be the first Amer.-trained singer to perform at the Metropolitan Opera (1899), as well as the first American to sing at Bayreuth.

cithara KITHARA.

citole a medieval flat-backed instrument, prob. identical to the GITTERN.

cittern *also,* **cithern** a fretted Renaissance flat-backed LUTE with wire strings and a pearlike shape, played with a plectrum. See GUITAR.

City Center NEW YORK CITY CENTER.

Clair de Lune [kler də lün] (Fr., moonlight) a poem by Verlaine, from *Fêtes galantes* (1869), set by many French composers, incl. Debussy and Fauré, and the inspiration for the third movement of the *Suite Bergamasque* by Debussy.

cláirseach CLÁRSACH.

clapper a CONCUSSION INSTRUMENT consisting of two or more objects that may be hinged or otherwise connected and are struck together to produce sound. A wide variety of materials may be used, incl. ivory, wood, metal, bone, etc. Cf. BONES.

Clapton, Eric (1945–) English rock and blues guitarist and singer, a prin-

cipal member of various rock groups, incl. the Yardbirds and Cream. After a bout with drugs, he formed his own groups in the 1970s.

claque [klak] (Fr.) a group of audience members hired or otherwise induced to support or find fault with an artist at a performance through applause, booing, etc.

clarabella also, **claribel, claribel flute** a wooden 8-foot ORGAN STOP with open pipes.

clarin a long trumpetlike wind instrument of Peru and Mexico.

clarina a wind instrument invented in 1891 by WILHELM HECKEL combining the qualities of clarinet and oboe.

clarinet a single-reed woodwind instrument with a cylindrical bore, made in a wide range of sizes and pitches from the soprano in E♭ to the contrabass in B♭. In some folk instruments the reed is carved from the same tube as the body of the instrument. Cf. BASSET HORN, CLARINETTE D'AMOUR, BASS CLARINET.

clarinette d'amour (Fr.) an 18th-c. CLARINET with a pear-shaped bell, made in various sizes.

clarino 1, the trumpet played in its high range without valves. See OVERBLOW. **2**, CLARION (1,). **3**, *also,* **clarin trumpet** the first trumpet part in an ensemble.

clarion 1, *also,* **clarino** the middle register of the clarinet. **2**, a medieval straight TRUMPET. **3**, a trumpetlike reed ORGAN STOP at 4-foot pitch.

Clark, Roy (1933–) Amer. country-music singer, songwriter and instrumentalist. In his youth he played for square dances, then accompanied various artists. Since the early 1960s he has produced a number of hit recordings and appeared on TV and in clubs.

Clarke, Henry Leland (1907–) Amer. composer, trained at Harvard and with Nadia Boulanger in Paris. He has taught at Vassar College, the U. of California at Los Angeles and the U. of Washington (Seattle). His works—which incl. operas, orchestral works and choral music and songs—often display an inventive approach to both harmony and text-setting.

Clarke, Jeremiah (?1674–1707) English organist and composer. He was organist of the Chapel Royal from 1700. His works incl. church music, odes and songs, music for the stage, and instrumental music. The famous Trumpet Voluntary, once ascribed to Purcell, but now thought to be Clarke's, appears to have originated in *The Prince of Denmark's March*, a work for trumpet and wind ensemble.

Clarke, Kenny (Spearman, Kenneth; Liaquat Ali Salaam) (1914–85) Amer. jazz drummer. He was associated with Charlie Parker and Dizzy Gillespie in the bop movement and was a founder-member of the MODERN JAZZ QUARTET. He developed the use of the RIDE CYMBAL as the principal pulse instrument, freeing the bass drum for more independent counter-rhythms.

clarone (It.) **1**, BASSET HORN. **2**, BASS CLARINET.

clàrsach ['klär-shäk] *also,* **clàirseach, clarseach, clarseth** (Gaelic) the ancient small HARP of Scotland and Ireland.

Clash, The British punk rock group formed in 1976 in London. Their songs, a mixture of rock and REGGAE, usu. deal with issues of political protest.

classical 1, a term referring to the period of Western art music from about 1770 to 1810, esp. the music of the Viennese composers (Haydn, Mozart, Beethoven). **2**, a term distinguishing "art music" from popular music, folk music, rock, jazz, etc. Cf. POPULAR MUSIC.

Classical Symphony the Symphony No. 1 in D major, Op. 25 (1916), by Prokofiev, so called because it is scored for a typical classical orch. and written in a Haydn-Mozart style with modernized harmonies.

classic jazz a term used to refer to early jazz, usu. up to the advent of bop, but sometimes more restrictively to refer to the jazz of the 1920s.

Claude de Sermisy SERMISY, CLAUDIN DE.

clausula 1, a medieval composition in descant style developed from a melismatic section of plainchant. **2**, an ornamented CADENCE (1,) of medieval music.

clavecin [kläv'sɛ̂] (Fr.) HARPSICHORD.

claves ['klä-väs] (Sp.) a CONCUSSION INSTRUMENT of Cuban origin consisting of small cylindrical wooden sticks struck together, used esp. as a rhythm instrument in Lat.-Amer. music.

clavicembalo [klä-vē'chem-bä-lō] (It.) HARPSICHORD.

clavichord a keyboard string instrument dating from as early as the 14th c. and having a rather soft tone, in which the strings are struck by metal hammers (*tangents*). There is no escapement, so the tangents continue to touch the strings until the key is released. This allows a slight modification of the pitch or a kind of tremolo (bebung) through varied pressure on the key. The clavichord can have a "fretted" or "unfretted" action, depending on whether each string serves several tangents or only one. Some instruments were fitted with pedals and used as practice instruments by organists. The clavichord is a descendant of the MONOCHORD and a precursor of the modern PIANO. Cf. BEBUNG.

clavicor a valved tenor HORN invented in Paris in 1837 and used in military bands until the end of the century.

clavicytherium an upright HARPSICHORD with a horizontal action, usu. operated by springs.

clavier 1, (Fr.) [klä'vyä] a keyboard. **2**, (Ger.) [klä'vēr] any instrument having a keyboard.

Clavier-Übung [-"ü-bûng] (Ger.) a name used by J.S. Bach for four publications of keyboard music. Parts I, II and IV are for harpsichord, and contain the partitas (I), the Italian Concerto and the French overture (II) and the Goldberg Variations (IV). Part III, for organ, contains organ chorales, fugues, and duets.

clavilux see COLOR ORGAN.

claviorgan an instrument combining a harpsichord and several ranks of organ pipes played from the same keyboard.

clawhammer style a two-finger style of banjo playing in which brush strokes are seldom used. Cf. FRAILING.

Clayton, Buck (Wilbur Dorsey) (1911–91) Amer. jazz swing trumpeter. He played with Count Basie from 1936 to 1943, then with various groups after the war, incl. Jimmy Rushing's and Eddie Condon's.

clef a sign placed on a staff, usu. at the beginning, to indicate the pitch of a line. Orig. the signs were actual letters (usu. F, C or G), but these gradually became stylized to the forms now in use. The C clef has become rare, except for notation of viola and cello parts and in historical editions. Cf. CHIAVETTE.

Clefs
middle C in various clefs

Clemens (non Papa), Jacobus (Clement, Jacob) (?1510–?1556) prolific Flemish composer. He is known to have lived in Ypres and to have taught in Bruges in the mid-1550s. His output includes a substantial number of sacred vocal works, incl. Mass settings, magnificats, motets, psalms ("Souterliedekens") and chansons.

Clementi, Muzio (1752–1832) Italian-born English composer, pianist, piano maker and teacher. In Vienna he participated in a celebrated contest with Mozart, in which both composers played their own compo-

sitions, improvised and read at sight works by Paisiello. Clementi was much more impressed with Mozart than Mozart was with him. From 1785 he remained in London, with the exception of a number of extended continental tours, until his death. He was widely esteemed as a teacher, and among his students were J.B. Cramer and John Field. He was also active, esp. after 1800, in his musical-instrument firm. Of Clementi's large output of keyboard and chamber music and orchestral works, his piano compendium *Gradus ad Parnassum* (1817–26) remains his best-known work, still used today for teaching.

Clemenza di Tito, La (It., The Mercy of Titus) opera seria in 3 acts by Mozart to a libretto by Caterino Mazzola, after a libretto by Metastasio (used by Gluck). Premiere, Prague 1791. Vitellia, daughter of the late emperor of Rome, wishes revenge on the current Emperor Titus for his refusal to marry her.

Clérambault, Louis-Nicolas [klā-rä′bō] (1676–1749) French organist and composer, stud. of André Raison and Jean-Baptiste Moreau. He held a number of positions in the French royal establishment, and in 1714 he became organist of a school near Versailles for poor but well-born girls. His works include cantatas and choral works, as well as songs, sonatas and symphonies.

Cleva, Fausto (Angelo) (1902–71) Italian-born Amer. conductor, educated at the Trieste Conservatory and the Verdi Conservatory in Milan. He came to the U.S. in 1920 and was chorus master, then conductor, at the Metropolitan Opera until his death.

Cleveland, The Reverend **James L.** (1932–91) influential Amer. gospel and soul singer, pianist and composer. He was the leader of the Southern California Community Choir and in 1968 organized the Gospel Singers Workshop Convention, a national organization of more than 25,000 members.

Cleveland, Jimmy (James) (1926–)
Amer. jazz trombonist, a member of
the Lionel Hampton band from 1949
to 1953, since then a free-lance recording artist.

Cleveland Institute of Music a music
conservatory founded in 1920, with
composer Ernest Bloch as its first director.

Cleveland Orchestra symphony
orch. founded in Cleveland in 1918
with Nikolai Sokoloff as its first conductor. Other conductors have been
Rodzinski, Leinsdorf, Szell, Maazel,
and Christoph von Dohnányi.

Cleveland Quartet Amer. string
quartet founded in 1968 at the Marlboro Festival, in residence at the
Cleveland Institute and then at
SUNY Buffalo, succeeding the Budapest Quartet. Since 1976 its members
have been on the faculty of the Eastman School.

Cliburn, Van (Harvey Lavan, Jr.)
(1934–) Amer. pianist, stud. of Rosina Lhévinne. He won the Tchaikovsky Competition in Moscow in
1958, but has performed little since
the mid-1960s. An international
piano competition is sponsored in his
name, est. in 1962 and held every four
years in Fort Worth, TX.

Clifton, William John HALEY, BILL.

Cline, Patsy (Hensley, Virginia Patterson) (1932–63) Amer. country-
music singer, best known for her
songs "I Fall to Pieces" and "Crazy"
(both 1961). She was elected to the
Country Music Hall of Fame in 1973.

clinker slang for a note missed or
played wrongly by an instrumentalist.

Clinton, George (1940–) Amer.
funk singer, head of various groups in
the 1970s and 1980s, incl. Parliament
and Funkadelic.

cloche [klosh] (Fr.) BELL; TUBULAR
BELLS.

clochette (Fr.) HANDBELL.

Clock, The the Symphony No. 101
in D major (1793) by Haydn, so called
from the tick-tock accompaniment in
the slow movement.

clog box CHINESE WOOD BLOCK.

clog dance *also,* **clogging dance** a step
dance of Irish and English origins
which became a folk dance of the Appalachian Mountains region. Music
for clog dances is fast, with driving
rhythms, in a duple or compound meter (6/8). Common tunes are "Old Joe
Clark," "Ragtime Annie," etc.

Clorindy, the Origin of the Cakewalk
musical by Will Marion Cook, libretto and lyrics by Paul Laurence
Dunbar. Premiere, New York 1898. A
black review set in the Louisiana of
the 1880s.

close CADENCE.

close harmony 1, *also,* **close position**
the arrangement of the tones of a
CHORD so that they are as close together as possible. See SPACING. **2,** a
sequence of chords in close position,
as found in certain vocal music, such
as BARBERSHOP.

close score a score in which two or
more parts are included on the same
staff. Cf. OPEN SCORE.

close shake a type of VIBRATO.

cluster a CHORD comprised of a collection of closely spaced pitches, either randomly selected or of a certain
defined set (as all black or all white
notes on the piano keyboard). Composition with clusters was first used
by Henry Cowell in the early 1910s
in his piano works.

Cluytens, André (1905–67) Belgian-
born French conductor, trained at the
Antwerp Royal Conservatory. He was
resident conductor of the Royal Theatre, Antwerp, then musical dir. of
the Toulouse Opera, the Opéra-
Comique in Paris and the Paris Conservatoire Orch. He was the first
French conductor to conduct at Bayreuth and was from 1959 assoc. with
the Vienna Staatsoper.

CMS *abbr.* COLLEGE MUSIC SOCIETY.

coach horn POST HORN.

Coasters, The Amer. rhythm-and-
blues vocal quartet formed in 1955 in
Los Angeles. The group disbanded in
the early 1970s, but individual members have led groups using the name
since then.

Coates, Albert (1882–1953) Russian-born English conductor and composer, stud. of Nikisch. He was principal conductor at the Marinsky Theater in St. Petersburg, then after 1919 he performed regularly with the London SO and at Covent Garden. He was musical dir. of the Rochester PO from 1923 to 1925. He was esp. noted for his conducting of the works of Scriabin and other Russian composers.

Cochran, Eddie (1938–60) Amer. rock singer and guitarist, an early master of studio OVERDUBBING and a virtuoso guitarist. His hits incl. "Summertime Blues" and "Three Steps to Heaven."

cocktail drum a modern form of BONGO DRUM.

cocoyé [kō-kō'yä] (Sp.) an 18th-c. Cuban instrumental and dance form.

coda (It., tail) the final, added section of a work or melody, following the completion of its formal design. In SONATA FORM, the coda follows the end of the recapitulation. The coda is often indicated by the sign (⊕).

codetta (It., little coda) a brief coda. In a FUGUE, a codetta is a section that links two entries of the theme, usu. coming after the answer and before the next entry of the subject.

Coffee Cantata a secular cantata, *Schweigt stille, plaudert nicht* (Be quiet, stop talking), BWV 211 (c. 1734), by J.S. Bach, about the pleasures of drinking coffee.

cogli ['kō-lyē], **coi, col, coll'** (It.) with.

cog rattle a SCRAPER that makes a ratchet-like sound by causing a flat piece of wood to flap against a notched cog wheel.

Cohan, George M(ichael) (1878–1942) Amer. composer, actor, lyricist, librettist, director and producer. He was known for his fast-paced vigor and his musicals with American themes and songs, as opposed to the European base for most of the operettas of the time. His songs incl. "Over There" and "Give My Regards to Broadway."

Cohn, Al(vin Gilbert) (1925–88) Amer. jazz tenor saxophonist and arranger. He played with a number of big bands in the 1940s, incl. those of Buddy Rich, Woody Herman and Artie Shaw; afterwards he performed as soloist and in small combos and was active as an arranger, esp. of Broadway shows.

Cohn, Arthur (1910–) Amer. composer and writer, trained at the Juilliard School. He was dir. of the Fleisher Music Collection (1934–52) and the Settlement School (1946–52) in Philadelphia. His writings incl. books on 20th-c. music.

coll'arco (It.) played with the bow, as opposed to PIZZICATO.

colascione [kō-lä'shō-nä] a European long-necked LUTE with 3 courses of metal strings and 24 movable frets.

Cole, Bob (Robert Allen) (1863–1911) Amer. composer, lyricist and entertainer. He wrote lyrics for a number of musicals, incl. *A Trip to Coontown* (1898) and *The Red Moon* (1909), as well as many hit songs, esp. "Under the Bamboo Tree" (1902).

Cole, Cozy (William Randolph) (1909–81) Amer. jazz drummer, trained at the Juillard School. He was active throughout his career as a successful studio musician and teacher. He played with many groups, incl. Cab Calloway's band, Louis Armstrong's All Stars and his own band.

Cole(s), Nat "King" (Nathaniel Adams) (1917–65) Amer. jazz singer and pianist, an important figure in the transition to bop and a highly influential performer. The King Cole Trio (1939–51) of piano, guitar and bass was copied by many later pianists.

Cole, Rossetter Gleason (1866–1952) Amer. composer, organist and teacher. He was president of the Music Teachers of North America, dean of the Illinois chapter of the American Guild of Organists and president of the Society of American Musicians.

Coleman, Cy (Kaufman, Seymour) (1929–) Amer. composer and pianist, best known for his Broadway scores for *Witchcraft* (1957) and *Sweet Charity* (1966).

Coleman, Ornette (1930–) Amer. jazz saxophonist and composer, largely self-taught (he studied briefly at the Lenox [MA] School of Jazz in 1959). His quartet, dating from 1959 with trumpeter Don Cherry, introduced the FREE JAZZ technique of jazz improvisation, which he later formulated as HARMOLODICS. He has been equally active as a composer and a performer, and in more recent years has adopted rock rhythms.

Coleridge-Taylor Choral Society a choral group for black singers founded in 1901 in Washington, D.C.

Coleridge-Taylor, Samuel (Taylor, Samuel Coleridge) (1875–1912) English composer of orchestral, vocal, theater and chamber music; educated at the Royal College of Music. He was permanent conductor of the Handel Society (1904–12). His best known work is the cantata *Hiawatha's Wedding Feast*, part of a trilogy *The Song of Hiawatha*. He was interested in developing his own black heritage and wrote many works with Negro subjects and themes.

Colgrass, Michael Charles (1932–) Amer. composer and percussionist, stud. of Milhaud, Ben Weber and Riegger, based in Canada since the 1970s. As a percussionist he has played jazz and classical music in a variety of ensembles and orchestras. His works, in an atonal idiom, frequently have a jazz flavor. He won the Pulitzer Prize in 1978 for his *Déjà Vu* for percussion and orch.

collage a term borrowed from the visual arts for a 20th-c. compositional technique involving the combining of disparate musical elements (different sound-producing agents, such as radios, quotations from various musical sources, etc.) in a single work.

colla parte *also*, **colla voce** (It.) of an accompaniment, to be played similarly to the solo part in tempo and phrasing.

collective composition a composition or collection of compositions produced by the collaboration of two or more composers. The most common examples are found in the theater and in commemorative works.

College Music Society an Amer. organization est. in 1957 to further communication and exchange of ideas between musicians working in the academic environment.

col legno ['lā-nyō] (It., with the wood) a direction in string writing to play with the wood of the bow bounced on or rosined and drawn across the string.

Collins, Judy (1939–) Amer. folk, rock and popular singer. She began as a folk singer involved in protest movements, but her later work has covered a variety of styles, incl. her two biggest hits, "Amazing Grace" and Sondheim's "Send in the Clowns."

coll'ottava (It., with the octave) an indication to play a passage adding the notes an octave below (or sometimes above) the notes written.

Colonel Bogey March (1914) by Kenneth J. Alford (a.k.a. Frederick J. Ricketts) (1881–1945), included in the film *The Bridge on the River Kwai* (1958).

Colonne, Edouard (Judas) (1838–1910) French violinist and conductor, educated at the Paris Conservatoire. He founded the Concerts Colonne in Paris in 1871 (orig. the Association artistique).

colophony *also*, **colophane** (Fr.) ROSIN.

color 1, in medieval music, ornamentation or repetition; esp., the repeated melody of an isorhythmic motet (see TALEA, ISORHYTHM). **2,** the special quality of a particular sound or sound complex, sometimes specifically related to visual color or colors. Some composers, notably Rimsky-Korsakov, Messiaen and Scriabin, have assigned colors to specific keys (e.g., C Major = white), but their lists differ significantly.

coloration 1, the coloring of notes or note-heads to indicate a change of duration in mensural or proportional notation. **2,** spontaneous or written out ornamentation. Cf. COLORATURA.

coloratura (It., coloring) **1**, florid ornamentation in vocal music. **2**, a singer specializing in singing coloratura, usu. a soprano.

color organ a device for projecting colored light on a screen in combinations to suggest the changes and themes of music. A number of such machines have been made since the 18th c.; one of the most successful was the Clavilux, made in 1925 by Thomas Wilfred. Such a machine is called for in the score of Scriabin's *Prometheus: the poem of fire* (1908–10).

col pugno [ˈpoo-nyō] (It., with the fist) an indication to use the fist or hand to produce a percussive effect on the piano keyboard.

Coltrane, John (William) (1926–67) Amer. jazz saxophonist. He played with Eddie Vinson, Dizzy Gillespie and Earl Bostic, but his most adventuresome work was with Miles Davis and Thelonious Monk in the late 1950s and with his own quartet in the 1960s.

Columbia-Princeton Electronic Music Center a center founded in 1951 in New York for the creation, performance and study of electronic music.

Columbia Symphony Orchestra symphony orch. formed by the Columbia Broadcasting System in 1958 in Los Angeles to make recordings with conductor Bruno Walter.

Columbia, the Gem of the Ocean Amer. patriotic song (1843) by David T. Shaw. The English have also claimed the work, under the title "Britannia, the Pride of the Ocean," first published in 1852. Unfortunately, because both texts end with the words *The Red, White and Blue*, the confusion remains, as these colors appear on the flags of both nations.

Combattimento di Tancredi e Clorinda, Il (It., The Combat between Tancred and Clorinda) a dramatic setting (1624) by Monteverdi of a passage from Tasso's *Gerusalemme liberata*, published as part of Monteverdi's *Eighth Book of Madrigals*. The work is distinguished by its use of STILE CONCITATO.

combination stop a preset selection of organ stops activated by a PISTON.

combination tone a tone heard by some listeners when two tones of widely differing frequency are sounded simultaneously. It is called a *difference tone* if its frequency equals the difference between the frequencies of the two tones producing it, a *summation tone* if its frequency is the sum of the two tones. Cf. RESIDUE TONE.

combinatoriality the study of the relationships between different arrangements of a SET of notes; specif., the concern as to whether the elements of a certain segment of a set, esp. a hexachord, may be found in analogous segments of other sets. The property is most often utilized by composers working with 12-note or other serial techniques wishing to find sections from different sets or rows, related by INVERSION or RETROGRADE transposition, not containing any of the same pitches and therefore available to be combined to form new but related sets.

combo in jazz and popular music, a small ensemble, usu. of three to five players.

comédie-ballet (Fr.) a 17th-c. French theatrical form invented by Lully and Molière, in which the acts of a play were separated by ballet interludes on subjects related to the subject of the play. It was a predecessor of the *opéra-comique*.

come prima [ˈkō-mäˈprē-mä] (It., as before) a direction to return to a previous tempo, mode of articulation, etc.

comes [ˈkō-mäs] (Lat.) ANSWER. Cf. DUX.

come sopra (It., as above) **1**, an indication to repeat certain earlier material. **2**, COME PRIMA.

come sta (It., as it stands) an indication to play exactly as written, without ornamentation or rhythmic alteration.

comic opera OPERA on a light or

comic theme, often with spoken dialogue. Cf. OPERA COMIQUE, OPERETTA, MUSICAL COMEDY, OPERA BUFFA.

Comissiona, Sergiu (1928–) Romanian conductor and violinist, educated at the Bucharest Conservatory. In 1959 he emigrated to Israel, where he founded the Israel Chamber Orch. His Amer. debut was with the Philadelphia Orch. in 1965. He has been music director of the Baltimore SO (1969–84), the Houston SO (1984–88) and several European orchestras.

comma 1, CAESURA; esp., a breath in vocal music. **2,** a minute difference between two versions of the same pitch, usu. resulting from differences in tuning. The *syntonic comma* is the difference between a just major 3rd and four just perfect 5ths less two octaves. The *Pythagorean comma* is the difference between twelve 5ths and seven octaves.

Commodores, The Amer. funk and pop sextet formed in 1968 in Alabama and led by singer-songwriter Lionel Richie. Their hits incl. "Three Times a Lady" (1978) and "Sail On" (1979).

common chord a major or minor TRIAD.

common measure *also,* **common meter, common time** duple or quadruple meter, esp. 4/4 time.

comodo *also,* **commodo** (It.) in a comfortable or convenient tempo.

compact disc a system of high-fidelity sound recording, utilizing a digitally-encoded disc that is read by a laser beam. Abbr., *CD*

comparative musicology ETHNOMUSICOLOGY.

compass RANGE (1,).

Compère, Loyset (?1445–1518) French composer of sacred and secular vocal music, a contemporary of Josquin des Pres. He was a member of the chapel of the Duke of Milan in the 1470s and joined the French court sometime in the early 1480s.

comping providing harmonic and structural support for another musician while he or she improvises a solo in a jazz performance.

compline the last of the daily services of the DIVINE OFFICE, falling between sunset and midnight. Also, *night song.*

Composers, Authors and Publishers Association of Canada a Canadian copyright collecting society, affiliated with ASCAP. Abbr., *CAPAC.*

Composers Collective of New York a group of composers formed in 1933 to support music for the working class. The group disbanded in 1938.

Composers' Forum an organization founded in 1935 in New York to further the rights of composers.

Composers String Quartet an Amer. string quartet formed in 1963 principally to perform contemporary music. It was initially quartet-in-residence at the New England Conservatory and, since 1974, at Columbia.

composition the act or process of creating a work of music.

compound interval an INTERVAL greater than an octave. Cf. SIMPLE INTERVAL.

compound meter *also,* **compound time** a meter containing three pulses within each beat, the most common examples being ⁶⁄₈, ⁹⁄₈ and ¹²⁄₈.

comprimario [kōm-prē'mä-ryō] (It.) a singer or dancer ranked just below the principal singers or dancers, analogous to a supporting role in theater and films.

computer music a term referring to music composed or performed with the aid of a computer. The computer can be used in a number of ways: a) it can help to produce compositional materials, through random number functions or various programs designed for specific tasks; b) it can actually "compose" a piece, using a set of predetermined algorithms; c) it can control a synthesizer or other tone-producing machine to produce sounds or combinations of sounds, either in live performance or in preparing a taped work; d) it can store sounds that have been transformed into digital information and manipulate the information in various ways if desired. Computers can also be used to produce music notation from information fed into it through a typewriter keyboard or from an external music source, by means of MIDI or other interface. Computers have also been used to aid in reconstruction of damaged recordings of the past. The potential of computers in music has just begun to be tapped.

Comte Ory, Le (Fr., Count Ory) comic opera in 2 acts by Rossini to a libretto in French by Scribe and Delestre-Poirson, based on a Picardy ballad. Premiere, Paris 1828. A complicated tale of disguise and amorous intrigue in which the Count Ory, a young rake, attempts to win the love of the Countess Adele.

con [kōn] (It.) with.

con brio ['brē-ō] (It.) with vigor and energy.

concentus (Lat., concord) **1**, the sound of instruments or voices playing together. **2**, the more elaborate part of a chant sung by the whole choir. Cf. ACCENTUS, PLAINSONG.

Concentus Musicus of Vienna Austrian ensemble founded in 1953 by Nikolaus Harnoncourt to perform baroque music on instruments of the period.

concert a public or private performance; sometimes restricted to mean an orchestral performance. Cf. RECITAL.

concertante *also*, **concertato** (It.) **1**, a composition of the 17th or 18th c. for an instrumental group with one or more soloists, or for solo group without orch. Cf. A CAPPELLA. **2**, CONCERTINO.

concertato motet a 17th-c. sacred vocal composition with instrumental accompaniment.

concert band SYMPHONIC BAND.

Concertgebouw Orchestra a Dutch symphony orch. founded in Amsterdam in 1888 under conductor Willem Kes. Subsequent conductors have been Mengelberg, Eugen Jochum, Haitink and Kondrashin.

concert grand a large GRAND PIANO

(usu. 9 feet long or more) designed for use in a concert hall.

concertina (It.) a small octagonal ACCORDION with button keys, which produces the same sounds on opening and closing strokes of the bellows.

concertino (It.) the solo instrumental group in a CONCERTO GROSSO—contrasted with RIPIENO or TUTTI.

concertmaster the leader of the first violins of an orch., by extension the leader of the string section and next below the conductor in rank in the ensemble. The concertmaster usu. directs the tuning of the orch. at rehearsals and concerts. Also, (Brit.) *leader.*

concerto 1, before 1650, a work for voices with organ or continuo. **2**, an instrumental work which contrasts a solo instrument or small group of instruments with a larger ensemble. The form of the instrumental concerto solidified in the 18th c. to three movements, usu. fast-slow-fast, with cadences for the solo instrument(s). The first movement is often in a modified SONATA FORM, and the last movement is frequently a RONDO or RONDO-SONATA.

concerto grosso a type of concerto in which a small group of instruments (the *concertino*) alternates with and is contrasted with a larger group (the *ripieno* or *tutti*).

concert pitch 1, the sounding pitch of a note played on a transposing instrument, as opposed to written pitch. **2**, the internationally approved standard of 440 cycles per second for the A above middle C (a'). Cf. KAMMERTON.

Concert spirituel [kō'ser spē-rē'tüel] (Fr., sacred concert) a concert series founded in Paris in 1725 by Anne Danican Philidor and continued until 1790.

concitato [kōn-chē'tä-tō] (It.) excited, agitated. Cf. STILE CONCITATO.

concord a subjective term for a pleasant combination of sounds. Cf. DISCORD.

Concord String Quartet string quartet founded in 1971 and winner of the

Naumburg Award in that year. The group has commissioned several composers; GEORGE ROCHBERG in particular has written a number of works for them.

Concord Sonata popular name for the Second Piano Sonata (1909–15) by Ives, entitled *Concord, Mass., 1840–1860*. The titles of the four movements are "Emerson," "Hawthorne," "The Alcotts" and "Thoreau."

concrete music see MUSIQUE CONCRÈTE.

concussion instruments one of a family of musical instruments in which pairs of similar objects are struck together to produce sound. The most common members are CYMBALS and CASTANETS.

Condon, Eddie (Albert Edwin) (1905–73) Amer. composer, guitarist, banjo player and leader. He was important in promulgating the Chicago jazz sound and produced numerous recordings. With his bands from 1938, and in his club after 1945, he showcased jazz and its most important performers.

conducting the control of a musical performance by physical gestures of hand or baton. Conducting began with an audible signal to give the beat (*tactus*), such as the sound of a stick hitting the floor. Early ensembles were led by one of their members, usu. a violinist leading with the bow or a keyboard player directing with head or hand signals. In the 19th c. the violinist's bow was replaced by a roll of paper and then by a baton. Modern conducting involves the use of fairly standardized patterns which convey to the players not only the beat, but also the meter, the dynamics, the articulation and the expression.

conductus a medieval vocal composition in one or more parts, the lowest of which consists of a Latin text set to a new melody (not derived from chant), which the other parts accompany. The text-setting was usu. syllabic, but the work sometimes ended with a melismatic phrase (*cauda*).

Cone, Edward T(oner) (1917–) Amer. composer and writer, stud. of Sessions. He has been on the faculty of Princeton U. since 1947 and was co-editor of *Perspectives of New Music* from 1965 to 1969.

confinal *also,* **confinalis** (Lat.) a secondary final, usu. the dominant, in the ecclestiastical modes. See MODE.

conga a ballroom circle or line dance of Cuban origin, accompanied by conga drums.

conga drums Cuban BARREL DRUMS, usu. used in pairs, having heavy vellum heads played with the hands and fingers.

conical drum a single- or double-headed DRUM whose top is larger in diameter than its base.

conjunct of a melodic line, moving by intervals of a major or minor second. Cf. DISJUNCT.

Conlon, James (1950–) Amer. conductor, stud. of Jean Morel. His conducting debut was in Spoleto, Italy, in 1971. He has conducted most major orchestras and opera companies in the U.S. and Europe. He has been music dir. of the Cincinnati May Festival since 1979, of the Rotterdam PO since 1983 and music dir. of the city of Cologne, Germany, since 1989.

Conn Amer. instr. manufacturing firm founded in 1875 in Elkhart, IN.

Connecticut Yankee, A musical by Richard Rodgers, lyrics by Lorenz Hart, book by Herbert Fields, based on Mark Twain's novel. Premiere, New York 1927. The Connecticut Yankee, Martin, is knocked on the head and dreams he is back in the days of King Arthur.

Conniff, Ray (1916–) Amer. jazz trombonist and arranger. He played with Bunny Berrigan, Bob Crosby and Artie Shaw before turning in the 1950s to arranging and choral conducting.

Consecration of the House, The (Ger., *Die Weihe des Hauses*) overture in C major, Op. 124 (1822), by Beethoven, written for the opening of the Josephstadt Theater in Vienna.

consecutives the occurrence of the

Conducting Patterns

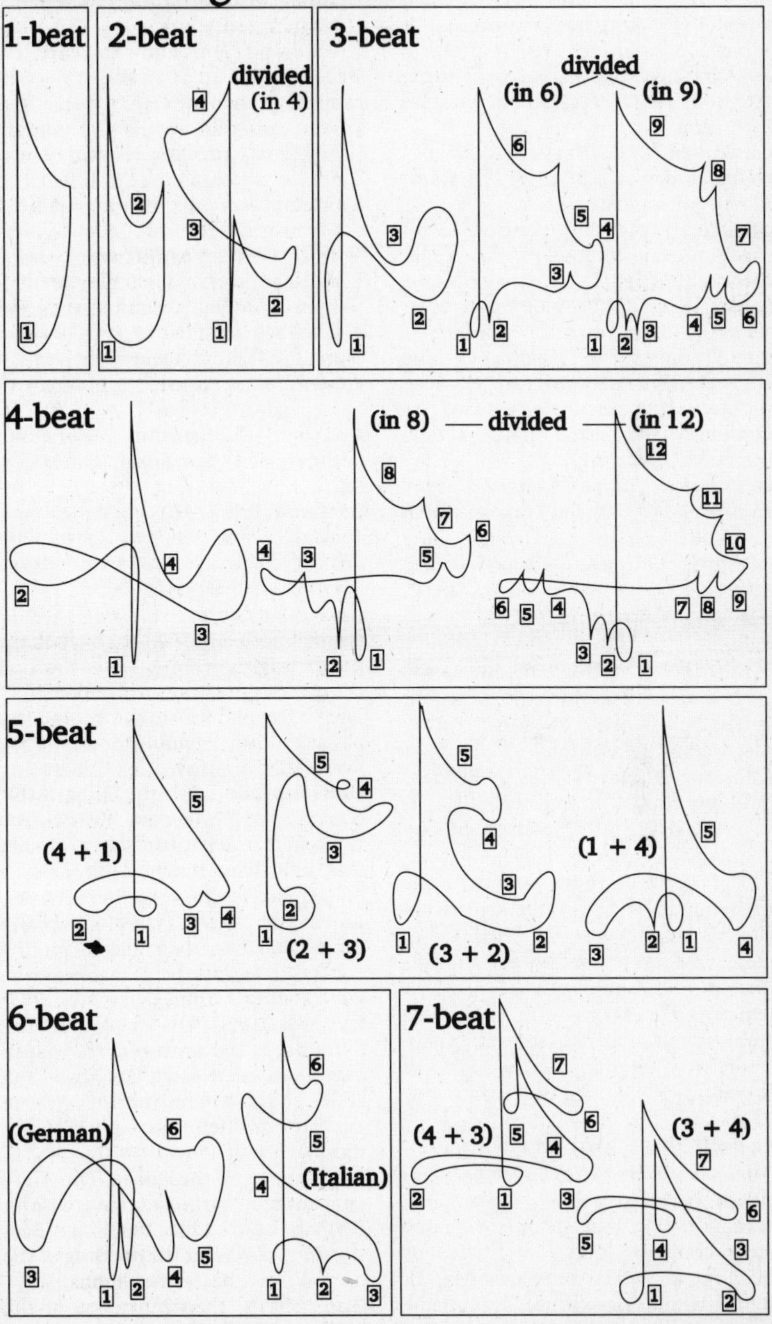

1-beat

2-beat

divided (in 4)

3-beat

divided
(in 6)   (in 9)

4-beat

(in 8) — divided — (in 12)

5-beat

(4 + 1)

(2 + 3)   (3 + 2)

(1 + 4)

6-beat

(German)

(Italian)

7-beat

(4 + 3)

(3 + 4)

same interval between two parts in successive chords. The use of consecutive fifths and octaves is frowned upon in traditional counterpoint. When consecutives result from a movement of two parts in the same direction they are called *parallel fifths* or *octaves*.

consequent see ANTECEDENT.

conservatory a school for the training of musicians.

console the main furniture unit of an organ containing the keyboard, pedals, pistons, etc.

consonance a harmonious concurrence of two or more sounds or pitches, opposed to DISSONANCE. The concept of what constitutes a harmonious concurrence has varied according to the period of history and the cultural setting.

con sordino (It.) with MUTE.

consort 1, esp. in the 16th and 17th c., a set of instruments of the same family to be played in concert. Cf. MIXED CONSORT, BROKEN CONSORT. **2,** any small instrumental or vocal group.

consort song an English song of the 16th and 17th c. for solo voice or voices and consort of viols or other instrumental ensemble.

Constant, Marius (1925–) Romanian-born French composer and conductor, stud. of Messiaen, Tony Aubin and Boulanger. He was a member of the electronic studio of the French radio and a founder in 1963 of the ensemble Ars Nova, dedicated to collective improvisation and the performance of 20th-c. music.

constructivism a term borrowed from the visual arts to refer to highly structured composition, such as found in the works of ANTON VON WEBERN.

Consul, The tragic opera in 3 acts by Menotti to his own libretto. Premiere, New York 1950. Set in a European country in the present, the story concerns John Sorel, who has been forced to leave his wife Magda, his baby and his mother, and escape over the border, and the unsuccessful attempt of Magda to rejoin him.

Contant, Alexis [kō'tä] (1858–1918) Canadian composer, stud. of Calixa Lavallé and Guillaume Couture. He was organist at St. Jean-Baptiste in Montreal for over 30 years. His works, most of which are unpublished, incl. the first Canadian oratorio, *Caïn* (1905).

Contemporary Chamber Ensemble a new music ensemble founded in New York in 1960 by Arthur Weisberg.

Contemporary Chamber Players contemporary music ensemble at the U. of Chicago founded in 1954 and directed by Ralph Shapey.

contemporary music see MODERN MUSIC.

Contes d'Hoffmann, Les [kōt dof'män] (Fr.) TALES OF HOFFMANN, THE.

continuo (It.) BASSO CONTINUO.

contrabass 1, of an instrument, pitched an octave below the normal bass range. **2,** DOUBLE BASS.

contrabass clarinet a large CLARINET pitched two octaves below the soprano B♭ clarinet. Also, *pedal clarinet*.

contrabassoon the largest BASSOON, pitched an octave below the standard bassoon and sounding an octave lower than written.

contrafactum (Lat.) the substitution of one text for another with almost no change in the musical setting. The technique usu. involves either the replacement of an older text with a newer one or of a secular text with a sacred one.

contralto see ALTO.

contrapuntal composed according to the practices of COUNTERPOINT. Sometimes the term is used to indicate a polyphonic texture with especially active and differentiated parts.

contrary motion the simultaneous movement of two parts in opposite directions.

contratenor (Lat.) *also,* **countertenor** in 14th- and 15th-c. music, an additional part written in the same range as the TENOR. —**contratenor altus**, (Lat.) a line in three-part polyphony placed just above the tenor.—**contra-tenor bassus**, (Lat.) a line in four-voice polyphony between the contratenor altus and the tenor.

contrebasse d'harmonie (Fr.) OPHICLEIDE (1,).

contredanse ['kō-trə"dãs] (Fr.) a French court dance developed from an English country dance for couples, usu. in duple meter.

contretemps [-tã] (Fr.) SYNCOPATION.

Converse, Frederick (Shepherd) (1871–1940) Amer. composer and teacher, stud. of Paine and Chadwick in Boston and of Rheinberger in Munich. He taught at Harvard College until 1907 then after the war at the New England Conservatory until his retirement in 1932. His first opera, *The Pipe of Desire* (1905), was the first Amer. opera performed in the Metropolitan Opera House. His works include tone poems, vocal works and chamber music.

Cook, Barbara (Nell) (1927–) Amer. singer and actress. She was the original Cunegonde in Bernstein's *Candide* (1956) and sang in the original production of *The Music Man* (1957). In recent years she has been a successful nightclub and stage singer.

Cook, Will Marion (1869–1944) Amer. composer, violinist and conductor. He studied at Oberlin U., with Joachim in Germany and with Dvořák in New York. In 1919 he toured the U.S. and Europe with his own orch. His works, mostly songs and stage musicals, make extensive use of Negro folk music, and incl. *Clorindy, or The Origin of the Cakewalk* (1898) and *In Dahomey* (1902).

Cooke, Sam (1935–64) Amer. gospel and soul singer and producer. He was a member of the Soul Stirrers for six years before developing his solo career.

Cooley, Spade (Donnell Clyde) (1910–69) Amer. country-music fiddler, singer and bandleader. His greatest success came in the 1940s and 1950s, when he made many recordings and hosted a television show in Los Angeles.

Coolidge, Elizabeth (Penn) Sprague (1864–1953) Amer. patron of the arts. She endowed the Library of Congress with funds to give concerts and to support musicological research, and also provided funds for an auditorium and an organ.

cool jazz a term used in the late 1940s and the 1950s to refer to a style of jazz playing with lighter tone and less impassioned improvisation, exemplified by the playing of Chet Baker, Stan Getz, Gerry Mulligan, Lee Konitz, and others, and by groups such as the Modern Jazz Quartet and the Dave Brubeck Quartet. Cf. WEST COAST SCHOOL.

coon song a type of comic song popular from the 1880s to World War I, characterized by lyrics in a dialect supposedly typical of Afr.-Amer. speech, usu. performed by white artists in vaudeville and written by both white and black composers.

Cooper, Alice (Furnier, Vincent) (1945–) Amer. hard-rock singer, famous for his theatrics and explicit lyrics.

Cooper, Stoney (Dale T.) (1918–77) Amer. country-music singer, fiddler and songwriter, for many years member of a popular duo with WILMA LEE.

Coperario, John COPRARIO, JOHN.

coperto (It., covered) used as an indication in drum music to use a mute, and in vocal music, to employ a darker, covered sound.

Copland, Aaron (1900–90) Amer. composer, pianist, conductor and writer, stud. of Goldmark and of Boulanger, who commissioned his Organ Symphony in 1929. In the 1920s he was active in the League of Composers and, with Sessions, sponsored a series of concerts of new music in New York (1928–31). He was a founder of the American Composers Alliance, of which he was president from 1937 to 1945. He taught at Harvard and was the first composer to deliver the Norton lectures there. Shortly after the Berkshire Music Center was founded Copland became chairman of the faculty, holding that position until 1965. He frequently appeared as guest conductor, usu. conducting his own works, which incl. *The Second Hurricane, The Tender Land* (operas), *Appalachian Spring, Billy the Kid, Rodeo* and other ballets, *Quiet City, El salón México, Lincoln Portrait, Fanfare for the Common Man,* chamber music, *In the Beginning, Canticle of Freedom* and other choral music, piano works, songs and film scores.

Coppélia (Fr.) ballet with music by Delibes based on a story by E.T.A. Hoffmann about a toymaker who creates lifelike dolls. Premiere, Paris 1870.

Coprario (Coperario, Cooper), **John** (?1580–?1626) English violist and composer of sacred and secular vocal and instrumental works, and of *Rules How to Compose,* a treatise on composing partsong (pre-1617).

copula an ORGAN STOP designed to bind the tone of other stops, such as reed and flue stops or loud and soft stops.

copyist a person who produces a finished score and/or instrumental parts from a composer's manuscript. In recent years, many copyists have used computers instead of traditional pen and ink for their work.

Coq d'or, Le [kok dor] (Fr., The Golden Cockerel) opera in 3 acts by Rimsky-Korsakov to a libretto in Russian by V.I. Bielski, after a fairy tale by Pushkin. A fantasy about an astrologer, a queen and a golden cockerel, and the trials of the imaginary King Dodon.

cor (Fr.) horn, usu. the FRENCH HORN.

cor anglais [ä′glä] (Fr.) ENGLISH HORN.

coranto (It.) a type of 16th-c. COURANTE.

corda (It., pl., *corde*) string. —**due corde,** (It., two strings) in piano music, an indication to depress the SOFT PEDAL part way, producing a result between the full sound of TRE CORDE and the muted sound of UNA CORDA. In string music, it is an indication to play the same tone on two strings si-multaneously. —**tre corde,** (It., three strings) in piano music, an indication to play without the SOFT PEDAL, thereby allowing all the strings (three, for most pitches) to sound. —**una corda,** (It., one string) in piano music, an indication to use the SOFT PEDAL, fully depressed.

Cordier, Baude (fl. early 15th c.) French composer of rondeaux, chansons and masses. His most familiar work is a chanson written in the shape of a heart.

Cordero, Roque (1917–) Panamanian composer and conductor, stud. of Mitropoulos, Krenek, Stanley Chapple and Leon Barzin. He taught at the National Institute of Music in Panama until 1966 and conducted the National Orch. Since then he has taught at Indiana U. and at Illinois State U. He has written orchestral, chamber, vocal and piano works in tonal and serial idioms.

Corea, Chick (Armando Anthony) (1941–) Amer. jazz pianist, composer, and drummer, specialist in Latin rhythms. He played with Stan Getz and Miles Davis, with whom he explored the use of electric keyboards and polytonal and nontonal improvisation, which he pursued with his own group, Circle (1970–71). He has also performed as a classical pianist and is an innovative composer.

Corelli, Arcangelo (1653–1713) Italian composer and violinist, whose works had a profound influence on string writing and performance. He spent the greater part of his career in Rome. The relatively small number of surviving works includes church and chamber sonatas as well as concerti grossi.

Corelli, Franco (Dario) (1921–) Italian tenor, educated in Pesaro. His Amer. debut was at the Metropolitan Opera in 1961. His large voice was well suited to the Italian *spinto* and *verismo* repertory of the late 19th c.

Corigliano, John (Paul) [kō-rē′lyä-nō] (1938–) Amer. composer, stud. of Luening, Giannini and Creston. He has been on the faculty of Lehman

College in New York and composer-in-residence of the Chicago SO. His works, in a generally conservative idiom, incl. concertos for violin, clarinet, oboe and flute; two operas; songs and chamber music.

Coriolan Overture orchestral work, op. 62 (1807), by Beethoven, written as an overture to a play by H.J. von Collin based on the same subject as Shakespeare's *Coriolanus*.

cori spezzati [spät′tsä-tē] (It., broken choirs) a technique of choral composition involving choral groups placed in different parts of a building. The term is used in particular in reference to music written for St. Mark's Basilica in Venice.

cornamusa (It.) **1**, BAGPIPE. **2**, a variety of SHAWM.

Cornelius, (Carl August) Peter (1824–74) German composer, stud. of Siegfried Dehn. He was a part of the circle around Liszt in Weimar and Wagner in Vienna. Of his many works, mostly for voice, he is best remembered for his opera *Der Barbier von Bagdad* (1855–8), which is still performed.

cornemuse (Fr.) BAGPIPE.

cornet 1, *also,* **cornett, cornetto** (It.) a six-keyed Renaissance wooden HORN played with a cup mouthpiece, used esp. for accompanying church choral music. Also, *zinke* (Ger.). **2**, a valved, brass HORN in B♭ similar to the trumpet, often used in combination with valveless, crooked trumpets in 19th-c. French orchestral compositions. The instrument is frequently used in jazz. Also, *cornopean, cornet-à-pistons* (Fr.). **3**, an ORGAN STOP.

corno (It.) FRENCH HORN.

corno di bassetto (It.) BASSET HORN.

corno inglese (It.) ENGLISH HORN.

cornopean a type of CORNET (2,).

cornu BUCCINA.

coronach a DIRGE sung or played on the bagpipes in Ireland and Scotland.

Coronation Anthem an anthem written for the coronation of a monarch. Famous examples incl. four anthems written by Handel in 1727 for George II (the best known of which is "Zadok the Priest") and "My heart is indit-

ing" by Purcell for James II in 1685.

Coronation Concerto either of two piano concertos, the D major, K. 537 (1788), or the F major, K. 459 (1788) by Mozart, so named because Mozart played them at the coronation of Emperor Leopold at Frankfurt in 1790.

Coronation Mass 1, the Mass in C major, K. 317 (1779), by Mozart, written for the annual coronation of the statue of the Virgin at the shrine of Maria Plain, in Austria. **2**, NELSON MASS.

Coronation of Poppea, The (It., *L'incoronazione di Poppea*) opera in 5 acts by Monteverdi to a libretto in Italian by Giovan Francesco Busenello. Premiere, Venice 1642. Ottavia's efforts to sabotage Nero's wedding to Poppea are unsuccessful; she is banished and Poppea is crowned.

corrente (It.) see COURANTE.

corrido [kō′rē-*thō*] (Sp.) a type of 20th-c. Mexican ballad and dance.

Corsair, The 1, (Fr., *Le Corsaire*) concert-overture, Op. 21 (1831–44), by Berlioz, based on Byron's poem. **2**, (It., *Il Corsaro*) opera in 4 acts by Verdi to a libretto by Piave based on Byron's poem. Premiere, Trieste 1848.

Cortés, Ramiro (1933–84) Amer. composer with Mexican roots, stud. of Cowell, Halsey Stevens, Dahl, Petrassi and Giannini. He was on the faculty of the U. of Southern California. His works incl. an opera, orchestral and chamber music.

Cortot, Alfred (Denis) (1877–1962) French pianist and conductor, stud. of Louis Diémer. He worked at Bayreuth from 1898–1901, after which he was active as a conductor in Paris. As a pianist, he was best known as member of a trio with Thibaud and Casals, formed in 1905. He was a founder of the École Normale de Musique, where he taught a celebrated course in interpretation. He produced a number of working editions of Chopin and Liszt, which combined the works themselves with technical exercises related to the music.

Cos Cob Press Amer. music publishers founded in 1929 to promote the music of serious Amer. composers.

Cosí fan tutte (It., All Women Are Like That) comic opera in 2 acts by Mozart, libretto in Italian by da Ponte. Premiere, Vienna 1790. Don Alfonso, an old cynic, wants to prove to his friends Guglielmo and Ferrando that their fiancées, Fiordiligi and Dorabella, are fickle and not to be trusted.

Cossotto, Fiorenza (1935–) Italian mezzo-soprano, educated at the Turin Conservatory, a constant presence at La Scala until the 1970s and in other major opera houses. Her roles incl. Azucena (*Il Trovatore*), Amneris (*Aida*) and Adalgisa (*Norma*).

Costeley, Guillaume (?1530–1606) French composer of chansons, motets and keyboard music, and composer to the court of Charles IX.

Costello, Elvis (McManus, Declan) (1955–) English new-wave rock singer and songwriter, noted for his intricate lyrics and clipped vocal delivery.

cotillon [kō-tē'yō] (Fr.) an 18th- and 19th-c. French square dance, similar to the QUADRILLE.

Cotrubas, Ileana (1939–) Romanian soprano, educated at the Bucharest Conservatory. Her Amer. debut was at the Chicago Lyric Opera in 1973. Her roles incl. Mélisande, Susanna (*The Marriage of Figaro*), and Mimì (*La Bohème*).

Cotten, Elizabeth ("Libba") (1893–1987) American folk singer, guitarist and banjoist, best known for her song "Freight Train," written at age 11.

Cotton Club nightclub in Harlem, New York, made famous in the 1920s and 1930s by the Duke Ellington band and other performers, incl. Cab Calloway. The club closed in 1940.

Cotton Pickers a famous jazz band led by William McKinney (1895–1969) in Detroit in the late 1920s.

coulé [koo'lā] (Fr.) a type of APPOGGIATURA.

Coulombe-Saint-Marcoux, Micheline SAINT-MARCOUX, MICHELINE COULOMBE.

Coulthard, Jean ['kōl-tärd] (1908–) Canadian composer, stud. of Vaughan Williams. She taught at the U. of British Columbia from 1947 until she retired in 1973. Her works, in a tonal, impressionist style, include orchestral, vocal and chamber works.

Council of Trent an important meeting of the Catholic Church (1545–63) which, among other decrees, outlawed the use of secular melodies in services.

counterexposition in FUGUE, a second EXPOSITION preceding the middle entries in related keys, preserving the original subject-answer relationships in the tonic key.

counterfugue a FUGUE in which the first answer is an inversion of the subject.

counterpoint 1, a term, dating (in its Latin form *contrapunctus*) from the 14th c., for polyphony composed according to a prescribed set of rules. The term is also used more generally to apply to polyphonic part-writing in which each part has a certain independence from the other parts in the texture. The rules of any contrapuntal system govern the accepted movement of parts relative to one another, i.e., what successions of vertical and horizontal intervals are acceptable and what dissonances are possible under what conditions. The principal types taught at present are 16th-century counterpoint (in the style of Palestrina); 17th-c. counterpoint, as formulated by Fux in his *Gradus ad Parnassum* (1725), also referred to as *species counterpoint;* and free style or harmonic counterpoint of the 18th c. (Baroque) and 19th c. (Romantic).

Species counterpoint, consisting of one or more contrapuntal voices against a *cantus firmus* in whole notes, is divided into five categories or species: a) note against note; b) two or three notes in the counterpoint against one in the *cantus firmus;* c) four or six notes in the counterpoint against one note in the *cantus firmus;* d) two notes in the counterpoint to one in the *cantus firmus,*

Species counterpoint against a cantus firmus
5th species

Cantus firmus

4th species

3rd species

2nd species

Invertible counterpoint

Inversion

(Beethoven, Symphony No. 3)

Techniques for varying a theme
Theme from
J.S.Bach, Art of the Fugue   Inversion

Retrograde   Retrograde inversion

Diminution   Augmentation

with each second note tied to the first of the next measure, i.e., syncopated; and e) a mixture of the four preceding species. More voices may be added against the *cantus firmus*, each in the same or differing species. See also IM-ITATION, FUGUE, CANON.

2, a polyphonic composition. **3**, in jazz, the term may refer either to melodic polyphony, common particularly in FREE JAZZ and in NEW OR-LEANS STYLE, or to multiple rhythmic layers, which are integral to jazz.

countersubject a second, contrasting theme in contrapuntal music. Specif., in FUGUE, a theme played against the subject, usu. first appearing against the first answer.

countertenor 1, *also*, **contratenor** a musical part between tenor and soprano. **2**, a MALE ALTO or a man singing a countertenor part in falsetto.

country and western music a hybrid Amer. popular music that emerged in the 1940s, combining elements of COUNTRY MUSIC and WESTERN MUSIC, epitomized in the music of Hank Williams and cowboy singers (Gene Autry, Roy Rogers).

country-dance a lively 17th-c. English social dance, usu. performed in a line and danced to a JIG or REEL. Cf. CONTREDANSE.

country blues a type of COUNTRY MUSIC incorporating elements of BLUES music, as exemplified in the early music of the Delmore Brothers.

Country Joe and the Fish Amer. folk-rock band formed in 1965 in San Francisco, a highly politicized group notorious for its lyrics. The Fish disbanded in 1970.

country music an Amer. style of popular music, derived from rural folk music (HILLBILLY music), itself derived from the music of British immigrants. The most usu. accompaniments are the fiddle, guitar and the banjo, although through the influence of WESTERN MUSIC, MOUNTAIN MUSIC and BLUEGRASS MUSIC, other instruments, such as the piano and drums, have become more and more common. The best known forum for commercial country music is the Grand Ole Opry in Nashville, TN, the recording capital of the country music industry. See also HONKY-TONK, ROCKABILLY, COUNTRY AND WESTERN MUSIC, COUNTRY ROCK.

country rock Amer. form of ROCK MUSIC incorporating some of the characteristic elements of COUNTRY MUSIC, as in the music of Linda Ronstadt, the Byrds, the Grateful Dead and others. Cf. OUTLAW COUNTRY.

coup [koo] (Fr.) blow, stroke.

coup d'archet [där'shā] (Fr.) a bow stroke. See BOWING.

coup de glotte [glot] (Fr.) GLOTTAL STOP.

Couperin, François [koo'pr̄e] ("Le Grand") (1668–1733) French composer, organist, harpsichordist and teacher, the most illustrious member of a family of musicians spanning three centuries. He studied with Jacques Thomelin, organist to the king, and obtained the position in 1693 when Thomelin died. He remained at court for the rest of his life, assuming in 1717 the position of king's harpsichordist as well. Couperin's compositions include sacred and secular vocal works, chamber music and many harpsichord works, models of the French keyboard suite. He also wrote in 1716 an important pedagogical work, *L'art de toucher le clavecin* (Fr., The Art of Playing the Harpsichord).

Couperin, Louis (?1626–61) French composer, harpsichordist and organist, uncle of François Couperin le Grand. Very little is known about his early life. From 1653 until his death he was organist at St. Gervais in Paris. His surviving works are all instrumental, for harpsichord, organ and chamber ensembles.

coupler a device for connecting, by mechanical or electrical means, two keyboards, two organ stops, etc.

couplet [koo'plā] (Fr.) an EPISODE that alternates with a main section, as in a RONDO.

courante [koo'rāt] (Fr., running, flowing) a dance and instrumental form which flourished from the late 16th c. to the mid-18th c., often as a movement of a dance suite, typically paired with an allemande. By the late 17th c. there were two types: the Italian *corrente*, homophonic, fast, in triple meter, usu. in binary form, with a clear harmonic and rhythmic structure; and the French *courante*, contrapuntal, majestic and grave, in triple meter, with rhythmic and metric complexity (often employing hemiola), having the slowest tempo of the French court dances of that time. Cf. CORANTO. See DANCE (*illus.*).

course a string (as of a lute) played alone, or together with one or more other strings tuned in unison or octave with it to produce greater volume.

courtaut [koor'tō] (Fr.) a Renaissance double-reed wind instrument with a double bore and six projecting tubes for fingerholes.

courting flute an end-blown native Amer. FLUTE of wood or cane used for serenading.

Couture, Guillaume [koo'tür, gē'yōm] (1851–1915) Canadian composer, stud. of Dubois. He was the first Canadian to study at the Paris Conservatoire and its first Canadian graduate. In Montreal he founded three concert societies, which he conducted. His works, few in number, incl. an oratorio, a cantata and works for organ, chamber ensemble and orch.

Covent Garden a theater in London, also known as the Royal Opera House, built in 1858, home since 1946 of the Royal Opera and the Royal Ballet.

cover 1, UNDERSTUDY. **2**, in popular music, the second and subsequent versions of a song, whether performed by the original artist or writer, or by another artist.

Coward, (Sir) **Noël (Pierce)** (1899–1973) English composer, songwriter, lyricist, librettist, actor and director. He was a highly versatile man of the theater, a creator of songs and shows, musical and non-musical, incl. an operetta, *Bittersweet* (1929).

cowbell a BELL with clapper suspended from the neck of a cow to signal its location; also, a similar bell without clapper used as a percussion instrument in bands and orchestras.

cowboy song a type of WESTERN MUSIC song describing the cowboy life, usu. accompanied by guitar.

Cowell, Henry (Dixon) (1897–1965) highly innovative and prolific Amer. composer, pianist and writer, stud. of Charles Seeger. He was the first

Amer. composer invited to the USSR. He was also interested in non-European music, and he collaborated with several ethnomusicologists in research. He founded the New Music Edition, an important disseminator of new works for almost 25 years. He taught music at the New School of Social Research in New York (1941–63), Peabody Conservatory (1951–56) and Columbia (1949–65). His pupils incl. Cage, Harrison and Gershwin.

In his book *New Music Resources* (1930) Cowell described his new techniques, which included clusters, counter-rhythms and harmonic innovations. His works (symphonies and other orchestral works, choral and solo vocal works, chamber and theater music, and piano works) give evidence of an ear searching for the right means for expression and the imagination to create a new one if none yet existed.

cow horn a bull's horn with the narrow end removed for blowing, called for in some operatic and orchestral scores.

Cox, Ida (1889–1967) Amer. blues singer, a popular recording and touring artist from the early 1920s until her retirement in the 1950s.

cps *abbr.* cycles per second.

crab canon a canon with a theme that is repeated backwards. See RETROGRADE.

crackle a type of ORNAMENT, the expressive delay of a melodic note.

cracovienne (Fr.) KRAKOWIAK.

cradle song LULLABY.

Cradle Will Rock, The political opera in 10 scenes by Marc Blitzstein to his own libretto, produced by Orson Welles. Premiere, New York 1937.

Craft, Robert (1923–) Amer. conductor and writer, educated at the Juilliard School. He was conductor of the Chamber Art Society in New York (1947–50) and the Monday Evening Concerts in Los Angeles (1950–68). As a conductor he has concentrated on early music and contemporary music, conducting for CBS the first recordings of the complete

works of Webern and most of the works of Schoenberg, as well as pioneering recordings of madrigals by Gesualdo. He is best known for his long association (from 1948) with Igor Stravinsky, for whom he was assistant, conductor, collaborator and biographer.

crash cymbal a single suspended CYMBAL struck with a drumstick.

Crawford (Seeger), Ruth (Porter) (1901–53) Amer. composer, stud. of Charles Seeger, whom she later married. In addition to her composition, which demonstrated a highly original, creative mind in a dissonant, atonal style, she was deeply involved in the transcription and arrangement of American folk music.

Cream Engl. blues-rock trio, active from 1966 to 1970, that mixed blues, pop and improvisation. Its members were guitarist Eric Clapton, bassist Jack Bruce and drummer Ginger Baker.

Creation Mass a popular name for the Mass in B♭ major (1801) by Haydn, which contains a theme from his oratorio *The Creation*.

Creation, The (Ger., *Die Schöpfung*) oratorio (1798) by Haydn to a German translation by Baron van Swieten of passages from the Book of Genesis and Milton's *Paradise Lost*.

Création du monde, La [krä-ä′syŏ dü mŏd] (Fr., The Creation of the World) ballet with music (1923) by Milhaud, dramatizing African mythology with music highly evocative of the black jazz of London and Harlem.

Creatures of Prometheus, The (Ger., *Die Geschöpfe des Prometheus*) ballet with music, Op. 43 (1800), by Beethoven, consisting of an overture and eighteen numbers, the Finale of which uses the same theme as the last movement of the EROICA SYMPHONY.

crecelle [krə′sel] (Fr.) COG RATTLE.

Crecquillon, Thomas [krä-kē′yŏ] (c1500–1557) Franco-Flemish composer, dir. of music to Charles V and later employed in various Flemish towns. He was best known as a chanson composer and also wrote masses, over 100 motets, psalm settings and lamentations.

Creedence Clearwater Revival Amer. rockabilly band formed in 1959 in California by brothers John and Tom Fogerty. They disbanded in 1972.

credo (Lat.) a part of the Ordinary of the Mass, the Nicene Creed.

Credo Mass the Mass in C major, K257 (1776), by Mozart.

Creole Jazz Band a famous jazz band led by KING OLIVER in Chicago in the early 1920s.

crescendo [krā'shen-dō] (It.) increasing in volume (<). Abbr., *cresc.*

crescendo pedal an organ pedal by means of which stops are gradually added automatically until FULL ORGAN is achieved.

Creshevsky, Noah (1945–) Amer. composer, stud. of Berio, Boulanger and Thomson. He has taught at the Juilliard School and Hunter College and, since 1969, Brooklyn College. His works employ indeterminacy and *musique concrète*, using speech as its basis.

Crespin, Régine (1927–) French soprano, educated at the Paris Conservatoire. Her Amer. debut was at the Metropolitan Opera in 1962 as the Marschallin (*Der Rosenkavalier*). She is esp. noted for her portrayal of heroic French and German roles.

Creston, Paul (Guttoveggio, Giuseppe) (1906–85) Amer. composer and teacher. He was largely self-taught as a composer and did not decide to make composition his career until 1932. He wrote many works for orch., as well as songs and chamber music.

crispatio (It.) a type of TRILL.

Cristofori, Bartolommeo (1655–1731) Italian instrument maker, the inventor of the FORTEPIANO.

Croce, Giovanni ['krō-chā] (?1557–1609) Italian composer and singer, stud. of Zarlino in Venice. He was assistant *maestro di cappello* at St. Mark's from the early 1590s, becoming *maestro* in 1603. He is known mainly for his sacred vocal works.

croche [krosh] (Fr.) EIGHTH NOTE.

Croche, Monsieur an imaginary person invented by Debussy to serve as his alter ego for his music criticism.

Crofoot, Alan (Paul) (1929–79) Canadian tenor and actor, trained at the Royal Conservatory, Toronto. He appeared in Broadway musicals (*Oliver!*) and in opera, making his Metropolitan Opera debut in 1978.

crook 1, a tube, usu. curved, inserted into the body of a brass instrument to lengthen it and thereby change its fundamental pitch. 2, a curved tube carrying the reed of a bassoon or English horn. Also, *bocal*.

crooning a popular music singing style characterized by use of half voice, suited for singing with a microphone.

Crosby, Bing (Harry Lillis) (1904–77) Amer. popular singer and actor, one of the first singers to employ CROONING, brother of BOB CROSBY. A drummer in high school, he then sang for a time in a vocal trio called The Rhythm Boys, but soon became a star of radio, films and (later) TV. He was highly successful and much imitated.

Crosby, Bob (George Robert) (1913–) Amer. singer, actor and bandleader, brother of BING CROSBY. In 1935 he was invited to front for a jazz orch., and his seven-year stay with the group established his reputation. He has also been a successful performer on radio and TV, and in films.

Crosby, John (O'Hea) (1926–) Amer. opera producer and conductor, founder of the Santa Fe Opera Company (1957), which he has led to an important position among Amer. companies. He was head of the Manhattan School of Music from 1976 to 1985.

Crosby, Stills and Nash Amer. folk-rock group formed in 1968 and joined for a time by Neil Young.

crossover the phenomenon of a work in one genre becoming a hit in another, as, a country-music song becoming a hit on the rock charts.

cross picking a style of guitar- and

mandolin-picking that imitates the finger-plucking style of the banjo.

cross relation FALSE RELATION.

cross rhythm the shifting of some of the beats in a metrical pattern to other than their normal positions.

crotals hollow spherical BELLS. Also, *antique cymbals.*

Crotch, William (1775–1847) English composer, organist and theorist. He was one of the most celebrated child prodigies of any era. From 1807 he was active as a teacher, conductor and composer. His works incl. oratorios, other sacred and secular vocal music, and keyboard works and concertos.

crotchet (Brit.) QUARTER NOTE.

crouth, crowd CRWTH.

crucifixus see MASS.

Crucible, The opera in 4 acts by Robert Ward to a libretto by Bernard Stambler based on the play by Arthur Miller. Premiere, New York 1961. A story of witchcraft set in 17th-c. Salem, MA.

Crumb, George (Henry) (1929–) influential Amer. composer, stud. of Finney. He has taught at the U. of Colorado and the U. of Pennsylvania. He won the Pulitzer Prize in 1968 for his *Echoes of Time and the River.* His works exhibit a keen ear for instrumental and vocal color.

crumhorn 1, a Renaissance double-reed instrument with a curved body. 2, an ORGAN STOP. Also, *cromorne, Krummhorn.*

crwth [krooth] *also,* **cruth, crouth, crowd** (Welsh) an ancient Celtish LYRE with a shallow body and a varying number of strings that were plucked or bowed.

csárdás ['chär-däsh] (Hung.) a Hungarian couple-dance that begins slowly and becomes increasingly more rapid, ending in a whirl.

C sharp the pitch (C♯) one half step above C, the enharmonic equivalent of D flat. See PITCH.

cuatro *also,* **quatro** (Sp.) a type of Cuban guitar with eight pairs of strings.

Cuban Overture rumba for orch. (1932) by Gershwin.

cu-bop a term for the fusion of Afro-Cuban music and Harlem bop, exemplified by the music of Machito and Chano Pozo.

Cucaracha, La (Sp., The Cockroach) Mexican song of unknown authorship, first published in 1916, but prob. dating from much earlier.

cuckoo a WHISTLE imitating the sound of a cuckoo bird.

Cuénod, Hugues (Adhémar) (1902–) Swiss tenor, trained at the Basel Conservatory. A specialist in character tenor roles, he also has sung lieder, French song, and baroque music, and recorded with Nadia Boulanger in the late 1930s.

Cugat, Xavier (1900–90) Spanish-born Amer. violinist and bandleader, famous for his popularizing of Latin dances. His band made many recordings and he also appeared in films.

Cui, César Antonovich (1835–1918) Russian composer and military engineer, stud. of Balakirev, a professor at the Engineering School at St. Petersburg from 1878. He was best known as a composer of opera, but he also wrote many solo vocal, choral, orchestral and chamber works.

cuivré [küē'vrä] (Fr.) brassy; as a direction for brass instruments, overblown (see OVERBLOW).

Cunning Little Vixen, The (Czech., *Príhody Lisky Bystrousky*) opera in 3 acts by Janáček to his own libretto. Premiere, Brno 1924. A fantasy about the pretty vixen Sharpears.

cup mute a metal MUTE for brass instruments, used to obtain a very soft, muffled tone.

cupo (It., hollow, gloomy) a direction used by Verdi for singers and instrumentalists, calling for an extremely soft, dark tone.

Curlew River miracle play by Britten to a libretto by William Plomer, based on a Jap. Noh play, *The Sumida River.* Premiere, Oxford Church, Suffolk 1964. The first of "three parables for church performance," the others being *The Burning Fiery Furnace* and *The Prodigal Son.*

curtal 1, DULCIAN. **2**, an ORGAN STOP imitating the sound of the dulcian.

Curtin (née Smith), **Phyllis** (1922–) Amer. soprano, stud. of Joseph Regneas. She has sung a wide variety of roles, incl. Violetta (*La Traviata*), Salome and the Mozart heroines. Since the late 1960s she has taught a master class at the Tanglewood Music Center. She taught at Yale from 1974 to 1983, then became dean of the Music School at Boston U.

Curtis Institute of Music a celebrated free conservatory founded in 1924 in Philadelphia by Mary Louise Curtis Bok.

Curzon, Sir **Clifford (Michael)** (1907–82) English pianist, stud. of Charles Reddie and Katherine Goodson. He is noted for his interpretation of the classical composers, both in solo performance and in chamber music.

cut time ALLA BREVE.

cyclic form music in which material from earlier sections or movements is reintroduced later, esp. near the end of the work. The technique is used in the later 19th c. as a means of achieving greater unity among movements.

cylindrical drum a single- or double-headed DRUM with a relatively long, narrow, cylindrical body.

cymbalon see CIMBALOM.

cymbals metallic CONCUSSION INSTRUMENTS, usu. of indefinite pitch. "Turkish" cymbals are made in the shape of round, thin plates which are struck together or with a mallet, or occasionally bowed with a cello or bass bow. They are produced in a variety of sizes to produce higher or lower sounds. "Chinese" cymbals are small, cup-shaped and thicker, and are often tuned. See SIZZLE CYMBAL, HI-HAT, CROTALS.

cythern see CITTERN.

czardas CSÁRDÁS.

Czerny, Carl (1791–1857) Austrian piano teacher, composer, pianist and writer, stud. of Beethoven and teacher of Liszt. He is best known for his piano studies and exercises, which are still in regular use by piano teachers.

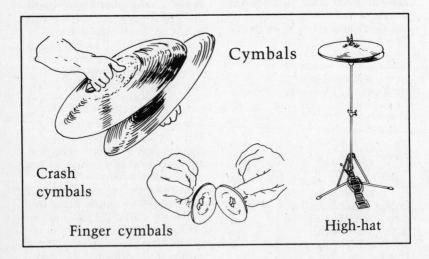

Cymbals

Crash cymbals

Finger cymbals

High-hat

D

D the second note of the scale of C major. See PITCH.

da camera (It.) see SONATA DA CAMERA.

da capo (It., from the head) a direction, usu. placed at the end of a section, to repeat the work, movement, etc., from the beginning. When the instruction is *da capo al fine* the section is repeated until the word *fine* (It., end) is encountered. The direction is used to avoid having to write out the repeated section a second time. See REPEAT. Cf. DAL SEGNO.

da capo aria an aria in tripartite A-B-A form; in the 17th and 18th c., the repeat of the A section usu. was performed with the solo part ornamented.

dada an avant-garde, iconoclastic movement of the late 1910s, largely in the literary and visual arts, concerned with the concepts of nonsense and communication. The term has been applied to certain musicians of that era, incl. JEF GOLISHEV and ERIC SATIE, and to musicians of the 1940s and 1950s, in particular, JOHN CAGE and the FLUXUS movement.

da-daiko (Jap.) a large Jap. 2-headed BARREL DRUM used in gagaku.

daff *also,* **duff** a FRAME DRUM of the Middle East and northern Africa, usu. round and often having jingles attached.

Dahl, Ingolf (1912–70) German-born American composer, conductor, pianist and educator. He fled the Nazis to California, where he wrote music for films, TV, etc. He was on the faculty of U. of S. California from 1945 and also taught at Middlebury College and the Berkshire Music Center. His students incl. conductor Michael Tilson Thomas.

daibyoshi (Jap.) a Jap. CYLINDRICAL DRUM used in Shinto worship.

Dalcroze JAQUES-DALCROZE.

Dalhart, Vernon (Slaughter, Marion Try) (1883–1948) Amer. baritone and country-music singer, trained at the Dallas Conservatory. After his beginnings as an opera singer, he recorded his first hillbilly hit in 1924, "The Prisoner's Song," which is one of the best-selling records of all time. He was elected to the Country Music Hall of Fame in 1981.

Dallapiccola, Luigi (1904–75) Italian composer, pianist and writer, stud. of Antonio Illersberg, Roberto Casiraghi and Vito Frazzi. He was professor at the Florence Conservatory from 1934 until his retirement in 1967. He was one of the most influential disciples of 12-tone composition and was also interested in early Italian music; he published editions of works of Monteverdi, Vivaldi and other baroque Italian composers. His works incl. *Il prigioniero, Ulisse* and other operas, *Canti di prigionia* and other choral and vocal works and chamber music.

Dallas Opera opera company founded in Dallas, TX, in 1957 as the Dallas Civic Opera by Nicola Rescigno and Lawrence Kelly.

Dallas Symphony Orchestra an orch. founded in 1900 by Hans Kreisig as the chamber orch. of the Dallas Symphony Club. It was expanded to full symphony size by Antal Dorati in 1945. Successive conductors were Walter Hendl, Paul Kletzki, Solti, Donald Johanos, Brusilow, Max Rudolf, Mata and Masur.

dal segno (It., from the sign) a direction to repeat from an earlier sign (𝄋), usu. until the indication *fine* (It., end) is reached (sometimes indicated by the instruction *dal segno al fine*). Abbr., *dal S*. See REPEAT.

Dameron, Tadd (Tadley Ewing Peake) (1917–65) Amer. jazz pianist, composer, arranger and bandleader. He was arranger for many important performers, incl. Coleman Hawkins, Sarah Vaughan, Fats Navarro and Dizzy Gillespie.

Damn Yankees musical by Richard Adler and Jerry Ross, book by George Abbot and Douglass Wallop, based on Wallop's novel *The Day the Yankees Lost the Pennant*. Premiere, New York 1955. A baseball enthusiast sells his soul to the devil for a chance to play ball.

Damnation of Faust, The (Fr., *La Damnation de Faust*) dramatic legend in 4 parts by Berlioz to a libretto in French by the composer, based on Goethe's *Faust*. Premiere, Paris 1846. The work began as a choral piece, *Eight Scenes from the Life of Faust*. It is performed both as a concert work and staged as an opera.

Damoiselle élue, La [dä-mwä'zel ä'lü] (Fr., The Blessed Damozel) lyric poem for soprano, chorus and orch. (1887) by Debussy, based on a French translation of the poem by Rossetti.

damper a felted block in a piano, harpsichord, etc., that rests on the string to keep it from sounding and is lifted when a key is depressed. —**damper pedal**, the pedal that controls the dampers in a piano by lifting them from the strings, allowing the strings to continue to sound. It is the pedal farthest to the right. Also, *sustaining pedal, loud pedal*.

Dämpfer ['demp-fər] (Ger.) MUTE.

Damrosch, Frank (Heino) (1859–1937) German-born Amer. conductor and teacher, son of LEOPOLD DAMROSCH. He was chorusmaster at the Metropolitan Opera (1865–91) and founder of the People's Choral Union and the Musical Art Society in New York, which he conducted until 1920.

Damrosch, Leopold (1832–85) German-born Amer. conductor, violinist and composer, stud. of Hubert Ries, S.W. Dehn and Böhmer. He came to

New York in 1871, where he founded the Oratorio Society, which his sons Walter and Frank also conducted. He was a founder and conductor of the New York Symphony Society from 1878 until his death and was responsible for the establishment of the German opera wing at the Metropolitan Opera in 1884.

Damrosch, (Johannes) Walter (1862–1950) influential German-born Amer. conductor, teacher and composer, son of LEOPOLD DAMROSCH. He was assistant conductor at the Metropolitan Opera from 1884 and conductor of the Oratorio and New York Symphony Societies his father had founded. He organized his own German opera company in 1894, which performed in New York and on tour for five years, after which he conducted the German operas at the Metropolitan for two years. He was also a conductor of the New York Philharmonic Society (1902–3). Interested in music education, he organized a bandmasters' training school for the American Expeditionary Force and was involved in the founding of the American Conservatory at Fontainebleau, France. He was the first to conduct a concert broadcast across the N. Amer. continent and was musical adviser to NBC from 1927. His works include operas (esp. *The Scarlet Letter*, 1896) and choral works.

dance 1, rhythmic movement performed to music, either by one person alone or by two or more persons together, usu. involving a more or less complex series of predetermined steps designed to fit with a certain metrical pattern. Music for the dance can range from folk melody (folk dance) to popular song (social dances, such as court dances, ballroom dances and disco) to extended works composed for choreographed dance (ballet, modern dance). The accompanying table illustrates some of the standardized rhythmic patterns for certain popular dances. 2, instrumental music inspired by the dance, such as the movements of the baroque

Characteristic Dance Rhythms

dance suite or the polonaises, mazurkas, etc., by Chopin.

dance band a small band for playing music in a steady tempo for social dancing. It can be as small as a trio (piano, bass, drums) or as large as 10–15 players, incl. brass, reeds and a rhythm section. In recent years the dance band has often been replaced by a disc jockey playing recorded music. Cf. DISCO.

dance of death in medieval and Renaissance art, the dance of Death, represented as a skeleton, leading the living to the grave. Many composers have written music evocative of this dance, incl. Liszt (*Totentanz*) and Saint-Saëns (*Danse macabre*).

Dance of the Seven Veils, The music for Salome's dance before King Herod in the opera SALOME by Richard Strauss.

dance song a song assoc. with—and sometimes describing the steps of—a particular dance, such as "Ballin' the Jack," "The Black Bottom" and "The Charleston."

dance suite see SUITE.

Daniel, The Play of either of two surviving medieval liturgical plays based on the Book of Daniel, one of which, by the students of Beauvais, contains notated music. Noah Greenberg's 1959 edition of the Beauvais version was first performed by the New York Pro Musica.

Daniel-Lesur (Lesur, Daniel Jean Yves) (1908–) French composer, stud. of Jean Gallon. He was a founder in 1936 of the group LA JEUNE FRANCE, professor of counterpoint at the Schola Cantorum, organist of the Benedictine Abbey of Paris and has been a government official concerned with the administration of music since the late 1960s. His works incl. an opera, orch. and chamber works, songs and works for piano and organ.

Daniels, Mabel Wheeler (1878–1971) Amer. composer, stud. of Chadwick and Ludwig Thuille. She was director of the Radcliffe Glee Club (1911–13) and head of music at Simmons College in Boston (1913–18). She wrote several operettas, choral and other vocal works, and orchestral and chamber works.

Dankworth, Johnny (John) (1927–) English composer, jazz clarinetist, saxophonist and bandleader. He was an important figure in British jazz through his small group, the Johnny Dankworth Seven, and his jazz orch. He has composed film scores, works for jazz orch. and works combining symphonic musicians and jazz players. He toured frequently with singer Cleo Laine, whom he later married.

Danse macabre a DANCE OF DEATH for orch., Op. 40 (1874), by Saint-Saëns, based on a poem by Henri Cazalis, which Saint-Saëns had orig. set as a song.

Danse sacrée et danse profane (Fr., Sacred and Profane Dances) work for harp and strings (1904) by Debussy.

Dante Sonata APRÈS UNE LECTURE DE DANTE.

Dante Symphony a work for female chorus and orch. (1857) by Liszt, the full title of which is *Eine Symphonie zu Dantes Divina Commedia* (Ger., A Symphony on Dante's Divine Comedy).

Danzi, Franz (Ignaz) (1763–1826) German cellist and prolific composer, trained at the Mannheim School of Music. Danzi's works include almost twenty Singspiels, orchestral, choral and other vocal works, and a large body of chamber music. His wind chamber music is still performed today.

Daphnis and Chloe (Fr., *Daphnis et Chloë*) ballet with chorus (1912) by Ravel, first choreographed by Michel Fokine, with settings by Léon Bakst. The story is based on Greek legend. Ravel extracted two orchestral suites from the score for concert performance.

Da Ponte, Lorenzo (1749–1838) Italian librettist and poet, author of three operas set by Mozart (*Le Nozze di Figaro*, *Don Giovanni*, and *Così fan tutte*), as well as of libretti for Martin y Soler and Salieri. Da Ponte had a colorful life; he was banned from teaching in Venice because of adultery. Late in life he emigrated to America, where he first was a grocer in New York, then a teacher of Italian at Columbia.

darabukka (Arab.) a small No. African GOBLET DRUM, usu. of pottery with a single skin head, held under the arm or resting on the leg and played with the hands.

dargason an English folk-dance tune dating from the 16th c., unusual in its lack of final cadence. It was used by Holst in his *St. Paul's Suite* in combination with the tune GREENSLEEVES.

Dargomïzhsky, Alexander Sergeyevich (1813–69) Russian composer, trained as an amateur pianist, violinist and singer. He incorporated Russian folk music and the natural intonation of Russian speech into his own works, coupled with a concern for "reality and truth." His best-known work is the incomplete opera *The Stone Guest*, a setting of a tragedy by Pushkin.

Darktown Follies of 1914 musical review by J. Leubrie Hill, containing the hit song "After the Ball," borrowed by Ziegfeld for his own *Follies*.

Darktown Strutters' Ball song (1917) by Shelton Brooks (1886–1975), inspired by a San Francisco ball. It was recorded in 1917 by the Original Dixieland Jass [*sic*] Band on what may have been the earliest commercial jazz recording made.

Darmstadt city in Germany, site (since 1946) of the Internationale Ferienkurse für Neue Musik (Ger., International Summer Courses for New Music), an important avant-garde music festival held every two years.

Dart, (Robert) Thurston (1921–71) English musicologist and keyboard player. He was editor of the *Galpin Society Journal*, secretary of the published series Musica Britannica and made over 90 recordings, most of them for L'Oiseau-Lyre, Monaco. He was artistic dir. of the Philomusica of London from 1954 and editor or joint

editor of numerous editions of the music of the 16th to 18th c.

Dartington Summer School a summer training school and concert festival held annually in August at Dartington Hall, Totnes, Devon, England. The festival began in 1948 at Bryanston School in Dorset and moved to Dartington in 1953.

daseian notation *also*, **dasian notation** a system of notation for ORGANUM, based on the use of Greek letters to designate the notes of the tetrachord.

date a professional musical playing engagement. Also, *gig*.

Daughter of the Regiment, The (Fr., *La fille du régiment*) comic opera in 2 acts by Donizetti to a libretto in French by Jules-Henri Vernoy de Saint Georges and Jean-Françaix-Alfred Bayard. Premiere, Paris 1840. Marie, the darling of the Grenadiers, wins her true love Tonio in spite of the machinations of the Marquise of Birkenfeld.

Davenport, (Jack) LaNoue (1922–) Amer. recorder player, editor and conductor. He was involved in the formation of the New York Pro Musica and played with them from 1960 to 1970. He has been editor of *Music for Recorders* and a member of the quartet Music for a While.

David, Ferdinand (1810–73) German violinist, composer and teacher, stud. of Spohr and Moritz Hauptmann. He led the Leipzig Gewandhaus orch. from 1836 until his death and taught at the Leipzig Conservatory from 1843 (Joachim was one of his first students). David wrote many works for violin (incl. concertos and concert pieces), songs and choral works, and produced or edited teaching works and collections for violin.

David, Johann Nepomuk (1895–1977) Austrian composer and teacher, stud. of Joseph Marx. His large body of works incl. orchestral works and concertos, sacred and secular choral and vocal music, organ works and chamber music.

Davidovsky, Mario (1934–) Argentinian-born Amer. composer, stud. of Guillermo Graetzer. He came to the U.S. in 1960 and has taught at the U. of Michigan, Yale and the City College of the City U. of NY. He is assoc. dir. of the Columbia-Princeton Electronic Music Center. Many of his works combine conventional instruments with recorded electronic sounds, esp. his series of works called *Synchronisms*. He won the Pulitzer Prize in 1971 for his *Synchronisms No. 6* for piano and tape.

Davidsbündlertänze ['dä-vits"bünt-lər"ten-tse] (Ger., Dances of the Davidsbündler) work for piano, op. 6 (1837) by Schumann. The Davidsbündler were members of an imaginary association invented by Schumann to fight against the Philistine Goliaths in music.

Davies, Dennis Russell (1944–) Amer. conductor, stud. of Jean Morel and Jorge Mester. He has been music dir. of the St. Paul Chamber Orch. (1972–80) and of the Württemberg State Opera, Stuttgart. He is known for his performance of contemporary works and has conducted many premieres.

Davies, Sir **Peter Maxwell** (1934–) English composer, stud. of Petrassi and Sessions. He was a founder of New Music Manchester (also known as the Manchester Group) in the early 1950s. In 1967 he co-founded, with Birtwistle, the Pierrot Players, which he later directed as the Fires of London. Among his many works for stage, films, chorus, orch. and chamber groups, the best-known are the opera *Taverner* (1962–8) and the theater piece *Eight Songs for a Mad King* (1969).

Davis, Andrew (Frank) (1944–) English organist and conductor, stud. of Franco Ferrara. He was assoc. conductor of the New Philharmonia from 1973, music dir. of the Toronto SO (1975–88) and has guest-conducted throughout Europe and the U.S.

Davis, Sir **Colin (Rex)** (1927–) English conductor, trained at the Royal College of Music. He became musical dir. of the Sadler's Wells Opera in 1957, introducing many new works to their repertory. He has been principal conductor of the BBC SO and principal guest conductor of the Boston SO and became musical dir. of Covent Garden in 1971. He was the first English conductor to appear at the Bayreuth Festival (1977).

Davis, "Lockjaw" (Eddie) (1922–87) Amer. jazz tenor saxophonist, a member of the Count Basie band several times from 1953 to 1973, in the interim periods leading his own groups.

Davis, Gary ("Blind Gary") (1896–1972) Amer. gospel and blues singer and guitarist, able to play unorthodox chords because of a wrist injury. A singer with a country string band in his early years, he became a minister in 1933 and played religious music almost exclusively thereafter.

Davis, Gussie (Lord) (1863–99) Amer. songwriter, who picked up his music training while working as a janitor at the Cincinnati Conservatory. His best-known ballad, "In the Baggage Coach Ahead," sold over a million copies.

Davis, Jimmie (James) **H(ouston)** (1902–) Amer. country-music, hillbilly and gospel singer, elected to the Country Music Hall of Fame in 1972. His early hits incl. "Nobody's Darlin' but Mine" (1935) and "You Are My Sunshine" (1940). He was also elected Governor of Louisiana for two separate terms.

Davis, Miles (Dewey) (1926–91) highly influential and innovative Amer. jazz trumpeter who came to prominence as a member of the Charlie Parker Quintet. In late 1948 he formed an unusual nonet composed of French horn, trumpet, trombone, tuba, alto and baritone saxes, piano, bass and drums, an early example of COOL JAZZ. Davis formed a quintet with John Coltrane in 1955 and later a sextet, adding Cannonball Adderley, introducing the concept of MODAL JAZZ. A new quintet, formed in 1963, developed another new approach, beginning with a regular tune, but continuing with improvisation in regular meters without prearranged harmonies. After 1968, Davis moved to longer works, with or without written themes, using unusual groupings of acoustic and electric instruments and incorporating elements of rock.

Davis, Sammy, Jr. (1925–90) Amer. popular singer and dancer of recordings, night clubs, on Broadway in *Mr. Wonderful* (1956) and *Golden Boy* (1968) and in films. He played the role of Sportin' Life in the film version of Gershwin's *Porgy and Bess* (1959).

Davison, Archibald T(hompson) (1883–1961) Amer. teacher and choral conductor, stud. of Widor. He taught at Harvard from 1909 until his retirement and directed the Harvard Glee Club (1912–33) and the Radcliffe Choral Society (1913–28). Among his contributions to music pedagogy are the *Historical Anthology of Music*, compiled in collaboration with Willi Apel, and the Concord Series of Educational Music, as well as a large number of editions of choral music and important works on choral conducting and composition.

Davison, Wild Bill (William Edward) (1906–89) Amer. jazz cornetist in Eddie Condon's house band from 1945. After 1965 he toured and recorded extensively in the U.S. and Europe as soloist and bandleader.

davul a double-headed CYLINDRICAL DRUM of the Middle and Near East, usu. played for dancing and processions.

Dawson, William Levi (1898–) Amer. composer and conductor, trained at the American Conservatory of Music in Chicago. He was dir. of music at the Tuskegee Institute and conductor of the Tuskegee Choir until he retired in 1955. His compositions usu. employ Negro folk songs and rhythms, and incl. the well-known *Negro Folk Symphony* (1934).

Db *abbr.* DECIBEL.

D.C. *abbr.* DA CAPO.

deaconing LINING OUT.

Dead Kennedys Amer. punk rock band formed in 1978 in San Francisco, headed by singer Jello Biafra.

Death and the Maiden (Ger., *Der Tod und das Mädchen*) a song (1817) by Schubert, to a text by Matthias Claudius. It is also the subtitle for the String Quartet in D minor (1824) by Schubert, the slow movement of which is based on the song.

Death and Transfiguration (Ger., *Tod und Verklärung*) tone poem (1890) by Richard Strauss, depicting a sick man nearing death.

Death in Venice opera in 2 acts by Britten to a libretto by Myfanwy Piper, based on the novel by Thomas Mann. Premiere, Aldeburgh 1973.

De Burgos, Rafael Frübeck FRÜBECK DE BURGOS, RAFAEL.

Debussy, (Achille-)Claude (1862–1918) influential French composer, stud. of Albert Lavignac, Franck and Ernest Guiraud. He won the Prix de Rome in 1884 with his cantata *L'enfant prodigue*, and his cantata *La damoiselle élue* was composed while he was in Rome. The years following his sojourn in Italy were personally difficult, while being highly productive musically, resulting in the *Prélude à l'après-midi d'un faune* (1894) and *Pelléas et Mélisande* (1902), among other works. He composed his ballet *Jeux* (1913) for Diaghilev's Ballets Russes, but its success was overshadowed by the premiere of Stravinsky's *Rite of Spring* two weeks later. For most of the remaining years of his life he was ill, producing relatively few works.

Debussy's compositions incl. *Pelléas et Mélisande* (opera), incidental music, *Nocturnes, La mer, Images* and other orchestral works, cantatas, choral works, sonatas for cello and violin, a piano trio, a trio for flute, viola and harp, many songs, *Préludes, Children's Corner, Études* and many other works for piano solo and numerous uncompleted projects.

decanal *also,* **decani** (Lat.) relating to or of the ecclesiastical or dean's (south) side of a church; contrasted with CANTORIAL.

deca-rock GLITTER ROCK.

decay the decline in intensity of a sound over time.

deceptive cadence see CADENCE. Also, *interrupted cadence, false cadence.*

decibel a unit for measuring loudness equal to 10 times the common logarithm of the ratio between two different signals. In general, any sound over 100 decibels is too loud for comfort, and at 200 decibels the threshold of pain is reached and damage to the eardrum may occur. Abbr. *dB.*

Decker, Franz-Paul (1923–) German conductor, trained at the U. of Cologne. He has been conductor of the Rotterdam PO (1962–8) and the Montreal SO (1967–75) and has guest-conducted orchestras throughout the world.

Deck the Hall Christmas carol, apparently a Welsh air, first publ. in 1784. The words commonly used with the tune are probably of American origin and date from much later.

declamation the relation between musical and verbal accent (stress) in text-setting and delivery. This relation becomes particularly significant in discussing a language, such as French, in which the use of stress is fundamentally different from that found in metrical music.

decrescendo (It.) becoming softer (>). Abbr., *decresc., decr.* Cf. DIMINUENDO.

Deep Purple English heavy-metal rock band, active from 1968 to the late 1970s, at one point considered the loudest rock band in the world.

Deering, Richard DERING, RICHARD.

De Falla see FALLA.

Defauw, Désiré [dəˈfō] (1885–1960) Belgian-born Amer. conductor and violinist, stud. of Johan Smit. He was conductor of the concerts of the Brussels Conservatory from 1926 to 1940, of the Montreal Société des Concerts Symphoniques (1940), of the Chicago SO (1943–7) and the Gary SO (1950–58).

DeFranco, Buddy (Boniface Ferdinand Leonardo) (1923–) Amer. jazz clarinetist and saxophonist. He has played with Gene Krupa, Charlie Barnet, Tommy Dorsey, Count Basie and Art Blakey and was leader of the Glenn Miller orch. (1966–74). He is esp. known for his facile technique.

De Gaetani, Jan (1933–89) Amer. mezzo-soprano, trained at the Juilliard School. She was a highly respected teacher at the Eastman School and the Aspen Festival and was noted for her performances of contemporary music, though her repertory embraced a wide variety of styles and periods.

degree the position of a note in a SCALE, usu. defined in relation to the DIATONIC SCALE. The degrees are identified by roman numeral, by name or by other means, such as Schenkerian notation.

dehors, en EN DEHORS.

De Koven, (Henry Louis) Reginald (1859–1920) Amer. composer, conductor and music critic, stud. of Suppé, Delibes and others. He was a critic for the *Harper's Weekly* and the *Chicago Evening Post* and was founder of the Philharmonic O. of Washington, D.C. He wrote a large number of songs, an orchestral suite, many operettas (the best known of which is *Robin Hood*) and two grand operas, the first, *The Canterbury Pilgrims*, premiered at the Metropolitan Opera (1917), the second, *Rip van Winkle*, at the Chicago Opera (1920).

Delage, Maurice (Charles) (1879–1961) French composer. He was strongly influenced by Ravel and Debussy and by music heard on his travels to the Orient. His small output incl. works for orch., voices with instruments, a string quartet and piano music.

Delalande, Michel Richard LALANDE, MICHEL-RICHARD DE.

De Larrocha, Alicia LARROCHA, ALICIA DE.

De la Rue, Pierre LA RUE, PIERRE DE.

Delibes, (Clément Philibert) Léo [dəˈlēb] (1836–91) French composer, stud. of Adolphe Adam. From 1856 to

1869 he wrote many light operettas, mostly for the Bouffes-Parisiens. After the success of his ballet *Coppélia* in 1870, he devoted himself to composition. The best-known fruits of this last period are the opera *Lakmé* (1883) and the ballet *Sylvia* (1876).

Delius, Frederick (Fritz) **(Theodore Albert)** (1862–1934) English composer. He worked in his father's wool business until 1884, then went to Florida to grow oranges. There he studied music with a certain Thomas Ward, then went to study at the Leipzig Conservatory in 1886, where he met Grieg, under whose guidance he devoted himself to music. His best known operas, *Koanga* (1895–7) and *A Village Romeo and Juliet* (1900–1), were completed around this time, as was *Sea Drift* (1904) for baritone, chorus and orch. Except for a wartime sojourn in England and brief journeys, Delius remained in France until his death. His works incl. 6 operas, incidental music, concertos for cello, piano and violin, *Hiawatha*, *Brigg Fair*, *In a Summer Garden*, *Appalachia* and other orchestral works, *Sea Drift* and many other choral works, 3 violin sonatas, a cello sonata and other chamber music and many songs.

della Casa, Lisa (1919–) Swiss lyric soprano, trained in Zürich. She has been a member of the Vienna Staatsoper since 1942 and sang at the Metropolitan Opera from 1953 to 1968. She is particularly noted for her performances of the operas of Richard Strauss, esp. *Arabella* and *Salome*.

Deller, Alfred (George) (1912–79) English countertenor. In 1950 he formed the Deller Consort, a small group devoted to the performance of early music, and in 1963 he founded the Stour Music Festival in Kent to provide a venue for the consort. A number of composers wrote works for him, including Britten, who intended the part of Oberon in *A Midsummer Night's Dream* for Deller. He made numerous recordings, both as soloist and with the Consort.

Dello Joio, Norman (1913–) Amer. composer and teacher, stud. of Wagenaar and Hindemith. He won the 1957 Pulitzer Prize for his *Meditations on Ecclesiastes* for string orch. He has taught at Sarah Lawrence College, the Mannes College of Music and Boston U. His works, which incorporate elements of popular music and jazz, incl. operas, ballets, choral, orchestral and chamber music.

Del Monaco, Mario (1915–82) Italian tenor, trained at the Pesaro Conservatory. His Amer. debut was at the Metropolitan in 1951. His powerful voice was at its best in the major Verdi roles.

Delmore Brothers Amer. country-music duo, performers on the Grand Ole Opry in the 1930s. Their music incorporated the influence of Afr.-Amer. blues and boogie-woogie.

de Los Angeles, Victoria LOS ANGELES, VICTORIA DE.

delta blues a style of BLUES characteristic of the Mississippi delta region in the 1920s and 1930s, typified in the work of such artists as SON HOUSE and CHARLIE PATTON.

Del Tredici, David (1937–) Amer. composer, trained at the U. of California at Berkeley and at Princeton. He has taught at Harvard, SUNY Buffalo and at the City College of NY. His works display a distinctive freedom and sense of humor, esp. his series of works based on Lewis Carroll's *Alice in Wonderland*. He won the Pulitzer Prize in 1980 for *In Memory of a Summer's Day*.

De Luca, Giuseppe (1876–1950) Italian baritone, stud. of Vinceslao Persichini in Rome. He sang a wide variety of roles at La Scala from 1903 to 1911. In 1915 he made his debut at the Metropolitan Opera, where he was principal baritone for 20 years, singing all the leading roles of the Italian repertoire.

demisemiquaver (Brit.) THIRTY-SECOND NOTE.

Dempster, Stuart (Ross) (1936–) Amer. trombonist and composer, trained at San Francisco State College. He has taught at the San Francisco Conservatory and at the U. of Washington (Seattle) and was first trombonist of the Oakland SO. He has encouraged the development and use of new sounds and techniques, and has been responsible for the commissioning and performing of new works, incl. Berio's *Sequenza V* (1966).

Demus, Jörg (1928–) Austrian pianist, stud. of Gieseking and Yves Nat. He is noted for his performance of late Classical and early Romantic repertoire, as well as for his interest in historical keyboard instruments. He has also performed frequently as an accompanist, working with such artists as singer Fischer-Dieskau and violinist Josef Suk.

Denisov, Edison (1929–) Russian composer and theorist, trained at the Moscow Conservatory, where he has taught since 1960. He also worked at the Experimental Studio of Electronic Music in Moscow (1968– 70). His compositions, though usu. serial, often emphasize a more diatonic harmonic style and make frequent use of Russian folk and peasant materials.

Denner, Johann Christoph (1655– 1707) German maker in Nuremberg of woodwind instruments, incl. oboes, recorders, bassoons and clarinets. He is credited with the invention of the clarinet and the rackett.

Density 21.5 solo flute work (1936) by Varèse, written to introduce the platinum flute (the specific gravity of platinum is approximately 21.5).

Denver Symphony Orchestra symphony orch. founded in 1934 under conductor Horace Tureman, who was succeeded by Vladimir Golschmann, Brian Priestman, Gaetano Delogu and Philippe Entremont. The orch. disbanded in 1989.

De Paur, Leonard (1915–) Amer. conductor, stud. of Cowell, Sergei Radamsky and Monteux. He was music dir. for a number of productions with Orson Welles in the late 1930s, worked on Broadway as a choral dir.,

then formed his own De Paur Chorus, with which he toured in the 1950s and 1960s. He has conducted the Symphony of the New World and recorded many works by Afr.-Amer. composers.

déploration [dā-plō-rä'syō] (Fr.) a work lamenting a death, usu. of a composer. The most famous examples are works dedicated to Binchois, Ockeghem and Josquin.

DePriest, James (Anderson) (1936–) Amer. conductor, stud. of Persichetti. He has been conductor of the Québec Symphony and of the Portland (OR) SO. Both of his legs were paralysed by an attack of poliomyelitis, which he contracted on a tour of the Far East.

derby mute a mute for brass instruments, shaped to resemble a derby hat and used for special effects.

de Reszke, Edouard (1853–1917) Polish bass, younger brother of JEAN DE RESZKE and stud. of Steller and Coletti. His career closely paralleled that of his brother, and he retired soon after him. His wide repertory encompassed the major French, German (Wagner) and Italian roles.

de Reszke, Jean (1850–1925) Polish tenor, older brother of EDOUARD DE RESZKE and stud. of Ciaffei and Cotogni. He began as a baritone, then switched to tenor. His Amer. debut was in Chicago in 1891. After his retirement in 1900, he taught for many years, his students incl. Maggie Teyte.

Dering, Richard (?1580–1630) English composer and organist. He was organist in Brussels in the early 1600s and was appointed organist to Queen Henrietta Maria of Belgium in 1625. He wrote music for the Anglican service in his earlier years, but he appears to have converted to Catholicism while in Europe and composed a body of instrumental and vocal music in the Italian manner.

derived set a 12-note SET derived from a smaller set (usu. a tetrachord or hexachord) by means of the usual transformations of inversion, retrograde and retrograde inversion.

Dermota, Anton (1910–89) Yugoslav tenor, stud. of Elisabeth Rado. He is best known for his performance of Mozart roles, but he had a very large repertory. He also performed frequently in recital.

des (Ger.) D FLAT.

De Sabata, Victor (1892–1967) eminent Italian conductor and composer, trained at the Milan Conservatory. After an early period dedicated to composition, he turned to conducting. He was conductor of the Monte Carlo Opera from 1918, then, from 1929, a regular conductor at La Scala, of which he was artistic director from 1953 to 1957. He conducted frequently in the U.S. in the 1950s.

descant *also,* **discant** **1,** a melody sung above the plainchant tenor. **2,** contrapuntal part music; esp., a type of medieval part-music having a melismatic plainchant tenor and characterized by note-against-note counterpoint and the use of RHYTHMIC MODES. Also, the art of composing such contrapuntal part music. Cf. ORGANUM, DESCANT STYLE. **3,** the upper voice (as the soprano) of contrapuntal part music. **4,** an additional counterpoint superimposed on a hymn tune, etc., and usu. sung by part of the soprano section.

descant style note-against-note counterpoint of the Middle Ages and Renaissance in which the tenor and descant generally move in contrary motion, interchanging consonances. Polyphony in descant style may be either composed or improvised. Three- and four-voice counterpoint (*tripla* and *quadrupla*) may be formed by writing successive descants to a single tenor, as in the motets of Pérotin. Cf. FABURDEN.

descant viol TREBLE VIOL; PARDESSUS DE VIOL.

Descarries, (Joseph Ernest) Auguste [dä-kä′rē] (1896–1958) Canadian composer, organist, pianist and teacher, stud. of Laliberté and others. He taught from 1944 at the Montreal Conservatory and the U. of Montreal,

and was founder of the chamber music ensemble Euterpe.

descort (Prov.) LAI.

descriptive music **1,** PROGRAM MUSIC. **2,** WORD PAINTING.

Déserts [dā′zer] (Fr.) work for orch. and tape (1954) by Varèse, the first work to combine recorded electronic sound with orch.

deses (Ger.) D double flat.

Desert Song, The musical by Sigmund Romberg, lyrics by Otto Harbach and Oscar Hammerstein II, book by Harbach, Hammerstein and Frank Mandel. Premiere, New York 1926. An English lady's adventures after she is abducted by an "Arab chieftain."

Des Marais, Paul (1920–) Amer. composer and teacher, stud. of Sowerby, Boulanger and Piston. He has taught since 1960 at the U. of California at Los Angeles. He has written an opera, *Epiphanies* (1964–8), and works for voice(s) and instruments.

Desmond (Breitenfeld), **Paul (Emil)** (1924–77) Amer. cool jazz alto saxophonist and composer, trained at San Francisco State U. He was a member of the Dave Brubeck quartet for much of his career, from 1951 until its dissolution in 1967. He also recorded as a soloist and in collaboration with Gerry Mulligan and others.

Des Prez, Josquin JOSQUIN DES PRES.

Dessane, (Marie Hippolyte) Antoine (1826–73) French-born Canadian organist, pianist, teacher and composer. From 1850 he was active in Quebec City as a producer of concerts and organist in various churches.

Dessau, Paul (1894–1979) German conductor and composer, stud. of Eduard Behm and Max Loewengard. During World War II he lived in the U.S., composing scores for films. He returned in 1948 to East Germany and set a number of Bertolt Brecht's plays. His works incl. operas and orchestral works, and employ such varied techniques as serial music, aleatory elements and diatonic harmonies.

Destinn (Kittl), **Emmy** (Destinnová, Ema) (1878–1930) Czech dramatic soprano, stud. of Marie Loewe-Destinn. Her Amer. debut was in 1908 at the Metropolitan Opera, where she sang regularly until 1916 and again after the war. She created the role of Minnie in Puccini's *La fanciulla del West* and was outstanding in a wide repertory, incl. Carmen, Salome and Senta (*The Flying Dutchman*).

détaché [dā-tä'shā] (Fr.) a nonlegato bowstroke. See BOWING.

Detroit Symphony Orchestra name for several different orchestras since 1875. The present Detroit SO was founded in 1914 by Weston Gales. Gabrilovich was the first permanent conductor, in 1919, and was succeeded by Franco Ghione, Karl Krueger, Paray, Ehrling, Ceccato, Herbig, and Neeme Järvi.

Dett, R(obert) Nathaniel (1882–1943) Canadian-born Amer. composer, pianist and conductor, trained at the Oberlin Conservatory, Harvard and other institutions, and with Boulanger in Paris. He was dir. of music at Hampton Institute from 1913 to 1931. His works, mostly for chorus or for piano solo, make extensive use of Afr.-Amer. folk music.

Dettingen Te Deum work for soloists, chorus and orch. (1743) by Handel, written to commemorate the British victory at Dettingen.

Deutsch, Max (1892–1982) Austrian-born French composer, conductor and teacher, stud. of Schoenberg. He settled in Paris in 1924, where he conducted many of the works of the Second Viennese School. After World War II he taught at the École Normale de Musique in Paris. He founded the Grands Concerts de la Sorbonne in 1960.

Deutsches Requiem, Ein GERMAN REQUIEM (2,).

Deutschland über Alles ['doich-länt 'ü-bər 'ä-ləs](Ger., Germany First of All) the German national anthem, a poem by Hoffmann von Fallersleben set to music by Haydn orig. composed to be the Austrian national hymn (see EMPEROR'S HYMN).

development the procedure of re-working material from earlier in a work by various means, incl. harmonic, contrapuntal, rhythmic or motivic variation. See SONATA FORM.

Devil and Daniel Webster, The folk opera by Douglas Moore to a libretto by Stephen Vincent Benét. Premiere, New York 1939. To save the soul of his friend Jabez, Daniel Webster debates with the Devil (Scratch).

Devil's Trill, The popular name for a violin sonata in G minor (1798) by Tartini. The work was supposedly inspired by a dream in which the composer sold his soul to the devil, who then gave a phenomenal violin performance which the composer tried unsuccessfully to write down. The trill alluded to in the title occurs in the last movement.

D flat the PITCH (D♭) a half step below D, the enharmonic equivalent of C sharp.

Diabelli, Anton (1781–1858) Austrian composer and publisher in Vienna. He was the publisher of Schubert and a friend and sometime publisher of Beethoven. The *Vaterländischer Künstlerverein* (Ger., Union of Artists of the Fatherland), a collection of variations by important Austrian composers on a waltz theme by Diabelli, was begun in 1819 and over 50 composers contributed works, the most famous of which was the *Diabelli Variations* for piano solo, Op. 120 (1823), by Beethoven, consisting of 33 variations on Diabelli's waltz.

Diabelli Variations see ANTON DIABELLI.

diabolus in musica (Lat., devil in music) the medieval name for the TRITONE.

Diaghilev, Sergei Pavlovich (1872–1929) Russian impresario. After several years of presenting Russian opera in Paris, he formed the Ballets Russes in 1909, which, during the two decades of its operation, was instrumental in introducing new music, stage design and choreography to Paris and to the world. Diaghilev commissioned many scores, incl. works by

Stravinsky (*The Firebird, The Rite of Spring*), Ravel (*Daphnis et Chloé*), Debussy (*Jeux*) and Richard Strauss (*Josephslegende*), and his productions were designed by leading artists of the time, among them Picasso and Cocteau.

dialogue a short 18th-c. English all-sung OPERA on a Cockney theme.

Dialogues of the Carmelites, The (Fr., *Les Dialogues des Carmélites*) tragic opera in 3 acts by Francis Poulenc to a libretto in French by Georges Bernac. Premiere, Milan 1957. The aristocrat Blanche de la Force joins the Carmelites during the French revolution and dies a martyr's death.

Diamond, David (Leo) (1915–) Amer. composer, stud. of Rogers, Boepple, Sessions and Boulanger. He settled in Florence in 1953, remaining there until 1965. He has taught at the Manhattan School of Music and at the U. of Buffalo. His extensive list of works includes ballets, film scores, orchestral works, vocal and choral music and instrumental works.

diapason 1, the octave in Greek music. **2**, a foundation pipe ORGAN STOP. **3**, the entire range of musical tones; also, the RANGE of an instrument or voice. **4**, a piece of wood in a harpsichord or clavichord which guides the movement of the keys. Also, *rack*. **5**, (Fr.) TUNING FORK.

diapason normal (Fr.) the standard of pitch adopted in 1859, establishing A above middle C (a') as 435 cps. Also, *French pitch, low pitch*. Cf. A.

diapente (Gk.) the INTERVAL of the fifth in ancient Greek music.

diaphony *also,* **diaphonia 1**, in ancient Greek theory, DISSONANCE, as opposed to *symphonia* or consonance; any interval other than the octave, perfect 5th or perfect 4th. **2**, two-part ORGANUM.

diastematic pertaining to a system of notation using NEUMES that relates the pitch of a note to its vertical position on the page, without the use of ruled lines.

diatessaron (Gk.) the interval of a fourth in ancient Greek music.

diatonic pertaining to an octave SCALE or MODE constructed of five tones and two semitones, in which the two semitones are as widely separated from one another as possible. Thus, the major and minor scales and the church modes are diatonic.

diatonic interval any INTERVAL that can be constructed between pitches of a diatonic scale, i.e., all the major, minor and perfect intervals. The tritone, although technically a diatonic interval, is sometimes considered to be an alteration of a perfect fourth or fifth and thus a chromatic interval. Cf. CHROMATIC INTERVAL.

Diaz, Justino (1940–) Amer. bass, stud. of Friedrich Jägel. He made his Metropolitan Opera debut in 1963 and has appeared there regularly since, specializing in a wide range of Italian roles.

Dibdin, Charles (1745–1814) English composer, actor, singer and writer, self-taught as a composer and a remarkable figure from the entertainment world. In 1776 he fled England for nonpayment of debts, but returned in 1778 to Covent Garden for several years, then formed his own company, which was soon in debt. In 1784 he was in debtors' prison. He later decided to go to India, but couldn't tolerate the sea travel. His final professional activity, probably his most successful, was presenting one-man "Table Entertainments" in a small theater off the Strand in London.

Dichter, Misha (1945–) Amer. pianist of Polish descent, born in Shanghai, stud. of Rosina Lhévinne. He is best known for his performance of 19th- and 20th-c. repertory.

Dichterliebe [diç'tər-lē-be] (Ger., Poet's Love) cycle of sixteen songs, Op. 48 (1840), by Schumann, a setting of poems by Heinrich Heine.

Dickens, Little Jimmy (James C.) (1920–) Amer. country-music singer, guitarist and songwriter. He has sung with the Grand Ole Opry from 1948 and is noted for his comic songs in praise of rural life and for his innovative use of backup instrumentation. He was elected to the Country Music Hall of Fame in 1983.

Dickenson, Vic(tor) (1906–84) Amer. jazz trombonist, singer and composer, a highly respected sideman with Count Basie, Eddie Condon, Lester Young and Sidney Bechet, among others, and leader of his own septet in the 1950s.

Diddley, Bo (McDaniel, Ellas) (1928–) Amer. rock-and-roll singer and guitarist, named after a type of one-stringed African guitar. He played with Chuck Berry on several recordings, then became famous with his first single, *Bo Diddley* (1955).

didgeridoo *also*, **didjeridoo** a large bamboo or wooden TRUMPET of the Australian aborigines.

Dido and Aeneas tragic opera in 3 acts by Purcell to a libretto by Nahum Tate based on Virgil's *Aeneid*. Premiere, London 1689. Dido dies, lamenting the loss of her beloved Aeneas.

Didone abbandonata (It., Dido abandoned) **1**, piano sonata in G minor, Op. 50 No. 3 (1821), by Clementi. **2**, violin sonata in G minor (1734) by Tartini.

dièse [dē′ez] (Fr.) SHARP.

dies irae [′dē-es ′ē-rā] (Lat., day of wrath) the SEQUENCE of the Roman Catholic Mass for the Dead. The melody has been used by many composers in settings of the Requiem, as well as in other works related to death, incl. Dukas's *The Sorcerer's Apprentice.*

diesis 1, (It.) SHARP. **2**, (Gk.) a term in Greek theory used for various intervals by different theorists.

Dietrich, Marlene (Maria Magdalene) (1901–92) singer and actress, trained at the Berlin Hochschule für Musik. Her husky, sensuous voice became famous in the film *Der blaue Engel* (The Blue Angel, 1930). During World War II she entertained the Allied troops, esp. with the song *Lili Marlene* and by playing the musical saw.

diferencias [dē-fä′rän-thē-äs] (Sp.) a 16th-c. Spanish term for VARIATIONS.

difference an ending formula for a PSALM TONE, usu. indicated in liturgical books by a melody above the letters EVOVAE. Also, *differentia* (Lat.).

difference tone see COMBINATION TONE.

dim. *abbr.* DIMINUENDO.

diminished of an INTERVAL, made smaller by a half step from minor or perfect.

diminished seventh chord a CHORD consisting of three superimposed minor thirds, thus dividing the octave into equal parts. The chord is harmonically unstable, capable of resolution to a triad on any degree of the chromatic scale; thus it makes a good pivot chord in MODULATION.

diminished triad a triad consisting of two superimposed minor thirds. See CHORD.

diminuendo (It.) becoming softer.

diminution 1, ornamental variation, often involving the breaking down of longer note values to a larger number of notes of shorter duration, hence the name. Cf. DIVISION (1,). **2**, repetition of a musical theme in smaller note values than orig. used; opposed to AUGMENTATION.

d'Indy, Vincent INDY, VINCENT D'.

Dion (DiMucci, Dion) (1939–) Amer. rock-and-roll singer. He recorded extensively with the group Dion and the Belmonts, formed in 1958, and also as a solo artist in the later 1960s and the 1970s.

direct a symbol (∿) placed at the end of a staff to indicate the first note of the following staff.

Dire Straits English rock band formed in 1977 in London under singer/guitarist Mark Knopfler.

dirge a burial or mourning song, or an instrumental work expressing mourning.

dirt in jazz, alteration of natural instrumental sound by use of mutes, "wa-wa" or other techniques.

dis (Ger.) D SHARP.

disis (Ger.) D double sharp.

discant DESCANT.

disc jockey an entertainer who selects and plays records on the radio, in a discothèque, for a dance, etc. On the radio, the selections are usu. separated by introductions and comments. See SCRATCHING.

disco a style of dance music of the 1970s whose main characteristic is a steady, thumped beat. Most disco music is on records, intended for dance halls employing a disc jockey rather than a live band. Its heyday followed the spectacular success of the film *Saturday Night Fever* (1977), but by 1980 the style's vogue had ebbed, leaving it still with a place in the dance halls but off the charts.

discord a harsh or unpleasant sound resulting from DISSONANCE, lack of ensemble or false intonation.

disjunct of a melodic line, proceeding by interval larger than a second. Cf. CONJUNCT.

displacement the repetition of a theme or motive in a different rhythmic position than its first statement, placing metric stresses on different parts of the melody.

dissonance a sound which, in the prevailing harmonic system, is unstable and must be resolved to a consonant, or stable, sound. Opposed to CONSONANCE. Cf. NONHARMONIC NOTE.

Dissonance Quartet the popular name for the string quartet in C major, K. 465 (1785), by Mozart, so called because of the unusual dissonances in the introduction.

Di Stefano, Giuseppe (1921–) Italian tenor, stud. of Luigi Montesanto. His Amer. debut was at the Metropolitan Opera in 1948. He sang a lighter repertoire in his earlier years, moving in the mid-1950s to the heavier roles, such as Don José (*Carmen*) and Radamès (*Aida*).

Distler, Hugo (1908–42) German organist and composer, stud. of Grabner and Ramin. His music—sacred and secular vocal works and instrumental chamber music—derives from a profound study of the forms and styles of the Baroque, esp., in his vocal music, the works of Schütz.

Distratto, Il (It., The Absent-minded

One) the Symphony No. 60 in C major (1774) by Haydn, derived from incidental music for a play of the same name.

dital a key on some HARP-GUITARS used to raise the pitch a half step.

dithyramb (Gk.) a song in honor of Dionysus (Bacchus).

Ditson, Oliver Amer. music publisher, whose roots date from the late 18th c. It was acquired by THEODORE PRESSER in 1937.

Dittersdorf, Carl Ditters von (1739–99) Austrian violinist and prolific composer of singspiels, symphonies and vocal and chamber works. His best-known works are his first singspiel, *Doktor und Apotheker* (1786), and his symphonies.

div. *abbr.* DIVISI.

diva ['dē-vä] (It.) a term sometimes used for a starring female opera singer, roughly synonymous with PRIMA DONNA and often having a pejorative connotation.

divertimento (It., diversion) an instrumental work, esp. of the 18th and 19th c., usu. in several movements, and designed for entertainment, as at a social gathering, banquet, etc.

divertissement [dē-ver-tēs'mä] (Fr., diversion) **1**, DIVERTIMENTO. **2**, a work comprising solos, ensembles and dances, used as part of a larger stage work and sometimes related to the action of the larger work. **3**, a stage work, often written for a specific occasion, such as a victory celebration.

divided stop a mechanism on a pipe organ allowing the use of different registrations for the treble and bass.

Divine Office the daily hours of the Roman Catholic Church, also known as the *canonical hours*. The individual hours, or offices, are matins (beginning after midnight), lauds (daybreak), prime (6 AM), terce (9 AM), sext (noon), none (3 PM), vespers (sunset) and compline (evening). Each office consists of psalms and canticles with antiphons, lessons and responsories, hymns, versicles and responses, and prayers. The ordering of the contents of the offices within the day and year follows a fixed pattern, or *cursus*. The entire Psalter is generally chanted each week. Prime, terce, sext and none together are known as the *lesser hours*. Each day in the liturgical calendar is measured from vespers to vespers.

divisi (It., divided, separate) a direction used as an instruction to a section of an orch. to divide several musical lines, often notated on the same staff, among the players. It is cancelled by *tutti* or *all'unisono*. Abbr., *div.*

division 1, a florid variation, esp. of the 17th and 18th c., in which the notes of a melody (*ground*) are divided into shorter, ornamental notes. Cf. DIMINUTION. **2**, a melismatic song or phrase of the same period. **3**, a group of organ stops played from the same manual.

division viol VIOLA DA GAMBA.

Dixie a "plantation song" (1859) by Daniel Decatur Emmett (1815–1904), first performed by Bryant's Minstrels and later associated with the Confederate cause in the Civil War.

Dixie Hummingbirds, The an Amer. gospel vocal quartet formed in 1928 in Greenville, SC. Their regular radio broadcasts and recordings made them the leading Southern black gospel quartet for more than fifty years.

Dixieland a style of jazz originating in New Orleans and standardized in the 1920s in Chicago, characterized by ensemble improvisations framing solos. The term is used either to cover both forms, or to refer to the Chicago developments as distinguished from the "genuine" New Orleans style.

Dixie to Broadway musical revue by George Meyer and Arthur Johnston, lyrics by Grant Clarke and Roy Turk. Premiere, New York 1924. The show also went to London and Paris and was a triumph for its star, Florence Mills.

Dixon, (Charles) Dean (1915–76) Amer. conductor, trained at the Juilliard School and Columbia U. He founded the New York Chamber Orch. in 1938 and in the early 1940s was the first black conductor to appear as guest conductor with the NBC SO, the New York PO and the Philadelphia Orch. He founded the American Youth Orch. in 1944. From 1949 to 1970 he conducted mainly overseas, being principal conductor of the Götebord SO (1953–60), the Hessian Radio SO in Frankfurt (1961–74), and of the Sydney SO (1964–7).

Dlugoszewski, Lucia [dloo-gō'shev-skē](1931–) Amer. composer, stud. of Felix Salzer and Varèse. She has written much music for the dance, and was musical dir. for the Eric Hawkins Dance Company. She has developed (and performed on) various percussion instruments.

do, doh (It., Sp.) the note C. See PITCH.

Dobbs, Mattiwilda (1925–) Amer. soprano, stud. of Lotte Lehmann and Bernac. She won first prize in the Geneva Competition for singers in 1951 and made her Metropolitan Opera debut in 1956.

Doblinger Austrian music publishers, founded in 1857 in Vienna. The firm has been an important supporter of modern music (it was Bruckner's publisher), as well as of church music and early music.

dobro a type of steel-string acoustic GUITAR having a large circular metal resonator on the belly and an internal tone chamber. It is popular with blues singers and is often played using a BOTTLENECK. Also, *resophonic guitar*.

Doctrine of the Affections AFFECTIONS, DOCTRINE OF THE.

Doctrine of Musical Figures FIGURES, DOCTRINE OF MUSICAL.

Dodds, "Baby" (Warren) (1898–1959) Amer. jazz drummer, brother of JOHNNY DODDS. He played and recorded with the important Chicago groups of the 1920s, incl. King Oliver, Louis Armstrong and Jelly Roll Morton, and was a pioneer of New Orleans jazz style and techniques. He introduced new effects on the snare drum, high hat and ride cymbal.

Dodds, Johnny (1892–1940) Amer.

jazz clarinetist and alto saxophonist, a leading player of the New Orleans style, brother of "BABY" DODDS. He played with Kid Ory in New Orleans, and with Fate Marable and King Oliver in Chicago. He recorded extensively with Louis Armstrong, Jelly Roll Morton and with his own groups.

dodecaphonic twelve-tone (see TWELVE-TONE MUSIC); sometimes erroneously used as a synonym for ATONAL.

dodecuple scale see TWELVE-TONE MUSIC.

Dodge, Charles (Malcolm) (1942–) Amer. composer, trained at the U. of Iowa, Tanglewood, Columbia and Princeton. He has composed extensively for computer-generated sounds, with or without instruments, as well as for orch. and chamber ensembles.

dogleg jack a harpsichord JACK used on instruments that lack manual coupling to permit playing several sets of strings from the same manual.

Dohnányi, Christoph von (1929–) Ger. conductor, stud. of Bernstein, grandson of Ernö Dohnányi. He has been music dir. in Lübeck, Kassel, Frankfurt and at the Hamburg Staatsoper, and chief conductor of the West German Radio SO in Cologne. He became music dir. of the Cleveland Orch. in 1984. He has conducted the premieres of several of Henze's operas and acclaimed productions of Schoenberg's *Moses und Aaron*.

Dohnányi, Ernö (Ernst von) (1877–1960) Hungarian pianist, composer, conductor and teacher, trained at the Budapest Academy. He concertized throughout Europe from 1897 to 1905, establishing his fame as the greatest Hungarian pianist since Liszt, then taught at the Berlin Hochschule (1905–15) at the invitation of Joachim. In 1915 he returned to Hungary and was instrumental in reshaping the musical life of his country, as teacher (and briefly, director) at the Budapest Academy. He was chief conductor of the Philharmonic Society from 1919 to 1945, during

which time he also made frequent tours to the U.S. In 1949 he emigrated to the U.S., joining the faculty of Florida State U. as pianist and composer. His pupils in Hungary incl. Géza Anda and Georg Solti.

Doktor Faust (Ger., Doctor Faust) opera in 3 tableaux by Busoni to his own libretto in German after Marlowe's *Doctor Faustus*. Premiere, Dresden 1925. The work was unfinished at Busoni's death and was completed by Philip Jarnach, Busoni's pupil. The story is from the original Faust legend and differs from Goethe's version.

Doktor, Paul (1919–89) Austrian-born Amer. violist, stud. of his father Karl, violist of the Busch Quartet. He came to the U.S. in 1948 and has taught at the Mannes College, the Philadelphia Academy and the Juilliard School. He was a founder and member of the Rococo Ensemble and the New York String Sextet.

dolce ['dōl-chā] (It.) sweet, soft.

dolcissimo [dōl'chēs-sē-mō] (It.) very softly and sweetly.

dolente, doloroso (It.) sorrowful.

Dolin, Samuel (Joseph) (1917–) Canadian composer, pianist and teacher, stud. of Reginald Godden and Weinzweig. He has taught at the Toronto Royal Conservatory of Music since 1945 and has taught many of Canada's composers. His own works, in a highly individual style, incl. 3 symphonies, a piano concerto, chamber works, music for two pianos and percussion, a concerto for oboe and cello, and choral works.

Dolly suite for piano duet about children (1896) by Fauré. The suite was orchestrated in 1912 by Henri Rabaud for use as ballet music.

Dolmetsch, (Eugène) Arnold (1858–1940) French-born English scholar, instrument maker and performer of early music, a major force in the revival of performance on original instruments. He worked at Chickering & Sons in Boston (1905–11), then in 1917 moved to Haslemere, England, which became a center for early music study and performance. The Dolmetsch Foundation was established in 1929 to further the study of early music. His third wife, **Mabel Dolmetsch** (1874–1963) made a special study of the court dances of the 16th to 18th c.

Dolmetsch, Carl (Frederick) (1911–) French-born English instrument maker and performer, esp. on the recorder, son of ARNOLD DOLMETSCH. He continued his father's researches and has been since 1947 musical dir. of the Haslemere Festival and of the Dolmetsch Foundation. He has given many recitals and has commissioned works for recorder by contemporary composers. He has also made many editions of recorder music and is general editor of the extensive series *Il Flauto dolce*.

Dolphy, Eric (1928–64) Amer. jazz alto saxophonist, flutist and clarinetist. He played with Chico Hamilton, Charles Mingus, Booker Little and John Coltrane. He was, after Ornette Coleman, an early proponent of FREE JAZZ.

Domaine musicale (Fr.) a concert society in Paris est. in 1954 by Boulez for the performance of 20th-c. music. It was active until 1973.

dömbra any of several types of Asian LUTE, predecessor of the BALALAIKA.

Domestic Symphony SYMPHONIA DOMESTICA.

dominant the fifth degree of the major or minor SCALE. Because it is also the fifth degree of the tonic triad and its own triad contains the two notes closest to the tonic, it is used in CADENCES to prepare the tonic.

dominant seventh chord the seventh CHORD built on the dominant triad by adding a minor seventh and having a strong tendency to resolve to the tonic triad. See CADENCE.

Domingo, Placido (1941–) Spanish tenor and conductor, stud. of Markevich. He began as a baritone singing *zarzuela* in Mexico. He sang with the Israeli National Opera (1962–65) and made his Amer. debut at the New York City Opera in 1966 and his Metropolitan Opera debut in 1968. After

many years as one of the world's leading tenors, he began conducting in 1973. He became musical dir. of the Los Angeles Music Center Opera Assoc. in 1986.

Dominicus Mass the Mass in C major, K.66 (1769), by Mozart.

Domino, Fats (Antoine) (1929–) Amer. rock-and-roll singer and pianist from New Orleans. He began playing barroom piano, in the company of the legendary Professor Longhair and Fats Waller, and played in the Dave Bartholomew band in the 1940s. His first solo record was in 1949, and he adapted to the rock-and-roll sound in the mid-1950s, when he produced a succession of hits, incl. "Ain't That a Shame" and "Blueberry Hill."

Donaldson, Walter (1893–1947) Amer. songwriter, lyricist and publisher. His best-known songs are "My Blue Heaven" and "Yes, Sir, That's My Baby."

Donath, Helen (1940–) Amer. lyric soprano, stud. of Paola Novikova. She has sung in Cologne, Hanover, Munich and throughout the world. Her roles include Pamina (*Magic Flute*), Sophie (*Der Rosenkavalier*) and Micaëla (*Carmen*).

Donato, Baldassare (?1530–1603) Italian composer and singer, a member of the choir at St. Mark's, Venice, and *maestro di cappella* from 1590. He was an influential composer of secular vocal music, esp. madrigals, which, because of their contrapuntal and harmonic simplicity, paved the way for the monodic developments of the early 17th c.

Donatoni, Franco (1927–) Italian composer. He studied with Pizzetti and at the Darmstadt summer courses. He has taught at the Milan Conservatory since 1969 and at the Accademia Chigiana and the U. of Bologna since 1970. His works, which have essayed serialism and aleatory writing, incl. orchestral and chamber music, a ballet and solo sonatas.

Don Carlos historical opera by Verdi to a libretto in French by Joseph Méry and Camille du Locle after the play by Friedrich Schiller. Premiere, Paris 1867; revised Italian version, premiere, Milan 1884. The story of the love between the Spanish Infante Don Carlos and his stepmother Queen Elisabetta de Valois.

Don Giovanni (It., Don Juan) comic opera by Mozart to a libretto in Italian by Lorenzo da Ponte. Premiere, Prague 1787. The life, loves and destruction of the rake Don Giovanni.

Donington, Robert (1907–90) English musicologist and performer, stud. of Arnold Dolmetsch. He was on the faculty of the U. of Iowa from 1964 and was a founder of the Galpin Society. His best-known works are his survey *The Instruments of Music* (1949) and the books on performance practice, *The Interpretation of Early Music* (1963) and *A Performer's Guide to Baroque Music* (1973).

Donizetti, (Domenico) Gaetano (Maria) [dō-nē'tset-tē] (1797–1848) Italian composer, stud. of Johannes Simon Mayr and Padre Mattei. He was in Naples from 1822 to 1832, during which time he produced over twenty operas. Of the many operas he produced between 1832 and 1838, the most successful were *L'elisir d'amore, Lucrezia Borgia* and *Lucia di Lammermoor*. In 1838 he moved to Paris, hoping to earn enough to retire from opera. The works written in Paris include *La fille du régiment* for the Opéra-Comique and *La favorite* for the Opéra. His final years, in Italy, produced several important works, esp. *Don Pasquale* and *Maria di Rohan*. In addition to his more than 60 operas, Donizetti produced a large body of sacred and secular vocal works, string quartets and other chamber music, and piano pieces.

Don Juan tone poem, Op. 20 (1888), by Richard Strauss, based on a poem by Nicolaus Lenau.

Donkey, The FIFTHS QUARTET.

Donovan, Richard Frank (1891–1970) Amer. organist, composer and teacher, trained at Yale and with Widor in Paris. He taught at Smith College and at Yale (until 1960) and was conductor of the New Haven SO from 1936 to 1951. His works incl. orchestral and chamber music, choral music and works for organ.

Don Pasquale comic opera in 3 acts by Donizetti to a libretto in Italian by Giacomo Ruffini. Premiere, Paris 1843. The rich old bachelor Don Pasquale wants to marry Norina who, however, is in love with Ernesto, Pasquale's nephew.

Don Quichotte [dō kē'shot] (Fr., Don Quixote) opera in 5 acts by Massenet to a libretto by Henri Cain, based on the play by Le Lorrain from the novel by Cervantes. Premiere, Monte Carlo 1910. Don Quichotte recaptures her necklace for his beloved Dulcinea, but she begs him to forget her, and he dies disillusioned.

Don Quixote 1, DON QUICHOTTE. **2**, symphonic poem, Op. 35 (1898), by Richard Strauss. Subtitled *Fantastische Variationen über ein Thema ritterlichen Charakters* (Ger., Fantastic Variations on a Theme of Knightly Character), the work tells of some of the knight's adventures, with Don Quixote represented by a solo cello and Sancho Panza by a solo viola.

Don Rodrigo opera in 3 acts by Ginastera to a libretto by A. Casona. Premiere, Buenos Aires 1964. The story of Don Rodrigo of Spain, who rapes the daughter of the governor of Ceuta.

Doobie Brothers a rock band formed in 1970 in San Jose, CA, which, after starting out with a country sound, developed into a jazz-influenced funk band. The group dispersed in 1982.

Doors, The influential hard rock band formed in 1965 in Los Angeles. The band's best-known member was singer Jim Morrison, whose alter ego, the Lizard King, appears in his lyrics. Morrison died in 1971 and the band broke up several years later.

doo wop a type of RHYTHM-AND-BLUES popular in the 1950s and 1960s using nonsense syllables in intricate harmonic arrangements. Classic examples are "Earth Angel" by the Pen-

guins and "Sh-Boom" by the Chords.
doppel (Ger.), **doppio** (It.) double.
Doppelleittonklang ["dop-əl'lĭt-tōn"kläng] (Ger., double-leading tone chord) an altered form of the major or minor triad, derived by replacing one of the notes in the chord by the notes lying a half step above and below it. In a minor triad the note usu. replaced is the 5th, in a major triad, the root.
Doppelschlag [-"shläk] (Ger.) a type of TURN.
Doppeltriller [-"tril-lər] (Ger.) a double TRILL.
Doppler, (Albert) Franz (1821–83) Polish flutist, composer and conductor, stud. of his father, an oboist. His works incl. operas and ballets, which were highly popular at the time, as well as orchestral and chamber works.
Dorati, Antal (1906–88) Hungarian-born Amer. conductor, stud. of Bartók, Kodály and Leo Weiner. He conducted at the Budapest Royal Opera, the Dresden Opera, the Münster Opera and the Ballets Russes de Monte Carlo, with which he toured extensively. He moved to Amer. in 1941 to become musical dir. of the American Ballet Theater. He was later musical dir. of the Dallas SO (1945–9) and the Washington National Symphony (1970–77). He has also been associated with the BBC SO, the Stockholm PO and the Royal PO in London.
dorian the authentic church mode with final on D. See MODE.
Dorian Toccata and Fugue popular name for the organ toccata and fugue in D minor, BWV 538, by J.S. Bach, erroneously so called because it is written without key signature.
Dorsey, Jimmy (James) (1904–57) Amer. swing jazz clarinetist, saxophonist and bandleader, brother of TOMMY DORSEY. He performed with a variety of groups and in studios, until forming the Dorsey Brothers Band with his brother Tommy in 1934. After the brothers split in 1935 he led a series of successful bands until the early 1950s. He was reunited with his brother in a film *The Fabulous Dorseys* in 1947 and in 1953 he rejoined Tommy's band, taking it over after his brother's death.
Dorsey, Thomas A. (1899–) Amer. gospel and blues songwriter and founder of the National Convention of Gospel Singers. In his early years he recorded blues and ragtime piano under the name Georgia Tom, touring with Ma Rainey and others.
Dorsey, Tommy (Thomas) (1905–56) Amer. swing jazz trombonist and bandleader, brother of JIMMY DORSEY, with whom he formed the Dorsey Brothers Band in 1934, taking over the Joe Haymes orch. in 1935 when he split with his brother. Over the years he built up a major jazz orch., which featured a succession of top singers, incl. Frank Sinatra and Jo Stafford.
dot 1, a sign added to a NOTE increasing its value by half. **2**, a sign placed over a note, alone or in combination with other signs, to indicate STACCATO articulation. See EXPRESSION.
dotted rhythm a rhythm in which longer, often dotted, notes alternate with shorter notes, resulting in an uneven rhythm. The degree of unevenness, i.e., the relation of the longer note to the shorter note or notes, has varied from era to era and varies from piece to piece, depending on the expression.

There are some specific circumstances requiring the modification of a notated dotted rhythm. When, in music of the Baroque, Classical and early Romantic periods, a dotted rhythm occurs against a triplet rhythm, in most cases the dotted figure is modified in performance to match the triplet. In the pompous style of the French overture and similar situations, dotted rhythms are usu. to be performed in an exaggerated manner, often called "double dotting," because the first note is lengthened in performance as though it were doubly dotted. Cf. NOTES INÉGALES.

double 1, applied to an instrument,

a term indicating that that instrument plays an octave lower. **2**, (Fr.) VARIATION, esp. of a melody, with no change to the accompanying harmonies. Cf. DIVISION. **3**, UNDERSTUDY. **4**, a singer singing two roles, or an instrumentalist playing more than one instrument, in the same piece.

double appoggiatura see APPOGGIATURA.

double bar two bar lines drawn through the staff to indicate the end of a section, a key change, etc. See BAR.

double bass the largest instrument of the VIOL family, having four strings tuned in fourths. It is an essential instrument of the orch., reinforcing the fundamental bass line; in jazz and dance bands, where it is usu. played pizzicato, it supplies both bass-line pitches and rhythm. There are two types of bass bow (see BOW). Also, *bass, contrabass, string bass, bass fiddle, bull fiddle.*

double bassoon CONTRABASSOON.

double-bémol ['doo-blǝ-bā'mol] (Fr.) DOUBLE FLAT.

double chorus two choruses, often spatially separated and singing antiphonally, in polychoral music. See CORI SPEZZATI.

double concerto a CONCERTO for two solo instruments and orch.

double counterpoint two-part INVERTIBLE COUNTERPOINT.

double-croche [-krosh] (Fr.) SIXTEENTH NOTE.

double-dièse [-dyez] (Fr.) DOUBLE SHARP.

double dot to place two dots after a note, lengthening its duration by three-quarters of its original length (♩.. = ♩ + ♪ + ♪).

double flat a chromatic alteration lowering the pitch of a note by two half steps (♭♭).

double fugue a FUGUE employing two subjects.

double harpsichord a two-manual HARPSICHORD. The term was sometimes used to indicate an instrument with an extended bass range.

double reed see REED.

double sharp a chromatic alteration raising the pitch of a note by two half steps (✗).

double stop on a string instrument, the STOPPING and bowing of more than one string at a time, producing chords of two or more notes.

double-strung of a stringed instrument, having two strings per pitch.

double time a jazz technique for increasing the apparent tempo of a performance by doubling the number of notes played.

double tonguing see TONGUING.

double whole note see BREVE.

doubling 1, in polyphonic music, the simultaneous repetition of a note by another part either at the unison or at an octave or more above or below. **2**, playing more than one instrument or singing more than one role in a work.

doucement [doos'mã] (Fr.) sweetly, softly.

doux [doo] (Fr.) sweet, soft.

Dowd, William (Richard) (1922–) Amer. harpsichord maker, stud. of John Challis. In 1949, in partnership with Frank Hubbard, he opened a workshop in Boston. When they disbanded in 1958, he opened his own business in Cambridge, MA, which continued to operate until 1989.

Dowland, John (1563–1626) English composer and lutanist, widely considered the finest lutanist of his time. He went to Denmark in 1598 to serve at the court of Christian IV, then returned to England in 1609. He was appointed one of the king's lutes in 1612. His works include several volumes of ayres, numerous lute works and instrumental chamber music for viols and lutes, the best known of which is his *Lachrimae or Seaven Teares* (1604).

downbeat the impulse (*thesis*) coinciding with the beginning of a bar in metered music, contrasted with UPBEAT.

down-bow a bow stroke beginning at the heel of the bow and proceeding toward the point; contrasted with UPBOW. See BOWING.

Downes, Edward O(lin) D(avenport)
(1911–) Amer. musicologist and
annotator, trained at Columbia, the
Manhattan School of Music and in
Paris and Munich, son of OLIN
DOWNES. He has been quizmaster for
the Metropolitan Opera radio broadcasts since 1958 (succeeding his father) and program annotator for the
New York Philharmonic since 1960.

Downes, (Edwin) Olin (1886–1955)
Amer. music critic, trained in New
York and Boston. He was music critic
of the *Boston Post* (1906–24) and of
the *New York Times* (1924–55) and
was the original quizmaster for the
Metropolitan Opera radio broadcasts.

drag 1, a descending portamento in
lute playing. **2**, a snare drum stroke,
usu. consisting of three or four grace
notes before the beat. **3**, a slow New
Orleans dance; a blues number in a
slow tempo. **4**, to play slower than the
prevailing tempo; be behind.

Drake, Earl R(oss) (1865–1916)
Amer. violinist and composer, stud.
of Joachim. He founded the Violinists' Guild, was head of the Gottschalk Lyric School in Chicago
(1893–7) and founded the Drake
School of Music in 1900. He composed two operas, works for violin
and piano and some orchestral pieces.

dramatic a term applied to various
voice types to indicate a stronger
voice suitable for heavier, more dramatic roles, as *dramatic soprano*,
dramatic tenor.

dramatic tenor *also*, **heroic tenor,
Heldentenor** (Ger.) see DRAMATIC.

drame lyrique [dräm lē′rēk] (Fr., lyric
drama) a term for a type of serious
opera with little or no spoken dialogue and on a more intimate scale
than grand opera, a development of
the more serious side of the *opéra-
comique*. Massenet's *Werther* was
called a *drame lyrique* by the composer and is a good example of the
type.

dramma giocoso [′dräm-mä jō′kō-zō]
(It., jocular drama) a comic opera
which mingles characters from serious opera with standard comic-opera

peasants and servants. The best
known example is Mozart's *Don Giovanni*.

dramma in musica (It., play set to music) a music drama; OPERA.

dramma per musica [per ′moo-zē-kä]
(It., play for music) a term for a libretto specifically intended to be set
to music.

drängend [′dreng-ənt] (Ger.) pressing,
urgent.

dreadnought guitar see JUMBO GUI-
TAR.

Dream of Gerontius, The oratorio,
Op. 38 (1900), by Elgar to a text from
the poem by Cardinal Newman.

Dream Quartet, The (Ger., *Ein
Traum*) the string quartet in F major,
Op. 50 No. 5 (1785), by Haydn.

Dreigroschenoper, Die [′drī-grō-
shən″ō-pər] (Ger.) THE THREEPENNY
OPERA.

Dresden amen a four-part setting of
the word *Amen* by J.G. Naumann
(1741–1801) for the Royal Chapel of
Dresden.

Dresden Philharmonic Orchestra an
orch. dating, under various names,
from 1870, a successor to the 300-
year-old Dresden Stadtkapelle. It was
given its current name in 1923 under
conductor Eduard Mörike, who was
succeeded by Paul Scheinpflug, W.
Ladwig and Paul van Kempen, who
brought the orch. to international
fame in the late 1930s. After World
War II its conductors have been Heinz
Bongartz, H. Förster, Masur, Herbig
and Herbert Kegel.

Dresden Staatskapelle the orch. of
the Dresden Staatsoper, performing
both as opera orch. and as highly acclaimed symphonic orch. The orch.
has had a succession of distinguished
conductors, incl. Fritz Busch and
Reiner before World War II, Sanderling and Blomstedt in the postwar
years.

Dresser, Paul (1857–1906) Amer.
songwriter, publisher and performer,
brother of novelist Theodore Dreiser.
He performed with the Billy Rose
Minstrels, then became involved in a
publishing venture which was suc-

cessful for a time. His songs are mostly sentimental ballads, the best known of which are "My Gal Sal" and "On the Banks of the Wabash."

Drifters, The Amer. rhythm-and-blues vocal quartet formed in 1953 in New York with Clyde McPhatter as lead singer; reformed in 1959 under Ben E. King. The group performed a gospel-style repertory which helped lead to the development of SOUL MUSIC.

Drinker, Henry S(andwith) (1880–1965) Amer. lawyer and amateur music scholar, best known for his performing translations of the vocal works of Brahms, Bach, Mozart, Schubert, etc. He established the Accademia dei Dilettanti di Musica (It., the Academy of Musical Amateurs), a mixed choir that met at his home in Philadelphia (1930–60) to study and perform vocal music of the 17th to 20th c. His wife, **Sophie Hutchinson Drinker** (1888–1968), was a champion of women in music.

drone 1, a musical part or instrument that sustains a pitch or other sound throughout a piece or section of a piece, usu. as accompaniment to a melody. Some instruments, such as the bagpipe or hurdy-gurdy, have built-in drones. **2**, BUMBASS.

Drucker, Stanley (1929–) Amer. clarinetist, stud. of Leon Russianoff. He has been first clarinet of the Indianapolis SO (1945–49) and of the New York Philharmonic (1960–) and has been on the faculty of the Juilliard School since 1968. He has produced a large body of teaching materials for clarinet.

Druckman, Jacob (1928–) Amer. composer, stud. of Persichetti, Mennin and Copland. He has taught at the Juilliard School, Bard College and Brooklyn College, and was appointed composer-in-residence with the New York PO in 1982. He has also worked at the electronic studios both at Yale and Brooklyn College. Some of his works explore the interaction of live musicians and recorded sounds, and he has written orchestral and choral

works and instrumental chamber music. His work *Windows* for orch. won the Pulitzer Prize in 1972.

drum a percussion instrument, probably the most prevalent musical instrument throughout history after the voice. In general, it consists of a membrane of skin or plastic stretched over an open frame of wood or other material. Drums are either beaten with the fingers, mallets or rattles (by far the most common form); rubbed; or plucked by means of a string attached to the membrane. The frame may be bowl-shaped, as in the kettledrum; tubular, with either or both ends covered with a membrane; or cylindrical in the form of a relatively narrow frame, usu. with membrane on both sides, such as the bass drum. See CYLINDRICAL DRUM, WAISTED DRUM, BARREL DRUM, CONICAL DRUM, TRAP, TALKING DRUM.

Drum-Roll Symphony (Ger., *Symphonie mit dem Paukenwirbel*) popular name for the Symphony No. 103 in E-flat major (1795) by Haydn, which opens with a kettledrum roll.

D.S. *abbr.* DAL SEGNO.

drumstick a wooden stick for beating a drum. The head of the stick may be of wood, felt, sponge, cork or other material, depending on the volume and tone quality of the sound desired.

D sharp the PITCH (D♯) a half-step above D, the enharmonic equivalent of E flat.

Drury Lane Theatre a London theater opened in 1663. The present theater on the site was built in 1812.

DuBarry Was a Lady musical by Cole Porter, book by Herbert Fields and B.G. DeSylva. Premiere, New York 1939. Louis Blore wins the Irish Sweepstakes and hopes to win May Daly, nightclub dancer.

Dubois, (François Clément) Théodore [dü'bwä] (1837–1924) French organist, composer and teacher, stud. of Benoit and Thomas, winner of the Prix de Rome in 1861. He replaced Saint-Saëns as organist of the Madeleine and taught at the Paris Conservatoire (1871–90), later becoming director

Drums

tuning screws

Kettledrum

Bongo drums

jingles

Tambourine

tuning pedal

Conga drum

Steel drum

snares

Bass drum

Snare drum (bottom view)

(1896–1905). Of his many stage, vocal and instrumental works, only the oratorio *Les sept paroles du Christ* (Fr., The Seven Words of Christ, 1867) has remained in the repertory, but his pedagogical treatises are still widely used.

Ducasse, Roger ROGER-DUCASSE, JEAN.

ductia a 13th-c. instrumental dance related to the ESTAMPIE.

Dudelsack ['doo-dǝl"säk] (Ger.) a German BAGPIPE with a chanter and two drones.

Dudelsky, Vladimir DUKE, VERNON.

due ['doo-ā] (It.) two.

Duenna, The comic opera by Prokofiev to a libretto in Russian by the composer and Mira Mendelssohn based on Sheridan's play. Premiere, Leningrad 1946. Mendoza, a rich fish merchant, wants to marry Louisa, but ends up marrying her governess.

duet an instrumental or vocal composition for two performers, usu. two solo instruments of more or less equal importance and interest. The term is usu. not used for the combination of a solo instrument with piano, although the term DUO is sometimes used in this sense.

duettino [doo-āt'tē-nō] (It.) a short
DUET.

Dufay, Guillaume (?1400–1474)
French composer, the leading composer of his day. By 1428 he was a
singer in the Papal Choir in Rome,
where he remained until 1433. He
was associated with the court of the
d'Este family in Ferrara, as well as
with the court of Savoy. He took up
permanent residence in Cambrai
sometime in the late 1430s, remaining there until his death. His position
of eminence was such that composers
traveled to see him in Cambrai,
among them Ockeghem and Tinctoris. His very large output of sacred and
secular vocal works includes Mass
settings, motets, hymns and rondeaus.

Duffalo, Richard (John) (1933–)
Amer. conductor and clarinetist,
trained at the Amer. Conservatory of
Music in Chicago and at the U. of
California. He was assoc. conductor
of the Buffalo PO (1962–6) and has
conducted many major orchestras in
Europe, esp. in contemporary works.
He has been artistic dir. of the Contemporary Music Conference at the
Aspen Festival from 1970 and on the
faculty of the Juilliard School from
1972. He was director of the short-
lived "Mini-Met" season in 1973.

dugazon [dü-gä'zō] (Fr.) a singer
specializing in SOUBRETTE roles.
The term comes from the soprano
Louise Rosalie Dugazon (1755–1821),
a leading singer at the Paris Opéra-
Comique.

dugdugi a Bengalese two-headed
WAISTED DRUM with a pottery body.

Dukas, Paul (Abraham) (1865–1935)
French composer, music critic and
teacher, stud. of Guiraud, friend of
Debussy and d'Indy. His surviving
works (he destroyed many of his compositions) include the opera *Ariane et
Barbe-Bleu* (Fr., Ariadne and Bluebeard), the ballet *La Péri*, a symphony
in C, a piano sonata in E-flat minor
and his best-known work, *L'apprenti
sorcier* (Fr., The Sorcerer's Apprentice), whose modernist harmonies

were to have a pronounced influence
on composers such as Stravinsky and
Schoenberg.

Duke Bluebeard's Castle BLUE-
BEARD'S CASTLE.

Duke, Vernon (Dukelsky, Vladimir
Alexandrovich) (1903–69) Russian-
born Amer. composer and songwriter,
trained at the Kiev Conservatory. For
his lighter music and songs he used
the pseudonym Vernon Duke, keeping his Russian name for his more serious works. He maintained both
styles into the 1960s. His most successful popular works were the musical *Cabin in the Sky* (1940), written
for an all-black cast and choreographed by Balanchine, and the music
for the film *April in Paris* (1952).

Dukes of Dixieland an Amer. jazz
group founded in 1948 in New Orleans by Fred and Frank Assunto.
They have made many recordings, occasionally with guest artists, incl.
Louis Armstrong.

dulcian 1, *also,* **curtal** early one-piece
form of the BASSOON, used as a substitute for the bass shawm. **2,** DUL-
CIANA.

dulciana a soft diapason ORGAN STOP
used for accompaniment of solo
stops.

dulcimer a BOARD ZITHER similar to
the PSALTERY and dating from the
15th c. It has no keyboard and is
played with hammers or by plucking.
Most dulcimers are portable, but
there are some concert models with
stands and damper pedals. See *illus.*,
p. 134. See CIMBALOM.

dulcitone a CELESTE-like instrument
in which hammers strike tuning
forks.

Dumbarton Oaks Concerto popular
name for the concerto in E-flat major
for 15 instruments (1938) by Stravinsky, named for the estate of R.W. Bliss
near Washington, D.C., where the
work was premiered.

dumka (Czech.; pl., *dumky*) a lament
or a slow movement that is elegiac or
melancholy.

Dumky Trio the piano trio in E minor, Op. 90 (1890–1), by Dvořák.

Appalachian dulcimer

Dulcimer

dump an 16th- and 17th-c. instrumental elegy or lament. Dumps were often written as memorials to persons mentioned in their titles.

Duncan, (Robert) Todd (1903–) Amer. baritone, trained at Butler U. and Columbia Teachers College. He was the first black member of the New York City Opera (from 1945) and the orig. Porgy in Gershwin's *Porgy and Bess* (1935). He also sang leading roles in Duke's *Cabin in the Sky* and Weill's *Lost in the Stars*. He has taught at Howard U., the Curtis Institute and privately, and has toured widely as a recitalist.

dunce notes see SHAPE-NOTE.

Dunn, Mignon (1931–) Amer. dramatic mezzo-soprano, stud. of Karin Branzell. She has sung at the Metropolitan Opera since 1958 in more than 50 roles, incl. Amneris (*Aida*), Brangäne (*Tristan and Isolde*) and Delilah.

Dunn, Thomas (Burt) (1925–) Amer. conductor, trained at the Peabody Conservatory, Harvard and the Amsterdam Conservatory. He was director of the Church of the Incarnation in New York and the Cantata Singers and founded the Festival Orch. of New York (1959–69). He was director of the HANDEL AND HAYDN SOCIETY in Boston (1967–87), where he presented programs covering a wide variety of periods and styles.

Dunstable, John (?1390–1453) English composer. Almost nothing is known of his life, but the fact that so much of his music survives is an indication of his fame in his own time. His surviving works incl. Mass settings and motets, many of them isorhythmic, and a few secular songs.

duo a DUET, esp. one for two instruments.

Duparc, (Marie Eugène) Henri (1848–1933) French composer, stud. of Franck. Between 1868 and 1884 he composed 13 songs (all other works he destroyed). He abandoned composition entirely in 1885, the victim of a neurasthenic condition resulting in a pathologically heightened sensitivity. This extreme sensitivity he also possessed as an artist, and his aesthetic sense was far in advance of his time.

duple meter *or* **time** two beats in a bar. See METER.

duplet a group of two notes played in the time normally required by three, thus usu. occurring in compound time. Duplets may be notated either with a bracket and a 2 (similar to triplet notation) or with dotted notes ($\frac{3}{4}$ ♩♩♩♩·♩·♩·♩♩.)

Du Pré, Jacqueline (1945–85) English cellist, stud. of William Pleeth, Tortelier and Rostropovich. Her playing career, which marked her as an expressive artist with a virtuosic technique, was cut short by multiple sclerosis in 1973. She was married to the pianist and conductor DANIEL BARENBOIM.

Dupré, Marcel (1886–1971) French organist, composer and teacher, stud.

of his father and of Guilmant, Vierne and Widor. He won the Prix de Rome in 1914. He performed the complete organ works of Bach in 1920 at the Paris Conservatoire, establishing his reputation. He was organist at St. Sulpice in Paris and, from 1926–54, professor at the Paris Conservatoire where his pupils included Messiaen and Alain. His many compositions for organ incl. not only the traditional liturgical and secular forms, but also symphonic works.

Duprez, Gilbert-Louis (1806–96) French tenor, famous for being the first tenor to sing a sustained high C in chest voice (in Rossini's *William Tell*). He was also an active teacher and composer.

dur (Ger.) MAJOR.

Durand [dü′rā] French music publishing firm founded by Marie Auguste Durand (1830–1909). The firm first issued most of the works of Debussy, Ravel, Fauré, Saint-Saëns and many other French composers, and the firm's *Édition classique* is a major collection of international masterworks.

Duran Duran English rock band formed in 1978 in Birmingham, whose style combined new wave and disco. Their name comes from a character in the Roger Vadim film *Barbarella*.

duration the length of a musical sound, traditionally indicated by use of proportional note shapes. In 20th-c. music duration is frequently indicated by nondurational note signs combined with spatial-temporal notation or by indications of the duration of a section, usu. in seconds. In ensemble music, new techniques have been developed for conductors to indicate such durations, such as conducting a large circle, which, when closed, marks off a unit of time. See NOTE, GRAPHIC NOTATION.

Durchführung [′doorç″fü-rûng] (Ger.) DEVELOPMENT.

durchkomponiert [-kōm-pō″nērt] (Ger.) THROUGH-COMPOSED.

durezza [doo′rāt-sä] (It., harshness) a term used in the 16th c. to describe DISSONANCE; later it came to denote a style of keyboard writing exploring chromaticism with discords and suspensions (*ligature*).

Duruflé, Maurice (1902–86) French organist and composer, stud. of Tournemire and Dukas. He was appointed organist of St. Etienne-du-Mont in 1930 and professor of harmony at the Paris Conservatoire in 1943, holding the post until 1969. His *Réquiem* (1947) is often performed.

Dushkin, Samuel (1891–1976) Polish born Amer. violinist, stud. of Auer and Kreisler. He is best known for his collaborations with Stravinsky, who wrote the Violin Concerto (1931) and *Duo concertante* (1932) for him, and who toured and recorded with Dushkin in the 1930s.

Dutilleux, Henri [dü-tē′yø] (1916–) French composer, stud. of Busser. He won the Prix de Rome in 1938. He worked at the French Radio (1943–63), taught at the École Normale de Musique (1961–70) and at the Paris Conservatoire (from 1970). His earlier works show the influence of Ravel, but his style later became very individualistic. His relatively small output includes two symphonies (the second was premiered in Boston by Münch), instrumental chamber music and songs.

Dutoit, Charles [dü′twä] (1936–) Swiss conductor. He studied at the Lausanne Conservatory and with Münch at Tanglewood. He has conducted the Lausanne Bach Choir, the Berne SO and the Zürich Tonhalle Orch. and has been musical dir. of the Montreal SO since 1978. He is noted for his performance of 20th-c. repertoire, esp. the works of Stravinsky.

Duval, Denise (1921–) French soprano, made famous by her role in Poulenc's *Les mamelles de Tirésias* (1947). She also sang in the Paris premiere of Poulenc's operas *Les dialogues des Carmélites* and *La voix humaine,* and was noted for her interpretation of Mélisande and other French roles. She retired in 1965.

dux (Lat.) SUBJECT. Cf. COMES.

Dvořák, Antonin (Leopold) (1841–1904) Czech composer, trained at the Prague Organ School, one of the outstanding composers of the Czech nationalist movement. In 1892 he became director of the National Conservatory of Music in New York. From this American stay resulted the Symphony No. 9 "From the New World"—inspired by spirituals sung to him at his request by a student at the conservatory, Harry T. Burleigh—as well as other "American" works. In 1896 he returned to the Prague Conservatory and spent his final years in Prague. Dvořák's extensive output includes works in all forms, of which his symphonies, chamber music and sacred and secular choral works (esp. the *Stabat Mater* and the *Requiem*) are most often performed.

dyad a two-note CHORD.

Dylan, Bob (Zimmerman, Robert Allan) (1941–) Amer. songwriter, singer and performer on guitar, harmonica and piano. He formed his own rock band in 1955, but under the influence of Woody Guthrie, Pete Seeger and others, he began to produce a more blues-oriented music and was an important figure in the folk-song revival of the 1960s. Several of his works became theme songs for protest movements, notably "Blowin' in the Wind" (1962) and "The Times They Are A-changin' " (1964). In the late 1960s he integrated rock style with folk, using an electric guitar and rock band accompaniment. His more recent music has returned to his earlier folk style, combined with country-music elements.

dynamics the aspect of musical expression concerned with changes in volume of a sound, esp. in time, as in *crescendo* and *diminuendo* or sudden contrasts between *piano* and *forte*, but also simultaneously, as in the balance between different parts of a polyphonic whole. It can be assumed that there have always been dynamic variations in the performance of music of all ages, but markings indicating such changes (in classical scores, traditionally in Italian) were rare until the 16th c. and were not highly developed until the late 17th c. Even at their most precise, however, dynamic markings can only partially indicate the shadings actually employed in performance, which have to be left to the discretion of the performer. See EXPRESSION MARKS.

Dzerzhinsky, Ivan (Ivanovich) (1909–1978) Russian composer, stud. of Mikhail Gnesin in Moscow and Asafiev in Leningrad, among others. His best-known work is the opera *Tikhiy Don* (Russ., Quiet flows the Don), a work recognized for its propaganda value by Stalin, who praised it.

E

E 3rd note of the scale of C major. See PITCH.

eagle rock an Afr.-Amer. jazz dance, performed to traditional jazz.

Eagles, The Amer. country-rock band formed in Los Angeles in 1971. The group disbanded in 1981 after a highly successful career.

Eames, Emma (Hayden) (1865–1952) Shanghai-born Amer. lyric soprano, stud. of Mathilde Marchesi in Paris. She made her debut in Paris as Juliet in Gounod's *Roméo et Juliette*, a role she studied, along with Marguerite in *Faust*, with the composer. Her Amer. debut was in New York in 1891, and she sang with the Metropolitan Opera until 1909. In her later years she concentrated on recitals and concert tours.

ear training the process of training one's ability to identify pitches and harmonies, to reproduce rhythms correctly and to sightsing. There are a number of standardized methods for teaching ear training, the most widely used of which is SOLFEGGIO.

early music a popular term for the music of earlier centuries, usu. understood to include the Middle Ages, Renaissance and Baroque.

Earth, Wind and Fire Amer. rock band formed in 1969 in Chicago by singer-drummer Maurice White, who had previously worked with Ramsey Lewis and Muddy Waters. Their music is eclectic, their stage shows elaborate.

East, Thomas (c1535–1608) English printer of music by Byrd, Morley, Dowland, Farnaby and many others.

East Coast jazz a hard-driving style of jazz of the 1950s and 1960s, characterized by dark, heavy timbres and blues melodic figures. The chief exponents of the style are Art Blakey, Horace Silver and Cannonball Adderley. Also, *hard bop, funky jazz, post-bop.*

Easter Oratorio oratorio, *Kommt, eilet und laufet*, BWV 249 (1732–5), by J.S. Bach, a revision by the composer of an earlier cantata (1725).

Easter Parade song (1933) by Irving Berlin from the Broadway show *As Thousands Cheer.*

Eastman School of Music a conservatory founded in 1912, assuming its present name in 1917 when George Eastman, of the Eastman Kodak Company, took over. The school became part of the U. of Rochester in 1921.

Easton, Florence (Gertrude) (1882–1955) English-born Canadian soprano, stud. of Elliott Haslam. She sang at the Berlin, Hamburg and Chicago Operas, and for 12 seasons (from 1917) at the Metropolitan Opera. She taught at the Juilliard School from the late 1930s and retired in 1943. Her roles incl. Santuzza (*Cavalleria rusticana*), Carmen and Isolde. She made many recordings in the 1920s and 1930s.

Eaton, John Charles (1935–) Amer. composer, stud. of Babbitt, Cone and Sessions. His early career was as a jazz pianist and he has taught at Indiana U. since 1971. His compositions make extensive use of microtonal tunings and of electronic media combined with conventional instruments. He has written several operas, chamber music and vocal works.

Ebony Concerto work for clarinet and jazz band (1946) by Stravinsky, written for Woody Herman. *Ebony stick* is a slang term for the clarinet.

Eccard, Johannes (1553–1611) German composer, trained at the Lateinschule in Mühlhausen and with Lassus in Munich. Eccard's compositions are largely concerned with the Lutheran chorale; he produced many chorale motets and four-part arrangements of chorale tunes. His works also incl. odes and occasional works.

eccentric dance a type of specialty, usu. solo, dancing performed to jazz music, involving contortions, shake dancing, etc.

échappée [ā-shä′pā] (Fr., escaped [note]) an unaccented NONHARMONIC NOTE falling between a note and its resolution, but approaching the resolution note from the opposite direction from that of the resolving note.

echo 1, the imitation in music of the natural echo, found both in vocal and in instrumental music, with answering a louder note or passage by its repetition in a very soft dynamic. Such effects are often inferred in music of earlier eras, such as the Baroque, when phrases or partial phrases are repeated, even if no specific dynamic indication is given. **2**, *also*, **echo song** a work making extensive use of the echo technique.

echo organ a division of an organ located away from the main pipes and fitted with softer stops appropriate for echo effects.

Eckhard, Jacob, Sr. (1757–1833) German-born Amer. organist, composer and teacher. His collection of service music and anthems for St. Michael's Church in Charleston, SC, is one of the earliest extant manuscripts containing Episcopal music.

Eckhardt-Gramatté, S(ophie)-C(armen) (Friedman-Kochevskoy, Sonia de) (1902–74) Russian-born Canadian violinist, pianist and composer. She studied piano with her mother (a student of Rubinstein), at the Paris Conservatoire and composition with Trapp in Berlin. She toured with Edwin Fischer in a piano duo in the 1920s. From 1939 to 1953 she lived in Vienna, winning many composition prizes and commissions, then came to Canada in 1953. Her works incl. orchestral concertos and sym-

phonies, chamber works and sonatas.

Eckstine, Billy (Eckstein, William Clarence; "Mr. B") (1914–   ) Amer. singer and bandleader, trained at Howard U. in Washington, D.C. He was with Earl Hines's band from 1939 to 1943, forming his own band in 1944, a visionary blend of blues and bop. Since 1947 he has performed as a solo popular singer.

eclogue a pastoral piece. The term orig. referred to a literary work, usu. in the form of a dialogue. During the 16th and 17th c., eclogues became important forms of music drama, esp. in Spain. In the late 19th c., the term was applied to piano pieces that incorporated pastoral features and dialogue techniques.

École d'Arceuil [ā′kol där′kœē] (Fr.) a circle of composers around Satie in the 1920s, generally anti-Romantic and anti-Wagner. The members were Désormière, Sauguet, Jacob and Cliquet-Pleyel. The name comes from a Paris suburb where Satie lived in his later years.

écossaise [ā-ko′sez] (Fr., Scottish) **1**, a dance in slow triple meter. **2**, a contredanse of the early 19th c. in quick duple meter, of obscure origins. Cf. SCHOTTISCHE.

Ecuatorial work for solo bass, brass, piano, organ, percussion and 2 ondes martenot (1934) by Varèse, one of the earliest works to employ electronic instruments.

Eddy, (Hiram) Clarence (1851–1937) Amer. organist and organ designer who toured extensively in the U.S., Canada and Europe. His virtuosic style elevated the standard of organ playing in America.

Eddy, Nelson (1901–67) Amer. baritone and actor. He sang with the Philadelphia Civic Opera and the Metropolitan Opera, but is best remembered for his roles in Hollywood film musicals, such as *Naughty Marietta* (1933).

Edinburgh Festival an annual summer festival of the arts in Edinburgh, Scotland, inaugurated in 1947 with Rudolf Bing as artistic director.

Edmonton Symphony Orchestra symphony orch. founded in 1920 under conductor Alberta Winston. It lasted until 1932, then was re-formed in 1952 under Lee Hepner. Subsequent conductors were Thomas Rolston, Brian Priestman, Lawrence Leonard, Pierre Hétu and Peter McCoppin.

Edvina, Louise (1878–1948) Canadian soprano, stud. of Jean de Reszke. She sang frequently in London and Paris, but relatively rarely in No. America. Her one appearance at the Metropolitan Opera was opposite Caruso in *Tosca*.

Edwards (née Gerlich), **Clara** (1887–1974) Amer. singer, pianist and composer. Her songs blend the styles of art song and parlor ballad, as in "Into the Night," sung by Ezio Pinza.

Edwards, Gus (1879–1945) Polish-born Amer. composer and impresario. He is best known for his "kiddie discovery shows" in which he promoted Eddie Cantor, George Jessel, Walter Winchell, Ray Bolger, etc. Edwards's life is the subject for the 1940 film *The Star Maker*. His songs incl. "School Days" and "By the Light of the Silvery Moon."

Effinger, Cecil (1914–90) Amer. composer and oboist, stud. of Wagenaar and Boulanger. He was first oboe in the Colorado Springs SO and the Denver SO, has taught at Colorado College and at the U. of Colorado (since 1948) and is the inventor of a music typewriter, the "Musicwriter."

E flat the PITCH (E♭) one half step below E, the enharmonic equivalent of D sharp.

Egk (Mayer), **Werner** (1901–83) German composer, stud. of Orff. He is best known for his theater works, which incl. a dozen operas and ballets, orchestral and vocal works, and a piano sonata.

Egmond, Max (Rudolf) van (1936–) Dutch baritone, trained in Holland. He is known primarily as a concert and recital singer, specializing in the music of the Baroque.

Egmont a tragedy by Goethe for which Beethoven wrote an overture and incidental music, Op. 84 (1810).

Ehrling, Sixten (1918–) Swedish conductor trained in Stockholm at the Royal Academy of Music. He has been conductor of the Stockholm Concert Society in the 1940s, music dir. of the Swedish Royal Opera (1953–70) and of the Detroit SO (1963–73), and head of conducting at the Juilliard School.

1812 Overture concert overture (1882) by Tchaikovsky, commemorating the retreat of Napoleon from Moscow. In its graphic depiction the score employs the Marseillaise and the Russian national anthem, and has optional parts for cannon and military band. The work is frequently played in the U.S. on the Fourth of July as accompaniment to fireworks.

eight-foot stop an ORGAN STOP which sounds the same pitch as written; so called because the lowest pipe of such a stop is approximately 8 feet long. Cf. FOUR-FOOT, SIXTEEN-FOOT.

eighth note a NOTE (♪) with the value of one-eighth of a whole note. Also, (Brit.) *quaver*.

eighth rest a REST (♇) having the value of an EIGHTH NOTE.

eilend ['ī-lənt] (Ger.) hurrying.

Eimert, Herbert (1897–1972) Ger. composer. He founded an electronic studio in Cologne (1951–62) and was coeditor with Stockhausen of the journal *Die Reihe*.

Eine kleine Nachtmusik KLEINE NACHTMUSIK, EINE.

Einem, Gottfried von (1918–) Austrian composer, stud. of Blacher. His best-known works have been for the theater or based on dramatic texts and incl. the operas *Dantons Tod* (1947) and *Der Prozess* (1953, based on the novel by Kafka), the ballet *Prinzessin Turandot* (1944) and the chorus *Das Stundenlied*, a setting of a text by Brecht.

Einleitung ['īn"lī-tûng] (Ger.) INTRODUCTION.

Einstein on the Beach mixed-media theater work in 4 acts by Glass to his own libretto, in collaboration with

Robert Wilson, the first part of a historical trilogy with *Satyagraha* and *Akhnaten*. Premiere, Avignon 1976.

eis [īs] (Ger.) E sharp.

Eisenbrandt, H(einrich) C(hristian) (Henry) (1790–1861) German-born Amer. manufacturer of woodwind and brass instruments, working mainly in Baltimore. His flutes and clarinets won several awards, incl. the silver medal at the Crystal Palace Exhibition in London, 1851. One of his jeweled clarinets is in the Smithsonian.

eisis (Ger.) E double sharp.

Eisler, Hanns (1898–1962) prolific German composer, stud. of Schoenberg and Webern. His choral and other vocal works of the 1920s, many in a diatonic brand of serialism, were very popular with left-wing European groups. In 1930 he began a lifelong collaboration with Brecht, producing in that year the teaching pieces *Die Massnahme* and *Die Mutter*. From 1937 to 1942 he taught at the New School for Social Research in New York, then moved in 1942 to Hollywood to teach at the U. of Southern California. In 1948 he was brought before the Committee on Un-American Activities and extradited, settling in Berlin. In his final years, Eisler wrote music for theatrical and large-scale public performance, as well as film scores and songs.

eisteddfod [ī'steth-vod] (Welsh) a Welsh competitive festival of music and literature dating from the Middle Ages.

ekphonetic notation a type of medieval notation used to facilitate the chanting of the lessons and Gospel in the Roman Catholic tradition. The musical indications are as yet undeciphered.

Elder, Mark (Philip) (1947–) English conductor, trained at Cambridge. He was an assistant conductor and chorus master at Glyndebourne (1970–2) and has conducted most British orchestras. He became musical dir. of the English National Opera in 1979.

Eldridge, (David) Roy (1911–89) Amer. swing jazz trumpeter and singer, a link between the swing era and modern jazz as well as between Louis Armstrong and Dizzy Gillespie. He played with Teddy Hill and Fletcher Henderson, then achieved national prominence as a soloist with Gene Krupa and Artie Shaw. In the 1960s he was often associated with Coleman Hawkins and from 1966 led his own quintet.

electric guitar an electrically amplified GUITAR. There are three fundamental types: a) the standard instrument, which may be an acoustic, hollow-body guitar with a pickup added or a solid-body instrument with no resonating chamber, pioneered in jazz and now standard in jazz and rock music; b) the so-called HAWAIIAN or STEEL GUITAR, a fretless instrument used primarily in country and western music; c) and the electrical bass guitar, a four-stringed instrument used as a replacement for the acoustic double bass.

The use of amplification has permitted the development of the guitar as a solo instrument in an ensemble, as pioneered by jazz guitarist CHARLIE CHRISTIAN. It also permits special effects, through electronic modification of the basic sound, as with the "fuzz" converter, the "wah-wah" effect, feedback and phasing.

electric jazz a general term for the jazz of the 1970s that employs electrical and electronic instruments and synthesizers in addition to the standard instruments. Also, *jazz-rock*. Cf. FUSION.

Electric Light Orchestra, The English rock band formed in Birmingham in 1971, whose music is characterized by an orchestral texture incorporating electronic effects and rich string sound. Abbr., *ELO*.

electric piano a piano or pianolike instrument that produces sound by electro-acoustic means, usu. without a soundboard, and amplifies it through a loudspeaker. The earliest instruments, which employed strings

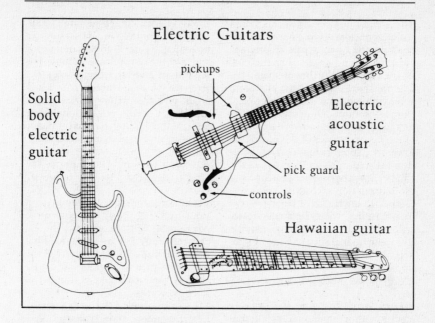

Electric Guitars

Solid body electric guitar

pickups

Electric acoustic guitar

pick guard

controls

Hawaiian guitar

and microphones, were made in the 1930s. Modern electric or electronic pianos do not use strings but synthesize the piano sound electronically. The highly complex nature of the grand piano sound has been particularly difficult to reproduce, and only recently have instruments begun to appear that closely approximate the acoustic instrument.

electric rock FUSION.

electronic instrument *also,* **electrophone** an instrument that produces its sound by means of synthesis or that modifies acoustically produced sound electronically. For examples, see TELHARMONIUM, THEREMIN, ONDES MARTENOT, TRAUTONIUM, ELECTRIC PIANO, ELECTRONIC ORGAN, ELECTRIC GUITAR.

electronic music *also,* **electroacoustic music** music produced by electronic means, usu. by means of a SYNTHESIZER with or without the aid of a computer. Electronically produced music can be composed of natural sounds manipulated electronically (MUSIQUE CONCRÈTE), or of electronically synthesized sounds recorded and combined on tape or produced

live in performance. Cf. COMPUTER MUSIC.

electronic organ an electronic instrument designed to imitate the sound of a pipe organ. There are several methods of production. The Hammond Organ (1935) produced each pitch separately by means of a tone

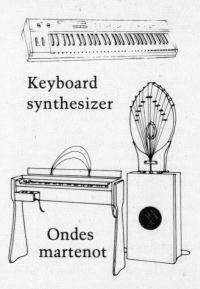

Keyboard synthesizer

Ondes martenot

wheel and allowed the combination of different notes of the harmonic series selected by drawbars to produce a complex tone. In another method, as used in the Wurlitzer organ, the vibrations of brass reeds are picked up and amplified. The most recent electronic instruments employ oscillators to produce the individual pitches of the upper register of the organ, the lower registers being derived electronically from them. Because of the smaller amount of space required and the elimination of tuning problems, electronic organs have been popular in situations where finances are restricted or, as in outdoor installations, where inability to control temperatures makes sensitive pipe organs impractical.

electrophone ELECTRONIC INSTRUMENT.

Electro String Instrument Company electric-guitar manufacturing company founded in 1930 in CA, best known for its Rickenbacker series, named after the company's founder, Adolph Rickenbacker.

elegy a song or instrumental work expressing lamentation or sorrow for the loss of someone through death.

Elegy for Young Lovers opera in 3 acts by Henze to a libretto by W.H. Auden and Chester Kallman. Premiere, Schwetzingen 1961 (in German). The poet Mittenhofer is responsible for the death of two young lovers.

Elektra (Ger., Electra) tragic opera in one act by Richard Strauss to a libretto in German by Hugo von Hofmannsthal based on the play by Sophocles. Premiere, Dresden 1909. Elektra, through the action of her brother Orestes, takes revenge on her mother and her mother's lover for the murder of Agamemnon, Elektra's father.

elevation a type of SLIDE (1,).

eleventh an INTERVAL composed of an octave and a fourth.

eleventh chord a NINTH CHORD with a third superimposed.

Elgar, Sir Edward (William) (1857–1934) English composer, largely self-taught as a musician. He was active in Worcester until 1890, conducting and playing with local groups. His reputation grew steadily, esp. on the strength of his cantata *The Black Night* and the oratorio *The Light of Life* (*Lux Christi*). His national fame was established by the performance in 1899 of the *Enigma Variations*. The *Sea Pictures* were premiered in the same year and the oratorio *The Dream of Gerontius* the following year.

The works produced in the London years from 1912 to 1923 included the ode *The Music Makers* and the orchestral study *Falstaff*. After his final move back to Worcester in 1923, he produced little new music but did record as conductor a large number of his own works.

Elias, Rosalind (1931–) Amer. mezzo-soprano, trained at the New England Conservatory and in Italy with Luigi Ricci. Her Metropolitan Opera debut was in 1954. She premiered the role of Erika in Barber's *Vanessa* and Charmian in his *Antony and Cleopatra*. She is noted esp. for her performance of Carmen and Baba the Turk (*The Rake's Progress*) and various travesti roles.

Elisir d'amore, L' [ā-lē′zēr dä′mō-rä] (It.) ELIXIR OF LOVE, THE.

Elijah (Ger., *Elias*) oratorio, Op. 70 (1846), by Mendelssohn, to a text from the Old Testament selected by Julius Schubring. First performed in Birmingham, England.

Elixir of Love, The (It., *L'Elisir d'amore*) comic opera in 2 acts by Donizetti to a libretto in Italian by Felice Romani. Premiere, Milan 1832. The peasant Nemorino finally wins the hand of his beloved Adina.

Elkan-Vogel Amer. music publisher founded in 1928 in Philadelphia. Composer Vincent Persichetti was chief editor from 1952 until his death. It was particularly noted as the Amer. agent for a number of important French publishers. The firm was acquired by Theodore Presser Co. in 1970.

Ellington, Duke (Edward Kennedy) (1899–1974) Amer. pianist, prolific composer, arranger and bandleader, noted for his innovative approach to scoring. His father was a butler at the White House. After his move to New York in 1923 his band played first at the Kentucky Club on Broadway, then at the famed Cotton Club in Harlem. From 1930 on he made many recordings and his experiments with extended jazz compositions also began in this period with the *Creole Rhapsody*. From 1943 to 1952 he presented a series of annual concerts at Carnegie Hall in New York, at which a number of large-scale works were tried out—esp. the five-section "tone parallel" entitled *Black, Brown and Beige*—encouraged as he was by the capabilities of the long-playing record.

In the last two decades of his life, he made many foreign tours and wrote several film scores, incl. the influential score for *Anatomy of a Murder* (1959), and concentrated on sacred music and full-length suites.

Ellington, Mercer (Kennedy) (1919–) Amer. jazz trumpeter, composer and arranger, son of DUKE ELLINGTON. He has led his own bands from 1939, was a road manager for Cootie Williams in the early 1940s and a radio disc jockey from 1962 to 1965, as well as working on and off for his father. He took over the Duke's band after his father's death.

Ellis, Don(ald Johnson) (1934–78) Amer. jazz trumpeter, composer and bandleader. He played with Charlie Barnet, Maynard Ferguson and George Russell as well as with his own trio. As a composer, he brought contemporary techniques to jazz, including microtonality and exotic time signatures, and revolutionized the use of the big band.

Elman, Mischa (1891–1967) Russian-born Amer. violinist, stud. of Leopold Auer. He came to the U.S. in 1911. In 1926 he formed the Elman String Quartet. He was esp. noted for his sensuous tone.

Elman, "Ziggy" (Harry Finkelman) (1914–68) Amer. jazz trumpeter and clarinetist from Philadelphia. He played with Benny Goodman (1936–40) and Tommy Dorsey (1940–47), then tried unsuccessfully to head his own band. In later years he worked in radio and films and made recordings.

El Salon Mexico SALON MEXICO, EL.

Elston, Arnold (1907–71) Amer. composer, stud. of Goldmark, Webern and Arthur Fiedler. He taught at the U. of Oregon (1941–58) and the U. of California at Berkeley (1958–71). His works incl. the chamber opera *Sweeney Agonistes* (1948–50), vocal and instrumental chamber music, and some orchestral works.

Elvira, Pablo (1941–) Puerto Rican baritone. His Metropolitan Opera debut was in 1979 as Tonio in *I Pagliacci*. He was a faculty member at Indiana U. from 1966 to 1974. Among his roles are Figaro, Tonio, Rigoletto and Germont (*La Traviata*).

Elwell, Herbert (1898–1974) Amer. critic, composer and teacher, stud. of Bloch and Boulanger. His best-known work, the ballet *The Happy Hypocrite*, was composed during his stay in Italy upon winning the American Prix de Rome (1923). He became head of composition at the Cleveland Institute of Music in 1928, retiring in 1948 to devote his time to composition and criticism.

embellishment non-structural decoration, either written or improvised, added to music for the purpose of producing variety. See ORNAMENTATION, IMPROVISATION.

embouchure [ä-boo'shür] (Fr.) **1**, the position of the mouth and lips in playing a wind instrument. **2**, the mouthpiece of a wind instrument.

Emerson, Billy (Redmond, William Emerson) (1846–1902) Belfast-born Amer. minstrel performer. His performing company—Emerson, Allen and Manning's Minstrels—was based in New York City during the late 1860s and early 1870s, then in San

Francisco during the later 1870s and 1880s.

Emerson, Lake and Palmer English progressive rock trio formed in 1970 that was famous for its flamboyant concerts, featuring dazzling light effects. The band broke up in 1979.

Emerson String Quartet quartet founded in 1976 as the professional continuation of a student ensemble at Juilliard. Its international debut was at the Spoleto Festival in 1981. The quartet specializes in 20th-c. chamber music.

Emmett (Emmit), Dan(iel Decatur) (1815–1904) Amer. composer and minstrel performer, noted mainly for his banjo tunes and WALK-AROUNDS. His most famous walk-around is "I wish I was in Dixie's land," first performed in 1859 by the entire cast of Dan Bryant's Minstrels at Mechanics Hall in New York.

Emperor Concerto a popular name for the Piano Concerto No. 5 in E-flat major, Op. 73 (1808), by Beethoven.

Emperor Jones opera in 2 acts by Gruenberg to a libretto by Kathleen de Jaffa, from the play by Eugene O'Neill. Premiere, New York 1933. A black ex-Pullman porter and escaped convict, ruler of a Caribbean island, is forced to flee when his people threaten revolt.

Emperor Quartet a popular name for the string quartet in C, Op. 76 No. 3 (1799), by Haydn, so called for its slow movement, which consists of variations on the EMPEROR'S HYMN.

Emperor's Hymn anthem with music (1797) by Haydn, orig. to a text by Lorenz Leopold Haschka, a patriotic Austrian hymn and the Austrian national anthem until 1947. The melody, with different words, was the national anthem of the Federal Republic of Germany (West Germany). Haydn's tune is also a popular hymn tune with various texts, one of which is "Glorious things of Thee are spoken." Cf. DEUTSCHLAND ÜBER ALLES.

empfindsamer Stil [emp'fint-zä-mər shtēl] (Ger., expressive style) an aesthetic of 18th-c. north Germany, epit-

omized in the works of C.P.E. Bach, according to which the main mission of music is to touch the heart through sensibility, sentimentality and *galanterie*. Cf. STYLE GALANT.

Empfindung [emp'fin-dûng] (Ger.) feeling.

Empire Brass Quintet chamber ensemble founded in 1971 at Tanglewood. Its international debut was at Carnegie Hall in 1976. The ensemble has been in residence at Boston U. since 1976.

emporté [ä-pôr'tä] (Fr.) passionate.

empressé [ä-pre'sä] (Fr.) hurrying.

enchaînez [ä-she'nä] (Fr.) ATTACCA.

en chamade [ä shä'mäd] (Fr.) a descriptive phrase indicating a rank of organ pipes (usu. a solo trumpet stop) placed horizontally in front of the organ case.

Encina, Juan del (1468–1529) Spanish poet, courtier and composer of villancicos, and an important early figure in the history of Spanish theater. He served the Duke of Alba in Salamanca until 1498, during which time most of his artistic work was produced. The rest of his life was spent in Rome and León.

encore **1,** a request (as by an audience, through clapping, shouting "encore," etc.) for further performance. **2,** a piece performed as the result of such a request, usu. after the completion of a scheduled program.

en dehors [ä də'or] (Fr., outside) an indication to emphasize or bring out a certain pitch or line.

endless melody a term coined by RICHARD WAGNER to describe a melody unhindered by interrupting cadences.

end pin **1,** a retractable steel or wooden spike, invented in the mid-19th c., attached to the bottom of a cello to support the instrument. **2,** a pin in the end of a guitar, mandolin, or other stringed instrument, used to secure a strap.

Enescu, George (Enesco, Georges) (1881–1955) Romanian composer, violinist, conductor and teacher, trained in Vienna and Paris. In 1902 he formed a piano trio with Louis Fournier and Alfredo Casella, and in 1904 he founded the Enesco Quartet. He taught at the École Normale in Paris, the American Conservatory at Fontainebleau, and the Accademia Chigiana in Siena, Italy. His students incl. Menuhin, Ferras and Grumiaux. He also worked to stimulate musical activity in his native Romania. His works incl. an opera (*Oedipe*), choral works and songs, five symphonies and other orchestral works, and chamber music.

Enfance du Christ, L' [lä'fäs dü krēst] (Fr., The Childhood of Christ) a sacred trilogy for soloists, chorus and orch., Op. 25 (1854), by Berlioz, who also wrote the text.

Enfant et les sortilèges, L' [lä'fä ä le sor-tē'lezh] (Fr., The Child and the Magic Spells) fantasy opera in 2 parts by Ravel to a libretto by Colette. Premiere, Monte Carlo 1925. The opera concerns an ill-behaved child who is first punished by the animals and inanimate objects that he has harmed but is ultimately saved by his concern for one of the animals when it is injured.

Engel, (A.) Lehman (1910–82) Amer. composer and conductor, stud. of Goldmark and Sessions. He wrote incidental music for many stage productions and was musical dir. of many others. He also worked for Columbia Pictures, the League of Composers, and the Composers and Lyricists Workshop. His nontheatrical music includes 2 symphonies, a piano sonata, a cello sonata and vocal works.

English Chamber Orchestra an orch. founded in 1948 as the Goldsborough Orch. and renamed in 1960. It was associated for many years with the Aldeborough Festival.

English flute RECORDER.

English guitar a type of 18th-c. CITTERN with a flat back and 6 courses of metal strings.

English horn a tenor OBOE, a transposing instrument playing a fifth lower than the oboe and with a darker, more muted tone. It is often used as a replacement for the oboe da caccia in baroque music.

English National Opera an opera company based in London, known until 1974 as the SADLER'S WELLS OPERA. Abbr., ENO.

English Opera Group an opera company founded in 1947 by Benjamin Britten and for which he wrote many of his chamber operas. It was taken over by Covent Garden in 1971 and renamed the English Music Theatre Company in 1975.

English Suites a set of six keyboard suites, BWV 806-11 (?1715), by J.S. Bach. Cf. FRENCH SUITES.

enharmonic 1, in ancient Greek music, of a scale or GENUS employing quarter tones. Of a tetrachord, comprising a major third and two quarter tones. Cf. CHROMATIC. **2**, designating notes written ("spelled") differently but sounding the same pitch on instruments tuned to the tempered scale. E.g. C♯ = D♭, B♯ = C = D♭♭.

enharmonic keyboard a keyboard having separate keys for various enharmonic equivalents and designed to accommodate tuning systems in which the written equivalents are not exactly the same pitch, as in MEANTONE TUNING, where there can be as much as a quarter-step difference between (for example) D♯ and E♭. The term is also used, somewhat inappropriately, for keyboards designed to play microtones.

Enigma Variations "Variations on an original theme for orchestra," Op. 36 (1898–9), by Elgar. The word *enigma* appears on the first page of the music and refers to the fact that each variation is a representation of the character of a friend of Elgar's, identified only by initials or nicknames. It also refers to the existence of a basic theme which is never heard but which underlies the entire set of variations.

enigmatic canon RIDDLE CANON.

enigmatic scale SCALA ENIGMATICA.

Eno, Brian (Eno, Brian Peter George St. John de Baptiste de la Salle)

(1948–) English rock musician, noted for his experiments in recorded live sounds (ambient music). He was a founder of the rock band Roxy Music in 1971, then in 1973 he concentrated on solo albums.

Enriquez(-Salazar), Manuel (1926–) Mexican violinist, teacher and composer, stud. of Ignacio Camarena, of Mennin at the Juilliard School and of Wolpe. He was one of the first No. Americans commissioned by the Donaueschingen Festival and is dir. of the Mexico City Conservatory.

En Saga SAGA, EN.

ensalada (Sp., salad) a type of 16th-c. Spanish QUODLIBET. Also, *fricasée* (Fr.).

ensemble 1, a musical grouping of more than two instruments or parts. **2**, the quality of togetherness in the concerted playing of a musical group.

Ensemble InterContemporain (Fr.) a chamber orch. founded in 1976 at IRCAM in Paris by Boulez and Peter Eötvös, specializing in the performance of 20th-c. music.

Entführung aus dem Serail, Die [ent′fü-rûng ows däm se′rī] (Ger.) ABDUCTION FROM THE SERAGLIO, THE.

entr'acte (Fr.) a musical piece performed between two acts of a play or opera.

entrée [ä′trä] (Fr.) in the 17th and 18th c.: **1**, a short composition in marchlike rhythm, usu. in two repeated parts, accompanying a procession in an opera or ballet. **2**, the opening movement of an opera, after the overture. **3**, a ballet movement in a divertissement.

entremés [en-tre′mäs] (Sp.) a type of 17th-c. Spanish comic INTERMEZZO, performed between the acts of a larger theatrical work.

Entremont, Philippe [′ä-trə-mõ] (1934–) French pianist and conductor, stud. of Marguerite Long. He has made many recordings, esp. of French music, and was conductor of the Denver SO from 1986 until its dissolution.

entry the beginning of a thematic statement anywhere in a work; also, the reentrance of a part that has been resting.

envelope an outline of the variations in amplitude of a sound in time as illustrated by a graph.

EP EXTENDED PLAY.

epicede *also*, **epicedium** a funeral song or ode; ELEGY.

epic opera a type of opera developed by Bertolt Brecht that is meant to function as a parable, not as an artistic statement, an example of which is the opera *Mahagonny*, a collaboration with composer Kurt Weill.

epilogue the final section of a piece; CODA.

épinette [ä-pē′net] (Fr.) **1**, SPINET. **2**, VIRGINAL.

épinette de Vosges [võzh] (Fr.) a long, shallow ZITHER, with only some of its strings fretted. It is stopped with a metal rod and plucked with a plectrum.

episode a subsidiary section of a piece, either derived from the main theme, as in a FUGUE, or based on new material, as in a RONDO.

epistle sonata an instrumental work intended to be performed during the Mass, probably between the Epistle and the Gospel. Mozart wrote seventeen, all of which are single allegro movements in sonata form with a short development.

epithalamium (Lat.) **1**, a marriage song in praise of the bride and groom. **2**, an instrumental work intended to be played at a wedding.

equale [ä′kwä-lä] (It.) a work for two or more equal voices or instruments.

equal temperament the division of the octave into twelve equal half steps. In actual practice, piano tuners do not adhere to strict equal temperament, but adjust the octaves in the highest and lowest registers to make them sound right. Cf. TUNING SYSTEMS.

equal voices two or more voices having the same compass.

Erard French piano- and harp-maker and music publisher founded in Paris in 1780 by Sébastien Erard (1752–1831). The firm was responsible for the introduction in piano construction of the double escapement and the agraffe (a metal device that bears down on the string) and for improvements in harp construction, most important of which was the double-action tuning mechanism.

Erb, Donald (1927–) Amer. composer, stud. of Marcel Dick and Bernard Heiden. He was composer-in-residence with the Dallas SO (1968–69), then composer-in-residence and professor of composition at the Cleveland Institute and now teaches at Indiana U. He frequently employs electronic sounds and aleatory techniques, as well as jazz elements, in his works.

Erbach, Christian (1570–1635) German organist, teacher and composer of canzonets, motets and organ music.

Erdödy Quartets the six string quartets, Op. 76 (1797), by Haydn, so named for their dedication to Count Joseph Erdödy, a councillor to the emperor.

Erede, Alberto (1909–) Italian conductor, stud. of Weingartner and Fritz Busch. He has been a staff conductor of the Glyndebourne Festival, chief conductor of the Turin Radio, and musical dir. of the New London Opera Company. He conducted at the Metropolitan Opera (1950–5), then was general music dir. in Düsseldorf. He has conducted at Bayreuth and has made many operatic recordings.

Erickson, Robert (1917–) Amer. composer and teacher, stud. of Krenek and Sessions. He has taught at several CA institutions, incl. (since 1967) the U. of California at San Diego. His works incl. chamber music, choral music, several concertos, and music for orch. and for tape.

Ernani tragic opera in 4 acts by Verdi to a libretto by Francesco Maria Piave after the play by Victor Hugo. Premiere, Venice 1844. Ernani finally wins the hand of Elvira through the clemency of the emperor but must kill himself when his rival Silva recalls a former promise.

ernst (Ger.) serious.

Eroica Symphony a popular shortening of the composer's own title for the Symphony No. 3 in E-flat Major, Op. 55 (1804), by Beethoven. The work was orig. dedicated to Napoleon, but Beethoven changed the dedication in a rage when Napoleon named himself emperor.

Eroica Variations 15 variations and a fugue in E-flat major for piano solo, Op. 35 (1802), by Beethoven. The theme is the same as that used in the last movement of the EROICA SYMPHONY, from which the variations get their nickname (although they were composed first).

Erwartung [er'vär-tûng] (Ger., Expectation) an operatic monodrama in one act by Schoenberg to a libretto by Marie Pappenheim. Premiere, Prague 1924 (but composed in 1909). The story of a woman searching for her lover, whose dead body she finds in a dark forest. The work is more often performed as a concert piece than as a stage work.

es (Ger.) E FLAT.

Escales [es'käl] (Fr., Ports of Call) symphonic tone poem in 3 movements (1922) by Ibert, depicting the ports of Palermo (Sicily), Nefta (Tunisia) and Valencia (Spain).

escapement the mechanism in the action of a piano that allows the hammer to rebound from the string after striking it before the key has been released.

escape note ECHAPPÉE.

Eschenbach, Christoph (1940–) German conductor and pianist, stud. of Hans Schmidt-Neuhaus and Eliza Hansen. He has concertized throughout the world, playing a wide repertoire from the Baroque through 20th-c. music. He became conductor of the Houston SO in 1989.

Eschig, Max(imilian) (1872–1927) French music publisher. He founded a publishing house in 1907 in Paris, specializing in foreign works.

eses (Ger.) E double flat.

E sharp the PITCH (E♯) one half step

above E, the enharmonic equivalent of F.

Esplanade Concerts an outdoor concert series of pops and light classics inaugurated in Boston in 1929 by ARTHUR FIEDLER.

espr., espress. *abbr.* ESPRESSIVO.

espressivo [ā-sprās′sē-vō] (It.) expressive, with feeling.

essence a dance in slow duple meter performed by black minstrels and characterized by a shuffling step; a precursor of the SOFT SHOE.

Estampes (Fr., Prints) a piano suite (1904) by Debussy depicting in its three movements *Pagodes* (Pagodas), *Soirée dans Grenade* (Evening in Grenada) and *Jardins sous la Pluie* (Gardens in the Rain).

estampie a slow, stomping Provençal round dance, popular from the 12th to 15th c., having repeated sections and a refrain, similar to the RONDEAU. Also, *stantipes.*

Esterházy a noble family of Hungary, noted for their support of music, and in particular, for their patronage of JOSEPH HAYDN. Their ancestral home was in Eisenstadt (part of Hungary until 1921, now in Austria) and their summer residence was in Esterháza (now Fertöd, Hungary).

Estes, Simon (1938–) Amer. bass-baritone, stud. of Charles Kellis. He won the silver medal at the Tchaikovsky Vocal Competition in Moscow in 1966 and has sung in the leading opera houses of the world, as well as in recital. He was the first Afr.-American to sing a major role at Bayreuth (1978).

Estey Organ Co. a firm of reed- and pipe-organ builders, founded in 1846 by H.P. Greene, then bought by Jacob Estey in 1848. The Estey Co. was dissolved in 1956.

estilo (Sp.) a type of Argentine solo song characterized by highly sentimental texts and accompanied by guitar.

estinto (It., dead) extremely soft.

estribillo [ās-trē′bē-lyō] (Sp.) the REFRAIN of various Spanish lyric forms.

Estro armonico, L' (It., Harmonic Caprice) the 12 violin concertos, Op. 3 (1712), by Vivaldi.

Ethiopian opera a 19th-c. term for MINSTREL SHOW.

ethnomusicology the study of the music in oral tradition (i.e., transmitted aurally rather than by writing), primarily of non-Western art music. Areas of study can include folk music of all cultures, music of non-literate and tribal cultures, and music in oral tradition of high cultures, such as the court music of Asian countries. The term was coined in 1950 and replaces the older term "comparative musicology."

ethos (Gk.) a term in ancient Greek music theory referring to the power of music to convey and foster ethical states; specif., the concept that each mode or key conveys a certain feeling or state of mind.

Etler, Alvin (Derald) (1913–73) Amer. oboist, composer and teacher, stud. of Hindemith. After an early career as a professional oboist, he devoted his time to teaching and composition. He taught at Yale and Smith College (MA) and wrote primarily orchestral and instrumental chamber music, esp. works involving winds.

étouffé [ā-too′fā] (Fr., damped) stopped (see STOPPING).

Etting, Ruth (1907–78) Amer. singer and actress, successful as a nightclub torch singer and on Broadway as a star in several editions of the *Ziegfeld Follies.*

étude [ā′tüd] (Fr.) STUDY.

Études d'exécution transcendante [ā′tüd dek-sā′kü-yō trā-sā′dāt] TRANSCENDENTAL ÉTUDES.

Études symphoniques [sē-fo′nēk] SYMPHONIC ÉTUDES.

etwas ['et-väs] (Ger.) somewhat, moderately.

Eugene Onegin romantic opera in 3 acts by Tchaikovsky to a libretto in Russian by the composer and K.S. Shilovsky, based on a poem by Pushkin. Premiere, Moscow 1881. Tatyana, spurned in her offer of marriage by her neighbor Onegin, marries Prince Gremin, leaving Onegin, now in love with her, alone and remorseful.

Eulenburg, Ernst (Emil Alexander) ['oi-lən-bûrk] (1847–1926) German music publisher, whose firm, founded in Leipzig in 1874, is known for its extensive catalog of miniature scores.

eunuch-flute an unusual 17th-c. MIRLITON consisting of a tube, open at one end and closed by a membrane at the other, which when sung into produces a nasal sound at the same pitch as the sung sound.

euouae *abbr.* EVOVAE.

euphone an 8- or 16-foot ORGAN STOP with a free reed producing a soft tone.

euphonium 1, a tenor BUGLE in C or B♭ with a mellow tone and sometimes a double bell, used in brass bands and military bands as a solo instrument. **2**, EUPHONE.

eurythmics see JAQUES-DALCROZE.

Euterpe an org. founded in Copenhagen in 1864 to perform works by young Scandinavian composers.

Evans, Bill (William John) (1929–80) Amer. jazz pianist and composer, a member for a short time of the Miles Davis Sextet (1958), since then performing as leader of his own trio. He is important as an innovator, both of improvisational styles and of harmonic freedom. His style originates in the post-bop language of Bud Powell, with little interest in the experimental idioms of the 1960s and 1970s. Evans has had a lasting influence on later jazz musicians, incl. Chick Corea, Herbie Hancock, Keith Jarrett and Steve Kuhn.

Evans, Sir **Geraint (Llewellyn)** (1922–) Welsh baritone, stud. of Fernando Carpi and Theo Hermann. He was esteemed as a singing actor, esp. in comic roles, such as Falstaff and Beckmesser (*Die Meistersinger*).

Evans, Gil (Green, Ernest Gilmore) (1912–88) Canadian-born jazz composer, arranger and bandleader, self-taught in music. He worked for Claude Thornhill in the early 1940s and extensively for Miles Davis in the 1950s; later he led an innovative and experimental rock-influenced big band.

Evans, Herschel (1909–39) Amer. jazz saxophonist and clarinetist. After some years with various bands, incl. Buck Clayton and Lionel Hampton, he joined the Count Basie Orchestra in 1936, becoming famous as one of the two battling saxes, the other being LESTER YOUNG.

evensong 1, the sixth of the seven CANONICAL HOURS. Cf. VESPERS. **2**, an evening worship service in the Anglican rite. Also, *evening prayer.*

Everett, Asa Brooks (1828–75) Amer. composer, teacher and tunebook compiler. He and his brother L.C. developed the "Everett System" for teaching elementary classes in music.

Everly Brothers an Amer. country-music and rockabilly duo of brothers Don (1937–) and Phil (1939–) Everly, made famous by their recordings of the songs "Bye Bye Love" and "Cathy's Clown." The duo split up in 1973, but reunited recently.

evovae *also*, **euouae** an abbreviation formed from the vowels of the closing words of the *Gloria patri* "seculorum, Amen," which are found in liturgical books of the Roman Catholic rite.

Ewing, Maria (Louise) (1950–) Amer. mezzo-soprano, stud. of Eleanor Steber and Jennie Tourel. Her Metropolitan Opera debut was in 1976 as Cherubino. She is noted for her entrancing stage personality as well as for her lyric voice.

exercise see STUDY.

experimental music a term sometimes used to describe the search for new and original modes of composition, esp. in the 20th c. Among the Amer. pioneers of experimental practice are Ives, Ruggles, Varèse and Cage.

exposition the opening section of a work which introduces the principal theme or themes. Cf. SONATA FORM, FUGUE.

expression 1, the part of musical performance that goes beyond the simple

Expression marks

(see also GLOSSARY, page 609)

reproduction of the pitches and notated rhythms of a work, i.e., DYNAMICS, TEMPO, ARTICULATION and PHRASING. A certain amount of the expression may be indicated in the score by means of EXPRESSION MARKS; the rest is provided by the performer according to his or her musical taste. **2**, the ability of a work to express a certain emotion, state of mind or abstract idea.

expression marks a general term for the various graphic symbols and verbal directions which indicate dynamics, articulation and phrasing in a musical score. Until the 20th c. most verbal directions were in Italian; more recently, composers have frequently used their native language. The range of tempos and esp. of loudness has gradually widened since the Baroque, when often only soft or loud were used, with no gradations indicated.

expressionism a term borrowed from the visual arts to identify an approach to musical expression that avoids the usual concepts of what is beautiful and allows any mode of expression suitable to represent the inner urges of the composer. The term is usually used to refer to the atonal (but not serial) compositions of the Second Viennese School.

extemporize improvise (see IMPROVISATION).

extended dominants DOMINANT SEVENTH CHORDS resolving to other dominant seventh chords, rather than to their expected target chords.

extended play a small phonograph record played at 45 rpm and having a duration of c. 8 minutes. *Abbr.*, EP. Cf. LONG-PLAYING RECORD.

extension organ an organ constructed in such a manner as to allow one rank of pipes to supply multiple octaves for a single key.

Eyeglass Duo the Duo in E-flat major for viola and cello (1796–7) by Beethoven, subtitled *mit zwei obligaten Augengläsern* (Ger., with two obbligato eyeglasses), prob. written to be played by himself and a friend, both of whom wore glasses.

eye music musical notation whose meaning is intended for appreciation by the eye rather than the ear. The most common historical type contrasts the black notes, symbolizing night, darkness and sadness with white notes symbolizing day, light and happiness. Other examples are the romantic 15th-c. rondeau by Baude Cordier, written in the shape of a heart and David del Tredici's 1971 "Mouse's Tale," in the score of which the wind and string parts look like a mouse's tail. Also, *Augenmusik* (Ger.).

F

F 1, fourth note of the scale of C major. See PITCH. **2**, *abbr.* FORTE. **3**, see F CLEF.

fa 1, fourth note of the Guidonian HEXACHORD. **2**, in the FIXED DOH system, the note F. See SOLMIZATION, PITCH.

Faber, Lothar (1925–) German virtuoso oboist and specialist in contemporary music, for whom many new works were written by Maderna, Berio and others. He was solo oboe in the Cologne Radio Orch. and has taught at the Accademia Chigiana in Siena.

Faber & Faber English book publisher, whose music publishing subsidiary, Faber Music, was founded in 1966.

Fabbri, Inez (Schmidt, Agnes) (1831–1909) Austrian-born Amer. soprano and impresario. In 1866, Fabbri gained an international reputation as a result of a publicity war with Adelina Patti in New York. After 1872 she sang exclusively in CA, and in the 1875–6 season she directed and sang in an astonishing 60 operas. After her singing career was over, she founded a company of German actors in San Francisco.

Fabray, Nanette (Fabares, Nanette Theresa) (1922–) Amer. singer and actress of Broadway (*High Button Shoes, Love Life*) and films (*The Band Wagon*).

faburden a style of English improvised polyphony, esp. of the 15th c., in which 3-voice texture is derived from a single melodic line. The plainchant is written out as the middle voice with an upper voice (the *faburden*) following at a perfect 4th above the chant and a lower voice following in parallel 3rds with the chant. Cadences and beginnings of phrases generally are limited to octave and fifth intervals. The words of the chant would be sung simultaneously in all 3 voices. Cf. FAUXBOURDON.

Façade poems by Edith Sitwell recited to musical accompaniment for flute, clarinet, saxophone, trumpet, cello and percussion (1923) by William Walton. The composer later derived two orchestral suites from the work.

facile (Fr., It.) simply, easily.

Fadette Ladies' Orchestra of Boston founded in 1888 by Caroline B. Nichols, the first professional all-woman orch. to achieve national recognition. The group provided performing experience for women, who were barred from the usual all-male orchestras.

fado (Port.) a mournful Portuguese folk song.

F-A-E sonata violin sonata in A minor (1853) written jointly by Albert Dietrich (1st mvt.), Schumann (2nd & 4th mvts.) and Brahms (3rd mvt.). The work was a greeting for Joachim, whose motto was *Frei aber einsam* (Ger., free but alone). Schumann used the movements he wrote as part of his Violin Sonata No. 3 in A minor.

fagotto (It.), **Fagott** (Ger.) BASSOON.

F.A.G.O. *abbr.* fellow of the AMERICAN GUILD OF ORGANISTS.

fah the subdominant of the current key (or its relative major, if the current key is minor), in TONIC SOL-FA.

Fahey, John (Aloysius) (1939–) Amer. folklorist, guitarist, composer and record producer. He founded the mail-order label Tacoma Records and produced rare recordings of traditional blues and country music as well as his own music. He went on to gain modest acclaim as a performer.

Fain (Feinberg), **Sammy** (1902–90) Amer. songwriter for stage and film, whose many projects include *Hellzapoppin'* (1938), *The Jazz Singer* (1953) and *Love Is a Many-Splendored Thing* (1955).

Fair at Sorochinsk, The opera in 3 acts by Mussorgsky to his own libretto in Russian based on an episode from Gogol's *Evenings on a Farm near Dedanka*. Premiere, in concert form, St. Petersburg 1911. The work was left incomplete at the composer's death and has been completed in various versions by Cui, Nicholay Tcherepnin and Josef Blatt. In the Ukraine in the mid-19th c., Tzigane, a gypsy, contrives to make possible the marriage of the peasant girl Parassia to the wealthy Cossack Gritzko.

Fairchild, Blair (1877–1933) Amer. composer, stud. of Widor. He settled in Paris in 1905 and his ballet pantomime, *Dame Libellule* (1919), was the first work by an Amer. composer to be performed at the Paris Opéra.

Fairfax, Robert Fayrfax, Robert.

fairground organ an elaborate Orchestrion used from the mid-19th c. in dance halls, skating rinks and, in a mobile form, in traveling fairs. It is equipped to imitate many orchestral sounds, including percussion.

Fairy Queen, The masque in 5 acts by Purcell to a libretto based on Shakespeare's *A Midsummer Night's Dream*. Premiere, London 1692. The score of the work was lost in 1700, and despite a reward of 20 guineas offered at the time for its recovery, it was not found until 1901, in the library of the Royal Academy of Music in London.

Faith, Percy (1908–76) Canadian-born Amer. conductor, arranger and composer. He recorded many albums for Columbia Records, collaborating with Tony Bennett, Rosemary Clooney, Johnny Mathis, etc. He also composed film scores, incl. *The Oscar* (1966) and *I'd Rather Be Rich* (1964).

fake to improvise, esp. in order to cover up a problem in performance, such as a memory slip.

fake book a collection of standard jazz and pop tunes with chord symbols (see Chord); used by dance- and jazz-band musicians as the basis for improvisation.

fa-la a colloquial English term of the 16th and 17th c. for a popular dance-like part song or ballad characterized by a refrain of nonsense syllables. Cf. Ballett.

falcon [fäl'kō] (Fr.) a type of dramatic soprano found in 19th-c. French grand opera of Meyerbeer, Halévy and others. The name is taken from a star of the Paris Opéra, Marie-Cornélie Falcon (1814–97). Cf. Dugazon.

Falla (y Matheu), Manuel de (1876–1946) Spanish composer, stud. of José Tragó at the Madrid Conservatory and later of Pedrell. He composed zarzuelas in the early 1900s, then went to Paris in 1907, where he made contact with Debussy and Ravel, whose influence combined with his Spanish heritage to produce his characteristic style. At the beginning of World War I he returned to Madrid, then moved to Granada and finally (in 1939) to Argentina, his home until his death. His principal work from 1926 was on the oratorio *Atlántida*, left incomplete. His other works incl. *La vida breve, El amor brujo, El retablo de maese Pedro* and other stage works, *Nights in the Gardens of Spain* for piano and orch., chamber music, piano works, *Seven Popular Spanish Songs* and other vocal works.

false cadence Deceptive cadence.

false relation an apparent conflict between two pitches chromatically separated by a half step, either in the same chord or in adjacent chords. The conflict is made acceptable by making the horizontal motion of each of

(Byrd)

the pitches melodically correct, so that the clash is produced by two voices pursuing their individually logical progressions. The intensity of this clash has been used by composers since the Renaissance as an expressive device.

falsetto (It., false voice) a singing voice extending above the normal singing range, esp. of a tenor, and having a weaker and less rich tone. The male falsettist—also called COUNTERTENOR or male alto—has been used for centuries in male choirs for the alto range, replaced only relatively recently by women in most situations. The technique is still used by men and women in popular music, esp. in the blues, country, gospel and soul music, and also in early music.

falsobordone (It., false bass) a type of chordal recitation used from the 15th to 18th c. primarily for singing psalms in the vesper service. Unlike FAUX-BOURDON, both the It. *falsobordone* and the Sp. *fabordón* use mainly root-position triads in four parts with all voices written out.

Falstaff comic opera in 3 acts by Verdi (his last, written at age 80), Italian libretto by Boito based on Shakespeare's *The Merry Wives of Windsor*. Premiere, Milan 1893. The portly Sir John Falstaff is taught a lesson when he tries to woo two women at once.

familiar style note-against-note homophonic writing in polyphonic music of the 15th and 16th c. See also DISCANT STYLE, LUXURIANT STYLE.

Famous Music Corporation New York firm of music publishers, founded in 1928.

Fanciulla del West, La GIRL OF THE GOLDEN WEST, THE.

Fanciulli, Francesco (1853–1915) Italian-born Amer. bandleader and composer. He succeeded Sousa as leader of the U.S. Marine Band in 1892 and wrote the *Grand March Inaugural* for Grover Cleveland's presidential inauguration. In 1897 he was named leader of the 71st Regiment Band of the New York National Guard and instituted a popular series of concerts in Central Park.

fancy see FANTASIA.

fandango (Sp.) **1**, a lively Spanish courtship dance in triple time performed by a man and a woman with castanets and accompanied by a guitar. See DANCE (*illus.*). **2**, a slow, lamenting gypsy song.

fandur Russ. three-string folk FIDDLE.

fanfare **1**, a flourish of trumpets. **2**, an orchestral passage featuring the brass section.

Fanfare for the Common Man work for brass and percussion (1942) by Copland, commissioned by Eugene Goossens as a wartime fanfare for the Cincinnati SO. Copland included the work in his Symphony No. 3.

Fanny musical by Harold Rome to a book by S.N. Behrman and Joshua Logan, based on a trilogy by Marcel Pagnol. Premiere, New York 1954. César's son, Marius, loves Fanny, but goes to sea; Fanny, being pregnant, agrees to marry César's friend Panisse. The role of César was created by opera star Ezio Pinza.

fantasia **1**, an instrumental composition, usu. for solo instrument, in a free and inventive manner, varying widely in form and style, as befits its name. The term has been in use at least since the 16th c., and the genre has played an important part in instrumental composition of every era. **2**, (*cap.*) an epoch-making animated film (1940) by Walt Disney, a visual cartoon rendering of eight classical selections: Bach's *Toccata and Fugue in D minor*, Tchaikovsky's *Nutcracker Suite*, Dukas's *The Sorcerer's Apprentice*, Stravinsky's *The Rite of Spring*, Beethoven's Symphony No. 6, Ponchielli's *Dance of the Hours* from *La Gioconda*, Mussorgsky's *Night on Bald Mountain* and Schubert's *Ave Maria*. The sound track was recorded by Leopold Stokowski and the Philadelphia Orch., and the narration was by Deems Taylor.

Fantasia on a Theme of Thomas Tallis work for two string orchestras (1909) by Vaughan Williams.

Fantasia on "Greensleeves" work for harp and string orch. (1934) by Vaughan Williams based on the song GREENSLEEVES. The work was originally an interlude in Vaughan Williams's opera *Sir John in Love*.

Fantasiestück also, **Phantasiestück** [fän-tä′zē″shtük] (Ger.) a short work, usu. for piano and part of a set of such pieces having a cyclic form, the main idea of the opening returning at the end. Cf. FANTASIA (1,).

Fantastic Symphony SYMPHONIE FANTASTIQUE.

Fantasticks, The musical by Harvey Schmidt, lyrics and book by Tom Jones, based on a play by Edmund Rostand. Premiere, New York 1960. A tale of two young lovers, brought together by their fathers and eventually united after trials and separations.

fantasy FANTASIA (1,).

fantinella (It.) a 16th- and 17th-c. form used for Italian songs and dances consisting of two repeated verses and a repeated refrain (*ripresa*).

farandole [fä-rä′dol] (Fr.) a lively Provençal chain dance in 6/8 time, performed on major religious holidays.

Farberman, Harold (1929–) Amer. composer and conductor, trained at the Juilliard School. He was a percussionist with the Boston SO, then conductor of the Oakland SO from 1971 to 1979 and founder in 1975 of the Conductors' Guild of the ASOL. His works span all genres and include two operas, chamber music and orchestral works.

farewell a 16th- to 18th-c. English term for a work lamenting the death of a person or, occasionally, for the concluding work of a set or movement of a work. Cf. DÉPLORATION.

Farewell Sonata see LES ADIEUX.

Farewell Symphony the Symphony No. 45 in F-sharp minor (1772) by Haydn, so called because of its final movement, which (according to one story) dramatized the desire of Prince Esterházy's musicians for a leave of absence by having them one by one put out their candles and leave the room.

Farinelli (Broschi, Carlo) (1705–82) the most famous Italian soprano castrato, prob. stud. of his father, Salvatore Broschi, and of Niccolà Porpora. After his early career in continental Europe. He went to London in 1734, where he created a sensation singing in the operas of Handel. In 1737, he left London for Madrid, where he served the Spanish monarchy for twenty years as singer and confidant to the king. He spent the last two decades of his life in retirement in Bologna.

Farkas, Ferenc (1905–) Hungarian composer and teacher, trained at the Budapest Academy of Music, where from 1949 to 1975 he was professor of composition and teacher of Ligeti, Petrovics and many others. His works include many stage and film scores, orchestral works, oratorios, cantatas, songs and chamber music.

Farkas, Philip (Francis) (1914–) Amer. horn player, stud. of Louis Dufrasne. He was principal horn of the Kansas City PO (1933–6), the Chicago SO (1936–41 and 1947–60), the Cleveland Orch. (1941–5 and 1946–7) and the Boston SO (1945–6). In 1960 he became professor at Indiana U. He has taught many of the current horn players in major U.S. orchestras.

Farlow, Tal(madge Holt) (1921–) Amer. jazz guitarist. He played with Red Norvo and Charles Mingus from 1949 to 1953 and with Artie Shaw's combo in the mid-50s. He is known for his fast execution in the early bop style, his gentle touch and his use of artificial harmonics.

Farmer, Art(hur Stewart) (1928–) Amer. jazz fluegelhorn and trumpet player. He played with the bands of Johnny Otis, Benny Carter, Wardell Gray and Lionel Hampton on the West Coast, and with Horace Silver and Gerry Mulligan in New York. He was co-leader of the Jazztet with Benny Golson and has led his own groups, moving to Europe in the 1970s.

Farnaby, Giles (?1565–1640) English composer, a joiner by trade, whose extant works include keyboard fantasias, vocal canzonets and psalm settings.

Farrant, Richard (?1530–80) English church musician and composer. He was a Gentleman of the Chapel Royal until 1564, when he became master of the choristers at St. George's Chapel at Windsor Castle. In 1569 he also obtained an equivalent post at the Chapel Royal. In addition to composing anthems and other church music he also produced plays.

Farrar, Geraldine (1882–1967) Amer. soprano, stud. of Mrs. J. H. Long, Emma Thursby and Lilli Lehmann. She sang at the Metropolitan Opera from 1906 until her retirement in 1922. She was best known for the roles Carmen and Butterfly.

Farrell, Eileen (1920–) Amer. soprano, stud. of Merle Alcock and Eleanor McLellan. Her opera debut was not until 1956; her earlier years were dedicated to concert and recital appearances. She was a member of the Bach Aria Group and was equally at home singing the blues.

Farrenc (Dumont), **(Jeanne-)Louise** (1804–75) French composer, pianist, teacher and scholar, stud. of Reicha. She was professor of piano at the Paris Conservatoire from 1842 until her retirement in 1873, the only woman to hold a permanent post of this rank in the 19th c. She was editor and compiler of the collection *Le trésor des pianistes* and made a significant study of early-music performance practice. Her works include a substantial body of music for the piano, as well as three symphonies and other orchestral works and chamber music.

farruca (Sp.) a Spanish gypsy dance.

farsa (It., farce) an 18th- or 19th-c. Italian intermezzo or afterpiece, performed during or after a spoken comedy.

Farwell, Arthur (1872–1952) Amer. composer, critic and editor, best known for his compositions, based on the music of Native Americans. He founded the Wa-Wan Press in 1901, dedicated to publishing the music of contemporary Amer. composers, and was chief music critic for *Musical America* from 1909 to 1914.

Fasch, Johann Friedrich (1688–1758) German composer, stud. at the Leipzig Thomasschule and then at the U. of Leipzig, where he founded a celebrated collegium musicum. Although most of the extensive body of his sacred vocal music is lost, much of his instrumental music remains and shows him to have been an important innovator in the development from the Baroque to early Classical style.

Faschingsschwank aus Wien ['fä-shingz"shvänk ows vēn] (Ger., Carnival Joke from Vienna) a set of five piano pieces, Op. 26 (1839), by Schumann.

fasola 1, a tetrachordal system of SOLMIZATION assigning the sequence of whole step-whole step (as in the first three notes of the major scale) to the syllables *fa sol la*, and *mi fa*, to half steps. The major scale was thus *fa sol la fa sol la mi fa* and the minor scale was *la mi fa sol la fa sol la*. **2**, a similar system often used in conjunction with SHAPE NOTE notation.

Fassbänder, Brigitte (1939–) German mezzo-soprano, trained at the Nuremberg Conservatory. Her Amer. debut was at the Metropolitan Opera in 1974. She is noted for her portrayal of *travesti* roles.

Fate Symphony popular name for **1**, the Symphony No. 5 in C minor, Op. 67 (1808), by Beethoven. **2**, the Symphony No. 4 in F minor, Op. 36 (1878), by Tchaikovsky.

Fauré, Gabriel(-Urbain) (1845–1924) French composer, organist, pianist and teacher, stud. of Louis Niedermeyer and Saint-Saëns. He was a founder of the Société nationale de musique (1871), which premiered many of his works. In 1896 he became chief organist at the Madeleine and composition teacher at the Paris Conservatoire, a post he had been refused four years earlier because Ambroise Thomas thought him too revolutionary. His pupils at the Conservatoire included Ravel, Roger-Ducasse and Nadia Boulanger. Fauré became director in 1905, and under his régime, which lasted until 1920, many reforms were initiated. From 1903 to 1921 he was music critic of *Le Figaro.* Fauré's influence on French composers of the early 20th c. was significant, both through his works and through his teaching at the Conservatoire. His works incl. *Pénélope* (opera), incidental music, a Requiem and other sacred vocal music, choral works, *Pelléas et Mélisande* suite, cantatas for violin and cello, a piano trio and piano quartet, chamber music, many piano works and songs, incl. the cycles *La bonne chanson, La chanson d'Ève,* and *L'horizon chimérique.*

Faust opera in 5 acts by Gounod to a libretto by Jules Barbier and Michel Carré, based on Goethe's play. Premiere, Paris 1859. The old philosopher Faust sells his soul to the devil in exchange for youth and the possession of Marguerite.

Faust Overture, A (Ger., *Eine Faust-Ouvertüre*) orchestral concert piece (1840) by Wagner, based on the drama by Goethe.

Faust Symphony, A (Ger., *Eine Faust-Symphonie*) symphony in three movements with chorus (1857) by Liszt. The movements are portraits of Faust, Gretchen and Mephistopheles.

fauxbourdon [fô-boor'dô] (Fr.) **1**, a style of vocal improvisation identified primarily with 15th-c. sacred music. Two voices—a discant and a tenor—are written in 6ths and octaves, with an improvised voice following at a 4th below the discant. In the late 15th c., a bass voice would be derived from the 2-part invention by singing in alternate 3rds and 5ths below the tenor. To this 3-voice texture a 4th voice might be added, singing in 3rds and 4ths above the tenor. Cadences were limited to fifth and octave intervals, and the words were sung simultaneously in all voices.

2, continental adaptation of the English FABURDEN, with the plainsong in the top part.

Favola d'Orfeo, La (It., The Fable of Orpheus) classic opera in 5 acts by Monteverdi to a libretto in Italian by Alessandro Striggio. Premiere, Mantua 1607. The story is the traditional myth of the musician Orfeo's attempt to bring his beloved Euridice back from death.

favola in musica (It., tale in music) a phrase found in 17th-c. scores indicating a dramatic work set to music, i.e., an opera.

favola per musica (It., tale for music) a term for a literary work designed to be set to music.

favorita (It.) a 16th- and 17th-c. Italian dance form based on the ROMANESCA harmonic pattern but in quicker note values.

Fay, Amy (Amelia Muller) (1844–1928) Amer. pianist, critic and teacher, stud. of Carl Taussig, Theodor Kullak and Liszt. She developed a format for giving concerts which she called "piano conversation," in which she supplemented her playing with discussions of the music. She founded the Artists' Concert Club in Chicago and was president of the New York Women's Philharmonic Society from 1903 to 1914.

Fayrfax, Robert (1464–1521) English composer of sacred Mass and motet settings, and secular vocal and instrumental music. He was a Gentleman of the Chapel Royal from 1497 and appears to have been a favorite of Henry VIII, who bestowed on him a number of awards and annuities.

F-clef a CLEF (𝄢) indicating the position on the staff of the F below middle C (f).

Federal Music Project see WPA.

feierlich ['fī-ər-liç] (Ger.) solemn, festive.

Felciano, Richard (James) (1930–) Amer. composer, stud. of Milhaud and Dallapiccola. He has taught at Lone Mountain College and at the U. of California at Berkeley. His works usu. involve electronic sounds and a great deal of flexibility for the performer. He has written theater pieces, orchestral works, chamber music and choral works.

Feldbrill, Victor (1924–) Canadian conductor and violinist, stud. of Kathleen Parlow and Pierre Monteux. He was assistant conductor of the Toronto SO (1956–7) and musical director of the Winnipeg SO (1958–68). He has taught at the U. of Toronto since 1972 and has been an important champion of the works of Canadian composers.

Feldman, Morton (1926–87) Amer. composer, stud. of Riegger and Wolpe. He was assoc. with John Cage and Earle Brown as well as with abstract expressionist artists in New York, all of whom were an important influence on his work. Both his earlier graphic scores and his later works in pitched notation but with freely notated rhythm are marked by a very limited dynamic range and a highly sensitive ear for instrumental color.

Feldmusik (Ger., field music), the players of military field music, esp. trumpeters and drummers; also, the music, such as fanfares, written for military use. In the 18th c. the term was also used for small wind bands which were technically reserved for military occasions, but might be used for other court functions as well.

Fellowes, Edmund H(orace) (1870–1951) English church musician, editor and musicologist, ordained as a minister in 1894. He was a minor canon at St. George's Chapel at Windsor Castle from 1897 until his death, where he also directed the choir for a short time. He is best known for his editions of English music of the 16th and early 17th c., esp. the Tudor Church Music series and the English Madrigal School.

feminine cadence a CADENCE or termination in which the final chord or note falls on a weak beat.

Fender firm of electric-guitar manufacturers named for its founder, Clarence Leo Fender (1909–91). The firm is best known for the Stratocas-

ter electric guitar, developed in 1954, the Mustang electric bass and the Fender-Rhodes electric piano.

Fender, Freddy (Huerta, Baldemar) (1936–) Mexican-Amer. rhythm-and-blues and country-music singer, composer and guitarist, best known for his songs "Wasted Days and Wasted Nights" (1959) and "Before the Next Teardrop Falls" (1974).

Fenice, Teatro la [fä'nē-chä] opera house in Venice opened in 1792.

Fennell, Frederick (1914–) Amer. conductor and teacher, trained at the Eastman School. He was on the faculty of Eastman from 1939 and formed the Eastman Wind Ensemble in 1952, a model for many similar organizations formed across the country. He was conductor-in-residence at the U. of Miami (1965–80) and was appointed conductor of the Kosei Wind Orch., Tokyo, in 1984.

Fennelly, Brian (1937–) Amer. composer and theorist, stud. of Powell, Martino, Forte, Perle and Schuller. He has taught at New York U. since 1968 and has been coeditor of the *Contemporary Music Newsletter*. His compositions incl. orchestral and chamber works in both atonal and serial idioms.

Fenyves, Lorand (1918–) Hungarian-born Canadian violinist, trained at the Liszt Academy in Budapest. In 1936 he emigrated to Israel to be concertmaster of the Palestine SO, where he founded the Fenyves Quartet and the Israel String Quartet. He has taught since 1966 at the U. of Toronto and at Banff and has performed extensively in Europe and No. America.

Ferencsik, János (1907–84) Hungarian conductor, trained at the Budapest National Conservatory. He was a conductor at the Budapest Opera from 1930, becoming its musical dir. as well as chief conductor of the Hungarian National PO in 1953. His Amer. debut was in 1962.

Ferguson, Maynard (1928–) Canadian-born jazz trumpeter, trombonist and bandleader, trained at the French Conservatory of Music in Montreal.

He worked (1950–53) with the Stan Kenton band, later leading his own bands in Europe and the U.S. He is particularly noted for his durability in the high register.

fermata (It., pause) prolongation of the value of a note or rest beyond its normal value; the sign indicating such a prolongation (∩). Also, *hold, pause, bull's-eye.*

Fernandes, Gaspar (?1570–1629) Portuguese-born Mexican composer, organist and singer. He was chapel master of Guatemala Cathedral (1599–1606) and of the Puebla (Mexico) Cathedral from 1606 until his death. His extant compositions incl. sacred vocal music and festal works.

Ferneyhough, Brian (1943–) English composer, stud. of Lennox Berkeley, Maurice Miles, Ton de Leeuw and Klaus Huber. He has taught at the Musikhochschule in Freiburg, the Darmstadt summer courses and, since 1987, at the U. of California, San Diego. His works are highly complex and contrapuntal, employing unusual time signatures and his own personal style of serialism.

Ferrabosco, Alfonso (I) (1543–88) Italian composer. He was in the service of Queen Elizabeth I of England from about 1562 until 1578, then, after 1582, of the duke of Savoy in Turin. His extant compositions incl. madrigals, instrumental fantasias and sacred vocal music.

Ferrabosco, Alfonso (II) (1578–1628) English composer, son (probably illegitimate) of Alfonso Ferrabosco (I). He was in the service of the royal chapel from childhood, becoming a king's musician and royal teacher under James I and composer to the king under Charles. He collaborated with the poet Ben Jonson on court masques and also produced motets and anthems as well as lute-songs, madrigals and instrumental works.

Ferrara, Franco (1911–85) Italian conductor and teacher. Because of a neurological ailment, he was unable to conduct in public, but he conducted the sound tracks for a number of films and taught a highly respected conducting class in Rome and Siena, where his pupils incl. Andrew Davis, Edo de Waart, Riccardo Muti and many others.

Ferrari, Luc (1929–) French composer, stud. of Cortot, Honegger and Messiaen. He was a founder of the Groupe de Recherches Musicales (1958) and has been a teacher of composition in Cologne and Montreal. His compositions incl. works for electronic media, piano works, chamber music and music for films and the broadcast media.

Ferras, Christian (1933–82) French violinist, stud. of Calvet and Enescu. He won the 1948 Scheveningen International Competition and the Prix Long-Thibaud and has concertized throughout the world.

Ferri, Baldassare (1610–80) Italian soprano, the first castrato to gain international fame, first at the court in Warsaw for thirty years, then for twenty years in Vienna.

Ferrier, Kathleen (Mary) (1912–53) English contralto, stud. of J. E. Hutchinson and Roy Henderson. She was known primarily as a concert and recital artist, her operatic roles being Lucretia in Britten's opera and the title role of Gluck's *Orfeo*. She performed frequently in concert with Bruno Walter and Sir John Barbirolli.

Festa, Costanzo (c1480–1545) Italian composer and singer. He appears to have served the French court until about 1517, when he joined the Papal Choir, remaining in the pope's service for the remainder of his life. A large body of Festa's works survive, an indication of his renown, and includes sacred and secular vocal works, in particular motets and madrigals, of which he was one of the earliest composers.

festa teatrale (It.) a type of baroque OPERA dealing with allegorical subjects and usu. composed for a specific celebration, as a marriage or birthday.

Festival Hall ROYAL FESTIVAL HALL.

Festival of Two Worlds opera festival

founded in 1958 in Spoleto, Italy, by Gian Carlo Menotti.

Festival Singers of Canada a 25-voice professional choir formed in 1954 by Elmer Iseler.

Feuermann, Emanuel (1902–42) Ukrainian-born Amer. cellist, stud. of Anton Walter and Klengel. He came to the U.S. in 1938 and taught at the Curtis Institute from 1941. He played in piano trios with Huberman and Schnabel as well as with Heifetz and Artur Rubinstein.

Févin, Antoine de (?1474–?1512) Franco-Flemish composer in the service of Louis XII. His surviving works incl. Mass and magnificat settings, motets and chansons.

ff *abbr.* FORTISSIMO.

fff *abbr.* FORTISSISSIMO.

fg. *abbr.* fagotto (see BASSOON).

f-hole see SOUND HOLE.

f-hole guitar a type of GUITAR with f-holes instead of the usual round sound hole, developed as an alternative to the banjo in jazz band rhythm sections. Also, *arch top guitar*.

fiato ['fya-tō] (It.) breath.

fibonacci series [fē-bō'nät-chē] a sequence of numbers in which each subsequent number is the sum of the two preceding numbers, as 1,2,3,5,8,13,... Like the GOLDEN SECTION, to which it is closely related, the series is frequently used by composers as a basis for pitch selection, formal design, etc.

ficta (Lat., false) a term for accidentals added to early music by editor or performer.

fiddle a term for any bowed, stringed instrument, though it is now generally restricted to instruments of the VIOLIN family. In country music, *fiddle* is the standard term for the violin, and there is a special style of playing associated with it, which, though it does not employ the fancier techniques of classical violin playing, has a virtuosity of its own. See REBEC, VIOL, CRWTH.

Fiddle Fugue popular name for the organ fugue in D minor, BWV 539 (c1720), by Bach, so called because it

is adapted from the solo violin sonata in G minor.

Fiddler on the Roof musical by Jerry Bock, lyrics by Sheldon Harnick, book by Joseph Stein, based on stories by Sholom Aleichem. Premiere, New York 1964. Set in a Jewish village in czarist Russia in 1905, it is the story of the family of the dairyman Tevye.

Fidelio opera in 2 acts by Beethoven to a libretto by Joseph von Sonnleithner, based on the play by Jean Nicolas Bouilly. Premiere, Vienna 1805. Florestan's wife Leonora, disguised as Fidelio, works in a jail, hoping to find a way to free her husband, a political prisoner.

Fiedler, Arthur (1894–1979) Amer. conductor and violinist, stud. of his father (a violinist with the Boston SO) and Willy Hess. He joined the Boston SO as a violist in 1918. In 1924 he formed the Boston Sinfonietta, which toured New England. In 1929 he organized the ESPLANADE CONCERTS and became, in the following year, conductor of the BOSTON POPS, which he conducted for almost 50 years.

Field, John (1782–1837) Irish composer and virtuoso pianist, stud. of Tommaso Giordani and Clementi. He lived in Russia for most of his life. Field introduced an expressive style of playing that led to Chopin, and he produced a large volume of works for solo piano, piano duet, and piano and orch.

Field-Hyde, Margaret (1905–) English soprano, best known for her performance of music of the early Baroque. She founded the Golden Age Singers in 1950, a group specializing in late Renaissance and early Baroque vocal music.

field holler an extemporized solo song sung by black Amer. field workers, usu. associated with cotton harvesting, but also sung by levee workers, rice and sugar plantation workers and mule skinners. It was described in 1853 as a "long, loud, musical shout, rising and falling and breaking into falsetto."

Fiery Angel, The (Russ., *Ongnennïy*

angel) opera in 5 acts by Prokofiev to his own libretto, based on the novel by Valery Bryusov. Premiere, Venice 1955, but composed in the 1920s.

fife a small six-holed transverse FLUTE, usu. made of wood in one piece and having a high, shrill tone. The modern fife in B♭ is pitched a third below the orchestral piccolo.

fifteenth 1, an INTERVAL spanning two octaves. **2**, a two-foot ORGAN STOP, sounding two octaves above normal pitch.

fifth an INTERVAL spanning four diatonic scale degrees. The PERFECT FIFTH spans three whole steps and a half step. The DIMINISHED FIFTH is one half step smaller and occurs in the major scale only between the fourth and seventh degrees. The fifth in equal temperament is slightly smaller than the pure fifth. Since ancient times the fifth has been considered to be consonant. See CIRCLE OF FIFTHS.

Fifths Quartet (Ger., *Quintenquartett*) popular name for the String Quartet in D minor, Op. 76 No. 2 (1797–8), by Haydn, so called because of the falling fifths in its first theme. Also, *Bell Quartet.*

Figaro see THE MARRIAGE OF FIGARO; THE BARBER OF SEVILLE.

figural *also,* **figurate** elaborate, florid. The term can refer to the elaboration or ornamentation of a melodic line, or, in a broader sense, to the elaboration of the music, i.e., through the use of polyphony. See MUSICA FIGURATA, DIVISION.

figuration melodic ornamentation, often patterned and extended through the use of relatively short "figures." The term is variable in use, but usu. implies ornamentation of a rather mechanical nature.

figured bass the bass part of a polyphonic composition for which numerical figures, usu. written below the notes, indicate desired harmonies. The term is usu. used in reference to music of the 16th and 17th c. Realization of the figures (i.e., improvised addition of the chords indicated

(Handel, Imeneo)

by the numbers) is generally provided by a continuo instrument such as organ, harpsichord or theorbo. Cf. BASSO CONTINUO.

Figures, Doctrine of Musical an aesthetic concept by which musical figures are seen to be analogous to rhetorical figures of speech. The concept is usu. applied to music of the Baroque. Cf. DOCTRINE OF THE AFFECTIONS.

fill music, usu. improvised, performed by an accompanying singer or instrument to fill the spaces between phrases of the lead soloist.

Fille du Régiment, La ['fē-yə dü rā-zhē'mā] THE DAUGHTER OF THE REGIMENT.

Fillmore, (James) Henry, (Jr.) (1881–1956) Amer. composer, arranger, bandleader and publisher. Pres. of the Amer. Bandmasters' Assoc. (1941–46), Fillmore formed his own professional band, which became known through radio broadcasts (1926–38). His compositions (256 miniatures and 774 arrangements) were published mainly by his family's firm, Fillmore Music House.

film music music composed or arranged to accompany a motion picture. In the days of silent films, the music was either improvised during the screening by a pianist or small instrumental group, or, in some cases, specially composed and played by an orch., which would travel with the film. Since the advent of sound films, film scores have run the gamut from simple background music to music of the highest quality by composers of note in the concert world. There has been an increased use of jazz in the scores of nonmusical films since the late 1940s, as well as a proliferation of the use of electronic musical techniques, in particular sampling and drum-machine sounds.

final *also*, **finalis** (Lat.) the last note of an ecclesiastical chant, or the last note in the tenor part of a polyphonic composition of the Middle Ages or Renaissance. The final is a determining factor in establishing the mode of a composition. Cf. MODE, CONFINAL, PLAINSONG.

finale [fē'nä-lā] (It.) the closing section or movement of a composition. In opera, the finale became in the late 18th and the 19th c. an extended ensemble section uniting a number of shorter solos, duets, etc., into a continuous whole which concluded an act or the work.

Finck, Heinrich (1445–1527) German composer and theorist. He seems to have spent much of his life in Poland, leaving there in 1510. He then probably worked in Bavaria and in Salzburg, moving to Vienna several years before he died. His compositional life was unusually long, spanning almost 60 years. His extant compositions are largely sacred vocal music—Mass settings, magnificats, motets—and a small number of secular songs.

fine ('fē-nā) (It., end) a term indicating the end of a composition or movement, esp. when this does not come at the end of the printed music, but earlier in the work after a partial repeat. See REPEATS (*illus.*).

Fine, Irving (Gifford) (1914–62) Amer. composer, conductor and teacher, stud. of Hill, Piston and Boulanger. He taught at Harvard (1939–50) and Brandeis (1950 until his death). He also was a member of the staff of the Berkshire Music Center (1946–57). His works incl. orchestral music, choruses, songs and chamber music in a style that ranges from dissonant to serial, strongly influenced by Stravinsky and Hindemith.

Fine, Vivian (1913–) Amer. composer and pianist, stud. of Ruth Crawford, Abby Whiteside, and Sessions. She has taught at New York U., the Juilliard School and at Bennington College (Vermont) and was a founder of the American Composers Alliance. Her works incl. dance pieces, several concertos, chamber and vocal music.

Fine Arts Quartet Amer. string quartet formed in 1946 in Chicago. It was the resident quartet of the American Broadcasting Company in Chicago from 1946 to 1954. Since 1963 the quartet has been resident at the U. of Wisconsin at Milwaukee.

Fingal's Cave see THE HEBRIDES.

fingerboard 1, the part of a stringed instrument against which the fingers press the strings to adjust the pitch. **2,** KEYBOARD.

finger cymbals small round CYMBALS attached to the fingers by straps and struck together in a manner similar to that used in playing castanets.

finger hole a hole in the body of a wind instrument which is covered or left uncovered, usu. by means of a mechanical key system, to produce different notes of the scale.

fingering the assignment of specific fingers or combinations of fingers to specific notes in the playing of an instrument. The principal development in the playing of keyboard instruments has been the increasing use of the thumb and fifth finger. Keyboard fingering is usually indicated by numbers placed above the notes, 1 indicating the thumb, 2 the index finger, and so on.

String fingering is also indicated by numbers over the notes, 1 for the index finger, 2 for the middle finger, and so on, with 0 indicating the open (unstopped) string. Occasionally the specific string desired is also indicated by Roman numeral or by letter.

Fingering for plucked stringed instruments is usu. indicated by means of TABLATURE, a graphic indication of where to place the fingers. Fingering for holed and keyed wind instruments is rarely indicated, it being up to the player to choose between alternate fingerings. When indications are given, in particular in modern works employing extended techniques, the fingering is often indicated by means of a graphic illustration of the instrument's keys and holes, marking with a black circle those to be closed, and with an open circle those to be left open. For valved wind instruments, numbers indicating the key to press are sometimes placed above the notes, but this is infrequent.

finger picking the plucking of a stringed instrument with the fingers, spec. a traditional guitar style by which the right-hand fingers pluck the melody while the thumb plucks an accompaniment bass figure.

Finian's Rainbow musical by Burton Lane, lyrics by E.Y. Harburg, book by Harburg and Fred Saidy. Premiere, New York 1947. The story of a crock of gold, an Irish immigrant named Finian, his daughter Sharon, and Og, a leprechaun.

Finlandia (Finn., *Suomi*) orchestral tone poem, Op. 26 No. 7 (1899) by Sibelius. It was orig. performed as the last of a series of pieces illustrating "Tableaux from the Past," but was later revised and performed separately as a concert work.

Finney, Ross Lee (1906–) Amer. composer and teacher, stud. of Donald Ferguson, Boulanger, Sessions and Berg. He taught at Smith College (MA) from 1929 to 1948 and at the U. of Michigan from 1949. His students incl. George Crumb and Roger Reynolds. His wide interests incl. Amer. folk music, and he has toured, singing folk songs to his own guitar accompaniment. He has worked in a variety of styles, experimenting with both traditional and serial techniques.

Finzi, Gerald (Raphael) (1901–56) English composer, stud. of Bairstow. During World War II he formed a quasi-amateur group, the Newbury String Players, which did readings of works by many young composers and provided a performance venue for young performers. A large percentage of his works are for voice and vocal ensembles.

fioritura [fyō-rē'too-rä] (It., flowering) embellishment of a vocal or instru-

mental line, either improvised or written out. Cf. FIGURATION, ORNAMENTATION.

fipple a wooden block containing an air channel (*flue*) and a flat, hard lip against which the air is directed, causing vibrations in the air column.

fipple flute WHISTLE FLUTE.

Fire Symphony the Symphony No. 59 in A major (c1769) by Haydn, possibly from incidental music written for a play of the same name.

Firebird, The (Russ., *Zhar Ptitsa*) ballet (1910) with music by Stravinsky written for the Ballets Russes, orig. choreographed by Michel Fokine. The story is derived from a Russian folk tale. Stravinsky extracted from the ballet a concert suite (1916), revised (with differing selections and orchestrations) in 1919 and 1945.

Firefly, The musical by Rudolf Friml, lyrics and book by Otto Harbach. Premiere, New York 1912. The story of an Italian street singer in New York who becomes a prima donna.

Fires of London a chamber ensemble formed as the Pierrot Players in 1967 by Dennis Russell Davies and Harrison Birtwistle. The name was changed in 1970 and Davies became sole director. The group has specialized in works involving mixed-media presentation.

Fireworks Music see MUSIC FOR THE ROYAL FIREWORKS.

firk a 17th-c. English dance, usu. in quick triple time and of a capricious or fanciful nature.

Firkušný, Rudolf (1912–) Czechborn Amer. pianist, stud. of Janáček, Vilém Kurz, Rudolf Karel and Josef Suk. His No. Amer. debut was in 1938 and he has taught at the Juilliard School and at Aspen. In addition to the standard 18th- and 19th-c. repertory, he has made a specialty of the piano works of Dvořák and Janáček and has premiered works by 20th-c. composers incl. Ginastera and Martinů.

first inversion see INVERSION.

first-movement form see SONATA FORM.

First Noel, The Christmas carol of unknown authorship, first appearing in print in the early 19th c.

fis (Ger.) F SHARP.

Fischer, Carl (1849–1923) Amer. music publisher, who founded a firm by the same name in 1872 in New York. In addition to an extensive catalogue of musical works, the firm has published *The Metronome*, a journal for bandleaders, since 1885, and the *Musical Observer* since 1907 (assimilated into the *Musical Courier* in 1913).

Fischer, Edwin (1886–1960) Swiss pianist, stud. of Hans Huber and Martin Krause. He was noted for his interpretation of the German repertory.

Fischer, Irwin (1903–77) Amer. conductor, composer and organist, trained at the American Conservatory in Chicago, where he taught from 1928, becoming dean in 1974. He wrote a number of orchestral works, as well as choral, piano, organ, vocal and chamber music.

Fischer, Johann Christian (1733–1800) German oboist and composer, stud. of Alessandro Besozzi. He played in the Dresden court orch., and traveled widely as a soloist. He was a frequent performer at the BACH-ABEL CONCERTS in London, and both Bach and Abel wrote music for him. He wrote concertos and sonatas for oboe and flute, and was a tutor for the oboe.

Fischer, Ludwig (1745–1825) German bass with an unusually wide range for whom Mozart wrote the role of Osmin in *The Abduction from the Seraglio*, Sarastro in *The Magic Flute* and several concert arias.

Fischer-Dieskau, Dietrich (1925–) German baritone, stud. of George Walter and Hermann Weissenborn. He has been principal baritone with the Berlin Städtische Oper and has appeared with the Vienna Staatsoper, the Bayreuth Festival and many other major opera houses, in German and Italian repertory, much of which he has also recorded. His greatest renown is as a lieder-singer, and he has performed and recorded most of the major lieder repertory, much of it in collaboration with pianist Gerald Moore.

Fisher, Avery (1906–) Amer. music patron and audio expert, founder of Fisher Radio. He funded the renovation of Philharmonic Hall in Lincoln Center, New York, which was renamed for him.

Fisher, Fred (1875–1942) German-born Amer. composer, lyricist and publisher, whose songs incl. "Peg o' My Heart" (1913) and "Chicago" (1922).

fisis (Ger.) F double sharp.

Fisk, Charles Brenton (1925–83) Amer. organ builder, whose company (founded in 1949) builds only organs with mechanical actions.

Fitzgerald, Ella (1918–) Amer. jazz and popular singer, made famous by her work with Norman Granz's "Jazz at the Philharmonic" tours. She is noted for her skill at SCAT SINGING and for the extraordinary quality of her voice. She has made hundreds of recordings.

Fitzwilliam Virginal Book a 17th-c. collection of keyboard music, mostly English, of the late 16th and early 17th c., copied by FRANCIS TREGIAN when he was imprisoned, 1609–19. It contains 297 works by Byrd, Bull, Morley and others.

Five, The MIGHTY HANDFUL, THE.

Five Pennies, The a jazz band, orig. a quintet, formed in the mid-1920s by trumpeter RED NICHOLS.

fixed do(h) a system of SOLFEGGIO in which the same syllable always refers to the same pitch, i.e., *doh* is always C, *re* is always D, etc., regardless of modulation. Cf. MOVABLE DO(H).

Fizdale, Robert (1920–) Amer. pianist who has made a career of performing music for two pianos with ARTHUR GOLD. The duo made its debut in 1944 at the New School for Social Research and is best known for its breadth of repertory, incl. commissions from Rorem, Barber, Randall Thomson, Brubeck, Mihaud, Poulenc and Tailleferre.

fl. *abbr.* FLUTE.

flagellant songs (Ger., *Geisslerlieder*) songs sung during the penitential rites of flagellants in the 13th and 14th c.

Flagello, Ezio (1931–) Amer. bass, stud. of Friedrich Schorr and John Brownlee. He has sung with the Metropolitan Opera since 1957 in a variety of roles, incl. both *buffo* and lyric parts.

Flagello, Nicolas (Oreste) (1928–) Amer. composer, conductor and pianist, stud. of Giannini and Mitropoulos. He appeared with opera companies in the U.S. and Europe, toured widely as an accompanist and taught for almost 30 years at the Manhattan School. His works incl. 7 operas, concertos for flute, violin and cello, 2 symphonies, other orchestral works and chamber music, songs and choral music.

flageolet a small 17th- to 19th-c. WHISTLE FLUTE similar to the treble RECORDER but with fewer holes and a cylindrical mouthpiece. Some composers in the 18th c., incl. Rameau and Handel, specified the instrument in certain works. It was also used to teach canaries to sing, and tunes were written for this purpose.

flageolet tones see HARMONICS.

Flagstad, Kirsten (Malfrid) (1895–1962) Norwegian soprano, stud. of Ellen Schytte Jacobsen and Dr. Gillis Bratt. Until 1932 she sang only in Scandinavia, appearing in opera, operetta, revues and musical comedy. Her Amer. debut was at the Metropolitan Opera in 1935, two years after her Bayreuth debut. In the following years she established a reputation as one of the greatest Wagnerian sopranos of all time. She retired from opera in 1953.

flam a side-drum drumbeat consisting of two strokes, the first of which is a quick grace note (♪♪).

flamenco (Sp.) a vigorous, rhythmic Gypsy dance style originating in Andalusia, Spain. The music accompanying such a dance encompasses a wide range of styles, the melodies usu. utilizing one of several modal scales typical of the region. There are two principal types of flamenco, the CANTE HONDO or *grande* and the CANTE CHICO.

Flanagan, William (1923–69) Amer. composer, stud. of Bernard Rogers, Burrill Phillips, Barber, Honegger, Copland and Diamond. For many years he was a music critic for the *New York Herald Tribune* and *Stereo Review*. Most of his works are for voice, incl. an opera (*Bartleby*) and songs as well as works for orch. and chamber music.

flare in jazz, a note or chord held at the end of a chorus, usu. with a crescendo, leading to a final tutti.

flat 1, a musical sign (♭) indicating a chromatic lowering of the PITCH of a note by a half step. 2, below the prevailing pitch level by a perceptible amount; said of an instrument, voice, etc.

flatpicking a guitar- and mandolin-picking style that utilizes a flat plastic plectrum.

flatté [flä′tä] *also*, **flattement** [′flat-mä] (Fr.) a type of MORDENT found in 17th-c. French viol music.

Flatt and Scruggs bluegrass and country music duo comprised of Lester Flatt (1914–79) and Earl Scruggs (1924–), playing guitar and banjo, respectively. They performed with the Grand Ole Opry from 1955 to 1969 and played regularly on national radio and TV. They are best known for their performances of "Foggy Mountain Breakdown" and "The Ballad of Jed Clampett" with the Foggy Mountain Boys band. The duo was elected to the Country Music Hall of Fame in 1985.

Flatterzunge [′flä-tər″tsûng-e] (Ger.) FLUTTER-TONGUE.

flautando, flautato [flow′tän-dō, -′tä-tō] (It., flute-like) a direction in string-playing calling for a flutelike tone, usu. produced by a light pressure of the bow over the fingerboard; in practice, synonymous with the more precise term SUL TASTO.

flautist (Brit.) FLUTIST.

flauto ['flow-tō] (It.) see FLUTE, RECORDER.

flauto dolce ['dōl-chā] (It.) RECORDER.

flauto piccolo (It.) PICCOLO.

flauto traverso (It.) FLUTE.

flebile ['flā-bē-lā] (It.) mournful, plaintive.

Fledermaus, Die ['flā-dər-mows, dē] (Ger., The Bat) comic opera in 3 acts by Johann Strauss, Jr., to a libretto in German by Carl Haffner and Richard Genée after a libretto by Mailhac and Halévy, based on a play by Roderich Benedix. Premiere, Vienna 1874. Dr. Falke plots revenge for a practical joke played on him by his friend Eisenstein.

Fleetwood Mac English blues and rock band, formed in 1967 and named (luckily) after the two most stable members of the group, drummer Mick Fleetwood and bassist John McVie. Their most successful records, *Fleetwood Mac* and *Rumours*, were recorded in the mid 1970s and sold over 15 million copies.

Fleisher, Edwin A(dler) (1877–1959) Amer. music patron, founder in 1909 of the Symphony Club of Philadelphia to provide training for young musicians in the performance of orchestral literature. Half of the rehearsal time was devoted to reading new or unfamiliar works. The music collected for this purpose formed the basis for the Fleisher Collection, given to the Free Library of Philadelphia in 1929 and now the world's largest collection of orchestral performance material.

Fleisher, Leon (1928–) Amer. pianist and conductor, stud. of Schnabel. He was the first American to win the Queen Elizabeth International Competition in Brussels and enjoyed an active international career until 1965, when his right hand became disabled. He began a career as a conductor, also concertizing with the repertory for left hand alone and teaching at the Peabody Conservatory. Since 1985 he has been artistic dir. of the Tanglewood Music Center.

Fleming, Robert (James Berkeley) (1921–76) Canadian composer, stud. of Howells, Benjamin and Willan. He worked with the Canadian Film Board as composer, conductor and music editor (1946–70), then went to Ottawa to teach at Carleton U. His works, in addition to the large body of music he composed for the Film Board, comprise mainly songs, ballets, and chamber works.

Flemish school see NETHERLANDS SCHOOL.

Flesch, Carl (1873–1944) Hungarian violinist and teacher, stud. of Marzick. From 1897 to 1902 he taught in Bucharest and was leader of the Queen's String Quartet. He settled in Berlin in 1908, where he gained a substantial reputation as a teacher and played in a trio with Schnabel and Hugo Becker.

flexatone a percussion instrument invented in 1922 consisting of a small, narrow, flexible metal sheet held by one end in a frame with a handle. When the frame is shaken, the sheet is struck alternately by small wooden balls attached to wires on either side of the sheet. The sheet can be bent by the thumb to produce different pitches. The instrument has been included in the scores of several composers, including Schoenberg, Khachaturian and Penderecki.

flicorno [flē'kôr-nō] *also*, **flicorno soprano** (It.) FLUGELHORN.

flicorno baritono [bā'rē-tō-nō] (It.) tenor TUBA in B♭.

Fliegende Holländer, Der ['flē-gən-də ho'len-dər] (Ger.) THE FLYING DUTCHMAN.

fliessend ['flē-sənt] (Ger.) flowing.

Flight of the Bumble Bee, The orchestral interlude from the opera *The Tale of Tsar Saltan* (1900) by Rimsky-Korsakov. It has been transcribed for various instruments, incl. the trumpet.

Flonzaley Quartet Amer. string quartet formed in 1902 in New York by a private patron, Edward J. DeCoppet, for the sole purpose of performing in his house, with the stipulation that they devote their time to rehearsing and playing together. From 1904 they began touring the U.S. and Europe and made some of the earliest quartet recordings. They disbanded in 1928.

Flood, The biblical musical drama by Stravinsky to a libretto by Robert Craft arranged from the book of Genesis and the York and Chester cycles of Miracle plays. Premiere, CBS-TV 1962; stage premiere, Santa Fe 1962. Noah's wife refuses to board the ark until persuaded by her sons.

florid ornamented, embellished. The term is applied to passage-work (divisions) or to the use of ornaments, such as trills, turns, etc.

Florio, Caryl (Robjohn, William James) (1843–1920) English-born Amer. composer, singer and choral conductor. The first boy soloist at Trinity Church, NY, later the dir. of music at the Vanderbilt estate in NC, he was a self-taught composer.

Florodora musical by Leslie Stuart, lyrics by Ernest Boyd-Jones, Paul Rubens and the composer, book by Owen Hall. Premiere, London 1899. An intricate tale of goings-on on a Philippine island and its owner, Cyrus Gilfain.

Flöte ['flø-te] (Ger.) FLUTE.

Flotow, Friedrich (Adolf Ferdinand) Freiherr von (1812–83) German opera composer, stud. of Reicha at the Paris Conservatoire. After 1838 his operas began to be performed throughout Europe. The best known were *Alessandro Stradella* and *Martha*, the latter remaining part of the repertory into the 20th c.

flourish 1, in stage music, a FANFARE. 2, a short PRELUDE or POSTLUDE, either improvised or written out.

Flower Drum Song musical by Richard Rodgers, lyrics by Oscar Hammerstein II, book by Hammerstein and Joseph Fields, based on a novel by Chin Y. Lee. Premiere, New York 1958. The story of "picture-bride" Mei Li in San Francisco and her intended husband Sammy Fong.

Floyd, Carlisle (1926–) Amer. opera composer, stud. of Ernst Bacon. He taught at Florida State U. (1947–

76) and has been at the U. of Houston since 1976. His works incl. the operas *Susannah* (1955), *Of Mice and Men* (1970) and *Willie Stark* (1981). For all of his operas Floyd is both composer and librettist.

flue pipe a stopped or open organ pipe employing a FIPPLE to produce its sound, similar to the WHISTLE FLUTE. Flue stops include the diapasons, principals, flutes, etc. Also, *labial pipe*.

Flügel (Ger.) GRAND PIANO.

flugelhorn a valved brass instrument in B♭ descended from the KEYED BUGLE and identical in compass to the cornet. It is used in continental and English bands and as a solo instrument in jazz. There is also a smaller version in E♭. Also, *Fluegelhorn*.

flute 1, a general term for a wide variety of instruments of Asian origin in which the sound is produced in a confined air column activated by a stream of air striking against the sharp edge of an opening to the confining tube. In modern usage, the term usu. refers to the transverse or side-blown flute (German flute), excluding the various members of the fipple or WHISTLE FLUTE family (recorders, flageolets, whistles and organ flue pipes) and VESSEL FLUTES. The modern transverse or concert flute is a tube of wood or, more commonly, metal, built in three sections comprising a *head joint, body* or *middle joint* and *tail* or *foot joint*. The head joint contains the mouthpiece, across which the player blows air. The body and tail joint are fitted with a key system devised by BOEHM. The flute family also includes the PICCOLO in C, the ALTO FLUTE in G, the BASS FLUTE in C, and the obsolete FLUTE D'AMOUR in A. Other sizes of transverse flute are sometimes found in concert bands. Cf. NOSE FLUTE. 2, a family of flue ORGAN stops.

flûte-à-bec [ä bek] (Fr., flute with a mouthpiece) see WHISTLE FLUTE, RECORDER.

flûte d'amour [dä'moor] (Fr.) a transverse FLUTE in A, a minor third below

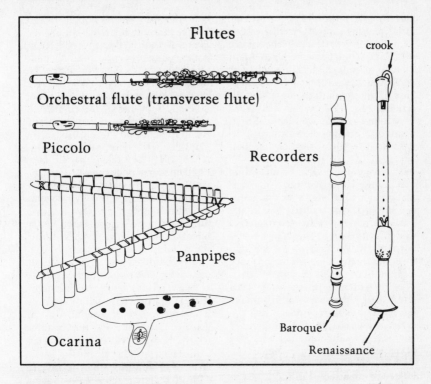

Flutes

crook

Orchestral flute (transverse flute)

Piccolo

Recorders

Panpipes

Ocarina

Baroque

Renaissance

the concert flute, used in the late 18th and early 19th c.

flutter-tonguing an effect produced on a wind instrument by rolling or trilling an "r" while blowing into the instrument. The effect is sometimes indicated by the abbreviation *Fltz.* or by a wavy line (~) over the notes to be so played and by strokes through their stems.

Fluxus an avant-garde arts coalition active in New York during the 1960s and 1970s, presenting concerts and theater music events of an experimental nature. Cf. DADA.

Flying Dutchman, The (Ger., *Der Fliegende Holländer*) romantic opera in 3 acts by Wagner to his own libretto in German, based on Heinrich Heine's adaptation of an old legend. Premiere, Dresden 1843. The Flying Dutchman is doomed to sail the seas until he finds a truly faithful love.

focus a term used in singing for the combination of factors that contrib-

ute to the production of an agreeable and resonant vocal sound, with little or no escaping air. Also, *placement*.

Foggy Mountain Boys Amer. bluegrass group founded in 1948 by FLATT AND SCRUGGS.

Foldes, Andor (1913–) Hungarianborn Amer. pianist and conductor, stud. of Tibor Szatmari, Leo Weiner and Dohnányi. He came to the U.S. in 1940 and became a citizen. He has specialized in the Viennese classics as well as the works of Bartók.

Foley, Red (1910–68) Amer. country-music and gospel singer, a star of the Grand Ole Opry from 1947; recorded regularly in Nashville. He was elected to the Country Music Hall of Fame in 1967.

folia *also,* **follia 1**, (Port.) a wild 17th-c. Spanish and Portuguese dance accompanied by guitar and *sonajas* (a percussion instrument consisting of metal discs attached to a wooden ring). The music is based on a bass pattern with a ritornello, the melody often making use of HEMIOLA. **2**, a Baroque development of the music of the FOLIA (1), slow and dignified, without the rhythmic offbeats of the earlier variety and with the bass harmonic pattern somewhat altered. See RENAISSANCE BASSES (*illus.*)

folk hymn a type of 18th-c. Amer. SPIRITUAL, usu. consisting of a religious text sung to a secular folk melody.

folk music the music of an ethnic community uninfluenced by popular and art music and transmitted through oral tradition, with the subtle changes that characterize that transmission. The concept is a particularly Western one, such distinctions being of lesser importance or not recognized by most non-Western cultures. In the later 19th and 20th c., the study of folk music has had a strong impact on the classical compositions of a number of composers in different cultures (see NATIONALISM). Cf. ETHNOMUSICOLOGY.

folk rock an attempt in the 1960s to combine folk-style songs (which usu. were not true folk songs but newly composed works imitating a folk style) with a rock or popular beat, as practiced by Bob Dylan, Simon and Garfunkel and others.

folk song a song, possibly once a work composed by a single person or by an ethnic group, that has entered oral tradition and has been passed on from generation to generation. The term is also used for newly composed works imitating the style of true folk songs.

follia FOLIA.

Fontane di Roma (It.) FOUNTAINS OF ROME.

foot 1, in poetry, a group of syllables forming part of a verse and containing a principal stressed syllable and one or more unstressed syllables. **2**, a standard measure for the air column in an organ pipe. The standard reference is the 8-foot C, two octaves below the bass staff; the 16-foot is an octave lower, the 4-foot an octave higher than the reference tone.

Foote, Arthur (William) (1853–1937) Amer. composer, organist and pianist, stud. of John Knowles Paine. He received from Harvard U. the first master's degree in music given in the U.S. and was one of the first musicians of note to receive all of his training in the U.S. He was organist at the Church of the Disciples in Boston (1878–1910) and taught at the New England Conservatory from 1920 until his death. His compositions incl. orchestral, chamber and choral works as well as songs.

footed drum a single-headed DRUM having legs, which are often cut from the wood body of the drum.

Forbes, Elliot (1917–) Amer. choral conductor and musicologist, trained at Harvard. He taught at Princeton (1947–58), then returned to Harvard, where he taught and conducted the Harvard Glee Club and the Radcliffe Choral Society. He edited the Harvard-Radcliffe Choral Music Series after 1959 and prepared the revised edition of Thayer's *Life of Beethoven*.

Ford, Thomas (c1580–1648) English composer, lutenist and viol player. He was in the service of the court as composer and viol player from 1611 until several years before his death. His extant works include anthems, part-songs and instrumental music, much of the latter published in his *Musicke of Sundrie Kinds* (1607).

foreground in Schenkerian analysis, the layer of musical analysis which most closely resembles the composition itself. The foreground sketch generally preserves the pitch content of the composition, usu. divesting it, however, of its rhythm, scoring and certain ornamental details. The foreground analysis takes account of short-range musical relationships, leaving longer-range, more comprehensive analyses to the MIDDLEGROUND and BACKGROUND sketches. See SCHENKER.

Forelle, Die (Ger.) THE TROUT.

For He's a Jolly Good Fellow a 19th-c. English text for the French satirical song "Malbrouk s'en va-t-en guerre," of unknown authorship and origin. Another text for the same melody is *The Bear Went over the Mountain*.

forlana *also*, **furlana** (It.) a lively north Italian dance in 6/8 or 6/4 time, which became a popular French court dance in the early 18th c.

formalism a term used in the USSR as an official criticism of certain music influenced too greatly by the Western developments of Stravinsky, Hindemith and others.

formant the relationship between frequency and amplitude in a sound-producing device (determined by the physical characteristics of the device), which defines the actual quality or timbre of the resulting sound.

formes fixes [form fēks] (Fr.) fixed forms of the French chanson, prominent during the 14th and 15th c. The most widely known are the RONDEAU (ABaAabAB), the BALLADE (aaB . . .) and the VIRELAI (AbbaA . . .).

Forrester, Maureen (1930–) Canadian contralto, stud. of Sally Martin, Frank Rowe and Bernard Diamant. She has sung internationally in concert and recital. Her operatic debut was in 1961 in Gluck's *Orfeo* and her operatic repertory incl. such roles as Erda, Ulrica (*Il Trovatore*) and the Witch in *Hansel and Gretel*. She has been chairman of the Voice Department at the Philadelphia Academy of Music and was head of the Canada Council from 1984 to 1989.

forte ['fôr-tā] (It.) loud; *abbr.f*

fortepiano (It.) an old term for PIANOFORTE. It is used currently to indicate the piano of the 18th and early 19th c. to distinguish it from the 20th-c. instrument.

forte-piano (It.) loud, then soft; *abbr.fp*

fortissimo (It.) very loud; *abbr.ff, fff.*

fortissississimo (It.) extremely loud; *abbr.fff*

Fortner, Wolfgang (1907–87) German composer and teacher, stud. of Grabner. He taught in Heidelberg, Darmstadt and elsewhere, his students including Henze. He was founder of the Heidelberg Chamber Orch. and the Heidelberg Musica Viva concerts; he also conducted the Munich Musica Viva from 1964. His many works in all genres utilize his own version of serial technique.

Forty-Eight, The THE WELL-TEMPERED CLAVIER.

Forza del Destino, La ['for-tsä] (It., The Force of Destiny) tragic opera in 4 acts by Verdi to a libretto by Francesco Maria Piave, based on a play by Angel de Saavedra. Premiere, St. Petersburg 1862. Don Alvaro accidentally kills the father of his beloved Leonora.

forzando, forzato [for'tsän-dō; -'tsä-tō] (It.) SFORZANDO. *Abbr. fz*

Foss (Fuchs), **Lukas** (1922–) German-born Amer. composer, conductor and pianist, stud. of Julius Goldstein, Noël Gallon and Felix Wolfes in Europe and of Virgil Thompson, Reiner, Koussevitzky and Hindemith in America. He has been conductor of the Buffalo PO and was founder of the Center for Creative and Performing Arts at SUNY Buffalo. Since 1971 he has been conductor of the Brooklyn Philharmonia and the Kol Israel Orch. of Jerusalem. His works have covered a wide range of styles, from neo-classical through improvisation to serial and graphic techniques.

Foster, Lawrence (Thomas) (1941–) Amer. conductor, stud. of Fritz Zweig. He was assoc. conductor of the San Francisco Ballet, assistant conductor of the Los Angeles PO and musical dir. of the Houston SO. He has guest-conducted in the U.S. and Europe, performing a wide variety of music with an emphasis on contemporary works.

Foster, Pops (George Murphy) (?1892–1969) Amer. jazz double-bass and tuba player from New Orleans. He played with King Oliver and Kid Ory and also with riverboat bands. He went to New York in 1929 to join King Oliver and then played with

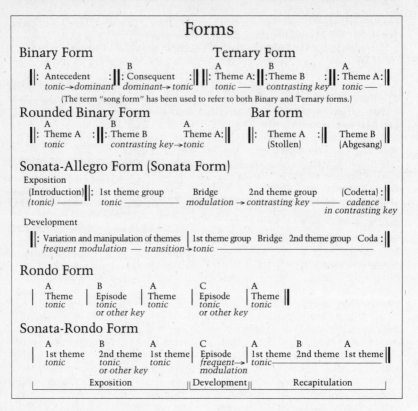

Forms

Binary Form

A — Antecedent (tonic→dominant) : Consequent (dominant→tonic) B

Ternary Form

A — Theme A (tonic —) : Theme B (contrasting key) : Theme A (tonic —)

(The term "song form" has been used to refer to both Binary and Ternary forms.)

Rounded Binary Form

A — Theme A (tonic) : Theme B (contrasting key→tonic) B — Theme A

Bar form

A — Theme A (Stollen) : Theme B (Abgesang)

Sonata-Allegro Form (Sonata Form)

Exposition

(Introduction) (tonic) — : 1st theme group (tonic) — Bridge (modulation → contrasting key) 2nd theme group — (Codetta) cadence in contrasting key :

Development

: Variation and manipulation of themes (frequent modulation — transition→tonic) 1st theme group   Bridge   2nd theme group   Coda :

Rondo Form

A — Theme (tonic)   B — Episode (tonic or other key)   A — Theme (tonic)   C — Episode (tonic or other key)   A — Theme (tonic)

Sonata-Rondo Form

A — 1st theme (tonic)   B — 2nd theme (tonic or other key)   A — 1st theme (tonic)   C — Episode (frequent→ modulation)   A — 1st theme (tonic)   B — 2nd theme   A — 1st theme

Exposition   Development   Recapitulation

Luis Russel's orch. for 11 years. In the late 1950s he played with Earl Hines in New York.

Foster, Stephen Collins (1826–64) Amer. songwriter, largely self-taught. His songwriting began in the late 1840s, and in 1850 he made an arrangement with Christy's Minstrels to give them exclusive first-performance rights to any song he produced. Despite the wide success of his works—which incl. sentimental ballads, minstrel songs and hymns—he died in poverty. His best-known songs incl. "Old Folks at Home" (1851, the state song of Florida), "Jeannie with the Light Brown Hair" (1854), "My Old Kentucky Home" (1853, the state song of Kentucky), and minstrel songs such as "Oh! Susannah" (1848) and "Camptown Races" (1850).

foundation stops a family of flue OR-GAN STOPS, usu. metal, with a strong fundamental tone and fewer overtones.

Fountain, Pete (Peter Dewey, Jr.) (1930–) Amer. jazz clarinetist and saxophonist. He became famous from his collaborations with Lawrence Welk in a Dixieland band drawn from Welk's orch. He opened his own club, Pete's Place, in New Orleans in the 1960s, where he frequently headlined, in addition to TV and radio appearances.

Fountains of Rome (It., *Fontane di Roma*) an orchestral tone poem (1916) by Respighi. Its four sections, each one depicting a different Roman fountain at a different time of day, are "The Valle Giulia Fountain at Dawn," "The Triton Fountain at Morning," "The Trevi Fountain at Noon" and "The Villa Medici Fountain at Sunset."

four-beat jazz synonym for SWING, contrasted with the preceding style of New Orleans jazz, known as "two-beat jazz."

four-foot stop an ORGAN STOP which sounds an octave higher than written.

Four Horsemen *also*, **Four Brothers** a term for the famous saxophone line in Woody Herman's Second Herd in the late 1940s, featuring Zoot Sims, Stan Getz, Serge Chaloff and Herbie Steward. The name came from a song written for Herman by Jimmy Giuffre.

Fournet, Jean [foor'nā] (1913–) French conductor, stud. of Philippe Gaubert. He was dir. of the Paris Opéra-Comique (1944–57) and taught at the École Normale until 1962. He became conductor of the Dutch Radio PO in 1961 and artistic dir. of the Rotterdam PO in 1968. He has specialized in the French operatic and symphonic repertory as well as in the works of Brahms.

Fournier, Pierre (Léon Marie) [foor'nyā] (1906–85) French cellist, stud. of Paul Bazelaire and André Hekking. He has taught at the École Normale de Musique and the Paris Conservatoire. Noted as a chamber musician, he has performed in chamber groups with Thibaud and Cortot, with Szeryng and Kempff and with Szigeti, Primrose and Schnabel. Numerous works have been written for him by Poulenc, Martin, Frank Martin and others.

fourniture [foor-nē'tür] (Fr.) **1,** a MIXTURE stop on the Great or Choir division of an organ, composed largely of fifth- and octave-sounding pipes. **2,** The BLOCKWERK of an organ without the principals and flutes.

four-note sol-fa see FASOLA.

fours a term in jazz for the practice of breaking up an improvised chorus into four-bar phrases, each taken by a different soloist. Also, *chase chorus*.

Four Saints in Three Acts surrealistic opera in 4 acts by Virgil Thomson to a libretto by Gertrude Stein. Premiere, Hartford, CT, 1934. A series of stylized vignettes concerning imaginary saints.

Four Seasons, The (It., *Le Quattro Stagioni*) a set of four violin concertos, Op. 8 Nos. 1–4 (1725), by Vivaldi, which depict, by means of vivid devices, the characteristics of each season.

Four Serious Songs (Ger., *Vier ernste Gesänge*) a set of four songs for low voice, Op. 121 (1896), by Brahms, his last composition, based on extracts from Luther's translation of the Bible.

Four Temperaments, The 1, a theme and variations for piano and strings (1940) by Hindemith. **2,** the Symphony No. 2, Op. 16 (1902), by Nielsen. Each of the four movements represents one of the four human temperaments—choleric, phlegmatic, melancholic and sanguine.

Four Tops, The Amer. vocal soul quartet formed in the early 1950s in Detroit and highly successful from the late 1960s with songs incl. "I Can't Help Myself" (1965).

fourth an INTERVAL spanning three diatonic scale degrees. The *perfect fourth* spans two whole steps and a half step. The *augmented fourth* is one half step larger than the perfect fourth and occurs in the major scale only between the fourth and seventh degrees. The *diminished fourth* is one half step smaller than the perfect fourth and is the enharmonic equivalent of the major third. During the Middle Ages, the perfect fourth was considered to be a consonance, although later Renaissance practice established it as a dissonance. However, 20th-c. harmonic practice has come to accept chords built on the fourth as stable and consonant.

Fox, Carol (1926–81) Amer. opera impresario, vocal stud. of Giovanni Martinelli and others. Determined to revive opera in Chicago, with conductor Nicola Rescigno and manager Lawrence Kelly she formed the Lyric Theatre of Chicago in 1954, using almost exclusively Italian artists, incl. Maria Callas in her American debut. Fox took sole control in 1956 and renamed the company the LYRIC OPERA OF CHICAGO.

Fox, Sam firm of music publishers, est. 1906, which pioneered the publication of film music. The firm became the exclusive publisher for Sousa's music from 1917 until his death in 1934.

Fox, Virgil (Keel) (1912–80) Amer. organist, trained at the Peabody Conservatory and with Marcel Dupré in Paris. He headed the Organ Dept. at Peabody (1938–42) and was organist at Riverside Church in New York (1946–65). He was a flamboyant recitalist, who traveled with a special electronic organ and light show and his own popularizing arrangements of the classics.

foxtrot a 20th-c. Amer. ballroom dance in duple time, derived from the ragtime dances of the early part of the century; its music could be either slow or fast (*quickstep*).

fp *abbr.* FORTE-PIANO.

Frager, Malcolm (1935–91) Amer. pianist, stud. of Carl Friedberg. He won the Leventritt Award (1959) and the Queen Elizabeth International Piano Competition in Brussels (1960). He has specialized in the works of Haydn, Mozart, Schubert and Beethoven, which he has sometimes performed on the fortepiano.

frailing a stroked banjo style of the Appalachian region.

frame drum a DRUM consisting of one or more membranes stretched over a frame of wood or other material. The membranes, of skin or plastic, may be pegged to the frame or may be attached by cords, often by a method allowing them to be tuned by tightening or loosening the cords. The modern BASS DRUM is an example of a frame drum, as is the TAMBOURINE.

Frampton, Peter (1950–) English rock guitarist and singer. In the late 1960s he was a member of the Herd and also Humble Pie. In 1973 he formed his own group, Frampton's Camel, with which he toured and recorded extensively.

Francaix, Jean [frä'se *or* -'seks] (1912–) French composer and pianist, stud. of Boulanger. As a virtuoso concert pianist, he toured extensively throughout Europe and the U.S., performing his own works. His large body of compositions touches every medium, incl. stage, film, orchestral, instrumental and vocal works, best known of which are his oratorio *L'apocalypse de St. Jean* (1939) and the opera *Le diable boiteux* (1937).

Francesca da Rimini tone poem, Op. 32 (1876), by Tchaikovsky, based on an episode from Dante's *Inferno*.

Francescatti, Zino (René) (1902–91) French violinist, taught by his parents. In addition to an active solo career, he performed in duo on tour with Ravel and, in his later years, with pianist Robert Casadesus.

Franck, César (-Auguste-Jean-Guillaume-Hubert) [fräk] (1822–90) Belgian-born French composer, organist and teacher. As organist at the basilica St. Clothilde from 1858 his extemporizations became well known. He became professor of organ at the Paris Conservatoire in 1872, a post he held until his death. His pupils there incl. Duparc, d'Indy and many others. Of Franck's extensive output, many works still remain in the standard repertory, incl. the Symphony in D minor (1886–8), the tone poem *Ce qu'on entend sur la montagne*, sacred vocal works (in particular, the *Panis angelicus*), the violin sonata and organ works.

Frank, Claude (1925–) German-born Amer. teacher and pianist, stud. of Schnabel. In addition to an active solo concert career, he has also appeared as a choral conductor, as a member of the Boston Symphony Chamber Players, and in piano duo with his wife Lilian Kallir. He has taught at Yale since 1972.

Franklin, Aretha (1942–) Amer. gospel, soul and popular singer, daughter of a Baptist minister. Through the years she has never been far from the top of the charts. Her many hits incl. "Respect," "Since You've Been Gone," "Day Dreaming" and "Jump to It."

Franklin, Benjamin (1706–90) Amer. statesman and music amateur, inventor of the "armonica," an improvement on the MUSICAL GLASSES. He played the harp, the guitar and the glass dulcimer and wrote a short treatise on music aesthetics.

Frank Music Corp. firm of music publishers founded by composer-lyricist FRANK LOESSER and specializing in the publication of music for musical theater.

Franz (Knauth), **Robert** (1815–92) German composer and organist, stud. of J.C.F. Schneider, but largely self-taught. Liszt was an ardent admirer and wrote a biography of Franz in 1872. Franz produced a large body of vocal and choral works, as well as numerous editions and arrangements of vocal works, esp. of J.S. Bach.

Frau ohne Schatten, Die [frow 'ō-ne 'shät-ən, dē] (Ger., The Woman without a Shadow) opera in 3 acts by Richard Strauss to a libretto in German by Hugo von Hofmannsthal. Premiere, Vienna 1919. The story of the cleansing and redemption of two couples: the dyer Barak and his wife and the Emperor and his half-supernatural Empress.

Frauenliebe und Leben ['frow-ən 'lē-bən ûnt 'lā-bən] (Ger., Woman's Love and Life) song cycle, Op. 42 (1840), by Schumann to words by Adalbert von Chamisso. The eight songs span a woman's life, from her first love to the death of her husband.

Frederick II (the Great), King of Prussia (1712–86) German monarch, intellectual, flutist and composer, stud. of Gottlieb Hayne and Quantz. He established the Berlin Opera under the direction of his general court musician C.H. Graun and developed a musical establishment with such illustrious musicians as C.P.E. Bach, Quantz and Agricola. In addition to the operas and intermezzi, there were regular performances of instrumental chamber music, often with Frederick as performer or composer. His works incl. 25 flute sonatas and four concertos.

free bass accordion a type of ACCORDION having for the left hand single-pitch buttons rather than chords, allowing the performance of both tonal and nontonal works.

free counterpoint part-writing following a free approach, as opposed to one strictly governed by imitation, invertibility, or a cantus firmus. See COUNTERPOINT.

Freed, Alan (1922–65) Amer. disc jockey, a significant force in bringing rhythm-and-blues to a wide audience and in integrating popular music concerts. From 1954 to 1959 he worked in New York for WINS and WABC until his alleged complicity in payola scandals resulted in his being fired.

Freed, Isadore (1900–60) Russian-born Amer. composer, stud. of Bloch, Josef Hoffman, d'Indy and Vierne. He taught at the Curtis Institute, Temple U. and the U. of Hartford. His works incl. the opera *The Princess and the Vagabond* (1948), orchestral and instrumental chamber music, and music for the Jewish sacred service.

Freedman, Harry (1922–) Polish-born Canadian oboist and composer, stud. of Weinzweig, Messiaen and Krenek. He played English horn with the Toronto SO from 1946 to 1969 and was composer-in-residence during his final year. His compositions, mostly written with serial techniques, are in all genres, incl. ballets, film scores, orchestral and choral works and chamber music.

free jazz an avant-garde jazz movement beginning in the 1960s involving improvisation through free association with no set harmonies or tonality, no bar lines and no preestablished melodic pattern. The movement was orig. championed by saxophonist Ornette Coleman, though similar tendencies were evident in the earlier work of Lennie Tristano, Charles Mingus and others. Also, *abstraction*.

Freeman, Bud (Lawrence) (1906–91) Amer. jazz tenor saxophonist, clarinetist and composer. His long career has alternated between years of solo concertizing and work with the bands of Red Nichols, Benny Goodman, Tommy Dorsey, Eddie Condon and others. With Coleman Hawkins, he was the most influential tenor saxophonist of the early 20th c.

Freeman, Harry Lawrence (1869–1954) Amer. composer and conductor, stud. of Johann Beck. He was one of the first Afr.-Amer. composers of opera; his first opera, *The Martyr*, was produced in Denver in 1893. His works incl. 14 operas, orchestral works, a ballet and songs.

Freeman, Paul (Douglas) (1936–) Amer. conductor, trained at the Eastman School, at the Berlin Hochschule für Musik and with Pierre Monteux. He has been assoc. conductor of the Dallas SO, conductor-in-residence of the Detroit SO and music dir. of the Victoria (Canada) SO (from 1979). He recorded a nine-album Black Composers Series for Columbia Records, conducts for Opera Ebony (since 1977) and is founder-conductor of the Chicago Sinfonia.

Freer, Eleanor Everest (1864–1942) Amer. composer, stud. of Benjamin Godard and Bernard Ziehn. She was known for her commitment to making music (esp. opera) accessible to the community and was a founding member of the Amer. Opera Society of Chicago in 1925. She composed 11 operas and over 150 songs.

free-reed see REED.

Freischütz, Der ['frī-shüts, där] (Ger., The Free-Shooter) romantic opera in 3 acts by Weber to a libretto by Friedrich Kind. Premiere, Berlin 1821. Max conspires with the devil to win the shooting contest and Agathe's hand.

Fremstad, Olive (1871–1951) Swedish-born Amer. mezzo-soprano, stud. of Lilli Lehmann. She sang at the Munich Opera (1900–3). Her U.S. debut was at the Metropolitan Opera in 1903 as Sieglinde. She specialized in the roles of Wagner, and also sang Carmen, Tosca and Salome.

French, Mrs. (fl. 1817–25) Amer. soprano, stud. of Benjamin Carr and Henri-Noel Gilles. She was described as the finest Amer. singer of her time, performing recitals of British and Amer. popular ballads and Italian and French songs.

French harp HARMONICA.

French horn see HORN.

French overture an introductory movement combining a slow, stately opening—characterized by a heavily dotted rhythm—with a lively, fugal second section. This type of movement, which originated in the 17th c. in the ballets of Lully, was much used as the opening of operas, ballets and instrumental suites.

French sixth an AUGMENTED SIXTH CHORD on the flattened sixth degree having both a major 3rd and an augmented 4th, as well as an augmented 6th. See CHORD (*illus.*).

French Suites the popular name for a set of six keyboard suites, BWV 812–17 (c 1722), by J.S. Bach. The first five appear in earlier versions in the Clavier-büchlein Bach prepared for his wife, Anna Magdalena Bach.

Freni (Fregni), **Mirella** (1935–) Italian lyric soprano, stud. of Campogalliani. Her Metropolitan Opera debut was in 1965, and she has sung regularly at La Scala and at Covent Garden. She is best known for her performance of Mimì (*La Bohème*), Micaela (*Carmen*), Susanna (*The Marriage of Figaro*), and such heavier roles as Desdemona (*Otello*) and Cio-cio-san (*Madama Butterfly*).

frequency the number of exact repetitions of a cyclical pattern, esp. the vibrations of a SOUND-producing body.

Frescobaldi, Girolamo (1583–1643) Italian composer and organist, stud. of Luzzaschi in Ferrara, active in Rome and Florence. Frescobaldi was famous in his own time both as an organist and as a composer, and his keyboard works chronicle the development from the late Renaissance to the Baroque. He also produced a significant body of sacred and secular vocal music.

fret a ridge of ivory, metal or other material on the fingerboard of a string instrument, used to mark the location of the pitches. On Western instruments, the distance between frets is usu. a semitone.

fricasée [frē-kä′sā] (Fr.) ENSALADA.

Frick, Gottlob (1906–) German bass, trained at the Stuttgart Conservatory. He is particularly noted for his interpretation of Wagnerian roles, as well as Rocco (*Fidelio*) and Gremin (*Eugene Onegin*). He retired in 1970.

Fricker, Peter Racine (1920–) English composer, trained at the Royal Conservatory of Music and, after the war, with Seiber. He became dir. of Morley College in 1952 and taught at the Royal Conservatory from 1955. In 1964 he went to the U. of California at Santa Barbara, where he later became chairman of the music department. His works are mostly in a free atonal style.

Fricsay, Ferenc (1914–63) Hungarian conductor, stud. of Kodály and Bartók. He conducted at the Budapest Opera and the Budapest PO. His U.S. debut was with the Boston SO in 1953 and he was for one season musical dir. of the Houston SO (1954) but returned the following year to Europe to conduct the Bavarian Staatsoper and the Berlin Radio Symphony Orch. He was particularly noted for his interpretations of the works of his teachers, Kodály and Bartók.

friction drum a DRUM whose membrane is made to sound by friction rather than by percussion, as by a stick, cord or thong passing through or in contact with the membrane. The instrument is found in Africa, Asia, Europe and So. America.

Friends and Enemies of Modern Music concert organization devoted to new music, founded in Hartford, CT, in 1929.

Friml, (Charles) Rudolf (1879–1972) Czech-born Amer. pianist and composer, stud. of Dvořák. He came to the U.S. in 1906 and made a reputation as an improviser and composer of character pieces, etc., some written under a pseudonym (Roderick Freeman). He is best known for his romantic operettas, which incl. *Rose-Marie* (1924) and *The Vagabond King* (1925).

friss [frish] (Hung.) the fast section of a csárdás or rhapsody; contrasted with LASSÚ. Cf. VERBUNKOS.

Frizzell, Lefty (1928–) Amer. honky-tonk singer, songwriter and guitarist, elected to the Country Music Hall of Fame in 1982. His hits incl. "I Want to Be with You Always" and "Always Late."

Froberger, Johann Jakob (1616–67) German composer, organist and keyboard player, stud. of Frescobaldi. His extant works are all for keyboard (with the exception of two vocal works) and exhibit Froberger's familiarity with the Italian and French styles. His influence on German music was felt well into the 18th c.

frog the movable device on a violin bow that secures the hair at the lower end of the bow stick and permits the regulation of its tension. The adjustable frog dates from the late 17th c. Also, *nut, heel.*

Frog Quartet (Ger., *Froschquartett*) a popular nickname for the string quartet in D major, Op. 50, No. 6, by Haydn. The theme of the last movement suggests to some the croaking of a frog.

From Bohemia's Meadows and Forests the fourth movement of MÁ VLAST by Smetana.

From My Life the String Quartet No. 1 in E minor (1876) by Smetana.

From the House of the Dead opera in 3 acts by Janáček to his own libretto, based on Dostoyevsky's prison novel. Premiere, Brno 1930.

From the New World the title of the Symphony No. 9 in E minor, Op. 95 (1893), by Dvořák, which was composed in America and attempts to reproduce some of the characteristics of popular American and Afr.-Amer. music.

Fromm Music Foundation a foundation established in Chicago in 1952 by the late philanthropist Paul Fromm (1907–87) to support the composition and performance of contemporary music. From 1964 to 1983 it funded the annual Tanglewood Festival of Contemporary Music; the Festival was moved to the Aspen School of Music in 1985. It also commissions works from Amer. composers, often assisting with their performance costs, and has sponsored recordings, seminars and the publication of *Perspectives of New Music*. It is now based at Harvard.

front to lead a jazz band, either as director or as headlining soloist.

front-line in a jazz band, the instrumentalists not in the rhythm section.

Frosch [frosh] (Ger.) Frog.

frottola (It.) a secular Italian part-song, flourishing in the late 15th and early 16th c., the most important forerunner of the 16th-c. Italian madrigal. In its specific definition, the frottola has the form ABAAB. More generally, the term refers to any popular polyphonic Italian form dating from c. 1470 to 1530. Cf. Strambotto, Canzone.

Frugoni, Orazio (1921–) Italian-born Amer. pianist, stud. of Scuderi, Casella and Lipatti. He was professor at the Eastman School of Music and has been dir. since 1967 of the Graduate School of Fine Arts at Villa Schifanoia in Florence.

Frühbeck de Burgos, Rafael (1933–) Spanish conductor, trained at the Munich Hochschule für Musik. He has been conductor of the Orquestra Nacional in Madrid (1962–), general music dir. in Düsseldorf (1966–71) and music dir. of the Montreal SO (1975–6). He has guest-conducted in Europe, Israel and the U.S. and recorded with the New Philharmonia, among other orchestras.

Fry, William Henry (1813–64) Amer. composer and critic, stud. of Leopold Meignen. He was European and later New York music critic of the *New York Tribune* (1846–52). His opera *Leonora* (1845) was the first grand opera composed in the U.S., and his *Notre Dame of Paris* was produced in Philadelphia in 1864, with Theodore Thomas making his operatic conducting debut.

Frye, Walter (fl. c.1450–75) English composer of Mass settings, motets, ballades and rondeaus, some of which provided cantus firmi for works by Josquin, Obrecht and others.

Fuchs, Joseph [fooks] (1900–) Amer. violinist and teacher, brother of Lillian Fuchs, stud. of Franz Kneisel. He was concertmaster of the Cleveland Orch. from 1926 to 1940, then pursued his solo career. He has been on the faculty of the Juilliard School since 1946 and has premiered a number of works, incl. the Piston Violin Concerto, which he commissioned.

Fuchs, Lillian (1903–) Amer. violist, composer and teacher, sister of Joseph Fuchs. She studied with Kneisel and Goetschius and was a member of the Perolé String Quartet. She has taught at the Manhattan School of Music, the Aspen Summer Institute and the Juilliard School. Her works incl. a *Sonata pastorale* (1956) for solo viola and 15 Characteristic Studies for violin and piano.

fuga ['foo-gä] (It.) Fugue.

fugato (It., fugued) in the style of a Fugue, but usu. less strictly carried out.

fuge Fuging Tune.

fughetta (It., small fugue) a short Fugue.

fuging tune also, **fuguing tune** an Amer. polyphonic hymn of the 18th and early 19th c., usu. in two sections, with the first being in block harmonies, the second employing imitation.

fugue a compositional technique involving the use of a single main theme that is treated imitatively. This procedure has been used with varying degrees of strictness in a variety of different forms since the 15th c.

A standard fugue begins with an *exposition*, in which the main theme (*subject*) is stated by each voice in turn, usu. entering at different pitch levels. The first statement is usu. unaccompanied. The second entry (*answer*) is generally at the interval of a fourth or fifth away from the first entry. The second and subsequent statements of the subject may be accompanied by another theme regularly associated with them (*counter-subject*). The exposition is followed by a section (*episode*) that may employ any number of devices and which may or may not be based on the subject or counter-subject. The alternation of episodes with subject-answer sections continues until the end of the fugue, which may be signaled by a *stretto*, or series of entries closer to each other in time than in the exposition.

There are as many variations on this standard procedure as there are fugues. However, a higher degree of strictness distinguishes the fugue from other forms of imitative counterpoint. Cf. CANON, ROUND, CATCH, FUGATO, STRETTO.

Fuleihan, Anis (1900–70) Cyprus-born Amer. composer, conductor and pianist, stud. of Alberto Jonas. He toured as a concert pianist and worked as a radio conductor in the 1930s. His works have been frequently performed by Amer. orchestras and are characterized by an oriental character and a moderate use of dissonance.

full anthem an ANTHEM for chorus without soloists and with optional instrumental accompaniment. Cf. VERSE ANTHEM.

full cadence *also*, **full close** PERFECT CADENCE.

Fugue

Exposition
Subject

Answer (real)

Countersubject

Episode

(J.S.Bach, Well-Tempered Clavier, Fugue II)

Subject

Subject

Stretto   Subject

Subject

(J.S.Bach, Well-Tempered Clavier, Fugue XVI)

Subject

Fuller, Blind Boy (Fulton, Allen) (?1909–41) Amer. blues singer and guitarist, best with fast ragtime themes, who had a gravelly voice and used washboard accompaniment. During his last years he played frequently with harmonica player Sonny Terry.

Fuller, Jesse (1896–1976) Amer. folk instrumentalist and songwriter, one of the best-known one-man bands, specializing in 12-string guitar and harmonica.

full orchestra ORCHESTRA.

full organ an organ played with most or all of the stops pulled. The term has different, more specific meanings for different schools of organ playing.

full score a score which contains all of the instrumental and/or vocal parts, esp. when the parts are all printed on separate staves.

functional harmony a type of harmonic practice based on the usu. relationships of chords in traditional tonal writing, esp. those between tonic, dominant and subdominant.

fundamental 1, the lowest note of a chord. **2,** the first harmonic, usu. the main sound of an instrument. On some instruments, however, esp. brass instruments, this note is practically unobtainable. Also, *pedal tone.* See HARMONICS.

fundamental bass an imaginary bass line composed of the roots (not necessarily the lowest notes) of a succession of chords.

funèbre [fü'ne-brə] (Fr.) funereal.

funeral march a slow, mournful march, such as one might play for a funeral procession. Many composers have written works in this character, such as the slow movements from Beethoven's Piano Sonata in A♭ major, Op. 26 (1800) and Chopin's Piano Sonata in B♭ minor, Op. 35 (1840).

Funeral Symphony (Ger., *Trauersinfonie*) the Symphony No. 44 in E minor (1772) by Haydn.

funk a term of uncertain origin indicating a style of Afr.-Amer. popular music characterized by heavy syncopation and extended vamping over one or two chords. The style came into prominence during the 1950s as a reaction to the intellectualism of cool jazz, and was exemplified by the music of Horace Silver and Art Blakey, which incorporated elements of blues and gospel into jazz. Later developments during the 1970s include STREET FUNK (Sly and the Family Stone, Kool and the Gang, and George Clinton's various groups) and then a fusion with DISCO in the late 1970s, typified by Chic's "Le Freak." An offshoot of the style in the early 1980s is HIP-HOP.

Funkadelic Amer. funk rock group formed in 1970 by George Clinton.

Funny Face musical by Gershwin, lyrics by Ira Gershwin, book by Paul Gerard Smith and Fred Thompson. Premiere, New York 1927. A complicated tale of a diary and a bracelet.

Funny Girl musical by Jule Styne, lyrics by Bob Merrill, book by Isobel Lennart. Premiere, New York 1964. The story of actress Fanny Brice (the role was created by Barbra Streisand).

Funny Thing Happened on the Way to the Forum, A musical by Stephen Sondheim, lyrics by the composer, book by Burt Shevelove and Larry Gelbart, based on plays by Titus Maccius Plautus. Premiere, New York 1962. A "scenario for vaudevillians" based on Plautus's characters.

fuoco, con ['fwo-kō, kōn] (It.) with fire, with passion.

Für Elise [für ā'lē-əe] (Ger., for Elise) the Bagatelle in A minor (1810) by Beethoven, first published in 1867, when the title (prob. erroneous) was added.

furiant (Czech.) a Bohemian dance whose meter alternates between ¾ and ²⁄₄, or its stylized equivalent, which regularizes the ²⁄₄ to ⁶⁄₈, resulting in a hemiola effect.

furlana [It.] FORLANA.

furniture a MIXTURE stop in a pipe organ. Cf. FOURNITURE.

furniture music a term coined by Eric Satie for BACKGROUND MUSIC.

Furtwängler, (Gustav Heinrich Ernst Martin) Wilhelm (1886–1954) German conductor, composer and author, stud. of Joseph Rheinberger and Max von Schillings. In 1922 he became conductor of the Berlin PO, with which orch. he continued to work for the rest of his career. He conducted the New York PO as guest conductor for three seasons (1925–27), but his highly individual interpretations were not well received by some of the critics and Toscanini was engaged in subsequent years instead. Furtwängler never conducted again in America. Although he did not cooperate with the Nazi regime, when the Chicago SO offered him the position of musical dir. in 1949, the outcry was sufficient to force the board to withdraw its offer.

Furtwängler fortunately has left a legacy of recordings that attest to his vision of music, quite different from the Toscanini approach. His works, although in a neo-Romantic style not now in vogue, cover a range of genres, incl. orchestral, choral and chamber music.

fusion a term for a composite musical type that combines two or more different styles. The most common use of the term is for the combination of jazz and rock (also called *jazz-rock* or *electric rock*) as pioneered by MILES DAVIS in the mid-1960s and the band Weather Report in the 1970s and 1980s, characterized by heavy amplification, strong rock rhythms and the use of synthesizers and electric piano.

futurism a movement in the visual arts, and to a lesser degree in music, initiated in Italy in the first decade of the 20th c. The musical manifestation of the movement was the experimental use of noises related to everyday experience, for the production of which machines were developed. The resulting sounds were prophetic of *musique concrète* and the electronic music of a later generation. The futurist movement died out by the end of the 1920s.

Fux, Johann Joseph (1660–1741) Austrian composer and theorist, trained in Graz at a Jesuit school. He became Kapellmeister to the Emperor Leopold I in 1698 and vice-Kapellmeister (later Kapellmeister) at St. Stephen's Cathedral in Vienna in 1705. He was an active teacher, as well as a prolific composer of church and secular music, incl. 20 operas, oratorios, masses, motets, and instrumental sonatas and partitas. His *Gradus ad Parnassum* was (and remains) one of the most important textbooks of COUNTERPOINT.

fuye (Jap.) a Jap. bamboo side-blown FLUTE.

fuzz an electronic modification of sound—most often of the electric guitar—to produce a rough, distorted tone. The device is usu. controlled by a foot pedal. Variants include the *fuzz-wah* and *fuzz-phaser*.

fz. *abbr.* FORZANDO.

G

G 1, fifth note of the scale of C major. See PITCH. **2,** see G CLEF.

Gabrieli, Andrea (Andrea di Cannaregio) (?1510–1586) Italian composer and organist, uncle of GIOVANNI GABRIELI. He made a significant contribution to every musical genre from the mass to ribald secular songs and instrumental ricercars. From 1566 he was organist at St. Mark's in Venice, where he remained until his death.

Gabrieli, Giovanni (c1555–1612) Italian composer and organist, nephew and student of ANDREA GABRIELI. In Venice he was organist at St. Mark's and at the Scuola Grande di St. Rocco, retaining both posts until his death. His life spanned the passage from the Renaissance into the early Baroque, and his works include compositions in both styles. His choral works, esp. the *Symphoniae sacrae*, are noted for their employment of large performing forces, divided into two or more choirs (see CORI SPEZZATI).

Gabrilovich, Ossip (1878–1936) Russian-born Amer. pianist, conductor and composer, stud. of Anton Rubinstein, Lyadov and Glazunov in St. Petersburg and Leschetizky in Vienna. His U.S. debut was in 1900; in 1918 he became conductor of the Detroit SO. His wife was Clara Clemens, a singer and daughter of Mark Twain.

Gaburo, Kenneth (Louis) (1926–) Amer. composer, trained at the Eastman School of Music, the U. of Illinois and at Tanglewood. He has taught at Kent State U., McNeese State U., the U. of Illinois and the U. of California at San Diego. He is conductor of the New Music Choral Ensemble, a virtuoso chamber group of 16 singers specializing in contemporary works. His works have covered a wide spectrum of media, incl. electronic works, theater music and TEXT-SOUND COMPOSITIONS.

Gadd, Steve (1945–) Amer. jazz drummer, trained at the Eastman School of Music. He played with Chick Corea, led his own trio (short-lived), then free-lanced in New York. He has played in rhythm sections on numerous albums, backing Paul McCartney, Barbra Streisand, Carla Bley and others and has been credited with being a creator of the prevalent 1980s fusion drum sound.

Gade, Niels (Wilhelm) (1817–90) Danish composer and violinist, stud. of A.P. Berggreen. In Copenhagen he reorganized the Musical Society, establishing a permanent orch. and choir. He was organist of the society from 1851 and director of the Copenhagen Academy of Music from 1866. His large output includes stage works, choral music, eight symphonies, tone poems, chamber music, songs and keyboard pieces.

gadulka a pear-shaped Bulgarian folk FIDDLE with three or four strings, played with the instrument resting against the knee or the belt.

Gaetani, Jan de DE GAETANI, JAN.

Gaffurius, Franchinus (1451–1522) Italian theorist and composer of motets and masses written for the Cathedral of Milan. In 1484 he became *maestro di capella* of the Milan Cathedral, a position he retained until his death. His three most significant treatises—*Teorica musicae* (1492), *Practica musicae* (1496) and *De harmonia musicorum instrumentorum opus* (1518)—offer a complete course of study in theoretical and practical music.

gagaku (Jap.) Japanese court music, played by an ensemble consisting of flutes, shawms, shōs, gongs, drums, biwas and kotos.

Gagliano, Marco da [gä'lyä-nō] (1582–1643) Italian composer, stud. of Luca Bati. In 1607 he founded the Accademia degli Elevati, which met weekly for readings and performances. His pastoral opera *Dafne* is a milestone in the early history of opera, providing an explicit link between the courtly INTERMEDIO and early opera. His large output of stage works, madrigals and monodies, and Latin and Italian sacred vocal works reflects the variety of music performed at the Medici court and at the Florence cathedral during his long tenure.

gagliarda (It.) GALLIARD.

Gagnier, J(ean)-J(osaphat) [gä'nyä] (1885–1949) Canadian conductor, composer and instrumentalist from Montreal. He conducted bands across Canada and in the U.S., founded the Montreal Little SO (1920) and reorganized the Montreal SO. He also founded the professional Gagnier Woodwind Quintet, all of whose members were from his family. From 1934 he was regional music director of the CBC.

Gagnon, (Frédéric) Ernest (Amédée) [gä'nyō] (1834–1915) Canadian organist and folklorist, organist at the Quebec Basilica and compiler of the series *Chansons populaires du Canada* (begun in 1865).

gaita [gä'ē-tä] (Sp.) a Span. BAGPIPE.

Gaîté parisienne [gä'tä pä-rē'zyen] (Fr.) ballet score (1938) arranged by Manuel Rosenthal for the Ballets Russes de Monte Carlo, comprised of tunes from works by Offenbach.

Galamian, Ivan (Alexander) (1903–81) Iranian-born Amer. violinist and teacher, stud. of Konstantin Mostras and Lucien Capet. He taught at the Curtis Institute, the Juilliard School and the Meadowmount School of Music, which he founded. A remarkably successful teacher, his students incl. Perlman, Zukerman, Zukofsky and Laredo, among many others.

galant [gä'lä] (Fr.) an 18th-c. term de-

noting light, pleasing music with simple melodies and accompaniments and performed in an elegant, stylish manner. Cf. STYLE GALANT.

Galanterie [gä-lä'trē] (Ger.) an 18th-c. term of unclear reference, apparently suggesting light, modish works. Cf. GALANT.

Galaxy Music Corporation Amer. music publishing firm, founded in 1931 in New York.

Galeazzi, Francesco [gä-lä'ät-sē] (1758–1819) Italian violinist, composer and theorist, whose treatise *Elementi teorico-pratici di musica* (1791 and 1796) is the most important Italian musical treatise of the 18th c. and an invaluable source of information on the Classical style.

Galilei, Vincenzo (c1520–91) Italian theorist, lutanist, singer and composer, an important figure in the development of monody, stud. of Zarlino in Venice and a member of the Florentine CAMERATA. His most influential work, *Dialogo della musica antica et della moderna* (1581), deals with the comparison between the music of the ancient world, i.e. Greece, and the music of his day. He was the father of the scientist Galileo Galilei.

gallant style STYLE GALANT.

gallarda [gä'lyär-dä] (Sp., elegant) a lively 16th- and 17th-c. Spanish dance in triple (or, more rarely, duple) meter, similar to the GALLIARD.

gallego [gä'lyē-khō] (Sp., from Galicia) a musical work, dance or instrument of Galicia, esp. a 16th- to 18th-c. variant of the VILLANCICO in Galician dialect.

Galli, Caterina (?1723–1804) Italian mezzo-soprano. She sang at the King's Theatre in London in 1742. In 1747 she was engaged by Handel for his Covent Garden oratorio season, and she sang opera and oratorio with him until 1754, performing mostly male roles.

galliard *also*, **gaillarde** [gä'yärd] (Fr.), **gagliarda** [gä'lyär-dä] (It.) a lively 16th- and 17th-c. court dance with hops and leaps, usu. in triple meter employing hemiola. It was often paired as an afterdance with the PAVANE. By the late 17th c. the galliard had become a slow piece. Also, *cinq pas* (Fr.).

Gallican rite the practice of monophonic liturgical chant used in the Christian churches of Gaul before Gregorian (Roman) chant was imposed during the reigns of Pepin (d. 768) and Charlemagne (d. 814). The Gallican tradition is defined primarily in contrast with Roman practice and is sometimes used in a general sense to indicate "non-Roman." No examples of notated Gallican chant survive.

Galli-Curci, Amelita (1882–1963) Italian soprano, largely self-taught as a singer. Her U.S. debut was in Chicago in 1916 as Gilda (*Rigoletto*), and she continued in Chicago for eight seasons. Her Metropolitan Opera debut was in 1921, and she sang there until her retirement in 1930. Her many recordings establish her as one of the greatest recording artists of the early period.

Galli-Marié, Célestine (Laurence) (1840–1905) French mezzo-soprano, stud. of her father, a tenor and conductor. She sang regularly at the Paris Opéra-Comique from 1862 to 1885, creating the title roles of Massenet's *Mignon* and Bizet's *Carmen*.

Gallus HANDL.

galop [gä′lō] (Fr.) a lively 19th-c. ballroom dance of German origin in duple meter and employing a side-to-side motion. Examples of the dance are to be found in a number of 19th-c. operas, notably in Ponchielli's *La Gioconda* (the Dance of the Hours) and in Offenbach's *Orphée aux enfers*. Also, *galopade* (Fr.).

galoubet [gä-loo′bā] (Fr.) a wooden PIPE of Provençal origin.

Galpin, Rev. **Francis W(illiam)** (1858–1945) English expert on early musical instruments. He wrote many books and articles on old instruments and had an extensive collection, which was sold to the Boston Museum of Fine Arts in 1916. His work has been commemorated by the Galpin Society, founded in England in 1946 by Thurston Dart, Robert Donnington and others. The *Galpin Society Journal* has been published since 1948.

Galuppi, Baldassare ("Il Buranello") (1706–85) Italian composer, conductor and instrumentalist, stud. of Antonio Lotti. His composition of *opera buffa*, for which he is best known, began in 1749. As musical dir. for Catherine the Great in St. Petersburg and Moscow, he not only produced Italian opera but wrote works for the Orthodox music service which had a profound effect on the development of service music in Russia.

Galway, James (1939–) Irish flutist, stud. of Geoffrey Gilbert, J.-P. Rampal and Marcel Moyse. He was an orchestral player for 15 years until 1975; since then he has pursued a highly successful solo career, performing on the flute and the penny whistle. He has taught at the Eastman School in Rochester.

Gamba, Piero (1936–) Italian conductor. He was musical dir. of the Winnipeg SO from 1970–81, then became principal conductor of the Adelaide (Austral.) SO.

gamba (It., leg) VIOLA DA GAMBA.

gamba bass a string pipe ORGAN STOP of 16-foot pitch.

gambang a wooden or bamboo XYLOPHONE of Java and Bali, found in the gamelan.

Gambler, The (Russ., *Igrok*) opera in 4 acts by Prokofief to his own libretto, based on the novel by Dostoyevsky. Premiere, Brussels 1929. A complicated tale, set in a European gambling spa, of Alexis's love for Pauline and the overwhelming power of the gambler's urge.

Game of Chance, A comic opera in 1 act by Seymour Barab to a libretto by Evelyn Manacher. Premiere, Rock Island, IL 1957. Three young women have their wishes granted, but none of them is satisfied.

gamelan *also*, **gamelang, gamelin** (Javanese) **1**, a percussion instrument of eastern Asia similar to the XYLO-

PHONE. **2**, an orch. of eastern Asian origin consisting of pitched and unpitched percussion instruments, spike fiddle, and sometimes flutes or other wind instruments.

gamma ut the note G in the HEXACHORD system.

gamme [gäm] (Fr.) SCALE.

gamut 1, a contraction of GAMMA UT. **2**, the entire range of the musical system encompassed by the GUIDONIAN HAND. **3**, the HEXACHORD system.

Ganelin Trio Russian jazz trio formed in 1971 by Vyacheslav Ganelin, keyboardist and composer. The trio performs a kind of abstract jazz, which often incorporates such disparate elements as nursery songs and European folk music.

ganga an African double-headed cylindrical SNARE DRUM.

gansa Balinese METALLOPHONE having a cradle-shaped box resonator, used as a melody instrument in a gamelan.

Ganz, Rudolph (1877–1972) German-born Amer. pianist, composer and conductor, stud. of Ferruccio Busoni, among others. He joined the faculty of the Chicago Musical College in 1901, where he taught for 61 years, serving also as director from 1929 to 1954. He toured extensively as a concert pianist, and from 1921 to 1927 he was conductor of the St. Louis SO.

ganza [gung'zä] (Port.) a type of Brazilian tube RATTLE used in Lat.-Amer. dance bands.

gapped scale an incomplete SCALE, i.e. one containing at least one interval larger than a whole tone. An example is the PENTATONIC SCALE.

Garant, (Albert Antonio) Serge (1929–86) Canadian composer, pianist and conductor, stud. of Champagne and Messiaen. He was professor of composition at the U. of Montreal from 1967 and music dir. of the Société de Musique Contemporaine du Québec since its founding in 1966. His works incl. a set of six *Offrandes*, all based on the theme of Bach's *Musical Offering*, which uses all but one of the 12 notes of the chromatic scale.

Garcia, José Maurício Nunes (1767–1830) Brazilian composer and ordained priest. He became chapel master of the Rio de Janeiro Cathedral in 1798, a position he held for 28 years. In 1808 he was appointed to the same position at the royal court. He was famous for his improvising skills.

García, Manuel (del Popolo Vicente Rodriguez) (1775–1832) famous Spanish tenor, composer and teacher, stud. of Antonio Riba. He was esp. noted as an interpreter of Rossini, whose operas he performed throughout Europe. His son, **Manuel (Patricio Rodriguez) García** (1805–1906) was a highly successful singing teacher and inventor of the laryngoscope (a device for observing the larynx) in 1855. His pupils included Jenny Lind and Julius Stockhausen.

Gardelli, Lamberto (1915–) Italian-born Swedish conductor. He studied in Pesaro and Rome and worked as an assistant to conductor Tullio Serafin. He has been resident conductor of the Swedish Royal Opera and of the Danish Radio SO. His U.S. debut was in 1964 at Carnegie Hall, followed two years later by his Metropolitan Opera debut.

Gardellino, Il (It.) popular name for two works by Vivaldi: **1**, the Concerto in D major for flute, oboe, violin, bassoon and cello. **2**, the Flute Concerto in D major, Op. 10 No. 3 (c1730).

Garden, Mary (1874–1967) Scottish-born Amer. soprano, trained in Chicago and in Paris. She created the role of Mélisande in Debussy's *Pelléas et Mélisande*. Her U.S. debut was in New York at Hammerstein's Manhattan Opera House in the American premiere of Massenet's *Thaïs*, but her principal affiliation in the U.S. was with the Chicago Grand Opera, where she sang for over 20 years (1910–32) and was dir. for one season (1921–22).

Gardiner, John Eliot (1943–) English conductor, stud. of Thurston Dart, Nadia Boulanger and George

Hurst. He founded the Monteverdi Choir in 1964 and the companion Monteverdi Orch. in 1968, and was music dir. of the Lyons Opera (1983–89). He has specialized in the music of the Baroque and Classical eras.

Garfunkel, Art (1941–) Amer. folk-pop singer and actor, known for his duo performances with Paul Simon in the 1950s and 1960s (see SIMON AND GARFUNKEL), thereafter more active as a film actor.

Garland, Ed(ward Bertram) "Montudi" (1885–1980) Amer. jazz bassist from New Orleans, a pioneer of jazz double bass. He played with King Oliver and Kid Ory, among others, after which he lived on the West Coast for 50 years, leading his own band and touring extensively.

Garland, Judy (Gumm, Frances Ethel) (1922–69) Amer. popular singer and actress, a professional in vaudeville from the age of two. She worked for Metro-Goldwyn-Mayer from 1935 to 1950 and made many memorable musical films, incl. *The Wizard of Oz* (1939), *Meet Me in St. Louis* (1944) and *A Star Is Born* (1954).

Garner, Erroll (Louis) (1923–77) Amer. jazz swing and bop pianist and composer, completely self-taught as a musician. He formed his own very successful trio in the mid-1940's, with which he made many recordings and appeared frequently on TV and radio. His compositions include the well-known song "Misty."

Garrick Gaieties, The musical revue by Richard Rodgers, lyrics by Lorenz Hart, with sketches by Kaye, Sullivan, Ryskind, Sorin, Jaffe, Green and Meiser. Premiere, New York 1925. Orig. presented as a fund-raiser, the show satirized the theater and the Theatre Guild. Two later versions appeared in 1926 and 1930.

Garrison, Jimmy (James Emory) (1934–76) Amer. jazz bassist from Miami. He was a member of Ornette Coleman's band at the Five Spot in New York, then joined John Coltrane's band (1961–6). During the fol-lowing decade he played and toured with various groups, taking a year off to teach at Bennington College and Wesleyan U.

Gaspard de la nuit [gäs'pär də lä nüe] (Fr., Gaspard of the Night) a set of three works for solo piano (1908) by Ravel, inspired by prose-poems by. Aloysius Bertrand, subtitled "Fantasies in the style of Rembrandt and Callot." The three pieces—the third of which is noted for its difficulty—are *Ondine*, a portrait of the water-nymph; *Le Gibet*, the gallows; and *Scarbo*, a clown.

Gasparini, Francesco (1668–1727) Italian opera composer and teacher, perhaps a stud. of Legrenzi. In addi-tion to more than 50 operas, com-posed between 1684 and 1724, he wrote cantatas, oratorios and his im-portant teaching work on keyboard harmony, *L'armonico pratico al cim-balo* (The Practical Harmonist at the Keyboard). He was the teacher of Do-menico Scarlatti, Quantz, Benedetto Marcello and others.

Gassenhauer ['gäs-ən"how-ər] (Ger.) a German street song or folksong. The term dates from the 16th c. to refer to a broad spectrum of urban popular or folk melodies, some of which were originally operetta- or opera-songs that entered the popular culture.

Gassmann, Florian Leopold (1729–74) Bohemian composer, perhaps a stud. of Padre Martini. He succeeded Gluck in 1763 in Vienna, where he remained for most of the rest of his life. He founded the oldest Viennese musical society, the Tonkünstler-So-zietät, and was the teacher of Salieri. Gassman produced over 20 operas, over 30 symphonies, oratorios (incl. *La Betulia liberata*) and a large vol-ume of chamber music.

Gastoldi, Giovanni Giacomo (c1550–1622) Italian composer, as-soc. for most of his life with Santa Barbara, the ducal chapel of the Gon-zaga family in Mantua. He was best known for his *balletti* (see BALLETTO), but composed a wide variety of sacred and secular music, primarily vocal.

The English fa-la madrigals of Thomas Morley and his contemporaries are modeled in large part on the *balletti* of Gastoldi.

Gatti-Casazza, Giulio (1869–1940) Italian opera impresario. He was the dir. of La Scala in Milan (1898–1908) and worked in conjunction with Arturo Toscanini. In 1908 he went with Toscanini to the Metropolitan Opera, of which he was dir. until 1935.

Gaudeamus Foundation Dutch philanthropic organization, founded in 1945 and dedicated to the support of new music, esp. the works of Dutch composers.

Gaudeamus igitur one of the oldest student songs, dating from perhaps as early as the 13th c. It is quoted by Brahms in his ACADEMIC FESTIVAL OVERTURE.

Gaveau French firm of piano and harpsichord makers founded in 1847 by Joseph Gaveau (1824–1903). ARNOLD DOLMETSCH was with the firm from 1911–14 and inaugurated their production of period spinets, harpsichords and clavichords. The firm combined in 1960 with ERARD.

gavotte (Fr.) *also,* **gavot 1**, a French peasant dance. **2**, a French court dance melody in moderate duple meter, always beginning on the third beat, and consisting of two repeated sections. The gavotte is frequently a movement of the baroque instrumental suite. Cf. DANCE (*illus.*).

Gay, John (1685–1732) English poet and playwright, inventor of the ballad opera. He wrote the libretto for Handel's *Acis and Galatea* and then, in 1728, produced *The Beggar's Opera*, the biggest theatrical success of the 18th c. and the first of a long series of operas employing popular tunes in English instead of elaborate arias in Italian.

Gay Divorce, The musical by Cole Porter, book by Kenneth Webb and Samuel Hoffenstein, based on a play by Dwight Taylor. Premiere, New York 1932. Novelist Guy Holden (created by Fred Astaire) is mistaken for a professional co–respondent in Mi-

mi's divorce case. The movie version (1934) was called *The Gay Divorcee*.

Gayane ['gä-yä-nə] ballet (1942) with music by Khachaturian, the story of a farm worker whose husband is executed for treachery. The score includes the well-known "Sabre Dance." The composer extracted two concert suites from the score.

Gaye, Marvin (1939–84) Amer. rock and soul singer and drummer from Washington, D.C., one of the most successful of the Motown recording artists.

Gazzaniga, Giuseppe [gät-sä'nē-gä] (1743–1818) Italian opera composer, stud. of Porpora and Piccinni. His best-known work is the one-act opera buffa *Don Giovanni* (1787), which was widely produced on the Continent and in England.

Gazzelloni, Severino [gät-säl'lō-nē] (1919–) Italian flutist, trained in Rome. He has taught at the Rossini Conservatory in Pesaro and at the Accademia Chigiana in Siena and was first flutist of the Italian Radio SO. He is esp. known for his performance of avant-garde works and has had many works composed for him.

Gebrauchsmusik [ge'browkhs-moo"-zēk] (Ger., music for use) music composed for use other than in concert, such as film music, school music, etc.; also, music that is socially useful and relevant. The term also implies that such music is intended for use by amateurs.

gebunden [ge'bûn-dən] (Ger.) LEGATO.

G clef a CLEF indicating the position on the staff of the G a fifth above middle C (g'). See CLEF (*illus.*).

gedackt *also,* **gedeckt** (Ger.) a labial pipe ORGAN STOP of flutelike quality.

Gédalge, André [zhä'dälzh] (1856–1926) French composer and teacher, esp. noted for his monumental treatise on the writing of fugues, *Traité de la fugue*. He was professor of counterpoint and fugue at the Paris Conservatoire from 1905 until his death.

Gedda (Ustinoff), **Nicolai (Harry Gustaf)** (1925–) Swedish tenor, trained in Leipzig and at the Stockholm Conservatory. His operatic debut was at the Stockholm Opera in 1952 and at La Scala in the same year. His Amer. debut was at the Metropolitan Opera in 1957. A very versatile performer, he has sung and recorded a wide range of roles from all periods.

gehend ['gā-ənt] (Ger.) ANDANTE.

Geige ['gī-ge] (Ger.) term orig. referring to any string instrument, but later reserved for the VIOLIN family (as opposed to the viols).

Geigenwerk [-gən"verk] (Ger.) a keyboard instrument similar to the HURDY-GURDY invented by Hans Haiden in the late 16th c. in which the strings are sounded by parchment-covered wheels operated by a foot pedal or crank.

The J. Geils Band Amer. rhythm-and-blues band formed in 1967 in Boston by guitarist Jerome Geils.

Geisslerlieder ['gīs-lər-] (Ger.) FLAGELLANT SONGS.

Geistertrio (Ger.) GHOST TRIO.

gekkin (Jap.) a fretted Japanese flat-backed LUTE having 4 strings tuned in pairs. Also, *moon guitar*.

gemächlich [ge'meç-liç] (Ger., leisurely) in a moderate, relaxed tempo; MODERATO.

Geminiani, Francesco (Xaverio) (1687–1762) Italian violin virtuoso, composer and theorist, stud. of Corelli and Alessandro Scarlatti. He went to London in 1714, where he remained for the rest of his life. His large output consists mainly of sonatas and concertos for the violin and concerti grossi, along with several important theoretical works, incl. *A Treatise of Good Taste in The Art of Musick* (1749), *The Art of Playing on the Violin* (1751) and *Guida armonica* (1754).

gemshorn 1, a medieval RECORDER made out of the horn of an ox or chamois and having a soft, husky tone. **2**, a labial pipe ORGAN STOP combining qualities of reeds and of string.

gender (Jav.) a Javanese METALLOPHONE having bamboo resonators for each bar, used in the gamelan.

Gendron, Maurice [zhā'drō] (1920–) French cellist and conductor, stud. of Gérard Hekking. He has taught at the Yehudi Menuhin School in England and at the Paris Conservatoire. He appeared several times in recital with Benjamin Britten and with Menuhin and as soloist under Pablo Casals, with whom he has also recorded.

general pause a rest of indeterminate length in all parts of an ensemble. Abbr., *GP*. Also, *cutoff*.

Generalbass [gā-nä'räl"bäs] (Ger.) thoroughbass (see BASSO CONTINUO).

Genesis English rock band formed in 1966, orig. as a "songwriter's collective" under the name "Garden Wall."

Gentlemen Prefer Blondes musical by Jule Styne, lyrics by Leo Robin, book by Anita Loos and Joseph Fields, based on the novel by Loos. Premiere, New York 1949. The story of gold-digger Lorelei and her friend Dorothy en route to Paris.

genus (pl., *genera*) one of the three basic TETRACHORDS in ancient Greek music.

Geographical Fugue one of several works for speaking chorus (*Gesprochene Musik*, 1930) by Toch.

George White's Scandals annual revue. Premiere, New York 1919. There were in all 11 editions of the revue in 13 years. The casts over the years incl. Rudy Vallée, Ethel Merman, Ray Bolger and many others. Composers incl. George Gershwin, Ray Henderson and Sammy Fain.

Georgia Minstrels a famous black minstrel troupe, organized in 1865 by Charles Hicks.

Georgian rite the medieval tradition of monophonic and polyphonic liturgical music in use in the Christian churches of Georgia in the Caucasus. The Georgian rite is related to the Byzantine tradition.

Gerhard, Roberto (1896–1970) Spanish composer, stud. of Granados, Pedrell and Schoenberg. He taught at the Ecola Normal de la Generalitat in Barcelona until the end of the Spanish

Civil War and later at King's College, Cambridge, taking British citizenship in 1960. He has also taught in the U.S. His works incl. ballets, an opera (*The Duenna*), 5 symphonies and other orchestral works, vocal and instrumental music, several works for electronic tape, and incidental music for film, theater, radio and TV.

Gericke, Wilhelm (1845–1925) Austrian conductor and composer, trained at the Vienna Conservatory. He was twice conductor of the Boston SO (1884–89, 1898–1906), whose repertory and season he expanded considerably.

German dance (Ger., *Deutsche*) a general 18th- and 19th-c. term for couple-dances in triple meter, including the LÄNDLER and the WALTZ. The music is usu. in two short phrases, both repeated, and in major keys.

German flute the transverse FLUTE, as opposed to the recorder (English flute).

Germania Musical Society an org. formed in 1848 by a group of young Berlin musicians to expand musical activities in the U.S. and to promote the music of German composers. It toured in the U.S. until 1854.

German Requiem 1, a nonliturgical service for the dead, deriving its text from the Lutheran Bible (see 2, below) or from a variety of Protestant liturgical sources and ceremonies. **2**, (Ger., *Ein Deutsches Requiem*) a choral cantata in seven movements for soprano, baritone, chorus and orchestra, Op. 45 (1866–9), by Brahms, written in memory of his mother. The text is not liturgical but is derived from Luther's translation of the Bible.

German sixth an AUGMENTED SIXTH CHORD consisting of the root, major third, perfect fifth and augmented sixth. The chord traditionally functions as a SECONDARY DOMINANT. See CHORD (*illus.*).

Gershwin, George (Gershvin, Jacob) (1898–1937) Amer. pianist, conductor and composer for Broadway, films and the opera and concert stage. The song "Swanee" (1919) was his first major success, recorded by Al Jolson. He produced during the 1920s and 1930s a number of successful musicals and four film scores, most of which were to lyrics by his brother Ira. His musical *Of Thee I Sing* was the first to win a Pulitzer Prize in drama. He also produced a number of works for the concert and opera stage, incl. *Rhapsody in Blue* (1924) for jazz band and piano, commissioned by Paul Whiteman; the Piano Concerto in F (1925) and *An American in Paris* (1928), commissioned by Walter Damrosch; and the opera *Porgy and Bess* (1935). He often appeared as a pianist performing his own music.

ges [gās] (Ger.) G FLAT.

Gesamtkunstwerk [ge'zämt"kûnstverk] (Ger., complete art work) a term coined by Wagner to refer to the music drama, which combines the musical, dramatic and visual arts as equals in one form.

Gesang [ge'zäng] (Ger.) SONG.

Gesang der Jünglinge [dār 'yüngling-e] (Ger., Song of the Youths) tape composition (1956) by Stockhausen, combining electronically produced sounds with an electronically manipulated child's voice (1956).

gesangvoll [-fol] (Ger.) CANTABILE.

Geschöpfe des Prometheus, Die [ge'shøp-fe däs prō'mā-tā-oos] (Ger.) THE CREATURES OF PROMETHEUS.

geschwind [ge'shvint] (Ger.) quick; ALLEGRO.

geses ['gā-səs] (Ger.) G double flat.

gestopft [ge'shtopft] (Ger.) STOPPED, as applied to the horn.

gestrichen [ge'shtri-çən] (Ger.) **1**, LEGATO. **2**, ARCO.

Gesualdo, Carlo [jā'zwäl-dō] (c1560–1613) Italian composer, prince of Venosa and count of Conza. In 1590, he murdered his wife and her lover, an act of passion which became widely publicized. Gesualdo composed both sacred and secular madrigals, and he is best known today for the highly chromatic style of his 5- and 6-part madrigals.

geteilt [ge'tīlt] (Ger.) DIVISI.

getragen (Ger.) SOSTENUTO.

Getz (Gayetsky), **Stan(ley)** (1927–91) Amer. jazz bop tenor saxophonist. In his early years he worked with a succession of major bands, incl. those of Stan Kenton, Benny Goodman and Woody Herman. In the 1960s and 70s he worked primarily with small groups. He has been a pioneer in the development of COOL JAZZ and the BOSSA NOVA jazz style.

Getzen Co. Amer. maker of brass instruments, est. in Elkhorn, WI, in 1939.

Gewandhaus Orchestra [ge'vänt-hows] an orch. in Leipzig associated with the Gewandhaus (Ger., Cloth Hall), a concert hall built in 1781.

Ghanaba (Warren, Guy) (1923–) drummer and composer from Ghana. He played with an African jazz group, the Tempos, during the 1940s, then, in 1950, with Kenny Graham's Afro-Cubists in London. In 1955 he came to Chicago to work with pianist Gene Esposito, then moved to New York in 1957 with his own trio. He has worked with Max Roach, Dizzy Gillespie and others, combining African music with jazz improvisation.

G flat the PITCH (G♭) a half step lower than G, the enharmonic equivalent of F sharp.

Ghent, Emmanuel (1925–) Canadian-born Amer. composer, stud. of Ralph Shapey. His works employ special electronic devices for coordination of performers and tape, and he has also worked with computer-generated composition.

Ghiaurov, Nicolai (1929–) Bulgarian bass, trained in Sofia, Leningrad and Moscow. His U.S. debut was at the Metropolitan Opera in 1965, and he has sung at all the major opera houses in the U.S. and Europe. Among his most noted roles are Philip (*Don Carlo*), Mephistopheles and Boris Godunov.

Ghitalla, Armando (1925–) Amer. trumpeter, stud. of William Vacchiano. He played with the Houston SO (1949–51) and the Boston SO (1951–79), becoming principal trumpet in 1965. He has been on the fac-ulty of the U. of Michigan since 1979.

ghost band a colloq. term for a band continuing to operate under the name of its deceased bandleader, such as the Count Basie orch. under Thad Jones and the Glenn Miller orch. under various leaders.

ghost notes notes played so softly that their presence is felt, rather than clearly heard; a device used esp. in ragtime piano music. Also, *shadow notes*.

Ghost Trio, The (Ger., *Geistertrio*) popular name for the piano trio in D major, Op. 70, No. 1 (1808), by Beethoven. The name refers to the eerie atmosphere of the slow movement.

Giannini, Vittorio (1903–66) Amer. composer, stud. at the Juilliard School and the American Academy in Rome. He taught composition and orchestration at the Juilliard School and the Manhattan School and was director of the North Carolina School of the Arts. He wrote eight operas (two orig. for radio), incl. *The Taming of the Shrew* (1952) and *The Servant of Two Masters* (1966) and orchestral, vocal and chamber works. His sister, **Dusolina Giannini** (1900–86), was a soprano who sang at the Metropolitan Opera (1936–41) and at other major opera houses.

Gianni Schicchi comic opera in 1 act by Giacomo Puccini to a libretto by Gioacchino Forzano, suggested by a passage in Dante. Premiere, New York 1918. The work is part of a triptych which also includes *Suor Angelica* and *Il Tabarro*. The death of Buoso Donati reveals that he wrote his relatives out of his will, but Schicchi finds a way around the problem to his own advantage.

Giant Fugue the organ chorale prelude "Wir glauben all an einen Gott" (Ger., We All Believe in One God), BWV 680 (c1710), by Bach.

Giants in the Earth tragic opera in 3 acts by Douglas Moore to a libretto by Arnold Sundgaard and the composer, based on the novel by O.E. Rölvaag. Premiere, New York 1951. Per and Beret Hansa, immigrants from

Norway, face the rigors and perils of pioneer life in Dakota Territory in the late 19th c.

Gibbons, Christopher (1615–76) English organist and composer, son of ORLANDO GIBBONS. During the Restoration he was appointed musician to Charles II and organist of the Chapel Royal and of Westminster Cathedral, posts he held until his death. He wrote anthems, consort music and keyboard music.

Gibbons, Orlando (1583–1625) English composer and organist, one of the most important musical figures in early 17th-c. England. He was a Gentleman of the Chapel Royal from about 1602, one of the king's virginal players from 1619 and organist of Westminster Abbey from 1623. His works incl. Protestant services, anthems and hymn tunes (*O Clap Your Hands, Lift Up Your Heads*), madrigals (*The Silver Swan*) and consort songs, and instrumental consort and keyboard music.

Gibbs, Mike (Michael Clement Irving) (1937–) Rhodesian jazz trombonist, pianist and composer, trained at the Berklee School of Music and the Lenox School of Jazz. He was an early exponent of the jazz-rock movement and his works combine elements of Messiaen, Gil Evans and others. He was composer-in-residence at Berklee (1974–83), then left to free-lance in New York. He has written film scores, ballets, and orchestral works.

Gibbs, Terry (Gubenko, Julius) (1924–) Amer. jazz vibraphonist from Brooklyn, NY. He played with Tommy Dorsey, Buddy Rich and Woody Herman, then led his own groups. In the 1960s he was musical dir. for various TV shows.

Gibson, Sir **Alexander (Drummond)** (1926–) Scottish conductor, stud. of Markevich and Paul van Kempen. In 1959 he became conductor of the Scottish National Orch., which he has made a significant force on the national music scene in England. His

Amer. debut was with the Detroit SO in 1970.

Gideon, Miriam (1906–) Amer. composer and teacher, stud. of Sessions and Lazare Saminsky. She has taught at Brooklyn College and the Jewish Theological Seminary in New York and at City College, City U. of New York. Her works incl. the opera *Fortunata* and a *Symphonia brevis.*

Gieseking, Walter (1895–1956) German pianist, stud. of Karl Leimer. His Amer. debut was in 1926. His repertory embraced a wide range of styles, from the Viennese classics to the 20th c., though he is perhaps best known for his performances and recordings of the works of Ravel and Debussy.

Gifford, Helen (Margaret) (1935–) Australian composer, stud. of Dorian Le Gallienne. Her works show the influence both of the eastern European composers, esp. Lutoslawski, and of the music of India and Indonesia, where she traveled in 1967 and 1971. Her works incl. the *Phantasma* for string orchestra, a Piano Sonata and *The Glass Castle* for soprano and orchestra.

gig [gig] slang term for a professional musical engagement or job.

giga ['jē-gä] (It.) JIG.

gigelira *also,* **gigalira** ['jē-gä"lē-rä] (It.) XYLOPHONE.

Gigli, Beniamino ['jē-lyē] (1890–1957) Italian tenor, trained at the Liceo Musicale in Rome. One of the great tenors of the early and mid-20th c., successor to Caruso, he made his Amer. debut in 1920 at the Metropolitan Opera, where he sang almost 30 roles during the next twelve seasons. He retired in 1956.

gigue [zhēg] (Fr.) JIG.

Gilbert, Henry F(ranklin Belknap) (1868–1928) Amer. composer, stud. of MacDowell. His works are notable for their use of exotic musical sources, folksong, Negro spirituals and jazz and incl. the tone poems *Comedy Overture on Negro Themes* and *The Dance in Place Congo.*

Gilbert, Kenneth (1931–) Canadian harpsichordist, organist, musicologist and teacher, stud. of Boulanger, Leonhardt and Ruggero Gerlin. In addition to regular performance on harpsichord as soloist and with orchestra, he has prepared scholarly editions of the harpsichord works of Couperin, D. Scarlatti and Rameau.

Gilbert, Sir **William S(chwenk)** (1836–1911) English poet, playwright and librettist, collaborator from 1875 with Sir ARTHUR SULLIVAN in producing the Savoy Operas.

Gilels, Emil (Grigorievich) (1916–85) Russian pianist, stud. of Reingbald and Heinrich Neuhaus. In 1938 he won the first prize of the Ysaÿe International Festival in Brussels. He was the first prominent Russian artist to appear in the U.S. after World War II (1955). His repertory embraced a wide range of styles.

Gillespie, Dizzy (John Birks) (1917–) Amer. jazz bop trumpeter, composer and bandleader. He played and recorded from 1939–41 with Cab Calloway's band. In the early 1940s he was one of the pioneers of the Bop style and was known for his intricate syncopated solos and innovative harmonies. In the late 1940s he was also a creator of AFRO-CUBAN JAZZ. He continues to tour with his own bands and has been a highly influential performer. Among his well-known songs are "Night in Tunisia," "Salt Peanuts," "Pickin' the Cabbage," and "Manteca."

Gillis, Don (1912–78) Amer. composer, trained at Texas Christian U., North Texas State, Louisiana State and Columbia. He has taught at Southern Methodist U., Dallas Baptist College, and the U. of South Carolina, and was program arranger for NBC in New York from 1944. His works incl. *Let us Pray* (cantata), *The Nazarene* (opera), piano concertos, etc.

gilly show a traveling carnival of the 1910s through the 1940s.

Gilmore, Patrick S(arsfield) (1829–92) Irish-born Amer. bandmaster, composer and impresario, noted for his band extravaganzas. He founded Gilmore's Grand Boston Band in 1859,

which, along with him, joined the Union Army in 1861. His first monumental concert-festival, the National Peace Jubilee, was in 1869 in Boston, with an orchestra of 1000, a chorus of 10,000 and six bands, performing in a specially built 50,000-seat auditorium. His World Peace Jubilee in 1872 was even bigger. His works incl. *When Johnny Comes Marching Home* (1863) and *Columbia* (1879).

gimel GYMEL.

Ginastera, Alberto (Evaristo) (1916–83) Argentine composer, trained at the Williams Conservatory and the National Conservatory. He taught at a number of schools in Argentina, his career being interrupted several times by political events in that country. He made frequent visits to the U.S. from 1945 and many of his numerous commissions came from this country. His works incl. *Don Rodrigo, Bomarzo, Beatrix Cenci* and other operas, a violin concerto, piano concertos, choral and vocal works and chamber music.

Gingold, Josef (1909–) Russianborn Amer. violinist and teacher, stud. of Vladimir Graffman and Ysaÿe. He was first violin of the NBC Orchestra under Toscanini (1937–43), concertmaster of the Detroit SO (1943–46) and of the Cleveland SO (1947–60) and a member of the Primrose String Quartet and the NBC String Quartet. He has taught at Western Reserve U. and since 1960 at Indiana U. His pupils incl. Jaime Laredo and Joseph Silverstein.

Gioconda, La [jō′kōn-dä] (It.) romantic opera in 4 acts by Ponchielli to a libretto in Italian by Tobia Gorrio (Arrigo Boito) based on Victor Hugo's play *Angelo, tyran de Padoue.* Premiere, Milan 1876. Barnaba, a spy for the Inquisition, plots to win for himself the love of the streetsinger La Gioconda.

giocoso [jō′kō-zō] (It.) jocose, lively.

Giordano, Umberto (1867–1948) Italian composer, trained at the Naples Conservatory. After several unsuccessful attempts at *verismo* operas in Naples, he moved to Milan, where he produced his two most popular and lasting works, *Andrea Chenier* (1896) and *Fedora* (1898). He never repeated these successes.

Gipps, Ruth (1921–) English conductor and composer, stud. of Vaughan Williams. Her works incl. 5 symphonies, concertos for piano and horn, sonatas for clarinet and violin and choral works.

Gipsy Baron, The (Ger., *Der Zigeunerbaron*) operetta in 3 acts by Johann Strauss Jr. to a libretto by Ignaz Schnitzer, based on Maurus Jókai's story *Saffi*. Premiere, Vienna 1885. Sandor Barinkay comes home to claim his ancestral lands and falls in love with a gipsy, Saffi.

giraffe an upright PIANO of the 18th and 19th c.

girl groups a term for the teenage DOO-WOP female vocal groups of the 1960s, such as the Chantels and the Ronettes.

Girl I Left Behind Me, The song, orig. printed in Dublin in the early 19th c., used at West Point Military Academy as the graduating class song.

Girl of the Golden West, The (It., *La Fanciulla del West*) opera in 3 acts by Puccini to a libretto by Guelfo Civinini and Carlo Zangarini, based on the play by David Belasco. Premiere, New York 1910. Minnie, owner of the Polka Saloon in Gold Rush California, twice saves the life of the outlaw Johnson and they ride off together to a new life.

Girl Crazy musical by George Gershwin, lyrics by Ira Gershwin, book by Guy Bolton and John McGowan. Premiere, New York 1930. Danny Churchill, a wealthy playboy, finds true love in postmistress Molly Gray and runs a dude ranch. The band for the show was the Red Nichols Orch., which included Benny Goodman, Glenn Miller, Jimmy Dorsey, Gene Krupa and Jack Teagarden.

gis (Ger.) G SHARP.

Giselle ballet in 2 acts with music by Adolphe Adam. Premiere, Paris 1841. Giselle, a peasant girl jilted by Duke Albrecht, becomes a Wilis, one of the spirits of girls who die before their intended marriages.

gisis (Ger.) G double sharp.

gitana, alla [jē′tä-nä] (It.) to be played in the gypsy manner.

gittern 1, a medieval fretted instrument with a flat back and gut strings, plucked with a plectrum. Also, *citole.* **2,** a 16th- and 17th-c. GUITAR.

Giuffre, Jimmy (James Peter) (1921–) Amer. cool jazz saxophonist, clarinetist and composer. In the 1940s he played with Jimmy Dorsey, Buddy Rich and Woody Herman. In the 1950s, after several years with Howard Rumsey and with Shorty Rogers, he formed his own trio with which, with several personnel changes, he has performed since. He was an important figure in the avantgarde jazz of the early 1960s and has been an active force in the FREE JAZZ movement.

Giulini, Carlo Maria (1914–) Italian conductor and violist, stud. of Bernardino Molinari. He formed the Milan Radio Orch. and conducted frequently at La Scala, becoming principal conductor in 1953. He has been principal guest conductor of the Chicago SO (1968–78), principal conductor of the Vienna SO (1973–76) and musical dir. of the Los Angeles SO (1978–84). He is noted for his lyricism and musical precision.

Giulio Cesare in Egitto (It., Julius Caesar in Egypt) historical opera in 3 acts by Handel to a libretto in Italian by Niccolo Haym. Premiere, London 1724. A complicated story of intrigue surrounding Caesar's meeting with Cleopatra.

giusto [′joo-stō] (It.) exact, just. See TEMPO GIUSTO.

Glagolitic Mass a setting of the Slavonic Mass for soloists, chorus, orchestra and organ (1927) by Janáček.

Glanville-Hicks, Peggy (1912–90) Australian composer, stud. of Vaughan Williams, Benjamin, Wellesz and Boulanger. She lived in the U.S. from 1942 to 1959 and was very active during this period in support of new music. She was a music critic for the *New York Herald Tribune* (1948–58) and then established The Artists' Company to produce new American operas. Her works incl. *The Transposed Heads, Nausicaa* and other operas, instrumental works, *13 Ways of Looking at a Blackbird, Letters from Morocco* and other vocal works.

Glareanus, Henricus (Loris, Heinrich) (1488–1563) Swiss theorist, esp. known for his work *Dodecachordon* (1547). See MODE.

Glass, Philip (1937–) Amer. composer and performer, trained at the U. of Chicago, the Juilliard School and with Nadia Boulanger. His study of Indian music in 1966–7 with Ravi Shankar and Alla Rakha has had a fundamental effect on his musical style, which has been described as minimalist. His works incl. *Einstein on the Beach, Satyagraha, Akhnaten* (opera trilogy), film music, vocal and instrumental chamber music.

glass harmonica a mechanical form of MUSICAL GLASSES invented (as the *armonica*) by Benjamin Franklin in 1761. The instrument is called for in Richard Strauss's *Die Frau ohne Schatten.*

Glazunov, Alexander (1865–1936) Russian composer, stud. of Rimsky-Korsakov. Glazunov was a member of the so-called BELYAYEV CIRCLE and taught at the St. Petersburg Conservatory (1899–1930), serving as dir. for most of his time there. He settled in Paris in 1932, after which he produced few works. His compositions incl. 9 symphonies, concertos, ballets, songs and instrumental chamber works.

Gleason, Frederick Grant (1848–1903) Amer. organist, composer and teacher, trained with Dudley Buck and in Europe. From 1897 he taught at the Hershey School of Music in Chicago. He was editor of the *Musical Bulletin* and the *Music Review* and a music critic of the *Chicago Tribune* and dir. of the Chicago Auditorium

Conservatory. He was a favorite composer of conductor Theodore Thomas.

glee an unaccompanied part-song, usu. for three or more solo male voices, popular in the 18th and 19th c. in England and the U.S.

glee club a singing group, usu. composed of men, for singing glees, part-songs, etc.

Glenn, (Evans) Tyree (1912–74) Amer. jazz trombonist, vibraphonist and singer from Texas. He worked with Benny Carter, Lionel Hampton and Cab Calloway before he joined Duke Ellington's band in 1947. He left Ellington to do studio work in 1951. He was with Louis Armstrong from 1965 to 1971, then led his own group.

Glière, Reinhold (Glier, Reyngold Moritsevich) (1875–1956) Soviet composer, stud. of Ippolitov-Ivanov and others. He taught at the Moscow Conservatory (1920–41) and was chairman of the organizing committee of the USSR Composers' Union. His works incl. *Krasnïy tsvetok* and other ballets, 6 operas, 3 symphonies and other orchestral works, vocal and instrumental chamber works.

Glinka, Mikhail Ivanovich (1804–57) Russian composer, whose musical education came largely from his association with his uncle's serf orch. and his limited school training. His nationalism was an important influence on Tchaikovsky and on the circle of composers around Balakirev. His works incl. 5 operas, orchestral and other instrumental works (incl. the *Symphony on two Russian themes*), choral music and songs.

gliss. *abbr.* GLISSANDO.

glissando an ascending or descending series of adjacent pitches produced by differing means on different instruments. On the harp and keyboard instruments, the intervening pitches are distinct; on most other instruments, they are not. *Abbr., gliss.* Cf. PORTAMENTO.

glitter rock a form of HARD ROCK glorifying fashion and sexuality; the term has little to do with the music performed.

Globokar, Vinko (1934–) Yugoslav composer and trombonist, stud. of Leibowitz and Berio. He formed a new music performance group at Buffalo U. in 1966, then joined the faculty at the Staatliche Hochschule für Musik in Cologne. He also was founder of the Free Music Group (1969) and the New Phonic Art quartet (1972). His virtuoso technique as trombonist has inspired a number of works written especially for him by Berio, Stockhausen and others. His works incl. *Voie* (chorus and orchestra), *Carrousel* (voices and inst. ensemble), other vocal, orchestral and instrumental chamber music.

Glocke (Ger.) BELL.

glockenspiel (Ger., play or set of bells) **1**, a percussion instrument consisting of metal bars tuned to the chromatic scale and played with two metal hammers. Cf. BELL-LYRA. **2**, CARILLON.

Glory, Hallelujah see BATTLE HYMN OF THE REPUBLIC.

glosa (Sp., gloss) **1**, VARIATION, usu. on a religious theme. **2**, ornamentation (see ORNAMENT).

glottal stop a type of attack in vocal music produced by quickly closing and reopening the false vocal chords.

Gluck, Alma (Fiersohn, Reba) (1884–1938) Romanian-born Amer. soprano, stud. in New York of A. Buzzi-Peccia. She sang with the Metropolitan Opera (1909–13) and then concentrated on recital and concert, combining popular ballad with serious music. She was the mother of music writer Marcia Davenport, and her second husband was violinist Efrem Zimbalist.

Gluck, Christoph Willibald (1714–87) German composer, trained in Reichstadt, Kreibitz and in Prague. He went to King's Theater in London in 1745, producing operas and becoming acquainted with Handel, then in 1750 settled in Vienna, where he was to remain for the rest of his life. Gluck's importance rests largely on his work to restore the balance of music and drama in opera, as outlined in his preface to his opera *Alceste* (1769). His works incl. *Orfeo ed Euridice, Alceste, Iphigénie en Aulide, Iphigénie en Tauride* and over 40 other operas, ballets, vocal and instrumental works.

Glückliche Hand, Die ['glük-li-çe hänt, dē] (Ger., The Favored Hand) opera in 1 act by Schoenberg to his own libretto. Premiere, Vienna 1924. The expression of one man's longing for the unattainable. Set for baritone, small chorus and two mimes.

Glyndebourne Festival Opera operatic festival founded in 1934 by John Christie and noted for its high standard of production, particularly of the works of Mozart. Musical directors have been Fritz Busch, Vittorio Gui, Pritchard and Haitink. Sir Rudolf Bing was the first manager, succeeded in 1949 by Moran Caplat.

Gobbi, Tito (1913–84) Italian baritone, stud. of Giulio Crimi in Rome. His Amer. debut was in 1948 in San Francisco, and he sang and directed regularly in Chicago from 1954. His performances of Scarpia (*Tosca*), Gianni Schicchi and Don Giovanni were particularly noteworthy. He made over 25 films and many recordings and was one of the greatest singing actors of his time.

goblet drum a single-headed DRUM in the shape of a goblet, with a narrow waisted body of pottery, metal or wood and a skin head, often glued to the rim of the body.

Godard, Benjamin (Louis Paul) (1849–95) French composer and violist, stud. of Henri Vieuxtemps and Henri Reber. He taught at the Paris Conservatoire (1887–95). Of his many works, the best remembered are his salon pieces, esp. his piano works.

God Bless America patriotic song (1939) by Irving Berlin. The song's chorus was actually written in 1918. There have been a number of other songs under the same title, incl. one by De Koven.

Godowsky, Leopold (1870–1938) Polish-born Amer. pianist and composer. He studied at the Berlin Hochschule and with Saint-Saëns in Paris. He lived and taught in the U.S. from 1890 to 1900 and then in Vienna until the outbreak of World War I, when he returned to the U.S. He suffered a partial paralysis in 1930, but continued to compose for piano.

God Rest You Merry, Gentlemen Christmas carol of unknown authorship, dating perhaps from the mid-18th c. The placement of the comma in the title varies.

God Save the King (Queen) the British national anthem. It is of unknown origin, perhaps attaining its present form in the mid-18th c. Cf. AMERICA.

Godspell rock musical by Stephen Schwartz, book by John-Michael Tebelak, based on the Gospel of Matthew. Premiere, NY 1971. The last days of Christ, with dramatized parables.

Goehr, (Peter) Alexander (1932–) German-born English composer, stud. of Hall at the Royal Manchester College and Messiaen and Loriod in Paris. He was program producer for the BBC until 1968. He has taught in the U.S. at the New England Conservatory and Yale and in England at Leeds and Cambridge. His works incl. *Shadowplay-2* and other theater works, orchestral, vocal, chamber and instrumental works.

goge an African single-string bowed FIDDLE or LUTE, used for accompaniment of songs.

Gold, Arthur (1917–90) Canadian pianist, stud. of Josef and Rosina Lhévinne. He is known as partner of pianist ROBERT FIZDALE in a duo formed in 1946. Their extensive repertory includes many 20th-c. works, among them a number of works which they have commissioned.

Goldberg, Szymon (1909–) Polish-born Amer. violinist and conductor, stud. of Carl Flesch. In addition to his extensive solo career, he has been concertmaster of the Dresden PO and the Berlin PO and played in a trio with Hindemith and Feuermann and a quartet with Victor Babin, Primrose and Nikolay Graudan. He became conductor and musical dir. of the Netherlands Chamber Orch. in 1955 and has taught at the Aspen Music Festival (1951–65).

Goldberg Variations "an aria with [30] variations for harpsichord," BWV 988 (1742), by J.S. Bach, the fourth part of the CLAVIERÜBUNG. The variations incl. canons at different intervals, two of which are in contrary motion, and a quodlibet (a piece incorporating popular tunes).

Golden Cockerel, The LE COQ D'OR.

Golden Gate Quartet Amer. vocal gospel quartet formed in the late 1920s in Virginia, noted for their performance of spirituals. They made very popular radio broadcasts in the 1930s and 1940s.

golden section the division of a quantity into 2 parts such that the ratio of the smaller to the larger is the same as that of the larger to the whole. The proportion has been used in the aural and visual arts since ancient times as pleasing to eye and ear. Many composers, incl. Berg and Bartók, have used the golden section in shaping their works. Cf. FIBONACCI.

Goldkette, Jean (1899–1962) French-born Amer. jazz pianist and leader. He created the Graystone Ballroom in Detroit and made it the home for his Victor Recording Orchestra, a collection of all-stars. During the 1920s he was one of the most important impresarios in the Midwest. The later part of his life he spent as an agent and performing classical piano music.

Goldman, Richard Franko (1910–80) Amer. bandmaster and composer, stud. of Boulanger and Riegger. His father, **Edwin Franko Goldman** (1878–1956), est. the Goldman Band in New York, of which Richard became conductor on his father's death. He taught at the Juilliard School (1947–60) and at the Peabody Conservatory (1968–77). He wrote music criticism for the *Musical Quarterly* (1948–68). He was important in restoring historic band works to the repertory, as well as in his support of contemporary composers.

Goldmark, Karl (Carl, Károly) (1830–1915) Hungarian opera composer, stud. of L. Jansa and Joseph Böhm. He was an important musical figure in Vienna, a music critic from 1860 and director of the Eintracht Choral Society. His works incl. *Die Königin von Saba* and 6 other operas; orchestral, choral, instrumental chamber music and songs.

Goldmark, Rubin (1872–1936) Amer. composer and teacher, stud. of Robert Fuchs and Dvořák. He taught privately and at the College Conservatory in Colorado Springs and at the Juilliard School, where his pupils included Copland and Gershwin.

Goldovsky, Boris (1908–) Russian-born Amer. conductor, pianist, lecturer and popularizer and producer of opera, stud. of Schnabel, Kreutzer, Ernö Dohnányi and Reiner. He directed the opera departments at the Cleveland Institute, the Berkshire Music Center and the New England Conservatory. He was founder of the Goldovsky Opera Institute and a touring company, the Goldovsky Grand Opera Theatre. His books include *Bringing Opera to Life* and *Accents on Opera*.

Goldsborough Orchestra see EN-GLISH CHAMBER ORCHESTRA.

goliard a wandering minstrel of the Middle Ages. Also, *vagante.* Cf. TROUBADOUR, TROUVÈRE.

Golishev, Efim (Jef) (1897–1970) Russian composer and painter, stud. of Auer and an important member of the DADA movement, both as painter and as musician. His musical works incl. two operas, film scores, vocal works and chamber music. He spent most of his last years in Brazil.

Golschmann, Vladimir (1893–1972) French-born Amer. conductor, trained at the Schola Cantorum in Paris. He conducted for the Ballets Russes, and was musical dir. of the Bériza Theatre in Paris, where he premiered a number of chamber operas by Ibert, Milhaud and others. He be-

came permanent conductor of the St. Louis SO in 1931, a post he held until 1956, after which he was made conductor emeritus. He was later musical dir. of the Tulsa SO (1958–61) and the Denver SO (1964–70). Throughout his career he championed the cause of new music.

Golson, Benny (1929–) Amer. jazz tenor saxophonist and composer. He has played with Lionel Hampton, Earl Bostic and Art Blakey and led his own Jazztet with Art Farmer. He also composed and arranged for many performers, incl. Dizzy Gillespie.

Gombert, Nicolas (?1495–?1560) Flemish composer, possibly a student of Josquin of whom he was an important successor. He sang in the court chapel of emperor Charles V from 1526, and was unofficial court composer. Gombert's motets are his most representative works, which also incl. Mass settings and chansons.

Gondoliers, The operetta in 2 acts by Sullivan to a libretto by W.S. Gilbert. Premiere, London 1889. Two gondoliers are being considered as heirs to the throne of Barataria until the rightful heir is found.

gong (Malay) a circular bronze plate of varying sizes and shapes used as a percussion instrument, struck with a padded hammer and yielding a subdued, highly resonant sound. Cf. TAM-TAM.

gong-ageng an instrument consisting of two suspended GONGS of slightly different pitches, used in the gamelan.

gong-chime set of small, tuned, high-pitched GONGS which are hung in a frame in order of pitch and played by one or more musicians. The gong-chime is used in the gamelan and other Asian orchestras.

gong drum a single-headed FRAME DRUM similar to a bass drum, but shallower.

gongue a concussion instrument consisting of two metal bells struck together to produce two separate pitches.

Gonsalves, Paul (1920–74) Amer.

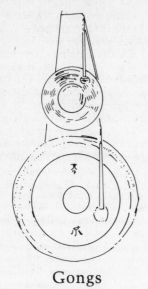

Gongs

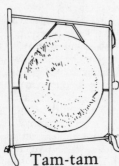

Tam-tam

jazz tenor saxophonist. He played with Count Basie and Dizzy Gillespie before joining the Duke Ellington orch., with which he remained for 24 years. He was known for the harmonic daring of his improvisations, anticipating the later FREE JAZZ movement.

Goodall, Reginald (1901–90) English conductor, trained at the Royal College of Music, London. He worked at Sadler's Wells Opera (1944–6) and Covent Garden from 1946 as a staff conductor. From 1961 to 1971 he was reduced to the role of repetiteur under Georg Solti, but returned to conducting at Sadler's Wells in the late 1960s and at Covent Garden in 1971. His performances of Wagner's operas were particularly noteworthy.

Goode, Richard (1943–) Amer. pianist, stud. of Nadia Reisenberg and Rudolf Serkin. He is best known as a chamber music pianist and has performed at the Marlboro Festival, with the Boston Symphony Chamber Players and with the Lincoln Center Chamber Music Society.

Good King Wenceslas Christmas carol, first published as a Latin spring song in the late 16th c., the present words added in 1853 by the Rev. J.M. Neale.

Goodman, Benny (Benjamin) **(David)** (1909–86) Amer. jazz swing bandleader, composer and clarinetist, the "King of Swing," stud. of James Sylvester and Franz Schoepp. He played with Ben Pollack's band from 1925 to 1929, becoming a leading free-lancer in New York. In 1934, he formed his first band, whose arrangements by Fletcher Henderson set the band's character and the standard for the swing era. In 1936 he formed a trio with pianist Teddy Wilson and drummer Gene Krupa, and a quartet, adding Lionel Hampton to the trio. In the 1940s the band underwent several permutations and was finally dissolved in 1949, though Goodman continued to tour and record with pick-up groups. The band over the years included many great jazz artists, among them Charlie Christian, Bunny Berigan, Zoot Sims, George Auld, Mel Powell, etc. Goodman was also a successful classical concert artist, whose recordings incl. the Mozart Clarinet Quintet and Clarinet Concerto, Belá Bartók's *Contrasts*, and concertos by Paul Hindemith and Aaron Copland, the latter three works commissioned by Goodman.

Good News! musical by Ray Henderson, lyrics by B.G. DeSylva and Lew Brown, book by DeSylva and Laurence Schwab. Premiere, New York 1927. Will Tom Marlowe, star football player, be allowed to play despite his failing scholastic average?

Goodrich, (John) Wallace (1871–1952)

Amer. conductor, organist and teacher, stud. of Chadwick, Widor and others. He taught at the New England Conservatory until 1942, meanwhile serving as organist in various Boston churches and conductor of the Worcester Festival, the Cecilia Society and the Boston Opera Company.

goofus a novelty instrument of the 1920s, a type of HARMONICA with saxophonelike keys, orig. manufactured by a French firm as the Couesnophone. The instrument was occasionally used by jazz musicians.

Goossens, (Sir) **(Aynsley) Eugene** (1893–1962) English conductor, violinist and composer, brother of LEON GOOSSENS, stud. of Charles Wood and C.V. Stanford. From 1916 he was assoc. with Sir Thomas Beecham, for whom he frequently substituted. He was conductor of the London Handel Society and conducted Covent Garden and the British National Opera Company. In 1923 he became conductor of the Rochester PO and in 1931 of the Cincinnati SO. He went to Australia in 1947 as conductor of the Sidney SO and dir. of the New South Wales Conservatorium.

Goossens, Leon (1897–1988) English oboist, brother of EUGENE GOOSSENS, stud. of William Malsch. He was principal oboe of the Queen's Hall Orch., the Covent Garden orch., the Royal Philharmonic Society and the London PO, but he was best known as a concert soloist, and many works were written for him.

gopak ['khō-päk] *also,* **hopak** (Russ.) a Ukrainian folk dance in duple meter characterized by stamping of the heels.

gora an African, stringed wind instrument, played by blowing on a quill attached to the string.

Gordon, Dexter (Keith) (1923–90) influential Amer. jazz bop tenor saxophonist, a major influence on John Coltrane and Sonny Rollins. He worked with Lionel Hampton, Fletcher Henderson and Charlie Parker in the 1940s. From 1962 he spent most of his time in Denmark,

returning to the U.S. to live in 1976. He appeared as star in the jazz film *Round Midnight* (1987).

Gorr, Rita (Geirnaert, Marguerite) (1926–) Belgian mezzo-soprano, stud. of Poelfiet and Jane Pacquot-d'Assy. Her Amer. debut was in 1962 at the Metropolitan Opera. She has sung in Paris, Bayreuth, at La Scala, Covent Garden, and is best known for her performances of Wagner and Verdi roles as well as French repertory.

gospel music *also,* **gospel** a body of Amer. religious song assoc. with the Protestant revivalism of the late 19th c. There are separate but interrelated traditions of white gospel and Afr.-Amer. gospel, the former developing from camp-meeting hymns, Sunday School hymns and shape-note singing, the latter from traditional preaching, singing and shouting, cross-fertilized by the blues, the spiritual, jazz and the Protestant hymn.

Gossec, François-Joseph (1734–1829) Dutch composer. He formed the Concert des Amateurs in 1769, which became one of Europe's finest orchestras. In 1773 he became a dir. of the Concert Spirituel, later (1780) assuming the same position with the Paris Opéra. During the Revolutionary decade he composed many republican works, including choruses, marches, and other works for large forces. After Napoleon's rise to power in 1799 Gossec composed few works, retiring in 1816.

Götterdämmerung, Die [gə-tər'de-mə-rûng, dē] TWILIGHT OF THE GODS, THE.

Gottschalk, Louis Moreau (1829–69) Amer. composer and pianist, stud. of François Letellier in New Orleans and in Paris of Camille Stamaty and Pierre Maleden. His performances of his own Creole piano works made him famous in Europe. He lived in the Caribbean islands from 1857 to 1861, then toured the U.S., leaving suddenly in 1865 to escape prosecution for seducing a young girl. He wrote piano concertos (esp. the *Grande tar-*

antelle), a large body of piano salon works, incl. the *Tournament galop* and the "Louisiana trilogy" (*Bamboula, La savane, Le bananier*), songs and several operas.

Goudimel, Claude (c1515–72) French composer and publisher, trained at U. of Paris. He died in the St. Bartholomew's Day Huguenot massacres. He is best known for his psalm settings.

Gould, Glenn (Herbert) (1932–82) iconoclastic Canadian pianist, composer and writer, stud. of Alberto Guerrero and Frederick Silvester. His U.S. debut was in 1955 in Washington, D.C. He made frequent concert appearances in the 1950s, but preferred the recording studio, and he eventually gave up live performance. He recorded a varied repertory, incl. Bach, Beethoven, Brahms and Schoenberg. His impeccable technique was accompanied by many mannerisms of performance and interpretation, including a tendency to sing as he played, even on his recordings.

Gould, Morton (1913–) Amer. composer and conductor, stud. of Abby Whiteside and Vincent Jones. He has toured widely as a conductor, but is best known for his works, which incl. musical comedies and ballets (*Fall River Legend*), many orchestral works (*American Salute, Soundings*) and works for piano.

Gounod, Charles (François) [goo'nō] (1818–93) French composer, stud. of J.F. Halévy and J.F. LeSueur. He won the Prix de Rome in 1839. He tried without much success to introduce the music of Palestrina and Bach to Paris and by 1850 he had decided to pursue a more traditional course for a French composer and write opera. His works incl. *Faust, Roméo et Juliette* and 10 other operas, incidental music, masses and other sacred music, choral music, songs, 2 symphonies, instrumental chamber music, and organ and piano works.

Goyescas 1, two sets of solo piano pieces (1911) by Granados, inspired by paintings by Goya. **2,** opera in 3 acts by Granados to a libretto in Spanish by Fernando Periquet, incorporating music from the piano pieces (1,). Premiere, New York 1916. Fernando and the toreador Paquiro fight a duel over Rosario, and Fernando dies in her arms.

grace note an ornamental note, usu. played quickly before a principal note and notated in a size smaller than the regular notes. In 20th-c. music, grace notes are often gestural, written to be played quickly as a group without being directed toward any principal note. See ORNAMENTS (*illus.*).

gradual 1, *also,* **responsorium graduale** (Lat.) a monophonic chant sung between the lessons of the liturgy in the Roman Mass. The gradual and alleluia (or tract) occur between the epistle and gospel. **2,** *also,* **liber gradualis** (Lat.) a liturgical book of the Christian Church containing chants for the Proper of the Mass, and, more recently, those of the Ordinary.

Gradus ad Parnassum (Lat., steps to Parnassus) **1,** a treatise on counterpoint (1725) by Fux. **2,** a collection of studies for piano (1817) by Muzio Clementi.

Graffman, Gary (1928–) Amer. pianist, stud. of Isabelle Vengerova, Vladimir Horowitz and Rudolf Serkin. He won the Rachmaninoff Prize in 1947 and the Leventritt Award in 1949. He specializes in the late Romantic and early 20th-c. repertory and has also performed frequently in chamber music with the Guarneri and Juilliard Quartets and in sonata recitals.

Grainger, (George) Percy (Aldridge) (1882–1961) Australian-born Amer. composer, pianist, folk-song collector and teacher, trained at the Hoch Conservatory in Frankfurt. He was a pioneer in collection of folk songs using the wax cylinder phonograph. He taught, for relatively brief periods, at Chicago Music College and at New York U. He also spent years collecting folk songs in Jutland and returned several times to Australia. In 1938 he inaugurated the Grainger Museum at the U. of Melbourne, to which he was to dedicate much of his time for the rest of his life.

Gramm (Grambsch), **Donald (John)** (1927–83) Amer. bass-baritone, trained at the Wisconsin College-Conservatory of Music, Chicago Musical College, and with Martial Singher in California. He sang for many years with the New York City Opera, the Opera Company of Boston, the Metropolitan Opera and other major opera companies. He was known for his versatility and intelligence and performed in many 20th-c. works.

Granados (y Campiña), Enrique (1867–1916) Spanish composer and pianist, trained in Barcelona and Paris. His first major success was his opera *Goyescas*, orig. intended for the Paris Opéra but ultimately premiered at the Metropolitan Opera in New York. He died tragically shortly thereafter, while attempting to save his wife after their boat had been torpedoed in the English Channel. He wrote zarzuelas, poemas, piano works, songs, chamber music and several works for orch.

gran cassa (It.) BASS DRUM.

grand GRAND PIANO.

grand détaché [grä dä-tä'shä] (Fr.) in bowing, a DÉTACHÉ with long bow-strokes.

Grand Duchess of Gerolstein, The (Fr., *La Grande Duchesse de Gérolstein*) comic opera in 3 acts by Offenbach to a libretto in French by Henri Meilhac and Ludovic Halévy. Premiere, Paris 1867. The Duchess finally resigns herself to marriage with the weakling Prince Paul—but not without many delays.

Grand Funk Railroad Amer. heavy-metal band formed in 1969 in Michigan. They toured extensively during their seven years of existence and sold over 20 million albums.

Grandi, Alessandro (c1580–1630) Italian composer of sacred vocal music, possibly stud. of Giovanni Gabrieli. In 1617 he joined the choir of St. Mark's, Venice, and served as Monteverdi's assistant after 1620. In 1627 he became *maestro* in Bergamo, where he died of the plague. He was an important composer in the new concertato style of the early Baroque.

Grandjany, Marcel (Georges Lucien) (1891–1975) French-born Amer. concert harpist, stud. of Henriette Renié. He came to the U.S. in 1924 and taught at the Juilliard School and at the Montreal Conservatory. He had tremendous influence as a teacher and his recordings testify to his sensuous tone and impeccable technique.

grand jeu [grä jø] (Fr.) a term used by French organ composers to denote a combination of ORGAN STOPS including bourdons, mutations and reeds.

Grand Ole Opry Amer. country-music variety show in Nashville initiated on radio in 1925 under the name "WSM Barn Dance" and renamed in 1927. Orig. broadcast from a studio without audience, the program is now housed in its own 4000-seat theater. Its founder, George D. Hay, was elected to the Country Music Hall of Fame in 1966.

grand opera 1, a term orig. used to signify French opera performed at the Paris Opéra (as well as the building itself). It was used in contrast to *opéra-comique*, a form of French music drama in which the musical numbers are separated by spoken dialogue, whereas grand opera features sung recitatives. Other characteristics of grand opera are that the plots are serious and heroic, chosen from history rather than mythology, and that the subjects are treated in grandiose proportions, employing the utmost resources of singing, orchestral music and staging. Examples are Meyerbeer's *Les Huguenots* (1836), Rossini's *Guillaume Tell* (1829) and Berlioz's *Les Troyens* (1858). **2,** fully sung OPERA of whatever origin performed with a certain magnificence, such as the larger works of Verdi, Massenet, Meyerbeer, etc.

grand piano a horizontal wing-shaped PIANO, the form considered best for concert use.

gran tamburo (It.) BASS DRUM.

Granz, Norman (1918–) Amer. jazz entrepreneur, famous for his long-lived touring series "Jazz at the Philharmonic," which began with a concert at the Philharmonic Auditorium in Los Angeles. The concerts were in the style of an informal jam session and were often recorded live. His series introduced many jazz greats to an international audience.

graphic notation while standard musical notation is, in fact, graphic, the term is usu. applied to notation which does not use the conventional symbols and words. Graphic notation systems—which date from experiments in the early 1950s of Feldman, Cage, Earle Brown and others—use new symbols to suggest new sounds or to avoid the specificity of conventional systems, or employ pictorial graphics to inspire the performer's improvisation.

Grappelli (Grappelly), **Stéphane** (1908–) French jazz violinist. In 1934 with guitarist Django Reinhardt he formed the Quintette du Hot Club in Paris. He lived in England c1940–48 after which he returned to Paris, from where he has continued to concertize. He has also performed with classical violinist Yehudi Menuhin.

Grateful Dead, The Amer. rock group, formed in 1965 in San Francisco. One of the longest-lived rock bands, and the only surviving psychedelic band, the group has been unusual in its concentration on live performance rather than recording. Over the years they have assembled a very devoted fan club, the Dead Heads.

Graun, Carl Heinrich (1704–59) German composer and tenor, studied at the U. of Leipzig. He joined the musical establishment of Crown Prince Frederick in 1736, becoming royal Kapellmeister in 1740 when Frederick acceded to the throne. Graun was responsible for hiring the singers and musicians for the new Berlin Opera House, which opened in 1742. His operas (the best known of which is *Montezuma*) are in the Baroque *opera seria* manner, but were also influenced by Gluck's reforms. He also wrote cantatas, songs, duets and instrumental works.

grave ['grä-vä] (It.) **1,** slowly, with solemnity. **2,** low or flat in pitch.

Graves, Milford Robert (1941–) Amer. jazz drummer, self-taught as a musician. He has been a member of the New York Art Quartet, the Jazz Composers' Orch. Association and Pieces of Time, an all-percussion quartet. He has been an important force in the free-jazz movement and a pioneer of extended percussion-only performance. He has taught at the Black Arts Repertory Theatre in New York and at Bennington College.

gravicembalo ["grä-vē'chem-bä-lō] (It.) HARPSICHORD.

Gray, Wardell (1921–55) Amer. jazz tenor saxophonist from Oklahoma. He played with Earl Hines, Benny Carter, Billy Eckstine, Benny Goodman and Count Basie and recorded frequently in partnership with saxophonist Dexter Gordon.

grazioso (It.) gracefully, with elegance.

Grease rock musical by Jim Jacobs and Warren Casey. Premiere, New York 1972. A nostalgic look at the '50s generation.

Great C Major Symphony the Symphony No. 9 in C major (c1825) by Schubert.

Great Fugue, The see GROSSE FUGE, DIE.

Great G Minor Fugue the Fantasia and Fugue in G minor, BWV 542 (c1717), by J.S. Bach.

Great Mass the Mass No. 3 in F minor (1867–8) by Bruckner.

Great Organ Mass the Mass in E♭ major (1774) by Haydn, with obbligato organ part.

great organ 1, the division of a pipe organ having the largest pipes and the loudest tone. Also, *Hauptwerk* (Ger.) **2,** a large organ, as opposed to a chamber organ.

Great Revival a period of religious

Graphic Notation

from *Sette Fogli, una collezione occulta*: "Manifesto per Kalinowski" for chamber orchestra by Sylvano Bussotti. © Copyright 1970 by Universal Edition. Copyright renewal assigned to G. Ricordi & C. Reprinted by permission of Hendon Music, Inc., Agents for G. Ricordi & C., Milan, Italy. →

from *Grande Aulodia* for flute and oboe solo with orchestra by Bruno Maderna. © Copyright 1963 by G. Ricordi & C. Reprinted by permission of Hendon Music, Inc., Agents for G. Ricordi & C., Milan, Italy. ↓

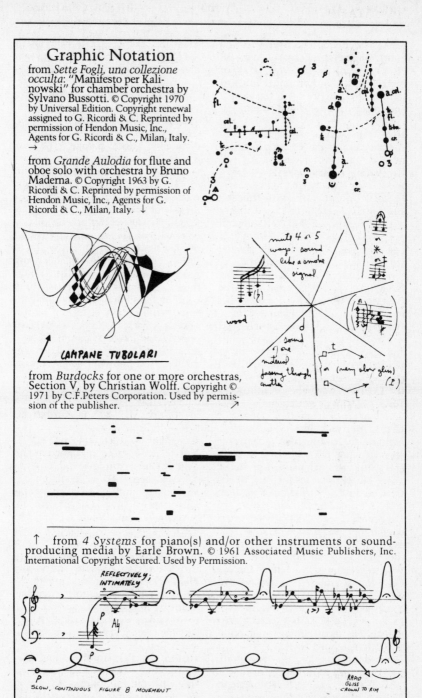

from *Burdocks* for one or more orchestras, Section V, by Christian Wolff. Copyright © 1971 by C.F.Peters Corporation. Used by permission of the publisher. ↗

↑ from *4 Systems* for piano(s) and/or other instruments or sound-producing media by Earle Brown. © 1961 Associated Music Publishers, Inc. International Copyright Secured. Used by Permission.

↑ from *The Crown of Ariadne* for solo harp with percussion by R. Murray Schafer. © Copyright 1980 Arcana Editions, Indian River, Ontario. Used with permission.

revivalism in the U.S. Midwest and South during the early 19th c., focused in camp meetings of 10,000 or more people. The principal musical form of the meetings was the simple and repetitive verse-and-refrain revival hymn.

great scale a scale ascribed to Guido Arezzo comprising seven hexachords from G to e″ (see HEXACHORD).

Grechaninov, Alexander (1864–1956) Russian composer. He studied at the Moscow Conservatory with Arensky and the St. Petersburg Conservatory with Rimsky-Korsakov. His liberal religious beliefs resulted in his use of instruments in his church music, which made it unusable in the Orthodox Church services. After the Revolution, he went first to Paris, then (in 1939) to the U.S. His works incl. operas and incidental music, symphonies and other orchestral works, liturgical vocal music, songs and instrumental chamber music.

Green, Freddie (Frederick William) (1911–87) Amer. jazz guitarist with the Count Basie orch. for almost 50 years (1937–85), where he was the mainstay of the rhythm section.

Green, Martyn (1899–1975) English baritone, best known as a character singer in the D'Oyly Carte Gilbert and Sullivan company for many years, where his roles incl. the Major General in *The Pirates of Penzance* and Ko-Ko in *The Mikado*.

Greenberg, Noah (1919–66) Amer. conductor and musicologist, a self-taught musician. He was choir dir. at St. Luke's Church in New York, which became the nucleus for his early music group Pro Musica Antiqua (1952), later known as the NEW YORK PRO MUSICA, an important force in the revival of early music performance. His most famous production was THE PLAY OF DANIEL.

Greensleeves an English tune, probably a dance tune dating from the 16th c., mentioned by Shakespeare in *The Merry Wives of Windsor* and popular as a melody for variations.

Greer, Sonny (William Alexander)
(1903–82) Amer. jazz drummer with the Duke Ellington orch. for 32 years until 1950, then with small bands headed by Johnny Hodges and others.

Gregorian chant the PLAINSONG sung as part of the Roman Catholic rite, said to have been written down by Gregory the Great (Pope Gregory I) as dictated to him by a dove, which sat on his shoulder.

Grétry, André-Ernest-Modeste (1741–1813) French composer, trained with various musicians in Liège and at the Collège de Liège in Rome. He was highly successful as a composer of *opéra-comique* (less so with serious opera) until the Revolution, after which he lost his court positions and produced little more music of significance. His works combined Italian forms and melodic style with sensitive setting of the French texts. His works incl. over 30 operas (incl. *Les deux avares, Zémire et Azor, Richard Coeur-de-Lion*), romances, revolutionary songs and instrumental works.

Grey (Katz), Joel (1932–) singer, dancer, actor, best known for his roles in *Cabaret* (1966) and *George M.* (1968) on Broadway.

Grieg, Edvard (Hagerup) (1843–1907) Norwegian composer, trained at the Leipzig Conservatory with E.F. Wenzel, Moscheles, Reinecke and others. His dedication to Norwegian nationalism was established by his contacts with Ole Bull and Rikard Nordraak in the mid 1860s. He became conductor of the Harmoniske Selskab in 1866 and was involved in the formation of the Norwegian Academy of Music. His works incl. incidental music, orchestral works (incl. the often performed Piano Concerto in A minor), many choral works and songs, works for piano solo and duet, chamber music.

Griffes, Charles T(omlinson) (1884–1920) Amer. pianist and composer, trained at Elmira College (NY) and in Berlin at the Stern Conservatory. He was dir. of music at the Hackley School, Tarrytown, NY from 1907 until his death. He wrote dance works, orchestral works (incl. arrangements of several of his piano pieces), chamber music, songs (incl. *Three Poems of Fiona MacLeod*), piano works (incl. *The White Peacock* and the Piano Sonata of 1917).

grind a basic Afr.-Amer. dance movement of the pelvis, common to many jazz dances.

Grisi, Giulia (1811–69) Ital. soprano, stud. of Marliani and Giacomelli. She sang in Italy until 1832, then left, never to sing there professionally again. She sang regularly thereafter in Paris and London, retiring in 1861. Her repertory included the major roles of Rossini, Bellini and Donizetti, and of Verdi and Meyerbeer as well. Her sister, **Giuditta Grisi** (1805–40), was a successful mezzo-soprano.

Grist, Reri (1932–) Amer. soprano, stud. of Claire Gelda. She began as a singer in musical comedy, then made her operatic debut in 1959 at Santa Fe. Her roles incl. Zerbinetta (*Ariadne auf Naxos*), the Mozart soubrettes and Adina (*L'Elisir d'amore*). She also sings frequently in recital and concert and has made many recordings.

Grofé, Ferde (Ferdinand) (**Rudolf von**) (1892–1972) Amer. composer, arranger and pianist. He played for 10 years as a violist with the Los Angeles SO, then worked as an arranger for Paul Whiteman from 1917 to 1933 and orchestrated Gershwin's *Rhapsody in Blue* for the band. He taught at the Juilliard School and conducted the New World Ensemble, a group performing on electric instruments, at the 1939 New York World's Fair. His works incl. orchestral suites (incl. *Grand Canyon Suite, Hudson River Suite*), arrangements and orig. works for jazz band, film scores (incl. *Minstrel Man*), other instrumental works.

grosse caisse [kes] (Fr.), **grosse Trommel** (Ger.) BASS DRUM.

Grosse Fuge, Der ['foo-ge] (Ger., The Great Fugue) fugue for string quartet, Op. 133 (1825), by Beethoven, orig.

intended to be the finale of his quartet in B-flat major, Op. 130. Because of its complexity, he replaced it in that work with a new finale and published the fugue separately.

ground *also*, **ground bass** a term used in 16th-c. England to indicate a bass melody, repeated many times in succession and accompanied by continuous variations in the upper parts. There are many examples of Renaissance instrumental grounds, such as the *passamezzo antico, passamezzo moderno, ruggiero, chaccone, passacaglia, folia*, etc. Examples of the use of ground basses in vocal music are the famous "Dido's Lament" from Purcell's *Dido and Aeneas* (1689), and Monteverdi's *Lamento d'Arianna* (1608). See RENAISSANCE BASSES (*illus.*)

ground harp an Afr. one-stringed instrument consisting of a string, attached to a flexible stave planted in the ground, and stretched to a soundboard held to the ground by weights. The string is stopped by one hand and plucked by the other.

ground zither an instrument of Asia and Africa consisting of a string stretched between posts set in the ground over a bark-covered resonating pit. The string is beaten with sticks.

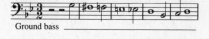

Ground bass

When I am laid, _ am laid____ in

earth, may my wrongs ____ cre – ate

etc.

(Purcell, Dido and Aeneas)

group a short melodic figure—sometimes having consistent dynamic, harmonic and rhythmic characteristics—used as a compositional unit by Stockhausen and others.

Group for Contemporary Music a contemporary music org. at Columbia U. founded in 1962 by Harvey Sollberger.

growl a technique used in playing wind instruments by which a guttural sound produced in the player's throat is transmitted through the instrument, resulting in a growling, dirty sound. The technique is much used in jazz, esp. in swing music.

Gruberova, Edita (1946–) Czech. coloratura soprano, who studied in Prague and Vienna. She made her debut with the Slovak National Theater and has sung at the Vienna State Opera, Bayreuth, Frankfurt Opera, the Chicago Lyric Opera and other major opera houses.

Gruenberg, Louis (1884–1964) Russian-born Amer. composer, stud. of Adele Margulies and Busoni. He was a founder of the League of Composers and his opera *The Emperor Jones* was produced in 1933 by the Metropolitan Opera. His works composed after 1920 make frequent use of jazz and Negro spirituals. After teaching at the Chicago Musical Coll. (1933–6), he moved to California and wrote film scores, three of which won Academy Awards. He wrote 10 operas, orchestral works (incl. *The Hill of Dreams*, 4 symphonies), vocal music (incl. *The Daniel Jazz*), chamber music.

Grumiaux, Baron **Arthur** (1921–86) Belgian violinist, stud. of Alfred Dubois and Enescu. He pursued a highly successful international solo career, interrupted only by the German occupation of Belgium. He taught at the Brussels Conservatory from 1949. He has made many recordings, of which those of Bach, Mozart and Beethoven are most noteworthy.

gruppetto *also*, **gruppo** (It., small group) a 16th-c. ORNAMENT similar to a trill. The term was also used later for a turn.

Guadagni, Gaetano (1725–92) Italian contralto castrato, a member of Handel's company in London and the creator of the role of Orfeo in Gluck's *Orfeo ed Euridice* (1764).

Guadagnini Italian family of violin makers from the early 17th to the beginning of the 20th c.

Guarneri Italian family of violin makers from the early 17th to the mid-18th c. The founder, Andrea Guarneri (c1626–98) was a student of Nicola Amati. The greatest violin maker of the family line was Giuseppe Guarneri the younger ("del Gesù") (1698–1744).

Guarneri String Quartet Amer. string quartet formed at the Marlboro Festival (VT) in 1964. The group has performed widely and made many recordings.

Guarnieri, (Mozart) Camargo (1907–) Brazilian composer, conductor and teacher, stud. of Baldi in São Paulo and Koechlin and Boulanger in Paris. He was conductor of the São Paulo SO from 1945, dir. of the São Paulo Conservatory from 1960 and a professor at the Santos Conservatory from 1964. His works incl. orchestral works (incl. 3 symphonies, violin concertos, *Abertura concertante*, several chôros), vocal and chamber music.

Gueden, Hilde (1917–88) Austrian soprano, trained at the Vienna Conservatory. She joined the Bavarian Staatsoper (Munich) in 1941. Amer. debut was at the Metropolitan Opera in 1960. Her wide repertory of roles incl. Anne Trulove (*The Rake's Progress*), Zerbinetta (*Ariadne auf Naxos*) and Sophie (*Der Rosenkavalier*).

Guédron, Pierre (1565–1621) French composer, singer and singing teacher. In 1588 he joined the French royal chapel and worked there until his death. He was a leading musician at the French court and one of the most important composers of *airs de cour* and *ballets de cour*. He is noted for his expressive, dramatic text settings, highly influenced by the *musique mesurée à l'antique* of Baïf. His *bal-*

lets mélodramatiques were important in the development of opera in France.

Guelph Spring Festival annual May festival of opera and concerts held in Guelph, Ontario, since 1968.

Guerre des bouffons, La [ger dã boo'fõ] (Fr.) BOUFFONS, WAR OF THE.

Guerrero, Francisco (1528–99) Spanish composer, stud. of Morales. He was *maestro di capilla* of Jaén Cathedral, then associate to the *maestro* of Seville Cathedral in 1551, where he became *maestro* in 1574. His works were published in Spain, Italy and France, and he traveled widely. He was one of the major composers of Spanish sacred music of his day and also a prolific composer of secular songs and works for vihuela.

Guess Who, The Canadian rock band formed in 1963 in Winnipeg. The group was most successful in the late 1960s and early 1970s, when it toured Canada and the U.S. and appeared on Canadian television regularly. They disbanded in 1976.

Gui, Vittorio (1885–1975) Italian conductor and composer, stud. at the Liceo di Santa Cecilia in Rome. He conducted in Italy from 1907 to 1928 and formed the Orchestra Stabile, of Florence, the forerunner of the Maggio Musicale. He conducted the BBC SO and the Royal PO and opera at Salzburg, Covent Garden and Glyndebourne. He never conducted in No. America.

Guido d'Arezzo (Aretinus) (?991–after 1033) one of the most important music theorists of the Middle Ages. His principal contributions to music theory were his method of sightsinging—which utilized the syllables ut, re, mi, fa, sol, la (see GUIDONIAN HAND)—and his introduction of the four-line staff. His *Micrologus* (c1026) is the earliest comprehensive treatise on musical practice to include discussions of both polyphonic music and plainchant. Next to Boethius's *De institutione musica*, Guido's *Micrologus* was the most copied and read instruction book on music in the Middle Ages.

Guidonian hand a system for teaching singers SOLMIZATION, in which each tone of the gamut is assigned to one of the joints of the left hand. The teacher would stand in front of his choir and point to the various joints of his hand while the singers sang the appropriate pitches.

Guildhall School a London conservatory founded in 1880.

Guillaume Tell [ge'yõm tel] (Fr.) WILLIAM TELL.

Guillaume de Machaut [dø mä'shõ] GUILLAUME DE MACHAUT.

Guilmant, (Félix) Alexandre [gē'mä] (1837–1911) French organist and composer of sacred vocal music and music for organ, stud. of his father. He taught at the Schola Cantorum (of which he was a co-founder) and at the Paris Conservatoire, where his pupils included Nadia Boulanger and Marcel Dupré.

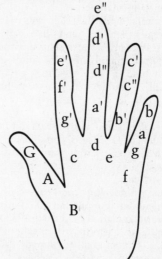

Guidonian hand

Letter names refer to relative positions in the sequence of hexachords, rather than to actual pitches.

guimbarde [gē'bärd] (Fr.) JEW'S-HARP.

Guiraud, Ernest [gē'rō] (1837–92) New Orleans-born French composer, stud. of Antoine-François Marmontel and Halévy. He won the Prix de Rome in 1859 and became close friends with Bizet during his stay in Rome. He wrote the accompanied recitatives in *Carmen* and the arrangement of the second suite from *L'arlésienne*. He also orchestrated Offenbach's *Les Contes d'Hoffmann*. From 1876, he taught at the Paris Conservatoire, where his pupils incl. Debussy and Dukas.

güiro ['gwē-rō] (Cuban) a Lat. Amer. percussion instrument consisting of a notched gourd scraped with a stick.

guitar 1, a fretted, flat-backed LUTE that is strummed or plucked. The modern acoustic guitar has six strings of gut or steel and a hollow resonating chamber with a round sound hole and a waisted shape. When used in jazz and popular music, the guitar is often fitted with an electric pickup (see ELECTRIC GUITAR), which is added to an acoustic guitar or built into a specially designed solid case without a resonating chamber.

Guitars of earlier centuries were generally smaller and had fewer strings and often a rose-shaped, rather than open, sound hole. Folk guitarists often use a twelve-string guitar, which is double strung, two strings per pitch. See GITTERN, LYRE GUITAR, UKULELE.

2, a medium-shallow STEEL DRUM, about 9" deep. Also, *second pan*.

guitarrón [gē-tär'rōn] (Sp.) a four-stringed BASS GUITAR used in Mexican music.

guitar violoncello ARPEGGIONE.

Gulbenkian Foundation a Portuguese organization founded in 1956 in accordance with the will of Calouste Sarkis Gulbenkian to support the arts, education and the sciences.

Gulda, Friedrich (1930–) Austrian pianist and composer, trained at the Grossmann Conservatory and the Vienna Academy of Music. He won the Geneva Competition in 1946 and founded the Classical Gulda Orchestra of the Vienna SO. In 1962 he shifted his emphasis to jazz and now mixes the two traditions in his recitals. He was also a founder of the Eurojazz Orchestra and the Internationales Musikforum at Ossiach.

Gurrelieder ['gû-re"lē-dər] (Ger., Songs of Gurre) a large cantata for soloists, three male choruses, a mixed chorus, narrator and large orchestra (1911) by Schoenberg. The text is based on a German translation of Danish poems by J.P. Jacobsen.

gusla ['goo-slə] (Serbo-Croatian) *also*, **gusle, gousle, guzla** a one-stringed Balkan folk FIDDLE with a round, concave body and a parchment sounding-surface.

gusli *also*, **guslee** ['goo-slē] (Russ.) a Russian keyboard stringed instrument similar to the zither usu. having 28 gut strings.

gutbucket BARRELHOUSE.

Guthrie, Arlo (1947–) Amer. folk singer from New York, son of WOODY GUTHRIE. He became famous for his song "Alice's Restaurant," which subsequently inspired a movie. He has performed with Judy Collins, Pete Seeger, the group Shenandoah and others.

Guthrie, Woody (Woodrow Wilson) (1912–67) influential Amer. folk-singer and songwriter. He was a street singer in the 1930s and traveled throughout the U.S. In the 1940s he was recorded by Alan Lomax for the Library of Congress and joined the Almanac Singers, a group organized by Pete Seeger. Many of his songs have become an integral part of the folk repertory, incl. "This Land Is Your Land," "So Long, It's Been Good to Know You" and "This Train Is Bound for Glory."

Guys and Dolls musical by Frank Loesser, book by Abe Burrows and Jo Swerling, based on Damon Runyon's short story *The Idyll of Miss Sarah Brown*. Premiere, New York 1950. Miss Sarah Brown of the Save-a-Soul

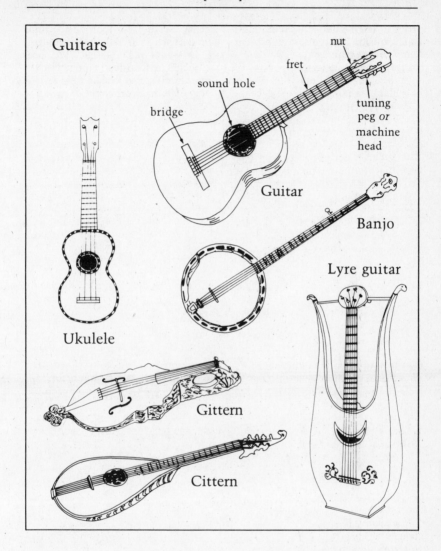

Guitars

nut

fret

sound hole

bridge

tuning peg *or* machine head

Guitar

Banjo

Lyre guitar

Ukulele

Gittern

Cittern

Mission loses her heart to gambler Sky Masterson, as does Nathan Detroit to Miss Adelaide.

gymel *also*, **gimel** ['jim-əl] a 15th- and 16th-c. English term indicating the temporary split of a single voice part into two parts of equal range.

Gypsy musical by Jule Styne, lyrics by Stephen Sondheim, book by Arthur Laurents, based on the autobiography of Gypsy Rose Lee. Premiere, New York 1959. The story of Rose, mother of vaudevillian Gypsy Rose Lee, and her attempts to enliven her life vicariously through the success of her daughter.

Gypsy music folk music of the Gypsies, an itinerant people believed to have originated in northern India. In the broader sense, any music performed and cultivated by Gypsies. Gypsy music today is assoc. mainly with Hungary. Gypsies have no ritual music, since they lack traditional festivities and customs that require special music. They use instruments only occasionally.

Gypsy Rondo last movement of the Piano Trio in G major (1795) by Haydn.

gypsy scale the harmonic minor SCALE with a raised fourth degree, i.e., C-D-E♭-F♯-G-A♭-B-C, so called because it occurs frequently in Hungarian Romantic music to impart a gypsy flavor. Also, *Hungarian gypsy scale.*

H

H 1, (Ger.) B (natural). **2**, *abbr.* HAUPTSTIMME.

Haas, Pavel (1899–1944) Czech composer, stud. of Janáček. He was executed by the Nazis during World War II. His works, which combine the influence of his teacher with Jewish chant, neoclassicism, and jazz, incl. a symphony, film scores, vocal works and chamber music.

Hába, Alois (1893–1973) Czech composer, theorist and teacher, trained at the Prague Conservatory (where he later taught) and privately with Franz Schreker and others. He founded the Opera of the 5th of May, was a pioneer in the use of MICROTONES in Western art music and invented several woodwind, brass and keyboard instruments to play quarter- and sixth-tones.

habanera [hä-vä′nä-rä, *not* -nyä-] (Sp., Havanan dance) a slow, seductive Cuban dance characterized by the rhythm of dotted eighth note, sixteenth note and two eighths throughout. One of the most famous examples is the aria "L'amour est un oiseau rebelle," sung by Carmen in Bizet's opera. See DANCE (*illus.*).

Habeneck, François-Antoine (1781–1849) French composer, violinist and conductor, stud. of Pierre Baillot. He was dir. of the Paris Opéra from 1821 to 1824 and conductor from 1824 to 1846. He premiered many works by Meyerbeer, Berlioz, Rossini and others and introduced the orchestral music of Beethoven to France. He taught at the Paris Conservatoire and founded the Société des Concerts du Conservatoire.

Hackbrett (Ger.) a Swiss DULCIMER.

Hackett, Bobby (Robert Leo) (1915–76) Amer. jazz cornetist, trumpeter and guitarist. He played with the bands of Louis Armstrong, Glenn Miller, Glen Gray, Eddie Condon and bands led by Jackie Gleason, among many others. In the mid-1950s he led his own band at the Henry Hudson Hotel in New York.

Hadley, Henry (**Kimball**) (1871–1937) Amer. conductor and composer, trained at the New England Conservatory. He was the first conductor of the San Francisco SO (1911–16) and in 1929 formed the Manhattan SO to perform works by Amer. composers. The Henry Hadley Memorial Library at the New York Public Library was endowed by the National Association for American Composers and Conductors (an org. he founded).

Haefliger, Ernst (1919–) Swiss tenor, stud. of Julius Patzak and Fernando Carpi. He has sung regularly at the Deutsche Oper in Berlin, but he is particularly noted for his recital work and as the Evangelist in the Passions of J.S. Bach.

Haendel, Georg Friederich see HANDEL.

Haendel, Ida (1924–) Polish-born British violinist, stud. of Mieczyslaw Michalowicz, Flesch and Enescu. She has toured widely in Europe, No. America and Russia, specializing in the concerto repertory. She has lived in Canada since 1952.

Haffner Serenade serenade in D major, K. 250 (1776), by Mozart, composed for the marriage of Elizabeth Haffner at Salzburg.

Haffner Symphony symphony in D major, No. 35, K. 385 (1782) by Mozart, orig. intended as part of a serenade.

Hagegård, Håkan (1945–) Swedish baritone. He became known through the Ingmar Bergman film of Mozart's *The Magic Flute* and has appeared at the Metropolitan Opera (since 1978) and other American and European opera houses.

Haggard, Merle (1937–) Amer. country-music singer and guitarist. He formed his own backing-group in the 1960s, the Strangers, with which he has toured extensively. He has written hundreds of songs, many of which have been recorded by other artists.

Hahn, Reynaldo (1874–1947) Venezuelan-born French composer and conductor, trained at the Paris Conservatoire with Théodore Dubois and Massenet. He was dir. of the Paris Opéra (1945–47) and also conducted at Salzburg and Cannes. His works incl. *Mozart, Ciboulette* and other operettas, operas, ballets, songs, orchestral and instrumental chamber music.

Haig, Al (Allan Warren) (1924–82) Amer. jazz pianist, among the first to adapt Charlie Parker's innovations to the piano. He performed with many of the bop greats, incl. Dizzy Gillespie, Charlie Parker and Stan Getz.

Hail! Columbia patriotic march (1798) with tune (orig. "The President's March") by Philip Phile, text by Joseph Hopkinson (son of statesman FRANCIS HOPKINSON).

Hail to the Chief a march song played (since the early 19th c.) to announce the arrival of the president of the U.S. The words (rarely used) are from *The Lady of the Lake* by Sir Walter Scott; the composer of the music is unknown.

Haine van Ghizeghem see HAYNE.

Hair rock musical by Galt MacDermot, lyrics and book by Gerome Ragni and James Rado. Premiere, New York 1967. An "American Tribal Love-Rock Musical" about the life style of East Village hippies, famous for the first-act finale in which the entire cast was nude.

hairpins familiar term for the symbols for *crescendo* (<) and *decrescendo* (>).

Haitink, Bernard (Johann Herman) (1929–) Dutch conductor, stud. of

Felix Hupka and Ferdinand Leitner. In 1961 he became the youngest principal conductor of the Concertgebouw Orch. He was also assoc. with the London PO from 1967 to 1979 and has been musical dir. of the Glyndebourne Festival since 1977 and of Covent Garden since 1987. He is particularly noted for his performance of the works of Mahler, Bruckner and Mozart.

halb [hälp] (Ger.) half.

Hale, Philip (1854–1934) Amer. music critic, trained at Yale and in Europe. He was critic for the Boston *Post*, the Boston *Journal* and the Boston *Herald* and editor of the *Musical Record*. He was also annotator for the programs of the Boston SO from 1901 to 1934.

Halévy, (Jacques-François-)Fromental (-Elie) ['ä-lä-vē] (1799–1862) French opera composer and teacher, stud. of L. Cherubini and winner of the Prix de Rome in 1819. He taught at the Paris Conservatoire from 1827, counting among his pupils Bizet and Gounod, and was *chef du chant* at the Théâtre-Italien and then at the Opéra. He was highly esteemed by Berlioz and Wagner, esp. as an orchestrator and for his dramatic effects. He wrote 40 operas (incl. *La Juive*), vocal works (esp. *Prométhée enchaîné*) and a few instrumental works.

Haley, Bill (Clifton, William John) (1925–81) Amer. rock bandleader. He led a country-music band in the 1940s and in 1953 formed the Comets, which became immensely successful in the early history of rock and roll. Their biggest hits were "Rock around the Clock" and "Shake, Rattle and Roll" (both 1954).

Half a Sixpence musical by David Heneker, book by Douglas Cross, based on H.G. Wells's *Kipps*. Premiere, London 1963. The career of orphan Arthur Kipps, a draper's apprentice, at the turn of the century.

half cadence, half-close IMPERFECT CADENCE.

half-diminished seventh chord a CHORD consisting of a root, minor third, diminished 5th and minor 7th. Cf. TRISTAN CHORD.

half-fall a type of APPOGGIATURA.

Halffter, Ernesto (Escriche) (1905–) Spanish composer and conductor, brother of RODOLFO HALFFTER and stud. of Falla, whose unfinished cantata *Atlántida* he completed. He was active as conductor both in Seville and in Lisbon. As a composer he has produced ballet music, film scores, orchestral suites, songs, chamber music and piano solos.

Halffter, Rodolfo (Escriche) (1900–) Spanish-born Mexican composer and teacher, brother of ERNESTO HALFFTER, largely self-taught but strongly influenced by Falla. His works incl. an opera, ballets, a violin concerto, orchestral suites, songs, chamber music and piano works.

half note a NOTE (♩) having half the value of a whole note. Also, (Brit.) *minim*.

half rest a REST (▬) having the value of a half note.

half-shake PRALLTRILLER.

half tone *also,* **half step** the smallest diatonic INTERVAL, represented in the C major scale by the distance between E and F and between B and C.

halil (Heb.) an ancient Jewish reed wind instrument similar to the Greek AULOS.

Hall, Adelaide (1895–) Amer. singer and actress, star on Broadway in *Blackbirds of 1928*, and *Brown Buddies* (1930) and a successful nightclub entertainer in the U.S. and England.

Hall, Tom T. (1936–) Amer. country singer and songwriter, best known for his song "Harper Valley P.T.A."

Hall and Oates highly successful Amer. rock duo formed in 1969 in Philadelphia by Daryl Hall and John Oates. Their hit singles incl. "Rich Girl" (1976) and "Private Eyes" (1981).

Halle, Adam de la ADAM DE LA HALLE.

Hallé, Sir Charles (Carl) (1819–95) German-born English conductor and pianist, stud. of Johann Rinck, Gott-fried Weber and George Osborne. He went to Manchester in 1848 and became conductor of the Gentleman's Concerts, which, in enlarged form, was to become the Hallé Orchestra, which he conducted for the rest of his life. He was also active in the founding of the Royal Manchester College of Music.

hallelujah ALLELUIA.

Hallelujah! the first all-black musical film (1929).

Hallelujah Chorus many works contain choruses based on the word *Hallelujah*, but the name usu. refers to the chorus which closes Part II of the oratorio *Messiah* (1742) by Handel.

Hallelujah Concerto the organ concerto in B♭ major, Op. 7 No. 3 (1751), by Handel.

halling (Norwegian) a lively Norwegian dance in duple time for 1 to 3 dancers, usu. accompanied on a HARDANGER FIDDLE.

hambone an Afr.-Amer. dance-song similar to JUBA. The CHARLESTON and other later dances borrowed some of the hand motions, such as crossing the hands on the knees.

Hamelle French music publishing firm, founded in 1877 by Julien Hamelle. Its catalogue incl. most of the earlier works of Fauré, Saint-Saëns, Franck, Debussy and Widor.

Hamilton, Lady Catherine (1738–82) English harpsichordist and composer, highly esteemed as a performer in her own time. Only one of her works, a minuet in C major, has survived.

Hamilton, Chico (Forestorn) (1921–) Amer. cool jazz drummer. He worked with Count Basie, Lester Young, Charlie Barnet and Gerry Mulligan. His own quintet, formed in 1955, was unusual in its inclusion of flute and cello and for its sophisticated, classical chamber-music style. More recently, he has been active as a writer of film music and commercial jingles.

Hamilton, Iain (Ellis) (1922–) Scottish composer, stud. at the Royal College of Music and at London U. He has taught at Morley College, London

U., Duke U. and Glasgow U., and has been visiting lecturer at several institutions. His works range from the tonal, romantic style of his earlier works to a Webern-influenced serialism and incl. *The Royal Hunt of the Sun, The Catiline Conspiracy* and other operas, incidental music, orchestral works, many songs, chamber music.

Hamilton, Jimmy (James) (1917–   ) Amer. jazz clarinetist, saxophonist and arranger. After working with the Teddy Wilson sextet and other groups, he joined the Duke Ellington orch. in 1943, remaining until 1968. Later he taught in the public schools in the Virgin Islands.

Hamilton Philharmonic Orchestra orch. founded in 1949 in Hamilton, Ontario. Its conductors have incl. Victor di Bello, Lee Hepner and Boris Brott.

Hamlisch, Marvin (1944–   ) Amer. composer, trained at the Juilliard School and Queens College, NY. He has written a number of film scores, receiving Academy Awards for *The Sting* (1973) and *The Way We Were* (1973), and he wrote the music for the hit Broadway musical *A Chorus Line* (1975). He has also written for television and appeared as a solo performer.

Hammerklavier (Ger., hammer keyboard) an obsolete German term for the piano, commonly used to refer to the piano sonata in B-flat major, Op. 106 (1817–8), by Beethoven, although the work's title, *Sonate für das Hammerklavier*, simply means "piano sonata."

Hammerschmidt, Andreas (?1611–75) Bohemian-born German organist and prolific composer of church music, the most representative composer of mid-17th-c. Ger. church music. He was organist in Freiberg and then in Zittau.

Hammerstein, Oscar (1846–1919) German-born Amer. producer, opera impresario, composer and lyricist, grandfather of OSCAR HAMMERSTEIN II. He built and managed the Man-

hattan Opera House (1906–10) and was producer of many shows, incl. *Naughty Marietta* (1910).

Hammerstein, Oscar (Greeley Clendenning) II (1895–1960) Amer. librettist, lyricist and producer. In addition to a long assoc. with composer Richard Rodgers, he also collaborated with Rudolf Friml, Jerome Kern and Vincent Youmans. He produced many Broadway shows, mostly in collaboration with Rodgers.

Hammond, Dame **Joan (Hood)** (1912–   ) New Zealand soprano, trained at the Sydney Conservatory, in London and in Vienna. She has sung with the Carl Rosa Opera Company, the Vienna Staatsoper and at other major opera houses. Her Amer. debut was with the New York City Center Opera in 1949. She was also greatly in demand as a concert soloist and recitalist and made many recordings.

Hammond organ an ELECTRONIC ORGAN invented in 1933 by Laurens Hammond (1895–1973). The instrument produces sound by means of ridged wheels revolving in a magnetic field. The timbres are controlled by drawbars which add overtones to the fundamental sound.

Hammond-Stroud, Derek (1929–   ) English baritone, stud. of Elena Gerhardt and Gerhard Hüsch. He is known as a recitalist and as an interpretor of comic baritone roles in opera, incl. Beckmesser (*Die Meistersinger*) and Papageno (*The Magic Flute*), as well as in operetta.

Hampton, Lionel ("Hamp") (1909–   ) pioneer Amer. jazz vibraphonist, drummer and bandleader. He joined the Benny Goodman orch. in 1936, then left to form his own band in 1940, with which he still performs. He is known for his extroverted solo style.

Hampton, Slide (Locksley Wellington) (1932–   ) Amer. jazz trombonist, tuba player and arranger. He has played with Lionel Hampton, Maynard Ferguson and Woody Herman, as well as leading his own bands. He is one of the few prominent left-handed trombonists.

Hancock, Herbie (Herbert Jeffrey) (1940–) Amer. jazz keyboard player and composer, trained at Grinnell College, obtaining degrees in electrical engineering and in composition. A child prodigy as a pianist (he played with the Chicago SO at the age of 11), he has worked with Donald Byrd, Eric Dolphy, Miles Davis and his own groups, featuring electronic sounds. His best-known works incl. "Maiden Voyage," "Chameleon," "Dolphin Dance" and "Speak Like a Child."

handbell a small BELL with a handle and usu. a clapper, tuned for use in musical performance.

Handel, George Frideric (Händel, Georg Friederich) (1685–1759) German-born English composer, stud. of F.W. Zachow, and one of the greatest composers of the Baroque. Born in Halle, he went to Hamburg in 1703, where his career as a composer of operas began. He then worked in Rome for the Marquis Francesco Ruspoli, where he composed secular cantatas, oratorios (incl. *La Resurrezione*) and instrumental works. In 1710 he became Kapellmeister to the Elector Palatine in Hanover.

Handel's first trip to London was in 1710 and his first Italian opera for London was *Rinaldo*, produced in 1711 with great success. In 1717 he became resident composer to the future duke of Chandos, for whom he wrote anthems, his masque *Acis and Galatea*, a *Jubilate* and a *Te Deum* in B♭, among many other works. He then became musical dir. of the Royal Academy of Music, an enterprise designed to establish Italian opera in London. It opened in 1720 and operated, in various guises and with interruptions, until 1737. From 1740 he composed mainly oratorios. His works incl. *Almira, Rinaldo, Giulio Cesare in Egitto, Orlando, Alcina, Serse* and 36 other operas, over 30 oratorios (incl. *Messiah, Samson, Israel in Egypt, Judas Maccabeus*), English and Latin church music, odes (*Alex-*

ander's Feast), cantatas and other vocal music, orchestral suites (incl. the *Music for the Royal Fireworks, Water Music*) and concerti grossi, concertos for various instruments, and instrumental sonatas and keyboard works.

Handel and Haydn Society a performing organization founded in Boston in 1815, perhaps the earliest oratorio society in the U.S.

hand horn an unkeyed HORN whose pitch is altered or modified by the player's hand inserted into the bell of the instrument.

Handl, Jacob ['hän-dəl] (Gallus, Jacobus) (1550–91) Slovenian composer, esp. of polychoral vocal works on sacred Latin texts, many of which are contained in his 4-vol. *Opus musicum* (1586–91). He was a singer in the chapel of Maximilian II under Philippe de Monte and choirmaster to the Bishop of Olomouc (1579–85), then Kantor in Prague.

hand organ a BARREL ORGAN operated by a hand crank.

hand piano LAMELLAPHONE.

Handstück ['hänt-stük] (Ger., hand piece) a didactic keyboard work used to develop a student's technical proficiency. Cf. ÉTUDE.

Handt, Herbert (1926–) Amer. tenor, conductor and impresario, trained at the Juilliard School and at the Vienna Academy. His singing debut was at the Vienna Staatsoper. He has conducted in Rome and specializes in the preparation and performance of unknown Italian works, esp. by composers from Lucca, where he founded the Associazione Musicale Lucchese.

Handy, W.C. (William Christopher) (1873–1958) Amer. trumpeter, bandleader and composer, sometimes called "The Father of the Blues." At the turn of the century he played in various brass bands and about 1914 became part owner of a publishing company in Memphis, TN, which published some of his own works, incl. "St. Louis Blues." He was one of the first composers to set jazz down on paper. He moved to New York in

1918, still continuing to tour with his bands and producing concerts of Afr.-Amer. music. His autobiography, *Father of the Blues*, is a fascinating account of turn-of-the-century America.

Hanon, Charles-Louis (1819–1900) French pianist and teacher, best known for his piano exercises, esp. the collection *Le Pianiste-virtuose* (Fr., The Virtuoso Pianist).

Hanover Square Rooms a London recital hall opened in 1775. The BACH-ABEL CONCERTS were held there until 1782, and the Salomon concerts, in which Haydn performed, were given there from 1791 to 1795.

Hansel and Gretel (Ger., *Hänsel und Gretel*) fairy tale opera in 3 acts by Humperdinck to a libretto by Adelheid Wette based on the Grimm fairy tale. Premiere, Weimar 1893. Hansel and Gretel are sent by their mother into the woods, where they get lost and are captured by a witch.

Hanslick, Eduard (1825–1904) German music critic, aesthetician and lecturer. He studied at Prague U. and with Tomášek. He was the first great professional music critic and was a pioneer in the teaching of music appreciation, best remembered now for his lengthy criticism of Wagner.

Hanson, Howard (1896–81) Amer. composer, conductor and teacher, trained at the Institute of Musical Art in New York and Northwestern U. He was dir. of the Eastman School from 1924 to 1964, where his pupils included Peter Mennin and Jack Beeson. He won the Pulitzer Prize in 1944 for his Symphony No. 4. He has conducted the Boston SO, the New York SO and other orchestras in the U.S. and Europe. His works incl. operas (incl. *Merry Mount*, 1933), choral works, 7 symphonies and other orchestral works, music for wind ensemble and chamber music.

happening a type of loosely structured musical theater popular in the 1950s and 1960s, usu. involving the interaction of the aural and visual arts

with a substantial amount of improvisation.

Happy Days Are Here Again song (1930) by Milton Ager, first performed in the film *Chasing Rainbows*, but known for its use as the campaign song of the Democratic party.

Harbison, John (Harris) (1938–) Amer. composer and teacher, stud. of Piston, Blacher and Sessions. He has taught at the Massachusetts Institute of Technology since 1969. He has been composer-in-residence at Reed College, with the Pittsburgh SO and the Los Angeles PO, and artistic chair for the St. Paul Chamber Orch. He won the Pulitzer Prize in 1987 for *The Flight into Egypt*. He has written 2 operas (*Winter's Tale*, *Full Moon in March*), ballets, orchestral music, chamber music, choral and solo vocal works.

Hardanger fiddle *also*, **Harding fiddle** a Norwegian FIDDLE with four stopped and four sympathetic strings used to accompany folksongs and dances such as the HALLING and SPRINGAR.

hard bop a term coined in the 1950s to refer to the BOP music of such musicians as Max Roach, Art Blakey and Sonny Rollins, as distinguished from COOL JAZZ.

hardingfele (Norwegian) a Norwegian folk violin similar to the HARDANGER FIDDLE.

hard rock an aggressive type of ROCK music characterized by loud blues-based music, heavily electrified, as in the music of The Doors, Lynyrd Skynyrd and the Jimi Hendrix Experience. Cf. HEAVY METAL.

Hardy, Hagood (1937–) Amer.-born Canadian composer, arranger and instrumentalist. He led a jazz group, the Montage, from 1969 to 1974, then composed and performed music for the film and broadcast media and appeared in concert in the U.S. and Canada.

Harfe (Ger.) **1**, HARP. **2**, *also*, **harfa** an ORGAN STOP that, when played staccato, imitates the sound of the harp.

harmolodics a theory espoused by

jazz saxophonist ORNETTE COLEMAN for a type of contrapuntal, improvised jazz in which every instrument is both a melody and a rhythm instrument.

harmonica 1, an instrument consisting of free metal reeds in individual channels, all encased in a housing that permits the reeds to be put in motion by the exhaling or inhaling of the player, unwanted holes being covered by the tongue. There are diatonic and chromatic models, the former being sold in various keys, the latter having a finger-operated slide which selects between two different sets of reeds, one tuned in C, the other in C♯. The harmonica is used as a teaching instrument and as a solo instrument in country, jazz, folk and occasionally classical music. Also, *mouth organ.* 2, MUSICAL GLASSES.

harmonic analysis the study of the relationships among the harmonies of a work. In traditional tonal music, this analysis involves determining the function of each chord in the harmonic sentence, esp. in relation to the arrival points (*cadences*) and in reference to the currently established key or tonality. Individual chords are usu. labelled with roman numerals to identify the position of their roots in the scale of the key. This type of analysis becomes more and more difficult in music of the later 19th c., as chromatic harmony becomes more developed, deliberately blurring the functional relationships. In nontonal music, the methods of harmonic analysis—when such analysis is appropriate—have to be determined from the harmonic language of a particular work. See HARMONY.

Harmonica

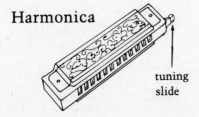

tuning slide

Harmonic Choir a vocal ensemble, formed in the late 1970s by composer DAVID HYKES, specializing in unusual vocal effects, incl. multiphonics and East-Asian chanting, and using JUST INTONATION.

harmonic minor scale a NATURAL MINOR SCALE whose 7th degree is raised a semitone.

harmonic rhythm the rhythm established by the harmonic changes in a work, as distinguished from the rhythm of the note changes. The term is sometimes used to refer to the speed of change (i.e., tempo) of the harmonies. A work having rapid note rhythms could have a static harmonic rhythm if the harmonies changed very seldom, as in many minimalist works. See HARMONY (*illus.*).

harmonics PARTIALS or OVERTONES that are present in varying strengths along with a fundamental tone and which provide the tonal color of a note. The ear is usually not consciously aware of harmonics, but in certain cases where certain harmonics are especially strong (as in a bell tone or some organ stops), they may be clearly distinguishable, sounding along with and perhaps stronger than the fundamental tone.

Harmonics provide the means for obtaining a chromatic scale on brass instruments. They are sometimes specifically called for by composers for special effects, indicated by a small circle over the note (°). In writing for strings, two methods for obtaining harmonics are used: The *natural harmonic* is obtained by pressing lightly on a string at a certain distance from the bridge. These harmonics are notated by the small circle placed over the note to be sounded or by a diamond-headed note in the position of the nodal point to be touched. The *artificial harmonic* is obtained by stopping a string completely at a cer-

Natural harmonic   Artificial harmonics

tain point and then pressing lightly with another finger between the stopping finger and the bridge. In this case the notation shows the main note to be stopped with a normal note head and the point to be lightly pressed as a diamond-headed note. As a rule, a harmonic has a softer, lighter tone than a fully stopped note.

harmonie [Fr., är·mo'nē; Ger., här·mō'nē-e] **1,** HARMONY. **2,** wind instruments, or, specif., brass instruments; also, a band composed of wind or brass instruments.

Harmonie der Welt, Die [dār velt] (Ger., The Harmony of the World) a symphony in 3 movements for orch. (1951) by Hindemith, based on the ideas of the Renaissance astronomer Johannes Kepler. The movements are entitled "Musica Instrumentalis" (Machine Music), "Musica Humana" (Human Music) and "Musica Mundana" (Worldly Music).

Harmoniemesse (Ger., wind-band mass) popular name for the Mass No. 14 in B flat (1802) by Haydn, so called because of the importance of wind instruments in the work.

Harmoniemusik (Ger.) music for wind or brass instruments; military band music.

Harmonious Blacksmith, The popular name for the air and variations in E major of the fifth suite from the first book of harpsichord suites (1720) by Handel. The name was added some years after Handel's death.

harmonium a type of REED ORGAN with compression bellows developed by Alexandre François Debain (1809–77) in Paris in the 1840s.

harmony 1, the combination of two or more tones, producing a CHORD. Harmony may be actual tones sounded simultaneously or implied (chords derived from the context of a melodic line). The term generally implies the presence of a tonality, and chords are said to contain harmonic and nonharmonic tones, depending on whether the tones are part of the current tonality. **2,** the study of the production of chords and the man-

ner in which chords function in relation to one another. See HARMONIC ANALYSIS.

harness bells JINGLES.

Harnoncourt, Nikolaus (1929–) Austrian cellist and conductor, stud. of Paul Grümmer and Emanuel Brabec. He played with the Vienna SO from 1952 to 1969, but he is best known for his work in early music. In 1953 he formed the CONCENTUS MUSICUS of Vienna to perform music of the Baroque on period instruments or reproductions and in period styles, and he has toured and recorded extensively with the group.

Harold in Italy (Fr., *Harold en Italie*) symphony with solo viola, Op. 16 (1834), by Berlioz. The title is a reference to *Childe Harold's Pilgrimage* by Byron, as the work represents in part a recollection of Berlioz' own

Harmony
(see also CHORDS, CADENCES, COUNTERPOINT)

(F. Chopin, Prélude, Op. 28 No. 6)

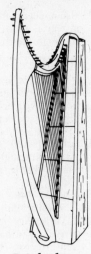

Irish harp

Pedal harp

travels in Abruzzi, with the solo viola representing Harold (Berlioz).

harp 1, a string instrument having an arched neck, a soundboard to which the neck is attached, and parallel strings of unequal lengths running from the neck to the soundboard. The strings are plucked with the fingers.

Until the mid-16th c. harps were usu. tuned to a diatonic scale. After that time, various methods were introduced to produce chromatic pitches by double- or triple-stringing. The modern chromatic harp is equipped with a double-action pedal mechanism developed by ERARD that permits the player to change quickly the pitch of each of the seven diatonic scale degrees (each of the seven pedals controlling all of the strings having the same pitch name) up by a semitone or a whole tone, thereby producing part of a chromatic scale. Cf. HARP-GUITAR, HARP-LUTE. **2**, JEW'S HARP. **3**, *also*, **mouth harp** HARMONICA.

Harper, Heather (1930–) British soprano, trained at Trinity College of Music. She has sung at Glyndebourne, at Bayreuth and frequently at Covent Garden and at the Teatro Colón in Buenos Aires. She appears frequently in concert and recital in a wide range of repertory. She is particularly assoc. with the operas of Benjamin Britten.

harp-guitar a type of GUITAR with a smaller body and a vaulted lutelike back, sometimes provided with keys (*ditals*) for making chromatic alterations (*dital harp*). Also, *harp-lute*.

harp-lute 1, a type of African folk LUTE whose 12 or more strings run over the two vertical sides of a rectangular bridge. **2**, HARP-GUITAR.

Harp Quartet, The popular name for the string quartet in E flat, Op. 74 (1809), by Beethoven, so called because of the harplike arpeggios in the first movement.

harpsichord a stringed keyboard instrument dating from the late 14th c. Its strings are plucked by natural or plastic quills (*plectra*) housed in a holder (JACK), which also incorporates its own felt damper and a spring mechanism activated by the player's finger on the key. The shape of the harpsichord is similar to that of the grand piano, with the strings running perpendicular to the keyboard. The instrument was popular well into the

Harpsichord

18th c., when it was eclipsed by the newly developed FORTEPIANO. A revival of interest in the harpsichord began in the late 19th c. Cf. VIRGINAL, SPINET.

harpsichord-piano an 18th-c. instrument combining the hammer action of the piano with the plucking action of the harpsichord.

harp stop BUFF STOP.

harp zither a type of stick ZITHER whose raffia strings run over a tall, vertical bridge in the center of the stick.

Harrell, Lynn (1944–) Amer. cellist, stud. of Leonard Rose. He was principal cellist of the Cleveland Orchestra from 1965, leaving in 1971 to concentrate on a solo and chamber music career. He has taught at Cincinnati U. and at the Juilliard School.

Harrell, Mack (1909–60) Amer. baritone, trained at the Juilliard School, father of LYNN HARRELL. He sang with the Metropolitan Opera from 1939 to 1954 and also appeared frequently in concert and recital and on the radio. He taught at the Juilliard School from 1945.

Harris, Bill (1916–73) Amer. jazz swing trombonist. He was a leading soloist with the Woody Herman band and also worked with Charlie Ventura, Chubby Jackson and Norman Granz's Jazz at the Philharmonic.

Harris, Charles K(assel) (1865–1930) Amer. songwriter and highly successful publisher, best known for his song "After the Ball" (1892).

Harris, Emmylou (1949–) successful Amer. country-music singer, whose early repertory mixed folk, country and rock. She has more recently concentrated on country and related genres.

Harris, Roy (1898–1979) Amer. composer, trained at the U. of California at Berkeley and privately with Farwell, Boulanger and others. He taught at the Juilliard School, the Westminster Choir School and UCLA, among other places. His music has a distinctly Amer. flavor and was strongly influenced by folk music. His works incl. 14 symphonies and many other orchestral works, music for band, a large body of choral music, ballets, solo vocal music, concertos and instrumental chamber music.

Harris, Wynonie (1915–69) Amer. blues singer, a vocalist with the bands of Lucky Millinder, Oscar Pettiford, Lionel Hampton and others and an important influence on early rock and roll.

Harrison, Lou (1917–) Amer. composer and writer, stud. of Cowell and Schoenberg. In a highly varied career he has taught at Black Mountain College and at San José State College, has studied Korean and Chinese courtly music, been an instrument builder and a ballet accompanist. He has written in a variety of styles, melody always being the most important consideration. His works incl. operas (incl. *Rapunzel*), ballets and incidental music, orchestral music, percussion music and other chamber music, choral and solo vocal works and instrumental sonatas.

Harshaw, Margaret (1909–   ) Amer. soprano and teacher, trained at the Curtis Institute. She was a noted Wagnerian singer, whose roles included Brünnhilde, Isolde and Kundry. She is a highly respected voice teacher, on the faculty of Indiana U. since 1962.

Hart, Lorenz (Larry) **(Milton)** (1895–1943) Amer. lyricist who collaborated with RICHARD RODGERS on many Broadway musicals, incl. *On Your Toes, Babes in Arms, The Boys from Syracuse* and *Pal Joey.*

Hartford Symphony Orchestra a civic orch. founded in Hartford, CT in 1934, preceded by the Hartford PO (1899–1924).

Hart House Orchestra chamber orch. in residence at the U. of Toronto from 1954 to 1971, formed by BOYD NEEL as a successor to his earlier English group.

Hart House Quartet distinguished Canadian string quartet founded in 1924 under the patronage of Vincent Massey, in residence at the U. of Toronto. The group was active until 1946.

Harth, Sidney (1929–   ) eminent Amer. violinist, conductor and teacher, stud. of J. Knitzer, Michael Piastro and Enescu and winner of the Naumburg Award in 1949. He has been concertmaster of the Louisville Orch., the Chicago SO, the Los Angeles PO and the New York PO and has taught at DePaul U. in Chicago, Carnegie-Mellon U. in Pittsburgh, the Mannes College of Music and SUNY at Stony Brook.

Hartmann, Karl Amadeus (1905–63) German composer, stud. of Joseph Haas, Scherchen and Webern. He founded the Musica Viva concert series in Munich after World War II, and his reputation as a composer dates from that time. He has written 8 symphonies, a chamber opera and other vocal works and instrumental chamber music.

Hartt School of Music conservatory in Hartford, CT, founded in 1920, now part of the U. of Hartford. It incorporates the Hartt Opera Theater, one of the first undergraduate opera programs in the U.S.

Harvard Musical Association a musical club and concert org. founded in Boston in 1837. It sponsored orchestral concerts from 1856 to 1882.

Harvard-Radcliffe Orchestra see PIERIAN SODALITY.

Harvey, Mary (Lady Dering) (1629–1704) English composer, esp. of lute songs, stud. of Henry Lawes.

Harwood, Elisabeth (Jean) (1938–90) English soprano, trained at the Royal Manchester College of Music. She sang at the major English opera houses, at La Scala and at the Metropolitan Opera (1975). Her roles included Gilda (*Rigoletto*), Susanna (*The Marriage of Figaro*) and Manon.

Háry János opera in a prologue, 5 parts and an epilogue by Kodály to a libretto by Béla Paulini and Zsolt Harsányi, based on a poem by János Garay. Premiere, Budapest 1926. A fantasy about Hungarian folklore figure János Háry and his love for the wife of Napoleon and a peasant girl.

Haskil, Clara (1895–1960) Romanian pianist. She studied in Bucharest and then in Paris with Cortot and Busoni. She is best remembered for her performances of Mozart, Beethoven and Schubert, and for her chamber music performances with Ysaÿe, Casals and others.

Haslinger Austrian music publishing firm, founded in 1803 as the Chemische Druckerey in Vienna. It was responsible for publishing many first editions of Beethoven and Schubert.

Hasse, Faustina see BORDONI, FAUSTINA.

Hasse, Johann Adolf (1699–1783) German singer and composer of *opera seria*. He sang in Hamburg and Brunswick until 1721, then spent the next nine years in Italy, where he was a great success composing *opera seria*. From 1731 he served as Kapellmeister to the Elector of Saxony, remaining until 1763, and set many texts by the poet Metastasio, who became a very close friend and collaborator. His reputation in his own time was substantial, but very little of his music is performed today. His wife was the singer FAUSTINA BORDONI. He wrote 60 operas, intermezzi, oratorios, cantatas, Mass settings and other sacred works, arias, concertos, instrumental chamber music and keyboard sonatas.

Hassler, Hans Leo (Haslerus, Johann) (1564–1612) German composer of sacred and secular vocal works and keyboard music, stud. of his father and Andrea Gabrieli. He is noted especially for his Latin choral works. He was chamber organist to the Fugger family in Augsburg, director of town music in Nuremburg and chamber organist to the Elector of Saxony. He was also involved in music publishing and mechanical instrument construction.

Hastings,   Thomas (1784–1872) Amer. composer, teacher and hymn writer. He was active throughout his life as a teacher in singing schools and in training music teachers. He composed nearly 1000 hymn tunes and compiled a large number of hymn tune collections. His best-known tune "Toplady" is the setting for the text "Rock of Ages."

Haubenstock - Ramati,   Roman (1919–   ) Polish-born Austrian composer, stud. of Artur Malawaki and Józef Koffler. He directed the music dept. of Kraków Radio from 1947 to 1950, then emigrated to Israel, where he has taught at the Academy of Music. His works explore variable forms and collages and the use of graphic scores and incl. *Amerika* (opera), orchestral works, *Credentials* and other vocal works, and instrumental chamber music.

Hauer, Josef Matthias (1883–1959) Austrian composer and theorist, who began composing at the age of 28. He claimed to be the first to discover and formulate rules for 12-tone composition, published in 1923. Rather than calling for a fixed arrangement of the 12 notes, Hauer divided them into a

trope of two unordered hexachords. Prior to World War II he wrote a large number of works in all forms based on his theories; after the war, he composed a series of *Zwölftonspiele* (12-tone Games) for various instrumental and vocal combinations. Other compositions incl. orchestral works, cantatas (incl. *Der Menschen Weg*) and other large vocal works, instrumental chamber music, songs and piano works and extensive theoretical writings.

Hauk, Minnie (Hauck, Amalia Mignon) (1851–1929) Amer. mezzo-soprano, stud. of Achille Errani and Maurice Strakosch. Several years after her debut (at 15) in Brooklyn in 1866, she went to Europe and sang in London, Paris, Russia, Vienna and Berlin. She first appeared at the Metropolitan Opera in 1890. Among her roles were Carmen and Manon.

haupt [howpt] (Ger.) principal, head (in compound words).

Hauptmann,   Moritz (1792–1868) German theorist and composer, stud. of Spohr and others. He taught theory at the Leipzig Conservatory and was a co-founder with Otto Jahn and Schumann in 1850 of the BACH GESELLSCHAFT, of which he was president until his death. His theory of harmony is based on the Hegelian principles of thesis, antithesis and synthesis.

Hauptstimme (-"shtim-me] (Ger., principal voice) in scores of Schoenberg, Berg and some later composers, a term indicating the part that is of principal importance at a certain moment, the next level of importance being the NEBENSTIMME. These voices are indicated by a special bracketlike sign made of the letters H (H⌐) and N (N⌐).

Hauptthema [-"tā-mə] (Ger.) principal theme.

Hauptwerk [-verk] (Ger., principal section) GREAT ORGAN.

Hausmusik ['hows-moo"zēk] (Ger., house music) a term dating from the 17th c. for music intended for performance in the home and generally referring to chamber music of moderate difficulty, marketed to the middle class.

Haussmann, Valentin (?1570–?1614) German composer, musician and poet, second of a line of musicians bearing the same name, trained at the Gymnasium Poeticum in Regensburg. Much of his career appears to have been spent in traveling throughout Germany and eastern Europe. He was important in the development of instrumental music, and he was one of the first composers in Germany to write specifically for the violin (as opposed to the viol).

hautbois (Fr.), **hautboy** [ō'bwä] OBOE.

haut-dessus ["ō-də'sü] (Fr., high treble) the highest part in an instrumental or vocal ensemble. When the part is divided, the lower voice is called the *bas-dessus*.

haute-contre ['ōt"kō-trə] (Fr.) a high tenor voice, prevalent in France in the 18th c., but still called for in some French opera of the 19th c. The voice was neither falsetto nor castrato, but a tenor voice placed unusually high.

Hawaiian guitar 1, a flat-bodied electric instrument similar to the STEEL GUITAR, with an unfretted neck and 6 to 8 steel strings. The instrument is held horizontally or placed on a stand, and the strings are plucked with a THIMBLE, the different pitches being obtained by sliding a metal bar ("steel") or a "bottleneck" tube on the raised strings. **2,** UKULELE.

Hawes, Hampton (1928–77) Amer. jazz pianist. He played with Shorty Rogers and Howard Rumsey before forming his own trio in the mid-1950s. After several years in prison for drug possession in the early 1960s he had difficulty regaining earlier successes, finding a somewhat better reception in Europe.

Hawkins, Coleman (Randolph) (1904–69) Amer. jazz tenor saxophonist known as the "father of jazz tenor saxophone playing." He played with the Fletcher Henderson band until 1934, then on the Continent for five years, returning to the U.S. in 1939 on the heels of his landmark recording of "Body and Soul," one of the best-known solos in jazz history. He then played with a number of bop ensembles and toured with Norman Granz's Jazz at the Philharmonic.

Hawkins, Erskine (Ramsay) (1914–) Amer. jazz swing virtuoso trumpeter and leader of a big band formed in the early 1930s, featured at the Savoy Ballroom in New York and active until the mid-1950s. More recently Hawkins has led small groups at clubs and festivals.

Hawkins, Sir **John** (1719–89) British music historian, antiquarian and attorney, rival of Charles Burney. He is best known for his *General History of the Science and Practice of Music* (1776), one of the first books in English on music history.

Haydn, (Franz) Joseph (1732–1809) Austrian composer, older brother of MICHAEL HAYDN, stud. of Porpora and others. In 1761 he was hired by Prince Paul Antony Esterházy, and he was to remain in the family's service until 1790. His activities were divided between the family seat at Eisenstadt and the summer palace called Eszterháza at Süttör. Haydn's work up to about 1775 was mainly instrumental court music; after that time he devoted himself increasingly to opera.

When his patron, Prince Nikolaus, died in 1790, Haydn was retained by the son, but with no duties (the son had no interest in music). Haydn very shortly thereafter went to London at the invitation of violinist Johann Peter Salomon. He went twice during the next decade, and his period in London was especially rich: compositions completed or conceived during that time incl. the 12 London symphonies, the oratorio *The Creation* and the English songs. Haydn's final years in Vienna were spent in further composition, the assembling of a catalog of his works and enjoyment of his eminent position.

Haydn lived and worked over a wide period which spanned the end of the Baroque, the Classical era and the beginnings of Romanticism. He was prominent in several genres of composition, in particular the development of the string quartet, the symphony and the sonata; but though he was very active as a composer of opera, his many works in that genre are rarely performed today. His works incl. *Il Mondo della luna, Orlando paladino* and other operas, incidental music, sacred and secular vocal music (incl. 14 Mass settings and 6 oratorios), 108 symphonies, string and wind chamber music (incl. almost 70 string quartets and works for the baryton, composed for Prince Esterházy), keyboard sonata, songs, folk-song arrangements, etc.

Haydn, (Johann) Michael (1737–1806) Austrian composer, younger brother of JOSEPH HAYDN. Trained as a choirboy, after his voice changed he lived hand-to-mouth for several years, becoming Kapellmeister to a Hungarian bishop in 1757. In 1763 he became court musician in the large musical establishment of Archbishop Schrattenbach in Salzburg. Haydn's well-known Requiem in C minor was composed for the Archbishop's funeral and played at Joseph Haydn's funeral as well. His works incl. a large body of sacred vocal music, secular songs, instrumental divertimenti, partitas, and other chamber music.

Haydn Quartets popular name for six string quartets written by Mozart from 1782 to 1785.

Haydn Variations VARIATIONS ON A THEME BY HAYDN.

Hayes, Isaac (1938–) Amer. songwriter, arranger and soul singer. He recorded in the early and mid-1960s with Otis Redding and others. His own records were highly successful, incl. the album *Hot Buttered Soul* and the music from the film *Shaft*. He formed his own band in the 1970s, but by the end of the decade he had lost his popularity. He has also appeared in several films.

Hayes, Roland (1887–1977) Amer. tenor, stud. of Arthur Hubbard, Sir George Henschel and Victor Beigel.

He was noted as a lieder singer and for his performance of spirituals.

Haynes, Roy Owen (1926–) Amer. jazz drummer. He has played with Luis Russell, Lester Young, Charlie Parker, Stan Getz and others. In the 1950s he was with Sarah Vaughan, Miles Davis and Thelonious Monk. More recently he has led his own Hip Ensemble.

Haynes, William S. (1864–1939) eminent Amer. flute maker, est. in Boston in 1900. He made wooden flutes until 1917 and began his manufacture of silver flutes in 1913. Cf. VERNE Q. POWELL.

Hayne van Ghizeghem (c1445–betw. 1472 and 1497) Burgundian composer of French chansons, mainly 3-voice rondeaux. He worked at the court of Charles the Bold and is best known for his chanson "De tous bien plaine," which is the foundation of many later Renaissance works.

Hb. *abbr.* hautbois (see OBOE).

head 1, in jazz, the first statement of the melody, which is followed by solos. **2,** *also,* **head arrangement** in jazz, an arrangement worked out collectively by a band and then memorized, or in some cases, performed spontaneously.

head-motif MOTTO.

head register see REGISTER (2,).

head voice a type of lighter vocal production in the upper or head register; distinguished from FALSETTO.

Heath, Percy (1923–) Amer. jazz bassist. He worked with Miles Davis, Dizzy Gillespie, Charlie Parker and others and was a founding member of the MODERN JAZZ QUARTET, with which he played from 1952 until 1974, and then again when it reformed in the 1980s. He is part of a musical family that includes his younger brothers drummer **Al(bert) "Tootie" Heath** (1935–) and saxophonist **Jimmy** (James Edward) **Heath** (1926–).

heavy metal a type of ROCK music characterized by heavy amplification, aggressive and hostile lyrics and an emphasis on the electric guitar. The style is represented by such bands as Led Zeppelin, Deep Purple, AC/DC and Black Sabbath. The term was originally coined by novelist William Burroughs. Cf. HARD ROCK.

Hebrides, The orchestral overture, Op. 26 (1830), by Mendelssohn, a result (with the Symphony No. 3) of a voyage to Scotland in 1829.

Heckel, Johann Adam (c1812–77) German instrument maker est. in 1831, specializing in double-reed instruments. He, his son **Wilhelm** (1856–1909) and grandson **Wilhelm Hermann** (1879–1952) did much to modernize the bassoon and contrabassoon and invented a number of instruments, incl. the HECKELPHONE and the HECKELCLARINA.

Heckelclarina a type of CLARINET invented for use in the premier of Wagner's *Tristan and Isolde* in 1865.

Heckelphone a baritone double-reed instrument invented in 1904 by WILHELM HECKEL. It is related to the oboe, but it uses a bassoon reed on a curved crook. In the orch. it is used in scores (usu. German) that call for it and as a substitute for the BARITONE OBOE.

heebie jeebies an eccentric jazz dance of the 1920s.

Hefti, Neal (1922–) Amer. trumpeter, composer and arranger for Earl Hines, Charlie Barnet, Woody Herman, Harry James and Count Basie (1950–62). More recently he has worked in television and films (he has composed the theme to the 1960s *Batman* TV series).

Heifetz, Jascha (1901–87) Russianborn Amer. violin virtuoso, stud. of Elias Malkin and Leopold Auer. He enjoyed a remarkable solo career into the early 1960s and played and recorded in outstanding chamber music ensembles with Emanuel Feuermann, William Primose, Artur Rubenstein, Bing Crosby and others. From 1962 he taught at the U. of Southern California.

Heiliger Dankgesang ['hī-li-gǝr 'dänk-ge"zäng] (Ger., Hymn of Thanksgiving) popular name for the middle movement of the string quartet in A minor, Op. 132 (1825), by Beethoven. The movement is subtitled "Hymn of Thanksgiving to the Divinity, from a Convalescent, in the Lydian Mode."

Heiligmesse ['hī-liç"me-se] (Ger., Holy Mass) the Mass Sancti Bernardi von Offida in B♭ major (1796) by Haydn.

Heiller, Anton (1923–79) Austrian organist and composer of sacred choral music, organ works and instrumental chamber music, trained at the Vienna Academy of Music. He was internationally known as a recitalist and taught at the Vienna Academy throughout his career.

Heinrich, Anthony Philip (Anton Philipp) (1781–1861) Bohemian-born Amer. composer, an important figure in 19th-c. Amer. musical life. After disastrous business ventures in Europe and then in the U.S., he devoted himself to music. He was perhaps America's first professional composer, dubbed the "Beethoven of America" by critics. He spent several extended periods in Europe, performing as soloist and as member of various orchestras. His descriptive orchestral and piano music often deals with Amer. themes, esp. related to Native Americans.

Heldenleben, Ein ['hel-dǝn"lā-bǝn, īn] (Ger., A Hero's Life) symphonic poem (1898) by R. Strauss, based on the composer's own life and including quotations from some of his own works.

Heldentenor (Ger., heroic tenor) DRAMATIC TENOR; the term is usu. restricted to Wagnerian roles.

helicon a large bass TUBA made in a circular shape for easier carrying in marching bands. Cf. SOUSAPHONE.

Heller, Stephen (István) (1813–88) Hungarian-born French pianist and composer, stud. of Franz Brauer and Anton Halm. After a hectic period of touring as a concert pianist, which led to a nervous collapse, he settled in 1830 in Augsburg to compose, then moved in 1838 to Paris, where he remained for the rest of his life, teaching piano and writing music criticism. Almost all of his works are for piano and incl. studies, variation sets, character pieces, sonatas and dances.

Hello, Dolly! musical by Jerry Herman, book by Michael Stewart, based on Thornton Wilder's play *The Matchmaker*, the story of a New York matchmaker in the late 19th c. Premiere, New York 1964.

Hellzapoppin revue by Sammy Fain, lyrics by Charles Tobias, sketches by Ole Olsen and Chic Johnson. Premiere, New York 1938. An elaboration of the vaudeville act of Olsen and Johnson.

Helmholtz, Hermann (Ludwig Ferdinand) von (1821–94) German scientist, preeminent in a variety of fields dealing with visual and aural perception, but known especially to musicians for his work in the study of ACOUSTICS, esp. concerning the overtone series and its importance to timbre.

Helps, Robert (Eugene) (1928–) Amer. pianist and composer, stud. of Abby Whiteside and Sessions. He has taught at the New England Conservatory, the Manhattan School of Music, Princeton, Stanford and the U. of California at Davis. He is particularly noted for his performance of 20th-c. piano music.

hemidemisemiquaver (Brit.) SIXTY-FOURTH NOTE.

hemiola *also*, **hemiolia 1,** in medieval music, the interval of a 5th. **2,** a rhythm resulting from a duple division of the meter in a section of predominantly triple divisions, or of a triple division of the meter in a section of predominantly duple divisions. The technique is common in Baroque music, esp. in the COURANTE.

Hempel, Frieda (1885–1955) German soprano, stud. of Selma Nicklass-Kempner. She sang regularly in Berlin until 1912 and in London after 1907. Her Amer. debut was at the Metropolitan Opera, where she sang from 1912 to 1919, after which she concentrated on a concert career, some-

Hemiola

(Dufay)

(Brahms)

times appearing as Jenny Lind in period costume.

Hen Symphony (Fr., *La Poule*) popular name for the Symphony No. 83 in G minor (1786) by Haydn, one of the Paris symphonies.

Henderson, (James) Fletcher (1897–1952) Amer. jazz swing bandleader. He formed his own band in the mid-1920s, which featured many outstanding soloists and was one of the leading bands of the time. After the group disbanded in 1934 he worked as an arranger for a number of bands, including Benny Goodman's.

Henderson, Ray (Brost, Raymond) (1896–1970) Amer. composer of Broadway musicals, usu. in collaboration with B.G. DeSylva and Lew Brown. His shows included *George White's Scandals, Good News!* and *Flying High.* Among his hit songs are "That Old Gang of Mine" and "Five Feet Two, Eyes of Blue."

Henderson, Skitch (Lyle Russell Cedric) (1918–) English-born Amer. conductor, composer, arranger and pianist, stud. of Schoenberg and Reiner. He worked as pianist and music dir. for Frank Sinatra, Bing Crosby and others in the 1940s, then worked in radio and television until the mid-1960s. In the 1970s and 1980s he has toured as a successful pops conductor with major U.S. orchestras.

Hendl, Walter (1917–) Amer. conductor and teacher, stud. of Reiner. He has conducted the New York PO, the Dallas SO, the Symphony of the Air, the Rochester PO and the Erie (PA) PO and has taught at Sarah Lawrence College and the Eastman School, of which he was director

(1964–72). While at Eastman he was musical adviser to the Rochester PO.

Hendricks, Jon (John Carl) (1912–) Amer. jazz singer, trained as a drummer. He is best known for writing lyrics to famous instrumental jazz solos, recorded both on his own and with the Dave Lambert Singers, which became Lambert, Hendricks and Ross. He has also written for and appeared with MANHATTAN TRANSFER.

Hendrix, Jimi (1942–70) Amer. rock guitarist, a pioneer in the use of the special effects available on the electric guitar, incl. feedback and distortion. In the early 1960s he played under the name Jimmy James with a number of leading musicians in New York, incl. B.B. King, Wilson Pickett and Curtis Knight. In 1966 he went to London and created the Jimi Hendrix Experience. He made celebrated appearances at the Monterey Pop Festival (1967) and at Woodstock (1969), and made many recordings at the Electric Lady studio which he built in New York.

Henle German music publisher, founded in 1948 in Munich by Günter Henle, an industrialist and amateur musician, with the aim of publishing "Urtext" (i.e., based on the original manuscripts) editions of music from the Classical and Romantic eras.

Henry VIII (1491–1547) king of England, composer, and a capable performer on the organ, virginal and lute. A small number of vocal and instrumental works ascribed to him survive.

Henry, Pierre (1927–) French composer, stud. of Boulanger and Messiaen. He worked with Pierre Schaeffer from 1949 in the development of MUSIQUE CONCRÉTE and from 1950 to 1958 headed the Groupe de recherche de musique concrète at the French radio. His collaboration with choreographer André Béjart (1954–71) resulted in a number of dance scores. He co-founded the Apsone-Cabasse Studio in 1958 to combine *musique concrète* with pure electronic sounds. His works are all works for tape and

incl. *Symphonie pour un homme seul, L'apocalypse de Jean, Concerto des ambiguités,* and *Ceremony.*

Henschel, Sir **(Isidor) George** (Georg) (1850–1934) German-born English conductor, composer and baritone, a stud. at the Leipzig and Berlin Conservatories. He was conductor of the Boston SO from 1881 to 1883, after which he settled in England, where he performed as a singer and taught at the Royal Conservatory of Music. He founded the London Symphony Concerts (1886–97) and directed the Handel Society of London.

Hensel, Fanny MENDELSSOHN, FANNY.

Henze, Hanz Werner (1926–) prolific German composer. He studied in Brunswick and, after the war, with Fortner. From 1953 to 1965 he lived in Italy, producing a number of important works, incl. the operas *Der junge Lord, Elegy for Young Lovers* and *The Bassarids.* He also taught at the Mozarteum in Salzburg during this time, and later in Havana. His more recent works reflect his commitment to socialism, esp. the solo cantatas *El Cimarrón* and *Versuch über Schweine* and the theater piece *We Come to the River.* His compositions incl. 15 operas, ballets, incidental music, a large number of orchestral works, incl. 6 symphonies, choral and solo vocal works, instrumental chamber music and sonatas.

Hepner, Lee (Alfred) (1920–) Canadian conductor, founder-conductor of the Edmonton SO, conductor of the Hamilton (Ont.) PO and guest conductor in No. America and Europe. He has taught at McMaster U. in Hamilton since 1961.

heptachord a seven-note SCALE, such as the modern major and minor scales.

heptatonic a term referring to any SCALE consisting of seven pitches to the octave.

Herbert, Victor (August) (1859–1924) Irish-born Amer. composer, cellist and conductor, trained at the Stuttgart Conservatory. He came to the

U.S. when he and his wife, singer Therese Foerster, were engaged by the Metropolitan Opera. He conducted the 22nd Regiment Band of the NY National Guard, the Pittsburgh SO (1898–1904) and his own Victor Herbert Orch. He was one of the founders of ASCAP and was an early participant in Edison's development of sound recording. He is best remembered for his more than 40 operettas, written between 1897 and 1920. His opera *Natoma* was premiered by the Philadelphia-Chicago Opera Company (1911) with Mary Garden and John McCormack. His works incl. 2 operas, over 40 operettas (incl. *Babes in Toyland, Naughty Marietta, Wonderland*), orchestral works, cello concertos, film scores (esp. *The Fall of a Nation*).

Herbig, Günther (1931–) German conductor, stud. of Hermann Abendroth, Karajan, Scherchen and Arvid Jansons. In Europe he has been conductor of the Weimar National Theater, the Berlin SO and the Dresden PO. In N. America he has been principal guest conductor of the Dallas SO, music dir. of the Detroit PO and music dir. of the Toronto SO.

Herbst, Johannes (1735–1812) Moravian-Amer. pastor and prolific composer of over 145 sacred songs and almost 200 anthems.

Herd a name used by clarinetist WOODY HERMAN for various bands he led in the 1940s and 1950s.

Herman, Jerry (Gerald) (1933–) Amer. songwriter and composer of Broadway musicals, best known for *Hello Dolly!* (1964) and *Mame* (1966).

Herman's Hermits English rock band formed in 1963 in Manchester. After several years of successful hits their vogue ended, and they disbanded in 1971. Their hits included "Mrs. Brown, You've Got a Lovely Daughter" and "Silhouettes."

Herman, Woody (Woodrow) **(Charles)** (1913–87) Amer. jazz clarinetist, saxophonist, vocalist and bandleader. In 1936 he formed his own band, which reached its greatest success in the mid-1940s and was noted for its originality and broad repertory. Stravinsky wrote his *Ebony Concerto* in 1945 for Herman's band.

Hermes ancient Greek god, son of Zeus and Maia. He is credited with fashioning a LYRE from the shell of a tortoise and for inventing the SYRINX (panpipes).

Hernried, Robert (Franz Richard) (1883–1951) Austrian-born Amer. composer, conductor and musicologist, trained at the Vienna Conservatory and the U. of Vienna. He came to the U.S. in 1939 and has taught at St. Ambrose College (IA), the State Teachers College in Dickinson, ND, St. Francis College in Fort Wayne, IN, and the Detroit Institute of Musical Art.

heroic tenor DRAMATIC TENOR.

Hero's Life, A HELDENLEBEN, EIN.

Hérodiade [ä'rō-dē-äd] (Fr., Herodias) tragic opera in 4 acts by Massenet to a libretto by Paul Milliet and Henri Gremont (Georges Hartmann) after the novel by Flaubert. Premiere, Brussels 1881. The story of Salome, Herod and John the Baptist, differing in its treatment of the relationship between John and Salome from the Oscar Wilde play set by R. Strauss (*Salome*).

Hérold, (Louis Joseph) Ferdinand (1791–1833) French composer of *opéras-comiques*, stud. of his father, C.P.E. Bach and Méhul. His first major success was *Almédan* (1826), which was followed (with lesser intervening works) in 1831 by *Zampa* and in 1832 by *Le Pré aux clercs*. He also wrote ballets, songs, 2 symphonies, 4 piano concertos, instrumental chamber music and sonatas, dances and character pieces for piano.

Herrera, Juan de (c1665–1738) Colombian composer of masses, lamentations, motets and villancicos, the most prolific composer of colonial Colombia. He was chaplain and choirmaster to the nuns of St. Inéz Convent (Bogotá) from 1690 and choirmaster of the Bogotá Cathedral from 1703, holding both posts until his death.

Herrmann, Bernard (1911–75) Amer. composer and conductor, trained at New York U. and the Juilliard School. He founded the New Chamber Orch. in 1931 and joined CBS Radio in 1934, becoming staff conductor of the CBS SO in 1938. He composed music for many films and guest-conducted a number of orchestras, incl. the New York PO and the London SO. His works incl. an opera, orchestral music, vocal works and film scores (incl. *Citizen Kane, Jane Eyre, Vertigo* and *Fahrenheit 451*).

Herschel, Sir **William** (Friedrich Wilhelm) (1738–1822) German-born English organist, violinist, oboist, composer and astronomer. He went to England in 1759 as a music copyist and music teacher, then to Bath in 1767 as organist and became dir. of the Bath orch. in 1776. By then he had become involved in astronomy; he was to discover the planet Uranus in 1781. After 1782 he pursued music only as an amateur.

Herseth, Adolph (1921–) Amer. trumpeter, stud. of Marcel LaFosse and Georges Mager. He became first trumpet of the Chicago SO in 1948 and has been important in the development of that orchestra's noted brass sound.

Hertz a unit of frequency equal to one cycle per second. Abbr., *Hz*.

Hertz, Alfred (1872–1942) German-born Amer. conductor, trained at the Hoch Conservatory in Frankfurt. He joined the Breslau Opera in 1899, then went to the Metropolitan Opera in 1902 as head of the German wing, remaining until 1915. He was conductor of the San Francisco SO from 1915 to 1930 and inaugurated the Hollywood Bowl summer concerts in 1922. He was a major musical figure in San Francisco until his death.

Hervé (Ronger, Florimond) (1825–92) French singer, composer and conductor, stud. of Auber, and often considered the creator of French operetta. In 1854 he opened his own theater, the Folies-Concertantes, and later toured with his own company. He was musical dir. at the Empire Theatre in London from 1886, and he performed and conducted there as well as at Covent Garden and the Gaiety. He wrote over 50 short theater pieces, operettas, songs, monologues, etc., and some church music under his real name.

Herz, Henri (Heinrich) (1803–88) Austrian pianist, composer and teacher, trained at the Paris Conservatoire and one of the most celebrated virtuosi of his day. He taught at the Conservatoire from 1842 to 1874, meanwhile conducting extensive concert tours of Europe and No. America. He was also involved in piano manufacturing and wrote many salon works and studies for piano.

heses (Ger.) B double flat.

Heseltine, Philip Arnold (1894–1930) Eng. composer, author and critic, stud. of Delius. He wrote music in all genres, but is best known for his songs, which are still in the repertory. His works were published under the pseudonym Peter Warlock.

hesitation waltz a Waltz in which the dancers intersperse gliding steps. Cf. Boston Waltz.

Hess, Dame **Myra** (1890–1965) English pianist, stud. of Tobias Matthay. She was noted both for her performances of the Classical and Romantic masterworks and for her work in chamber music, and she was very popular in the U.S. During World War II she instituted a series of concerts at the London National Gallery, performing for no fee.

heterophony the performance of the same melody by two or more voices or instruments with minor variations in rhythm or pitch among the players.

Hétu, Jacques (Joseph Robert) [ā'tü] (1938–) Canadian composer and teacher, stud. of Pépin, Papineau-Couture and Foss. His works incl. 3 symphonies, concertos for piano and violin, chamber music, piano and choral works.

Hétu, Pierre (1936–) Canadian conductor and pianist, trained at the

U. of Montreal, in Paris and elsewhere. He has been assistant conductor of the Montreal SO, music dir. of the Kalamazoo SO, assoc. conductor of the Detroit SO and artistic dir. of the Edmonton SO and has guest-conducted opera and in concert.

Heugel [ø'zhel] French music publishing firm founded in 1839 and basing its reputation in the 19th c. on the theater music of David, Offenbach, Thomas and others. In addition to its extensive catalogue, the firm publishes *Le pupitre*, a collection of editions of early music.

Heure espagnole, L' [lør es-pä'nyōl] (Fr., The Spanish Clock) comic opera in 1 act by Ravel to a libretto by Franc-Nohain. Premiere, Paris 1911. Concepción, wife of the clockmaker Torquemada, entertains her lovers while her husband winds the government's clocks.

Hewitt, James (1770–1827) English-born Amer. composer, conductor and publisher, active in Boston and New York. He conducted the Park Street Theater orch. in New York and was organist at Trinity Church (Episcopal). He also published music and sold musical instruments.

hexachord a series of six notes. In the Guidonian system, the standardized hexachords consists of six notes separated by whole tones except for a half step between the third and fourth notes. The six notes are always named *ut, re, mi, fa, sol, la*, regardless of the exact pitch of the beginning note. The system for naming the pitches, described by GUIDO D'AREZZO, is a series of overlapping hexachords and combines the name of the pitch with its scale degree name(s). The lowest scale begins on G, the first note of which is *gamma ut*, the second *a re*, and so on. The second hexachord starts on the fourth degree of the first scale and includes both names, hence *c fa ut, d sol re*, etc. Hexachords are labeled "natural," "hard" or "soft," depending on the quality of the pitch B, i.e., the natural hexachord contains no B, the

hard hexachord contains a B♮ and the soft hexachord contains a B♭ on fa.

hexatonic a term referring to any SCALE consisting of six pitches to the octave.

Hexenmenuet ['hex-an-] (Ger.) the 3rd movement of the string quartet in D minor, Op. 76 No. 2, by Haydn.

Hexenscheit [-"shīt] (Ger.) a German or Swiss strummed ZITHER.

Heywood, Eddie (Edward, Jr.) (1915–89) Amer. jazz pianist, arranger, composer and bandleader. In the late 1930s he worked with various bands, incl. those of Benny Carter and Zutty Singleton, then led a successful sextet in New York. In his later years he concentrated on composition, his most popular number being "Canadian Sunset."

hibernicon a type of bass HORN invented in 1823 in Ireland.

hichiriki a Japanese bamboo OBOE, the principal melody instrument of the GAGAKU orch.

Hidalgo, Juan (c1612–85) Spanish composer. He was appointed to the royal chapel as a harpist and harpsichordist in 1631 and remained there until his death. In collaboration with Pedro Calderón de la Barca, Hidalgo wrote the first Spanish opera, *La púrpura de la rosa*, for which the music is no longer extant, and the first surviving Spanish opera, *Celos aun del aire matan* (1660).

hidden fifths, octaves see CONSECUTIVES.

hi see HIGH.

Higginbotham, J.C. (Jack) (1906–73) Amer. jazz trombonist. He worked with Luis Russell from 1928 to 1931, played in Fletcher Henderson's band, then returned to Russell as backup for Louis Armstrong. In the 1940s he toured with "Red" Allen, settling in the 1950s at the New York Metropole jazz bar.

High Button Shoes musical by Jule Styne, lyrics by Sammy Cahn, book by George Abbott and Phil Silvers, based on a novel by Stephen Longstreet. Premiere, New York 1947. The story of a family in New Jersey in

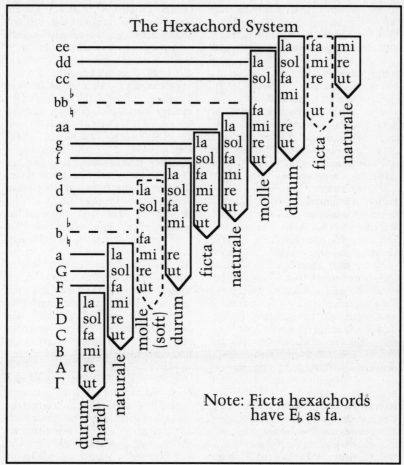

The Hexachord System

Note: Ficta hexachords have E♭ as fa.

1913 and its encounter with a con art-ist.

high fidelity *also*, **hi-fi** a term, now largely out of use, for sound repro-duction very faithful to the original.

highlife *also*, **hi-life** an Afr. dance of the early 20th c. in simple duple me-ter and strict tempo. It is usu. accom-panied by drums, castanets, maracas and claves.

high-hat *also*, **hi-hat** a percussion in-strument combining two CYMBALS, one stationary with the concave side facing up, the other above the first, facing down. The upper cymbal is brought into contact with the lower cymbal with a foot-controlled pedal. The instrument is used in jazz for rhythmic effects. Also, *sock cymbal*.

High Mass a Mass of which all sec-tions, excluding the Epistle and Gos-pel, are sung rather than recited. Cf. MISSA SOLEMNIS.

Hildegard of Bingen (1098–1179) German abbess, mystic and writer. Her lyrical and dramatic poetry (on sacred subjects) has survived in mon-ophonic musical settings.

Hill, Edward Burlingame (1872–1960) Amer. composer, stud. of Paine, Widor and Chadwick. He taught at Harvard from 1908 until his retirement in 1940. His works are strongly influenced by French impressionism and incl. 3 sympho-nies, tone poems, concertos, instrumental chamber music and vocal music.

Hill, Uri K(eeler) (1780–1844) Amer. voice and instrumental teacher and composer of hymn tunes and secular songs. His publishered collections inc. *The Vermont Harmony* (1801). His son, **Ureli Corelli Hill** (1802–75), was a violinist, composer (stud. of Spohr) and conductor of the New York Sacred Music Society and the New York Philharmonic Society.

hillbilly music derogatory historical term for MOUNTAIN MUSIC. See COUNTRY MUSIC.

Hiller, Ferdinand (von) (1811–85) German composer, conductor and teacher, stud. of Alois Schmitt and Hummel. He conducted the Leipzig Gewandhaus Orch., then ran a series of concerts in Dresden and later in Düsseldorf. In Cologne he reorganized the music school and directed the Gürzenich concerts, remaining a significant force in the musical scene until his death. His works incl. 6 operas, oratorios and other works for chorus and orchestra, symphonies, concertos, overtures, instrumental chamber music and many works for piano solo.

Hiller, Johann Adam (1728–1804) German composer and writer. Most of his professional life was spent in Leipzig, where he ran a series of subscription concerts, directed the Grosses Concert, founded a song school and wrote theater works which were the foundation for the German Singspiel. In 1781 he became conductor of the Leipzig Gewandhaus concerts and in 1789 Kantor of the Thomaskirche.

Hiller, Lejaren (1924–) Amer. composer, stud. of Sessions and Babbitt. He directed the experimental music studio at the U. of Illinois from 1958 to 1968, then went to SUNY at Buffalo. He was co-producer of the *Illiac Suite*, the first work composed with a computer, and wrote chamber music (incl. works combining tape and instruments), electronic works and music for theater, films and TV.

Hillis, Margaret (1921–) Amer. choral conductor, stud. of Robert Shaw. She has taught at the Juilliard School and the Union Theological Seminary, and was chorus master of the American Opera Society (1952–68). In 1957 she founded the Chicago SO Chorus, of which she is dir. She has also conducted the Santa Fe Opera, the Kenosha Civic Orch. and the Chicago Civic Orch. She was a founder of the American Choral Foundation in 1954.

hímení Polynesian adaptation of "hymn," indicating hymn-tune style. In Hawaii, the term applies to any song not used for the HULA.

Hindemith, Paul (1895–1963) influential German composer, conductor, violist, theorist and teacher, trained at the Hoch Conservatory in Frankfurt. He played in the Rebner Quartet and the Frankfurt Opera Orch. in the early 1920s. In 1923 he became involved with the Donaueschingen Festival, which under his guidance achieved international prominence. He taught at the Berlin Hochschule für Musik from 1927, also continuing to perform.

His music was boycotted by the Nazi regime, and when he was supported by Furtwängler, the conductor was relieved of his posts. Hindemith left Germany in 1937, going first to Switzerland and then (1940) to the U.S., where he joined the faculty at Yale and taught until 1953, when he retired to Zürich. He wrote theater works (esp. the operas *Hin und Zurück*, *Cardillac*, and *Mathis der Maler*), many concertos and instrumental sonatas, songs (esp. "Das Marienleben" in two very different versions), chamber music and school music.

Hinderas, Natalie (Henderson) (1927–87) Amer. pianist, stud. of Samaroff and Steuermann. She toured widely, specializing in the classical music of African-Americans.

Hines, Earl (Kenneth) ("Fatha") (1905–83) Amer. jazz pianist, a master of the STRIDE PIANO style and of his own "trumpet style," modeled after the playing of Louis Armstrong. Originally from Pittsburgh, he moved to Chicago in 1923, playing with several local bands and with Carroll Dickerson's band on tour. He became the band's director under Louis Armstrong in 1927 but soon moved to Jimmie Noone's band, with which he made a number of recordings. He led his own band at the Grand Terrace in Chicago from 1928 to 1938 and other bands until 1948, after which he worked with Louis Armstrong's All-Stars. His later years he spent with smaller groups. Hines was one of the most influential pianists in jazz, spanning the development from ragtime to swing to bop.

Hines (Heinz), **Jerome (Albert Link)** (1921–) Amer. bass and composer, stud. of Gennaro Curci. His debut was with the San Francisco Opera in 1941 and he first sang with the Metropolitan Opera in 1946. He has sung at Bayreuth and the Bolshoi Opera and at most major American and European houses. His roles include Boris Godunov, Philip II (*Don Carlos*) and Don Giovanni.

Hin und Zurück [hin ünt tsoo'rük] (Ger., There and Back) opera in 1 act by Hindemith to a libretto by Marcellus Schiffer. Premiere, Baden-Baden 1927. Halfway through the opera, the action and the musical themes reverse themselves, making a palindrome; hence the title.

hip-hop a type of Afr.-Amer. urban art of the 1970s and 1980s, incorporating elements of RAP and FUNK music, BREAK DANCING and street art (graffiti).

Hirt, Al(ois Maxwell) (1922–) Amer. jazz trumpeter, trained at the Cincinnati Conservatory of Music. He played with the New Orleans SO and the bands of Horace Heidt, the Dorseys and the Dukes of Dixieland. His work has been successful both in the jazz and the popular markets.

Hirt auf dem Felsen, Der [hērt owf däm 'fel-sən] (Ger.) THE SHEPHERD ON THE ROCK.

his (Ger.) B SHARP.

Histoire du soldat, [ē'stwär dü sol'dä] (Fr.) THE SOLDIER'S TALE.

historia 1, medieval term for the antiphons and responsories of the divine office for an entire day. **2,** from the period of the Reformation, any biblical story, or any musical setting of a biblical story. The genre is best represented in the *Historiae* by Schütz and Distler.

historicus the narrator in a musical setting of a biblical story. Also, *testo* (It.).

H.M.S. Pinafore operetta in 2 acts by Sullivan to a libretto by W.S. Gilbert. Premiere, London 1878. Through a twist of fate, Josephine narrowly escapes being married to Sir Joseph Porter so that she can marry her true love, Ralph.

Hoboe (Ger.) archaic for OBOE.

Hoboken, Anthony van (1887–1983) Dutch bibliographer and collector, stud. of Schenker. He is best known for his thematic catalogue of the works of F.J. Haydn.

hochet [o'shä] (Fr.) a RATTLE.

hocket *also,* **hoquet** [o'kä] (Fr.) a musical device primarily assoc. with the 13th and 14th c., consisting of contrasting sounds and silences between two or more vocal lines, resulting in a "hiccup" effect.

Hodes, Art (Arthur W.) (1904–) Russian-born Amer. jazz and blues pianist, writer, lecturer and editor of the magazine *The Jazz Record* (1944–47). He has played in a variety of bands and has appeared widely as a soloist in the U.S. and Europe.

Hodges, Johnny (John Cornelius) ("Rabbit," "Jeep") (1906–70) Amer. jazz alto saxophonist, stud. of Sidney Bechet. He played with the Duke Ellington orch. almost without interruption from 1928 until his death and was famous for his lush tone.

hoedown orig. applied in the 19th c. to various Afr.-Amer. dances, the term is now used primarily to refer to folk dances and square dances in duple meter or to the parties at which they are danced. Cf. BREAKDOWN.

Hoffmann, E(rnst) T(heodor) A(ma-

deus) (Ernst Theodor Wilhelm) (1776–1822) German writer, critic and composer. He studied music, painting and law in Königsberg and was a Prussian civil servant in Plock. He established a reputation as a writer of tales exhibiting a sense of the fantastic; he also wrote music criticism (primarily for the *Allgemeine musikalische Zeitung*) and a substantial body of music. His tales have provided the basis for a large number of works by other composers, the best known of which are the *Kreisleriana* by Schumann and the opera *Les Contes d'Hoffmann* by Offenbach.

Hoffman, Richard (1831–1909) English-born Amer. pianist, teacher and prolific composer of salon music, stud. of Moscheles, Anton Rubinstein and others.

Hoffmeister, Franz Anton (1754–1812) Austrian composer and music publisher. He published his own works and the works of many other composers, incl. Clementi, Beethoven, Haydn and Mozart.

Hoffnung, Gerard (1925–59) German-born British artist, musician and humorist, noted for his cartoons and for the Hoffnung Music Festival, which he inaugurated in 1956.

Hofhaimer, Paul (1459–1537) Austrian organist and composer, largely self-taught. He was organist for Duke Sigmund of Tyrol at Innsbruck and also served King Maximilian I. From 1519 he was organist at the Salzburg Cathedral. He was highly regarded both as an organist and as a teacher. Only a small part of his output has survived, incl. some songs and instrumental and organ works.

Hofkapelle ['hōf-kä"pel-ə] (Ger.) court CHAPEL.

Hofmann, Josef (Casimir) (1876–1957) Polish-born Amer. pianist and composer (under the pseudonym Michael Dvorsky). After his international debut at the age of 7 he became the sole private pupil of Anton Rubinstein, and his public reappearance coincided with Rubinstein's death in 1894. He was dir. of the Curtis Institute (1926–38) and the first professional musician to make a recording, having cut several cylinders at Edison's laboratory in 1887.

Hofmannsthal, Hugo von (1874–1929) Austrian poet, dramatist and librettist, best known for his long collaboration with Richard Strauss, which produced, among others, the operas DER ROSENKAVALIER and ARIADNE AUF NAXOS.

Hoftanz ['hōf"tänts] (Ger., court dance) a sedate 16th-c. German couple dance related to the BASSE DANSE.

Hofweise ['hōf"vī-ze] (Ger., courting song) a medieval courtship song usu. in binary form with a refrain.

Hogan, Ernest (Crowders, Reuben) (1865–1909) celebrated Amer. minstrel and ragtime composer, star of the musical *Rufus Rastus* (1902). He is unfortunately remembered esp. for his hit song "All Coons Look Alike to Me" (1890), which began the much-criticized craze of the COON SONG.

Hogwood, Christopher (Jarvis Haley) (1941–) English harpsichordist, stud. of Puyana and Leonhardt. He was a founding member of the Early Music Consort, in Cambridge, England, and in 1973 of the Academy of Ancient Music. Since 1987 he has been conductor of the Handel and Haydn Society in Boston and dir. of music of the St. Paul Chamber Orch.

Hohlflöte ['hōl"flø-te] (Ger.) an open wood flute pipe ORGAN STOP with a hollow tone, usu. at 8-foot pitch.

Hohner, M(atthias) ['hō-nər] the world's largest manufacturer of harmonicas and accordians, est. in 1857. It is also one of the largest publishers of music for accordian and harmonica.

Hoiby, Lee (1926–) Amer. composer, stud. of Egon Petri and Gian Carlo Menotti. He is best known for his operas, esp. *Summer and Smoke* (1971).

Holiday, Billie (Fagan, Eleanora) ("Lady Day") (1915–59) Amer. jazz singer. She sang and recorded with

Benny Goodman, Teddy Wilson, Count Basie and Artie Shaw, establishing a reputation as the outstanding jazz singer of the first half of the 20th century. Her life story was dramatized in the 1972 film *Lady Sings the Blues*.

Holland, Charles (1909–87) Amer. tenor, stud. of May Hamaker Henley and Georges Le Pyre. He sang in Hall Johnson's *Run Little Chillun'*, Thomson's *Four Saints in Three Acts*, then moved to Europe, where he was the first black singer to sing at the Paris Opéra-Comique, and pursued a highly successful operatic career. He returned to the U.S. in the 1970s.

holler a type of declamatory blues song, a development of the unaccompanied work song of Afr.-Amer. slaves and workers (see FIELD HOLLER).

Holliger, Heinz (1939–   ) Swiss oboist and composer, stud. of Pierre Pierlot and Boulez. He was principal oboist of the Basel SO (1960–3) before pursuing a solo career. He is noted esp. for his mastery of new effects in the performance of 20th-c. music. Many composers have written works for him, incl. Berio, Penderecki and Stockhausen.

Holly, Buddy (Holley, Charles Hardin) (1938–59) Amer. rock singer and musician, who, in the two years during which he recorded before being killed in an airplane crash, made a number of hits that have been an important influence on later singers. Among his best-known songs are "That'll Be the Day" and "Peggy Sue."

Hollywood Bowl an outdoor theater in Los Angeles, site of an annual summer concert series est. in 1922.

Holmès, Augusta (Mary Anne) (1847–1903) French composer, stud. of Henri Lambert and Franck. Her works, which show the strong influence of Wagner and her teacher Franck, incl. operas, symphonic poems, choral works and songs.

holograph a manuscript written in the hand of its composer or author. Also, *autograph*.

Holst, Gustav(us Theodore von) (1874–1934) English composer, stud. of Charles Stanford. He taught at St. Paul's Girls School in Hammersmith, at Morley College and at the Royal College of Music, but from about 1925 he devoted himself to composition. He is best known for his orchestral suite *The Planets*, still widely performed, his cantata *The Hymn of Jesus* and his opera *Sāvitri*. His daughter, **Imogen (Clare) Holst** (1907–84), was a writer, conductor and administrator, whose works show the influence of early music and folk music.

Holyoke, Samuel (Adams) (1762–1820) Amer. composer and compiler of tunebooks, trained at Harvard College. He was a singing teacher in New England and compiled a number of psalm books, incl. the *Harmonia americana*, the *Columbian Repository* and the *Christian Harmonist*, which contain many of his over 600 works.

Holz [hōlts] (Ger.) wood.

Holztrompete (Ger.) **1**, a wooden TRUMPET. **2**, an instrument created to play the shepherd's melody in Act III of Wagner's *Tristan and Isolde*, comprising an English horn bell, a cup mouthpiece and a single valve. The part is now usu. played on the English horn.

Home, Sweet Home a song with music by Henry R. Bishop, orig. set to different words, which appeared for the first time with the present text in the opera *Clari, or The Maid of Milan* (London, 1823). The text is by John Howard Payne.

Homme armé, L' [lum ar'mä] (Fr., the armed man) a 15th-c. melody said (prob. erroneously) to have been composed by Antoine Busnois. The tune serves as the cantus firmus for over 30 polyphonic works written during the 15th to 17th c., incl. masses by Dufay, Busnois, Josquin, Ockeghem, Obrecht and Compère. (See *illus.*, p. 234.)

homophony a term usu. referring to part-writing in which all the parts

L'hom – me, l'hom – me, l'homme ar – mé,

l'homme ar–mé, L'homme ar–mé doibt on doub ter,

Fine

doibt on doub–ter.　On a fait par–tout cri–er

Que chas–cun se

1.

2.

viegne ar– mer D'un hau–bre–gon de　fer.

D.C. al Fine

move together in the same rhythm, as opposed to the contrapuntal style. Also, *block harmony*. Cf. MONO-PHONY, POLYPHONY.

Honegger, Arthur (Oscar) (1892–1955) Swiss composer. He studied at the Zurich Conservatory and with Capet, Gédalge, d'Indy and Widor at the Paris Conservatoire. He was a member of LES SIX but had little affinity with the others of the group. He taught at the École Normale de Musique in Paris. Of his large body of works in all genres, the most frequently performed are the "dramatic psalm" *Le roi David* (King David), the Christmas cantata *Une cantate de Noël*, the oratorio *Jeanne d'Arc au bûcher* and the orchestral *mouvements symphoniques* (*Rugby* and *Pacific 231*).

Höngen, Elisabeth (1906–) German mezzo-soprano, stud. of Hermann Weisenborn and Ludwig Horth. She was a member of the Vienna Staatsoper from 1943 and a frequent performer at Salzburg, Bayreuth and Covent Garden. Her U.S. debut was in 1952 at the Metropolitan Opera.

honky-tonk 1, a style of music dating from the 1940s related to COUNTRY MUSIC, characterized by a loud, heavy beat and the use of electric instruments, first made popular by Ernest Tubb. **2,** an upright, out-of-tune piano such as one might find in a barroom.

Honolulu Symphony Orchestra orch. founded in Honolulu in 1900. Its music directors have been F. A.

Ballaseyus, Fritz Hart, George Barati, Robert LaMarchina and Donald Johanos.

hoofer a professional dancer.

hook harp a diatonic HARP fitted with a row of hooks at the neck which permit the player to raise the pitch of each string by a semitone. A later development in the design allows the player to operate the hooks from a foot pedal.

Hooker, John Lee (1917–) Amer. blues singer and guitarist, consistently popular since the late 1940s. He is noted for his original lyrics and his rich voice, which formed a link between blues and rock and roll. He appeared at the Newport Folk Festival in 1959, but he has also appeared and recorded with Canned Heat and other groups.

hootenanny an informal party for folk dancing and singing, assoc. mainly with rural No. America.

hopak GOPAK.

Hopekirk, Helen (1856–1945) Scottish-born Amer. pianist and composer, trained at the Leipzig Conservatory. She performed with the Boston SO in 1883 and taught at the New England Conservatory from 1897.

Hopkins, Lightnin' (Sam) (1912–82) Amer. blues singer and guitarist from Texas, the most recorded traditional blues artist in history. He spent much of his early life as a street singer and was strongly influenced by his work with BLIND LEMON JEFFERSON. Later he recorded with Brownie McGhee and Sonny Terry, among others.

Hopkinson, Francis (1737–91) Amer. keyboard player, composer and statesman, a member of the Continental Congress and a signer of the Declaration of Independence. He claimed to be the first native-born American to "produce a Musical Composition" (the claim is based on his *Seven Songs* of 1788).

hoquet [o'kā] (Fr.) HOCKET.

hora a folk dance of Romanian origin in moderate ⅔ or ⁶/₈ time, highly popular in Israel.

hora lunga a type of Romanian folk

music, consisting of continuous variations of a highly ornamental melody performed vocally or instrumentally. Also, *doina*.

Horenstein, Jascha (1899–1973) Russian-born Amer. conductor, stud. of Joseph Marx and Franz Schreker. He began as an assistant to Furtwängler, then was chief conductor of the Düsseldorf Opera (1928–33) until he was forced by the Nazis to leave. He came to the U.S. in 1940. He was known for his performances of the works of Mahler and Bruckner, and as a champion of 20th-c. music he introduced a number of important works to the U.S., including Berg's *Wozzeck* and Busoni's *Doktor Faustus*.

horn 1, in jazz, any wind instrument. **2,** a wind instrument whose reed is the lips of the player. Primitive horns were usu. made from the horn or tusk of an animal and were end-, or more rarely, side-blown. More advanced instruments are blown by means of a small, cupped mouthpiece attached to a curved conical tube, usu. coiled in circles and ending in a flared bell. The early horn without valves had a set of *crooks* of different lengths which could be inserted into the tubing to change its length and consequently its fundamental tone. The valveless, or natural, horn could achieve a diatonic scale only in the top octave or by stopping the horn with the hand (see STOPPING). The valved horn has three or more valves which serve to open or close tubes of varying lengths and thus change the length of the overall tube, allowing the production of the chromatic scale. **3,** *also,* **French horn** the modern orchestral horn. The single horn is usually pitched either in B♭ or in F. (There is also a high horn in F alto which is used primarily for high Baroque and Classical horn parts.) The double horn combines the B♭ and F horns, employing a fourth valve to switch between the two sets of tubing. In the past, horn parts were written in C, with a written indication as to the actual pitch of the part ("horn in F," "horn in E," etc.), the player making the transposition. Modern parts are universally written in F. **4,** ENGLISH HORN. (Horns, in senses 2 and 3, are illustrated on pp. 236–37.)

horn band a late- 18th- and early 19th-c. type of WIND BAND composed entirely of hunting horns, each player playing (initially) only one note, later two or three.

Horne, Lena (Calhoun) (1917–) Amer. singer and actress. She began as a dancer in Harlem's Cotton Club, then was successful as a singer with the Charlie Barnet orch. She has appeared in films (*Cabin in the Sky*, *Stormy Weather*, *The Wiz*) and on Broadway (*Jamaica*), and has made many recordings.

Horne, Marilyn (1934–) Amer. mezzo-soprano, stud. of Lotte Lehmann. She was the voice of Dorothy Dandridge in *Carmen Jones* in 1954, the year of her operatic debut in Los Angeles. In 1961 she began a memorable association with soprano Joan Sutherland, performing bel canto repertory. Her Metropolitan Opera debut was in 1970. She has also been an active concert artist and made many recordings.

horn fifths a two-part chord progression playable on natural trumpets and horns, consisting not only of fifths, but of a major third, a perfect fifth and a minor sixth. The progression is found not only in brass music (as in the trumpet calls of Rossini's *William Tell* overture) but also in music for other instruments evoking the sound of the natural horn or trumpet.

horn fifths

(Rossini, William Tell overture)

hornpipe 1, a single reed wind instrument possibly of Celtic origin consisting of a pipe of wood or bone with fingerholes, the mouthpiece and/or bell often of animal horn. Cf. PIBGORN, STOCKHORN. **2,** a lively British sailors' dance in ¾ for a single dancer accompanied by the hornpipe.

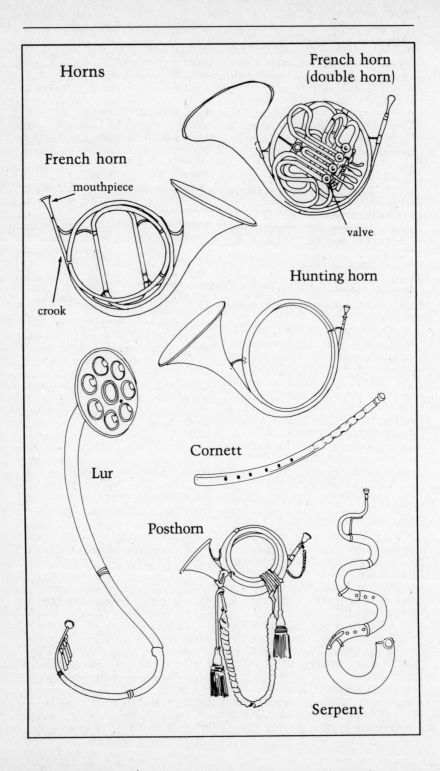

Horns

French horn
(double horn)

French horn

mouthpiece

valve

crook

Hunting horn

Lur

Cornett

Posthorn

Serpent

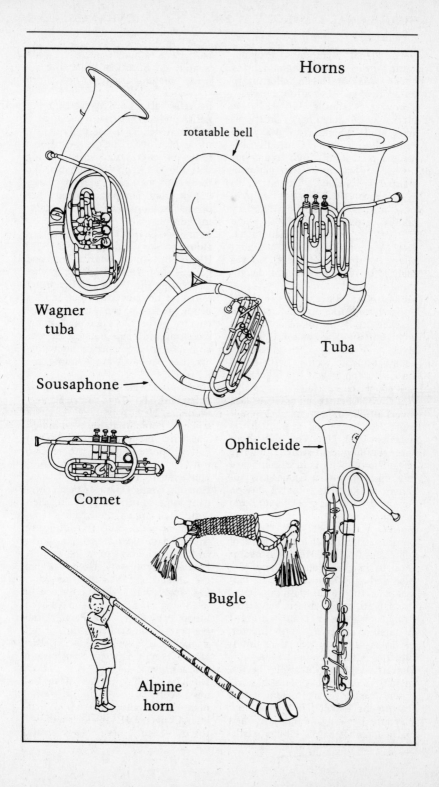

Horns

Wagner
tuba

rotatable bell

Tuba

Sousaphone

Cornet

Ophicleide

Bugle

Alpine
horn

Horn Signal Symphony popular name for the Symphony No. 31 in D major (1765) by Haydn, referring to the work's fanfares for four horns.

Horowitz, Vladimir (1904–89) remarkable Ukranian-born Amer. pianist, stud. of Sergei Tarnowsky and Felix Blumenfeld. He initially became a pianist to earn a living, but his success was immediate and substantial. He became a U.S. citizen in 1944. From 1936 he performed publicly only at intervals, separated by periods of retirement (1953–65 and since 1970). He had a phenomenal technique joined to a very individualistic interpretive approach. He was married to Wanda Toscanini, daughter of the conductor.

Horszowski, Mieczyslaw (1892–) Polish-born Amer. pianist, stud. of Leschetizky. From his beginnings as a child prodigy, he has toured extensively and performed frequently in chamber music recitals with Pablo Casals, Joseph Szigeti and others. He still concertizes actively.

Hot Club of France an assoc. of jazz lovers formed in Paris in 1932 to promote "real jazz" and to publish the magazine *Jazz Hot*. The club sponsored the unique all-string Quintette of the Hot Club of France, composed of violinist STÉPHANE GRAPPELLI, guitarists DJANGO REINHARDT, Joseph Reinhardt and Roger Chaput, and bassist Louis Vola.

Hotter, Hans (1909–) German-born Austrian bass-baritone, stud. of Matthäus Roemer. He performed at Breslau, Prague, Hamburg and Munich and sang frequently at Covent Garden, the Metropolitan Opera (from 1950) and Bayreuth. He retired from the stage in 1972, but continued to pursue a career as a stage director. He is highly respected as an interpreter of both opera and lieder.

Hotteterre, Jaques(-Martin) ("Le Romain") (1674–c1763) French composer, teacher, instrumentalist and instrument maker. He was a flute player in the king's employ in Paris and a member of the Grands Haut-

bois. He is famous especially for his treatise on flute (and oboe and recorder) playing, *Principes de la flûte traversière* (1707).

hourglass drum a WAISTED DRUM of Africa and the Far East, wide at both ends and slender in the middle, usu. made of wood. The leather drumheads are often attached by a lacing that allows the player to control the tension of the heads, thereby changing the pitch. These variable-pressure drums are sometimes called "talking" drums.

hours see DIVINE OFFICE.

House, Son (Eddie James, Jr.) (1902–88) Amer. blues singer and guitarist from Mississippi. He was active during the 1930s as a performer noted for his powerful voice and his biting guitar playing. He was rediscovered in the 1960s and made many recordings and appearances. He was an important influence on later singers, incl. Muddy Waters and Bonnie Raitt.

House of Flowers musical by Harold Arlen with a book by Truman Capote. Premiere, New York 1954. A tale of two rival bordellos in the West Indies. The orig. production starred Pearl Bailey, Juanita Hall and Diahann Carroll.

house music HAUSMUSIK.

Houston Grand Opera an opera company founded in 1955 by Walter Herbert. The company has made a reputation for performing, in addition to the standard repertory, Amer. works and unusual works from the past.

Houston Symphony Orchestra an orch. founded in 1913, disbanded during World War I, then re-formed in 1930. The music directors have been Julian Paul Blitz, Paul Berge, Uriel Nespoli, Frank St. Leger, Ernst Hoffman, Efrem Kurtz, Stokowski, Barbirolli, Previn, Lawrence Foster and Comissiona.

Hovhaness (Chakmakjian), **Alan (Vaness) Scott** (1911–) prolific Armenian-Amer. composer, stud. of Frederick Converse. His music has shown the influence of his major interests:

music of the Far East, Armenian music and mysticism. He has written a large body of works in all forms, incl. operas, ballets, symphonies and tone poems, works for chamber orchestra, string ensemble and wind ensemble, sacred vocal works and instrumental chamber music.

How do you do? the string quartet in G major, Op. 33 No. 5 (1781), by Haydn, one of the "Russian" quartets.

How to Succeed in Business Without Really Trying musical by Frank Loesser, book by Abe Burrows, Jack Weinstein and Willie Gilbert, based on the book by Shepherd Mead. Premiere, New York 1961. The satirical story of the rise of J. Pierpont Finch from window cleaner to presidency of a wicket company.

Howe, Elias (1820–95) Amer. music publisher, who began by selling fiddle tunes door-to-door. In 1850 he sold his catalog to Oliver Ditson and left the business for ten years. In 1860 he reopened in Boston as a music and rare-instruments dealer.

Howells, Herbert (Norman) (1892–1983) English composer, teacher and writer, stud. of Charles Stanford and Charles Wood. He taught at the Royal College of Music from 1920, was Holst's successor at the St. Paul's Girls' School and was professor at London U. from 1950. He is especially noted for his work *Hymnus Paradisi* for voices and orchestra and for his songs.

Howlin' Wolf (Burnett, Chester Arthur) (1910–76) influential Amer. blues singer. He began as a street singer in Mississippi, then moved to Chicago in 1952, where he made many recordings. He appeared in the 1960s and 1970s at various festivals and recorded with Eric Clapton, Ringo Starr, B.B. King and others.

hptw. *abbr.* Hauptwerk (see GREAT ORGAN).

Huang, Cham-Ber (1925–) Amer. harmonica player born and educated in Shanghai. He has developed several kinds of harmonica, incl. the "chordomonica," which is capable of playing a melody and chordal accompaniment simultaneously. He has premiered many new works and has made many arrangements for harmonica.

Hubbard, Frank (Twombly) (1920–76) Amer. harpsichord maker, trained at the Dolmetsch school and with Hugh Gough. He collaborated with William Dowd from 1949 to 1958, afterwards working independently. He produced a popular harpsichord kit and wrote an important book on his art, *Three Centuries of Harpsichord Making* (1965).

Hubbard, Freddie (Frederick DeWayne) (1938–) Amer. trumpeter, fluegelhorn player, composer and pianist. In the late 1950s he worked with Eric Dolphy, Sonny Rollins, Quincy Jones and others. He played on the epoch-making Ornette Coleman album *Free Jazz* in 1960, was a member of Art Blakey's Jazz Messengers 1961–4, then joined Max Roach. He experimented in the late 1970s with jazz-rock fusion but was not successful and has returned to acoustic sound. He has been an important influence on younger players.

Hubbell, Raymond (1879–1954) Amer. composer of songs and musicals for the Hippodrome and for Broadway, incl. several editions of the *Ziegfeld Follies*.

Huber, Klaus (1924–) Swiss composer and violinist, stud. of Willy Burkhard and Blacher. He has taught at the Zürich and Lucerne Conservatories and, from 1961, at the Basel Musical Academy. His works have been performed frequently at the festivals of the ISCM and have won many awards. He has written orchestral works (incl. *Tenebrae*), works for voice, incl. *Des Engels Anredung an die Seele* (The Angel's Address to the Soul) and instrumental chamber music.

Huberman, Bronislaw (1882–1947) Polish violinist, stud. of Markees (a Joachim student) and Charles Grigorovich. A child prodigy who played at the age of 13 in Adelina Patti's farewell concert in Vienna, he successfully made the transition to adult virtuoso and toured Europe and the U.S. extensively. He was a co-founder with William Steinberg of the Palestine SO.

Hucbald (c840–930) medieval monk, music theorist, composer, teacher and hagiographer, the author of the first systematic treatise on Western music theory, *De harmonica institutione* (880).

Huggett Family a Canadian vocal and instrumental family ensemble based in Ottawa specializing in early music and folk music. They have been touring since 1969.

Huguenots, Les ['hü-gə-nō] (Fr., The Huguenots) opera in 5 acts by Meyerbeer to a libretto by Eugène Scribe and Émile Deschamps. Premiere, Paris 1836. In 16th-c. France a Huguenot nobleman, Raoul de Nangis, loves a Catholic woman, Valentine, with tragic results.

Huddersfield Choral Society a famous amateur choral society in Yorkshire, England, founded in 1836. Its conductors have included Malcolm Sargent and John Pritchard.

Hufnagel *also,* **Hufnagelschrift** (Ger., hobnail script) a style of German medieval chant notation, so-called from the resemblance of one of its signs to a horseshoe nail.

hula a type of Hawaiian dance characterized by gestures of the upper torso, arms and hands to interpret mood and feeling.

Hume, Tobias (?1570–1645) English composer, viol player and professional soldier. His extant works are contained in two volumes of music for viol and lyra viol.

Humfrey, Pelham (1647–74) English composer of service music, odes, sacred and secular songs and masques. He was a chorister in the Chapel Royal from about 1660 (with John Blow and others) and later a Gentleman of the Chapel Royal and a musician for the lute. He became Master of the Children of the Chapel Royal

in 1672. He traveled on the mainland in the mid-1660s and incorporated in his works the latest French and Italian styles.

Hummel, Johann Nepomuk (1778–1837) Austrian composer, pianist, conductor and teacher, stud. of Mozart, Haydn, Albrechtsberger and Salieri. He was an outstanding child prodigy who toured widely after his study with Mozart, returning to Vienna in 1793. In 1804 he became konzertmeister to Prince Esterházy, composing for the chapel, teaching, and assembling the Haydn archive. He was Kapellmeister in Stuttgart from 1816 to 1818, then moved to the same post in Weimar, where he conducted the court theater while making major trips to France, the Netherlands, Russia, Poland and (in 1830 and later) London.

He produced a large body of works in all genres, incl. operas and incidental music, ballets, sacred and secular vocal music, instrumental chamber music, orchestral overtures and dances, and many works for solo piano.

hummels a fretted Swedish board ZITHER.

humoreske *also,* **humoresque** a composition of fanciful or capricious character; CAPRICCIO.

Humperdinck, Engelbert (1854–1921) German composer and teacher, trained at the Cologne Conservatory and the Royal Music School in Munich. He assisted Wagner at Bayreuth in the early 1880s, then moved frequently, holding a variety of teaching posts. He taught at the Hoch Conservatory in Frankfurt from 1890 on and shortly thereafter produced the principal work for which he is known, the opera *Hänsel und Gretel*, which began as a series of songs for his sister. He moved to Berlin in 1900 to teach composition. His works incl. 10 operas, incidental music, choral works, many songs and a small body of instrumental music.

Hungarian Dances a set of 21 dances for piano duet (1852–69) by Brahms, some of which he later orchestrated.

Hungarian gypsy scale. GYPSY SCALE.

Hungarian Rhapsodies a series of works for solo piano (1851–3, 1871–86) by Liszt, six of which were later orchestrated.

Hungarian String Quartet a string quartet founded in Budapest in 1935, resident in the U.S. from 1950. It disbanded in 1970.

Hunt Cantata popular name for the Cantata No. 208, "Was mir behagt, ist nur die muntre Jagd!" (What pleases me is only the joyous hunt!) (c1713) by J.S. Bach, written for the birthday of the duke of Saxe-Weissenfels.

Hunter, Ivory Joe (1914–74) Amer. blues singer, pianist and songwriter, who combined rhythm-and-blues with country music, later singing as a member of the Grand Ole Opry.

Hunt Quartet the popular name for: **1**, the string quartet in B♭ major, K. 458 (1784), by Mozart, so called because of the similarity of the opening theme to the sound of hunting horns. **2**, (Fr., *La Chasse*) the divertimento for string quartet in B♭, Op. 1 No. 1 (c1758), by Haydn.

Hunt Symphony (Fr., *La chasse*) popular name for the Symphony No. 73 in D major (c1781) by Haydn. The title refers to the hunt sounds in the 4th movement, orig. written as the overture to his opera *La fedeltà premiata*.

Hunter, Rita (Nellie) (1933–) English dramatic soprano, stud. of Edwin Francis, Redvers Llewellyn and Eva Turner. She has sung regularly at Sadler's Wells, the Metropolitan Opera (debut 1972), Covent Garden and in other major houses. Her roles incl. Brünnhilde, Leonora (*Il Trovatore*) and Amelia (*A Masked Ball*).

hurdy-gurdy 1, a BOX ZITHER in which a rosined wheel, turned by a hand crank, bows the strings, whose pitches are varied by a set of mechanical keys. The instrument usually has one or more unkeyed drone strings. **2**, BARREL ORGAN. **3**, a mechanical PIANO played in the

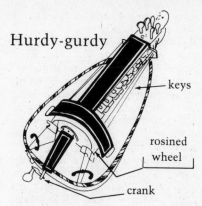

Hurdy-gurdy — keys — rosined wheel — crank

streets and operated with a hand crank.

Hurst, George (1926–) British conductor, trained at the Royal Conservatory in Toronto. He has taught at the Peabody Conservatory (1947–55) and has been conductor of the York SO (PA), the BBC Northern SO (1958–68) and the Western Orchestral Society.

Hurt, Mississippi John (1894–1966) Amer. blues singer and guitarist who performed most of his life as an amateur in relative obscurity. After making a few recordings in 1928, he returned to anonymity until 1963, when he was rediscovered and appeared at the Newport Folk Festival and on television, and made a number of new recordings.

huruk a wooden WAISTED DRUM of India.

Husa, Karel (1921–) Czech-born Amer. composer and conductor, trained at the Prague Conservatory and in Paris with Boulanger, Honegger and others. He lived in Paris until 1954, after which he came to the U.S. to teach and conduct at Cornell U. He won the Pulitzer Prize in 1969 for his String Quartet No. 3. Husa's works, which sometimes employ quartertones, incl. music for orchestra and wind ensemble and chamber music. He is particularly known for his works for concert band, such as *Music for Prague* and *Apotheosis of This Earth*.

husla (Serbic) a bowed string instrument of eastern Europe related to the medieval FIDDLE.

Huston, Scott (1916–) Amer. composer and teacher, stud. of Bernard Rogers and Howard Hanson. He has taught at the Cincinnati College-Conservatory of Music since 1952. His works incl. 4 symphonies, concertos, vocal music and instrumental chamber music, and employ both tonal and atonal techniques.

Hutchinson Family a celebrated Amer. singing family, active in the mid-1800s, touring the U.S. and Great Britain with Alpine songs, glees and laments, often with instrumental accompaniment.

hybrid chord a term used in jazz theory for a harmony resulting from a triad or seventh chord being played over an unrelated bass note.

hydraulis *also*, **hydraulos** (Gr.) an ancient Greek and Roman pipe ORGAN using hydraulic pressure to force air through the pipes.

Hykes, David (Bond) (1953–) Amer. singer and composer, trained at Antioch College and Columbia U. He studied Indian and other Asian musics privately. He founded the unusual vocal group the HARMONIC CHOIR and has also written works for dulcimer and other instruments.

hymn a sacred or secular song in praise of gods or heroes. Historically, the category has included psalms, canticles, sequences and other liturgical tropes. Most hymn melodies (or *tunes*) are relatively simple, employing syllabic text setting; some hymns, however, have more than one melody for a given text and sometimes more than one text is set to a given melody. Polyphonic settings of hymns, incl. Lutheran chorales, generally are written in chordal style and are often based on preexisting plainsong melodies, usu. modified to conform to a metrical pattern. Cf. SPIRITUAL, CAMP MEETING SPIRITUAL.

hymnal a collection of HYMNS, often including other service music as well.

Hymn of Praise (Ger., *Lobgesang*) the Symphony-cantata No. 2 in B♭ major, Op. 52 (1840), by Mendelssohn.

hypodorian the second church MODE, the plagal mode on D.

hypolydian the sixth church MODE, the plagal mode on F.

hypomixolydian the eighth church MODE, the plagal mode on G.

hypophrygian the fourth church MODE, the plagal mode on E.

I

Ian, Janis (Fink, Janis Eddy) (1951–)
Amer. rock singer and songwriter of
such hits as "Society's Child" (written when she was 14), "At Seventeen" and "Stars."

Iannaccone, Anthony (Joseph)
(1943–) Amer. composer, stud. of
Giannini, Diamond and others. Since
1971 he has taught at Eastern Michigan U., where he founded an electronic music studio. He has written
a number of works for wind ensembles, as well as 2 symphonies, chamber music and songs.

Ibach German firm of piano and organ makers, founded in Kluse in 1794
by Johannes Adolph Ibach (1766–
1848).

Iberia 1, see IMAGES (2,). **2,** a set of
12 piano pieces in four volumes
(1906–8) by Albéniz with characteristic Spanish rhythms and melodies.

Ibert, Jacques (François Antoine)
[ē'ber] (1890–1962) French composer, stud. of Paul Vidal. He won the
Prix de Rome in 1919 for his cantata
Le poète et la fée. His stay in Rome
produced, among other works, his
popular orchestral suite *Escales*
(1922). He later returned to Rome to
direct the Académie de France (1937–
60). His works incl. 7 operas (incl.
L'aiglon and *Barbe-bleue*, the latter
for radio), ballets, incidental music
and film scores, songs, symphonic
poems, cantatas, instrumental chamber music (incl. a string quartet) and
piano works.

Ibrahim, Abdullah (Brand Dollar)
(1934–) So. Afr. jazz pianist, composer, instrumentalist and vocalist.
He sang and played with groups in So.
Africa until 1962, when he moved to
Europe. Under the aegis of Duke Ellington he came to the U.S. in 1965
and became involved with the free-
jazz movement in New York. In 1968
he returned to Africa and to a more
traditional style of music making, incorporating Afr. rhythms and melodies. After a festival in So. Africa
breaking the rules of apartheid, he
was forced to leave, settling in New
York. In the 1980s he has led his
own group, Ekaya ("home"), and produced a multi-media musico-dramatic collage called *Kalahari Liber-
ation Opera*.

ictus a term borrowed from prosody
to refer to metrical ACCENT (which
may or may not coincide with the
musical accent).

idée fixe [ē'dā fēks] (Fr., obsession) a
term coined by Berlioz to refer to a
musical idea used "obsessively" in
a work. Berlioz applied the term specifically to the main theme of his
Symphonie fantastique (1830), which
represents the obsession of an artist
for his beloved.

idiophone an instrument (such as a
bell, rattle, a gong and certain drums)
whose source of sound is the vibration of its own material unmodified
by any special tension (such as that
of strings or membranes). Idiophones
may be stamped, shaken, struck,
rubbed, scraped or plucked to produce
their characteristic sounds.

Idomeneo opera seria in 3 acts by
Mozart to a libretto in Italian by Abbé
Giambattista Varesco, based on Dan-
chet's libretto for *Idoménée* by André
Campra. Premiere, Munich 1781. In
return for safe passage in the midst of
storms, Idomeneo, King of Crete,
vows to Neptune to sacrifice the first
person he meets on his safe return
home, who turns out to be his son
Idamante.

I'd Rather Be Right musical by Richard Rodgers, lyrics by Lorenz Hart,

book by George S. Kaufman and Moss Hart. Premiere, New York 1937. The only stage musical in which actor George M. Cohan appeared that he did not write himself. A satire about a young couple, Peggy and Phil, and their imaginary experiences with President Franklin D. Roosevelt.

idyll a pastoral or romantic composition.

illustrative music see PROGRAM MUSIC.

Images [ē'mäzh] (Fr., images) **1,** two sets of piano pieces (1905–7) by Debussy. **2,** a set of three symphonic poems (1909) by Debussy: *Gigues* (Jigs), *Iberia* and *Rondes de printemps* (Round Dances of Spring). *Iberia* is in three sections: *Par les rues et par les chemins* (By the Streets and Byways), *Les Parfums de la nuit* (The Fragrances of the Night) and *Le Matin d'un jour de fête* (The Morning of a Festival Day).

I Married an Angel musical by Richard Rodgers, lyrics by Lorenz Hart, book by Rodgers and Hart, based on a play by Janos Vaszary. Premiere, New York 1938. The first musical directed by Joshua Logan, the play is a satirical fantasy about a Budapest banker who marries an angel.

Imbrie, Andrew (Welsh) (1921–) Amer. composer, teacher and pianist, stud. of Pauline and Leo Ornstein and Sessions. He has taught at the U. of California at Berkeley and at the San Francisco Conservatory and has received many commissions and awards, including two Guggenheim grants and the Naumburg Recording Award. His works incl. *Angle of Repose* (opera, 1976), 3 symphonies, concertos for flute, piano, violin and cello, 3 string quartets, other chamber music and songs.

imbroglio (It., mixture) a simultaneous mixture of contrasting rhythms, as in Mozart's *Don Giovanni*, where three different dance orchestras play simultaneously in three different meters (see POLYMETER). The technique is frequently employed in 20th-c. music, as in the works for multiple orchestras of Ives, Stockhausen and others.

imitation 1, repetition of the melodic contour and rhythm of a passage in one part by another part, frequently at a different pitch level and with varying degrees of fidelity to the original. The exactness of the repetition can range from perfect reproduction (strict imitation, as in CANON and FUGUE) to distant similarity or echoing (free imitation, the more frequent current use of the term). The technique has played an important role in Western music since the Middle Ages and became an important structural element of compositions of the 16th and 17th c. employing *imitative technique,* in which the form of the work consisted in a series of "points of imitation" (see POINT, 1,) that succeeded or dovetailed with one another. See also COUNTERPOINT. **2,** one of a group of terms (PARODY, PARAPHRASE, free imitation, CANTUS FIRMUS) which classify the degree to which one composition is based on a preexistent model. The distinctions among categories often overlap, but imitation is usu. considered to be partway between cantus firmus technique and parody. Thus, an imitation mass will make some use of a preexisting cantus firmus while at the same time borrowing from the model's polyphonic texture. Masses which are based on preexisting material are often called by the name of the model, as in *Missa L'homme armé,* etc.

imperfect cadence a CADENCE which concludes on the dominant, usually preceded by the tonic (I–V). Also, *half cadence, half close.*

imperfect consonance the INTERVAL of a major or minor 3rd or 6th or their compounds (10th, 13th, etc.). Cf. PERFECT CONSONANCE.

Imperial popular name for **1,** the Mass in D minor (1798) by Haydn. Also, *Nelson Mass, Coronation Mass.* **2,** the Symphony No. 53 in D major (1778) by Haydn.

Impresario, The (Ger., *Der Schau-*

spieldirektor) comic opera in 1 act by Mozart to a libretto in German by Gottlob Stephanie the Younger. Premiere, Vienna 1786. Two prima donnas vie for a position with an operatic company.

impressionism a term borrowed from painting which refers to a style (as in works of Monet) that attempts through the use of light, color and blurring to produce a kind of naturalism, as opposed to realism. In music the term is used to refer to a style that produces a similar sensation of indefiniteness by means of certain instrumental techniques and harmonies, and an emphasis on color and timbre rather than on form. The most common use of the term is in French music of the late 19th and early 20th c., in particular the music of Debussy.

Impressions, The Amer. rock and soul vocal ensemble formed in 1957 in Chicago, led (from 1961) by Curtis Mayfield. They were one of the most popular vocal groups of the 1960s.

impromptu an improvisatory composition, usu. for solo instrument. The term was first used in the early 19th c. and composers of works of this sort incl. Schubert, Chopin and Schumann.

improvisation the creation of music while it is being performed. (In a sense, all performance involves improvisation, since no notational system yet devised is more than an approximate indication of execution.) The extent of the creation can range from the addition of a few notes to the creation of the form and content of a complete work. Improvisation in art music is usu. produced within a stylistic framework defined either by a composer or by convention, and this framework can be quite specific, particularly in non-Western music, which tends to incorporate a large degree of improvisation within very clearly defined guidelines.

In Western art music, there are certain areas that have traditionally been left to improvisation—such as cadenzas, ornaments and some sacred service music—though this tradition was stronger in earlier centuries, the tendency in current times being to compose such elements prior to performance. The use of improvisation as an integral element of a musical work has become common in certain types of contemporary music; the performer is provided with tools—a set of pitches to use, a graphic indication of contour, dynamic, rhythm, tempo or emotion—and instructed to invent (see ALEATORY).

Improvisation is common in popular and folk music and is an integral part of JAZZ and jazz-related styles (such as some ROCK music).

See ORNAMENTATION, CADENZA.

IMS INTERNATIONAL MUSICOLOGICAL SOCIETY.

in alt a term in vocal music indicating the notes that lie in the octave above the highest line of the treble staff. The notes in the second octave above the staff are *in altissimo*. Cf. ALT VOICE.

incidental music music composed for a dramatic work, or music incorporated into a dramatic work for which it was not originally written. Such music is not the dominant element in the work but illustrates or comments on the action, provides color or fills time (as between scene changes).

incipit ['in-chə-pət] (Lat., [here] begins) the opening music or words of a composition or text.

Incoronazione di Poppea, L' [ēn-ko-ro-nä'tsyō-nä dē pop'pä-ä] (It., The Coronation of Poppea) historical opera in 5 scenes by Monteverdi to a libretto by Giovanni Francesco Busenello. Premiere, Venice 1642. Ottone, Nero's general, loves Poppea, who has given herself to Nero.

In Dahomey musical revue by Will Marion Cook with lyrics by Paul Lawrence Dunbar and Alex Rogers, featuring the comic duo Bert Williams and George Walker, the first all-black show to play at a major Broadway theater. Premiere, New York 1903.

indeterminate music see ALEATORY.

India, Sigismondo d' (?1582–1629) Italian composer and singer of noble birth. He was dir. of chamber music for the duke of Savoy at Turin and later at the Este court at Modena. He was an important composer of secular vocal music, esp. monody and madrigals, and also wrote sacred vocal works.

Indianapolis Symphony Orchestra orch. founded in Indianapolis, IN, in 1930. Its conductors have been Ferdinand Schaefer, Fabien Sevitsky, Izler Solomon, John Nelson and Raymond Leppard.

industrial rock a type of loud, aggressive ROCK music influenced by environmental noise and using, in addition to electronic instruments, such industrial equipment as pipes, oil drums, power drills, etc., as sound producers.

Indy, (Paul Marie Théodore) Vincent d' [dɛ̃'dɛ̃, vɛ̃'sã] (1851–1931) French composer, teacher and writer. He studied with Lavignac and at the Paris Conservatoire and was one of the first members of the Société nationale de musique. In 1894 he co-founded the Schola Cantorum in Paris, which he directed after 1900 and which was famous for its rigorous training. One result of his teaching experience was the monumental *Cours de composition musicale* (1903–31), a four-volume compendium of the composer's art. He was a devoted admirer of Wagner and of César Franck, and his works from all but the last years of his life show their influence. His works incl. *Fervaal* (opera, 1889–93), *L'étranger* (opera, 1903), *Symphonie sur un chant montagnard français* (1886), *Le chant de la cloche* (cantata, 1879–83), songs and instrumental chamber music.

inflection 1, in PLAINCHANT, a deviation from the reciting note, usu. to clarify the divisions of the text. Cf. MEDIANT, PSALM TONE. **2,** a deviation from the standard pitch for expressive purposes (e.g., the "BLUE NOTE" of jazz) or for ornamentation.

Ingegneri, Marc' Antonio [ēn-jä'nye-rē] (c1545–92) Veronese composer, teacher of Claudio Monteverdi and possibly a student of Vincenzo Ruffo and Cipriano de Rore. He was *maestro di cappella* at the Cremona Cathedral c1580. He is known primarily for his 5-voice madrigals.

ingungu a So. Afr. FRICTION DRUM played with a stick through the skin head.

inharmonic a transient pitch in the sound of an organ pipe or instrument, not a multiple of the fundamental or the first harmonic, contributing to the characteristic timbre.

Ink Spots, The Amer. popular vocal quartet formed in 1934 by four porters at New York's Paramount Theater. Their hits incl. "If I Didn't Care" (1939) and "To Each His Own" (1946).

innig ['in-iç] (Ger.) heartfelt.

innomine the name given to many English polyphonic instrumental compositions of the 16th and 17th c. that use a cantus firmus based on the benedictus section of John Taverner's *Missa Gloria tibi trinitas*.

Institut de recherche et de coordination acoustique/musique (Fr., Institute for Research and Coordination of Acoustics and Music) an institute for the study of composition, electronic and computer techniques, acoustics and instrument building founded in Paris in 1976 under the direction of Pierre Boulez. Abbr., *IRCAM*.

Institute of Musical Art a conservatory founded in New York in 1905. It became the JUILLIARD SCHOOL OF MUSIC in 1923.

instrument orig. a Ger. term for a keyboard string instrument, the word now applies to any device for making music.

instrumentation 1, the ensemble of instruments for which a composition is intended. **2,** the arranging of a composition for a certain group of instruments. Cf. ORCHESTRATION.

intabulation *also,* **intavolatura** (It.), **Intabulierung** (Ger.) an arrangement written in TABLATURE of a vocal work for a keyboard or plucked string instrument.

Intégrales [ɛ̃-tā'gräl] (Fr.) work for small orchestra and percussion (1925) by Varèse.

Interlochen Arts Academy an important summer training program for young musicians est. in 1928 in Interlochen, MI, as the National Music Camp. It became affiliated with the U. of Michigan in 1941.

interlude a short work played between sections of a larger musical work or of a play or other nonmusical event. In a concert work, an interlude usu. provides a transition between movements. In a dramatic work such as an opera, interludes are usu. instrumental works covering the time required for a scene change, or they may be provided to suggest an action not easily represented on stage (such as a storm) or to comment on an action or situation. See INTERMEZZO, ENTR'ACTE.

intermède [ɛ̃-ter'med] (Fr.) a short entertainment, usu. combining music and dance, inserted between the acts of a French opera or play. It may or may not have any relationship with the story of the principal work. Cf. INTERMEDIO, INTERMEZZO.

intermedio [ēn-ter'mä-dyō] (It.) an entertainment, usu. combining music and dance, inserted between the acts of Italian plays during the Renaissance and of Italian operas in the early 17th c. Early *intermedii* were sometimes comprised of instrumental music played out of sight of the audience but later were often very lavish dramatic spectacles. They were one of the principal precursors of opera. Cf. INTERMEZZO.

intermezzo 1, a short, usu. light, composition played between the acts of an opera or ballet; esp., in the 18th c., a comic interlude performed between the acts of an opera seria. **2,** a short movement coming between major sections of an extended instrumental work. **3,** a short instrumental composition, often for solo piano.

Intermezzo comic opera in 2 acts by R. Strauss to his own libretto. Premiere, Dresden 1924. A conductor and his wife experience domestic difficulties when she finds a misdirected love letter from a servant.

Internationale, L' [lɛ̃-ter-nä-syō'näl] (Fr.) a revolutionary song with music by Pierre Degeyter (1848–1932) and words by Eugène Pottier (1816–87). The text was written in 1871 in Paris; the music was added in about 1888. The song was the official anthem of the Soviet Union from 1917 to 1944.

International Composers' Guild an organization founded in 1921 in New York by Edgard Varèse and Carlos Salzedo to support performance of contemporary music. It was disbanded in 1927.

International Folk Music Council an organization founded in 1947 in London to further the study and preservation of folk music and dance. Its presidents have included Vaughan Williams, Jaap Kunst, Kodály and Willard Rhodes.

International Music Council an organization created by UNESCO in 1949 to support musical research, composition and performance throughout the world.

International Musicological Society an organization founded in 1927 in Basle, Switzerland, to promote the historical and theoretical study of music. Abbr., *IMS*. Cf. AMS.

International Society for Contemporary Music an organization founded in 1922 to promote contemporary music. Abbr., *ISCM*.

interpretation the individual decisions required of a performer to resolve questions of performance not clearly determined by notation. The decisions can include dynamic level, tempo, articulation and *rubato* and are strongly influenced by contemporary stylistic preferences and performance practices. In performing music of earlier periods, intelligent interpretation requires research into current knowledge of the PERFOR-

MANCE PRACTICE of the period in question.

interrupted cadence DECEPTIVE CADENCE.

interval the distance between two pitches, considered a *harmonic* interval when between two pitches sounded simultaneously and a *melodic* interval when between two successive pitches.

The most common method of naming intervals is based on the diatonic scale, whether or not the prevailing context is diatonic. Thus the distance between C and D (ascending) is a second, between C and F a fourth, and so on. Interval names may be qualified by the modifiers MAJOR, MINOR, PERFECT, DIMINISHED and AUGMENTED. This system is based on the half-tone chromatic scale, and there is no standardized naming system in Western music for smaller divisions of the octave. Two intervals which, when combined, make up an octave are said to be *inversions* of each other (such as the perfect fourth and perfect fifth). Intervals wider than an octave are described as *compound intervals*

Intervals

(such as the thirteenth, an octave wider than a sixth).

Intervals can also be defined according to the ratio of their frequencies. Thus, an octave is in a ratio of 2:1, the fifth 3:2, the fourth 4:3, etc. These ratios are ideals and may or may not be encountered in actual practice, depending on the system of TUNING in use. In the tempered scale (see TEMPERAMENT), none of the intervals is "pure" with respect to its ratios except the octave.

The application of set theory (see SET) to the naming and manipulating of intervals has resulted in a description of the relationships between one PITCH CLASS and another. Still considering the octave as divided into twelve semitones, the distance between the pitch class C and the pitch class D, written (C, D), forms an *interval class* of two semitones. The inverse of the interval (D, C) is an interval class of 10 semitones. In an alternate method, the pitch succession (C, D) forms an interval class of 2 semitones, but the descending interval succession (D, C) forms an interval class of −2 semitones (the minus sign indicating a descending interval). The absolute interval class of the two intervals, i.e., ignoring the direction, would be the same. The set-theory approach to intervals allows certain kinds of analysis to be performed both on the nontonal music of today and on earlier music, revealing in some cases relationships more difficult to demonstrate by earlier methods.

In the Steppes of Central Asia (Russ., *V srednei Azii*) popular title for an orchestral tone poem (1880) by Borodin, which depicts the passage of a caravan. The work was composed as accompaniment for a tableau vivant.

Intimate Letters (Czech, *Listy dů věné*) the String Quartet No. 2 (1928) by Janáček.

intonation 1, the initial melodic phrase of a chant, usu. sung by the priest or cantor before the choir or people begin to sing. See PLAIN-

CHANT. **2,** a term used to describe the relationship between the pitch of a singer or instrumentalist and a reference pitch. The performer is said to be *on pitch* or *in tune* (and therefore have good intonation) if the two tones correspond, and *flat* or *sharp* (bad intonation) if the performer's pitch is respectively lower or higher than the reference. Cf. JUST INTONATION, TUNING.

intonazione [ēn-tō-nä′tsyō-nä] (It.) a short 17th- or 18th-c. prelude similar to a TOCCATA played in a church service before a vocal work to establish its tonality.

intrada [ēn′trä-dä] (It.) an INTRODUCTION or PRELUDE in 16th- and 17th-c. instrumental music. Also, *entrée* (Fr.), *entrada* (Sp.).

introduction an opening section, usu. slow, often found at the beginning of a symphony, sonata, quartet, etc. It is sometimes, but not always, related thematically to the rest of the work.

introit 1, the first chant of the Proper of the Mass, consisting of an antiphon followed by a verse and the Gloria Patri. The verse and Gloria Patri are sung to the same melodic formula, of which there are eight, one for each ecclesiastical mode. **2,** an instrumental work replacing all or part of the sung introit.

invention a short, imitative instrumental composition, usu. for keyboard. The most familiar examples are the 15 two-part works by J.S. Bach, which he called *Inventio.* (The three-part works usu. published with them were called *sinfonia*s by Bach, though they are often referred to as inventions.) Cf. RICERCAR.

inversion 1, (of an interval) the lowering of the upper or the raising of the lower tone by an octave. **2,** (of a chord) the shifting of the root tone to a position other than the lowest in the chord. **3,** the repetition of a melody with ascending intervals converted to corresponding descending intervals and vice versa. See COUNTERPOINT. **4,** the transposition (switching) of an upper and a lower part. **5,** *also,* **inverted pedal** the shift of a PEDAL TONE from the bass to an upper or intermediate part.

inverted mordent an ambiguous term referring either to an upper or lower MORDENT.

invertible counterpoint a technique for constructing a polyphonic texture in which the parts may be arranged in any vertical order by inverting the intervals between the parts. Invertible counterpoint in two, three or four parts is often called *double, triple* or *quadruple counterpoint,* respectively. The most common interval for inversion is the octave, but other intervals, such as the tenth, are found as well. The difficulty inherent in the technique is that the rules of consonance and voice-leading must be observed in both the original and inverted state(s). See COUNTERPOINT.

Invitation to the Dance (Ger., *Aufforderung zum Tanz*) piano piece, Op. 65 (1819), by Weber, consisting of an introduction, a dance and a coda. The work was orchestrated in 1841 by Berlioz (as *L'invitation à la valse*) and later by the conductor Felix Weingartner.

invitatory the opening chant of MATINS in the Divine Office.

Ioannidis, Yannis (1930–) Greek composer, trained at the Athens Conservatory and the Vienna Academy of Music. He became a Venezuelan citizen in 1968 and has taught at the Caracas Conservatory and Caracas U. He founded the Caracas Chamber Orchestra in 1971 but returned to Athens in 1976. His works incl. *Figuras* for string orch., *Metaplassis A* and *B* for orchestra, instrumental chamber music and choral works.

Iolanta opera in 1 act by Tchaikovsky to a libretto by his brother Modest, based on the Danish story "Kong Renés Datter" by Henrik Hertz. Premiere, St. Petersburg 1892. The opera was intended as a companion piece for the ballet *Nutcracker.* Iolanta, blind from birth but unaware of it, is

cured by faith and her love for Vau-
démont.

Iolanthe operetta in 2 acts by Sullivan to a libretto by W.S. Gilbert. Premiere, London and New York 1882.
A satire on British politics in which
the entire House of Lords must be
turned into fairies so that Strephon,
a half-mortal and half-fairy, can
marry a shepherdess.

ionian mode the authentic MODE on
C, identical to the MAJOR mode.

Ionisation [ē-ō-nē-zä'syō] (Fr.) work
for percussion and sirens (1931) by
Varèse.

Iphigenia in Aulis (Fr., *Iphigénie en
Aulide*) classical opera in 3 acts by
Gluck to a libretto in French by Bailli
du Roullet based on a drama by Racine. Premiere, Paris 1774. Iphigenia
is destined for sacrifice by her father
Agamemnon but is saved by the goddess Diana to serve as her priestess.

Iphigenia in Brooklyn musical parody (1965) by P.D.Q. Bach (Peter
Schickele) of the operas of Gluck and
of Classical and Baroque opera in general.

Iphigenia in Tauris (Fr., *Iphigénie in
Tauride*) classical opera in 4 acts by
Gluck to a libretto in French by Fran-
çois Guillard, based on the drama by
Euripides. Premiere, Paris 1779. In
this sequel to *Iphigénie in Aulide*,
Iphigenia learns of the death of her
father and saves Orestes from sacri-
fice at the hands of Thoas, King of
Scythia.

Ippolitov-Ivanov, Mikhail (1859–
1935) Russian composer, teacher and
conductor, trained at the St. Petersburg Conservatory. He taught at the
Academy of Music in Tbilisi and,
from 1893, at the Moscow Conservatory. He conducted frequently at
the Mamontov Opera and the Bolshoi
Theater and was conductor of the
Russian Choral Society from 1895 to
1901. He wrote 7 operas, *Caucasian
Sketches* for orchestra, choral works,
instrumental chamber music and
songs.

IRCAM *abbr.* INSTITUT DE RECHER-
CHE ET DE COORDINATION ACOUS-
TIQUE/MUSIQUE.

Irene musical by Harry Tierney, lyrics by Joseph McCarthy, book by
James Montgomery, based on his play
Irene O'Dare. Premiere, New York
1919 (revival 1973). A Cinderella
story about a poor New York girl who
ends up with a Long Island millionaire.

Irish harp a type of diatonic HARP
used in Ireland until the 19th c., having a soundbox made of a hollowed
piece of willow. See CLÀRSACH.

Irish jig a solo dance involving elaborate movements of the feet, with the
body and arms relatively stationary.
It is danced to a tune called a PORT
(2,), usu. in 6/8 time (*single* or *double
jig*) or 9/8 time (*slip* or *hop jig*).

Irma La Douce musical by Marguerite Monnot, lyrics and book by Julian
More, Monty Norman and David Heneker, based on a French show. Premiere, London 1958. The prostitute
Irma is wooed by Nestor, a poor student who masquerades as a rich man.

Irwin, May (Campbell, Ada May)
(1862–1938) Canadian-born Amer.
singer and actress in vaudeville and
on Broadway, infamous for her rendition of COON SONGS in Afro.-Amer.
dialect.

Isaac, Heinrich (Arrigo d'Ugo)
(c1450–1517) Flemish composer of
masses, motets and other sacred and
secular vocal music, in the service of
the Medici in Florence from 1484 to
1493 and of the Emperor Maximilian
I from 1497 until his death, spending
much of that time in Italy. He was
highly esteemed as a singer and as a
composer.

Isabella Leonarda (1620–1704) Italian composer, abbess of the convent
at Novara where she composed and
published motets, masses and other
sacred vocal music.

ISCM *abbr.* INTERNATIONAL SOCIETY
FOR CONTEMPORARY MUSIC.

Iseler, Elmer (1927–) Canadian
conductor and editor, founder of the
Festival Singers of Canada and the Elmer Iseler Singers, important profes-

sional vocal ensembles that have performed throughout Canada, Europe and the U.S. He became conductor of the Toronto Mendelssohn Choir in 1963. In both capacities he has been a strong supporter of Canadian music and has initiated many commissions.

Isle of the Dead, The (Russ., *Ostrov myortvïkh*) symphonic poem (1909) by Rachmaninov, inspired by a painting by Arnold Böcklin. The work is written largely in ⅝ meter.

isometric a term designating compositions in which all voices move in approximately the same rhythm, as in works in strict chordal style (see FAMILIAR STYLE).

isorhythm a term coined in the early 20th c. to refer to the use in the motets of the 14th and 15th c. of a single rhythmic pattern (see TALEA), repeated throughout a vocal work in one voice (usu. the tenor). Examples of the technique can be found in the works of Machaut, de Vitry and Dunstable.

Israel in Egypt oratorio (1739) by Handel based on a text from the Book of Exodus.

Israel Philharmonic Orchestra orch. founded in 1936 in Tel Aviv (orig. called The Palestine Symphony).

Israel Symphony symphony in 3 movements with soloists and chorus (1916) by Bloch. The first two movements together make Part One, devoted to Yom Kippur. The third movement is devoted to the feast of Succoth.

istesso tempo, 1' (It., in the same tempo) a direction to continue at the same tempo despite changes of meter or note value. Also, *medesimo tempo*.

Istomin, Eugene (1925–) Amer. pianist, stud. of Rudolf Serkin. He has had an active international solo career, but is probably best known for his chamber music playing, esp. with the Busch Chamber Players and in trio with violinist Isaac Stern and cellist Leonard Rose.

Italiana in Algieri, L' (It.) ITALIAN GIRL IN ALGIERS, THE.

Italian Concerto a work in F major in three movements for harpsichord solo (1735) by J.S. Bach, published as the 2nd part of his CLAVIERÜBUNG. It imitates the style and contrasts of the contemporary Italian orchestral concerto by use of the two harpsichord manuals.

Italian Girl in Algiers (It., *L'Italiana in Algieri*) comic opera in 2 acts by Rossini to a libretto by Angelo Anelli. Premiere, Venice 1813. Isabella, the chosen Italian new wife for Mustapha, the Bey of Algeria, is saved from the harem by Lindoro, and Mustapha returns to his first wife Elvira.

Italian overture a type of instrumental introduction found in Italian opera and oratorio of the 18th c. It was normally in three movements (fast-slow-fast) and was a precursor of the classical symphony. Cf. FRENCH OVERTURE.

Italian Quartet see QUARTETTO ITALIANO.

Italian Serenade a work in one movement for string quartet (1887) by Hugo Wolf, subsequently (1892) arranged by the composer for small orchestra.

Italian sixth an AUGMENTED SIXTH CHORD consisting of root tone, major third and augmented sixth. Cf. GERMAN SIXTH, FRENCH SIXTH, TRISTAN CHORD.

Italian Songbook see ITALIENISCHES LIEDERBUCH.

Italian Symphony the Symphony No. 4 in A major, Op. 90 (1833), by Mendelssohn, inspired by a trip to Italy. The last movement is a SALTARELLO.

Italienisches Liederbuch (Ger., Italian Songbook) settings (1890–6) by Hugo Wolf of 46 anonymous Italian poems in German translation by Paul Heyse.

Iturbi, José (1895–1980) Spanish conductor and pianist, trained at the Valencia Conservatory and the Paris Conservatoire. He taught at the Geneva Conservatory until 1923, then toured extensively, settling in the U.S. in 1929. He was conductor of the Rochester PO from 1936 to 1944 and appeared in a number of films.

Ivan Susanin opera in 4 acts and an epilogue by Glinka to a libretto by Georgy Fyodorovich Rozen. Premiere, St. Petersburg 1836. In 1612 a Russian, Susanin, is hired by the Polish forces to lead their march on Russia, which he successfully sabotages. The opera was originally produced under the title *A Life for the Tsar*.

Ives, Burl (1909–) Amer. folksinger. He has performed and promoted folk music in all media. He hosted a radio program, "The Wayfaring Stranger" (1940–2), appeared on Broadway in *Sing Out, Sweet Land* (1945), has made many recordings and compiled several collections of folksongs. He also appeared in a number of films in the late 1950s.

Ives, Charles (Edward) (1874–1954) Amer. composer. He studied with his father, **George Ives** (1845–94), who was an inventive instrumentalist, bandmaster and teacher. He also studied with Cornelius Griggs and Horatio Parker at Yale. He was from the beginning an experimenter, esp. in his combining of apparently disparate musical materials. In 1899 he joined the Mutual Insurance Co., working during the day and composing at night. He was organist at First Presbyterian Church in Bloomfield, NJ, and then at Central Presbyterian Church in New York. His courtship of Harmony Twitchell—who supplied many of his song texts—inspired him to create a wealth of works, incl. the *Three-page Sonata* (1905), the *Set for Theatre Orchestra* (1906), and his best-known work, *The Unanswered Question* (1906). The next decade produced the *Concord Sonata*, *The Fourth of July*, *Three Places in New England* and the monumental *Fourth Symphony*. He continued throughout his composing career to write songs, which display an astonishing breadth of styles and moods. Ives stopped composing in 1926, only revising and finishing earlier works after that time, and retired from his insurance work in 1930. He won the Pulitzer Prize in 1947 for his Third Symphony. His works incl. 4 symphonies, works for theater orchestra, 4 violin sonatas, piano works, choral works (*Harvest Home Chorales*, psalm settings), songs (*Charlie Rutlage, Watchman, The Children's Hour, Tom Sails Away, The Housatonic at Stockbridge*, etc.).

ivories slang term for the piano keys and, by extension, the piano.

Izenzon, David (1932–79) Amer. jazz bassist and composer, best known for his work in avant-garde jazz, esp. with the Ornette Coleman trio. He also led his own quintet in New York in the 1960s. In the 1970s he became a psychotherapist.

J

Jaches de Wert WERT, GIACHES DE.

jack an upright wooden piece in any of several keyboard instruments, incl. the harpsichord, which transmits the action of the key to the string by means of a plectrum or hammer.

Jackson, George K(nowil) (1757–1822) English-born Amer. composer and teacher, stud. of James Nares. He came to the U.S. about 1795, worked in New York from 1801 to 1812, then moved to Boston, where he was active as a performer, teacher, composer, music seller and as a consultant to the HANDEL AND HAYDN SOCIETY.

Jackson, George Pullen (1874–1953) Amer. folk-song scholar and teacher, educated at Vanderbilt U., the U. of Chicago and elsewhere. He taught at Vanderbilt from 1918 and founded the Nashville SO in 1920. He studied the music of the large southern singing groups, which he published in several collections.

Jackson, Isaiah (Allen) (1945–) Amer. conductor, trained at the Juilliard School and with Boulanger in Paris. He has been assoc. conductor of the Rochester PO and music dir. of the Flint (MI) SO. He has also con-ducted the Vienna SO, the Toronto SO and the Royal Ballet at Covent Garden.

Jackson, Judge (1883–1958) Amer. composer and tunebook compiler. He composed many shape-note hymns, which he published in *The Colored Sacred Harp* (1934), the first new collection in shape notation published in the 20th c.

Jackson, Mahalia (1911–72) Amer. gospel singer. She came to Chicago in 1927 and sang with the Greater Salem Baptist Church choir and toured with the Johnson Gospel Singers. From the mid-1930s she toured with Thomas A. Dorsey, singing and promoting his songs. She sang at the inauguration of President John F. Kennedy in 1961.

Jackson, Michael (Joe) (1958–) Amer. rock singer and songwriter, member of the Jackson 5, a highly successful black pop soul vocal group. He has concentrated on solo work since 1979. His album *Thriller* (produced by Quincy Jones) sold over 30 million copies.

Jackson, Milt(on) ("Bags") (1923–) Amer. bop jazz vibraphonist and composer. He began as a member of Dizzy Gillespie's sextet, then, in 1951, founded the Milt Jackson Quartet, which a year later became the innovative MODERN JAZZ QUARTET. He is noted as the creator of a legato, arioso style on the vibraphone.

Jacob, Gordon (Percival Septimus) (1895–1984) English composer and teacher, stud. of Stanford and Howells. From 1926 to his retirement in 1966 he taught at the Royal College of Music, where his pupils included Imogen Holst and Malcolm Arnold. He wrote several books on instrumentation and edited the Penguin scores series. His works incl. sym-

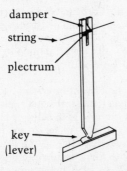

damper
string
plectrum
key
(lever)

harpsichord jack

phonies, concertos for various instruments, songs and instrumental chamber music.

Jacob de Senleches (fl. 1378–95) French composer and shawm player, best known for his composition in the intricate, complicated style of the ARS SUBTILIOR. His works incl. ballades and virelais (esp. *La harpe de mélodie*).

Jacobi, Frederick (1891–1952) Amer. composer and conductor, stud. of Rubin Goldmark, Bloch and Paul Juon. He was assistant conductor at the Metropolitan Opera (1913–17), then moved west to study American Indian music (his First String Quartet and several other works are based on Indian themes). He taught at the master School of United Arts in New York and at the Juilliard School. His works incl. *The Prodigal Son* (opera), Jewish service music, orchestral works (2 symphonies, cello concerto), instrumental chamber music, songs and solo piano music.

Jacobs, Paul (1930–83) Amer. pianist and harpsichordist, trained with Ernest Hutcheson and at the Juilliard School. He performed with the Composers' Forum in New York, the Domaine Musical in Paris and the Darmstadt and Dartington schools. He became pianist for the New York PO in 1962 and their harpsichordist in 1974 and taught at Brooklyn College. He was particularly noted for his performance of 20th-c. music and appeared frequently in duo with pianist URSULA OPPENS.

Jacob's Dream popular name for the second movement of the Piano Trio in E♭ minor (1795) by Haydn, possibly orig. a separate work.

Jacopo da Bologna (fl. 1340–60) Italian composer and theorist. He served at the Visconti court in Milan, then at the La Scala court in Verona, then once again in Milan. Of his music, a number of madrigals have survived, as well as a 3-voice motet and a theoretical work on mensurated melody.

Jacques, (Thomas) Reginald (1894–

1969) English organist and composer, trained at Queen's College, Oxford, where he became organist and dir. of music in 1926. He was conductor of the Oxford Orchestral Society from 1930 to 1936 and of the London Bach Choir for thirty years and was founder of the Jacques Orch. in 1936. He was coeditor with David Willcocks of the *Carols for Choirs* collections.

Jacques de Liège (?1260–?1330) Flemish music theorist, author of the treatise *Speculum musicae*, the largest surviving medieval treatise on music.

Jacquet, Illinois (Jean-Baptiste) [zhä′ket] (1922–) Amer. jazz tenor saxophonist and bassoonist. He played with Lionel Hampton, Cab Calloway and Count Basie, toured with Norman Granz's Jazz at the Philharmonic and from the late 1940s led his own groups.

Jacquet de la Guerre, Elisabeth-Claude [zhä′kä də lä ger] (?1666–1729) French composer and harpsichordist. A child prodigy, she was watched over by Louis XIV. After 1704 she gave a series of concerts in her home and performed at the Théâtre de la Foire. Her works incl. *Cephale et Procris* (opera), cantatas, songs, harpsichord works and sonatas for violin and viola da gamba.

Jacquet of Mantua (Colebault, Jacques) (1483–1559) French composer and singer. He served at the Este court in Ferrara, then settled in Mantua, where he became *maestro di cappella* of the Cathedral of SS. Peter and Paul. Despite his noble patronage, he died in debt. His surviving works are nearly all sacred, comprising motets and Mass-settings, esp. PARODY Masses.

Jagdmusik [′yäkt-moo″zēk] (Ger., hunt music) musical signals relating to the hunt, esp. horn calls, or music imitating these sounds. Cf. JIRKING.

Jagel, Frederick (1897–1982) Amer. tenor with the Metropolitan Opera from 1927 to 1950 and at other leading houses in the U.S. and S. America.

He later taught at the New England Conservatory.

Jagger, Mick (Michael Phillip) (1943–) English rock singer, lead vocalist of the ROLLING STONES.

Jahreszeiten, Die (Ger.) ['yä-res"tsī-tən, dē] SEASONS, THE.

jale ['yä-lä] (Ger.) a method of solmization introduced in Germany in 1959, using the syllables *ja, le, mi, ni, ro, su, wa, ja* to represent the ascending degrees of the major scale. The repeated vowels occur at the semitones. Chromatic semitones are similarly handled.

jaltarang an Indian form of MUSICAL GLASSES employing porcelain bowls filled with water and beaten with bamboo sticks.

jam to improvise on an instrument with a group, esp. outside of one's regular job. See JAM SESSION.

Jamaica musical by Harold Arlen, lyrics by E.Y. Harburg. Premiere, New York 1957. The show was a vehicle for LENA HORNE, one of her relatively few Broadway appearances.

Jamal, Ahmad (Jones, Fritz) (1930–) influential Amer. jazz pianist. He formed his first group in about 1949 and has since toured and recorded with various of his own ensembles, usu. a trio or quartet.

James, Dorothy (1901–82) Amer. composer and teacher, stud. of Hanson, Willan and Krenek, among others. She taught at Eastern Michigan U. (1929–69) and wrote music criticism for the *Ypsilanti Press.* Her works incl. *Paolo and Francesca* (opera), many choral works and songs and instrumental chamber music.

James (Hawkins), **Etta** (c1938–) Amer. soul singer, best known as a concert artist in duo with Johnny Otis and on her own in singles incl. "All I Could Do Was Cry" (1960).

James, Harry (**Haag**) (1916–83) Amer. jazz trumpeter and bandleader, stud. of Everett James. He played with Ben Pollack in 1936 and with Benny Goodman (1937–8), then formed his own highly successful band, whose popularity dipped briefly in the bop era, but rebounded in the 1960s and early 1970s. James was a supreme trumpet virtuoso, recording a series of *tours de force* in the early 1940s, incl. "Carnival of Venice" and "Trumpet Rhapsody."

James, Philip (**Frederick Wright**) (1890–1975) Amer. composer and conductor, stud. of Goldmark and Herbert, among others. He began as a choir dir. and organist, then taught at New York U. and Columbia. He conducted the Victor Herbert Opera Company and was involved in the founding of the New Jersey SO, which he conducted until 1929. He was also conductor of the Brooklyn Orchestral Society (1927–30) and the Bamberger Little Symphony (1929–36). His works incl. 2 symphonies, works for small orchestra, symphonic poems, choral cantatas and instrumental chamber music.

jam session a group improvisation session, esp. in jazz. Such sessions have become rarer, in part as a result of the decreasing reliance on standard tunes as a basis for improvisation. See JAM.

Janáček, Leoš (Leo Eugen) ['yä-nə-chek, 'lä-osh] (1854–1928) Czech composer, trained with Pavel Křižkovský, at the Czech Teachers' Institute and at the Prague and Vienna conservatories. He founded an organ school in Brno, which he directed from 1881. In the late 1880s he began writing opera, the form for which he is now best known. His third opera, *Jenůfa* (1904), completed when the composer was 50, showed the results of the development of his theory of "speech-melody." From 1908 to 1916, he produced a number of chamber and vocal works, then *Jenůfa* was performed at the Prague National Opera and Janáček became internationally known and published. In the late 1920s he retired from the organ school and taught classes in Brno for Prague U. At the time of his death he was working on his last opera, *From the House of the Dead.* His works incl. *Jenůfa, Kátya Kabanová, The*

Cunning Little Vixen, The Makropulos Affair, From the House of the Dead and 6 other operas, incidental music, a folk ballet, choral works and cantatas (incl. the *Glagolitic Mass*), orchestral works (incl. *Taras Bulba, Sinfonietta*) chamber music (incl. 2 string quartets, violin sonata), solo piano music and folk-song arrangements.

Janáček String Quartet Czech quartet formed in 1947 in Brno. In addition to the quartets of Janáček the quartet plays a wide repertory of classic and modern works, which they perform from memory.

Janequin, Clément ['yä-nə-kē, klā'mä] (?1485–1558) French composer. During his career he held a series of minor posts in Angers, Paris and elsewhere, but never maintained a regular position with a cathedral or a court. His surviving output is almost entirely secular "Parisian" chansons, of which the best known are the programmatic chansons "Le chant des oiseaux," "Les cris de Paris" and "La bataille."

Janigro, Antonio (1918–89) Italian cellist and conductor, stud. of Alexanian and Casals. He taught at the Zagreb Conservatory until 1953, when he became conductor of the Zagreb Radio SO and formed the Solisti di Zagreb. He also taught at the Düsseldorf Conservatory and was conductor of the Orch. dell'Angelicum in Milan and of the Saar Radio Chamber Orch.

Janis (Yanks), **Byron** (1928–) Amer. pianist, stud. of Adele Marcus, Joseph and Rosina Lhévinne and Horowitz. He is best known for his performances of Russian repertory.

janissary music *also*, **janizary music** **1,** military band music modeled on Turkish military bands, featuring fifes, oboes, drums, cymbals, triangles and Turkish crescents. (A Janissary was a member of an elite corps of Turkish troops established in the 14th c. as the Sultan's guard and abolished in the early 19th c.) **2,** orchestral music imitating this sound, very popular in the 18th c. (as in Mozart's *The Abduction from the Seraglio*).

Janko keyboard a piano keyboard invented in 1882 by Hungarian engineer and musician Paul von Janko (1856–1919). The keyboard has 6 rows of keys with three keys to each note, with each row offset at wholestep intervals. The advantages of the system are that all major and minor scales are fingered alike and the octave span is much shorter than on a conventional keyboard. The system also compensates for the unequal lengths of the fingers.

Jannequin, Clément JANEQUIN, CLÉMENT.

Janowitz, Gundula (1939–) German soprano, trained at the Styrian Conservatory at Graz. She has sung at the Vienna Staatsoper, Bayreuth, the Salzburg Festival and other major European houses. Her roles incl. the Countess (*The Marriage of Figaro*), the Empress (*Die Frau ohne Schatten*) and Donna Anna (*Don Giovanni*).

Janowski, Marek (1940–) Polish conductor, trained in Cologne and Siena. He has been associated with the Deutsche Oper in Berlin, the Munich Staatsoper and the Dresden Staatskapelle and has conducted at the Metropolitan Opera, Chicago Lyric Opera and San Francisco Opera and throughout Europe. He has been music dir. in Freiburg, Dortmund and Cologne.

Janssen, Werner (1899–) Amer. conductor and composer, stud. of Converse, Chadwick, Weingartner, Scherchen and Respighi. He was invited to become the first Amer. conductor of the New York PO and has been music dir. of the Baltimore SO (1937–39), the Janssen SO in Los Angeles (1940–52), the Portland SO (1947–9) and the San Diego SO (1952–4). He composed music for the Ziegfeld Follies and other revues, as well as for more than 45 films. Many of his works incorporate jazz elements.

Jaques-Dalcroze, Emile (1865–1950) Swiss teacher and composer, stud. of

Fauré, Delibes, Bruckner and Fuchs. He is famous for the development of *eurythmics*, a system of "rhythmic gymnastics" for coordinating music and body movement in teaching the fundamentals of music.

jarabé [khä-rä′bā] (Sp.) a Lat. Amer. dance in quick ⁶⁄₈ or ¾ meter, dating from the late colonial period.

jarana [khä′rä-nä] (Sp.) **1**, a type of song and dance indigenous to the Yucatán peninsula of Mexico. **2**, a type of GUITAR having five double courses of strings.

Jarboro, Caterina (1903–86) Amer. soprano, trained in Paris and Milan, the first Afr.-Amer. to appear with an Amer. opera company (Chicago Opera Co. in 1933).

Jarman, Joseph (1937–) Amer. jazz woodwind player, vocalist and percussionist. In Chicago he performed with the AACM from 1965 and joined the AEC in 1969.

Jarnach, Philipp (1892–1982) French-born German composer, stud. of Albert Lavignac in Paris. He is best known for his work with the music of Ferruccio Busoni, for whom he prepared several vocal scores and whose *Doktor Faustus* he completed after the composer's death.

Jarre, Maurice (1924–) French percussionist and composer, stud. of Honegger. He was dir. of music for the Théâtre National Populaire in Paris and his ballet *Notre Dame de Paris* was successful at the Paris Opéra in 1964. He has written many film scores and received Oscars for his music for *Lawrence of Arabia* (1963) and "Lara's Song" from *Doctor Zhivago* (1965).

Jarrett, Keith (1945–) Amer. jazz pianist, composer and soprano saxophonist. After an early start as a child prodigy, he joined Art Blakey's JAZZ MESSENGERS in 1965 and the Charles Lloyd quartet the following year. In 1969 he formed his own trio and also worked with Miles Davis. He is one of the most influential jazz pianists of the 1980s. He has also produced totally composed music, incl. *The Celestial Hawk* for piano and orchestra. He is perhaps best known for his concerto-length improvised piano works.

JATP JAZZ AT THE PHILHARMONIC.

jawbone a beaten RATTLE of African origin, orig. the jawbone and teeth of a mule. Also, *quijada*. Cf. VIBRA-SLAP.

Jay and the Americans Amer. rock vocal quintet formed in Brooklyn in 1961, whose hits incl. "Come a Little Bit Closer" (1964) and "Cara Mia" (1965, 1980). They disbanded in 1970.

jazz a complex art form derived from certain folk, African and slave music (such as field hollers and work songs) influenced by contact with Western functional harmony (as exemplified in the SHAPE-NOTE hymns of the early 19th c. and the music of the brass and army bands found on plantations and in the cities). The characteristics of the form (none of which are invariably present) are improvisation, a regular metrical pulse, use of the BLUE-NOTES and the small modifications of the regular pulse known as SWING (2,).

Jazz has evolved over the years through a number of stages, beginning in the late 19th c. with RAGTIME and BLUES. The late 1910s saw the development of the so-called NEW ORLEANS JAZZ style, sometimes called DIXIELAND. This was essentially a group improvisation effort, with more emphasis placed on the ensemble than on the individual performer. Jazz for larger orchestra (big band) was also developed during this period, but its heyday came later, in the 1930s, with the development of SWING. The 1940s were dominated by BOP, whereas the 1950s countered with COOL JAZZ and WEST COAST JAZZ and the earthier HARD BOP. The avant-garde movement of the 1960s and 1970s produced FREE JAZZ and FUSION (jazz-rock), as well as THIRD STREAM (first theorized in the 1950s), an attempted synthesis of jazz and classical art music. In the 1980s there has been a return by some players to the roots of jazz (Dixieland and Swing).

Jazz at the Philharmonic orig. the name of a benefit concert organized by Norman Granz and held in Los Angeles in 1944. From 1946 to 1957 the name was used for a national (later international) tour of jazz all-stars under Granz's sponsorship. Many of the concerts were recorded for later release. Abbr., *JATP*.

jazz band a group of instruments assembled to play jazz music, usu. consisting of one or more solo instruments (most common are saxophone, trumpet, clarinet or trombone), combined with a rhythm section consisting of piano, plucked double bass, guitar or banjo and traps.

jazz eighths eighth notes as commonly played in jazz, i.e., with a swing rhythm, the first note longer and more heavily stressed than the second. This style is conventional and is not shown in the notation.

jazzbo a makeshift jazz instrument of the 1930s consisting of a kazoo inserted in the body of another instrument, such as a trombone or saxophone, to provide resonance.

Jazz Messengers, The a cooperative formed in 1954 by Art Blakey, Horace Silver and others which, despite frequent changes in personnel (except for Blakey), has remained the principal representative of the style usu. known as HARD BOP. The group has been important as a training ground for young jazz musicians.

jazz-rock see FUSION.

Jazz Workshop an experimental jazz ensemble of varying personnel and size organized by CHARLES MINGUS in the mid-1950s.

Jeanie with the Light Brown Hair song by Stephen C. Foster. The "Jeanie" of the title refers to Foster's wife, Jane McDowell.

Jeanne d'Arc au bûcher [zhän därk ō bü'shä] (Fr., Joan of Arc at the Stake) oratorio (1938) by Arthur Honegger to a text by Paul Claudel. Some of the parts (esp. Joan's) are spoken.

Jefferson, Blind Lemon (?1897–1930) Amer. blues singer and guitarist. He started as a street singer and sang with Huddie Ledbetter in Dallas. He moved to Chicago in 1925, where he made many recordings, establishing him as the most influential blues singer of his time.

Jefferson Airplane Amer. psychedelic rock band formed in 1965 in San Francisco, headed soon after its founding by vocalist Grace Slick. The group disbanded in 1972. An attempt at revival was made in 1974 under the name Jefferson Starship.

Jeffreys, George (?1610–85) English composer. He was organist to Charles I at Oxford during the English civil war, then steward to Sir Christopher Hatton at Kirby (1646–85). His works—which incl. Latin and English service music, sacred and secular songs, and some instrumental fantasias—represent a melding of the Italian declamatory style with earlier polyphonic techniques.

Jehan des Murs (c1300–c1350) French theorist and scientist, important for his highly influential writings on musical proportions and mensural notation.

Jelinek (Elin), **Hanns** (1901–69) Austrian composer and teacher, stud. of Schoenberg but largely self-taught. During most of his career he earned his living as a bandleader and composer of film scores. His works after 1933 are in the 12-note serial style, and he wrote a textbook on the technique.

Jenkins, Florence Foster (1868–1944) Amer. soprano and philanthropist, remembered for her concerts and recordings of vocal music, which demonstrated more enthusiasm than technical mastery.

Jenkins, John (1592–1678) English composer and instrumentalist. He was a theorbo player in the King's Musick after 1660 but was seldom actually at court. He is noted for his consort music, esp. for viols, and also wrote sacred and secular vocal works.

Jenkins, Newell (Owen) (1915–) Amer. conductor and musicologist, trained with Carl Orff and Jacques Barzun. He founded the Yale Opera Group in New Haven, the Piccola Accademia Musicale in Florence and the Clarion Concerts in New York.

Jenks, Stephen (1772–1856) Amer. composer and compiler. He published 10 collections of sacred music, incl. the *Delights of Harmony* (1803–6), and made drums and tambourines.

Jenůfa opera in 3 acts by Janáček to a libretto in Czech by the composer, based on a story by Gabriella Preissová. Premiere, Brno 1904. Laca is in love with Jenůfa, who is in love with Laca's brother Stewa.

Jephtha 1, oratorio (1650) by Carissimi with a text largely from the ninth chapter of Judges. **2**, oratorio (1752) by Handel to a libretto by Thomas Morell.

Jeremiah Symphony the Symphony No. 1 for mezzo-soprano and orchestra (1943) by Bernstein to a text from the Bible. Its three movements are entitled "Prophecy," "Profanation" and "Lamentation."

Jeremiáš, Otakar (1892–1962) Czech composer and conductor, trained at the Prague Conservatory. He was conductor of the Prague radio SO from 1929 and of the Prague National Theater from 1945. He was a prolific composer, esp. of vocal music, including an opera (1922–7) based on Dostoyevsky's *The Brothers Karamazov.*

Jeritza, Maria (Jedlitska, Marie) [ye′rĕ-tsä] (1887–1982) Czech soprano, trained at the Prague Conservatory. She joined the Vienna Volksoper in 1911 and the Staatsoper in 1912. Her Metropolitan Opera debut was in 1921 in Korngold's *Die tote Stadt;* she sang there regularly until 1933. Her roles incl. Jenůfa, Tosca, Ariadne and Sieglinde.

Jerome of Moravia (Hieronymus de Moravia) (fl. 1272–1304) music theorist and Dominican friar, author of the *Tractatus de musica*, one of the most important chant treatises of the Middle Ages.

Jessye, Eva (1895–) Amer. choral conductor and composer, the first Afr.-Amer. woman to gain international renown as a choral dir., trained at Western U. and Langston U. and with Will Cook and Goetschius. In the mid-1920s she formed the Original Dixie Jubilee Singers, which became the Eva Jessye Choir and toured widely and performed on radio. She was choral dir. for the operas *Porgy and Bess* and *Four Saints in Three Acts* and the film *Hallelujah* and has published many collections of choral works and spirituals.

Jesus, Joy of Man's Desiring (Ger., *Jesu, bleibet meine Freude*) a chorale from the church cantata No. 147, *Herz und Mund und Tat und Leben*, for trumpet, oboe, strings and organ (1723) by J.S. Bach. It is often heard in a piano transcription by MYRA HESS. The chorale melody is "Werde Munter" (1641) by Johann Schop.

Jesus Christ Superstar musical by Andrew Lloyd Webber, lyrics by Tim Rice, book by Tom O'Horgan, based on the New Testament. Premiere, New York 1971. Called a "rock opera," the work treats the last seven days of Christ.

jeté [zhə′tä] (Fr., thrown) a bouncing bowstroke, usu. from two to six ricochets, indicated by staccato dots and a slur. See BOWING.

Jeter-Pillars Orchestra a jazz orchestra formed in Ohio in 1934 by saxophonists James Jeter and Hayes Pillars, which provided an important training ground for a number of young musicians who later became famous, incl. Charlie Christian, Jimmy Blanton and Jo Jones.

Jethro Tull English progressive-rock band formed in 1968 by vocalist, flutist and guitarist Ian Anderson. The band combines elements of folk, classical and rock music.

jeu [zhø] (Fr.) ORGAN STOP.

Jeu de cartes [zhø də kärt] (Fr., Card Game) ballet in "3 deals" (1937) by Stravinsky to his own libretto, choreographed by George Balanchine.

Jeune, Claude le LE JEUNE, CLAUDE.

Jeune France, La [zhøn fräs] (Fr.) a

group of composers formed in Paris in 1936 by Daniel-Lesur, Messiaen, Jolivet and Baudrier in opposition to the then prevalent neoclassical movement.

Jeunehomme Concerto [zhø'nom] popular name for the Piano Concerto in E♭ major, K.271 (1777), by Mozart, named for the French pianist who played it in Salzburg.

Jeunesses Musicales [zhə'nes müzē'käl] (Fr., musical youth) an international organization founded in 1940 in Belgium to promote live music in schools and universities and among working youth.

Jeux [zhø] (Fr., Games) *poème dansée* (danced poem) (1912) by Debussy to a scenario by NIJINSKY, who also was the choreographer. The story involves a game of tennis.

Jeux d'eau [dō] (Fr., fountain) innovative and virtuoso piano work (1902) by Ravel.

Jeux d'enfants [dã'fã] (Fr., Children's Games) suite of 12 pieces for piano duet (1871) by Bizet. Some of the pieces were orchestrated by Bizet in 1873 as *Petite suite d'orchestre*. Others have been orchestrated by Karg-Elert and H. Finck.

jew's harp a lyre-shaped instrument of metal, bamboo, or other material, held between the teeth with a protruding metal tongue played by the finger to produce a variety of tones. The instrument is frequently used in bluegrass music. Also, *jew's trump.*

J. Geils Band see GEILS.

jig 1, one of several related British dances, all characterized by leaping. See HORNPIPE, IRISH JIG, MORRIS JIG, JIGG. See also GIGUE. **2**, Afr.-Amer. dancing.

Jig Fugue the Fugue in G major for organ, BWV 577, composer unknown,

formerly erroneously attributed to J.S. Bach.

jigg a type of entertainment of the mid-16th to mid-19th c. combining music, dance and drama in a short burlesque comedy for two to five characters sung to popular tunes and interspersed with dancing. The form probably originated in Great Britain but was soon popular on the Continent as well.

jim-jams HEEBIE-JEEBIES.

jingle a short rhymed lyric set to music and used in a commercial advertisement.

Jingle Bells song by James Pierpont (1822–93), first published in 1857, a perennial Christmas favorite.

jingles a cluster of small bells or other rattling objects, usu. arranged on a leather strap or a wooden handle or worn on the body, which are shaken to produce a tremolo or a rhythmic sound. Pitch is rarely specific. In orchestral use, jingles usu. are employed to imitate sleigh bells, etc. Cf. TURKISH CRESCENT.

jingling Johnny TURKISH CRESCENT.

Jirák, K(arel) B(oleslav) (1891–1972) Czech composer, stud. of Vítězslav Novák and Joseph Foerster. In the 1930s he toured as a conductor, promoting Czech music and headed the music department of Czech radio from 1930 to 1945. In 1947 he came to Chicago to teach at Roosevelt U., where he remained until his death. His works incl. *Žena a bů* (opera, The Woman and the God), 6 symphonies, choral works, string quartets, chamber music, instrumental sonatas, many songs and works for solo piano (esp. the cycle *Na rozhraní*, On the boundary).

jirking a 16th- and 17th-c. technique in natural horn playing of adding one or two neighboring overtones as grace notes to repeated-note calls. Also, *tayauté.*

jitterbug see LINDY.

jive 1, a style of 1940s Afr.-Amer. jazz characterized by a very easygoing swing and witty, sophisticated lyrics. **2**, a term sometimes used to

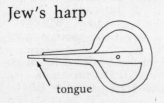

Jew's harp

tongue

refer to particularly "hot" jazz or to the dancing associated with it, such as the LINDY.

Joachim, Joseph (1831–1907) Austro-Hungarian violinist, conductor, composer and teacher, stud. of Joseph Böhm, Ferdinand David and Moritz Hauptmann. He was concertmaster under Liszt from 1850 to 1852, then violinist to King George V at Hannover. He moved to Berlin in 1868 to direct the Hochschule für Ausübende Tonkunst. He was a devoted supporter of the music of Brahms, which he performed as violinist and as conductor throughout Europe. His many works, principally concertos and string chamber music, are rarely performed today.

Joachim, Otto (1910–) German-born Canadian composer, viola player and teacher, trained in Düsseldorf and Cologne. From 1934 to 1949 he lived in the Far East, having fled the Nazi regime, then settled in Montreal. He founded the Montreal String Quartet and the Montreal Consort of Ancient Instruments and from 1956 taught at McGill U. and the Quebec Conservatory. He has worked both with aleatory and 12-tone serial techniques, sometimes combining the two, and he has also composed electronic works.

Joachim Quartet string quartet founded in Berlin in 1869 by JOSEPH JOACHIM. The group lasted until Joachim's death in 1907 and was esp. noted for its performances of the Viennese classics, in particular the late Beethoven quartets.

Jobert [zhō'ber] French music publishing firm founded in 1922 by Jean Jobert. Its catalogue includes many of the important works of Debussy.

Jobin, Raoul [zhō'bɛ̃] (1906–74) Canadian tenor, trained in Quebec and Paris. He sang at the Paris Opéra and Opéra-Comique from 1937 to 1957 and joined the Metropolitan Opera in 1939. After his retirement he taught in Canada. His son, **André Jobin** (1933–) is also an operatic tenor.

Jochum, Eugen ['yō-kəm, 'oi-gən] (1902–87) distinguished German conductor, stud. of Wolfgang von Waltershausen and Siegmund von Hausegger. He became musical dir. of the Berlin radio in 1932 and general music dir. of the Hamburg Staatsoper and Hamburg PO in 1934 and from 1949 headed the Bavarian Radio SO in Munich. He frequently conducted the Berlin PO, the Concertgebouw Orch. and at Bayreuth, as well as in the Americas.

jodel ['yō-dəl] (Ger.) YODEL.

Johannes de Garlandia (fl. c1240) music theorist, author of *De plana musica* and *De mensurabili musica*, two of the most significant treatises on early polyphonic music.

Johannes de Muris JEHAN DES MURS.

John Brown's Body song written in 1861, shortly after the attack on Fort Sumter. The BATTLE HYMN OF THE REPUBLIC is sung to the same tune. The John Brown of the title is not the antislavery crusader, but a sergeant at Fort Warren in Massachusetts.

John, Elton (Hercules) (Dwight, Reginald Keith) (1947–) English rock singer. His stage name was borrowed from an early band he worked with, and it later became his legal name. He worked for several years in collaboration with lyricist Bernard Taupin, producing many hit records. His Amer. debut was in 1970, and he made many successful tours in the 1970s.

Johnny Johnson anti-war musical by Weill, story by playwright Paul Green. Premiere, New York 1938. The story of an idealistic soldier who tries to put the military out of business with laughing gas.

John of Afflighem (Johannes Afflighemensis) (fl. c1100) music theorist and author of *De musica*, an important chant treatise of the Middle Ages.

Johnson, "Blind" Willie (c1902–c1950) Amer. gospel guitarist and singer. His recording career in the late 1920s was brief but has influenced many other gospel singers.

Johnson, Bunk (Geary) (1889–1949)

Amer. jazz trumpeter, whose career was marred by alcoholism. He played with various groups in the South until around 1930, then was rediscovered in 1939. In the early 1940s he made many recordings, but his work in the later 1940s was again interrupted by his drinking.

Johnson, Edward (Di Giovanni, Edoardo) (1878–1959) Canadian tenor and opera impresario, trained in New York. He appeared on Broadway before going to Italy to study in 1909. He returned to the U.S. in 1919 to become leading tenor of the Chicago Opera, then joined the Metropolitan Opera in 1922, where he sang until 1935. He was general manager of the Metropolitan from 1935 to 1950, after which he returned to Canada.

Johnson, Frank (1792–1844) Martinique-born Amer. cornetist, violinist, composer and bandmaster. His was the first dance orchestra to tour England, performing for Queen Victoria. He developed the "promenade concert" concept in the U.S. and wrote many dances and marches.

Johnson, (Francis) Hall (1888–1970) Amer. choral conductor, violinist and composer. His first small choral group, the Hall Johnson Choir, was formed in 1925 and he was choral dir. for Marc Connely's *The Green Pastures* in 1930. After producing his folk play, *Run Little Chillun'*, on Broadway in 1933, Johnson went to Hollywood and worked on several films. He later organized the Festival Chorus of New York City in 1946.

Johnson, Hunter (1906–) Amer. composer and teacher, trained at the U. of North Carolina and the Eastman School. He has taught at the U. of Michigan, the U. of Manitoba, Cornell U., the U. of Illinois and the U. of Texas. His works frequently incorporate jazz elements and incl. the ballet *Letter to the World*, a symphony, piano sonata, chamber music and songs.

Johnson, James P(rice) (1894–1955) Amer. jazz composer, conductor and pianist, composer of "The Charles-

ton," and "father of the Harlem 'stride' piano." He wrote a number of large-scale works, incl. operas, operettas and musical comedies (*Runnin' Wild, Sugar Hill*) and orchestral works (*Harlem Symphony, Jasmine Concerto*).

Johnson, J.J. (James Louis) (1924–) Amer. jazz bop trombonist and composer. He played with Benny Carter, Count Basie and co-led bands with trombonist Kai Winding. He was an important innovator in jazz trombone. He has written a number of works for large jazz orchestra; from the 1960s through the late 1980s he was a respected composer of film and TV scores.

Johnson, James Weldon (1871–1938) Amer. lyricist, diplomat and writer, brother of J. ROSAMUND JOHNSON and collaborator with ROBERT COLE on more than 200 songs, incl. "Under the Bamboo Tree" (1902) and "The Congo Love Song" (1903). Among his many writings is *Black Manhattan* (1930), a history of black theater and musical theater in New York.

Johnson, J(ohn) Rosamond (1873–1954) Amer. composer and singer, brother of JAMES WELDON JOHNSON, trained at the New England Conservatory. He was instrumental in the development of Negro musical theater, writing in an operetta style rather than the earlier minstrel format. He taught at the Music School Settlement in New York and toured with the Rosamond Johnson Quintet. His songs incl. "Lift Every Voice and Sing" (1899).

Johnson, Lonnie (Alonzo) (?1899–1970) Amer. blues guitarist and vocalist. He worked as a staff musician for Okeh Records, recording with Louis Armstrong, Duke Ellington and others. In the 1930s he worked with various groups and led his own ensembles. In the 1960s he lived and worked in Toronto.

Johnson, Robert (I) (c1500–c1560) Scottish composer of Latin and English sacred music and consort music.

Johnson, Robert (II) (c1583–?1633)

English composer and lutanist. He was lutanist to the king from 1604 until his death, adding in 1628 the position of composer for the "lute and voices." He wrote many songs for plays and music for court masques, as well as sacred and secular vocal music and music for the lute.

Johnson, Robert (III) (c1912–1938) Amer. blues singer and guitarist, an important representative of the Mississippi blues tradition.

Johnson, Tom (1939–) Amer. composer and critic, stud. of Morton Feldman. He was influential as music critic for the *Village Voice* in New York (1971–83) and has written experimental works, incl. *The Fournote Opera* (1972) and *Risks for Unrehearsed Performers* (1977–).

Johnston, Ben(jamin Burwell) (1926–) Amer. composer, stud. of Milhaud, Rolf Libermann, Luening, Partch, Cage and others. His works employ a wide variety of contemporary techniques (incl. microtones and aleatory procedures) and incl. 4 string quartets, songs, instrumental chamber music, ballets and chamber operas (*Carmilla, Gertrude*).

Joio, Norman Dello NORMAN DELLO JOIO.

Joke Quartet the String Quartet in E♭ major, Op. 33 No. 2 (1781), by Haydn. The title refers to the unusual ending of the last movement.

Jolas, Betsy (Illouz, Elizabeth) (1926–) French composer, trained at Bennington College and in Paris with Olivier Messiaen. Her father founded the magazine *Transition*, and she grew up in an artistic milieu. She has worked for the French radio (1955–70) and assisted Messiaen in his composition class since 1971. Her works incl. *D'un opéra de voyage* (1967), *O Wall* (mini-opera), *Quatuor II* (soprano, string trio) and chamber music.

Jolie fille de Perth, La [zho'lē 'fē-yə də pert] (Fr., The Fair Maid of Perth) opera in 4 acts by Bizet to a libretto by Jules-Henri Vernoy de St-Georges and Jules Adenis, based on the novel *The Fair Maid of Perth* by Sir Walter Scott. Premiere, Paris 1867. The story of the love of Henry Smith, an armorer, for Catherine Glover, daughter of a glovemaker of Perth.

Jolivet, André [zho-lē'vä] (1905–74) French composer, stud. of his mother and, much later, Edgard Varèse. He was a member of the group Jeune France, founded in 1936 to promote new music. From 1943 to 1959 he was dir. of music for the Comédie Française, and he taught composition at the Paris Conservatoire from 1966 to 1970. His music has a personal, nonserial atonal style. He has written ballets and marionette plays, orchestral works, instrumental concertos (incl. works for ondes martenot, percussion, violin, trumpet, piano, harp), 3 symphonies, cantatas and other vocal works, instrumental chamber music and incidental music for plays.

Jolson, Al (Yoelson, Asa) (?1886–1950) Amer. singer and actor, celebrated for his blackface roles and his "Mammy" songs. He appeared on the stage and in films, including the first full-length talking film, *The Jazz Singer* (1927). At one time he was married to singer Ruby Keeler.

Jommelli, Niccolò (1714–74) Prolific Italian composer, trained in Naples and with Padre Martini in Bologna. He wrote his first operas in 1737 for Naples. In 1743, he became musical dir. for the Ospedale degli Incurabili in Venice, for which he wrote much sacred vocal music, and later served at the Papal Chapel. For the duke of Württemberg he established a first-rate operatic company and one of the finest orchestras in Europe. He returned to Naples in 1769. Jommelli was an important force in the modernization of opera from the earlier succession of arias and recitatives to a more unified whole. His works combine the best elements of the French, German and Italian styles and incl. over 50 serious operas, over 20 comic operas and intermezzi, other theatrical works, oratorios, cantatas, passion settings and instrumental chamber music.

Jones, Charles (1910–) Canadian-born Amer. composer, stud. of Wagenaar. He has taught at Mills College, the Music Academy of the West, the Juilliard School, Mannes College and the Aspen Music School. His many works are generally in a neoclassical style.

Jones, Elvin (Ray) (1927–) Amer. jazz drummer, brother of Hank and Thad Jones. He has played with the Donald Byrd Quintet, with John Coltrane, and as leader of his own bands. His style emphasizes the role of the drummer as improviser and is characterized by the use of simultaneous, metrically contrasting rhythms.

Jones, Grandpa (Louis Marshall) (1913–) Amer. country-music banjoist, guitarist, and songwriter. He acquired his nickname when in his 20s. He was a member with Merle Travis of the popular gospel quartet, the Brown's Ferry Four, and was a regular on the Grand Ole Opry from the late 1940s. He was elected to the Country Music Hall of Fame in 1978.

Jones, Gwyneth (1936–) Welsh soprano (she began as a mezzo-soprano), trained by Ruth Packer, Maria Carpi, and in Siena and Zürich. She has sung regularly at the Welsh National Opera, Covent Garden, Bayreuth and other leading European houses. Her Metropolitan Opera debut was in 1972 as Sieglinde. Her roles incl. Wagnerian heroines, Donna Anna (*Don Giovanni*), Salome and Desdemona (*Otello*).

Jones, Hank (Henry) (1918–) Amer. jazz drummer, brother of Thad and Elvin Jones. He was the founder of the Detroit school of pianists, then moved to New York in 1944, where he worked with Coleman Hawkins and Ella Fitzgerald and was an important recording session pianist. He also toured with Jazz at the Philharmonic.

Jones, Inigo (?1573–1652) English architect and set designer. Through his collaborations with such composers as Alfonso Ferrabosco II, Giovanni Coperario, Nicolas Campion, Nicholas Lanier and William and Henry Lawes, Jones's work in staging English masques greatly influenced the beginnings of opera in England.

Jones, Jo(nathan) (1911–85) Amer. jazz drummer. He played with Walter Page and Bennie Moten, then joined the Count Basie band, remaining until 1948. After that he played freelance and with his own trio. He developed the high-hat cymbal ride style and was an important influence on the development of bop drumming.

Jones, Philly Joe (Joseph Rudolph) (1923–85) Amer. jazz drummer and pianist. He has played with many groups, incl. Miles Davis, Gil Evans and Bill Evans. He lived in Europe from 1967 to 1972, returning then to Philadelphia to perform with his own groups. He was esp. noted for his rimshot technique and brush work.

Jones, Quincy (Delight, Jr.) (1933–) American composer, arranger and trumpeter. His first work as an arranger was for Lionel Hampton, then he worked for Dizzy Gillespie's big band. He has since then worked freelance for such artists as Sarah Vaughan, Billy Eckstine, Michael Jackson and Frank Sinatra and has written scores for over 40 films.

Jones, Robert (fl. 1597–1615) English composer of ayres, madrigals and anthems, trained at Oxford.

Jones, Rufus (1936–) Amer. jazz drummer with the Duke Ellington orch., introduced African, Lat.-Amer., and oriental rhythms.

Jones, Sissieretta (Joyner, Matilda) (1868–1933) Amer. soprano, founder of the Black Patti Troubadors, an opera touring company (she was dubbed "the Black Patti" in comparison with ADELINA PATTI).

Jones, Spike (Lindley Armstrong) (1911–65) Amer. bandleader and drummer, known for his musical humor and his use of unorthodox instruments (such as washboards, auto pumps, etc.). He appeared frequently on television and also made several films.

Jones, Thad(deus Joseph) (1923–86) Amer. jazz trumpeter, brother of Elvin and Hank Jones. He played with the Count Basie band (1954–63), then worked as a free-lance arranger and studio player. The Thad Jones-Mel Lewis orch. (1965–78) began as a rehearsal band and established an international reputation. He emigrated to Denmark in 1978.

Jongen, (Marie-Alphonse-Nicholas-) Joseph (1873–1953) Belgian organist and composer, trained at the Liège Conservatory, where he taught from 1902. In 1920 he was appointed to the Brussels Conservatory and became conductor of the Concerts Spirituels. Most of his music is instrumental, incl. symphonies, concertos, tone poems and instrumental chamber music.

jongleur [zhō'glœr] (Fr.) **1**, an accompanist for a troubadour. **2**, a strolling medieval musician available to recite or sing for hire.

Jonny spielt auf ['zho-nē shpēlt owf] (Ger., Johnny Strikes Up) opera in 2 parts by Ernst Krenek to his own libretto. Premiere, Leipzig 1927. The opera incorporates jazz elements and tells the story of the leader of a jazz band who steals a violin with which he becomes successful as a jazz musician.

Joplin, Janis (1943–70) Amer. blues singer who made her name as a member of the group Big Brother and the Holding Company (1966–69), then left to form her own group, the Kozmic Blues Band. She died at 27 of a heroin overdose.

Joplin, Scott (1868–1917) Amer. composer and pianist. He is famous for his RAGTIME compositions (he was called the "King of Ragtime" in the late 1890s), the best known of which are the "Maple Leaf Rag" and "The Entertainer." He also wrote more extended works; his second opera, *Treemonisha*, was finally performed in 1972 (his first opera, *The Guest of Honor*, has been lost). He

was awarded the Pulitzer Prize posthumously in 1976.

Jordan, Louis (1908–75) Amer. jazz singer, alto saxophonist and bandleader, an early influence on rock and roll and from 1938 leader of the rhythm-and-blues band Tympany Five.

Joshua oratorio (1744) by Handel to a libretto by James Miller.

Josquin des Pres (Josquin Desprez) [zhos'kɛ̃ dā prā] (c1440–1521) Franco-Netherlandish composer, possibly the greatest composer of the Renaissance. Little is known of his life before 1459, when he was a singer at the Milan Cathedral, remaining until 1472. Shortly thereafter he entered the service of the Sforzas in Milan and Rome, singing at times in the Papal Chapel as well, until the early 1500s. He joined the ducal chapel in Ferrara sometime before 1503, leaving during an outbreak of the plague in late 1503 for France. He was provost of Condé from then until his death. Josquin's surviving works incl. 18 Mass settings written in a variety of compositional styles, a large number of motets and some chansons.

Josten, Werner (Erich) (1885–1963) German-born Amer. conductor and composer, stud. of Rudolf Siegel and Jaques-Dalcroze. He taught at Smith College (MA) (1923–49) and conducted the orchestras of Smith and Amherst College and the Pioneer Valley Orchestra. He wrote 3 ballets, *Jungle* for orchestra, 2 symphonies, choral works (incl. *Ode for St. Cecilia's Day*), chamber music and songs.

jota ['khō-tä] (Sp.) a Spanish folk dance in rapid 3/4 time danced by a couple using castanets and heel taps as accompaniment.

Joubert, John (Pierre Herman) (1927–) So. Afr.-born English composer, trained at the Royal Academy of Music. He has taught at the U. of Hull (1950–62) and the U. of Birmingham (1962–). His works, in an accessible and imaginative style, incl. 6 operas, 2 symphonies, a substantial body of choral music, chamber music and songs.

Joy to the World song by Lowell Mason (1792–1872) with lyrics by Isaac Watts, first published in 1839. Mason, a music teacher and hymn-tune composer, credited the music to Handel, who may have provided inspiration, if not actual notes.

juba a 19th-c. Afr.-Amer. improvised dance of African origin accompanied by handclapping and body slapping ("patting juba" or "clapping juba").

Jubilee musical by Cole Porter, book by Moss Hart. Premiere, New York 1935. Members of a bored royal family pose as common people in a series of adventures. The show included the songs "Begin the Beguine" and "Just One of Those Things."

jubilee a type of joyous SPIRITUAL describing the happiness of Heaven after the tribulations of the world.

Jubilee Singers Amer. group of spiritual singers, est. in 1871 at Fisk U. in Nashville, TN, by George L. White, for the purpose of fund-raising. It was disbanded in 1880.

jubilus a melismatic section of the ALLELUIA of the Roman Mass, sung on the syllable "ia" of the word "alleluia" before the verse. Since its beginnings in the 4th c. the textless jubilus was considered to be a direct expression of the soul in music.

Judas Maccabaeus oratorio (1747) by Handel to a libretto by Thomas Morell.

jug band a type of Afr.-Amer. instrumental ensemble of the 1920s and 1930s consisting of one or two top-blown jugs, strings and harmonica or kazoo.

Juilliard School of Music a conservatory in New York City est. in 1905 as the Institute of Musical Art. The present name was adopted in 1923.

Juilliard String Quartet Amer. string quartet founded in 1946 by William Schuman, then president of the Juilliard School of Music in New York. The group has been of major importance in the support of Amer. composers. The quartet has been in resi-

dence at the Library of Congress since 1962.

Juive, La [zhüēv] (Fr., The Jewess) opera in 5 acts by Halévy to a libretto by Eugène Scribe. Premiere, Paris 1835. In 15th-c. Constance, Cardinal Brogni condemns to death the Jewess Rachel, who he too late learns is his daughter.

juke box a mechanical phonograph, invented in the late 19th c. in the U.S. as an arcade novelty and later, in the 1930s, common in restaurants, becoming an important factor in the dissemination of popular music.

Julius Caesar (in Egypt) (It., *Giulio Cesare in Egitto*) historical opera in 3 acts by Handel to a libretto in Italian by Niccolo Haym. Premiere, London 1724. The role of Caesar, orig. written for a castrato, is now often performed in a transposed version by a baritone. The story concerns the relationship between Caesar and Cleopatra and various plots to kill Caesar and Cleopatra's brother Ptolemy.

Jullien, Louis Antoine [zhü'lyē] (1812–60) French conductor and composer. A colorful figure, he studied at the Paris Conservatory. He went to England in 1838, conducting a series of concerts at the Drury Lane Theatre and at Surrey Gardens, then toured the U.S. in 1853 at the invitation of P.T. Barnum, giving 214 concerts in less than a year. His showmanship included the use of a jeweled baton handed to him on a silver platter. Most of his own works are lost.

Jumbo musical by Richard Rodgers, lyrics by Lorenz Hart, book by Ben Hecht and Charles MacArthur. Premiere, New York 1935. This combination of musical comedy and circus, a sort of *Romeo and Juliet* under the big top, was a success but had a short run because of its high cost.

jumbo guitar a large folk GUITAR; dreadnaught.

jump band a type of small BAND (7–9 players) popular in the 1930s which combined jazz and blues, while imitating the power of the big bands. The style, with its heavy up-beat and repetition, was a predecessor of RHYTHM-AND-BLUES.

jump blues a type of Afr.-Amer. music for small group in the 1940s, a predecessor of RHYTHM-AND-BLUES.

Jumping Frog of Calaveras County, The opera in 1 act by Lukas Foss to a libretto by Jean Karsavina, based on the story by Mark Twain. Premiere, Bloomington, IN, 1950. A stranger engages in a jumping contest with Smiley's jumping frog, Daniel Webster.

Junge Lord, Der ['yüng-e] (Ger., The Young Lord) comic opera in 2 acts by Henze to a libretto by Ingeborg Bachmann from a fable, "The Sheik of Alexandria and His Slaves," by Wilhelm Hauff. Premiere, Berlin 1965. Strange events ensue when the Englishman Sir Edgar and his entourage arrive in Hulsdorf-Gotha.

Jupiter Symphony popular name for the symphony No. 41 in C major, K.551 (1788), by Mozart.

Jürgens, Jürgen (1925–) German conductor, stud. of Kurt Thomas and Konrad Lechner. Since 1955 he has conducted the Hamburg Monteverdi Choir, with which he has made many recordings of works ancient and modern. He directs the Akademische Musikpflege and teaches at Hamburg U.

Jurinac, Sena (Srebenka) (1921–) Yugoslav-born Austrian soprano, stud. of Milka Kostrenčić. She sang with the Vienna Staatsoper from 1945, and also appeared at Glyndebourne and Salzburg, where she made a lasting impression with her performances of Mozart roles. Her roles also incl. the Marschallin (*Der Rosenkavalier*), Electra and Cio-cio-san (*Madama Butterfly*).

Justiniana GIUSTINIANA.

just intonation *also,* **pure intonation** a TUNING system that produces harmonic intervals tuned to eliminate all beats. On a keyboard instrument, such a tuning is possible only with compromise or the construction of a special keyboard.

JVC Jazz Festival see NEWPORT JAZZ FESTIVAL.

K

K. *abbr.* see KÖCHEL.

Kabalevsky, Dmitri Borisovich (1904–87) Russian composer, pianist, teacher and writer, trained at the Moscow Conservatory, where he taught after 1932. He was active in various Soviet composers' organizations and was principal editor of the journal *Soviet Music* in the 1940s. His works incl. concertos for piano and violin, 4 symphonies, *Komediantï* (The Comedians) for small orchestra, cantatas and oratorios, other choral works and songs, instrumental chamber music and solo sonatas.

Kaddish Symphony the Symphony No. 3 for soprano, female speaker, chorus and orchestra (1961–3) by Bernstein, written partly in Hebrew and partly in Aramaic and dedicated to the memory of President John F. Kennedy.

Kadosa, Pál (1903–83) Hungarian composer, pianist and teacher, stud. of Arnold Székely and Kodály. He taught at the Fodor Conservatory and the Goldmark School of Music in Budapest and, after the war, at the Budapest Academy. His works show the influence of Stravinsky as well as Hindemith and his compatriots Bartók and Kodály. His works incl. 8 symphonies, concertos for violin, viola and piano, 2 operas, choral works, chamber music and solo sonatas.

Kagel, Mauricio (Raúl) (1931–) Argentinian composer, performer and filmmaker, self-taught as a composer. In 1969 he became dir. of the Institute of New Music in Cologne and was one of the founders of the Cologne Ensemble for New Music. His works have employed a wide range of techniques, from serialism to aleatory and theatrical "happenings."

Kaiserquartett [-kvär"tet] (Ger.) EMPEROR QUARTET.

Kajanus, Robert (1856–1933) Finnish composer and conductor, stud. of Reinecke and Hans Richter. He founded the Helsinki Orchestral Society in 1882 and conducted it for the rest of his life. He is esp. noted for championing the works of Sibelius.

kakaki a long metal west African TRUMPET used principally in ceremonial music.

kakko Japanese BARREL DRUM with two deerskin heads, used in GAGAKU.

kalengo KALUNGU.

kalevala (Finnish) epic songs of 14th-c. Finland used by many Finnish composers, incl. Sibelius, as a source of texts and stories.

Kalkbrenner, Frédéric (Friedrich Wilhelm Michael) (1785–1849) German-born French composer, pianist and teacher, trained at the Paris Conservatoire. He lived in England from 1814 to 1824, establishing his reputation as a piano virtuoso, then in Paris, from where he toured Europe and where he became active as a teacher. His works, most of which involve the piano, incl. concertos, chamber music with winds and strings, solo sonatas and duets and several collections of études.

Kalliope the Greek muse of heroic poetry and stringed instruments. Cf. CALLIOPE.

Kalliwoda, Johann Wenzel (Kalivoda, Jan Křtitel Václav) (1801–66) Bohemian composer and violinist, trained at the Prague Conservatory. He played under Weber for five years, then conducted the orch. of the Prince of Fürstenberg in Donaueschingen until his retirement. He was a prolific composer of symphonies, overtures and chamber music, and also wrote operas and choral music.

Kálmán, Imre (Emmerich) (1882–1953) Hungarian operetta composer, trained at the Budapest Academy of Music. He spent most of his compositional life in Vienna, becoming a U.S. citizen in 1942. Among his most popular works were the operettas *Tatárjárás* (The Gay Hussars, 1908) and *Der Zigeunerprimas* (The Gypsy Violinist, 1912).

Kalmus, Edwin F. (1893–) Austrian-born Amer. music publisher, founder in 1926 of the firm of the same name, one of the largest music publishing houses in the U.S.

kalungu an Afr. 2-headed WAISTED DRUM with tunable head, used for communication. Also, *talking drum.*

kamancha (Arab.) a bowed SPIKE FIDDLE of the Middle East.

kameso a type of tube RATTLE used in Lat.-Amer. bands.

Kaminsky, Max (1908–) Amer. Dixieland jazz trumpeter, stud. of Max Schlossberg. He has played with Joe Venuti, Tommy Dorsey, Artie Shaw and Eddie Condon and led his own groups. He was a specialist in the use of the plunger mute.

Kammer- (Ger.) chamber.

Kammersänger(in) [-"seng-ər(-in)] (Ger.) chamber singer; an honorary title bestowed in Germany and Austria on distinguished singers.

Kammerton [-tōn] (Ger.) **1,** CAMMERTON. **2,** in current German usage, concert pitch (a' = 440 CPS).

Kanawa, Kiri Te TE KANAWA, KIRI.

Kander, John (Harold) (1927–) Amer. composer of Broadway musicals, stud. of Beeson, Luening and Douglas Moore. Among his shows, produced in collaboration with lyricist Fred Ebb, are *Cabaret* (1966), *Zorba* (1968) and *Funny Lady* (1975).

kanoon (Turk.) see ZITHER.

Kansas City jazz a style of big-band music represented by the bands of Bennie Moten and his successor Count Basie and Jay McShann and characterized by blues motives, repetitive riffs, virtuoso soloists and a flexible, relaxed rhythm section.

Kansas City Philharmonic Orchestra orch. founded in 1934 under conductor Karl Krueger. Later conductors have been Efrem Kurtz, Hans Schwieger, Jorge Mester and Maurice Peress. The orch. disbanded in 1972 and has been replaced by the Kansas City Symphony under conductor William McGlaughlin.

kantele *also,* **kantela** ('kän-tə-lə) (Finn.) **1,** a traditional Finnish bowed folk LYRE once having 5 strings but now having as many as 30. **2,** a Finnish BOARD ZITHER.

Kantor (Ger.) **1,** a solo singer in liturgical music. Also, *Cantor.* **2,** in Germany, the dir. of music in a Lutheran church and often the head of an educational establishment connected with the church.

kanun (Turk.) see ZITHER.

Kapelle [kä'pe-le] (Ger.) CHAPEL.

Kapellmeister [-"mī-stər] (Ger.) the musical director of a CHAPEL.

Kaplan, Abraham (1931–) Israeli-born Amer. conductor, trained at the Juilliard School. He was conductor of the Kol Israel Chorus and the Haifa Oratorio Society in Jerusalem and founded the Camerata Singers in New York. He has been dir. of choral music at the Juilliard School since 1961 and has taught at the Berkshire Music Center, at Boston U. and at the Union Theological Seminary in NY.

Karajan, Herbert von (1908–89) Austrian conductor and opera impresario, stud. of Franz Schalk, a major force in mid-20th-c. symphonic and opera performance and recording. He worked at the Städtisches Theater in Ulm (1929–34), then became Generalmusikdirektor at Aachen. After the war he was made concert dir. for life of the Gesellschaft der Musikfreunde in Vienna and conducted the London PO, La Scala and the Vienna PO. He became music dir. of the Berlin PO in 1955 (resigning the post shortly before his death in 1989) and made his U.S. debut on tour with that orchestra. In 1956 he became artistic dir. of the Salzburg Festival and a year later of the Vienna Staatsoper.

karaoke [kä-rä'ō-kā] (Jap., empty orchestra) the pratice of singing a song with a prerecorded accompaniment from which the original vocal line has been electronically removed.

Karelia overture, Op. 10, and orchestral suite, Op. 11 (1893), by Sibelius, a tribute to the Finnish province of Karelia. The movements are "Intermezzo," "Ballade" and "Alla Marcia."

Karg-Elert, Sigfrid (1877–1933) German composer, pianist, organist and theorist, trained at the Leipzig Conservatory, where he later taught.

Karlins, M(artin) William (1932–) Amer. composer and teacher, stud. of Frederick Piket, Giannini, Richard Hervig and Philip Bezanson. He has taught at Northwestern U. since 1967. Most of his compositions are instrumental, incl. many works for woodwinds (esp. saxophone).

Karpeles, Maud (1885–1976) English folk music scholar. Introduced to folk music study by CECIL SHARP, she served as his assistant until his death and was active in the English Folk Dance Society. She published Sharp's collection of English folk songs and made an extensive collection of the folk songs of Newfoundland. She was secretary of the International Folk Music Council for 15 years.

Karr, Gary (Michael) (1941–) Amer. double bass player, stud. of Harman Reinshagen, Warren Benfield and Stuart Sankey. He founded the International Institute for the String Bass in 1964 and has commissioned a number of works for the instrument.

Kasemets, Udo (1919–) Estonian-born Canadian composer, pianist, conductor and teacher, trained at the Tallinn Conservatory. He was the founder and conductor of the Toronto Bach Society and editor of the Canavangard new score series. His works have incl. conventional scores, esp. for voices, and nonconventional scores designed for differing realizations using different instrumental or electronic forces such as his *Cas-*

cando (1965) for 1 to 128 performers.

Katchen, Julius (1926–69) Amer. pianist, stud. of his grandmother. His wide repertory embraced the Classical and Romantic masterworks as well as contemporary works.

Katerina Ismailova tragic opera in 4 acts by Shostakovich to a libretto by himself and A. Preys, after a novel by Nicolai Lyeskov. Premiere, Leningrad 1934, as *Lady Macbeth of Mtsensk*. A revised version, made to conform to government restrictions, had its premiere in Moscow in 1962. Katerina, unhappy in her marriage with Zinovy, gives in to the seduction of Sergei, with tragic results.

Katims, Milton (1909–) Amer. conductor and violist, stud. of Leon Barzin and Herbert Dittler. He was violist and assistant conductor at the New York radio station WOR (1935–43), then played principal viola under Toscanini at NBC. He became music dir. and conductor of the Seattle SO in 1954 and dir. of the School of Music at the U. of Houston in 1976.

Katya Kabanova tragic opera in 3 acts by Janáček to a libretto in Czech by Vincenc Cervinka, after the Russian play *The Storm* by Alexander Ostrovsky. Premiere, Brno 1921. Katya finds temporary escape from her provincial life in an affair with Boris.

Kawai Japanese piano manufacturer est. in 1925.

Kay, Connie (Kirnon, Conrad Henry) (1927–) Amer. jazz drummer. He played with Miles Davis, Cat Anderson and Lester Young and did studio work before joining the Modern Jazz Quartet in 1955, remaining with the group through its disbanding and eventual reunion.

Kay, Hershy (1919–81) Amer. composer and orchestrator. He wrote a number of ballets (incl. *Stars and Stripes, Cakewalk*) and orchestrated scores for many Broadway musicals (incl. Bernstein's *On the Town*) and films (*Peter Gunn*).

Kay, Ulysses (Simpson) (1917–) Amer. composer, nephew of KING

OLIVER, trained at the U. of Arizona, at the Eastman School of Music and with Paul Hindemith at Yale. He has taught at the City U. of New York since 1968. His works incl. *Jubilee* (opera), orchestral works, cantatas and other choral works, film scores (*The Quiet One*) and television scores.

Kaye, Danny (Kominsky, David Daniel) (1913–87) Amer. singer, actor and comedian in clubs, in films (*Up in Arms, A Song Is Born*) and on Broadway (*Lady in the Dark, Two by Two*). He frequently appeared with U.S. symphony orchestras in comic routines to aid in fund raising.

kazachok [kä-zä′chok] (Russ.) a Russian folk couple dance in 2/4 meter depicting the peasant-warriors of the Cossack territory.

kazoo *also,* **gazoo** an instrument consisting of an open tube with a side hole covered by a membrane into which a person hums or sings, producing an amplified vocal sound with a pronounced buzz. The instrument was formerly used in jazz ensembles. Also, *mirliton, zarah, eunuch flute, Tommy talker*.

Kb. *abbr.* (Ger.) Kontrabass (see DOUBLE BASS).

Keats, Donald (Howard) (1929–) Amer. composer, stud. of Hindemith, Luening and Cowell. He has taught at U. of Denver since 1975. His works incl. 2 symphonies, a piano concerto, a piano sonata and songs.

Keeler, Ruby (Ethel Hilda) (1909–) Canadian-born Amer. singer, dancer and actress in Broadway musicals (*No, No, Nanette*) and films (*42nd Street, Gold Diggers of 1933*).

keen a LAMENT or wail for the dead. Cf. CORONACH.

Keene, Christopher (1946–) Amer. conductor. He has been music dir. of the American Ballet Co., ArtPark, the Syracuse SO and the Spoleto Festival. He founded the Long Island PO and has been musical dir. of the New York City Opera since 1988. He is esp. known for his performances of 20th-c. repertory.

Kegelstatt Trio [′kä-gəl″shtät] the trio for piano, clarinet and viola, K.498 (1786), by Mozart, supposedly written while the composer was bowling (Ger. *Kegel*, bowling pin).

Kehraus [′kä-rows] (Ger., sweeping out) in German-speaking countries, the last dance at a ball. The traditional tune for the *Kehraus*, the 17th-c. *Grossvater-Tanz* (Grandfather Dance), was used by Schumann in the final pages of his piano cycles *Papillons* and *Carnaval*.

Keilberth, Joseph (1908–68) German conductor, trained in Karlsruhe. He was music dir. of the Staatstheater in Karlsruhe, then of the German PO in Prague, the Dresden Staatsoper, the Hamburg PO, and the Bayerische Staatsoper in Munich. He also conducted at Bayreuth and at Salzburg and made many recordings.

Kelemen, Milko (1924–) Yugoslav composer, trained at the Zagreb Academy of Music and with Messiaen and Fortner. He has taught at the Zagreb Academy, at the Düsseldorf Conservatory and the Stuttgart Musikhochschule and has been an important figure in promoting avantgarde music in Yugoslavia. His own works, in an individual atonal style, incl. 3 operas, ballets, orchestral works (some involving electronic sounds), instrumental chamber music and songs.

Kell, Reginald (Clifford) (1906–81) English clarinetist, stud. of Haydn Draper. He was principal clarinet of the Royal PO, the Royal Opera House, the London PO, the London SO, the Liverpool PO and the Philharmonia Orchestra, then emigrated to the U.S. in 1948. He developed a new clarinet style in England involving the use of vibrato, made many recordings and published clarinet methods and studies.

Kelley, Edgar Stillman (1857–1944) Amer. organist, composer and writer, trained in Chicago and Stuttgart. He worked in the San Francisco area, then conducted a touring operetta company on the East Coast. He taught in Berlin and at the Cincinnati Conservatory.

Kelley, Peck (John Dickson) (1898–1980) Amer. jazz pianist, famous for his band Peck's Bad Boys, which toured Texas in the early 1920s. Except for a brief, unsuccessful period in St. Louis, he stayed in Texas, leading his own groups and refusing to record.

Kellogg, Clara (Louise) (1842–1916) Amer. soprano, stud. of Achille Errani and Claudia Muzio. She sang frequently in New York and Boston, and in London from 1867. In 1873 she organized the English Opera Co. to perform opera in English. She retired in 1887.

Kelly, Gene (Curran, Eugene) (1912–) Amer. dancer, choreographer, actor, singer and director. After his success as the lead in *Pal Joey* on Broadway, he made many film musicals, incl. *On the Town* (1949), *An American in Paris* (1951) and *Singin' in the Rain* (1952).

Kelly, Michael (1762–1826) Irish tenor, composer and theater manager, stud. of Arne, Finaroli and Aprile. He spent four important years in Vienna, creating the parts of Don Curzio and Don Basilio in *The Marriage of Figaro* of Mozart, then went to London in 1787, where he was highly successful. He composed nearly 50 operas, as well as some songs and country dances, and wrote a fascinating autobiography, *Reminiscences* (1825).

Kelly, Wynton (1931–71) Amer. jazz pianist. He worked with Dizzy Gillespie, Lester Young, Charles Mingus and Miles Davis, then established his own trio. An influential pianist among pianists, he is relatively unknown to the general public.

Kelpius, Johannes (1673–1708) German hymn book compiler. He came to America in 1694, and his early-18th-c. hymnbook is the earliest surviving musical manuscript of the colonies.

Kelterborn, Rudolf (1931–) Swiss composer and conductor, trained at the Basle Music Academy. After 1968

he taught at the Zürich Musikhochschule. His many works developed from an early neo Baroque style to a later atonal, quasi-serial, technique.

kemanak a Balinese metal CLAPPER.

Kempe, Rudolf (1910–76) distinguished German conductor, trained at the Dresden Musikhochschule. After World War II he was musical dir. of the Dresden Opera, the Bavarian Staatsoper in Munich, the BBC SO and other groups. His Metropolitan Opera debut was in 1954 and his first Bayreuth appearance was in 1960. In 1961 he became principal conductor of the Royal PO in London and was named conductor for life in 1970.

Kempff, Wilhelm (1895–1991) German pianist, stud. of Robert Kahn and Heinrich Barth. His Amer. debut was in 1964. In addition to his distinguished reputation as a solo pianist he has an outstanding reputation as a teacher.

Kendall, Ned (Edward) (1808–61) Amer. keyed bugle player and bandmaster, founder of the Boston Brass Band in 1835 and noted for his virtuoso high-register playing.

kĕndang an Indonesian double-headed laced DRUM.

Kenins, Talivaldis (1919–) Latvian-born Canadian composer and teacher, stud. of Tony Aubin and Messiaen. He emigrated to Canada in 1951 to join the music faculty of the U. of Toronto. His works incl. 5 symphonies, concertos, choral works and instrumental chamber music.

Kennan, Kent Wheeler (1913–) Amer. composer and teacher, stud. of Hanson. He won the Prix de Rome (1936) and studied with G. Pizzetti in Rome. He has taught at Kent State U. and at the U. of Texas. His works are mainly in a neoclassical style.

Kennedy Center for the Performing Arts major performing arts complex in Washington, D.C., opened in 1971.

kenong a Javanese GONG.

Kent bugle KEYED BUGLE.

Kenton, Stan(ley Newcomb) (1912–79) outspoken Amer. jazz bandleader, pianist and arranger noted for his innovative arrangements and for his various jazz orchestras. He was also active as a teacher and workshop leader on university campuses.

Kentucky dulcimer APPALACHIAN DULCIMER.

Keppard, Freddie (1889–1933) Amer. jazz cornetist. He led his own groups in New Orleans, then moved to Los Angeles in 1912, forming the Original Creole Orchestra. In 1918 he resettled in Chicago.

Kerker, Gustave Adolph (1857–1923) German-born Amer. composer. He came to the U.S. in 1867, became music dir. of the Casino Theatre in New York in 1879 and wrote more than 20 musicals and operettas for this and other theaters, the best known of which was *The Belle of New York* (1897).

Kerle, Jacobus de (?1532–91) Netherlands composer and organist. He was a singer and organist at Orvieto until 1562, then worked at Ypres Cathedral, Augsburg Cathedral and Cambrai Cathedral, finally settling in 1583 in Prague. His surviving music, all sacred vocal works and madrigals, is in the Franco-Netherlandish style.

Kerll, Johann Kaspar von (1627–93) German composer and organist, stud. of Giovanni Valentini, Carissimi and possibly Frescobaldi. He was court organist in Brussels until 1656, when he became Kapellmeister to the Bavarian Elector in Munich. He was later organist to the imperial court. Kerll was active as a teacher and numbered among his pupils Pachelbel and perhaps Fux. He was particularly noted as a keyboard player and for his keyboard and sacred music.

Kern, Jerome (David) (1885–1945) Amer. composer, trained at the New York College of Music and at Heidelberg U. He is considered the "father" of the modern musical theater. His over 40 Broadway productions incl. *The Cat and the Fiddle* (1931), *Roberta* (1933) and *Show Boat* (1927), the first musical to become part of the repertory of an opera company. He also wrote many film scores.

Kerr, Harrison (1897–1978) Amer. composer and teacher, stud. of James H. Rogers and Boulanger. He taught at the U. of Oklahoma (1949–69) and served on the editorial boards of New Music Edition and New Music Quarterly Recordings. His works incl. *The Tower of Kel* (opera, 1958–60), 3 symphonies, a violin concerto, instrumental sonatas, choral works and songs.

Kertész, István (1929–73) Hungarian-born German conductor, stud. of Kodály, Somogyi and Leó Weiner. He worked at the Budapest Opera before moving to Germany in 1956. He was music dir. at Augsburg (1958–63) and Cologne (from 1964) and conducted frequently in England, becoming principal conductor of the London SO in 1965. He recorded extensively, incl. the complete symphonies of Dvořák.

Kessel, Barney (1923–) Amer. jazz guitarist. He played with the bands of Charlie Barnet and Artie Shaw, then concentrated on studio work and recording under his own name. He has toured with Oscar Peterson, Jazz at the Philharmonic, Herb Ellis and others.

Ketèlbey, Albert W(illiam) (Vodorinski, Anton) (1875–1959) English conductor and composer, trained at Trinity College in London. He is best known for his descriptive works such as *In a Monastery Garden* (1915). He also wrote music for silent films.

kettledrum a VESSEL DRUM with a single, tunable skin stretched over the open end of a hemispherical body made of metal, clay or wood; an ancestor of the modern orchestral TIMPANI.

key 1, the tonal center of a composition, as defined by the relationship between the notes of a scale to a certain note called the tonic or key note. Cf. TONALITY. **2**, PITCH, as in *off key* (out of tune) and *on key* (at standard pitch or in tune). Cf. INTONATION. **3**, a balanced or spring-mounted lever which, when pressed by a finger or hand, activates a sounding mechanism, such as an air valve in an organ, a jack in a harpsichord or a cover for a hole in a wind instrument. Keys are usu. ordered for convenience in a horizontal layout (see KEYBOARD).

keyboard a set of keys or levers activating the mechanism of a piano, organ, etc. Early keyboards were simple and usu. operated by the hand, rather than the fingers. For some time, keyboards were purely diatonic, with only the B♭ added. Arrangement of the keys in a manner similar to the current standard, in two rows with the sharps and flats grouped by two and three in the back row, dates from the 15th c. A number of different experimental designs for the keyboard have been developed over the centuries, usu. in order to accommodate a certain scale (as in instruments designed to play microtones) or, in recent years, to reduce the domination of the C major scale (cf. JANKO KEYBOARD). Also, *fingerboard*.

keyed bugle *also*, **key bugle** an early 19th-c. BUGLE having keys controlling side holes, rather than valves, and usu. having from 5 to 12 keys and a 2-octave range. The instrument is called for in a number of opera scores of the early 19th c. Also, *Royal Kent bugle, Kent bugle.* Cf. REGENT'S BUGLE.

keyed trumpet an 18th- and early 19th-c. TRUMPET fitted with keyed side holes rather than valves and having a softer tone than the valve trumpet.

key note TONIC.

key signature the set of sharps or flats placed at the beginning of a composition to define the tonality of the composition. The signature affects all pitches of the same name in whatever octave unless overridden by an accidental or a new key signature. It is usu. placed directly after the clef or, if in the middle of a staff, after a double bar. The same signature is used for a major key and its relative minor; e.g., B♭ major and g minor share the same signature of two flats. In music

prior to the late 18th c. minor key signatures were often written with one less flat or one less sharp than in the modern system. Nontonal music usu. does not use the key signature, or, in some cases, may use nonstandard signatures, sometimes combining flats and sharps.

key trumpet KEYED TRUMPET.

keywork the collective term for the keys of an instrument, usu. referring to woodwind or brass instruments.

Kfg. *abbr.* (Ger.) Kontrafagott (see CONTRABASSOON).

Khan, Chaka (Stevens, Yvette Marie) (1953–) Amer. soul singer, whose name combines an Afr. word for fire (*chaka*) and a boyfriend's name. She was lead singer for the band Rufus until 1978; she since then has concentrated on solo performance.

Khatchaturian, Aram Il'yich (1903– 78) Soviet composer, trained at the Gnesin Music Academy and later with Nicolay Myaskovsky. He was active in the Union of Soviet Composers in the late 1930s and later taught at the Gnesin Institute and the Moscow Conservatory. His works combine his Armenian heritage with the academic discipline of Rimsky-Korsakov, and incl. concertos for vi-

Key Signatures
(C = major, c = minor)

C   a   G   e   D   b   A   f♯

E   c♯   B   g♯   F♯ d♯

C♯ a♯   F   d   B♭ g

E♭ c   A♭ f   D♭ b♭

Mixed

G♭ e♭   C♭ a♭

olin and piano, *Gayane* (ballet and suites), *Spartak* (ballet and suites), chamber music, and film scores.

Khovanshchina (Russ., The Khovansky Plot) historical opera in 5 acts by Mussorgsky to a libretto by the composer and V.V. Stassov. Premiere, St. Petersburg 1886. There are versions edited by Rimsky-Korsakov and by Dimitri Shostakovich. The struggle between three factions in the time of Peter the Great: Old Russia, the Sectarians and the New Russia.

Khrennikov, Tikhon (1913–) Soviet composer, stud. of Mikhail Gnesin and Vissarion Shebalin. He was assoc. with the Vakhtangov Theater from 1934, for which he composed incidental music. He taught at the Moscow Conservatory from 1963 and has appeared as a soloist playing his own piano concertos. His works incl. *Mat'* (Mother) and other operas, operettas and ballets, 3 symphonies, concertos for piano, violin and cello, orchestra suites, songs and film scores.

khumbgwe a So. Afr. VESSEL FLUTE.

Killebrew, Gwendolyn (1939–) Amer. mezzo-soprano, trained at the Juilliard School and the Metropolitan Opera Studio. She has been a member of the Deutsche Oper am Rhein in Düsseldorf since 1976 and has appeared at Bayreuth and in other European and American houses. Her roles incl. Amneris (*Aida*) and Orfeo in Gluck's opera.

Kim, Earl (Eul) (1920–) Korean-Amer. composer, stud. of Schoenberg and Sessions. He has taught at Princeton and, since 1967, at Harvard. His relatively limited output consists of works of an extreme delicacy in an atonal but usu. not dodecaphonic style.

kin (Chin.) an ancient Chinese ZITHER having silk strings. Cf. KOTO.

Kincaid, William (1895–1967) Amer. flutist, stud. of Georges Barrère. He played in the New York SO (1914–18), then joined the Philadelphia Orchestra in 1921 as solo flutist, remaining until 1960. He taught at the

Curtis Institute of Music for most of his career.

Kinderszenen ['kin-dərs"tsā-nən] (Ger.) SCENES FROM CHILDHOOD.

Kindertotenlieder [-"tō-tən"lē-dər] (Ger., Songs on the Death of Children) cycle of five songs with orchestra (1901–4) by Mahler to poems by Friedrich Rückert.

King, B.B. (Riley B.) (1925–) Amer. blues singer and guitarist (the initials B.B. come from "Blues Boy," his name as disc jockey for a radio station in Memphis). His music combines elements of jazz, rhythm and blues and gospel, forming a basis for rock and roll.

King (Klein), **Carole** (1942–) Amer. rock and popular singer and songwriter. Before she began recording in 1960, she wrote "You Make Me Feel Like a Natural Woman" and "One Fine Day," among other hits, for various singers and groups. Her own recordings incl. *Tapestry* (1971), which sold over 13 million copies.

King, Dennis (Pratt, Dennis) (1897–1971) Amer. actor and baritone, romantic star of *Rose-Marie* and *The Vagabond King* among many other Broadway shows.

King, James (1925–) Amer. tenor, stud. of Martial Singher and Max Lorenz. He has sung in all major opera houses in the U.S. and Europe, specializing in heroic repertory, incl. Bacchus (*Ariadne auf Naxos*), Florestan (*Fidelio*) and Lohengrin.

King, Pee Wee (Kuczynski, Julius Frank Anthony) (1914–) Amer. country-music singer, songwriter, accordion player and bandleader, leader of the Golden West Cowboys, a staple of the Grand Ole Opry. His best-known song is "Tennessee Waltz" (1946). He was elected to the Country Music Hall of Fame in 1974.

King and I, The musical by Richard Rodgers, lyrics and book by Oscar Hammerstein II, based on Margaret Landon's novel *Anna and the King of Siam*. Premiere, New York 1951. The idea for the musical was originally proposed by Gertrude Lawrence, the first Anna. Anna, governess of the Siamese king's children, exerts a great influence on the king.

King Arthur dramatic opera in five acts by Purcell to a libretto by John Dryden. Premiere, London 1691. A complicated story of the conflict between King Arthur of the Britons and the Saxon Oswald.

King Crimson English art rock group formed in 1969 and known for their dissonant, complex music.

King Curtis (Ousley, Curtis) (1934–71) Amer. rhythm-and-blues saxophonist, famous for his studio work with such musicians as Eric Clapton, the Coasters and Aretha Franklin.

King David (Fr., *Le Roi David*) dramatic psalm (1921) by Honegger to a libretto by R. Morax based on a biblical text.

King Musical Instruments Amer. brass instrument maker founded in 1893 in Cleveland. It became a subsidiary of Seeburg Co. in 1965 and has acquired the French woodwind manufacturer Strasser-Marigaux-Lemaire.

King Priam tragic opera in 3 acts by Sir Michael Tippett to a libretto by the composer, after Homer. Premiere, Coventry 1962. A retelling of the story of the Trojan War.

King's Singers British vocal ensemble formed in 1968 by (with one exception) a group of choral scholars at King's College, Cambridge. Its wide repertory ranges from Renaissance to barbershop and contemporary works.

Kingston Trio Amer. folk-popular vocal group formed in San Francisco in 1957.

kinnor ['kē-nôr] (Heb.) an ancient Jewish lyre.

Kipnis, Alexander (1891–1978) Ukrainian-born Amer. bass, trained in Warsaw and Berlin. He was leading bass with the Berlin Charlottenburg Opera (1919–30), then at the Berlin Staatsoper until 1934. He sang regularly at the Bayreuth and Salzburg festivals, in Chicago (1923–32) and at the Metropolitan Opera (1940–6). He

was also a successful recitalist and lieder singer.

Kipnis, Igor (1930–) Amer. harpsichordist, son of ALEXANDER KIPNIS. He studied at Harvard, but was largely self-taught as a performer. His debut as harpsichordist was not until 1959, and he has since toured widely. He has taught at the Berkshire Music Center and at Fairfield (CT) U.

Kirbye, George (?–1634) English composer. He worked as a domestic musician for Sir Robert Jermyn. His surviving works consist of madrigals, several sacred vocal works and psalm settings published in Thomas East's 1592 psalter.

Kirchner, Leon (1919–) Amer. composer, conductor and pianist, stud. of Schoenberg, Bloch and Sessions. He has taught at the U. of Southern California, at Mills College and (since 1961) at Harvard. He has appeared as pianist and conductor, both performing his own works and the music of other eras. His works have a very individual style. He won the Pulitzer Prize in 1967 for his Third String Quartet. His works incl. *Lily* (opera), 2 piano concertos, *Music for orchestra*, 3 string quartets, a piano sonata and songs.

Kirk, Andy (Andrew Dewey) (1898–) Amer. jazz baritone saxophonist and tuba player. He joined Terrence Holder's Dallas band Dark Clouds of Joy in 1925 and was leader from 1929, when the band moved to Kansas City. The band toured widely until its breakup in 1948.

Kirk, Rahsaan Roland (1936–77) Amer. jazz tenor saxophonist, instrumentalist and composer, noted for his use of unusual instruments (incl. manzello, stritch and nose flute) and simultaneous performance on several instruments. He worked with Charles Mingus, then with his own groups. His style was original but incorporated jazz influences of the past.

Kirkman family of English harpsichord (and later piano) makers. The firm was est. in England in the 1730s by Jacob Kirkman (1710–92) and continued in operation until 1898, when it was bought by the Collard Company.

Kirkpatrick, John (1905–91) Amer. pianist and scholar, stud. of Boulanger and Louta Nouneberg. He has taught at Monticello College, Mount Holyoke College, Cornell and Yale (where he is curator of the Ives Collection). As a pianist, he has premiered many works of American composers and is noted for his performances of and writings on the works of Charles Ives.

Kirkpatrick, Ralph (Leonard) (1911–84) Amer. harpsichordist and pianist, stud. of Landowska and Boulanger. He toured widely performing the works of Bach, Domenica Scarlatti, etc. He also performed on the clavichord and the fortepiano, edited the sonatas of Domenico Scarlatti and taught at Yale and the U. of California at Berkeley.

Kirnberger, Johann Philipp (1721–83) German composer and theorist, trained in Sondershausen and with J.S. Bach in Leipzig. He joined the service of Princess Anna Amalia of Prussia in 1758 and remained until his death. His theoretical works are wide-ranging and are based, in part, on J.S. Bach's method. His own works incl. songs, cantatas, instrumental sonatas and trio sonatas.

Kirov Theater theater in St. Petersburg (Leningrad), opened in 1833.

Kirsten, Dorothy (1917–) Amer. soprano, stud. of Astolfo Pescia in Rome. She sang with the Metropolitan Opera from 1945 and also appeared in films. Her roles incl. Mimì (*La Bohème*), Tosca and Nedda (*I Pagliacci*).

Kismet musical by Robert Wright and George Forrest, based on musical themes by Borodin; book by Charles Lederer and Luther Davis, based on the play by Edward Knoblock. Premiere, New York 1953. A day in the life of a poet in ancient Baghdad.

Kiss Amer. heavy-metal rock band formed in New York in 1972. The group is known more for its outlan-

dish makeup, costuming and mock-threatening image than for its music.

Kiss Me, Kate musical by Cole Porter, book by Bella and Sam Spewak, based in part on Shakespeare's *Taming of the Shrew*. Premiere, New York 1948. The on-stage and off-stage happenings in and around Ford's Theatre, Baltimore, during a tryout of a musical version of Shakespeare's *The Taming of the Shrew*. The idea was suggested by a real-life situation involving Alfred Lunt and Lynn Fontanne.

kit a small unfretted bowed VIOLIN used from the 16th to 19th c., esp. by dancing masters. It is much narrower than the violin or viol and can be classified either as a small member of the viol family, or a relative of the REBEC. The kit usu. had four strings and was sometimes tuned like a violin, although more often it was tuned in 4ths, 5ths and octaves.

Kitchener-Waterloo Symphony Orchestra orch. founded in Kitchener, Ont., in 1944 by Glenn Kruspe, its conductor until 1960. Subsequent conductors have been Frédérick Pohl and Raffi Armenian.

kithara *also,* **cithara** an ancient Greek LYRE, also adopted by the Romans.

Kitt, Eartha (1928–) Amer. popular singer and actress best known as a nightclub singer. She has also appeared on Broadway (*New Faces of*

Kit

1952), in film and on radio and television.

Klang [kläng] (Ger.) sound; sonority.

Klangfarbenmelodie (Ger., tone-color-melody) used esp. in reference to the music of Schoenberg and Webern, the term indicates an analogous relationship between a succession of timbres applied to a given pitch and a succession of pitches. Thus, one might invoke timbre, or tone-color, as a structural element of a composition.

Klappe ['klä-pe] (Ger., lid) **1**, KEY (3,). **2**, VALVE.

Klarinette (Ger.) CLARINET.

Klavier [klä'vēr] (Ger.) **1**, KEYBOARD. **2**, CLAVICHORD. **3**, PIANO.

Klavierauszug [-"ows-tsook] (Ger.) piano arrangement, esp. of the orchestral accompaniment of an opera or oratorio with the vocal parts left unchanged.

Klavierstück [-"shtük] (Ger.) piece for solo piano or piano with orchestra.

Klavierübung [-"ü-bûng] (Ger.) STUDY for solo piano.

Kleiber, Carlos (1930–) German-born Argentinian conductor, son of ERICH KLEIBER. He has been conductor of the Potsdam Opera, the Deutsche Oper am Rhein, the Zürich Opera and the Stuttgart Staatsoper. He has also conducted regularly at the Bavarian Staatsoper in Munich, the Vienna Staatsoper and at Bayreuth. He is known for his perfectionism and attention to detail.

Kleiber, Erich (1890–1956) Austrian conductor, trained in Prague at the conservatory and university. He became Generalmusikdirektor of the Berlin Staatsoper in 1923, leaving in 1934 in protest to the Nazi regime. During the prewar years he conducted widely in S. America, and, in the early 1950s, regularly at Covent Garden and elsewhere in Europe. He conducted premieres of many new works, among them Janáček's *Jenůfa* and Berg's *Wozzeck*.

Klein, Lothar (1932–) German-born Canadian composer, stud. of Paul Fetler, Petrassi and Blacher. He has taught at the U. of Minnesota, the U. of Texas and (since 1968) the U. of Toronto. His works incl. *Symmetries for Orchestra* and *Three Chinese Laments*, works for chamber orchestra and vocal music.

Klein, Manny (Emmanuel) (1908–) Amer. jazz trumpeter, stud. of Max Schlossberg. He has spent most of his professional life as a studio musician, recording in all styles and making film scores (he played the trumpet solos for Montgomery Clift in *From Here to Eternity*).

kleine Flöte ['klī-ne 'flø-te] (Ger.), PICCOLO.

kleine Nachtmusik, Eine ['näkht-moo"zēk] (Ger., A Little Night Music) serenade in 4 movements for string orchestra, K. 525 (1787), by Mozart.

kleine Trommel ['trâ-məl] (Ger.) SIDE DRUM.

kl.Fl. *abbr.* (Ger.) kleine Flöte (see PICCOLO).

kl.Tr. *abbr.* (Ger.) *kleine Trommel (see* SIDE DRUM*)*.

Klemperer, Otto (1885–1973) German conductor and composer, stud. of James Kwast, Ivan Knorr and Pfitzner. He was musical dir. of the Cologne Opera, the Wiesbaden Opera and the subsidiary Staatsoper at the Kroll Theater, where he was a major force in the development of 20th-c. opera. He emigrated to the U.S. in 1933, becoming music dir. of the Los Angeles PO (1933–39). He then led the Budapest Opera (1947–50) and the Philharmonia Orch. of London (1955–72). He was particularly noted for his control of the overall concept of a work and his avoidance of sentimentality. Of his compositions, many of which he destroyed, a large number remain as yet unperformed.

Klenau, Paul (August) von (1883–1946) Danish composer and conductor, stud. of Otto Malling, F. Hillmer, Thuille and, much later, Schoenberg. He founded the Danish Philharmonic Society, which he conducted until 1926, then moved to Vienna to conduct the Konzerthausgesellschaft. He retired to Denmark in 1940. His works incl. 6 operas, 3 ballets, 7 symphonies, songs with orchestra and chamber music.

klezmer (Yiddish) a professional instrumental musician of the Jewish and German ghettos of eastern Europe. The services of a band of *klezmorin* are generally used for weddings, circumcision feasts and other special occasions.

Klien, Walter (1928–91) Austrian pianist, stud. of Josef Dichler, Michelangeli and Hindemith. He has toured widely and made many recordings, incl. the complete solo piano works of Brahms and Mozart and many of the sonatas of Schubert and Haydn. He has also accompanied both singers and instrumentalists in concert and on records.

Klindworth, Karl (1830–1916) German pianist, conductor and teacher, stud. of Liszt. From 1854 to 1868 he was in London, performing as a pianist and conductor. He taught at the Moscow Conservatory (1868–82) where he also produced the piano-vocal scores of Wagner's *Ring*. He returned to Germany in 1882 as conductor of the Berlin Philharmonic and the Wagner Society in Potsdam.

Kluge, Die ['kloo-ge, dē] (Ger., The Wise Woman) comic opera in 1 act by Orff to his own libretto based on a Grimm fairy tale, "The Farmer's Clever Daughter." Premiere, Frankfurt 1943. The farmer's daughter saves his life and becomes queen through her wisdom.

Knaben Wunderhorn, Des ['knäbən 'vûn-dər"horn, däs] (Ger., The Youth's Magic Horn) a collection of German folk poems from which Mahler chose texts for a number of songs as well as for vocal sections of his second, third and fourth symphonies.

Knabe Amer. piano manufacturing firm founded in Baltimore in 1837 by William Knabe (1803–64). It became part of the American Piano Co. in 1911.

knackers BONES.

Knappertsbusch, Hans ['knäpərts"bûsh] (1888–1965) German conductor, stud. of Fritz Steinbach. He directed opera in Elberfeld, Leipzig, Dessau and then in Munich until his life contract was nullified by the Nazi regime in 1936. He conducted in Vienna at the Staatsoper and Vienna PO during the war, then returned to Munich. He conducted frequently at Bayreuth during the 1950s, and his recordings from this period are highly regarded.

knee-lever a device operated by the knee on various keyboard instruments to provide a variety of functions, such as loudness control on a reed organ or change of register on a harpsichord.

Knepper, Jimmy (James M.) (1927–) Amer. jazz trombonist and arranger, esp. known for his work with Charles Mingus's Jazz Workshop. He has also worked with Claude Thornhill, Stan Kenton, Benny Goodman, the Thad Jones-Mel Lewis band and the Lee Konitz nonet. He is noted for his virtuoso technique and extended range on the trombone.

Knickerbocker Holiday musical by Kurt Weill, lyrics and book by Maxwell Anderson. Premiere, New York 1938. The show was Walter Huston's only Broadway musical appearance. The story of the reign of Governor Stuyvesant in New Amsterdam in 1647 is used to comment on the theme of democracy versus totalitarianism.

Knight, Gladys (M.) (1944–) Amer. soul singer, leader of the vocal group Gladys Knight and the Pips, which was formed in 1952 in Atlanta.

Knipper, Lev (1898–1974) Russian composer, trained in Moscow at the Gnesin School of Music and in Freiburg and Berlin. He was allied with the avant garde in the 1920s but adjusted his approach to be in line with socialist-realist policies of the 1930s. His works incl. the opera *Severniÿ veter* (The North Wind), 14 symphonies (the Fourth Symphony contains "Meadowland," which became popular as a song and concert work), and a number of orchestral suites.

Knot Garden, The opera in 3 acts by Sir Michael Tippett to his own libretto. Premiere, London 1970. A number of complex personal relationships are studied and modified through interaction with the psychoanalyst Mangus.

Knoxville, Summer of 1915 work for soprano and orchestra (1947) by Barber to a text inspired by the novel *A Death in the Family* by James Agee.

Knussen, (Stuart) Oliver (1952–) English composer, stud. of John Lambert and Schuller. He has been coordinator of contemporary music activities at Tanglewood since 1986. His works incl. 3 symphonies, songs and chamber music, and the opera *Where the Wild Things Are* (1979–80).

Koanga tragic opera in 3 acts by Delius to a libretto by C.F. Keary after George Washington Cable's novel, *The Grandissimes*. Premiere, Elberfeld 1904. The story, told by a Louisiana slave, of an African prince who is to marry a mulatto slave girl.

koboro an Ethiopian CONICAL DRUM.

Koch, Helmut (1908–75) German choral conductor, stud. of Max Friedman and Scherchen. He was founder of the Berlin Chamber Orch., the vocal ensemble Solistenvereinigung and the Berlin Radio Choir in East Germany. He directed the Berliner Singakademie from 1963. He is esp. known for his performances and recordings of Handel's oratorios.

Köchel, Ludwig (Alois Ferdinand) von (1800–77) Austrian botanist, mineralogist and bibliographer, who prepared a schematic catalogue of the works of Mozart. His numbering system, expanded and corrected since his time by musicologist Alfred Einstein and others, is indicated in identifications of Mozart's works by "K."

Koczwara, František KOTZWARA, FRANZ.

Kodály, Zoltán (1882–1967) Hungarian composer, teacher and ethnomusicologist, trained at the Budapest Academy of Music. Early in his career he became interested in Hungarian folk song and made many collecting tours, often in collaboration with composer Belá Bartók. He taught at the Budapest Academy of Music from 1906, and from 1921 he made many performing tours, conducting his own works. He also became deeply involved in music education in Hungary, esp. in choral music training, for which he wrote many exercises and choruses. Kodály's importance in the musical life of Hungary and the preservation of its folk heritage cannot be overstated. His works incl. *Háry János* (opera and suite), 6 other operas, *Galántai táncok* (Dances of Galánta) and other orchestral works, *Psalmus Hungaricus*, *Missa Brevis* and many other choral works with and without instruments, songs and chamber music.

Koechlin, Charles (Louis Eugène) ['kœç-lɛ̃] (1867–1950) French composer, teacher and musicologist, stud. of Massenet and Fauré. In his lifetime he was better known as an orchestrator, theorist and teacher than as a composer, and his substantial output is largely unknown and unperformed today. His pupils incl. Poulenc and Tailleferre.

Koffman, Moe (Morris) (1928–) Canadian flutist, saxophonist, clarinetist, bandleader, composer and arranger. His reputation was established by his recording of the "Swinging Shepherd Blues" (1958). He has played regularly at George's Spaghetti House in Toronto. He toured with his own group in the 1950s and 1960s, then joined the BOSS BRASS in 1972.

Kogan, Leonid (Borisovich) (1924–82) Soviet violinist, trained at the Moscow Conservatory. He performed widely as soloist, in duet with his wife, violinist Elizaveta Gilels, and in trio with pianist Emil Gilels and cellist Rostropovich. His repertory incl. many modern works, some of which were dedicated to him.

Köhler, (Christian) Louis (Heinrich) (1820–86) German composer, remembered for his piano studies, which are still used world-wide.

Kolb, Barbara (1939–) Amer. composer and clarinetist, stud. of Arnold Franchetti, Schuller and Foss. She was the first Amer. woman to win the Rome Prize and has received many commissions. Her works incl. *Trobar Clus* (1980) for chamber orchestra and tape, works for piano and other instruments, with and without electronic sounds and many songs and other vocal works.

Kolisch, Rudolf (1896–1978) Austrian-born Amer. violinist, stud. of Ševčik and Arnold Schoenberg. Because of a childhood injury, he learned to play with his hands reversed, bowing with the left hand. In 1922 he formed the Kolisch Quartet, which was famous for its performances of new music as well as standard repertory, most of which was performed from memory. The group disbanded in 1939. Kolisch taught at the U. of Wisconsin (1944–67) and the New England Conservatory of Music (1967–78).

Kollo, René (1937–) German tenor, stud. of Elsa Varena. His U.S. debut was in 1976 as Lohengrin. He has appeared in both lyric and dramatic roles throughout Europe, esp. at Bayreuth and Salzburg.

Kol Nidre (Aramaic, all the vows) **1**, an Aramaic prayer for Yom Kippur; also, a traditional melody for singing or chanting the prayer. **2**, a work for cello and orchestra (1880) by Max Bruch.

Kondrashin, Kirill (1914–81) Soviet conductor, stud. of Nikolay Zhilyayev and Boris Khaikin. He was conductor at the Malïy Theater in Leningrad, then at the Bolshoi Theater in Moscow. From 1960 to 1975 he was artistic dir. of the Moscow PO, assuming the same position with the Amsterdam Concertgebouw Orch. in 1979.

Konitz, Lee (1927–) Amer. cool jazz alto saxophonist, closely assoc. with pianist Lennie Tristano. He has also worked with Claude Thornhill, Stan Kenton and Miles Davis and led his own bands, ranging from trio to nonet format.

Kontakte [kōn'täk-te] (Ger., Contacts) important work for piano, percussion and electronic sounds (1960) by Stockhausen.

Kontarsky, Alfons (1932–) German pianist, brother of ALOYS KONTARSKY, stud. of Maurits Frank and Eduard Erdmann. He has performed in duo with his brother, concentrating on contemporary music, and also in a trio with violinist Saschko Gawriloff and cellist Klaus Storck. He has taught at Darmstadt and Cologne.

Kontarsky, Aloys (1931–) German pianist, brother of ALFONS KONTARSKY, stud. of Maurits Frank and Eduard Erdmann. In addition to his performances with his brother, he has also performed as soloist, particularly in the works of Stockhausen, and in duo with cellist Siegfried Palm. He has taught at Darmstadt and Cologne.

Kontrabass ['kōn-trä"bäs] (Ger.) DOUBLE BASS.

Kontrapunkt [-pûnkt] (Ger.) COUNTERPOINT.

Konzert [kon'tsert] (Ger.) CONCERT.

Konzertina (Ger.) CONCERTINA.

Konzertmeister [-"mī-stər] (Ger.) CONCERTMASTER.

Konzertstück [-"shtük] (Ger., concert-piece) a work for solo instrument(s) and orch., usu. more limited in scope than a concerto. A famous example is Weber's *Konzertstück* in F major for piano and orch.

Kool Jazz Festival see NEWPORT JAZZ FESTIVAL.

kora a West African, 21-string, plucked HARP-LUTE with a large leather-covered gourd resonator.

Korner, Alexis (1928–84) French-born English jazz and blues guitarist, pianist and vocalist. In the late 1940s his blues quartet played as part of Chris Barber's band concerts and later in the SKIFFLE group. In the early 1960s he formed Blues Incorporated, which was the blues source for many young English musicians of the time, and in the 1970s he hosted a jazz radio program on BBC.

Kornett [kôr'net] (Ger.) CORNET.

Korngold, Erich Wolfgang (1897–

1957) Hungarian-born Amer. composer, son of the Austrian music critic Julius Korngold. A child prodigy composer, his early works were championed by Mahler, Schnabel, Puccini and other noted musicians. His best-known work, the opera *Die tote Stadt*, was composed when he was 20. He taught at the Vienna Staatsakademie from the mid-1920s until 1934, when he moved to Hollywood, where he wrote 19 film scores, two of which won Oscars (*Robin Hood* and *Anthony Adverse*). His many works, in a lush Romantic style, incl. 5 operas, orchestral works, chamber music and songs.

Kostelanetz, André (1901–80) Russian-born Amer. conductor. He came to the U.S. in 1922 and worked for the CBS radio network from 1930. He was principal conductor of the New York PO promenade concerts and was well known for popularizing classical music. He was married to singer LILY PONS.

koto (Jap.) a long Japanese ZITHER having 13 silk strings stretched over movable bridges. The instrument is used in the GAGAKU orchestra and has also been written for by 20th-c. composers, incl. Cowell. Cf. KIN.

Kotoński, Włodzimierz (1925–) Polish composer and musicologist, trained at the Warsaw Conservatory and at Darmstadt. He has taught at the Warsaw Conservatory since 1967. His works incl. orchestral and chamber music, works for electronic tape and a piano sonata.

Kotschmar, Hermann (1829–1909) German-born Amer. composer, organist and teacher, active in Portland (ME) from 1849 and an important teacher (his pupils incl. John Knowles Paine).

Kotzwara, Franz (Koczwara, František) (1730–91) Bohemian instrumentalist and composer, active primarily in England. His published music consists of instrumental sonatas, trios and quartets for various combinations of strings, woodwinds and keyboard.

Koussevitzky, Serge (1874–1951) eminent Russian-born Amer. conductor and double bassist. He played bass with the Bolshoi Theater Orchestra, then made his conducting debut with the Berlin PO, which he hired for the occasion. In 1909 he founded the music publishing house Éditions Russes de Musique, which published music of Stravinsky and Scriabin, among others, and in the same year formed his own orchestra, which toured Russian cities and towns. With another orchestra formed by him he toured the major European cities. In 1924 he went to the U.S. as conductor of the Boston SO, where he remained for 25 years. During his tenure he commissioned many important works, including Stravinsky's *Symphony of Psalms* and Bartók's *Concerto for Orchestra*. In 1935 he established the summer concerts at TANGLEWOOD near Lenox (MA), and, five years later, the Berkshire Music Center. In 1941 he established the Koussevitzky Music Foundation in memory of his first wife to commission works from composers of all nationalities.

Koven, Reginald de DE KOVEN, REGINALD.

Kraft, Leo (1922–) Amer. composer and teacher, stud. of Karl Rathaus, Randall Thompson and Boulanger. He has taught at Queens College (NY) and has been president of the American Music Center. In addition to his works in all genres except stage music, he has written many music-theory and ear-training textbooks.

Kraft, William (1923–) Amer. composer and percussionist. He studied at Columbia U. and with Morris Goldenberg and Saul Goodman. He was percussionist with the Los Angeles PO (1955–81) and has directed the Los Angeles Percussion Ensemble and Chamber Players. He has been composer-in-residence with the Los Angeles PO and dir. of the New Music Group. He has written works for orchestra, chamber orchestra and wind ensemble, sonatas and other chamber music, songs, film scores and works for instruments and slides.

kräftig ['kref-tiç] (Ger.) powerfully, vigorously.

Krainik, Ardis (1929–) Amer. opera impresario and mezzo-soprano, General Manager of LYRIC OPERA OF CHICAGO since 1981 (General Director since 1987). She sang with the company in the mid-1950s and worked in its administration since its founding in 1954.

krakowiak [krä'kō-vē-äk] (Pol.) a Polish folk dance combining the polka with older round- and square-dance elements.

Krasner, Louis (1903–) Russian-born Amer. violinist, stud. of Eugene Gruenberg, Frederick Converse, Carl Flesch and others. He was concertmaster of the Minneapolis SO (1944–9) and then taught at the U. of Syracuse until 1972. He has been a champion of new music and commissioned the Berg Violin Concerto, which he premiered, along with a number of other important works.

Kraus, Alfredo (1927–) Spanish tenor, stud. of Mercedes Llopart. He has sung at all major opera houses, where his light, elegant singing has made him one of the leading lyric tenors of his generation. His roles incl. Alfredo (*La Traviata*), Werther and Don Ottavio (*Don Giovanni*).

Kraus, Lili (1905–86) Hungarian-born Amer. pianist, stud. of Kodály, Bartók, Steuermann and Schnabel, taught at the Vienna Conservatory and Texas Christian U., Fort Worth. She was noted for her performances of the Viennese classics, esp. Mozart.

Krause, Tom (1934–) Finnish baritone, trained at the Vienna Academy. He has sung regularly at Hamburg and has also appeared at Bayreuth, Glyndebourne and at other major European houses. His U.S. debut was at the Metropolitan Opera in 1971. He is also noted as a recitalist.

Krauss, Clemens (1893–1954) Austrian conductor. He worked at the Vienna Staatsoper and in Frankfurt. He directed the Berlin Staatsoper (1935–37), then the Munich Opera (1937–

43), in both cases replacing other conductors who had resigned in protest to the Nazi regime. During his final years he conducted the radio concerts of the Vienna PO. He was noted as an interpreter of the music of Richard Strauss, a close friend.

Krebs, Johann Ludwig (1713–80) German composer and organist, stud. of his father and of J.S. Bach. He was organist of the Marienkirche in Zwickau, at the castle at Zeitz and at the court of Prince Friedrich of Gotha-Altenburg. He was known as a virtuoso and an expert on organ construction. His works show influences of his teacher, J.S. Bach, and of the evolving *galant* style, and incl. many works for solo organ and harpsichord, trio sonatas and other chamber music, and sacred vocal works.

Kreisler, Fritz (1875–1962) Austrian-born Amer. violinist and composer, stud. of Jacques Auber, Joseph Hellmesberger Jr. and J.L. Massart, entering the Vienna Conservatory at the age of 7. He had no violin instruction after the age of 12, yet his matchless technique seemed effortless. He moved to the U.S. in 1939. As a composer, he produced an operetta, cadenzas and many short works for violin, some of which he wrote in the style of various 18th-c. composers to whom he ascribed the works, admitting his authorship only many years later, to the indignation of some critics and the amusement of others.

Kreisleriana (Ger.) a suite of eight piano pieces dedicated to Chopin, Op. 16 (1838), by Schumann, named after a pen name used by E.T.A. Hoffman for his contributions to the *Allgemeine Musikalische Zeitung*.

Krell, William (1873–1933) Amer. bandleader and composer of the first published instrumental work with the word *rag* in its title, *The Mississippi Rag*. He conducted a popular dance band in Chicago from the 1890s.

Krenek, Ernst (1900–91) prolific Austrian-born Amer. composer and conductor, stud. of Schreker. After an initial dissonant period, he gradually adopted a more diatonic idiom, sometimes incorporating jazz elements, as in his successful opera *Jonny spielt auf* (1925–6). He later adopted a version of 12-note serialism. He moved to the U.S. in 1938, teaching at Vassar College, Chicago Musical College, Dartmouth College and elsewhere. In the 1960s he wrote a number of operas, incl. several for television, and produced a number of books and articles on music, incl. texts on counterpoint and music appreciation, and musicological studies. His works incl. 21 operas, ballets and incidental music, many choral works, 5 symphonies, concertos, works for small orch. and wind band, chamber music, songs, works for solo piano.

Kreutzer, Rodolphe (1766–1831) famous French violinist, composer and teacher, stud. of Stamitz. He joined the king's music in 1785 and quickly est. himself as a leading virtuoso. He taught at the Institut National de Musique and its successor, the Paris Conservatoire. He met Beethoven, but the latter's so-called Kreutzer sonata (see KREUTZER 1,) was dedicated without the violinist's knowledge and does not appear to have been played by him. In 1810 he broke his arm, which ended his solo career, though he continued to play in ensembles. He became conductor of the Opéra in 1817, holding the post until 1824. As a composer, he produced over 50 operas and ballets, 19 violin concertos, chamber music, and sonatas and duos for violin, as well as études and caprices.

Kreutzer popular name for **1**, the sonata for violin and piano in A major, Op. 47 (1802–3), by Beethoven, composed for the mulatto violinist George Augustus Polgreen Bridgetower, who performed it with the composer at the piano (cf. KREUTZER, RODOLPHE). The finale was orig. composed for the Sonata in A major, Op. 3 No. 1. **2**, the String Quartet No. 1 (1923–4) by Janáček, a work apparently inspired by Tolstoy's novel *Kreutzer-sonata* (1904).

Krieger, Johann Philipp (1649–1725)

prolific German composer and organist. He studied in Nüremberg, Denmark and in Italy. He was Kapellmeister at the court in Weissenfels for most of his life. A large part of his enormous output is lost, but fortunately from 1684 he maintained a catalogue of works performed at the court, covering almost 50 years. His younger brother, **Johann Krieger** (1652–1735), was organist and choir dir. at Zittau for 53 years and also produced a significant body of vocal music and operas. He wrote over 2000 cantatas, instrumental sonatas, sacred and secular vocal works and almost 20 operas (all lost, except for librettos and a few arias).

Krips, Josef (1902–74) Austrian conductor, stud. of Mandyczewski and Weingartner. He was assoc. for much of his career with Vienna. Later he was principal conductor of the London PO (1950–54), the Buffalo PO (1954–63), the San Francisco SO (1963–70), and the Cincinnati May Festival (1954–60). He also conducted at Covent Garden, Salzburg, the Metropolitan Opera and the Deutsche Oper, Berlin.

Kroll, William (1901–80) Amer. violinist, stud. of Henri Marteau and Franz Kneisel. He was noted as a chamber music player in the Elshuco Trio, the Coolidge Quartet and the celebrated **Kroll Quartet** (1944–69). He taught at the Institute of Musical Art (NY), the Peabody Conservatory, the Cleveland Institute, the Mannes College, Queens College (NY) and Tanglewood.

Kronos Quartet Amer. string quartet formed in Seattle in 1973 specializing in contemporary music. The quartet has commissioned many new works and has toured widely in No. America and Europe. Since 1982 it has been in residence at the U. of S. California.

krummhorn (Ger.) *also*, **krumhorn** CRUMHORN.

Krumpholtz, Jean-Baptiste (1742–90) Bohemian harpist, composer and instrument maker. From 1773 he played under Haydn in the Esterházy

orch., but drowned himself in the Seine when his wife eloped with a lover. He produced an important body of works for the harp, still part of the repertory, and effected major mechanical improvements to the instrument.
Krupa, Gene (1909–73) Amer. jazz drummer and bandleader. After playing with the McKenzie-Condon Chicagoans and doing studio work, he joined the Benny Goodman orch. (1935–38) and made his name as a flamboyant performer. He led his own bands until 1951, then toured with Jazz at the Philharmonic and taught.

Kubelik, Rafael (Jeronym) (1914–) Czech-born Swiss conductor and composer, son of Czech violinist Jan Kubelik (1880–1940). He studied at the Prague Conservatory. He was conductor of the Czech PO (1934–48), the Brno Opera (1939–41), the Chicago SO (1950–53) and Covent Garden (1955–8), and has guest-conducted throughout Europe and the U.S. In 1961 he became principal conductor of the Bavarian Radio SO in Munich. For a brief time he was the Metropolitan Opera's first musical director. His compositions include 2 operas, symphonies, concertos and choral works.

Kubik, Gail (Thompson) (1914–84) Amer. composer, trained at the Eastman School, the American Conservatory in Chicago, and Harvard. He won the Pulitzer Prize in 1952 for his *Symphony Concertante*. He has worked in radio, television and film and has composed much music for these media. His works also incl. orchestral, choral and chamber music.

Kuerti, Anton (Emil) (1938–) Austrian-born Canadian pianist and composer, stud. of Serkin, Loesser and Horzowski, among others. He has toured widely and performed with orchestras in Europe and No. America. He is equally noted as a soloist, chamber music pianist and accompanist. In 1980 he founded the Festival of the Sound in Parry Sound (Ont.).

Kuhlau, (Daniel) Friedrich (Rudolph)

(1786–1832) German-born Danish composer and pianist, stud. of C.F.G. Schwenke in Hamburg. He went to Copenhagen in 1810 to escape Napoleon's troops and became court chamber musician in 1813, establishing a reputation as a virtuoso concert pianist. Notwithstanding his many works for flute, he was not a flutist, nor did he play the instrument. His works incl. 5 operas (incl. *Lulu*, based on the same source as *The Magic Flute*), a piano concerto, chamber music, esp. with flute, works for solo piano and piano duet, songs.

Kuhnau (Cuno, Kuhn), **Johann** (1660–1722) German composer, theorist, keyboard player and scholar, stud. of Christoph Kittel and Alexander Heringk in Dresden. In 1682 he became organist at the Thomaskirche in 1684, assuming the post of Kantor at the Thomasschule in 1701. A large number of cantatas, Latin sacred vocal music and keyboard music survive; his secular vocal music is lost. He also wrote a novel on the life of a 17th-c. musical charlatan, *Der musickalische Quack-Salber*.

Kuijken Early Music Group a Belgian early music performing ensemble consisting of three brothers—gambist **Wieland Kuijken** (1938–), viol player **Sigiswald Kuijken** (1944–) and flutist and recorder player **Barthold Kuijken** (1949–). The group frequently performs with other musicians incl. Gustav Leonhardt, Alfred Deller and Frans Bruggen. The ensemble is known for its high quality of musicianship, attention to detail, historical scholarship and purity of sound. Each brother also performs and records separately.

kujawiak (koo'yä-vē-äk]) (Pol.) a Polish couple-dance in moderate triple time with displaced accents, similar to the MAZURKA.

kulintang 1, a GONG-CHIME consisting of eight gongs hung in a row. **2,** an ensemble combining four or five kulintangs.

Kullak, Theodor (1818–82) German pianist and teacher, stud. of Czerny.

He was a co-founder of the Stern Conservatory in Berlin and founder of the Neue Akademie der Tonkunst, which became the largest private musical institute in Germany. His pupils incl. Scharwenka and Moszkowski. His methods are still in use, esp. the *Schule des Oktavenspiels* (The School of Octave-playing).

kultrun a small Chilean KETTLEDRUM, filled with seeds or stones.

Kunst der Fugue, Die [kûnst dār 'fooge] (Ger.) ART OF THE FUGUE, THE.

Kunzel, Erich (1935–) Amer. conductor, trained at Harvard and Brown Universities and with Monteux. He taught at Brown and was conductor with the Cincinnati SO from 1965 to 1974. He founded the Cincinnati Pops in 1977 and is best known as a conductor of light classics and jazz.

Kupferman, Meyer (1926–) Amer. composer and clarinetist, self-taught as a composer. He has taught at Sarah Lawrence College since 1951. His works incl. 25 *Infinities* for various ensembles, all based on the same 12-note series, symphonies (incl. *Symphony of the Yin-Yang*), film scores, choral and vocal works, and chamber music.

Kurka, Robert (Frank) (1921–57) Amer. composer, stud. of Otto Luening and Darius Milhaud. His works, which show the influence of his Czech heritage, incl. *The Good Soldier Schweik* (opera), 2 symphonies, works for small orchestra, string quartets, sonatas, piano works and songs.

Kurtz, Efrem (1900–) Russian-born Amer. conductor, trained in St. Petersburg and Berlin. He was musical dir. of the Stuttgart PO (1924–33) and conducted tours for the dancer Anna Pavlova, then became musical dir. of the Ballets Russes de Monte Carlo (1933–41). He served as musical dir. of the Kansas City PO (1943–47) and the Houston SO (1948–54), thereafter free-lancing throughout the world.

Kurz, Selma (1874–1933) Austrian soprano, stud. of Johannes Ress. She sang regularly in Vienna and at Covent Garden. In the U.S. she sang only in recital. Her principal roles were Violetta (*La Traviata*), Gilda (*Rigoletto*) and Oscar (*Un Ballo in Maschera*).

K.V. *abbr.* (Ger.) Köchel-Verzeichnis (see KÖCHEL).

kwela (Zulu) S. African urban music, usu. blending guitars, flutes and bass.

Kyle, Billy (William Osborne) (1914–66) Amer. jazz pianist and arranger, pianist for Louis Armstrong's All Stars from 1953. He was considered one of the best band pianists.

kyrie eleison one of the sections of the Mass Ordinary (see MASS). The Kyrie occurs immediately after the INTROIT, and is the only section of the Mass to have a Greek text.

L

la 1, the note A. See PITCH. **2,** the sixth and last degree of the Guidonian HEXACHORD. **3,** IN THE TONIC SOL-FA system, the raised submediant of the current key (or of the relative major, if the current key is minor). See SOLMIZATION, LAH.

La Barbara, Joan (1947–) Amer. singer and composer of music that frequently combines live and electronic sounds. She has developed new vocal techniques, incl. circular breathing and multiphonics, and has premiered new works by Cage, Lucier and her husband, Morton Subotnick.

La Barre, Michel de (c1675–c1744) French flutist and composer, a member of the royal chamber music. His flute suites published in 1702 were the first solo pieces for transverse flute to appear in print. In addition to 13 books for solo flute and flute duet, he produced trio sonatas, two ballets and vocal music.

labial pipe FLUE PIPE.

Lablache, Luigi (1794–1858) Italian bass, trained in Naples. He sang in Palermo for two years, then at La Scala in Milan for six years, then joined the royal chapel in Vienna. From 1830 to 1852 he sang regularly in London at the King's Theatre and at the Théâtre-Italien in Paris. He is best known for his portrayal of comic roles, and he created the role of Don Pasquale in Donizetti's opera.

Lacy, Steve (Steven Lackritz) (1934–) Amer. jazz composer and soprano saxophonist. He played traditional jazz for many years, then worked with Cecil Taylor and Jimmy Giuffre before undertaking a rigorous examination of compositions by Thelonious Monk. In the late 1960s he worked in Rome, experimenting with electronic music. He has been based in Paris since 1967, playing with various groups and recording extensively.

Laderman, Ezra (1924–) Amer. composer and teacher, stud. of Wolpe and Luening. He has taught at Sarah Lawrence College and at SUNY, Binghamton. He has been president of the American Music Center and of the Composers' Commissioning Program of the National Endowment of the Arts. His works incl. 4 operas (incl. *Sarah*, a television opera), 3 symphonies, piano concertos, oratorios, songs and chamber music.

Lady, Be Good! musical by George Gershwin, lyrics by Ira Gershwin, book by Guy Bolton and Fred Thompson. Premiere, New York 1924. The story of two dispossessed dancers (originally played by Fred and Adele Astaire) who come into money.

Lady Day popular name for jazz singer BILLIE HOLIDAY.

Lady in the Dark musical by Kurt Weill, lyrics by Ira Gershwin, book by Moss Hart. Premiere, New York 1941. A fashion magazine editor tries psychoanalysis to regain her self-confidence.

Lady Macbeth of Mtsensk see KATERINA ISMAILOVA.

LaFaro, Scott (1936–61) virtuosic Amer. jazz double bassist, a performer with Chet Baker, Bill Evans and Ornette Coleman and an important innovator in the free-jazz style.

La Forge, Frank (1879–1953) Amer. pianist, teacher and composer, stud. of Leschetizky and others. He taught in Berlin for some years, then returned to the U.S. to perform, primarily as an accompanist, always performing from memory. He also taught voice (Tibbett was a pupil) and wrote songs and piano works.

Lagacé, Bernard (1930–) Canadian organist, stud. of Conrad Letendre, André Marchal and Anton Heiller. He has taught at the Quebec Conservatory since 1957 and has given many recitals in Europe and No. America.

lah in TONIC SOL-FA, the submediant of the current key (or, if the key is minor, the submediant of its relative major). See SOLMIZATION, LA.

lai [lā] (Fr.) a medieval song form in which each stanza has a unique form and musical setting. The term encompasses a wide variety of poems, broadly divisible into the lyric lai and the narrative lai (*lai breton*). The most famous composer of lais was undoubtedly GUILLAUME DE MACHAUT. Also, *leich, descort.*

Laine, Cleo (Campbell, Clementina Dinah) (1927–) English contralto, whose wide repertory encompasses jazz, popular and contemporary classical repertory. She is particularly noted for her scat singing.

Laine, Frankie (LoVecchio, Frank Paul) (1913–) Amer. popular singer, whose style combines crooning with jazz techniques. His hits incl. "Mule Train" (1949) and "High Noon" (1952).

Lake George Opera Festival a summer opera season in Lake George, NY, founded in 1962.

Lakmé [läk'mā] (Fr.) opera in 3 acts by Delibes to a libretto by Edmond Gondinet and Phillipe Gille, based on Gondinet's play *Le Mariage de Loti.* Premiere, Paris 1883. Lakmé, daughter of a Hindu priest, falls in love with a British soldier.

Lalande, Michel-Richard de [lä'lād] (1657–1726) French composer, organist and harpsichordist. He became one of the four royal organists in 1683, assuming full control in 1714. He is best remembered as a composer of the *grand motet,* a late Baroque form combining elements of opera and motet. He also produced many ballets and divertissements for the royal court, as well as symphonies and airs.

Lalo,   Edouard(-Victoire-Antoine)

(1823–92) French composer, stud. of Habeneck, Julius Schulhoff and J.-E. Crèvecoeur. He was a founder and member of the Armingaud Quartet (1855), formed to promote the quartets of Beethoven, Mozart and Haydn in France. Most of his important compositions date from after 1870, principally orchestral music and opera (the opera *Le roi d'Ys* is his best-known work). He also composed a number of chamber works and songs. His son, **Pierre Lalo** (1866–1943), was an important French music critic.

Lamb, Joseph F(rancis) (1877–1960) Amer. ragtime composer, stud. of Scott Joplin. His works were composed from 1909 to 1919 and after 1949; in the interim he worked in the textile trade. His best works are for piano (*American Beauty Rag,* the *Alaskan Rag* and *Champagne and Bohemia*) and he also wrote songs.

Lambeg drum a large double-headed DRUM beaten with bamboo canes, used in fife-and-drum bands in Ulster county, Ireland.

Lambert, (Leonard) Constant (1905–51) English composer, conductor and writer, trained at the Royal College of Music. He conducted the Camargo Society, the Vic-Wells Ballet and guest-conducted occasionally at Covent Garden, Sadler's Wells and elsewhere. His most important works are for the ballet (his *Romeo and Juliet* was the first English work performed by Diaghilev's Ballets Russes). He also wrote songs, choral works, orchestral music, incidental music and film scores, and a book of criticism, *Music Ho! A Study of Music in Decline* (1934).

lamellaphone a type of instrument found esp. in Africa whose sound is produced by the plucking of a thin tongue of metal, wood or other material. Cf. SANSA.

lament a musical work expressing grief over the loss of a person, esp. a loved one, through death or leave-taking. Laments may be vocal or instrumental. They form a part of every culture's musical heritage. Also, *dé-*

ploration, tombeau, plainte (Fr.). Cf.
LAMENTO.

Lamentatione (It.) title for the Symphony No. 26 in D minor (1770) by Haydn.

lamentations verses of mourning of the prophet Jeremiah as found in the Old Testament. Portions of these verses form a part of the Roman Catholic liturgy for Maundy Thursday, Good Friday and Holy Saturday and settings appear as early as the 15th c. The text has been frequently set by composers up to the present day.

lamento (It.) a lament; esp. a type of lamenting aria found in early Italian opera, often composed over a ground bass which descends by step over the interval of a fourth. See GROUND.

La Montaine, John (1920–) Amer. composer, stud. of Rogers, Hanson, Wagenaar and Boulanger. He was pianist for the NBC SO under Toscanini and taught briefly at the Eastman School. His works incl. several operas, concertos for piano and flute, symphonies and other orchestral works, songs and chamber music. He won the Pulitzer Prize in 1959 for his Piano Concerto.

Lamoureux, Charles [lä-moo′rø] (1834–99) French conductor and violinist, trained at the Paris Conservatoire. Made wealthy by marriage, he organized his own performances of oratorios in the mid-1870s, then in 1881 founded the weekly Concerts Lamoureux, through which he pursued his support of the music of Wagner. His effort in 1887 to produce *Lohengrin* was unsuccessful because of a strong anti-German protest, but a decade later he produced *Tristan und Isolde* at the Nouveau-Théâtre.

lancers a 19th-c. square dance, a variant of the QUADRILLE, danced to popular songs.

Landi, Stefano (1586–1639) Italian composer, singer and teacher. He worked in Rome for most of his career, joining the Papal Choir in 1629. His surviving works incl. two operas (*La morte d'Orfeo, Il Sant' Alessio*),

motets, psalms and secular madrigals and arias.

Landini, Francesco (c1325–97) Italian composer, organist, singer and instrument maker, son of the painter Jacopo Del Casentino. Little is known about him except that most of his life was spent in Florence, where he was probably organist at the monastery of Santa Trinità and at the church of St. Lorenzo. His surviving works consist entirely of secular virelais, ballatas and madrigals.

Landini cadence a cadence in which the sixth scale degree (*Landini sixth*) is interposed between the leading tone and the tonic, a procedure common both in the works of FRANCESCO LANDINI and in 15th- and 16th-c. polyphony in general. See CADENCE (*illus.*).

Ländler [′lend-lər] (Ger.) an Austrian couple-dance in triple time, slower than the waltz. The style of the Ländler was often imitated in works by Haydn, Mozart, Brahms, Bruckner and Mahler. Also, *Dreher* (Ger.), *Tyrolienne, Styrienne* (Fr.).

Landowska, Wanda (1879–1959) Polish keyboard player, stud. of Jan Kleczyński, Alexander Michałowski and Heinrich Urban. From the turn of the century she concentrated on the harpsichord, commissioning from Pleyel an instrument built to her specifications. She taught at the Berlin Hochschule für Musik, the Paris École Normale, and at the École de Musique Ancienne, which she founded in 1925. She was largely responsible for the revival of interest in the harpsichord and in the development of a modern technique on the instrument. Poulenc and Falla wrote harpsichord concertos for her.

Lane, Burton (Kushner, Morris Hyman) (1912–) Amer. composer of songs, musicals and film scores. His best-known works are the musicals *Finian's Rainbow* (1947) and *On a Clear Day You Can See Forever* (1965).

Lane, Louis (1923–) Amer. conductor, stud. of Rogers, Martinů and

Sarah Caldwell. He has been assoc. conductor of the Cleveland Orchestra, the Dallas SO and the Atlanta SO and has guest-conducted extensively. His programs often specialize in contemporary Amer. music.

Lang, B(enjamin) J(ohnson) (1837–1909) Amer. pianist, organist, teacher, composer and conductor, stud. of Liszt and others. He was an influential force in Boston musical life from the early 1860s as an organist, teacher and conductor, esp. of choral music (he was conductor of the Apollo Club and the Cecilia Society).

Lang, Eddie (Massaro, Salvatore) (1902–33) Amer. jazz guitarist, orig. trained as a classical violinist. For many years he performed on guitar in duet with violinist Joe Venuti. He also played with Red Nichols, Paul Whiteman, the Dorsey brothers and Bing Crosby, among others.

Lang, Josephine (Carolin) (1815–80) German composer and singer of lieder, stud. of Mendelssohn.

Lang, Margaret Ruthven (1867–1972) Amer. composer of songs and instrumental works, daughter and stud. of B.J. LANG. Her songs were performed by many leading singers, and she was the first woman in the U.S. to have a work performed by a major symphony orch. (Boston SO, 1893). She stopped composing in 1917.

Langdon, Michael (1920–91) English bass, best known for his portrayal of Baron Ochs (*Der Rosenkavalier*), which he has sung in many major opera houses. His roles also incl. Don Basilio (*The Barber of Seville*), Claggart (*Billy Budd*) and Osmin (*The Abduction from the Seraglio*). He retired from opera in 1977.

Langlais, Jean (1907–) French organist and composer, stud. of Marchal, Dupré, Tournemire and Dukas. He was organist of St. Pierre de Montrouge, then, after 1945, of St. Clothilde, and he taught at the Institution des Jeunes Aveugles. He has frequently toured in the U.S. and has written a large body of works for organ alone and with other instru-

ments, as well as sacred choral works.

langleik (Norwegian) a Norwegian folk BOARD ZITHER with one melody string and drone strings, played with a plectrum.

langsam ['läng-zäm] (Ger.) slow(ly).

langspil (Icelandic) an Icelandic bowed BOARD ZITHER.

langueur [lä'gœr] (Fr.) a type of VIBRATO.

Lanier, Nicholas (1588–1666) English composer, singer, lutanist and painter, the first Master of the King's Music in 1625. He wrote masques in collaboration with Ben Jonson and composed a large number of songs, many of which unfortunately have not survived.

Lansky, Paul (1944–) Amer. composer, trained at Queens College and Princeton, where he has taught since 1969. His works utilize a 12-tone tonal style based on theories of George Perle and incl. chamber works and computer-generated music.

Lanza, Mario (Cocozza, Alfredo Arnold) (1921–59) Amer. tenor and actor. He began in opera and concert but made his name in films, esp. in his portrayal of Enrico Caruso (*The Great Caruso*).

Lara, Agustin (1900–70) Mexican songwriter, many of whose songs, incl. "Granada," achieved international popularity.

Laredo, Jaime (Eduardo) (1941–) Bolivian-born Amer. violinist, stud. of Ivan Galamian. In 1959 he was the youngest ever to win the Queen Elisabeth Competition in Brussels. He has toured extensively and plays regularly at the Marlboro Festival.

largamente (It.) broadly.

large [lärzh] (Fr.) LARGO.

larghetto [lär'gät-tō] (It.) rather slow, but faster than LARGO.

largo (It.) **1**, slow, broad, slower than LENTO, faster than GRAVE. **2**, (cap.) popular name for the aria "Ombra mai fu" from Handel's opera *Serse*, frequently performed in various instrumental arrangements.

larigot [lä-rē'gō] (Fr.) a foundation ORGAN STOP pitched two octaves and a fifth above the fingered pitch. Also, *nineteenth*.

Lark Ascending, The a romance for violin and orchestra (1914, rev. 1920) by Vaughan Williams. The title comes from a poem by George Meredith.

Larkins, Ellis Lane (1923–) distinguished Amer. jazz pianist, trained at the Peabody Conservatory and the Juilliard School. For most of his career he led his own trio in New York in addition to working as a studio musician.

Lark Quartet popular name for the string quartet in D, Op. 64 No. 5 (1789), by Haydn, supposedly so named because of effects in the first violin that resemble the song of the lark.

Larrocha (y de la Calle), Alicia de (1923–) Spanish pianist, stud. of Frank Marshall. Her Amer. debut was in 1955 in Los Angeles. She teaches at the Marshall Academy at Barcelona. She is noted for her performances of Spanish works as well as the repertory of the Romantic and Classical eras.

Larsen, Libby (Elizabeth Brown) (1950–) Amer. composer, trained at the U. of Minnesota. She was cofounder of the Minnesota Composers Forum and has been composer-in-residence with the Minnesota Orchestra. She has written several operas, orchestral and chamber works and works for voice(s) with various instrumental ensembles.

Larsson, Lars-Erik (Vilner) (1908–86) Swedish composer, trained at the Stockholm Conservatory and in Germany. He worked for Swedish radio (1937–53) and has taught at the Stockholm Conservatory (1947–59) and Uppsala U. (1961–6). His works incl. many orchestral and chamber music works, 2 operas, a ballet, film scores, choral works and songs.

La Rue, Pierre de (c1460–1518) Flemish composer and singer. He sang at Siena Cathedral and 's-Hertogenbosch Cathedral and was a member of the Burgundian court chapel until 1508, when he returned to the Netherlands. His surviving works incl. many Mass settings, other sacred vocal music, motets and chansons.

LaSalle Quartet Amer. string quartet formed in 1949 by students from the Juilliard School. The quartet was in residence at Colorado College, then at the College Conservatory of Music at the U. of Cincinnati. The LaSalle is best known for its renditions of 20th-c. masterworks, and many composers have written works for the ensemble.

La Scala see SCALA, TEATRO ALLA.

Laschi (Mombelli), **Luisa** ['lä-skē] (c. 1760–c1790) Italian soprano, active principally in Vienna. She was the original Countess in Mozart's *Le nozze di Figaro* and Zerlina in *Don Giovanni*.

Lasso, Orlando di (1532–94) Flemish composer. In 1556 he joined the court of Duke Albrecht of Bavaria in Munich, a position he held until his death and which was passed on to his sons. Lasso was famous throughout Europe in his own time, and his works were widely published. His immense output incl. sacred vocal music, madrigals, chansons and German lieder.

lassú ('lä-shoo) (Hung.) the slow introductory section of a CSÁRDÁS or rhapsody; contrasted with FRISS. Cf. VERBUNKOS.

Lassus, Roland de LASSO, ORLANDO DI.

Lateef, Yusef (Evans, William) (1921–) Amer. jazz tenor saxophonist, flutist and oboist. He has worked with Roy Eldridge, Dizzy Gillespie, Charles Mingus and Cannonball Adderley and has also led his own groups. In the early 1980s he lived and taught in Nigeria, but moved back to the U.S. later in the decade.

Lateiner, Jacob (1928–) Cuban-born Amer. pianist, trained at the Curtis Institute and with Schoenberg. He has performed throughout Europe and the U.S., specializing in the works of Beethoven and of contemporary Amer. composers, such as Sessions and Carter.

laud a hymn of praise.

lauda *also,* **lauda spirituale** (It.) an Italian religious song not based on liturgy, usu. having a refrain (*ripresa*) and verses. Early forms (13th and 14th c.) are usu. monophonic, later forms are often polyphonic.

Lauder, Sir **Harry (Maclennan)** (1870–1950) popular Scottish music-hall singer and composer, whose stage *persona* was usu. a stereotypical Scotsman with brogue and kilt. He composed much of his own musical material.

Laudon Symphony, The the symphony no. 69 in C (1778) by Haydn, composed in honor of the Austrian field marshal Ernst von Laudon.

lauds the second of the daily services which comprise the DIVINE OFFICE of the Roman Catholic church, usu. sung at daybreak.

launedda a Sardinian triple CLARINET with two drone pipes and one melody pipe.

Lauri-Volpi, Giacomo (1892–1979) Italian tenor, stud. of Antonio Cotogni and Enrico Rosati. He sang regularly at La Scala and at the Metropolitan Opera from 1922 and made many recordings. His roles incl. Calaf (*Turandot*), the Duke (*Rigoletto*) and Arnold (*Guillaume Tell*). He retired in 1959.

Lavallée, Calixa (1842–91) Canadian composer and pianist, trained in Montreal and later at the Paris Conservatoire. In his early years he toured and taught in Canada and the U.S. and for a brief time was in charge of the New York Grand Opera House (a minstrel-show theater). He returned to Canada in 1875 to teach and compose. His song *O Canada*, now the national anthem of Canada, was written for St. John the Baptist Day celebrations in 1879. His surviving works (most of his unpublished works are lost) incl. the operas *TIQ* and *The Widow*, some orchestral and chamber music and songs.

lavolta (It.) VOLTA.

Law, Andrew (1749–1821) Amer. tunebook compiler and organizer of SINGING-SCHOOLS. He traveled widely in the eastern U.S., promoting his many publications and teaching his system of staffless SHAPE NOTE notation.

Lawes, Henry (1596–1662) English singer and composer of ayres, older brother of WILLIAM LAWES. He joined the Chapel Royal in 1626 and the king's musicians in 1631. He was also a successful teacher of singing. His works incl. anthems and psalm settings, and many songs and ayres.

Lawes, William (1602–45) English composer and musician, younger brother of HENRY LAWES and stud. of John Coperario. He was in the service of Prince (later King) Charles and a member of his personal guard. He produced a substantial body of works for viols, keyboard, and other instruments, and sacred and secular vocal music, much of the latter for inclusion in dramatic works.

Lawrence, Gertrude (Klasen, Gertrud Alexandra Dagmar Lawrence) (1898–1952) English actress, singer and dancer; as singer best known for her roles in *Lady in the Dark* and *The King and I*. Several musicals in the late 1920s were written for her, notably by the Gershwin brothers (*Oh, Kay!* and *Treasure Girl*).

Lawrence, Robert (1912–81) Amer. conductor, commentator and critic. He conducted in Italy in the mid-1950s, then led the Phoenix SO, the Ankara SO and the American Opera Society. He founded the Friends of French Opera in 1961 and was a regular commentator on the Metropolitan Opera broadcasts. He taught at the Peabody Conservatory.

lay LAI.

layer one of various levels of polyphonic representation of a work in Schenkerian analysis (see SCHENKER).

Layton, Billy Jim (1924–) Amer. composer, stud. of F.J. Cooke, Carl McKinley, Porter, Gombosi and Piston. He taught at Harvard until 1966, then at SUNY Stony Brook. His relatively small output includes several works for orch., a string quartet, studies for violin and piano, *Dylan Thomas Poems* for chorus and brass sextet, and other chamber music.

Lazarof, Henri (1932–) Bulgarian-born Amer. composer, trained in Sofia, Jerusalem, Rome and at Brandeis U. He has taught at the U. of California at Los Angeles. His works, atonal and sometimes serial, are mostly instrumental, some incorporating electronic tape.

Leadbelly (Ledbetter, Huddie) (1885–1949) Amer. blues singer and guitarist. Twice sentenced for murder, he was discovered and recorded by Alan Lomax in the 1930s. He worked frequently with Blind Lemon Jefferson and harmonica player Sonny Terry. Of his many songs, "Good Night Irene" and "Rock Island Line" are among the best known.

leader 1, CONDUCTOR. **2**, (Brit.) CONCERTMASTER.

leading motive LEITMOTIF.

leading tone *also*, **leading note** the seventh degree of a major scale, or the raised seventh degree of a minor scale, a half step beneath the tonic and hence tending toward it. Also, *subtonic*.

lead sheet a simplified or outline version of a popular song used as a basis for improvisation.

League of Composers an org. founded in 1923 in New York to encourage the composition and performance of new music. From 1924 to 1947 it published the periodical *Modern Music*. It merged with the ISCM in 1954.

Lear (née Shulman), **Evelyn** (1928–) Amer. soprano, trained at the Juilliard School and at Tanglewood. She has performed regularly at the Deutsche Oper in Berlin, at the Metropolitan Opera (since 1967) and at other major houses. She is particularly noted for her portrayal of the title role of Alban Berg's *Lulu*, as well as many standard roles, incl. Tosca, Mimì and the Countess (*The Marriage of Figaro*). She is married to baritone THOMAS STEWART.

Le Beau, Luise Adolpha (1850–1927) German pianist and composer of an opera (*Hadumoth*), vocal and orchestral works, and an autobiography about the obstacles confronting a woman composer.

Lebègue, Nicolas-Antoine (c1631–1702) French composer, organist and harpsichordist. By 1664 he was organist at St. Merry, a position he held until his death, and in 1678 he added the title of organist to the king. He was noted in his time as a virtuoso organist and harpsichordist, as an expert on organ building and as a teacher. He left a substantial body of works for harpsichord and for organ as well as some sacred choral works.

Lebensstürme ['lā-bəns"shtür-me] (Ger., Life's Storms) the Allegro in A minor for piano duet, Op. 144 (1828), by Schubert.

lebhaft ['lāp-häft] (Ger.) lively, brisk. Cf. VIVACE.

Leclair, Jean-Marie (1697–1764) French violinist, dancer and composer, a major force in the establishment of the French school of violin playing. He was noted for his adaptation of the Italian sonata style to the French taste. His surviving music is largely for violin, either solo, in concerto, or in chamber music combination with other instruments.

Lecocq, (Alexandre) Charles [lə'kok] (1832–1918) French composer of operetta, stud. of Bazin and Halévy. He shared first place with Bizet in a competition organized by Offenbach which involved setting the libretto for *Le docteur Miracle* (Bizet's version is occasionally performed today). Lecocq wrote more than 50 operettas, as well as songs, choruses and works for solo piano.

leçons de ténèbre [la'sō də tā'ne-brə] (Fr.) a Baroque name for settings of the LAMENTATIONS of Jeremiah.

lectionary a liturgical book of lessons to be read or chanted during the MASS or DIVINE SERVICE.

Ledbetter, Huddie LEADBELLY.

ledger lines extra lines added above or below the staff to permit writing notes that exceed the range of the staff. Often the OTTAVA sign (8va) is used to avoid excessive use of ledger lines. Also, *leger lines.*

Leduc, Alphonse [lə'dük] (1804–68) French music publisher, founder of a publishing firm in Paris in 1841, best known for its pedagogical publications for voice and solfège.

Led Zeppelin English heavy-metal rock band formed in 1968 and active until the early 1980s. They have produced a number of hits, among them "Stairway to Heaven" and "Whole Lotta Love."

Lee, Brenda (Tarpley, Brenda Mae) (1944–) Amer. popular and country-music singer, who established an international career in pop music before she was 20. In recent years she has concentrated on country-music hits. Her songs incl. "I'm Sorry" (1960) and "Nobody Wins" (1973).

Lee, Peggy (Egstrom, Norma Dolores) (1920–) Amer. popular singer, songwriter and actress. She sang with various swing bands, incl. Benny Goodman's, and also appeared in films (*Pete Kelly's Blues*).

Lee (Leary), **Wilma** (1921–) Amer. bluegrass guitarist, singer, organist and songwriter. She appeared regularly with her husband Stoney Cooper on the "Jamboree" radio program in Wheeling, WV, from 1947, later becoming a star of the Grand Ole Opry. After her husband's death, she continued to perform and record.

Leeman, Cliff (Clifford) (1913–86) Amer. jazz drummer. He played with Artie Shaw, Glenn Miller, Tommy Dorsey, Charlie Barnet and Woody Herman. In the 1940s he worked both with big bands and in the studio. In later years he played with Eddie Condon, the Dukes of Dixieland and many others.

Lees, Benjamin (1924–) Amer. composer, born in China of Russian parents, stud. of Halsey Stevens, Dahl and Antheil. He lived and worked in Europe from 1954 to 1962, returning to the U.S. to teach at the Peabody Conservatory and to compose. His works are relatively free from the influence of schools, utilizing a highly chromatic but fundamentally tonal style, and incl. *The Oracle* and *The Gilded Cage* (operas), choral and orchestral works, piano sonatas and pieces and instrumental chamber music.

Leeuw, Ton de (1926–) Dutch composer and teacher, stud. of Badings, Messiaen and Hartmann. He teaches at the Amsterdam Conservatory and has worked for Dutch radio as a producer. He has written operas and stage works, some for television or radio, orchestral works, instrumental chamber music, some with electronic tape, works for solo piano and songs.

legato (It., tied) smooth, connected; opposed to STACCATO. This articulation is often indicated by a curved line over or under the notes to be so played. In string playing, *legato* may be indicated whether or not the notes are to be played in the same bow stroke, as long as no separation is heard between the notes (the unslurred *legato* bowstroke is called, somewhat confusingly, *détaché*). See BOWING.

Legends see LEMMINKÄINEN SUITE.

leger 1, [lə'zhā] (Fr.) light; may be an indication of tempo or of character. **2,** see LEDGER LINES.

leggero *also,* **leggiero** [led'ge-rō] (It.) lightly, gracefully; usu. an indication of character.

Leginska (Leggins), **Ethel** (1886–1970) English-born Amer. pianist, conductor and composer, stud. of Leschetizky, Bloch and others. She concertized actively until 1926, then concentrated on conducting (until about 1935) and composing. In her later years she taught piano in Los Angeles.

legit [lə'jit] referring to music, a slang term meaning classical, not jazz, pop, etc.

legni ['lā-nyē] (It.) woodwind instruments or the woodwind section of an orchestra.

legno, col COL LEGNO.

legomania a style of ECCENTRIC

DANCING consisting of high kicks and wiggles. Also, *rubberlegs*.

Legrand, Michel [lə'grã] (1932–) French conductor and composer, stud. of Henri Chaland and Boulanger. He has worked principally in jazz and popular music, making many recordings and composing film scores (he has won four Oscars).

Legrenzi, Giovanni (1626–90) Italian composer and organist at St. Maria Maggiore in Bergamo and the Accademia dello Spirito Santo at Ferrara. He became chorus master at the Conservatorio dei Mendicanti in Venice in the late 1670s, moving to St. Mark's in 1681. He wrote 19 operas, 7 oratorios, sacred and secular vocal music and instrumental sonatas.

Lehár, Franz (Ferencz) (1870–1948) Hungarian-born Austrian conductor and composer, trained at the Prague Conservatory. He was a bandmaster until 1902, producing instrumental dances and marches, and then conducted at several theaters in Vienna. The tremendous success in 1905 of his operetta *Die lustige Witwe* (The Merry Widow) was followed by, among others, *Zigeunerliebe* (Gypsy Love) and *Das Land des Lächelns* (The Land of Smiles). His last operetta was written in 1934, after which he concentrated on publishing activities. His works incl. *Kukuška* (opera), 40 operettas, film scores, instrumental marches and dances, orchestral works, songs and works for solo piano.

Lehmann, Lilli (1848–1929) German soprano, stud. of her mother, singer Marie Loewe. Her London debut was in 1880, and her U.S. debut was at the Metropolitan Opera in 1885. After leaving the Metropolitan in 1899, she sang for ten years at the Salzburg Festival, of which she was artistic director. She was famous for her interpretive skill in opera as well as in recital, and also as a teacher. Her pupils included Geraldine Farrar and Olive Fremstadt. Lilli's younger sister, **Marie Lehmann** (1851–1931), was also a singer at Bayreuth, Berlin and elsewhere.

Lehmann, Liza (Elizabetha Nina Mary Frederica) (1862–1918) English singer and composer, stud. of Jenny Lind and others. She was a successful recital artist, but is best known for her song cycle *In a Persian Garden* (1896).

Lehmann, Lotte (1888–1976) German soprano, stud. of Mathilde Mallinger. She sang from 1916 to 1938 in Vienna, where she established herself as a leading interpreter of the roles of Strauss, Puccini, Massenet and others. She also sang regularly at Covent Garden from 1924 to 1938, performing a wide range of roles. Her Amer. debut was in Chicago in 1930, and she sang regularly at the Metropolitan from 1934 to 1945. Equally revered as a recital artist, she continued to perform in concert until 1951 and to teach after her retirement from the stage.

Lehrer, Tom (Thomas Andrew) (1928–) Amer. songwriter, humorist, performer and mathematics teacher. Since the early 1950s he has recorded and toured, performing his own songs, which are sometimes biting satires on contemporary issues.

Lehrstück ['lär″shtük] (Ger., teaching piece) a work intended for amateur performers and designed to raise artistic and political consciousness. The term may have been coined by Bertolt Brecht, who wrote a number of works in the genre in collaboration with Weill, Hindemith, Eisler and other composers. Cf. GEBRAUCHS-MUSIK.

Leibowitz, René (1913–72) Polish-born French composer, conductor and musicologist, stud. of Schoenberg, Webern and Ravel. He conducted the chamber ensemble of the Orchestre National of the French Radio from 1937 and founded the International Festival of Chamber Music. He is esp. noted for his support in France, through writings (esp. *Schönberg et son école*) and performances, of the works of the Second Viennese School.

His own works, which employ a rigorous serial technique, incl. 5 operas, orchestral works, instrumental chamber music, works for solo piano (incl. 2 sonatas), choral works and songs.

Leich [līç] (Ger.) LAI.

Leider, Frida ['lī-dər] (1888–1975) German soprano, trained in Berlin. She was the principal dramatic soprano of the Berlin Staatsoper from 1923 to 1938, specializing in Wagner, Mozart, Strauss and Verdi. She also sang regularly at Covent Garden and, from 1928 to 1932, in Chicago. Her Metropolitan Opera debut was in 1933, but she sang there for only two years. Many of her finest roles are preserved on records.

Leigh, Mitch (Mitchnick, Irwin) (1928–) Amer. songwriter, stud. of Hindemith, best known for his Broadway musical *Man of La Mancha* (1965).

Leinsdorf (Landauer), **Erich** (1912–) Austrian-born Amer. conductor, stud. of Paul Pisk and others in Vienna. He began as rehearsal pianist for Webern, then as assistant to Bruno Walter at Salzburg. He went to the Metropolitan Opera in 1937 as assistant conductor, taking charge of the German wing in 1939. He was conductor of the Rochester PO (1947–55) and of the Boston SO (1962–9). Since then he has free-lanced throughout the world, known for his thorough preparation and innovative programming.

leitmotiv ['līt-mō"tēf] (Ger., leading motive) *also*, **leitmotif** a musical theme associated by a composer with a certain idea, feeling, object or character and used throughout a work as its representative. It may be repeated exactly or altered for various reasons, as long as it is still recognizable enough to recall the earlier association. Incipient uses of motives for this purpose appear in late 18th-c. opera, and the term was orig. coined by F.W. Jähns in discussion of the operas of Weber. The technique is usu. associated most fully with Wagner,

who used it extensively in his works from *The Flying Dutchman* on. It has also been used by composers since Wagner's time, notably Janáček and Berg.

Leitner, Ferdinand (1912–) German conductor, stud. of Franz Schreker and Julius Prüwer. He has been conductor of the Nollendorf Theater in Berlin, the Hamburg Staatsoper, the Munich Staatsoper and the Stuttgart Opera, of which he became musical dir. in 1950. Since 1969 he has been principal conductor of the Zürich Opera. He has also conducted frequently in Munich, Hamburg, Chicago and Buenos Aires, specializing in the operas of Wagner and Richard Strauss.

Leittonwechselklang ['līt-tōn"vek-səl-kläng] (Ger., leading-tone change chord) a CHORD formed from a major triad by lowering the tonic a minor 2nd and keeping the 3rd and 5th fixed, or from a minor triad by raising the 5th a minor second and keeping the tonic and 3rd fixed.

Le Jeune, Claude (Claudin) (c1528–1600) French composer. A Protestant, he lived under the protection of several Huguenot nobles. He was an active participant in the Académie de Poésie et de Musique of Antoine Baïf and Thibault de Courville and was a leading exponent of MUSIQUE MESURÉE. Around 1580 he became the Master of the Children at the court of François of Anjou and later a composer to the king. Many of his works survive, most of them published shortly after his death by Pierre Ballard; they incl. psalm settings, *airs mesurés*, sacred and secular chansons, madrigals, several instrumental works.

Lélio, ou le Retour à la Vie (Fr., Lelio, or the Return to Life) lyric monodrama for narrator, soloists, chorus and orch., Op. 14b (1831–2), by Berlioz, orig. written as a sequel to the SYMPHONIE FANTASTIQUE.

Lemminkäinen Suite (Finn., *Lemminkäis-sarja*) set of four tone poems, Op. 22 (1895, rev. 1897–1900), by Sibelius, based on the Finnish epic, the *Kalevala*. The four works are *Lemminkäinen and the Maidens of Saari*, *Lemminkäinen in Tuonela*, *The Swan of Tuonela* (often performed separately) and *Lemminkäinen's Homecoming*.

Lemoine [lə'mwän] French music publishing firm, founded in 1772 in Paris and specializing in ballet, opera and teaching materials.

Léner Quartet string quartet formed in 1918 by Hungarian violinist Jenö Léner (1894–1948), esp. noted for its blend and ensemble in the performance of Mozart, Beethoven and 19th-c. classics.

Lengnick English music publishering firm founded in 1893 by Alfred Lengnick, at that time British agent for Simrock, whose catalog the firm later acquired. The company was acquired by Schott in 1904.

Leningrad Philharmonic Orchestra orch. formed in 1924 (successor to the St. Petersburg court orch., founded in 1882). Its conductors have been Emil Cooper, Nikolay Malko, Alexander Gauk, Fritz Stiedry and Evgeny Mravinsky.

Leningrad Symphony popular name for the Symphony No. 7 (1941) by Shostakovich, which attempts to portray the German siege of Leningrad during World War II.

Lennon, John (Ono) (Winston) (1940–80) English rock singer and songwriter, a member of the BEATLES and, with Paul McCartney, its main songwriter. After the breakup of the Beatles in 1970, he recorded and appeared alone and with his wife Yoko Ono, esp. in support of the peace movement.

Lenox Quartet Amer. string quartet formed in 1958 at the Berkshire Music Center, specializing in 20th-c. repertory.

lent [lä] (Fr.), **lento** ['len-tō] (It.) slow; faster than LARGO, slower than ADAGIO.

Lentz, Daniel K(irkland) (1942–) Amer. composer, trained at Brandeis U. and the Berkshire Music Center.

He is founder of the California Time Machine, a performing group, and the LENTZ ensemble in Los Angeles. His works exhibit a very individual style, in some technical aspects similar to MINIMALISM, presenting a slow but definite development of material, often for mixed media and displaying a dark sense of humor.

Lenya (Lenja), **Lotte** (Blamauer, Karoline Wilhelmine) (1898–1981) Austrian-born Amer. actress and singer, wife of composer KURT WEILL and best known as interpreter of his songs. She appeared in his *The Threepenny Opera* and *Mahagonny*, among others, as well as in the musical *Cabaret*.

Leo, Leonardo (Ortensio Salvatore de) (1694–1744) Italian composer and teacher, stud. of Nicola Fago. He became an organist of the viceroy's chapel in Naples in 1713 and chapel master for the Marchese Stella and St. Maria della Solitaria. He wrote serious and comic operas for theaters in Naples, Rome, Venice and elsewhere, and a substantial body of oratorios.

Leonarda, Isabella ISABELLA LEONARDA.

Leoncavallo, Ruggero (1857–1919) Italian composer and librettist, stud. of Lauro Rossi. Frustrated over his inability to have his first opera performed, he wrote the libretto and music for the *verismo* opera *Pagliacci*, deliberately aiming to outdo the success of Mascagni's *Cavalleria rusticana*. In this he succeeded, but his version of *La Bohème* was eclipsed by Puccini's and his next opera, *Zazà*, was only a modest success. He is remembered now chiefly for his one operatic success and for some songs, the best known of which is "Mattinata."

Leonhardt, Gustav (Maria) (1928–) Dutch organist, harpsichordist and conductor, specialist in early music and stud. of Eduard Müller. He has taught at the Vienna Academy of Music and the Amsterdam Conservatory, where he is also organist of the Waalse Kerk. He has appeared and recorded frequently with the Vienna

Concentus Musicus and with his own Leonhardt Consort, formed in 1955.

Léonin ['lā-ō-nē] (Magister Leoninus) (fl. c1163–90) French musician, credited with the creation of the MAGNUS LIBER ORGANI and with the development of the first rational rhythmic system and a notation to express it.

Leonore Overture any one of three overtures written by Beethoven for his opera FIDELIO, named for the heroine of the opera. *Leonore No. 1*, perhaps the original overture, was never performed. *Leonore No. 2* was used at the first performance of the opera in 1805. *Leonore No. 3* replaced *Leonore No. 2* at the performance of the revised opera in 1806. For the final revised version of the opera in 1814 Beethoven wrote a fourth overture, known as the *Fidelio* overture. The *Leonore No. 3* overture is frequently performed as a concert work and is sometimes inserted in performances of the opera before the last scene.

L'Epine, (Francesca) Margherita de (c1683–1746) Italian soprano, active primarily in England at Drury Lane and at the Queen's Theatre. She sang in a number of operas by Handel, Domenico Scarlatti, Pepusch (whom she married c1718) and others, and was extremely popular in her time. She retired in 1719 and turned to teaching.

Leppard, Raymond (John) (1927–) English conductor, harpsichordist and music editor, trained at Cambridge. A specialist in the music of the 17th and 18th c., he taught at Trinity College, Cambridge, until 1967. He has conducted opera in the leading English houses and at Glyndebourne as well as in No. America. He has frequently conducted the English Chamber Orchestra and was conductor of the BBC Northern SO (1973–80). He has produced performing editions of Monteverdi's operas and of works by Cavalli and has made a number of recordings.

LeRoy, Adrian (c1520–98) French lu-
tanist, composer and music publisher. In 1551 he established, with his cousin Robert Ballard, a music publishing firm, which in 1553 became the French royal music printer. The firm of LeRoy and Ballard published works of many important composers of the time, incl. Orlando de Lasso, Arcadelt and Goudimel, and also printed pedagogical works for the lute, cittern and guitar.

Les Adieux (Fr.) see ADIEUX, LES.

Leschetizky, Theodor (Leszetycki, Teodor) (1830–1915) Polish pianist, composer and teacher, stud. of Czerny. He taught at the St. Petersburg Conservatory under Anton Rubinstein (1862–78), then returned to Vienna. He also toured as pianist and conductor. His pupils incl. Schnabel, Paderewski and Elly Ney.

lesser hours the four hours of the DIVINE OFFICE of the Roman Catholic church which are performed during full daylight: prime (6 am), terce (9 am), sext (noon), and none (3 pm).

lesson 1, ÉTUDE. **2**, in 17th- and 18th-c. England, a sonata or one of a set of instrumental pieces, usu. for keyboard instrument. Also, *port.*

Lesur, Daniel see DANIEL-LESUR.

Let's Face It! musical by Cole Porter, book by Herbert and Dorothy Fields, based on the play *The Cradle Snatchers*. Premiere, New York 1941. Three Southampton matrons hire three gigolos to check on their husbands' affairs.

Let's Make an Opera entertainment for children by Britten to a libretto by Eric Crozier. Premiere, Aldeburgh, England, 1949. An opera, *The Little Sweep*, is planned and rehearsed.

letter notation any of various systems of notation using letters instead of graphic note symbols, used chiefly for theoretical purposes. Cf. TABLATURE.

Levant, Oscar (1906–72) Amer. pianist and composer, stud. of Sigismund Stojowski and Schoenberg. As a pianist, he played with various jazz bands and later championed the works of Gershwin. His own works incl. many songs and film scores as well as a piano concerto and some chamber music. He also wrote two books of memoirs noted for their caustic wit.

levare [lä′vä-rä] (It.) **1**, UPBEAT. **2**, take off (as a stop, mute, etc.).

Leveridge, Richard (c1670–1758) English bass and composer of songs, a leading singer in London in both English and Italian opera at Henry Purcell's company until about 1700, then at Lincoln's Inn Fields and Covent Garden, retiring in 1751.

Levi, Hermann (1839–1900) German conductor, stud. of Moritz Hauptmann and Julius Rietz. He was conductor in Saarbrücken, Mannheim, Rotterdam and Karlsruhe before becoming court Kapellmeister in Munich in 1872. He was noted as an interpreter of Schumann, Brahms and Wagner and was the first conductor of Wagner's *Parsifal* at Bayreuth.

Levine, James (1943–) Amer. conductor and pianist, stud. of Rosina Lhévinne, Rudolf Serkin and Jean Morel. He was assistant conductor of the Cleveland Orchestra (1964–70) and has conducted at the Metropolitan Opera since 1971, becoming principal conductor in 1973 and music dir. in 1975. He was dir. of the Cincinnati May Festival and has been dir. of the Ravinia Festival since 1973. He has taught at the Aspen Music School, the Cleveland Institute, Oakland U. and elsewhere. He is equally active as pianist and as conductor of opera and orchestral concert repertory in Europe and the Americas.

Levy, Edward (Irving) (1929–) Amer. composer, stud. of Babbitt, Shapey, Wolpe and others. He has taught at Yeshiva U. since 1967. Most of his works are for instrumental ensembles.

Lévy, Ernst (1895–1981) Swiss composer and pianist, stud. of Petri, Raoul Pugno and Huber. He founded the Choeur Philharmonique in Paris in 1928, then came to the U.S. in 1941, where he taught at the New England Conservatory, Bennington College, the U. of Chicago, MIT and Brooklyn College. He retired to Switzerland in 1966. He wrote 15 symphonies, cantatas, chamber music and keyboard works.

Levy, Marvin David (1932–) Amer. composer, stud. of Philip James and Luening. His opera *Mourning Becomes Electra* (1967) was commissioned and premiered by the Metropolitan Opera. His works incl. 4 operas, a symphony, piano concerto, chamber music and the oratorio *For the Time Being*.

Lewenthal, Raymond (1926–) Amer. pianist, stud. of Samaroff and Cortot. He specializes in unusual repertory, esp. neglected works of the 19th c., in particular the music of Alkan.

Lewis, George (George Louis Francis Zeno) (1900–68) Amer. jazz clarinetist and alto saxophonist. In the 1920s and 1930s he was a bandleader in New Orleans. From 1941 he recorded extensively for William Russell, often collaborating with Bunk Johnson. In the 1950s he was a symbol of revivalism and made some successful tours with his band.

Lewis, George (1952–) Amer. composer and virtuoso trombonist, trained with Dean Hey and Muhal Abrams and at Yale. He has been active in the AACM, working closely with member Anthony Braxton, and has been a leading figure in the avant garde of jazz. He was the music dir. of the Kitchen (NY) from 1980 to 1982 and teaches at Columbia College in Chicago. His works combine jazz improvisation and electronic and computer music and incl. works for various chamber ensembles.

Lewis, Henry (1932–) Amer. conductor. He founded the Los Angeles Chamber Orchestra and was music dir. of the New Jersey SO (1968–76). He has guest-conducted with most major U.S. orchestras and in Europe and has conducted at the Metropolitan Opera and other houses. He was married to mezzo-soprano Marilyn

Horne, with whom he made a number of recordings.

Lewis, Jerry Lee (1935–) Amer. rock singer and pianist. His music was at first an amalgam of country and gospel, but his hits began when he moved toward rock and roll, recording in the late 1950s "Whole Lotta Shakin' Going On" and "Great Balls of Fire." He returned in the late 1960s to country music and became very popular again. He continues to tour with an act incorporating all the various styles of his career.

Lewis, John (Aaron) (1920–) Amer. jazz pianist and composer, stud. at the U. of New Mexico. He played with Dizzy Gillespie's band, then worked with Miles Davis. In 1952 he took over musical direction of the MODERN JAZZ QUARTET. He has taught in Lenox, MA, and directed the Monterey Jazz Festival (1958–64). His works incl. several film scores, works for jazz quartet and jazz band, and a ballet.

Lewis, Meade (Anderson) "Lux" (1905–64) Amer. jazz boogie-woogie pianist. He played in Chicago bars in the 1920s, then was rediscovered in 1935, when his best-known work, "Honky Tonk Train Blues," orig. recorded in 1927, was reissued. He was for a time teamed with pianists Albert Ammons and Pete Johnson.

Lewis, Mel(vin Sokoloff) (1929–90) Amer. jazz drummer. He worked with Stan Kenton, Hampton Hawes, Gerry Mulligan, Benny Goodman and Dizzy Gillespie before forming with Thad Jones an all-star band of studio players that toured throughout the 1960s and 1970s. Lewis assumed complete control of the band in 1980.

Lewis, Ramsey (1935–) Amer. rock and jazz pianist, trained in Chicago as a classical pianist. He formed the Ramsey Lewis Trio in 1956, which continues to tour with varying personnel. He has also played with Max Roach, Sonny Terry and others.

Lewis, Robert Hall (1926–) Amer. composer, trained at the U. of Rochester and with Boulanger in Paris. He has taught at Goucher College and Johns Hopkins U. Most of his works are for instruments, incl. 3 symphonies, 3 string quartets, many chamber music works and several works for chorus.

Lewis Family Amer. bluegrass gospel singing group comprising various members of the family of Pauline and Roy Lewis. Active since the early 1950s, they have produced a popular TV show in Augusta, GA, since 1954 and made many recordings.

lexical music see TEXT-SOUND COMPOSITION.

Leyrac (née Tremblay), **Monique** (1928–) French-Canadian singer and actress. She has sung in N. Amer. and Europe in cabarets, on the stage and on radio and television, specializing in French and French-Canadian repertory. She has also appeared in *The Threepenny Opera* at the Stratford Festival and elsewhere.

L.H. *abbr.* left hand (as in piano music).

Lhévinne, Josef (1874–1944) Russian pianist, stud. of Vasily Safonov, and husband of ROSINA LHÉVINNE. He taught in Tiflis, at the Moscow Conservatory and from 1922 at the Juilliard School in New York. His distinguished solo career concentrated on the virtuoso repertory of the 19th c.

Lhévinne, Rosina (Bessie) (1880–1976) eminent Russian pianist and teacher, wife of JOSEF LHÉVINNE. She taught at the Juilliard School from 1922, where her pupils incl. James Levine, John Browning and Van Cliburn.

Liadov LYADOV.

Liberace, (Walter) (Wladziu Valentino) (1919–87) Amer. pianist. In 1940 he performed with the Chicago SO, playing Liszt's Second Piano Concerto, but soon concentrated on popular music. His carefully crafted stage appearances and performances were highly successful.

liber gradualis (Lat.) GRADUAL.

Liber Usualis (Lat., Book of Common Practice) a collection of chants, prayers and lessons for the Roman Catholic Church year, issued by the monks of the monastery at SOLESMES in 1896.

libretto (It., small book) the words or text of an opera, musical comedy, etc.; a book containing such a text.

licenza [lē'chen-tsä] (It., licence) **1**, CADENZA. **2**, rhythmic or expressive freedom, as in the direction *con alcuna licenza* (with some freedom).

Licht [liçt] (Ger., light) cycle of 7 operas (begun in 1977) by Stockhausen. A work in progress, the completed cycle will comprise one opera for each of the days of the week.

lick a term in jazz and popular music for a rhythmic or melodic phrase that is used habitually by a player in improvisation. A player's "licks" are his basic musical vocabulary. Cf. BREAK.

Lidholm, Ingvar (Natanael) (1921–) Swedish composer and violist, trained with Rosenberg and Seiber. He was dir. of chamber music for Swedish Radio (1956–65) and taught at the Stockholm Music High School from 1965. His works, most in a 12-tone serial style, incl. an opera, a ballet, orchestral works, vocal works (esp. the *A cappella-bok*, an extensive series of works of increasing difficulty) and chamber music.

Liebermann, Rolf (1910–) Swiss composer and opera manager. He has managed the Hamburg Staatsoper (1959–73) and the Paris Opéra (1973–80). His works, most of which were written before 1959, incl. 4 operas (*The School for Wives* was premiered in Louisville, KY), vocal works, a concerto for jazz band and other orchestral works and a piano sonata.

Liebesfuss ['lē-bəs"foos] (Ger., love foot) PAVILLON D'AMOUR.

Liebeslieder [-"lē-dər] (Ger., Songs of Love) a set of eighteen waltzes for vocal quartet and piano duet, Op. 52 (1868–9), by Brahms. A second set of 15 waltzes, the *Neue Liebeslieder*, Op. 65, was published in 1874. Brahms also published both sets for piano duet without voices as Op. 52a (1874) and Op. 65a (1877), and an arrangement of nine of the songs with

orchestral accompaniment was published in 1870.

Liebestod [-"tōt] (Ger., love-death) popular title for Isolde's death scene at the end of Wagner's *Tristan und Isolde*, but applied by Wagner to the love duet in Act 2.

Liebesträume [-"troi-me] (Ger., Dreams of Love) Liszt's title for his piano arrangement (1850) of three of his songs: "Hohe Liebe" (High Love), "Gestorben war ich" (I Had Died), and "O lieb, so lang du lieben kannst" (O Love, as long as you can love), the best known of the three.

Liebling, Estelle (1880–1970) Amer. soprano and singer, stud. of Mathilde Marchesi and Selma Nicklass-Kempner. She performed with a number of European and U.S. opera companies (Metropolitan Opera, 1903–4) and toured with Sousa's band, giving over 1600 concerts. From 1930 she concentrated on teaching (Beverly Sills was a pupil) and preparing editions of coloratura repertory.

Lied [lēt] (Ger., song; pl., *Lieder*) a German folk or art song, which may be mono- or polyphonic. The term is often applied specifically to the German art song of the 19th c., as exemplified in the works of Schubert, Schumann, Brahms, Wolf, etc., but also indicates songs written in the German vernacular from any historical period.

Lieder eines fahrenden Gesellen ['lē-dər 'ī-nəs 'fä-rən-dən ge'zel-ən] (Ger.) SONGS OF A WAYFARER.

Liederkreis [-"krīs] (Ger.) **1**, SONG CYCLE. **2**, a musical club devoted to performance and enjoyment of song. **3**, a song cycle, Op. 24 (1840), by Schumann.

Lieder ohne Worte ['ō-ne 'vor-te] (Ger.) SONGS WITHOUT WORDS.

Liederspiel [-"shpēl] (Ger., songplay) a type of 19th-c. German entertainment based on the composition of new melodies to preexisting and current lyric poetry, usu. without ensembles or choruses. The principal composer working in the form was J.F. Reichardt. Schumann's *Span-*

isches Liederspiel is not related to this genre, the title notwithstanding.
Liedertafel [-"tä-fəl] (Ger., song-table) a 19th-c. male singing society.
Lied von der Erde, Das [fon dār 'ār-de] (Ger.) SONG OF THE EARTH, THE.
Lieutenant Kijé orchestral suite in five movements, Op. 60 (1934), by Prokofiev, derived from his score for a 1933 film spoof of the tsarist bureaucracy in which Lieutenant Kijé, whose name derives from the Tsar's misreading of a phrase, must be created to satisfy the rule of the Tsar's infallibility.
Life for the Czar, A IVAN SUSANIN.
ligature 1, a type of NEUME which indicates a group of notes to be sung to one syllable. Ligatures often also indicate rhythm. The most common forms are the *pes*, indicating a rise of a step; the *clivis*, indicating a descent of a step; and the *torculus*, indicating a rise and then fall of a step. **2**, the metal band securing the reed of a clarinet or saxophone to the mouthpiece.

Ligatures

(see MENSURAL NOTATION for note values)

Ligeti, György (Sándor) (1923–) Hungarian-born Austrian composer, stud. of Ödön Farkas, Pál Kadosa and Sándor Veress. He has taught at the Budapest Academy and worked at the West German Radio electronic studios in Cologne. He has taught at the Stockholm Academy of Music and at the Hamburg Musikhochschule. His early works employ a tonal language, but from the mid-1950s on, his works employ a technique of chromatic clusters, removing to a large degree the elements of harmony and rhythm. Later works utilize microintervals and modified tunings. His compositions incl. *Apparitions* (1959), *Atmosphères* (1961), *Aventures* (1962) *Lux aeterna* (1966), *Le grand macabre* (music theater, 1978), chamber music and concertos.

light classics a vague and mildly derogatory term for works in the European art music tradition which are relatively undemanding of the listener and "pleasant" to listen to. The term is usu. applied to classical music which is included in pops programs. The word "light" is also appended to other music terms (opera, etc.) with a similar connotation.
Lightfoot, Gordon (1938–) Canadian singer and songwriter. Orig. a pianist, he switched to guitar in 1960 and has made a successful career both as performer and as songwriter.
Lightfoot, Terry (Terence) (1935–) English jazz clarinetist, alto saxophonist, singer and bandleader. He worked with Kid Ory in 1959, then formed his own band, which has toured and performed in clubs since the early 1960s.
Li'l Abner musical by Gene de Paul, lyrics by Johnny Mercer, book by Norman Panama and Melvin Frank, based on the comic strip by Al Capp. Premiere, New York 1956. The hill folk of Dogpatch become involved with a government plan to use their town for atomic tests.
Lillie, Beatrice (Gladys) (1894–1989) Canadian-born actress, singer, and comedienne. She appeared in numerous London and Broadway revues.
Lili'uokalani (Kamaka'eha Paki, Lydia) (1838–1917) Hawaiian composer, pianist, organist and conductor, briefly queen of Hawaii (1891–3). Her works incl. the popular song "Aloha 'oe" and the Hawaiian anthem, "He mele lahui Hawaii."
lilt 1, (Scots) sing in a cheerful way; a spirited song without words. **2**, a rhythmical cadence or swing.
lilting a type of Gaelic singing with nonsense syllables, used to accompany dancing. The same tradition is found in French Canada, called *turlutage* or *mouth music*.
Lily opera by Kirchner to his own libretto, based on Saul Bellow's novel *Henderson, The Rain King*. Premiere, New York 1977.
Lincoln Center for the Performing

Arts a performing arts complex in New York, opened in 1962. The complex comprises the Metropolitan Opera House, the New York City Opera, the New York State Theater, Avery Fisher Hall, a library and the Juilliard School.

Lincoln Portrait, A work for narrator and orchestra (1942) by Copland, based on Lincoln's letters and speeches and incorporating "Camptown Races" by Stephen Foster and other traditional melodies.

Lind (Lind-Goldschmidt), **Jenny** (Johanna Maria) (1820–87) Swedish soprano, the "Swedish nightingale," stud. of Isak Berg. Her operatic debut with the Royal Opera in Stockholm was in 1838 and from 1844 she appeared in opera houses in Germany, Austria and Denmark. Her U.S. debut was in 1850, when she toured with Julius Benedict and baritone Giovanni Belletti under the management of Phineas T. Barnum, performing 93 concerts in less than a year. She lived in England from 1858 until her death, retiring to teach in 1883. She was best known for her performance of Amina (*La Sonnambula*), Marie (*The Daughter of the Regiment*) and Alice (*Robert le diable*) and as a concert artist.

lindy also, **lindy hop** an Amer. social dance of the 1920s and 1930s, performed to fast, syncopated jazz music in duple meter. Also, *jitterbug*.

linear counterpoint a term emphasizing the horizontal or melodic aspect of COUNTERPOINT, as opposed to the vertical or harmonic aspect.

lining out a method for performing hymns in which a leader reads out the words or melody, or both, a line at a time, before they are sung by the congregation. Also, *deaconing*.

linke Hand (Ger.) left hand.

Linley, Thomas (1733–95) English composer, harpsichordist and singing teacher, stud. of Thomas Chilcot and William Boyce. He directed concerts in Bath in the mid-18th c. that incl. himself and some of his children, who were also well-trained musicians. He was a dir. at Drury Lane from 1774 until his death. His surviving works incl. 12 operas and numerous songs. His son **Thomas Linley** (1756–78) demonstrated an extraordinary musical precocity as a composer and a violinist. He trained with Boyce and with Nardini in Florence. From 1773 to 1778 he was leader at Drury Lane and composed during these years a large volume of works which, to judge from the small amount that have survived, were of a remarkably high quality.

Linz Symphony popular name for the symphony No. 36 in C, K. 425 (1783), by Mozart, composed and first performed in Linz.

lion's roar a type of STRING DRUM consisting of a rosined cord passed through a membrane.

lip to modify (esp., raise) the pitch on a woodwind or brass instrument by adjustment of the embouchure: *lip up* or *down*. Cf. LIP REED INSTRUMENT.

Lipatti, Dinu (Constantin) (1917–50) Romanian pianist and composer, taught at home (because of ill health) by Floria Musicescu. He also studied in Paris with Cortot, Münch, Dukas and Boulanger. He established himself as a major technician and interpreter, but because of the effects of a rare form of cancer, which eventually caused his death, he preferred recording to live performance.

Lipkin, Seymour (1927–) Amer. pianist and conductor, stud. of David Saperton, Serkin and Horszowski. He has concertized widely as a pianist and has conducted at the New York City Opera, the New York PO, the Huntington SO and the Joffrey Ballet. He has taught at the Berkshire Music Center, the Curtis Institute and the Manhattan School.

lip reed instrument an instrument using the lips to cause vibration in the air stream; esp., the brass instruments.

Lipscomb, Mance (1895–1976) Amer. blues guitarist, singer and fiddler. He was not discovered until the early 1960s, and thus when he made his first recordings he was well over

60 years old. Before this time he had played only for friends and co-workers at dances and outings. Until forced by ill health to retire in 1974, he appeared at folk festivals and in several documentary films, in addition to making recordings.

lira ['lē-rä] (It.) **1**, LYRE. **2**, see LIRA DA BRACCIO, LIRA DA GAMBA. **3**, LIRA ORGANIZZATA. **4**, a Greek folk FIDDLE.

lira da braccio ['brät-chō] (It., arm lira) a Renaissance FIDDLE similar in shape to the violin but with a lower bridge, a leaf-shaped pegbox, five stopped strings and two drones.

lira da gamba (It., leg lira) a bass LIRA DA BRACCIO, played between the knees. The instrument had nine to 14 stopped strings and two drone strings.

lira organizzata [ōr-gä-nē'dzä-tä] (It.) a HURDY-GURDY incorporating one or two ranks of organ pipes in its body. The hand crank operates both the rosined wheel that bows the strings and the bellows that sounds the pipes.

lirica a Yugoslavian folk FIDDLE with a pear-shaped body, a wide neck and three strings.

lirico spinto (It.) see SPINTO.

lirone [lē'rō-nä] (It.) LIRA DA GAMBA.

List, Eugene (1918–85) Amer. pianist, stud. of Samaroff. He taught at the Eastman School of Music and at New York U. He was noted for his championship of unusual music of the past and of new music. He frequently performed with his wife, violinist Carroll Glenn.

List, Garrett (1943–) Amer. composer and trombonist, trained at the Juilliard School and with Hall Overton. He has been a member of The Ensemble and Musica Elettronica Viva in New York and was music dir. of the Kitchen. His works combine jazz with contemporary art music techniques and include orchestral and chamber music works and works for voice(s) with chamber ensembles.

l'istesso (It.) ISTESSO.

Liston, Melba Doretta (1926–) Amer. jazz trombonist and arranger. She played with Gerald Wilson and Count Basie, then joined Dizzy Gillespie's band. She has also worked with Quincy Jones, Randy Weston, and with various all-women groups, has written liner notes and has taught in the U.S. and Jamaica.

Liszt, Franz (Ferencz) (1811–86) Hungarian virtuoso pianist, conductor and teacher, stud. of Czerny and Salieri in Vienna and with Reicha and Paer in Paris. In 1848, he assumed a full-time position as Director of Music Extraordinary in Weimar, which, under his influence as conductor and teacher, became the center of the German avant-garde in music, known as the "New German school." His support of Wagner and his living arrangements with his new mistress, Carolyne Sayn-Wittgenstein, were more and more frowned upon, and in 1858, after an unfavorable demonstration, he resigned his post. He went to Rome several years later and took minor orders of the church, but never became a priest. From 1869 until his death he made regular journeys between Rome, Weimar and Budapest to give master classes and occasionally to perform.

Liszt produced an extraordinary body of works for chorus, orchestra, solo piano and solo voice. He was the inventor of the orchestral tone poem (as well as of the term); his piano transcriptions of works by his contemporaries are remarkable for their versatility and technical mastery. As a pianist he was the greatest performer of his time and perhaps of all time, and he played a repertory of tremendous breadth. As a conductor, he was an ardent supporter of the new developments in music. His works incl. *Don Sanche* (opera), many oratorios and other sacred choral works, secular cantatas, works for men's chorus, orchestral tone poems (*Les Préludes*, *Prometheus*, *Mazeppa*, *Hamlet*), piano concertos, chamber music, many works for piano solo (*Transcendental Études*, *Années de pélérinage*, dances), works for organ, many songs and transcriptions for various media of operatic, vocal and orchestral repertory.

litany a liturgical prayer, or the procession during which such a prayer is chanted. The three major litanies (litania romana, italica, gallicana) all contain three distinct sections: an invocation of Christ or the Trinity, invocations of the saints, etc., and a series of supplications. Polyphonic settings of litanies began to be composed in the 16th c.

lithophone resonant stone slabs or plaques used as a tuned percussion instrument. A Western version of this is the *rock harmonica*, developed by the firm Richardson and Sons, which has a range from five to seven chromatic octaves.

Litolff, Henry (Charles) (1818–91) French composer and pianist, stud. of Moscheles. He concertized in England and Europe in the 1840s. In 1851 he founded the publishing firm Henry Litolff Verlag (taken over by Peters in 1940). In 1855 he became Kapellmeister at the court of Saxe-Coburg-Gotha, then moved to Paris in 1858, remaining there until his death. His works incl. operas, oratorios, orchestral overtures, 5 *concertos symphoniques* for piano and orch., works for violin and orchestra, chamber music, works for solo piano and songs.

Little Anthony (Gourdine, Anthony) (1940–) Amer. soul singer, leader from 1958 of Little Anthony and the Imperials, which continued to perform into the 1970s.

Little C Major the Symphony No. 6 in C major (1817–8) by Schubert.

Little G Minor the fugue in G minor for organ, BWV 578 (c1705), by Bach.

Little Hours see LESSER HOURS.

Little Mary Sunshine musical by Rick Besoyan. Premiere, New York 1959. A "New Musical About an Old Operetta," set in the Rockies. It concerns a romance between Little Mary and Captain Big Jim Warington of the Forest Rangers.

Little Night Music, A 1, KLEINE NACHTMUSIK, EINE. **2**, musical by Ste-

phen Sondheim, book by Hugh Wheeler, based on Ingmar Bergman's film *Smiles of a Summer Night*. Premiere, New York 1973. A sophisticated look at love among the social classes.

Little Organ Mass the Missa brevis in B♭ major (c1775) by Haydn.

Little Richard (Penniman, Richard) (c1935–) Amer. rock pianist and singer, an important figure in the early history of rock and roll. His biggest hits were in the late 1950s and incl. "Tutti Frutti," "Long Tall Sally" and "Good Golly, Miss Molly."

Little Russian Symphony popular name for the symphony No. 2 in C minor, Op. 17 (1873), by Tschaikovsky, so called because it quotes Ukrainian (Little Russian) folk tunes.

Little Sweep, The see LET'S MAKE AN OPERA.

Little Walter (Jacobs, Marion Walter) (1930–68) Amer. blues singer and harmonica player, a pioneer in the use of amplified harmonica. He performed as a street musician in Chicago, later accompanying Muddy Waters, Leroy Foster and others.

liturgical drama a type of medieval play with music based on Biblical stories and used as part of the official liturgy.

liturgy the rites and procedures of the Christian Church or other religious services.

lituus a Roman military TRUMPET having a detachable mouthpiece and shaped approximately like a letter J.

lizard a tenor CORNET (1,).

Liza musical revue by Irving C. Miller, book by Maceo Pinkard, the first Negro show to play on Broadway during the regular season and the first to present the Charleston. Premiere, New York 1922.

Lizzie Borden opera in 3 acts by Beeson to a libretto by Kenward Elmslie, based on an idea by Richard Plant. Premiere, New York 1965.

Lloyd, David (1920–) Amer. tenor, trained at the Minneapolis College of Music and the Curtis Institute. He was assoc. for many years with the

New York City Opera and sang in many other houses in No. America and abroad. He directed the Lake George Opera Festival from 1974 to 1980 and has taught at the U. of Illinois in Urbana since 1971.

Lloyd Webber, Andrew (1948–) English composer, a student for a time at the Royal College of Music. He has enjoyed a remarkable success as a composer for musical theater, producing *Jesus Christ Superstar* (1971), *Joseph and the Amazing Technicolor Dreamcoat* (1977), *Evita* (1979), *Cats* (1982), *The Phantom of the Opera* (1988), several film scores and a *Requiem*.

Lobgesang ['lōp-ge"zäng] (Ger.) the symphony-cantata No. 2 in B♭ major for soloists, chorus and orchestra, Op. 52 (1840), by Mendelssohn.

Lobkowitz Quartets the string quartets in G major and F major, Op. 77 (1799), by Haydn, dedicated to the Austrian patron Prince Franz Joseph Lobkowitz (1772–1816), to whom Beethoven also dedicated a number of works.

Locatelli, Pietro Antonio (1695–1764) Italian composer and violinist. In 1729 he moved to Amsterdam, which was to become his permanent home, taught violin and directed an amateur ensemble. He also published his own chamber music. His works incl. concerti grossi, sonatas for violin and flute and violin concertos.

Locke, Matthew (1621–77) English composer, stud. of Edward Gibbons, William Wake and John Lugge. From 1653 he was active as a composer of theater music and contributed to the music for *The Siege of Rhodes*, arguably the first English opera. In 1660, at the time of the Restoration, he was appointed composer to the king and organist to the queen and wrote music for the king's coronation. His compositions, and perhaps he himself, exerted an influence on Henry Purcell, who succeeded him in one of his royal appointments. He wrote songs and incidental stage music, Latin motets, songs and services,

English anthems, secular songs, consort music, harpsichord works, music for wind instruments.

locked hands a style of jazz piano playing in which the right hand plays the melody, harmonized by a four-note chord, while the left hand doubles the melody an octave below.

loco (It., in its place) used as an indication that the notes following it are to be played at the notated level, countermanding previous OTTAVA indications.

locrian a classical Greek term used to define the diatonic scale beginning on B. The mode was not used in Gregorian chant, because its dominant or fifth degree is a tritone away from the tonic B, a forbidden interval.

Loeffler, Charles Martin (1861–1935) French-born Amer. composer and violinist, trained in Berlin and Paris. In 1881 he came to the U.S., first playing under Leopold Damrosch, then in the Boston SO, remaining there until 1903, after which he devoted his time to teaching and composition. A highly educated man and an aristocrat, he composed in an impressionist style and incorporated jazz elements in some of his works.

Loeillet, Jean-Baptiste [lœ'yā] (John Loeillet of London) (1680–1730) Flemish composer, harpsichordist, oboist and flutist. He moved to London around 1705, where he played in the Drury Lane orch. and at the Queen's Theatre, Haymarket. He also presented weekly concerts at his house and established a reputation as an excellent teacher of the harpsichord. His surviving works incl. keyboard suites (lessons), sonatas for various wind instruments and trio sonatas.

Loeillet, Jean-Baptiste (Loeillet de Gant) (1688–c1720) Flemish composer in the service of the archbishop of Lyons. His works incl. recorder sonatas and trio sonatas.

Loesser, Frank (Henry) ['le-sər] (1910–69) Amer. composer, lyricist and producer, best known for his musicals *Guys and Dolls* (1950), *The*

Most Happy Fella (1956), and *How to Succeed in Business Without Really Trying* (1961), for which he won a Pulitzer Prize. He was president of Frank Music Corp. in New York. His brother, **Arthur Loesser** (1894–1969), was a concert pianist who taught at the Cleveland Institute.

Loewe, (Johann) Carl (Gottfried) ['lœ-və] (1796–1869) German composer and singer, stud. of Daniel Türk. He taught at the Stettin Gymnasium and seminary from 1820 until his death. Over the years he made a number of recital tours which were highly successful. He is best known for his many songs, but he also wrote oratorios, operas, choral works, symphonies, chamber music and solo piano works, many of which are programmatic.

Loewe, Frederick [lō] (1904–88) Austrian-born Amer. composer and pianist, stud. of Ferruccio Busoni and Eugène d'Albert. He came to the U.S. in 1924, and after some failures produced many hit Broadway musicals, all in collaboration with lyricist Alan Jay Lerner, incl. *Brigadoon* (1947), *Paint Your Wagon* (1951), *My Fair Lady* (1956) and *Camelot* (1960).

Loewenguth Quartet ['lø-vən"güt] French string quartet, formed in Paris in 1929 by violinist Alfred Loewenguth (1911–). After 1945 the quartet toured extensively in the U.S. and S. America as well as in Europe, performing a wide repertory and making many recordings.

Logothetis, Anestis (1921–) Greek-born Austrian composer. He was trained at the Vienna Music Academy and has worked at the Cologne electronic studios (1957). His more recent compositions have employed graphic notation, allowing great freedom of interpretation.

Lohengrin romantic opera in 3 acts by Wagner to a libretto by the composer based on a medieval legend. Premiere, Weimar 1850. Elsa of Brabant is defended in trial by combat by a mysterious knight, Lohengrin, servant of the Holy Grail.

L'Oiseau-Lyre ['lwä-zō lēr] (Fr.) *also,* **Lyrebird Press** French firm of music publishers, founded by Australian patron Louise B.M. Dyer in Paris in 1932 and now headquartered in Monaco. The firm has specialized since its founding in lavishly produced special editions. The firm has also produced recordings of rare and previously unrecorded music.

Lomax, Alan (1915–) Amer. folksong scholar, trained at Harvard, the U. of Texas and Columbia U. He has produced numerous radio programs on folk music and was dir. of folk music for Decca Records in the late 1940s. He has compiled many collections of folk songs and poetry and has studied certain folk performers in depth.

Lombard, Alain (1940–) French conductor, trained at the Paris Conservatoire. He has been conductor of the Lyons Opera, the Strasbourg PO and the Opéra du Rhin. His Amer. debut was with the American Opera Society in 1963, and he conducted at the Metropolitan Opera in 1967.

Lombardo, Guy (Gaetano Alberto) (1902–77) Canadian-born Amer. bandleader. His dance orchestra, the Royal Canadians, was organized in 1917. From 1929 to 1962 they played at the Roosevelt Grill in New York, made many recordings and frequent TV and radio appearances and toured extensively. Their New Year's Eve performances were a perennial favorite (in later years, broadcast from the Waldorf-Astoria Hotel, in New York).

Londonderry Air a melody of uncertain origin from the county of Derry (formerly Londonderry), Ireland, first published in 1855. Among the many lyrics to have been set to the tune, probably the best known is *Danny Boy* (1913).

London (Burnstein), **George** (1919–85) Canadian-born Amer. bass-baritone, stud. of Hugo Strelitzer, Nathan Stewart, Enrico Rosati and Paola Novikova. Making his professional debut in 1941, he first sang at the Metropolitan Opera in 1951. He was the

first non-Russian to sing Boris Godunov at the Bolshoy Opera and he
sang frequently at Bayreuth, his roles
incl. Wotan in the complete *Ring*
cycle of Wagner. He abandoned opera
for medical reasons in 1967 and was
active for the rest of his life as a producer and administrator.

London Academy of Music London
conservatory founded in 1861 by
Henry Wylde and closed in 1939.

London College of Music London
conservatory founded in 1887.

London Philharmonic Orchestra
London orch. founded in 1932 by Sir
Thomas Beecham. After Beecham's
departure, the orch. continued as a cooperative. Its conductors since 1949
have been Eduard von Beinum, Adrian Boult, John Pritchard, Bernard
Haitink and Georg Solti.

London Sinfonietta London chamber
orch. founded in 1968 by David Ath-
erton for the purpose of performing
20th-c. music.

London Symphony 1, one of the
twelve symphonies, Nos. 93 to 104
(1791–95), by Haydn, composed for
J.P. Salomon on the occasion of
Haydn's two visits to London in
1790–91 and 1794–95. Also, *Salomon symphonies*. **2**, the symphony
No. 2 in C major (1912–13) by
Vaughan Williams, revised in 1920
and 1933.

London Symphony Orchestra a self-
governing London orch. founded in
1904 by players breaking away from
the QUEEN'S HALL ORCHESTRA. Its
principal conductors have been Hans
Richter, Nikisch, Elgar, Hamilton
Harty, Krips, Monteux, Kertesz,
Previn and Abbado. It was the first
English orch. to tour No. America and
has made a large number of recordings.

long *also*, **longa** (Lat.) a note having
twice the value of a BREVE. Its use
dates from the early 13th c.

Long, Marguerite (Marie Charlotte)
(1874–1966) French pianist, stud. of
Antoine Marmontel. She taught at
the Paris Conservatoire from 1906 to
1940 and founded her own school in
1920. She premiered several works of

Ravel (*Le Tombeau de Couperin* and
the G-major piano concerto) and
wrote interpretative books on the
piano music of Fauré, Debussy and
Ravel. In 1943 she founded with
Jacques Thibaud an international violin and piano competition.

Long Beach Women's Symphony
women's orch. founded in Long
Beach, CA, in 1925 under conductor
Eva Anderson.

longhair a derogatory term for a composer, performer or lover of classical
music.

Longo, Alessandro (1864–1945) Italian pianist and composer, stud. of
Beniamino Cesi and Paolo Serrao. He
is primarily known for his edition of
the keyboard sonatas of Domenico
Scarlatti, which organizes the sonatas
into suites related by their tonalities.
He was an active piano teacher and
produced many pedagogical works.

long-playing record (*trade-name*) a
disc played at a speed of 33-⅓ revolutions per minute with very narrow
grooves (*microgrooves*). *Abbr.*, *LP*. Cf.
EXTENDED PLAY.

longways a folk dance in which couples face each other in two parallel
lines, men on one side, women on the
other.

Longy, (Gustave-)Georges(-Léopold)
['lō-zhē] (1868–1930) French oboist,
composer, conductor and teacher,
stud. of Georges Gillet. He was first
oboist of the Boston SO (1898–1925)
and founder of the Longy School of
Music. He conducted a number of
Boston musical organizations, incl.
the Boston Orchestral Club.

Longy School of Music conservatory
in Boston founded in 1916 by
GEORGES LONGY.

lontano [lōn'tä-nō] (It.) *also*, **da lontano** to sound as if coming from a distance; in opera, usu. intended to be
performed offstage in the wings. Also,
von ferne (Ger.).

lontar a Balinese bamboo CLAPPER.

Loomis, Harvey Worthington (1865–
1930) Amer. composer, stud. of Dvořák. He was a prolific composer, his
output including two operas, inciden-

tal music and works based on American Indian melodies. Only a few of his works have been published.

Lopatnikoff, Nikolai (Lvovich) (1903–76) Russian-born Amer. composer and pianist, trained at the St. Petersburg and Helsinki Conservatories and privately with Toch. He came to the U.S. in 1939 and taught at the Hartt College of Music and at Carnegie-Mellon U. He was commissioned by Koussevitzky, who also published a number of his works. He wrote *Danton* (opera), *Melting Pot* (ballet), 4 symphonies, concertos and other orchestral works, chamber music, works for solo piano.

Lorengar, Pilar (1928–) Spanish soprano, trained in Madrid. She began singing in *zarzuelas*, then sang opera at Aix-en-Provence, at Covent Garden and at Glyndebourne, where she appeared frequently between 1955 and 1960. She also sang regularly at the Deutsche Oper in Berlin. Her Metropolitan Opera debut was in 1966.

Loriod, Yvonne (1924–) French pianist and ondes martenot player, stud. of Lazare Lévy, Messiaen (whom she later married) and Milhaud. Since 1943 she has premiered all of Messiaen's works that include piano, as well as important works of other 20th-c. composers. She has taught at the Paris Conservatoire and at Darmstadt.

Lortzing, (Gustav) Albert (1801–51) German opera composer, in large measure self-taught. He wrote his first comic opera in Leipzig in 1833; it was eventually produced in a number of European cities. His second comic opera, and the one for which he is best known today, was *Zar und Zimmermann* (Tsar and Carpenter, 1839). In all, he wrote about 20 operas and singspiels, incidental and other theater music, songs and miscellaneous vocal works.

Los Angeles, Victoria de (1923–) Spanish soprano, trained at the Barcelona Conservatory. She won the Geneva Competition in 1947 and soon became internationally known as a concert and opera artist. She sang frequently in Madrid, at Covent Garden and in the U.S. at the Metropolitan Opera, and at most major international houses. Her roles incl. Manon, Butterfly and Desdemona (*Otello*). She is esp. known for her performance of Spanish songs.

Los Angeles Chamber Symphony chamber orch. founded in Los Angeles in 1969. Its conductors have been Marriner, Gerard Schwarz and Iona Brown.

Los Angeles Philharmonic Orchestra orch. founded as the Los Angeles SO in 1898 with Harley Hamilton as its first conductor. The name was changed to its present form in 1919. Its conductors have included Rodzinski, Klemperer, Wallenstein, von Beinum, Mehta, Giulini, Previn, and Sallinen.

Lost in the Stars musical by Weill, lyrics and book by Maxwell Anderson and Alan Paton, based on Paton's novel *Cry, the Beloved Country*. Premiere, New York 1949. In Johannesburg, S. Africa, Absalom Kumalo accidentally kills a white man in a robbery attempt.

Lotti, Antonio (c1667–1740) Italian composer, possibly born in Germany, stud. of Legrenzi. He began as a singer at St. Mark's in Venice, becoming organist and then *maestro di cappella* in 1736. He composed much sacred music for the basilica. From 1692 he also wrote over 30 operas and intermezzi for the Venetian theaters and occasional works for the Doge's banquets and other events.

loudness the attribute of a SOUND determining the magnitude of the sensation the sound produces, measured in DECIBELS, PHONS or SONES. On high fidelity equipment, the "loudness" control actually adjusts the relative level of the bass portion of the sound to compensate for different volume levels.

loud pedal DAMPER PEDAL.

Louise romantic opera in 4 acts by Gustave Charpentier to his own libretto. Premiere, Paris 1900. Louise, in love with the artist Julien, runs away from home to Paris to be with him.

Louisiana Purchase musical by Irving Berlin, book by Morrie Ryskind, based on a story by B.G. DeSylva. Premiere, New York 1940. Political shenanigans in Louisiana.

Louisiana Story orchestral suite derived from a film score (1948) by Virgil Thomson. A second suite from the same score is entitled *Acadian Songs and Dances*.

Louisville Orchestra orch. founded in Louisville, KY, in 1937. The orch. initiated in 1948 a project which commissioned and recorded over 100 works until the project was discontinued in 1960. Conductors of the orch. have been Robert Whitney, Jorge Mester, Akiro Endo and Lawrence Leighton Smith.

loure [loor] (Fr.) a French dance in slow triple time. Bach composed several *loures* for keyboard, one of which appears in the fifth French Suite, another in the Partita in E major.

louré [loo'rā] (Fr.) a legato bowstroke; portato. See BOWING.

lourer [loo'rā] (Fr.) produce a type of NOTES INÉGALES, achieved by making the first note of each beat slightly longer than the others.

Lourié, Arthur Vincent (1892–1966) Russian-born Amer. composer, trained at the St. Petersburg Conservatory. He made early experiments in serial techniques around 1915, then later experimented with quartertones and with modal harmonies. His works incl. *The Feast during the Plague* (opera-ballet), *The Blackamoor of Peter the Great* (opera), 2 symphonies, a large body of choral and solo vocal works, chamber music, music for solo piano.

Louvin Brothers Amer. country-music duo composed of mandolinist Ira Loudermilk and guitarist Charlie Loudermilk. They joined the Grand Ole Opry in 1955 and made over 100 recordings. The duo disbanded in 1963.

Love for Three Oranges, The fantasy opera in 4 acts by Prokofief to a libretto in Russian by the composer, based on the comedy by Carlo Gozzi. Premiere, Chicago 1921. A play within a play, in which a prince finds happiness despite the machinations of the sorceress Fata Morgana.

lozhky ['lozh-kē] (Russ., spoons) a Russian instrument similar to the TURKISH CRESCENT.

Lübeck, Vincent (1654–1740) German composer, teacher and organist at SS. Cormas and Damian, near Hamburg, from 1675 to 1702, then at St. Nicolai in Hamburg until his death. He was also famous in his own time as an expert on organ building. Very few of his works survive: nine for organ, a collection for harpsichord and several chorale arrangements.

Luboff, Norman (1917–87) Amer. composer, arranger, and choral conductor, active in radio, TV, and films. His choral ensemble, the Norman Luboff Choir, made more than 75 albums and toured the U.S. and Europe.

Lucas, Clarence (1866–1947) Canadian composer and conductor, trained in Paris. He taught at the Toronto College of Music, conducted the Hamilton (Ont.) Philharmonic Society in 1889 and worked in New York as a music critic from 1906–23. His many works are conservative in style and incl. operas, choral and orchestral works, music for piano and songs.

Lucia di Lammermoor (It.) tragic opera in 3 acts by Donizetti to a libretto in Italian by Salvatore Cammarano, based on Sir Walter Scott's novel *The Bride of Lammermoor*. Premiere, Naples 1835. Lucia of Lammermoor and Edgardo of Ravenswood, whose families are locked in a feud, exchange vows of love, but Lucia's brother Enrico has other plans for her.

Lucier, Alvin (Augustus Jr.) (1931–   ) Amer. composer, trained at Yale and Brandeis U. He has taught at Brandeis and Wesleyan U. and was a co-founder of the Sonic Arts Union. Since the 1960s he has specialized in electronic and environmental music.

Luders, Gustav (Carl) (1865–1913) German-born Amer. composer. He came to the U.S. in 1888 and conducted popular concerts and light opera in Milwaukee and Chicago. He is remembered for his operettas, the best known of which is *The Prince of Pilsen* (1902).

ludus paschalis (Lat.) a medieval Latin church play dealing with the story of the Resurrection.

Ludwig, Christa (1928–) German mezzo-soprano, stud. of Felice Hüni-Mihaček. She sang with the Frankfurt, Darmstadt and Hannover operas and appeared at the Salzburg Festival and the Vienna Staatsoper, where she sang regularly from 1955. Her Metropolitan Opera debut was in 1959 and she has also sung in Chicago and throughout Europe. Her roles incl. Octavian (*Der Rosenkavalier*), Amneris (*Aida*) and Brangäne (*Tristan und Isolde*).

Luening, Otto (Clarence) (1900–) Amer. composer, conductor, flutist and teacher, trained in Munich and Zürich and privately with Jarnach and Busoni. His highly varied musical life has included playing flute at the Zürich Opera, conducting opera at the Eastman School and elsewhere, providing music for silent films and stage managing. He has taught at the Eastman School, the U. of Arizona, Bennington College, Columbia and the Juilliard School. His many works incl. an opera (*Evangeline*), orchestral works, electronic works, a substantial body of chamber music and vocal music.

Luftpause ['lûft"pow-ze] (Ger., breath-break) CAESURA.

lullaby a cradle song; also, a vocal or instrumental work having a quiet, lulling character.

Lully, Jean-Baptiste (Lulli, Giovanni Battista) (1632–87) Italian-born French composer, violinist and dancer, stud. of Nicolas Métru and Nicolas Gigault. In 1653 he entered the service of King Louis XIV and became, in 1656, director of the "petits violons," a chamber group formed from the larger *grande bande*, or "24 violons du roi." From 1664 he collaborated frequently with the major dramatists of France, Corneille and esp. Molière. A royal privilege granted in 1672 established Lully's control over theatrical performance in the kingdom and soon established a new musical genre, the *tragédie lyrique*. In 1681 he became *secrétaire du roi*. He died as the result of an injury to his toe caused by his sharpended conducting cane and a fast-spreading gangrene, which he refused to halt by amputation of the toe. He wrote 15 *tragédies lyriques*, ballets, *comédies-ballets*, motets, instrumental music (suites, divertissements).

Lulu tragic opera in 3 acts by Alban Berg to his own libretto adapted from two plays by Frank Wedekind. Premiere, Zürich 1937. The third act remained uncompleted at Berg's death; it was reconstructed in 1974 by Friedrich Cerha. Scenes from the life of Lulu, a woman beyond good and evil, who in the end dies at the hand of Jack the Ripper.

Lunceford, Jimmie (James Melvin) (1902–47) Amer. jazz swing bandleader. He organized his first band, the Chickasaw Syncopators, in 1927, which later became the Jimmie Lunceford Orch. and made many recordings. The group, with its star trumpeter Sy Oliver, was highly influential in the 1930s.

lunga (It., long) a word placed over a rest or fermata, indicating a longer pause or hold than might otherwise be expected.

lur a Scandinavian Bronze Age HORN consisting of a long, conical tube curved into the shape of an S ending in a bronze disc.

lusingando (It.) caressing.

lustig ['lûs-tiç] (Ger.) merry, jolly.

Lustige Witwe, Die ['lûs-ti-ge 'vit-ve, dê] MERRY WIVES OF WINDSOR, THE.

Lustigen Weiber von Windsor, Die ['lûs-ti-gen 'vī-bər fon 'vind-sər, dê] MERRY WIVES OF WINDSOR, THE.

lutanist a player of the LUTE.

lute a wooden, plucked or bowed CHORDOPHONE consisting of a resonator permanently attached to a neck across which the strings pass. Technically, the violin is a lute, although in common usage the term is usu. employed in referring only to other plucked instruments of the category, which also includes the GUITAR family of instruments, which have a boxlike body. The European lute, to which the term more commonly refers, has a vaulted body and a flat soundboard with a sound hole, usu. elaborately carved. The neck is fretted, and has a pegbox that is usu. angled to the neck. The strings, often 12 in number, are usu. of gut and are arranged in paired courses. The instrument was orig. played with a plectrum, more recently with the fingertips. The lute enjoyed a height of popularity in Europe from the 16th to 18th c. Cf. THEORBO, SITAR, SAMISEN, UD, ARCHLUTE, HARP LUTE.

lute-harpsichord a HARPSICHORD equipped with gut strings to imitate the sound of the lute.

lute song also, **lute ayre** a song for voice and lute, popular esp. in the late 16th and early 17th c. in England. The lute part was usu. written in tablature. See AYRE.

lute stop a row of harpsichord jacks set to pluck the strings very close to the bridge, producing a very penetrating sound. The term is often confused with BUFF STOP.

luthéal [lü-tā′äl] (Fr.) a device invented in 1919 to produce a harpsichordlike sound using a grand piano. It was written for by Ravel in several works, but never became popular.

luthier [lü′tyā] (Fr.) a maker of lutes, or, frequently, a maker of string instruments.

Lutoslawski, Witold (1913–) Polish composer and pianist, trained at the Warsaw Conservatory with Witold Maliszewski and others. He has appeared throughout Europe and No. America as pianist and conductor of his own works and has taught courses at Tanglewood, Dartington, the Co-

penhagen Conservatory and elsewhere. His works, which are widely performed, display both a complete command of form and an acute ear for tonal color. He has written 2 symphonies, *Venetian Games,* a violin concerto, *3 poems of Henry Michaux* for chorus and orch., other choral and solo vocal music, chamber music and works for piano.

Lutyens, (Agnes) Elisabeth (1906–83) English composer, trained at the Royal College of Music. She developed her own form of serialism, largely in isolation from the developments of the Second Viennese School. A prolific composer, she produced music in all genres, with an emphasis on vocal and chamber music.

Luxon, Benjamin (1937–) English baritone, trained at the Guildhall School of Music. He sang frequently with the English Opera Group and at Glyndebourne (from 1972). He is also noted as a recital and concert artist.

luxuriant style florid COUNTERPOINT of the 15th and 16th c.

Luzzaschi, Luzzasco [loot′tsä-skē] (?1545–1607) Italian composer, organist and teacher, prob. a stud. of Rore and Brumel. He joined the Este court in Ferrara in 1561 and eventually was in charge of the duke's musical establishment. Around 1570 he took charge of the singing ladies (*concerto delle donne*), who performed a secret repertory reserved for the duke. He was well considered in his own time as a composer, as an instrumentalist and as a teacher, numbering among his pupils Girolamo Frescobaldi. His surviving works consist of madrigals, concerted vocal music, sacred vocal works and works for organ.

Lvov, Alexey Fyodorovich (1798–1870) Russian composer and violinist. From 1837 he was dir. of the imperial court chapel choir. He also toured Europe, establishing a reputation as a virtuoso. His works incl. 3 operas, a violin concerto, caprices for violin solo and sacred choral works. His best-known work is the

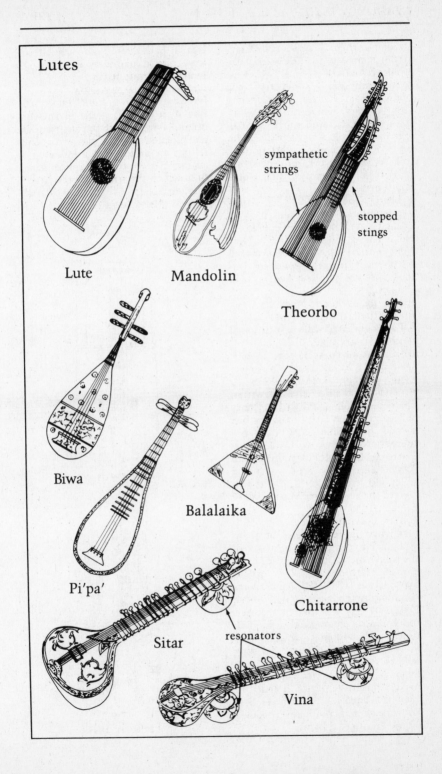

Lutes

Lute

Mandolin

sympathetic strings

stopped stings

Theorbo

Biwa

Balalaika

Pi'pa'

Chitarrone

Sitar

resonators

Vina

Russian anthem "God save the Tsar" (1833), composed for Tsar Nicholas I.

Lyadov, Anatoly (1855–1914) Russian composer, conductor and teacher, trained at the St. Petersburg Conservatory, where he was a brilliant but erratic student. He specialized in short, characteristic pieces for orch. or piano and orchestrations of folk songs and works of other composers. He also wrote choral works and songs.

Lybbert, Donald (1923–) Amer. composer and teacher, stud. of Wagenaar, Carter, Luening and Boulanger. He taught at Hunter College, New York, until 1980. His works incl. 2 operas, instrumental works for various ensembles, piano sonatas and song cycles.

lydian the authentic MODE on F, the fifth of the eight church modes.

lydian augmented scale a scale based on the LYDIAN mode.

lydian flat seven scale the LYDIAN scale with a lowered seventh degree.

Lynn (Webb), **Loretta** (1935–) Amer. country singer and songwriter. She began singing and writing songs at 18 and by the early 1960s she had several hits. Since 1970 she has toured regularly with Conway Twitty. Her autobiography, *Coal Miner's Daughter* (1976), was a best seller and a successful film. She was elected to the Country Music Hall of Fame in 1988.

Lynyrd Skynyrd Amer. southern rock group formed in Florida in 1966, a popular touring group until six of the band's members were killed in an airplane crash in 1977.

Lyon, James (1735–94) Amer. composer and tunebook compiler, whose *Urania* (1761) was the first Amer. tunebook to contain English fuguing tunes and anthems, which were models for later New England tune writers.

Lyon & Healy Amer. instrument maker and music dealer, founded in 1864 in Chicago. The firm is best known as a maker of harps, modeled on the Erard pedal harp.

lyra 1, BELL LYRE. **2**, an early Greek LYRE, played mainly by amateurs.

lyrachord LYRICHORD.

lyra viol VIOLA BASTARDA.

lyraway written in lute TABLATURE.

lyre 1, a CHORDOPHONE of ancient origin having four to ten strings that are plucked with a plectrum. The strings are attached to a frame consisting of two arms and a crossbar from which the strings stretch to the sounding body. Cf. KITHARA, ROTE, LYRA. **2**, MUSIC LYRE.

Lyres

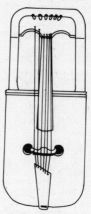

Crwth

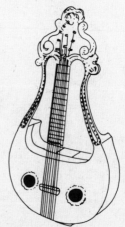

French lyre

Lyrebird Press OISEAU-LYRE, L'.

lyre guitar a GUITAR having a lyre-like shape.

lyric 1, *also,* **lyrical** smooth, sweet; melodic. **2,** the text of a vocal composition. **3,** a light, flexible voice; contrasted with DRAMATIC and SPINTO.

lyrichord a form of SOSTENENTE PIANO invented by Roger Plenius in 1741.

Lyric Opera of Chicago opera company founded in Chicago in 1954 as The Lyric Theatre by Carol Fox, Nicola Rescigno and Lawrence Kelly. The company was renamed in 1956. Ardis Krainik has been the company's general director since 1981.

Lyric Suite string quartet in six movements (1926) by Berg. The composer later arranged part of the suite for string orchestra.

Lyttleton, Humphrey (1921–) English jazz trumpeter, clarinetist, bandleader and broadcaster. He formed his own band in 1948, based on the remains of George Webb's Dixielanders, and quickly established a reputation through appearances and recordings. In the 1960s he became involved in radio and television. He has also written an important multi-volume autobiography, *I Play As I Please* (1954).

Lytton, Sir **Henry** (1867–1936) English baritone, a leading singer for over thirty years performing with the D'Oyly Carte Company in Gilbert and Sullivan operettas.

M

ma in TONIC SOL-FA, the lowered MEDIANT of the current key (or, if that key is minor, of its relative major).

Ma, Yo-Yo (1955–) French-born Amer. cellist, stud. of Leonard Rose. He has performed with major orchestras internationally, appears in recitals and chamber music performances, and has participated frequently in the Marlboro Music Festival.

Maag, (Ernst) Peter (Johannes) (1919–) Swiss conductor, trained at the Zürich, Basel and Geneva conservatories. He was assistant to Ernest Ansermet before becoming principal conductor in Düsseldorf and general music dir. in Bonn. He has been principal conductor at the Vienna Volksoper, in Parma and in Turin and has recorded extensively. He is esp. known as an interpreter of Mozart.

Maazel, Lorin (Varencove) (1930–) French-born Amer. conductor and violinist, stud. of Vladimir Bakaleinikoff. He first conducted the New York PO when he was nine and made his recital debut at age 15. He joined the Pittsburgh SO in 1948 and was apprentice conductor from 1949 to 1951. He was the first American to conduct at the Bayreuth Festival and made his Metropolitan Opera debut in 1962. He has been artistic dir. of the Deutsche Oper in Berlin, the Berlin Radio SO and the Vienna Staatsoper. From 1972 to 1982 he was music dir. of the Cleveland Orchestra and assumed the same position with the Pittsburgh SO in 1985.

Mácal, Zdeněk (1936–) Czech conductor, trained at the Brno Conservatory and the Janáček Academy. His Amer. debut was with the Chicago SO in 1972. He has been conductor of the Moravian PO and the Cologne Radio SO and became music dir. of the Milwaukee SO in 1985.

macaronic text a text mixing two or more languages.

Macbeth tragic opera in 4 acts by Verdi, libretto by Francesco Piave and Andrea Maffei, based on Shakespeare's play. Premiere, Florence 1847. Political intrigue in medieval Scotland.

McBride, Robert (Guyn) (1911–) Amer. composer and instrumentalist, stud. of Luening. He has taught at U. of Arizona and Bennington College. He has been a member of the League of Composers Woodwind Quintet and has appeared as soloist on various instruments. He has also performed extensively in jazz bands, and his works (ballets, orchestral works, choral works, chamber music) often reflect this experience.

McCartney, (James) Paul (1942–) English rock singer, guitarist and songwriter, a founding member of the BEATLES and founder of the band Wings in 1971.

McCormack, John (1884–1945) Irish-born Amer. tenor, stud. of Vincenzo Sabatini. He made his Metropolitan Opera debut in 1909, then abandoned the opera stage c1918 to concentrate on concert and recital performance. He became an Amer. citizen in 1917 but returned to Ireland in the late 1920s.

McCracken, James (Eugene) (1926–88) Amer. tenor, stud. of Wellington Ezekiel. His debut was at Central City, CO, in 1952, and he debuted at the Metropolitan Opera a year later. Among his best roles were Otello, Radamès (*Aida*) and Don José (*Carmen*).

McCurdy, Alexander (1905–83) Amer. organist, stud. of Lynwood Farnam. He was organist at the Second

Presbyterian Church in Philadelphia (1927–71) and taught at the Curtis Institute and the Westminster Choir College. He was organ editor of *The Étude* from 1946–57.

McDonald, Harl (1899–1955) Amer. composer, pianist, conductor and teacher, trained at the U. of S. California and in Leipzig. He taught at the Philadelphia Musical Academy and at the U. of Pennsylvania and from 1939 to 1955 was manager of the Philadelphia Orchestra. His works are principally for instruments, incl. orchestral works, piano pieces, 2 piano trios and 2 string quartets.

MacDowell, Edward (Alexander) (1860–1908) Amer. composer, pianist and teacher, trained in Paris and Frankfurt. In the 1880s he taught piano privately in Frankfurt and Wiesbaden, then returned to the U.S. and settled in Boston, concentrating on composing and appearing as solo pianist, establishing his reputation as one of the leading figures in Amer. musical life. He taught at Columbia from 1896 to 1903 and also conducted the Mendelssohn Glee Club. In his last years he worked on behalf of the American Academy of Arts and Letters, of which he was a founder, and other organizations. He wrote 2 piano concertos, orchestral suites, many songs and part songs and works for solo piano (*Woodland Sketches, Sea Pieces*, 4 sonatas).

MacDowell Colony a retreat established in 1907 for creative artists (composers, writers and visual artists) built around the New Hampshire summer home of EDWARD MAC-DOWELL.

Mace, Thomas (c1612–?1706) English composer, singer and lutanist, active in Cambridge, England. He is best remembered for his defense of the English musical tradition in *Musick's Monument* (1676).

Macero, Teo (Attilio Joseph) (1925–) Amer. jazz composer, saxophonist and producer, trained at the Juilliard School. In the 1950s he composed classical works in an atonal jazz style and performed with bassist Charles Mingus. He joined Columbia Records in 1957 and has produced many recordings, esp. those of Miles Davis and Thelonious Monk.

McEwen, Sir John (Blackwood) (1868–1948) Scottish composer and teacher, trained at Glasgow U. and the Royal Academy of Music in London. He was a prolific composer in all genres and was perhaps the first composer in England to utilize SPRECHSTIMME.

MacFarren, Sir George (Alexander) (1813–87) English composer, stud. of Charles Lucas and Cipriani Potter. He taught at the Royal Academy of Music and conducted from 1845 at Covent Garden. A prolific composer, he produced works in all genres, incl. 19 operas (incl. *Robin Hood* and *King Charles II*), oratorios and cantatas, 9 symphonies, overtures, chamber music and piano works.

McGregor, Chris (1936–) S. Afr. jazz pianist and composer. In 1962 he formed the Blue Notes, who left So. Africa for good in 1964 to go to Europe. Their music combined African and free-jazz elements. In 1970 the group was enlarged and became the Brotherhood of Breath.

Machaut, Guillaume de [mä'shō, gē'yōm də] (c1300–77) French composer and poet. He was secretary of the king of Bohemia from about 1323 to 1346 and of various high French nobles, incl. Charles V, after the Bohemian king's death. His large output represents the height of the French ARS NOVA, and incorporates the rhythmic innovations of Philippe de Vitry. He composed the first complete mass ordinary and was the first composer to make a complete edition of his compositions, which incl. the *Messe de Nostre Dame*, motets, ballades, rondeaux, lais and virelais.

machete [mä'chä-tä] (Port.) a small, four-stringed, Portuguese guitar, a predecessor of the UKULELE. Also, *cavaquinho*.

machicotage [mä-shē-kō'täzh] (Fr.) the insertion of ornaments between the principal tones of certain sections of plainchant. The practice was usu. reserved for certain singers known as *machicots*; it was common in the Middle Ages and has persisted in some areas into modern times.

machine head a mechanical device such as a tuning peg, rachet, etc., used to adjust and maintain the pitch of a string on a musical instrument.

machine stop a mechanism found on certain English harpsichords of the later 18th c. allowing a pedal to control two or more registers, overriding their individual hand stops.

mächtig ('meç-tiç) (Ger.) **1,** powerful; loud. **2,** very; *mächtig bewegt,* very lively.

McHugh, (James Francis) Jimmy (1894–1969) Amer. pianist and composer of scores for Cotton Club reviews, films and Broadway plays, including, with lyricist Dorothy Fields, *The Blackbirds of 1928* and many successful songs for films.

McKenna, Dave (David J.) (1930–) Amer. jazz pianist. He has played with a number of major bands, incl. those of Woody Herman, Gene Krupa and Eddie Condon, as well as with combos led by Bobby Hackett, Stan Getz, Zoot Sims and others. He has also made a number of solo recordings.

Mackenzie, Sir **Alexander (Campbell)** (1847–1935) Scottish composer, violinist and conductor, trained in Germany and at the Royal Academy of Music. In 1879 he went to Florence to devote himself to composition, producing a number of successful choral works, then, in 1888, became principal of the Royal Academy of Music, a post he held until his death. His works incl. operas and incidental music, cantatas and oratorios (*The Rose of Sharon, The Dream of Jubal*), orchestral suites, overtures, etc., chamber music, many songs and arrangements of Scottish folk melodies.

Mackerras, Sir **(Alan) Charles (MacLaurin)** (1925–) Amer.-born Australian conductor and oboist, stud. of Michael Mudie and Václav

Talich. He was on the staff of Sadler's Wells Opera, then became principal conductor of the BBC Concert Orch. He conducted frequently at Covent Garden from 1963, became principal conductor at the Hamburg Staatsoper in 1966, then musical dir. of Sadler's Wells in 1970. He has recorded extensively and is esp. known for his interpretation of the operas of Janáček.

McKinley, Ray (Raymond Frederick) (1910–) Amer. jazz drummer, singer and bandleader. He played with the Jimmy Dorsey band until 1939, then formed a big band with trombonist Will Bradley. He later joined the Glenn Miller band and took over after Miller's death. He retired in 1965.

McKinney's Cotton Pickers Amer. jazz ensemble formed in Ohio in the early 1920s, led from 1927 to 1931 by arranger DON REDMAN, under whose leadership they made many recordings.

McKuen, Rod (Marvin) (1933–) Amer. composer, singer and poet, writer of over 100 songs, many of them influenced by the style of the French *chansonniers*. He has written film scores, musicals, ballets, orchestral suites and piano music.

McLaughlin, John (1942–) English jazz guitarist and composer, noted for his astonishing technique. In the 1960s he experimented with free jazz and became interested in Eastern philosophy. He worked in the late 1960s with Miles Davis, then formed his own Mahavishnu Orch. in 1970, which went through several incarnations, and the quartet Shakti, composed of guitar, violin, tabla and percussion. He has written many works in a variety of styles, including a guitar concerto which he performed with the Los Angeles PO.

MacMillan, Sir **Ernest (Alexander Campbell)** (1893–1973) eminent Canadian conductor, composer, organist and teacher; trained in Toronto, Edinburgh and Oxford. He was an important figure in almost every area of Canadian musical life. He was organist at Timothy Eaton Memorial Church in Toronto from 1919 to 1925 and co-founder of the annual performances of the Bach *St. Matthew Passion*. He was principal of the Toronto Conservatory of Music (1926–42) and, from 1927, dean of the Faculty of Music at the U. of Toronto, which named its new opera theater, built in 1964, after him. He conducted the Toronto SO (1931–51), which he built into a fully professional orchestra, and the Toronto Mendelssohn Choir (1942–57). He was also a founder of the Canada Council in 1957.

MacNeil, Cornell (1922–) Amer. baritone, stud. of Friedrich Schorr. He began in Broadway musicals, then created the role of John Sorel in Menotti's *The Consul*, beginning a long and distinguished operatic career. He is esp. noted for his performance of Verdi baritone roles.

Macon, Uncle Dave (1870–1952) Amer. country-music banjo player and singer, a popular vaudevillian and recording artist in the 1920s and 1930s. He was elected to the Country Music Hall of Fame in 1966.

Maconchy, Elizabeth (1907–) English composer, trained in London and Prague. She has composed in all genres, but is particularly known for her chamber music, esp. her string quartets. She has also written 7 operas, orchestral works, choral and solo vocal music and piano pieces.

McPartland, Jimmy (James D.) (1907–91) Amer. jazz trumpeter and cornettist, a principal member of the Chicago Austin High Gang. He worked with Ben Pollack and Eddie Condon and toured extensively. In the 1960s he played at the Metropole in New York, then toured and played at festivals in the 1970s and 1980s. He was married for a time to MARIAN McPARTLAND.

McPartland (née Turner), **Marian** (**Margaret**) (1920–) English-born Amer. jazz pianist. She came to the U.S. with her then husband JIMMY McPARTLAND and played in various piano bars and concertized. In recent years she has hosted a popular radio program, on National Public Radio, "Piano Jazz."

Macque, Giovanni de (?1548–1614) Flemish composer, organist and teacher, stud. of Philippe de Monte and organist of the chapel of the Spanish Viceroy in Naples from 1594. His works divide stylistically between his periods in Rome and in Naples, the Roman works being more conservative. His many works incl. motets, madrigals and other secular vocal music, instrumental ricercars and canzonas.

McRae, Carmen (1922–) Amer. jazz singer and pianist. She sang with the bands of Benny Carter, Count Basie and Mercer Ellington, then performed with her own trio.

McTell, Blind Willie (c1898–1959) Amer. blues singer, guitarist and songwriter, blind from birth. He performed as a street musician in Atlanta for most of his life and made many recordings.

Macurdy, John (1929–) Amer. bass, stud. of Avery Crew and Goldovsky. He sang with the New York City Opera (1959–62) and the Metropolitan Opera (1962–), as well as at major opera houses elsewhere in the U.S. and in Europe. His roles incl. Sarastro (*The Magic Flute*) and Arkel (*Pelléas et Mélisande*).

Madama Butterfly (It., Madame Butterfly) tragic opera in 3 acts by Puccini to a libretto by Luigi Illica and Giuseppe Giacosa, based on a play by David Belasco, from a story by John Luther Long. Premiere, Milan 1904. The Japanese geisha Butterfly is married, then abandoned, by an American naval officer.

Maddy, Joe (Joseph) (**Edgar**) (1891–1966) Amer. conductor and educator. He taught in various high schools and at the U. of Michigan. He was organizer of the National High School Orchestra (1926) and creator in 1928 of the National Music Camp at Interlochen, MI (see INTERLOCHEN ARTS ACADEMY).

Maderna, Bruno (1920–73) Italian composer, conductor and teacher, an important influence as performer and teacher on Italian postwar music. He studied with Bustini, Malipiero, Guarnieri and Scherchen. He settled in Darmstadt in the 1950s and taught at the summer courses. He also taught at the Milan Conservatory, the Berkshire Music Center and the Dartington Summer School. He conducted the Darmstadt International Chamber Ensemble and the Radio Milan SO. His works, which make frequent use of aleatory procedures, incl. *Satyricon* (opera), concertos for piano, oboe, flute; other orchestral works, various vocal works, chamber music and works for electronic tape.

madrigal 1, a 14th-c. Italian poetic and musical form. By mid-century, its form was stable: two or three three-line stanzas followed by a one- or two-line refrain or *ritornello*, usu. with a change of time signature for the *ritornello*. The poetry consists in a free alternation of seven- and eleven-syllable lines falling into one of a variety of formal rhyme schemes. The musical style is two-part florid counterpoint and, for the most part, both voices are texted. Phrases are separated by cadences and often a change of mode. The extant repertory consists of approximately 200 pieces, and the genre died out completely by 1420. **2**, a 16th-c. Italian poetic and musical form, consisting of a single stanza of free verse with a free rhyme scheme in alternating seven- and eleven-syllable lines. The term is also often used generically to indicate musical settings of sonnets, ballate, canzoni, ottave rime, etc. The late 16th c. witnessed the development of the concerted madrigal (madrigal for voices and instruments), a form which continued well into the 17th c.

madrigal comedy a term probably coined by Alfred Einstein to refer to a type of Italian Renaissance theatrical entertainment consisting in a series of madrigals or other secular vocal pieces held together by a story to which the texts relate. The most famous example is *L'Amfiparnaso* (1597) by Orazio Vecchi.

madrigale arioso an Italian secular SONG form which combines the free treatment of a madrigal with the formulaic setting of an aria.

madrigale spirituale (It., spiritual madrigal) a madrigal composed to a devotional but not liturgical text. Cf. LAUDA.

madrigaletto a light MADRIGAL of the 16th c.

madrigalism a term referring to the musical devices used in 16th- and 17th-c. madrigals for WORD-PAINTING or as a MANNERISM.

Maelzel, Johann Nepomuk (1772–1838) German inventor of mechanical instruments, incl. the Panharmonicon and the METRONOME.

maestoso [mä-ä′stō-zō] (It.) majestic, stately.

maestro [mä′ā-strō] (It., master) a title used as a term of respect for conductors, music coaches, etc.

maestro di cappella (It.) a musician in charge of a CHAPEL (2,); not necessarily synonymous with "choirmaster." Also, *Kapellmeister* (Ger.).

maestro di musica (It., music master) a music teacher.

magadis (Gk.) an ancient Greek twenty-stringed harplike instrument having the capability of playing in octaves.

magadize to sing or play in octaves.

Maganini, Quinto (1897–1974) Amer. conductor, composer and flutist, stud. of Georges Barrère, Domenico Brescia and Boulanger. He played in the San Francisco SO and the New York SO, then worked as conductor of the New York Sinfonietta, the Maganini Chamber SO and the Norwalk (CT) SO.

Maggio Musicale Fiorentino [′mäd-jō moo-zē′kä-lä] (It., the May Music Festival of Florence) a concert and opera festival founded in 1933 by G.M. Gatti. Permanent conductors have included Bruno Bartoletti and Riccardo Muti.

maggiore [mäd′jō-rä] (It., major) a term usu. signalling the return to major tonality after a section or movement in minor. Cf. MINORE.

Magic Flute, The (Ger., *Die Zauberflöte*) opera in 2 acts by Mozart to a libretto by Emanuel Schikaneder. Premiere, Vienna 1791. A parable of good versus evil as the young prince Tamino proves himself worthy of the hand of Pamina.

magnificat [mä′nyē-fē-kät] (Lat., he praises) the biblical canticle beginning "My soul doth magnify the Lord" (Luke 1:46–55) which is sung in the Roman Catholic church at the end of the vespers service. An antiphon usu. accompanies the canticle. The magnificat has been a part of the church service since the Middle Ages. Well-known settings were composed by Monteverdi, J.S. Bach, Mozart and Penderecki.

Magnus Liber organi (Lat.) the *Magnus Liber organi de graduali et antifonario*, a 12th-c. liturgical book of graduals and alleluias for the Mass and responsories for the Vespers service, traditionally said to have been compiled by Magister Leoninus (see LÉONIN) and later revised by Magister Perotinus (see PÉROTIN).

magraphah (Heb., shovel) a Jewish organlike instrument of the early Christian era.

Mahagonny see RISE AND FALL OF THE CITY OF MAHAGONNY.

Mahavishnu Orchestra Amer. jazz-rock fusion ensemble formed in 1971 by JOHN MCLAUGHLIN, incorporating elements of Indian music. The group was active until 1976.

Mahler, Gustav (1860–1911) influential Austrian composer and conductor, stud. of Julius Epstein, Robert Fuchs and Franz Krenn at the Vienna Conservatory. His conducting career began at a series of small opera houses, incl. Kassel (1883–5), where he had an unhappy affair with one of the singers which led to the composition of the cycle *Lieder eines fahrenden Gesellen* (Songs of a Wayfarer). He conducted for a year at the Deutsches Landestheater in Prague and for two years at the Neues Stadttheater in Leipzig. While in Leipzig he completed Weber's opera *Die drei Pintos*, and a series of successful performances provided money and fame for him. Three years at the Budapest Royal Opera were followed by a longer stay at the Stadttheater in Hamburg, where he conducted as many as 19 operas in a month. The pinnacle of his career was his ten years at the Vienna Court Opera (1897–1907), during which time he also provided some support for the emerging composers in Schoenberg's circle. His final years were spent at the Metropolitan Opera. His works, which display a supreme command of vocal and instrumental writing, incl. *Das klagende Lied* (cantata), song cycles (*Lieder eines fahrenden Gesellen, Kindertotenlieder*), 10 symphonies (incl. *Das Lied von der Erde*) and many songs with piano or orchestra.

Maid as Mistress, The SERVA PADRONA, LA.

Maiden's Prayer, The salon piece for piano (publ. 1856) by Tekla Badarzewska (1834–61), which became internationally popular and was published in many different arrangements.

mainstream jazz a vague term given different meanings by different writers, nearly always excluding avantgarde or experimental jazz of the then-current period. It is often (and was originally) used to refer to the small-group swing jazz of the 1950s.

majeur [mä′zhœr] (Fr.) MAJOR.

Majo, Gian Francesco (de) (1732–70) Italian composer of opera seria, stud. of his father, uncle and great-uncle. He worked, as did his father, at the royal chapel in Naples. His music was praised by Mozart and other contemporaries and incl. over 20 operas, cantatas, oratorios, motets and a harpsichord sonata.

major one of the two principal modes of Western music since the 17th c., the other being MINOR. See MAJOR SCALE, TONALITY.

major interval the distance between the key note of a major scale and any other note in the scale, other than those called *perfect*; one half step larger than a minor interval. See INTERVAL.

major key a tonality based on a MAJOR SCALE.

major scale a SCALE having half steps between the 3rd and 4th and the 7th and 8th degrees.

major seventh chord a MAJOR TRIAD with an additional major seventh.

major triad a three-note CHORD composed of a fundamental tone with its major third and a perfect fifth.

malagueña [mä-lä′gä-nyä] (Sp.) **1**, a Spanish gypsy folk tune. The music is usu. written over a repeated chord pattern of descending root-position minor triads. **2**, a Spanish couple dance similar to the FANDANGO, native to the province of Málaga.

Malcolm, George (John) (1917–) English pianist, harpsichordist and conductor, trained at the Royal College of Music. He was master of music at Westminster Cathedral (1947–59) and has performed frequently on piano and harpsichord with various groups in London and conducted in London and on the Continent.

male alto a male singer employing FALSETTO; countertenor.

Malgoire, Jean-Claude (1940–) French oboist and conductor. In 1966 he founded La Grande Écurie et la Chambre du Roy for the performance of Baroque music and the Florilegium Musicum de Paris for the performance of medieval and Renaissance music. He has been an important force in early music in France.

Malibran (née Garcia), **Maria(-Felicia)** (1808–36) French-born Spanish mezzo-soprano, sister of PAULINE VIARDOT, stud. of her father, tenor MANUEL GARCIA. She performed with her father and sister in London and New York until 1827, then sang in London and Paris until 1832, after which she appeared frequently in Italy. Her death at 28 resulted from a riding accident. She was noted for her performances of roles by Bellini, Rossini and Donizetti.

malinconico (It.) melancholy: a mark of expression.

Malipiero, Gian Francesco (1882–1973) prolific Italian composer and musicologist, trained in Bologna and the Liceo Musicale in Venice, which he directed from 1939 to 1952. He collaborated with ALFREDO CASELLA in the Società Italiana di Musica Moderna and the Corporazione delle Nuove Musiche. He developed an early interest in music of the Italian Renaissance and Baroque and produced a complete edition of Monteverdi's works, a monumental first step in Monteverdi scholarship. He was also in charge of the edition of Vivaldi's works produced by the Istituto Italiano Antonio Vivaldi. He wrote over 30 operas, 6 ballets, many orchestral works, vocal works with orch., songs, chamber music, piano pieces.

Malko, Nikolay (1883–1961) Russian-born Amer. conductor, trained at the St. Petersburg Conservatory and with Felix Mottl in Munich. He was chief conductor of the Leningrad PO, then left in 1929 for western Europe, guest-conducting in many cities in Europe and S. America, esp. in Copenhagen. In 1940 he settled in Chicago, continuing to conduct internationally and teaching at various schools. His books on conducting have had wide circulation, esp. *The Conductor and his Baton* (1950).

mallet instruments percussion instruments played with mallets, esp. the MARIMBA, XYLOPHONE and VIBRAPHONE.

Malotte, Albert Hay (1895–1964) Amer. composer and organist, stud. of Georges Jacob in Paris. He was music dir. for Walt Disney and wrote a number of film scores, but he is best remembered for his setting of the Lord's Prayer (1935).

Mamas and the Papas, The Amer. psychedelic folk-pop vocal group formed in New York in 1965. Among their hits were the songs "Monday,

Monday" and "California Dreamin' " (1966). The group disbanded in 1968 but was revived briefly in 1982.

mambo a ballroom couple-dance of Cuban origin derived from the RUMBA; it is the source of other Latin American dances, such as the CHA CHA CHA. See DANCE (*illus.*).

Mame musical, music and lyrics by Jerry Herman, book by Robert E. Lee and Jerome Lawrence, based on their play *Auntie Mame*, adapted from the novel by Patrick Dennis. Premiere, New York 1966. The story of how an unconventional, pleasure-seeking lady raises her nephew.

Mamelles de Tirésias, Les [mä'mel də tē'rä-zē-äs] (Fr., The Bosoms of Thérèse) comic opera in 2 acts by Poulenc to a libretto by Guillaume Apollinaire, from his own play. Premiere, Paris 1947. A series of sketches dealing with the battle of the sexes.

Ma mère l'oye [mä mer lwä] (Fr.) MOTHER GOOSE SUITE.

Mamlok, Ursula (1928–) German-born Amer. composer and teacher, trained in Berlin and in New York with Szell, Giannini, Shapey and others. She has taught at New York U. and the Manhattan School. Her works incl. several concertos, many chamber music works and vocal works.

Mana-Zucca (Zuckermann, Augusta) (1885–1981) Amer. composer and pianist, stud. of Alexander Lambert. Her songs were performed by many leading artists in the 1920s and 1930s and several of her concertos have been performed by U.S. orchestras. Her memoirs and her accounts of her European travels make interesting reading.

Mance, Junior (Julian Clifford, Jr.) (1928–) Amer. jazz pianist. He played with Gene Ammons, Lester Young, Cannonball Adderley and Dizzy Gillespie and formed his own trio around 1960. He is esp. known as an accompanist of such artists as singers Joe Williams and Aretha Franklin.

Mancinelli, Luigi (1848–1921) Ital-ian composer and conductor, trained with his brother Marino and in Florence. From 1874 he was conductor at the Teatro Apollo in Rome, where he established a substantial reputation, esp. for Wagner. He left Italy in 1886 under mysterious circumstances. He became chief conductor at Covent Garden in 1888, remaining until 1905. He was also chief conductor at the Madrid Opera and in 1893 at the Metropolitan Opera in New York. He was a highly esteemed conductor and also composed a substantial number of works, incl. 4 operas, some orchestral works, incidental music, cantatas and songs.

Mancini, Henry (1924–) Amer. conductor and composer, trained at the Juilliard School and with Krenek and Castelnuovo-Tedesco. He has composed for television and scored over 100 films, winning three Oscars.

mandola [män'do-lä] (It.) **1,** *also,* **mandora** (It.), **mandore** a pear-shaped, four-course LUTE of the 16th and 17th c., a predecessor of the MANDOLIN. Also, *lutina.* **2,** a tenor MANDOLIN.

mandolin a pear-shaped fretted LUTE having four to six pairs of strings played with a plectrum. The instrument appeared in the 17th c. and is still in use in folk music and occasionally in chamber and orchestral music.

mandore *also,* **mandora** (It.) MANDOLA.

Manfred 1, incidental music, Op. 115 (1848–9), by Schumann, intended for performance with Byron's poem. **2,** symphony, Op. 58 (1885), by Tchaikovsky, inspired by Byron's poem.

Mangelsdorff, Albert (1928–) German jazz trombonist, trained at the Frankfurt Conservatory. From 1958 he led his own groups, traveling in 1964 to Asia, which led to the incorporation of elements of Indian and other Asian music in his works. He has developed the playing of chords on the trombone and combining lip playing with vocal sounds.

Manhattan Opera House an opera theater in New York opened in 1906.

Manhattan School of Music a conservatory in New York founded in 1917.

Manhattan Transfer Amer. vocal quartet formed in 1969 in New York specializing in popular vocal music from the 1920s to the present, esp. vocal versions of jazz instrumental recordings.

Mann, Herbie (Herbert Jay Solomon) (1930–) Amer. jazz flutist, saxophonist and composer. After a decade working in TV and playing with the Mat Mathews Quintet and the Pete Rugolo Octet, he formed the Afro-Jazz Sextet in 1959, and toured Africa and S. America. He has incorporated many folk and popular elements into his music, which has given it a wide popular appeal.

Manne, Shelly (Sheldon) (1920–84) Amer. jazz drummer. He played with Stan Kenton and Woody Herman in the 1940s, then settled on the West Coast, where he worked as a studio musician and made many recordings with his group Shelly Manne and his Men. He also operated Shelly's Manne-Hole, a prominent Los Angeles night club.

mannerism a term borrowed from art history to describe the tendency in music of the late 16th c. toward a preoccupation with style, emphasis on detail and extreme chromaticism. Noted composers of mannerist music were Marenzio and Gesualdo.

Mannes College of Music a conservatory in New York founded in 1916 by Amer. conductor and violinist David Mannes (1866–1959), orig. as the David Mannes School. The school was directed for many years by Mannes's son Leopold (1899–1964).

Mannheim School a term referring to the 18th-c. styles of violin playing, and precise ensemble work within the orchestra that exploited dynamic effects, developed at the court of Mannheim. The leading composers of the Mannheim School were Johann Stamitz, Franz Xaver Richter, Ignaz Holzbauer and Anton Filtz. Melodic figures peculiar to the style incl. the orchestral sigh (an appoggiatura with anticipated resolution) and the "Mannheim rocket" (a rising triadic theme).

mano (It.) hand.

Man of La Mancha musical by Mitch Leigh, lyrics by Joe Darion, book by Dale Wasserman, based on the novel by Cervantes. Premiere, New York 1965. Several adventures of Don Quixote, in love with the servant girl Aldonza, whom he calls Dulcinea.

Manon [mä′nō] tragic opera in 5 acts by Massenet to a libretto by Henri Meilhac and Philippe Gille, based on a novel by Abbé Prévost. Premiere, Paris 1884. The story of Manon Lescaut's ill-fated love of the young Chevalier Des Grieux. Cf. Manon Lescaut.

Manon Lescaut [les′kō] tragic opera in 4 acts by Puccini to a libretto by Ruggiero Leoncavallo and others based on a novel by Abbé Prévost. Taken from the same novel as Massenet's Manon, Puccini's opera deals with the periods of the story falling between the acts of the former work.

Mantovani, (Annunzio Paolo) (1905–80) Italian-born English violinist and conductor. He began as a concert violinist, turning to lighter music in the 1930s, then achieved wide popularity in the 1950s with his unique string-orch. sound.

manual a Keyboard played by the hands.

manualiter [mä-noo′ä-lē-ter] (Lat.) an indication that a piece for organ (or a section of a piece) is to be played on the manuals only. Cf. Pedaliter.

manzello (Sp.) an archaic type of Spanish Saxophone.

Manziarly, Marcelle de (1899–1989) French composer, pianist and conductor, stud. of Boulanger and Weingartner. She taught and performed both in Paris and the U.S., appearing as conductor and pianist, often in her own works, which include La Femme en flèche (chamber opera), a piano concerto, chamber music, piano music, choral works and songs.

Manzoni Requiem popular name for

the Requiem Mass (1874) by Verdi, dedicated to the memory of the Italian poet and novelist Alessandro Manzoni.

Mara (née Schmeling), **Gertrud Elisabeth** (1749–1833) German soprano, stud. of Paradisi. Until 1784 she sang in Germany, being at first in the service of Frederick the Great. In London she appeared with success in opera (she sang Cleopatra in Handel's *Giulio Cesare*) and concert until 1802, when she returned to the Continent.

Marable, Fate (1890–1947) Amer. jazz pianist and leader of a Mississippi riverboat band from the late 1910s until his retirement in the early 1940s. Many musicians later to be famous played in his band, incl. Louis Armstrong and Baby Dodds.

maracas (Sp.) a pair of dried gourds or similar containers, filled with seeds or pebbles, that have handles by which they are shaken for use as a percussion instrument. Cf. CABACA.

Marais, Marin [mä're, mä'rē] (1656–1728) French composer and bass viol player, stud. of Sainte-Colombe and Lully and a member of the royal orch. for most of his life. Marais published five volumes of works for bass viol and also composed four operas, inspired no doubt by his long association with Lully.

Marbeck MERBECKE.

marcando, marcato (It.) strongly accented.

Marcello, Alessandro (1669–1747) Italian composer, brother of BENEDETTO MARCELLO. He was a noble musical amateur, and most of his relatively small output was published under the pseudonym Eterio Stinfalico. His best-known work is his Oboe Concerto in D minor, orig. ascribed to Vivaldi and then to Alessandro's brother Benedetto. J.S. Bach made an embellished keyboard transcription of the work.

Marcello, Benedetto (1686–1739) Italian composer and theorist, brother of ALESSANDRO MARCELLO and stud. of Gasparini. In addition to his musical activities he was an active public servant, holding a variety of important posts in Brescia. His output, mainly vocal music, incl. an opera, cantatas, serenatas, motets, oratorios and instrumental concertos and sonatas.

march music with a strong, regular metrical pattern and repetitive rhythms, orig. designed to accompany military processions.

Marchal, André(-Louis) [mär'shäl] (1894–1980) French organist, blind from birth, stud. of Eugène Gigout. He was organist at St. Germain-des-Prés and at St. Eustache and toured extensively in Europe and the U.S. He was a very active teacher, privately, at Fontainebleau and in master classes.

Marchesi (Marchesini), **Luigi** (1755–1829) Italian castrato and composer, stud. of Albuzzi and Caironi. He was castrated at his own request. His fame was established in Naples at the Teatro S Carlo and later in Milan and Turin, where he joined the court. From 1788 to 1790 he sang regularly in London, but later he sang almost exclusively in Italy.

Marchesi (de Castrone) (née Graumann), **Mathilde** (1821–1913) German mezzo-soprano and teacher, stud. of Nicolai and Manuel García. A successful concert artist, she was, however, best known for her teaching, counting among her many famous pupils Nellie Melba, Mary Garden and Emma Calvé.

marching band a BAND, usu. composed of woodwinds, brass and drums, that performs while marching. Some marching bands, esp. high school and collegiate groups, execute elaborate marching patterns. Marching bands played an important part in the development of jazz, beginning with 19th-c. brass bands playing ragtime and performing at functions such as funerals.

marcia ('mär-chä) (It.) MARCH.

Marenzio, Luca (c1553–99) Italian singer and composer, a musician in the service of the Gonzaga family in Mantua, possibly a stud. of Giovanni

Contino. Marenzio spent most of his professional life in Rome. He was and is best known for his many madrigals and villanellas, and he also wrote motets and other sacred vocal compositions.

mariachi (mä-rē'ä-chē) (Span.) a group of itinerant Mexican folk musicians, usu. consisting of violinists, guitarists and singers. Also, a musician belonging to such a group or the music performed by them.

Maria Golovin tragic opera in 3 acts by Menotti to his own libretto, commissioned by NBC. Premiere, Brussels 1958. The story concerns Maria's ill-fated love for the blind Donato.

Marian antiphon one of a group of ANTIPHONS dating from the 13th c., based on texts in honor of the Virgin Mary and sung after Vespers (see DIVINE OFFICE). Cf. ALMA REDEMPTORIS MATER, SALVE REGINA, AVE MARIA, REGINA CAELI.

Marian motet a motet composed in honor of the Virgin Mary, intended for performance during the divine office, esp. at vespers. See also MARIAN ANTIPHON.

Mariano, Charlie (Carmine Ugo) (1923–) Amer. jazz saxophonist, flutist and nagaswaram player, trained at the Berklee School. He worked with Stan Kenton, Shelly Manne and others in Los Angeles, then formed a quartet with pianist Toshiko Akiyoshi, to whom he was married at that time. He worked with Charles Mingus in 1962, taught at Berklee (1965–71), then spent the next decade in Europe, where he worked with a number of different groups.

Mariazeller Mass the Mass No. 8 in C major (1782) by Haydn.

Marienleben, Das (Ger., Life of Mary) song cycle, Op. 27 (1922–3), by Hindemith to 15 poems by Rilke. The work was extensively revised (1936–48) on the basis of new harmonic theories. The composer also orchestrated some of the songs (1938–59).

marimba a primitive XYLOPHONE of Africa and Central America with res-

onators, often of calabash, beneath some or all of the wooden bars. The modern orchestral version of this instrument uses metal tube resonators beneath each bar. Also, *xylorimba*.

marimba gong a MARIMBA with metal bars.

Marines' Hymn, The a text of unknown authorship set to music from Offenbach's operetta *Geneviève de Brabant* (1868). The poem ("From the Halls of Montezuma to the Shores of Tripoli . . .") refers to the Mexican War and to the war against the Barbary Pirates of No. Africa.

marinera a social dance of northern S. America, performed to melodies in 6/8 meter with refrain.

marine trumpet TRUMPET MARINE.

Marinuzzi, Gino (Giuseppe) (1882–1945) Italian conductor and composer, trained in Palermo. He made his reputation conducting the Italian repertory and works of Richard Strauss and Wagner, in Italy and Argentina. He directed the Bologna Conservatory (1915–18) and was artistic dir. of the Chicago Opera Association (1919–21).

Mario, Giovanni Matteo, Cavaliere di Candia (1810–83) Italian tenor, husband of soprano GIULIA GRISI. He was renowned in a wide repertory of French and Italian roles, esp. in operas by Meyerbeer and Verdi.

Mario (Tillotson), **Queena** (1896–1951) Amer. soprano, stud. of Oscar Saenger and Marcella Sembrich. She sang with the Metropolitan Opera from 1922 to 1938, as well as with the San Francisco Opera and other companies. She taught at the Juilliard School from 1942.

Markevich, Igor (1912–83) Russian-born Italian conductor and composer, stud. of Cortot, Boulanger and Scherchen. His professional conducting debut was in 1930 with the Concertgebouw Orch. He was musical dir. of the Maggio Musicale in Florence from 1944, and he was also resident conductor of the Stockholm SO, the Concerts Lamoureux in Paris, the Spanish Radio and Television Orchestra and the Monte Carlo Orchestra. His U.S. debut was with the Boston SO in 1955.

Marlboro Music Festival Amer. chamber music festival founded in 1950 by Rudolf Serkin, Adolf and Hermann Busch and Marcel and Louis Moyse. It takes place each summer in Marlboro, VT, and a group called Music from Marlboro, comprised of musicians from the festival, has toured annually since 1965. Illustrious instrumentalists who have participated incl. Casals, Schneider and Horszowski.

Marlowe (Sapira), **Sylvia** (1908–81) Amer. harpsichordist, trained at the École Normale in Paris and with Boulanger and Landowska. She performed regularly on the radio and later in concerts and recordings. She taught at the Mannes College of Music from 1948, commissioned new works from a number of composers and made editions of works by Couperin.

Marpurg, Friedrich Wilhelm (1718–95) German theorist, composer and critic, best known as editor of three music periodicals and writer of theoretical treatises.

Marriage of Figaro, The (It., *Le nozze di Figaro*) comic opera in 4 acts by Mozart to a libretto in Italian by Lorenzo da Ponte, based on a French comedy by Beaumarchais. Premiere, Vienna 1786. Figaro's impending marriage to Susanna is complicated by the claims of their employer, the Count Almaviva, to the right to a first night with the bride.

Marriner, Sir **Neville** (1924–) English violinist and conductor, trained at the Royal College of Music (where he taught from 1949 to 1959), the Paris Conservatoire and later with Pierre Monteux. He played in the Martin String Quartet and was a cofounder with Thurston Dart of the Jacobean Ensemble. He was a member of the Philharmonia Orch. and the London SO. In 1959 he formed the Academy of St. Martin-in-the-Fields, with which he has made many recordings and established an international reputation. He has been musical dir. of the Los Angeles Chamber Orch. and the Minnesota Orch. and has guest-conducted in Europe and the U.S.

Marsalis, Wynton (1961–) Amer. trumpet virtuoso, equally at home in jazz and classical music, trained with John Longo, at Tanglewood and at the Juilliard School. He played with Art Blakey's Jazz Messengers and with Herbie Hancock, then formed his own quintet. He was the first instrumentalist to win Grammies in Jazz and Classical Music in the same year. His brother, **Branford Marsalis** (1960–), plays soprano and tenor saxophone and has played with Art Blakey, Omar Hakim and Herbie Hancock, the rock singer Sting, and his brother, also leading his own quartet.

Marschner, Heinrich August (1795–1861) German composer, trained in Zittau and Leipzig. In the 1820s he joined the staff of the Leipzig Stadttheater and became conductor of the Hannover court theater. His operas *Der Vampyr* (1827) and *Hans Heiling* (1831–2) are still occasionally performed today. He wrote 14 operas, incidental music, 2 symphonies, overtures, chamber music, piano works, choral works and songs.

Marseillaise, La [mär-se'yez] patriotic song and French national anthem (1792), music and lyrics by royalist officer Claude Rouget de Lisle (1760–1836), orig. written for the war between France and Prussia. The title refers to the volunteers from Marseilles who took part in the storming of the Tuileries in 1792.

Marshall, Lois (Catherine) (1925–) Canadian soprano, stud. of Weldon Kilburn and Emmy Heim. She has performed with Toscanini, Beecham and since 1971 in duet with Maureen Forrester. She was a member of the Bach Aria Group for many years. In recent years she has performed mezzo-soprano and alto roles.

Marteau sans maître, Le [mär'tō sä 'me-trǝ] (Fr., The Hammer without a

Master) highly influential work in nine sections for contralto and chamber ensemble (1955) by Boulez, a setting of poems by René Char.

martelé [mär-tə'lä] (Fr.) **martellato** (It.) detached and strongly accented. Cf. DÉTACHÉ, BOWING.

martenot, ondes ONDES MARTENOT.

Martha ['mär-tä] comic opera in 4 acts by Flotow to a libretto by W. Friedrich, based on a ballet by Vernoy de Saint-Georges. Premiere, Vienna 1847. Two ladies of the court go in search of adventure posing as servants to farmers.

Martin, Dean (Crocetti, Dino Paul) (1917–) Amer. singer and actor, partner with Jerry Lewis in a highly successful comedy duo in the 1950s, then a popular crooner in the 1960s and 1970s on TV and recordings.

Martin, Frank (1890–1974) Swiss composer, stud. of Joseph Lauber. He taught at the Jaques-Dalcroze Institute and the Technicum Moderne de Musique in Geneva and at the Cologne Hochschule für Musik. He has also performed as a pianist and harpsichordist. His works incl. *Monsieur de Pourceaugnac* (opera), ballets, incidental music, *Le vin herbé* (oratorio) and other choral works, *6 Monologe aus "Jedermann"* (song cycle) and other songs, orchestral works and chamber music.

Martin, Mary (Virginia) (1913–90) Amer. singer, dancer and actress, best known for her roles in Broadway musicals and films incl. *South Pacific* (1949), *Peter Pan* (1954) and *The Sound of Music* (1959). She first made her name in the Cole Porter musical *One Touch of Venus* (1943) singing "My Heart Belongs to Daddy."

Martinello, Giovanni (1885–1969) Italian tenor, trained in Milan. He sang frequently at Covent Garden, La Scala, the Metropolitan Opera (debut 1912), Chicago and San Francisco. He was Caruso's successor as performer of heroic and dramatic roles and even sang one performance of Tristan in Chicago with Kirsten Flagstad. He continued singing into his 82nd year.

Martini, Padre Giovanni Battista (Giambattista) (1706–84) Italian teacher, composer and writer. He was *maestro di cappella* at St. Francesco in Bologna from 1725 until his final years and became a priest in 1729. He was one of the most famous teachers of his century, his pupils including Mozart, J.C. Bach, Grétry and Jommelli. He wrote a large body of sacred and secular vocal music and instrumental works (sinfonias, concertos, sonatas). His many writings incl. a history of music and works on counterpoint.

Martini, Johann Paul Aegidius ("el Tedesco") (1741–1816) German composer, theorist, teacher and organist. He was an inspector of the Paris Conservatoire from 1798 and also taught composition there from 1800. He is best known as a composer of opera (*Henry IV*), but also as the first composer in France to publish songs with piano accompaniment. Among his treatises, *Mélopée moderne* (or *L'art du chant*) is the most noteworthy.

Martini, Padre MARTINI, GIOVANNI BATTISTA.

Martino, Donald (James) (1931–) Amer. composer, stud. of Bacon, Sessions, Babbitt and Dallapiccola. He has taught at Princeton, Yale, the New England Conservatory and Harvard. He won the Pulitzer Prize in 1974 for his *Notturno* for chamber ensemble. He has written concertos (for piano, cello, clarinets), *Paradiso Choruses* (for chorus, orchestra and tape), instrumental chamber music and songs.

Martinon, Jean [mär-tē'nō, zhä] (1910–76) French conductor and composer, stud. of Roussel and Munch. He was in a Nazi labor camp during the war, then, when released, returned to France to conduct the Concerts du Conservatoire in Paris and, from 1946, the Bordeaux SO. He was principal conductor of the Concerts Lamoureux, the Israel PO, the City of Düsseldorf, the Chicago SO (1963–9), the French National Radio

Orch. and the Hague Orch. His works incl. a ballet, an opera, 4 symphonies, choral works, chamber music, piano music and songs.

Martinů, Bohuslav (Jan) (1890–1959) Czech composer, trained at the Prague Conservatory and later with Roussel in Paris. He stayed in Paris until 1940, when forced to leave by the Nazis. He was in the U.S. from 1941 to 1953, during which time he composed six symphonies and television operas and taught at Princeton, then returned to Europe. Martinů's music, much of which is unpublished, was quickly produced and is of a very original style, frequently employing Czech folk melody. He wrote 16 operas, 11 ballets, many orchestral works and concertos, choral music, songs, chamber music and piano works.

Martín y Soler, Vicente (1754–1806) Spanish composer, prob. a stud. of Padre Martini. He was in Madrid by about 1775, where his first *zarzuela* was performed. In 1785 he moved to Vienna, where he began a fruitful collaboration with LORENZO DA PONTE, which produced, among other works, his best-known opera, *Una cosa rara* (1786). Most of his final years were spent in St. Petersburg at the court of Catherine II. He wrote over 20 operas, ballets and sacred and secular vocal works.

Martirano, Salvatore (1927–) Amer. composer, stud. of Elwell, Rogers and Dallapiccola. He has taught at the U. of Illinois at Urbana since 1963. His works are noteworthy for their original use of popular elements and sound experimentation, frequently using nonstandard notation. He has written a number of works for electronic tape, as well as chamber, choral and orchestral music.

Marx, Joseph (1882–1964) Austrian composer, teacher and critic, trained in philosophy at Graz. He taught at the Vienna music academy from 1914, becoming dir. in 1922. During the 1930s he wrote criticism for the *Neues Wiener Journal* and later for the *Wiener Zeitung*. Although he wrote music in all genres except theater music, he is best known for his many songs.

marziale (It.) martial.

Mascagni, Pietro (1863–1945) Italian composer and conductor. He studied at the Milan Conservatory but was dismissed for lack of application to his work. After he had spent some years conducting several small touring opera companies, his opera *Cavalleria rusticana* was one of the winners in a contest run by the publisher Sonzogno and Mascagni and was in a short time world famous. None of his later works was able to recapture its success. During the Fascist period he was the official composer of the Italian government. His works incl. *Cavalleria rusticana*, *L'amico Fritz*, *Iris*, *Il piccolo Marat* and 13 other operas, many songs, choral works and various instrumental works.

mascherata [mä-skä′rä-tä] (It., masquerade) **1**, a Renaissance theatrical entertainment consisting of pantomime with music performed on a parade or carnival float. Cf. MASQUE. **2**, a type of VILLANELLA intended for performance during Carnival.

masculine cadence a phrase ending on a strong beat. See CADENCE.

Masked Ball, The (It., *Un ballo in maschera*) opera in 3 acts by Verdi to a libretto by Antonio Somma, based on an earlier libretto by Scribe for Auber's opera *Gustave III, ou Le Bal masqué*. Premiere, Rome 1859. Originally set in Sweden but moved to colonial Boston because of political censorship, the story concerns the secret love between Riccardo, governor of Boston, and Amelia, wife of Riccardo's secretary, Renato.

Mason, Daniel Gregory (1873–1953) Amer. composer, writer and teacher, grandson of LOWELL MASON. He was trained at Harvard and with Chadwick and d'Indy. He taught at Columbia U. from 1905 to 1942. As a writer on music, he produced a number of historical texts and studies. His works incl. *Chanticleer* (overture) and other orchestral works, songs, chamber music and piano music.

Mason, Edith (Barnes) (1893–1973) Amer. soprano, stud. of Enrico Bertran and Edmond Clément. She sang with the Boston Opera, the Metropolitan Opera, Paris Opéra, La Scala and in Salzburg and in Chicago from 1921, where her roles incl. Sophie (*Der Rosenkavalier*) and Gilda (*Rigoletto*). She retired in 1939.

Mason, Lowell (1792–1872) Amer. conductor, composer and educator, stud. of Frederick L. Abel. He was famous as an innovator in public-school music instruction and music teacher training. In Boston he was choirmaster of the Bowdoin Street Church and then of the Central Church, music dir. of the Handel and Haydn Society and superintendent of music in the public schools. He produced a number of collections of sacred and secular music as well as pedagogical materials.

Mason, Marilyn (May) (1925–) Amer. organist, stud. of Palmer Christian, Boulanger and Duruflé. She has taught at the U. of Michigan at Ann Arbor and toured throughout the world. She is noted for her performance of new music and has commissioned works from Cowell, Krenek and Alec Wyton, among others.

Mason & Hamlin Amer. piano and reed organ maker, founded in 1854 by Henry Mason (1831–90), son of Lowell Mason, and Emmons Hamlin (1821–85). The company later became part of the Aeolian American Corporation.

masque *also*, **mask** a 16th- and 17th-c. English form of theatrical entertainment featuring a masked dance and combining poetry, music and ornate sets. The entertainment often included the presentation of a token to a royal personage. The best-known type was the court masque such as those written by poet Ben Jonson in the early 17th c. A related form, the theater masque, is considered to be an antecedent of English Opera and

found its highest form in the works of Purcell.

Mass the ritual celebrating the Eucharist, primarily in the Roman Catholic church. The Mass consists of two parts, the Ordinary and the Proper, the former of which remains constant throughout the year, the latter changing for each date and service. The two parts are further divided into sections or movements: The Mass Ordinary is comprised of the Kyrie, Gloria, Credo, Sanctus, Agnus Dei. The Mass Proper includes the Introit, Gradual, Alleluia or Tract, Sequence, Offertory, Communion. See also Requiem mass, Missa brevis, Missa solemnis.

Masselos, William (1920–) Amer. pianist, stud. of Carl Friedberg and David Saperton. He is noted for his performances of music by 20th-c. composers, incl. Ives, Copland and Ben Weber.

Massenet, Jules (Emile Frédéric) (1842–1912) French opera composer, stud. of Reber and Thomas. He won the Prix de Rome in 1863 and joined the faculty of the Conservatoire in 1878, where his students included Gustave Charpentier, Hahn and Pierné. His first opera to be performed was *La Grand'-tante* in 1867 and he produced over 27 more during his career, of which *Manon*, *Werther*, *Thaïs*, *Cendrillon* and *Don Quichotte* are still in the standard repertory. He also wrote incidental music, 3 ballets, orchestral and chamber music, piano works, choral music and many songs.

Massey Hall concert hall in Toronto, built in 1894 by industrialist Hart A. Massey as a gift to the city.

mässig ('mes-siç) (Ger., moderate) Moderato.

Master Peter's Puppet Show (Sp., *El Retablo de maese pedro*) opera in 1 act by Falla to his own libretto, based on an episode in *Don Quixote* by Cervantes. Stage premiere, Paris 1923. Thinking the puppets are real persons needing help, Don Quixote intervenes in Master Peter's puppet show and ruins it.

Mastersinger Meistersinger.

Mastersingers of Nuremberg, The
MEISTERSINGER VON NÜRNBERG, DIE.

Masterson, (Margaret) Valerie
(1937–) English soprano, stud. of
Adelaide Saraceni. Her debut was in
Salzburg, after which she sang Gilbert
and Sullivan operettas for four years
with the D'Oyly Carte Opera. She
joined the Sadler's Wells Opera in
1971 and has also sung at Covent
Garden, the Paris Opéra and in the
U.S.

Masur, Kurt (1927–) German con-
ductor, trained at the Leipzig Con-
servatory. He has worked at the Halle
National Theater, the Erfurt City
Theater and the Leipzig City Theater.
He has been music dir. of the Dresden
PO, the Komische Oper in Berlin, the
Leipzig Gewandhaus Orch. and the
New York PO. He has made many
recordings, principally of 19th-c. rep-
ertory.

Mata, Eduardo (1942–) Mexican
conductor and composer, trained at
the Mexican National Conservatory
and at Tanglewood. He conducted
and taught at the U. of Mexico from
1965, founding an orch. there, and
also conducted the Guadalajara Orch.
He has been principal conductor of
the Phoenix (AZ) SO (1974–7) and the
Dallas SO (since 1977).

matachin [mä-tä'shē] (Fr.) a men's
battle dance dating from the 16th c.,
performed in teams as a theatrical
dance. Also, *les bouffons* (Fr.).

Mather, (James) Bruce (1939–) Canadian composer, pianist and teacher,
stud. of Beckwith, Morawetz, Milhaud, Messaien and Leland Smith. He
has taught since 1966 at McGill U. in
Montreal. His works incl. *The White
Goddess* (cantata), orchestral works,
chamber music (incl. the series of
Madrigals for various voices and instruments), piano music and film
scores.

Mathis, Edith (1938–) Swiss soprano, trained at the Lucerne Conservatory. She has sung at Cologne,
Glyndebourne, Covent Garden, Salzburg and the Munich Festival as well
as in concert. Her roles incl. Pamina

(*Die Zauberflöte*), Zdenka (*The Bartered Bride*) and Mélisande.

Mathis der Maler (Ger., Mathias the
Painter) **1**, political opera in 7 scenes
by Hindemith to his own libretto
based on the life of the 16th-c.
painter, Mathias Grünewald. Premiere, Zürich 1938. Episodes from
the life of a painter. **2**, symphony
(1934) by Hindemith, musically related to the opera (1,).

**Matin, Le Midi, Le Soir et La Tem-
pête, Le** [mä'tẽ, lə mē'dē, lə swär ä lä
tä'pet] (Fr., Morning, Midday, Evening and the Tempest) symphonies
No. 6 in D major, No. 7 in C major,
and No. 8 in G major (1761) by Haydn,
composed for Prince Esterházy and
based on an undisclosed program.

matins one of the daily services
which comprise the DIVINE OFFICE of
the Roman Catholic liturgy. Matins
is the longest service of the office, beginning after midnight, often around
3 AM. Also known in medieval and
Renaissance sources as *vigils*.

Matlock, Matty (Julian Clifton)
(1907–78) Amer. jazz clarinetist, saxophone player and arranger. He
played and arranged for Ben Pollack,
Bob Crosby and free-lanced, specializing in Dixieland scoring. He arranged the music for the "Pete Kelly's
Blues" radio and TV series and film.

Matrimonio segreto, Il [mä-trē'mō-
nē-ō sä'grä-tō, ēl] (It., The Secret Marriage) comic opera in 2 acts by Cimarosa to a libretto by Giovanni Ber-
tati, after the play *The Clandestine
Marriage* by George Colman and
David Garrick. Premiere, Vienna
1792. Complications arise when Carolina keeps secret her marriage to Pa-
olino.

Matthäus-Passion [mä'tä-oos pä'-
syōn] (Ger.) ST. MATTHEW PASSION.

Mattheson, Johann (1681–1764) German composer, organist, theorist,
critic and lexicographer. A child prodigy, he began as a singer. He was music dir. of the Hamburg Cathedral
from 1715 until 1728 when increasing deafness forced him to resign. In
addition to his compositions—8 op-

eras, over 20 oratorios and passion settings, sonatas and suites for keyboard—he produced many works of literature, articles, treatises and translations.

mattinata (It.) morning song.

Mattinata, La (It.) a popular Italian song (1904) by Leoncavallo.

Matton, Roger (1929–) Canadian composer and ethno-musicologist, stud. of Champagne, Boulanger and Messaien. Folk music and jazz have had a significant effect on his works, which incl. a Te Deum, two concertos for two pianos and orch. and *Horoscope* for orch. He has taught at Laval U. in Quebec.

Mauceri, John (1945–) Amer. conductor, trained at Yale and at the Berkshire Music Center. He has been conductor of the Yale SO and the American SO and has guest conducted worldwide. He is best known as an opera conductor and has been music dir. of the Scottish Opera since 1987.

Maurel, Victor (1848–1923) French baritone, stud. of Vauthrot and Duvernoy. He sang regularly at La Scala and the Paris Opéra, as well as at Covent Garden and in New York at the Academy of Music and the Metropolitan Opera, and created the role of Tonio in *Pagliacci*. He taught in New York from 1909 until his death and wrote a number of books on singing and opera staging.

Má Vlast (Czech., My Country) set of six symphonic poems (1874–9) by Smetana, depicting the Czech countryside and scenes from Czech history. The sections are Vyšehrad (the citadel of Prague), The Moldau, Šárka (the leader of the Bohemian amazons), From Bohemia's Fields and Groves, Tábor (the stronghold of the leader of the Hussites) and Blaník (a mountain in S. Bohemia.)

Mavra comic opera in 1 act by Stravinsky to a libretto in Russian by Boris Kochno after Pushkin's "The Little House in Kolomna." Premiere, Paris 1922. The young hussar Vasili masquerades as a female cook to be near his girlfriend Parasha.

Maw, (John) Nicholas (1935–) English composer, stud. of Berkeley, Steinitz, Boulanger and Deutsch. His music is an interesting synthesis of Webernesque serialism and Bartókian pantonalism. His works incl. *One Man Show* and *The Rising of the Moon* (operas), choral works, chamber music and songs.

maxixe [məˈshēsh] (Port.) a Brazilian popular dance similar to the POLKA, originating in the late 19th c. in Rio de Janeiro.

Maxwell Davies, Peter DAVIES, PETER MAXWELL.

Mayfield, Curtis (1942–) Amer. rhythm-and-blues singer, guitarist and songwriter, leader of THE IMPRESSIONS until 1970, then a solo performer. He made the soundtrack for the film *Superfly* (1972), which produced several hit singles.

Mayr, (Johanns) Simon (1763–1845) German composer, stud. of Carlo Lenzi and Ferdinando Bertoni. Most of his serious operas were written for La Scala in Milan, and his works also received performances in Rome and Naples as well as in Germany and England. From 1802 he worked in Bergamo, where he taught Donizetti and others. He became blind in 1826 but continued to teach and compose. He was one of the most important opera composers in Italy before Rossini. He wrote over 60 operas, oratorios and cantatas, many sacred and secular vocal works, works for orch., chamber music, keyboard works.

Maytime musical by Sigmund Romberg, lyrics and book by Rida Johnson Young, based on the Viennese operetta *Wie ernst im Mai*. Premiere, New York 1917. A World War I hit, it is a sentimental tale of the love between rich Ottilie and poor Richard.

Mayuzumi, Toshirō (1929–) Japanese composer, trained at the National U. of Fine Arts and Music in Tokyo and with Aubin in Paris. He introduced many contemporary techniques to Japan, incl. *musique con-*

crète, aleatory methods and serial organization. His works incl. *Kinkakuji* (opera), ballets, musicals, incidental music, choral works, electronic music, many orchestral and chamber works.

Mazeppa (Russ.) opera in 3 acts by Tchaikovsky to a libretto by the composer and Viktor Burenin, based on Pushkin's poem *Poltava*. Premiere, Moscow 1884. Tragedy results when Mazeppa abducts Maria to thwart the wishes of her father.

mazurka *also*, **mazourka** (Russ.) a Polish country dance in moderate triple time, usu. having a slide and hop to the side. The three varieties are the *mazur*, the *obertas*, and the KUJA-WIAK. The music of the mazurka has two or four parts, each repeated, and is usu. played on the *duda* (a type of bagpipe). The instrumental mazurka was made popular esp. by Chopin.

Mazzocchi, Domenico (1592–1665) Italian composer, for many years in the service of the Aldobrandini family in Rome. He wrote several operas, but he is best known for his cantatas, madrigals, and sacred works. His brother, **Virgilio Mazzocchi** (1597–1646) was also a composer, stud. of Domenico and a noted chapel master at several Roman churches.

Mazzoleni, Ettore (1905–68) Italian-born Canadian conductor and teacher, trained at Oxford and the Royal Conservatory of Music in London. From 1929 he was conductor of the orch. at the Toronto Conservatory, later becoming principal in 1945. He was also assoc. with the Toronto SO and the Festival Opera Company (predecessor of the Canadian Opera Company).

MCA Music Amer. music publisher, founded in New York in 1965.

MC5 Amer. rock group founded in Detroit in 1965 and active until 1972; a predecessor of the punk rock of the 1970s.

m.d. *abbr.* (Fr., *main droite*) right hand.

me [mā] the mediant of the current key (or, in minor, its relative major) in TONIC SOL-FA.

meane **1**, in English polyphony of the 15th to 17th c., a vocal part usu. in the alto range below the highest part. **2**, a cantus firmus derived from plainsong.

meantone *also*, ¼-**comma mean tone** a system of tuning keyboard instruments based on the equivalence of a whole tone to one half of a pure major third. The thirds in meantone tuning are "pure."

measure **1**, the space between two bar lines. Also, (Brit.) *bar*. **2**, a 16th- and 17th-c. English term for a series of choreographed dance steps in moderate duple time having the length of a musical STRAIN.

mechanical instrument an instrument which produces sound by mechanical means, usu. automatically, without the intervention of a performer. Such devices are usu. programmed by means of a punched card, sheet or metal disc or a cylinder having raised pegs attached to it. In the case of the punched medium, the holes either allow air to pass or permit a lever to protrude, thereby activating a mechanism (such as a reed). The pegs on the cylinder contact levers which in turn activate a sounding mechanism. See MUSIC BOX, PLAYER PIANO, AEOLIAN HARP, HYDRAULIS. Cf. ELECTRONIC INSTRUMENT.

medesimo tempo (It., the same tempo) ISTESSO TEMPO, L'.

medial cadence **1**, a CADENCE ending on the MEDIANT. **2**, a CADENCE in which the penultimate chord is in inversion. Also, *inverted cadence*.

mediant the third DEGREE of the major or minor scale, halfway between the tonic and the dominant. In the church modes (see MODE), the scale step is a third below the tenor.

mediation a cadence between the two reciting tones in Gregorian and Anglican chant, occurring halfway through a PSALM TONE. See PLAINSONG.

Medium, The melodrama in 2 acts by Menotti to his own libretto. Premiere, New York 1946. A medium, Madame Flora, becomes obsessed with the reality of her own fraudulent séances.

medley a performance chaining together a number of (usu. related) songs or other musical works.

Medtner METNER.

Mehta, Zubin (1936–) Indian conductor, stud. of Hans Swarowsky. He has been conductor of the Montreal SO, the Los Angeles SO and the New York PO, and has also conducted at the Metropolitan Opera and most major international orchestras. His father, **Mehli Mehta** (1908–) is a conductor, violinist and founder-conductor of the Bombay SO.

Méhul, Etienne-Nicolas (1763–1817) French composer, stud. of Wilhelm Hanser and Jean-Frédéric Edelmann. He began writing comic opera in 1790 and joined the staff of the new Institut National de Musique in Paris in 1793. He produced a number of civic works during the Revolutionary period and also wrote works for Napoleon. In his later years he concentrated on symphonic composition. He was esp. noted for his innovative orchestration. Méhul wrote over 30 operas, ballets, choral cantatas and other works, songs, 5 symphonies, chamber music and keyboard sonatas.

Meier, Gustav (1929–) Swiss-born Amer. conductor, stud. of Paul Müller and de Carvalho. He moved to the U.S. in 1958 and joined the faculty of Yale three years later. He has also taught at the Eastman School and the U. of Michigan. He is esp. noted for his conducting of 20th-c. music.

Meistergesang ['mī-stər-ge"zäng] (Ger., master-singing) the Meistersinger tradition.

Meisterlied [-"lēt] (Ger.) a song of a Meistersinger, always having an odd number of stanzas (the minimum is three), usu. based on preexistent tunes (*Töne* or *Weisen*) in BAR form.

Meistersinger [-"zing-ər] (Ger., Mastersinger) a member of one of the 15th- or 16th-c. German guilds of craftsmen united for the cultivation of music and poetry.

Meistersinger von Nürnberg, Die (Ger., The Mastersingers of Nuremberg) comic opera in 3 acts by Wagner to his own libretto. Premiere, Munich 1868. The cobbler Hans Sachs (a famous 16th-c. Meistersinger) helps Walther win the hand of Pogner's daughter Eva.

mejorana [mä-kho'rä-nä]] (Sp., marjoram) a Panamanian dance and its music, accompanied by the *mejoranera*, a small, short-necked five-string guitar.

Melachrino, George (Miltiades) (1909–65) English composer, conductor and arranger, famous for his 50-piece orch., the Melachrino Strings, formed in 1945.

Melba, Dame **Nellie** (Mitchell, Helen Porter) (1861–1931) Australian soprano, stud. of MATHILDE MARCHESI. Her brilliant career incl. regular performances at Covent Garden, the Metropolitan Opera, the Chicago Opera and La Scala. Her best-loved roles included Mimì (*La Bohème*), Gilda (*Rigoletto*) and Lucia. She made many recordings, spanning over 20 years of singing.

Melchior, Lauritz (Hommel, Lebrecht) (1890–1973) Danish Wagnerian heroic tenor, stud. of Paul Bang and Vilhelm Herold. He sang at the Metropolitan Opera from 1926 to 1950 as well as at Bayreuth and Covent Garden and also appeared in later years on Broadway, on radio and in films. He made many recordings, beginning in 1913.

melisma [mə'liz-mə] (Gk., song) a group of notes sung to the same syllable. The opposite of *melismatic* is *syllabic*, i.e., each syllable having a note. See MELODY.

mellophone a circular ALTHORN designed for use in marching bands and also used in jazz bands. Not to be confused with MELOPHONE.

melodeon AMERICAN ORGAN.

melodic minor scale a minor SCALE with an ascending form having half steps between the 2nd and 3rd and the

7th and 8th degrees and a descending form with half steps between the 6th and 5th and the 3rd and 2nd degrees. Also, *jazz minor scale.*

mélodie [mā-lō′dē] (Fr., melody) a 19th- or 20th-c. French song, a descendant of the ROMANCE and the German LIED; a setting of a serious lyric poem, usu. for voice and piano. Particularly noteworthy are the *mélodies* of Gounod, Massenet, Fauré, Debussy and Ravel.

melodrama 1, a type of drama consisting of recitation performed with a musical background, formalized in the 18th c. and reaching its height in the 19th c. Mozart included melodramas in two of his operas (*The Abduction from the Seraglio* and *Zaïde*), and the form was also used by Beethoven, Berlioz, Cherubini, Verdi and a number of 20th-c. composers. Distinct from MELODRAMMA. **2,** a play or musical drama characterized by excessive theatricality or sensationalism.

melodramma (It.) a dramatic text intended to be set to music. Distinct from MELODRAMA.

melody a succession of musical tones, usu. with a definite rhythm and having a characteristic musical shape. The 20th-c. concept of "absolute melody" defines melody as free from the influence of its accompanying voices and unconstrained by considerations of pitch or instrumentation.

melophone a portable ACCORDION shaped like a guitar and having a keyboard. Not to be confused with MELLOPHONE.

melopoeia (Gk.) MELODY; also, the art of writing melody.

Melos a monthly journal for new music founded by Scherchen and published 1920–34 and 1946–74.

Melos Ensemble an English ensemble formed in London in 1950, orig. to perform the larger works of 19th- and 20th-c. chamber music.

Melos Quartet German string quartet formed in Stuttgart in 1965.

membranophone an instrument having a tightly stretched membrane as its vibrating medium, as a drum or kazoo.

Memphis Minnie (Douglas, Minnie) (1896–1973) Amer. country-blues singer and guitarist. From 1928, when she moved to Chicago, she made a celebrated series of blues recordings, many with her husband, mandolinist Joe McCoy, and held "Blue Monday" parties for almost 30 years. She returned to Memphis in 1957.

Memphis Blues, The song (1912) by W.C. Handy, orig. a campaign song for Mayor "Boss" Crump of Memphis, TN, entitled "Mr. Crump."

Memphis Slim (Chatman, Peter) (1915–) Amer. blues singer and pianist in the BARRELHOUSE style. He was accompanist to Big Bill Broonzy in the 1940s, then led his own groups. Since the early 1960s he has lived in Paris and performed regularly throughout Europe.

Mendelssohn(-Bartholdy) (Hensel), **Fanny (Cäcilie)** (1805–47) German composer and pianist, sister of FELIX MENDELSSOHN, stud. of Ludwig Berger, C.F. Zelter and Marie Bigot. Her compositions include songs, choral works (cantatas, oratorios) and piano works, most of which have never been published. She kept a diary that provides much important information on her brother's life.

Mendelssohn(-Bartholdy), (Jakob Ludwig) Felix (1809–47) German composer and pianist, stud. of Ludwig Berger and C.F. Zelter. He was accomplished not only as a musician, but also as a poet and artist. The principal influences on him as a composer were the works of Bach, Handel and Mozart, rather than those of his contemporaries. By the time he was eighteen he had produced a substantial body of works, incl. the still popular overture to *A Midsummer Night's Dream.* Until 1835 he traveled frequently and widely on the Continent and in England, performing and conducting his works. He then became conductor of the Leipzig Gewandhaus Orch., where he introduced many 18th- and early 19th-c. classics, incl. Schubert's C major Symphony. He also supervised the founding of the Leipzig Conservatory in 1843. Mendelssohn's influence on 19th-c. music composition and performance was far-reaching despite anti-Semitic trends. His music was suppressed throughout the Nazi era. Mendelssohn's works incl. operas (*Loreley*), incidental music, oratorios (*St. Paul, Elijah*), sacred and secular cantatas, 12 Sinfonias for strings, 4 symphonies, overtures and other orchestral works, concertos for violin and piano, chamber music, many keyboard works, choral works, songs and duets.

Mengelberg, (Josef) Willem (1871–1951) Dutch conductor, trained at the Cologne Conservatory. He became conductor of the Amsterdam Concertgebouw Orch. in 1895, making it into one of the leading orchestras of Europe. He was esp. noted for his performances of Mahler and of Strauss, who dedicated the tone poem *Ein Heldenleben* to the conductor. He also guest-conducted elsewhere in Europe and with the New York PO. Because he conducted in Germany during the occupation of Holland, he was forbidden to conduct after 1945 in Holland and spent his last years in Switzerland.

Mennin (Mennini), **Peter** (1923–83) Amer. composer and teacher, stud. of Norman Lockwood, Hanson and Rogers. He taught at the Juilliard School, was dir. of the Peabody Conservatory (1958–62) and then returned to Juilliard as president in 1962 and initiated the founding of the American Opera Center and the Contemporary Music Festival. His works incl. 9 symphonies and other orchestral works, concertos for violin, flute and piano, songs, choral works, sonatas, chamber music.

meno ['mā-nō] (It.) less.

meno mosso ['mōs-sō] (It.) less lively, slower.

Menotti, Gian Carlo (1911–) Italian-born Amer. opera composer and director, trained at the Milan Conservatory and at the Curtis Institute with Rosaio Scalero. His first opera to be performed, *Amelia Goes to the Ball*, was produced by the Metropolitan Opera in 1936. Among his successful operatic works have been *The Old Maid and the Thief* and *Amahl and the Night Visitors* (both commissioned by NBC), *The Medium* and *The Consul* (winner of the Pulitzer Prize in 1950) and *The Saint of Bleecker Street*. He has also written choral works, concertos for piano and violin, a symphony, chamber music and songs. His music combines a conservative musical language with a strong sense of the theatrical. In 1958 he founded the Festival of Two Worlds in Spoleto, Italy, with which he has continued to maintain close connections.

mensural notation a system of notation developed in the 13th c. consisting of single notes and ligatures having definite time values, thereby permitting the notation of independent voice parts in a polyphonic texture. The exact value of the notes depended on the *mensuration sign*, which indicated whether to make a duple or triple division of the breve and semibreve. From the mid-15th c. the system is known as *white mensural notation* on account of the use of white (hollow) note shapes instead of the older black ones.

mensuration the relationships among the note values in MENSURAL NOTATION.

mensuration canon a CANON in which a single written part is read simultaneously in different mensurations. Also, *fuga*.

mento a Jamaican folk dance music in duple meter similar in rhythm to a slow rumba. It is accompanied by an ensemble of various melody instruments, drums and other percussion, and guitars or banjos.

menuet [mə'nüä] (Fr.) MINUET.

menuetto (It.) a term for the instrumental MINUET found in some 18th-c. non-Italian works.

Menuhin, Yehudi (1916–) Amer.

Mensural notation

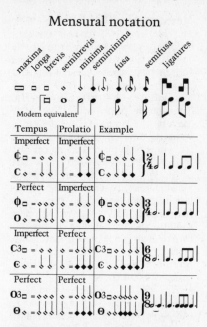

Tempus	Prolatio	Example

"Bagatelle without Tonality," was publ. posthumously.

Mer, La (Fr., The Sea) three orchestral sketches (1905) by Debussy, depicting the varying moods of the sea. The movements are "De l'aube à midi sur la mer" ("From Dawn to Noon on the Sea"), "Jeux de vagues" ("The Play of the Waves") and "Dialogue du vent et de la mer" ("The Dialogue of the Wind and the Sea").

Merbecke, John ['mär-bek] (c1510–c1585) English composer and writer, an organist at St. George's Chapel, Windsor, for most of his life. He is best remembered for *The Booke of Common Praier Noted* (1550), the first musical setting of services from the 1549 Prayer Book. A devoted Calvinist, he also produced a concordance of the English Bible and wrote sacred vocal works, only a few of which survive.

Mercadante, (Giuseppe) Saverio (Raffaele) (1795–1870) Italian opera composer and teacher, stud. of Furno, Tritto and Zingarelli. After 1818 he concentrated on vocal music, composing his first opera in 1819 and producing an average of three operas a year for the next decade. However none of his operas have remained in the repertory. He was dir. of the Naples Conservatory from 1840 until his death. He became blind by 1862 but continued to compose by dictation. He wrote 60 operas, ballets, cantatas, masses, hymns, sinfonias, songs and duets, chamber music.

Mercer, Johnny (John Herndon) (1909–76) Amer. composer and lyricist of songs, Broadway musicals and film scores. He composed several hit songs ("I'm an Old Cowhand," "Something's Gotta Give"), but he was best known as a lyricist, collaborating with a number of composers, incl. Arlen, Kern, Mancini and Richard A. Whiting. He was a co-founder of Capitol Records.

Mercure, Pierre (1927–66) Canadian composer and conductor, stud. of Champagne, Boulanger, Dallapiccola and others. He was a bassoonist in the

violinist and conductor, stud. of Louis Persinger, Enescu and Adolf Busch. He was a remarkable child prodigy and became a concert artist of great breadth as well as an international statesman for music. Since 1959 he has lived in England, where he has been assoc. with several musical institutions, most notably the Bath Festival and a school for musically talented children at Stoke d'Abernon. Many composers have written works for him, incl. Bartók and Walton. His sister **Hepzibah Menuhin** (1920–81) appeared frequently as a pianist in recital with her brother. Another sister **Yalta Menuhin** (1922–) is also a pianist.

Mephistopheles MEFISTOFELE.

Mephisto Waltzes four waltzes by Liszt depicting a character from *Faust* by Lenau. The first, for orch. (1861), was orig. entitled "Der Tanz in der Dorfschenke," the second of *Two Episodes from Lenau's Faust*. The second, also for orch., was written in 1880–81. The third and fourth, both for piano, were written in 1883 and 1885 respectively; the latter, entitled

Montreal SO for several years and later a producer of music for the CBC French television network. His works, which explore avant-garde techniques, incl. ballets, orchestral works (*Kaléidoscope, Lignes et points*), works for electronic tape and film scores.

merengue [mä'rän-gä] (Sp.) a ballroom couple-dance, orig. from the Dominican Republic, popular in the U.S. in the mid-1950s.

Merman, Ethel (Zimmermann, Ethel Agnes) (1909–84) Amer. actress and singer, famous for her strong voice and dynamic personality. She appeared in many Broadway musicals, incl. *Girl Crazy* (1930), *Annie Get Your Gun* (1946), *Call Me Madam* (1950) and *Hello, Dolly!* (1970).

Merola, Gaetano (1881–1953) Italian-born Amer. conductor and impresario. After years of conducting at the Metropolitan Opera and with the San Carlo Opera in San Francisco, he founded the San Francisco Opera, of which he was general dir. for 30 years. He held a similar position with the Los Angeles Grand Opera Association (1924–31).

Merrill, Robert (1917–) Amer. baritone, stud. of Samuel Margolis. He sang for thirty years at the Metropolitan Opera, celebrating his 500th performance in 1973.

Merriman, Nan (Katherine-Ann) (1920–) Amer. mezzo-soprano, stud. of Alexia Bassian. After working in films, she made her operatic debut in 1942 in Cincinnati. She has sung at Glyndeboune and La Piccola Scala, has recorded with Karajan and Toscanini and has appeared frequently on the concert stage. She retired in 1965.

Merry Widow, The (Ger., *Die lustige Witwe*) operetta in 3 acts by Léhar to a libretto by Viktor Léon and Leo Stein, based on Henri Meilhac's comedy *L'Attaché*. Premiere, Vienna 1905. A plot is hatched—and ultimately succeeds—to keep a wealthy widow's money within the country by arranging for her to marry a local noble.

Merry Wives of Windsor, The (Ger., *Die lustigen Weiber von Windsor*) comic opera in 3 acts by Otto Nicolai to a libretto in German by Salomon Mosenthal, based on Shakespeare's play. Premiere, Berlin 1849. Falstaff, a middle-aged knight, is thwarted in his amorous pursuits.

Merula, Tarquinio (c1594–1665) Italian composer, organist and violinist. He served for a time as organist to the king of Poland but spent most of his professional life in Cremona. He was a composer in tune with the latest developments, esp. the work of Monteverdi, and composed an opera, motets, psalm settings, madrigals, canzonettas and instrumental canzonas.

Merulo, Claudio (1533–1604) Italian composer, organist and publisher, stud. of Tuttovale Menon and Girolamo Donato. He was organist at St. Mark's in Venice and a member of the doge's chapel for almost 30 years. His last years were spent as organist to the duke of Parma and the company of the Steccata. His works incl. madrigals and motets, but he is best known for his instrumental toccatas, canzonas and ricercars.

Mesplé, Mady (1931–) French soprano, trained at the Toulouse Conservatory. She has sung at the Opéra-Comique, the Brussels Opera, in Aix-en-Provence, and elsewhere in Europe and the U.S. She is esp. noted for her performance of contemporary repertory.

messa di voce ['mes-sä dē 'vō-chä] (It., placing of the voice) in vocal music, a gradual crescendo and decrescendo on a sustained tone, a technique common to *bel canto* style. Not to be confused with *mezza voce*.

Messager, André (Charles Prosper) (1853–1929) French composer, conductor, pianist, organist and administrator, stud. of Fauré and Saint-Saëns. He was organist at St. Sulpice and at St. Paul-St. Louis in Paris, and conducted at the Eden-Théâtre in Brussels and the Folies-Bergère in Paris. His first operetta was written in 1885 and he composed more than 20, incl. *Les P'tites Michu* (1897) and *Véronique* (1898), which are considered classics of the French repertory. He was musical dir. of the Opéra-Comique (1898–1903) and later dir. of the Opéra, and he also conducted the Societé des concerts du Conservatoire. In addition to operetta, he wrote ballets, cantatas and works for piano and was in demand as an orchestrator, arranger and conductor (he conducted the premiere of Debussy's *Pelléas et Mélisande*).

messe (Fr.) MASS.

Messiaen, Olivier (Eugène Prosper Charles) [me'syɛ̃] (1908–92) highly influential French composer and teacher, trained at the Paris Conservatoire, where he taught from 1941 until his death. Earlier he taught in Paris at the École Normale de Musique and the Schola Cantorum. He formed the group La Jeune France in 1936 with Daniel Lesur, Yves Baudrier and Jolivet, but the war interrupted its activities. He was imprisoned in Silesia during the war and wrote his *Quatuor pour la fin du temps* (Quartet for the end of time) while a prisoner. His passion for birdsong had a major effect on his works, many of which contain imitations or evocations of bird calls. His influence as a teacher was extensive, and his pupils included Boulez, Loriod and many of France's younger composers. His works exhibit a profound interest in rhythmic organization and harmony; he outlines his techniques in his book *Techniques de mon langage musical* (1944). His works incl. *Turangalila-symphonie, Oiseaux exotiques, Sept haikaï, Couleurs de la cité céleste* (orchestra), songs, *Visions de l'amen, Catalogue d'oiseaux* and *Vingt regards sur l'enfant Jésus* (piano), works for organ, *Le merle noir* (flute) and chamber music.

Messiah oratorio (1742) by Handel to a libretto selected from the Bible by Charles Jennans and the composer.

Mester, Jorge (1935–) Mexican-born Amer. conductor, stud. of Jean

Morel. He has conducted widely in Europe and the U.S. He was musical dir. of the Louisville Orch. (1967–79), with which he premiered and recorded many new works. He has also been musical advisor of the Kansas City PO and music dir. of the Pasadena (CA) SO. He taught at the Juilliard School until 1967 and after 1980.

mesto (It.) sad.

mesuré [mə-zü'rā] (Fr., in time) an 18th-c. French marking indicating either TEMPO GIUSTO or A TEMPO. Cf. MUSIQUE MESURÉE.

metallophone a PERCUSSION INSTRUMENT which utilizes tuned metal bars, usu. arranged in either single or double rows.

metamorphosis Cf. TRANSFORMATION, THEMATIC.

Metastasio, Pietro (Trapassi, Antonio Domenico Bonaventura) (1698–1782) Italian poet and librettist, author of opera, oratorio and other dramatic texts whose works have been set more often than that of any other writer in the history of opera.

meter the arrangement of the rhythmic units of a composition so as to produce a regular pattern of beats (see BEAT), which are then grouped in measures (see MEASURE). The number of beats in a measure is indicated by the TIME SIGNATURE.

Metheny, Pat (1954–) Amer. jazz guitar virtuoso. He taught at the Berklee School and at the U. of Miami while still in his teens. He played

Frequently used meters

with Gary Burton, then formed his own group, which has become immensely popular. He has recorded with Ornette Coleman and many others and written several film scores.

Metner (Medtner), **Nikolay Karlovich** (1880–1951) Russian composer and pianist, stud. of Pabst, Safonov and others, but largely self-taught as a composer. He taught at the Moscow Conservatory until 1921, then left Russia, settling in Paris in 1925 and moving to London in 1935. He was highly regarded as a pianist and concertized in Europe and No. America, but his principal interest was in composition. His works incl. 3 piano concertos, a large number of sonatas and characteristic pieces for solo piano, chamber music and over 100 songs.

metric modulation a 20th-c. compositional technique which expedites the change from one meter to another by means of ambiguous rhythmic situations, roughly analogous to MODULATION from one harmony to another by means of a pivot chord. The shift is usu. marked by a new time signature and an indication of the equivalent note values.

weight

Metronome

Metric modulation

metrical psalm PSALM, METRICAL.

metronome an instrument which emits an audible or visible signal to mark regular intervals of time, calibrated in units of beats per minute, used to determine the exact tempo for a musical work or section. Until recently, metronomes employed a spring-driven pendulum with a movable weight mounted on a calibrated flat steel shaft. More recent metronomes employ electronic means, such as the vibration of quartz, to determine the pulse, which is indicated by a click or a blinking light.

Metropolitan Conservatory conservatory est. in 1886 in New York. It became the Metropolitan College of Music in 1891 and the American Institute of Applied Music in 1904.

Metropolitan Opera opera company in New York founded in 1883. The company moved in 1966 from its original opera house on 39th St. to a building in the Lincoln Center complex.

Mexican Hayride musical, music and lyrics by Cole Porter, book by Herbert and Dorothy Fields. Premiere, New York 1944. A clownish numbers racketeer flees to Mexico.

Meyer, Joseph (1894–1987) Amer. songwriter and composer of Broadway musicals. His hits incl. "If You Knew Susie," "Crazy Rhythm" and "California, Here I Come."

Meyerbeer (Meyer Beer), **Giacomo** (Jakob Liebmann) (1791–1864) German composer, stud. of Zelter and B.A. Weber in Berlin and Abbé Vogler in Darmstadt. In his youth he est. a reputation as a fine pianist, but his attempts at German opera failed. From 1816 to 1825 he was in Italy, where he wrote a series of Italian operas that greatly improved his reputation, but it was the production of *Robert le Diable* at the Paris Opéra in 1831 that raised him to the first rank of composers of French opera. In 1842 he became general music dir. in Berlin, and, in fact, he never lived in Paris, visiting only when necessary for productions of his works. He wrote 17 operas (*Robert le Diable, Les Hu-*

guenots, *Le Prophète, L'Africaine*), incidental music, choral works, instrumental works and songs.

Meyerowitz, Jan (1913–   ) German-born Amer. composer and teacher, stud. of Gmeindl and Zemlinsky in Berlin, and Respighi, Casella and Molinari in Rome. He has taught at Brooklyn College and at the City College of the City U. of New York. His works employ an essentially tonal style, and his operas remain within the traditions of 19th-c. Italian opera.

mezza, mezzo ['med-zä] (It.) half.

mezza voce (It.) with medium volume, half voice; used as an indication in vocal music. Not to be confused with *messa di voce*.

mezzo forte (It.) moderately loud; a dynamic level between *piano* and forte. It is sometimes considered to be synonymous with *mezzo piano*. *Abbr., mf*.

mezzo piano (It.) moderately soft; a dynamic level between piano and *forte*. It is sometimes considered to be synonymous with *mezzo forte*. *Abbr., mp*.

mezzo-soprano *also,* **mezzo** a woman's voice between soprano and alto, with a normal range from a to f♯".

mezzo-soprano clef a C CLEF placed on the second line from the bottom of the 5-line staff.

mf *abbr.* MEZZO FORTE.

m.g. *abbr.* (Fr., *main gauche*) left hand.

mi [mē] **1**, the third degree of the Guidonian HEXACHORD. **2**, (Fr., It., Sp.) the note E.

Michelangeli, Arturo Benedetti (1920–   ) Italian pianist, stud. of Giuseppe Anfossi. He has est. a reputation as one of the finest pianists of his time, and he has toured throughout Europe and No. and S. America. He has taught in Bologna and in Florence and was founder and for five years artistic dir. of the International Pianists' Academy in Brescia.

microtone a musical interval smaller than a semitone. Use of microtones in non-Western art music has a long history, and microtones occur in Western popular and folk music (the BLUE NOTE in jazz is an example), but in Western art music the usage essentially begins in the 20th c. Because of the difficulty of obtaining precise microtones on conventional instruments, composers have had to employ unusual tunings or, in some cases, have designed and constructed instruments for the purpose. The advent of electronics has facilitated the development of microtonal composition. Some of the early experimenters with microtones were Ives, Hába and Carillo.

middle c a popular name for the musical note c', so called because of its position between the two staves of the GRAND STAFF used for keyboard writing.

middleground a term in Schenkerian analysis (see SCHENKER) for the layer between the foreground and background and linking the two.

MIDI ['mid-ē] acronym for Musical Instrument Digital Interface, a standardized system for encoding and transmitting musically related data between computers and/or instruments.

Midi, Le see MATIN, LE MIDI ET LE SOIR ET LA TEMPÈTE, LE.

Midsummer Night's Dream, A 1, incidental music, Op. 21 (1826) and Op. 61 (1842), by Mendelssohn to the play by Shakespeare. **2**, opera in 3 acts by Britten to a libretto by the composer and Peter Pears based on the Shakespeare play. Premiere, Aldeburgh 1960.

Mighty Handful, The (Russ., *moguchaya kuchka*) a group of 19th-c. Russian composers based in St. Petersburg. The members of the group were Balakirev, Borodin, Cui, Mussorgsky and Rimsky-Korsakov, who had the common aim of creating a distinctive nationalist school of Russian music. Also, *The Five*.

Mignon [mē'nyō] (Fr.) romantic opera in 3 acts by Thomas to a libretto by Michel Carré and Jules Barbier, based on Goethe's novel *Wilhelm*

Meister. Premiere, Paris 1866; revised version in Italian with recitatives, London 1970.

Mikado, The operetta in 2 acts by Sullivan to a libretto by W.S. Gilbert. Premiere, London 1885. Nanki-Poo, son of the Emperor of Japan, has been promised to the elderly Katisha but falls in love with Yum-Yum, ward of Titipu's Lord High Executioner, Ko-Ko.

Mikrokosmos (Gr., microcosm) a progressively graded set of 153 short piano pieces (1926, 1932–9) by Bartók, providing instructional material for a large variety of rhythmic and technical problems through music of a very high quality.

Milán, Luis de (c1500–c1565) Spanish composer and writer, in the service of the ducal court of Valencia for at least part of his life. His book of music for vihuela, *El maestro* (1536), is noteworthy both for being the first collection of guitar music and for having the first instances of verbal tempo indications in a printed volume. The collection contains both instrumental and vocal music.

Milanese chant see AMBROSIAN CHANT.

Milanov (née Kunc), **Zinka** (1906–89) Yugoslav soprano, trained at the Zagreb Conservatory. She was the leading soprano at the Zagreb Opera from 1928 to 1935, then sang at the Metropolitan Opera from 1937 to 1966, portraying Verdi and Puccini heroines. She also sang in San Francisco and Chicago, but rarely in Europe.

Miley, Bubber (James Wesley) (1903–32) Amer. jazz trumpeter with the Duke Ellington orch. until 1929. He then worked with other bands and led his own orch. He was noted for his use of mutes and the "growl" tone.

Milhaud, Darius [mē′ yō *or* mē′lō] (1892–1974) prolific French composer, trained at the Paris Conservatoire. He spent several years in Brazil as secretary to poet Paul Claudel, and the Lat.-Amer. influence is frequently found in his music. He was a member of the group LES SIX and participated in several joint works. He was also strongly influenced by jazz, and polytonality was a dominant element of his style. He taught at Mills College, the Aspen School and, after the war, at the Paris Conservatoire. His works incl. 15 operas (*Christophe Colomb*, *La Mère coupable*), ballets (*Le Boeuf sur le toit*, *La Création du monde*), many orchestral works and concertos, choral works, songs, chamber music and works for piano.

military band an instrumental group composed of woodwinds, brass and percussion. The term orig. applied to regimental bands; more recently, it has been used to refer to any such grouping, whether military or civilian. Cf. JANISSARY MUSIC.

Military Symphony popular name for the Symphony No. 100 in G major (1794) by Haydn, the eighth Salomon symphony. The name comes from the inclusion of military band instruments plus a trumpet call in the second movement.

Miller, (Alton) Glenn (1904–44) Amer. bandleader, trombonist, composer and arranger. He played with the Dorsey Brothers and Ray Noble and arranged for the Casa Loma Orch. before forming his own orchestras in 1937 and 1938, the second of which was highly successful. He joined the Army in 1942, where he assembled a service band. He disappeared during a wartime airplane flight.

Miller, Marilyn (Reynolds, Mary Ellen) (1898–1936) Amer. actress, singer and dancer. She began in vaudeville, then became a very popular musical-comedy actress of the 1920s, appearing in several editions of the *Ziegfeld Follies*, in *Sally* (1920), *Rosalie* (1928) and *As Thousands Cheer* (1933), among other Broadway shows.

Miller, Mitch(ell William) (1911–   ) Amer. oboist and conductor, trained at the Eastman School. He played in the CBS SO and free-lanced in the late 1930s and early 1940s, then worked as a producer for Columbia records. In the 1960s he developed a very popular "Sing Along" series of record albums and television programs with home participation.

Miller, Roger (Dean) (1936–) Amer. country-music singer, songwriter and guitarist. Beginning as a backup musician in Nashville, he became enormously popular in the 1960s as a solo recording artist.

Miller, Steve (1943–) Amer. poprock composer, guitarist and leader of the Steve Miller Blues Band, formed in 1966.

Millöcker, Karl (1842–99) Austrian composer and flutist, trained at the Vienna Conservatory. Until 1883 he conducted in various Viennese theaters, incl. the Theater an der Wien, and composed. The best known of his 18 operettas is *Der Bettelstudent* (The Beggar Student, 1882), which is still in the repertory in Germany and Austria. He also wrote songs and incidental music.

Milnes, Sherrill (Eustace) (1935–) Amer. baritone, stud. of Andrew White and Hermanus Baer. He sang with Boris Goldovsky's Boston Opera company and the Baltimore Civic Opera before his New York City Opera debut in 1964 and his Metropolitan Opera debut the following year. He has sung with every major opera company and has recorded extensively. His wide repertory includes the leading Verdi baritone roles, Don Giovanni and Escamillo (*Carmen*).

Milstein, Nathan (1904–) eminent Russian-born Amer. violinist, stud. of Pyotr Stolyarsky. He appeared frequently with pianist Vladimir Horowitz, and the two left Russia together in 1925. The duo was sometimes joined by fellow émigré, cellist Grigor Pyatigorsky. Milstein became an American citizen in 1949.

Milwaukee Symphony Orchestra orch. founded in 1958 under conductor Harry John Brown. Subsequent conductors have been Schermerhorn, Foss and Mácal.

Mingus, Charles (1922–79) Amer. jazz double-bass player, composer and pianist. In the 1940s he played with Louis Armstrong, Kid Ory, Lionel Hampton, Red Norvo and Billy Taylor. In the 1950s, after working with Charlie Parker, Bud Powell and others, he formed his own Jazz Workshop, which established his reputation as an important and risk-taking composer, with such then avantgarde works as *Pithecanthropus erectus* (1956) and *The Black Saint and the Sinner Lady* (1963).

miniature score a musical score, esp. a full orchestral score, printed pocketsize for study.

minim 1, in MENSURAL NOTATION, a note equal to either a half or a third of a semibreve. **2,** (Brit.) HALF NOTE. **3,** (Brit.) HALF REST.

minimalism a vague term for music which employs rudimentary materials (often simple diatonic scales and triads), generally nondissonant, static and nonmodulating harmony and repetitive rhythmic and melodic figures, in deliberate contrast with the complex forms and devices of much 20th-c. art music (such as that of the Second Viennese School). The term covers a number of very different musical styles and has generally been resisted by those composers to whom it has been applied, such as Philip Glass, Terry Riley, Steve Reich and John Adams.

Mini-Met short-lived project (1973) of the Metropolitan Opera to produce small-scale productions, esp. of 20th-c. repertory.

Minneapolis Symphony Orchestra see MINNESOTA ORCHESTRA.

Minnelli, Liza (May) (1946–) Amer. actress, singer and dancer, daughter of JUDY GARLAND. She was star of the film version of *Cabaret* and is a performer in nightclubs, concerts and on television.

minnelied ['mi-ne"lēt] (Ger.) a song sung by the minnesingers.

Minnesang [-"zäng] (Ger.) the German tradition of the MINNESINGER.

minnesinger *also,* **Minnesänger** [-"zeng-ər] (Ger.) one of the 12th- to 14th-c. class of aristocratic German lyric musician poets, analogous to the

French *trouvères*, whose works dealt with love and beauty.

Minnesota Opera resident opera ensemble founded in Minneapolis as the Center Opera in 1962 and renamed in 1964. The company is noted for its performance of contemporary works, esp. the works of Dominick Argento.

Minnesota Orchestra orch. founded in 1901 as the Minneapolis SO under musical dir. Emil Oberhoffer. The name was changed in 1968. Conductors of the orch. have included Henri Verbrugghen, Ormandy, Mitropoulos, Dorati, Skrowaczewski, Marriner and de Waart.

minor one of the two principal modes of Western music since the 17th c., the other being MAJOR. It is distinguished from the major by its lowered third degree and, in some forms, lowered sixth degree (see MINOR SCALE). See TONALITY, SCALE.

minore [mē'nō-rā] (It., minor) a term used to indicate a change to minor tonality, usu. when the predominant tonality is major, as for a section of a set of variations. Cf. MAJORE.

minor interval an interval a semitone smaller than a MAJOR INTERVAL but having the same number of diatonic steps.

minor key a tonality based on a MINOR SCALE.

minor scale a SCALE having, in its natural form, half steps between its second and third degrees and its fifth and sixth degrees. In practice, there are several forms: the *harmonic minor* scale has half steps between the seventh degree and the octave (to produce a leading tone); the *ascending melodic minor* scale is the same as the harmonic minor with the sixth degree raised; the *descending melodic minor* scale is identical to the natural minor.

minor seven, flat five chord HALF-DIMINISHED SEVENTH CHORD.

minor seventh chord a MINOR TRIAD with an additional minor seventh.

minor sixth chord a MINOR TRIAD with a major sixth added.

minor triad a three-note CHORD built of a fundamental tone with its minor third and a perfect fifth.

minstrel a professional entertainer of the 12th to 17th c., esp. a professional, secular musician. Also (until the 16th c.) *jongleur* (Fr.). See also MINSTREL SHOW.

minstrel show a type of 19th-c. popular Amer. entertainment featuring black performers or white performers in black face presenting sketches of stereotyped Negro situations and personalities, such as the plantation slave or dandy. The shows were often presented by small traveling groups— of which the best known were the Virginia Minstrels, Christy's Minstrels and the Bryant Minstrels—consisting of instrumentalists on banjo and percussion instruments who also sang and danced.

Minton, Yvonne (Fay) (1938–) Australian mezzo-soprano, trained at the Sydney Conservatory. She has sung at Covent Garden, the Cologne Opera, Chicago Lyric, the Metropolitan Opera and at Bayreuth and has recorded extensively. Her repertory includes several Wagnerian roles, Dorabella (*Così fan tutte*) and Octavian (*Der Rosenkavalier*) as well as concert works.

Minton's Playhouse an important night spot in Harlem, New York. During the 1940s saxophonist Teddy Hill led the house band and attracted other progressive jazz musicians, whose after-hours jam sessions spurred the development of BEBOP.

minuet *also*, **minuetto** [mē-noo'et-tō] (It.), **menuet** [mə'nüe] (Fr.) a French 17th- and 18th-c. court and social dance in slow triple meter which, in stylized instrumental form, became an integral part of dance suites, the sonata, the symphony, etc., usu. paired with a TRIO.

Minute Waltz popular name for the waltz in D-flat major, Op. 64, No. 1 (1847), by Chopin, so named because it seems to go by so quickly that it takes only a minute.

Miracle, The popular (and erroneous) name for the Symphony No. 96 in D major (1791) by Haydn, so called because of the legend that at its first performance a chandelier fell and barely missed the audience. The accident did, in fact, occur, but it was at the premiere of Haydn's Symphony No. 102.

Miraculous Mandarin, The (Hung., *A csodálatos mandarin*) pantomime in 1 scene by Bartók to a libretto by M. Lengyel. Premiere, 1926 (composed in 1918). The lurid story of a mandarin, the customer of a prostitute working with three thugs, who will not die until he has been embraced by her. Bartók also fashioned an orchestral suite from the score (1927).

Miranda, Carmen (1909–55) Portuguese-born Amer. singer and actress, known as the "Brazilian Bombshell." She appeared in the 1940s on Broadway, in films and in night clubs presenting S. Amer. novelty songs and dances.

mirliton a device which by means of a thin membrane modifies the tonal quality of sound fed into it. The best-known modern mirliton is the KAZOO. See also EUNUCH-FLUTE.

mirror canon or **fugue** a CANON or FUGUE that can be played backwards or inverted as if read in a mirror.

Mischakoff, Mischa (1896–1981) Russian-born Amer. violinist, stud. of S. Korguyev. He settled in the U.S. in 1921 and was concertmaster, successively, of the New York SO, the Philadelphia Orchestra, the Chicago SO, the NBC SO and the Detroit SO. He taught at the Juilliard School and Wayne State U. in Detroit and led the Mischakoff String Quartet.

miserere (Lat., have mercy) the first word of psalms 50, 55, 56 and other liturgical texts. Psalm 50 is one of the seven penitential psalms and therefore has many polyphonic settings, esp. from the 16th and 17th c. Miserere settings are an important part of the Roman Catholic office for the dead.

missa (Lat.) MASS.

missa brevis (Lat., short Mass) **1**, a complete setting of the Ordinary of the MASS in which all movements are brief. Brevity is achieved through omission of text or simultaneous presentation of successive clauses of text. **2**, a musical setting of the Kyrie and Gloria only, intended for use in the Lutheran service. This form was prevalent during the 17th and 18th c.

missa dominicalis (Lat., Lord's Day Mass) a Mass for use on Sundays. In the Roman Catholic tradition, the missa dominicalis uses chants from Mass XI of the Roman Gradual ("In dominicis infra annum"). The earliest example dates from c1500; the missa dominicalis was especially favored by German composers of the 16th c.

missa lecta (Lat., read mass) Low Mass, a Mass in which the liturgy is spoken throughout, although a few hymns may be introduced. Cf. MISSA SOLEMNIS.

missa pro defunctis REQUIEM MASS.

missa solemnis (Lat., solemn Mass) **1**, High Mass, a celebration of the Eucharist in which all sections of the Mass except the Epistle and Gospel are sung either in chant or polyphony. Cf. MISSA LECTA. **2**, the Mass in D major, Op. 123 (1819–23), by Beethoven.

Miss Julie opera in 2 acts by Rorem to a libretto by Kenward Elmslie based on the play by August Strindberg. Premiere, New York 1965.

misura [mē′zoo-rä] (It.) **1**, MEASURE. **2**, METER. **3**, BEAT.

Mitchell, Howard (1911–88) Amer. conductor and cellist, stud. of Felix Salmond. He was principal cellist of the National SO in Washington, D.C. (1933–41), then became its conductor in 1949. He remained until 1969, when he assumed the conductorship of the SODRE SO in Montevideo, Uruguay.

Mitchell, Joni (Anderson, Roberta Joan) (1943–) Canadian-born Amer. pop singer, guitarist and songwriter. Her many hit songs, recorded by herself and others, incl. "Both Sides Now," "Big Yellow Taxi" and "Woodstock." She has experimented with various styles, incl. rock and jazz (with bassist Charles Mingus).

Mitchell, Roscoe (1940–) innovative Amer. jazz instrumentalist, singer and leader. After playing with Henry Threadgill and Richard Abrams, he was involved in the formation of the AACM. In the 1960s he led his own groups, forming, in 1969, the ART ENSEMBLE OF CHICAGO.

Mitropoulos, Dimitri (1896–1960) Greek-born Amer. conductor, composer and pianist, trained in Athens and Brussels and in Berlin with Busoni. He conducted and taught in Greece in the late 1920s, then began to guest-conduct in Europe in the 1930s. His Amer. debut was in 1936 with the Boston SO. He was conductor of the Minneapolis SO (1937–49), then of the New York PO (1949–58). From 1954 until his death he also conducted regularly at the Metropolitan Opera. He used no baton and always conducted from memory in contemporary as well as traditional scores.

mixed consort BROKEN CONSORT.

mixed media a term describing an event or work employing several different artistic media, such as film, music, dance, etc. Also, *multimedia*.

mixed voices choral forces including both men and women.

mixolydian the seventh church MODE, the authentic mode on G.

mixture *also*, **mixture stop 1**, an ORGAN STOP having more than one pipe for each key, usu. producing octaves and fifths. Cf. PARTIAL. **2**, the main diapason mixture stop.

mizmār a name for various reed woodwind instruments of the Arab world.

MLA MUSIC LIBRARY ASSOCIATION.

Mlle. Modiste musical by Victor Herbert, lyrics and book by Henry Blossom. Premiere, New York 1905. The story of the stagestruck Fifi, who becomes the toast of Paris.

MM. (Ger., *Metronom Maelzel*) *abbr.* Maelzel's METRONOME; used to precede an indication relating a note value to a metronome setting, as MM. ♩ = 60.

Mobley, Hank (Henry) (1930–86) Amer. tenor saxophonist. He played with Max Roach, Tadd Dameron, Dizzy Gillespie, Horace Silver and Miles Davis in the 1950s and early 1960s, then with various groups until his retirement in 1975.

mobile form a compositional device in which music is composed in sections whose order of performance is decided by the performer. The technique dates principally from the 1950s, though examples of its use can be found as early as Mozart.

mock trumpet an early form of the 18th-c. CHALUMEAU (2,).

mod. *abbr.* MODERATO.

modal jazz a type of jazz improvisation of the late 1950s and early 1960s based on other modes than the traditional major and minor of bop. See MODE.

modal rhythm see RHYTHMIC MODES.

mode 1, in MENSURAL NOTATION, the proportional relationship between a longa and a brevis. **2**, INTERVAL (early Middle Ages). **3**, a designation for types of scales or melodies, indicating the range, pitch center and the whole- and half-step relationships between the notes. When applied to Gregorian chant, eight modes (*Church modes*) are distinguished:

  1. Dorian (the authentic mode with its final on D)
  2. Hypodorian (the plagal mode with its final on D)
  3. Phrygian (authentic, final on E)
  4. Hypophrygian (plagal, final on E)
  5. Lydian (authentic, final on F)
  6. Hypolydian (plagal, final on F)
  7. Mixolydian (authentic, final on G)
  8. Hypomixolydian (plagal, final on G)

Authentic modes have a range of approximately one octave, from the final (analogous to the TONIC in tonal music) to the octave above. Plagal modes also have a range of approximately one octave, with the final di-

Medieval Church Modes

Glareanus's 12 Modes

7. Mixolydian (G-G, final:G)
8. Hypomixolydian (D-D, final:G)
9. Aeolian (A-A, final:A), equivalent to the natural minor scale
10. Hypoaeolian (E-E, final:A)
11. Ionian (C-C, final:C), equivalent to the major scale
12. Hypoionian (G-G, final:C)

Modes with a final on B were avoided in order to avoid the *diabolus in musica*, the tritone interval from B to F.

Zarlino retained GLAREANUS's 12 modes, but renumbered them so that the sequence started with the C modes as 1 and 2. He also refuted the naming of the modes as Ionian, etc.

During later centuries, the word "mode" was used to indicate scales and melodies outside of the standard major/minor tonal system. Use of modes in tonal music, esp. during the 19th c., evoked an exotic flavor, often recalling ethnic folk tunes.

The concept of mode is further applied to scales used in the music of non-Western cultures, such as the ragas of India. Such concepts of mode are quite different from Western uses of the term. See also MODAL JAZZ.

Mode de valeurs et d'intensités [mod də vä'lœr zā dɛ̃-tā-sē'tā] (Fr., mode of durations and volumes) piano work (1949) by Messiaen, the third of his *Four Studies on Rhythm*. The work uses an array of 36 pitches, each having its own duration, volume and articulation.

mode of limited transposition a mode which can be transposed only a limited number of times before the same collection of pitches is produced; for example, the whole-tone scale.

moderato [mō-dā'rä-tō] (It.) moderate, restrained.

moderator pedal *also,* **muffler pedal** a pedal that moves a strip of felt between the hammers and strings of a piano to mute the sound. It is usu. either the middle or left pedal and is now found only on uprights. It is used when the SOFT PEDAL is called for.

modernism a term used mainly in America in the 1930s to describe the

viding the range into two parts, usu. a 4th plus a 5th.

During the Renaissance, a 12-mode system was introduced by GLAREANUS:

1. Dorian (D-D, final:D)
2. Hypodorian (A-A, final:D)
3. Phrygian (E-E, final:E)
4. Hypophrygian (B-B, final:E)
5. Lydian (F-F, final:F)
6. Hypolydian (C-C, final:F)

work of composers such as Varèse and Cage who sought to expand the frontiers of music. Cf. POST-MODERNISM.

modern jazz an imprecise term usu. used to refer to the BOP jazz of the 1950s. It means something different to each person who uses it.

Modern Jazz Quartet Amer. jazz ensemble established in 1954 (though the group had recorded earlier) by Milt Jackson, John Lewis, Kenny Clarke and Percy Heath. The group was noted for its collective improvisation and for the compositions of pianist Lewis. The quartet disbanded in 1974, but it has come together on various occasions in recent years.

modern music 1, a term used to refer to the music of the current time or, sometimes, more generally, the music of the 20th c. Also, *contemporary music*. 2, (*cap*.) an important journal of contemporary music published from 1925 to 1946 by the League of Composers in New York.

modinha (mō'dē-nyə) (Port.) a sentimental Portuguese art song, usu. accompanied by the guitar.

modo (It.) 1, MODE. 2, manner, style.

modulation 1, in tonal music, the movement from one key to another, usu. accomplished by means of a chord which functions in either key (*pivot chord*). 2, in telecommunications, the superimposition of a "program" signal on a "carrier" wave. The two most common methods of modulation, familiar from radio, are *amplitude modulation* (in which the height of the carrier wave is made to conform to the program variations) and *frequency modulation* (the frequency of the carrier wave is modified). Other common types are ring modulation (see RING MODULATOR), PULSE MODULATION and PHASE MODULATION.

modulator an electronic device used to modulate sound signals. See MODULATION.

Moeck German music publisher and instrument manufacturer, esp. known for its recorders and recorder

Modulation

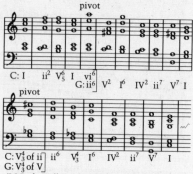

C: I   ii^2 V$^6_5$ I   vi^6
G: ii^6 V^2 I^6 IV^2 ii^7 V^7 I

C: V$^4_3$ of ii   ii^6 V$^4_3$ I^6 IV^2 ii^7 V^7 I
G: V$^4_3$ of V

(J.S.Bach, Well-Tempered Clavier, Bk. I No. 1) (reduced to chords)

music. The firm was est. in 1925 at Celle.

Moennig ['me-nig] Amer. family of instrument dealers and repair specialists in Philadelphia.

Moevs, Robert (Walter) (1920–) American pianist and composer, stud. of Piston and Boulanger. He has taught at Harvard and Rutgers. His works incl. a ballet, various works for orch., a concerto for piano and percussion, chamber music, choral works and songs.

Moffo, Anna (1935–) Amer. soprano, stud. of Eufemia Giannini-Gregory, Luigi Ricci and Mercedes Llopart. Her Amer. debut was at the Chicago Lyric Opera in 1957, and she first sang at the Metropolitan Opera two years later. She has also sung in all the major opera houses of Europe. Her many roles incl. Violetta (*La Traviata*), Manon, Mélisande and Gilda (*Rigoletto*).

mojiganga [mō-khē'gäng-gä] (Sp.) a short 17th- or 18th-c. Spanish comic or satiric theatrical piece, performed at the conclusion of a dramatic production.

Moldau, The see MÁ VLAST.

Mole, Miff (Irving Milfred) (1898– 1961) innovative Amer. jazz trombonist, noted for his recordings with the Original Memphis Five and Red Nichols's groups. During the 1930s he played with the NBC RO and with the bands of Paul Whiteman and Benny Goodman.

Molinari-Pradelli, Francesco (1911–) Italian opera conductor and pianist, stud. of Ivaldi, Nordio and Bernardino Molinari. He has conducted at most major European opera houses and made his Amer. debut in 1957 at San Francisco. His Metropolitan Opera debut was in 1966. He also performs and records as a pianist.

moll (Ger.) MINOR.

Moll, Kurt (1938–) German bass, stud. of Emmy Mueller. Since 1970 he has performed with many European opera companies, incl. the Salzburg and Bayreuth festivals, and in N. Amer. His repertory includes the leading Wagner bass parts, Osmin (*The Abduction from the Seraglio*) and Baron Ochs (*Der Rosenkavalier*).

molto (It.) very.

Moment Musical [mô′mä mü-zē′käl] (Fr.) a term coined by a Viennese publisher for each of a set of six piano pieces, Op. 94 (1823–7), by Schubert. The term was later used by other composers, incl. Rachmaninov.

Monaco, Mario del DEL MONACO, MARIO.

Monday Group a group of composers, students of Rosenberg, who met in Stockholm on Mondays at the home of Blomdahl in the late 1940s.

Mondonville, Jean-Joseph Cassanéa de [mô-dô′vēl] (1711–72) French composer, violinist and conductor. He was a violinist of the royal chapel, becoming *intendant* in 1744. He was very active as a performer, both solo and in collaboration with other important instrumentalists and singers. As a composer he wrote operas and ballets, motets and instrumental sonatas.

monferrina (It.) a 19th-c. English country dance of Piedmontese origin.

Moniuszko, Stanislaw (1819–72) Polish composer, trained in Minsk and Berlin. In the mid-1840s he began to write dramatic music, but his first major success came in 1858 in Warsaw when his revised opera *Halka* was performed to acclaim; he wrote in all over 20 operas and operettas. He also produced some orchestral works, other vocal music, several collections of songs for home use and a textbook on harmony (he taught at the Music Institute in Warsaw from 1864).

Monk, Meredith (1943–) Amer. composer, film maker and singer, founder in 1978 of the Meredith Monk Vocal Ensemble and a highly regarded composer for music theater.

Monk, Thelonious (Sphere) (1917–82) highly original Amer. jazz bop-era pianist and composer, considered the most important jazz composer following Duke Ellington. His unique piano style was characterized by crushed notes and clusters and heavily accented playing. His groups used saxophonists Sonny Rollins and John Coltrane and later Charlie Rouse. A number of his compositions have become classics, most notably the song "Round about Midnight" (1944).

Monk, William Henry (1823–89) English composer and organist. He was organist and choirmaster at the church of St. Matthias in Stoke Newington, professor of vocal music at King's College, London, and editor of *Hymns Ancient and Modern* (1861). The hymn tune "Eventide," to which "Abide with Me" is sung, is his composition.

Monn (Mann), **Matthias Georg** (1717–50) Austrian composer and organist, one of the most important of the early Viennese symphonists. He is credited with having composed the first four-movement symphony with a third-movement minuet, and his use of formally distinct sections in his symphonies was an important step toward the use of sonata form in the symphony. He also was important in the development of the classical concerto. He wrote 21 symphonies, concertos for harpsichord and violin, string quartets and other chamber music, keyboard sonatas and suites and choral works.

monochord 1, an ancient one-stringed instrument used to demonstrate the mathematical relations of musical tones. **2**, a similar instrument of the late Middle Ages having several strings for sounding chords. **3**, TRUMPET MARINE.

Monod, Jacques(-Louis) [mō′nō] (1927–) French conductor, pianist and composer, stud. of Messiaen and Leibowitz. He also studied at the Juilliard School, at Columbia and in Berlin. He has performed frequently as pianist, solo and in recital with soprano Bethany Beardslee (his wife for some years). As a conductor he is noted as an interpreter of 20th-c. music. His own works incl. songs, chamber music and orchestral works.

monodrama strictly speaking, a MELODRAMA for a single performer, though the term is sometimes used for a sung dramatic work for one performer (such as Schoenberg's *Erwartung*).

monody 1, music consisting of a single line; see also MONOPHONY. **2**, a 20th-c. term for an Italian, accompanied, solo song, usu. secular, a form which was popular during the first half of the 17th c. The principal types are the concerted madrigal and strophic aria. The earliest printed examples are found in Caccini's *Le nuove musiche* of 1601–2.

monophony music for a single voice or part, usu. unaccompanied, such as plainsong. Contrasted with POLY-PHONY and HOMOPHONY.

monothematic a term describing a work based on a single theme. Some famous examples are Bach's *Art of the Fugue* and *Musical Offering* and Berlioz's *Symphonie fantastique*.

monotone a single unvarying pitch, such as a reciting tone.

Monroe, Bill (William) **(Smith)** (1911–) Amer. country-music mandolin player, singer and composer. He gained a reputation in the 1930s as a hillbilly singer on radio, then formed the Blue Grass Boys in 1938 and joined the Grand Ole Opry a year later. His style was the basis for what has since been called BLUE-GRASS MUSIC.

Monsieur Croche (Fr.) CROCHE, MONSIEUR.

Monte, Philippe de (Filippo di) (1521–1603) Flemish composer. His youth was spent in Italy. In the early 1550s he served in the London chapel of Philip II of Spain. In 1567 he joined the service of the Emperor Maximilian II in Vienna and spent the rest of his life at the Hapsburg court. He is best known for his secular vocal works (madrigals, chansons), a large number of which were published starting in 1554. He also published collections of motets and sacred madrigals.

Montemezzi, Italo (1875–1952) Italian composer, trained at the Milan Conservatory. In his final years he lived in California. He is known for one work, the opera *L'amore dei tre re* (1913), which is still widely performed. He wrote 6 other operas and some choral works.

Monteux, Claude [mō′tø, klōd] (1920–) Amer. conductor and flutist, son of PIERRE MONTEUX and stud. of Georges Laurent. He played with the Kansas City PO in the late 1940s. His conducting began with the Ballets Russes, and he has conducted throughout Europe and Scandinavia. He has been conductor of the Columbia (OH) Orchestra and the Hudson Valley (NY) PO and was a member of the Harpsichord Quartet.

Monteux, Pierre (1875–1964) French-born Amer. conductor and violinist, trained at the Paris Conservatoire. He played as violist in the Quatuor Geloso and in various orchestras. In 1911 he became conductor of the Ballets Russes, leading the premieres of Stravinsky's *Petrushka* and *The Rite of Spring*, Ravel's *Daphnis et Chloé* and Debussy's *Jeux*, among other works. He moved to the U.S. in 1916, conducting at the Metropolitan Opera and then becoming conductor of the Boston Symphony in 1920. From 1924 to 1934 he was second conductor of the Amsterdam Concertgebouw orch., during which time he also founded the Orchestre symphonique de Paris, which he conducted until 1938. He was conductor of the San Francisco SO from 1936 to 1952. His final post was with the London SO. Monteux founded a conducting school in Paris in 1932, moving it to Maine in 1936; his pupils there incl. many now distinguished conductors.

Monteverdi, Claudio (Giovanni Antonio) (1567–1643) outstanding Italian composer, one of the most important in the history of Western art music, stud. of Marc' Antonio Ingegneri. By the age of 16 he had already publ. a volume of motets and a book of sacred madrigals. He joined the service of the duke of Mantua c1590 as a string player, and he soon est. a firm reputation as a composer. His first opera, *L'Orfeo*, was produced in 1607 and was shortly thereafter followed by *L'Arianna*. In 1612 he assumed the post of *maestro di cappella* of St. Mark's in Venice, a post he held until his death. Of the eight operas known to have been completed by him, three survive: *L'Orfeo* (1607), *Il ritorno d'Ulisse in patria* (1640), and *L'incoronazione di Poppea* (1642), his last opera; the others were destroyed in a library fire. He also published 8 volumes of madrigals and canzonettas and many sacred vocal works, including the much-performed Vespers of 1610. Monteverdi was as much an innovator in the early development of opera as he was a master at assimilating the techniques and styles before and around him.

Montgomery, Kenneth (1943–) British conductor, stud. of Boult, Celibadache and Pritchard. He has worked at Glyndebourne, Sadler's Wells Opera, Covent Garden, the Netherlands Opera and in No. America. On the concert stage he has conducted the Bournemouth SO and the Netherlands RO, among others.

Montgomery, Wes (John Leslie) (1925–68) Amer. jazz guitarist. He played briefly with Lionel Hampton (1948–50), later forming a group, the Mastersounds, with his brothers. In the 1960s he toured with his own group and played with the Wynton Kelly trio. His last years brought him much popular success in recordings and TV appearances. His playing combined the best features of his predecessors, Charlie Christian, Django Reinhardt and Barney Kessel.

Montoya, Carlos (1903–) noted Span. guitarist, esp. well known for his work in flamenco style, both as solo performer and as composer.

Montreal Symphony Orchestra orch. founded in Montreal in 1934 under Athanase David as Les Concerts Symphoniques. The name was changed in 1954. Conductors of the orch. have included Defauw, Klemperer, Markevich, Mehta, Decker, Frühbeck de Burgos and Dutoit.

Montsalvatge, Xavier [mō-säl'väzh] (1912–) Spanish composer and critic, trained at the Barcelona Conservatory. Since 1936 he has written over 20 ballet scores. He has been critic for the weekly *Destino* of Barcelona and the *Vanguardia española* and has taught in Barcelona at the San Jorge Academy, the Destino Seminary and the Conservatory. His eclectic style encompasses the traditions of Spanish and Catalan music as well as those of traditional European art music. He has written 3 operas, over 20 ballets, works for orch., songs and song cycles, chamber music, works for keyboard and guitar, film scores.

mooche [moosh] a shuffling jazz dance step of the 1920s. Also, *Congo grind*.

Moody Blues English art-rock band formed in Birmingham in 1964, noted for their use of the Mellotron, an orchestral synthesizer.

Moog, Robert A(rthur) (1934–) Amer. inventor, creator of the Moog synthesizer and other electronic instruments. His synthesizer was made famous by the recording *Switched-On Bach* by Walter Carlos, who collaborated with Moog on the design of the instrument.

Moonlight Sonata popular name for

the piano sonata in C sharp minor, Op. 27, No. 2 (1801) by Beethoven, apparently due to an association of the mood of the first movement with moonlight on Lake Lucerne.

Moore, Dorothy Rudd (1940–) Amer. composer, stud. of Mark Fax, Boulanger and Chou Wen-chung. She has taught at the Harlem School of the Arts, NYU and Bronx Community College and was a co-founder of the Society of Black Composers. Her works incl. a symphony, the opera *Frederick Douglass* (1979–85), chamber music and songs.

Moore, Douglas S(tuart) (1893–1969) Amer. composer, organist, teacher and writer, stud. of d'Indy, Bloch and Boulanger. He taught at Columbia from 1926 to his retirement in 1962. He is best known for his operas, several of which have entered the standard repertory: *The Devil and Daniel Webster* (1938), *The Ballad of Baby Doe* (1956) and *Carrie Nation* (1966). He won the Pulitzer Prize in 1951 for his opera *Giants in the Earth*. He also wrote orchestral works, chamber music and songs, as well as scores for several documentary films.

Moore, Gerald (1899–1987) English pianist, stud. of Mark and Michael Hambourg. From 1925 until his retirement in 1967 he accompanied virtually every major instrumentalist and singer in concert and in an extensive list of recordings. He also gave lecture-recitals on the art of accompaniment throughout the world and wrote several popular books, incl. *The Unashamed Accompanist* (1943) and *Am I too Loud? Memoirs of an Accompanist* (1962).

Moore, Grace (1898–47) Amer. actress and soprano, stud. of Marafioti and Berthélemy. She sang in opera, musical comedy and films with equal finesse. Her Metropolitan Opera debut was in 1928, and she sang there until 1939. She also sang at the Opéra-Comique in Paris and Covent Garden.

Moore, Undine Smith (1905–88) Amer. composer and teacher, trained at the Juilliard School, the Eastman School and elsewhere. She taught at Virginia State College from 1927 until her retirement in 1972 and founded the Black Music Center. Her works incl. chamber music, many choral works (incl. the oratorio *Scenes from the Life of a Martyr*, 1982) and songs.

Moorman, (Madeline) Charlotte (1933–) Amer. cellist and performance artist noted for her collaboration with composer Nam June Paik in works dealing with sex and violence.

Morales, Cristóbal de (c1500–53) Spanish composer. After holding several positions in his native Seville and elsewhere in Spain, he joined the Papal Choir in Rome around 1535, leaving to return to Spain in 1545. His extant works, many published in Rome or Venice, incl. Mass settings, magnificats, motets and other sacred and secular vocal music.

Moran, Robert (Leonard) (1937–) Amer. composer, stud. of Apostel, Milhaud and Berio. He has taught in San Francisco and directed the West Coast New Music Ensemble. His best-known works employ a wide variety of means and performing forces and often utilize indeterminate notation.

Morath, Max (Edward) (1926–) Amer. ragtime pianist, specializing in one-man shows presenting social history through music and anecdotes. He has made many recordings of vocal and piano music of the early part of the 20th c.

Moravian music the music, principally sacred, of the Moravian religious sect, est. in the 18th c. in Pennsylvania (esp. Bethlehem) and North Carolina. Music played an important part in the Moravian service, usu. performed by male chorus accompanied by organ and other instruments. The most common forms were hymns, anthems and solo songs.

Morawetz, Oskar (1917–) Czech-born Canadian composer, pianist and conductor, stud. of Karel Hoffmeister,

Julius Isserlis and Lazare Lévy. He emigrated to Canada in 1940 and has taught at the U. of Toronto since 1958. His works incl. *Carnival Overture*, 2 symphonies, concertos for harp, brass quintet and violin, *From the Diary of Anne Frank* (for soprano and orch.), many vocal works, chamber music and piano works.

morbido ['mor-bē-dō] (It.) soft, tender.

morceau [mor'sō] (Fr., piece) a short musical work.

mordent 1, a melodic ORNAMENT consisting of rapid alternation between a principal tone and an auxiliary tone a half or whole step above (*upper modent, Pralltriller*) or below (*lower mordent, Schneller*). **2**, ACCIACCATURA.

Morel, Jean (1903–75) French conductor and teacher, stud. of Isidore Philipp, Noël Gallon, Pierné and Hahn. He taught at the American Conservatory in Fontainebleau (1921–36) and at the Juilliard School (1949–71). He conducted in Europe and No. and S. America, incl. opera at New York City Center and the Metropolitan Opera.

Morello, Joe (Joseph A.) (1928–) Amer. cool jazz drummer. He worked with Glen Gray, Stan Kenton and the Marian McPartland trio before joining the Dave Brubeck Quartet in 1956.

morendo (It., dying away) becoming gradually softer and slower. Cf. CALANDO.

Moresca (It.) *also,* **morisca, morisco 1**, a stylized battle dance of the Renaissance. Cf. MORRIS DANCE. **2**, a type of VILLANELLA parodying Moorish dialect.

Morgan, Helen (1900–41) Amer. actress and torch singer of vaudeville, Broadway musicals, and nightclubs. She starred in *Show Boat* (1932) and *Sweet Adeline* (1929).

morisca *also,* **morisco** MORESCA.

Morley, Thomas (c1557–1602) English composer, organist and theorist, principal exponent of the Elizabethan madrigal, stud. of Byrd. He was or-ganist at St. Paul's and a Gentleman of the Chapel Royal. His works incl. service music, anthems, psalms and motets, madrigals and ayres, keyboard music and instrumental chamber music. He also pub. collections of works by other composers (*The Triumphes of Oriana*) and a popular book of instruction, *A Plaine and Easie Introduction to Practicall Musicke* (1597).

Moross, Jerome (1913–83) Amer. composer, trained at Juilliard and at NYU. He was active as a theater and film composer and arranger and as a composer for the concert stage. His film scores incl. *Hans Christian Andersen* (1952) and *The Cardinal* (1963), and he orchestrated scores for Copland and others. His own works incl. ballets, 2 operas, a symphony and chamber music.

Morris dance *also,* **morris** an English folk dance related to the MORESCA, performed as a traditional part of English pageants.

Morrison, Van (1945–) Irish rock singer, songwriter and guitarist, noted for his originality and visionary lyrics. He formed two short-lived groups, Them (1963) and the Caledonia Soul Orchestra (1972), but most of his career he has performed and recorded with pickup groups, often with jazz musicians.

Morrow, Charlie (Charles Geoffrey) (1942–) Amer. composer and producer, stud. of Sydeman. He was a founder of the NEW WILDERNESS PRESERVATION BAND. His works incl. outdoor events, usu. for large performing forces, theater works, orchestral and chamber music, tape works and film scores.

Morton, Jelly Roll (Ferdinand Joseph) (1890–1941) Amer. jazz pianist, composer and raconteur. Born in Mississippi, he was first successful in Los Angeles (1917–22), then in Chicago (from 1923), making an extensive series of recordings based in ragtime. He was perhaps the first important jazz composer; some of the best-known of his many compositions are "King

Porter Stomp" (1906), "Jelly Roll Blues" (1905) and the "Kansas City Stomp" (1919).

Moscheles, Ignaz (1794–1870) Czech-born German pianist, conductor and composer, stud. of B.D. Weber in Prague and Albrechtsberger and Salieri in Vienna. He pursued a highly successful concert career, then settled in London in 1825, where he taught piano and conducted the Philharmonic Society. In 1846 he moved to Leipzig to teach at the conservatory. The majority of his own works are for piano, and he also wrote songs, chamber music and a symphony and produced editions of works by Beethoven, Haydn, Clementi and others.

Moryl, Richard (1929–) Amer. composer and conductor, stud. of Blacher and Berger. He founded the New England Contemporary Music Ensemble and the Charles Ives Center for American Music. He has written works in all genres, frequently employing tape or mixed media.

Moscow Chamber Orchestra small chamber orch. formed in Moscow in 1956 by conductor Rudolf Barshai.

Moscow Philharmonic Orchestra orch. formed in Moscow in 1931.

Moses and Aaron (Ger., *Moses und Aron*) opera in 3 acts by Schoenberg to his own libretto. Premiere, Zürich 1957. The work was left incomplete at the composer's death, the music for Act III not yet having been composed, and the opera is performed in its incomplete form. Moses has the word of God but cannot communicate it and uses Aaron as his spokesman, with unfortunate results.

mosso (It., agitated) rapid, animated; found most often in the phrases *più mosso* (faster) and *meno mosso* (slower).

Most Happy Fella, The musical by Frank Loesser, based on Sidney Howard's play *They Knew What They Wanted*. Premiere, New York 1956. The operalike musical tells the story of the love of Tony, a winegrower, for a waitress, Rosabella.

Moten, Bennie (Benjamin) (1894–

1935) Amer. jazz pianist and bandleader. Through his groups, beginning with a trio in 1918, he established the so-called "Kansas City" orchestral style. His band formed the nucleus for the Count Basie orch. after his death.

motet in the broadest sense, a polyphonic sacred vocal composition. Throughout the Middle Ages and Renaissance, the motet was one of the highest forms of musical composition, and the history of Western music during this time may be traced in its development.

The genesis of the motet lies within the 12th-c. settings of organum in the MAGNUS LIBER ORGANI. The 13th-c. motet generally consists of a textless tenor line taken from preexisting Gregorian chant, plus one or two added lines with texts in either Latin or French. These added texts generally elucidate the meaning of the original chant text.

Late 13th-c. developments in the motet repertory include the dissolution of modal rhythm in favor of rhythmic notations in which the rhythm of a note is determined by its shape rather than by melodic context; and the introduction of secular tenors taken from the French chanson repertory. Bilingual double motets, in which one voice above the tenor has a Latin text and the other a French text, become prevalent.

14th-c. motets begin to show isorhythmic structures (see ISORHYTHM), a formal procedure which continues well into the 15th c.

Mid-15th-c. chanson-motets in three parts, based on the treble-dominated compositional style of the French chanson, are prevalent. These motets, often written in honor of saints (saints' motets) or the Virgin Mary (Marian motets), are often intended for use during the divine office.

Late 15th-c. motets are generally composed in four parts, consisting of a cantus firmus tenor taken from some preexistent tune, a bass line below the tenor and two voices above; all voices set the same text. These

motets are usu. written for special occasions. In Milan collections of motets are used in place of the movements of the Mass (*motetti missales*).

The 16th-c. motet repertory is
marked by an explosion of compositional techniques such as IMITATION,
PARAPHRASE and PARODY the existing
cantus firmus technique. The number of voices in a motet ranges from
four to 36, with a preference for 5–6
voices during the latter half of the
century. Late in the century, polychoral motets are written for the
unique performing conditions at St.
Mark's Cathedral in Venice, and the
expansion of polychoral techniques
engenders the concertato principle of
the Baroque.

motetti missales (Lat., motets for the
Mass) motets which were used as
substitutions for the movements of
the Mass in late 15th- and early 16th-
c. Milan. Also, *substitution Mass*.

motetus (Lat.) the voice to be composed first in motets of the 13th, 14th
and early 15th c., situated directly
above the tenor. Previous to the introduction of French poetry into the
motet repertory, this voice was
known as the *duplum*.

Mother Goose Suite (Fr., *Ma mère
l'oye*) a suite of five pieces for piano
duet (1908) by Ravel based on Perrault's fairy tales. The five pieces are
"Pavan of the Sleeping Beauty,"
"Tom Thumb," "The Ugly Little Empress of the Pagodas," "Conversation
between Beauty and the Beast," and
"The Fairy Garden." The work was
orchestrated by Ravel in 1912 and
also made into a ballet by the addition
of new passages linking the movements.

Mother of Us All, The historical opera in 2 acts by Virgil Thomson to a
libretto by Gertrude Stein. Premiere,
New York 1947. A vignette-pageant
centering on the life and ideals of Susan B. Anthony.

Mothers of Invention a rock performing group orig. formed as The
Muthers in 1964 by FRANK ZAPPA.

motif (Fr.) *also*, **motive** a melodic

and/or rhythmic musical idea used as
a building block for themes.

moto (It.) motion, movement.

moto perpetuo (It., perpetual motion)
a type of work in which a rapid, often
repetitive, figuration is maintained
over a period of time as if it could
continue forever. Cf. MOTOR
RHYTHM.

motor rhythm a term for a type of
rhythmic organization which main-
tains a constant rhythmic pulse for
an extended period with machinelike
regularity. The term is sometimes applied to baroque music. Cf. MOTO
PERPETUO.

Motown (from "Motortown," a nickname for Detroit, MI) a variety of
Afr.-Amer. popular music of the
1960s and later, a blend of blues, gospel and rock characterized by sophisticated arrangements recorded with
large orchs. The style was epitomized
in the recordings of Motown Records,
one of the first large Amer. music
firms owned and run by African-
Americans.

Mottl, Felix (Josef) (1856–1911) Austrian conductor and composer, stud.
of Bruckner. He conducted at Karlsruhe from 1881 and at Bayreuth from
1886 (he had worked there as an assistant since 1876). He also conducted Wagner's operas at Covent
Garden and at the Metropolitan Opera. In addition to his conducting,
Mottl was active as an arranger and
prepared the piano-vocal scores of
Wagner's operas.

motto theme *also*, **motto** a recurring
theme usu. related to a specific idea
or action. Also, *head-motif*. Cf. LEIT-
MOTIV.

mountain music the folk music of
so. Appalachian region and the rural
South and West of the U.S. Also, *old
time music*. See COUNTRY MUSIC.

Mount of Olives, The CHRIST ON THE
MOUNT OF OLIVES.

Moussorgsky MUSSORGSKY.

mouth organ *also*, **mouth harp** HAR-
MONICA.

mouthpiece the section of a woodwind or brass instrument which comes into contact with the mouth and which, in some reed instruments, holds the reed.

Mouton, Jean (1459–1522) French composer of vocal music. For most of his professional life he was attached to the French court and was court composer for part of that time. He is noted for his motets, of which more than 100 survive, as well as for his chansons and Mass settings.

mouvement [moov'mā] (Fr.) MOVEMENT.

movable doh a SOLMIZATION system in which the syllables may be transposed to any key and refer to the scale degrees of the current tonality, as opposed to the FIXED-DO SYSTEM, in which each syllable always refers to the same pitch class.

movement a self-sufficient section of a work, distinguished by its character, its tonality, its tempo or its position in the work.

movie music FILM MUSIC.

movimento (It.) MOVEMENT.

Moyse, Marcel (Joseph) (1889–1984) French flutist, stud. of Paul Taffanel, Lucien Capet and others. He was first flute of the Pasdeloup Orch., the Société des concerts du Conservatoire and the Opéra-Comique and taught at the Paris Conservatoire. He made many recordings, wrote teaching works for the flute and, in trio with his son **Louis Moyse** (1912–) and his daughter-in-law, was a founder of the Marlboro Festival in Vermont.

Mozarabic chant a type of Spanish Christian liturgical chant in use during the Middle Ages on the Iberian peninsula.

Mozart, (Johann Georg) Leopold (1719–87) Austrian composer, theorist and violinist in the court of the prince-archbishop of Augsburg. He was the father of W.A. MOZART and from 1760 he dedicated himself to the education of his children, esp. his son, and produced few more compositions. Leopold's own works incl. numerous symphonies, sacred music, divertimentos and serenades, keyboard music, concertos, dances and an important work on violin playing.

Mozart, (Johann Chrysostom) Wolfgang Amadeus (1756–91) brilliant Austrian composer, son of LEOPOLD MOZART and master of every musical medium of his time, in particular opera, concerto, symphony and string chamber music. A child prodigy, he was taken on lengthy performing journeys to France, Italy and England, where he and his sister performed at the local courts. He was in the service of the prince-archbishop of Salzburg from 1769, then moved to Vienna when he was discharged in 1781 and led the life of an independent musician, giving lessons and concerts. In 1782 he married Constanze Weber, a relative of Carl Maria von Weber. Mozart did obtain ultimately an appointment as a chamber musician at the Viennese court, for which he wrote numerous dances and other entertainment music, but he died a pauper's death and was buried in an unmarked grave. Mozart's works incl. *Bastien und Bastienne, Zaïde, The Abduction from the Seraglio, The Magic Flute* (singspiels), *Idomeneo, La Clemenza di Tito* (opera seria), *Der Schauspieldirektor, The Marriage of Figaro, Così fan tutte, Don Giovanni* (comic operas), ballets, 41 symphonies, instrumental dances, marches, serenades, cassations, etc., concertos for piano, violin, horn, flute, trumpet, oboe and clarinet, chamber music for strings and winds, violin sonatas, keyboard sonatas and variation sets, Mass settings (incl. the *Missa in C minor*), *a Requiem*, other sacred vocal music, secular choral music, songs and part-songs.

Mozarteum conservatory in Salzburg founded in 1841.

Mozart fifths consecutive fifths formed by the resolution of the German 6th chord to the dominant. See CHORD (*illus.*).

mp *abbr.* MEZZO PIANO.

ms *abbr.* **1**, (Lat., *mano sinistro*) left hand. **2**, manuscript.

Muck, Karl (1859–1940) German conductor, noted esp. for his performances of Wagner's operas and of the works of Bruckner. He was musical dir. of the Deutsches Landestheater in Prague (1886–92), the Berlin Opera (1908–12), the Boston SO (1912–22) and the Hamburg PO (1922–30). He also conducted at Bayreuth, Covent Garden and in Görlitz, where he directed the Silesian Music Festival (1894–1911).

Mudarra, Alonso (c1510–80) Spanish composer and vihuelist. From 1546 he was assoc. with the Seville cathedral, where he was a canon. His known works are contained in a volume published in 1546 and (transcribed for keyboard) in a later collection published by Venegas de Henestrosa.

Muddy Waters (Morganfield, McKinley) (1915–) Amer. blues singer and guitarist. First recorded in Mississippi, he moved to Chicago in 1943 and made a number of recordings using electric guitar in collaboration with harmonica player Little Walter, pianist Otis Spann and guitarist Jimmy Rogers.

Muffat, Georg (1653–1704) French-born German organist and composer, father of GOTTLIEB MUFFAT, stud. of Lully and others. He became organist and chamber musician to the Archbishop Gandolf in Salzburg in 1677, then Kapellmeister at the court of the bishop of Passau. During his service to Gandolf he visited Italy, where he was profoundly influenced by the work of Pasquini and Corelli. Muffat's works—consisting of orchestral suites, concerti grossi, instrumental sonatas, toccatas, etc.—represent a result of the cross-fertilization of the French, Italian and German styles.

Muffat, Gottlieb (Theophil) (1690–1770) German organist and composer, son of GEORG MUFFAT. He stud-

ied at the Viennese court under Fux and became court organist in 1717, receiving several promotions thereafter. His works are all for keyboard, comprising organ preludes, ricercars, fugues, canzoni and versets.

Mullican, Moon (Aubrey) (1909–67) Amer. hillbilly pianist. His nickname came from playing piano in a bordello at night. From 1939 he made many recordings, incl. "Jolé Blon" and "I'll Sail My Ship Alone," and later performed with the Grand Ole Opry.

Mulligan, Gerry (Gerald Joseph) (1927–) influential Amer. cool jazz baritone saxophonist, composer and arranger. He worked with Gene Krupa, Claude Thornhill and Miles Davis as instrumentalist and arranger; led his own larger groups, then formed his own group with trumpeter Chet Baker.

multimedia MIXED MEDIA.

multiphonics a term describing multiple simultaneous tones produced on a wind instrument from a single fingering. The technique is frequently called for in contemporary scores, the composer usu. providing the fingerings required to produce the desired sound; it is also used in jazz by such artists as John Coltrane and Albert Mangelsdorff.

multitonality POLYTONALITY.

Mumma, Gordon (1935–) Amer. composer, horn player and performer, trained at the U. of Michigan. He has collaborated with Robert Ashley in mixed-media events and co-founded the Cooperative Studio for Electronic Music in Ann Arbor and the Sonic Arts Union in New York. He has also worked with Merce Cunningham's dance company as composer and performer. Most of his works are for tape or require electronic manipulation of live sounds.

Münch, Charles (1891–1968) French conductor and violinist, stud. of Flesch and Lucien Capet. He taught at the Strasbourg Conservatory and was concertmaster of the Leipzig Gewandhaus Orch. (1926–33). From 1933 he was musical dir. of the Société Philharmonique de Paris and the Société des concerts du Conservatoire, and taught at the École Normale de Musique. He was conductor of the Boston SO from 1948 to 1962, then returned to France, co-founding L'Orchestre de Paris in 1967. He was a champion of new repertory, esp. French, and conducted many premiere performances.

Münchinger, Karl (1915–) German conductor, stud. of Abendroth. In 1945 he founded the Stuttgart Chamber Orch., with which he has toured and recorded extensively. He is esp. noted for his performances of the music of J.S. Bach.

Mundy, John (c1555–1630) English composer and organist, son of WILLIAM MUNDY. He was organist at St. George's Chapel, Windsor, for more than 40 years. His surviving works incl. psalm settings, anthems, motets and instrumental fantasias and in nomine settings.

Mundy, William (c1529–91) English composer, father of JOHN MUNDY. He became a Gentleman of the Chapel Royal in 1564. He composed service music, anthems, motets and instrumental works.

Munich Bach Choir and Orchestra choral society in Munich founded by conductor Karl Richter.

Munich Philharmonic Orchestra orch. formed in 1924 from the private Kaim orch. Its conductors have incl. Pfitzner, von Hausegger, Kabasta, Hans Rosbaud and Rudolf Kempe.

Munrow, David (John) (1942–76) English instrumentalist, specialist on early wind instruments. He directed his own recorder ensemble, had his own radio series, "Pied Piper" (1971–6), and was co-founder of the Early Music Consort of London (1967), which he directed until his untimely death.

Munsel, Patrice (Beverly) (1925–) Amer. soprano, stud. of William Herman and Renato Bellini. Her Metropolitan Opera debut was in 1943, when she was 18, and she sang with the company until the late 1950s, then concentrated on musical comedy.

murky bass also, **murky** a style of 18th-c. keyboard bass writing consisting of alternating octaves played over an extended period of time. Cf. ALBERTI BASS.

Murphy, Turk (Melvin) (1915–87) Amer. jazz trombonist and composer. He played for ten years with Lu Watters's Yerba Buena Jazz Band in San Francisco, forming his own successful band after their breakup. He later played at his own club, Earthquake McGoon's, in San Francisco. He was an articulate spokesman for classic jazz.

Murray, Anne (1946–) Canadian country-pop singer, the first Canadian female singer to earn a gold record in the U.S. She sang regularly in the early 1970s with Glen Campbell and then enjoyed a number of hits as a solo artist, incl. "You Needed Me," "Snowbird" and "Walk Right Back."

Murray, Sunny (James Marcellus Arthur) (1937–) Amer. free-jazz drummer, trained at the Manhattan School of Music. He worked regularly with pianist Cecil Taylor, the New York Contemporary Five and the Albert Ayler band.

musette 1, a small 18th-c. bagpipe. **2,** also, **musette pipe** a small, high-pitched OBOE. **3,** a pastoral, dancelike piece for orch. or keyboard suggesting the sound of the bagpipe. **4,** a reed ORGAN STOP.

Musgrave, Thea (1928–) Scottish composer, stud. of Gál, Boulanger, Copland and others. She is best known as a composer and conductor of opera, and she was the first woman to conduct her own composition with the Philadelphia Orch. Her works incl. *The Voice of Ariadne* and *Mary, Queen of Scots* and other operas, various concertos and orchestral works, songs and choruses and instrumental chamber music, sometimes involving taped sounds.

music sound organized in space and time. A more specific definition would depend on the definer and the period of history, as the concept of what constitutes music has changed greatly over time. At present the term has a rather broad scope, esp. in its use by avant-garde classical, jazz and rock musicians.

Musica Elettronica Viva an important electronic music ensemble active in Rome from 1966 to 1971.

Musica enchiriadis one of the earliest musical treatises to discuss the organizational principles of composed polyphony. Often attributed to Hucbald of St. Amand, the treatise is said to have been written c900.

musica figurata (It.) **1,** contrapuntal music with rhythmically independent parts (as opposed to note-against-note counterpoint). **2,** ornamented melody in plainchant.

musica ficta *also,* **musica falsa** (Lat., false music) tones foreign to the mode introduced into plainchant or polyphonic modal music. The term is also applied to the accidentals so added, whether written in the source or added later by performer or editor. Editorial *ficta* are usu. indicated by a small accidental sign placed over the note in question or by placing the accidental in parentheses before the note.

musical MUSICAL COMEDY.

musical bow a bow-shaped string instrument consisting of a flexible piece of wood curved by the tension of the string(s) attached to both ends. A resonator of some sort is attached to the wood and the string is plucked or bowed.

musical box MUSIC BOX.

musical clock a MECHANICAL INSTRUMENT connected to a clockwork, producing music at timed intervals regulated by the clock.

musical comedy *also,* **musical** a 20th c. form of musical theater popular in English-speaking countries. The form is a development of OPERETTA and the distinction between the two forms is not always clear. The term *musical play* is sometimes used to refer to musicals of a more serious nature. Some of the most important composers of musicals have been George Gershwin, Jerome Kern, Richard Rodgers, Leonard Bernstein and Stephen Sondheim.

musical glasses an 18th- and 19th-c. instrument consisting of tuned drinking glasses played by rubbing the edges with a dampened finger. The glasses were orig. tuned by varying the amount of water they contained. Mozart, Beethoven, and others wrote music for the instrument. A mechanical form, invented by Benjamin Franklin (who dubbed it the *armonica*), contains glass bowls of graduated sizes mounted to turn on an axis, moistened by a water reservoir and played with the fingers. Also, *glass harmonica.*

Musical Joke, A (Ger., *Ein musikalischer Spass*) the divertimento in F for 2 horns and strings, K 522 (1787), by Mozart, a parody of the work of the second-rate composers of his time.

Musical Offering, A (Ger., *Ein musikalisches Opfer*) a set of contrapuntal pieces on a theme of Frederick the Great (1747) by J.S. Bach. The work consists of two fugues, several canons and a trio sonata for flute, violin and harpsichord. The initial letters of the inscription—*"Regis Iussu Cantio Et Reliqua Canonica Arte Resoluta"* (by order of the king, a theme and other things worked out by canon)—spell out the word *ricercar.*

musical play see MUSICAL COMEDY.

musical saw a handsaw bent to produce pitches when hit with a hammer or bowed with a violin bow.

musical theater see MUSIC THEATER.

music appreciation a type of music education intended to introduce an unknowledgeable audience to music, esp. Western art music.

musica reservata (Lat., reserved music) a term which indicates mid-16th- and 17th-c. music that was reserved for the enjoyment of a specific noble patron. Such musical compositions and their performance would usu. be kept a secret, although death of the patron generally released the compositions from their reserved status, as in the case of Willaert's *Musica Nova* of 1559, which was presumably collected earlier as *musica reservata* under the name of *La Peccorina*.

Musica Transalpina two volumes of Italian madrigals with English singing translations published by Nicholas Yonge in 1588 and 1597 which significantly influenced the development of the English madrigal school.

music box **1**, a box containing clockwork for producing music. **2**, Juke box.

Music Box Revue musical revue by Irving Berlin. Premiere, New York 1921. The revue, which opened the Music Box Theater, had four annual editions.

music drama a term sometimes used to refer to Opera in which music, drama and the staging are of equal importance and conceived to produce a unified whole. See Gesamtkunstwerk.

music hall a type of 19th- and early 20th-c. British musical entertainment similar to Vaudeville, combining musical acts, popular song and drinking.

Musici, I ['moo-zē-chē, ē] (It., the musicians) Italian chamber ensemble of strings and harpsichord formed in 1952 by students from the Accademia di St. Cecilia in Rome. Their repertory includes music of the Italian and German Baroque as well as contemporary works.

Music Library Association Amer. association formed in 1931 to promote the growth of and communication among music libraries in the U.S. Abbr., *MLA*.

music lyre Music stand.

Music Man, The musical by Meredith Willson, from a story by Willson and Franklin Lacey. Premiere, New York 1957. A bogus instr. salesman invades River City, Iowa, and fleeces the citizens until he falls in love with the local librarian.

musico ['moo-zē-kō] (It., musician) **1**, a professional musician. **2**, a Castrato.

musicology the study of music, usu. the history and theory of music.

music stand a small frame or easel with or without extendable legs and often foldable for portability, used for holding music so that it can easily be read by a musician while playing. Also, *music lyre*.

music theater **1**, a general term for a stage presentation combining drama and music. See Opera, Musical comedy, Music drama, Minstrel show, Revue. **2**, a vague term used to distinguish small-scale operatic works, as well as primarily musical works that involve an element of dramatic action or staged performance, from grand opera and its implied excesses.

music therapy the treatment of various physical or psychological illnesses by using music to structure the attention of the patient.

musikalischer Spass, Ein Musical joke, a.

musikalisches Opfer, Ein Musical offering, a.

musique concrète recorded natural sounds and noises, often manipulated electronically, used to create all or part of a musical composition. See Electronic music.

musique mesurée à l'antique [mü'zēk mə-zü'rä ä lä'tēk] (Fr., measured music in the manner of antiquity) a concept devised by Antoine de Baïf for the musical setting of *vers mesurés*, in which the quantitative principles of Latin and Greek were applied to French poetry. Chief exponents of the musical style were Claude le Jeune and Jacques Mauduit.

Mussorgsky, Modest Petrovich (1839–81) highly original Russian composer, stud. of Anton Herke and Balakirev. For much of his life he was in the government service. As a composer he planned much more than he completed; in fact, *Boris Godunov* was the only opera he completed himself. His aim was naturalism and the avoidance of "art for art's sake." Consequently, his orchestration and his harmony had a roughness that others, such as Rimsky-Korsakov, have tried to smooth out. The tendency in recent years, however, has been to return to the original rough-hewn form of his works. Mussorgsky's works incl. *Boris Godunov, Khovanshchina, Sorochintsy Fair* (operas), choral works, *Night on Bald Mountain* and other orchestral works, keyboard works and songs (*The Nursery, Songs and Dances of Death*, many others).

Mustel French harmonium manufacturer founded in 1855 by Victor Mustel (1815–90). His instruments incorporated two new techniques: the "double expression," by which the volume of upper or lower registers can be separately controlled by knee pedals; and the *harpe éolienne*, a tremolo stop produced by two ranks of vibrators tuned slightly higher and slightly lower than the desired pitch level. The company manufactures the Mustel organ as well as celestes and keyboard glockenspiels.

muta (It.) change.

mutation stop a pipe ORGAN STOP producing a pitch a fifth, twelfth, or more above the upper octave of the indicated note. Also, *overtone stop*.

mute a device used to muffle or otherwise modify the sound of a wind or string instrument. For brass instruments, the device is placed in the bell of the instrument. A variety of mutes is available to produce different effects; the most common mutes are the HARMON MUTE, the CUP MUTE, the STRAIGHT MUTE, the SOLOTONE MUTE, the DERBY MUTE and the PIXIE. Mutes for string instruments are placed over the bridge of the instrument to reduce the vibrations conveyed to the sounding body. Mutes are not usually used on woodwind instruments, but such makeshift devices as socks have been used to cover the bell.

mute cornet a straight CORNET (1,) with a built-in mouthpiece and a softer tone, used for consort playing.

Muti, Riccardo (1941–) Italian conductor, trained at the Naples and Milan conservatories. He has been principal conductor of the Maggio Musicale in Florence, the New Philharmonia Orch. and the Philadelphia Orch. (since 1980) and has conducted all major orchestras in Europe and the U.S. in a wide repertory which embraces music of the 18th–20th c.

Muzak (*trademark*) a company founded in 1934 which produces taped background music for use in offices, restaurants, etc.; also, the music produced.

Muzio, Claudia (1889–1936) Italian soprano, daughter of a stage director and a chorister, stud. of Annetta Casaloni. She sang frequently at the Metropolitan Opera (1916–22) and the Chicago Opera (1922–30), as well as in S. America and Italy, and made many recordings. Her repertory included the leading Puccini and Verdi roles.

My Country *also*, **My Fatherland** MÁ VLAST.

My Fair Lady musical by Frederick Loewe, lyrics and book by Alan Jay Lerner, based on Bernard Shaw's *Pygmalion*. Premiere, New York 1956. The adaptation of Shaw's play about a Cockney girl who becomes genteel, had been turned down by practically every other major Broadway figure when Lerner accepted the challenge and produced one of the most successful musicals of all time.

Myaskovsky, Nikolai (1881–1950) Russian composer, stud. of Glier, Krïzhanovsky, Lyadov and Rimsky-Korsakov. He taught at the Moscow Conservatory from 1921 and was a charter member of the Moscow Composers' Collective. His music, considered advanced for its time, includes over 25 symphonies, concertos for violin and cello, string quartets, sonatas, choral music and songs.

My Old Kentucky Home song (1853) by Stephen Foster; the state song of Kentucky.

mystic chord a name coined by Scriabin for the CHORD C-F♯-B♭-E-A-D. The chord, constructed of fourths, was used in his tone poem *Promethée* and is sometimes called the "Promethean chord."

N

N *abbr.* Nebenstimme (N).

Nabokov, Nicholas (1903–78) Russian-born Amer. composer, stud. of Vladimir Rebikov, Yalta, Busoni and Juon. He came to the U.S. in 1933 and taught at Wells College, St. John's College (Annapolis) and the Peabody Conservatory. He also worked for the Voice of America and was active as an organizer of contemporary music festivals. His works incl. 2 operas, 5 ballets, 3 symphonies, choral music and songs.

Nabucco [nä'boo-kō] (It.) opera in 4 acts by Verdi to a libretto in Italian by Temistocle Solera based on the play *Nabucodonosor* by Auguste Anicet-Bourgeois and Francis Cornu. Premiere, Milan 1842. In 6th-c. Jerusalem, Nabucco, King of Babylon, saves his daughter Fenena from execution by praying to Jehovah for help.

nachlassend ['näkh"läs-ənt] (Ger.) Ritardando.

Nachschlag [-shläk] (Ger., afterstrike) **1,** a musical Ornament consisting of one or several short notes played with and in the time of the preceding main note. **2,** the closing note(s) of a trill.

Nachspiel [-shpēl] (Ger., afterplay) Postlude.

Nachtanz [-tänts] (Ger., afterdance) the second of a pair of dances, usu. based on the same musical material as the first dance and in a quick, triple meter. Examples incl. the *galliard*, the *piva* and the *tourdion*.

Nachtmusik ['näkht-moo"zēk] *also,* **Nachtstück** [-shtük] (Ger., night music) Nocturne.

Nachtmusik, Eine kleine Kleine Nachtmusik, Eine.

nafir (Arabic) an end-blown straight Trumpet of the Arab world dating from around the 10th c.

nagaswaram a Shawm of s. India.

Nagel German music publisher founded in 1835 in Hannover.

Nägeli, Hans Georg (1773–1836) Swiss composer and music publisher. He founded a music shop and lending library around 1790 in Zürich and began publishing shortly thereafter, his catalog incl. works of Beethoven, Clementi, Bach, Handel and others. He was founder of several singing organizations in Zürich and traveled giving lectures on musical aesthetics.

nail violin *also,* **nail fiddle, nail harmonica** an unusual 18th-c. musical instrument invented by Johann Wilde consisting of a semicircular sounding board with nails of varying lengths driven into it around its edge and bowed to produce different pitches.

nakers ['nā-kərz] small medieval Kettledrums, usu. used in pairs, worn around the player's waist and played with drumsticks.

Nancarrow, Conlon (1912–) Amer.-born Mexican composer, stud. of Slonimsky, Piston and Sessions. In addition to chamber music, he has written a number of works for player piano, its mechanical nature permitting him to create complex rhythms.

Nance, Ray (Willis) (1913–76) Amer. jazz trumpeter, violinist, singer and dancer. In the 1930s he had his own

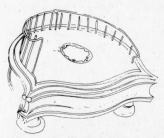

Nail violin

band in Chicago then joined the Duke Ellington orch. from 1940 to 1963.

Nänie ['ne-nē-e] (Ger., dirge) choral ode with orch., Op. 82 (1880–1), by Brahms, to a text by Schiller.

Nanton, Joe (Irish, Joseph N.; "Tricky Sam") (1904–46) Amer. jazz trombonist with the Duke Ellington orch. from 1926, a master of the plunger-mute "growl" style.

naqara [nä'kä-rä] (Arabic) NAKERS.

Nardini, Pietro (1722–93) Italian violinist and composer, stud. of Tartini. During the 1740s and 50s he est. his reputation as a performer and teacher, famous for his tone. He was leader of the ducal orch. in Stuttgart and from 1770 music dir. at the ducal court in Florence. His compositions incl. violin concertos, sonatas for solo violin and string chamber music.

Narváez, Luis de (fl. 1530–50) Spanish composer and vihuela player, attached for some time to the chapel of Philip II of Spain. Aside from two motets, his extant works are for solo vihuela and incl. fantasias, variations and arrangements.

Nashville sound *also*, **Nashville pop** country or pop music produced in Nashville, TN; spec., country music heavily influenced by pop and rock music, a mixture intended to produce a more marketable product. The style is characterized by lush backup strings and vocal choruses.

Nashville Symphony Orchestra orch. founded in 1946 by Walter Sharp (after attempts in 1904 and 1920). Its conductors have included William Strickland, Guy Taylor, Willis Page, Thor Johnson, Michael Charry and Kenneth Schermerhorn.

Nat, Yves (1890–1956) French pianist and composer, stud. of Louis Diémer. He performed throughout Europe and the Americas, specializing in the works of Beethoven and Schumann. He also appeared as accompanist for such artists as Enescu and Ysaÿe. After 1934 he taught at the Paris Conservatoire.

national anthem a song, hymn, march, fanfare or anthem sanctioned by a country as its representative music for official occasions. Like the flag or crest, the anthem is a symbol of its country.

National Arts Centre Orchestra orch. founded in Ottawa, Canada, in 1969, the only fully state-supported orch. in No. America. Many works have been commissioned for the ensemble. Its conductors have been Mario Bernardi, Franco Mannino and Gabriel Chmura.

National Association of Negro Musicians org. founded in Chicago in 1919 to promote interest in Afr.-Amer. music. Abbr., *NANM*.

National Association of Teachers of Singing org. founded in 1944 in Cincinnati, OH, to promote high standards in the teaching of singing. Abbr., *NATS*.

National Barn Dance a country-music radio program broadcast from Chicago on WLS from 1924 to 1960 and on WGN from 1960 to 1970 and carried nationally over the NBC network from 1936.

National Conservatory of Music in America conservatory founded in 1885 in New York by Jeannette Thurber. Despite a distinguished faculty (Dvořák was dir. from 1892 to 1895), the school closed in the late 1920s.

National Endowment for the Arts American governmental agency founded in 1965 in Washington, D.C., as part of the National Foundation on the Arts and the Humanities to provide financial support for the arts. Abbr., *NEA*.

National Federation of Music Clubs a large org. founded in 1898 in Springfield, IL, representing over 5000 musical organizations in the U.S. and Puerto Rico. It sponsors an annual National Music Week and gives scholarships and other awards. Abbr., *NFMC*.

National Institute for Music Theater org. est. in 1969 in Washington, D.C., as the National Opera Institute to encourage the development of music theater in the U.S.

nationalism a movement, occurring

at different times in different countries, focusing on the special musical characteristics of a country and its peoples. The movement is often accompanied by a renewed interest in the folk music of the nation, which is collected and studied and elements of which then become incorporated into the country's art music. During the 19th-century Romantic era there were a number of such movements, especially in Russia (Glinka and others), Hungary (Bartók, Kodály) and Finland (Sibelius), and in the 20th century in America (Ives, Copland, and others).

National Music Camp INTERLOCHEN ARTS ACADEMY.

National Music Council a national org. of music organizations, acting as a forum for the discussion of relevant issues and as an adviser to Congress.

National Opera Association 1, org. founded in 1955 in Washington, D.C., to support opera composition and production. **2**, an opera company in Raleigh, NC, founded in 1948.

National Opera Institute see NATIONAL INSTITUTE FOR MUSIC THEATER.

National Orchestral Association org. founded in 1930 in New York to maintain a training orch. for young musicians. Its music dir. have incl. Leon Barzin, John Barnett and Alvaro Cassuto.

National Peace Jubilee a highly successful five-day musical extravaganza organized in 1869 in Boston by PATRICK GILMORE, held in a specially built 3½-acre coliseum. A ten-day sequel, the World's Peace Jubilee held in 1872, was as much a failure as the first was a success.

National Symphony Orchestra orch. founded in Washington, D.C., in 1931. Its conductors have been Hans Kindler, Howard Mitchell, Antal Dorati and Mstislav Rostropovich.

National Youth Orchestra of Canada a summer training orchestra for highschool- and college-age musicians founded in 1960 by Walter Susskind.

natural a musical sign (♮) placed before (or, editorially, over) a note to indicate the cancellation of a previous sharp or flat (appearing either as an accidental or as part of the key signature) that would have affected the note so marked. During the Middle Ages and Renaissance, a SHARP sign sometimes performed the same function.

natural harmonic see HARMONICS.

natural horn (trumpet) an elementary form of the horn (trumpet) without keys or valves, producing only the pitches in the harmonic series of its fundamental tone.

natural minor scale see MINOR SCALE.

natural notes notes of the harmonic series of a brass instrument obtainable without use of valves, slides or keys.

Naughty Marietta musical by Victor Herbert, lyrics and book by Rida Johnson Young. Premiere, New York 1910. The adventures of Marietta, a Neapolitan who comes to New Orleans and finds true love.

Naudot, Jacques-Christophe [nō'dō] (c1690–1762) French flutist, composer and teacher, known for his many sonatas and concertos for flute and his chamber music for flutes and other instruments.

Naumann, Johann Gottlieb ['nowmän] (1741–1801) prolific German composer and conductor, trained in Dresden, where he spent most of his professional career. His works incl. over 25 operas and other stage works, oratorios and cantatas, Mass settings, songs and solo cantatas, orchestral sinfonias and concertos, chamber music and sonatas for keyboard and for glass harmonica.

Naumburg, Walter W(ehle) (1867–1959) American arts patron. The Walter W. Naumburg Foundation, established in 1924, sponsors annual auditions for performance debuts and is a supporter of recordings and other projects.

Navarra, André(-Nicolas) (1911–88) French cellist, stud. of J. Loeb and

Charles Tournemire. He was a member of the Krettly String Quartet (1929–35), then toured the world as a soloist. He taught at the Paris Conservatoire (from 1949), the Accademia Chigiana in Siena, the Vienna Hochschule für Musik and the Detmold Academy.

Navarro, Fats (Theodore) (1923–50) Amer. jazz bop trumpeter. He played with Andy Kirk, Howard McGhee, Billy Eckstine, Coleman Hawkins and Tadd Dameron. A master of the bop style, Navarro incorporated elements of swing into his playing and is best remembered for the ease of movement in his improvisations.

Nazareth Scottish hard-rock band formed in 1969.

nay a rim-blown FLUTE of Africa and the Near East.

NBC Symphony Orchestra orch. formed in 1937 for Arturo Toscanini and disbanded in 1954 when he retired. Toscanini made many historic broadcasts and recordings with the orch.

NEA NATIONAL ENDOWMENT FOR THE ARTS.

Neapolitan sixth chord a first-inversion major triad based on the lowered second degree of the major scale. It usu. functions like a subdominant (it has the same bass note), preceding a V-I cadence. See CHORD (*illus.*).

Nebenstimme [′nä-bən″shti-me] (Ger., voice) see HAUPTSTIMME.

Neblett, Carol (1946–) American soprano, student of William Vennard, Lotte Lehmann and Pierre Bernac. Her opera debut was with the New York City Opera in 1969. She has sung with leading opera companies and orchestras in roles including Minni (*The Girl of the Golden West*) and Senta (*The Flying Dutchman*).

neck the part of a string musical instrument, usu. narrow, which extends from the body and to which are attached the fingerboard, the pegbox and the strings. See VIOLIN.

Neel, (Louis) Boyd (1905–81) English conductor. He founded the Boyd Neel

Orch. in 1932, which played throughout the world until 1952. In 1953 he went to Canada, became dean of the Royal Conservatory of Music of Toronto and founded the Hart House Orch., which he conducted until his death.

Nef, Isabelle (Lander) (1898–1976) Swiss pianist and harpsichordist, stud. of Philipp, d'Indy and Landowska. She toured throughout the world and taught at the Geneva Conservatory. She also made many recordings.

negrilla [nä′grē-lyä] (Sp.) a VILLANCICO illustrative of the life and music of black people. Also, *canario*.

Negro spiritual see SPIRITUAL.

neighbor note an auxiliary NONHARMONIC NOTE approached by interval of a second from its principal note.

Neikrug, Marc (Edward) (1946–) Amer. composer and pianist, son of the eminent cellist and teacher George Neikrug, stud. of Giselher Klebe. His works incl. several operas, concertos for piano, clarinet and violin, and chamber music.

Nelson Mass *also,* **Lord Nelson Mass** popular name for the Mass in D minor (1798) by Haydn, who titled the work *Missa in Angustiis* (Mass in Time of Need). It is sometimes called the *Imperial Mass* in England.

Nelson, John (1941–) American conductor, student of John Morel. He has been music director of the Indianapolis SO (1976–87) and the Caramoor Festival and a guest conductor at the Metropolitan Opera and elsewhere. He has also taught at the Juilliard School.

Nelson, Willie (Hugh) (1933–) Amer. country and western singer, songwriter and guitarist. He has toured extensively with his band throughout the South and West, has made many recordings and has appeared in several films. His records incl. "On the Road Again," "Georgia on My Mind," "Crazy" and "Honeysuckle Rose."

Nelsova, Zara (Nelson, Sara) (1918–) Canadian-born Amer. cell-

ist, stud. of Herbert Walenn and Casals. She has toured extensively, both
as soloist and in duo with her husband, pianist Grant Johannesen. She
is known for her performance of
20th-c. literature and has had works
written for her by Bloch, Barber and
others.

neo-bop a term for the 1970s revival
of Bop, a reaction against free jazz and
modal jazz.

neo-Classical a style of composition
prevalent in the 1920s and 1930s (and
later) which represented a return to
the forms and thematic techniques of
the Classical period, combined with
dissonant tonal or even atonal harmonies. The principal composer in
the style was Stravinsky, who wrote
many works aptly described as "neo-
Classical," incl. *Pulcinella* (1919–20)
and *The Rake's Progress* (1948–51).

neo-Gallican chant a style of chant
used by a Catholic liturgical movement in France from the 1750s to the
1900s.

neo-Romanticism 1, term for a
movement in Western art music
starting in the late 1960s to relate to
and draw inspiration and sometimes
material from the music of the Romantic era. The movement coincides
with a return to tonal writing. The
tendency can be seen in certain works
of a number of composers, incl. Rochberg and Berio. Also, *new Romanticism*. **2**, a term applied to music of
the 1930s and 1940s by Hindemith,
Prokofiev, and others.

Netherlands Wind Ensemble Dutch
woodwind and brass ensemble
founded in 1960 by students of the
Amsterdam Conservatory.

Neue Bach-Gesellschaft See Bach-
gesellschaft.

neue Sachlichkeit ['noi-e 'zäkh-liç-
kīt] (Ger., new objectivity) a term for
a movement related to Neo-classicism emphasizing the avoidance of
the subjective expression of Romanticism.

Neues vom Tage ['noi-əs fom 'tä-ge]
(Ger., News of the Day) comic opera
in 2 acts by Hindemith to a libretto

by Marcellus Schiffer. Premiere, Berlin 1929. A newly married couple, Eduard and Laura, become "News of the
Day" when they quarrel and decide
to seek a divorce.

Neuhaus, Max ['noi-hows] (1939–)
Amer. avant-garde composer and percussionist, trained at the Manhattan
School. He has performed with such
artists as Boulez and Stockhausen,
but since 1968 he has concentrated
on composing. Many of his works are
sound installations, usu. in highly
public locations.

neuma ['noo-mä] (Lat.) **1**, Neume.
2, a passage of chant without text;
Melisma.

Neumann, Václav (1920–) Czech
conductor and violinist, trained at the
Prague Conservatory. He has held positions with the Czech PO, the Leipzig Gewandhaus Orch., the Leipzig
Opera and the Stuttgart Staatsoper
and is esp. noted for his performances
of Czech repertory, incl. the operas of
Janáček.

neumatic style the setting of plainchant text with one Neume (combining two to four notes in one symbol)
per syllable, intermediate between
syllabic style (one note per syllable)
and *melismatic style* (many notes per
syllable).

neume a graphic notational sign used
mainly during the Middle Ages which
represents pitch and, in some systems, rhythm.

Neusiedler, Hans (c1508–63) German composer, lutanist and lute

Neumes

9th-10th c.

11th-13th c.

modern notation

maker in Nuremberg. He publ. three collections of graded lute music, incl. arrangements, preludes and dances. His son **Melchior Neusiedler** (1531–90) was also a composer, lutanist and lute maker.

Nevada (Wixom), **Emma** (1859–1940) Amer. soprano. Her first operatic successes were in Europe; her Amer. debut was in 1884 in New York. Her roles incl. Amina (*La Sonnambula*) and Lucia, and she also appeared frequently in oratorio. Her daughter, **Mignon Nevada** (1886–1971) was also a soprano, who sang in Italy, England and France such roles as Ophelia (*Hamlet*), Lakmé and Mimì.

Nevin, Ethelbert (Woodbridge) (1862–1901) Amer. composer, trained in Boston and Berlin. He taught and performed in Boston and in Europe and composed songs and works for piano.

Nevin, Arthur (Finlay) (1871–1943) Amer. composer and conductor, brother of ETHELBERT NEVIN, trained in Boston and Berlin. He taught in Pennsylvania until 1910, then at the U. of Kansas and in Memphis, TN. He was interested in the music of the Blackfoot Indians, which influenced his opera *Poia* (1909). He also wrote one other opera, some vocal works and instrumental chamber music.

new age 1, a style of popularized jazz designed for easy listening. **2**, a type of recorded rock or popular music of the 1970s and 1980s making extensive use of noninstrumental electronically synthesized sounds and other high-tech developments and characterized by soft dynamics and relaxed performance.

Newborn, Phineas, Jr. (1931–89) Amer. jazz pianist. He worked and recorded with Charles Mingus, Roy Haynes and others and with his own quartet.

New England Conservatory conservatory founded in 1867 in Boston by Eben Tourjée, by 1878 the largest music school in the U.S. Directors of the school have included Carl Faelton, Chadwick, Harrison Keller, Gunther Schuller, and Lawrence Lesser.

New England Holidays symphony in 4 movements, assembled from four separate works by Ives. The titles of the movements are "Washington's Birthday" (1909), "Decoration Day" (1912), "Fourth of July" (1911–13) and "Thanksgiving and/or Forefathers' Day" (1904).

New England School term introduced by H.W. Hitchcock (1969) for **1**, (*First New England School*) a group of composers or compilers of tune books, active in New England in the late 18th and early 19th c. **2**, (*Second New England School*) a group of composers active in Boston in the late 19th c., incl. Paine, Parker, Chadwick, Beach, etc. Most were trained in Europe and wrote in the European tradition.

New England Triptych orchestral work (1956) by William Schuman, subtitled "Three Pieces for Orchestra After William Billings." The movements, elaborations of Billings's melodies, are "Be Glad Then, America," "When Jesus Wept" and "Chester."

newgrass a popular term for BLUEGRASS MUSIC performed in a more commercial style and incorporating electric instruments.

Newman, Alfred (1900–70) Amer. composer and conductor, stud. of Goldmark, George Wedge, William Daly and Schoenberg. He conducted on Broadway, but soon moved to Hollywood (1930), where he composed scores for over 200 films and was nominated for the Academy Award 45 times, winning nine Oscars. His scores incl. *Street Scene* (1931), *Wuthering Heights* (1939) and *The Robe* (1953).

Newman, Anthony (1941–) Amer. organist, harpsichordist and composer, stud. of Cochereau, Boulanger and Kirchner. He has taught at the Juilliard School, SUNY Purchase and Indiana U. He is an active performer, esp. of Baroque music, and has also composed for chamber ensembles and solo instruments.

Newman, Joe (Joseph Dwight) (1922–) Amer. jazz trumpeter. He played for two years with Lionel Hampton, then joined Count Basie's band, where he stayed for the better part of 20 years. After leaving Basie in 1961 he was involved in Jazz Interactions, a jazz advocacy organization, which he headed for a time and for whose orch. he wrote a number of extended jazz compositions.

New Moon, The musical by Sigmund Romberg, lyrics by Oscar Hammerstein II, book by Hammerstein, Frank Mandel, and Laurence Schwab, based on a true story. Premiere, New York 1928. Robert, an 18th-c. French nobleman wanted for murder, comes to America and establishes a colony on the Isle of Pines.

new music 1, a term variously used to refer to music recently written, music of the current c. or avant-garde music. Cf. MODERN MUSIC. **2**, (cap.) a publishing company founded by Henry Cowell in 1927. Its journal, *New Music*, published new works, usu. by American composers, of artistic but not necessarily commercial interest. The company also produced recordings and sponsored performances. Substantial financial assistance was provided by the composer Charles Ives.

New Orleans jazz a style of jazz dating from before World War I, characterized by small ensembles and group improvisation, related to DIXIELAND JAZZ. The ensemble typically incl. trumpet (usu. the leader), clarinet, trombone, guitar or banjo, drums, piano and bass, and the repertory consisted primarily of blues, rags and marches.

New Orleans Philharmonic Symphony Orchestra orch. founded in New Orleans in 1936. Its conductors have included Arthur Zack, Ole Windingstad, Massimo Freccia, Alexander Hilsberg, James Yestadt, Werner Torkanowsky, Leonard Slatkin, Philippe Entremont and Maxim Shostakovich.

New Orleans Rhythm Kings an Amer. jazz band founded in Chicago in the early 1920s, disbanding by the end of the decade.

New Philharmonia Orchestra PHILHARMONIA ORCHESTRA.

Newport Jazz Festival an important summer jazz festival held in Newport, RI, from 1954 to 1971, after which it moved to New York. Because of corporate sponsorship in the 1980s it was renamed the Kool Jazz Festival then, more recently, the JVC Jazz Festival.

new thing FREE JAZZ.

new wave 1, a style of pop-rock music developed in the mid-1970s as an alternative to HARD ROCK; a milder form of PUNK ROCK. Representative bands incl. Talking Heads, the Cars and Blondie. Cf. NO WAVE. **2**, FREE JAZZ.

New World Records recording company formed in 1975 under a grant from the Rockefeller Foundation to record a comprehensive representation of American music for free distribution to libraries and educational institutions. The project encompassed more than 100 recordings. The project has been completed, but the company has continued to produce recordings.

New World Symphony popular name for the Symphony No. 9 (No. 5 in an older numbering) in E minor, Op. 95 (1893), by Dvořák, subtitled by the composer "From the New World" and written while he was in America.

New York City Opera opera company founded in 1943 in New York as the City Center Opera Company, performing since 1966 at the New York State Theater in Lincoln Center. The company has maintained a reputation for using young American singers and concentrating on ensemble production rather than highlighting star singers. It was the first major American opera co. to employ black singers as principals. Its directors have incl. Laszlo Halász, Josef Rosenstock, Erich Leinsdorf, Julius Rudel, Beverly Sills and Christopher Keene.

New York College of Music conservatory founded in New York in 1878 and absorbed by NYU in 1968.

New York Dolls Amer. glitter-rock group founded in New York in 1971, a precursor of the PUNK ROCK movement.

New York Philharmonic Orchestra orch. founded in New York in 1842, the oldest orch. in continuous existence in the U.S. Its distinguished series of music directors has included Theodore Thomas, Seidl, Walter Damrosch, Mahler, Furtwängler, Toscanini, Erich Kleiber, Walter, Barbirolli, Rodzinski, Mitropoulos, Bernstein, Boulez, Mehta, and Mazur.

New York Pro Musica influential Amer. early music ensemble founded as the Pro Musica Antiqua in 1952 by Noah Greenberg.

New York Woodwind Quintet Amer. woodwind quintet formed in 1947 in New York. The group has premiered many new works and has toured extensively. From 1954 to 1969 the quintet was in residence at the U. of Wisconsin.

New York Symphony orch. founded in New York in 1878 by Leopold Damrosch and later also conducted by his son Walter. It was the first U.S. orch. to tour Europe (1920).

ngoma [əng'gō-mə] an Afr. KETTLEDRUM.

nguru [əng'goo-roo] a Maori wooden VESSEL FLUTE.

Niblock, Phill (1933–) Amer. filmmaker and composer of electronic music. He frequently makes use of conventional instrumental sounds, esp. sustained tones, joined and manipulated electronically. He has taught at CUNY Staten Island since 1976.

Nichols, Red (Ernest Loring) (1905–65) Amer. jazz cornetist and bandleader. He worked primarily with his own groups in the 1920s and 1930s (see THE FIVE PENNIES), having as sidemen over the years a number of important musicians, incl. Jimmy Dorsey, Benny Goodman and Artie Shaw.

nickelodeon a coin-operated player piano or juke box of the 1920s.

Nicolai, (Carl) Otto (Ehrenfried) (1810–49) German conductor and composer, stud. of Zelter and Bernhard Klein. His principal work was in Berlin and in Vienna, where in 1842 he founded the Vienna Philharmonic Concerts with the court opera orch. He is best remembered for his opera *The Merry Wives of Windsor* (1849). Other works incl. operas, choral music, songs, overtures and chamber music.

Nicolet, Aurèle (1926–) Swiss flutist, stud. of Marcel Moyse and Yvonne Drappier. He was principal flute in the Berlin PO under Furtwängler and has taught in Berlin, Freiburg and Basle. Many works have been written for him.

Nicolini (1673–1732) Italian alto castrato. He sang for many years in Italy, then in London from 1708, returning to Italy in 1717. Handel wrote the parts of Rinaldo and Amadigi for him.

Nielsen, Carl (August) (1865–1931) Danish composer, trained with his father and at the Copenhagen Conservatory. He was a violinist of the royal chapel (1889–1905), then became a conductor at the Royal Theater (1908–14), after which he was assoc. with the Copenhagen Conservatory. Nielsen wrote music in all genres, but he is best known as a symphonist and writer of songs. His works incl. 6 symphonies, concertos for flute, violin and clarinet, 2 operas, incidental music, cantatas and other choral works, songs and chamber music.

niente ['nyen-tä] (It.) nothing, silence.

Nigg, Serge (1924–) French composer, stud. of Messiaen and Leibowitz. He was one of the first French serialists, and he mixed serial techniques with polytonal and modal elements. His works are primarily instrumental, incl. several concertos, orchestral works, sonatas for piano and violin and other chamber music.

Night Flight (It., *Volo di Notte*) opera in 1 act by Dallapiccola, based on the novel *Vol de Nuit* by Saint-Exupéry, an autobiographical account of a night flight of a mail plane over the Andes. Premiere, Florence 1940.

Night on Bald Mountain, A orchestral tone poem (1867) by Mussorgsky, a depiction of a witches' sabbath on Mt. Triglaf near Kiev. The orchestration was "revised" by Rimsky-Korsakov, the version most frequently heard today.

Nightingale, The 1, opera in 3 acts by Stravinsky to a libretto by the composer and Stepan Mitusov after the fairy tale by Hans Christian Andersen. Premiere, Paris 1914. **2,** SONG OF THE NIGHTINGALE.

Nights in the Gardens of Spain (Sp., *Noches en los Jardines de España*) symphonic impressions in 3 movements for piano and orch. (1915) by Falla.

Nikisch, Arthur (1855–1922) Hungarian conductor and violinist, trained at the Vienna Conservatory. He played in the Vienna Court Orch., then joined the Leipzig Opera. He conducted the Boston SO from 1889 to 1893, returning to Europe to become conductor of the Leipzig Gewandhaus Orch. and the Berlin PO, shortly thereafter also becoming conductor of the Hamburg Philharmonic concerts. In his day he was the outstanding conductor of Romantic music.

Niles, John Jacob (1892–1980) Amer. singer, folk singer, collector and composer. His training was as an opera singer, but most of his life was spent in the service of folk music. He collected more than 1000 tunes, largely from the Appalachian region, and wrote songs that have been mistaken for folk songs, such as "I Wonder as I Wander" and "Black Is the Color of My True Love's Hair."

Nilsson (Svennsson), **(Märta) Birgit** (1918–) Swedish soprano, stud. of Joseph Hislop. She sang at the Swedish Royal Opera from 1942 and at the Bayreuth festival from 1957 to 1970. Her Covent Garden debut was in 1957 and her U.S. debut in 1956 in San Francisco and 1959 at the Metropolitan Opera. She was famous for her performances of Wagnerian heroines as well as for her portrayals of Electra and Turandot.

Nilsson, Bo (1937–) prolific Swedish composer, largely self-taught as a composer. He has written for both instrumental and vocal forces in a serial style, sometimes employing electronic means.

Nimsgern, Siegmund (1940–) German baritone, stud. of Sibylle Fuchs. He has sung throughout Europe and in the U.S. at the Metropolitan Opera, Chicago Lyric and elsewhere. His roles incl. Don Giovanni, Iago (*Otello*) and Amfortas (*Parsifal*).

Nin-Culmell, Joaquín María (1908–) Amer. composer, pianist and conductor, stud. of Dukas and Falla. In addition to an active concert career, he has taught at Williams College and at the U. of California at Berkeley. His works, in all genres, employ a neo-Classical style incorporating with Spanish elements.

nineteenth an INTERVAL spanning 2 octaves and a fifth.

ninth an INTERVAL spanning an octave and a second.

ninth chord a DOMINANT SEVENTH CHORD with a minor ninth added.

Ninth Symphony although many composers wrote at least nine symphonies, the title usu. refers to the Symphony No. 9 in D minor by Beethoven, also known as the Choral Symphony.

Nin (y Castellanos), Joaquín (1879–1949) Cuban composer and pianist. He studied with Moszkowski in Paris, then returned to Cuba in 1910. He toured widely, performing Bach and early Spanish keyboard music on the piano, being opposed to the use of the harpsichord.

Nitty-Gritty Dirt Band Amer. folkrock group formed in 1966 in California. Renamed the Dirt Band in 1976, it was the first U.S. rock group to tour the Soviet Union (1977).

Nixon, Marni (McEathron, Margaret Nixon) (1930–) Amer. soprano, stud. of Carl Ebert, Jan Popper and Goldovsky. She has worked extensively in film, TV, musical comedy, opera and concert and has recorded many contemporary works.

Nixon, Roger (1921–) Amer. composer, stud. of Schoenberg, Sessions and others. He has taught at San Francisco State College since 1960. His works incl. an opera, works for band and orch., chamber music, and many songs.

Nixon in China historical opera in 2 acts by John Adams to a libretto by Alice Goodman based on President Richard Nixon's epochal trip to China in 1972. Premiere, Houston 1987.

Noack, Fritz (1935–) Amer. organ builder. He worked with Charles Fisk and the Estey Organ Co., then opened his own business in 1960. He has specialized in mechanical tracker-action organs and positive organs.

Noble, Ray(mond Stanley) (1903–78) English composer and bandleader. He came to the U.S. in 1934 and worked in Los Angeles as a broadcaster and bandleader. His songs incl. "The Very Thought of You" and "You'd Be So Easy to Love."

Noble, T(homas) Tertius (1867–1953) English organist and composer, trained at the Royal Conservatory of Music. He was organist of Ely Cathedral and York Minster and then of St. Thomas's Church in New York, where he was in charge of reestablishing a cathedral liturgical tradition, incl. the founding of a celebrated choir school.

Noces, Les [nos, lä] (Fr.) WEDDING, THE.

noch einmal [nokh 'ĭn-mäl] (Ger.) once again.

Noches en los Jardines de España ['nō-chäs än lōs khär'dē-nes dä ä'spä-nyä] (Sp.) NIGHTS IN THE GARDENS OF SPAIN.

nocturn a division of the hour of matins. Three nocturns comprise the MATINS service.

nocturne ['nok-türn] (Fr., night piece) a short, dreamy work, usu. for piano. Also, *notturno* (It.), *Nachtstück* (Ger.).

Nocturnes, (Fr.) three tone poems for women's chorus and orchestra (1899) by Debussy. The titles of the works are *"Nuages"* (Clouds), *"Fêtes"* (Festivals) and *"Sirènes"* (Sirens).

node the point, line or surface in a vibrating body (as an instrument string) that is free from vibration. See OVERTONE (*illus.*).

Noehren, Robert (1910–) Amer. organist, composer and organ builder, stud. of Gaston Dethier and Lynnwood Farnam. He invented a punched-card system for controlling all the pistons of an organ. He has been active as a recitalist and designer and has been organist and choirmaster.

noel [nō'el] a nonliturgical song of Christian joy; esp., a Christmas CAROL. Also, *nowell.*

noire [nwär] (Fr., black) QUARTER NOTE.

noise a collection of sounds having no perceptible pitch and no conventional musical meaning. *White noise* is noise containing an even distribution of all frequencies. *Colored noise* is white noise that has had some frequencies filtered out. Also, *static.* Cf. MUSIC.

Nolan, Bob (1908–80) Amer. country singer and songwriter, a founder of the SONS OF THE PIONEERS.

nondiatonic not utilizing pitches from the major (ionian) scale.

none one of the lesser hours of the DIVINE OFFICE of the Roman Catholic church. The hour of none begins around 3 PM.

nonet 1, a group of nine solo instruments or voices. **2,** music written for such a group.

nonfunctional harmony harmonic writing in which chords do not fulfill their traditional functions (esp. the dominant-to-tonic resolution).

nonharmonic note in traditional part-writing, a note that is not consonant with the other notes of the chord with which it is sounded and that must therefore be resolved to a note that is consonant in the next chord. The following are the most common types of nonharmonic notes: the *passing tone* or *note*, which connects two pitches by conjunct motion by itself or paired with another note; the *anticipation*, an unaccented note or chord that belongs to and is repeated in the following chord; the *échappée*, which intervenes between two notes and is approached by the opposite direction from that of the resolution; the *cambiata*, similar to the *échappée*, which intervenes between two notes but is approached in the same direction; the *auxiliary note* (or *chord*), sometimes known as the *neighbor note* (or *chord*), which ornaments a main note (or chord) a second above or below it and which returns to that note (or chord); and the *appoggiatura*, a nonharmonic note occurring on a strong beat (if the note is not articulated on that beat, it is known as a *suspension*). A passing note, when on a strong beat, is often called an *appoggiatura*, an *accented passing note* or a *nota cambiata*. See table.

non legato a series of notes, separately articulated or bowed.

Non nobis domine (Lat.) a 16th-c. riddle canon in 3 parts, attributed to William Byrd. There are several possible solutions to the riddle.

Nono, Luigi (1924–90) Italian composer, stud. of Malipiero, Maderna and Scherchen. He taught at Darmstadt, where his music first attracted international attention (1954–60) and gave seminars throughout Europe and S. America. His works incl. stage works (*Intolleranza, Al gran sole carico d'amore*), a ballet, vocal works with or without instrumental or electronic accompaniment (incl. *Il canto sospeso*), and works for electronic tape.

No, No, Nanette musical by Vincent Youmans, lyrics by Irving Caesar and Otto Harbach, book by Harbach and Frank Mandel, based on the play *My*

Nonharmonic Notes

Lady Friends by Mandel and Emile Nyitray. Premiere, London 1925. The story of a New York Bible publisher who helps the careers of three girls in three different cities.

nonquartal harmony a term applied to music of the 15th c. in which the vertical interval of a 4th is treated as a dissonance. Nonquartal harmony may be seen in opposition to FAUX-BOURDON, a style of music made up largely of first-inversion chords, with an interval of a fourth occurring between the two upper voices.

noodling informal improvisation on an instrument, as in warming up.

Noone, Jimmie (1895–1944) Amer. jazz clarinetist from New Orleans. He played with Freddie Kleppard, King Oliver and Doc Cook, then led his own band in the 1930s at the Apex Club in Chicago. He was an important—and acknowledged—influence on Benny Goodman and others.

Nordheim, Arne (1931–) Norwegian composer. He studied at the Oslo Conservatory and for eight years was a music critic. From 1962 he was deeply involved with composition employing electronics alone or in combination with live instruments.

Nordica (Norton), **Lillian** (Lilian)

(1857–1914) Amer. soprano, stud. of John O'Neill and Antonio Sangiovanni. She began her operatic career in Europe, toured the U.S. in 1885, then sang principally in England, in opera and oratorio. Her wide range of roles incl. Marguerite (*Faust*), Cherubino (*The Marriage of Figaro*) and Isolde.

Nørgård, Per (1932–) Danish composer. He studied in Copenhagen and with Boulanger in Paris. He has taught at the Copenhagen and Århus conservatories and has been an active leader of young composers in Denmark. He has written works in all genres, some employing tape.

Nørholm, Ib (1931–) Danish composer, trained at the Copenhagen Conservatory. He has taught at that conservatory and served as organist at several churches. His works, which cover all genres, incl. 3 operas, works for orch., many works for chorus or solo voice, chamber music and works for solo piano or organ.

Norma tragic opera in 4 acts by Bellini to a libretto by F. Romani, based on the tragedy by L.A. Soumet. Premiere, Milan 1831. Norma, a high priestess of the Druids, has secretly married Pollione, who now loves Adalgisa; Norma magnanimously offers herself as a sacrifice to the gods and is joined on the pyre by a repentant Pollione.

Norman, Jessye (1945–) Amer. soprano, stud. of Carolyn Grant, Elizabeth Mannion and others. She is equally acclaimed as an operatic and concert artist, esp. in works of Strauss, Wagner, Berlioz and Mahler and the Second Viennese School.

Norrington, Roger (Arthur Carver) (1934–) English conductor, stud. of Sir Adrian Boult. He founded the Heinrich Schütz Choir in 1962, which later became the Schütz Choir of London. He is esp. known for his performances of Baroque and Classical repertory.

North, Alex (1910–91) Amer. conductor and composer. A composer of widely varied experiences, he has worked in the Soviet Union, the U.S. and Mexico. His *Revue* for clarinet and orch. was premiered by Benny Goodman with the New York PO. In the 1940s and 1950s he wrote many film scores, the best known of which were for *A Streetcar Named Desire* (1951), *Viva Zapata!* (1952), *The Long, Hot Summer* (1958) and others, some with jazz elements or unusual instruments. He has also written ballets, incidental music, and vocal and instrumental concert music.

North Carolina School of the Arts a state-supported school for the performing arts in Winston-Salem, NC, founded in 1965.

Northwestern University School of Music conservatory (part of Northwestern U., Evanston, IL) founded in 1895 under Peter C. Lutkin. It was one of the first music schools in the U.S. to grant music degrees.

Norvo, Red (Norville, Kenneth) (1908–) Amer. jazz xylophonist and vibraphonist. He played with Paul Whiteman and Charlie Barnet, then led his own orch. with his wife, MILDRED BAILEY. During the late 1940s he played with Benny Goodman, then in the 1950s he led various groups with such bop greats as Tal Farlow, Jimmy Raney and Charles Mingus. In the 1970s and 1980s he toured widely in Europe.

Norwegian Dances four orchestral dances, Op. 35 (1881), by Grieg.

nose flute a side- or end-blown FLUTE sounded by breath from one nostril instead of from the mouth, the other nostril being plugged (as with a rag) or closed with a finger. The instrument is common in the Polynesian islands.

No Strings music and lyrics by Richard Rodgers, book by Samuel Taylor. Premiere, New York 1962. An innovative musical, the story of an interracial romance between a black fashion model and a novelist.

nota cambiata ['nō-tä käm-bē'ä-tä] (It., changed note) **1,** *also,* **Berardian cambiata** an accented passing note (see NONHARMONIC NOTE). **2,** *also,*

Fuxian cambiata an unaccented NON-HARMONIC NOTE left by leap of a third downwards. Also, *changing note*.

notation a means for representing musical sounds, whether graphic, literal, verbal or pictoral. See the accompanying illustration for some traditional and nontraditional methods of notation. See also BRAILLE NOTATION, NEUME, SHAPE NOTE, SOLMIZATION, TABLATURE, TONIC SOL-FA, MENSURAL NOTATION, GRAPHIC NOTATION, PROPORATIONS.

notch flute *also*, **notched flute** an end-blown FLUTE with a V- or U-shaped notch cut in the rim of its blowhole.

note 1, a single sound of a specific PITCH and duration. Also, *tone*. **2**, the sign representing this sound.

note blanche [not blāsh] (Fr.) HALF NOTE.

note noire [nwär] (Fr.) QUARTER NOTE.

note row ROW.

Notation
(see also NOTES AND RESTS, CLEFS, EXPRESSION MARKS, ABBREVIATIONS)

Notes and Rests

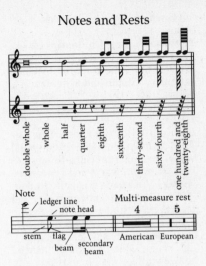

notes inégales [not zē-nā'gäl] (Fr., unequal notes) a rhythmic convention of the 16th- to 18th c., esp. in France, specifying that values notated as equal be played as alternately long and short rhythms.

note value the duration of a certain sound as indicated by a specific graphic sign. See NOTES (*illus.*).

Notre Dame school modern name for a group of musicians in Paris in the late 12th and early 13th c., thought to be assoc. with the Cathedral of Notre Dame. See LÉONIN, PÉROTIN.

Notte, La ['not-tā, lä] (It.) title for three works by Vivaldi: the bassoon concerto in B♭ major, RV501; the flute concerto in G minor, RV439; and the quartet for flute, violins and bassoon in G minor, RV104.

notturno [nōt'toor-nō] (It., nocturnal) an 18th-c. SERENADE or DIVERTIMENTO to be performed in the late evening.

Nourrit, Adolphe [noo'rē] (1802–39) French dramatic tenor, stud. of García. Rossini, Auber, Halévy and others composed major roles for him. He was considered a great actor as well as one of the great tenors.

novachord an early form of electronic piano using vacuum tubes to produce tones imitating the sound of the piano, organ, violin, etc. It was invented in 1939 by Laurens Hammond.

Novaës (Pinto), **Guillomar** (1895–1979) Brazilian pianist, stud. of Isidor Philipp, esp. known for her interpretations of Chopin and Schumann.

Novák, Jan (1921–) Czech composer, trained at the Brno Conservatory and at Tanglewood. He lived in Brno until 1968; since then he has lived in Italy. He has written choral works, chamber music, a ballet, several orchestral works and concertos.

Novák, Vítězslav (Augustin Rudolf) (1870–1949) Czech composer and teacher. He studied at the Prague Conservatory in Dvořák's master class. He became active in collecting folk songs, which greatly influenced and revitalized his composition. He wrote in all genres, with instrumental and choral music predominating earlier in his career and stage works appearing in his later years.

novelette (Fr.) a free-form romantic work for piano, usu. having a number of contrasting sections.

Novello, Clara (Anastasia) (1818–1908) English soprano, daughter of VINCENT NOVELLO. A celebrated concert singer before she was 21, she then studied opera in Italy and appeared for a short while on the operatic stage. From 1851 she enjoyed a successful oratorio career, retiring in 1860. She was a close friend of Rossini.

Novello, Ivor (Davies, David Ivor) (1893–1951) British composer of songs and musical comedies, the best known of which was *The Dancing Years* (1939). He also wrote the popular wartime song "Keep the Home Fires Burning."

Novello, Vincent (1781–1861) English composer, organist, conductor and publisher, organist for the Portuguese embassy chapel in London for 25 years. His publishing activities began in 1811 and specialized in vocal scores of works by Haydn, Mozart and others.

Novello & Co. English music publisher based in London, founded in 1829 by Alfred Novello (1810–96), son of VINCENT NOVELLO.

Novello-Davies, Clara (1861–1943) Welsh singing teacher and choral conductor, mother of IVOR NOVELLO. She founded and conducted the Welsh Ladies' Choir, which toured Europe and the U.S. with great success.

novelty piano a term of the 1920s for various types of piano music based on RAGTIME.

Nowak, Lionel (1911–) Amer. pianist and composer, stud. of Edwin Fischer, Herbert Elwell, Sessions and Porter. He has taught at Fenn College, Converse College, Syracuse U. and Bennington College. His works incl. music for the dance, concertos, chamber music, songs and works for right hand alone.

no wave an avant-garde variety of PUNK ROCK developed in New York in the late 1970s and characterized by the rough, loud, often atonal music of such groups as Captain Beefheart and DNA.

Noye's Fludde (Old Eng., Noah's Flood) a Chester miracle play in 1 act with music by Britten. Premiere, Aldeburgh 1958. Designed to be performed by professionals and children, the play tells the story of Noah and his ark.

Nozze di Figaro, Le ['not-sä dē 'fē-gä-rō, lä] (It.) MARRIAGE OF FIGARO, THE.

nuance [nü'äs] (Fr.) variety of dynamic, articulation, tempo, etc.; usu. in the phrase *sans nuance* (Fr.), uniform, expressionless.

Nuits d'été, Les [nüē dä'tä, lä] (Fr., Summer Nights) cycle of six songs, Op. 7 (1841), by Berlioz to poems from *La comédie de la mort* by Théophile Gautier. The songs were later orchestrated by the composer, forming one of the first orchestral song cycles. The six songs are "Villanelle," "Le spectre de la rose" (the specter of the rose), "Sur les lagunes" (on the lagoons), "Absence," "Au cimetière" (in the cemetery) and "L'île inconnue" (the unknown island).

number 1, a work performed, esp. a song in jazz or popular music. **2**, a self-sufficient section within an opera, usu. consisting of a recitative or scena and an aria or ensemble.

number opera a term for an opera consisting of a series of NUMBERS (2,), as opposed to an opera in which each act consists of a continuous musical texture. Among the finest examples of the form are the 18th-c. operas of Handel and Mozart, the 19th-c. operas of Rossini and Donizetti, and some 20th-c. operas such as Stravinsky's *The Rake's Progress* (1951).

nunc dimittis [nûnk di'mi-tis] (Lat.) the canticle of Simeon, "Lord, now lettest thou thy servant depart in peace" (Luke ii:29–32), sung during compline in the divine office of the Roman Catholic rite and during evensong in the Protestant Anglican rite.

nun's fiddle TRUMPET MARINE.

Nuove musiche, Le ['nwo-vā 'moo-sē-kā, lā] (It., the new music) an innovative collection of monodic songs by Giulio Caccini, publ. in 1602 with an important explanatory foreword by the composer.

nuovo ['nwo-vō] (It.) new. **—di nuovo**, [dē] (It.) again.

nut 1, in string instruments, the grooved ridge of wood or ivory over which the strings pass, near the upper end of the fingerboard below the pegbox. See VIOLIN. **2**, FROG.

Nutcracker, The ballet, Op. 71 (1892), by Tchaikovsky based on a fairy tale by E.T.A. Hoffman and first choreographed by Ivanov. Tchaikovsky arranged an orchestral suite from the ballet, consisting of a Miniature Overture, March, Dance of the Sugar-Plum Fairy, Russian Dance (Trepak), Arab Dance, Chinese Dance, Dance of the Flutes and Waltz of the Flowers.

nyckelharpa (Swed.) a Swedish, folk, bowed FIDDLE whose strings are stopped mechanically by means of keys.

Nygaard, Jens (1931–) Amer. pianist and conductor. He conducted the series "Music in Our Time" at Columbia and founded the Westchester, NY, Chamber Chorus and Orchestra. He also co-founded the Jupiter SO and has been conductor of the Naumburg SO and the Rutgers U. SO.

Nyro, Laura (1947–) Amer. rhythm-and-blues and gospel singer and songwriter. She has had a number of successful albums, incl. *Eli and the Thirteenth Confession* (1968) and *New York Tendaberry* (1969) and has had songs recorded by Barbra Streisand, the Fifth Dimension and others.

O

O 1, Open. **2,** in Mensural notation, a sign for *perfect time*, or triple division of the breve.

obbligato [ōb-blē'gä-tō] (It., obligatory) not to be omitted; the term usu. refers to a prominent part played by a solo instrument accompanying a principal melody.

oberek *also,* **obertas** (Polish) a Polish folk dance related to the Mazurka and with acrobatic and march steps in a quick triple meter.

Oberlin, Russell (Keys) (1928–) Amer. countertenor and teacher, a founding member of the New York pro musica and a frequent performer in opera and concert. Since 1971 he has taught at Hunter College in New York.

Oberlin College Conservatory of Music a conservatory founded in 1865 at Oberlin College, Oberlin, OH, by John P. Morgan and George W. Steele.

Oberwerk ['ō-bər"verk] (Ger., upper section) the upper manual and chest of a German Organ, sometimes equipped with shutters.

oblique motion in Counterpoint, the movement of one part in one direction against a stationary second part.

oboe 1, a soprano double-reed woodwind instrument developed in the 17th c. from the treble Shawm, prob. by the Hotteterre family. The instrument has three sections and a conical bore. The player forces air through a small opening between two shaped pieces of cane (a *reed*) mounted on a *staple* and held tightly by the lips, causing the cane to vibrate. **2,** a family of instruments similar to the oboe, incl. the English horn, Oboe d'amore, Baritone oboe and Musette.

oboe da caccia [dä 'kät-chä] (It., oboe of the hunt) a tenor Oboe, forerunner of the English horn.

oboe d'amore [dä'mō-rā] (It., oboe of love) an alto Oboe in A with a pear-shaped bell and a darker tone than the oboe, pitched a minor 3rd lower.

Oborin, Lev (1907–74) Russian pianist and teacher, stud. of Elena Gnesina and Konstantin Igumnov. He won the first Warsaw Competition in 1927 and toured widely. He taught at the Moscow Conservatory, where his pupils incl. Ashkenazy.

obra ['ō-brä] (Sp.) a musical work.

Obraztsova, Elena (1937–) Russian mezzo-soprano, trained at the Leningrad Conservatory. Her U.S. debut was in San Francisco in 1957, and she has also sung at the Metropolitan Opera, Chicago Lyric and La Scala, in addition to the Bolshoi Opera. Her roles incl. Carmen, Marfa (*Khovanshchina*) and Hélène (*War and Peace*).

Obrecht, Jacob (c.1450–1505) Franco-Flemish composer of masses, motets and chansons, one of the most important contemporaries of Josquin des Prez. His principal positions were at Cambrai cathedral, Notre Dame at Antwerp and in his home town of Bergen op Zoom.

O'Brien, Eugene (1945–) Amer. composer, stud. of Robert Beadell, B. A. Zimmermann, John Eaton and Xenakis. He has taught at the Cleveland Institute since 1973. His works incl. a symphony, concertos, works for chamber ensemble and vocal works, among them an *Elegy for Bernd Alois Zimmermann (Pss.)*.

O Canada! national anthem of Canada (1880), with music by Calixa Lavallée (1842–91) to a French text by Adolphe-Basile Routhier. The anthem was approved in 1967 but not officially adopted until 1980. The accepted English translation (1908) is by Robert Stanley Weir.

ocarina [ō-kä′rē-nä] (It., little goose) a VESSEL FLUTE with a whistle head, made in various shapes of terracotta or plastic, having a mouthpiece and finger holes. Also, *sweet potato.*

occasional music music written for performance at or on a specific occasion, such as a wedding or coronation.

Ochs, Phil(ip David) (1940–76) Amer. folk singer and songwriter. He performed in the 1960s as a protest singer with Bob Dylan and others so much that he was banned from radio and TV for a time. During the 1970s he lived mostly abroad. His recordings incl. *All the News that's Fit to Sing* (1964) and *I Ain't Marchin' Anymore* (1965).

Ockeghem, Johannes (Jean, Jehan) (c1415–1497) Franco-Flemish composer, one of the masters of the later 15th c. From the mid-1440s he was in the service of the Bourbon court for about a decade, then joined the French court of Charles VII. His surviving works incl. masses, motets and chansons. Josquin wrote the déploration *Nymphes des bois* in honor of Ockeghem upon his death.

Octandre [ok′tā-dr] (Fr.) work in 3 movements for wind septet and double bass (1924) by Varèse, named after the flower, which has eight stamens.

octave 1, an INTERVAL comprising 8 diatonic degrees. The octave is the simplest acoustic interval, having a ratio of 2:1, and represents the interval between a note and its first overtone (see HARMONICS). It is the only interval that is pure in the tempered system. **2**, a note an octave above or below another note. **3**, a CHORD comprising two notes separated by an octave. **4**, an ORGAN STOP producing tones an octave above the fingered pitch.

octavin a single-reed ww. instrument invented in 1894, having elements of the saxophone, clarinet and bassoon and a sound similar to that of the soprano saxophone.

octet 1, a group of eight players, often of instruments of the same family, as a wind octet. **2**, a work written for such a group.

octobass a large DOUBLE BASS with three strings stopped mechanically by fingered keys and pedals.

October, To the Symphony No. 2 in B major (1927) by Shostakovich.

octotonic of a SCALE, consisting of eight notes to the octave; esp., consisting of eight notes alternating whole steps and half steps.

octuor [′ok-tüôr] (Fr.) OCTET.

o-daiko (Jap.) Jap. double-headed WAISTED DRUM used in Shinto rites.

O'Day, Anita (Colton, Anita Belle) (1919–) Amer. jazz singer. She appeared frequently with the Gene Krupa and Stan Kenton bands, then became a successful solo artist. She is esp. noted for her scat improvising.

O'Day, Molly (Williamson, LaVerne) (1923–) Amer. country-music singer and instrumentalist specializing in religious works. A successful recording artist in the 1940s, she retired from music in the early 1950s to be an evangelist.

ode 1, a CANTICLE of the Eastern Orthodox church. **2**, in classical antiquity, a lyric poem intended to be sung. During the Renaissance, a number of composers set Horatian odes to music in a humanistic attempt to reconstruct Greek musical practices. The English ode, dating from the mid-17th c., was an extended cantata, usu. a song of praise to the reigning monarch or to St. Cecilia (see ST. CECILIA'S DAY).

Ode to Napoleon Buonaparte work for speaker, strings and piano, Op. 41 (1942), by Schoenberg, based on a poem by Byron against Napoleon. The work tacitly invited comparison between Hitler and Napoleon.

Ode to the West Wind a cello concerto (1953) by Henze in five sections which correspond to the five stanzas of Shelley's poem that inspired it.

Odetta (Gordon, Odetta Holmes Felious) (1930–) Amer. folk singer and guitarist, an influential recording and concert artist from the mid-1950s. She has toured throughout the world and has appeared on TV and in films.

Odhecaton A a collection of chansons (*Harmonice musices Odhecaton A*) published by Petrucci in 1501 in Venice, the first printed collection of polyphonic music. It contains 96 chansons by Josquin, Ockeghem, Busnois and others.

Oedipus Rex ['e-di-pûs reks] (Lat., Oedipus the King) opera-oratorio in 2 acts by Stravinsky to a libretto in French by Jean Cocteau translated into Latin by J. Danielou, based on Sophocles' play. Premiere, Paris 1927.

œuvre ['œvr] (Fr.) a musical work.

offbeat a weak beat of a metrical pattern, not the first beat (*downbeat*). The offbeat preceding the downbeat is called the UPBEAT. Cf. AFTERBEAT.

Offenbach, Jacques (Jacob) (1819–80) German-born French composer and cellist, the most important force in establishing operetta as an international genre. He studied in Cologne and in Paris, then joined the orch. of the Opéra-Comique, where he played until 1838, after which he performed as a cello virtuoso soloist. He became conductor of the Théâtre Français in 1850, then opened his own Bouffes Parisiens in 1855, which enjoyed great success. He spent his final years working on his opera *Les Contes d'Hoffmann*, left unfinished at his death. His works incl. *La Vie Parisienne, La Grande-Duchesse de Gérolstein, La Périchole, Orphée aux Enfers* and over 90 other operettas, *Les Contes d'Hoffmann* (opéra-comique), German and French songs, ballets, vaudevilles, works for accompanied and solo cello, dance music.

offertory one of the chants of the Proper of the MASS. It is sung after the Mass of the Catechumens and begins the Communion of the Faithful.

office, divine DIVINE OFFICE.

Of Mice and Men tragic opera in 3 acts by Carlisle Floyd to his own libretto, based on the Steinbeck novel and play. Premiere, Seattle 1970. The story of two migrant workers, George and Lennie, in the Salinas Valley of California.

Of Thee I Sing musical by George Gershwin, lyrics by Ira Gershwin, book by George S. Kaufman and Morrie Ryskind. Premiere, New York 1931. In this satire of political and cultural institutions, John P. Wintergreen runs for president on a platform of Love.

Ogdon, John (Andrew Howard) (1937–89) English pianist and composer, stud. of Egon Petri, Denis Matthews and others. He was a co-winner of the Tchaikovsky Competition in 1962. He performed a very broad repertory, equally rich in Viennese classics, the Romantics and 20th-c. music.

Ogdon, Will (Wilbur Lee) (1921–) Amer. composer and musicologist, stud. of Krenek, Sessions and Manfred Bukofzer in the U.S. and Honegger in Paris. He has taught at the U. of Texas at Austin, Wesleyan U. at Bloomington (IL) and at the U. of California at San Diego. His works incl. an opera, songs with instruments and chamber music.

Ohana, Maurice (1914–) French composer and pianist, stud. of Daniel-Lesur, Casella and others. His wide range of interests has included study of medieval and ancient African and Mediterranean music. In 1947 he founded a new music group in Paris, Zodiaque, and also worked with Dutilleux and Pierre Schaeffer. He has taught at the École Normale de Musique in Paris. His works incl. a chamber opera, *Autodafé* (opera), works for dance, radio and film scores, *Llanto por Iganacio Sanchez Majias* (oratorio), songs, instrumental chamber music and concertos.

Oh, Boy! musical by Jerome Kern, lyrics by P.G. Wodehouse, book by Guy Bolton and Wodehouse. Premiere, New York 1917. One of the seven "Princess Theatre musicals," the story is one of marital misunderstanding with a happy ending.

Oh, Kay! musical by George Gershwin, lyrics by Ira Gershwin, book by Guy Bolton and P.G. Wodehouse. Premiere, New York 1926. Kay (orig. played by Gertrude Lawrence), the sister of a titled English bootlegger, comes to Long Island to be near playboy Jimmie Winter.

Ohlsson, Garrick (1948–   ) Amer. pianist, stud. of Rosina Lhévinne. He was the first American to win the Warsaw Chopin Competition (1970). He is esp. known for his performances of works of Scriabin and Chopin.

Oiseau de feu, L' [lwä'zō də fø] (Fr.) FIREBIRD, THE.

Oiseau-Lyre, L' L'OISEAU-LYRE.

Oiseaux exotiques [wä'zō zeg-zō'tēk] (Fr., exotic birds) orchestral tone poem (1956) by Messiaen, recreating the sounds of over forty different bird calls.

Oistrakh, David (1908–74) Russian virtuoso violinist and conductor, stud. of Pyotr Stolyarsky. In addition to a distinguished solo career in the Soviet Union and abroad, he taught from 1934 at the Moscow Conservatory. He was noted for his performance of new works, and many Russian composers wrote for him. His son, **Igor Oistrakh** (1931–   ), who studied with him, is also a gifted violinist and performed many times with his father in violin duo or with his father conducting.

Ojai Festival an annual spring festival of concerts given since 1947 at Ojai, CA, emphasizing rare works of Western music.

okedo (Jap.) a Jap. folk CYLINDRICAL DRUM used in the Kabuki theater.

Oklahoma! musical by Richard Rodgers, lyrics and book by Oscar Hammerstein II, based on Lynn Rigg's play *Green Grow the Lilacs*. Premiere, New York 1943. In the Indian Territory in the early 1900s, Curly and Jud are rivals for the hand of Laurey Williams. The title song is the state song of Oklahoma.

Olcott, Chauncey (Chancellor John) (1858–1932) Amer. singer, composer and lyricist, a popular performer in operetta, esp. in Irish roles. He wrote "My Wild Irish Rose" (1899) and the lyrics for "When Irish Eyes are Smiling" (1912) and "Mother Machree" (1911). He also wrote the scores for several operettas.

Old American Opera Company the Amer. arm of William Hallam's London opera troupe, formed in 1752 in VA.

Old Folks at Home song (1851), also known as "Swanee River," by Stephen Foster, written for Christy's Minstrels. It is the state song of Florida.

old-folks concert a type of 19th-c. entertainment reviving the practices and tunes of 18th-c. hymnody, as exemplified in the New England SINGING-SCHOOL.

Old Hall MS a MS collection of late 14th-c. and early 15th-c. sacred music, compiled by a single scribe in the early 15th c. and containing mostly works by English composers.

Old Harp Singers hymn singers who use the 1848 Tennessee tunebook *The Harp of Columbia*. Cf. SACRED HARP SINGERS.

Old Hundredth hymn tune by Louis Bourgeois, written in 1551 for Psalm 134 in the Genevan Psalter; later, in 1560 and thereafter, it was used to set the English translation of Psalm 100, "All people that on earth do dwell."

Old Maid and the Thief, The comic opera in 1 act by Menotti to his own libretto. Premiere, NBC radio 1939; stage premiere, Philadelphia 1941. The elderly Miss Todd falls in love with an escaped prisoner and tries to protect him from the police.

old way of singing a term for a type of Protestant hymn singing, related to LINING OUT, in which the congregation sings in an extremely slow tempo, with rhythmic drive, sometimes ornamenting individual notes. The practice probably originated in the 16th c. and is still found in some regions of the U.S.

olio 1, a series of specialty acts, usu. serving as the finale to a minstrel or burlesque show. **2,** MEDLEY.

oliphant *also,* **olifant** a medieval end-blown HORN of Eastern origin carved from an elephant tusk, used for ceremonial purposes or as a reliquary.

Oliver! musical by Lionel Bart, based on Charles Dickens's novel *Oliver Twist*. Premiere, London 1960.

Oliver, King (Joseph) (1885–1938) influential Amer. jazz cornetist and bandleader from New Orleans. In 1922 in Chicago he formed his Creole Jazz Band, of which Louis Armstrong was for a while a member. After the group disbanded in 1927, he worked in New York and toured with various groups.

Oliver, Sy (Melvin James) (1910–88) Amer. composer and arranger. He worked with Jimmie Lunceford and Tommy Dorsey and later led his own band, playing for some years at the Rainbow Room in New York. He also arranged scores for TV and films.

Olivero, Magda (Maria Maddalena) (c1913–) Italian soprano, trained at the Turin Conservatory and with Ghedini. She sang throughout Italy until 1941, then retired for almost ten years, until the composer Cilea convinced her to return to the stage in 1951. Her U.S. debut was in Dallas in 1967; she did not sing at the Metropolitan Opera until 1975, when she was over 60. Her roles incl. Tosca, Minnie (*The Girl of the Golden West*) and Adriana Lecouvreur.

Oliveros, Pauline (1932–) Amer. composer, instrumentalist and performer, stud. of Paul Koepke, Robert Erickson and William Palmer. She has taught at the U. of California at San Diego and has been active in the development of electronic music and mixed media works. Her own works employ these forces as well as acoustic instruments and incl. theater and film scores, chamber music, vocal music and music for electronic tape.

olla podrida ['ō-lyä pō'thrē-thä] (Sp., rotten pot) PASTICCIO.

ombgwe a So. Afr. VESSEL FLUTE.

omnitonic horn an early 19th-c. HORN with a number of different crooks built into its coils, selected by a slide and dial.

ONCE an assoc. of avant-garde composers and artists formed in the late 1950s by Robert Ashley and active until around 1970. The group produced an annual festival in Ann Arbor, MI.

ondes martenot [ōd mär-tə'nō] *also,* **ondes musicales, ondium martenot** (Fr., Martenot's *or* musical waves) an ELECTRONIC INSTRUMENT, invented in Paris in 1928 by Maurice Martenot (1898–1980), capable of producing MICROTONES, played either from a keyboard or with a sliding ribbon controller. The transducer (speaker) is equipped with sympathetic strings, which add duration and color to the sound. The instrument produces one pitch at a time; chords are not possible. A number of composers have written for the ondes martenot, incl. Messiaen, Varèse and Jolivet.

one-step a type of ballroom dance of the 1910s associated with RAGTIME music and made popular by the dancing team of Vernon and Irene Castle.

ongarese, all' [äl-lōn-gä'rä-zä] (It.) in the Hungarian style; an indication to play in the Gypsy manner.

On Hearing the First Cuckoo in Spring one of a pair of works for small orchestra (1912) by Delius, using the clarinet to evoke the cuckoo and incorporating a Norwegian folk tune, "In Ola Valley." The other work is *Summer on the Night River* (1911).

On the Town musical by Leonard Bernstein, lyrics and book by Betty Comden and Adolph Green, from an idea by Jerome Robbins. Premiere, New York 1944. Based on the ballet *Fancy Free*, the story covers a day in the life of three sailors in New York.

On Your Toes musical by Richard Rodgers, lyrics by Lorenz Hart, book by Rodgers, Hart and George Abbott. Premiere, New York 1936. The show includes an early use of ballet as a central element, in the extensive "Slaughter on Tenth Avenue," with choreography by Balanchine. In the story, an ex-vaudeville hoofer takes the lead in a modern ballet.

One Touch of Venus musical by Kurt

Weill, lyrics by Ogden Nash, book by S.J. Perelman and Ogden Nash, based on *The Tinted Venus* by F. Anstey. Premiere, New York 1943. A statue of Venus comes to life and falls in love with a barber. The part of Venus, played by Mary Martin in her first Broadway starring role, was orig. intended for Marlene Dietrich.

op. *abbr.* OPUS.

op. posth. *abbr.* OPUS POSTHUMOUS.

open not muted; in horn writing, a direction to discontinue hand stopping. See OPEN NOTE (3,).

open fifth a root-position triad which is lacking a third.

open form a musical form that does not end with a conclusive ending formula or cadence.

open harmony OPEN POSITION.

open note 1, a NOTE with an outline head, such as a half note. 2, *also,* **open tone** a natural harmonic tone on a brass instrument. 3, an unstopped note, as on the horn or a stringed instrument (see OPEN STRING), indicated by the sign (°) over the note.

open position *also,* **open harmony** an arrangement of the notes of a chord in which the upper parts encompass an octave or more. Opposed to CLOSE HARMONY.

open score a SCORE in which each instrumental part has its own staff. Cf. CLOSE SCORE.

open shake MORDENT.

open string an unstopped string on a stringed instrument. Also, *open note.*

Oper (Ger.) OPERA.

opera (It., work) a type of musical dramatic work in which the characters sing all or most of their lines. The form is generally considered to have originated in early 17th-c. Italy. The distinction commonly made between opera and MUSICAL COMEDY or MUSIC THEATER and between opera and OPERETTA is not always clear-cut. Musical comedy and operetta are usu. lighter in subject matter and musical treatment, and the proportion of dialogue to sung text is generally higher than in opera. Music theater may place a higher degree of importance

on the dramatic element than that in many opera productions. Nevertheless, all the forms share the special attribute of opera, which is that it combines the visual, aural and performing arts in one elaborate unity.

Until the mid-19th c. most operas consisted of several acts, each composed of a sequence of arias and ensembles connected by plot-advancing dialogue or RECITATIVE (see NUMBER OPERA). During the 19th c. there was a gradual development toward more through-composed works, where the distinction between set pieces and recitative tended to blur more and more.

Outstanding opera composers of the 17th c. incl. Monteverdi and Lully; of the 18th c., Gluck, Handel and Mozart; of the 19th c., Rossini, Bellini, Berlioz, Donizetti, Massenet, Meyerbeer, Pergolesi, Tchaikovsky, Verdi and Wagner; of the 20th c. Barber, Berg, Britten, Henze, Janáček, Maxwell Davies, Menotti, Puccini and R. Strauss.

In addition to those mentioned above, other relatives of opera are: BALLAD OPERA, COMÉDIE-BALLET, DIVERTISSEMENT, INTERMEZZO, MASQUE, MELODRAMA, PUPPET OPERA, OPÉRA-BALLET, SERENATA, SINGSPIEL, VAUDEVILLE and ZARZUELA.

opéra-ballet (Fr.) a type of late 17th-c. and early 18th-c. French OPERA consisting of a prologue and several acts or entrées, each independent but related to the general topic of the work.

opéra bouffe [boof] (Fr.) a type of OPÉRA-COMIQUE with spoken dialogue between the numbers, developed by Offenbach in the mid-19th c.

opera buffa ['boo-fä] (It.) 18th-c. Italian comic opera with sung recitative rather than spoken dialogue.

opéra-comique [ko'mēk] (Fr.) 18th-c. and 19th-c. French OPERA with spoken dialogue. The term orig. referred to comic opera, but later came to cover romantic works and tragedies as well.

Opéra-Comique (Fr.) **1,** SALLE FA-

VART. **2**, (Théâtre National de l'Opéra-Comique) opera company formed in 1801 through the amalgamation of the Favart and Feydeau companies. It has had as its home several theaters, the latest being the Salle Favart, sometimes known as the Opéra-Comique.

opera house a theater designed primarily for opera or where opera is performed.

opera semiseria ["sä-mē'sä-rē-ä] (It.) a type of melodramatic Italian opera falling between tragedy and comedy, between grand opera and operetta. The form was current from the late 18th c. through the 19th c.

opera seria (It., serious opera) a term used to refer to Italian heroic or tragic opera of the 18th and early 19th c.

Opera Theatre of St. Louis opera company in St. Louis, MO, founded by Richard Gaddes in 1976. It is esp. known for its productions of American opera.

operetta (It., little opera) a form of light OPERA with spoken dialogue, short songlike arias and dance, developed in the mid-19th c. and flourishing into the first quarter of the 20th c. in the U.S. and to the present in Europe. The most noted composers in the form incl. Offenbach and Adam in France, the Johann Strausses and Franz Lehár in Germany and Austria, Gilbert and Sullivan in England and Rudolf Friml and Sigmund Romberg in the U.S. The term was sometimes used in the 17th and 18th c. for shorter, less serious operas. Cf. MUSICAL COMEDY.

ophicleide **1**, an obsolete bass KEYED BUGLE invented in 1821. The instrument was written for by Verdi, Wagner, Schumann and other composers of the Romantic era. **2**, a reed ORGAN STOP of 8- or 16-foot pitch.

Oppens, Ursula (1944–) Amer. pianist, stud. of Rosina Lhévinne, Leonard Shure and Guido Agosti. She was a founding member of SPECULUM MUSICÆ, and has performed with the Chamber Music Society of Lincoln Center. She is esp. noted for her performance of contemporary music.

opus (Lat., work; pl., *opera*, opuses) a term most commonly used in the numbering of a composer's compositions. The practice of assigning opus numbers began in the 19th c. Abbr., *op.* —**opus posthumous**, (Lat.) a work published after the composer's death.

oral tradition the process of passing information from generation to generation by word of mouth (often through apprenticeship), rather than in writing. It is the common means of transmission of folk music and of much of the musical convention of earlier centuries.

oratorio (It., prayer hall) an extended musical composition based on a sacred or scriptural subject, similar to OPERA in form but involving no stage action or scenery. The form developed in Italy along with opera in the early and mid-17th c., in settings of texts in either Latin or Italian by composers such as Carissimi, Stradella and A. Scarlatti. In Protestant Germany, the most common example of oratorio was the setting of the Passion story (see HISTORIA), as in works by Schütz, Telemann, Bach and others. The English oratorio, as made famous by Handel's many works in the form, made extensive use of the chorus. Other composers to use the form incl. Marc-Antoine Charpentier, Haydn (*The Creation* and *The Seasons*), Mendelssohn (*Elijah*), Liszt, and in the 20th c., Elgar (*The Dream of Gerontius*), Walton (*Belshazzar's Feast*), Tippett (*A Child of Our Time*), Schoenberg (*Die Jakobsleiter*), Stravinsky (*Oedipus Rex*) and Penderecki (*St. Luke Passion*).

Orbison, Roy (Kelton) (1936–89) Amer. rockabilly singer, songwriter and guitarist, popular in the U.S. and England from the mid-1950s. His music alternated between country ballads and rhythmic rock. He was known for his very high falsetto singing.

orchestra a term, dating (in modern

times) from the late 17th c., for an instrumental ensemble, usu. restricted to mean an ensemble composed of a section of bowed strings with more than one player to a part along with woodwind, brass and percussion instruments. In the 17th and 18th c. the term *chapel*, as used in court and ecclesiastical establishments, often meant the same thing. The modern symphony orch. usu. contains from 40 to 100 players (see also CHAMBER ORCHESTRA). The orchestral ensemble can function as a soloist in concert or as an accompanist, as in concertos, opera and ballet. Cf. BAND, ENSEMBLE.

orchestration the ARRANGING of music for an orch. or similar ensemble, with attention to the proper use of the individual instruments and the artful combination of the various instrumental sounds into a harmonious whole. See also INSTRUMENTATION.

Orchestre de la Suisse Romande (Fr.) orch. founded in 1918 in Geneva by conductor Ernest Ansermet.

Orchestre de Paris (Fr.) orch. founded in Paris in 1967, as successor to the Orchestre des concerts du Conservatoire, under conductor Charles Münch. Other principal conductors

of the orch. have been Karajan, Solti and Barenboim.

orchestrion a late-18th- and 19th-c. MECHANICAL INSTRUMENT capable of imitating the full orch. by means of organ pipes.

Ordinary the Ordinary of the Mass is comprised of chants which retain the same texts throughout the liturgical year. Technically the term applies to certain chants of the Mass and office, but it most often refers to the Kyrie, Gloria, Credo, Sanctus and Agnus Dei chants of the Mass. The "Ite, missa est" is sometimes included in the Ordinary. Composers of polyphony, from the 14th c. on, usu. set the chants of the Ordinary, and such settings could be performed throughout the year. Cf. MASS, PROPER.

ordre ['or-drə] (Fr.) an 18th-c. term for a set of harpsichord pieces in the same key; used by François Couperin and others. It was often synonymous with SUITE.

Oregon Amer. eclectic jazz chamber group formed in 1970 from members of the Paul Winter Consort, each of whom plays a variety of instruments. The group improvises collectively, combining elements of jazz, Western and Indian classical music and folk

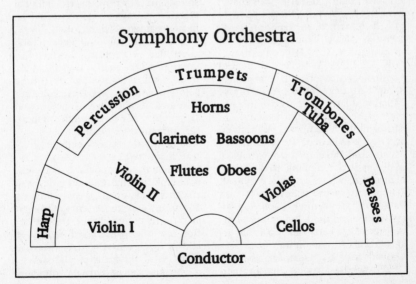

Symphony Orchestra

music. In the mid-1980s the group added electric instruments (notably synthesizers).

Oregon Symphony Orchestra orch. founded in Portland, OR, in 1896 as the Portland SO, renamed in 1967. Its conductors have included Carl Denton, Willem van Hoogstraten, Werner Janssen, James Sample, Theodore Bloomfield, Piero Bellugi, Jacques Singer, Lawrence Leighton Smith and James DePriest.

Orfeo ed Euridice (It., Orpheus and Eurydice) classical opera in 3 acts by Gluck to a libretto by Raniero da Calzabigi. Premiere, Vienna 1762. The classic tale of the attempt of the singer Orpheus to reclaim his wife Eurydice from death.

Orfeo, La Favola d' (It., The Fable of Orpheus) classical opera in 5 acts by Monteverdi to a libretto by Alessandro Striggio. Premiere, Mantua 1607. One of the earliest operas, it tells the tale of Orpheus, who (in this version) at first loses Eurydice but then is transported by Apollo to Olympus to dwell with her in immortality.

Orejón y Aparicio, José de (1706–65) Peruvian composer and organist, employed for most of his life at Lima Cathedral, first as chorister, then as organist, finally (and briefly) as chapel master. His surviving works, some of which remained in repertory well into the 19th c., consist of cantatas, motets and a Good Friday Passion.

Orff, Carl (1895–1982) influential German composer and teacher. He studied at the Munich Academy of Music and later with Max Kaminski. He taught at the Güntherschule in Munich, of which he was co-founder, and at the Staatliche Hochschule für Musik and developed an extensive body of teaching materials, *Orff-Schulwerk*, which is widely used in Europe and in the U.S. He was conductor of the Munich Bach Society (1930–33) and made a number of arrangements of early music for that organization. As a composer he is best known for his *Carmina burana* (1937), whose driving rhythm and primitive force are characteristics of many of his works. His other works incl. *Die Kluge* (opera), other stage works, *Rota* (written for the Munich Olympic Games, 1972) and choral works.

Orford Quartet string quartet formed in 1965 at a summer school in Mount Orford, Quebec. It has been quartet-in-residence at the U. of Toronto from 1968 and tours regularly in Europe and No. America.

organ 1, a wind instrument consisting of tuned pipes sounded by air under pressure, which is provided by a bellows and released by sliders, levers or a keyboard. The earliest forms of the instrument date from antiquity (see HYDRAULIS). Early organs were operated by sliders acting like valves to open or close the flow of air to each pipe. Later organs replaced that cumbersome method with levers and then keys. A simple organ may have only one set or *rank* of pipes, one pipe for each pitch. Larger organs have hundreds of ranks of pipes, each rank activated by a *stop* controlled by a *piston*. The stops are mechanically connected so that they can be combined in various ways by *couplers* to produce different combinations of sounds. In larger organs, the ranks of pipes are assigned to sections (the most common of which are the Swell, Great, Choir, Solo and Pedal), each controlled by a separate keyboard or *manual* of the organ and each having its own characteristics, whether it be solo stops, pedal stops, etc. The addition of electric-powered action and air pumping has rendered the modern instrument more flexible.

A distinction is made between electric organs with a TRACKER ACTION, in which the key operates the pipe-sounding mechanism directly, the electricity being used only for air pumping, and those employing an electric relay action, the tracker action often being preferred because it allows the organist control over the speed with which the pipe speaks.

The pipes of which the organ is

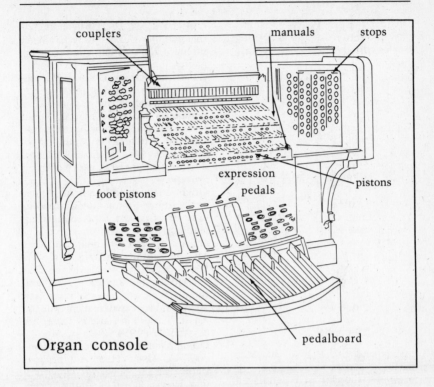

couplers   manuals   stops

expression
pedals   pistons

foot pistons

Organ console   pedalboard

composed are of three main types: open flue pipes, stopped flue pipes and reed pipes. The first two types are WHISTLE FLUTES. Through the use of different shapes and materials (wood, metal) a wide variety of tone colors can be achieved. Nevertheless, certain periods of history have produced organs of fairly uniform design. The baroque organ has a preponderance of bright, reedy stops for clarity; the Romantic organ concentrates on darker, flue pipes for richness. See HARMONIUM, REGAL, PORTATIVE ORGAN, POSITIVE ORGAN. See ORGAN PIPES (*illus.*).

2, ELECTRONIC ORGAN.

organ chorale an organ work based on a Protestant CHORALE melody.

organ hymn a type of hymn performance in which the organ plays the odd- or the even-number verses in alternation with the congregation or choir.

organized sound a 20th-c. alternative term for MUSIC.

organistrum HURDY-GURDY.

organ Mass a Mass in which the Ordinary and Proper are performed *alternatim* between the organ and singers. Usu. the choir sings plainchant rather than polyphony, and the organ versets are often based on the plainchant they replace.

organ point PEDAL POINT.

organ score 1, an OPEN SCORE of a contrapuntal organ work. 2, an OPEN SCORE of a vocal and instrumental work from which the organ reproduces the voice parts. 3, a reduction for organ of an orchestral work.

organ shake TREMULANT.

Organ Solo Mass the Missa Brevis in C major, K.259 (1777), by Mozart.

organ stop 1, a lever on an organ which activates a rank of pipes, producing a specific timbre and volume, but not affecting pitch. 2, the rank of pipes itself.

Organ Symphony the Symphony No. 3 in C Minor, Op. 78, for organ, 2

Organ pipes

Flue   Reed

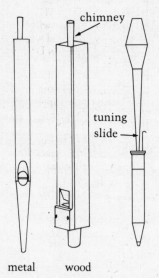

chimney

tuning
slide

metal   wood

pianos and orch. (1886) by Saint-Saëns.

organum the earliest type of medieval polyphony, consisting of a tenor part, usu. derived from Gregorian chant, and a duplum part, which, in its earliest form, moved in parallel motion to the chant (*parallel organum*). A third (triplum) and/or fourth (quadruplum) voice might be added by doubling the tenor and/or duplum at the octave, thereby creating any one of a variety of types of composite organum. During the 11th c. a kind of polyphony developed in which the tenor and duplum move freely, often in contrary rather than parallel motion, and often in different rhythms, allowing for 2–3 notes to be sung in the duplum against one note in the tenor. This is known as free organum. Later developments of florid or melismatic organum are associated with 12th-c. schools of style such as ST. MARTIAL.

Orgel ['or-gəl] (Ger.), **orgue** [org] (Fr.) ORGAN.

Orgelbüchlein [″büç-lĩn] (Ger., little

organ book) a collection of short chorale preludes (1708–17) by J.S. Bach, intended for teaching the art of ornamenting and varying a chorale tune. The orig. plan envisaged preludes for the year, 164 in all, but it was never completed.

orguinette [or-gē′net] (Fr.) a small crank-operated portable REED ORGAN.

Oriental America musical (1896) produced by John Isham, the first production with a black cast to open on Broadway.

Original Dixieland Jazz Band Amer. jazz ensemble formed in Chicago in 1916, the first jazz band to make recordings.

Orioles Amer. rhythm-and-blues vocal group formed in 1948 as the Vibranaires, often considered the first rhythm-and-blues vocal group and the first doo-wop singers. They sang on TV and appeared frequently at the Apollo Theater in Harlem. The group disbanded in 1954.

Orloff, Vladimir (1928–) Russian-born Canadian cellist and teacher, trained at the Bucharest Conservatory. He was a member of the Vienna PO in the mid-1960s and toured Europe and No. America. He came to Canada in 1971 to teach at the U. of Toronto and has concertized extensively across Canada.

Ormandy, Eugene (Blau, Jenö) (1899–1985) Hungarian-born Amer. conductor and violinist, trained at the Budapest Royal Academy. He came to the U.S. in 1921 and played in a theater orch., then conducted programs of light classics for radio and for the Philadelphia Orch.'s summer concerts. He became conductor of the Minneapolis SO in 1931 and then of the Philadelphia Orch. in 1938, remaining until 1980, developing the orch.'s famous string sound. He conducted the first orchestral concert televised in America (before Toscanini by several hours) and made a large number of recordings.

ornament a formula used to embellish a musical phrase, either improvised or intended to have the feeling

Ornaments
(see also NONHARMONIC NOTES)

Appoggiaturas

Slide

Trills and shakes

Trill with resolution

Half-trill (Pralltriller)   Inverted mordent (Schneller)

Mordent   Ribattuta

Turns

Springer   Trillo

Grace notes

of improvisation. Ornaments fall into several well defined types, which are illustrated in the accompanying table: appoggiaturas; trills, shakes and vibrato; melodic ornaments, such as turns and divisions; and combinations of the preceding.

Ornithoparcus, Andreas (c1490–c1535) German theorist of the 16th c., a disciple of Erasmus, best known for his treatise *Musicae activae micrologus*, published in 1517 in Leipzig. The *Micrologus* was widely read and used as a textbook and was translated into English by JOHN DOWLAND in 1609.

Ornstein, Leo (1892–) Russian-born Amer. composer and pianist, stud. of Bertha Fiering Tapper. A controversial performer of his own experimental works, he retired from performance in 1920 to concentrate on composition and to teach, first at the Philadelphia Musical Academy and then at his own Ornstein School of Music. Many of his works are for piano; he has also written songs, sonatas and other chamber music, a piano concerto, *Evening Song of the Cossack* for chamber orch. and the *Lysistrata Suite* for orch.

orpharion a wire-strung bass CITTERN with slanting frets.

Orpheus in the Underworld (Fr., *Orphée aux Enfers*) comic opera in 2 acts by Offenbach to a libretto in French by Hector Crémieux and Ludovic Halévy. Premiere, Paris 1858. A parody of the Orpheus legend.

orphica a small portable PIANO of the early 18th c., designed for outdoor use.

Ortiz, Diego [ōr′tēth] (c1510–c1570) Spanish composer and theorist, noted for his *Trattado de glosas* (1553), the first treatise on ornamentation for bowed string instruments.

Ory, Kid (Edward) (1886–1973) Amer. jazz trombonist, composer and bandleader from New Orleans. He led a highly influential band in the 1910s and produced the first jazz recording to be made by black artists. After a period of retirement, he toured in the 1940s and 1950s, retiring to Hawaii in 1966. Among his own songs was the very popular "Muskrat Ramble."

Osborne Brothers, The Amer. country-music vocal duo, noted for their intricate harmonies and instrumental virtuosity, important in popularizing BLUEGRASS music in the 1950s.

oscillator an electronic device that produces a wave form, used as the building block of synthesized sounds. Cf. SYNTHESIZER.

ossia (It., or let it be) or else (indicating an alternate version). Also, *oppure, ovvero* (It.).

ostinato (It., obstinate) **1**, a musical figure repeated, usu. at the same pitch, throughout a composition. **2**, GROUND.

Otello (It., Othello) tragic opera in 4 acts by Verdi to a libretto by Arrigo Boito, based on Shakespeare's tragedy. Premiere, Milan 1887. Otello's jealousy concerning his wife Desdemona is aroused by false rumors planted by the quintessential villain, Iago.

ôtez *also*, **ôter** [ō'tā] (Fr.) remove (as, a mute).

ottava (It.) OCTAVE.—**ottava alta**, (It.) to be played at the octave above. Usu. indicated by the sign 8^(va) above the note or passage. Also, *ottava sopra* (It.). —**ottava bassa**, (It.) to be played at the octave below. Usu. indicated by the sign 8^(va) below the note or passage. Also, *ottava sotto* (It.).

ottavino (It.) **1**, PICCOLO. **2**, a soprano CLARINET. **3**, a small VIRGINAL.

ottoni [ōt'tō-nē] (It.) BRASS INSTRUMENTS.

Oubradous, Fernand ['oo-brə-doo] (1903–86) French bassoonist and conductor, founder of the Trio d'anches de Paris, a professor at the Paris Conservatoire and an active editor and publisher of French music of the 18th c.

Ours, L' [loors] (Fr.) see BEAR, THE.

out-chorus in jazz, the final chorus of an arrangement, usu. for the full band.

outi a Greek round-backed plucked bass LUTE.

outlaw country a type of COUNTRY MUSIC of the 1970s influenced by rock music, developed as an alternative to the Nashville sound. Proponents of the movement incl. Willie Nelson, David Coe and Waylon Jennings.

ouvert [oo'ver] (Fr., open) **1**, the first ending of a repeated musical section (the second is called *clos*). **2**, on the horn, open (see OPEN NOTE 3,).

ouverture [oo-ver'tür] (Fr.) OVERTURE.

overblow to blow into a wind instrument with more than usual force to change the pitch, usu. producing an OVERTONE instead of the fundamental tone.

overdubbing a technique, used extensively in sound films and in studio work, of recording different parts of a work separately and then superimposing them electronically, allowing one performer to play several simultaneous parts or to add an instrument to a pre-existing recording.

overstringing a type of piano stringing in which some of the bass strings pass diagonally over the strings of the middle range, thus allowing for a shorter piano case.

Over There patriotic song (1917) by George M. Cohan.

Overton, Hal (1920–72) Amer. composer, stud. of Persichetti, Riegger and Milhaud. He was a jazz performer and arranger, working with Stan Getz, Teddy Charles and Thelonious Monk. He taught at the Juilliard School, the New School in New York and Yale. His own works are influenced by jazz and incl. 3 operas, several symphonies, string quartets, sonatas for viola and cello and other chamber music.

overtone one of the tones which, along with the FUNDAMENTAL, comprise a musical tone. See HARMONICS.

overture a work, usu. for orch., intended as the introduction to a dramatic work or for independent concert performance. See FRENCH OVERTURE.

Owens, Buck (1929–) Amer. country music singer and instrumentalist, creator of the so-called California sound and a highly popular recording artist in the 1960s and 1970s.

Overtone Series

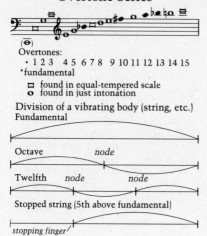

(☺)
Overtones:
· 1 2 3   4 5 6 7 8   9 10 11 12 13 14 15
·fundamental

▫ found in equal-tempered scale
○ found in just intonation

Division of a vibrating body (string, etc.)
Fundamental

Octave   node

Twelfth   node   node

Stopped string (5th above fundamental)

stopping finger

Oxford Symphony popular name for the Symphony No. 92 in G major (1788) by Haydn, so called because it was performed on the occasion of his receiving an honorary degree from Oxford, although in fact it had been written three years earlier.

Ozawa, Seiji (1935–) Manchurian-born Japanese conductor. He studied at the Toho School in Tokyo under Hideo Saito, at Tanglewood and with Karajan. He was assistant conductor of the New York PO, and was music dir. of the Ravinia Festival (Chicago), the Toronto SO and the San Francisco SO before becoming music dir. of the Boston SO in 1973. He is known esp. for his performance of large-scale orchestral works of the late 19th and early 20th c.

P

p *abbr.* PIANO (1,).

Pacchiarotti, Gasparo (1740–1821) famous Italian soprano castrato. He sang in every important theater on the Continent (including the opening of La Scala in 1778 and of La Fenice in 1792) and in England with consistent success. He retired to Padua in 1793.

Pace, Charles Henry (1886–1963) Amer. gospel composer and publisher. He formed the Pace Jubilee Singers in 1925 to perform and record his and other composers' works and founded two publishing houses in Pittsburgh.

Pachelbel, Johann (1653–1706) German composer and organist, stud. of Kaspar Prentz. He was organist at Erfurt, then at St. Sebald in his home town of Nuremberg. He was a prolific composer, producing a large number of organ works, keyboard suites and variations and vocal music (arias, motets, concertos), incl. the widely performed canon from the Canon and Gigue in D major for three violins and continuo. One of his sons, **Charles Theodore Pachelbel** (1690–1750), was an organist in Boston, MA, and Charleston, SC.

Pachmann, Vladimir de (1848–1933) Ukrainian pianist, stud. of his father and Joseph Dachs. He had a distinguished career, marred only by a certain eccentricity in his performance manner.

Pacific 231 evocative tone poem (1923) by Honegger; inspired by a famous locomotive.

Pacini, Giovanni (1796–1867) Italian composer of opera, vocal music and chamber music, stud. of Padre Mattei and Bonaventura Furlanetto. He was a remarkably prolific and gifted composer, producing over 85 operas, as well as cantatas, oratorios, other sacred and secular vocal music and instrumental works.

Paderewski, Ignace (Ignacy) **Jan** (1860–1941) eminent Polish pianist and composer, trained at the Warsaw Conservatory and with Leschetizky in Vienna. He was active during the First World War and after the Nazi invasion of Poland in relief efforts for his homeland. All the while he pursued an intensive concert schedule, finding time to compose as well, producing an opera, a symphony, a piano concerto, songs and many works for piano solo.

padoana (It.) any of several different 16th- and 17th-c. dances.

Padovano, Annibale (1527–75) Italian composer and organist at St. Mark's, Venice, and then at the court of Archduke Karl II of Austria in Graz. His extant works consist of ricercars and toccatas, as well as motets and madrigals.

pad 1, a small flat disc used to face the heads of keys on wind instruments and assure a tight closure, which is essential for proper intonation. The pads are of leather or synthetic material. **2,** *also,* **practice pad**, a disc of rubber or other material used by percussionists for silent practice of drumming patterns.

paean a Gk. choral hymn in praise of Apollo.

Paër, Ferdinando (1771–1839) Italian opera composer, stud. of Francesco Fortunati and Gaspare Ghiretti. In 1797 he became dir. of the Kärntnertor Theater in Vienna, and in 1807 Napoleon, an admirer, appointed him his *maître de chapelle* in Paris, from which followed his directorship of the Opéra-Comique and the Théâtre Italien, posts he held until 1827.

He composed over 50 operas (incl. *Camilla* and *Achille*), cantatas, oratorios, masses, motets, several symphonies and chamber music.

Paganini, Niccolò (1782–1840) Italian virtuoso violinist and composer, stud. of Giacomo Costa and Paër. He spent a decade in Lucca as concertmaster of the national orch., composing, teaching and playing concerts, then embarked on a free-lance solo career. He established new heights of virtuosity, reflected in the demands of his many works for violin, best known of which are the caprices and concertos.

Paganini variations any of several works based on the theme of Paganini's Caprice No. 2 in A minor. Among them are Brahms's *Variations on a Theme of Paganini*, Op. 35, for piano (1862), Rachmaninov's *Rhapsody on a Theme of Paganini*, Op. 43, for piano and orch. (1934), and works by Lutoslawski, Blacher and Schumann.

Page, Hot Lips (Oran Thaddeus) (1908–54) Amer. jazz trumpeter and singer from Texas, strongly influenced by Louis Armstrong. He played with the bands of Bennie Moten, Count Basie and Artie Shaw and made numerous solo recordings. He was noted for his improvisational singing.

Page, Patti (Fowler, Clara Ann) (1927–) Amer. popular singer with a country-music manner, some of whose hits incl. "Tennessee Waltz" and "How Much Is That Doggy in the Window?"

Page, Walter (Sylvester) (1900–57) Amer. jazz bassist and bandleader. After a stint with the Bennie Moten band he founded his own Blue Devils. Later he played with the Count Basie orch.

Pagliacci [pä'lyät-chē] (It., Clowns) tragic opera in 2 acts by Leoncavallo to his own libretto. Premiere, Milan 1892. The actor Canio is highly jealous of his young wife, Nedda, and kills her and her lover after a play-within-a-play reenacts the story of her infidelity.

Paik, Nam June (1932–) Korean composer, trained with Fortner and with Stockhausen in Cologne. In 1964 he moved to the U.S. and has taught at the California Institute for the Arts since 1970. His works incl. *Hommage à John Cage*, which involves the destruction of two pianos during the performance.

Paillard, Jean-François [pä'yär] (1928–) French conductor, founder in 1959 of the Jean-François Paillard Chamber Orch., which specializes in rare works from the 17th and 18th c.

Paine, John Knowles (1839–1906) Amer. composer, organist and teacher, trained in the U.S. and in Berlin. He joined the faculty of Harvard in 1863, becoming a major force in Boston musical life as well. His works incl. 2 operas, incidental music, choral works and songs, 2 symphonies, several tone poems, chamber music and works for solo organ and piano.

paired imitation term for either of two contrapuntal techniques: a) a pair of canonic voices is imitated by another pair; b) a pair of voices stating two simultaneous themes is imitated by another pair. Both techniques are common in the works of Josquin des Prez and of other 15th- and 16th-c. composers. See IMITATION.

Paisiello, Giovanni (1740–1816) prolific Italian composer of opera and sacred and secular vocal music, trained in Naples. He was *maestro di cappella* to Catherine II of Russia (1776–83), then became theater music composer to the King of Naples. He went to Paris in 1802 at Napoleon's behest, then returned to Naples when Napoleon's brother became king. He wrote over 80 operas, incl. lesser-known versions of *The Barber of Seville* and *La serva padrona*.

Pajama Game, The musical by Richard Adler and Jerry Ross, book by George Abbott and Richard Bissell, based on Bissell's novel *7½ Cents*. Premiere, New York 1954. The superintendent of a pajama factory falls in love with the head of the workers' grievance committee.

Palestine, Charlemagne (Martin, Charles) (1945–) Amer. composer, pianist and video artist, stud. of Subotnick. He performs mainly his own music, which involves unusual pianistic and vocal techniques.

Palestrina opera in 3 acts by Pfitzner to his own libretto about the great Renaissance composer. Premiere, Munich 1917. Palestrina, inspired by a vision of nine great composers, composes the *Missa Papae Marcelli*.

Palestrina, Giovanni Pierluigi da (1525–94) prolific Italian composer of sacred vocal music and madrigals, trained in Rome at St. Maria Maggiore. Most of his professional life was spent in Rome, either at the Vatican or at St. Peter's, and that his reputation was substantial elsewhere in Europe is apparent from the offers from other monarchs for his services. He wrote over 100 masses, almost 400 motets, over 100 other sacred works and almost 150 madrigals; most of his music was publ. during his lifetime. His works have been used for centuries as models of contrapuntal writing.

palindrome 1, a literary term for a word or phrase that reads the same backwards and forwards. A musical equivalent of the technique has been used, esp. in nontonal music, by various composers, incl. Hindemith, Berg and Webern. **2**, (cap.) popular name for the Symphony No. 47 in G major (1772) by Haydn.

Pal Joey musical by Richard Rodgers, lyrics by Lorenz Hart, book by John O'Hara, based on his *New Yorker* short stories. Premiere, New York 1940. Entertainer Joey gives up the virtuous Linda for the wealthy Vera.

pallet a valve in a pipe organ windchest which allows air to pass to a selected pipe or pipes.

Palm, Siegfried (1927–) German cellist and teacher, stud. of Enrico Mainardi. He has been principal cello in the orchestras of Lübeck, the Ham-

burg Radio and the Cologne Radio and has taught at the Staatliche Hochschule für Musik in Cologne. In 1977 he became general manager of the Deutsche Oper in Berlin. He is noted for his performance of 20th-c. music and for his development of cello techniques. He has played in various chamber ensembles, incl. the Hamann Quartet.

Palmer, Robert (Moffat) (1915–) Amer. composer and teacher, stud. of Rogers, Harris, Copland and Quincy Porter. He has taught at the U. of Kansas and at Cornell. His works incl. a piano concerto, 2 symphonies, other orchestral works, songs, 4 string quartets, 3 piano sonatas, other sonatas for various instruments and a *Toccata Ostinato* for solo piano.

Palmgren, Selim (1878–1951) Finnish composer, pianist and conductor, trained in Helsinki, Germany and Italy. He was conductor of various groups in Finland, then toured as pianist and accompanist and taught at the Sibelius Academy in Helsinki. He is best known for his piano works; he also wrote a large number of songs, an opera and 5 piano concertos.

pan a STEEL DRUM.

Panama Hattie musical by Cole Porter, book by Herbert Fields and B.G. DeSylva. Premiere, New York 1940. Panama City nightclub owner Hattie must be approved by an eight-year-old before she can marry divorcé Nick Bullett.

Pan American Association of Composers short-lived support organization for composers (1928–34) founded by Varèse and supported anonymously by Ives.

Pandean pipes PANPIPES.

pandiatonicism *also*, **pandiatonism** a term coined by Nicolas Slonimsky for the free use of notes from the diatonic rather than the chromatic scale without traditional resolutions.

pandora 1, BANDORA. **2**, a bass CITTERN with a scalloped outline.

pandura *also*, **pandoura 1**, BANDORA. **2**, BANDURA. **3**, an ancient LUTE-like instrument with a long neck.

pandurina an 18th-c. Milanese MANDOLIN.

panharmonicon an ORCHESTRION invented by J.N. Maelzel in 1805.

panpipes a primitive wind instrument consisting of a graduated series of clay, wood or stone flutes bound together or carved from a single block. Also, *Pandean pipes, mouth organ, syrinx.*

pantaleon *also,* **pantalon** a large DULCIMER invented about 1700; it has about 250 gut and metal strings and is played with wooden mallets.

pantalon stop a device found on some clavichords that allows the strings to sound sympathetically after the key has been released.

pantomime a dramatic entertainment involving mime supported by music and by stage machinery. The genre, descended from the commedia dell'arte, began in England in the early 18th c. and was popular in the U.S. in the late 18th and early 19th c.

pantonality **1**, a term coined by Rudolf Réti in 1958 for an extension of TONALITY with rapidly changing key centers but not discarding tonal intervallic relationships. Such techniques are found in the late Romantic works of Wagner, Debussy and others. **2**, a term for the property of a scale or melodic fragment allowing it to be played in more than one key.

pants role TRAVESTI.

Panufnik, Andrzej (1914–91) Polish-born English composer, pianist and conductor, stud. of Sikorski and Weingartner. He has been conductor of various orchestras in Poland and England, but since 1959 he has concentrated on composition. His works incl. *Miss Julie* (ballet), symphonic music, concertos for violin and piano, chamber music and choral and solo vocal works.

Papillons [pä-pē'yō] (Fr., Butterflies) a set of 12 piano pieces, Op. 2 (1832), by Schumann.

Papineau-Couture, Jean [pä-pē'nō koo'tür] (1916–) Canadian composer and teacher, stud. of Quincy Porter and Boulanger. He taught at the U. of Montreal from 1951 to 1973; among his students were Jacques Hétu and André Prévost. His works incl. 2 ballets, orchestral works, a series of *Pièces concertantes* for various instruments, choral and solo vocal works, chamber music and works for piano.

Parade [pä'räd] (Fr.) a "realistic ballet" in 1 act with music by Satie to a libretto by Jean Cocteau. Premiere, Paris 1917, with Massine as choreographer and Picasso as designer.

Paradis, Maria Theresia von (1759–1824) Austrian composer, pianist, organist and singer; blind from youth. Based in Vienna, she concertized widely in Europe and England. She wrote 3 operas, several cantatas, songs, 2 piano concertos and piano sonatas, all written down in her own system of notation.

Paradise and the Peri, The (Ger., *Das Paradies und die Peri*) oratorio for soloists, chorus and orch., Op. 50 (1843), by Schumann to a text adapted from Thomas Moore's *Lalla Rookh.*

parallel fifths *or* **octaves** see CONSECUTIVES.

parallel keys *or* **modes** major and minor keys having the same tonic, as C major and C minor. Cf. RELATIVE KEYS.

parallel motion in COUNTERPOINT, the simultaneous movement of two or more parts in the same direction, separated by the same interval(s).

parallel organum see ORGANUM.

parameter any one of the various aspects of music, as tempo, pitch or pitch class, loudness, etc. In serial music, any or all parameters may be determined by serial procedures (see SERIALISM).

paraphrase **1**, a compositional technique, prevalent in the 15th and 16th c., in which a new composition is based on preexisting material from another polyphonic work. One voice of the source is given greater importance than the others and occurs in its entirety in the new composition; material from the other voices is used occasionally. Cf. PARODY. **2**, a relatively free musical TRANSCRIPTION.

Paray, Paul (M.A. Charles) (1886–1979) French composer and conductor, winner of the Prix de Rome in 1911. He was conductor of the Concerts Lamoureux, the Monte Carlo Orch. and the Concerts Colonne from 1933 and after the war. From 1952 to 1963 he was principal conductor of the Detroit SO.

pardessus de viole [pär-də'sü] (Fr.) a small VIOL higher in pitch than the treble viol.

Paris popular name for: **1**, the Symphony No. 31 in D major, K.297/300a (1778), by Mozart, written in Paris. **2**, the symphonies Nos. 82–87 (1785–6) by Haydn, written on commission for the Concerts de la Loge Olympique in Paris.

Parisot, Aldo (Simoes) (1920–) Brazilian cellist and teacher, stud. of Ibere Gomes Grosso. He has toured throughout the world and is known for his performances of Bach, the Viennese classicists and contemporary repertory. Several composers have written works for him. He has taught at the Peabody Conservatory, the New England Conservatory, Mannes College, the Banff Center for the Arts and Yale (since 1958).

Parker, Charlie (Charles Christopher) ("Bird," "Yardbird") (1920–55) Amer. jazz bop alto saxophonist from Kansas City. In the late 1930s and early 1940s he played in the bands of Jay McShann, Earl Hines and Billy Eckstine, also jamming in celebrated late-night sessions. From 1945 he led his own groups in New York and Hollywood. He was the most influential and innovative of the bop musicians, because of his improvisational style, his harmonic daring, his rhythmic complexity, his fast, driving tempos and his dry, biting tone.

Parker, Horatio (William) (1863–1919) Amer. composer, organist and music educator, stud. of Chadwick and Josef Rheinberger. He worked in New York until 1893, then taught at Yale, where his students incl. Ives, Sessions and Quincy Porter. He

founded and conducted the New Haven SO and Choral Society. His works incl. 2 operas, incidental music, a concerto for organ, orchestral and chamber music, much choral music (incl. the widely performed *Hora novissima*), many songs, church music, and works for solo piano.

Parker, Junior (Herman) (1927–71) Amer. blues vocalist and harmonica player. He played with Sonny Boy Williamson and Howlin' Wolf, then in Memphis joined the Beale Streeters. In 1952 he formed the Blue Flames and recorded extensively.

parlando also, **parlante** (It., speaking) of vocal music, performed in a manner suggesting speech. Cf. SPRECHSTIMME.

Parliament one of several funk groups led by singer GEORGE CLINTON.

Parlow, Kathleen (1890–1963) Canadian violinist, stud. of Henry Holmes and Leopold Auer. She toured extensively until 1941, when she settled in Toronto to teach and lead her own string quartet.

Parma, Ildebrando da see PIZZETTI.

Parnas, Leslie (1931–) Amer. cellist, stud. of Piatigorsky. He was principal cellist of the St. Louis SO (1954–62), then concentrated on solo and chamber music performance. He was a founder of the Chamber Music Society of Lincoln Center and a frequent participant at the Marlboro Festival. He has taught at Boston U. and the St. Louis Conservatory.

parody 1, a compositional technique, prevalent in the 16th c., in which a new composition is based on a preexisting polyphonic work. The entire texture of the model is used in the new composition, interspersed with sections of newly composed material. Cf. PARAPHRASE. **2**, an imitation of a musical composition, esp. one in which the text is altered comically.

parody mass a mass of the 16th c. which employs parody technique (see PARODY 1,). Each movement usu. begins and ends with polyphonic material from the model.

Parrenin Quartet French string quartet founded in 1942 in Paris by violinist Jacques Parrenin (1919–). The quartet concentrated on 20th-c. repertory, in particular on the works of the Second Viennese School.

Parry, Sir **(Charles) Hubert (Hastings)** (1848–1918) prolific English composer and teacher, stud. of Henry Hugo Pierson. He taught at the Royal College of Music from its creation in 1883 and became its dir. in 1894. He wrote a large number of works in all genres, the best-known work of which is probably *Jerusalem* (1916) for unison voices and orch.

Parsifal religious opera in 3 acts by Wagner to his own libretto based on medieval legend and a poem by Wolfram von Eschenbach. Premiere, Bayreuth 1882. A parable of the struggle between evil, represented by Klingsor, and good, represented by the knights of the Holy Grail, in which salvation comes in the form of the Guileless Fool, Parsifal.

part 1, the line or lines of music of a work realized by one performer or group of performers, as the piano part, the violin part, etc. The term also refers to the separate volume containing the part. **2**, a line or voice of a polyphonic texture, as the top part, the tenor part, etc. **3**, a formal section of a composition.

partbook a volume containing a single complete instrumental or vocal PART (1,).

Partch, Harry (1901–74) Amer. composer, performer and instrument maker. He developed instruments to play his 43-note tuning system based on JUST INTONATION. His works incorporate elements of Amer. folk, African and Asian music. Except for the voice, he utilized almost exclusively instruments he invented or modified himself.

parte (It.) PART (3,).

partial OVERTONE, esp. the overtones making up the sound of a bell.

partial signature a key signature found in some, but not all, of the voices of a composition. The term usu. refers to the ♭ in music of the 13th and 14th c.

particella [pär-tē′chel-lä] (It.) SHORT SCORE.

partie [pär′tē] **1**, (Ger.) SUITE; PARTITA. **2**, (Fr.) PART.

partimento (It., division) in the late 18th and early 19th c., keyboard exercises for figured bass playing.

partita (It.) **1**, a set of musical variations. **2**, SUITE.

partition [pär-tē′syō] (Fr.) *also*, **partitur** (Ger.), **partitura** (It.) a full score showing each instrumental or vocal part on a separate staff.

part music music, esp. vocal music, for several voices or instruments having independent parts.

Partos, Oedoen (1907–77) Israeli composer, violinist and teacher, stud. of Jenö Hubay and Kodály. In 1938 he went to Israel to be concertmaster of the Palestine SO and violist of the Israel Quartet, while continuing to tour. He taught at the Rubin Academy of Tel-Aviv U. from 1951. His works are largely for instruments, but he also wrote some songs and choral works.

part-song a vocal composition, usu. in 4 parts and predominantly homophonic, often unaccompanied. Cf. *prick song*.

part-writing the writing of part-music or COUNTERPOINT with an emphasis on each line as melody rather than on the resulting harmonic texture.

pasamala a jazz dance song of the early 20th c. performed to ragtime music.

Pasatieri, Thomas (1945–) Amer. composer, stud. of Giannini, Persichetti and Milhaud. He is best known for his songs and operas in a neo-Romantic idiom, incl. *The Seagull* (1974), *Inez de Castro* (1976) and *The Trial of Mary Lincoln* (TV opera, 1972).

Pasdeloup, Jules-Etienne [′pä-də-loo] (1819–87) French conductor. He was founder in Paris of the Société des Jeunes Artistes in 1852 to perform the music of young composers, the Concert populaire in 1861 and the Société des Oratorios in 1868. Through his projects he expanded the audience for classical music in Paris.

pasillo [pä'sē-lyō] (Sp.) an 18th-c. Latin-Amer. dance derived from the Austrian waltz and surviving as a slow dance-song or a faster instrumental dance.

paso doble ['pä-sō 'dō-blä] (Sp., double step) a Latin-Amer. dance in 6/8 time assoc. with the bullfight.

paspy PASSEPIED.

Pasquini, Bernardo (1637–1710) Italian composer, organist and harpsichordist, stud. of Cesti and Loreto Vittori. He was organist at St. Maria in Aracoeli and in the service of Prince Giambattista Borghese. He was noted in his time as a virtuoso keyboard player and composer, but he also wrote 15 operas as well as oratorios, cantatas and other vocal music.

Pass, Joe (Passalaqua, Joseph Anthony Jacobi) (1929–) Amer. jazz guitarist. He free-lanced in relative obscurity until 1973, when his first unaccompanied album was recorded. Since then he has accompanied singers and played with Oscar Peterson, among others. He is unusual among jazz guitarists because of his virtuosity as a finger picker.

passacaglia [päs-sä'kä-lyä] *also,* **passacaglio** (It.) **1,** a dance tune of Spanish or Italian origin. **2,** baroque instrumental variations in slow triple time composed on a ground bass. **3,** a dance performed to a passacaglia (1,). Cf. CHACONNE.

passacaille [pä-sä'kī] (Fr.) PASSACAGLIA.

passage 1, a section of a composition. **2,** PASSAGGIO.

passage-work a section of a work with rapid scale or arpeggio figures.

passaggio (It.) **1,** an ornamental figure or section (see ORNAMENT). **2,** the range of the voice in which the transition from one REGISTER to another takes place. The term usu. refers to the transition from full voice to head voice. **3,** PASSAGE (1,).

passamezzo *also,* **pass'e mezzo** (It.) a 16th- and 17th-c. Italian dance in duple meter, similar to the PAVAN but nearly twice as fast. It was usu. followed by a galliard or a saltarello. 17th-c. passamezzos are usu. for lute or keyboard and consist of variations on a ground. The two main types of passamezzo are the *passamezzo antico* and the *passamezzo moderno,* different in their chord schemes. See RENAISSANCE BASSES (*illus.*).

passecaille [pä-sə'kī] (Fr.) PASSACAGLIA.

passepied [-pyā] (Fr.) a 17th- and 18th-c. French court dance in triple or compound triple meter, similar to the MINUET and often found in instrumental suites.

passing note *also,* **passing tone** a NONHARMONIC NOTE stepwise filling in the space between two principal notes.

Passione, La [pä'syō-nä] (It.) popular name for the Symphony No. 49 in F minor (1768) by F.J. Haydn.

Passion music settings of the story of the Crucifixion as related in the Gospels. Polyphonic settings have been composed since the 15th c.

Pasta, Giuditta (Maria Costanza) (1798–1865) Italian operatic soprano, stud. of Giuseppe Scappa. She was highly successful in Italy, France and England, particularly in the operas of Rossini (some of which she performed with the composer conducting), Bellini and Donizetti. Her roles incl. Desdemona (Rossini's *Otello*), Tancredi and Anna Bolena.

pasticcio [pä'stēt-chō] (It., hodgepodge) a musical work made up of extracts from other works, often by other composers. Also, *potpourri, olla podrida.* Cf. MEDLEY.

pastiche [pä'stēç] (Fr.) PASTICCIO.

pastorale (Fr.) **1,** a type of OPERA of the 16th and 17th c. having a plot based on or evocative of rural life. **2,** an instrumental or vocal work with a pastoral character.

Pastorale 1, piano sonata No. 15 in D major, Op. 28 (1801) by Beethoven. **2,** name given to three harpsichord sonatas by Domenico Scarlatti: K415 in D major, K446 in F major and K513 in C major.

Pastorale d'été [dā-tā] (Fr., Summer Pastorale) an orchestral tone poem (1920) by Honegger.

Pastoral Symphony 1, popular name for the Symphony No. 6 in F major, Op. 68 (1808) by Beethoven, subtitled "Recollections of Country Life." The movements are "The Awakening of happy feelings on arriving in the country," "Scene by the stream," "Merry gathering of the peasants," "Storm," and "Shepherd Song; Happy and thankful feelings after the storm." **2**, title of the Symphony No. 3 (1921) by Vaughan Williams.

pastorella (It., shepherdess) a 17th- to 19th-c. church composition for Christmas to be performed by the choir with soloists and a small orch. The form is found principally in Germany and eastern Europe.

Pastorella, La (It.) concerto in D major for recorder, oboe, bassoon, violin and basso continuo, RV95, by Vivaldi.

pastourelle [pä-stoo'rel] (Fr.) a French lyric poem of the late Middle Ages consisting of a love debate between a knight and a shepherdess.

Patanè, Giuseppe (1932–89) Italian opera conductor. He conducted in most major opera houses in Europe and at the Metropolitan and San Francisco Operas in the U.S. He also conducted many major orchestras.

patent notes note shapes used in SHAPE NOTE notation.

Pathétique [pä-tā'tēk] **1**, popular name for the Piano Sonata No. 8 in C minor, Op. 13 (1797) by Beethoven. **2**, popular name for the Symphony No. 6 in B minor, Op. 74 (1893), by Tchaikovsky.

Patience operetta in 2 acts by Sullivan to a libretto by W.S. Gilbert. Premiere, London 1881. A satire on the aesthetic movement in England in which two poets compete for the affections of a milkmaid.

patter song a song in which rapid declamation is used humorously. Patter songs are most often found in the op-

erettas of Gilbert and Sullivan and the operas of Rossini and Donizetti.

Patti, Adelina (Juana Maria) (1843–1919) Italian coloratura soprano, stud. of Ettore Barilli and Emmanuele Muzio. As a child she toured with violinist Ole Bull and pianist Louis Gottschalk, then made her operatic debut at the age of 16 in New York. She had a remarkable career, surrounded by factual and fictional legends, retiring in 1906. Her roles incl. Amina (*La Sonnambula*), Violetta (*La Traviata*) and Rosina (*The Barber of Seville*). She made many recordings, mostly when she was in her 60s.

Patti, Black see JONES, SISSIERETTA.

patting intricate rhythmic patterns, prob. derived from African drumming, performed with the hands as an accompaniment to various Afr.-Amer. dances, esp. the JUBA (*patting Juba*).

Patton, Charley (c1887–1934) Amer. blues singer and guitarist from Mississippi, known esp. from his recordings, made during the last five years of his life.

Patzak, Julius (1898–1974) Austrian tenor, self-taught as a singer. He sang with the Munich Opera (1928–45), then with the Vienna Opera and in England. He taught at the Vienna Music Academy and the Mozarteum in Salzburg.

Pauken ['pow-kən] (Ger.) TIMPANI.

Paukenmesse [-"me-se] (Ger., Timpani Mass) popular name for the *Missa in tempore belli* in B♭ major (1782) by Haydn.

Paul, Les (Polfus, Lester) (1915–) Amer. guitarist and inventor, leader of the Les Paul Trio in the 1930s and popular performer in duo with his wife, Mary Ford, in the 1950s. He pioneered in the development of guitar amplification, multitrack recording, overdubbing and various types of guitar pickups.

Paulus, Stephen (Harrison) (1949–) Amer. composer, stud. of Paul Fetler and Argento. He was co-founder of the Minnesota Composers Forum and has been composer-in-residence of the Minnesota Orch. His operas *The Village Singer* (1979) and *The Postman Always Rings Twice* (1982) were premiered by the Opera Theater of St. Louis. He has also written works for chamber orch., many songs, chamber music and tape works.

Paumgartner, Bernhard (1887–1971) Austrian musicologist, conductor and composer, stud. of Guido Adler and Eusebius Mandyczewski. He was dir. of the Salzburg Mozarteum from 1917 to 1959, excluding the war years, and was closely involved with the Salzburg Festival. He was also very active as a music editor and was an expert on Mozart.

pausa ['pow-zä] (It.) *also*, **pause 1**, REST. **2**, FERMATA. Cf. LUFTPAUSE.

pause [pōz] (Fr.) half-note REST.

Pause ['pow-ze] (Ger.) REST. Cf. CAESURA.

pavane *also*, **pavan, pavin** a 16th- and 17th-c. English court DANCE of Italian origin in duple meter and of slow and stately tempo, often used as a processional or wedding march. The pavan-saltarello-piva was a common grouping; the most usual in the 16th c. is pavan-galliard. By mid-16th c. the dance was giving way to the PASSAMEZZO; later, it gained new significance as an English keyboard idiom.

Pavarotti, Luciano (1935–) immensely successful Italian tenor, stud. of Arrigo Pola and Ettore Campogalliani. His U.S. debut was in 1965 in Miami; his Metropolitan Opera debut was two years later. In addition to his most famous operatic roles— Rodolfo (*La Bohème*), Cavaradossi (*Tosca*), Calaf (*Turandot*) and the Duke (*Rigoletto*)—he excels in the performance of Italian songs.

pavillon [pä-vē'yō] (Fr.) the BELL of a wind instrument.

pavillon d'amour [dä'moor] (Fr.) the bulbous lowest section of an English horn, oboe d'amore and several now obsolete instruments. Also, *Liebesfuss* (Ger.).

pavillon chinois [shē'nwä] (Fr.) TURKISH CRESCENT.

Paz, Juan Carlos (1901–72) Argentinian composer and theorist, trained in Buenos Aires and in Paris with d'Indy. He was a founder of several organizations in support of new music, incl. the Grupo Renovación, the Conciertos de la Nueva Música and the Agrupación Nueva Música. His works, always searching for a new musical language, are primarily instrumental, for orch., chamber ensemble and solo piano.

Peabody Conservatory music conservatory founded in 1857 in Baltimore, MD, with an endowment from George Peabody. It is part of the Peabody Institute and affiliated with Johns Hopkins U. Its directors have included Reginald Stewart, Peter Mennin, Richard Franko Goldman, Elliott W. Galkin and Robert O. Pierce.

Peacock, Gary (1935–) Amer. jazz double-bass player. He performed with Bud Shank, Bill Evans, Miles Davis and Albert Ayler, in avant-garde recordings and performances in the early 1960s and with his own groups after 1977.

Pearl, Minnie (Cannon, Sarah Ophelia) (1912–) Amer. country-music singer and comedienne, who derived her rural character from an actual person in Alabama. She joined the Grand Ole Opry in 1940 and appeared regularly on the TV program "Hee Haw." She was elected to the Country Music Hall of Fame in 1975.

Pearl Fishers, The (Fr., *Les Pêcheurs de perles*) romantic opera in 3 acts by Bizet to a libretto by Eugène Cormon and Michel Carré. Premiere, Paris 1863. The illicit love between a Brahmin priestess, Leîla, and a fisherman, Nadir, is aided by his comrade and rival, Zurga.

Pears, Sir **Peter (Neville Luard)** (1910–86) English tenor, stud. of Elena Gerhardt and Dawson Freer. He sang in various vocal groups until 1936, when a long association began with composer Benjamin Britten. He sang with the Sadler's Wells Opera from 1943 and was a founder of the English Opera Group in 1946 and the

Aldeburgh Festival in 1948, where he taught until his death. He was esp. noted for his performances of the Evangelist in the Bach Passions, of various Mozart roles and of the roles written for him by Britten.

Peasant Cantata popular name for the secular cantata No. 212, "Mer hahn en neue Oberkeet" (We have a new overseer) (1742) by J.S. Bach to a text by Picander.

peau de buffle [pō də büfl] (Fr.) a harpsichord register with plectra made of buff leather.

Pêcheurs de perles, Les [pe'shœr də perl] (Fr.) PEARL FISHERS, THE.

ped. *abbr.* PEDAL.

pedal a foot-operated lever used on various instruments for various purposes, as for expression on the piano, organ, etc.; to change stops on the harpsichord, organ, etc.; to tune the harp and timpani; to pump air for the harmonium, etc.; or to sound the bass drum or hi-hat cymbal in a jazz and popular-music percussion set.

pedal board a pedal keyboard operated by the feet, esp. on an organ or harpsichord.

pedal clarinet CONTRABASS CLARINET.

pedal guitar a STEEL GUITAR having pedals and sometimes knee levers used to change the pitch of a note before or while it is being sounded. Many have two necks, each with its own set of strings tuned to a different open chord.

pédalier [pā-dä'lyä] (Fr.) PEDAL BOARD.

pedaliter (Lat.) an indication that a work for organ is to be played by both hands and feet. Cf. MANUALITER.

pedal piano a PIANO with an attached pedal board.

pedal point a sustained note in the bass, usu. the tonic or dominant and often occurring toward the end of a work. Also, *organ point*.

pedal tone *also*, **pedal note** one of the FUNDAMENTAL notes of a brass instrument, sometimes called for in instrumental scores.

Pedrell, Felipe (1841–1922) Spanish composer and musicologist, largely self-taught. Most of his works were composed before 1880, after which he concentrated on historical study and writing on Spanish liturgical music. His works incl. operas (esp. *Los Pirineos*, a trilogy), several orchestral works, choruses, songs and works for piano solo.

Peerce, Jan (Perelmuth, Jacob Pincus) (1904–84) Amer. tenor, stud. of Giuseppe Boghetti. His operatic career began late, in 1938, and his Metropolitan Opera debut was three years later. He sang in every major U.S. and European opera house, with the Bolshoi Opera in 1956 and on Broadway in *Fiddler on the Roof*. He taught at the Mannes College of Music from 1981.

Peer Gynt incidental music (1874–75) by Grieg for the play by Henrik Ibsen. The composer arranged two orchestral suites from the score, Ops. 46 and 55 (1876), but the various numbers are performed in widely differing orders and combinations.

Peerson, Martin (c1571–1651) English organist, virginalist and composer of ayres, motets, anthems, and keyboard and consort music.

Peer-Southern Amer. music publishing firm est. in 1928 as Southern Music Publishing Co. and combined in 1960 with Peer International Corp. The firm has concentrated on jazz, country music and contemporary music, and published works of many important Amer. composers, incl. Ives, Cowell and Wolpe.

Peeters, Flor (1903–86) Belgian composer, organist and teacher, studied at the Lemmens Institute in Mechelen, where he taught until 1931. He also taught at the Ghent, the Tilburg and Antwerp conservatories and was organist at the Cathedral of St. Rombout in Mechelen. He is best known for his many organ works, but he also wrote much sacred choral music, an organ concerto and chamber music.

peg *also*, **tuning peg** a wooden pin used to regulate the pitch of a string in a string instrument.

pegbox the portion of the head of a string instrument which holds the tuning pegs.

Peking Opera (Chin., *ching-chü*) a type of Chinese theater founded in Peking in the late 18th c., typically having very simple settings with complex costumes and stage action and stereotyped characters. The companies were exclusively either men or women until the early 20th c. The Peking Opera was reformed in 1949 to conform with Communist ideals.

Pelléas et Mélisande [pø-lā'äs ä mā-lē'zäd] play (1892) by Maurice Maeterlinck in which Prince Golaud kills his brother Pelléas, after Pelléas falls in love with Goland's wife, Mélisande. The play has inspired a number of musical works, incl. **1**, tragic opera in 5 acts by Debussy. Premiere, Paris 1902. **2**, incidental music (1898) by Fauré; also, a suite derived from the score by the composer. **3**, symphonic poem, Op. 5 (1902–3) by Schoenberg. **4**, incidental music, Op. 46 (1905), by Sibelius.

Pelletier, (Louis) Wilfred (1896–1982) Canadian conductor and educator, stud. of Isidore Philipp and Widor in Paris. He joined the Metropolitan Opera in 1917 as coach and assistant conductor, becoming a regular conductor in 1932. He was a founder of the Montreal SO in 1935 and of their children's concerts series. He retired in 1970.

Penderecki, Krzystof (1933–) Polish composer, trained at the Kraków Conservatory, where he later taught. He frequently travels to conduct his own works, which have won many awards. His music utilizes a rich palette of colors, with large blocks of sound, clusters and innovative scoring. His opera *Paradise Lost* (1978) was commissioned by the Lyric Opera of Chicago. His works incl. *The Devils of Loudon* and *Paradise Lost* (operas), incidental music, *Threnody for the Victims of Hiroshima, De natura sonoris* (orch.), chamber music, and music for tape.

Pendergrass, Teddy (1950–) Amer. soul singer, drummer and songwriter. He played with the Cadillacs and Harold Melvin and the Blue Notes, then had success as a solo recording artist.

penillion an improvised Welsh song with words sung to a familiar tune and accompanied on the harp.

Pennario, Leonard (1924–) Amer. pianist, stud. of Olga Steeb and Toch. He has toured extensively and performed in trio with Heifetz and Piatigorsky.

penny whistle a small, high-pitched, metal WHISTLE FLUTE made popular in the 1980s by flutist James Galway. Also, *tin whistle.*

pentachord 1, an ancient five-stringed instrument. **2**, a diatonic SCALE with five notes to the octave.

pentatonic a term referring to any SCALE consisting of five notes to the octave, esp. a major scale of which the fourth and seventh tones are omitted (thus eliminating minor 2nds). Pentatonic scales are common in folk music and have been used by many composers.

Pentland, Barbara (Lally) (1912–) Canadian composer, stud. of Cécile Gauthiez, Frederick Jacobi, Wagenaar and Copland. She taught at the U. of British Columbia from 1949 to 1963, then concentrated on composition. Her works, in all genres except stage music, have developed from a lush, romantic style in the 1930s to a Webernesque serialism and beyond in the 1970s. Her works incl. 3 symphonies, *Variations concertantes* (piano, orch.), 3 string quartets and other chamber music, songs and choral works and many works for solo piano.

Pépin, (Jean-Josephat) Clermont [pä'pɛ̃] (1926–) Canadian composer, pianist and teacher, trained in Montreal, Philadelphia, Toronto and Paris. He taught at the Montreal Conservatory from 1955 to 1964, then was its dir. from 1967 to 1972. His works make inventive use of instrumental groups and performance placement of instruments and incl. 4 symphonies, 2 piano concertos, choral and solo vocal works, works for string quartet, sonatas and works for solo piano.

Pepper, Art(hur Edward) (1925–82) Amer. jazz alto and tenor saxophonist. He played with Benny Carter, Stan Kenton, Jack Montrose, Buddy Rich and Don Ellis, successfully combining the lighter West Coast sound with the passion of bop.

Pepping, Ernst (1901–81) German composer, stud. of Gmeindl. He taught at the Spandau Church Music School and at the Hochschule für Musik in Berlin. His works, which remain within traditional forms and techniques, are mainly sacred and secular choruses and organ works, but he also wrote several symphonies, a piano concerto, chamber works and works for piano.

Pepusch, Johann Christoph (1667– 1752) German composer, theorist and antiquarian. He was in the service of the Prussian court until about 1700, then moved to London, where he worked at Drury Lane Theatre and was music dir. for the duke of Chandos. He was also a founder of the Academy of Ancient Music. He wrote the bass lines and the overture for *The Beggar's Opera* and produced several other ballad operas after it, hoping to recapture its success. He also wrote *A Treatise on Harmony* and other theoretical works.

Perahia, Murray (1947–) Amer. pianist, stud. of Artur Balsam and Horzowski. He has toured widely, specializing in Mozart and late Romantic repertory, and has performed frequently as a chamber music musician and as accompanist.

percussion instruments strictly used, the term refers to tuned or untuned IDIOPHONES or MEMBRANO-PHONES which are struck by beaters or sticks to produce sound. However, in current usage the term usu. encompasses all idiophones and most membranophones, no matter how sounded, whether by percussion, friction, concussion, being shaken, plucked or stamped (see illus., p. 404).

perdendosi [per′den-dō-sē] *also,* **perdendo** (It.) dying away.

Perera, Ronald (Christopher) (1941–) Amer. composer, stud. of Kirchner and Gottfried Koenig. He has taught at Syracuse U., Dartmouth College and Smith College. He has specialized in electronic and computer music and most of his works involve taped sounds.

Peress, Maurice (1930–) Amer. conductor and trumpeter, trained at NYU and the Mannes College. He began as a trumpeter, then became Bernstein's assistant with the New York PO. He has been music dir. of the Corpus Christi SO, the Austin SO and the Kansas City PO and has conducted at the Vienna Staatsoper and the San Francisco Opera.

perfect 1, designating the intervals of the unison, fourth, fifth and octave. See INTERVAL. 2, designating a note value in MENSURAL NOTATION which equals three of the next lower denomination.

perfect cadence the dominant chord followed by the tonic chord in root position (V-I). Also, *full cadence, authentic cadence, full close.* See CADENCE.

perfect consonance the INTERVAL of a major or minor 4th or 5th or their compounds (11th, 12th, etc.). Cf. IMPERFECT CONSONANCE.

perfect pitch ABSOLUTE PITCH.

performance art a type of theatrical art involving solo or small ensemble performance combining visual arts (incl. video art), music (often rock) and stage action. Such performances often have elements of Dada and other experimental movements of the early 1900s and sometimes resemble the improvised "happenings" of the 1960s.

performance practice a term for the combination of elements which constitutes a musical performance: instrumentation, style, convention, expression, etc. Since these elements can be only imperfectly specified in a musical score, it is difficult for later generations—which no longer have

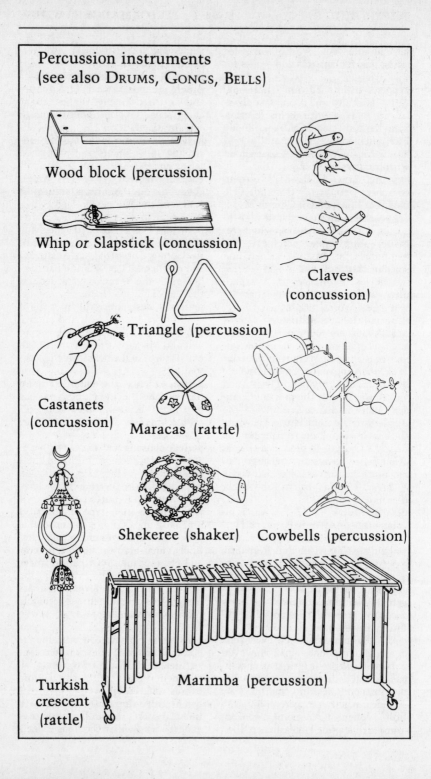

Percussion instruments
(see also DRUMS, GONGS, BELLS)

Wood block (percussion)

Whip *or* Slapstick (concussion)

Claves (concussion)

Triangle (percussion)

Castanets (concussion)

Maracas (rattle)

Shekeree (shaker)

Cowbells (percussion)

Turkish crescent (rattle)

Marimba (percussion)

the unwritten conventions of the time to help them—to produce a historically accurate performance of a work of the past. Scholars attempt, through study of the few written clues that may be available, to throw some light on what the scores do not clarify. Cf. STYLE.

performing rights societies organizations which collect fees for the performance of works registered by their members and protect their members against unauthorized performances of their works. There are four such organizations in the U.S.: the American Society of Composers, Authors and Publishers (ASCAP), Broadcast Music, Inc. (BMI), Sesac, Inc. and the Harry Fox Agency, Inc.

Pergolesi, Giovanni Battista (1710–36) Italian composer, trained in Naples under Gaetano Greco, Leonardo Vinci and Francesco Durante. For the short period of his professional life he served a succession of Neopolitan nobles and produced a remarkable volume of work, which brought him fame only after his death. His works incl. serious and comic operas (esp. *La serva padrona*), a *Stabat mater* and other sacred vocal music, cantatas, arias, instrumental concertos and sonatas.

Peri, Jacopo (1561–1633) Italian composer, singer and organist, one of the first opera composers. He held posts as organist and singer in churches in Florence and at the Medici court, where he later concentrated on composition, and maintained close connections with Mantua as well. In addition to *Dafne* (lost) and *Euridice* (1600), his best-known work, he wrote several other operas, oratorios, ballettos, intermedios and songs.

Périchole, La comic opera in 3 acts by Offenbach to a libretto by Henri Meilhac and Ludovic Halévy. Premiere, Paris 1868. The streetsingers Paquillo and La Périchole survive the machinations of the love-struck viceroy of Lima.

period a musical section or phrase, comparable to a grammatical sentence, delineated by the completion of the musical sense, usu. by a full cadence. A period is often composed of two parts, an antecedent and a consequent (see ANTECEDENT).

Perkins, Carl (1932–) Amer. rockabilly singer and songwriter, better known for his songs recorded by others, incl. the Beatles. His biggest hit was "Blue Suede Shoes" in 1956.

Perkins, Henry S(outhwick) (1833–1914) Amer. composer and music educator, founder of the Chicago National College of Music (1891) and an organizer of the Music Teachers National Assoc. (1876) and the Illinois Music Teachers Assoc. (1886).

Perkins, John MacIvor (1935–) Amer. composer and teacher, stud. of Boulanger, Gerhard, Arthur Berger and others. He has taught at the U. of Chicago, Harvard and Washington U. in St. Louis. His relatively small list of works incl. *Andrea del Sarto* (opera), instrumental works and songs.

Perle, George (1915–) Amer. composer and theorist, stud. of Wesley Laviolette and Krenek. He has taught at the U. of Louisville, the U. of California at Davis and Queens College in NY. He developed a concept of "12-tone tonality" combining serial techniques with the use of tonal centers. He won the Pulitzer Prize in 1986 for his *Wind Quintet IV*. He has also written several important books on the Second Viennese School, incl. *The Operas of Alban Berg* (1980–85). His works incl. 3 symphonies, 2 serenades for chamber orch., cello concerto, much chamber music, piano works and songs.

Perlea, Jonel (1900–70) Romanian conductor, trained in Munich and Leipzig. He conducted in Bucharest, in Italy, in the U.S. at the Metropolitan Opera (briefly), at the Manhattan School of Music and for the Connecticut SO.

Perlman, Itzhak (1945–) Israeli-born. Amer. violinist, trained in Tel-Aviv and in New York with Galamian and DeLay. He lost the use of his legs at the age of four as a result of poliomyelitis. He won the Leventritt Competition in 1964 and has since toured throughout the world and recorded extensively. He has taught at Brooklyn College and held master classes at various music festivals.

Pérotin (fl. early 13th c.) Parisian composer of organum, conductus and discant, credited with having revised the MAGNUS LIBER ORGANI of Léonin and with writing the first examples of four-voice polyphony (*Sederunt principes, Viderunt omnes*).

perpetual canon CIRCULAR CANON.

perpetuum mobile (Lat.) MOTO PERPETUO.

Perrault, Michel (1925–) Canadian composer, conductor and teacher, stud. of Boulanger and Honegger. He has been assistant conductor of the Montreal SO and musical dir. of Les Grands Ballets Canadiens. His works incl. ballets, concertos, orchestral music, chamber music and works for jazz ensemble.

Perry, Julia (Amanda) (1924–79) Amer. composer, stud. of Boulanger and Dallapiccola. Her works, mostly in a neoclassical style, incl. 4 operas, 12 symphonies (incl. *Soul Symphony*), cantatas and other vocal works and chamber music.

Perséphone [per-sä'fon] (Fr.) danced melodrama in 1 act by Stravinsky to a libretto by André Gide. Premiere, Paris 1934. The legend of Perséphone, daughter of the goddess of agriculture.

Persichetti, Vincent (1915–87) Amer. composer, conductor and pianist, stud. of Harris, Nordhoff and Reiner. He taught at Combs College, the Philadelphia Conservatory and the Juilliard School. He also worked for the publisher Elkan-Vogel from 1952. He composed in all genres except stage works in a variety of styles depending on the work.

Persinger, Louis (1887–1966) Amer. violinist, pianist and teacher, stud. of Hans Becker, Ysaÿe, Nikisch and others. He formed his own string quartet in 1917 in San Francisco, where he

also directed the Chamber Music Society and taught (Yehudi Menuhin and Isaac Stern were among his pupils). He later taught at the Cleveland Institute and the Juilliard School.

Perspectives of New Music a semi-annual journal devoted to 20th-c. music (esp. 12-tone serial music), est. in 1962 at Princeton.

pes 1, a medieval English term analagous to TENOR (2). A pes can be formed of two voices, as in the two-part rondellus that accompanies the round "Sumer is a cumin in." **2**, a NEUME representing two notes, the first lower than the second.

pesante [pä'zän-tä] (It.) heavy, weighty.

Peter and the Wolf a "tale for children" for narrator and orch., Op. 67 (1936), by Prokofiev, in which each character is represented by a different instrument or instrumental section of the orch.—bird (flute), duck (oboe), cat (clarinet), grandfather (bassoon), wolf (horns) and Peter (strings).

Peter Grimes tragic opera in 3 acts by Britten to a libretto by Montagu Salter, after the poem "The Borough" by George Crabbe. Premiere, London 1945. Commissioned by the Koussevitzky Music Foundation. The hypocrisy of a small fishing town drives the fisherman Peter Grimes to suicide.

Peter, Paul and Mary Amer. folk trio formed in 1961, often active in support of political causes. Their hits incl. "Leaving on a Jet Plane" (1969) and "Puff, the Magic Dragon" (1963). They disbanded in 1970, then reformed in 1982.

Peters German firm of music publishers in Leipzig founded in 1800 by Hoffmeister and Kühnel and purchased by Carl Friedrich Peters (1779–1827) in 1814. The firm published works of Bach, Mozart, Haydn and Beethoven, as well as of lesser-known composers.

Peters (Petermann), **Roberta** (1930–) Amer. soprano, stud. of William Hermann. She sang with the Metropolitan Opera from 1950 and at other houses around the world as well as on film and in musical comedy. Her roles incl. Gilda (*Rigoletto*), Despina (*Così fan tutte*) and Lucia.

Peterson, Oscar (Emmanuel) (1925–) Canadian jazz bop pianist, composer and leader noted for his extraordinary technical skill. He frequently performed in Norman Granz's Jazz at the Philharmonic tours. He usu. works in a trio with bass and guitar or bass and drums, and has accompanied many solo artists.

Petit, Buddy (1897–1931) Amer. jazz cornetist from Louisiana, co-leader with Jimmie Noone from 1916 of a band in New Orleans and a colleague of Louis Armstrong. He worked briefly with Jelly Roll Morton on the West Coast.

petite flûte [ptēt] (Fr.) PICCOLO.

Petrassi, Goffredo (1904–) Italian composer, organist and teacher, stud. of Vincenzo di Donato, Bustini and Molinari. In Rome he taught at the Conservatorio and Accademia di St. Cecilia and he has given master classes at the Mozarteum, Tanglewood and elsewhere. His works incl. ballets, operas (*Il cordovano* and *Morte dell'aria*), 8 concertos for orch., choral works (*Coro di morti*), songs, chamber music and works for piano solo.

Petri, Egon (1881–1962) Dutch-born German pianist, stud. of Busoni, naturalized Amer. in the 1940s. He was noted esp. for his performance of Bach and Liszt. In the U.S. he taught at Cornell and Mills College in CA.

Petrides, Frédérique Joanne (Mayer, Frédérica Jeanne Elisabeth Petronille) (1903–83) Belgian-born Amer. conductor, stud. of Crickboom, Gösta Andreasson and Paul Stassevitch. In 1933, she founded the all-female Orchestrette of New York, whose influential newsletter she edited.

Petrillo, James C(aesar) (1892–1984) Amer. trumpeter and labor leader, president of the Chicago local of the AFM in 1922 and national president in 1940.

Petrushka *also*, **Petrouchka** ballet (1911) with music by Stravinsky to a libretto by Alexandre Benois, written for Dyaghilev's Ballets Russes and first choreographed by Fokine. The composer extracted an often-played orchestral suite in 1914 (revised 1947) and also made a piano arrangement of 3 movements. The ballet tells the story of a love triangle among three puppets: Petrushka, a Ballerina and a Moor.

Petrushka chord a CHORD used in the ballet PETRUSHKA, combining a C-major chord with an F♯-major chord, an example of POLYTONALITY.

Petrucci, Ottaviano (dei) (1466–1539) 16th-c. Italian music printer and publisher, the first to print music with movable type (*Odhecaton A*, 1501).

Pettiford, Oscar (1922–60) Native Amer. jazz bop bassist and bandleader. He played with Charlie Barnet's band, trumpeters Roy Eldridge and Dizzy Gillespie, and with Duke Ellington, then led his own big band in the mid-1950s. He was an important influence on later bop bassists Charles Mingus and Ray Brown.

petto, voce di ['pet-tō, 'vō-chē dē] (It.) CHEST VOICE.

Petty, Tom (Thomas) (1952–) Amer. rock singer, guitarist and songwriter, leader of the rock band Heartbreakers, formed in Los Angeles in 1975.

Peyer, Gervase de DE PEYER, GERVASE.

peyote drum a type of WATER DRUM usu. consisting of a soaked buckskin hide stretched over an iron kettle and struck with a single beater. The drum is used in certain Native American religious ceremonies.

Pezel (Petzold), **Johann Christoph** (1639–94) German composer and civic musician in Leipzig and later in Bautzen. He wrote music for various wind and string groups, as well as some vocal music (much of which is lost).

pf *abbr.* pianoforte (see PIANO 2,).

Pfitzner, Hans (Erich) (1869–1949) German composer, pianist and conductor, stud. of Iwan Knorr and James

Kwast. He taught at the Stern Conservatory in Berlin, then moved to Strasbourg, where he taught and conducted. He is best remembered for his opera *Palestrina* (1912–15). He also wrote other operas, choral music and songs, several symphonies, concertos (for violin, cello and piano) and chamber music.

Phalèse, Pierre [fä'lez] (c1510–c1575) Antwerp music printer and publisher of the 16th c. The Phalèse family maintained the publishing house until 1674.

Phantasie (Ger.) FANTASIA.

phantasy the required title for one-movement chamber music compositions entered in an English competition est. in 1905 by Walter Cobbett.

phase music a compositional process assoc. with MINIMALISM, involving the repetition of the same material simultaneously by different instruments, but in phase with each other only part of the time.

phaser an electronic processor used to produce a special undulating sound effect through a PHASE SHIFT (2,) in the signal from an electric guitar or other instrument.

phase shift 1, the effect in PHASE MUSIC when two or more polyphonic parts gradually move out of synchronization with one another. 2, a shift in the direction of an electronic signal produced by a PHASER.

Philadelphia Orchestra orch. founded in 1900 in Philadelphia, PA. Its music dir. have been Fritz Scheel, Karl Pohlig, Stokowski, Ormandy and Muti. It performs at the ACADEMY OF MUSIC.

Phile, Philip (?–1793) Amer. violinist and composer, concertmaster of the orch. of the Old American Company from c1784 and composer of "The President's March," later used to set the text "Hail Columbia."

Philharmonia Orchestra orch. founded in London in 1945 by producer Walter Legge for public performance and recording. The orch. reorganized as the New Philharmonia Orchestra under conductor Otto

Klemperer, then went back to its original name in 1977.

philharmonic 1, formerly, a lover of music. 2, a musical org., esp. a symphony orch.

Philidor, François-André-Danican (1726–95) French composer and chess master, one of an extensive family of musicians, stud. of Campra. He supported himself at first by music copying and teaching, but later by his chess playing. As a composer he was most successful in writing *opéra-comique*, among them *Tom Jones* (1765) and *Ernelinde* (1767).

Philipp, Isidor (1863–1958) Hungarian-born French pianist and teacher, trained at the Paris Conservatoire. A successful concert artist, he was however most noted as a teacher at the Paris Conservatoire until 1934 and in New York during World War II.

Philippe de Vitry VITRY, PHILIPPE DE.

Philippot, Michel Paul (1925–) French composer, stud. of Dandelot and Leibowitz. He has taught at the Paris Conservatoire and at the U. of São Bernardo do Campo in Brazil. As a composer, he advocates the application of scientific principles to music, and his works involve rigorous use of systems.

Philips, Peter (1561–1628) English composer and organist. A Catholic, he fled England in 1582, settling in Antwerp. He joined the chapel of Archduke Albert as organist in 1597, becoming a member of the royal chapel when the archduke married Isabella of Spain. Philips was a prolific composer, and many of his works were published in his lifetime. He wrote motets, madrigals, keyboard works and works for various instrumental ensembles.

Phillips, Burrill (1907–88) Amer. composer, pianist and teacher, stud. of Hanson and Rogers. He taught at the Eastman School, the U. of Illinois, the Juilliard School and Cornell. His works incl. ballets, *Selections from McGuffey's Reader* and other orch. works, choral works, piano sonatas, string quartets and other chamber music.

Phillips, Harvey (Gene) (1929–) Amer. tuba player and administrator, trained at the Juilliard School. After many years of playing in various orchestras, incl. those of the New York City Ballet and the Metropolitan Opera, he became assistant to the president of the New England Conservatory, then joined the faculty of Indiana U. He is noted for his virtuoso technique and smooth tone.

Philosopher, The popular name for the Symphony No. 22 in E♭ major (1764) by Haydn. So named because of the solemn character of the first movement.

Philosophic popular name for the Symphony No. 6 in A major (1879–81) by Bruckner.

Phoenix Symphony Orchestra orch. founded in Phoenix, AZ, in 1947 under John Barnett. Subsequent conductors have been Robert Lawrence, Leslie Hodge, Guy Taylor, Phillip Spurgeon, Eduardo Mata and Theo Alcantara.

phon a unit of LOUDNESS.

phonograph a mechanism for reproducing sound recorded on discs or (formerly) cylinders by means of a metal or gem stylus agitated by variations in the walls of a spiral groove. A development in 1957 permitted the recording of two simultaneous channels in the same groove, resulting in STEREOPHONIC sound.

phrase a linguistic term applied to short musical units, usu. longer than a MOTIF but shorter than a PERIOD, delineated in some way such as by a cadence or melodic contour. It can apply either to a melodic unit (see PHRASING) or to a complete polyphonic unit.

phrasing the grouping and articulation of a group of notes so as to form a logical unit or PHRASE.

phrygian the authentic MODE on E, the third of the eight church modes.

phrygian cadence a CADENCE in which the lowest part arrives on the final or tonic from above by a semitone.

piacere, a [pyä'chā-rā, ä] (It.) A PIACERE.

piacevole [pyä'chā-vō-lä] (It., pleasant) peaceful, relaxed.

Piaf, Edith (Giovanna) (1915–63) French singer in cabaret, films, TV, radio and operetta. Her many songs incl. "Mon légionnaire," "La Vie en rose" and "Le Vagabond."

pianette (Fr.) PIANINO.

piangendo [pyän'gen-dō] (It.) plaintively.

pianino (It.) a small upright PIANO (2,).

pianissimo (It.) very softly. Abbr., *pp* (or sometimes, erroneously, *ppp*), p^{mo}.

pianississimo (It.) extremely softly. Abbr., *ppp, pppp*, etc.

piano (It.) **1**, softly. Abbr., *p*. **2**, *also*, **pianoforte** a keyboard string instrument in which the strings are struck by felt-covered hammers that rebound after striking the string, allowing the string to continue sounding until the key is released. The rebound is made possible by a mechanism called an *escapement*. When the key is released, a damper falls upon the string to stop the sound. Most pianos have two or three pedals, which usu. function as follows: The left, soft or *una corda* pedal moves the hammers so that they strike only one string, making for a softer sound. The right or *loud* pedal keeps the dampers raised above all the strings, even when all the keys have been released. The middle or *sostenuto* pedal, found only on some pianos, functions similarly to the right pedal, but allows the player to choose which dampers will remain off the strings.

The piano was developed in the early 18th c. by an Italian, Bartolommeo Cristofori (1655–1731). Pianos are made in various shapes and sizes, the principal variants being the SPINET, the tail or GRAND PIANO, the SQUARE PIANO and the UPRIGHT PIANO. For predecessors of the piano, see CLAVICHORD and HARPSICHORD.

piano-accordion an ACCORDION with

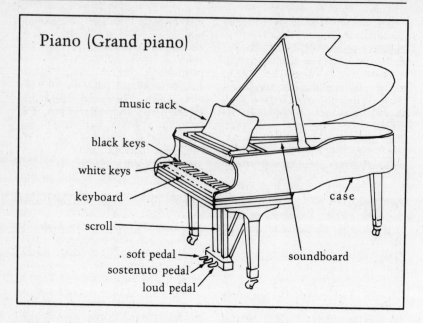

Piano (Grand piano)

music rack
black keys
white keys
keyboard
scroll
soft pedal
sostenuto pedal
loud pedal
case
soundboard

a keyboard for the right hand corresponding to the middle register of a piano.

piano arrangement an ARRANGEMENT for piano solo of a work orig. written for another instrument or ensemble.

piano concerto a CONCERTO for piano and orch.

piano duet **1**, a work for two pianists playing at one piano, one playing the upper half of the keyboard, the other the lower. The music is notated either with both parts together, the top system being the *primo*, the bottom being the *secondo*; or with the *primo* part on the right-hand page, the *secondo* part on the left-hand page. **2**, a work for two pianists, each at his/her own instrument.

pianoforte PIANO (2,).

piano player **1**, pianist. **2**, the mechanism in a PLAYER PIANO that operates the keys and hammers.

piano quartet a chamber work for piano with three other instruments, usu. violin, viola and cello; also, the ensemble itself.

piano quintet a chamber work for piano with four other instruments,

usu. a string quartet; also, the ensemble itself.

pianola **1**, (*trademark*) PLAYER PIANO. **2**, a piano equipped with a PIANO player (2,).

piano reduction a PIANO ARRANGEMENT of a work orig. written for instrumental ensemble or orch. Also, *piano score*.

piano sonata a SONATA for solo piano.

piano trio a work for piano with two other instruments, usu. violin and cello; also, the ensemble itself.

Piatigorsky, Gregor (1903–76) Russian-born Amer. cellist and composer, stud. of Alfred von Glehn and Anatol Brandukov. He played in the Lenin Quartet and was principal cellist of the Bolshoi Theater orch. After leaving the Soviet Union in 1921, he became principal cellist of the Berlin PO, then left in 1928 to pursue his solo career, which was spectacularly successful. He played in famous trios with Horowitz and Milstein and with Heifetz and Rubinstein and was cofounder of the Heifetz-Piatigorsky Concerts in Los Angeles, dir. of chamber music at the Berkshire Music

Center and on the faculty of the U. of S. California.

piatti ['pyät-tē] (It.) CYMBALS.

Piazzolla, Astor (1921–) Argentine composer, stud. of Boulanger, noted for his exploration of the tango as a medium for classical art music.

pibgorn *also,* **pibcorn** an obsolete Welsh single-reed wind instrument similar to the HORNPIPE.

pibroch *also,* **piobaireachd** ('pē-bräk) theme and variations on a traditional theme for Scottish bagpipe.

Picardy third a major third used as part of a major chord at the end of a work written predominantly in the minor mode. Also, *tierce de Picardie* (Fr.).

Piccini, Niccolò (1728–1800) prolific Italian opera composer, stud. of Leo and Durante. He was highly successful as a composer of comic and serious operas, esp. in Naples and Rome, until 1775. He then went to Paris, becoming part of a famous conflict between his own supporters and supporters of Gluck. He enjoyed success in Paris for a decade, then once again fell from public favor. The final years of his life were spent in indigence and anonymity. His works incl. over 100 operas, several oratorios, sacred and secular vocal music, and instrumental sonatas.

piccolo *also,* **piccolo flauto** (It., small) a small FLUTE pitched an octave above the standard concert flute. It is notated an octave lower than it sounds.

piccolo trumpet a small high TRUMPET pitched in D or E♭ or equipped to play in either key with a valve for switching.

piccolo violoncello a small 18th-c. CELLO, tuned like the standard cello, often with an extra treble string, used as a solo instrument and sometimes called for in the cantatas of J.S. Bach.

picco pipe a type of small RECORDER with two finger holes and a thumb hole, capable of playing a chromatic range of three octaves.

pick 1, PLECTRUM. **2,** a young dancer, usu. black, employed as an adjunct to a performing act in a minstrel show at the turn of the 20th c.

Picker, Tobias (1954–) Amer. composer and pianist, stud. of Wuorinen and Elliott Carter. He has been composer-in-residence for the Houston SO and has received many commissions. His works, which show a fresh originality, incl. a piano concerto, chamber music and works for solo piano.

Pickett, Wilson (1941–) Amer. soul singer and songwriter from Alabama. He sang with the Falcons, a rhythm-and-blues group in Detroit, then later with Booker T. and the MGs, their first hit being "In the Midnight Hour." He continues to tour and to record.

pickup 1, UPBEAT. **2,** a microphone, esp. a small microphone attached to an instrument.

pickup group a band, orch., etc., put together for a specific appearance or recording, not working together on a regular basis.

Picou, Alphonse (Floristan) [pē'koo] (1878–1961) Amer. Dixieland jazz clarinetist from New Orleans. He played with various groups until the 1930s and again in the 1950s, when traditional jazz enjoyed a revival.

Pictures at an Exhibition piano suite (1874) by Mussorgsky, inspired by sketches and watercolors by Victor Hartmann. The suite has been orchestrated several times, the most popular being the one made by Maurice Ravel in 1923, a commission by Serge Koussevitsky. The sections/pictures (separated by a kind of refrain, the "Promenade") are: "Gnomus" (The Gnome); "Il Vecchio Castello" (The Old Castle); "Tuileries"; "Bydlo" (Cattle); "Ballet of the Chicks in Their Shells"; "Two Polish Jews, One Rich, the Other Poor"; "Limoges—The Marketplace"; "Catacombs"; "With the Dead in a Dead Language"; "The Hut on Fowl's Legs"; and "The Great Gate of Kiev."

piece a musical composition; work.

pièce croisée [pyes krwä'zā] (Fr., crossed work) a harpsichord work to be played on two manuals, in which the hands constantly cross each other in the same range.

piede ['piā-dā] (It.) the second section of the 14th-c. Italian BALLATA.

Pierce, Webb (1926–91) Amer. honky-tonk singer and guitarist, a highly successful recording artist from the 1950s to the 1970s. His tunes incl. "Back Street Affair" and "Missing You."

Pierian Sodality musical organization at Harvard, founded in 1808, which sponsors the Harvard-Radcliffe Orch. and other activities.

Pierlot, Pierre (1921–) French oboist, trained at the Paris Conservatoire, winner of the Geneva Competition in 1949. He was a founder of the Quintette à vent français and of the Ensemble baroque de Paris and has taught at the Paris Conservatoire since 1969. He has made numerous recordings of Baroque and Classical repertory.

Pierné, (Henri-Constant-) Gabriel (1863–1937) French composer and conductor, stud. of Franck and Massenet. He was organist at St. Clotilde in Paris and conductor of the Concerts Colonne (from 1910) and the Ballets Russes. He wrote operas, ballets, orchestral suites, tone poems, choral works, songs and chamber music.

Pierrot Lunaire [pye'rō lü'ner] (Fr.) epochal melodrama, Op. 21 (1912), by Schoenberg, a setting of 21 poems by Albert Guiraud in a German translation by Otto Erich Hartleben. The instruments for which the work is scored—flute (doubling piccolo), clarinet (doubling bass clarinet), violin (doubling viola), cello, piano—has become a standard instrumental grouping for contemporary ensembles.

Pierrot Players contemporary music ensemble formed in 1967 in London by Davies and Birtwistle, then reformed in 1970 as Fires of London under Davies' sole direction.

piffero *also*, **piffaro** (It.) **1**, an ancient Italian shepherd SHAWM. **2**, FIFE.

Piguet, Michel (1932–) Swiss oboist and recorder player, one of the principal modern performers on the Baroque oboe. He played with the Zürich Tonhalle Orch. and co-founded the Ricercare Ensemble. He has taught at the Basel Schola Cantorum and at the Zürich Conservatory.

Pijper, Willem (1894–1947) Dutch composer and teacher, stud. of Wagenaar. He was a music critic in Utrecht and taught at the Amsterdam and Rotterdam conservatories. His compositional technique is based on the "germ-cell" principle, in which the work grows from a single chord or motif. His works incl. *Halewijn* (opera), incidental music, 3 symphonies, concerto for piano, violin and cello, choral works and songs, 5 string quartets, sonatas, and works for piano solo.

Pilkington, Francis (c1570–1638) English composer. An ordained minister, he sang in the choir of Chester Cathedral until his death. His surviving works consist mainly of ayres, madrigals, pastorals and lute music.

pincé [pĕ'sā] (Fr., plucked) a type of trill or mordent. See ORNAMENT.

pincement [pĕs'mā] (Fr.) a type of MORDENT.

pincullo [pēn'koo-yō] (Sp.) a S. Amer. WHISTLE FLUTE made of wood, cane or bone with three to seven holes.

Pines of Rome, The (It., *Pini di Roma*) orchestral tone poem in four sections (1924) by Respighi, depicting the pine trees of four sections of Rome. It incorporates a recording of the song of a nightingale.

ping pong a shallow STEEL DRUM.

Pini-Corsi, Antonio (1858–1918) Italian baritone, a specialist in the comic roles of Rossini and Donizetti. He created the role of Ford in Verdi's *Falstaff*, Schaunard in Puccini's *La Bohème* and Happy in *The Girl of the Golden West*. His Metropolitan Opera debut was in 1899.

Pink Floyd English acid-rock band formed in London in 1965. They were one of the first bands to use a light and slide show in their performances. Among their most successful works were the album *The Dark Side of the Moon* (1973) and the score for the film *The Wall* (1982).

Pinkham, Daniel (Rogers, Jr.) (1923–) Amer. composer, harpsichordist and organist, stud. of Copland, Honegger, Barber, Boulanger, Landowska and Biggs. He has taught at the New England Conservatory since 1959 and is music dir. of King's Chapel in Boston. A prolific and widely performed composer, he has written choral and solo vocal works, concertos for violin and organ, 3 symphonies, chamber music, music for recorded tape and film scores.

Pinnock, Trevor (1946–) English harpsichordist, trained at the Royal College of Music. He has played with the Galliard Harpsichord Trio and the English Concert.

Pins and Needles musical by Harold J. Rome, with sketches by Marc Blitzstein et al. Premiere, New York 1937. The cast consisted of amateur performers from the International Garment Workers Union.

Pinza, Ezio (Fortunato) (1892–1957) Italian bass, trained at the Bologna Conservatory. After singing in Italy for a decade, he joined the Metropolitan Opera in 1926, where he sang until 1948. His roles incl. the main Italian and French bass roles. In his later years he appeared on Broadway and in films, his biggest success being *South Pacific* (1948).

piobaireachd (Welsh) PIBROCH.

p'i-p'a ('pē-pä) (Chin.) a 4-stringed Chinese LUTE having silk strings and 12 frets and plucked like a guitar.

pipe 1, a small WHISTLE FLUTE, usu. with three holes and accompanied by the TABOR. **2**, an AEROPHONE consisting of a tube of metal, wood or other material, stopped (one end closed) or open, with or without finger holes. See ORGAN.

pipe and tabor a pair of medieval instruments consisting of the PIPE (1,) and TABOR, played by one or two persons, usu. providing music for dancing.

pipe organ see ORGAN.

Pippin musical by Stephen Schwartz, book by Roger O. Hirson, revised by Bob Fosse. Premiere, New York 1972. An account of the life of Charlemagne's son Pippin who, after yearning for glory, finally settles down to a normal married life.

piqué [pē'kā] (Fr.) **1**, a type of STACCATO. **2**, a type of SAUTILLE bowstroke executed without change of bow direction.

Pique-Dame [pēk-däm] (Fr.) QUEEN OF SPADES, THE.

Pirates of Penzance, The operetta in 2 acts by Sullivan to a libretto by W.S. Gilbert. Premiere, Paignton 1879. Frederic's sense of honor is tested when he is forced to help a gang of pirates defeat the forces of order, despite his love for Mabel, daughter of the Major-General.

Pisaroni, (Rosamunda) Benedetta (1793–1872) Italian contralto famous for her performance of the music of Rossini, who wrote several roles for her.

Pisk, Paul A(madeus) (1893–90) Austrian-born Amer. composer, pianist and musicologist, stud. of Schoenberg and Schreker at the U. of Vienna. He taught at the Vienna Volkshochschule, the New Vienna Conservatory and the Austro-Amer. Conservatory at Salzburg. After coming to the U.S. in 1936, he taught at the U. of Redlands (CA), the U. of Texas at Austin and Washington U. in St. Louis. He wrote at length about the Second Viennese School. His own works incl. ballets, orchestral works, choral works and songs, and chamber music.

piston 1, part of the VALVE in a brass instrument. **2**, a push-button on an organ console used to activate a preselected registration. See STOP.

Piston, Walter (Hamor, Jr.) (1894–1976) Amer. composer and teacher. He came to music in his late 20s and studied with Davison, Boulanger and Dukas. He taught at Harvard from 1926 until 1960, during which time he produced several widely used textbooks, incl. *Harmony* (1941), *Coun-*

terpoint (1947) and *Orchestration* (1955). The large majority of his works are for instrumental ensembles. Piston won the Pulitzer Prize twice, in 1948 for his Symphony No. 3 and in 1961 for his Symphony No. 7. His works incl. 8 symphonies, concertos (for violin, flute, viola and clarinet), many other orchestral works, 5 string quartets, sonatas for various instruments and other chamber music.

pitch the position of a specific sound in the SCALE, usu. definable by reference to the frequency of its fundamental wave (which sometimes, as in the case of difference in tones, can be determined only by the listener). Until recent times there has not been a standard pitch for Western music, and the frequency of a' has varied from as low as 360 CPS to as high as 510 CPS (a variance of 3 whole tones), depending on the region, the time of year and the particular instrument or organ in question.

The current accepted standard for concert music is a' = 440 CPS, though there is more deviation from this standard in practice than there is conformity to it, generally erring on the higher side. For the performance of baroque music on period instruments, the generally accepted compromise is a' = 415 CPS, about a semitone below the concert standard. See also KAMMERTON, CHOR-TON.

Pitch notation has become graphically standardized for conventional music (see accompanying illustration), along with several common

systems of nomenclature. The first, known as Helmholtz pitch notation, is the system employed in this dictionary. For earlier systems, see HEXACHORD, SOLMIZATION. Also, *tone*.

pitch bend a 20th-c. technique in string and esp. woodwind playing by which the pitch of a note is raised or lowered slightly at the end of the note for ornamental or expressive purposes. In classical music, the technique is usu. indicated by a line under or over the note, curving up or down to indicate the direction of the bend. The technique is common in jazz.

pitch class the set of all the pitches of the same name, regardless of octave; e.g., all c's are of pitch class C.

pitchpipe a device for determining a certain pitch, as for giving pitches to a singing group. Orig. pitchpipes were wooden instruments similar to a recorder with a graduated stopper for choosing the pitch desired. More recent pitchpipes are usu. reed instruments, often circular, providing a full chromatic octave. In many cases, such blown pitchpipes have been replaced by electronic instruments, usu. tunable to different pitch standards.

Pitfield, Thomas B(aron) (1903–) English composer, poet, visual artist and teacher of composition at the Royal Manchester College of Music. His works are in a pleasant, quasi-18th-c. style, and incl. orchestral and choral works and chamber music.

Pittel, Harvey (1943–) Amer. sax-

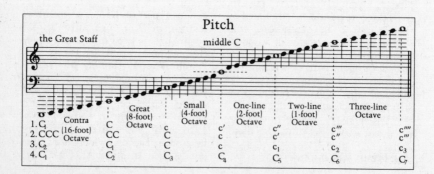

ophonist, stud. of Kalman Bloch, Franklyn Stokes, Frederick Hemke and Joseph Allard. He has taught at the U. of S. California, California State U., Boston U., the Mannes College and the U. of Texas at Austin. He has performed baroque and contemporary works in recital and with orch. in the U.S. and Europe.

Pittsburgh Symphony Orchestra orch. founded in 1895 as the Pittsburgh Orchestra. Under that name, its music directors were Frederick Archer, Victor Herbert and Emil Paur. It disbanded in 1910, then reappeared in 1926 as the Pittsburgh SO. Subsequent music directors have been Antonio Modarelli, Reiner, William Steinberg, Previn and Maazel. The orch. performs in Heinz Hall for the Performing Arts and at the Ambler Festival.

più (It.) more.

piùttosto (It.) rather.

piva ['pē-vä] (It., bagpipe) **1**, an ancient Italian BAGPIPE or SHAWM. **2**, a 15th- and 16th-c. Italian court dance in triple meter, a type of quick BASSADANZA. As a dance it faded in the mid-15th c., only to reappear in lute music in quick triple meter at the beginning of the 16th c.

pivot chord a chord which can be analyzed as part of more than one tonality and which serves as a connection between two tonalities. See MODULATION. Cf. METRIC MODULATION.

pixie mute a small mute used in conjunction with a PLUNGER MUTE for an especially choked sound.

pizz. *abbr.* PIZZICATO.

Pizzetti, Ildebrando (da Parma) (1880–1968) Italian composer, conductor and critic, stud. of Telesforo Righi. He taught at the Parma Conservatory and the Istituto Musicale in Florence and later became dir. of the Milan Conservatory and a teacher at the Accademia di St. Cecilia in Rome. His many works, which are predominantly vocal, incl. *Assassinio nella cattedrale* (based on a work by T.S. Eliot) and other operas and incidental music, cantatas, orchestral works, choral and solo vocal works, chamber music and music for solo piano.

pizzicato [pēt-sē'kä-tō] (It.) an indication for string players to pluck rather than bow the strings. The plucking is usu. by the right hand, but sometimes left-hand pizzicato is indicated, either simultaneously or in alternation with bowed notes. In 20th-c. music a hard pizzicato (also called "Bartók pizzicato") is often indicated, in which the string slaps back against the fingerboard. It is indicated by the sign (♂) placed over the note(s) to be so plucked. Abbr., *pizz.*

placement FOCUS.

plagal cadence a CADENCE proceeding from the subdominant chord to the tonic (IV-I), rather than from the dominant.

plagal mode a MODE having the 4th scale step as the keynote; e.g., the 2nd, 4th, 6th and 8th church modes.

plainchant musical ['plĕ-shä mü-zē'käl] (Fr.) a type of reformed, accompanied PLAINSONG in use in France from the 17th to 19th c.

plainsong *also*, **plainchant** the non-metrical monophonic chant used in the liturgy of the Roman Catholic church and certain other Christian churches. It is sung in unison and based on the ecclesiastical modes (see MODE) and usu. unaccompanied. The principal types of plainchant in use today are GREGORIAN CHANT, AMBROSIAN CHANT and BYZANTINE CHANT. Cf. ANGLICAN CHANT.

plainte [plɛ̃t] (Fr.) **1**, a type of VI-

Plainsong

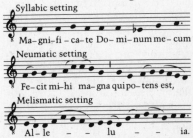

Syllabic setting

Ma–gni–fi – ca–te Do–mi–num me–cum

Neumatic setting

Fe–cit mi–hi ma–gna qui po–tens est,

Melismatic setting

Al–le — — lu — – ia.

BRATO. See ORNAMENT. **2**, a work expressing lament.

plain tune in late 18th-c. Amer., a syllabic setting of a sacred poem in three- or four-part harmony. The melody is usu. in the tenor voice.

Plançon, Pol(-Henri) [plä′sō] (1851–1914) French bass, stud. of Louis-Gilbert Duprez and Giovanni Sbriglia. He sang at the Paris Opéra from 1883 to 1892, made his London debut in 1891 and his Metropolitan Opera debut in 1893. He sang at Covent Garden until 1904 and at the Metropolitan until 1908, specializing in the leading bass roles in the French and Italian repertory, incl. Mephistopheles (*Faust*) and Le Cid. He made many recordings in the first decade of the 20th c.

planctus a medieval song of lamentation.

Planets, The orchestral suite, Op. 32 (1917), by Gustav Holst, each movement representing a different planet of the solar system (excluding the Earth and the then undiscovered Pluto). The seven sections are "Mars, the Bringer of War," "Venus, the Bringer of Peace," "Mercury, the Winged Messenger," "Jupiter, the Bringer of Jollity," "Saturn, the Bringer of Old Age," "Uranus, the Magician" and "Neptune, the Mystic."

plantation song *or* **melody** a type of song popular in the 19th c. in minstrel shows and vaudeville and as domestic music.

Platters, The Amer. rock-and-roll vocal quartet formed in 1953 in Los Angeles. Their many hits incl. "Only You" (1955), "The Great Pretender" (1956) and "My Prayer" (1956).

player piano a piano containing a mechanical PIANO PLAYER (2,) and storing information for performance on punched paper rolls (*piano rolls*) or on a punched metal disk. Modern versions of the player piano are operated by computer and use tape cassette or floppy disk for storage. Piano rolls were an early recording outlet for pianists, esp. in jazz. Also, *pianola*. Cf. WELTE.

Playford, John (1623–86) the most important English music printer and publisher of the mid-17th c. Among his more renowned publications are John Dowland's *A Musicall Banquet*, *The Whole Book of Psalmes* and *The English Dancing Master*. His son, **Henry Playford** (c1657–c1707), took over the business upon John's death.

Play of Daniel DANIEL, PLAY OF.

plectrum (pl., plectra) a small, thin piece of quill, wood, ivory, metal or plastic, used to pluck the strings of the lute, guitar, etc. Also, *pick*.

plein jeu [plɛ̃ jø] (Fr., full registration) **1**, an organ mixture stop including the unison, octave and fifth. **2**, FULL ORGAN.

plenary mass a complete musical setting of both the Ordinary and Proper of the Roman Catholic Mass. The Requiem mass is a plenary mass; other examples are rare.

Pleskow, Raoul (1931–) Austrian-born Amer. composer, stud. of Karol Rathaus and Luening. He taught at C.W. Post College from 1959, where he was a colleague of Wolpe, who influenced him greatly. His works incl. bagatelles and movements for orch. and for various other instruments, songs, choral works and chamber music.

Pleyel, Ignace Joseph (1757–1831) Austrian composer, piano maker and music publisher, stud. of Vanhal and Haydn. He was Kapellmeister to Count Erdödy, then held the same position for the Strasbourg Temple Neuf. He opened a publishing house in Paris, which built a large and distinguished catalogue in its 39 years of existence and issued the first miniature scores. In 1807 he founded the Pleyel piano manufacturing firm, which also developed a chromatic harp and was important in the revival of interest in the harpsichord at the beginning of the 20th c. His works incl. several operas (incl. a puppet opera), various vocal works, many symphonies and concertos and a large number of chamber music works for various combinations.

plica (Lat.) a type of curved, two-note NEUME.

Plishka, Paul (Peter) (1941–) Amer. bass, stud. of Armen Boyajian. He has sung with the Metropolitan Opera since 1965 and at most leading opera houses in the world, performing both serious and comic roles.

pneuma ['noo-mə] (Gk., wind) **1**, a LIGATURE in medieval music representing a long, florid melody sung to one syllable. **2**, NEUME.

pneumatic action an action in a pipe ORGAN operated by compressed air, which is produced by a bellows.

pochette [po'shet] (Fr.) KIT.

poco (It.) little.

pochissimo [pō'kēs-sē-mō] (It.) very little.

poem, symphonic SYMPHONIC POEM.

Poème [po'em] (Fr.) work for violin and orch., Op. 25 (1896), by Chausson.

Poem of Ecstasy the Symphony No. 4 in one movement, Op. 54 (1908), by Scriabin.

Poet and Peasant (Ger., *Dichter und Bauer*) comedy (1846) by K. Elmar, with songs by Suppé. The overture is often performed separately.

Pohjola's Daughter tone poem, Op. 49 (1906), by Sibelius, based on a Finnish legend about the courtship of a fairy coquette by an old man, who must accomplish a series of tasks to win her.

poi ['pō-ē] (It.) then.

point 1, an English term used in music of the 16th to 18th c. for a THEME or passage suitable for imitation. The music resulting from the working-out of the imitation is called a *point of imitation*. **2**, an isolated note in a composition. See POINTILLISM. **3**, the upper end of the violin bow. Also, *tip*.

point d'orgue [pwē dorg] (Fr.) PEDAL POINT.

pointe [pwēt] (Fr.) POINT (3,). —**à la pointe**, (Fr.) at the point of the bow.

pointer (Fr.) a term used in French music of the 17th and 18th c. to indicate that notes which are notated equally should be played as if dotted, i.e., the first note of each two-note

group should be lengthened, the second shortened. Cf. NOTES INÉGALES.

Pointer Sisters Amer. rock vocal quartet (later trio) formed about 1970 in Oakland (CA) by Ruth, Anita, Bonnie and June Pointer. Their broad repertory of pop, jazz, country and rhythm-and-blues numbers helped them get exposure on TV and at the Grand Ole Opry, though their greatest success has been with the pop audience. Their hits incl. "Fairytale," "Fire" and "Slow Hand."

point of imitation see POINT (1,).

pointillism a term in painting for the technique of applying tiny dots or strokes of color which, when viewed from a distance, produce a united, luminous whole. The term is applied in music to a style of the 1950s generally considered to have been inspired by Webern in which a work is formed of many seemingly isolated notes and groups of notes rather than of traditionally connected phrases. See POINT (2,).

pointing in Anglican chant, the use of marks in the text to indicate where the text corresponds to changes in the plainchant melody.

polacca (It.) POLONAISE.

Pollack, Ben (1903–71) Amer. Dixieland jazz drummer and bandleader. He formed his own band in 1926, which employed a number of soon-to-be-great jazz musicians, incl. Benny Goodman, Jimmy McPartland and Jack Teagarden. He had problems in the 1930s due to personality conflicts, but was again successful in the 1960s.

Police, The English rock group formed in 1977 by Stewart Copeland, STING and Andy Summers.

poliphant a 17th-c. English plucked LUTE having a scalloped shape and about 40 wire strings.

Polish Symphony popular name for the Symphony No. 3 in D major, Op. 29 (1875) by Tchaikovsky.

polka a lively couple-DANCE in duple time of Polish origin consisting of three steps and a hop.

Pollikoff, Max (1904–84) Amer. vi-

olinist, stud. of Auer. An ardent supporter of contemporary music, he est.
in New York in 1954 a chamber music concert series, Music in Our
Time, which in its 20-year history
presented more than 250 works by
20th-c. composers, sometimes in an
unusual format by which several
pieces would be performed at the
same time in different rooms, the audience being free to wander.

Pollini, Maurizio (1942–) Italian
pianist, stud. of Carlo Lonati and
Carlo Vidusso. He won the Warsaw
Chopin competition in 1960 and has
toured Europe and the U.S. regularly.
He has an unusually wide repertory,
ranging from Bach to 20th-c. masterworks, incl. the piano works of
Schoenberg and Boulez's Second Sonata.

polo (Sp.) a Spanish folk dance in a
quick ⅜ time.

polonaise [po-lo'nez] (Fr.) a stately
19th-c. Polish DANCE in moderate ¾
time. Its characteristic rhythm is an
eighth note followed by two six-
teenths and then four eighth notes.
Also, *polacca* (It.).

Polovtsian Dances dance music from
Act II of *Prince Igor* (1890) by Borodin,
much of which was used in the musical KISMET.

polychoral performed by a choral ensemble divided into two or more
groups; ANTIPHONAL.

polychord a chord composed of two
or more separately recognizable
chords. Cf. POLYTONALITY.

polymeter the simultaneous presence, in different parts, of different
meters, common in medieval and
20th-c. music but rare in the intervening centuries. A famous 18th-c.
example is the simultaneous use of
three dances in different meters in the
finale to Act I of Mozart's opera *Don
Giovanni*.

polyphony music in more than one
part, esp. music in which the parts
have relatively independent melodic
and rhythmic character. Cf. HETERO-
PHONY, HOMOPHONY, MONOPHONY.

polyrhythm 1, POLYMETER. 2, the

Polymeter

(Mozart, Don Giovanni)

Polyrhythm

(Berlioz, Symphonie   (Brahms, Capriccio
fantastique, 5th mvt.)   in D minor)

conflict of two or more rhythms
within the same meter, a common
feature of jazz as well as of contemporary classical music. Also, *cross-
rhythm*.

polytonality the technique of writing
music in two or more different but
simultaneous keys, producing a jarring effect while retaining the essential feeling of tonality. The most frequent occurrence is of two keys
(*bitonality*). Aside from isolated examples in earlier music, the technique belongs to the 20th c., esp. in
the works of Milhaud, Prokofiev,
Ives, and others.

pommer (Ger.) **1**, BOMBARDON. **2**, a
name for the larger types of SHAWM,
incl. the tenor, bass and great bass.

Pomo d'oro, Il (It., the Golden Apple)
opera in 5 acts by Cesti to a libretto
by Francesco Sbarra, based on the
myth of Paris and the Golden Apple.
Premiere, Vienna 1667. Written for
the wedding of Leopold I, emperor of
Austria, to the Spanish infanta,
Margherita.

Pomp and Circumstance set of 5
marches for orch., Op. 39 (1901–30),
by Elgar. The first is the most often
performed.

Ponce, Manuel (Maria) (1882–1948) Mexican composer and pianist, stud. of Cipriano Ávila and Vicente Mañas. He worked and taught in Mexico City for most of his life, with sojourns in Havana and Paris. He is best known for his songs and piano works, but also wrote concertos for piano and violin, chamber music and works for guitar.

Ponchielli, Amilcare [pōng'kye-lē] (1834–86) Italian composer, trained at the Milan Conservatory. He worked in Cremona for most of his life, then after 1881 he joined the faculty of the Milan Conservatory and worked in Bergamo at St. Maria Maggiore. He is known primarily for his opera *La Gioconda* (1876), the only one of his works to have remained in the repertory. He wrote 11 operas, ballets, sacred and secular choral works, a symphony, works for band, chamber music and music for solo piano.

Pons, Lily (Alice Joséphine) (1898–1976) French-born Amer. coloratura soprano, stud. of Alberti di Gorostiaga. She made her Metropolitan Opera debut in 1931, and sang there for over 25 years. She also appeared in films and in concert, esp. with her husband, conductor ANDRÉ KOSTELANETZ.

Ponselle (Ponzillo), **Rosa (Melba)** (1897–1981) Amer. soprano, stud. of Anna Ryan. Her Metropolitan Opera debut—also her operatic debut—was in 1918 as Leonora in Verdi's *La forza del destino*. She sang at the Metropolitan for 19 seasons, retiring in 1937. She also sang in England and in Italy. She was later artistic dir. of the Baltimore Civic Opera and an active teacher. Her wide repertory included Norma, Violetta (*La Traviata*) and Elisabetta (*Don Carlo*); she never sang any Puccini or Wagner. She was esp. noted for her beauty of tone. Her sister, **Carmela Ponselle** (1892–1977), was a mezzo-soprano who also sang at the Metropolitan Opera (1925–35).

ponticello [pōn-tē'chel-lō] (It.) **1**, the bridge of a bowed string instrument.

2, of the voice, a change in REGISTER; break. See SUL PONTICELLO.

Ponty, Jean-Luc ['pō-tē, zhǎ lük] (1942–) French violinist and composer, trained at the Paris Conservatoire. He played in the Orchestre Lamoureux, then switched to jazz and fusion. He has worked with Frank Zappa, George Duke and as a free lance, heading his own group, playing the amplified violin and baritone violin (violectra).

Poole, Charlie (Cleveland) (1892–1931) Amer. country-music singer and banjo player from No. Carolina who made many recordings in the 1920s and toured with the North Carolina Ramblers.

Poot, Marcel (1901–) Belgian composer and teacher, trained at the Brussels Conservatory and the Royal Flemish Conservatory in Antwerp. He was a founder, with other students of Paul Gilson, of the Synthétistes (1925–30), a mutual support group for composers. He taught at the Brussels Conservatory and was a co-founder of the *Revue musicale belge*, also serving as a music critic for several Belgian newspapers. He has written in all genres in a style that is reminiscent of Prokofiev.

Pop, Iggy (Osterberg, James Newell) Amer. punk rock singer, leader of the Stooges, a group formed 1967 in Ann Arbor. After the band broke up in 1970, he worked frequently with David Bowie, producing a number of albums, incl. *Lust for Life* (1977).

pop music see POPULAR MUSIC.

Popp, Lucia (1939–) Czech-born Austrian coloratura soprano. She has sung at the Vienna Staatsoper, the Metropolitan Opera (debut 1967) and throughout Europe, as well as in recital and concert. Her roles include the Queen of the Night (*The Magic Flute*), Oscar (*A Masked Ball*) and Despina (*Così fan tutte*).

Popper, David (1843–1913) Austrian cellist and composer, stud. of Julius Goltermann in Prague. He toured widely, then played principal cello with the Vienna Court Opera and in the Hellmesberger Quartet. From 1896, he taught at the Budapest Royal Conservatory and played in the Hubay Quartet. Most of his works are for cello, and some are still in the repertory.

pops a term usu. referring to LIGHT CLASSICS. The typical pops concert, modeled after European 19th-c. promenade concerts, is an orchestral concert of light classics accompanied by refreshments. In the U.S. the pops orchestra of the Boston SO (the BOSTON POPS) has served as a model for other similar groups.

popular music a term used to refer to music that is accessible to and enjoyed by the general public, as distinguished (presumably) from music intended for or enjoyed by a more musically sophisticated or experienced listener. The term usu. excludes classical music, folk music, jazz and even rock, though isolated works from any of those genres may become "popular music" through simplification, repeated exposure, arrangement, etc. Among the characteristics of popular music are relatively simple harmony, a memorable melody and shortness.

Porgy and Bess ['por-gē] opera in 3 acts by Gershwin to a libretto by Du Bose Heyward based on the play *Porgy* by Du Bose and Dorothy Heyward, and lyrics by Ira Gershwin. Premiere, New York 1935. A melodrama of Negro life in Charleston, SC, and the love between the crippled beggar Porgy and Crown's mistress Bess.

Porpora, Nicola (Antonio) (1686–1768) Italian composer and singing teacher, trained in Naples, where he taught until 1721, his pupils incl. the castrati Farinelli and Caffarelli. His many works, mostly vocal, incl. almost 50 operas, many cantatas, oratorios, sacred choral works, sinfonias and concertos.

port 1, (Scot.) LESSON (2,). **2,** an Irish jig tune, usu. in 6/8 or 9/8 meter and having repeated sections.

Porta, Costanzo (1528–1601) Italian composer and teacher, stud. of Wil-

laert. His posts incl. *maestro di cappella* in Padua and in Ravenna. His surviving works consist largely of motets, masses and other sacred vocal works, and madrigals. In his time he was a highly respected composer and renowned as a teacher.

portamento (It.) **1,** an unbroken slide produced by a voice or instrument in passing from one note to another. Also, *port de voix* (Fr.). **2,** PORTATO.

portative organ a small portable pipe ORGAN once used in processions. The right hand played the short keyboard, the left hand operated the bellows. Cf. *positive organ*.

portato (It.) semidetached BOWING. Also, *portamento*.

port de voix [por də vwä] (Fr., carrying of the voice) **1,** a baroque appoggiatura, esp. one that resolves upward. See ORNAMENT. **2,** PORTAMENTO (1,).

Porter, Cole (Albert) (1891–1964) Amer. theatrical songwriter, trained at Harvard and with d'Indy in Paris. His work was characterized by witty lyrics, double entendres, and complex melodies. He wrote music for over 25 Broadway musicals, incl. *Gay Divorce* (1932), *Anything Goes* (1934), *DuBarry was a Lady* (1939) and his masterpiece, *Kiss Me, Kate* (1948); many of the shows also became films. He also wrote songs directly for films, the best known being *High Society* (1956).

Porter, (William) Quincy (1897–1966) Amer. composer, violinist and teacher, stud. of Parker, David Smith, d'Indy and Bloch. He taught at the Cleveland Institute, Vassar College, the New England Conservatory and Yale. An active chamber music player, his best works are for that medium. He also wrote 2 symphonies, concertos for viola and harpsichord, other orchestral works, incidental music and songs. He won the Pulitzer Prize in 1954 for his Concerto for Two Pianos and Orchestra.

Porter, Walter (c1590–1659) English composer, lutanist and tenor, stud. of Monteverdi. He was a Gentleman of the Chapel Royal and, from 1639, master of the choristers at West-minster Abbey. His works incl. mo-tets, madrigals and ayres.

pos. *abbr.* Posaune (see TROMBONE).

Posaune [pō′zow-ne] (Ger.) TROM-BONE.

position 1, see SPACING. **2**, the place-ment of the hand (usu. the left hand) on the fingerboard of a stringed in-strument such as the violin. A change from one position to another is called a *shift*. **3**, one of the seven defined degrees of extension of the trombone slide, each successive position low-ering the pitch downward by a semi-tone.

positive organ *also,* **positif 1**, a small stationary pipe ORGAN. Also, *cham-ber organ.* Cf. PORTATIVE ORGAN. **2**, a division of an organ used to comple-ment the great organ. Also, *choir organ.*

Posse [′po-se] (Ger., farce) *also,* **Pos-senspiel** [′po-sən″shpēl] from the 17th to 19th c. in Germany and Au-stria, a farce with music, spec., a play with less music than a Singspiel.

post-bop HARD BOP.

Postcard from Morocco fantasy opera in 1 act by Argento to a libretto by John Donahue. Premiere, Minneapo-lis 1971. Seven travelers in a wait-ing room reveal their innermost thoughts, fears and desires.

post horn a straight or coiled HORN in various keys used in the 18th and 19th c. as a coachman's horn. Some post horns were keyed or valved and equipped with crooks and tuning slides. Also, *coach horn.*

Posthorn Serenade the serenade for orch. in D major, K. 320 (1779), by Mozart.

postlude 1, the closing section or phrase of a composition. Cf. CODA. **2**, a piece played at the conclusion of a church service.

post-minimalism a type of music of the 1980s influenced by the tech-niques of MINIMALISM but with a much greater range of expression and variety of harmony and rhythm.

post-modernism a musical reaction in the 1960s to the deliberate avant-garde stance of MODERNISM.

potpourri [pō-poo′rē] (Fr., rotten pot) MEDLEY.

Poule, La [pool] (Fr.) HEN SYMPHONY.

Poulenc, Francis (Jean Marcel) [poo′lɛ̃k, frä′sēs] (1899–1963) French composer and pianist, stud. of Ri-cardo Viñes and Koechlin. Often crit-icized for the simplicity of his writing, he was nonetheless a mas-ter in particular of vocal writing, strengthened by his long assoc. with baritone Pierre Bernac, for whom he wrote many songs. His style, full of verve and humor, is unmistakable. His works incl. *Les mamelles de Ti-résias, Dialogues des carmélites, La Voix humaine* (operas), 5 ballets (incl. *Les Biches*), incidental music, film scores, concertos for piano and for or-gan, *Concert champêtre* for harpsi-chord, *Litanies à la vierge noire, Gloria* and other choral works, many songs, incl. the cycles *Tel jour, tel nuit, Le travail du peintre* and *La courte paille,* chamber music and works for piano solo (incl. *Trois mouvements perpetuels*).

Pousseur, Henri (Léon Marie Thérèse) [poo′sœr, ä′rē] (1929–) Belgian com-poser, teacher and theorist, trained at the Liège and Brussels conserva-tories. From 1949 to 1958 he taught school and composed, then founded the Studio de Musique Electronique in Brussels. He taught in Cologne and Basle and lectured in the U.S. and Eu-rope. Since 1971 he has taught at the Liège Conservatory. He has written extensively about music. His many works incl. the opera *Votre Faust,* or-chestral works (incl. *Couleurs croi-sées,* based on the song "We shall overcome"), chamber music and works for tape.

Powell, Bud (Earl) (1924–66) Amer. bop jazz pianist influenced by Art Ta-tum, Thelonious Monk and Nat "King" Cole, and especially by Dizzy Gillespie and Charlie Parker. He was an important figure in jazz piano who influenced many later musicians. He played with Charlie Parker and then with his own trios in the 1940s and early 1950s; thereafter his appearances were sporadic, due to recurrent mental instability.

Powell, John (1882–1963) Amer. composer and pianist, stud. of Leschetizky and Navrátil. He toured the U.S. and Europe in the first quarter of the century, then was active in Virginia musical life, esp. in folk music, which is an important element in his own works.

Powell, Mel(vin) (1923–) Amer. composer and teacher, stud. of Wagenaar, Toch, Reisenberg and Hindemith. He has taught at the Mannes College, Yale and the California Institute of the Arts. He was active for some years as a jazz pianist, most notably with Benny Goodman. His works are mostly for instrumental ensembles with or without taped sounds, but he has also written songs (esp. *Haiku Settings*). He won the Pulitzer Prize in 1990 for his work *Duplicates* for two pianos and orch.

Powell, Verne Q. (1879–1968) Amer. flute maker. He worked with WILLIAM S. HAYNES until 1926, then started his own business, producing flutes and piccolos in silver, gold and platinum.

Power, Leonel (c1380–1445) English composer and theorist, a contemporary of Dunstable, assoc. with Christ Church, Canterbury. His extant works are all sacred vocal works, Masses and Latin motets.

Pozo, Chano (Pozo y Gonzales, Luciano) (1915–48) Cuban drummer, singer and dancer, known for his brief but significant work with Dizzy Gillespie in incorporating Lat.-Amer. music into jazz.

pp *abbr.* **1,** PIANISSIMO. **2,** *più piano* (It., softer).

ppp *abbr.* PIANISSISSIMO.

practice chanter a double-reed WINDCAP INSTRUMENT used as a practice substitute for a bagpipe chanter. It has the same fingerings and tuning but sounds an octave lower.

praeludium (Lat.) PRELUDE.

Praetorius, Hieronymus (1560–1629) German composer, organist and music editor, trained in Hamburg and Cologne. He was organist at St. Jacobi in Hamburg from 1582 until his death. He composed a large number of Masses and motets, many of them polychoral, and organ works.

Praetorius, Michael (1571–1621) German composer, theorist and organist and choirmaster to the duke of Brunswick. He wrote a large quantity of vocal and instrumental music, but he is best remembered for his monumental treatise on music, *Syntagma Musicum* (1614–15), which gives invaluable information on instruments and compositional practices of the time.

Prague Symphony popular name for the Symphony No. 38 in D major, K.504 (1786), by Mozart.

Prallender (Ger.) a type of TRILL, usu. executed on the lower note of a descending second and tied to the preceding note. See ORNAMENT.

Pralltriller (Ger., rebound trill) an ORNAMENT consisting of the alternation of a principal note with its upper neighbor. Also, *inverted mordent.*

Pran Nath, Pandit (1918–) Indian singer and composer. He taught at Delhi U. in the 1960s, then est. the Kirana Center for Indian Classical Music in New York, teaching a broad range of Western musicians, incl. Lee Konitz, La Monte Young and Terry Riley.

Pratt, Paul (Charles) (1890–1948) Amer. ragtime composer and pianist. from about 1905 to 1920 he composed rags and recorded piano rolls for player pianos. His best-known work was the "Hot House Rag." After 1920 he worked as accompanist and conductor on Broadway.

Prausnitz, Frederik (William) (1920–) German-born Amer. conductor, trained at the Juilliard School. He has conducted at the New England Conservatory, was music dir. of the Syracuse SO and taught at the Peabody Conservatory. He is noted for his performances of 20th-c. music and has made many recordings.

precentor 1, the leader of congregational singing when there is no choir. **2,** CANTOR.

precipitando [prä-chē-pē'tän-dō] *also,* **precipitato** [-'tä-tō] (It.) rushing; rushed.

preclassical a term referring to the period between the Baroque and Classical eras, roughly from about 1730 to 1770, the period of the Rococo or galant style.

prefatory staff a portion of staff (or tablature) preceding the clef, time signature, etc., used in scholarly editions to indicate the original pitch, clef and note values of the piece being edited. See SCORE.

prelude 1, an introductory instrumental section or movement. 2, a piece played preceding the start of a church service. 3, a short concert work, usu. for piano or orch.

Prélude à l'Après-midi d'un faune (Fr.) PRELUDE TO "THE AFTERNOON OF A FAUN."

prélude non mesuré [prä'lüd nō mə-zü'rä] (Fr.) a type of 17th-c. harpsichord prelude written in notes of indeterminate duration. The interpretation of these sections is left to the performer.

Préludes, Les ['prä-lüd, lä] (Fr.) symphonic poem (1854) by Liszt, orig. written (1848) as an overture to a choral work, *Les quatres élémens*, then reworked as a tone poem after a poem by Lamartine.

Prelude to "The Afternoon of a Faun" (Fr., *Prélude à l'après-midi d'un faune*) orchestral tone poem (1892) by Debussy inspired by the symbolist poem by Stéphane Mallarmé. The work shocked contemporary listeners because of its apparent lack of conventional formal design and its harmonic freedom.

preparation the presentation of an accented NONHARMONIC NOTE as a consonant note in the preceding chord to mitigate its dissonance. See SUSPENSION.

prepared piano a piano which has been modified in some way to produce special effects, such as by placing objects between or on the strings to alter their sound.

Preservation Hall a dance hall in New Orleans built in 1861 and popular since the turn of the century as a center of jazz performance.

Presley, Elvis (Aaron) (1935–77) influential Amer. rock singer, guitarist and actor. He began as a country-music singer, recording in Memphis and appearing on the Grand Ole Opry and elsewhere. In 1955 he signed with RCA Victor and his first recording, "Heartbreak Hotel," was a No. 1 hit on all charts, after which he had a string of hits, incl. "Love Me Tender," "Jailhouse Rock" and "Hound Dog." He also made a number of films and appeared on TV.

Presser, Theodore Amer. firm of music publishers founded in 1883 in Philadelphia by Theodore Presser (1848–1925). The firm publishes the works of many Amer. composers.

pressez [pre'sā] (Fr.) hurry; usu. synonymous with ACCELERANDO.

presto ['pre-stō] (It., ready) quick, faster than ALLEGRO.

prestissimo [pre'stē-sē-mō] (It.) very fast.

Preston, Simon (John) (1938–) English organist, harpsichordist and conductor, trained at King's College, Cambridge. He has toured as an organist, performing music of all periods, and has conducted a number of recordings of music by Haydn and others. He has been dir. of the choir at Christ Church, Oxford, since 1970 and organist at Westminster Abbey since 1981.

Pretenders, The English new-wave rock group formed in 1978 and led by guitarist/songwriter Chrissie Hynde. By 1982 half of the original group had died.

Prêtre, Georges (1924–) French conductor, stud. of Cluytens. He has specialized in opera, conducting in French regional houses, at the Paris Opéra and throughout the world. He has conducted and recorded most of Poulenc's works and was a frequent collaborator with opera singer Maria Callas.

Previn, André (George) (Priwin, Andreas Ludwig) (1929–) German-born Amer. conductor, pianist and composer, stud. of Castelnuovo-Tedesco, Toch and Monteux. He began as a jazz pianist, making many recordings on the West Coast, and was a musical dir. for MGM in the late 1940s and early 1950s. He won four Academy Awards for film scores. He has been musical dir. of the Houston SO, principal conductor of the London SO, and musical dir. of the Pittsburgh SO (1976–84), the Royal PO (from 1985) and the Los Angeles PO (1985–9). His own compositions incl. scores for musicals, a symphony for strings, chamber music and concertos for cello and guitar.

Prévost, André [prä'vō] (1934–) Canadian composer and teacher, stud. of Pépin, Messiaen and Dutilleux. He has taught at Montreal U. since 1964. His orchestral scores are esp. noteworthy for their color and inventiveness. He has also written choral works, sonatas for various instruments, 2 string quartets and other chamber music.

Prey, Hermann (1929–) German baritone, trained at the Berlin Music Academy. He has sung regularly at the Vienna Staatsoper and the Bavarian Staatsoper. His U.S. debut was at the Metropolitan Opera in 1960, and he has sung frequently at Bayreuth, Salzburg and Covent Garden. He is equally esteemed as a lieder singer.

Price (née Smith), **Florence Bea(trice)** (1888–1953) Amer. composer and teacher, trained at the New England Conservatory and later in Chicago with Leo Sowerby and others. Her Symphony in E minor was performed by the Chicago SO in 1933, and she was the first black woman to win fame as a symphonist. She combined 19th-c. European techniques with elements of Negro folk heritage. Her works incl. 4 symphonies, concertos for violin and piano, tone poems, chamber music, choral works, many songs and spirituals and works for solo piano and organ.

Price, (Mary Violet) Leontyne (1927–) Amer. soprano, trained at the Juilliard School. She made her operatic debut in Virgil Thomson's *Four Saints in Three Acts*, then sang for several years as Bess in Gershwin's *Porgy and Bess*. She sang at major opera houses in the U.S. and Europe, esp. in major Verdi roles, retiring from the operatic stage in 1985. She has also been active as a recital artist and has been extensively recorded.

Price, Lloyd (1933–) Amer. rock and rhythm-and-blues singer and songwriter. He has written a number of hits, incl. "Lawdy, Miss Clawdy" and "Ain't It a Shame" and has been successful as a pop music entrepreneur.

Price, Margaret (Berenice) (1941–) Welsh soprano, trained at the Trinity College of Music. She has sung at all major houses in Europe and the U.S., specializing in the lyric roles of Mozart. She is also a highly regarded recitalist. Her U.S. debut was in 1959 in San Francisco.

Price, Ray (Noble) (1928–) Amer. country-music singer and guitarist. He worked for some years with the Cherokee Cowboys, formerly Hank Williams' band, making many recordings in a honky-tonk style. He later became more pop oriented, adopting a crooning vocal style.

prick 1, *also,* **prick song** in the 15th and 16th c., written music, esp. polyphonic music. Cf. PART SONG. **2,** DESCANT. **3,** DOT.

Prigioniero, Il [prē-jō'nye-rō, ēl] (It., The Prisoner) psychological opera in 1 act by Dallapiccola to a libretto by the composer from plays by Count Villiers de l'Isle-Adam and Charles de Coster. Premiere, Turin 1949. The Prisoner's final torture is "hope."

Prima, Louis (1911–78) Amer. jazz trumpeter from New Orleans. He played in New York with Pee Wee Russell in the 1930s, then opened his own Famous Door club in Hollywood and appeared in films. In the 1960s he incorporated more pop and rock music into his jazz and toured the major clubs coast-to-coast.

prima ['prē-mä] (It.) first.

prima donna ['don-nä] (It.) the principal female singer, as in an opera. Cf. PRIMO UOMO.

prima prattica (It., first practice) a term, perhaps coined by G.C. Monteverdi (Claudio's brother) referring to music which follows traditional 16th-c. rules of counterpoint, as distinguished from *seconda prattica*, in which the text is paramount and can justify special effects of voice leading and dissonance.

prima volta (It.) the first time, as of a repeated phrase.

prime 1, one of the lesser hours of the DIVINE OFFICE of the Roman Catholic church. It begins around 6 A.M. **2**, UNISON.

primo uomo (It.) the principal male singer, as in an opera. Cf. PRIMA DONNA.

Primrose, William (1903–82) Scottish-born Amer. violist, stud. of Ysaÿe. He played in the London String Quartet and was principal violist of the NBC SO (1937–42). He formed the Primrose Quartet in 1939 and the Festival Quartet in 1954. He taught at the Aspen School, the U. of S. California, Indiana U., the Banff Centre and the Tokyo U. of Fine Arts and Music. Bartók's viola concerto was written for him, and a number of other composers also wrote works for him.

Prince (Nelson, Prince Rogers) (1960–) Amer. rock singer and songwriter, noted for suggestive lyrics and for his inventive melodies and arrangements. In recent years he has concentrated on recordings (*Prince*, *Controversy* and *Purple Rain*), which he produces himself and on which he plays many of the instruments.

Prince Igor romantic opera in 4 acts by Borodin to a libretto by the composer based on a play by Stassov, itself based on a 14th-c. Russian poem. Premiere, St. Petersburg 1890. The opera was completed by Rimsky-Korsakov, Liadov and Glazounov.

principal 1, a fugue SUBJECT. **2**, an ORGAN STOP an octave above the open diapason.

Pritchard, Sir **John (Michael)** (1921–89) English conductor, trained in Italy. He was assoc. with the Glyndebourne Opera from 1947 to 1978 and was musical dir. from 1969. He was also musical dir. of the Royal Liverpool PO and the London PO, principal conductor of the Cologne Opera and chief guest conductor of the BBC SO. He became musical dir. of the San Francisco Opera in 1988.

Prix de Rome [prē də rōm] (Fr.) an annual award given by the Académie des Beaux-Arts in Paris from 1803 to 1968 for study in Rome. The American Academy in Rome offers a similar award to Amer. composers.

Pro Arte Quartet Belgian string quartet formed in 1912, noted for its performance of modern music. It has been in residence at the U. of Wisconsin since 1940.

processional 1, a type of liturgical book originating in the 11th c. that contains the chants for liturgical processions. Such processionals often contain chants not found in other liturgical books. **2**, music written to be played for a procession, esp. during a church service.

process music a compositional technique assoc. with MINIMALISM, in which simple materials are subjected to processes such as gradual changes in rhythm, harmony, dynamics or timbre; ceaseless repetition, or phase shifts.

Procope, Russell (1908–81) Amer. jazz alto saxophonist and clarinetist. He played in the bands of Benny Carter, Chick Webb and Fletcher Henderson and others. In the 1940s he worked in John Kirby's sextet, then, after the war, joined Duke Ellington, staying for 28 years.

Procul Harum English classical rock band, formed in London, 1966. Their biggest hit was their first recording, "A Whiter Shade of Pale" (1967).

Prodigal Son, The church opera in 1 act by Britten, to a libretto by William Plomer after a New Testament fable. Premiere, Suffolk 1968. Third of the three "parables for church performance," the others being *Curlew River* and *The Burning Fiery Furnace*.

professor a slang term for a piano player in ragtime, vaudeville, minstrel shows, etc.

Professor Longhair (Byrd, Henry Roeland) (1918–80) Amer. rhythm-and-blues pianist and singer from New Orleans. He made his first recordings in 1949 and was a formative influence on Fats Domino, James Booker and many others.

program music music which attempts to represent an extra-musical idea, scene, story, etc., without use of words. The program may be simply a generalized situation (Beethoven's Symphony No. 6, *Pastoral*) or may consist of a story, even with plot and characters (Berlioz's *Symphonie fantastique*). Cf. TONE POEM, SYMPHONIC POEM.

progression a succession of notes or chords having harmonic or melodic cohesion. See HARMONY, SEQUENCE (2,).

progressive country a type of COUNTRY MUSIC incorporating elements of rock music, characterized by extensive use of electric instruments and a rock beat. Examples of the style may be found in the recordings of Willie Nelson, Linda Ronstadt and others. Also, *country rock*.

progressive jazz experimental jazz of the 1950s, esp. big-band jazz (the term was coined by Stan Kenton), which used a more complex, often dissonant, musical language. The term has also been assoc. or equated with COOL JAZZ and with later movements, such as FUSION.

progressive rock a type of ROCK music of the 1970s integrating rock instruments and formats with classical motifs in extended works. Among the bands associated with the genre are Genesis, Nice, and Emerson, Lake and Palmer. Also, *art rock*.

progressive tonality a term for the 20th-c. technique of beginning a tonal work in one key and ending in another (the term does not refer to a simple change of mode, as from minor to major).

Prokofiev, Serge (Sergeyevich) (1891–1953) prolific and influential Russian composer and pianist, trained with Glière and at the St. Petersburg Conservatory with Rimsky-Korsakov, Lyadov, Nikolay Tcherepnin and Anna Esipova. The prerevolution years in Russia saw the creation of his ballet *Chout* and the opera *The Gambler*, the *Classical Symphony*, 2 piano concertos and 4 piano sonatas. He went to the U.S. in 1918 and devoted much of his time to completing the opera *The Love for Three Oranges* for the Chicago Opera. He was in Paris from 1922 to 1936, writing his Second and Third Symphonies, more piano concertos and sonatas, the ballets *The Steel Step* and *The Prodigal Son* and the music for the film *Lieutenant Kijé*. In 1936 he returned to Moscow, where he remained until his death. The works of this final period incl. the ballet *Romeo and Juliet* and *Cinderella*, the opera *War and Peace* and *The Story of a Real Man*, more symphonies, concertos and sonatas and the film scores *Alexander Nevsky* and *Ivan the Terrible*.

prolation in MENSURAL NOTATION, the relationship between the semibreve and minim, i.e., the duple or triple division of the semibreve.

prologue a scene introducing a dramatic work, often explaining the work which is to come.

promenade concert an informal orchestral concert during which the audience stands and, in some cases, moves around. Cf. POPS.

Promethean chord MYSTIC CHORD.

Prometheus the Symphony No. 5, *The Poem of Fire*, Op. 60 (1911), by Scriabin. The work, in one movement, includes a substantial solo part for piano, a wordless chorus and a COLOR ORGAN.

Promises, Promises musical by Burt Bacharach, lyrics by Hal David, book by Neil Simon, based on the film *The Apartment*, by Billy Wilder and I.A.L. Diamond. Premiere, New York 1968. To secure business advancement,

Baxter lends his apartment to executives for their extramarital affairs.

Pro Musica Antiqua Belgian ensemble of singers and instrumentalists formed in 1933 by Safford Cape to specialize in early music. The group disbanded in 1974.

Proper the Proper of the Mass consists of the chants of the Roman Mass which have different texts according to the liturgical occasion. The types of chants included in the Mass Proper are the Introit, Gradual, Offertory, Alleluia or Tract and Communion. The Tract replaces the Alleluia during penitential seasons such as Lent. Polyphonic settings of the Proper are far less common than settings of the ORDINARY, with some notable exceptions such as Isaac's *Choralis Constantinus*.

proportional notation 1, TIME-SPACE NOTATION. **2,** MENSURAL NOTATION.

proportions in MENSURAL NOTATION, the augmentation or diminution of normal note values, indicated by time signatures. The three most common were *proportio dupla* (twice as fast), *proportio tripla* (three times as fast), and *proportio sesquialtera* (three in the space of two).

Proportz (Ger., proportion) a 16th- and 17th-c. AFTER-DANCE derived from its preceding duple-meter dance (e.g., a pavan or allemande) by applying *proportio sesquialtera* (see PROPORTIONS) to the melody of the former dance, i.e., three notes of the *Proportz* equal two notes of the preceding dance.

prosa a text for a SEQUENCE.

prosula (Lat. diminutive of *prosa*, prose) a medieval term indicating a text added to the notes of a melisma in Gregorian chant. Eventually, the term came to indicate a specific style and form of music in which both music and text might be newly composed.

Prussian popular name for **1**, 6 keyboard sonatas (1740–2) by C.P.E. Bach. **2**, 6 string quartets, Op. 50 (1787) by F.J. Haydn. **3**, 3 string quartets, K.575 in D major, K.589 in B♭

major and K.590 in F major (1789–90) by Mozart, his last works in the genre.

ps. *abbr.* PSALM.

psalm 1, name given to the poems of the Hebrew Book of Praises, otherwise known as the Biblical psalms. **2**, a musical setting of one of the Biblical psalms. Psalms are performed according to rigid musical formulas, often in an alternatim style between cantor and choir or congregation. Polyphonic settings of psalms are typical in Protestant churches after the Reformation and often take the form of strophic homophonic harmonizations (metrical psalms). Abbr., *ps*.

psalmodikon a one-stringed bowed ZITHER used from the 17th to 19th c. in Scandinavia to regulate choral singing.

psalmody 1, in Protestant churches, service music, incl. hymns, psalms and anthems. **2**, the singing of psalms.

psalms, metrical translations or paraphrases of the Biblical psalms in verse, intended to be sung to tunes or hymns in which the rhythm and meter are specified. The style flourished in the 17th c.

psalm tone the music to which psalm texts are chanted, consisting of an *intonation*, a *reciting note* (tenor), a *mediation*, a second intonation, a second reciting note and an *ending*. See *illus.*, p. 428.

psalter a printed book of psalms intended and often modified for singing or reciting in a church service.

psalterer a bowed string instrument of the late 17th c. used to support choral singing in church. Cf. PSALMODIKON.

psaltery a type of BOARD ZITHER developed from the Middle Eastern QANUN, usu. having a trapezoidal shape and strings passing over movable bridges, played with the fingers.

psychedelic rock ACID ROCK.

Ptolemy, Claudius (after 83–161) Greek mathematician, geographer, astronomer and music theorist. He was the author of the 3-vol. treatise *Harmonika*, which is the most dis-

Psalm Tone

Psalm 39 (4th Tone, D and c endings)

Initium   *Tenor*   *Flexa*   *Tenor*   *Mediatio*

Spe - rá - vi, sperávi in Dó - mi - no, † et incli - ná - *vit se* **ad** me, ˙

Tenor   *Terminatio*   *Differentia*

et exaudivit *cla - mó - rem* **mé** - um.   *cla - mó - rem* **mé** - um.

tinguished music treatise from antiquity that survives. Ptolemy's basic rule was that all judgments are based on both reason and empirical observation.

Puccini, Giacomo (1858–1924) Italian opera composer, stud. of Fortunato Magi and Carlo Angeloni (both of whom had studied with Puccini's father) and of Ponchielli at the Milan Conservatory. His first opera, *Le Villi*, was written for Sonzogno's one-act opera competition. His next opera, *Edgar*, was a failure, but he was highly successful with his third work, *Manon Lescaut*, and the operas which followed—*La Bohème*, *Tosca* and *Madama Butterfly*—are still among the most often performed operas worldwide. After a lapse of six years, Puccini produced *La Fanciulla del West* (The Girl of the Golden West) for the Metropolitan Opera. The opera has had only modest acceptance, and Puccini's attempt at operetta, *La Rondine*, was also less than a hit. Nevertheless, his final two works, the trio of operas *Il Trittico* (*Il Tabarro*, *Suor Angelica* and *Gianni Schicchi*) and the unfinished *Turandot* have both become part of the standard repertory. The latter work was completed after Puccini's death by Franco Alfano. Puccini also wrote songs, some sacred vocal music (mostly early works) and chamber music.

Puckett, Riley (1894–46) Amer. country music singer and guitarist from Georgia, the leader for many years of the string band Skillet Lickers and an influential recording artist in the 1920s and 1930s.

pu-ilu a Hawaiian bamboo CLAPPER.

Pulcinella ballet (1919) with neoclassical music by Stravinsky, based on melodies by Giovanni Battista Pergolesi, orig. choreographed by Massine with sets by Picasso. The composer extracted an orchestral suite in 1922.

Pult [pûlt] (Ger.) MUSIC STAND.

Punch and Judy tragi-comic opera in 1 act by Birtwistle to a libretto by Stephen Pruslin. Premiere, Aldeburgh 1968. The two sides of Punch are violence and the search for the ideal woman.

punk rock orig., a type of Amer. rock of the 1960s, a reaction to the BRITISH INVASION. The term now refers to British rock music of the 1970s, characterized by outrageous clothing and behavior and raw, simplistic musical style, often played by untrained musicians, as exemplified by the Sex Pistols and the Buzzcocks.

puppet opera a type of opera performance by a puppet theater, popular from the 17th c. in Italy and France, less so in England and the U.S. A number of composers have written for the genre, incl. Haydn, Pleyel, Falla and Britten.

Purcell, Henry (1659–95) prolific English composer, organist and singer, who in his short lifetime established himself as perhaps the greatest of all English composers. As a boy he was a member of the Chapel Royal, then became composer for the violins and organist at Westminster Abbey. He was also an organ maker and keeper of the king's instruments. His works incl. *Dido and Aeneas, The Fairy Queen* and other operas, incidental music for over 40 plays, many anthems and other service music, odes and other occasional pieces, songs and catches and works for solo harpsichord. Purcell's brother, **Daniel Purcell** (c1660–1717), was also a composer of theater music, vocal works and chamber music.

purfling an inlaid border on a musical instrument, as on a violin.

Puritani, I [poo-rē'tä-nē, ē] (It., The Puritans) historical opera in 3 acts by Bellini to a libretto by Count Carlo Pepoli, based on a play by F. Ancelot and X.B. Saintaine. Premiere, Paris 1835. A story of love between a Puritan woman, Elvira, and a Stuart sympathizer, Lord Arthur Talbot.

Purlie musical by Gary Geld, lyrics by Peter Udell, based on the Ossie Davis play *Purlie Victorious.* Premiere, New York 1970.

putorino a sideblown Maori wooden TRUMPET.

Puyana, Rafael (1931–) Colombian harpsichordist, stud. of Landowska. He has toured throughout Europe and No. and S. America, presenting a wide range of repertory from the 16th c. to the present.

puzzle canon RIDDLE CANON.

pyramid piano a vertical GRAND PIANO of the 19th c.

Pythagorean tuning a tuning of the scale using pure 4ths and 5ths, based on the theories of the Greek philosopher Pythagoras (c582–c500 BC).

Q

qanun (Arab.) a Turkish plucked BOARD ZITHER dating from the Middle Ages.

quadran pavan the passamezzo moderno. See PASSAMEZZO.

quadrille [kä'drēl] (Fr.) a 19th-c. square dance for couples, usu. in a lively 6/8 or 2/4 meter.

quadrupla (Lat.) in MENSURAL NOTATION, a proportional diminution of note values by a ratio of 4:1.

quadruple counterpoint see INVERTIBLE COUNTERPOINT.

quadruple meter *or* **time** four beats to the measure. See METER.

quadruplet a group of four notes performed in the time ordinarily occupied by three notes of the same type.

quality tone one of the notes of a chord that, along with the root, provide its essential character, as the lowered third degree of the minor triad.

Quantz, Johann Joachim (1697–1773) German flutist, oboist, flute maker, composer and writer, stud. of Zelenka, Gasparini and others. He was oboist in the Polish chapel of Augustus II, then in 1727 joined the Dresden court chapel. From 1728 he taught flute to Prince Frederick, remaining in his service when Frederick became king of Prussia. His works incl. sonatas, trio sonatas and concertos for flute, some vocal works and the highly influential treatise on flute playing, *Versuch einer Anweisung, die Flöte traversiere zu spielen* (On Playing the Flute, 1752).

quartal harmony a harmonic system based on the interval of a fourth, as opposed to the TERTIARY HARMONY of the major-minor system.

quarter note a note (♩) occupying one fourth of the time of a WHOLE NOTE. Also, (Brit.) *crotchet*.

quarter rest a rest with the value of a QUARTER NOTE. See NOTES AND RESTS (*illus.*).

quarter-tone *or* **-step** an interval one half the size of a HALF STEP. Many 20th-c. composers have written works utilizing quarter-tones (which are a common feature of some non-Western musics), either for occasional coloring of a predominantly diatonic texture or as the principal musical language for a work. Important composers to use quarter-tones incl. Hába, Carrillo, Bloch, Blackwood and Eaton. While no standard notation yet exists for quarter-tones, the chart below gives some of the most frequently encountered signs. Cf. MICROTONE, BLUE NOTE.

Quarter-tone Notation

1/4 up	3/4 up	1/4 down	3/4 down

quartet 1, a work composed for four instruments, each having its own individual part; esp. a work for string quartet. **2,** a group of four instruments or voices, or combination thereof.

Quartet for the End of Time (Fr., *Quatuor pour la fin du temps*) work in eight movements for violin, clarinet, cello and piano (1940) by Messiaen, written while the composer was in a German prison camp in Silesia. The instrumentation was chosen to match the players available in the camp.

Quartetto Italiano (It.) Italian string quartet founded in 1945, noted for meticulous preparation, esp. of the works of French impressionism and 20th-c. Italy.

Quartetto serioso the string quartet in F minor, Op. 95 (1810), by Beethoven.

Quartetsatz [kvär'tet"zäts] (Ger.,

quartet movement) an allegro movement in C minor for string quartet (1820) by Schubert, intended to be the first movement of a larger work.

quasi ['kwä-zē] (It.) approximately, almost, as if.

quaternaria (Lat.) a LIGATURE comprising four notes.

quatro (Sp.) CUATRO.

quattro ['kwät-trō] (It.) four.

Quattro stagioni, Le [städ'zhō-nē] (It.) FOUR SEASONS, THE.

quatuor [kä'tüor] (Fr.) QUARTET.

quaver 1, (Brit.) EIGHTH NOTE. **2,** TRILL.

Queen of Spades, The (Russ., *Pikovaya dama*) tragic opera in 3 acts by Tchaikovsky to a libretto by his brother Modest revised by the composer, based on a story by Pushkin. Premiere, St. Petersburg 1890. In the story, set in St. Petersburg at the end of the 18th c., Herman seeks to win his beloved Lisa by learning the gambling secrets of the Countess, with tragic results after a supernatural intervention.

Queen, The (Fr., *La Reine*) popular name for the Symphony No. 85 in B♭ major (1785) by Haydn. The title refers to Marie Antoinette, queen of France.

Queler (Rabin), **Eve** (1936–) Amer. conductor, stud. of Joseph Rosenstock, Susskind, Slatkin and others. She worked at the New York City Opera and the Metropolitan Opera, then in 1968 formed her own Opera Orch. of New York, which specializes in rarely performed operas. She has conducted many orchestras in the U.S. and Europe and has made a number of recordings.

quena a S. Amer. NOTCHED FLUTE made of bone.

Quicksilver Messenger Service Amer. acid rock band formed in 1965 in San Francisco, more successful as a concert band than with recordings. They disbanded in the mid-1970s.

quickstep 1, a lively MARCH tune, usu. intended to accompany a military march in quick time. **2,** a fast version of the FOXTROT.

Quiet City a short work for English horn, trumpet and strings (1939–40) by Copland, orig. part of an incidental score for Irwin Shaw's play *Quiet City*.

quijada [kē'khä-da] (Sp.) JAWBONE.

Quilico, Louis (1929–) Canadian baritone, stud. of Lina Pizzolongo and Martial Singher. His Metropolitan Opera debut was in 1972. He has sung frequently with the Metropolitan Opera and the Canadian Opera Company, as well as with other major companies in No. America and Europe. He has taught since 1970 at the U. of Toronto. His son, **Gino Quilico** (1955–), is also a successful operatic baritone.

quilisma a NEUME providing an ornamental connection between two notes, usu. a third apart.

quill the PLECTRUM of a harpsichord, usu. made from a bird's feather.

Quilter, Roger (1877–1953) English composer, stud. of Iwan Knorr in Frankfurt. He is best known for his many songs and light orchestral works.

quint 1, an interval of a FIFTH. **2,** a pipe ORGAN STOP sounding a fifth higher than the indicated pitch, sometimes used in conjunction with a pipe a fifth lower to produce a combination tone an octave below the lower note. **3,** the smallest VIOLA DA BRACCIO. **4,** the E string of a violin. **5,** QUINTON. **6,** (Ger.) an indication that an instrument should play a fifth lower than normal.

Quintenquartett (Ger.) FIFTHS QUARTET.

quintet 1, a work composed for five instruments, each having its own individual part; esp. a work for STRING or WOODWIND QUINTET. **2,** a group of five instruments or voices, or a combination thereof.

quinto (Sp.) a small CONGA DRUM.

quintole *also,* **quintolet** [kē-to'lä] (Fr.) QUINTUPLET.

Quintón, José I(gnacio) (1881–1925) Puerto Rican composer and pianist. He taught at the Coamo Municipal

Academy of Music. His music, mostly for chamber ensemble, is in the Romantic idiom.

quinton an 18th-c. five-stringed VIOL.

quintuor [kɛ̃'tüor] (Fr.) QUINTET.

quintuple meter *or* **time** five beats to the bar. As a regular METER, it is rare in Western music but relatively common in folk music.

quintuplet a group of five notes performed in the time ordinarily occupied by four notes of the same type.

quintus (Lat., fifth) in polyphonic vocal music, a fifth part of unspecified range.

quodlibet (Lat., what you please) a musical medley or fantasia, usu. humorous, combining familiar tunes and texts. The tunes can be connected sequentially or superimposed (*simultaneous quodlibet*). A famous example of the latter is the last movement of J.S. Bach's *Goldberg Variations*, which combines two German songs with the theme of the variations. Also, *cento.*

Quog an avant-garde music theater group org. in New York in 1970 by composer Eric Salzman.

quotation the use in a work or improvisation of a theme, motif, etc., taken from another work.

R

R *abbr*. RITARDANDO.

Ra, Sun SUN RA.

ra the lowered second degree of the prevailing key (or of its relative major, if the key is minor) in TONIC SOL-FA.

Raaff, Anton (1714–97) German tenor, stud. of Bernacchi. He sang in Madrid and Naples before joining the Bavarian court in 1770. Mozart wrote the title role of *Idomeneo* for him.

rabab (Arab.) a bowed LUTE, FIDDLE or SPIKE FIDDLE.

rabana an Indonesian FRAME DRUM.

Rabin, Michael (1936–72) Amer. violinist, stud. of Galamian. He toured widely, performing Romantic repertory, and made a number of recordings.

race record a term of the 1920s and 1930s for music recorded specifically for the Afr.-Amer. market, a predecessor of RHYTHM-AND-BLUES. The term covered a wide stylistic range, incl. jazz, blues and gospel music, both vocal and instrumental.

Rachmaninov, Sergei (1873–1943) Russian composer, pianist and conductor, educated at the Moscow Conservatory with Nikolai Zverev. He gained considerable success in all three aspects of his career. Most of his works were written before he left the U.S.S.R. in 1918 to pursue his performing career. He made many U.S. tours as pianist, playing his own works and a relatively small repertory of works by other composers. His final years were spent in Beverly Hills, CA.

Rachmaninov's works incl. *Aleko* (1892), *Francesca da Rimini* (1900) and other operas, 4 piano concertos, 3 symphonies, *The Isle of the Dead* (symphonic poem), *Rhapsody on a Theme of Paganini* for piano and orch., *Symphonic Dances*, choral works, many works for piano solo (incl. 33 Études-tableaux and Prelude in C♯ Minor) and songs.

rackett (Ger.) an obsolete Renaissance and Baroque double-reed bass instrument of the OBOE family consisting of a tube bent in short lengths and enclosed within a wooden cylinder. Higher-pitched versions of the instrument were also made. Also, *sausage bassoon*.

Radetzky March march (1848) by Johann Strauss the elder, named in honor of an Austrian field marshal.

radical bass an imaginary bass line produced by taking in succession the roots (not necessarily the lowest notes) of all the chords in a progression. See HARMONY (*illus*.).

radio ballad a type of documentary program developed for the BBC combining narrative and songs, some recorded on location.

Radziwill, Prince **Antoni Henryk** (1775–1833) Polish composer, singer, cellist and guitarist, a friend of Beethoven, Chopin and other composers of the time, a number of whom dedicated works to him. His house in Poznán was a center of cultural life in the early 19th c. His own works incl. songs, chamber music and incidental music to Goethe's *Faust*.

Raeburn, Boyd(e Albert) (1913–66) Amer. jazz bandleader noted for his bop groups of the late 1940s and the avant-garde arrangements they played, influenced by European impressionism.

Raff, (Joseph) Joachim (1822–82) German composer and teacher, largely self-educated. From 1856 to 1877 he composed and taught in Wiesbaden, then went to Frankfurt to head the Hoch Conservatory, where he taught Edward MacDowell, among others. His works incl. 11 symphonies, concertos for violin, cello and piano, several operas, choral works and songs, chamber music and a large number of works for piano.

rag a work in RAGTIME style.

raga (Sanskrit) a traditional melody or mode of Hindu music, consisting of a fixed series of notes associated with moods, times of year or ceremonies.

Rage over a Lost Penny, Vented in a Caprice a *rondo a capriccio* in G major for piano, Op. 129 (1795), by Beethoven.

ragtime a type of popular music prevalent in the U.S. from the late 19th c. to the end of World War I. Characteristics of ragtime are a syncopated rhythm in duple or quadruple meter and a series of 16-bar themes, usu. alternating between strains in the tonic and in the subdominant. In piano rags the left hand is predominantly accompanimental, alternating lower octaves on the main beats and midrange chords on the off beats, while the right hand is predominantly syncopated. Ragtime music was written for all instrumental and vocal combinations, though we are most familiar today with the piano works, which were played by "piano professors." Of the many composers who wrote and played ragtime music, the best known today incl. Scott Joplin (*Maple Leaf Rag*), Eubie Blake, Joseph Lamb, and Jelly Roll Morton.

Raimondi, Ruggero (1941–) Italian operatic bass, stud. of Teresa Pediconi and of Piervenanzi. He has sung at every major opera house in Europe and made his Metropolitan Opera debut in 1970. He is esp. known for his performance of early Verdi and Mozart operas.

Raindrop popular name for the Prelude in D♭ major, Op. 28 No. 15 (1836), by Chopin.

Rainey, Ma (Pridgett, Gertrude) (1886–1939) Amer. blues and jazz singer. She made many recordings in the mid 1920s and toured with the Georgia Jazz Band. Her best-known recordings incl. "Ma Rainey's Black Bottom" (1927) and "See See Rider" (1924).

Rainier, Priaulx (1903–86) S. Afr. composer, educated at the S. Afr. College of Music in Capetown and the Royal Academy of Music in London. Until 1935 she supported herself by teaching and playing, then concentrated on composition. Her works, in a very personal tonal style, incl. orchestral music, concertos for violin and cello, a Concertante Duo (for oboe, clarinet and orch.) instrumental and vocal chamber music and songs.

Rain Sonata the Violin Sonata No. 1 in G major, Op. 78 (1878–79), by Brahms.

Raisa, Rosa (Burchstein, Rose) (1893–1963) Polish-born Amer. dramatic soprano, stud. of Barbara Marchisio in Naples. Discovered by Cleofonte Campanini, she sang regularly in Chicago and Covent Garden and under Toscanini at La Scala. She opened a singing school in Chicago in 1937.

Raisin musical by Judd Woldin and Robert Brittan, libretto by Robert Nemiroff and Lorraine Hansberry, based on the latter's *A Raisin in the Sun*. Premiere, New York 1973. A black family tries to move to the Chicago suburbs.

Rake's Progress, The opera in 3 acts by Stravinsky to a libretto by W.H. Auden and Chester Kallmann, suggested by William Hogarth's drawings. Premiere, Venice 1951. The story, with a modern score modeled on the style of Mozart, is a parallel to the Faust legend, pitting Tom Rakewell against the Devil (Nick Shadow).

raking a technique for playing broken chords on the lute.

Rákóczy March patriotic Hungarian tune by an unknown composer, first printed in 1820. The tune is named after the leader of the revolt against Austria (1703–11) and was used by Liszt, Berlioz and others.

Raksin, David (1912–) important Amer. film composer, stud. of Isadore

Freed and Schoenberg. He worked for several years for Charlie Chaplin, then worked free-lance, producing over 100 film scores. His works incl. scores for the films *Forever Amber* and *Carrie*, and the highly popular song "Laura."

ralentir [rä-lä′tēr] (Fr.) slow down.

rall. *abbr.* RALLENTANDO.

rallentando [räl-län′tän-dō] (It.) slowing down; RITARDANDO. Cf. RITENUTO. Abbr., *rall.*

Rameau, Jean-Philippe [rä′mō] (1683–1764) French composer and theorist. He went to Paris in 1722, and by 1726 he had published several books of harpsichord music and two important theoretical treatises, the *Traité de l'harmonie* (Treatise on Harmony) and the *Nouveau système de musique théorique* (the New System of Music Theory), which firmly established his reputation. His first opera was performed in 1733, when he was 50. His works incl. *Hippolyte et Aricie* and *Castor et Pollux* (tragédies lyriques), *Les Indes galantes* (opéra-ballet), *La Princesse de Navarre* (comédie-ballet), over 20 other stage works, sacred and secular vocal music, keyboard suites, chamber music (*Pièces de clavecin en concert*) and theoretical works.

Ramey, Samuel (Edward) (1942–) Amer. bass-baritone, stud. of Arthur Newman and Armen Boyajian. He has sung with the New York City Opera (since 1973) and with the Metropolitan Opera (since 1984) and has appeared with practically every major international opera company. His wide repertory incl. Don Giovanni, Mephistopheles (*Faust*) and Philip II (*Don Carlo*).

ramkie a S. Afr. unfretted folk GUITAR with four strings and a gourd resonator.

Rampal, Jean-Pierre (Louis) (1922–) French flutist, educated at the Marseilles and Paris Conservatories. He played first flute at the Vichy Opéra and the Paris Opéra before establishing a highly successful solo concert and recording career. He was founder of the Quintette à Vent Française (1945) and the Ensemble Baroque de Paris (1953).

Ran, Shulamit (1949–) Israeli-born composer and pianist, educated in Tel Aviv and at the Mannes College in New York, student of Nadia Reisenberg, Dello Joio and Dorothy Taubman. She also studied with Ralph Shapey in 1976. She has performed as piano soloist with the New York PO and the Israel PO and has taught at the U. of Chicago since 1973. Her compositions incl. works for piano and orch., chamber ensembles (incl. *For an Actor: Monologue for Clarinet*), voice, and solo piano. She won the 1991 Pulitzer Prize for her *Symphony*.

R & B RHYTHM-AND-BLUES.

Randall, J(ames) K(irtland) (1929–) Amer. composer, stud. of Leonard Shure, Elwell, Thad Jones, Sessions and Babbitt. He has taught at Princeton since 1958 and has been actively involved in computer synthesis since the early 1960s. Since 1980 he has concentrated on improvised performance, recorded on videotape under a project called INTER/PLAY.

Rands, Bernard (1934–) English-born Amer. composer, stud. of Dallapiccola, Roman Vlad, Maderna, Boulez and Berio. He has taught at Princeton, the U. of Illinois, York University in England and at the U. of California, San Diego. He was awarded the Pulitzer Prize in 1984 for his song cycle *Canti del sole* (1982). His works incl. *Wildtrack 1, 2* and *3* for orch., *Ceremonial* and *Requiescant*, works for chamber ensemble, pieces for piano and songs.

Raney, Wayne (1921–) Amer. country-music harmonica player, responsible in large part for popularizing country harmonica, esp. in his performances with the DELMORE BROTHERS.

range 1, the set of pitches covered by a voice or instrument from its lowest to its highest note, or the interval between the two extremes. Also, *compass.* **2,** the lowest and highest notes

in a particular work, or the interval between them. Cf. TESSITURA.

rank a complete set of organ pipes of the same type and controlled by a single STOP. A stop may include more than one rank, so as to produce an undulating effect (e.g., *voix celeste*) or to provide higher overtones (as a mixture).

Rank, Bill (William C.) (1904–79) Amer. jazz trombonist. He played regularly with Bix Beiderbecke and with Paul Whiteman (1927–37), then led his own bands.

ranket 1, RACKETT. **2**, a reed organ pipe having a covered tone and sounding at 8- or 16-ft. pitch.

Rankl, Karl Franz (1898–1968) Austrian-born English conductor and composer, stud. of Schoenberg and Webern. Before World War II he conducted at various German opera houses, then he came to England, where in 1946 he was in charge of reestablishing the opera at Covent Garden. From 1950 to 1955 he conducted the Scottish Orch., then accepted the directorship of the Sydney Opera.

rant a gay tune, esp. a dance tune similar to a JIG.

ranz des vaches [räs dä väsh] (Fr., procession of cows) a type of Swiss melody played on the alphorn or sung by herdsman to call cattle home.

rap a type of Afr.-Amer. rock music dating from the late 1970s consisting of written or improvised verbal rhymes recited to a rock or funk background. Rap is often used as an accompaniment for break dancing and disco. Cf. SCRATCHING.

Rape of Lucrezia, The tragic opera by Britten to a libretto by Ronald Duncan, after the play *Le Viol de Lucrèce* by André Obey. In 6th-c. Rome the chaste Lucretia stabs herself to death after being ravished by the libertine Prince Tarquinius.

Raphling, Sam (1910–) Amer. composer, trained in Chicago and in Germany. He has written in all classical genres, but he has specialized in works involving wind instruments.

rappresentativo, stile (It.) STILE RAPPRESENTATIVO.

Rappresentazione di anima e di corpo, La [räp-rä-zän-tät'syō-nä] (It., The Representation of Soul and Body) opera-oratorio by Emilio dé Cavalieri. Premiere, Rome 1600. The work is usu. considered to be the first oratorio.

rappresentazione sacra (It.) a Renaissance religious play with music, a forerunner of OPERA and ORATORIO. Also, *sacra rappresentazione*.

Rascals, The Amer. soul group, also known as the Young Rascals, formed in 1964 in New York. Among their hits were "Good Lovin' " (1966) and "Groovin' " (1967). The group disbanded in 1972.

rasch [räsh] (Ger.) fast; PRESTO.

rasgado [räs'gä-*thō*] (Sp.) an arpeggio in guitar playing produced by sweeping the thumb across the strings.

Raskin, Judith (1928–84) Amer. soprano, stud. of Anna Hamlin. She sang with the New York City Opera, the Metropolitan Opera and Glyndebourne, and she made frequent appearances in recital and concert. She taught at the Manhattan School and the Mannes College in New York.

raspa (Sp.) a Cuban SCRAPER having a hollow resonator.

Rasumovsky see RAZUMOVSKY.

rataplan a verbal representation of the sound of an iterating instrument such as a snare drum.

ratchet COG RATTLE.

Rathaus, Karol (1895–1954) Polish-born Amer. composer, educated in Vienna and Berlin. He came to the U.S. in 1938 and taught at Queens College, where a new music building (1960) was named after him. His works, in a dissonant tonal style, incl. 3 symphonies, a piano concerto, overtures and other orchestral works, songs, an oratorio, string quartets and other chamber music, and works for solo piano.

Ratsche ['rät-she] (Ger.) RATTLE.

rattle a percussion instrument found in several different forms, the most common of which are a container (such as a gourd) with noise-making contents (such as seeds) or a stick with clashing objects attached.

Rattle, Simon (Denis) (1955–) English conductor, educated at the Royal Academy of Music in London. He was assistant conductor of the Bournemouth SO, then assoc. conductor of the Royal Liverpool PO and assistant conductor of the BBC Scottish SO. He has also conducted the Glyndebourne Opera and orchestras in Europe and U.S.

Rauschpfeife ['rowsh"pfī-fe] (Ger.) a 16th- and 17th-c. Ger. reed-cap SHAWM.

Ravel, (Joseph) Maurice [rä'vel] (1875–1937) French composer, conductor and pianist, educated at the Paris Conservatoire with Fauré and Gédalge. In his early years in Paris he was a member of LES APACHES and a dandy. He was also a founding member of the Société Musicale Indépendante (1909). His prewar years were marked by his assoc. with Stravinsky, his first opera (*L'Heure espagnole*) and ballet (*Daphnis et Chloé*). During the war he was a transport driver. He refused the Légion d'honneur in 1920 and largely withdrew from Parisian society, producing his second opera (*L'enfant et les sortilèges*), the everpopular *Boléro* and *La Valse* and orchestrations of his own and other composers' works. His final years were marred by the rapid deterioration of his health caused by Pick's disease.

Ravel's works incl. *L'Heure espagnole* and *L'Enfant et les sortilèges* (operas), *Daphnis et Chloé, Boléro* and other ballets, *Shéhérazade, La Valse*, two piano concertos, songs (incl. *Trois poèmes de Stéphane Mallarmé, Chansons madécasses, Histoires naturelles*), 2 violin sonatas, a string quartet, a piano trio and solo piano works (incl. *Pavane pour une infante défunte, Sonatine, Ma Mère l'Oye* for piano duet, *Valses nobles et sentimentales, Le Tombeau de Couperin*).

Ravenna rite a type of Roman Catholic liturgical chant assoc. with Ravenna, Italy, until the early 11th c.

Ravenscroft, Thomas (c1590–c1635) English composer, theorist and editor, educated at Gresham College. He published several important 17th-c. music collections incl. *The Whole Book of Psalmes* (1621), *Pammelia* (1609), the earliest English collection of rounds, and his own *Brief discourse . . .* (1614).

Ravinia Park an entertainment park built north of Chicago in 1904, site of many musical and theatrical events since its founding and home since 1936 of the annual summer Ravinia Festival (a series of concerts by the Chicago SO and visiting groups). Recent music directors have been Seiji Ozawa and James Levine.

ravvivando (It.) reviving.

Rawls, Lou (1935–) Amer. rock singer and recording artist, whose hits incl. "You'll Never Find Another Love Like Mine" (1976) and "Love Is a Hurtin' Thing" (1966).

Rawsthorne, Alan (1905–71) English composer and pianist, stud. of Frank Merrick, Carl Fuchs and Egon Petri. His works incl. 3 symphonies, concertos for clarinet, piano, oboe and violin, *A Canticle of Man* and other choral works, songs, chamber music and film scores.

ray the supertonic of the current key (or its relative major, if the key is minor) in TONIC SOL-FA.

Ray, Johnnie (John Alvin) (1927–90) Amer. popular singer, orig. a rhythm-and-blues artist. His most successful songs were "Cry" and "The Little White Cloud That Cried" (1951) and "Just Walking in the Rain" (1956).

Razor Quartet the string quartet in F minor, Op. 55 No. 2 (1788), by Haydn, supposedly so called because Haydn gave the quartet to an English publisher in return for two English razors.

Razumovsky Quartets the three string quartets, Op. 59 (1805–6), by Beethoven, dedicated to Count Razumovsky, the Russian ambassador to Vienna. Also, *Russian Quartets*.

re 1, [rā] the second degree of the Guidonian HEXACHORD. **2**, (Fr., It., Sp.) the note D. **3**, [rē] the raised supertonic of the current key (or of the relative major, if the key is minor) in TONIC SOL-FA. See PITCH.

Read, Daniel (1757–1836) Amer. composer and tunebook compiler. His tunes appeared in various late 18th-c. hymnbooks and his own *The American Singing Book* (1785).

Read, Gardner (1913–) Amer. composer, stud. of Hanson, Rogers and Pizzetti. He has taught at the St. Louis Institute, the Kansas City Conservatory, the Cleveland Institute and for 30 years at Boston U. (until his retirement in 1978). He is noted as an orchestrator and has written several widely used books on the subject. His works incl. *Villon* (opera), 4 symphonies, concertos for piano, cello and violin, *Quiet Music*, three *Sonoric Fantasies* for chamber orch., also vocal music, chamber music, works for solo piano and solo organ.

real answer see ANSWER.

realism see VERISMO.

realization 1, the interpretation of compositional details left by the composer to the performer's discretion. Most often the term is used to indicate the BASSO CONTINUO player's interpretation of a FIGURED BASS. **2**, the performance of a score written for one instrument or group of instruments at another instrument, as the realization of an orchestral score at the piano.

Reardon, John (1930–87) Amer. baritone, stud. of Martial Singher and Margaret Harshaw. He sang regularly at the New York City Opera and the Metropolitan Opera, performing a wide repertory of roles of the 19th and 20th c., a number of them in premieres.

rebab an Arabic FIDDLE of the Middle Ages having one to three strings and found in the gamelan.

rebec *also*, **rebeck, ribible** a lute-shaped medieval FIDDLE related to the rebab.

Rebikov, Vladimir (1866–1920) Russian composer, trained at the Moscow

Conservatory. His works were unusual for their time because of their extensive use of the whole-tone scale. He wrote operas, orchestral works and piano music as well as numerous articles on music.

rebop BOP.

recapitulation the third section of SONATA FORM in which the material of the EXPOSITION is repeated, more or less exactly, usu. in the tonic key.

rechte Hand ['reç-te hänt] (Ger.) right hand.

récit [rā'sē] (Fr.) **1**, a 17th- and 18th-c. term for a composition for solo voice or instrument. **2**, one of the four manuals of the French classical organ.

recit. *abbr.* RECITATIVE.

recital a 19th-c. term for a CONCERT given by a solo performer or, sometimes, a small group of performers, as opposed to an orchestral concert.

recitative *also*, **recitativo** [rā-chē-tä'tē-vō] (It.) a vocal passage delivered in a speechlike manner. If accompanied by BASSO CONTINUO only, it is called *recitativo secco* or *semplice* (dry or simple recitative); when accompanied by orch., it is called *recitativo accompagnato* or *stromentato* (accompanied or orchestrated recitative). Cf. STILE RECITATIVO.

Secco recitative

Be – hold, a vir – gin shall con – ceive,

Continuo

Accompanied recitative

Thy re – buke hath bro – ken his heart;

Strings

(G.F. Handel, Messiah)

Recitative Quartet the string quartet in G major, Op. 17 No. 5 (1771) by Haydn, so named for the adagio movement, written in an operatic style with a recitative and aria.

recitativo accompagnato [äk-kōm-pä′nyä-tō] *also,* **accompagnato** (It.) see RECITATIVE.

recitativo arioso (It.) **1,** a RECITATIVE combining speechlike and more expressive melodic music. **2,** instrumental music in *arioso* style.

recitativo secco [′sek-kō *or* **semplice** [′sem-plē-chā] (It., dry or simple recitative) see RECITATIVE.

reciting note the note (tenor) on which most of a psalm verse is sung. See PSALM TONE.

recorder 1, a wooden WHISTLE FLUTE prevalent during the Renaissance and baroque periods. The instrument is made in various sizes, the most common being: *sopranino, soprano, descant, treble, alto, tenor, bass* and *great bass.* The recorder has eight finger holes, sometimes with keys, and a wide, tapering bore. In recent times it has been widely used for teaching music to young children; the teaching instruments are often made of plastic. Also, *English flute.* **2,** a pipe ORGAN STOP similar in tone quality to the recorder; *Blockflöte* (Ger.).

recoupe [rə′koop] (Fr.) an after-dance of the BASSE DANSE.

Redding, Otis (1941–67) Amer. soul singer and songwriter. One of his best-known recordings, "The Dock of the Bay" (1968), was released after his premature death.

Redman, Don (Donald Matthew) (1900–64) Amer. jazz composer, arranger, saxophonist and bandleader, a pioneer in the evolution of large orch. arranging. He played in and arranged for Fletcher Henderson's band in the early 1920s, then became music dir. of McKinney's Cotton Pickers. In 1931 he formed his own band. During the 1940s he arranged for the big bands and for radio and TV, then worked for Pearl Bailey in the 1950s.

Red Mill, The musical by Victor Herbert, lyrics and book by Henry Blos-som. Premiere, New York 1906. Two impoverished Americans in Holland try to get money to return home.

redowa [′re-də-və] (Czech) a 19th-c. Bohemian ballroom dance either in ¾ waltz time or ²⁄₄ polka time.

Red Poppy, The (Russ., *Krasnïy mak*) ballet (1927) by Glière to a story about the revolutionary movement in China.

reed a thin, narrow, flexible sheet of metal, vegetable tissue (cane or reed) or plastic that is made to vibrate by means of an airstream directed against the reed and produced by a bellows or the player's lungs. A *beating* reed vibrates against the ridges of an opening which it covers (a *single* reed) or against another reed (*double* reed); examples are the clarinet or saxophone reed and the pipe-organ reed pipe (single) or the oboe reed (double). Most woodwind reeds are made from cane (experiments with plastic have yet to produce consistently acceptable substitutes) and are shaved to make the vibrating tip thinner and hence able to vibrate more easily. A *free* reed vibrates within an opening and sometimes is simply cut from the surrounding material of the resonating tube. Examples of free-reed instruments are the mouth organ and the accordion.

Reed, Alfred (1921–) Amer. composer and conductor, educated at the Juilliard School and Baylor U. He has taught and conducted at the U. of Miami and has worked for the NBC and ABC networks. He has written many works for band, as well as orchestral works and chamber music.

Reed, Lou (1942–) Amer. rock singer, songwriter and guitarist. He was a founder of the group VELVET UNDERGROUND and member until 1970, then turned to solo performance. His biggest hit, "Walk on the Wild Side" (1973), was recorded early in his career.

reed-cap instrument a single- or double-reed wind instrument whose reed is covered by a cap pierced with a hole through which the player blows,

Reed instruments

Double-reed   Single-reed

scrape

reed

staple

(oboe)

mouthpiece

(clarinet)

Bassoon   crook

Saxophone

Oboe   bocal

English horn

bell

Renaissance Double-reeds

reedcap

Rackett   Shawm   Krummhorn   Clarinet   Bass clarinet

causing the reed to vibrate. Examples incl. the krummhorns and some shawms.

reed organ a keyboard wind instrument having free metal reeds activated by air under pressure or (in the *American organ*) under suction. Small versions of the reed organ were transported West by the pioneers and were frequently used by traveling evangelists. Cf. HARMONIUM, CABINET ORGAN.

reed pipe see REED; ORGAN.

reel 1, a lively Scottish highland dance in ¼ time with gliding movements. **2,** VIRGINIA REEL.

Reeves, Jim (James Travis) (1923–64) Amer. country-pop singer, a representative of the NASHVILLE SOUND. From the mid-1950s he appeared on the Louisiana Hayride (where he began as an announcer) and the Grand Ole Opry and toured extensively. He was elected to the Country Music Hall of Fame in 1967.

Reformation Symphony the Symphony No. 5 in D minor, Op. 107 (1830), by Mendelssohn, composed to celebrate the 300th anniversary of the Augsburg Confession of the Lutheran Church. The last movement is based on Martin Luther's chorale, "Ein' feste Burg" (A mighty fortress).

refrain a recurring verse or phrase that comes back, esp. at the end of a division of a song. Also, *chorus, burden*.

regal 1, a small portable organ of the 16th and 17th c. having reed pipes (later also flue pipes) activated by a bellows operated by one hand while the other hand plays a keyboard. Cf. BIBLE REGAL. **2,** a group of pipe organ stops similar to reed stops.

regent's bugle a type of KEYED TRUMPET with a tuning slide.

Reger, Max(imilian) (1873–1916) prolific German composer, pianist and organist, stud. of Adalbert Lindner and Hugo Riemann. He was a professor at Leipzig U. from 1907 to 1911, where his pupils incl. Szell and Weinberger. He conducted the court orch. in Meiningen for three years,

then settled in Jena, where he spent his last years. His works are characterized by a strong feeling for harmony and counterpoint (he was nicknamed "the second Bach") and by a remarkable musical density. His works incl. concertos for violin and for piano, orchestral works, songs and choral works (*Psalm 100*, works for male chorus), sonatas, quartets, clarinet quintet, string sextet and other chamber music, many works for solo piano and organ, and arrangements.

reggae ['reg-ā] a type of 1960s urban popular music of Jamaican origin, a successor to ROCK STEADY, characterized by a strong offbeat rhythm in ⁴⁄₄ or ¹²⁄₈ time and short ostinatos in the accompaniment. Cf. ROCKERS, SKA.

Regina opera in 3 acts by Marc Blitzstein to his own libretto, based on Lillian Hellman's *The Little Foxes*. Premiere, New York 1949. The domineering Regina seeks to control the Giddens family business in a small town in the South.

register 1, a section of the compass of a voice, instrument, composition, etc. **2,** an area of the vocal range. The principal areas are the *lower* or *chest register*, the *middle register*, the *upper* or *head register* and *falsetto*. **3,** a set of pipes in an ORGAN having the same quality. Also, *stop*.

registration combination of stops prearranged on an organ, harpsichord, etc., for the performance of a particular work or portion of a work.

Regnart, Jacob (Jacques) (c1540–99) Dutch composer of German songs and Latin sacred vocal music. He was in the service of the Hapsburg court from the late 1550s in Prague, Vienna and Innsbruck. Much of his music was published in his lifetime and widely disseminated.

rehearsal a preconcert practice session.

Reich, Steve (Stephen) (**Michael**) (1936–) Amer. composer, educated at the Juilliard School with Persichetti and Bergsma and at Mills College with Milhaud and Berio. He studied Afr. drumming in Ghana and the gamelan in California. Considered one of the first minimalist composers (see MINIMALISM), his works usu. consist in permutations of simple materials, such as a single chord, motif or rhythmic idea. In 1966 he formed the group Steve Reich and Musicians to perform his music. His works incl. *Pulse Music; Four Organs* for electronic organs and maracas; *Drumming* for women's voices and drums; *Variations for Winds, Strings and Keyboards; Vermont Counterpoint* for flute and tape; and *The Desert Music* for chorus and orch.

Reicha, Antonín (1770–1836) prolific Czech composer, theorist and teacher. He studied with his uncle, Josef Reicha (1752–95), who was a cellist, composer and conductor. From 1801 to 1808 he lived in Vienna, where he formed a close friendship with Haydn; the rest of his life was spent in Paris. He taught at the Paris Conservatoire from 1818, his pupils incl. Liszt, Berlioz and Franck. Reicha produced a large body of chamber music, of which only the wind quintets remain in the repertory, almost 20 operas, symphonies, concertos and overtures, choral and solo vocal works and works for piano and organ solo. His theoretical works on harmony, counterpoint and composition were widely used in the 19th c.

Reichardt, Johann Friedrich (1752–1814) German composer and writer, educated in his home city of Königsberg. He served at the Royal Berlin Opera for most of his career and produced a substantial body of operas, vocal and instrumental music, and theoretical and historical writings. His daughter, **Louise Reichardt** (1779–1826), was a singer, composer, conductor and voice teacher.

Reimann, Aribert (1936–) German composer and pianist, stud. of Blacher and Pepping. His compositional style was influenced by Webern and the music of India, though he later abandoned serialism. He has performed widely as solo pianist and accompanist, notably for baritone Fischer-Dieskau. His works incl. *Lear* and other operas, concertos for violin and piano, and vocal and chamber music.

Reinagle, Alexander (1756–1809) English-born Amer. composer, pianist, arranger, conductor and impresario. From 1790 until his death he was musical dir. of the New Company in Philadelphia and Baltimore and wrote many stage works and airs for the operas he produced there. He also wrote four piano sonatas (possibly the first piano pieces written in America), chamber music, and choral and vocal works.

Reine, La [ren] (Fr.) QUEEN, THE.

Reinecke, Carl (Heinrich Carsten) (1824–1910) German composer, pianist, conductor and teacher, stud. of his father. He was court pianist in Copenhagen from 1846, then worked for shorter periods in Barmen and Breslau. In 1860 he settled in Leipzig to teach at the Conservatory, of which he was dir. from 1897, and to conduct the Gewandhaus Orch. His works, in the style of Schumann and Brahms, are still represented in the repertory and incl. 6 operas, 3 symphonies, overtures, concertos for various instruments, chamber music (much of it with piano), works for solo piano and songs.

Reiner, Fritz (1888–1963) Hungarian-born Amer. conductor, stud. of István Thomán and Bartók. He was musical dir. of the Dresden court opera, the Cincinnati SO (1922–31), the Pittsburgh SO (1938–48) and the Chicago SO (1953–62), and also frequently conducted at the Metropolitan Opera. From 1931 to 1941 he taught at the Curtis Institute, where his pupils incl. Bernstein and Foss. He was noted for his attention to rhythmic detail and for his small, precise beat.

Reinhardt, Django (Jean Baptiste) (1910–53) Belgian gypsy jazz guitarist, the first European to exert a strong influence on Amer. jazz. He was cofounder in 1934 with violinist Stéphane Grappelli of the Quintet of the Hot Club de France.

Reisenberg (Sherman), Nadia (1904–83) Lithuanian-born Amer. pianist, stud. of Leonid Nikolayev. Her Amer. debut was in 1922, and she performed frequently with the New York PO and other orchestras in the U.S. and abroad. She taught at the Curtis Institute, the Mannes College and the Juilliard School.

Reizenstein, Franz (Theodor) (1911–68) German-born English composer and pianist, stud. of Hindemith, Vaughan Williams and Solomon. He taught at the Royal Academy of Music in London and the Royal Manchester College of Music. His works, which clearly show the influence of Hindemith, are predominantly for chamber music combinations but also incl. concertos for piano and violin, overtures and songs.

réjouissance [rā-zhwē′säs] (Fr., rejoicing) a lively movement of the 18th-c. suite.

relative keys keys with the same key signature, such as C major and A minor. The major key is a minor third above its relative minor.

relative pitch the ability to identify a certain pitch by relation to other pitches. Contrasted with ABSOLUTE PITCH.

relish an ORNAMENT or grace in early English music.

Reményi, Ede (Eduard) (1828–98) Hungarian violinist, stud. of Joseph Böhm. He was exiled from Hungary in 1848 for his part in the Kossuth revolution and did not return until 1860. He toured frequently in the U.S., where he lived during several periods of his life. He was esp. noted for the gypsy fervor of his playing.

Renaissance in music history, the period from about 1430 to about 1600, characterized by the development of musical techniques which lead from the successive conception of voices in polyphony (as in 15th-c. cantus firmus technique) to the simultaneous conception of voices necessary for PARODY technique and compositions based on points of imitation (see POINT). The era is also known for the

development of vocal and instrumental virtuosity, and an increasing independence of instrumental music from vocal models.

Reno, Don(ald) (1927–84) Amer. country-music singer and banjo player. He was a member of the Blue Grass Boys from 1948, then in 1952 formed the Tennessee Cutups with Red Smiley.

REO Speedwagon Amer. hard-pop group formed in 1967 in Champaign, IL. A popular touring group, their most successful album was *Hi-Infidelity* (1980), which incl. the hit single "Keep on Lovin' You."

repeat the restatement of a musical phrase, section, movement, etc., usu. not written out but indicated by the sign (‖) at the beginning of the section and (:‖) at the end. See also DA CAPO, DAL SEGNO.

repetiteur [rā-pā-tē′tœr] (Fr.) a singing coach, esp. one that coaches singers in operatic roles.

répétition [rā-pā-tē′syō] (Fr.), **ripetizione** [rē-pā-tēt′syō-nā] (It.) REHEARSAL.

reports points of imitation (see POINT).

reprise [rə′prēz] (Fr.) **1,** a musical repetition; esp., a RECAPITULATION. **2,** the second section of a binary form in 17th-c. French music.

reproaches a series of Good Friday

Renaissance Basses

Ruggiero

Passamezzo antico

Passamezzo moderno

Folia

Romanesca

Repeats

chants reproaching man for his unfaithfulness to God. Also, *improperia* (Lat.).

reproducing piano a type of PLAYER PIANO which records and plays back not only the pitches and durations, but also other elements of a particular performance, such as dynamics, pedaling, etc.

Requiem Mass in the Roman Catholic service, the Mass for the Dead. The name is derived from the first words of the Introit: "Requiem aeternam dona eis, Domine." The Requiem consists of settings from both the Proper and Ordinary and is therefore a type of PLENARY MASS. The separate movements are the Introit; Kyrie, Gradual and Tract; Sequence (Dies Irae); Offertory; Sanctus and Benedictus; Agnus Dei; and Communion (Lux Aeterna). On solemn occasions, the responsory "Libera me, Domine" follows the Communion. This essential structure was established by the 14th c. In addition to the Requiem Mass, there is also an Office of the Dead, which has seldom been set by composers. The oldest extant Requiem setting is by Ockeghem (c1470); other famous settings have been made by Mozart (left unfinished at his death and completed by F.X. Süssmayer), Berlioz and Verdi. Brahms's *A German Requiem*, like other German Requiems, is based on scripture and does not derive from the Roman Catholic liturgy.

rescue opera a type of opera whose plot involves the rescue of a leading character at the last moment by the heroic effort of another. The genre was popular esp. in France in the decades after the French Revolution. The most famous example is Beethoven's *Fidelio*.

reservata MUSICA RESERVATA.

res facta *also*, **resfacta** (Lat., created thing) a medieval and Renaissance term for music which is written down, as opposed to improvised music.

reshoto (Russ.) a Russian FRAME DRUM with jingle disks.

residue tone a tone heard when several harmonically related tones are sounded together quietly. Its pitch is directly related to the pitch level of the tones sounded (in distinction to *difference tone*). See COMBINATION TONE.

Resnik, Regina (1922–) Amer. mezzo-soprano and stage dir., stud. of Rosalie Miller. She sang with the Metropolitan Opera from 1944, as well as at Bayreuth, Vienna, Chicago, San Francisco, Covent Garden and other major houses. Her roles incl. Mistress Quickly (*Falstaff*), Leonora (*Il Trovatore*) and Laura (*La Gioconda*).

resolution 1, the consonant tone to which a dissonant tone moves (*resolves*). **2,** the act of resolving a DISSONANCE.

resonance an oscillation in a sound-producing body that occurs when the frequency of the sound source is close to the frequency of the body. The oscillation can enhance the principal sounds or, in certain circumstances, dampen them.

resonator a body used to produce a sound-enhancing RESONANCE in a musical instrument, such as the body of a violin, the tube of the flute or the tubes beneath the bars of a xylophone.

Respighi, Ottorino (1879–1936) Italian composer, pianist and violinist, educated at the Bologna Liceo Musicale and with Rimsky-Korsakov in Russia. He taught at the Conservatory of St. Cecilia in Rome from 1913 to 1926, then devoted himself to composing and private teaching. He wrote 8 operas, ballets and chamber music, but he is best known for his orchestral works, esp. the tone poems *Fontane di Roma* (1914–16) and *Pini di Roma* (1923–4) and his songs (incl. "Nebbie" and "Nevicata").

respond 1, RESPONSORY. **2,** RESPONSE.

response a verse said or sung by the congregation in answer to a VERSICLE. Also, *respond*.

responsorial referring to a type of chanting in which the verses are sung by a soloist or cantor and the refrain or *response* is sung by the congregation and/or choir. Cf. ANTIPHONAL.

responsory a type of RESPONSORIAL chant used for matins and vespers services and following the lessons. Also, *respond*.

rest a silence of a definite length, usu. indicated by a notational symbol or a direction. Most rests are indicated by a sign corresponding to a certain note value. However, in 20th-c. music the length of a rest is sometimes given in time units or illustrated by proportional spacing in the score (see TIME-SPACE NOTATION). In orchestral parts, multiple measures of rest are usu. combined into one measure with a number indicating the number of measures of silence represented. See NOTES AND RESTS (*illus.*).

resultant 1, COMBINATION TONE. **2,** *also*, **resultant bass** ACOUSTIC BASS.

Resurrection Symphony popular name for the Symphony No. 2 in C minor for soprano, contralto, chorus and orch. (1888–94) by Mahler.

Retablo de Maese Pedro, Il (Sp.) MASTER PETER'S PUPPET SHOW.

retardation a suspension which resolves upward. See NONHARMONIC NOTE.

retenu [rə-tə'nü] (Fr.) RITENUTO.

Rethberg, Elisabeth (Sättler, Lisbeth) (1894–1976) German soprano, stud. of Otto Watrin. She sang for seven years with the Dresden Opera, then joined the Metropolitan Opera in 1922, remaining with the company for twenty years. She also sang in Italy and England and at the Salzburg Festival. Her many roles incl. Aida, Elisabeth (*Tannhäuser*) and the Countess (*The Marriage of Figaro*).

retransition the part of a SONATA FORM at the end of the development which prepares for the RECAPITULATION.

retrograde the form of a theme or melody in which the notes are rendered backward, with or without the original rhythms. The technique is common in canon and in serial music, rarer in noncanonic tonal music. A famous example is the final, fugal movement of Beethoven's *Hammerklavier Sonata*, in which one exposition is based on the theme in retrograde. See COUNTERPOINT.

retrograde inversion a combination of the techniques of RETROGRADE and INVERSION in which the notes of a theme are rendered backward with the original intervals inverted.

Reubke, (Friedrich) Julius (1834–58) German composer, pianist and organist, educated at the Berlin Conservatory and with Liszt. He is remembered for two works, the Piano Sonata in B♭ minor and the Organ Sonata in C minor, both masterpieces of German Romantic music.

Reutter, Hermann (1900–85) German composer, teacher and pianist, educated at the Munich Academy. He was active as an accompanist for many singers, working with Hans Hotter and Elisabeth Schwarzkopf, among others; as a composer; and as a teacher at the Stuttgart Musikhochschule and the Hoch Conservatory in Berlin. Best known for his songs in a late Romantic style, he also wrote operas and ballets, concertos for piano and violin, choral works, chamber music and many songs.

Revel, Harry (1905–58) English-born Amer. songwriter and pianist, composer of Broadway revues and Hollywood film scores. His songs incl. "Did You Ever See a Dream Walking?" (1934) and "You Hit the Spot" (1936).

reverberation the reflecting back and forth of a sound wave between the surfaces of a space, like the walls of a room. The time required for a reverberating sound wave to become inaudible is an important consideration in acoustical design.

Revolutionary Étude the Étude in C minor, Op. 10 No. 12 (1830), by Chopin. The reason for the name is unknown.

revue a theatrical entertainment consisting of a series of sketches, usu. based on a common theme but not contributing to a common plot. The form was esp. popular in the first three decades of the 20th c., as in the *Ziegfeld Follies*, the George White *Scandals*, the *Blackbirds* and the *Garrick Gaieties*, and survives in television and theatrical specials of recent years.

Revueltas, Silvestre (1899–1940) Mexican composer and violinist, educated in Mexico, Austin, TX, and Chicago. After holding various posts in the U.S., he became assistant conductor of the Mexico SO and taught at the conservatory in Mexico City. His works combine a modern dissonant idiom with tunes and rhythms reminiscent of Mexican folk music.

Reynolds, Roger (Lee) (1934–) Amer. composer, stud. of Finney and Gerhard. He was a co-founder of the ONCE performance group in Ann Arbor, MI, and of concert series in Japan and Europe. He has taught at the U. of California, San Diego, since 1969. He has written theater works (*The Emperor of Ice Cream*), orchestral music (some involving computer con-

trol), chamber music, vocal works and tape works. He was awarded the Pulitzer Prize in 1989 for his orchestral work *Whispers Out of Time*.

rf. *also*, **rfz.** *abbr.* RINFORZANDO.

R.H. *abbr.* right hand.

Rhapsodie espagnole ['räp-sō-dē es-pä'nyōl] (Fr., Spanish Rhapsody) a four-movement suite for orch. (1907) by Ravel. The movements are the "Prelude to the Night," a malagueña, a habanera and "Feria" (Fiesta).

rhapsody a work in the style of a FANTASY or IMPROVISATION, often—esp. in the later 19th c.—heroic or emotional.

Rhapsody in Black a revue by Mann Holiner and Alberta Nichols, starring Ethel Waters. Premiere, New York 1931.

Rhapsody in Blue work for piano and orch. (1924) by Gershwin, written for Paul Whiteman's band and orchestrated by Ferde Grofé.

Rhapsody on a Theme of Paganini work for piano and orch., Op. 43 (1934), by Rachmaninov, consisting of 24 variations on a theme from Paganini's *24 Caprices for Violin Solo*, Op. 1.

Rheinberger, Joseph (Gabriel) (1839–1901) German composer, conductor, organist and teacher. He studied with Philipp Schmutzer and at the Munich Conservatory. He was conductor of the Munich Choral Society, a professor at the Munich Conservatory and court Kapellmeister. A prolific composer, Rheinberger's many works in all genres have not remained in the repertory; he is remembered primarily as the teacher of Wolf-Ferrari, Furtwängler and many others.

Rheingold, Das ['rīn-golt] (Ger., The Rhinegold) epic opera in 1 act by Wagner to his own libretto, the first opera of THE RING OF THE NIBELUNGEN. Premiere, Munich 1869. The Nibelung dwarf Alberich renounces love and steals the Rhinegold to forge an ill-fated ring.

Rhenish Symphony popular name for the Symphony No. 3 in E major,

Op. 97 (1850), by Schumann, inspired by a visit to Cologne.

Rhodes, Harold (1910–) Amer. teacher and inventor. He established the Harold Rhodes School of Popular Piano in 1930, which he developed into a nationwide chain. In 1942 he invented for the U.S. Air Corps a small piano that could be made from various scrap materials. His real success, however, was his electric piano, developed in collaboration with Leo Fender and marketed since 1965 as the Rhodes (or Fender-Rhodes) electric piano.

rhumba Rumba.

rhythm the distinctive grouping of sounds and silence in time, based on duration of tone, strong and weak stresses and other factors (such as harmony, melodic contour, etc.). Rhythm is often regulated by meter or some other form of regular pulse such as a Tactus. With melody and harmony, it is one of the principal elements of music.

rhythm-and-blues a type of Afr.-Amer. popular music of the 1940s to the 1960s, a successor to the Race records of the 1920s and 30s and the predecessor of Soul music. It is a combination of blues and jazz styles, esp. Swing, and is characterized by blues-type melodies accompanied by a prominent and heavily syncopated rhythm section. Rhythm-and-blues was the first black music to become widely popular with white audiences and paved the way for Rock. Among the many performers of the genre were Joe Turner, Muddy Waters, B.B. King, Chuck Berry and Ray Charles and the vocal groups the Platters and the Drifters. Also, *Harlem jump.*

rhythmic modes a medieval system of rhythmic notation by which the duration of an individual note is determined by its position among long and short values. The modes, of which there were six (see example), were notated using a preexistent system of ligatures.

rhythmicon a mechanical instrument invented in 1931 by Henry

Rhythmic Modes

Cowell and Leon Theremin capable of producing complex combinations of beat patterns. To demonstrate the machine, Cowell wrote a concerto for rhythmicon and orch.; the work was not premiered, however, until 1971 with the rhythmicon part realized on a computer.

rhythm section the section of a band or orch. that provides the rhythmic pulse. It usu. consists of traps, a plucked bass instrument and sometimes a guitar or banjo. The piano is sometimes considered to be part of the rhythm section.

ribible Rebec.

Ricci, Ruggiero (Rich, Woodrow Wilson) (1918–) Amer. violinist, stud. of Louis Persinger, Michel Piastro, Georg Kulenkampff and Paul Stassevitch. He plays a wide classical and jazz repertory, specializing in late 19th-c. virtuoso works, and has toured the world. He has taught at Indiana U. and at the Juilliard School.

Rice, Edward Everett (1848–1924) Amer. composer of musical burlesques, the most popular being *Evangeline* (1874) and *Adonis* (1884).

Rice, Thomas Dartmouth ("Daddy") (1808–60) Amer. minstrel performer, the first to present a solo act in blackface. He was also the creator of Ethiopian opera, a genre consisting of blackface farces separated by songs.

ricercar [rē-cher'kär] *also,* **ricercare** (It., research) **1,** a contrapuntal instrumental work of the 16th c. analogous to the vocal Motet. **2,** in the 18th c., an academic fugue.

Rich, Buddy (Bernard) (1917–87) Amer. jazz drummer and bandleader. He played with the bands of Artie Shaw, Tommy Dorsey and Bunny

Berigan in late 1930s and early 1940s, as well as leading his own groups, then joined Harry James in 1953. In 1966 he formed a second big band, which toured successfully until 1974. He was noted for his technical virtuosity.

Rich, Charlie (1932–) Amer. country-music singer, pianist and songwriter. He found his biggest success in the 1960s and 1970s with songs such as "Set Me Free" and "The Most Beautiful Girl" and the album *Behind Closed Doors* (1973).

Richie, Lionel (1950–) Amer. soul singer and songwriter, leader of the COMMODORES until 1982. His speciality is slow, romantic ballads. He has also produced albums and wrote the theme song for the film *Endless Love* (1981).

Richter, Hans (1843–1916) Austro-Hungarian conductor, educated at the Vienna Conservatory. He was an assistant to Bülow and worked with Wagner in the preparation of the scores of the *Ring* and *Die Meistersinger*. He conducted regularly at Bayreuth and in England, where he founded the Richter Concerts and was conductor of the Birmingham Music Festival and the Hallé Orch.

Richter, Karl (1926–81) German conductor, organist and harpsichordist, stud. of Rudolf Mauersberger, Karl Straube and Günther Ramin. He became organist of the Leipzig Thomaskirche in 1947 and taught at the Munich Hochschule für Musik from 1951, also founding the Munich Bach Choir and Orch. With these groups he toured widely and recorded many of the works of J.S. Bach and other baroque composers.

Richter, Svyatoslav (1915–) Russian pianist, stud. of his father, but largely self-taught. He later studied with Heinrich Neuhaus. Until 1960 he performed only in the Soviet Union and in eastern Europe; in that year he made his U.S. debut in Chicago. His technique and interpretive powers are consummate and best shown in the 19th-c. Romantic masterworks and the 20th-c. literature by Prokofiev and Rachmaninoff. He also appears as a chamber music pianist and has accompanied singers in recital and in recordings.

ricochet in string BOWING, a bouncing staccato played in one stroke.

Ricordi Italian firm of music publishers founded in Milan in 1808 by Giovanni Ricordi (1785–1853). The Ricordi family and the firm had a significant influence on Italian composition in the 19th and early 20th c. Their extensive catalogue covers all periods and styles.

Ridderbusch, Karl (1932–) German bass. He studied in Essen and sang with the Essen Opera from 1963 to 1965, then moved to the Deutsche Oper in Düsseldorf. He sang regularly at Bayreuth, the Metropolitan Opera, Covent Garden and the Vienna Staatsoper, appearing in the major bass roles of Wagner, Verdi, Beethoven, etc. He is also noted for his performance in concert repertory.

Riddle, Nelson (1921–85) Amer. conductor, composer and arranger. He arranged and conducted for a number of eminent popular singers, incl. Frank Sinatra, Peggy Lee, Linda Ronstadt and Ella Fitzgerald. He worked extensively in TV and films, winning an Academy Award for his score for *The Great Gatsby* (1975).

riddle canon a canon in which the entrances are indicated by symbols or cabalistic devices. Also, *enigma canon*.

ride cymbal a suspended cymbal used in jazz since the 1930s to mark the regular metric accents or afterbeats.

Rider, The popular name for the string quartet in G minor, Op. 74 No. 3 (1793), by Haydn.

Ridout, Godfrey (1918–) Canadian composer, stud. of Ettore Mazzoleni, Healey Willan and Charles Peaker. He taught at the Toronto Conservatory from 1940 and then at the U. of Toronto from 1948. He composed and conducted many film scores for the National Film Board of Canada and has provided music for many CBC radio programs. His works incl. *Ballade* for viola and orch. and other orchestral works, choral music, songs and chamber music.

Riegger, Wallingford (Constantin) (1885–1961) Amer. composer, stud. of Alvin Schroeder and Percy Goetschius. His works are forceful and dissonant, in both atonal and twelve-tone idioms and incl. *New Dance* (1935), *With my Red Fires* (1936) and other ballets, 3 symphonies (his Symphony No. 3 won several prestigious awards in 1948), many other orchestral works (*Quintuple Jazz, Dichotomy, Variations*), 2 string quartets and other chamber music, songs and choral works and arrangements.

Riemenschneider, (Charles) Albert (1878–1950) Amer. organist, conductor and scholar. He taught at the Baldwin-Wallace College Conservatory of Music (and at the Wallace Kollegium, its predecessor) from 1896 and in 1933 established the Baldwin-Wallace College Bach Festival, modeled on the BETHLEHEM BACH FESTIVAL. He is best remembered for his editions of works by Bach, esp. the chorales.

Rienzi romantic grand opera in 5 acts by Wagner to his own libretto, based on the novel by Edward Bulwer-Lytton. Premiere, Dresden 1842. Set in Rome in the mid-14th c., the opera tells the story of Cola di Rienzi, an Italian patriot who attempted in vain to restore the old Roman system of government.

Ries, Ferdinand (1784–1838) German pianist and composer, stud. of his father. In his youth he earned his living copying music, then he went to Vienna to study with Beethoven. In the first decade of the 19th c. he toured extensively, then settled in London for eleven years, retiring in 1824 to the Rhineland. He was a prolific composer in all forms, writing operas, 8 symphonies, overtures, concertos, choral and vocal music, chamber music and a large body of works for piano solo.

Rieti, Vittorio (1898–   ) Amer. composer of Italian descent, stud. of Giuseppe Frugatta and Respighi. In the 1920s and 1930s he divided his time between Paris and Rome. He wrote music for the Ballets Russes and was a founder of the modern chamber music group La Sérénade in Paris. He moved to the U.S. in 1940 and taught at the Peabody Conservatory, the Chicago Musical College, Queens College (NY) and the New York College of Music. His music, predominantly in a neoclassical idiom, incl. operas, ballets, concertos, orchestral works, chamber music and songs.

riff in popular music and jazz, a short rhythmic ostinato pattern repeated with no melodic variation, usu. as an accompaniment to a solo. It apparently came to jazz from West Afr. through New Orleans marching band music and it has become a part of rhythm-and-blues and rock as well.

Rifkin, Joshua (1944–   ) Amer. musicologist, pianist, composer and conductor, educated at the Juilliard School, New York U. and Princeton. He has taught at Brandeis and worked for over ten years for Nonesuch Records. He was an important force in the revival of interest in ragtime music, though his principal area of musicological research is Renaissance and Baroque music.

rigaudon [rē-gō′dō] (Fr.) *also*, **rigadoon** a lively 17th and 18th c. French jumping DANCE in duple time, derived from folk dances of several regions of France. In instrumental form it was often a part of the Baroque dance suite.

Righteous Brothers a white soul duo formed in 1962 by Bill Medley and Bobby Hatfield. Their hit songs incl. "You've Lost that Lovin' Feeling" (1964) and "(You're My) Soul and Inspiration" (1965). The duo disbanded in 1968.

Rigoletto tragic opera by Verdi to a libretto by Francesco Maria Piave, based on Victor Hugo's play *Le Roi s'amuse*. Premiere, Venice 1851. The court jester Rigoletto seeks vengeance on his lord, the Duke of Mantua, for seducing his daughter, but it is his daughter, not the Duke, who is killed.

Rihm, Wolfgang [rēm] (1952–) German composer, stud. of Searle, Stockhausen, Huber and Fortner. He has taught at the Hochschule für Musik in Karlsruhe. His works, in an expressionist style, incl. several operas, 3 symphonies, works for voice and orch., concertos, chamber music and songs.

Riisager, Knudåge (1897–1974) prolific Danish composer of music in all genres, trained in Copenhagen and Leipzig. He was dir. of the Royal Danish Conservatory (1956–67).

Riley, Terry (Mitchell) (1935–) Amer. composer and performer, educated at the U. of California, Berkeley. He was a member of FLUXUS in 1961, then experimented in Paris at the ORTF studios. His work *In C* (1964) employs 53 motifs played by an indeterminate number of players with improvised patterns of repetition to create a constantly shifting texture of coincidence and divergence. The piece is considered a seminal work in the development of MINIMALISM. Like several other composers whose interests lie in this direction, he has studied Indian music.

Rilling, Helmuth (1933–) German organist, conductor and teacher, trained in Stuttgart. He has taught in Frankfurt since 1966 and is dir. of the Stuttgart Bach Choir. He travels extensively to give master classes on choral music.

rim shot a technique in drumming, used in jazz and occasionally in classical percussion, of hitting the side of a drum and the head with the drumstick at the same time, producing a sharp, cracking sound.

Rimsky-Korsakov, Nikolai (1844–1908) Russian composer, stud. of Théodore Canille and Balakirev. Trained as a naval officer, he taught from 1871 at the St. Petersburg Conservatory, resigning his naval commission and taking the post of In-

spector of Naval Bands. In 1881 Rimsky-Korsakov took charge of organizing the late Mussorgsky's manuscripts, in the process "improving" the harmony and orchestration; he did similar work on Borodin's *Prince Igor* upon Borodin's death. In the final 15 years of his life he wrote 12 operas and many songs, as well as his highly influential *Principles of Orchestration* (1913) and the autobiographical *Chronicle of My Musical Life* (1909).

rinforzando [rēn-fôr′tsän-dō] *also,* **rinforzato** [-′tsä-tō] (It., reinforcing) an indication to play with a greater volume of sound.

Ring des Nibelungen, Der (Ger.) RING OF THE NIBELUNG, THE.

ring modulator a basic electronic device for modifying a sound signal by modulating it with a carrier signal, resulting in a single output signal representing the sum and the difference of the two input signals. See SYNTHESIZER.

Ring of the Nibelungen, The (Ger., *Der Ring des Nibelungen*) a four-day stage festival by Wagner based on 12th-c. German mythology. Premiere (as a cycle), Bayreuth 1876. See DAS RHEINGOLD; DIE WALKÜRE; SIEGFRIED; GÖTTERDÄMMERUNG.

ring shout an Afr.-Amer. circle dance-song characterized by a jerking motion and accompanied by guitar, mandolin or jew's harp.

rip in jazz, an ornamental, rapid glissando up to a note, with the final note played heavily accented and short.

ripieno [rē′pyä-nō] (It.) **1,** a supplementary group added to swell the sound of an orch. **2,** TUTTI.

Riposo, Il [rē′pō-zō] (It., rest) the violin concerto in E major, RV270, by Vivaldi.

ripresa [rē′prä-zä] (It.) **1,** REPEAT. **2,** the refrain of a 14th-c. FROTTOLA or BALLATA. **3,** a term for small instrumental segments (usu. four measures in length) that are played before, after and/or between the repetitions of music for a song or dance of the 16th and 17th c. The ripresa is similar to the RITORNELLO, although the latter term came to indicate entire instrumental sections which alternated with other music.

Rise and Fall of the City of Mahagonny, The (Ger., *Der Aufstieg und Fall der Stadt Mahagonny*) opera in 3 acts by Kurt Weill to a libretto by Bertolt Brecht. Premiere, Leipzig 1930. A symbolic satire on the human condition, detailing man's weaknesses through the interaction of convicts, miners and prostitutes. The orig. form of the opera, *Das Songspiel Mahagonny* (The Mahagonny Songcycle), which contained much of the same music, was a series of vignettes paralleling some of the scenes of the full opera.

risoluto [rē-zō'loo-tō] (It.) decisive.

Ristenpart, Karl (1900–67) German conductor, educated at the Stern Conservatory. From 1946 he was conductor of the RIAS Chamber Orch., which he founded in Berlin, and of the Saar Radio Chamber Orch.

rit. *abbr.* **1,** Ritardando. **2,** Ritenuto.

ritardando (It.) a gradual slowing down; Rallentando. Cf. Ritenuto. Abbr., *rit.*

Ritchie, Jean (1922–) Amer. folk singer, songwriter, guitarist and dulcimer player, educated at the U. of Kentucky. She came from a family whose folk-song repertory was recorded by the Library of Congress. From the late 1940s she has performed across the country, recorded and appeared on radio and TV.

Ritchie, Stanley (**John**) (1935–) Australian-born Amer. violinist, educated in Paris and at Yale. He has been concertmaster of the New York City Opera Orch., assoc. concertmaster of the Metropolitan Opera orch., a member of the New York Chamber Soloists and of the Philadelphia String Quartet, and a founder of the Aston Magna Music Festival. He is a virtuoso on both modern and period violin and performs with his wife, harpsichordist Elizabeth Wright, as the Duo Geminiani. He has taught at Indiana U. and the Juilliard School.

Rite of Spring, The (Fr., *Le Sacre du printemps*) ballet with music (1913) by Stravinsky. Its first performance in Paris caused a famous riot because of the unprecedented ferocity of its rhythm and its harmonic clashes. The work is in two sections, "The Adoration of the Earth" and "The Sacrifice." It is more often performed now as a concert work than as a ballet.

riten. *abbr.* Ritenuto.

ritenuto (It.) held back in tempo; immediately slower, as opposed to gradually slowing down. Cf. Rallentando, Ritardando. Abbr., *riten.*

ritmo (It.) Rhythm.

ritornello (It.) **1,** a short passage in a vocal or instrumental work, usu. functioning as a refrain. Cf. Ripresa (2,). **2,** a Tutti passage in a concerto.

Ritter, Tex (Woodward Maurice) (1905–74) Amer. country-music singer, songwriter and historian, educated at the U. of Texas. He began as a singing actor on Broadway, at the same time appearing on various radio programs of Western music and recording cowboy songs. In the mid-1930s and the 1940s he made over 60 Western films, then returned to radio in the 1950s and 1960s, hosting the "Town Hall Party" on NBC and then joining the Grand Ole Opry. He was elected to the Country Music Hall of Fame in 1964.

Ritual Fire Dance an orchestral tone poem (1915) by Falla, extracted from his ballet *El Amor Brujo.*

Rivers, Sam (Samuel Carthorne) (1930–) Amer. jazz saxophonist, flutist, pianist and composer, trained at the Boston Conservatory. He has played with Miles Davis and Cecil Taylor and has led his own groups. He has worked in all styles but has largely avoided the electronic jazz of the 1970s.

River Suite orchestral suite in four movements (1937) by Virgil Thomson, extracted from the score for a documentary film about the Mississippi River. The movements are "The Old South," "Industrial Expansion in the Mississippi Valley," "Soil Erosion and Floods" and "Finale." In the work Thomson quotes several traditional American melodies.

Roach, Max(well) (1925–) Amer. jazz drummer and composer, educated at the Manhattan School of Music. He participated in the early bop experiments with Charlie Parker and performed with Parker's quintet and with Miles Davis in the late 1940s. He has led his own groups since the 1950s, incl. an accomplished and influential quintet with trumpeter Clifford Brown and (in the 1980s) an unusual ensemble combining a string quartet (in which his daughter plays cello) with a jazz combo. In recent years he has been active as a composer for jazz ensembles, Broadway and films, and has taught at the U. of Massachusetts, Amherst, and at the Lenox (MA) School of Jazz. He received a MacArthur Foundation grant in 1988.

Roberta musical by Jerome Kern, lyrics and book by Otto Harbach, based on *Gowns by Roberta* by Alice Duer Miller. Premiere, New York 1933. The show tells the story of the romance between an American fullback and a Russian princess and incl. the song "Smoke Gets in your Eyes."

Robert le Diable [rŏ'ber lə dyäbl] (Fr., Robert the Devil) opera in 5 acts by Meyerbeer to a libretto by Eugène Scribe and Germain Delavigne. Premiere, Paris 1831. Robert of Normandy wins his beloved Isabella despite the machinations of his father, the Devil.

Robbins, Marty (Robinson, Martin David) (1925–82) Amer. country-music singer, guitarist and songwriter. His repertory was very wide, embracing all the country-music genres and some pop music. His hits incl. "Singing the Blues" (1956) and "A White Sport Coat" (1957), which became his trademark song. He was elected to the Country Music Hall of Fame in 1982.

Robertson, Eck (Alexander Campbell) (1887–1975) Amer. country-music

fiddler. Until 1922 he tuned pianos, played trick fiddle in fiddlers' contests and accompanied silent films. He then went to New York with Henry C. Gilliland, another fiddler, to make the first commercial country-music recordings.

Roberts, Luckey (Charles Luceyth) (1887–1968) Amer. jazz stride pianist and composer, orig. a dancer and acrobat on Broadway, then composer of musical comedies. From the 1920s he led his own band at social functions in New York and owned a Harlem bar.

Robeson, Paul (1898–1976) Amer. bass-baritone and actor, educated at Rutgers and Columbia U. Law School. His stage debut was in 1921 and his concert debut in 1925. He was famous both for dramatic and singing roles on stage and in films, and esp. for his rendition of spirituals and of the song "Ol' Man River" from the film version of *Show Boat*. After a tour of the USSR in the 1940s he expressed his support for communism, which effectively ruined his career in the U.S., but he continued to perform successfully abroad.

Robin Hood musical by Reginald De Koven, lyrics and book by Harry B. Smith. Premiere, Chicago 1890. The opera contains "Oh, Promise Me," which was very popular as a concert song.

Robinson, Anastasia (c1692–1755) English soprano (later a contralto, as a result of illness), stud. of Croft, Sandoni and Baroness Lindelheim. She created roles in a number of operas by Handel, Bononcini and others.

Robinson, Bill "Bojangles" (Luther) (1878–1949) Amer. jazz dancer and entertainer in vaudeville and, in his later years, on Broadway in *Blackbirds of 1928* and *Hot Mikado* (1939) and in films (*Stormy Weather*). He was famous for a dance routine performed on a flight of stairs.

Robinson, Earl (Hawley) (1910–) Amer. composer and songwriter, stud. of Copland and Eisler. He worked in the 1940s and 1950s as a film composer but was blacklisted for his socialist views. He received an Academy Award in 1946 for his score for *The House I Live In*. His cantata *Ballad for Americans* (1938) was premiered by Paul Robeson on radio. He also wrote folk operas and musicals, songs and concertos for banjo and piano.

Robinson, Faye (1943–) Amer. soprano, stud. of Ruth Stewart and Ellen Faull. She has sung frequently with New York City Opera since her debut in 1972, as well as with other companies in the U.S., Europe and S. Amer. Her roles incl. Micaela (*Carmen*), Liù (*Turandot*) and the soprano roles in *The Tales of Hoffmann*.

Robinson, Smokey (William) (1940–) Amer. rhythm-and-blues singer and songwriter, founder of the vocal group THE MIRACLES and one of the early successes of Motown Records. With the Miracles he recorded such hits as "Shop Around" (1960) and "Ooo Baby Baby" (1965); after going solo in 1972, he was successful again with "Cruisin'" (1979) and other songs.

Robison, Carson J(ay) (1890–1957) Amer. country-music singer, guitarist and songwriter. He went to New York in 1924 to work as a studio musician, then teamed up with Vernon Dalhart on a number of recordings. After they split up in 1928, he worked alone or with other partners, recording songs primarily in cowboy or country style.

Rochberg, George (1918–) Amer. composer, stud. of Hans Weisse, Szell and Leopold Mannes. He later studied at the Curtis Institute and the U. of Pennsylvania. He has taught at the Curtis Institute (1947–54) and at the U. of Pennsylvania (since 1960); in the intervening years, he worked for publisher Theodore Presser. A long-standing relationship with the Concord String Quartet produced six works in the 1970s. His compositions incl. *The Confidence Man* (opera), *Phaedra* (melodrama), 5 symphonies, concertos for oboe and violin, 7 string quartets, a string quintet and piano quartet, other chamber music, piano works, songs and choral works.

Rochester Philharmonic Orchestra orch. founded in 1921 in Rochester, NY, as the Eastman Theatre Orch. and used until 1929 to accompany silent films. From 1923 it also gave symphony concerts under its present name, conducted by Eugene Goossens. Subsequent conductors have included Leinsdorf, Zinman and Jerzy Semkow.

rock a type of Amer. popular music, the current stage of a development beginning with SOUL MUSIC and RHYTHM-AND-BLUES and passing through rock-and-roll.

Rock-and-roll emerged in the mid-1950s as rhythm-and-blues began to attract a white as well as a black audience. It was popularized by recordings and the radio, and in particular by disc jockey Alan Freed, who claimed to have coined the term. The early greats of rock-and-roll came both from country music and from rhythm-and-blues and incl. Bill Haley, Buddy Holly, Jerry Lee Lewis, Chuck Berry, Fats Domino and the most successful of all, Elvis Presley.

As had folk music in earlier decades, rock became assoc. in the 1960s and 1970s with political and social protest, principally concerning the Vietnam War and the sexual and drug revolutions (see PUNK ROCK, ACID ROCK). In the late 1970s and the 1980s these issues were less prominent, and the music became more generally oriented toward the usual themes of popular culture: love, school, life. Other forms of music have influenced rock: country right from the start, but also jazz (FUSION) and classical (ART ROCK).

Rock has kept pace with the development of electronic instruments and sounds, so that synthesizers, electronic drums, etc., have become an integral part of current rock music. This trend is also seen in the tremendous popularity of the rock video, a short quasi-dramatic rendering of a rock song, orig. produced by recording companies for promotion purposes, but becoming an art form in its own right. See also, ROCKABILLY, RAP.

rockabilly a style of rock-and-roll created in the 1950s as a combination of COUNTRY MUSIC and the BLUES, epitomized in the early work of Elvis Presley, Jerry Lee Lewis and Johnny Cash.

rock-and-roll *also,* **rock-'n'-roll** see ROCK.

Rockefeller, Martha Baird (1895–1971) Amer. philanthropist and pianist, stud. of Schnabel. She was an active recitalist and soloist until her retirement in 1931. In 1951 she married John D. Rockefeller, Jr., and after his death devoted much of her inheritance to the support of music through a fund in her name, terminated in 1982.

rockers a style of REGGAE characterized by driving rhythm, extensive use of dubbing and minimal instrumental accompaniment.

rock-'n'-rouge see GLITTER ROCK.

rock steady a mid-1960s style of Jamaican music, a successor to SKA and precursor of REGGAE. It had a relaxed beat, complex rhythms and lyrics about social issues.

Rococo a term borrowed from art history and applied, with little precision, to 18th-c. music, esp. in France, more usually covered by the term GALANT. The music was characterized by a lightness, grace and refinement, in reaction to Baroque music.

Rodgers, Jimmie (James Charles) (1897–1933) Amer. country-music singer, guitarist and songwriter, often called the Father of Country Music. A railroad worker until 1925, he made his first recordings in 1927 and became one of the first country music superstars, though he never appeared at the Grand Ole Opry. He was the first performer elected to the Country Music Hall of Fame (1961).

Rodgers, Richard (**Charles**) (1902–1979) Amer. composer, producer and librettist. As a composer, Rodgers worked for almost 40 years with only two librettists, Lorenz Hart and Oscar Hammerstein II, creating many hit musicals, including *The Boys from Syracuse* (1938) and *Pal Joey* (1940) with Hart and then *Oklahoma!* (1943), *Carousel* (1945), *South Pacific* (1949), *The King and I* (1951) and *The Sound of Music* (1959) with Hammerstein. Among his many other works are the scores for the TV series *Victory at Sea* (1952) and *Winston Churchill, the Valiant Years* (1960). Rodgers's daughter **Mary Rodgers** (1931–) is also a composer and wrote the score for the musical *Once Upon a Mattress* (1967).

Rodrigo, Joaquín (1901–) Spanish composer, blind from youth, stud. of Antich and Dukas. He has taught at Madrid U. since 1947. His most-performed works are for guitar, esp. the *Concierto de Aranjuez* (1939), which established his reputation, and the *Fantasia para un gentilhombre* (1954). He has also written concertos for other instruments, ballets and songs and many works for guitar, solo and duet.

Rodriguez, Robert Xavier (1946–) Amer. composer and teacher, stud. of Hunter Johnson, Kent Kennan, Halsey Stevens, Dahl and Boulanger. He has taught at the U. of Texas at Dallas since 1975 and was composer-in-residence with the Dallas SO from 1982 to 1985. He has written in most genres, incl. 4 operas, instrumental music for a variety of combinations, chamber music, choral music and songs.

Rodzinski, Artur (1892–1958) Polish-born Amer. conductor, stud. of Joseph Marx, Franz Schreker, Emil Sauer and others. He came to the U.S. in 1925 as an assistant to Stokowski in Philadelphia, where he also headed the Opera and Orchestral Departments of the Curtis Institute. He was conductor of the Los Angeles PO (1929–32) and then of the Cleveland Orch. (1933–43), which he built to international prominence. He took over the New York PO in 1943, again producing a marked improvement, but left in 1947 in a disagreement with the board. He was musical dir. of the Chicago SO for one season, after which he worked as a guest conductor in the U.S., Latin America and Europe. A renowned orch. builder, he was chosen by Toscanini to assemble and train the NBC SYMPHONY ORCHESTRA.

Roger-Ducasse, Jean(-Jules Aimable) (1873–1954) French composer and teacher, stud. of Fauré. He taught at the Paris Conservatoire until 1940. He wrote 3 operas, orch. works, choral and vocal music, chamber music (incl. a piano quartet and 2 string quartets) and works for solo piano.

Rogers, Bernard (1893–1968) Amer. composer and teacher, orig. trained as an artist. He studied music with Farwell, Bloch and Goetschius. He worked for several years for the magazine *Musical America*, taught at the Hartt School of Music, then joined the faculty of the Eastman School, where he remained until his retirement in 1967. His students incl. Diamond, Argento and Ussachevsky. His treatise on orchestration, *The Art of Orchestration* (1951), is a standard text. He has written *The Warrior* and 4 other operas, 5 symphonies, tone poems, works for chamber orch., oratorios and cantatas and other choral works, songs and chamber music.

Rogers, Kenny (Ray, Kenneth) (1941–) Amer. country-music singer and guitarist. He worked with a variety of groups and styles, incl. the New Christy Minstrels and his folkrock band Kenny Rogers and the First Edition, before settling on country music in the late 1970s.

Rogers, Nigel (David) (1935–) English tenor and conductor, trained at King's College, Cambridge, and in Rome, Milan and Munich. He has specialized in music of the Renaissance and the Baroque, esp. the operas of Monteverdi and English and Italian monody. He teaches at the Schola Cantorum in Basle.

Rogers, Roy (Slye, Leonard) (1911–) Amer. country-music singer, a founder of the Sons of the Pioneers in 1933. He assumed his stage name in 1938 and made more than 100 Western films. He was elected to the Country Music Hall of Fame in 1988.

Rogers, Shorty (Rajonsky, Milton M.) (1924–) Amer. jazz trumpeter, composer, arranger and bandleader. He played and arranged for the Woody Herman band in the late 1940s, then, after a short stint with Stan Kenton, he led a series of bands in Los Angeles, some of which experimented with nontonal harmonies. He has also recorded some important film scores, incl. for *The Man with the Golden Arm* (1955).

Rogg, Lionel (1936–) Swiss organist, trained at the Geneva Conservatory, where he has taught since 1960. He is renowned as an interpreter of Bach.

Rohrflöte ['rōr"flø-te] (Ger.) a flute ORGAN STOP having closed, metal pipes with *chimneys* (narrow tubes at the top of each pipe which add harmonics to the tone).

Roi David, Le [rwä dä'vēd] (Fr.) KING DAVID.

Roldán, Amadeo (1900–39) Cuban composer, conductor, violinist and teacher, trained at the Madrid Conservatory. He settled in Havana in 1921, where he conducted the Havana PO, founded the Havana String Quartet and taught at the Havana Conservatory. A major figure in Havanan musical life, he incorporated Cuban folk music into his works, which incl. ballets, tone poems, songs and chamber music.

roll 1, a rapid succession of beats on a drum or other percussion instrument. **2,** on a keyboard instrument, TREMOLO.

Rolling Stones English rock group, formed in 1962 in London. They probably have enjoyed the most consistent, sustained success of any rock group. Their music is derived largely from rhythm-and-blues and most of it is composed by members Mick Jagger and Keith Richard.

Rollins, Sonny (Theodore Walter;

"Newk") (1929–) Amer. jazz tenor saxophonist, with John Coltrane the major tenor influence after Coleman Hawkins and Lester Young. Until the mid-1950s he worked with a number of important bop musicians, in particular Miles Davis and Max Roach. He has since then led his own combos, producing a series of innovative recordings, incl. several with a piano-less trio and several unaccompanied solos and cadenzas.

Rollo an imaginary character created by composer Charles Ives as a symbol for proper, conformist gentility in music.

Rolón, José (1883–1945) Mexican composer, stud. in Paris of Gédalge, Boulanger and Dukas. He is esp. known as a symphonic composer. His works incl. symphonies, ballets, tone poems and a piano concerto.

Roman Carnival, The (Fr., Le *Carnaval romain*) a concert overture, Op. 9 (1844), by Berlioz, based on material from his opera *Benvenuto Cellini* (1834–8) and his solo scena *Cléopâtre* (1829).

romance (Fr., Sp.) **1**, a short ballad-like vocal work dating from as early as the 15th c. **2**, an instrumental work in the style of a vocal romance, written in a variety of formal structures, incl. the rondo and tripartite ABA forms.

romanesca a bass pattern with a flexible harmonic rhythm used in Italy in the later 16th and earlier 17th c. as a basis for vocal and instrumental music. See RENAISSANCE BASSES (*illus.*).

Roman Festivals (It., *Feste Romane*) a tone poem (1928) by Respighi evoking festivals of different eras of Roman history. The four sections are "Circenses" (from the days of the Empire), a Christian-era "Jubilee," "October Festival" and "Epiphany Eve."

Romantic a term used to refer to music in which sensibility is considered more important than form and to the period in Western music during which this aesthetic principle was dominant, roughly coinciding with the 19th c. Musical characteristics of the period incl. a broad expansion of the harmonic language, a heightened awareness of psychological implications and the expression of human feelings, an increased use of instrumental color for the sake of expression and sensuality rather than for the articulation of form, a preoccupation with nature and with the past, esp. the heroes of the past, a greatly increased interest in national characteristics and causes and the development of the solo concerto.

Romantic Symphony a subtitle for the Symphony No. 4 in E♭ major (1874–86) by Bruckner.

romanza [rō′män-tsä] (It.), **Romanze** [-tse] (Ger.) ROMANCE.

Romberg, Sigmund (1887–1951) Hungarian-born Amer. conductor and composer of operettas, trained in Vienna. He came to the U.S. in 1909 and worked as a café pianist and bandleader. Of his almost 60 operettas, the most popular, written in the 1920s, were *The Student Prince* (1924), *The Desert Song* (1926) and *The New Moon* (1928). After the war he wrote film scores and conducted his own orch.

Rome, Harold (Jacob) (1908–) Amer. composer and lyricist of many Broadway shows, the earlier works having strong socio-political themes. His most successful were *Pins and Needles* (1937), *Wish You Were Here* (1952) and *Fanny* (1954).

Romeo and Juliet (Fr., *Roméo et Juliette*) **1**, tragic opera in 5 acts by Gounod to a libretto in French by Jules Barbier and Michel Carré, based on Shakespeare's drama. Premiere, Paris 1867. **2**, dramatic symphony for soloists, chorus and orch., Op. 17 (1839), by Berlioz to a text by Emile Deschamps, based on Shakespeare's drama. **3**, ballet with music (1938) by Prokofiev. The composer extracted two concert suites from the score.

rondeau 1, one of the 14th- and 15th-c. French FORMES FIXES having the generalized form ABaAabAB. The rondeau became the form for French chansons at the end of the 15th c. favored by such composers as Busnois, Ockeghem and Compère. **2,** RONDO.

rondellus (Lat.) a 13th-c. technique for composing three-voice counterpoint based on the exchange of parts by two or all of the three voices:

Voice 1: a b c a . . .
Voice 2: c a b c . . .
Voice 3: b c a b . . .

Cf. VOICE-EXCHANGE.

rondo a formal design common in both single- and multimovement forms and based on the alternation between a main thematic section, usu. in the principal key of the movement, and a series of contrasting sections (episodes or *couplets*), usu. in related keys. The form developed from an earlier French form called a *rondeau*, itself probably derived from folk sources. The rondo form is typically found as the final movement of three- and four-movement sonata-type works (symphonies, sonatas, concertos, quartets, etc.). Frequently these finales are in a modified type of rondo, the SONATA-RONDO FORM, which combines the alternation scheme of the rondo with a harmonic pattern derived from SONATA FORM. See FORM (illus.).

rondo-sonata form SONATA-RONDO FORM.

Ronstadt, **(Maria) Linda** (1946–) Amer. popular, country-rock and rock singer. She found success in 1974 with *Heart Like a Wheel* and later recordings under producer Peter Asher. She has also appeared as Mabel in Gilbert and Sullivan's *Pirates of Penzance* and as Mimì in a version of Puccini's *La Bohème*.

root in TERTIARY HARMONY, the lowest note of a chord when the notes are arranged as a rising sequence of thirds. The root is the note after which the chord is named and which determines its function in the harmonic progression.

Root, **George Frederick** (1820–95) Amer. composer and teacher, stud. of Artemas Johnson and George Webb. He taught under Lowell Mason in Boston and New York, after 1850 composing dramatic cantatas for the students to perform. He also wrote songs, hymns and gospel songs, which had great success.

Rore, **Cipriano da** (c1515–65) Flemish composer of motets, madrigals and chansons. From the late 1540s he was in Italy, in the service of the court in Ferrara until 1559, then in Parma until his death. He was credited by Monteverdi with being the first composer to write in the style of the seconda prattica (see PRIMA PRATTICA). He was a pupil of Willaert and teacher of Luzzaschi. His best-known composition is the madrigal "Ancor che col partire."

Rorem, **Ned** (1923–) Amer. composer and writer, stud. of Sowerby, Honegger, Virgil Thomson and others. He has taught at the Curtis Institute and elsewhere, but has earned his living chiefly from composing. He won the Pulitzer Prize in 1976 for his orchestral suite *Air Music*, but he is best known for his vocal works, esp. his songs. He has also written 7 operas, several symphonies, chamber music and choral works; as well as a number of diaries and collections of essays.

rosalia (It.) a pejorative term, from the name of a popular song, for the repetition of a passage a step or half step higher, a simple form of variation. Also, *Cousin Michel* (Fr.), *Schusterfleck* (Ger.).

Rosamunde incidental music, D. 797 (1823), by Schubert, for the play *Rosamunde, Princess of Cyprus* by Wilhelmine von Chézy. The so-called Overture to *Rosamunde* is not the work originally used for that purpose, but was written by Schubert three years earlier as the overture to *The Magic Harp*. The original overture to *Rosamunde* was taken from his opera *Alfonso and Estrella* (1822).

Rosbaud, **Hans** (1895–1962) Austrian conductor, trained at the Hoch Conservatory in Berlin. His conducting positions incl. at the Mainz Städtische Musikschule, the Frankfurt Radio, the Munich PO, the Zürich

Tonhalle Orch. and the Southwest German Radio Orch. He was famous as an interpreter of 20th-c. works, esp. those of Schoenberg, Berg and Stravinsky.

rose a decoration of the circular sound hole of a guitar, harpsichord, etc.

Rose, **(Knols) Fred** (1897–1954) Amer. country-music and popular songwriter. His country-music career began in the late 1930s, when he wrote songs for Western films. After his move to Nashville, he co-founded the first country-music publishing house; he later worked for MGM as a producer. He was elected to the Country Music Hall of Fame in 1961.

Rose, Leonard (Joseph) (1918–84) Amer. cellist, stud. of Walter Grossman, Frank Miller and Felix Salmond. He was asst. principal cellist of the NBC SO (1938–9) and principal of the Cleveland Orch. (1939–43) and the New York PO (1943–51), after which he concentrated on a solo and chamber music career. He taught at the Curtis Institute and the Juilliard School and taught many of today's leading cellists, incl. Yo-Yo Ma and Lynn Harrell. From 1961 he performed frequently in trio with pianist Eugene Istomin and violinist Isaac Stern.

roseau [rō′zō] (Fr.) the reed plant used for making woodwind instrument reeds. Cf. ANCHE.

Roseingrave, Thomas (1688–1766) English organist and composer. He was organist at St. George's church in London from 1725 to the early 1750s, then spent his final years in Dublin. He was noted as a composer for the harpsichord and organ and as a virtuoso organist. He was also a staunch supporter of Domenico Scarlatti and edited a number of his sonatas.

Rose-Marie musical by Rudolf Friml and Herbert Stothart, lyrics and book by Oscar Hammerstein II and Otto Harbach. Premiere, New York 1924. The story, set in Canada, concerns the romance between a singer and a fur trapper.

Rosen, Charles (Welles) (1927–) Amer. pianist, writer and scholar, stud. of Moriz Rosenthal, Hedwig Kanner-Rosenthal and Karl Weigl. As a pianist he has toured widely, performing a broad repertory, with emphasis on Beethoven and the 20th c. He is probably best known as the author of *The Classical Style* (1971), a highly perceptive study of the Classical era, and *Sonata Forms* (1980). He has taught at SUNY, Stony Brook, and has been guest lecturer at various institutions. He has been on the faculty of the U. of Chicago since 1987.

Rosenberg, Hilding (Constantin) (1892–1985) prolific Swedish composer, conductor and teacher, stud. of Ellberg and Scherchen. From 1926 he was intimately involved in theater and opera, and much of his output was theatrical. He also was highly influential as a teacher, numbering among his many pupils Blomdahl and Sven-Erik Bäck. His works incl. 15 operas, much incidental music, several ballets, oratorios and cantatas, 8 symphonies, concertos for various instruments, 4 string concertos, 12 string quartets, chamber music, piano works and songs.

Rosenboom, David (1947–) Amer. composer, performer and instrument inventor, stud. of Binkerd, Martirano and Hiller. He has taught at York U. in Toronto, Mills College (CA) and the San Francisco Art Institute. He has written works for instruments alone or combined with electronic sounds and has specialized in works utilizing electrical signals produced by the human body (such as brain waves).

Rosenkavalier, Der [′rō-zən-kä-vä″lēr] (Ger., The Chevalier of the Rose) romantic opera in 3 acts by Richard Strauss to a libretto by Hugo von Hofmannsthal. Premiere, Dresden 1911. Octavian, the young lover of the Feldmarschallin, is smitten by the young fiancée of the boorish Baron Ochs and contrives to free her from his clutches and win her hand.

Rosenthal, Manuel (1904–) French conductor and composer, stud. of Ravel. He has been conductor of the Orchestre National in Paris, the Seattle SO (1948–51) and the Liège Orch. (1964–7) and has taught at the Paris Conservatoire. He is esp. known as an interpreter of 20th-c. French repertory. His own works incl. operas, orchestral works, choruses, chamber music and songs.

Rosenthal, Moriz (1862–1946) Ukrainian pianist, stud. of Joseffy and Liszt. He toured widely and was noted as a virtuoso technician. His last years were spent in New York as a teacher.

rosin a transparent resin applied to the hairs of a string instrument bow to provide additional friction. Also, *colophony, colophane* (Fr.).

Rosolino, Frank (1926–78) Amer. jazz trombonist and singer. He played with Gene Krupa's band, the Georgie Auld quintet and the Stan Kenton orch. and as a free lance in recording sessions in Los Angeles.

Ross, Diana (1944–) Amer. soul and popular singer, leader of the vocal group THE SUPREMES until 1969, then a successful solo artist. In the early 1970s she appeared in several films, incl. the film biography of Billie Holiday.

Ross, Hugh (Cuthbert Melville) (1898–1990) English-born Amer. choral dir. and organist, stud. of Mengelberg and Vaughan Williams. He directed several choral groups in Winnipeg in the 1920s, then moved to New York to conduct the Schola Cantorum (1927–71), meanwhile teaching at the Manhattan School and the Berkshire Music Center and guest-conducting worldwide.

Rosseter, Philip (c1567–1623) English composer and lutanist at the court of James I and a manager of the theatrical group Children of Whitefriars (later, Children of the Queen's Revels) until 1617. His extant works incl. ayres and works for lute.

Rossi, Luigi (1598–1653) Italian composer, lutanist, harpsichordist and singing teacher, stud. of Giovanni de Macque in Naples. From about 1620 he was in Rome as organist of St. Luigi dei Francesi and in service to a series of noble households. His fame rests largely on his more than 300 chamber cantatas. He also wrote oratorios, 2 operas and instrumental chamber music.

Rossi, Michelangelo (1602–56) Italian violinist, organist and composer of keyboard works, principally in Rome. He was noted as a virtuoso violinist and also wrote an opera, *Erminia sul Giordano* (1637).

Rossi, Salamone (c1570–c1628) Italian composer and instrumentalist in Mantua. An important work is his *Hashirim asher lish'lomo* (The Song of Solomon, 1622–3), which, curiously, contains no texts from the Song of Solomon; perhaps the title is a pun on the composer's name. He published five books of 3- to 5-voice madrigals and canzonets and four books of instrumental works for various combinations.

Rossi-Lemeni, Niccolà (1920–91) Italian bass, stud. of Xenia Macadon (his mother) and Carnevali-Cusinati. His U.S. debut was in 1951 in San Francisco; he also sang in Chicago and New York as well as throughout Europe. His roles incl. Boris Godunov, Philip II (*Don Carlo*) and Mephistopheles (*Faust*). He taught at the U. of Indiana from 1980.

Rossignol, Le [ro-sē'nyōl] (Fr.) NIGHTINGALE, THE (1,).

Rossini, Gioacchino (Antonio) (1792–1868) Italian opera composer, trained in Bologna; the greatest composer of his day and one of the most successful composers in history. Rossini's first commission was in 1810, and between then and his operatic retirement in 1829 he produced 39 operas, 14 of which were comic (incl. *Il Barbiere di Siviglia, La Cenerentola* and *L'Italiana in Algieri*) and the rest serious (incl. *Tancredi, Semiramide* and *Guillaume Tell*). Although most of his modern reputation rests on the comic operas, which are more frequently performed today, his historical importance rests more with the serious operas, esp. those produced late in his career. From the late 1830s he lived in Italy in ill health, producing mostly incidental sacred vocal works, then returned to Paris in 1855. During his final years in Paris his health returned and he composed the *Péchés de vieillesse* (Sins of Old Age), comprising piano works, songs, ensembles and the *Petite messe solennelle*.

Rostropovich, Mstislav (1927–) Russian cellist, pianist and conductor, trained at the Moscow Conservatory. He has toured widely as a cellist, famous for his robust tone and dramatic performances. He became musical dir. of the National SO in Washington, D.C., in 1977 and has guest-conducted in the U.S. and Europe. His wife is singer GALINA VISHNEVSKAYA.

Roswaenge, Helge (1897–1972) Danish tenor. He sang regularly at the Berlin Staatsoper, at Salzburg, Covent Garden, and in Vienna and Munich (he never sang opera in the U.S.). His roles incl. Tamino (*The Magic Flute*) and Don José (*Carmen*).

rota 1, ROUND. **2,** HURDY-GURDY.

Rota, Nino (1911–79) Italian composer, stud. of Pizzetti and Casella. He taught from 1939 at the Bari Conservatory. He is best known for his film scores, esp. those for Zeffirelli and Fellini. His works also incl. 10 operas, several ballets, choral works, concertos (for cello, piano and trombone) and chamber music.

rote a medieval Anglo-Saxon LYRE.

Rothwell (Barbirolli), **Evelyn** (1911–) English oboist, stud. of Leon Goossens. After playing principal oboist with several orchestras, she has concentrated on a solo career. Many works have been dedicated to her and she has produced several widely used books on oboe repertory and technique. She was married to the conductor JOHN BARBIROLLI.

roto-tom a small, single-headed DRUM without shell or with a very shallow shell. It has a tunable head and is sometimes used as a substitute for a conventional tom-tom, side drum or bass drum.

Rouet d'Omphale, Le [roo'ā dō'fäl] (Fr., Omphale's Spinning Wheel) orchestral tone poem, Op. 31 (1871), by Saint-Saëns, a story of the seduction of Heracles by Omphale, queen of Lydia.

roulade a rapid musical ORNAMENT, esp. in vocal music, usu. sung to a single syllable and embellishing a melody.

round 1, a perpetual CANON at the unison, serious or frivolous. "Row, row, row your boat" and "Frère Jacques" are popular examples. Cf. CATCH. **2,** *also,* **round dance** a country circle dance.

rounded binary form a modification of the BINARY FORM in which all or part of the first section is repeated at the end of the second (AABABA).

roundelay 1, a simple SONG. **2,** a ROUND dance.

Rounseville, Robert (Field) (1914–1974) Amer. opera singer, who also appeared in several Broadway musicals, incl. *Candide* (1956) and *Man of La Mancha* (1965).

Rouse, Charlie (Charles) (1924–88) Amer. jazz tenor saxophonist. He played with a number of important bands, incl. those of Dizzy Gillespie, Duke Ellington and Count Basie, then played for a decade with the Thelonious Monk Quartet. In his later years he free-lanced with various small groups.

Rouse, Christopher (Chapman) (1949–) Amer. composer, stud. of Husa, Robert Palmer and others. He has taught at the U. of Michigan and the Eastman School and has been composer-in-residence with the Indianapolis SO. His works incl. *The Infernal Machine* (1981) and other orchestral works, a string quartet, vocal music and works for percussion ensemble.

Rousseau, Jean-Jacques [roo'sō]

(1712–78) Swiss philosopher and composer. Of his small output of musical works, the most important were *Le Devin du village* (1752), a precursor of the *opéra-comique*, and *Pygmalion* (1770), a *scène lyrique* with dialogue, a precursor of the melodrama. He also wrote several important treatises on music, the *Lettre sur la musique française* (1753; a denunciation of French opera), and a dictionary of music (1768).

Roussel, Albert (Charles Paul Marie) (1869–1937) French composer. He trained as a naval cadet, only turning to music in 1894. He studied with Gigout and at the Schola Cantorum, where he taught for ten years. His works incl. *Bacchus et Ariane* (opera), a ballet, incidental music, 4 symphonies, tone poems, a piano concerto, chamber music, works for piano and many songs.

rovescio, a *or* **al** [rō′ve-shō] (It.) by INVERSION or RETROGRADE.

row a SET of nonrepeating pitches (usu. twelve) arranged in a fixed sequence and used as the basic compositional material in TWELVE-TONE MUSIC and in serial music (see SERIALISM).

Roxelane, La (Fr.) the Symphony No. 63 in C major (1781) by Haydn. The slow movement is a set of variations on the melody of an aria written by Haydn for a stage character named Roxelane.

Roy, Klaus George (1924–) Austrian-born Amer. writer and composer, trained at Boston and Harvard universities. He was music critic for the *Christian Science Monitor* (1950–57) before becoming program annotator for the Cleveland Orch.

Royal Academy of Music London conservatory of music founded in 1822.

Royal Albert Hall large London concert hall built in 1871, with a seating capacity of 10,000 persons, home of the Henry Wood Promenade Concerts.

Royal College of Music London musical college founded in 1882 as suc-

cessor to the National Training School of Music.

Royal Festival Hall concert hall complex in London built in 1951 and the site of most orch. concerts. The principal hall in the complex is the Queen Elizabeth Hall.

Royal Fireworks Music a suite of dances for large wind orch. (1749) by Handel, written to accompany fireworks in celebration of the end of the War of the Austrian Succession. Handel later added string parts to the score.

royal kent bugle KEYED BUGLE.

Royal Opera House COVENT GARDEN.

Rozhdestvensky, Gennady (1931–) Soviet conductor, stud. of his father and Lev Oborin. He has been conductor of the Bolshoi Opera and the Symphony Orch. of All-Union Radio and Television, artistic dir. of the Stockholm PO and chief conductor of the BBC SO in London and has toured extensively. He has championed 20th-c. Soviet music.

Rózsa, Miklós (1907–) Hungarian-born Amer. composer, educated at the Leipzig Conservatory. He is best known as a composer of film scores, both in England and in Hollywood; films for which he has provided music incl. *Spellbound* (1945), *The Asphalt Jungle* (1950), *Quo Vadis?* (1951), *Ben-Hur* (1959) and *Dead Men Don't Wear Plaid* (1981). He has also written orchestral and chamber music, concertos for piano, viola, cello and violin, a symphony, songs and choral works.

ruan (Chin.) a Chinese flat-backed, long-necked LUTE with a drumlike body.

rubato *also*, **tempo rubato** (It., stolen time) **1**, freedom or irregularity of speed in a phrase, often against a steady accompaniment; hence, **2**, a type of AGOGIC ACCENT.

rub-board a metal WASHBOARD hung from the player's shoulders and played by running a metal object over the ridges.

Rubini, Giovanni-Battista (1795–1854) Ital. tenor, the first noncastrato male to achieve international renown, esp. noted for his performance of roles in operas by Donizetti and Bellini.

Rubbra, (Charles) Edmund (1901–86) English composer, pianist and teacher, stud. of Cyril Scott, Holst and R.O. Morris. He taught at Oxford U. and the Guildhall School of Music. His works incl. 11 symphonies, concertos for violin, viola and piano, many choral works, sonatinas for various instruments, 4 string quartets and songs.

Rubinstein, Anton (1829–94) Russian pianist, composer and teacher, trained in Russia and Berlin. He established a reputation as one of the leading virtuosos of his time. He founded the Russian Musical Society in 1859 and the St. Petersburg Conservatory in 1862, then conducted the Vienna Philharmonic Concerts in 1871. He continued to tour until the late 1880s. He was a prolific composer of works in all genres, but only the piano works and songs are still performed outside the USSR.

Rubinstein, Artur (1887–1982) Polish-born Amer. pianist, trained in Warsaw and Berlin. He toured extensively until 1932, when he withdrew for some years to restudy his repertory and solidify his technique, then pursued an illustrious career until his retirement from the concert stage in 1976. He was noted for his performance of the Romantic masters, esp. Chopin.

Ruby, Harry (Harold) (1895–1974) Amer. songwriter and lyricist, a longtime collaborator with lyricist Bert Kalmar. They wrote a number of hit songs, incl. "Three Little Words," and "Who's Sorry Now?" as well as scores for Broadway and films, among them several of the Marx Brothers' movies.

Ruckers a family of Flemish harpsichord makers active in Antwerp from about 1580 to 1670.

Rückpositiv ['rük-po-zi"tēf] (Ger., back positive [organ]) a small organ placed at the organist's back, the second principal manual of a major or-

gan. Its function was replaced in the 18th c. by the *Oberwerk*.

Ruddigore operetta in 2 acts by Sullivan to a libretto by W.S. Gilbert. Premiere, London 1887. A satire on the Gothic novel, the story of a family cursed by its first baronet.

Rudel, Julius (1921–) Austrian-born Amer. conductor, trained at the Vienna Academy and the Mannes College of Music in New York. He joined the New York City Opera in 1943 and became dir. in 1957, producing and conducting a wide range of operatic repertory. He remained there until 1979, then was musical dir. of the Buffalo PO until 1985. He continues to guest-conduct opera and concert in the U.S. and Europe.

Rudolf, Max (1902–) German-born Amer. conductor, trained at Frankfurt U. He was conductor of the German theater in Prague and in Göteborg, Sweden. He then came to the U.S. and conducted at the Metropolitan Opera from 1945 to 1958. He has been musical dir. of the Cincinnati May Festival and head of opera and conducting at the Curtis Institute. He is the author of a popular conducting textbook, *The Grammar of Conducting* (1950).

Ruffo, Titta (Titta, Ruffo Cafiero) (1877–1953) Italian baritone, stud. of Venceslao Persichini, Senatore Sparapani and Lelio Casini. His Amer. debut was in 1912 in Philadelphia; his Metropolitan Opera debut was in 1922. He also made several films. He retired from performance in 1931.

Rugby the Symphonic Movement No. 2 (1928) by Honegger, written to suggest the aggressive action of a rugby game.

ruggiero [rood'je-rō] (It.) a melodic and harmonic bass pattern used as a basis for songs and variations in the early 17th c. The term suggests an association with Ariosto's epic poem *Orlando Furioso*. See RENAISSANCE BASSES (*illus.*).

Ruggles, Carl (Charles) **Sprague** (1876–1971) Amer. composer, stud. of George Hill, Josef Claus and Paine.

He was founder in 1907 of the Winona SO in MN and of the orch. at the Rand School in New York and taught at the U. of Miami (1938–1943). The 1920s and 1930s were his most productive years in music; in later years, he concentrated on painting and on revising his previous works. Ruggles's style was uniquely his own, founded on a nontonal, contrapuntal idiom. He wrote relatively few works, incl. *The Sunken Bell* (opera), *Men and Angels, Men and Mountains* and *Sun-treader* (for orch.), *Evocations* (piano).

Rugolo, Pete (1915–　) Amer. jazz arranger and composer, stud. of Milhaud. He was a collaborator of Stan Kenton in the late 1940s, then became involved in writing for films and television.

Rührtrommel ['rür"trom-əl] (Ger.) TENOR DRUM.

Ruins of Athens, The (Ger., *Die Ruinen von Athen*) play by August von Kotzebue for which Beethoven wrote incidental music for chorus and orch., Op. 113 (1812).

Rule Britannia ode (1741) by Arne with a text by either James Thomson or David Mallet, written in commemoration of the accession to the English throne of the House of Hanover (1714).

Rumanian Rhapsodies two orchestral works (1901) by Enescu.

rumba *also,* **rhumba** a ballroom DANCE derived from an Afr.-Cuban recreational dance. The dance is accompanied by claves or maracas and its music often incorporates jazz elements. It has spawned the MAMBO, CHA CHA CHA and other Latin ballroom dances.

run a series of short contiguous notes (esp. in piano music) such as a scale passage or figural ornamentation, played rapidly.

Run, Little Chillun' musical by Hall Johnson, based on the works of Zora Neale Hurston. Premiere, New York 1933. A beautiful African woman tempts the son of a pastor to leave his wife and religion.

Runnin' Wild musical revue by James P. Johnson, lyrics by Cecil Mack, book by Flournoy Miller and Aubrey Lyles. Premiere, New York 1923. The show introduced "The Charleston."

rural blues COUNTRY BLUES.

Rusalka opera in 3 acts by Dvořák to a libretto by Jaroslav Kvapil. Premiere, Prague 1901. The water nymph Rusalka falls in love with a prince and wants to become human.

Rush, Loren (1935–　) Amer. composer, stud. of Erickson. He has been an active promoter of new-music concert series and performing groups on the West Coast since the late 1950s and has taught at the San Francisco Conservatory and at Stanford. His relatively small output incl. a number of works combining live performers with computer-processed music, such as *Song and Dance* (1975).

Rush, Otis (1934–　) Amer. blues singer, guitarist and harmonica player, based in Chicago. His music, influenced by B.B. King, incl. such hits as "I Can't Quit You, Baby" (1956) and "So Many Roads, So Many Trains" (1960). He has also toured extensively.

Rushing, Jimmy (James Andrew) (1903–72) Amer. blues and jazz singer. He sang with the bands of Walter Page and Bennie Moten, then enjoyed substantial success with Count Basie (1935–50). In later years he worked free-lance and toured with various bands.

Ruslan and Lyudmila opera in 5 acts by Glinka to a libretto by Valeryan Fyodorovich Shirkov, based on Pushkin's poem. Premiere, St. Petersburg 1842. Ruslan is aided by a fairy in his search for Lyudmila. The overture to the opera is often excerpted for concert performance.

Russell, (George) Alexander (1880–1953) Amer. organist and composer, trained at Syracuse U. and in Europe. From 1910 to 1952 he worked as organist and dir. of musical activities for the John Wanamaker department stores in New York and Philadelphia. For part of that time he was also dir.

of music for Princeton. His own works were much performed in his time.

Russell, Anna (Russell-Brown, Claudia Ann) (1911–   ) English-born Canadian contralto and comedienne, stud. of Vaughan Williams. From the 1940s she performed a one-woman show parodying serious music with such skits as her version of Wagner's *Ring* and "How to Write Your Own Gilbert and Sullivan Opera." She retired several times after 1981.

Russell, George (Allan) (1923–   ) Amer. jazz composer, arranger, pianist and theorist, stud. of Stefan Wolpe. He has worked as an arranger for Dizzy Gillespie, Lee Konitz and others and has taught at various institutions in the U.S. and abroad. His theory of composition, outlined in his important text *The Lydian Chromatic Concept of Tonal Organization* (1953), determines the importance of intervals by grading them on their distance from a central note.

Russell, Henry (1812–1900) English composer, singer and pianist, stud. of Rossini and Bellini. He came to Rochester, NY, in the mid-1830s to work as organist and to teach at the Rochester Academy, but then toured the U.S. successfully as a one-man show, singing and accompanying himself at the piano. He returned to England in 1845 and continued to sing and compose until his last years. His HOUSEHOLD SONGS can be said to have established the popular song in the U.S. Examples are "Woodman, Spare that Tree" (1837) and "The Old Arm Chair" (1840).

Russell, Lillian (Leonard, Helen Louise) (1861–1922) Amer. soprano and actress, stud. of Leopold Damrosch. From 1880 to her retirement in 1912 she was a popular vaudeville, operetta and musical star, appearing in a variety of shows, incl. Gilbert and Sullivan's *Patience* and Offenbach's *La belle Hélène*.

Russell, Pee Wee (Charles Ellsworth) (1906–69) iconoclastic Amer. jazz clarinetist. He played with many leading performers from Bix Beiderbecke in the 1920s to Red Nichols and Louis Prima in the 1930s, then appeared regularly for several decades with Eddie Condon in New York and on tour. He was one of the most important Dixieland performers.

Russian bassoon an obsolete 19th-c. upright SERPENT similar in shape to the bassoon.

Russian Easter Festival (Russ., *Svetlïy prazdnik*) overture, Op. 36 (1888), by Rimsky-Korsakov, using authentic church melodies to evoke the grandeur of Russian Easter celebrations.

Russian Quartets 1, 6 string quartets, Op. 33 (1781), by Haydn, dedicated to a Russian grand duke who was visiting Vienna. **2**, RAZUMOVSKY QUARTETS.

Russo, William (1928–   ) Amer. composer and arranger, stud. of Lee Konitz, Lennie Tristano, John J. Becker and Karel Jirák. He has led various jazz orchestras, incl. his own Russo Orch. (1958–61) and the London Jazz Orch. (1962–5), and was composer-arranger for the Stan Kenton orch. (1950–4). He teaches at Columbia College in Chicago. He has also worked in films and has written several widely used textbooks on jazz composition. His works incl. operas, ballets and rock cantatas, works for jazz orch., concertos, works for small jazz ensemble, studies and other works for trombone.

Russolo, Luigi (1885–1947) Italian composer, painter and inventor. He was one of the most outspoken of the FUTURIST musicians of the 1910s and the inventor of various machines ("noise intoners") to amplify and "tune" the noises of daily experience. He also developed an "enharmonic bow" to obtain unusual sounds from string instruments. His machines were unfortunately destroyed during the World War II bombings of Paris.

Rust, Friedrich Wilhelm (1739–96) German violinist, pianist and composer, stud. of W.F. Bach, C.P.E. Bach and others. For most of his career he was in the service of Prince Leopold III of Dessau, and he greatly expanded the musical life of the city during his tenure. He wrote a substantial body of chamber music works, as well as several stage works, choral music and songs.

Rustica, Concerto alla the violin concerto in G major, RV151, by Vivaldi.

Rustle of Spring (Ger., *Frühlingsrauschen*) a popular piano work (1896) by Sinding, one of a set of six, Op. 32.

Ruy Blas a play by Victor Hugo for which Mendelssohn reluctantly (he hated the play) wrote a song, "Lied aus 'Ruy Blas,' " Op. 77 (1839) and an overture, Op. 95 (1839), at the request of the Leipzig Theatrical Pension Fund.

Ryom, Peter (1937–) Danish musicologist. He has produced the most complete catalog (1973) of the music of Vivaldi. His numbers are usu. preceded by an "RV."

Rysanek, Leonie (1926–) Austrian dramatic soprano, stud. of Alfred Jerger and Rudolf Grossmann. Since her formative years in various German opera houses, she has appeared regularly at the Metropolitan Opera (since 1959), the Vienna Staatsoper and at Bayreuth. Her roles incl. Sieglinde (*Die Walküre*), Elsa (*Lohengrin*), Turandot and the leading Strauss roles.

Rzewski, Frederic (Anthony) (1938–) Amer. composer and pianist, stud. of Thompson, Piston, Sessions, Babbitt and Dallapiccola. He has spent most of his professional career in Europe as a performer and teacher and as a co-founder and member of the electronic ensemble Musica Elettronica Viva (MEV) in Rome. He has been esp. interested in collective improvisation and the incorporation of folk melodies in his works.

S

S. *abbr.* **1**, SEGNO. **2**, SINISTRA. **3**, SUBITO.

Sabata, Victor de DE SABATA, VICTOR.

saccadé [sä-kä′dä] (Fr., jerked) an accented bowstroke. See BOWING.

Sacher, Paul (1906–) [′zä-khar] Swiss conductor, stud. of Weingartner and Karl Nef. In 1926 he founded the Basle Chamber Orch. to perform the music of the pre-Classical and contemporary periods, and over the years he has commissioned many works. He also founded the Schola Cantorum Basiliensis in 1933 to promote research in early music.

Sachs, Hans [zäks] (1494–1576) German poet, Meistersinger and shoemaker, the subject of Wagner's opera *Die Meistersinger von Nürnberg.*

sackbut 1, the medieval TROMBONE. **2**, a loud, chorus reed ORGAN STOP of 16-foot pitch imitating the sound of the trombone.

sacra rappresentazione (It.) RAPPRESENTAZIONE SACRA.

Sacred Harp Singers hymn singers who use the 1844 shape-note tunebook *The Sacred Harp.* Cf. OLD HARP SINGERS.

Sacre du printemps, Le [′sä-krə dü prē′tä] (Fr.) RITE OF SPRING, THE.

Sadler's Wells orig. a pleasure garden in London, whose music hall later became the Sadler's Wells Theatre, opened in 1765 and reconstructed in 1931. It was the home of the Sadler's Wells Opera until 1968, when the company moved to the Coliseum. In 1974 the company became the ENGLISH NATIONAL OPERA.

Saga, En (Finn., A Tale) orchestral tone poem, Op. 9 (1892), by Sibelius, evoking the romance and savagery of heroic legend.

Sahl, Michael (1934–) Amer. composer, stud. of Sessions, Babbitt and others. He has held a variety of positions, incl. that of music dir. for Judy Collins and for WBAI-FM (NY). His music is geared toward a nonconcert environment and is influenced by jazz and popular music. His works incl. 5 operas, 5 symphonies, a violin concerto, a string quartet, a piano sonata, chamber music and film scores.

St. Anne Fugue the fugue in E♭ from the *Clavierübung,* Part III (1739), by J.S. Bach, so called because it is based on the hymn-tune of that name ascribed to William Croft (1678–1727).

St. Cecilia Mass the first of two masses in C major (1766) by Haydn, both dedicated to St. Cecilia, the patron saint of music. The second is the so-called MARIAZELLER MASS.

St. Cecilia's Day November 22, date of a celebration initiated in England by the Musical Society in 1683 and observed annually for 30 years in honor of the patron saint of music. Many composers wrote odes for this occasion, incl. Purcell, Blow and Clarke. Some of the texts written for these occasions, esp. those by John Dryden, were later set for different occasions by Handel and others.

Sainte-Marie, Buffy (Beverly) (1941–) Canadian popular singer, guitarist and songwriter of native Indian descent. Her repertory embraces country music, native Indian music and folk music.

Saint-Georges, Joseph Boulogne, Chevalier de [sē′zhorzh] (c1739–99) French composer and violinist from Guadeloupe. He settled in Paris in 1749 and was prob. a student of Gossec. He founded the Concert de la Loge Olympique in 1781, and it was for this orch. that Haydn's Paris Symphonies were written. During the

Revolution he commanded the Légion National du Midi, a corps comprised of black soldiers. His works incl. 7 operas, violin concertos, symphonies, chamber music and some songs.

St. John Passion popular name for the *Passion According to St. John* (1723) by J.S. Bach.

St. Louis Blues song (1914) by W.C. Handy, claimed by its publisher to be "The First Successful 'Blues' Published."

St. Louis Opera see OPERA THEATER OF ST. LOUIS.

St. Louis Symphony Orchestra the second-oldest orch. in the U.S., founded in 1881 as the St. Louis Choral Society and operating under various names until it assumed its present one in 1907. Its conductors have incl. Alfred Ernst, Max Zach, Rudolf Ganz, Vladimir Golschmann, Eleazar de Carvalho, Walter Susskind, George Semkow and Leonard Slatkin.

St. Louis Woman musical comedy by Harold Arlen, book by Arna Bontemps and Countee Cullen, based on Bontemps's novel *God Sends Sunday*. Premiere, New York 1936. Pearl Bailey made her Broadway debut, and Ruby Hill played the title role.

Saint-Marcoux, Micheline Coulombe [sɛ̃-mär′koo, mē-shə′lēn koo′lōb]] (1938–1985) Canadian composer and teacher, stud. of Champagne, Tremblay, Pépin and Pierre Schaeffer. She was a founder of the Groupe international de musique électroacoustique de Paris in 1969. In Québec from 1971 until her death, she was active as an organizer of concerts of electronic music and dance and appeared a number of times on the CBC. Her works incl. several pieces for orch., chamber music for various instrumental ensembles (sometimes with tape) and electronic works.

St. Mark Passion the *Passion According to St. Mark* (1731) by J. S. Bach. Most of the music is lost.

St. Martial a monastery at Limoges, France, important for its extensive collection of medieval manuscripts containing both monophonic and polyphonic music.

St. Martin-in-the-Fields ACADEMY OF ST. MARTIN-IN-THE-FIELDS.

St. Matthew Passion popular name for the *Passion According to St. Matthew* (1729) by J.S. Bach.

Saint of Bleecker Street, The tragic opera in 3 acts by Menotti to his own libretto. Premiere, New York 1954. Annina, known as the saint of Bleecker Street because of the stigmata on her hands, desires to become a nun before her impending death.

St. Olaf Lutheran Choir chorus founded in 1912 at St. Olaf College, MN, by F. Melius Christiansen (1871–1955) who developed a choral sound, which has been widely imitated, characterized by a straight tone and uniform color.

St. Paul (Ger., *Paulus*) oratorio, Op. 36 (1836), by Mendelssohn to a text drawn by J. Schubring from the Acts of the Apostles.

St. Paul Chamber Orchestra professional chamber orch. founded in 1959 in St. Paul, MN, by Leopold Sipe. Subsequent conductors have been Davies, Zuckermann and Hogwood.

Saint-Saëns, (Charles) Camille [sɛ̃′sä] (1835–1921) French composer, organist, pianist and writer, trained at the Paris Conservatoire from the age of 13. He was organist at the church of St. Merry and then at the Madeleine (1857–76), during which time he championed the cause of new music and the rediscovery in France of Bach, Mozart and Handel. He also cofounded the Société nationale de musique in 1871 to promote and perform new music by French composers. After 1888 he traveled widely in Europe and, in 1915, to America. He is best remembered for his opera *Samson et Dalila* (1877) and for *Le Carnaval des animaux* (1886), a trifle he wrote in a few days and which he suppressed during his lifetime. His works incl. 13 operas, ballets and incidental music, 3 symphonies, tone poems (esp. *Danse macabre*, 1874), concertos for various instruments, sacred and secular choral music, chamber music, songs, and works for solo piano and solo organ.

saint's motet a motet in honor of a saint, for performance during the divine office or votive service.

Salabert [sä-lä'ber] French music publishing firm founded in Paris in 1896 by Edouard Salabert.

salicet a soft-toned string ORGAN STOP of 4- or 2-foot pitch.

salicional an ORGAN STOP similar to the SALICET but at 8-foot pitch.

salicus a NEUME standing for three notes, the second of which is an ORISCUS.

Salieri, Antonio (1750–1825) Italian composer, stud. of his brother Francesco, Giuseppe Simoni, Giovanni Pescetti and others. He became court composer and conductor of Italian opera in Vienna in 1774, adding the post of court Kapellmeister in 1788. He resigned as dir. of opera in 1790, but composed operas for the court until 1804. He was active in the musical life of Vienna and important as teacher of Beethoven, Schubert, Liszt and many others. The stories of his enmity towards Mozart appear to be unfounded. Salieri wrote over 40 operas; oratorios, masses and other service music, secular cantatas, songs and other vocal music, concertos and sinfonias and chamber music.

Sallinen, Aulis (1935–) Finnish composer, stud. of Oskar Merikanto and Joonas Kokkonen. He taught at the Sibelius Academy in Helsinki until 1981. His works, largely atonal, sometimes serial, incl. 2 operas, a ballet, 4 symphonies, concertos for violin and cello, choral works, 4 string quartets and chamber music.

salmo (Sp.) TAMBOURIN DE BÉARN.

Salmond, Felix (Adrian Norman) (1888–1952) English cellist, trained at the Royal College of Music, London, and in Brussels. From 1922 he toured extensively in No. America, specializing in 20th-c. repertory. He was also a respected teacher at the Juilliard School and at the Curtis Institute, where his pupils incl. Bernard Greenhouse and Leonard Rose.

Salome [sä-lō'mä] psychological opera in 1 act by Richard Strauss to his own libretto based on Hedwig Lachmann's translation of Oscar Wilde's French play. Premiere, Dresden 1905. Salome demands as payment for her dance before Herod the head of the prophet John the Baptist.

Salomon, Johann Peter (1745–1815) Ger. violinist and composer. He went to London (1780), where he remained, active as a violinist and concert promoter. A founder of the Philharmonic Society (1813), he directed its first concert. He arranged for Haydn's visits to London in the 1790s, commissioning the LONDON SYMPHONIES. He was a prolific composer but none of his works entered the repertory.

Salonen, Esa-Pekka (1958–) Finnish conductor, composer and horn player. He has been principal conductor of the Swedish Radio SO and principal guest conductor of the Oslo PO and the London Philharmonia Orch. In 1992 he becomes Music Director of the Los Angeles PO.

Salomon Symphonies see LONDON SYMPHONY (1,).

Salon Mexico, El [sä'lōn 'mä-hē-kō] (Sp., Mexican Dance Hall) an orchestral tone poem (1936) by Copland, full of evocative references to Mexican music. Copland called it a "modified potpourri."

salon music music written for or played in a *salon*, an 18th- and 19th-c. social and artistic gathering in a private residence, often held on a regular basis. Esp. popular were songs and works for solo piano, but works for small orch. were also performed in the salons of wealthier patrons.

salpinx a Greek ivory TRUMPET.

salsa (Sp., sauce) a type of Cuban popular music dating from the 1940s, a precursor of AFRO-CUBAN JAZZ, incorporating elements of the principal Lat.-Amer. dances, such as the mambo and cha cha cha. It has a characteristic two-bar rhythm (*clave*). See DANCE (*illus.*).

saltando (It.) ARCO SALTANDO.

saltarello (It., little hop) **1,** an Italian

dance in quick triple time with a hop step at the beginning of each measure. The saltarello is an afterdance, usu. following a pavan, passamezzo or quarternaria. Musical material for the saltarello is usu. derived from the preceding dance. Cf. GALLIARD. 2, *also,* **salterello** a harpsichord JACK.

saltato (It.) SAUTILLÉ.

Salve Regina (Lat., Hail, Queen [of Mercy]) one of the four most popular MARIAN ANTIPHONS.

Salzburg Festival a major annual music festival dating from the late 19th c., held during the summer in Salzburg, Austria (Mozart's birthplace). During the Festival month, orchestral and chamber music concerts and opera are presented throughout the city.

Salzburg Mozarteum a college of music founded in 1841 in Salzburg, Austria, by Franz von Hilleprandt, devoted to the encouragement of all music, esp. church music.

Salzedo, Carlos (Léon) (1885–1961) French-born Amer. harpist and composer, trained at the Paris Conservatoire. He came to the U.S. in 1909 to play with the Metropolitan Opera and founded the Trio Lutèce with flutist Georges Barrère and cellist Paul Kéfer. He taught at Curtis from 1924 and ran a harp colony in Maine from 1931. He wrote a number of works for harp, incl. two concertos.

Salzman, Eric (1933–   ) Amer. composer and critic, trained at Columbia and Princeton. He wrote for various New York newspapers and worked for WBAI-FM. In 1970 he founded QUOG, a new music ensemble composed of singers, instrumentalists and dancers. His works sometimes use mixed media and music theater elements, combined with extensive improvisation.

Samaroff (née Hickenlooper), **Olga** (1882–1948) Amer. pianist and teacher, trained at the Paris Conservatoire. She retired from performance in 1924 because of an arm injury and taught at the Juilliard School and the Philadelphia Conservatory until her death, her pupils including Rosalyn Tureck and Alexis Weissenberg.

samba (Sp.) a lively Brazilian couple DANCE of Afr. origin in $\frac{4}{4}$ time. In the original folk dance the dancing is always accompanied by singing in which a soloist alternates with a chorus. Cf. BOSSA NOVA, DANCE (*illus.*).

Saminsky, Lazare (1882–1959) Russian-born Amer. composer, conductor and writer, stud. of Lyadov and Rimsky-Korsakov. He came to New York in 1920, where he was a founder of the League of Composers, the music dir. of Temple Emanu-El (1924–56) and dir. of the annual Three Choirs Festival. His works incl. 3 operas, 5 symphonies, tone poems, Hebrew services and other choral music, songs and chamber music.

samisen *also,* **shamisen, samsien** (Jap.) a Jap. flat-backed, plucked LUTE similar to a banjo, with three silk or nylon strings and several tunings for different performance situations.

Sammartini, Giovanni Battista (1701–75) Italian composer and oboist, brother of GIUSEPPE SAMMARTINI and an important figure in the development of the Classical style. He spent his career in Milan, where he was *maestro di cappella* for many of the city's churches, incl. the ducal chapel. He taught at the Collegio de' Nobili, where his pupils incl. Gluck, and also influenced (through his conducting) such musicians as J.C. Bach and Boccherini, who played under him. He was a founder of the Philharmonic Society in Milan in 1758 and his works were published in Paris and London and performed throughout Europe. His wrote 3 operas, oratorios and cantatas, 76 symphonies, concertos for violin and oboe, overtures, sonatas for various instruments, string quartets and other chamber music, songs and arias.

Sammartini, Giuseppe (1695–1750) Italian oboist and composer, brother of G.B. SAMMARTINI. Raised in Milan, he went to London about 1728, where he remained for the rest of his life, appearing as oboe soloist, playing in Handel's orch. and serving as tutor to the children of the Prince of Wales. He was considered the greatest oboist of his day. His works incl. concerti grossi, overtures, oboe concertos and sonatas, many trio sonatas and other chamber music, cantatas and arias.

sampler a machine that digitizes and stores analog information, such as the sound of a particular instrument, which can then be manipulated electronically for various purposes. Also, *digital sampler*.

samsien SAMISEN.

Samson oratorio (1743) by Handel to a text by Newburgh Hamilton, based on poems by Milton.

Samson and Delilah (Fr., *Samson et Dalila*) Biblical opera in 3 acts by Saint-Saëns to a libretto in French by Ferdinand Lemaire, based on the Book of Judges. Premiere, Weimar 1877 (in German). The Biblical story of the seduction of Samson by the Philistine priestess Dalilah.

Samuel, Gerhard (1924–) German-born Amer. conductor and composer, stud. of Hindemith, Koussevitzky and others. He has been assoc. conductor of the Minneapolis SO and the Los Angeles PO and music dir. of the Oakland (CA) SO and of the San Francisco Ballet. He has taught at the Cincinnati College-Conservatory of Music and at the California Institute of the Arts. In each city in which he has worked, he has been an active force in the musical life, a founder of organizations and a supporter of avant-garde music. As a composer, he has written orchestral works, choral works and chamber music.

San Antonio Symphony orch. formed in 1939 in San Antonio, TX. Its conductors have incl. Max Reiter, François Huybrechts, Lawrence Leighton Smith and Sixten Ehrling.

Sanctus (Lat., holy) the second chant of the Mass Ordinary, sung after the Preface and before the Canon of the Mass. The Sanctus is the oldest chant of the Mass.

sand drum a percussion instrument

made by tunneling out sand to form a hole partly covered by a small bridge which is beaten with the hands.

Sanderling, Kurt (1912–) German conductor. He was in Russia from 1936 to 1960 as conductor of the Moscow Radio SO and the Leningrad PO. He has also been conductor of the East Berlin SO and the Dresden Staatskapelle, and has guest-conducted throughout Europe.

Sanders, Robert L(evine) (1906–74) Amer. composer and teacher, trained in Chicago, Rome and Paris. In Chicago he held a variety of posts, incl. that of organist at the First Unitarian Church. He taught at Indiana U. (1938–47) and at Brooklyn College (1947–72). His works, in a dissonant tonal idiom, incl. a ballet, 2 symphonies, a violin concerto, *Saturday Night* for orch., works for chorus, sonatas and other instrumental chamber music.

Sanders, Samuel (1937–) Amer. pianist, trained at the Juilliard School, where he has taught since 1963. He is renowned as an accompanist for singers and instrumentalists (incl. Perlman, Rostropovich and Jessye Norman) and as a chamber music pianist. He has also taught at SUNY Purchase, and elsewhere.

Sándor, György (1912–) Hungarian-born Amer. pianist, stud of Bartók and Kodály. He came to the U.S. in 1939. He has toured and recorded extensively a wide repertory ranging from J.S. Bach to contemporary works and has made many editions of piano music. He has taught at S. Methodist U., the U. of Michigan and the Juilliard School.

sandunga (Sp.) a type of Mexican dance-song accompanied by an orch. of marimba and winds.

San Francisco Opera opera company founded in 1923 by conductor GAETANO MEROLA and performing in the War Memorial Opera House since 1934. Since Merola's death in 1953 the company's directors have been Kurt Herbert Adler, Terence A. McEwen and Lotfi Mansouri.

San Francisco Symphony Orchestra orch. est. in 1911 under conductor Henry Hadley. Subsequent music directors have incl. Alfred Hertz, Monteux, Enrique Jorda, Krips, Ozawa, de Waart and Blomstedt.

sansa an Afr. plucked instrument consisting of a set of tongues of metal or cane held by a lateral bar over a resonating chamber. The tongues are tuned by sliding them to different positions under the bar and are plucked by the thumbs. Also, *thumb piano.*

Santana Amer. jazz-rock band formed in 1967 in San Francisco by Mexican-born guitarist and singer Carlos Santana (1947–). Their hits incl. "Evil Ways" (1969) and "Black Magic Woman" (1970).

Santa Fe Opera opera company founded by John O. Crosby in 1956 as the Opera Association of New Mexico and performing during an annual summer festival. The company presents a varied repertory, frequently premiering new works and specializing in the operas of R. Strauss.

santur *also,* **santour** (Arab.) a Middle Eastern DULCIMER.

saraband *also,* **sarabande** a stately court DANCE of the 17th and 18th c., resembling the MINUET, in slow triple time, with an accent on the second beat and trochaic rhythms. It is often found in the Baroque and Classical instrumental dance suite. Both slow and fast versions of the sara-

bande were known in the 17th c., although the slower variety gained preeminence.

sarangi a No. Indian bowed folk FIDDLE with three or four strings, a boxlike shape and a varying number of sympathetic strings.

Sarasate (y Navascuéz), Pablo (Martín Melitón) de (1844–1908) Spanish virtuoso violinist and composer, stud. of M.R. Sáez in Madrid and of Delphin Alard in Paris. His sweet tone and effortless virtuosity made him a favorite throughout Europe and the Americas and many composers dedicated works to him. As a composer, he produced a number of violin works, interesting primarily for their technical demands.

Saratoga Festival annual summer festival in Saratoga Springs, NY, founded in 1937. The Philadelphia Orch. and the New York City Ballet are resident. Dennis Russell Davies has been dir. since 1985.

sardana (Sp.) a Catalan circle dance in $\frac{6}{8}$ time, traditionally accompanied by the fife and drum. Cf. FARANDOLE.

Sargent, Sir (Harold) Malcolm (Watts) (1895–1967) English conductor. He assisted Beecham with the London PO, then conducted the Hallé Orch., the Liverpool PO and the BBC SO and was chief conductor of the Promenade Concerts from 1948 until his death. He was particularly known as a choral conductor and led the first performance of Walton's *Belshazzar's Feast* (1931).

sarinda an Indian folk FIDDLE.

sarod (Hindi) a plucked LUTE of No. India with two resonators.

saron (Javanese) a METALLOPHONE having seven bronze plates, used in the Javanese gamelan.

sarrusophone a baritone, double-reed brass instrument similar to the bassoon and often replacing it or the contrabassoon. It was invented in 1856 by a French bandmaster who envisaged a full range of such instruments intended to replace oboes and bassoons in military bands.

Sarum rite a modified form of the

Sansa (thumb piano)

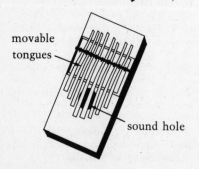

movable tongues

sound hole

Roman Catholic rite used in the Middle Ages at Salisbury Cathedral in England.

SATB *abbr.* soprano, alto, tenor, bass: an indication of four-part choral music.

Satchmo nickname for LOUIS ARMSTRONG; probably derived from "Satchelmouth," used to describe his large oral musculature.

Satie, Erik (Alfred Leslie) [säˈtē] (1866–1925) French composer. He entered the Paris Conservatoire in 1879 but was dismissed in 1882 for failing to attain the required standard. He lived the bohemian life in Montmartre until the late 1890s, a close friend of Debussy and active in various avant-garde, and sometimes outrageous, projects. From 1898 to 1910 he lived in relative obscurity in the suburbs of Paris, played café piano and studied at the Schola Cantorum. His ballet PARADE, designed by Picasso and presented by Diaghilev, caused a scandal at its premiere. He is seen now as an innovator and precursor of such modern movements as MINIMALISM. His works incl. *Uspud, Parade, Mercure, Relâche* and other ballets, *Socrate* (symphonic drama), songs, chamber music and piano works (incl. *3 Gymnopédies, 3 Gnossiennes, 3 Morceaux en forme de poire* and *5 Nocturnes*).

Satz [zäts] (Ger.) **1**, a musical setting. **2**, MOVEMENT. **3**, THEME.

saudades [sowˈdä-däs] (Port.) melancholy, nostalgia; used as a title of works by Milhaud and others.

Sauer, Emil von [ˈzow-ər] (1862–1942) German pianist, stud. of Nikolay Rubinstein and Liszt. A successful concert artist, he is best remembered today as an editor of the piano works of Brahms and others.

Sauguet, Henri(-Pierre) [sōˈgä] (1901–89) French composer, stud. of Paul Combes and Canteloube. He was a member of the ÉCOLE D'ARCUEIL and a successful composer in most genres in a tonal idiom. His works incl. *La Chatte* and many other ballets, *Les Caprices de Marianne*

and 5 other operas, 2 piano concertos, 4 symphonies, symphonic poems, chamber music, choral works, many songs and music for films, radio and TV.

Sauret, Emile [soˈrä] (1852–1920) French violinist and composer, stud. of de Beriot and perhaps of Vieuxtemps and Wieniawski. He concertized throughout Europe and No. Amer. and taught at the Royal Academy of Music and at Trinity College of Music in London and at the Chicago Musical College. He also performed in trio with pianist Rudolf Ganz and cellist Bruno Steindel.

sausage bassoon RACKETT.

Sauter, Eddie (Edward Ernest) (1914–81) Amer. jazz composer and arranger, trained at the Juilliard School. He was an arranger for the bands of Red Norvo, Artie Shaw, Benny Goodman and others, and also wrote original music for those groups. He later led the Sauter-Finegan Orch., noted for its novel, even unique, arrangements.

sautillé [sō-tēˈyä] (Fr.) a rapid, bouncing bowstroke played in the middle of the bow, one note to a stroke, usu. indicated with dots above the notes. Also, *arco saltando, saltato* (It.). Cf. SPICCATO, BOWING.

Savage, Henry W(ilson) (1859–1927) Amer. impresario, important producer of opera in English, as well as of musical comedies and plays. He was responsible for the Amer. premiere of Puccini's *Madame Butterfly* (1906) and productions of Léhar's *The Merry Widow* (1907), Wagner's *Parsifal* (which toured the U.S. for almost a year) and many other works.

Savoy Ballroom a famous dance hall in Harlem (NY) opened in 1926 and active until 1959, during which time almost 250 big bands played there, incl. those of Ellington, Whiteman, Rudy Vallee and Chick Webb.

Savoy operas the operettas of GILBERT AND SULLIVAN, many of which were first performed at the Savoy Theatre in London, built in 1881 by

Richard D'Oyly Carte for their presentation.

saw, musical a folk instrument consisting of a flexible hand saw bowed with a string-instrument bow or struck with a soft mallet and bent to produce different pitches. Henri Sauguet wrote a work, *Plainte* (1949), for the instrument.

Sawallisch, Wolfgang [sä'vä-liç] (1923–) German conductor and pianist, trained at the Munich Academy. He has been music dir. at Aachen, Wiesbaden, Cologne, and, since 1971, at the Bavarian Staatsoper in Munich. He first conducted at Bayreuth in 1957. He has also been assoc. with the Vienna SO and the Hamburg PO and has performed frequently as pianist with singers and occasionally as soloist.

Sax, Adolphe (Antoine Joseph) (1814–94) highly innovative Belgian wind-instrument maker. He moved from Brussels to Paris in 1842, establishing his workshop, and produced a wide variety of wind instruments, of which the most successful were the saxophones and the saxhorns.

saxhorn one of a family of valved brass instruments patented by Adolphe Sax in 1845, having a conical bore and characterized by a wide range and full tone. Saxhorns are used extensively in military brass bands.

saxophone 1, a metal, single-reed instrument invented c1840 by Adolphe Sax. It has a conical bore like an oboe but uses a clarinet reed and is made in various sizes esp. for use in military bands and in jazz. It is also called for by some orchestral composers. See REED INSTRUMENTS (*illus.*). **2**, a flue or reed pipe ORGAN STOP imitating the sound of the saxophone.

saxtuba a bass SAXHORN.

Sayão, Bidú (Balduina) (**de Oliveira**) [sä'yäoo, bi'doo] (1902–) Brazilian soprano, stud. of Jean de Reszke in France. Her U.S. debut was in 1935; she first sang with the Metropolitan Opera two years later and appeared with the company regularly for 15 years. She retired from the stage in 1958. Her roles incl. Gilda (*Rigoletto*), Mimì (*La Bohème*) and Susanna (*The Marriage of Figaro*).

scabellum (Lat.) an ancient CLAPPER of Greece and Rome played with the foot.

Scaggs, Boz (William Royce) (1944–) Amer. rock and blues singer and songwriter. He lived in Europe in the 1960s, then returned to the U.S. in 1967, performing with the Steve Miller Band. After 1969 he concentrated on solo recordings strongly influenced by soul music. In 1980 he provided music for the score of the film *Urban Cowboy*.

scala enigmatica (Lat., enigmatic scale) an unusual SCALE used by Verdi in his *Ave Maria* for chorus (1898), the first of the *Quattro pezzi sacri* (Four Sacred Pieces). The scale, which resembles a whole-tone scale, is C-D♭-E-F♯-G♯-A♯-B-C.

Scala di seta, La (It., The Silken Ladder) opera in 1 act by Rossini to a libretto by Giuseppe Foppa, after the play *L'Échelle de Soie* by François Antoine Eugène de Planard. Premiere, Venice 1812. To guard the secret of their marriage, Dorvil must use a silken ladder to enter the apartment of his wife, Giulia, in her guardian's house.

Scala, Teatro alla theater in Milan, usu. known as La Scala, built in 1778. The name comes from the church which preceded the theater on the site, which in turn was named after a 14th-c. member of the ruling Visconti family, Regina della Scala.

scale a sequence of notes in ascending or descending order of pitch, usu. beginning and ending on the fundamental note of a tonality or mode and considered to have a compass of one or more octaves. Western music usu. makes use of one of two types of scales, DIATONIC (principally the MAJOR and MINOR scales) or CHROMATIC.

Other scales less frequently encountered are the WHOLE-TONE SCALE, consisting entirely of whole tones; and scales of differing numbers

of notes within the octave, such as the PENTATONIC SCALE, which has five notes within the octave, the HEPTATONIC scale (seven notes) and the OCTOTONIC scale (eight notes).

scale degree a note occupying a certain position in a scale, usu. defined in relation to the DIATONIC scale. Scale degrees may be referred to by their numerical position in the scale (second, third, etc.), by pitch names (see PITCH) or by names implying their harmonic function within the scale, as TONIC, SUPERTONIC, MEDI-

ANT, SUBDOMINANT, DOMINANT, SUBMEDIANT, LEADING TONE.

scaling 1, the relationship between the length and the diameter of an organ pipe, the length affecting the pitch level, the diameter its tonal quality. **2**, in string instruments, the relationship between pitch and string length. In general, strings tend to be shorter than expected as the pitch gets lower, compensation being made in tension and string diameter to achieve the desired pitch and quality.

scandicus (Lat.) a NEUME representing three ascending notes.

Scarlatti, (Pietro) Alessandro (Gaspare) (1660–1725) prolific Italian composer, considered the founder of the Neapolitan school of composers, father of DOMENICO SCARLATTI and possibly a stud. of Carissimi. He was in Rome until 1684 in the service of Queen Christina of Sweden and several important cardinals. In 1684 he went to Naples to serve the marquis del Carpio, remaining until 1702 and composing at least 40 and perhaps as many as 70 operas in addition to large numbers of sacred vocal works. He wrote in all nearly 80 operas, oratorios, a large volume of cantatas, madrigals, sacred vocal music, vocal chamber music, concerti grossi, sonatas and keyboard works.

Scarlatti, (Giuseppe) Domenico (1685–1757) Italian composer, harpsichordist and teacher, son of ALESSANDRO SCARLATTI. After several years in Naples and Venice, he entered the service of the exiled Polish queen Maria Casimira and later other nobles in Rome. He went to Portugal in 1719 to serve at the patriarchal chapel, moving to Madrid in 1728 in the train of the infanta. There he served until his death, evidently sharing authority with the eminent castrato FARINELLI. While Scarlatti produced a number of operas, oratorios, cantatas and other vocal music, as well as sinfonias, he is remembered for his nearly 600 harpsichord sonatas, which exerted an important influence on keyboard writing.

scat singing a technique of jazz singing in the manner of an instrument, using meaningless syllables. Noted practitioners incl. Louis Armstrong (who may have created the technique), Ella Fitzgerald and Cab Calloway. A similar technique has also been used with success by the SWINGLE SINGERS and others in vocalizing classical instrumental works of the Baroque and other periods. Cf. VOCALESE.

Scelsi, Giacinto ['shel-sē, ja'chēn-tō] (1905–89) Italian composer, stud. of Egon Koehler and Walter Klein. His music is known for its extreme changes in style, which characterize the spiritual development of the composer; his late works show antirationalist tendencies. Although he wrote for orch., voice, chorus, chamber ensembles and piano, only eleven chamber works have been published.

scena ['shä-nä] (It.) **1**, a scene in an opera, esp. one having a free formal construction comprised of various elements, such as recitative, arioso, choral interpolations, etc. **2**, an independent vocal work like an operatic SCENA (1,).

scenario an opera LIBRETTO.

Scenes from Childhood (Ger., *Kinderszenen*) suite for solo piano, Op. 15 (1838), by Schumann, consisting of 13 easy pieces. The descriptive titles were added later by the composer.

Schäffer, Boguslaw (1929–) prolific Polish composer, theorist and teacher, trained at the Kraków Conservatory, where he has taught since 1963. He has also worked at the Experimental Studio of the Polish Radio in Warsaw. His works have employed serial and aleatory techniques and mixed-media presentation and incl. music for happenings, *Musica ipsa*, *Scultura* and other orchestral works, concertos, works for chamber orch., string quartets and other chamber music, songs, works for jazz ensemble and electronic works.

Schaeffer, Pierre (1910–) French composer, theorist and teacher, trained as a scientist. His work as a technician for French Radio gradually led to the founding of the Studio d'essai, the home of his experiments that led to MUSIQUE CONCRÈTE. He was a founder of the Groupe de recherche de musique concrète in 1951, later reformed as the Groupe de recherches musicales. He has taught since 1968 at the Paris Conservatoire. His works are for tape and involve the manipulation of natural, recorded "sound objects."

Schafer, R. Murray (1933–) Canadian composer and teacher, stud. of Alberto Guerrero, Weinzweig and others. He founded the Ten Centuries Concerts in Toronto in 1961 and since 1962 has taught at Simon Fraser U., where he established the World Soundscape Project to study the relationship of man to his acoustic environment. His works incl. *Loving/ Toi, Patria, Apocalypse* and other stage works, *Son of Heldenleben* for orch. and tape, other works for orch., 2 string quartets, works for voice and various instruments and works for tape.

Schalmei [shäl'mī] (Ger.) a German SHAWM with a reed-cap and a single key.

Scharwenka, (Franz) Xaver (1850–1924) Polish-born German pianist, composer, conductor and teacher, stud. of Kullak. He toured extensively from 1874, and in 1881 in Berlin organized a concert series and opened his own conservatory. From 1891 he split his time between New York and Berlin, making many tours of the U.S. and Canada. His works are mostly for piano, incl. 4 concertos, chamber music and dances. He also wrote an opera, *Kataswintha* (1896).

Schauspieldirektor, Der ['show-shpēl-di-rek"tor] (Ger.) IMPRESARIO, THE.

Scheherezade 1, symphonic suite, Op. 35 (1888), by Rimsky-Korsakov, based on stories from the *Arabian Nights*. **2**, (Fr., *Shéhérazade*) cycle of three songs for voice and orch. or piano (1903) by Ravel to poems by Tristan Klingsor. The titles are "Asie" (Asia), "La Flûte enchantée" (The Enchanted Flute) and "L'Indifférent" (The Indifferent One).

Scheibe, Johann Adolph ['shī-be] (1708–76) German composer, critic and theorist, largely self-taught. After several years in Hamburg as a music critic, he went to Copenhagen to serve at the Danish court, which he did, with a lengthy interruption, until his death. Most of his works (concertos, cantatas, oratorios, serenades) are lost; the surviving works incl. an Easter oratorio and cantata, songs, violin and harpsichord sonatas and a flute concerto.

Scheidt, Samuel [shīt] (1587–1654) German organist and composer, stud. of Sweelinck and a link between the traditional contrapuntal style and the new Italian concertato style. He spent his life in Halle, first in service at the court of the margrave of Brandenburg, then as dir. of music to the town. He wrote a large volume of German and Latin sacred vocal music, organ and harpsichord chorales and dances, as well as other instrumental dances and symphonies.

Schein, Johann Hermann [shīn] (1586–1630) German composer and poet, trained at the Schulpforta near Naumburg. He was Kantor at the Thomasschule in Leipzig from 1616 until his early death. He is principally known for his sacred and secular vocal works, and he also wrote instrumental suites and canzonas.

Schelle, Johann (1648–1701) German composer, Kantor of the Leipzig Thomaskirche from 1677 until his death and responsible for the introduction of the Gospel and chorale cantatas into the Lutheran service.

Schellen ['shel-ən] (Ger.) JINGLES.

Schelling, Ernest (Henry) (1876–1939) Amer. pianist, conductor and composer, trained at the Paris Conservatoire. He concertized in Europe and No. and S. America and was briefly conductor of the Baltimore Symphony.

Schelomo (Heb., Solomon) Hebrew Rhapsody for Cello and Orch. (1916)

by Bloch, in which the cello represents the voice of King Solomon.

Schenk, Johann (Baptist) (1753–1836) Austrian teacher and composer of Singspiele, stud. of Wagenseil. He apparently assisted Beethoven with his composition exercises for Haydn. His works also incl. cantatas and other sacred vocal music, symphonies, concertos and chamber music.

Schenker, Heinrich (1868–1935) Polish-born Austrian theorist, noted for his theory of tonal music based on the concepts of the harmonic scale-step and large-scale structure. Although he was never affiliated with a university, Schenker was known as a gifted teacher, with Felix Salzer and Oswald Jonas among his pupils. His theoretical work culminates in the treatise *Der freie Satz* (1935), which enumerates a system by which tonal music is divulged as a series of layers leading from the foreground, or surface of the piece, further and further into the background, or deeper structural levels of the composition. Schenkerian analysis reveals long-range linear relationships as well as harmonic relationships.

Scherchen, Hermann (1891–1966) German conductor, largely self-taught, throughout his career an ardent supporter of new music. He founded the Neue Musikgesellschaft in Berlin (1918), the Scherchen Quartet (1918) and the Ars Viva Orch. (after World War II). He was conductor of East German Radio Orch., the Zürich Radio Orch. and the Winterthur Musikkollegium and edited the journals *Melos* and *Musica viva* (Brussels). His U.S. debut was in 1964.

Scherman, Thomas (Kielty) (1917–79) Amer. conductor, stud. of Carl Bamberger and Max Rudolf. In 1947 he created the Little Orch. Society in New York, which he conducted for most of his career.

Schermerhorn, Kenneth (de Wirt) (1929–) Amer. conductor, trained at the New England Conservatory and at the Berkshire Music Center. He has been music dir. of the Amer-

ican Ballet Theater, the New Jersey SO, the Milwaukee SO, the Nashville SO and the Hong Kong PO.

scherzando [sker'tsän-dõ] (It.) playful, jesting.

scherzetto [-'tsät-tõ] (It.) a short SCHERZO or scherzolike piece.

Scherzi, Gli ['sker-tsē, lyē] RUSSIAN QUARTETS (1,).

scherzo ['sker-tsõ] (It., joke) a lively, sometimes humorous, instrumental work in quick triple time and usu. in ternary form, often the third movement in a four-movement symphony, sonata, quartet, etc.

Scherzo Capriccioso [kä-prēt'tchõ-zõ] concert scherzo, Op. 66 (1883), by Dvořák.

scherzoso [-zõ] (It.) SCHERZANDO.

Schickele, (Johann) Peter (1935–) Amer. composer and humorist, stud. of Harris, Persichetti, Bergsma and Milhaud. He has taught at the Juilliard School and has composed music in a broad range of styles, many of them performed by his "chamber-rock-jazz" trio, Open Window, founded in 1967. In 1965 he introduced the fictional Baroque composer "P.D.Q. Bach," under which name he has written many parodic works and toured widely, performing with orchestras and in concert.

Schicksalslied ['shik-säls"lēt] (Ger.) SONG OF DESTINY.

Schifrin, Lalo (Boris) (1932–) Argentinian-born Amer. composer and jazz pianist, stud. of Juan Carlos Paz and Messiaen. He has directed his own jazz band in Argentina and played with Dizzy Gillespie's quintet, but he is best known as a composer of film and TV scores. His works incl. ballets, concertos, chamber music and works for jazz and rock band.

Schikaneder, Emanuel (1751–1812) Austrian dramatist, actor, singer and composer, author of a large number of librettos and plays, best known for his libretto *The Magic Flute* (1791), set by Mozart, in which he played the role of Papageno.

Schillinger, Joseph (1895–1943) Rus-

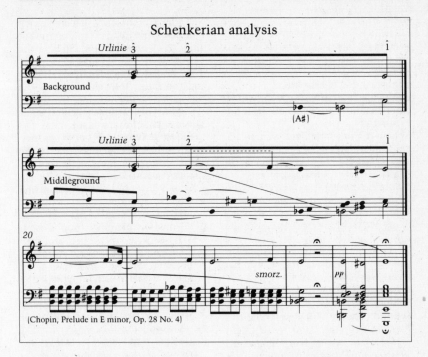

(Chopin, Prelude in E minor, Op. 28 No. 4)

sian-born Amer. composer, teacher and theorist, known for his system of composition, which he conveyed to his many students, among them Glenn Miller and George Gershwin.

Schindler, Kurt (1882–1935) German-born Amer. conductor, composer and music editor. He came to the U.S. in 1905 to conduct the Metropolitan Opera and formed the MacDowell Chorus, later renamed the Schola Cantorum of New York. He also worked as an editor for G. Schirmer and Oliver Ditson and was involved in collecting and recording Spanish folk music.

Schiøtz, Aksel (Hauch) [shøts] (1906–75) Danish tenor, known esp. for his performance of Lieder. His career as a tenor was ended in 1950 by a brain tumor, though he was later able to sing again as a baritone for some years. He taught at the universities of Minnesota, Toronto and Colorado and at the Royal Danish School of Educational Studies.

Schipa, Tito (Raffaele Attilio Ama-deo) ['skē-pä] (1888–1965) Italian lyric tenor, stud. of A. Gerunda and E. Piccoli. He sang with the Chicago Grand Opera from 1919 to 1932, as well as the Metropolitan Opera and at leading Italian houses. His repertory included Des Grieux (*Manon*) and Nemorino (*The Elixir of Love*).

Schippers, Thomas (1930–77) Amer. conductor, trained at the Curtis Institute and with Olga Samaroff. He was music dir. of Menotti's Festival of Two Worlds and later of the Cincinnati SO, and also conducted at the New York City Opera, the Metropolitan Opera, Bayreuth and La Scala. He taught at the Cincinnati College-Conservatory of Music.

Schirmer, E.C. firm of music publishers est. in Boston in 1921 by Ernest Charles Schirmer (1865–1958), nephew of Gustave Schirmer, founder of G. SCHIRMER.

Schirmer, G., Inc. one of the largest music publishers in the U.S., founded in New York in 1866 by Gustave Schirmer (1829–93). The firm has published the *Musical Quarterly* since 1915.

schisma ['skiz-mə] term for various intervals smaller than a semitone, a type of COMMA (2,).

Schlag [shlak] (Ger.) BEAT.

Schlaginstrument *also*, (pl.) **Schlagzeug** [-tsoik] (Ger.) PERCUSSION INSTRUMENT.

Schleifer ['shlī-fər] (Ger.) SLIDE.

schleppen ['shlep-ən] (Ger.) to drag; usu. used in the negative: *nicht schleppend*, without dragging.

Schlick, Arnolt (c1460–c1525) German organist and composer, active in Heidelberg as organist for the palatine court. He was famous in his day as an organist and as an organ tester, and he wrote an important treatise on organ building and playing. A number of his works for organ survive.

Schluss [shlûs] (Ger., end) CADENCE.

Schlüssel ['shlüs-əl] (Ger.) KEY; CLEF.

Schmidt, Daniel W(inslow) (1942–) Amer. composer and instrument maker, stud. of Subotnick and Ki Wasitodipura (Javanese music). He has directed gamelans at the U. of California at Berkeley and at Sonoma (CA) State College and has written for gamelan as well as for electronic and mixed-media presentation. He has designed and built instruments for gamelan and for other uses.

Schmidt, Harvey (Lester) (1929–) Amer. composer of musicals, incl. *The Fantasticks* (1960) and *110 in the Shade* (1963); co-founder of the experimental Portfolio Studio (NY).

Schmidt-Isserstedt, Hans (1900–73) German conductor and composer, mus. dir. of the Deutsche Oper in Berlin and the North German SO in Hamburg and principal conductor, Stockholm PO (1955–64). He was esp. known for performance of the music of Mozart and of 20th-c. repertory.

Schmieder, Wolfgang (1901–) German librarian, known esp. for his catalog of the works of J.S. Bach. His numbers are usu. preceded by the letters "BWV" (Bach-Werke-Verzeichnis).

Schmitt, Florent (1870–1958) French composer and music critic, trained at the Paris Conservatoire. He won the Prix de Rome on his fifth attempt, in 1900, and he traveled extensively during the following two decades. His substantial body of works in all genres shows his ear for orchestral color and sensual chromaticism.

Schnabel, Artur (1882–1951) Austrian-born Amer. pianist, one of the most eminent interpreters of the modern age, stud. of Leschetizky. He lived in Berlin until 1933, performing as soloist and in concert with his wife, contralto Therese Behr. He also performed in chamber groups with Casals, Feuermann, Szigeti and others. He taught at the State Academy in Berlin in the late 1920s, then came to the U.S. in 1939 and taught at the U. of Michigan. His own compositions incl. three symphonies, a piano concerto, string quartets and other chamber music, and songs.

Schneider, (Abraham) Alexander (1908–) Lithuanian-born Amer. violinist and conductor, trained in Frankfurt. He was twice a member of the BUDAPEST STRING QUARTET (1932–44, 1955–67). He collaborated with Casals at the Prades Festival and has been active as performer and conductor with the Mostly Mozart Festival (NY).

schnell [shnel] (Ger.) quick, fast; PRESTO.

schneller (Ger.) **1**, MORDANT. **2**, faster.

Schnitger German family of organ builders, the most famous of whom was Arp Schnitger (1648–1719).

Schnittke, Alfred (1934–) German-born Russian composer, trained in Vienna and at the Moscow Conservatory. He is one of the leading experimentalists of the former Soviet Union. His works incl. 4 symphonies, concertos, a requiem, and many choral and chamber music works.

Schoeck, Othmar (1886–1957) Swiss composer, pianist and conductor, trained at the Zürich Conservatory and with Reger. He conducted various choral groups in Zürich and orchestral concerts at St. Gall and appeared in concert as an accompanist. His works incl. 9 operas, concertos for horn and cello, many choral and other vocal works, songs, 2 string quartets and other chamber music.

Schoenberg (Schönberg), **Arnold (Franz Walter)** (1874–1951) Austrian composer, theorist and teacher of seminal importance in the development of 20th-c. music, stud. of Zemlinsky. The development in his works from the highly expressive chromaticism of *Gurrelieder* (1900–1) through the atonal conciseness of *Pierrot lunaire* (1912) to the serial neoclassicism of the Wind Quintet (1923–4) provoked, with few exceptions, general incomprehension.

In his earlier years in Vienna Schoenberg made a living making arrangements and orchestrations, teaching lessons (his most illustrious students were ALBAN BERG and ANTON WEBERN) and working in cabarets (see ÜBERBRETTL). He received support and occasional financial assistance from Mahler. He moved to Berlin in 1911 and taught at the Stern Conservatory. During World War I he taught at the Schwarzwald School in Vienna, then, in the early 1920s, founded the Society for Private Musical Performances, which between 1919 and 1921 presented performances of many new and avant-garde works in arrangements for piano or chamber ensemble. From 1925 to 1933 he taught at the Prussian Academy of the Arts in Berlin, then moved to the U.S. He taught in Boston for one year, then on the West Coast at the U. of California at Los Angeles. He wrote several important didactic works on harmony, counterpoint and composition.

Schoenberg's works incl. *Erwartung, Die glückliche Hand, Von Heute auf Morgen, Moses und Aron* (operas), *Gurrelieder, Friede auf Erden, Kol Nidre, Modern Psalm* and other choral works, *Pelleas und Melisande,* concertos for piano, violin and cello, 2 chamber symphonies, *Verklärte Nacht* for string sextet, 4 string quartets, *Serenade* for wind/string septet, many songs, canons and piano works.

schola cantorum ['skō-lä] (Lat., school for singers) **1**, since the 7th c., a school for teaching singing (orig., Gregorian chant). **2**, (*cap. S, C*) a famous school founded by d'Indy in Paris in 1894.

Schöne Müllerin, Die ['shö-ne 'mü-lə-rin] (Ger., The Beautiful Miller's Daughter) cycle of twenty songs (1823) by Schubert to poems from the *Müllerlieder* of Wilhelm Müller. The poems tell the story of a courtship ending in tragedy.

Schoolmaster, The popular name for the Symphony No. 55 in E♭ major (1774) by Haydn, perhaps named for the somewhat pedantic nature of the slow movement.

school opera SCHULOPER.

Schöpfung, Die ['shöp-fûng] (Ger.) THE CREATION.

Schorr, Friedrich (1888–1953) Hungarian-born Amer. bass-baritone, stud. of Adolf Robinson. He was the leading Wagnerian bass-baritone of the early 20th c., singing regularly at Bayreuth in the 1920s, at Covent Garden until 1933 and at the Metropolitan Opera from 1924 to 1943.

Schott German music publisher founded in Mainz in 1770 by Bernhard Schott (1748–1809). The firm has been the principal publisher of Beethoven, Wagner and many other important 19th- and 20th-c. composers.

Schottische ['skot-ti-she] (Ger., Scottish) a 19th-c. round dance with gliding and hopping steps, similar to, but slower than, the POLKA. Also, *German polka.* Cf. ÉCOSSAISE.

Schradieck, (Carl Franz) Henry (1846–1918) German-born Amer. violinist and teacher, stud. of Hubert Héonard and Ferdinand David. He came to the U.S. in 1883 to teach at the Cincinnati College of Music. He later taught at the National Conservatory in New York, the South Broad

Street Conservatory in Philadelphia and the American Institute of Applied Music in New York. A number of his pedagogical works are still in use.

Schrammel Quartet orig. a late 19th-c. quartet consisting of 2 violins, clarinet and bass that played in Vienna and eventually toured the U.S. The clarinet was replaced by an accordion, and the term *Schrammel quartet* has come to refer to this combination.

Schreker, Franz (1878–1934) Austrian composer, conductor and teacher, stud. of Robert Fuchs in Vienna. He is known primarily as an opera composer, and his opera *Der ferne Klang* (1901–10) had a demonstrable influence on the *Wozzeck* of Berg, who prepared the vocal score of Schreker's opera.

Schröder-Devrient, Wilhelmine ['shrø-dər-də"vrēnt] (1804–60) German soprano, stud. of Giuseppe Mozatti and Aloys Mieksch. She sang at the Dresden Hoftheater from 1822 to 1847 and elsewhere in Europe and England. She was esp. known for her acting abilities.

Schroeder, Gene (Eugene Charles) (1915–75) Amer. pianist, a member of Eddie Condon's band for almost 20 years from the mid-1940s. He then played with the Dukes of Dixieland.

Schubert, Franz (Seraph Peter) (1797–1828) Austrian composer, stud. of Michael Holzer and Salieri. In his short lifetime he produced masterworks in a number of genres and established himself as one of the greatest songwriters in Western musical history. Until 1818 he taught school near Vienna, then became music master to the children of Count Johann Esterházy. After he left the Esterházy position he earned money from private publication of his songs (when the commercial publishers would not take them) and from contributions from dedicatees. The last years of his life finally saw his reputation begin to be established and more of his works published by such firms as Artaria and Diabelli, but he was still unable to secure a permanent position at court.

Schubert wrote 16 operas and Singspiels; incidental music to *Rosamunde*; 6 masses and other sacred vocal music; works for mixed, male and female choruses; 9 symphonies; overtures; string quartets and trios, a string quintet, *Die Forelle* (piano quintet), wind/string octet, violin sonatas; dances, sonatas and fantasies for piano solo, piano duets; and more than 600 songs, incl. the cycles *Die schöne Müllerin* and *Die Winterreise* and the posthumous collection *Schwanengesang.*

Schuller, Gunther (Alexander) (1925–) Amer. composer, conductor, horn player, administrator, publisher and teacher, a major and tireless figure in all aspects of 20th-c. musical life. He studied at the St. Thomas Choir School, then played principal horn in the Cincinnati SO (1943–5) and the Metropolitan Opera orch. (1945–59). He has taught at the Manhattan School, Yale School of Music and the New England Conservatory, of which he was president from 1967 to 1977. He has also served in various capacities at the Berkshire Music Center, incl. dir. from 1974 to 1984. He has conducted in No. America and Europe, specializing in contemporary music, was an important force in the revival of interest in ragtime music and early Amer. classical music and founded two companies to publish and distribute neglected works of American composers. He has been intensely interested in jazz since the 1950s and has completed two volumes of a history of jazz. He coined the term THIRD STREAM to describe the fusion between jazz and classical art music and has written works in this style. In addition he has managed to produce a substantial and significant body of works in various genres, incl. *The Visitation, The Fisherman and his Wife* (operas), concertos for horn, piano, cello and other instruments, *Seven Studies on Themes of Paul Klee, American Trip-*

tych and other orchestral works, music for chamber ensembles, songs and scores for film and television.

Schuloper ['skool"ō-pər] (Ger., school opera) an opera written for use in schools and sometimes for performance by schoolchildren. Examples are Weill's *Der Jasager* and Hindemith's *Wir bauen eine Stadt*, both written in 1930. The former is a didactic work for professional performance, the latter is designed for performance by children.

Schuman,   William   (Howard) (1910–92) Amer. composer, teacher and administrator. He studied privately with various teachers, incl. Wagenaar, Adolf Schmid and Harris and won the first Pulitzer Prize in music in 1943 for his *Secular Cantata No. 2, A Free Song*. He taught at Sarah Lawrence College (1935–45) and has been president of the Juilliard School (1948–62) and of the Lincoln Center for the Performing Arts (1962–9). His works incl. *The Mighty Casey* (opera), ballets, 10 symphonies, concertos (for piano, violin and viola), *Variations on "America," American Festival Overture*, overtures for orch. and wind band, songs and choral works and 4 string quartets.

Schumann (née Wieck), **Clara (Josephine)** (1819–96) German pianist and composer, highly acclaimed both as child prodigy and as mature adult performer. She was married to ROBERT SCHUMANN. After her husband's death she toured extensively and became important as a teacher. She maintained a lifelong friendship with Brahms and was a devoted interpreter of his music. Her own compositions incl. many works for piano, two concertos, a piano trio, songs and cadenzas for concertos by Beethoven and Mozart.

Schumann, Elisabeth (1888–1952) German soprano, stud. of Natalie Hänisch, Marie Dietrich and Alma Schadow. She sang with the Hamburg Stadttheater until 1919, then moved to the Vienna Staatsoper, remaining until 1937, after which she lived in New York. Her light, high soprano was esp. prized in the works of Mozart and Strauss and in recital. She made many recordings.

Schumann,   Robert   (Alexander) (1810–56) German composer, pianist and writer, stud. of Friedrich Wieck and Heinrich Dorn. He trained as a pianist, but his right hand became crippled in 1832, prob. as a result of disease. In 1834 he began his assoc. with the new music journal, *Neue (Leipziger) Zeitschrift für Musik*, which would be his principal literary and critical outlet (aside from his assiduously kept diary). Literary associations were always important to him, and they appear in his musical work in his fondness for musical ciphers (such as his works based on the letters ASCH and ABEGG) and in the many fictional characters he invented for his imaginary antiphilistine organization, the DAVIDSBUND.

He married pianist Clara Wieck (see CLARA SCHUMANN) in 1840. For a time he was music dir. in Düsseldorf, but continuing problems with the chorus were aggravated by the onset of the neurological illness which would eventually cause his death. In late 1856 he died in an asylum near Bonn.

Schumann's works incl. *Genoveva* (opera), incidental music for Byron's *Manfred, Das Paradies und die Peri, Der Rose Pilgerfahrt* and other choral works for mixed voices, men's chorus and women's chorus, 4 symphonies, concertos for piano, violin and cello, overtures, chamber music for various instruments, piano works (*Album für die Jugend, Carnaval, Albumblätter, Symphonic Études*, sonatas, many characteristic pieces) and songs (incl. the song cycles *Liederkreis, Frauenliebe und -leben, Dichterliebe, Spanisches Liederspiel*).

Schumann-Heink (née Rössler), **Ernestine** (1861–1936) Czech-born Amer. contralto, stud. of Franz Wüllner, G.B. Lamperti and others. She sang with the Dresden and Hamburg operas until 1897 and at Bayreuth until 1914. Her Metropolitan Opera debut was in 1899, and she sang regularly with the company until 1903, thereafter concentrating on concert tours and recordings, esp. of Wagnerian repertory.

Schuppanzigh, Ignaz (1776–1830) Austrian violinist and conductor, leader of several string quartets (one assembled for Count Rasumovsky) that introduced a number of the quartets of Beethoven.

Schütz, Heinrich (1585–1672) eminent German composer, stud. of Giovanni Gabrieli and Monteverdi. In 1615 he entered the service of the elector of Saxony in Dresden, at first on loan from the landgrave, but after 1617 he was in the elector's sole service. When Saxony entered the Thirty Years' War he spent several years in Denmark (1633–4 and 1642–4), returning to Dresden in 1645. When the elector died in 1657, Schütz was finally relieved of daily duty and assigned a pension. His final fifteen years were spent composing, with occasional visits to other courts in Wolfenbüttel, Zeitz and elsewhere.

Schütz was justly famous in his own time but largely forgotten after his death until rediscovered in the mid-19th c. His position has since then been assured as the most important German composer of the 17th c., in part for his role in bringing the Italian style of composition to Germany, and he was probably the first to attain true international renown. His lost opera *Dafne* (1627) was the first German opera.

Of Schütz's works over 500 survive (probably less than half of his total output), incl. madrigals, polyphonic psalm settings (*Psalmen Davids*), motets, an Easter oratorio, a Christmas oratorio, *The Seven Last Words*, a Requiem, and unaccompanied Passions according to St. John, St. Matthew and St. Luke.

Schuyler, Philippa Duke (1931–67) Amer. pianist and composer, stud. of Hoffman, Wittgenstein and others. She toured throughout the world and also wrote books about her travels. Her compositions incl. *Manhattan Nocturne* (1943), *Rhapsody of Youth* (1948) and *Nile Fantasy* (1965).

schwach [shväkh] (Ger.) weak; soft.

Schwanendreher ['shvä-nən"drä-ər] (Ger., The Swan-Turner) concerto for viola and chamber orch. without violins or violas (1935) by Hindemith, premiered by the Concertgebouw Orch. with the composer as soloist. The work is based on German folk tunes and tells the story of a traveling fiddler.

Schwanengesang [-ge"zäng] (Ger., Swan Song) a set of 14 songs (1828) by Schubert, collected and published posthumously, with the title supplied by the publisher. The songs are unrelated except by their late date.

Schwantner, Joseph (1943–) Amer. composer, stud. of Bernard Dieter, Alan Stout and Anthony Donato. He has taught at the Eastman School of Music since 1970 and was composer-in-residence with the St. Louis SO (1982–84). He won the Pulitzer Prize in 1979 for his orchestral work *Aftertones of Infinity*. His works, which demonstrate his special interest in sonority, incl. orchestral works, instrumental chamber music and works for voice with various instrumental ensembles.

Schwartz, Arthur (1900–84) Amer. composer of Broadway revues and musicals, most written in collaboration with lyricist Howard Dietz, incl. *The Band Wagon* (1931) and *A Tree Grows in Brooklyn* (1951).

Schwartz, Elliott (Shelling) (1936–) Amer. composer and writer, stud. of Luening, Beeson and Creston. He has taught at the U. of Massachusetts at Amherst and at Bowdoin College and has been active in various national organizations, incl. Asuc and Cms. His works are primarily for instruments, sometimes involving taped sounds and synthesizers.

Schwarz, Gerard (1947–) Amer. conductor and trumpeter, stud. of Vacchiano and Creston. He was a member of the American Brass Quintet, the American SO and the New York PO, but since 1976 he has concentrated on conducting, founding the "Y" Chamber SO in New York in 1977 and also conducting the Los Angeles Chamber Orch. (1978–85) and the Seattle Symphony from 1983. He has appeared regularly with the Mostly Mozart Festival in New York.

Schwarzkopf, Elisabeth (1915–) Polish-born German soprano, stud. of Maria Ivogün. She is noted as a recital and concert artist, one of the leading Lieder singers, and has also sung a number of operatic roles (esp. the Marschallin in *Der Rosenkavalier* and the Countess in *The Marriage of Figaro*) at Covent Garden, La Scala, San Francisco, the Metropolitan Opera and other major houses. She has recorded many of her best roles and a large Lieder repertory.

Schwebung ['shvā-bûng] (Ger.) VIBRATO.

Schweitzer, Albert (1875–1965) Alsatian organist, theologian, philosopher, humanitarian and physician, a noted Bach scholar and editor of Bach's organ works. He concertized in Europe when on leave from his African hospital and was interested in the restoration of old organs.

Schwung [shvûng] (Ger.) swing, spirit.

sciolto ['shol-tō] (It., loose) **1**, with freedom. **2**, detached, nonlegato.

scoop to slide up to a pitch from below; the term is usu. applied in singing, where it is considered an undesirable mannerism.

scordatura (It., faulty tuning) the use of unusual tuning of a string instrument to achieve pitches not normally available, to produce special effects (such as new tonal colors or greater brilliance) or to simplify certain technical passages. The notation is usu. similar to that of a transposing instrument, i.e., the pitches notated are the pitches to be fingered, not the sounding pitches.

score a manuscript or printed representation of a musical work in staff notation with barlines to show vertical alignment. Cf. FULL SCORE, PIANO SCORE, VOCAL SCORE, OPEN SCORE, CLOSE SCORE, MINIATURE SCORE.

scoring the arrangement of a work for ensemble by assigning the parts to the various instruments. Cf. ORCHESTRATION, INSTRUMENTATION.

scorrendo *also,* **scorrevole** (It.) flowing, gliding.

Scotch snap a rhythmic figure in which a dotted note is preceded, not followed, by its complementary shorter note (as ♫). Also, *Scotch catch.*

Scott, James (Sylvester) (1885–1938) Amer. ragtime composer and pianist. From the early 1900s to 1922 he composed rags and toured as a performer. Later he played for silent films and led a dance band.

Scott, Tony (Anthony Sciacca) (1932–) Amer. clarinetist, saxophonist, composer and arranger, an experimenter with free jazz and atonality. He was a sideman with Buddy Rich, Charlie Ventura and Claude Thornhill, among others, and has led his own groups from the mid 1950s. In the early 1960s he was in the Far East, incorporating elements of Eastern music into his jazz. Since 1970 he has lived in Italy.

Scotti, Antonio (1866–1936) Italian baritone, stud. of Ester Trifari-Paganini. He sang regularly at the Metropolitan Opera and Covent Garden from 1899 until his retirement in 1933. His roles incl. Scarpia (*Tosca*) and Falstaff, as well as the lyric roles of Donizetti and Bellini.

Scottish Fantasy a concerto for violin

Scordatura

Normal tuning (Accordatura)　Scordatura tuning　*written*

IVIIIIII　IVIIIIII

sounds

(Biber, "Mystery" Sonata)

and orch., Op. 46 (1880), by Bruch, based on Scottish melodies.

Scottish Symphony popular name for the Symphony No. 3 in A minor, Op. 56 (1842), by Mendelssohn, inspired by his 1829 visit to Holyrood Castle in Edinburgh.

Scotto, Renata (1934–   ) Italian soprano, stud. of Emilio Giriardini and Mercedes Llopart. She has sung regularly at La Scala, Covent Garden and the Metropolitan Opera as well as at other major houses in a wide variety of roles ranging from Cio-cio-san (*Madame Butterfly*) to Amina (*The Elixir of Love*). She has been noted for her interpretative skill and dramatic intensity.

scraper an IDIOPHONE consisting of a rough, corrugated surface in any of various shapes scraped by a hard object of wood, metal, plastic or other material.

Scratch Orchestra an unusual orch. of amateurs and professionals founded in 1969 by English composer CORNELIUS CARDEW to perform new music. The orch. later concentrated on revolutionary and protest music.

scratching **1**, a technique used by disc jockeys of rotating a record back and forth beneath a stationary stylus to produce a rhythmic scratching sound. **2**, a group of techniques used by disc jockeys to produce continuous music from a succession of recordings, usu. employing multiple variable-speed turntables. The techniques incl. transition without break from one recording to another, using variable speed controls to match the tempos of the two songs, and rapid alternation between two recordings to intermix portions of two songs. Cf. HIP-HOP.

Scriabin, Alexander (1872–1915) eccentric Russian composer and pianist, stud. of Taneyev, Safonov, Arensky and Zverev. He pursued an active concert career despite his unusually small hands. From the turn of the century he became increasingly preoccupied with mystical philosophies, resulting in a shift of direction in his compositions. His works combine an acute awareness of sensuality and color in music and of the relationship between music and visual stimulation and incl. 3 symphonies, *Le Poème de l'extase*, *Prométhée*, many works for solo piano (incl. 10 sonatas, études, impromptus, preludes) and chamber music. Cf. COLOR ORGAN.

Scruggs, Earl (Eugene) see FLATT AND SCRUGGS.

Scruggs-picking a banjo technique using the thumb and first and second fingers, developed by Earl Scruggs.

Scythian Suite concert suite for large orch., Op. 20 (1915), by Prokofiev, drawn from an unfinished ballet *Ala and Lolly*.

sea shanty SHANTY.

Searle, Humphrey (1915–82) English composer and writer, trained at the Royal College of Music and with Webern in Vienna. He worked for the BBC in the 1940s and for Sadler's Wells Ballet in the 1950s. His own works, most of which employ a strict 12-tone serial technique, incl. 3 operas (all to his own librettos), ballets, symphonies and other works for orch., chamber works, many choral works and songs.

Seasons, The **1**, (Ger., *Die Jahreszeiten*) secular oratorio for soprano, tenor and bass soloists, chorus and orch. in four parts (1801) by Haydn on a text translated and adapted by Baron van Swieten from James Thomson's poem. The English text most often used in performance is not the original poem, but a translation of van Swieten's German text. The four parts correspond to the four seasons. **2**, ballet (1900) by Glazunov, with choreography by Petipa. **3**, see FOUR SEASONS, THE.

Sea Symphony, A the Symphony No. 1 for soprano, baritone and orch. (1903–9) by Vaughan Williams, a setting of poems by Walt Whitman.

Seattle Opera opera org. founded in 1964 under general dir. Glynn Ross. In 1975 the company inaugurated a summer presentation of Wagner's complete *Ring* cycle in German and English.

Seattle Symphony Orchestra orch. founded in 1903 and reorganized in 1926. Music directors have incl. Hadley, Beecham, Rosenthal, Katims and Schwarz.

sec [sek] (Fr.) *also,* **secco** ['sek-kō] (It.) dry, short.

secco recitative see RECITATIVE.

second the INTERVAL between any two adjacent diatonic scale degrees. A *major second* is equal to a whole tone, a *minor second* equals a semitone, an *augmented second* is a major second increased by a chromatic semitone, and a *diminished second* (the term is rarely used) is a minor second reduced by a chromatic semitone (the same as an ENHARMONIC equivalent).

second inversion see INVERSION.

second pan GUITAR (2,).

seconda prattica (It.) see PRIMA PRATTICA.

seconda volta (It.) second time, as of a repeated phrase. See VOLTA.

secondary dominant in tonal harmony, a chord functioning as a DOMINANT to a degree other than the tonic of the prevailing tonality, as a dominant seventh chord on the sixth degree cadencing to the second degree (VI-II). The term is sometimes used to refer specifically to the dominant of the dominant (V of V). Also, *applied dominant.*

secondo (It., second) the lower part of a DUET.

second touch a special effect available on some organ manuals by which additional pressure on a manual or pedal key activates additional stops to provide accent, color, etc.

Second Viennese School a term for Schoenberg and the composers who studied with him in Vienna (or in Germany) in the early 20th c., esp. Webern and Berg. The term presupposes an earlier "first school" of composers active in Vienna during the late 18th and early 19th c., i.e., Haydn, Mozart, Beethoven and Schubert.

section a group of instruments of the same type functioning as a unit in a larger ensemble, as the string section of an orch.

Sedaka, Neil (1939–) Amer. popular singer and songwriter, a longtime collaborator with lyricist Howard Greenfield. Their hit songs incl. "Breaking Up Is Hard to Do" (1962) and "Laughter in the Rain" (1974).

Seefried, Irmgard (1919–88) German-born Austrian soprano, trained at the Augsburg Conservatory. She sang in all the major opera houses of Europe and the Americas, specializing in the soubrette roles of Mozart and Strauss. She also appeared frequently in concert and recital.

Seeger, Charles (Louis) (1886–1979) Amer. composer, musicologist and teacher, trained at Harvard. He taught at the U. of California at Berkeley, in New York at the Institute of Musical Art and the New School for Social Research. He was later active in the Federal Music Project, the Pan-American Union, the AMS (of which he was a founder) and the Society for Ethnomusicology. His second wife was composer RUTH CRAWFORD.

Seeger, Pete(r R.) (1919–) Amer. folk singer, guitarist, banjoist and songwriter, son of CHARLES SEEGER. He was a founder of the ALMANAC SINGERS in 1941 and the WEAVERS in 1949. He has made many recordings of folk music and children's songs and has appeared widely in concert, esp. in support of various political causes.

Seeger, Ruth Crawford CRAWFORD, RUTH.

Seger, Bob (Robert) (1945–) Amer. hard rock and soul singer, songwriter and guitarist, achieving national prominence with his albums *Live Bullet* and *Night Moves* (both 1976).

segno ['sā-nyō] (It., sign) a sign or symbol, esp. one used for the beginning or end of a repeat (𝄋). Cf. DAL SEGNO.

Segovia, Andrés (1893–1987) Spanish guitarist, completely self-taught. He was largely responsible for the renewed popularity of classical guitar, through his own virtuoso performances, his enrichment of the repertory with arrangements and commissions and his encouragement of young guitarists. He has taught in Siena, Berkeley and elsewhere.

segue ['se-gwā] (It., it follows) **1**, a transition from one musical section to another. **2**, ATTACCA.

seguidilla [sā-gē'dē-lyä] (Sp.) a Spanish dance of varying steps and character in moderate triple time and usu. accompanied by guitar and castanets. A famous example is sung by Carmen in Bizet's opera. Cf. BOLERO.

Seiber, Mátyás (György) (1905–60) Hungarian-born British composer, conductor and teacher, stud. of Kodály. Highly respected as a teacher, he taught at the Hoch Conservatory in Frankfurt from 1928, then in England at Morley College from 1942. He was active as a conductor, esp. of his own works, and founded the Dorian Singers in 1945. His works incl. an opera and several other dramatic works, works for orch. and for jazz band, *Ulysses*, (for tenor, chorus and orch.), choral works, songs and chamber music.

Seidl, Anton (1850–98) Hungarian conductor, assistant to Wagner at Bayreuth, then conductor at the Metropolitan Opera and of the New York PO. He was esp. noted for his performances of Wagner and Bruckner and conducted the world premiere of Dvořák's Symphony No. 9 in E minor, *From the New World*.

seis [sās] (Sp.) an unaccompanied S. Amer. dance-song.

Selby, William (c1738–98) English composer and organist. He was active in Boston from 1771 as an organizer of concerts and as organist at various churches, notably Stone Chapel.

Selika (née Smith), **Marie** (Williams, Mrs. Sampson) (c1849–1937) Amer. soprano, trained in San Francisco, Boston and England. She was successful as a concert artist in the late 19th c., touring with her husband.

Selmer French wind instrument

manufacturer founded in Paris in 1885 by Henri Selmer.

SEM *abbr.* SOCIETY FOR ETHNOMUSICOLOGY.

Sembrich, Marcella (Kochánska, Prakseda Marcelina) (1858–1935) Polish-born Amer. lyric soprano, stud. of G.B. Lamperti. She sang at most major opera houses in Europe and the U.S. and was a regular at the Metropolitan Opera from 1883 till her retirement from opera in 1909. She continued to sing in concert until 1917. Her roles incl. Susanna (*The Marriage of Figaro*) and Violetta (*La Traviata*).

semibreve (Brit.) WHOLE NOTE.

semichorus 1, a passage to be sung by a portion of the singers of a chorus. **2**, the group performing such a passage.

semi-opera a type of spoken English Restoration drama with subsidiary musical scenes performed by secondary characters. The most noted examples are by Purcell and include *King Arthur* (1691) and *The Fairy Queen* (1692).

semiquaver (Brit.) SIXTEENTH NOTE.

Semiramide [sā-mē'rä-mē-dā] (It., Semiramus) tragic opera in 2 acts by Rossini to a libretto in Italian by Gaetano Rossi after Voltaire. Premiere, Venice 1823. Rossini's last *opera seria*, a story of incest in Babylon.

semitone HALF TONE.

Semkow, Jerzy (1928–) Polish conductor, trained in Kraków and Leningrad and with Erich Kleiber, Walter and Serafin. He has been music dir. of the St. Louis SO and the Rochester PO and has appeared with other leading orchestras in No. Amer. and Europe.

Semper Paratus song (1928) by Capt. Francis Saltus von Boskerck, the official march of the U.S. Coast Guard.

semplice ['sem-plē-chā] (It.) simply.

sempre ['sem-prā] (It.) always.

Senesino (Bernardi, Francesco) (c1680–c1755) Italian contralto castrato. After Senesino sang in Italy for almost 15 years, Handel brought him to London where he was a star at the King's Theatre (1720–8), singing in virtually all the operas produced there during that period. He sang again in London in the mid-1730s, then returned to Italy, where he probably retired around 1740.

Senfl, Ludwig (c1486–1543) Swiss composer, probably a stud. of Isaac in Augsburg. He was a member of the Emperor Maximilian's chapel until 1519, then in 1523 joined the court chapel of Duke Wilhelm of Bavaria. His extensive output, mainly vocal music, includes Mass settings, motets and other sacred works, odes and a large number of German Lieder.

sennet in Elizabethan theater, a fanfare on cornets or trumpets signaling the ceremonial entrance or exit of actors.

senza ['sen-tsä] (It.) without.

septet *also*, **septette 1**, a group of seven musicians **2**, the music for such a group.

septolet [sep-to'lä] (Fr.) SEPTUPLET.

septuor [sep'tüor] (Fr.) SEPTET.

septuplet a group of seven notes to be played in the time of four or six of the same notated value. Also, *septolet, septimole.*

sequence 1, a medieval Latin chant of extended length, usu. syllabic, setting a text intended for a specific use, such as *Victimae paschali laudes*, an Easter sequence. **2**, a short musical phrase which is repeated at successively higher or lower pitch levels, either exactly or modified to conform to the current tonality. Cf. ROSALIA.

sequencer an electronic device used to produce repetitions of the same musical material. The device actually

Sequence (2,)
Non-modulating Modulating
(exact repetition)

↖ repeated unit ↗

stores only the information about the sounds, not the sounds themselves, which are recreated on playback (often with modifications) by a synthesizer.

Serafin, Tullio (1878–1968) Italian conductor, trained at the Milan Conservatory. He was principal conductor at La Scala in the 1910s and 1920s, then a conductor at the Metropolitan Opera from 1924 to 1934, at the Rome Teatro Reale until 1943 and at the New York City Opera and the Chicago Lyric Opera in the 1950s. He continued to conduct into his 80s. He was an outstanding interpreter of Italian opera and a supporter of American music and conductors.

Serebrier, José (1938–) Uruguayan-born Amer. conductor and composer, trained at the Montevideo Conservatory and with Giannini, Monteux and Dorati. He has been assoc. with various U.S. orchestras, incl. the Minneapolis SO, the American SO and the Cleveland Orch. (as composer-in-residence) and was the founder of the International Festival of the Americas (1984). His works are mainly for instruments and some involve mixed-media presentation.

serenade 1, a courting or love song, often accompanied by guitar or other plucked instrument. **2**, a type of instrumental DIVERTIMENTO for various instrumental ensembles, usu. performed outdoors in the evening.

serenata (It.) **1**, a pastoral CANTATA, usu. written for a specific event. **2**, SERENADE.

Serenata notturna (It., Nocturnal Serenade) the serenade for strings and timpani, K. 239 (1776), by Mozart.

serialism a method of composition by which a short series of notes, durations, dynamics, timbres, etc., is manipulated by various means (esp. RETROGRADE, INVERSION or RETROGRADE INVERSION) to provide all the notes, etc., for an entire work or section. Any number of the parameters of a work may be treated serially, the most common being pitch and dura-

Serialism

Row (Melodic series)
(N.B. Notes are natural unless preceded by an accidental.)

O (original)

1 2 3 4 5 6 7 8 9 10 11 12

R (retrograde)

1 2 3 4 5 6 7 8 9 10 11 12

I (inversion)

1 2 3 4 5 6 7 8 9 10 11 12

RI (retrograde inversion)

1 2 3 4 5 6 7 8 9 10 11 12

Rhythmic series

1 2 3 4   5 6   7 8 9   10 11 12

Dynamic series

mf fp ff ppp f p ffff mp pp sf pppp fff

1 2 3 4   5 6 7 8   9 10 11 12

Example of Total Serialism

(Notes in the left hand with stems down are the
inversion of the melody and the
retrograde of the rhythms of the
right-hand melody. Chords with stems up
are a verticalization of the retrograde inversion.)

tion. Cf. TWELVE-TONE MUSIC, TOTAL
SERIALISM.

series an ordered succession of notes,
durations, etc., used as compositional
material. See SERIALISM, ROW.

serious music a condescending (and
erroneous) term usu. used to distinguish CLASSICAL MUSIC from other
types of music (jazz, rock, etc.).

Serkin, Peter (1947–) Amer. pianist, son of RUDOLF SERKIN, stud. of his
father and Horszowski. He performs
a wide repertory of styles, incl. 20th-
c. music. He was a co-founder in 1973
of the chamber ensemble Tashi and
has also performed with other chamber and orchestral ensembles.

Serkin, Rudolf (1903–91) Austrian-
born Amer. pianist, stud. of Richard
Robert, Joseph Marx and Schoenberg.
His U.S. debut was in 1933 in recital
with violinist Adolf Busch, with
whom he frequently collaborated in
duo performance. He taught at the
Curtis Institute from 1939 and was a
founder of the Marlboro Festival. He
was noted for his bold interpretations
of the Classical and Romantic repertory.

Serly, Tibor (1901–78) Amer. composer, violist, teacher and theorist,
stud. of Kodály, Leó Weiner and Hubay. He played in the Cincinnati SO,
the Philadelphia Orch. and the NBC
SO and has conducted his own works
with various orchestras. He was a
supporter of Bartók during the composer's last years in the U.S. and reconstructed the viola concerto from
Bartók's sketches. Some of his own
works are based on his "modus las-
civius," an alternative to 12-tone serialism.

Sermisy, Claudin de (c1490–1562)
French composer of chansons, Mass
settings and other sacred vocal music.
He apparently served a succession of
French kings and worked at the
Sainte-Chapelle. He was highly re-
garded as a composer of both sacred
and secular music.

Serocki, Kazimierz (1922–81) Polish
composer and pianist, stud. of Sikorski, Boulanger and Levy. He toured as
a concert pianist until 1951, then concentrated on composition. His works
incl. 2 symphonies (one with soloists
and chorus), concertos, songs and
choral works, chamber music for
trombones and percussion and works
for piano.

serpent an 18th- and 19th-c. bass
wooden HORN having a cupped

mouthpiece, a long, serpentine, conical tube with fingerholes and a strong, rough sound. It is related to the CORNET (1,).

Serva padrona, La (It., The Maid Mistress) comic opera in 1 act by Pergolesi to a libretto by Gennaro Antonio Federico. Premiere, Naples 1733. The maid Serpina intrigues to make her employer, the bachelor Uberto, marry her.

service an Anglican liturgical office set to music; specif., a setting of the canticles for matins, evensong and certain other offices.

SESAC Inc. an Amer. music licensing agency founded in 1931.

sesquialtera 1, in MENSURAL NOTATION, a rhythm of three minims in the space of the two preceding. Cf. HEMIOLA. **2**, a mixture ORGAN STOP having a brilliant tone produced by two ranks of pipes reinforcing the high harmonics.

session musician *also,* **sessionist** an instrumentalist (or, more rarely, vocalist) hired to play in a recording session for records, film, TV or commercial advertising. Also, *studio musician.*

Sessions, Roger (Huntington) (1896–1985) eminent Amer. composer and teacher, stud. of Parker and Bloch. He taught at Smith College, the Cleveland Institute, the U. of California at Berkeley and for many years at Princeton, where he was also a co-director of the Columbia-Princeton Electronic Music Center. With Copland he ran the Copland-Sessions Concerts of Contemporary Music in New York (1928–31) and was active in the American branch of the ISCM. He won a Pulitzer special citation in 1974 and a Pulitzer Prize for his Concerto for Orch. in 1982. He taught many of America's most distinguished young composers, incl. Kirchner, Del Tredici, Martino and Babbitt. Sessions's works incl. *The Trial of Lucullus* and *Montezuma* (operas), incidental music for *The Black Maskers*, 8 symphonies, a concerto for piano and a double concerto

for violin and cello, choral works (incl. *When Lilacs Last in the Dooryard Bloom'd*), songs, string quartets and sonatas for piano.

sestina a form of Italian verse set by composers of frottole and madrigals. Each stanza consists of six lines with a rhyme scheme of abcdef. Every stanza has not only the same rhyme scheme, but the rhyming words are always identical.

set a term borrowed from mathematics for a collection of notes used as a compositional element which may be modified in various ways. In TWELVE-TONE MUSIC the specific set of pitches is called a ROW. Cf. RETROGRADE, INVERSION, COMBINATORIALITY, SERIALISM.

Ševčík, Otakar ['shev-chik] (1852–1934) Czech violinist and teacher, trained at the Prague Conservatory. He taught in Kiev, Prague, Vienna and Písek, developing a widely followed teaching method based on the semitone system.

Seven Deadly Sins, The (Ger., *Die sieben Todsünden der Kleinbürger*) *ballet chanté* (sung ballet) in seven scenes with songs (1933) by Weill to a text by Bertolt Brecht.

Seven Last Words, The 1, orchestral work in seven movements (1785) by Haydn, composed for the Cathedral of Cadiz as interludes between the sermons on Good Friday. Haydn later made arrangements of the work for string quartet (1787) and as an oratorio for soloists, chorus and orch. (1795–6). **2**, oratorio for soloists, chorus and instruments (1645) by Schütz. **1776** musical by Sherman Edwards, book by Peter Stone, based on a concept by Edwards. Premiere, New York 1969. The story of John Adams's efforts to break down the opposition to independence in prerevolutionary America.

seventh an INTERVAL covering seven diatonic scale steps, as, from C to B. A *major seventh* is a semitone smaller than an octave, a *minor seventh* is a whole tone smaller than an octave, a *diminished seventh* is a minor seventh reduced by a chromatic semitone, and an *augmented seventh* is the enharmonic equivalent of an octave.

seventh chord a four-note CHORD composed of a triad and a seventh. The *major seventh chord* has a major triad and a major seventh; the DOMINANT SEVENTH CHORD, a major triad and a minor seventh; the *minor seventh chord*, a minor triad and a minor seventh; and the DIMINISHED SEVENTH CHORD, a diminished triad and a diminished seventh.

Severinsen, Doc (Carl Hilding) (1927–) Amer. trumpeter and bandleader, lead trumpet in a number of swing bands, then popular bandleader on television, esp. for the "Tonight" show. He has given many trumpet clinics and toured extensively.

Sex Pistols English punk-rock band formed in 1975 in London. The band, headlined by Johnny Rotten (John Lydon) and later Sid Vicious (John Ritchie), provoked outrage and broke up in 1978 during its first U.S. tour.

sext 1, one of the LESSER HOURS of the divine office of the Roman Catholic church, occurring at about 12 noon. **2,** SIXTH.

sextet *also,* **sextette 1,** a composition in six parts. **2,** the group playing such a work.

sextolet *also,* **sextole** SEXTUPLET.

sextuor [sex'tüor] (Fr.) SEXTET.

sextuplet a group of six notes played in the time of four notes of the same notated value.

sf. *abbr.* SFORZANDO.

sfogato [sfō'gä-tō] (It., let out) **1,** light, airy. **2,** with a high, light tone.

sforzando [sfor'tsän-dō] *also,* **sforzato** [-'tsä-tō] (It.) **1,** accented. Abbr., *sf.,* *sfz.* **2,** an organ piston which instantly adds additional stops for sudden dynamic effects.

sforzando-piano (It.) an indication to apply a *sforzando* accent and then immediately become softer. Abbr., *sfp.*

sfp. *abbr.* SFORZANDO-PIANO.

sfz. *abbr.* SFORZANDO.

shag Amer. jazz dance popular in the 1930s and 1940s.

shake 1, TRILL. **2,** a slow, lascivious jazz dance popular in the first third of the 20th c.

shaker a percussion instrument used esp. in dance bands, consisting of a container filled with a rattling material such as beans or pebbles.

shakuhachi (Jap.) a Japanese end-blown bamboo FLUTE with four holes and a wide bore.

Shalyapin CHALIAPIN.

shamisen SAMISEN.

Shanet, Howard (1918–) Amer. conductor and writer, stud. of Koussevitzky and Honegger, among others. He has taught at Hunter College (NY) and Columbia and has been conductor of the Music-in-the-Making concerts in New York and the String Revival string orch.

shango a dance of Trinidad, a predecessor of the MAMBO.

shank a short tube inserted between the mouthpiece and the main tubing of a brass instrument to adjust the pitch.

Shankar, Ravi (1920–) Indian sitar player and composer, very popular in the U.S. in the late 1950s and 1960s, teacher of and collaborator with many Western musicians, incl. Yehudi Menuhin and George Harrison of the Beatles.

shanty *also,* **shantey, chantey** a work song sung by or about sailors. The songs were separated into various categories, depending on which task (hauling, pumping, etc.) the song was intended to accompany. Also, *sea shanty.*

shape-note notation a system of notation using note shapes to indicate scale degree (or name in a system of solmization). The most common systems were the four-note FASOLA system and various seven-note systems. Shape-note notation was used from the beginning of the 19th c. primarily for hymn singing and is still in use in some parts of the U.S. Other terms for the shape note are *patent note,* *character note, buckwheat note.*

fa sol la fa sol la mi fa

Shapero, Harold (Samuel) (1920–)
Amer. composer and teacher, stud. of
Slonimsky, Piston, Krenek, Hindemith and Boulanger. He has taught at
Brandeis since 1951, where he also
founded an electronic music studio.
His works, primarily instrumental,
have embraced a variety of styles and
media, incl. 12-note serialism, jazz
and electronic sounds.

Shapey, Ralph (1921–) Amer. composer and conductor, stud. of Wolpe.
Since 1954 he has conducted the Contemporary Chamber Players at the U.
of Chicago, where he also taught
(1964–91). He has also appeared as
guest conductor with a number of
U.S. orchestras, usu. performing his
own works. Between 1969 and 1976
he protested against conditions in the
musical world by refusing to permit
his music to be performed. His works
incl. *Double Concerto* for violin and
cello, *Grotou* and *Sinfonie concertant*
and other orchestral works, 7 string
quartets, a chamber symphony, many
works for instrumental chamber ensembles, works for piano and songs
for voice(s) with instruments.

Shaporin, Yuri (1887–1966) Russian
composer and teacher, trained (at the
age of 26) at the St. Petersburg Conservatory. In the 1920s and 1930s he
was musical dir. of several Leningrad
theaters and was a co-founder of the
Association for Contemporary Music. From 1939 he taught at the Moscow Conservatory. His works incl.
the opera *The Decembrists*, incidental music for theater and films, several orchestral works, choral music,
songs, sonatas and other works for
piano.

sharp 1, a musical sign (♯) indicating
a chromatic raising of the PITCH of a
note by a half step. In medieval notation the sharp sign is used as a NAT-
URAL sign as well to cancel a preceding flat. Cf. DOUBLE SHARP. **2**, above
the prevailing pitch level by a percep-

tible amount; said of an instrument,
voice, etc.

Shavers, Charlie (Charles James)
(1917–71) Amer. jazz swing trumpeter and arranger. He first established a reputation as performer and
arranger in the John Kirby Sextet,
then worked with Tommy Dorsey
until the late 1950s. He later played
in studio bands and small groups. He
was noted for his bravura playing and
improvisation.

Shaw, Alice J. (1856–1918) Amer.
virtuoso whistler, much in demand as
a concert artist in the early 20th c.

Shaw, Artie (Arshawsky, Arthur Jacob) (1910–90) Amer. jazz swing
bandleader, clarinetist and composer.
After playing with various bands and
in the studios, he formed his first
band in 1936, an unusual combination of strings, clarinet and rhythm
section, to which he later added other
winds and a singer. For the next
twenty years he led a variety of
groups, establishing a major following and a reputation to rival that of
Benny Goodman.

Shaw, Robert (Lawson) (1916–)
Amer. conductor, trained at Pomona
College (CA) and later with Monteux
and Rodzinski. He organized and conducted the Fred Waring Glee Club,
the Collegiate Chorale (New York)
and his own Robert Shaw Chorale
(1948–67). He was assoc. with the
San Diego SO and the Cleveland
Orch., then became music dir. of the
Atlanta SO (1967–87). His mastery of
choral groups is universally recognized.

Shaw, Woody (Herman) (1944–89)
Amer. jazz trumpeter. He performed
in a variety of groups with such performers as Eric Dolphy and Horace
Silver and co-led a quintet with drummer Louis Hayes. He was known for
his cerebral yet fiery improvisations.

shawm *also*, **shalm** an early one-
piece double-reed instrument made
in a range of sizes from high treble to
great bass, a predecessor of the OBOE.
The Renaissance shawm usu. had a

REEDCAP covering the reed. Cf. POMMER.

Shawnee Press Amer. firm of music publishers founded in 1939 in Pennsylvania by conductor FRED WARING.

Shchedrin, Rodion (1932–) Russian composer, stud. of Shaporin, a successful composer within the guidelines of the Soviet system. His works incl. the opera *Not Love Alone* (1961), the ballet *The Little Humpbacked Horse* (1956), 2 symphonies, 2 piano concertos, string quartets, cantatas and works for piano. His orchestral work *Chimes* (1967) was written for the New York PO.

Shearing, George Albert (1919–) English bop pianist, blind from birth. He is noted for his use of the LOCKED HANDS style of playing, utilized in a quintet consisting of piano, vibraphone, guitar, bass and drums. He has also performed classical concertos with orch. He was the composer of "Lullaby of Birdland" (1952).

Shebalin, Vissarion Yakovlevich (1902–63) Russian composer and teacher, stud. of Myaskovsky at the Moscow Conservatory, where he taught after 1928. Official and critical acceptance of his music in the USSR were not always forthcoming; he was ousted from the Conservatory for several years in the late 1940s in a purge. His works incl. *The Taming of the Shrew* (opera), ballets, a musical, incidental music, 5 symphonies, orchestral suites and concertos, several cantatas, 9 string quartets, sonatas and works for piano and guitar.

Shéhérazade (Fr.) SCHEHERAZADE.

shekeree [shā-kāerā] (Sp.) a large CABAÇA.

sheng a Chinese HARMONICA dating from the 6th c. B.C. and used in Confucian ceremonial music. It consists of 17 bamboo pipes controlled by fingerholes and mounted on a copper wind chest.

Shepherd, Arthur (1880–1958) Amer. composer, conductor and teacher, stud. of Goetschius and Chadwick. He taught at the New England Conservatory (1909–20), then was active in Cleveland as teacher at Western Reserve U., as a music critic and in various capacities with the Cleveland Orch. He wrote works in all genres except stage music, incl. 5 string quartets, 2 symphonies, a violin concerto, choral music and songs.

Shepherd, John SHEPPARD, JOHN.

Shepherd on the Rock, The (Ger., *Der Hirt auf dem Felsen*) song for soprano, clarinet and piano (1828) by Schubert, a setting of a poem by Wilhelm Müller.

Shepp, Archie (Vernon) (1937–) Amer. free jazz saxophonist, a collaborator with Cecil Taylor, Bill Dixon and Don Cherry and a teacher at SUNY, Buffalo, and the U. of Massachusetts. From the mid-1960s he has led his own groups.

Sheppard, John (c1515–c1560) English composer, a Gentleman of the Chapel Royal from about 1545. His surviving works incl. Mass settings, motets and anthems.

Shere, Charles (1935–) Amer. composer and critic, stud. of Berio and Erickson. He has taught at Mills College and was a music producer for several radio stations in the San Francisco area. His music is experimental, incl. the opera *The Bride Stripped Bare by Her Bachelors, Even* (1964); text works for chorus; chamber music and works for small orch.

Sherman, Russell (1930–) Amer. pianist, stud. of Edward Steuermann. He has taught at Pomona College, the U. of Arizona and the New England Conservatory and is highly respected for his virtuosity and profoundly imaginative interpretations.

Sherry, Fred (Richard) (1948–) Amer. cellist and conductor, stud. of Leonard Rose and Channing Robbins. A champion of new music, he founded SPECULUM MUSICAE, was a founding member of TASHI and is a performer with the Chamber Music Society of Lincoln Center.

Shifrin, Seymour (1926–79) Amer. composer and teacher, stud. of Luening. He has taught at the U. of California at Berkeley and at Brandeis.

Most of his works are for smaller instrumental ensembles or vocal forces, incl. 5 string quartets, a cello sonata, a chamber symphony and songs.

shift the displacement of the stopping hand (usu. the left) on the fingerboard of a string instrument from one position to another.

shimmy an Amer. dance of the 1910s and 1920s involving a rapid gyration of the torso, incorporated into a number of ballroom dances, incl. the Charleston and the Lindy.

Shirley, George (Irving) (1934–) Amer. lyric tenor, stud. of Thelmy Georgi and Cornelius Reid. His Metropolitan Opera debut was in 1961, and he also sang at Glyndebourne, Covent Garden, Santa Fe and the New York City Opera, among many other houses. He has been very active as a teacher and coach.

Shirley-Quirk, John (1931–) English bass-baritone, stud. of Roy Henderson. He has sung regularly with the English Opera Group and other English opera companies and in opera and concert in the U.S. (his Metropolitan Opera debut was in 1974).

shiwaya a S. Afr. VESSEL FLUTE made from a hollow fruit shell.

shō a Japanese harmonica similar to the SHENG, used in the gagaku orch.

shofar *also,* **shophar** (Heb.) a ram's horn blown as a trumpet, orig. as a battle signal, now used in religious services. Its provenance and use are strictly regulated by the Talmud.

Shore, Dinah (Frances Rose) (1917–) Amer. popular singer, esp. noted as a radio and television artist, having her own TV show in the 1950s.

Shorter, Wayne (1933–) Amer. jazz saxophonist and composer. He was a member of the JAZZ MESSENGERS (1959–63) and of Miles Davis's quintet (1964–70), then co-founded the jazz-rock group Weather Report. He is equally important as performer and composer, using pantonal or nontonal harmonies.

short octave a special tuning for the incomplete lowest octave of some early keyboard instruments, eliminating less often used notes and replacing them with other, lower, more frequently used ones. In general, the diatonic white keys are tuned normally, and the chromatic black keys are retuned to lower diatonic notes. Some short-octave instruments use split keys to produce two different notes. Also, *broken octave.*

short score a condensed orchestral score omitting the less important parts or compressing several parts onto the same staff. The term is also used for a composer's working sketch on a few staves indicating intended orchestration. Also, *compressed score.*

Shostakovich, Dmitri (1906–75) Russian composer, trained at the Petrograd Conservatory with Glazunov and others. During his distinguished career he had several major stylistic conflicts with the Soviet authorities but managed to reconcile his artistic requirements with those of the state, remaining a dominant figure in Soviet musical life. He is best known for his symphonies, a number of which are directly related to major events in Soviet history. He also produced orchestrations of Mussorgsky's *Khovanshchina, Boris Godunov* and *Songs and Dances of Death.* His works incl. 15 symphonies, orchestral suites, operas (incl. *Lady Macbeth of Mtsensk* and *The Nose*), ballets, many film scores, incidental music, an operetta, choral works, songs, 15 string quartets, sonatas for cello and viola, a piano quintet and works for piano solo.

Shostakovich, Maxim (1938–) Russian conductor and pianist, son of DMITRI SHOSTAKOVICH, trained at the Moscow Conservatory. He has conducted the Moscow PO and the USSR State SO on tour and has appeared as guest conductor with a number of orchestras in Europe and the U.S.

shout a style of loud, forceful blues singing dating from the SWING era. The term is sometimes used for instrumental music with a similar style.

Show Boat musical by Jerome Kern, lyrics and book by Oscar Hammerstein II, based on the novel by Edna Ferber. Premiere, New York 1927. Magnolia and Ravenal fall in love and act in showboat productions on the Mississippi in the mid-1880's.

shuffle an Afr.-Amer. dance characterized by a flat-footed, dragging step and foot tapping.

Shuffle Along musical by Noble Sissle and Eubie Blake, book by Flournoy Miller and Aubrey Lyles. Premiere, New York 1921. The story of a three-way race for the mayoralty of Jimtown, Dixieland. The longest-running musical produced, written and acted by blacks, presented in a run-down lecture hall north of the Broadway theater district.

Shumsky, Oscar (1917–) Amer. violinist and conductor, stud. of Auer and Zimbalist. He played with the NBC SO under Toscanini and in the Bach Aria Group and was leader of the Primrose Quartet. He was music dir. of the Stratford Festival in Ontario (1959–67) and conductor of the Westchester SO. He has taught at the Peabody Conservatory, the Curtis Institute and the Juilliard School.

Shure, Leonard (1910–) Amer. pianist, stud. of Schnabel, for whom he worked as an assistant. He has performed with all of the major Amer. orchestras and has been an active chamber music pianist. He has taught at the Longy School (Cambridge, MA), the New England Conservatory, the Mannes College and Boston U. and his pupils incl. many now prominent musicians, incl. Ursula Oppens, George Cleve and Pinchas Zukerman. He is assoc. in particular with the standard Classical and Romantic repertory.

si the note B in the SOLFEGGIO system. Also, *ti*.

Sibelius, Jean (Johann) **(Julius Christian)** (1865–1957) Finnish composer and violinist, stud. of Wegelius, of Albert Becker in Berlin and of Goldmark and Fuchs in Vienna. His reputation as Finland's leading composer was established in the late 19th c., and an international reputation followed. He was esp. noted as a symphonic composer. He wrote almost no music after the mid-1920s, his last major work being the tone poem *Tapiola* (1926). Sibelius wrote 7 symphonies, incidental music (*Pelléas and Mélisande, Belshazzar's Feast*), tone poems (*Lemminkäinen Suite, Finlandia, En saga*), many choral works and songs, chamber music (incl. the string quartet *Voces Intimae*) and works for piano.

siciliana [sē-chē'lyä-nä] *also*, **siciliano** (It.), **sicilienne** [sē-sē'lyen] (Fr.) **1**, a Sicilian rustic dance in 6/8 or 12/8 time similar to the PASTORALE, in which the dancers are joined with handkerchiefs. **2**, a stylized, instrumental form of the dance found in the baroque dance suite, opera, etc.

side drum a shallow, two-headed FRAME DRUM used in orchestras and military bands.

sideman any instrumentalist in a band aside from the bandleader.

Sidlin, Murray (1940–) Amer. conductor, stud. of Celibidache and Husa. He has been music dir. of the New Haven SO, the Tulsa PO and the Long Beach (CA) SO and resident conductor of the Aspen Music Festival.

Siegfried opera in 3 acts by Wagner to his own libretto, the third section of the cycle *The Ring of the Nibelung*. Premiere, Bayreuth 1876. The hero Siegfried, who knows no fear, forges the sword Nothung, kills the giant Fafner and the dwarf Mime, shatters the spear of the Wanderer (Wotan) and claims Brünnhilde from the magic fire.

Siegfried Idyll a chamber work (1870) by Wagner based on themes from his opera *Siegfried*. The work was composed as a birthday present for his second wife, Cosima.

Siegmeister, Elie (1909–91) Amer. composer and conductor, stud. of Bingham, Riegger, Stoessel and Boulanger. He taught at Hofstra U. (1949–76), was a founder of the American Composers Alliance and a member of the Composers Collective of New York. His compositions often incorporate elements of jazz and blues as well as Amer. folk and popular music. His works incl. 6 operas, a ballet, a musical (*Sing Out, Sweet Land*), 6 symphonies, concertos (for piano, clarinet, flute and violin), works for band, choral and solo vocal music, chamber music (3 string quartets, 5 violin sonatas) and works for piano.

Siepi, Cesare (1923–) Italian bass, a member of the Metropolitan Opera from 1950 to 1974, where he sang the major Italian lyric bass roles, as well as Boris Godunov, Mephistopheles (*Faust*) and Mozart's Figaro.

sigh SLIDE (1,).

sighting *also,* **sight** a Middle English term for the technique of improvising a DISCANT above or below plainchant.

sight-reading the action of reading or the ability to read music at sight without prior rehearsal or practice.

sight-singing the performance at sight of vocal music (see SIGHT-READING).

signal a short musical figure for

Trumpet Signals

Reveille

Charge

Taps

To the Colors

trumpet or drum, used as a call to a certain action. The most common use is military, as in a call to charge, retreat, etc. Cf. SENNET, FANFARE (1,).

signature see KEY SIGNATURE, TIME SIGNATURE.

signature tune a melody, song, etc., chosen as the theme music of an orch., performer or performing ensemble.

Silbermann, Gottfried (1683–1753) one of a family of German builders of keyboard instruments.

Silence popular name for *4'33"* for any instrument(s) (1952) by Cage, in which the performer does not play at all for the duration of the work.

Silent Night song with music by Franz Gruber (1787–1863) and words by Joseph Mohr (1792–1848), used as a Christmas carol.

Sills, Beverly (Silverman, Belle Miriam) (1929–) Amer. soprano and opera dir., stud. of Estelle Liebling. She sang regularly with the New York City Opera from 1955, becoming dir. in 1979. Her Metropolitan Opera debut was not until 1975, four years before her retirement from the stage. As a performer, she was esp. noted for her portrayal of bel canto roles.

Silver, Horace (Ward Martin Tavares) (1928–) Amer. jazz bop pianist, composer and bandleader, known for his funky, simple, tuneful phrases. He toured with Stan Getz, then freelanced in New York. He was a member and co-leader of the JAZZ MESSENGERS (1953–5) before forming his own quintet, which served as a training ground for many young players. Among his own compositions that have become standards are "Señor Blues" and "Doodlin'."

Silverman, Stanley J(oel) (1938–) Amer. composer, stud. of Kirchner, Milhaud, Cowell and Ussachevsky. He has been active in music theater for most of his career, serving as music dir. of the Vivian Beaumont Theater (NY) and the New York Shakespeare Festival, among other positions. In addition to much incidental music, he has written operas (incl. *Elephant Steps, Dr. Selavy's Magic Theatre* and *Madame Adare*), film scores and chamber music.

Silverstein, Joseph (1932–) Amer. violinist and conductor, stud. of Zimbalist, Gingold and Mischakoff. He was a member of the Boston SO from 1955 to 1983, becoming concertmaster in 1962 and assistant conductor in 1971. He won the Naumburg Foundation Award in 1960. He has taught at the New England Conservatory, Boston U. and the Berkshire Music Center and has concertized extensively. He was music dir. of the Worcester SO, principal guest conductor of the Baltimore SO and has been artistic dir. of the Utah SO since 1983.

sim. *abbr.* SIMILE.

similar motion the simultaneous movement in the same direction of two or more parts in a polyphonic texture.

simile ['sē-mē-lā] (It., like) **1**, a term directing that a certain indicated articulation, phrasing, bowing, etc., is to be continued, even though the marking is not repeated. Abbr., *sim*. **2**, *also*, **simile mark** a sign (usu. •/•) indicating the repetition of a preceding measure or phrase as often as the sign occurs.

Simionato, Giulietta (1910–) Italian mezzo-soprano, stud. of Locatello and Palumba. She sang regularly at La Scala from 1946, as well as at Covent Garden, Chicago Lyric (1954) and the Metropolitan Opera (from 1959), specializing in bel canto repertory. She retired in 1966.

Simmons, Calvin (Eugene) (1950–82) Amer. conductor and pianist, stud. of Rudolf Serkin and Max Rudolf. He was assistant conductor of the San Francisco Opera and the Los Angeles PO and became music dir. of the Oakland SO three years before his untimely death. He also conducted a number of major orchestras in No. America and at Glyndebourne.

Simon, Carly (1945–) Amer. popular singer and songwriter. After early years as a folk singer she attained suc-

cess in the popular field, incl. the hits "You're So Vain" (1972) and "Nobody Does It Better" (1977).

Simon, Paul (1942–) Amer. popular singer, guitarist, songwriter and actor, best known as half of the duo SIMON AND GARFUNKEL and writer of most of their hits, incl. "Bridge over Troubled Water" (1970) and "Mrs. Robinson" (1968). He has also had substantial success as a solo artist ("Second Avenue").

Simon and Garfunkel Amer. popular and folk duo, formed by PAUL SIMON and ART GARFUNKEL in 1964 and active until the early 1970s.

Simoneau, Léopold (1918–) Canadian tenor, stud. of Salvator Issaurel and Paul Althouse. A specialist in Mozart roles, he has sung at most major European opera houses and festivals and at the Metropolitan Opera. He has taught at the Montreal Conservatory and was artistic dir. of L'Opéra du Québec.

Simone Boccanegra (It.) opera in 3 acts by Verdi to a libretto in Italian by Francesco Maria Piave, revised by Boito, based on a play by Antonio Gutiérrez. Premiere, Venice 1857; revised version Milan 1881. A complex story of intrigue and love in Venice.

simple interval an INTERVAL of an octave or less. Contrasted with COMPOUND INTERVAL.

simple meter *also*, **simple time** a METER whose main beats are divisible by 2. Contrasted with COMPOUND METER.

Simple Symphony string symphony in 4 movements in the Classical style, Op. 4 (1934), by Britten.

Simpson, Christopher (c1605–69) English composer, viol player and theorist, best known for his didactic works *The Division-Violist* (1659) and *A Compendium of Practical Musick* (1665).

Simrock German music publishing firm founded in 1793 by Nicolaus Simrock (1751–1832).

Sims, Ezra (1928–) Amer. composer, stud. of Kirchner, Milhaud and Porter. After years as a computer programmer with the Harvard Music Library, he was music dir. of the New England Dinosaur Dance Theatre and their new music ensemble Dinosaur Annex, both of which groups performed his music. His works incl. both instrumental and tape music, the latter utilizing microtones and collage techniques.

Sims, Zoot (John Haley) (1925–85) Amer. jazz tenor saxophonist, a member of the orchestras of Benny Goodman, Gerry Mulligan, Woody Herman (he was one of the Four brothers) and Stan Kenton and a frequent collaborator with Al Cohn.

Sinatra, Frank (Francis Albert) (1915–) Amer. popular singer and actor. He became famous as a singer with Harry James and esp. Tommy Dorsey in the early 1940s. After a slump in the early 1950s he achieved a comeback in films (*From Here to Eternity, Guys and Dolls, Man with the Golden Arm*) and recordings. His artistry combines operatic, jazz and popular crooner styles.

Sinding, Christian (August) (1856–1941) prolific Norwegian composer, trained at the Leipzig Conservatory. He spent much of his career in Germany and also taught briefly at the Eastman School. His works, popular in his own time, have been largely forgotten, with the exception of some songs and piano pieces.

sinfonia (It., symphony) **1**, an instrumental Canzone (2,) of the 17th c. **2**, a type of orchestral composition of Italian origin similar to a Prelude and found in 17th-c. vocal music and as an overture (usu. in three movements) in 18th-c. opera. Cf. Overture.

Sinfonia Antarctica the Symphony No. 7 for soprano, small women's chorus and orch. (1949–52) by Vaughan Williams.

sinfonia concertante (It.) Symphonie concertante.

sinfonietta 1, a small orch., esp. a string orch.; **2**, a short symphony or other orchestral work, esp. for small string or chamber orch.

Singher, Martial (Jean-Paul) [sĕ'ger] (1904–90) French-born Amer. baritone and teacher, stud. of Juliette Fourestier. He sang in Paris for many years at the Opéra and the Opéra-Comique. After coming to the U.S. in 1941 he sang at the Metropolitan Opera until 1959 and taught at the Mannes College, the Curtis Institute and the Music Academy of the West. His many pupils incl. Donald Gramm and Louis Quilico.

singing the production of musical sounds with the voice. In previous centuries singing of art, popular and folk music was largely limited to conventional musical sounds. 20th-c. composers, however, have incorporated many unconventional vocal noises into their works, requiring singers to broaden their technical resources. Cf. Sprechstimme, Parlando.

singing birds a clockwork bird that produces birdlike sounds by means of a small organ pipe. The machine may also produce motions, flapping its wings, etc.

singing in tongues a form of ecstatic, improvised singing in incomprehensible (and probably invented) language, forming part of the services of various Pentecostal churches of the 19th and 20th c.

singing saw Saw, musical.

singing-school a series of instructional sessions popular in 18th- and 19th-c. Amer. for teaching vocal technique, sight-reading and hymn-singing.

single a phonograph record with one song to each side, as opposed to an album.

Singleton, Zutty (Arthur James) (1898–1975) Amer. jazz drummer from New Orleans, an early proponent of wire brushes and other innovative techniques, and known for his recordings with Louis Armstrong, Jelly Roll Morton and Barney Bigard, among others. In later years he played in Dixieland bands in New York.

Singspiel ['zing-shpēl] (Ger., singplay) a type of German dramatic musical work dating from the late 16th c. and esp. popular in the 18th c., similar to opera, but having spoken dialogue interspersed with popular or folk songs, or art music in such a style. The term was sometimes used in a broader sense to refer to any dramatic work including vocal music.

sinistra *also,* **mano sinistra** [sē′nē-strä] (It.) left hand.

Sinopoli, Giuseppe (1946–) Italian composer and conductor, stud. of Maderna, Stockhausen and Swarowsky. In Venice he taught at the Conservatory and was founder of the Bruno Maderna Ensemble for contemporary music. He has since then established a successful conducting career and has appeared with orchestras and opera companies in the U.S. and Europe.

si placet (Lat.) see AD LIBITUM.

Sissle, Noble (Lee) (1889–1975) Amer. singer, composer and lyricist, best known for his collaborations with EUBIE BLAKE which produced such musicals as *Shuffle Along* (1921) and *Chocolate Dandies* (1924).

sistro (It.) **1**, SISTRUM. **2**, a type of GLOCKENSPIEL mounted in a small frame, usu. with a handle and called for in some 18th-c. Italian opera scores.

sistrum (Lat.) a metal RATTLE, esp. an ancient Egyptian idiophone having a thin, metal frame and numerous small, metal rods that jingle against it when shaken.

sitar *also,* **sittar** a long-necked, plucked Hindu LUTE, usu. having a gourd resonator, five melody strings (as well as drone and sympathetic strings) and movable frets. The instrument has been utilized since the 1960s in some Western art and popular music.

sit in in jazz, to join in performance or jam session with a band or group of which one is not a regular member.

Sitzprobe [′zits″prō-be] (Ger.) in opera, a musical rehearsal with orch. but with no stage action.

Six, Les [sēs] (Fr.) French group of composers formed about 1918 under the influence of Satie, devoted to incorporating the influence of everyday life, popular music and jazz in a music of brevity and honesty. The composers were Auric, Durey, Honegger, Milhaud, Poulenc and Tailleferre; their spokesman was Jean Cocteau. The group presented concerts for the three years of its existence.

Six Characters in Search of an Author symbolic opera in 3 acts by Weisgall to a libretto in English by Denis Johnston, based on the play by Luigi Pirandello. Premiere, New York 1959. Six representative characters from an unfinished opera intrude upon a rehearsal and reveal their interrelationships.

six-four chord a TRIAD in second inversion, i.e. containing the fourth and sixth from the bass note. In functional harmony the chord is unstable and must be resolved, usu. by the sixth and fourth resolving to the fifth and third above the bass.

sixteen-foot stop a pipe ORGAN STOP producing tones an octave below the notated pitch.

sixteenth note a NOTE (♪) having one-sixteenth the duration of a whole note. It is written with two flags or beams.

sixth an INTERVAL covering six diatonic scale steps, as from C to A. A *major sixth* equals three whole tones plus a semitone, a *minor sixth* equals three whole tones, an *augmented sixth* (rare as a melodic interval) is a semitone larger than a major sixth, and a *diminished sixth* (rare) is a semitone smaller than a minor sixth.

sixth chord a TRIAD in first inversion, i.e. containing the third and sixth from the bass note. Consecutive sixth chords are a characteristic of certain medieval techniques, such as FABURDEN. Also, *six-three chord.* Cf. NEAPOLITAN SIXTH CHORD, AUGMENTED SIXTH CHORD, GERMAN SIXTH, FRENCH SIXTH, ITALIAN SIXTH.

six-three chord SIXTH CHORD.

sixty-fourth note a NOTE having one sixty-fourth the duration of a whole note, written with four flags or beams. See NOTES AND RESTS (*illus.*).

sizzle cymbal a Turkish CYMBAL used esp. in popular music, having small, loose rivets inserted around the inside of the rim that produce a sizzling sound when the cymbal is struck.

ska a type of Jamaican popular dance music of the late 1950s, a fusion of MENTO and RHYTHM-AND-BLUES; a predecessor of ROCK STEADY and REGGAE.

Skaggs, Ricky (1954–) Amer. country-music singer, guitarist and mandolinist. He played with various groups, incl. the Stanley Brothers and the Country Gentlemen, before forming his own group, Boone Creek. He has also led Emmylou Harris's Hot Band. His work is known for its relative freedom from pop influence.

Skalkottas, Nikos (1904–49) Greek composer and violinist, stud. of Jarnach, Schoenberg and Weill. He lived in Berlin until 1933, when financial and personal problems drove him to return to Athens, leaving his music behind him. In Athens he worked as a back-desk violinist and composed at night. He wrote a substantial body of both tonal and serial works, almost exclusively for orch., chamber ensemble or solo piano.

sketch **1**, a short composition for piano. **2**, preliminary musical material written down as part of the compositional process.

skiffle orig., a type of musical entertainment of the 1930s incl. blues, boogie-woogie and other styles. During the mid-1950s folk revival in the U.S. and England, skiffle bands, often composed of amateurs, were formed that used folk instruments such as guitar, harmonica, washboard and kazoo. Professional bands in England usu. employed a more conventional combination of guitars and drums. The major hit of the style was "Rock Island Line" (1956), performed by Lonnie Donegan.

Skillet Lickers Amer. country-music string band formed in 1926 by fiddlers Gid Tanner and Clayton McMichen and guitarist Riley Puckett. The group was active until about 1934 and made very successful recordings of rustic comedy numbers and traditional songs.

Skilton, Charles Sanford (1868–1941) Amer. composer, trained at Yale and the Berlin Hochschule für Musik. He taught at several different institutions, incl. the U. of Kansas, and was esp. interested in the music of Native Americans, which influenced his own works. His compositions incl. 3 operas, orchestral suites, cantatas and songs, 2 string quartets and other chamber music.

skins colloquial term for drums.

Skryabin SCRIABIN.

Skrowaczewski, Stanislaw [skrō-vä'chev-skē] (1923–) Polish-born Amer. conductor and composer, trained in Kraków and with Boulanger and Paul Kletzki in Paris. He has been music dir. of the Minneapolis SO (1960–79) and the Hallé Orch. (from 1983) and has conducted at the Metropolitan Opera and elsewhere in the U.S. and Europe.

slancio, con ['slän-chō] (It.) with dash or vigor.

slap in jazz, a vigorous attack, such as plucking a string so that it slaps against the fingerboard on the double bass or vigorous blowing on a saxophone that causes the reed to slap against its seat.

slapstick WHIP.

Slatkin, Leonard (1944–) Amer. conductor, stud. of Susskind and Morel. Except for two years in New Orleans, he has been assoc. with the St. Louis SO from 1968, becoming music dir. in 1979, and he has also appeared as a guest conductor with many major orchestras. He has championed American music and initiated a number of commissions.

Slåtter Norwegian peasant fiddle dance-tunes, transcribed for piano by Grieg as his Op. 72.

Slaughter on Tenth Avenue ballet with music by Richard Rodgers, part of the musical *On Your Toes* (1936).

Slavonic Dances two sets of orchestral dances, Op. 46 (1878) and Op. 72 (1886), by Dvořák.

Sleeping Beauty, The ballet in 3 acts (1890) with music by Tchaikovsky to a book by choreographer Marius Petipa and Ivan Vsevolojsky, after fairy tales by Charles Perrault.

sleigh bells a type of orch. JINGLE consisting of a number of small bells attached to a strap with a handle, used to imitate the sound of real sleigh bells.

slentando [zlän'tän-dō] (It.) RALLENTANDO.

Slezak, Leo (1873–1946) Austrian-Czech tenor, stud. of Adolf Robinson and Jean de Reszke. He sang with the Vienna Staatsoper (1901–33), the Metropolitan Opera (1909–12) and at Covent Garden and was also highly regarded as a singer of Lieder.

slide **1**, an ORNAMENT consisting of two grace notes approaching a main note in conjunct motion from the same direction. **2**, a term for a GLISSANDO whose exact character depends on the instrument being played. On a string instrument, the slide is usu. a result of a SHIFT of position; it may also be used as a special effect. Slides are also possible on brass instruments equipped with a SLIDE (3,), such as the slide trombone and slide trumpet. **3**, a telescopic joint on a slide TRUMPET or slide TROMBONE, used to lengthen the tubing and produce different fundamental pitches.

slide guitar see STEEL GUITAR.

slider action an early type of pipe-organ mechanism for controlling air supply to a pipe by means of a hand-operated wooden tongue.

slide trombone see TROMBONE.

slide trumpet see TRUMPET.

slide whistle SWANNEE WHISTLE.

slit drum a type of DRUM made from a length of wood or bamboo hollowed out through a slit carved along one side. Slit drums are found in all sizes from lap-size to very large and are generally used for ceremonies and signaling.

slow drag a type of SHUFFLE of the late 19th and early 20th c., danced by couples to slow, sensual music.

slur **1**, a curved line over two or more consecutive notes indicating that they should be played connected (legato). In general, slurs indicate the desired result and not necessarily the exact articulation (bowing or breathing) for the player to observe. In certain types of baroque music, slurring may indicate presence or absence of NOTES INÉGALES. **2**, SLIDE (1,).

Sly and the Family Stone Amer. rock band formed in 1967 by singer and guitarist **Sly Stone** (Stewart, Sylvester) (1944–   ) and active until the late 1970s. Their many hits incl. "Everyday People" (1968) and "There's a Riot Goin' On" (1971).

Smallens, Alexander (1889–1972) Russian-born Amer. conductor, trained at the New York Institute of Musical Art and the Paris Conservatoire. He was conductor of the Chicago Opera (1919–23) and the Philadelphia Civic Opera (1924–31) and assistant conductor of the Philadelphia Orch. (1927–34). He later conducted the Lewisohn Stadium concerts and was music dir. of Radio City Music Hall. He retired in 1958.

Smalley, Roger (1943–   ) avant-garde English composer and pianist, trained at the Royal College of Music and in Cologne with Stockhausen, whose piano works he frequently performs. Many of his works involve tape or electronic manipulation of live sounds.

smear a GLISSANDO, esp. on the slide trombone.

Smetana, Bedřich (Friedrich) (1824–84) prolific Czech. nationalist composer and pianist, stud. of Josef Proksch. Until the mid-1850s he taught in Prague at his own music institute, founded in 1848. He moved to Götebord, Sweden, in 1856, where he opened a school, gave concerts and composed. He returned to Czechoslovakia in 1861, and in 1866 he became principal conductor of the Provisional Theater in Prague. His final ten years were marked by increasing deafness and other symptoms of syphilis. Smetana's works incl. *The Bartered Bride, Dalibor, Libuše, The Kiss* and *The Devil's Wall* (operas), tone poems (incl. *Ma Vlast*), 2 string quartets, a piano trio, choral works, songs and many piano works.

Smit, Leo (1921–　) Amer. composer and pianist, stud. of Vengerova and Nabokov. He has taught at Sarah Lawrence College, UCLA and SUNY, Buffalo. His works incl. 3 symphonies, a piano concerto, 2 ballets, 2 operas, chamber music and choral works.

Smith, Arthur (Leroy) (1898–1971) Amer. country-music fiddler, singer and songwriter, noted for his use of blue notes, double stops and slides. He appeared on the Grand Ole Opry from 1927 and was a founder of the Dixieliner String Band. After World War II he played and recorded with various artists, incl. the Delmore Brothers.

Smith, Arthur ("Guitar Boogie") (1921–　) Amer. country-music guitarist and banjoist, a member of the Rambler Trio. He was one of the first to record the boogie-woogie guitar style, a forerunner of rock-and-roll.

Smith, Bessie (Elizabeth) (1894–1937) Amer. blues and jazz singer, "Empress of the Blues." In the late 1920s and early 1930s she established her reputation, recording blues and jazz standards that featured Clarence Williams, Louis Armstrong and many others.

Smith, Gregg (1931–　) Amer. conductor and composer, trained at UCLA. He has taught at Ithaca College, the Peabody Conservatory, Barnard College and the Manhattan School. He is best known as conductor of the Gregg Smith Singers, an influential chamber choir, formed in 1955, which has performed and recorded a wide repertory from the Renaissance to the 20th c.

Smith, Hale (1925–　) Amer. composer, trained at the Cleveland Institute of Music. He taught at the U. of Connecticut from 1970 until his retirement in 1984. His works incl. *Blood Wedding* (opera), several orchestral works, a cello sonata, chamber music, songs and choral works.

Smith, Huey "Piano" (1934–　) Amer. rock-and-roll pianist and songwriter, a member of the vocal group the Clowns.

Smith, Jabbo (Cladys) (1908–　) Amer. jazz trumpeter, trombonist and singer, a talented artist of the late 1920s and 1930s in the bands of Charlie Johnson and James P. Johnson (and distinguished in recordings with Ellington). From about 1940 to 1970 he worked odd nonmusical jobs in Milwaukee, reappearing in the 1970s to play at Preservation Hall and elsewhere.

Smith, Jimmy (James Oscar) (1925–　) Amer. jazz organist, known as the "Father of Jazz Organ." He was one of the first to use the electric organ as a complete jazz instrument in small combos. He has continued to tour in the 1980s.

Smith, John Stafford (1750–1836) English composer, stud. of Boyce and a Gentleman of the Chapel Royal. He is remembered as the composer of the song "To Anacreon in Heaven," which in 1814 provided the tune for "The Star-Spangled Banner."

Smith, Julia Frances (1911–89) Amer. pianist and composer, trained at the Juilliard School and New York U. She performed in concert and recital until the 1960s and composed works in all genres.

Smith, Lawrence Leighton (1936–　) Amer. conductor and pianist, stud. of Leonard Shure and Ariel Rubstein. He has been conductor of the Oregon SO, the San Antonio SO and the Louisville Orch. and is also active as an accompanist.

Smith, Leland C(layton) (1925–　) Amer. composer, clarinetist, bassoonist and teacher, stud. of Milhaud, Sessions and Messiaen. He has taught at Mills College, the U. of Chicago and at Stanford (since 1958), where he has done extensive research on computerized music printing and composition.

Smith (née Robinson), **Mamie** (1883–1946) Amer. jazz singer, the first black jazz-blues singer to record. Her recording of "Crazy Blues" in 1920 was a major success and was followed by many others, as well as film appearances.

Smith, N(athaniel) Clark (1877–1933) Amer. conductor, composer and teacher, trained at the Guildhall School and the Chicago Musical College, during which time he formed an Afr.-Amer. symphony orch. and a Ladies' Orch. He later taught at the Tuskegee Institute and at various high schools in Chicago and St. Louis and organized the Pullman Porter Band for Pullman railroad employees.

Smith, Pine Top (Clarence) (1904–29) Amer. jazz pianist and singer, said to be the inventor of the term *boogie-woogie*, used for his recording of "Pine Top's Boogie Woogie" (1928).

Smith, Stuff (Hezekiah Leroy Gordon) (1909–67) Amer. jazz swing violinist and singer, a long-time collaborator with trumpeter Jonah Jones in performance at the Onyx Club in New York in the late 1930s and 1940s.

Smith, Willie "The Lion" (William Henry Joseph Bonaparte Bertholoff) (1897–1973) Amer. jazz stride pianist and composer, made famous by recordings issued in the mid-1930s and later. His compositions were performed in the 1940s by Tommy Dorsey, Artie Shaw and others.

Smith Brindle, Reginald (1917–) English composer, stud. of Pizzetti and Dallapicolla. He taught at the U. of Bangor (Wales) and the U. of Surrey. He has written works in a wide variety of genres and styles, concentrating on instrumental music, incl. a number of works for guitar and guitar ensembles.

smorz. *abbr.* SMORZANDO.

smorzando [smor'tsän-dō] (It.) dying away; becoming gradually softer and slower. Abbr., *smorz.* Cf. MORENDO.

SMPTE time code ['simp-tē] a standard developed by NASA and the So-

ciety of Motion Picture and Television Engineers for synchronization of audio and visual information, multiple recorders, etc.

Smyth, Dame **Ethel (Mary)** (1858–1944) English composer, trained in Leipzig at the Conservatory and privately. She is best known for her operas, incl. *Der Wald* (1899–1901), *The Wreckers* (1903–4) and *The Boatswain's Mate* (1913–4). She also wrote a mass, songs, a concerto for violin and horn, and chamber music.

Snape Maltings an opera house and concert hall in ALDEBURGH, England, opened in 1967.

snare drum a SIDE DRUM having one or more strings of gut or metal (*snares*) stretched across its lower head to produce a rattling effect when the drum is played. See DRUMS (*illus.*)

Snow, Hank (Clarence Eugene) (1914–) Canadian country-music singer, guitarist and songwriter. He initially made his name broadcasting from Halifax, NS, then joined the Grand Ole Opry in 1950. He recorded for RCA from 1936 to 1981 and was the first Canadian artist elected to the Country Music Hall of Fame (1979).

soave [sō'ä-vä] (It.) gentle, sweet.

soca a style of Lat.-Amer. popular music combining elements of SOUL and CALYPSO.

society band a jazz band, usu. with strings added, used primarily for accompanying society dances.

Society for Ethnomusicology an Amer. org. est. in 1955 in Philadelphia to advance study and research in the field of ethnomusicology. Abbr., *SEM.*

Söderström, (Anna) Elisabeth (1927–) Swedish soprano, trained in Stockholm. She has sung regularly with the Swedish Royal Opera, as well as in most major international opera houses. Her roles incl. the Marschallin (*Der Rosenkavalier*), the Countess (*The Marriage of Figaro*) and Mélisande. Her Metropolitan Opera debut was in 1959.

soft pedal a pedal on a piano that shortens the length of stroke of the hammer (on some upright pianos) or reduces the number of strings struck by the hammer (on grand pianos) to soften the sound. The latter type is also known as the *una corda* pedal. Cf. MODERATOR PEDAL.

soft rock a type of ROCK music characterized by slower, gentler rhythms and a softer dynamic. The term has also been applied to FOLK-ROCK.

soft shoe a type of Afr.-Amer. SHUFFLE similar to tap dancing, but without metal plates on the shoes.

soggetto [sŏd'jet-tō] (It., subject) **1**, a canon or fugue SUBJECT of moderate length. Cf. ANDAMENTO, ATTACCO. **2**, SOGGETTO CAVATO.

soggetto cavato (It., excavated subject) a musical theme derived from the letters, syllables or vowels of a name, such as ASCH or B-A-C-H, or Josquin's *Missa Hercules Dux Ferarriae*, based on the soggetto cavato re-ut-re-ut-re-fa-mi-re (D-C-D-C-D-F-E-D), derived from the vowels of the title.

soh the dominant of the current key (or of its relative major, if the current key is minor) in TONIC SOL-FA.

Soir, Le see MATIN, LE.

sol 1, the note G in the SOLFEGGIO system. **2**, the fifth degree of the Guidonian HEXACHORD.

Soldier's Tale, The (Fr., *Histoire du soldat*) tragicomedy in 2 acts by Stravinsky to a libretto in French by C.F. Ramuz. Premiere, Lausanne 1918. A soldier puts himself in the Devil's power, in the end losing his soul.

Soler (Ramos), Padre **Antonio** (1729–83) Spanish composer, organist and theoretician, stud. of Domenico Scarlatti and José de Nebra. He was a Jeronymite monk in the Escorial community, serving the royal family from the early 1750s. He is remembered for his many keyboard sonatas and for his treatise *Llave de la modulación . . .* (Key to modulation . . . , 1762). He also wrote a large body of sacred and secular vocal music.

Solesmes [so'lem] A Benedictine abbey in France dating from the 11th c. and noted for research in the notation and performance of Gregorian chant, culminating in the continuing series of publications *Paléographie musicale* (1880–).

sol-fa see TONIC SOL-FA.

solfeggio [sŏl'fed-jō] (It.), **solfège** [sol'fezh] (Fr.) a system for teaching sight-reading and ear-training using SOLMIZATION syllables, usu. do (or ut), re, mi, fa, sol, la, ti (or si). The term has also been used for untexted vocal exercises used in voice teaching.

Sollberger, Harvey (Dene) (1938–) Amer. flutist, composer, conductor and teacher, stud. of Baron, Luening and Beeson. He was co-founder of the Group for Contemporary Music, of which he is a dir., and has taught at Columbia, the Manhattan School and Indiana U., where he directs a contemporary music ensemble. Most of his own works involve the flute, usu. in combination with other wind instruments.

solmization the use of syllables to represent the tones of a musical scale, primarily used in sight-singing and

Solmization

memorization. Cf. GREAT SCALE, GUIDONIAN HAND, TONIC SOL-FA, SOLFEGGIO.

solo (It., alone) a piece for one performer, with or without accompaniment. In an ensemble context, the term may refer to a predominant line or to a section to be played by only one instrument or singer of a section.

Solomon (Cutner, Solomon) (1902–88) English pianist, stud. of Mathilde Verne (a pupil of Clara Schumann). He performed widely from the mid-1920s until 1965, when a stroke ended his career. He was highly respected as a sensitive interpreter as well as a virtuoso technician.

solo organ a pipe organ division consisting of SOLO STOPS.

solo sonata in the Baroque, a sonata for solo instrument and basso continuo (or occasionally for a single instrument alone). In more recent times, the term may refer to a work for solo instrument and piano or for a single instrument alone.

solo stop an ORGAN stop designed to be used for solo, melodic performance and not as part of a chorus.

Solovox (tradename) an electronic instrument with its own keyboard used to imitate various orchestral instruments to play a melody line with piano accompaniment.

Solti, Sir **Georg** (1912–) Hungarian-born British conductor, stud. of Dohnányi, Bartók and Kodály. He has been conductor of the Bavarian Staatsoper, general music dir. of the city of Frankfurt, and music dir. of Covent Garden (1961–71), the Chicago SO (1969–91) and the Salzburg Festival. He has also been assoc. with the Dallas SO, the Orchestre de Paris, the Paris Opéra and the London PO. He has made many recordings, incl. the first complete *Ring* cycle, and has won more than 20 Grammy awards.

Sombrero de tres picos (Sp.) THREE-CORNERED HAT, THE.

Somers, Harry (Stewart) (1925–) Canadian composer and pianist, stud. of Weinzweig and others. For most of his career he has supported himself through commissions and through work for CBC radio and TV. His works incl. an opera (*Louis Riel*), several ballets, a symphony, 2 piano concertos, many songs and choruses, 3 string quartets, 5 piano sonatas, 2 violin sonatas and chamber music.

sommeil [so'me-ē] (Fr., sleep) a conventional scene found in 17th- and 18th-c. stage works and occasionally in other forms, usu. consisting of an orchestral prelude and a vocal ensemble about sleep and frequently involving appropriate deities such as Morpheus.

Somogi, Judith (1937–88) Amer. conductor, stud. of Max Rudolf. She was assistant conductor at the New York City Opera, where she also conducted a number of productions, and she appeared with various orchestras and opera companies in the U.S. She was the first woman to conduct at a major Italian opera house and was principal conductor at the Frankfurt Opera from 1982 until her death.

son (Sp.) a type of Spanish folk dance-song accompanied by guitar ensemble.

sonajero [sō-nä'hä-rō] (Sp.) a type of Mexican RATTLE with a wooden frame.

sonata (It., sounded) an instrumental work, usu. in two, three or four movements and for one or more solo instruments or small chamber ensemble. The term orig. denoted instrumental rather than vocal music with little suggestion of form.

The Baroque sonata, used in church and for court functions, could be for solo instrument or for one or more solo instruments with basso continuo (or occ. fully written accompaniment) and usu. had several movements of contrasting tempi and natures, the most common schemes being slow-fast-slow-fast or fast-slow-fast. Cf. SONATA DA CAMERA, SONATA DA CHIESA.

The Classical sonata was more often for a solo melody instrument combined with a keyboard or other chord-playing instrument, in three or four movements, with the first nearly always fast and extended, the middle movement(s) slow and/or dancelike, and the last movement again fast. Formally the first movement was often in the elaborate binary form known as SONATA FORM, the slow movement in a simple binary form, the dance movement in ternary form, and the last movement in a rondo or other form. Substitutions were frequent, such as a variation form for one of the movements. The movements were conceived with a logical harmonic relationship between them.

Using the Classical sonata as a basis, composers of the Romantic era developed freer forms. Movements were melded together or eliminated, a cyclic structure was often superimposed and more daring harmonic relationships were attempted, while the instrumentation remained essentially the same. A similar development continued into the 20th c., while the strong harmonic connotations that had developed in the form in the Classical and Romantic eras made the transition to atonality difficult, though composers in the neo-Classical style made frequent use of the term. Atonal sonatas tend to have formal elements which are deliberately reminiscent of the tonal sonata. Cf. SONATINA.

sonata-allegro form SONATA FORM.

sonata da camera (It., chamber sonata) a 17th- or 18th-c. instrumental work for one or more solo instruments and basso continuo, a forerunner of the DANCE SUITE, consisting of several movements, most with dance names.

sonata da chiesa (It., church sonata) a 17th- or 18th-c. instrumental work, possibly orig. used as part of church ritual, consisting of three or four movements, usu. slow-fast-(slow)-fast, for one or more melody instruments and continuo. See SONATA.

sonata form a type of rounded, binary form developed in the Classical period and a primary building block for sonatas and sonata-type works (symphonies, quartets, etc.) from then to the 20th c. The standard sonata has two parts, the second one of which is divided into two sections. The first part (*exposition*) may begin with an introduction, then present a first theme group in the tonic key, followed by a second theme group in another key (usu. the dominant or relative of the orig. key), which ends the first half. The exposition is often repeated.

The second part is divided into the *development* and the *recapitulation*. The development in most cases draws on musical material from the exposition (and occ. the introduction), only rarely introducing new thematic material, and returns by a circuitous route to the tonic key. The recapitulation repeats the material of the exposition more or less exactly but entirely in the tonic key. The movement will usu. end with a CODA.

There are as many variations on the form as there are examples. 20th-c. composers working in an atonal style have sometimes used the thematic and developmental techniques of sonata form, but the lack of the tonal relationships that are basic to the form make the transition difficult. Also, *sonata-allegro form, first-movement form*. See FORMS (*illus.*).

sonata-rondo form a type of SONATA FORM incorporating elements of the RONDO. In its most common manifestation, in the exposition the second theme group (the first episode of the rondo) is followed by a return of the first theme group, sometimes in the key of the second theme group. Then comes a second episode, which may be a true development or be based on new material. A recapitulation follows, which often only repeats the material of the first episode, but in the tonic key, followed by the first theme group once more and a coda, or the coda alone. See FORMS (*illus.*).

sonatina 1, a short SONATA. **2,** a type

of Sonata form with shortened or omitted development section.

Sondheim, Stephen (Joshua) (1930–) highly successful Amer. composer and lyricist, stud. of Babbitt. As lyricist he has collaborated with Bernstein (*West Side Story*, 1957, and *Candide*, 1973), Styne (*Gypsy*, 1959) and Rodgers (*Do I Hear a Waltz?*, 1965). As a composer, his most successful shows have been *Company* (1970), *A Little Night Music* (1973), *Sweeney Todd* (1979) and *Sunday in the Park with George* (1984).

sone a subjective unit of Loudness based on the individual listener's threshold of hearing.

song 1, the act or process of singing. **2**, a work intended to be sung, esp. a work for one or more voices, accompanied or unaccompanied. The most common use of the term is for a work for solo voice with piano accompaniment. Cf. Chanson, Lied, Canzone. **3**, in popular music, a musical work, whether instrumental or vocal.

song cycle a set of songs, related by subject matter and usu. musically, as through key relationships, sharing motifs, style, etc. The form is essentially a 19th- and 20th-c. development. Some well-known examples are *Die schöne Müllerin* and *Die Winterreise* of Schubert, the *Dichterliebe* of Schumann, the *Kindertotenlieder* and *Lieder eines fahrenden Gesellen* of Mahler, *La Bonne Chanson* of Fauré and *A Charm of Lullabies* of Britten.

song form a rather misleading and vague term for a form used frequently for songs and short instrumental works, which may be simple Binary form, Rounded binary form or Ternary form. See Forms (*illus.*).

Song of Destiny (Ger., *Schicksalslied*) work for chorus and orch., Op. 54 (1871), by Brahms with words taken from a poem by Friedrich Hölderlin.

Song of Norway musical by Robert Wright and George Forrest, adapted from melodies by Edvard Grieg; book by Milton Lazarus, based on a play by

Homer Curran. Premiere, New York 1944. The dramatization of an episode in the life of composer Edvard Grieg.

Song of Orpheus a fantasy for cello and orch. (1961) by William Schuman, inspired by some verses from Shakespeare's *Henry VIII*.

Song of the Earth, The (Ger., *Das Lied von der Erde*) song cycle in six movements for tenor and mezzo-soprano with orch. (1908) by Mahler, who orig. intended the work to be his ninth symphony, but hesitated because of superstition to name it so (Beethoven and Schubert had died after completing their ninth symphonies). The text, taken from a German translation of six 8th-c. Chinese poems, deals with life's joys and sadness.

Song of the Night, The the Symphony No. 7 in E minor (1905) by Mahler, an unusual work in five movements with a first movement, a finale, a scherzo-type movement at the center, and two eerie "nightmusics" as the second and fourth movements.

Songs of a Wayfarer (Ger., *Lieder eines fahrenden Gesellen*) set of four songs with orch. (1884) by Mahler, settings of texts by the composer telling the story of a youth forsaken by his beloved. Music from three of the songs reappears in his First Symphony (1888).

Songspiel ['zong"shpēl] (Ger.) an English-German term coined by Weill and Bertolt Brecht for a theatrical cabaret show. The term was first applied by Weill to the orig. version of his opera Mahagonny.

songster 1, a name often given to 18th- and 19th-c. collections of songs or song lyrics, usu. published in pocket size. **2**, a singer; specif., an Afr.-Amer. singer in the Reconstruction era who performed ballads, minstrel songs and dance tunes, sometimes with a backup group of instrumentalists.

Songs without Words (Ger., *Lieder ohne Worte*) title given by Mendelssohn to eight books of piano works (1830–45) by himself and his sister Fanny.

songwriter a person who writes the music and/or the lyrics of a song. The term is usu. understood to refer to writers of popular songs in the 20th c. Cf. LYRICIST.

Sonnambula, La [sōn'näm-boo-lä] (It., The Sleepwalker) opera in 2 acts by Bellini to a libretto by Felice Romani. Premiere, Milan 1831. Through a misunderstanding resulting from Amina's sleepwalking, her marriage to Elvino is threatened.

sonnerie [son'rē] (Fr.) **1**, SIGNAL. **2**, a CARILLON.

sonore [so'nōr] (Fr.), **sonoramente** (It.) sonorously, resonantly.

Sons of the Pioneers Amer. country-music group, orig. formed as the Pioneer Trio in 1933 by lead singer ROY ROGERS, singer/songwriter Robert Clarence Nolan and tenor Tim Spencer, joined in 1944 by fiddler Hugh Farr. There were many changes to the group's personnel in the 1940s and 1950s; the original group was elected to the Country Music Hall of Fame in 1980.

son bouché [sō boo'shā] (Fr.) STOPPED NOTE.

son étouffé [sō nä-too'fä] (Fr.) damped note; usu. used for the harp.

Sontag, Henriette (Gertrud Walpurgis) (1806–54) German soprano, stud. of Anna Czegka in Prague. She was one of the outstanding sopranos of the mid-19th c., singing in the premieres of Beethoven's Ninth Symphony and the *Missa solemnis* and creating the role of Euryanthe in Weber's opera.

Sonzogno, Edoardo (1836–1920) Italian music publisher. He began publishing music in 1874 and inaugurated a contest for new operas in 1883. The 1884 prize was won by Mascagni's *Cavalleria rusticana* and the opera's enormous success established the reputations of both Mascagni and Sonzogno.

sop. *abbr.* SOPRANO.

Sophie Elisabeth, Dutchess of Bruns-wick-Lüneburg (1613–76) German composer of Singspiels and sacred songs, occasional student of Schütz.

sopra (It., above, over) a term used in piano music to indicate that one hand should cross over the other.

sopranino (It.) an instrument higher in pitch than the soprano instrument of the same family.

soprano (It.) **1**, the highest female voice, usu. ranging from c' to a" (and often higher). Cf. BOY SOPRANO, CASTRATO. **2**, one of the highest instruments in a family, playing approximately the same range as the vocal soprano (1,).

soprano clef the C CLEF on the first line of the staff, formerly used for notating soprano vocal lines.

Sor (Sors), **(Joseph) Fernando (Macari)** (1780–1839) Spanish guitarist and composer, active in Madrid until 1813, then in London and Paris. He performed widely and is best known for his compositions for guitar. He also wrote operas, ballets, symphonies, chamber music and vocal music.

sord. *abbr.* sordino (see MUTE).

sordine 1, a cone-shaped trumpet MUTE. **2**, *also*, **sourdine** a soft, low-pitched TRUMPET formerly used to give the signal to march in battle. **3**, a 17th-c. Italian KIT.

sordino (It.) MUTE.

sordone (It.) *also*, **sordun** a large Renaissance double-reed instrument similar to a BASSOON.

Sospetto, Il the Violin Concerto in C minor, RV199, by Vivaldi.

sostenente piano an experimental type of PIANO designed to make a sustained sound, usu. by means of a rosined wheel or mechanical bows.

sostenuto (It.) sustained.

sostenuto pedal an optional pedal on a piano that, when depressed, sustains selected notes or chords. It is usu. the middle pedal on a grand piano, but is often called the *third pedal* (not present on many European pianos). Distinguished from the sustaining or DAMPER PEDAL.

sotto (It.) beneath.

sotto voce ['vō-chā] (It.) very softly;

under the breath; used in instrumental and vocal music.

soubrette [soo'bret] (Fr.) in opera, a light lyric SOPRANO that sings supporting roles, usu. the intriguing maid, such as Despina in Mozart's *Così fan tutte.*

soul see SOUL MUSIC.

soul music a style of Afr.-Amer. secular popular music, combining elements of RHYTHM-AND-BLUES and GOSPEL MUSIC and dating from the 1960s, as in the music of Ray Charles and Dinah Washington. The term "soul" has also been used in jazz for a quality of performance reflecting the influence of black gospel music, seen in the work of such musicians as Milt Jackson and Horace Silver.

sound a sensation received by the auditory sense. Musical sound has traditionally been taken to mean pitched sound having a pleasing character, though in the 20th c. this definition has been considerably broadened to include any sound used in a musical context.

Sound is produced by causing vibrations (*sound waves*) initiated by a reed, membrane, string, the vocal cords, etc. to be transmitted through the air (or other medium) and received by the ear, a microphone, etc. The pitch of the sound depends on the frequency of the vibrations (*cycles per second*).

The essential characteristics of a sound are its beginning (*attack*); its continuation (*envelope*), usu. consisting of a series of relatively small changes in its amplitude; and its ending (*decay*). The *timbre* of the sound is defined by its components, i.e., the relative intensity of the fundamental tone and of the HARMONICS which occur simultaneously with that tone, which can range from a fundamental with no audible harmonics to *white noise*, in which the fundamental and all harmonics are of equal intensity. The timbre will also be affected by the FORMANTS of the amplification system, whether it be a simple speaking horn or an elaborate electronic system.

Systems of electronic or electromechanical synthesis of sound patterns have used a variety of means to produce the components of musical sound, with much success in the realm of noninstrumental electronic sounds; the successful re-creation of instrumental sound remains largely elusive, except by means of SAMPLING.

soundboard a resonant board in an instrument so placed as to reinforce the instrument's tones by sympathetic vibration.

sound hole an opening in the belly of a string instrument to increase resonance and volume. Cf. C-HOLE, F-HOLE, ROSE.

Sound of Music, The musical by Richard Rodgers, lyrics by Oscar Hammerstein II, book by Howard Lindsay and Russel Crouse, based on Maria Von Trapp's book, *The Trapp Family Singers.* Premiere, New York 1959. The story, set in Austria in 1938, of the TRAPP FAMILY and their escape after the German invasion.

soundpost a wooden post in a string instrument, set under the bridge to transmit its vibrations to the soundboard.

sound sheet *also,* **song sheet** a recording pressed on flexible vinyl for inclusion in a book, magazine, etc.

soupir [soo'pēr] (Fr.) **1,** a MORDENT. **2,** a QUARTER REST.

sourdine [soor'dēn] (Fr.) **1,** SORDINE (2,). **2,** SPINET. **3,** MUTE.

Sousa, John Philip (1854–1932) Amer. bandmaster, composer and lyricist, known as "The March King." He led the U.S. Marine Corps Band from 1880 to 1892, then formed his own band, gaining many players from the band of the late PATRICK GILMORE. Sousa's Band became immensely popular, touring No. America annually and Europe on several occasions. Sousa composed operettas, one of which, *El Capitan* (1895), has been revived in recent years. He also wrote a large number of songs and marches, incl. "Guide Right," "The Stars and Stripes Forever!" and "The

Salvation Army," as well as orchestral and chamber music.

sousaphone a large, circular bass TUBA with a flaring upright bell, later made rotatable.

soutenu (Fr.) SOSTENUTO.

Souterliedekens ["soo-tər'lē-də-kəns] (Dutch, Little Songs from the Psalter) a collection of rhymed Dutch psalms published in 1540 and set by various composers, the best known of which was Clemens non Papa.

Southerners, The musical by Will Cook, Broadway's first interracial musical. Premiere, New York 1902.

southern white rock a style of HARD ROCK combining country, blues and soul music, played by bands such as the Allman Brothers and Lynyrd Skynyrd.

South Pacific musical by Richard Rodgers, lyrics by Oscar Hammerstein II, book by Hammerstein and Joshua Logan, based on stories in James Michener's book *Tales of the South Pacific*. Premiere, New York 1949. A pair of love stories—a sailor and a Polynesian girl, and a French planter and a Navy nurse.

Souzay (Tisserand), **Gérard (Marcel)** (1918–) French baritone, stud. of Bernac, Lotte Lehmann and others. He is esp. noted as a recital artist and has performed extensively the Lieder and chanson repertory with pianist Dalton Baldwin. He has also performed on occasion in opera.

Sowerby, Leo (1895–1968) Amer. composer and organist, based for most of his career in Chicago as teacher at the American Conservatory of Music and organist and choirmaster at the Episcopal Cathedral of St. James. He received the Pulitzer Prize in 1946 for his cantata *Canticle of the Sun*. His works incl. concertos for piano, violin and organ, 5 symphonies, many choral works, chamber music, organ and piano music, and songs.

spacing the vertical arrangement of the notes of a chord with respect to the intervals between them. The spacing is determined by the placement of the three upper notes of the chord; the chord is in *close position* if they fall within an octave, otherwise it is in *open position*. Cf. CLOSE HARMONY.

spagane a S. Afr. wooden CLAPPER.

Spagna, La a BASSE DANSE tune often used as the cantus firmus for 16th and 17th c. works, esp. instrumental music and pedagogical exercises.

spagnoletta (It.) a 16th- and 17th-c. dance, the harmonic pattern of which was used as the basis for instrumental works and songs.

Spalding, Albert (1888–1953) Amer. violinist and composer, stud. of Augustin Lefort in Paris. He toured extensively until his retirement in 1950 and was noted for his refinement and interpretative powers.

Spanier, Muggsy (Francis Joseph) (1906–67) Amer. jazz cornetist and bandleader. He played in the orchestras of Ted Lewis and Ben Pollack in the 1930s, then formed his own Ragtime Band, which had a short but influential life. In the 1950s and 1960s he performed in various small Dixieland groups.

Spanisches Liederbuch ['spä-ni-shəs 'lē-dər-bookh] (Ger., Spanish Songbook) a collection of songs (1890) by Wolf, a setting of 44 Spanish poems of the 16th and 17th c. in German translation.

Spanish Hour, The HEURE ESPAGNOLE, L'.

Spanish Rhapsody RHAPSODIE ESPAGNOLE.

spasm band a type of Afr.-Amer. folk band of the early 20th c. in New Orleans, similar to a WASHBOARD BAND.

Spatzenmesse ['shpät-sən"me-se] (Ger., Sparrow Mass) the Missa Brevis in G major, K.220/196b (1775–6), by Mozart.

Spaur Mass [shpowr] the Missa Brevis in C major, K.258 (1776), by Mozart.

speaker key a key on a woodwind instrument which facilitates the production of the upper harmonics by opening or closing the *speaking hole*. Also, *register key*.

speaking stop an ORGAN STOP that produces a sound when activated, rather than operating a coupler, tremolo, etc.

Speaks, Oley (1874–1948) Amer. composer and baritone, best known for his many songs for voice and piano, incl. "On the Road to Mandalay" (1907) and "Hark, Hark, my Soul" (1923).

species counterpoint see COUNTERPOINT.

Speculum Musicae (Lat., mirror of music) a chamber music ensemble formed in 1971 in New York for the performance of contemporary music. The group won the first Naumburg Chamber Music Award in 1972 and has been in residence at Columbia since 1982.

speech song SPRECHSTIMME.

spezzato [spāt′sä-tō] (It., divided) see CORI SPEZZATI.

Spialek, Hans (1894–1983) Austrian-born Amer. composer, arranger and orchestrator of Broadway shows, incl. works by Rodgers and Porter.

spianato (It.) smooth, even.

spiccato [spēk′kä-tō] (It., detached) to be performed with a springing or bouncing bow. Also, ARCO SALTANDO. Cf. SAUTILLÉ.

Spiegel, Laurie (1945–) Amer. composer, stud. of Druckman. She has been esp. interested in the application of computers to music and has worked at Bell Telephone Laboratories and the WNET Experimental Television Laboratory. Many of her works involve electronics and film or videotape. She has also written ballets and instrumental works.

Spies, Claudio (1925–) Chilean-born Amer. composer and teacher, stud. of Boulanger, Fine and Piston. He has taught at Swarthmore College (1958–70) and Princeton (since 1970). He has written a number of vocal and choral works with instruments, as well as chamber music and *Tempi* and *Eights and Fives* for orchestra.

spike fiddle a type of folk FIDDLE whose neck pierces the body and projects as a spike at the base.

spinet 1, a small HARPSICHORD, often with a contoured (*bentside*) case and strings parallel to the keyboard, similar to the VIRGINAL. **2**, a compact, upright piano or electronic organ.

Spinners, The Amer. soul vocal group formed in 1957 in Detroit, esp. popular in the mid-1970s with such hits as "I'll Be Around" (1972) and "The Rubberband Man" (1976).

Spinning Song (Ger., *Spinnerlied*) a type of song portraying a character singing while spinning, usu. with an accompaniment of rapid, flowing figuration imitating the motion of the spinning wheel. Among many examples from the 19th c. are Senta's aria in Wagner's *The Flying Dutchman*, Schubert's song *Gretchen am Spinnrade* and the Song without Words in C major for piano, Op. 67 No. 4 (1845), by Mendelssohn.

spinto *also*, **lirico spinto** (It., pushed [lyric]) the heaviest form of the LYRIC voice, capable of more power and drama than the standard lyric. The term is usu. applied to tenors or sopranos and refers to such roles as Mimì in *La Bohème* or Alfred in *La Traviata*.

spiritoso (It.) vivacious, lively. Also, *con spirito*.

spiritual a type of Amer. revivalist folksong arising in the late 18th c.

The Afr.-Amer. spiritual is usu. one of two types, the sorrowful, slow song of suffering, or the lively or exhortatory song of jubilation. Either type may employ BLUE NOTES, syncopation and counterrhythms. Spirituals were usu. sung in unison, often in a call-and-response pattern, and accompanied by dancing. Cf. JUBILEE.

The white spiritual tradition includes the folk hymn, the sacred ballad and the CAMP MEETING SPIRITUAL. The first two are virtually indistinguishable from their secular folk counterparts except for their texts. The tunes are often modal, as are their harmonizations, and the rhythms are squarer than in the Afr.-Amer. spiritual, though the two often share sources.

Spitalny, Phil(ip) (1890–1970) Ukrainian-born Amer. bandleader and composer. After coming to the U.S. in 1895 he conducted theater orchestras and dance bands, then formed an All-Girl Orch. in 1934, which remained active until the early 1950s, performing on its own radio show from 1935 to 1948.

Spohr, Louis (Ludwig) (1784–1859) prolific German composer, conductor and violinist, trained in Brunswick and by Franz Eck, a teacher in the tradition of the Mannheim school. Spohr was concertmaster in Gotha, theater dir. at the Theater an der Wien and opera dir. in Frankfurt, then settled in Kassel in 1822, where he directed the court orch., the opera and (from 1847) all music of the city. His works incl. 13 operas, 9 symphonies, 15 violin concertos, 4 clarinet concertos, almost 40 string quartets, chamber music for many combinations, oratorios and other choral works and songs.

Spontini, Gaspare (1774–1851) Italian opera composer and conductor, trained in Naples. He was in Paris from 1803 to 1819, during which time he held various posts, incl. composer to the Empress Joséphine and dir. of the Théâtre-Italien. From 1819 to 1842 he served as general music dir. to King Friedrich Wilhelm III (and later his successor) in Berlin, enduring much factionalism. His final years were spent in Paris. Spontini's works incl. *La Vestale, Fernand Cortez, Alcirod, Agnes von Hohenstaufen* and 19 other operas, cantatas, songs, choral works and occasional instrumental works.

Sprechstimme ['shpreç"shti-me] (Ger., speech-voice) *also,* **Sprechgesang** [-ge"zäng] (Ger., speech-song) a vocal style between speaking and singing, first used by Humperdinck (in his incidental music to *Königskinder,* 1897) but fully exploited by Schoenberg and Berg in such works as *Pierrot lunaire* and *Wozzeck.* Berg also indicates a transition from speaking to singing through inter-mediate stages. A variety of notational devices have been used to indicate the technique.

Sprechstimme | half sung

sprezzatura ["sprät-sä'too-rä] (It.) a term for a type of expression and rubato used in the performance of monodic music of the early 17th c.

springar (Norw.) a Norwegian folk dance.

Springer ['shpring-ər] (Ger.) **1,** NACHSCHLAG. **2,** JACK.

Spring Sonata the violin sonata in F major, Op. 24 (1801), by Beethoven.

Springsteen, Bruce (1949–) Amer. rock singer and songwriter. He led several bands in the late 1960s, incl. Steel Mill and the Bruce Springsteen Band. His biggest success to date has been his album *Born in the USA* (1984), and his energetic and exuberant stage performances have made him a popular artist on tour.

Spring Symphony the Symphony No. 1 in B♭ major, Op. 38 (1841), by Schumann.

square 1, a term in popular music, esp. jazz, for someone unable to appreciate or render the "swing" of jazz or for music which lacks the complex syncopations of Afr.-Amer. styles. **2,** a medieval and Renaissance term indicating use of the duplum or triplum voice of a FABURDEN as the cantus firmus of a newly composed polyphonic work (composing "on the square").

square dance a type of Amer. social dance performed by groups of four couples facing each other in a square. The groups perform a series of steps announced by a *caller;* many of the steps are derived from French social dances of the 19th c. The dance is usu. accompanied by fiddle, guitar, banjo or piano, alone or in combination, playing popular and traditional songs.

square piano a horizontal piano with an oblong case in which the strings run parallel to the keyboard, similar to the CLAVICHORD, of which it is a descendant.

SSA *abbr.* soprano, soprano, alto: a common form of three-part women's chorus.

Stabat Mater a poem used in the Roman Catholic liturgy as both a sequence and hymn. Although it was removed from the liturgy in the 16th c. by the Council of Trent, the Stabat Mater was later reinstated as part of the Feast of Seven Sorrows. Important settings incl. those by Josquin, Palestrina, Lasso, Mozart and Verdi.

stacc. *abbr.* STACCATO.

staccato (It., detached) a type of articulation in which each note so marked is separated from the following note and may receive a greater or lesser accent, depending on the notation and the context. Normal staccato is usu. indicated by a dot over or under the note; vertical dashes or wedges are also found, usu. indicating a stronger accent. Dots under a slur usu. indicate either SPICCATO or a staccato played with a pressed bow. (For other meanings of slurs with dots, see PORTATO and BEBUNG.)

Stacy, Jess (Alexandria) (1904–) Amer. jazz swing pianist. He played with Benny Goodman and Bob Crosby in the 1940s and has found renewed success in the 1970s and 1980s. He is noted for his right-hand tremolo and improvisatory skills.

Stade, Frederica von VON STADE, FREDERICA.

Staden, Johann (1581–1634) German composer and highly respected organist, mostly in Nuremberg. His surviving works incl. sacred and secular vocal music and instrumental dances and suites.

Stadler Quintet popular name for the quintet for clarinet and strings, K.581 (1789), by Mozart, named for the clarinetist **Anton Stadler** (1753–1812), a member of the Viennese court orch., for whom the work was written and who first performed it.

Stadtpfeifer ['shtät"pfī-fər] (Ger., town piper) in German-speaking countries, a professional musician employed by a town government. Cf. WAIT (1,).

staff *also,* **stave** a set of lines serving as a guide for writing notes and indicating their relative position. For most music the five-line staff has been standard since about the 13th c., a CLEF being used to indicate the position of a reference note. For chant notation, a four-line staff has been in use since the 12th c. The *grand staff* used for keyboard writing is actually an eleven-line staff with the middle line (middle c′) left out (see PITCH).

staff notation musical notation employing a STAFF.

stage band 1, THEATER ORCHESTRA. **2,** BANDA.

Stainer, Sir **John** (1840–1901) English composer and musicologist, founder of the Oxford Philharmonic Society, which he conducted, and of the Musical Association. He wrote many works for the cathedral, but is best remembered for his scholarly editions and studies.

Stamitz, Johann (Wenzel Anton) (1717–57) Czech composer, violinist and teacher, trained at Prague U. He served at the Mannheim court from about 1741 until his death. One of the most important early Classical symphonists, he wrote a large number of orchestral works and concertos, instrumental sonatas and other chamber music and sacred vocal music.

stamped pit in Oceania and elsewhere, a hole in the ground covered with bark on which dancers stamp during ceremonial dancing, producing a deep, thudding sound.

Stamps, V(irgil) O(liver) (1892–1940) Amer. composer, singer and publisher of gospel hymns in round and SHAPE NOTE notation. He also organized singing schools and broadcast a weekly radio program to promote gospel hymn singing.

standard a popular song or instr. work, which, in a nonlegal sense, has passed into general use and is considered part of the common repertory.

Ständchen ['shtent-çən] (Ger.) SERENADE.

Stanford, Sir **Charles Villiers** (1852–1924) prolific English composer, conductor and teacher, trained at Trinity College, Cambridge, and in Leipzig with Reineke and Papperitz. He taught at the Royal College of Music and at Cambridge from the mid-1880s until his death, exerting a strong influence on a generation of composers, among them Vaughan Williams and Britten. At various times he was conductor of many musical organizations, incl. the London Bach Choir and the Leeds Triennial Festival. He wrote a large volume of works in almost every genre, but it is his church music that has survived.

Stanley Brothers Amer. bluegrass duo formed by singer/guitarist Carter Stanley (1926–66) and singer/banjoist/songwriter Ralph Stanley (1927–), backed by the Clinch Mountain Boys. The duo recorded and performed in concert and on radio until Carter's death, after which Ralph has continued to record and perform, instituting an annual bluegrass festival in Virginia in 1973.

stantipes (Lat.) ESTAMPIE.

Starer, Robert (1924–) Austrian-born Amer. composer, trained at the Jerusalem Conservatory and with Jacobi and Copland in the U.S. He taught at the Juilliard School (1949–74) and at Brooklyn College (from 1963) and has written *Rhythmic Training* (1969). His works incl. 4 operas, 7 ballets, 3 symphonies, 3 concertos for piano, choral works and songs, chamber music and 2 piano sonatas.

stark [shtärk] (Ger.) loud, strong.

Starker, Janos (1924–) eminent Hungarian-born Amer. cellist, trained at the Budapest Academy. He was principal cellist of the Budapest Opera, the Dallas SO, the Metropolitan Opera orch. and the Chicago SO, then joined the faculty of Indiana U. and concentrated on teaching and solo performance. He has also made editions of a number of standard cello works and has performed in various chamber groups.

Starr, Ringo (Starkey, Richard) (1940–) English rock singer, drummer and actor, a member of the BEATLES. Since the breakup of the group, he has made several albums, incl. the hit singles "Photograph" and "No No Songs," and appeared in films.

Stars and Stripes Forever!, The march (1897) by Sousa, written on shipboard while the composer was en route to the U.S. from England.

Star-Spangled Banner, The poem (1814), orig. entitled "Defence of Fort M'Henry," by Francis Scott Key (1780–1843), written during the English bombardment of Fort McHenry, MD. The tune which sets it was written in 1779 as "The Anacreontic Song" by JOHN STAFFORD SMITH and was used to set many other patriotic American texts. The song became the official anthem of the U.S. in 1931.

stasimon (Gk.) a choral number performed between the scenes of ancient Greek tragedy.

Statler Brothers Amer. country-music vocal quartet formed in the 1950s. They performed with Johnny Cash in the 1960s, then recorded and performed on their own, singing gospel and country songs.

stave STAFF.

steam organ *also*, **steam piano** CALLIOPE.

Steber, Eleanor (1916–90) Amer. soprano, stud. of William Whitney at the New England Conservatory and of Paul Althouse. She sang with the Metropolitan Opera from 1940 to 1966 and at other major American and European houses. She also appeared frequently in recital and concert. She taught at the Cleveland Institute, the Juilliard School and Brooklyn College. Her roles incl. Arabella, Vanessa and Donna Anna (*Don Giovanni*).

steel band an ensemble composed of STEEL DRUMS of various sizes, orig. developed in Trinidad.

steel drum a tuned, metal IDIOPHONE also called a *pan*, developed in Trinidad in the 1940s. It is made from an oil drum that has been shortened, compartmentalized and tuned to produce a scale when struck with a rubber-headed mallet. The drums come in various sizes, the most common of which are the melody or tenor pan (*ping pong*), the rhythm pan (incl. the guitar pan and the second pan) and the bass pan (*tuned boom*). See DRUMS (*illus.*).

steel guitar *also*, **Hawaiian guitar** a type of fretless ELECTRIC GUITAR played with a movable metal slide (*steel*) held in the left hand to stop the strings while the right hand plucks them. The instrument is usu. tuned to a major chord. The *pedal steel guitar* has a special pedal tuning system and is supported on a stand.

Steely Dan Amer. progressive rock group formed in 1972 in Los Angeles by Walter Becker and Donald Fagen and named after an object in William Burroughs' novel *Naked Lunch*. The band, which disbanded c1980, was noted for the high quality of its recordings.

Stefano, Giuseppe di DI STEFANO, GIUSEPPE.

Steffani, Agostino (1654–1728) Italian composer and diplomat, stud. of Ercole Bernabei in Rome. He was court organist to the elector of Bavaria in Munich, and later became dir. of chamber music. From 1688 he served the duke of Hannover as Kapellmeister and as emissary to various foreign courts. When he left to join the service of the elector Palatine in Düsseldorf in 1703, he essentially gave up music. Steffani is best remembered for his operas and his chamber duets.

Steg [shtāk] (Ger.) BRIDGE (1,).

Stein, Leon (1910–) Amer. composer and writer, stud. of Sowerby and Frederick Stock. He taught for most of his career at DePaul U. (Chicago), and produced several major didactic works. His works incl. 2 operas, 4 symphonies, concertos, 4 string quartets, chamber music and choral works.

Steinberg, William (Hans Wilhelm) (1899–1978) German-born Amer. conductor, stud. of Abendroth in Cologne. Before World War II he conducted regularly at the Frankfurt Opera and the Berlin Staatsoper. In 1936 he co-founded and conducted the Palestine Orch., then came to the U.S. to be assoc. conductor of the NBC SO under Toscanini. He was later music dir. of the Buffalo PO, the Pittsburgh SO, the London PO and the Boston SO.

Steiner, Max(imilian Raoul Walter) (1888–1971) Austrian-born Amer. conductor and composer, godson of Richard Strauss. Before World War I he conducted operettas and musical comedies in Europe, then came to the U.S. and conducted on Broadway. From 1929 he worked in Hollywood as a composer of dramatic film scores, incl. *King Kong* (1933), *Dark Victory* (1939), *Casablanca* (1943) and *The Fountainhead* (1949).

Steinway and Sons Amer. firm of piano makers est. in New York in 1853 by Heinrich Steinweg (1797–1871), responsible for several crucial developments in piano design. Of esp. importance was the development of the cast-iron frame with overstrung strings at high tension and large, machine-covered hammers with heavy felts which permitted considerable flexibility of touch.

Stenhammer, (Karl) Wilhelm (Eugen) (1871–1927) Swedish composer, conductor and pianist, essentially self-taught. He performed extensively in Sweden as soloist and in chamber ensembles and was briefly artistic dir. of the Stockholm Philharmonic Society and for many years of the Göteborgs Orkesterförening. He is best known for his vocal works, esp. his songs and choral music.

stentando *also*, **stentato** (It.) with difficulty or suffering.

Steppenwolf Amer. hard-rock and heavy-metal band, formed in 1967 in Los Angeles and active until 1976. Their biggest hit was "Born to Be Wild" (1968), from their first album.

stereophonic a term referring to a

sound recording and reproducing system designed to provide the illusion of depth in recorded sound by the use of two (or more) separately and simultaneously recorded sound tracks that are played back through separate speakers. Cf. HIGH FIDELITY.

Stern, Isaac (1920–) Russian-born Amer. violinist, stud. of Louis Persinger and Naum Blinder. An outstanding virtuoso, he has played throughout the world as soloist and in chamber ensembles, esp. in trio with pianist Eugene Istomin and cellist Leonard Rose. He has also been an important figure in the musical life of Israel and was instrumental in 1960 in saving New York's Carnegie Hall from being razed.

stesso ['stäs-sō] (It.) same.

Steuermann, Edward (Eduard) (1892–1964) Polish-born Amer. pianist and composer, stud. of Vilém Kurz, Busoni and Schoenberg. He taught in Europe and at the Juilliard School (from 1952), numbering among his pupils Alfred Brendel, Lili Kraus and Russell Sherman. He was a distinguished interpreter of contemporary and standard repertory and played in the premiere performances of many of Schoenberg's works, as well as those of Berg and Webern.

Stevens, Cat (Georgiou, Steven) (1947–) English rock singer and songwriter, active during the late 1960s and 1970s, after which he abandoned music. His hits incl. "Wild World" (1971) and "Morning Has Broken" (1971).

Stevens, Halsey (1908–) Amer. composer, musicologist and teacher, stud. of Berwald and Bloch. He has taught at Syracuse U., Dakota Wesleyan U., Bradley Polytechnic Institute, the U. of Redlands (TN) and the U. of S. California. He is a noted expert on the music of Bartók and has written music in all genres except stage music.

Stevens (Steenberg), **Risë** (1913–) Amer. mezzo-soprano, stud. of Anna Schoen-René and Marie Gutheil-Schoder. She sang with the Metropolitan Opera from 1938 to 1961 and also appeared in a number of films and in concert. She was president of the Mannes College from 1975 to 1978.

Stewart, Rod (1945–) Scottish rock singer and songwriter. He sang for several years with the Jeff Beck Group, then joined The Faces and also made solo recordings. His recording of "Maggie Mae" (1971) was the first single to be simultaneously on the charts in England and the U.S., and the album from which it came was the first album to do so.

Stewart, Thomas (James) (1928–) Amer. baritone, trained at the Juilliard School, husband of soprano EVELYN LEAR. He has sung regularly at Bayreuth, the Metropolitan Opera and elsewhere in Europe and the U.S. His repertory includes Wagnerian roles, as well as Ford (*Falstaff*) and Eugene Onegin.

Stich-Randall, Teresa (1927–) Amer. soprano, trained at the Hartt School of Music and Columbia. In the late 1940s she sang under Toscanini and created the role of Gertrude Stein in Thomson's *The Mother of Us All* (1947). She was the first American to be made a KAMMERSÄNGERIN and has sung with the Metropolitan Opera, the Chicago Lyric Opera and at other major opera houses. She is well known as a recital and concert artist.

stick zither a type of ZITHER consisting of one or more strings stretched between the ends of a fretted stick attached to one or more gourd resonators. Cf. VINA.

Stierhorn ['shtēr"horn] (Ger., cow horn) **1**, an ancient bugle HORN. **2**, a straight, conical brass instrument called for by Wagner in his *Ring* cycle.

stile antico ['stē-le an'tē-kō] (It., old style) a Baroque term for a style of composition which imitates the music of Palestrina; opposed to STILE MODERNO. Cf. PRIMA PRATTICA.

stile concitato [kōn-chē'tä-tō] (It., agitated style) a term coined by Monteverdi to describe a style of composition used to express agitation from anger, excitement, etc. One of the characteristics of the style was rapid, measured repetition of a single note or chord. An example of the style may be found in Monteverdi's *Il Combattimento di Tancredi e Clorinda*.

stile moderno (It., modern style) a Baroque term for church music in the then current style, as opposed to STILE ANTICO.

stile rappresentativo (It., representative style) the style of composition used in the earliest operas of Caccini, Peri and Monteverdi, constituting a kind of text declamation heightened by music. Development of this style was a conscious attempt to re-create the emotive properties of ancient Greek music.

Still, William Grant (1895–1978) distinguished Amer. composer, trained at Oberlin College and with Varèse and Chadwick. His *Afro-American Symphony* (1930) was the first symphony by a black American to be played by a major orch., and his opera *Troubled Island* (1934) was the first opera by a black American produced by a major opera company (the New York City Opera, but with white singers in blackface). Still's works incl. *Blue Steel, The Pillar* and other operas, ballets, 5 symphonies, symphonic poems, orchestral suites, chamber works, choruses, songs and arrangements of spirituals.

Stilwell, Richard (1942–) Amer. baritone, stud. of Frank St. Leger and Daniel Ferro. He made his name singing Pelléas, a role he has sung with many companies. He has sung at Glyndebourne, Covent Garden, the Metropolitan Opera, La Scala and most major opera houses in roles ranging from the Count (*Marriage of Figaro*) to Billy Budd in Britten's opera.

Stimme ['shti-me] (Ger.) voice, part.
Stimmung ['shti-mûng] (Ger.) **1**, mood. **2**, TUNING.

Sting (Sumner, Gordon) (1951–) English rock singer, songwriter, bassist, saxophonist, keyboard player and actor, member of the band The Police. His stage name came from a yellow and black jersey he often wore. Sting has also appeared in several films.

sting VIBRATO in lute playing.

Stitt, Sonny (Edward) (1924–82) Amer. jazz saxophonist. He played in the bands of Tiny Bradshaw, Billy Eckstine and Dizzy Gillespie in the 1940s, then worked with Gene Ammons and Miles Davis in the 1950s and 1960s. After years as an alto saxophonist in the shadow of Charlie Parker, he shifted to tenor in the 1950s, though he continued to play alto.

stochastic a term borrowed from probability theory to refer to the production of essentially random elements according to a certain process. The technique has been used most extensively in composition by XENAKIS.

Stock, David (Frederick) (1939–) Amer. composer and conductor, trained at Brandeis, in Paris and at the Berkshire Music Center. He has taught at the Cleveland Institute, the New England Conservatory, Antioch College and the U. of Pittsburgh, where he has also been conductor of the Pittsburgh New Music Ensemble and the Carnegie SO. He has written almost exclusively for instruments, a notable exception being his work *Scat* (1971) for soprano, flute, bass clarinet, violin and cello.

Stock, Frederick (Friedrich August) (1872–1942) German-born Amer. conductor, trained at the Cologne Conservatory. He joined the Chicago SO in 1895, becoming assistant conductor in 1899 and succeeding Theodore Thomas as conductor in 1905, a post he held for the rest of his life. He also established the Chicago Civic Orch. (1920), a training orch., and conducted the first commercial recordings made by a U.S. orch. under its regular conductor.

stock arrangement a published band arrangement, as opposed to one written esp. for a particular band.

stockhorn *also*, **stock-and-horn** an obsolete 18th-c. single-reed instrument resembling the melody pipe of a bagpipe.

Stockhausen, Karlheinz (1928–) German composer and theorist, stud. of Schroeder and Martin in Cologne and with Messiaen in Paris. He was also strongly influenced by his summer at Darmstadt in 1951. From 1953 he worked at the electronic music studio in Cologne and has continued to produce both instrumental/vocal works and electronic works, exploring the characteristics of both media. In recent years he has become interested in dramatic music and opera. He has also taught in Cologne, where he founded the Cologne Institute for New Music, and has written articles on new music. Stockhausen's works incl. *Zeitmasse* for woodwind quintet, *Gruppen* for 3 orchestras, *Gesang der Jünglinge* (electronic), *Zyklus* for percussion, *Kontakte* (electronic), *Momente* and *Prozession* for instruments and electronics, *Aus den sieben Tagen* (text piece) and *Licht* (opera).

Stoessel, Albert (Frederic) (1894–1943) Amer. violinist, composer and conductor, trained in Berlin. Following years of concertizing, he became conductor of the Oratorio Society of New York, the Chautauqua Institution and the Worcester (MA) Music Festival, posts he held until his death. He taught at New York U. and the Juilliard School and guest-conducted various U.S. orchestras. He wrote many works for orch., chorus and chamber ensembles, as well as books on violin playing and conducting.

Stokowski, Leopold (Anthony) (1882–1977) English-born Amer. conductor, trained at the Royal College of Music and at Oxford. After four years as music dir. of the Cincinnati SO he became conductor of the Philadelphia Orch. (1912), a post he held for 25 years. He championed works by American composers and made many recordings as well as several films, incl. the epoch-making *Fantasia* (1941). After leaving Philadelphia he was assoc. with various or-

chestras, incl. the Houston SO and the American SO, and conducted frequently in Europe.

Stolz, Robert (Elisabeth) (1880–1975) Austrian conductor and composer of operettas and film musicals.

stomp a jazz dance characterized by heavy foot stamping.

stomping a heavy left-hand Vamp used in the Barrelhouse style of piano playing.

Stone, Sly see Sly and the family stone.

stop 1, a Register of an organ or harpsichord, usu. controlled by a lever, knob or pedal. **2**, the controlling device itself. Cf. Organ stop.

stopped modified by Stopping; esp., an indication in horn music, either with the word or with a sign (+), that the note or notes so marked should be stopped with the hand. It is canceled by the term Open or the sign (°). Also, *chiuso* (It.).

stopped note a note on a string instrument or horn produced by Stopping.

stopped pipe a Flue pipe of an organ of which one end is closed by a cap or stopper, lowering the fundamental by an octave and eliminating the even-numbered Overtones.

stopping 1, on a string instrument, the act of pressing the string hard against the fingerboard (or a fret) to shorten its length and so produce a pitch higher than its fundamental pitch. **2**, on the horn, controlling the opening of the bell with the closed fingers of the right hand. The technique lowers the harmonics produced, while also significantly changing the tonal quality of the notes.

Stop the World—I Want to Get Off musical by Leslie Bricusse and Anthony Newley. Premiere, London 1961. An allegorical story of an everyman who marries the boss's daughter, rises to the top, and in his old age reflects on the shallowness of his life.

stop-time a technique of accompaniment (of a solo, a dance, etc.) consisting of heavy chords and rhythmic punctuation at the beginning of every bar (or every other bar), the rest of the bar remaining silent except for the soloist.

Storace, Stephen (John Steven) (1762–96) English composer of operas, dialogue operas, songs and chamber music, possibly a student of Mozart. His dialogue opera *The Haunted Tower* (1789) was one of the most successful English operas of the 18th c. His sister **Nancy** (Anna) **Storace** (1765–1817) was a soprano highly popular in comic opera of the time, portraying Susanna (*The Marriage of Figaro*) and inspiring Mozart to write a concert aria for her. She sang at Drury Lane until her brother died, then toured on the continent.

Stormy Weather 1, musical film (1943) featuring Bill "Bojangles" Robinson, Lena Horne and an all-black cast. **2**, song (1933) by Harold Arlen, words by Ted Koehler, part of the *Cotton Club Parade—22nd Edition*. The song was written for Cab Calloway but introduced by Ethel Waters.

Storyville a center for jazz and legalized prostitution in New Orleans from 1897 until it was closed in 1917. Also, *The District*.

Stothart, Herbert (1885–1949) Amer. conductor and composer of Broadway musicals (usu. in collaboration with others, such as *Rose-Marie* with Friml and *Song of the Flame* with Gershwin) and film scores (*Treasure Island, Mutiny on the Bounty, National Velvet*, etc.).

Stout, Alan B(urrage) (1932–) Amer. composer and teacher, trained at Peabody Conservatory and Johns Hopkins. He has taught at Northwestern since 1963. He has written many vocal works, mainly sacred, as well as 4 symphonies, chamber music and works for organ.

Stradella, Alessandro (1644–82) Italian composer, perhaps a student of Ercole Bernabei. In Rome he was in the service of Queen Christina of Sweden, leaving in 1677 for Venice and then for Turin, where he was almost killed as the result of one incidence

of his apparently constant philandering. By 1678 he was in Genoa, where he remained until his death. His works incl. 7 operas, numerous intermezzi and other stage works, oratorios, mass settings, motets, many Italian cantatas, songs, arias and canzonettas, instrumental sinfonias and sonatas.

Stradella accordion an ACCORDION with buttons for the left hand representing chords, usu. arranged in six rows. Also, *standard-bass accordion*.

straight a term in popular music and jazz referring (not necessarily with derogatory intent) to European-style fully composed music.

straight mute the standard MUTE for brass instruments, used to soften the sound without undo alteration of the tone.

Stradivari, Antonio (1644–1737) Italian string instrument maker in Cremona, generally considered the greatest violin maker of all time, a student of NICOLA AMATI, for whom he worked until about 1680. He made significant modifications of the design of the instrument, improving its tone and projection.

strain term in popular music for THEME or CHORUS (3,).

strascinando [strä-shē′nan-dō] (It.) heavily slurred.

Stratas, Teresa (Strataki, Anastasia) (1938–) Canadian soprano of Greek descent, stud. of Irene Jessner. Since her debut in 1959 with the Canadian Opera, she has sung regularly at the Metropolitan Opera, La Scala, Salzburg and other major European houses. Her roles incl. Mimì (*La Bohème*), Violetta (*La Traviata*) and Mélisande.

strathspey a Scottish dance similar to, but slower than, the REEL, in duple or quadruple time characterized by the SCOTCH SNAP.

Straus, Oscar (1870–1954) Austrian conductor and composer of operettas, stud. of Hermann Grädener and Bruch. Of his over 40 operettas, still popular in Austria, esp. *The Chocolate Soldier* (1908) gained success in the U.S. He also wrote ballets, film scores and cabaret songs for the ÜBERBRETTL, where he worked at the turn of the century.

Strauss, Johann (Baptist), Jr. (1825–99) Austrian composer, conductor and violinist, son of JOHANN STRAUSS, SR. He studied with Joseph Drechsler and Anton Kohlmann. He formed his own orch. in 1844 and after his father's death merged his father's orch. with his. He toured extensively between 1850 and 1890, gaining the title of "The Waltz King" and traveling as far as New York. He wrote innumerable waltzes and other dances (among them *Stories of the Vienna Woods; Wine, Women and Song; The Beautiful Blue Danube* and the *Centennial Waltzes*, written for the centennial celebrations in the U.S.) and operettas (*Die Fledermaus, A Night in Venice, The Gypsy Baron, Vienna Blood*).

Strauss, Johann (Baptist), Sr. (1804–49) Austrian composer, conductor and violinist, stud. of Polischansky and Ignaz von Seyfried. He formed his own orch. in 1825 and soon won favor for his works, later going on foreign tours to England and throughout Europe. His works incl. dance numbers of all types (waltzes, galops, cotillons, quadrilles, marches, polkas, etc.), the most famous being the "Radetzky March," Op. 228 (1848).

Strauss, Richard (Georg) (1864–1949) German conductor and prolific composer of opera and orchestral music, stud. of Friedrich Wilhelm Meyer in Munich. His "Serenade for 13 Winds," written when he was 17, was performed by the Dresden Court Orch. and by the prestigious Meiningen Court Orch. under von Bülow, whose assistant he became in 1885. In the following years he held posts in Munich and Weimar, eventually becoming chief conductor of the Munich Opera. In 1905 his opera *Salome* was premiered, an enormous success whose earnings helped to keep him in comfort for the rest of his life. His extraordinarily produc-

tive collaboration with the poet Hugo von Hofmansthal began a few years later.

Strauss was a regular conductor of the Berlin Opera until 1918, then enjoyed a similar assoc. with the Vienna Staatsoper until 1924. After Hofmannsthal's death Strauss collaborated with novelist Stefan Zweig and archivist Josef Gregor. Strauss's activities and stance in Germany during the Nazi period have frequently been criticized; though he was essentially an apolitical man, he evidently made some unfortunate decisions. Postwar reconciliation was initiated by Beecham two years before the composer's death with a festival of his music. His mastery as an orchestrator has been rarely matched and his collaborations with Hofmannsthal stand among the outstanding operatic creations of the 20th c.

Strauss's works incl. *Salome, Elektra, Der Rosenkavalier, Ariadne auf Naxos, Die Frau ohne Schatten, Intermezzo, Arabella, Capriccio* and other operas, *Josephs-Legende* (ballet), *Symphonia domestica*, tone poems (*Don Juan, Death and Transfiguration, Thus Spake Zarathustra, Don Quixote, A Hero's Life*), concertos for horn and for oboe, many songs (incl. the *Four Last Songs*), choral works and chamber music.

stravaganza [strä-vä'gän-tsä] (It.) a term for a work in any form having unusual or extraordinary features of style, melody, harmony, etc.

Stravaganza, La the 12 Violin Concertos, Op. 4, by Vivaldi.

Stravinsky, Igor (Feodorovich) (1882–1971) Russian-born Amer. composer, stud. of Akimenko, Vassily Kalafaty and Rimsky-Korsakov. In 1909 began the assoc. with impresario Serge Dyagilev that was to establish his international reputation, beginning with the ballet *The Firebird* and followed by *Petrushka*. His third ballet for the Ballets Russes was *The Rite of Spring*, whose premiere occasioned one of the most celebrated theatrical scandals of recent history.

He spent the years of World War I in Switzerland, then relocated in France, celebrating his arrival with the ballet *Pulcinella*. His time in Paris, 1920–39, was the period of his NEOCLASSICAL compositions, incl. the opera *Oedipus Rex*, the cantata *Symphony of Psalms* (commissioned by the Boston SO for its 50th anniversary) and the chamber work *Duo concertante* for violin and piano.

Stravinsky came to the U.S. in 1939, settling in Hollywood. The first part of this lengthy final period continued the neo-Classicism of Paris, esp. in the *Symphony in Three Movements*, the Mass, the Cantata and the opera *The Rake's Progress*. In the last two decades of his life he gradually adopted serial techniques, perhaps under the influence of his colleague Robert Craft, realizing them fully in his ballet *Agon*.

For much of his career, esp. the later years, Stravinsky appeared frequently as conductor of his own works. In his American years he also produced new, sometimes significantly altered, editions of his Russian and Parisian works. The influence of his music, esp. the Parisian ballets and the neo-Classical works, has been extensive and pervasive, establishing him as one of the giants of 20th-c. composition.

Stravinsky's works incl. *The Nightingale, Mavra, Oedipus Rex, The Rake's Progress, The Flood* and other musical theater works; *The Firebird, Petrushka, The Rite of Spring, Pulcinella, Apollon musagète, The Card Party, Agon* and other ballets; concertos for piano and violin, the *Dumbarton Oaks* concerto for chamber orch., *Symphony in Three Movements, Ebony Concerto* for jazz band, *Movements* for piano and orch., *Variations* for orch., *Symphony of Psalms*, Mass, Cantata, *Canticum sacrum, Threni, Requiem Canticles* and other choral works; many songs; Octet, Septet, *Duo concertante* and other chamber music; and works for solo piano.

Strayhorn, Billy (William) (1915–67) Amer. jazz pianist, composer and arranger. He played with and arranged for Duke Ellington's orch. from 1939 until his death. His works for the band incl. "Take the A Train," "Passion Flower" and "Raincheck." He also collaborated with Ellington on many large-scale compositions, esp. suites.

street cries calls of street vendors, usu. short musical motifs, used from time to time by composers as material for vocal works, from Janequin's *Les Cris de Paris* (c1550) to the vendors in Gershwin's *Porgy and Bess* (1935).

street funk a type of FUNK popular in the 1970s and exemplified in such groups as Parliament and Kool and the Gang.

street organ see BARREL ORGAN.

street piano HURDY-GURDY (3,).

Street Scene musical by Weill to a libretto by Langston Hughes, based on the play by Elmer Rice. Premiere, New York 1947.

Streich [shtrīç] (Ger.) **1**, in compound words, string, as, *Streichquartett*, string quartet; *Streicher*, strings or string section. **2**, BOWSTROKE.

Streich, Rita (1920–87) German coloratura soprano, stud. of Dongraf-Fassbänder, Maria Ivogün and Erna Berger. In the late 1940s she sang at the Berlin Staatsoper, then joined the Vienna Staatsoper. She sang at many international opera houses and festivals and appeared frequently in recital.

Streisand, Barbra (Joan) (1942–) Amer. singer, actress and comedienne in films (incl. *Hello Dolly!* and *Yentl*), recordings, and on Broadway (*Funny Girl*).

strepitoso [strä-pē′tō-zō] (It.) impetuous, noisy.

Strepponi, Giuseppina (Clelia Maria Josepha) (1815–97) Italian soprano, trained at the Milan Conservatory, later Verdi's second wife. From her debut in 1834 to her retirement in 1846 she was highly popular in such roles as Amina (*La Sonnambula*) and Lucia (*Lucia di Lammermoor*).

stretta (It.) STRETTO (2,).

stretto (It.) **1**, in FUGUE and other imitative counterpoint, the presentation of two or more statements of the subject in close canon, usu. found (when present at all) at the end of the work. **2**, a term for a speeding up of the tempo at a climactic section of a work, movement or section. Cf. STRINGENDO.

Strich [shtriç] (Ger., bow, line) **1**, BOWSTROKE. **2**, BARLINE.

Strickland, Lily (Theresa) (1887–1958) Amer. composer, trained at the Institute of Musical Art in New York. Her music—operettas, cantatas, suites, piano works and songs—was strongly influenced by Afr.-Amer. music, Native Amer. music and the music of India. Her song "Lindy Lou" was a popular recital encore piece.

strict counterpoint COUNTERPOINT conforming to rigid rules of consonance, dissonance and part-writing; esp., species counterpoint. Contrasted with FREE COUNTERPOINT.

stride piano a style of jazz piano derived from RAGTIME, popular esp. in the 1910s and 1920s and characterized by the "stride bass" (see WALKING BASS), rapid tempos and virtuoso right-hand technique. Representatives of the style incl. James P. Johnson, Willie "The Lion" Smith and Fats Waller. Also, *Harlem stride, Harlem school*.

Striggio, Alessandro (c1535–c1590) Italian composer and instrumentalist, best known for his intermedii, such as those for the comedy *La Cafanaria*, performed at the wedding of Francesco de' Medici and Johanna of Austria in 1565. His son, also named Alessandro Striggio, was a famous poet and is best remembered as the librettist of Monteverdi's opera *Orfeo* (1607).

Strike Up the Band musical by George Gershwin, lyrics by Ira Gershwin, book by Morrie Ryskind, based on a book by George S. Kaufman. Premiere, New York 1930. A political satire concerned with a war between the U.S. and Switzerland over tariffs on chocolate.

string 1, the sounding medium of a STRING INSTRUMENT, made of gut, metal, silk, plastic or other material, stretched to produce a certain fundamental pitch and bowed, struck or plucked by hand, bow, plectrum or mechanical means. On some instruments, such as the guitar or violin, the string may be shortened by STOPPING to produce pitches above the fundamental. Gut strings are frequently wrapped with a thin winding of metal wire to strengthen the string. **2**, a family of bright-toned, flue ORGAN STOPS.

string. *abbr.* STRINGENDO.

string bass CONTRABASS.

string drum a type of FRICTION DRUM in which a string of cord or gut is passed through a hole in the membrane and pulled or whirled to cause vibration.

stringed instrument also **stringed instrument** an instrument whose sound is produced by a stretched string. See CHORDOPHONE.

stringendo [strēn'jen-dō] (It.) quickening the tempo.

string quartet 1, a solo string ensemble composed of two violins, viola and cello, one of the major chamber music ensembles since the Classical era and the medium for some of the greatest works of composers since that time. **2**, a work composed for this combination, usu. in the three- or four-movement form of the SONATA.

string quintet 1, a solo string ensemble, usu. consisting of a STRING QUARTET with an extra viola or cello. **2**, music written for this combination.

string trio 1, a solo string ensemble consisting of a violin, a viola and a cello. **2**, music written for this ensemble.

strings the string section of an orch.

strisciando [strē'shän-dō] (It.) **1**, in a smooth or slurred manner. **2**, GLISSANDO.

stritch a type of SAXOPHONE occasionally used in jazz.

stroke 1, in English music for virginals, a line that is drawn through the stem of a note to indicate one of various ORNAMENTS. Its exact meaning is unknown. **2**, a blow on a drum; drumstroke.

stromentato (It.) *abbr.* recitativo stromentato (see RECITATIVE).

stromento (It.) STRUMENTO.

strophic a term applied to songs in which all text stanzas are set to the same music; opposed to THROUGH-COMPOSED.

Strouse, Charles (Louis) (1928–) Amer. composer of Broadway musicals incl. *Bye Bye Birdie* (1960), *Applause* (1970) and *Annie* (1977) and film scores, incl. *Bonnie and Clyde* (1967).

struggle a jazz shuffle-dance of the 1920s.

strumento (It.) INSTRUMENT. Also, *stromento*.

strut a jazz dance step used in many early dances such as the cakewalk.

Stück [shtük] (Ger.) PIECE.

Student Prince in Heidelberg, The operetta by Sigmund Romberg, lyrics and book by Dorothy Donnelly, based on the play *Old Heidelberg* by Rudolf Bleichman. Premiere, New York 1924. The sentimental story of the Student Prince Karl Franz's brief romance with a Heidelberg waitress.

studio musician SESSION MUSICIAN.

studio upright a large UPRIGHT PIANO.

study a didactic instrumental work, most often for keyboard instrument, designed to emphasize a certain technique or problem. The best examples of the type also have inherent musical value as well, as found in the studies of Schumann, Chopin, Debussy and many other composers. Also, *étude* (Fr.).

Sturm und Drang [shtûrm ûnt dräng] (Ger., storm and stress) a late 18th-c. German literary movement reflected in music of the time, emphasizing the power of the arts to move the emotions and rouse to action, esp. against social injustice.

style 1, the manner in which a work is performed, esp. the idiosyncracies of performance of a certain performer, or the performance conventions of a certain period or geographical area. Cf. PERFORMANCE PRACTICE. **2**, the characteristic mode of expression, i.e. the details of musical language, that distinguish one work or composer from another.

style brisé [stēl brē'zā] (Fr., broken style) the use of arpeggiated chords in keyboard music.

style galant [gä'lā] (Fr.) a term for a late 18th-c. compositional style characterized by simplicity, homophonic writing and ornamented periodic melodies, performed with grace and designed to please. The style is represented in the works of Domenico Scarlatti, François Couperin and J.C. Bach, among others.

style luthé [lü'tā] (Fr., lute style) STYLE BRISÉ.

Styne, Jule (Julius Kerwin) (1905–) English-born Amer. composer and pianist, trained at the Chicago College of Music. After early careers as concert pianist, bandleader and vocal coach, he became a highly successful composer of Hollywood and Broadway musicals. His hits incl. *Gentlemen Prefer Blondes* (1949), *Gypsy* (1959) and *Funny Girl* (1964) and the songs "I Don't Want to Walk Without You" and "Three Coins in the Fountain."

subdominant the fourth DEGREE of the major or minor scale, so called from its position a fifth below the tonic, analogous to the position of the dominant above the tonic.

subito ['soo-bē-tō] (It.) suddenly, immediately.

subject a theme used as the basis for a composition or a section of a composition. See FUGUE, ANDAMENTO, SOGGETTO.

submediant the sixth DEGREE of the major or minor scale, so called from its position a third below the tonic, analogous to the position of the mediant above the tonic.

Subotnick, Morton (1933–) Amer. composer and teacher, stud. of Milhaud and Kirchner. He has taught at Mills College, NYU. and the California Institute of the Arts and has been music dir. of the Anne Halprin Dance Company and the Electric Circus, among other organizations. Most of his works explore the relationships between conventional sounds and synthesized sounds, incl. the use of electronic manipulation of live sounds in real time. His best-known works incl. *Silver Apples of the Moon* (1967), created on a Buchla synthesizer, a series called *Play!*, and *Two Life Histories* (1977). He has also written instrumental chamber music and incidental scores.

substitute chord a chord that can replace another chord without a change of harmonic function, the most common being the supertonic (II) and subdominant (IV) chords either of which can substitute for the other.

substitution mass a collection of motets used to replace the traditional movements of the Mass during the late 15th and early 16th c. See MOTETTI MISSALES.

subtonic the seventh degree of the major or minor scale, the note below the tonic. See LEADING TONE.

Suisse Romande, Orchestre de la (Fr.) orch. founded in 1918 in Geneva by conductor Ernest Ansermet.

suite a set of instrumental works related in some manner and intended to be performed together. Common forms are the dance suite and suites extracted from a dramatic work, such as a ballet or opera. In many cases, the works are related tonally as well as in character. The dance suite of the Baroque and Classical eras, a development from the SONATA DA CAMERA, had a fairly consistent format, usu. beginning with a prelude or other form of introduction, followed by a series of stylized dances (*allemande, courante, sarabande, gigue,* for ex-

ample), varying in tempo and character. Also, *dance suite.*

suivez [süē'vä] (Fr., follow) **1**, ATTACCA. **2**, COLLA VOCE; COLLA PARTE.

Suk, Josef (1874–1935) Czech composer and violinist, trained at the Prague Conservatory with various teachers, incl. Dvořák, whose daughter he married. Suk taught at the Prague Conservatory from 1922, where his students incl. Reiner and Martinů. He wrote mainly instrumental music for orch., piano and chamber ensembles. His grandson **Josef Suk** (1929–) is a concert violinist of international renown.

Sullivan, Sir **Arthur S(eymour)** (1842–1900) English composer and conductor, trained at the Royal Academy of Music and at the Leipzig Conservatory. He conducted various organizations in England and was principal of the National Training School. Although he wrote a large body of works in all forms, especially sacred and secular vocal works, he is remembered mainly for his many comic operettas written in collaboration with playwright William S. Gilbert.

Sullivan's works incl. *Trial by Jury, The Sorcerer, HMS Pinafore, The Pirates of Penzance, Patience, Iolanthe, The Mikado, Ruddigore, The Yeoman of the Guard, The Gondoliers* and other operettas, operas and incidental music, *The Golden Legend* and other oratorios, orchestral and chamber works, service music, hymn tunes, songs and choral works.

Sullivan, Maxine (Williams, Marietta) (1911–) Amer. jazz singer and instrumentalist with Claude Thornhill in the late 1930s, then a performer in several films, on Broadway, in clubs and at festivals.

sul ponticello [pōn-tē'chel-lō] (It., on the bridge) a direction in string playing to bow close to (or occasionally on) the bridge of the instrument, producing a thin, nasal sound.

sul tasto *also,* **sulla tastiera** (It.) a direction in string playing to bow over or near the fingerboard, producing a flutelike tone. Cf. FLAUTANDO.

Sumac, Yma (Chavarri, Emperatiz) (1927–) Peruvian-born Amer. singer, noted for her remarkable range (from low contralto to high coloratura) and exotic repertory, specializing in S. Amer. folk songs in colorful arrangements. She was promoted as an Inca princess.

Sumer is icumen in a medieval four-voice ROTA dating from about 1250, orig. composed in motet style over a texted PES tenor. Also, *Reading* ['reding] *rota*. See CANON

summation tone see COMBINATION TONE.

Summer and Smoke opera in 2 acts by Lee Hoiby to a libretto by Lanford Wilson, based on the play by Tennessee Williams. Premiere, St. Paul, MN 1971.

Sun Quartets the 6 Quartets, Op. 20 (1772), by Haydn, so called because of an elaborate image of the sun appearing on one of the printed editions of the quartets.

Sun Ra (Blount, Herman) (1914–) Amer. jazz composer, keyboard player and bandleader. He formed the Myth-Science Arkestra in the early 1950s, creating a unique style and exerting a significant influence on avant-garde jazz.

Sunrise Quartet the string quartet in Bb major, Op. 76 No. 4 (1797), by Haydn.

Sun-Treader monumental orchestral work (1931) by Carl Ruggles, premiered in Paris in 1932 but not performed in the U.S. until 1966. The title comes from the poem "Pauline" by Robert Browning.

Suor Angelica (It., Sister Angelica) tragic opera in 1 act by Puccini to a libretto in Italian by Giovacchino Forzano. Premiere, New York 1918. Part of the triptych which includes *Il Tabarro* and *Gianni Schicchi*. Sister Angelica, doing penance for having an illegitimate child, takes poison when she hears her child has died.

superdominant SUBMEDIANT.

supertonic the second DEGREE of the

major or minor scale, the note above the tonic.

Suppé, Franz von (1819–95) Austrian opera composer and conductor, trained in Vienna. He is best known today for the overtures to several of his operas, heard frequently in pops concerts, incl. *Poet and Peasant* and *Light Cavalry*. He wrote well over 200 stage works as well as sacred choral music, symphonies and chamber music.

Supremes, The Amer. female soul vocal trio composed of DIANA ROSS, Florence Ballard and Mary Wilson. They recorded many hit singles in the mid-1960s, incl. "Where Did Our Love Go?" and "Stop! In the Name of Love." The group continued for a time after Ross left to pursue a solo career but disbanded in the late 1970s.

surf music a type of popular music of the early 1960s celebrating the S. California surfing and sunning culture with music characterized by high harmony vocals and guitar. The quintessential representatives of the genre are the BEACH BOYS.

Surinach, Carlos (1915–) Spanish-born Amer. conductor and composer, trained in Barcelona, Düsseldorf and Berlin. He has been most successful as a composer for the dance, having created works for the Joffrey Ballet and Martha Graham, among others.

Surprise Symphony the Symphony No. 94 in G major (1791) by Haydn, so named for an unexpected punctuating chord in the theme of the slow movement.

Survivor from Warsaw cantata for speaker, men's chorus and orchestra, Op. 46 (1947), by Schoenberg. The text, in English, German and Hebrew, describes Nazi atrocities against the Jews.

Susannah tragic opera by Carlisle Floyd to his own libretto. Premiere, Tallahassee, FL 1955. The Apocrypha story of Susannah and the Elders transposed to a primitive Tennessee mountain valley.

Susato, Tielman (c1500–c1564)

Flemish composer and printer of many important anthologies of chansons, motets and Flemish songs as well as of the *Souterliedekens* of Clemens non Papa.

suspension in part-writing, a dissonance tied over from the previous chord and resolving, usu. downward, after the new chord is sounded. An upward-resolving suspension is sometimes called a *retardation*. Cf. NON-HARMONIC NOTE.

Susskind, (Jan) Walter (1913–80) Czech-born English conductor, stud. of Suk, Hába and Szell, whom he assisted at the German Opera in Prague. He was music dir. of the Scottish Orch., the Toronto SO, the Aspen Festival and the St. Louis SO. He was also founder of the National Youth Orch. of Canada. He was esp. noted for his innovative programming.

Süssmayr, Franz Xaver (1766–1803) Austrian composer, trained in Kremsmünster and in Vienna with Mozart and Salieri. He was Kapellmeister of the German opera in Vienna from 1794. He was a successful composer of operas and Singspiele, though none of his works has survived in the repertory. He is remembered principally for his work in completing Mozart's *Requiem*.

sustaining pedal DAMPER PEDAL.

Sutherland, Dame **Joan** (1926–) Australian soprano, stud. of John and Aida Dickens, Clive Carey and of her husband, RICHARD BONYNGE, who directed her work toward the bel canto repertory for which she is famous. She has sung in all major opera houses in Europe and No. America as well as in her native Australia.

Sutherland, Margaret (Ada) (1897–1984) Australian composer and pianist, trained in Melbourne, London and Vienna. She was active from 1935 as composer, performer and teacher, championing the music of Australian composers. Her works incl. an opera, several ballets, orchestral concertos and concerti grossi, choral works, songs and much chamber music.

Suzuki, Shin'ichi (1898–) Japanese violin teacher, creator of the famous Suzuki method of instruction on violin and other instruments, based on the premise that any child can develop a high level of skill.

Sw. *abbr.* SWELL (2,).

Swan, Alfred J(ulius) (1890–1970) American composer and musicologist, trained at Oxford and at the St. Petersburg Conservatory. He taught at Swarthmore and Haverford colleges from 1926 until his retirement in 1958. His specialties were Russian music and the music of the Eastern Orthodox liturgy.

Swan Lake ballet with music (1876) by Tchaikovsky, orig. choreographed by Petipa and Ivanov.

swannee whistle a WHISTLE with a movable slide allowing a continuous variation of the pitch, used as a toy and in the orch. for special effects. Also, *slide whistle*.

Swan of Tuonela work for English horn and orch., the third movement of the LEMMINKÄINNEN SUITE by Sibelius.

Swanson, Howard (1907–78) Amer. composer, trained at the Cleveland Institute and with Boulanger in Paris. His song "The Negro Speaks of Rivers" (1942) and others were frequently performed in recital by Marian Anderson. He wrote 3 symphonies, the *Short Symphony*, piano sonatas, a trio (for flute, oboe and piano) and many songs.

Swan Song SCHWANENGESANG.

Swarowsky, Hans (1899–1975) Austrian conductor, stud. of Schoenberg, Webern, Weingartner and R. Strauss. He held posts at various German houses in the 1930s, worked as an opera manager during the war and became permanent conductor of the Vienna Staatsoper in 1957. He taught at the Vienna Academy of Music from 1946, where his pupils incl. Abbado and Mehta. He was a highly respected interpreter of late Romantic composers and the Second Viennese School.

Swarthout, Gladys (1900–69) Amer. contralto, trained in Chicago, where she made her operatic debut in 1924. She sang regularly at the Metropolitan Opera from 1929 to 1945 and also appeared in films. Her roles incl. Carmen, Mignon and Adalgisa (*Norma*).

Sweelinck, Jan Pieterszoon (1562–1621) prolific Netherlands composer, organist and teacher. He was organist at the Oude Kerk in Amsterdam from about 1580 until his death. He was famous as a teacher and taught students from the Netherlands and Germany. As a composer he wrote a large number of vocal works—the secular music on French or Italian texts, the motets on Latin texts—and an equally important set of fantasias, toccatas and variations for keyboard and lute.

Sweeney Todd, the Demon Barber of Fleet Street musical/opera by Sondheim, book by Wheeler, after a 19th-c. melodrama by C. Bond. Premiere, New York 1979.

Sweet Adelines an organization of female barbershop quartets. The name comes from a song by Henry W. Armstrong ("Sweet Adeline," 1903) which was a favorite of barbershop quartets and whose title refers to the famous opera singer Adelina Patti.

Sweet Charity musical by Cy Coleman, lyrics by Dorothy Fields, book by Neil Simon, based on the film *Nights of Cabiria* by Federico Fellini, Tullio Pinelli, and Ennio Flaiano. Premiere, New York 1966. A New York dime-a-dance hostess gets involved romantically with an Italian screen star.

sweetening Mordent.

sweet potato Ocarina.

swell 1, an increase in loudness; esp. an increase in loudness followed by a corresponding decrease, indicated by the symbol (<>). 2, a mechanical device on the organ for producing a graded crescendo or diminuendo, usu. by opening and closing shutters enclosing the pipes by means of a pedal or lever. Usu. only one section of an organ (*swell organ*) is so equipped. Similar mechanisms on harpsichords and pianos never achieved any popularity.

swell organ see Swell (2,).

swing 1, a style of jazz popular in the 1930s and 1940s emphasizing large ensembles (big bands) and a greater degree of solo improvisation. The music tended to have a more even stress on the four beats of the bar and the repertory was largely drawn from popular, Tin Pan Alley songs. Among the many popular bands of the time the most famous were those of Benny Goodman, Count Basie, Fletcher Henderson, Artie Shaw, the Dorsey brothers and Duke Ellington. Cf. Mainstream jazz. 2, a quality of jazz performance characterized by a subtle interplay of regular pulse, cross-rhythms and gentle syncopation.

Swingle Singers French pop vocal group formed in 1962 by Ward Swingle (1927–), performing scat arrangements of Baroque and Classical instrumental repertory. The group was replaced in 1973 by an English group, Swingle II, whose repertory covered a broader range of styles.

Swing Mikado one of several modernized versions for black performers of the operetta by Gilbert and Sullivan, produced in New York in 1939. A competing version produced by Mike Todd, *Hot Mikado*, opened at about the same time.

swipe a type of constantly expanding chord progression in barbershop singing.

Sydeman, William (Jay) (1928–) Amer. composer, stud. of Sessions, Petrassi, Salzer and others. He taught at the Mannes College (1959–70), during which time he wrote works in the then current atonal and aleatory idioms. In more recent years, he has produced more accessible works, influenced by his study of Eastern philosophy and religion.

syllabic style in plainsong, the setting of a text with one note per syllable.

Sylphides, Les ballet (1909) adapted from the piano music of Chopin, choreographed by Fokine.

sympathetic string in certain stringed instruments, strings that are not played but sound in sympathy with the same note sounded on one of the played strings. Stringed instruments having sympathetic strings incl. the viola d'amore, the baryton and the Hardanger fiddle. Cf. ALIQUOT SCALING.

symphonia 1, any of various medieval instruments, incl. the hurdy-gurdy. **2**, an orchestral work; SYMPHONY. **3**, CONSONANCE.

Symphonia domestica (Lat., Domestic Symphony) orchestral work (1904) by R. Strauss, an autobiographical work supposedly commenting on the composer's private life.

symphonic band also, **concert band** a large wind band formed to give concerts rather than for marching.

symphonic jazz a term dating from the 1920s for jazz-influenced music for orch., a predecessor of THIRD STREAM music. The term can apply either to music by jazz or popular composers scored for conventional orchestral forces (such as Ellington's *Creole Rhapsody*) or to works deliberately fusing jazz and classical elements and forms (Milhaud's *La Création du monde*, Gershwin's *Rhapsody in Blue*).

symphonic poem an orchestral work attempting by musical means to convey a narrative story or visual image to the listener. The program can range from a general idea, as in *Ce qu'on entend sur la montagne* by Liszt, to a complete story, as in Richard Strauss's *Don Juan* and *Till Eulenspiegel* or Berlioz's *Symphonie fantastique*. Often the inspiration for the work may come from a preexistent poem or other literary work (Debussy's *Prélude à l'après-midi d'un faune*, based on a poem by Stéphane Mallarmé, is a famous example, as are the numerous works based on Byron's *Manfred*). Cf. TONE POEM.

Symphonie espagnole [se-fo'ne espä'nyŏl] (Fr., Spanish Symphony) a work in five movements for violin and orch., Op. 21 (1874), by Lalo.

symphonie concertante [kŏ-ser'tät] (Fr.) a type of CONCERTO for two or more solo instruments with orch.

Symphonie fantastique [fä-täs'tēk] (Fr., Fantastic Symphony) orchestral work in five movements, Op. 14 (1830), by Berlioz, subtitled *Épisode de la vie d'un artiste* (Episode in an Artist's Life). The movements are entitled "Rêveries—Passions" (Daydreams—Passions), "Un Bal" (a ball), "Scène aux champs" (Scene in the Country), "Marche au supplice" (March to Execution) and "Songe d'une nuit de Sabbat" (Dream of a [witches'] Sabbath).

symphonium a type of HARMONICA invented in 1829 by Charles Wheatstone.

symphony 1, SINFONIA. **2**, an extended instrumental passage occurring in a vocal work. **3**, an extended work for orch., usu. employing the three- or four-movement form of the SONATA; also, a similar work for organ. **4**, symphony orch. (see ORCHESTRA).

Symphony 1933 the Symphony No. 1 (1933) by Roy Harris.

Symphony of a Thousand the Symphony No. 8 in E♭ major for soloists, boy choir, chorus and orch. (1906) by Mahler, so called (rather inflatedly) because of the large forces required to perform it.

Symphony of Psalms symphony in three movements for chorus and orch. (1930) by Stravinsky on texts from the Psalms, commissioned by Koussevitzky for the 50th anniversary of the Boston SO.

Symphony on a French Mountain Air concerto in three movements for piano and orch., Op. 25 (1886), by d'Indy.

syncopation a temporary shifting of the rhythmic accent from an accented beat to a normally unaccented beat. The note so accented (*syncope*) is often held over into the following strong beat. See RHYTHM.

synthetic scale in jazz theory, a scale composed of parts of other scales.

synthesizer a machine which gen-

Syncopation

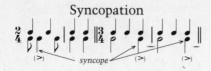

erates sounds electronically and is usu. capable of performing a wide variety of modifications on the sounds created.

Syracuse Symphony Orchestra the name for a number of short-lived orchestras in Syracuse NY dating from 1892. The present orch. was formed in 1961. Its conductors have included Karl Kritz, Prausnitz, Keene and Akiyama.

syrinx 1, PANPIPE. **2,** the mouthpiece of the aulos.

system two or more musical staves, usu. joined together by a line or brace at the left end, representing the whole musical texture of a line of music.

system music a method of composition involving extensive use of motivic repetition; most often encountered in minimal music (see MINIMALISM).

Szell, George (Georg) (1897–1970) Hungarian-born Amer. conductor, stud. of Mandyczewski, Foerster, Reger and Richard Robert. He joined the staff of the Berlin Staatsoper in 1915, was musical dir. of the German Opera and Philharmonic in Prague and conductor of the Scottish Orch. He conducted at the Metropolitan Opera in the mid-1940s, then led the Cleveland Orch. from 1946 to 1970, creating one of the finest orchestral ensembles in the world.

Szeryng, Henryk (1918–88) Polish-born Mexican violinist, stud. of Flesch and Boulanger. He was active during the war working with the Polish government in exile to find homes for refugees in Mexico. He also gave over 300 concerts for Allied troops overseas. From 1946 he lived and taught in Mexico, performing music of native Mexican composers, and continued to tour extensively from 1954.

Szigeti, Joseph (1892–1973) Hungarian-born Amer. violinist, stud. of Hubay in Budapest. His Amer. debut was in 1925 under Stokowsky. He toured extensively in the 1930s and 1940s and performed with Bartók and Stravinsky. After 1960 he concentrated on teaching and writing about the violin and its repertory.

Szokolay, Sandor (1931–) Hungarian composer, stud. of Szabó and Farkas in Budapest, where he taught after 1966. His major work has been the opera *Blood Wedding* (1962–64) based on a play by Lorca.

Szymanowska (née Wolowska), **Maria Agata** (1789–1831) Polish pianist and composer, trained in Warsaw. She concertized widely in Europe and Russia until 1828, thereafter devoting herself to teaching. Most of her works are for solo piano or voice.

Szymanowski, Karol (Maciej) (1882–1937) Polish composer, trained in Warsaw. He was a founder in 1905 of the Young Polish Composers' Publishing Co. in Berlin to encourage new Polish music. In the 1920s he spent much time abroad, returning in 1927 to become dir. of the Warsaw Conservatory (later the Warsaw Academy of Music), resigning in 1932. He spent his last years composing in relative penury. His works incl. *King Roger* and 3 other operas, *Harnasie* (ballet), 2 violin concertos, 4 symphonies, *Stabat Mater*, 2 string quartets, many songs, choral works and piano pieces.

T

T. *abbr.* TUTTI.

ta the flattened leading tone of the current key (or of the relative major, if the current key is minor) in TONIC SOL-FA.

Tabarro, Il (It., The Cloak) *verismo* opera in 1 act by Puccini to a libretto by Giuseppe Adami after the play *La Houppelande* by Didier Gold. Premiere, New York 1918. The first opera of IL TRITTICO. Barge owner Michèle kills the lover of his wife Giorgetta.

tabla a pair of single-headed Indian drums, a wooden barrel-drum on the right (*dhaya* or *tabla*) and a clay or copper kettledrum on the left (*bhaya*), tuned to different pitches and used to accompany vocal and instrumental music.

tablature 1, any of various systems of notation dating back to the 14th c. that indicate which finger, fret, etc., to use by letters, numbers or other signs rather than by means of notes on a staff. Tablature was used esp. for keyboard and plucked string instruments and is still in use for guitar, lute and other similar instruments, esp. in popular music. **2**, TONIC SOL-FA notation.

table BELLY.

table-book a musical SCORE printed in such a way that the performers can read their parts when seated around a table.

tab show *or* **tabloid show** a type of VAUDEVILLE road show of the late 19th and early 20th c.

Tabulatur [tä-boo-lä-toor'] (Ger.) TABLATURE.

tabor *also*, **tabour** a small SIDE DRUM with a soft calfskin head and one or more snares, used to accompany the fife, both usu. being played by the same person. Cf. *tabret, tambourine.*

tabret TAMBOURINE.

Tabuteau, Marcel [tä-bü'tō] (1887–1966) French oboist, stud. of Georges Gillet. He came to the U.S. in 1905, playing first oboe with the New York SO (1905–14), the Metropolitan Opera orch. (1908–14) and the Philadelphia Orch. (1914–54). He taught at the Curtis Institute from 1924, where he produced a generation of distinguished oboists.

tacet ['tä-sət] (Lat., he is silent) an indication not to play, usu. for the duration of a movement.

tactus the BEAT in 15th- and 16th-c. music, indicated by regular movements of the hand, a stick, etc., and usu. corresponding to the semibreve.

Taddei, Giuseppe (1916–) Italian baritone, trained in Rome. Until 1942 he sang mostly in Rome; since the war he has appeared throughout Europe and in the U.S. (Chicago). His wide repertory includes both dramatic and comic roles.

Tafelklavier ['tä-fəl-klä"vēr] (Ger., table piano) SQUARE PIANO.

Tafelmusik [-moo-zēk'] (Ger., table

Tablature

Lute (French)

(D. Gaultier)

Guitar

Woodwind (oboe)

music) a term used in the 16th and 17th c. for music intended for feasts and banquets. Cf. DIVERTIMENTO.

Taffanel, (Claude) Paul (1844–1908) eminent French flutist, trained at the Paris Conservatoire, where he later taught a famous class. He played and conducted at the Opéra Comique and the Société des concerts du Conservatoire and was a founder of the Société des instruments à vent in 1879.

tag in popular music and jazz, a short coda-like addition to the end of a song, often improvised.

Tagelied ['tä-gə"lēt] (Ger., day song) a song of the Minnesingers announcing daybreak. Cf. ALBA.

Tagliabue, Carlo [tä-lyä'boo-ä] (1898–1978) Italian baritone, stud. of Gennai and Guidotti. He sang regularly at La Scala from 1930 and in the U.S. from 1937 as well as at other major international opera houses. He retired in 1960.

Tagliavini, Ferruccio [-'vĕ-nĕ] (1913–) Italian tenor, stud. of Bassi and Brancucci. His Metropolitan Opera debut was in 1947 and he sang there until 1962. He was esp. known for his performance of bel canto roles.

taiko Jap. double-headed folk BARREL DRUM.

tailgate style a style of jazz trombone playing developed in New Orleans in the early 1900s, characterized by smears, growls, and other evocative sounds.

taille [tī] (Fr., tenor) **1**, the TENOR in vocal music. **2**, a tenor instrumental part, as for the tenor viol, the viola or the English horn. **3**, OBOE DA CACCIA.

Tailleferre, Germaine ['tī-yə-fer, zher'men] (1892–1983) French composer, trained at the Paris Conservatoire, a member of LES SIX. Her works incl. 6 operas, ballets, orchestral works, sonatas for violin, harp and clarinet, other chamber music and songs.

tailpiece the piece of wood or metal to which the strings are attached at the lower end of a stringed instrument.

tailpin ENDPIN.

Tajo, Italo ['tī-yō] (1915–) Italian bass, stud. of Nilde Bertozzi in Turin. He performed in Italy and England and made his U.S. debut in Chicago in 1946. He taught at the Cincinnati College-Conservatory of Music from 1966 to 1988 and appeared on Broadway in the mid-1950s in *Fanny* and *Kiss Me, Kate*. He has sung a wide repertory of roles, specializing in later years in character parts.

take in music recording, a version of a work that is actually being recorded (as opposed to a rehearsal).

Takemitsu, Toru (1930–) Japanese composer, stud. of Yasuji Kiyose. He has written in a variety of styles, experimenting with most contemporary techniques, and has also written new works for traditional Japanese instruments. His compositions incl. a number of orchestral works and concertos (incl. *November Steps*, for biwa, shakuhachi and orch.), chamber music, works for piano, tape works and film scores. He also produced several musico-dramatic "events" in Tokyo in the 1960s.

Takt (Ger.) **1**, METER. **2**, MEASURE. **3**, BEAT.

Tal (Gruenthal), **Josef** (1910–) prolific Israeli composer, pianist and teacher, trained in Berlin. He taught at the Israel Academy of Music from 1936 to 1952 (he was dir. from 1948) and at Hebrew U. from 1950, where he heads the Electronic Music Center. His works incl. 6 operas, 3 symphonies, concertos (for flute, piano, viola and cello), string quartets, piano works, chamber music and works combining instruments with taped sounds.

tala a rhythmic unit in Indian music, repeated cyclically and performed by the hands, a drum or other percussion instrument.

talamba a Yugoslav KETTLEDRUM.

Talbot, Howard (Howard Munkitrick) (1865–1928) American-born English composer of London musicals, especially *A Chinese Honeymoon* (1899) and *The Arcadians* (1909).

talea (Lat., cutting) a rhythmic pattern that is repeated any number of times (and often using proportional relationships in diminution and/or augmentation) to form the basis of an isorhythmic motet. The *talea* is often combined with a COLOR (1), the length of which may or may not correspond to the length of the *talea*. Both *color* and *talea* usu. occur in the tenor part of the motet. See ISO-RHYTHM.

Tales from the Vienna Woods (Ger., *Geschichten aus dem Wienerwald*) orchestral waltz, Op. 325 (1868), by Johann Strauss Jr.

Tales of Hoffmann, The (Fr., *Les Contes d'Hoffmann*) opera in 3 acts by Offenbach to a libretto by Jules Barbier based on stories of E.T.A. Hoffmann. Premiere, Paris 1881. The opera, which was left incomplete at the composer's death, has been performed in several different versions. The story concerns the poet Hoffmann, his love for the opera singer Stella, who embodies three women (an automaton, a courtesan and an artist) and his antagonist Lindorf, who finally wins her.

Talich, Václav (1883–1961) Czech conductor, trained in Prague. He was chief conductor of the Czech PO (1919–41) and the Slovak PO (1949–52), retiring in 1956. He was a noted interpreter of a wide repertory, esp. the works of Janáček, Smetana and Dvořak and contemporary Czech.

talking drum a drum used for wordless communication; esp. the KALUNGU.

Talking Heads Amer. new-wave and funk-rock band formed in 1975 in New York and headed by singer/guitarist David Byrne.

tallharpa ['täl-här-pä] a Swedish folk bowed LYRE.

Tallis, Thomas (c1505–85) English composer, singer and organist, a Gentleman of the Chapel Royal from about 1542. In 1575 he received, with William Byrd, an exclusive license to print and publish music, a venture which was not financially successful.

He wrote a large amount of music for both the Latin and English services, as well as secular part music, keyboard works and consort music. His best-known work is prob. the 40-voice motet "Spem in alium." The IN NOMINE cantus firmus is derived from Tallis's *Missa in Gloria tibi Trinitas*.

Talma, Louise (1906–) French-born Amer. composer, stud. of Philipp and Boulanger. She taught at Hunter College (1928–79) and at Fontainebleau and has received many awards. Her works progressed from a neo-Classical style in the 1940s to a serial style in the 1950s. She has written many vocal works, incl. the opera *Alcestiad*, chamber music and works for orch.

talon (Fr.) FROG.

Talvela, Martti (Olavi) (1935–89) Finnish bass, trained in Stockholm and a frequent performer at Bayreuth as well as at other international opera houses.

Tamagno, Francesco [tä'mä-nyō] (1850–1905) Italian tenor, stud. of Pedrotti. He pursued a highly successful career in Italy, London and Buenos Aires, esp. in the heroic Verdi roles, incl. Otello and Don Carlo.

Tamberlik, Enrico (1820–1889) Ital. dramatic tenor, esp. noted for his performance of Verdi roles such as Manrico (*Il Trovatore*) and Ernani.

tamborito (Sp.) a Panamanian dance-song of Afr.-Hispanic origin.

tambour [tä'boor] (Fr.) *also*, **tambor** [täm'bor] (Sp.) DRUM.

tambour de basque [bäsk] TAMBOURINE.

tamboura (Pers.) an unfretted Asian LUTE used as a drone instrument to accompany singing. Also, *tanbur*.

tambourin [tä-boo'rē] **1**, (Provençal) a lively Provençal dance in quick duple meter, often with a drone bass, orig. accompanied by the tambourine. **2**, (Fr.) an 18th-c. French character piece in a lively duple meter found in opera, ballet, keyboard dance suites, etc., based on the TAMBOURIN (1,).

tambourin de Béarn [bä'ärn] (Fr.) an odd STRING DRUM consisting of six gut strings stretched over a wooden sounding box. The strings are struck with a stick held in the right hand as the performer plays a small three-hole pipe, fingered by the left hand.

tambourine a small FRAME DRUM, esp. one with a single head and loose metal disks at the side that jingle when the drum is played. Also, *timbrel.*

tambour militaire [mē-lē'ter] (Fr.) SIDE DRUM.

tambura **1**, a Yugoslav long-necked LUTE. **2**, an Indian drone LUTE with four strings and a movable bridge.

Tamburini, Antonio (1800–76) Ital. bass-baritone, noted both in serious and buffo roles of Donizetti, Bellini, etc. He retired in 1859.

tamburo (It.) DRUM.

tamburone (It.) BASS DRUM.

tampon a two-headed DRUMSTICK used for playing rolls on the bass drum when one hand must be used for another purpose, as for playing the cymbals.

tam-tam **1**, TOM-TOM. **2**, a tuned bronze GONG.

tanbur TAMBOURA.

Tancredi opera in 2 acts by Rossini to a libretto by Gaetano Rossi, based on Voltaire's *Tancrède*. Premiere, Venice 1813. Tancredi returns home from exile in Sicily in time to prevent the marriage of his beloved Amenaide to his rival Orbazzano. The original happy ending, in which the lovers are united, was changed for the opera's second production to Voltaire's ending, in which Tancredi dies, but audiences preferred Rossini's original version.

Taneyev, Sergey (1856–1915) Russian composer and pianist, stud. of Tchaikovsky, Nikolay Rubinstein and others. He taught at the Moscow Conservatory from 1878 and became dir. in 1885, resigning in 1889 to concentrate on composition. He was generally unsympathetic to the nationalist movement, retaining a more broadly European style. His works incl. an opera (*Oresteya*), 4 symphonies, a piano concerto, string chamber music, piano works, many choral works and songs. He also wrote a treatise on counterpoint and made arrangements and orchestrations of works of Tchaikovsky and others.

tangent a flat-ended brass wedge mounted perpendicular to the end of a clavichord key that strikes the string to produce a sound and terminates its vibrating length, thus fixing the pitch.

tangent piano a type of mid-18th-c. piano using harpsichord-type jacks and wooden tangents.

Tanglewood an eight-week series of summer concerts begun in 1934 in Stockbridge, MA, but held in Lenox at the Tanglewood estate since 1938. The Boston SO is the resident orch. The Tanglewood Music Center, est. in 1940 as the Berkshire Music Center, is a training institution held on the estate during the festival.

tango an Argentinian ballroom DANCE in ¼ time with elaborate posturing and a characteristic rhythm. The dance was orig. created by the Gauchos of the Argentine pampas.

Tanguay, Eva (1878–1947) Amer. vaudeville singer and dancer, famous for her audacious and blatantly sexual dancing and singing.

Tannhäuser ['tän"hoi = zər] **1**, German Minnesinger and composer (c1205–c1270). **2**, romantic opera in 3 acts by Wagner to his own libretto, based on medieval legend concerning the historical Tannhäuser (1,). Premiere, Dresden 1845. The opera was revised for a later Paris production (1861) with the addition of ballet music and other changes.

Tansman, Alexandre (1897–1986) Polish-born French composer, conductor and pianist, trained at Warsaw U. He toured extensively as a pianist and conductor and composed in a wide variety of styles and genres, incl. film scores.

tanto (It.) so much; used in tempo indications.

Tanz [tänts] (Ger.) dance.

Tanzhalle [-"hä-le] (Ger.) dance hall.

tap dance a type of Amer. theatrical

dance of the 20th c., combining elements of the Irish jig, English clog dance and Afr.-Amer. dance. The dance is performed with metal plates (taps) attached to the toe and heel of the shoes to sound the rhythm of the feet. Cf. SOFT SHOE.

tape recorder music music conceived for performance by means of recorded tape composed of electronically produced sounds or of electronically manipulated natural sounds. See ELECTRONIC MUSIC, MUSIQUE CONCRÈTE.

Tapiola pastoral tone poem, Op. 112 (1925), by Sibelius, evoking the domain of Tapio, the Finnish mythical forest god.

tar 1, a Turkish FRAME DRUM with jingle disks. 2, a type of Middle Eastern long-necked LUTE.

tarabuka a Greek GOBLET DRUM.

Tarack, Gerald (1929–) Amer. violinist, stud. of Galamian, Max Senofsky and others. He has been concertmaster of the Puerto Rico SO, Clarion Concerts and the Mostly Mozart Orch. and has led his own Tarack Chamber Players from 1974. He was a founding member of the Beaux Arts String Quartet and has taught at Brooklyn College, Queens College (NY) and at SUNY, Stony Brook. His broad repertory has included performance with various jazz artists, and he has been assoc. with several major dance companies.

tarantella (It.) also, **tarentelle** [tärä'tel] (Fr.) a quick so. Italian couple folk DANCE in 6/8 time accompanied by tambourines.

Taras Bulba orchestral rhapsody in 3 movements (1918) by Janáček, based on a work by Nicolay Gogol, telling a story of love and heroism during a war between the Cossacks and the Poles. The movements are "The Death of Andri," "The Death of Ostapov" and "The Prophecy and Death of Taras Bulba."

tarbouka DARABUKKA.

tardamente (It.) slowly.

tardo (It.) slow.

tarentelle (Fr.) TARANTELLA.

Tarlton, Jimmie (Johnny James Rimbert) (1892–1979) Amer. country-music singer and guitarist, one of the earliest artists to record on the acoustic steel guitar. He performed extensively in duo with singer/guitarist Tom Darby.

tarogato (Hung.) 1, a Hungarian woodwind instrument using a clarinet reed and having a bell similar to that of the English horn. In the early 18th c. it was assoc. with the Rákóczy freedom movement in Hungary. 2, a type of SHAWM.

taro-patch fiddle a large UKULELE.

Tarr, Edward H(ankins) (1936–) Amer. trumpeter and musicologist, stud. of Voisin, Herseth and Leo Schrade. He has specialized in the realization of early trumpet music on modern instruments and reconstructions and has published work on the history of the trumpet. He has taught at the Basel Conservatory and the Schola Cantorum Basiliensis.

Tartini, Giuseppe (1692–1770) influential Italian composer, violinist, teacher and theorist. By 1721 he was employed at St. Anthony's Basilica in Padua, a post he held until 1765. In addition to his fame as a violin virtuoso, he is noted for his discovery of the difference tone (see COMBINATION TONE) and his theoretical writings, as well as for his many concertos and sonatas for violin and string ensembles, esp. the DEVIL'S TRILL sonata. He founded a famous violin school ("School of Nations") in Padua in 1728.

Tartiniana either of two works for solo violin and small orch. (1951, 1956) by Dallapiccola, based on melodies by Giuseppe Tartini.

Tartini's tone difference tone (see COMBINATION TONE.

Tartöld ['tär-tœlt] (Ger.) a 16th-c. RACKETT having a metal body in the shape of a dragon, the tail of which is the crook.

Tashi (Tibetan, good fortune) chamber music ensemble founded in New York in 1972 by pianist Peter Serkin, clarinetist Richard Stoltzman, violinist Ida Kavafian and cellist Fred

Sherry. The instrumentation is based on the *Quatuor pour la fin du temps* of Messiaen.

tastar (It.) a type of 16th-c. lute work in free prelude style intended to test the tuning of the strings and establish the mode or tonality of the works to follow. Also, *tañer* (Sp.).

tastiera [täs′tye-rä] (It.) **1,** KEYBOARD. **2,** FINGERBOARD.

tasto (It., key, fret) **1,** the KEY of a keyboard instrument. **2,** FINGERBOARD. See SUL TASTO, TASTO SOLO.

tasto solo (It., single key) an instruction in FIGURED BASS not to play chords above the bass.

Tate, Buddy (George Holmes) (1913–) Amer. tenor saxophonist. He played in a number of different southwestern bands before joining Count Basie in 1939. He stayed nine years, then moved to the Celebrity Club in Harlem, where he played for over 20 years. His recent years he has spent as a free-lancer, working in the U.S. and in Europe.

tattoo *also,* **tatto** a call to quarters preceding taps, orig. a drum call, later enhanced with fifes. Cf. SIGNAL.

Tatum, Art(hur) (1910–56) innovative and influential Amer. jazz pianist from Toledo, OH. His virtuoso technique and highly developed improvisational skills were displayed throughout the U.S. and England. He formed a trio with double bass and guitar in 1943, then in the 1950s made many appearances and recordings under producer Norman Granz. His art combined the stride piano technique with a harmonic sophistication and blinding speed, making him an important precursor of bop.

Tauber, Richard (Seiffert, Ernst) (1891–1948) Austrian-born English tenor, stud. of Carl Beines. He sang opera at the Dresden Opera and in Berlin, Munich and Salzburg, but was even more successful as a singer in operetta, esp. Lehár's *The Land of Smiles.*

Tausig, Carl (1841–71) Polish pianist and composer, stud. of Liszt. He was highly regarded as a virtuoso in a var-

ied repertory from Scarlatti to the late Romantic works. He also produced several important didactic works for piano.

Taverner opera in 2 acts by Maxwell Davies to his own libretto based on the life of composer JOHN TAVERNER. Premiere, London 1972. The opera treats some themes by Taverner in a contemporary fashion. Taverner is accused of heresy by the abbot and tried for heresy; he then accuses and tries the abbot.

Taverner, John (c1490–1545) English composer of sacred vocal music. He was choir master at Christ Church, Oxford, then at St. Botolph, Boston (England). Most of his sacred vocal works—mass and magnificat settings and motets—appear to have been written in the 1520s.

tayauté [tä-yō′tä] (Fr.) see JIRKING.

Taylor, Billy (William) (1921–) Amer. jazz pianist, composer and teacher. He has worked with many artists, incl. Dizzy Gillespie, Don Redman and Stuff Smith, and has led his own trio since the early 1950s. He has also produced a number of didactic works on jazz piano, given many performance clinics and written a doctoral dissertation on the history of jazz piano.

Taylor, Cecil (Percival) (1933–) Amer. avant-garde jazz pianist and composer, trained at the New England Conservatory. He has been the leader of various small groups with such artists in them as Steve Lacy, Buell Neidlinger and Jimmy Lyons, and although his music is somewhat forbidding to the general audience, incorporating clusters and irregular rhythms, and snippets of poetry and dance, he has consistently won critical praise.

Taylor, (Joseph) Deems (1885–1966) Amer. composer and critic, stud. of Oscar Coon. He was music critic for several papers and a dir. of ASCAP for over thirty years. He was a successful composer in his time—two of his operas received multiple performances at the Metropolitan Opera—but his works have not survived the test of time. He wrote *The King's Henchman* and *Peter Ibbetson* and other operas and operettas, *A Christmas Overture* and other orchestral works, choral music and songs, as well as a number of books on music and musicians, incl. *Of Men and Music* (1937), *The Well Tempered Listener* (1940) and *Music to my Ears* (1949).

Taylor, James (Vernon) (1948–) Amer. pop singer, guitarist and songwriter, noted for his despairing lyrics and understated tone. His first successes came in the early 1970s with "You've Got a Friend" and "Carolina in My Mind." He has recorded with Simon and Garfunkle and with his former wife Carly Simon. His sister **Kate** and brothers **Alex** and **Livingston** are also singers.

Taylor, Raynor (1745–1825) English-born Amer. composer, organist and teacher. Although successful in London, he came to America in 1792, settling in Philadelphia, where he served as organist at St. Peter's Church and wrote music for the Chestnut Street Theater. He was also an influential teacher and a music dealer. His works incl. *The Ethiop* (opera), chamber music, songs and anthems.

Taylor, Samuel Coleridge COLERIDGE-TAYLOR, SAMUEL.

Taylor-Greenfield, Elizabeth (1809–76) Amer. soprano, born a slave in Mississippi. She established her reputation in the northeastern U.S. in the early 1850s, nicknamed "The Black Swan" and likened to Jenny Lind, but made her greatest successes in England. She taught in Philadelphia until her death.

t.c. *abbr.* TRE CORDE.

Tchaikovsky, Piotr Ilyich (1840–93) Russian composer, trained at the St. Petersburg Conservatory. After graduation he taught at the Moscow Conservatory with the encouragement of Nikolay Rubinstein. In later years he made a number of conducting tours to Europe and, in 1891, to the U.S. He died by his own hand under unclear circumstances. Tchaikovsky's music, primarily for orchestra and the stage, is esp. esteemed for its melodic skill, the dark cast of the harmonies and orchestration and the use of Russian folk melody. His works incl. *Undine, Eugene Onegin, Mazeppa, The Queen of Spades, Iolanta* and other operas, *The Sleeping Beauty, Swan Lake, The Nutcracker* and other ballets, 6 symphonies, tone poems, overtures (incl. the perennial favorite "1812 Overture"), piano concertos, a violin concerto, choral works, string quartets, *Souvenir de Florence* (string sextet), piano works and songs.

Tcherepnin, Alexander (1899–1977) Russian composer, conductor and pianist, son of NICOLAY TCHEREPNIN. He studied in Paris with Isidor Philipp and Paul Vidal and toured as pianist from the 1920s to the 1940s. From 1950 to 1964 he taught at De Paul U. in Chicago. He wrote a large number of works in all genres, incl. operas, ballets, 4 symphonies, 6 piano concertos, songs and chamber music.

Tcherepnin, Ivan (1943–) French-born Amer. composer, son of ALEXANDER TCHEREPNIN, stud. of Kirchner, Pousseur, Boulez and others. He has taught at the San Francisco Conservatory, Stanford and Harvard and was co-dir. of Alea II, a new music ensemble at Stanford. Most of his works are electronic or for live instruments combined with electronic sounds.

Tcherepnin, Nikolay (1873–1945) Russian conductor and composer, stud. of Rimsky-Korsakov. He conducted the first season of Diaghilev's Ballets Russes in Paris and was later conductor of the National Conservatory of Tbilisi. From 1921 he lived in Paris and guest-conducted in Europe and the U.S. His works, in the tradition of his teacher Rimsky-Korsakov, incl. operas, a number of ballets, tone poems, many choral and vocal works, chamber music and piano works.

Tcherepnin, Serge (1941–) French-born Amer. composer and instrument maker, son of ALEXANDER

Tcherepnin, stud. of Boulanger, Kirchner, Stockhausen and others. He has taught at New York U. and the Valencia (CA) School of Music and is the designer and manufacturer of the Serge synthesizer.

tbn. *abbr.* Trombone.

Teagarden, Jack (Weldon Leo) (1905–64) Amer. jazz trombonist and singer from Texas. One of the finest jazz trombonists (and blues singers), he played with a number of bands, incl. Peck's Bad Boys, Louis Armstrong, Eddie Condon and Paul Whiteman. He was one of the famous Three t's. He later led a number of small bands in the 1940s and 1950s. He was esp. noted for his beautiful tone.

Tear, Robert (1939–) Welsh tenor, trained at King's College, Cambridge. He has sung a number of roles for the English Opera Group and at Covent Garden and has appeared in many international opera houses and in concert. He is esp. esteemed for his interpretation of the Evangelist in Bach's Passions.

Tebaldi, Renata (1922–) Italian soprano, stud. of Carmen Melis. She sang regularly at La Scala until 1959. Her U.S. debut was in San Francisco in 1950 and she sang at the Metropolitan Opera (1955–74), Chicago Lyric Opera, in Dallas and elsewhere. Her roles incl. Aida, Mimì (*La Bohème*) and Tosca.

technopop term for a variety of rock music of the 1980s specializing in the use of the most advanced electronic equipment and effects.

tedesca [tä′de-skä] (It., in the German style) usu. used in the phrases *danza tedesca* or *alla tedesca*, referring to 15th- and 16th-c. dances in quick triple time; Allemande.

Te Deum (Lat., Thee God [we praise]) the chant or a setting of the chant sung at the close of Matins on Sundays and feast days. Polyphonic settings of the Te Deum abound, most notably those by Haydn, Berlioz and Verdi. Settings in English and German (as for Protestant services) incl. works by J.S. Bach, C.P.E. Bach, Bux-

tehude and Purcell. Walton's 1953 setting in English was sung at the coronation of Elizabeth II.

Te Deum Symphony the incomplete Symphony No. 9 (1903) by Bruckner. The composer suggested replacing the unfinished last movement with his *Te Deum* (1881–4).

Teitelbaum, Richard (Lowe) (1939–) Amer. composer and performer, trained at Yale and in Italy with Petrassi and Nono. His wide compositional and performing interests have included electronic music using the Moog synthesizer, biofeedback music, collective improvisation and computer-controlled performance.

Te Kanawa, Dame **Kiri** (1944–) New Zealand soprano, stud. of Vera Rosza. She has sung regularly at Covent Garden since 1970 and has appeared at Glyndebourne, the Metropolitan Opera (debut 1974) and most major opera houses. Her U.S. debut was in San Francisco in 1972. Her roles incl. the Countess (*The Marriage of Figaro*), Desdemona (*Otello*) and Mimì (*La Bohème*). She has also recorded popular songs and several musicals by Bernstein.

Telemann, Georg Philipp (1681–1767) highly prolific German composer, instrumentalist, singer and theorist, trained with Benedikt Christiani, at the Gymnasium Andreanum in Hildesheim and at the U. of Leipzig. His many musical activities in Leipzig incl. the organization of a student collegium musicum, the directorship of the Leipzig Opera and the position of organist at the Neue Kirche. In 1705 he became Kapellmeister in Sorau, around 1708 he moved to the court at Eisenach and in 1712 he became city dir. of music in Frankfurt am Main.

In 1721 he moved to Hamburg, where he would remain as Kantor of the Johanneum and musical dir. of the churches until his death. His position required two cantatas a week and a Passion every year, as well as ceremonial music, etc. In later years he cut back on his composition and concentrated on theoretical work.

As a composer Telemann represented an important link between the baroque and Classical eras. His works, still widely performed today, incl. c20 operas, sacred and secular cantatas, oratorios, almost 50 Passion settings, masses, motets, psalms, occasional music, songs, instrumental concertos, orchestral overtures and symphonies, a large quantity of instrumental chamber music, keyboard and lute suites, and fantasies.

Telephone, The comic opera in 1 act by Menotti to his own libretto. Premiere, New York 1947. Because Lucy spends all her time on the phone, Ben has to call her up himself to propose marriage.

telharmonium a keyboard instrument designed c1900 by Thaddeus Cahill to transmit music over telephone wires. Also, *dynamophone*.

tema ['tā-mä] (It.) THEME.

Temianka, Henri (1906–) Scottish-born Amer. violinist and conductor, stud. of Hess, Flesch, Rodzinski and others. He briefly held orchestral positions but concentrated on a solo career. He founded the Paganini String Quartet in 1946 and the California Chamber SO in 1960 and has taught at the U. of California at Santa Barbara and at California State U. in Long Beach.

temperament the modification of the tones of a scale made up of pure intervals to produce a fixed scale of twelve pitches equally spaced so as to permit less jarring modulation from one key to another. Of the many tempered tuning systems developed since the mid-15th c., the most widely used are MEAN-TONE TEMPERAMENT, EQUAL TEMPERAMENT and JUST INTONATION. See TUNING SYSTEMS.

Tempest, The the piano sonata in D minor, Op. 31 No. 2 (1802), by Beethoven.

Tempesta di Mare, La 1, the violin concerto in E♭ major, RV253, Op. 8 No. 5, by Vivaldi. **2**, the concerto for flute and orch. in F major, RV433, Op. 10 No. 1, by Vivaldi.

temple block CHINESE WOOD BLOCK.

Templeton, Alec (Andrew) (1909–63) Welsh-born Amer. composer, pianist and satirist, blind from birth. He was trained in London. He was best known as a radio and recording artist, esp. for his satirical sketches and musical parodies.

tempo the rate of speed of a musical passage, indicated by a suggestive word or phrase or by a precise indication such as a METRONOME marking. In popular music a fast tempo is referred to as *up tempo*, a slow one as *down tempo*. Out of tempo playing can mean RUBATO or can suggest a poor sense of rhythm. For a list of standard tempo indications, see EXPRESSION MARKS; Glossary (p. 609).

tempo giusto ['joo-sto] (It., strict time) a tempo marking of variable meaning, suggesting that the performer adopt a traditional tempo for the type of work involved (as for a dance movement) or a tempo that seems correct. The marking is also used to mean strict tempo after a section in free time.

tempo ordinario (It.) COMMON TIME.

tempo primo (It.) an indication to return to the original tempo after a temporary change.

tempo rubato (It.) RUBATO.

temporale [tām-pō'rä-lā] (It., storm) **1**, a storm scene in a 19th-c. opera, esp. in the operas of Rossini. **2**, see PROPER.

Tempora Mutantur (Lat., Times are Changing) the symphony No. 64 in A major (c1773) by Haydn.

Temptations, The Amer. male gospel and soul vocal quintet formed in 1962 in Detroit. In the late 1960s their style changed to psychedelic soul. Their many hits incl. "My Girl" (1965), "Just My Imagination" (1971) and "Papa Was a Rolling Stone" (1972).

tempus (Lat., time) in MENSURAL NOTATION the relationship between the semibreve and the breve, i.e. the double or triple division of the breve.

ten. *abbr.* **1**, TENUTO. **2**, TENOR.

Tender Land, The opera in 3 acts by Copland to a libretto by Horace Everett. Premiere, New York 1954. A story of love and disillusionment on a Midwestern farm.

Tenney, James (Carl) (1934–) Amer. composer, pianist and conductor, stud. of Steuermann and others. He has performed as soloist and with the Steve Reich and Philip Glass ensembles and has been a dir. of the Tone Roads concert series in New York and Los Angeles. He has taught at the California Institute of the Arts and York U. (Toronto). He has done extensive research in computer and microtonal music and his own works often incorporate electronic media.

Tennstedt, Klaus (1926–) German conductor, trained at the Leipzig Conservatory. He held various positions in East Germany in the 1950s and 1960s, then moved to Sweden in 1971. His U.S. debut was in Boston in 1974 and he first appeared with the Metropolitan Opera in 1983. He has been principal conductor of the London PO since 1983. He is esp. noted for his performances of Bruckner and Mahler.

tenor **1**, the highest natural, adult, male voice, having a range from about c to a'. **2**, the melodic part, usu. the cantus firmus, in medieval part music. **3**, the principal reciting tone in plainsong. **4**, an instrument having approximately the range of a vocal tenor.

tenor banjo a BANJO with a shorter neck and no fifth string.

tenor clef the C CLEF on the fourth line of the staff.

tenor cor a valved HORN in F invented c1860 in Paris having half the tube length of the standard F horn and hence requiring less advanced lip technique. Also, *mellophone.*

tenor drum a medium-sized DRUM without snares used in the symphony orch.

tenore di forza ['for-tsä] (It.) HEROIC TENOR.

tenore di grazia ['grä-tsya] (It.) LYRIC TENOR.

tenor guitar a small, four-string GUITAR tuned higher than the regular guitar.

tenor horn an alto SAXHORN in E♭ used in military and brass bands.

Tenorlied [-lēt] (Ger., tenor song) a type of 15th- and 16th-c. German part-song consisting of a cantus firmus derived from an existing Lied melody and two or three contrapuntal parts. It was orig. performed as a solo song with instruments with only the cantus firmus line being sung.

tenor Mass a Mass setting in which the same cantus firmus appears in the tenor of each section. Cf. CANTUS FIRMUS MASS.

tenoroon a small BASSOON pitched a 5th higher than the standard bassoon.

tenor saxophone a type of SAXOPHONE in B♭ used as a melody instrument, esp. in jazz. Also, *melody saxophone.*

tenor tuba a TUBA in B♭ similar in range to the cello, used in orchestras and bands.

tenor violin a now obsolete term referring to a viola or small cello.

tenth an INTERVAL encompassing nine diatonic steps (an octave and a third).

tenuto (It.) of a note, held, sustained (for its full value). Cf. STACCATO.

teponaztli a pre-16th-c. Mexican SLIT DRUM.

terce one of the lesser hours of the DIVINE OFFICE of the Roman Catholic church. It begins around 9 AM.

ternary form a three-part form, usu. abbreviated ABA, in which the two outer sections are related thematically and/or harmonically (the second A may be simply an exact repeat of the first), the middle (B) section providing contrast. The minuet-trio-minuet of the Classical sonata is an example of the form. Cf. ROUNDED BINARY FORM. See FORM (*illus.*).

Terpsichore the muse of choral dance and song, whose symbol is the lyre.

terraced dynamics a type of dynamic

organization in which sections of a musical form are differentiated by relatively sharp contrasts in dynamic level, without transitional crescendos or diminuendos connecting them. The technique is considered to be a characteristic of baroque music.

territory band a term for jazz dance bands of the 1920s and 1930s in the Midwest and West that were based in regional centers and serviced the surrounding areas.

Terry, Clark (1920–) Amer. jazz trumpeter and fluegelhorn player. He played with Charlie Barnet, Count Basie and for almost a decade with the Duke Ellington band. He was influential in the transition from swing to bop and popularized the use of the fluegelhorn. Since the 1960s he has led various groups and been active in studio work, esp. with the Tonight Show band in the 1960s.

Terry, Sonny (Teddell, Saunders) (1911–86) Amer. harmonica player and blues singer, blinded as a child. From 1934 he performed with singer Blind Boy Fuller, then from 1940 almost until his death he worked with guitarist Brownie McGhee, touring extensively and making over 30 records.

tertian 1, relating to mean tone temperament, in which the thirds are perfectly in tune. **2**, an ORGAN STOP consisting of two sets of metal pipes tuned a third apart. **3**, referring to a harmonic system based on thirds, as in the major-minor tonal system, as opposed to QUARTAL harmony or other systems. Also, *triadic harmony*.

terzet *also*, **terzetto** [ter'tset(-tō)] (It.) TRIO.

Teschemacher, Frank (1906–32) Amer. jazz clarinetist, alto saxophonist and violinist. He played with dance bands in Chicago in the 1920s as well as with Jimmy McPartland and Red Nichols.

tessitura (It., texture) the range of a melody or voice part, esp. the register in which the most of a work or part

lies (which may or may not be near the extremes of its range).

testo (It., text) **1**, LIBRETTO. **2**, in the 17th c., a narrator or soloist in a musical work. **3**, the narrative portions of a text, such as the Evangelist in the German Passions.

testudo (Lat., tortoise) **1**, the Greek LYRE. **2**, LUTE.

tetrachord 1, a four-stringed instrument. **2**, a basic grouping of notes in ancient Greek music—echoed in medieval and Renaissance music theory—consisting of four diatonic notes within the compass of a perfect fourth. **3**, a four-note SCALE. **4**, the INTERVAL of the perfect fourth.

Tetrazzini, Luisa (Luigia) (1871–1940) Italian soprano, trained in Florence. She sang in principal opera houses of Europe and No. and S. America from the 1890s until her retirement in the mid-1930s. Her U.S. debut was at the Manhattan Opera in 1908. She was esp. known for her performances of Lucia, Gilda (*Rigoletto*) and Marie (*The Daughter of the Regiment*).

Texas Tommy an Afr.-Amer. theatrical dance performed to ragtime music.

Tex-Mex music popular music of the Amer. Southwest, combining MARIACHI and COUNTRY MUSIC.

text-sound composition a genre of composition using words and/or phonemic sounds to create "quasi-musical" works. Examples of the genre may be seen in works of Beth Anderson and Charles Amirkhanian, among others.

texture a term referring to the various aspects of the vertical organization of a work, i.e., the number and nature of the parts, how the parts are combined, instrumentation, etc. (e.g., homophonic or polyphonic texture).

Teyte (Tate), Dame **Maggie** (1888–1976) English soprano, stud. of Jean de Reszke. She was one of the first singers chosen by Debussy for the part of Mélisande and sang many of his chansons with the composer accompanying. She sang frequently in England with Beecham and others, and in Chicago, Boston and New York. She was renowned as a recitalist in French repertory, performing with Gerald Moore.

Thaïs [tä'ēs] (Fr.) opera in 3 acts by Massenet to a libretto by Louis Gallet, based on a novel by Anatole France. Premiere, Paris 1894. The monk Athanaël succeeds in converting the courtesan Thaïs to a pious life, only to fall in love with her when she is on her deathbed.

Thalberg, Sigismond (Fortuné François) (1812–71) Swiss pianist and composer, stud. of Hummel, Moscheles and others, and one of the great piano virtuosi of the 19th c. He toured extensively from the early 1830s, gaining fame after an extended controversy between Liszt and himself. His Amer. debut was in 1856 and during the next two years he gave over 300 concerts across the country, performing mostly his own works.

Tharpe, Sister Rosetta (1915–73) Amer. gospel and soul singer and guitarist. She sang in Harlem at the Holy Roller Church, and later appeared with Count Basie, Cab Calloway, Lucky Millinder and Benny Goodman. She also toured Europe in the 1960s.

theater music any music written for performance in a theater (as opposed to the concert hall, church or chamber). Cf. BALLET, OPERA, MUSICAL COMEDY, INCIDENTAL MUSIC.

theater orchestra a CHAMBER ORCHESTRA of about 20 players, such as might be used in a theater pit. Ives wrote several works for theater orchestras of varying instrumentation.

theater organ 1, a large pipe organ of the 17th to 19th c. used to accompany theatrical entertainments, concerts, opera, etc., often as a replacement for an orch. 2, a large organ used in Amer. movie houses to accompany silent films or provide entertainment between orch. breaks. Such organs often had special effects, incl. percussion, whistles, etc. Also, *cinema organ*.

Thebom, Blanche (1918–) Amer. mezzo-soprano, stud. of Margarete Matzenmauer and Edyth Walker. Her Metropolitan Opera debut was in 1944, and she sang there until her retirement in 1970.

thematic catalogue a musical index listing works by their opening notes or principal melodies. Methods of representation vary from standard notation to letters or computer codes.

theme a melody or motif on which a work or section of a work is based. In a serial work, the theme (if there is one) may or may not be identical with the row itself. Cf. SUBJECT.

theme group the SUBJECT of a fugue or the main or subsidiary themes of a SONATA FORM.

theorbo a large 17th-c. ARCHLUTE having two sets of pegs, one of which carries long bass strings played as open strings.

theremin an electronic melody instrument invented by a Russian, Léon Thérémin c1920. It is played by moving one hand between two electrodes while the other hand controls the dynamics. (Keyboard and fingerboard versions were also produced.) A number of composers wrote for the instrument, incl. Varèse and Fuleihan.

Theresienmesse [te'rä-zē-ən"me-se] (Ger.) the Mass No. 12 in B♭ major (1799) by Haydn.

thesis DOWNBEAT. Opposed to ARSIS.

Thibaud, Jacques (1880–1953) French violinist, stud. of Belgian violinist Martin Marsick. During the 1898–91 seasons he performed regularly with the Concerts Colonne, then toured extensively for many years. He was a member of several chamber ensembles, the most famous being a trio with pianist Cortot and cellist Casals in the 1930s.

Thielemans, Toots (Jean Baptiste) (1922–) Belgian-born Amer. jazz harmonica player, guitarist, whistler and composer. He played with Charlie Parker, Benny Goodman, George Shearing, Quincy Jones and others, and led his own group in the 1960s. He has also written scores for films and TV. His song "Bluesette" (1962) was an international hit.

thimble a type of guitar PLECTRUM.

third 1, an INTERVAL covering three diatonic steps. **2,** MEDIANT. **3,** a harmonic INTERVAL of two tones a major or minor third apart.

third inversion a seventh CHORD with the seventh in the bass.

third stream a term coined by Gunther Schuller for music which combines Western art music with elements of jazz or other popular or ethnic music, in particular incorporating their improvisational and rhythmic characteristics. Many composers have written works in this genre, incl. Schuller, Babbitt, Steve Lacy, Alec Wilder and Ran Blake. Cf. SYMPHONIC JAZZ.

thirteenth an INTERVAL encompassing eleven diatonic steps (an octave and a sixth).

thirteenth chord an ELEVENTH CHORD with a thirteenth added, containing all the notes of the diatonic scale.

thirty-second note a NOTE with three flags or beams having the value of one thirty-second of a whole note. Also, (Brit.) *demisemiquaver.* See NOTES AND RESTS (*illus.*).

thirty-second rest a REST (𝄾) having the value of a thirty-second note.

thirty-two foot stop a pipe ORGAN STOP producing a pitch two octaves below the notated pitch.

This Is the Army musical by Irving Berlin. Premiere, New York 1942. An all-male, all-soldier revue offering a view of army life as seen through the eyes of selectees.

Thomas, (Charles Louis) Ambroise (1811–96) French composer, trained at the Paris Conservatoire under Dourlen and LeSueur. He won the Prix de Rome in 1832. From 1837 he produced twenty operas and *opéras-comiques,* of which *Mignon* (1866) and *Hamlet* (1868) have remained in the repertory. *Mignon* received over 1000 performances at the Opéra-Comique between its premiere and Thomas's death. Thomas taught at the Conservatoire from 1856, later becoming its dir. He was noted for his inflexibility.

Thomas, Isaiah (1749–1831) Amer. tunebook publisher and printer based in Worcester, MA.

Thomas (Tomashevsky), **Michael Tilson** (1944–) Amer. conductor and pianist, trained with Dahl and at Bayreuth and the Berkshire Music Center. He held several positions with the Boston SO in the early 1970s, was music dir. of the Buffalo PO (1971–79) and dir. of the Young People's Concerts of the New York PO (1971–76). He has also been assoc. with the Los Angeles PO and has guest-conducted with most major orchestras in the U.S. and Europe. He has been an active advocate of 20th-c. music.

Thomas, Theodore (Christian Friedrich) (1835–1905) German-born Amer. conductor. He came to the U.S. in 1845, playing shortly thereafter in various New York orchestras, incl. the New York Philharmonic Society from 1854, and was co-founder of a monthly chamber music series at Dodworth Hall in New York. His conducting debut was in 1859 and by 1862 he was conductor of the Brooklyn Philharmonic. In the following years he conducted concerts in a variety of venues, including the famous Central Park Garden, and formed the Theodore Thomas Orch., which made regular tours throughout the U.S. and Canada. He was dir. of the Cincinnati May Festival from its founding in 1873 until his death and inaugurated similar festivals in other cities. He conducted the New York PO from 1877 to 1891, then founded the Chicago Orch. in 1891 (forerunner of the Chicago SO), spearheading the drive which finally produced Orch. Hall in Chicago, opened the year before his death.

Thomasschule (Ger.) a celebrated school in Leipzig whose Kantors have incl. such eminent musicians as Schein, Schelle, Kuhnau and J. S. Bach.

Thompson, Hank (Henry William) (1925–) Amer. country-music singer, songwriter, harmonica player, guitarist and bandleader. His Western swing band, the Brazos Valley Boys, was formed in 1946 and made many hit recordings and successful tours.

Thompson, Lucky (Eli) (1924–) Amer. bop tenor saxophonist. He played with a number of bands in New York and on the West Coast, incl. Don Redman, Lionel Hampton, Count Basie and Stan Kenton. He retired from music in the mid-1970s.

Thompson, Randall (1899–1984) Amer. composer and teacher, trained at Harvard and with Bloch. He taught at UCLA, the Curtis Institute, the U. of Virginia in Charlottesville, Princeton and at Harvard from 1948 until his retirement in 1965. He wrote a large number of sacred and secular choral works (incl. *Alleluia*, composed for the opening of the Berkshire Music Center), two operas, a ballet, 3 symphonies, *A Trip to Nahant* (orchestral fantasy) and chamber music.

Thomson, Virgil (Garnett) (1896–1989) Amer. composer and critic, trained at Harvard and with Boulanger in Paris. He lived in Paris from 1925 to 1940, where he wrote his opera *Four Saints in Three Acts* (1927) in collaboration with Gertrude Stein. He returned to the U.S. in 1940 to be music critic of the *New York Herald Tribune*, a post he held for 14 years. His second Stein opera, *The Mother of Us All* (1946), was written during this time, as was his score for the documentary film *Louisiana Story*, which won him the 1949 Pulitzer Prize. Thomson's music was noted for its diatonicism and its use of popular and folk music. He wrote 3 operas, ballets, 3 symphonies, many orchestral works and suites, musical portraits, many choral works, songs, chamber music, piano pieces, film scores (incl. for *The Goddess* and *Louisiana Story*) and incidental music.

Thorne, Francis (1922–) Amer. composer and pianist, stud. of Hindemith, Diamond and others. He worked as a jazz pianist in the 1950s and served at several important philanthropic organizations, incl. the Thorne Music Fund, which he founded, and the Naumburg Foundation. He was also a co-founder of the American Composers Orch. He has written several operas, 5 symphonies and other orchestral works, instrumental sonatas and chamber music and songs.

Thornhill, Claude (1909–65) Amer. jazz and popular bandleader, pianist, composer, and arranger. With his arranger, Gil Evans, he was a precursor of the COOL JAZZ style.

Thornton, Big Mama (Willie Mae) (1926–84) influential Amer. blues singer. During the 1940s she toured with Sammy Green's Hot Harlem Revue, then joined the touring show of Johnny Otis. She was an important influence on Elvis Presley, Janice Joplin and others (Presley had a major hit—as she had—with her song "Hound Dog"). She continued to perform through the 1970s.

thoroughbass BASSO CONTINUO.

Three Blind Mice a three-voice ROUND of unknown authorship, first published in 1609.

Three Choirs Festival an annual English six-day festival of choral and orchestral music dating from the early 18th c. and based in the cathedrals of Gloucester, Worcester and Hereford.

Three-Cornered Hat, The (Sp., *Sombrero de tres picos*) dramatic ballet in 1 act with music by Falla, orig. choreography by Leonide Massine with scenery and costumes by Picasso. Premiere, London 1919.

Three Dog Night Amer. rock band formed in 1968, consisting of three vocalists and instrumental backing. Their hits incl. "Joy To The World" (1971) and "Black and White" (1972).

Three Musketeers, The musical by Rudolf Friml, lyrics by Clifford Grey, book by William Anthony McGuire, based on Dumas's novel. Premiere, New York 1928. The story of d'Artagnan's first meeting with the Three Musketeers and his romance with Constance.

Threepenny Opera, The (Ger., *Die Dreigroschenoper*) satiric opera in 3 acts by Weill to a libretto in German by Bertolt Brecht, based on THE BEGGAR'S OPERA. Premiere, Berlin 1928. The opera tells the story of the crimes of the gangleader Macheath and the love of Polly Peachum for him.

Three Page Sonata a short piano sonata in one movement (1905) by Ives, based on the B-A-C-H motive.

Three Pictures for Orchestra three tone poems by Virgil Thomson: *The Seine at Night* (1947), *Wheat Field at Noon* (1949) and *Sea Piece with Birds* (1952).

Three Places in New England three orchestral tone poems (1914) by Ives, also called the First Orchestral Set. The three works are "Boston Common," "Putnam's Camp, Redding, Connecticut" and "The Housatonic at Stockbridge." The first work incorporates several songs, incl. "Old Black Joe" and "Marching Through Georgia."

Three T's popular name for three brass players in Paul Whiteman's band in 1936: trombonist JACK TEAGARDEN, saxophonist FRANKIE TRUMBAUER and trumpeter Charlie Teagarden.

Threni: id est Lamentationes Jeremiae Prophetae (Lat., Threnodies: that is, the Lamentations of the Prophet Jeremiah) work for soloists, chorus and orch. (1958) by Stravinsky, his first fully 12-tone work.

threnody a vocal or, more rarely, instrumental LAMENT.

Throckmorton, Sonny (1940–) Amer. country-music singer and songwriter. From the late 1970s he produced a number of hit songs incl. "Knee Deep in Loving You" and "Middle Age Crazy."

through-composed 1, of a song, having a different setting for each strophe or stanza (cf. STROPHIC). **2**, of an opera, not clearly divided into arias and recitatives, like the later operas of Wagner.

thrush a slang term for a singer, esp. a singer with a band.

Thuille, Ludwig (Wilhelm Andreas Maria) (1861–1907) Austrian composer, stud. of Josef Rheinberger and others. He taught in Frankfurt am Main and later in Munich, also conducting various ensembles. His works incl. several operas, choral works, songs and many instrumental chamber works.

thumb piano SANSA.

thunder machine any of various devices for creating the sound of thunder, the most common of which are recorded sound effects or a THUNDER SHEET.

thunder sheet a large, suspended iron sheet used in theaters that when struck or shaken approximates the sound of thunder.

thunderstick BULL-ROARER.

Thus Spake Zarathustra (Ger., *Also sprach Zarathustra*) symphonic tone poem (1896) by Richard Strauss, after a text by Nietzsche. Zarathustra is the Persian prophet Zoroaster. The work was popularized by its use in Stanley Kubrick's film *2001: A Space Odyssey* (1968).

ti 1, the note B in the FIXED-DO SYSTEM. **2**, the subtonic or leading tone in the MOVABLE-DO SYSTEM.

Tibbett, Lawrence (1896–1960) Amer. baritone, stud. of Frank La Forge and others. He sang regularly with the Metropolitan Opera from 1923 to 1950 and also appeared in films, on Broadway (*Fanny*) and on radio.

tibia 1, an ancient Roman double-reed instrument similar to the Greek AULOS. **2**, an ancient flute, orig. made from an animal's leg bone. **3**, a flute ORGAN STOP.

Tichatschek, Joseph Alois (1807–86) Czech tenor, a leading singer in Vienna and Dresden, esp. in Wagnerian roles. He created the roles of Rienzi and Tannhäuser.

tie a curved line connecting two notes of the same pitch resulting in a single note of their combined durations. The sign is also used to connect notes across a bar line and to produce a note value for which there is no single note symbol (e.g. ♩‿♪). Cf. SLUR.

tiento ['tyen-tō] (Span., touch) a 16th-c. Spanish organ composition similar to the RICERCAR using imitative counterpoint.

tierce [tyers] (Fr.) **1**, THIRD. **2**, the tone two octaves and a major third above a given tone; also, an ORGAN STOP producing tones this interval above the fingered note.

tierce de Picardie [də pē-kär'dē] (Fr.) PICARDY THIRD.

tiktiri an Indian double CLARINET.

Tiller Girls a female dance troupe of the 1920s, predecessors of the Radio City Music Hall Rockettes.

Till Eulenspiegel's Merry Pranks ['oi-lən"shpē-gəl] (Ger., *Till Eulenspiegels lustige Streiche*) an orchestral tone poem, Op. 28 (1895), by Richard Strauss, based loosely on the exploits of a legendary medieval prankster who was hanged for his misdeeds.

Tillman, Floyd (1914–) Amer. honky-tonk singer, guitarist and songwriter. He played with Adolph Hofner and the Blue Ridge Playboys and later appeared regularly at the Grand Ole Opry and the Ozark Jubilee. He was elected to the Country Music Hall of Fame in 1984.

timbal *also,* **tymbal** KETTLEDRUM.

timbales a pair of small singleheaded CYLINDRICAL DRUMS tuned like bongos and used primarily in Lat.-Amer. dance bands.

timbre *also,* **timber** the color or tonal quality of a sound, determined by its overtones.

timbrel a small hand drum; TAMBOURINE.

time METER.

time point a term coined by Babbitt to refer to the metrical starting point of sound (not its duration), indicated by its position in the numeration of metrical units (such as sixteenthnotes) starting from 0. By referring to each sound by its time point, one can construct a set of time points for a melody and compute and relate the distances between time points the way one does with intervals (a mea-

sure being the equivalent of an octave).

time signature an indication of METER placed at the beginning of a composition and at the beginning of any measure where there is a change in the prevailing meter. The signature is usu. a fraction whose numerator is the number of beats and whose denominator is the unit of beat (2 = 𝅗𝅥, 4 = ♩, 8 = ♪, etc.). In certain 20th-c. scores novel forms of time signatures have been used, employing note symbols rather than numbers for the denominator or using proportional signs.

Unusual Time Signatures
(see also METER)

time-space notation a system of rhythmic NOTATION first used by Earle Brown that indicates the duration of events by means of horizontal lines related to a fixed scale. The technique is most often used for the notation of tape parts in scores combining recorded and live events.

timpani a set of KETTLEDRUMS, usu. two to four, played by one player in an orch.

Timpany Five a popular Amer. JUMP BAND of the 1940s led by saxophonist Louis Jordan.

timp-tom a shallow single-headed tunable TOM-TOM.

Tinctoris, Johannes (c1435–c1511) Franco-Flemish theorist and composer of sacred and secular vocal music. He is best known for his theoretical writings on many aspects of music notation, composition, etc., such as the *Liber de arte contrapunctus* (The Art of Counterpoint) of 1477. For most of his life he was in the service of King Ferdinand I of Naples.

Tin Pan Alley popular name for the

music-writing and -publishing industry in New York from the late 19th
c. to about 1950.

tin whistle PENNY WHISTLE.

Tiomkin, Dimitri (1894–1979) Russian-born Amer. composer and pianist, stud. of Glazunov, Busoni and
others. He toured as a pianist in the
1920s, giving the European premiere
of Gershwin's Concerto in F in Paris
in 1928. From 1937 to 1968 he wrote
film scores in Hollywood, his first
being for *Lost Horizon* (1937); others
incl. *It's a Wonderful Life* (1947),
High Noon (1952), *Dial M for Murder*
(1954) and *The Guns of Navarone*
(1961). He won four Academy
Awards.

tiple (tē′plä) (Sp.) **1**, a soprano GUI-
TAR. Also, *tipple*. **2**, a large, steel-
stringed UKULELE **3**, a Catalan keyed
SHAWM.

Tippett, Sir **Michael (Kemp)**
(1905–) English composer, trained
at the Royal College of Music and
later with R.O. Morris. Until 1932 he
was a schoolteacher; he then worked
at Morley College in London as a conductor and later dir. of music, resigning in 1951 to take a position with
the BBC. His recognition came late,
when he was in his 40s, but he is now
considered one of England's most important and original composers. His
works incl. *The Midsummer Marriage, King Priam, The Knot Garden,
The Ice Break* and other operas, choral works (incl. *A Child of our Time,
The Mask of Time*), 4 symphonies, a
piano concerto, songs, 4 string quartets, 3 piano sonatas and other chamber music.

tipping TONGUING.

tipple TIPLE (1,).

Tip-Toes musical by George Gershwin, lyrics by Ira Gershwin, book by
Guy Bolton and Fred Thompson. Premiere, New York 1925. The adventures of a vaudeville dancer stranded
in Palm Beach with her two uncles.

tirana (Sp.) an Andalusian dance-
song of the late 18th and 19th c. in a
syncopated ⁶/₈ or ³/₈ time.

Tiranna, La (It., the tyrant) the string

quartet in G major, G223 (1792), by
Boccherini.

tirata (It.) a scalelike ORNAMENT connecting main notes separated by an
interval wider than a third. Also, *run,
cascata.*

Titan the Symphony No. 1 in D major (1884–8, rev. 1893–6) by Mahler.
The work orig. was in five movements, but an andante movement
("Blumine") was discarded in the revision.

Titus, Alan (1945–) Amer. baritone, stud. of Schiøtz and Hans
Heinz. He has sung in the premieres
of a number of Amer. works, incl.
Bernstein's Mass and Hoiby's *Summer and Smoke*, and has sung with
most major Amer. opera companies,
as well as in Europe. His Metropolitan Opera debut was in 1976.

ti-tzu (Chinese) a Chinese side-
blown FLUTE having a vibrating membrane (as in a mirliton).

Tjader, Cal (Callen Radcliffe, Jr.)
(1925–82) Amer. jazz vibraphonist
and drummer. He played with Dave
Brubeck and George Shearing in the
early 1950s, then formed his own
Latin-Amer. music quintet, which
toured widely and made many recordings.

tlalpanhuéhuetl a Mexican FOOTED
DRUM.

toasting a type of rhythmic recitation of improvised poetry often found
in the ROCKERS style of reggae.

T.O.B.A. *abbr.* Theater Owners'
Booking Association, a group of
theaters formed in 1920 by Sherman
Dudley as a circuit for Afr.-Amer.
vaudeville performers. The circuit ultimately included more than 80 theaters in the South, Southwest and Midwest, and lasted until the early 1930s.
Also, *Toby.*

toccata (It., touched) a fantasia-like
composition, usu. for keyboard instrument and brilliant in style, designed to show off the manual dex-
terity of the performer. Toccata-like
passages are often incorporated into
other forms, such as the sonata, or

combined with more rigorous styles, as in the toccata and fugue.

Toch, Ernst [tokh] (1887–1964) Austrian-born Amer. composer, pianist and teacher, self-taught as a composer. He taught in Mannheim and Berlin until his forced emigration in 1933. From 1936 he taught at the U. of S. California. His Third Symphony won the Pulitzer Prize in 1956. His works incl. 7 symphonies, other orchestral works, *The Last Tale* (opera), choral works (incl. works for speaking chorus), songs, 13 string quartets and other chamber music, works for piano and film scores.

toddle a 1920s dance performed to Dixieland music.

Tod und Verklärung [tōt ûnt fer'klerúnk] (Ger.) DEATH AND TRANSFIGURATION.

Tokyo String Quartet string quartet founded in New York in 1969 by four Japanese string players studying at the time at the Juilliard School. Since 1977 it has been in residence at Yale. The group has won many awards and toured and recorded extensively.

Tomášek, Václav Jan Křtitel (1774–1850) Czech composer and teacher, largely self-taught as a musician. During the first two decades of the 19th c. he free-lanced as composer and teacher, establishing himself as a major force in Prague's musical life. His works incl. 2 operas, orchestral dances and piano concertos, choral music, a large number of songs and works for piano solo.

Tomasi, Henri (Frédien) (1901–71) French composer and conductor, trained at the Paris Conservatoire. He won the Prix de Rome in 1927. He was noted for his colorful orchestration and exotic inspiration. His works incl. 2 operas (*L'Atlantide, Miguel de Mañara*), ballets, choral works, concertos for various instruments and chamber music.

Tomasini, (Alois) Luigi (1741–1808) Italian composer and violinist in the service of the Esterházy family, perhaps a stud. of Haydn and Leopold Mozart. He is best known for his large output of chamber works for strings. He also wrote several violin concertos and 3 symphonies.

tombeau [tō'bō] (Fr., tomb) an instrumental work commemorating the death of a real or imaginary person.

Tombeau de Couperin, Le (Fr., Couperin's Tomb) baroque-style piano suite (a TOMBEAU to François Couperin) in six movements (1917) by Ravel, each section of which is dedicated to the memory of a World War I victim. Four of the movements were orchestrated in 1919 by the composer.

Tomkins, Thomas (1572–1656) English composer of madrigals, anthems, service music, consort music and keyboard suites, perhaps a stud. of Byrd. He was assoc. with Worcester Cathedral and was a Gentleman of the Chapel Royal, becoming an organist there in 1621.

Tomlinson, Arthur pen name for CHARLES T. GRIFFES.

Tommasini, Vincenzo (1878–1950) Italian composer, trained in Rome and in Berlin with Bruch. Independently wealthy, he wrote for his own enjoyment. His early works are in a chromatic style strongly influenced by Debussy; his later works are more neoclassical in style. He wrote several operas and ballets, orchestral tone poems and concertos, 3 string quartets and other chamber music and songs.

tom-tom 1, a small single- or double-headed CYLINDRICAL drum of varying shape beaten with the hands or drumsticks and used in modern jazz ensembles. Cf. ROTO-TOM, TIMP-TOM. **2**, TAM-TAM.

ton [tō] (Fr.) **1**, TONE. **2**, FRET.

tonada [tō'nä-thä] (Sp.) a meditative Spanish folksong or melody.

tonadilla [tō-nä'thē-lya] (Sp.) a short 18th-c. Spanish INTERMEZZO written to be performed between the acts of a play, usu. a solo song with guitar accompaniment; later, a short, comic opera.

tonal answer in a fugue, an ANSWER which has been modified to remain in the tonic key. (A REAL ANSWER may or may not remain in the tonic, depending on the composition.)

tonality the system of relationships between pitches and chords, usu. serving to establish a central note or harmony (the *tonic*) which is the focal point of a work or section of a work. Also, *key.*

tonary a liturgical book of the Roman Catholic church which classifies Gregorian antiphons, responsories and various other chants according to the eight PSALM TONES.

Tondichtung ['tōn"diç-tûng] (Ger.) TONE POEM.

tone 1, a musical sound or PITCH. 2, WHOLE TONE. 3, a recitation formula in Gregorian chant. Cf. PSALM TONE. 4, a broad term used by both singers and instrumentalists to refer to the qualities that make up a performer's sound. 5, NOTE.

tone cluster CLUSTER.

tone color TIMBRE.

tone poem an orchestral work suggested by or suggestive of poetic or literary subjects or sentiments. See SYMPHONIC POEM.

tone row see ROW.

tonette a small, plastic RECORDER with a range of just over an octave, used in elementary school education.

tonguing on a mouth-blown wind instrument, the attack or articulation of a note by use of the tongue. Articulation is usu. produced by forming the consonant T, which is combined in double- and triple-tonguing with the consonant K (T-K and T-K-T—or T-T-K—respectively). Also, *tipping.* Cf. FLUTTER-TONGUING.

tonic 1, the first degree of a major or minor scale. Also, *keynote.* 2, the tonal center of the harmonic or melodic TONALITY.

tonic accent an accent produced as a result of higher pitch, rather than because of stress or longer duration.

tonicization in tonal harmony, the treatment for a brief time of a note other than the keynote as a tonic, as by approaching it from its dominant. A tonicization is usu. considered to be too brief to constitute a MODULATION.

tonic sol-fa a system of SOLMIZATION and notation invented by John Curwen in the mid-19th-c. based on key relationships and utilizing the SOL-FA syllables or their first letters. Chromatic alterations are indicated by changing the vowel of the sol-fa name, "e" (pronounced "ē") for sharps and "a" (pronounced "â") for flats. Rhythmic values are indicated by use of bar lines and colons (which precede weak beats). Minor keys are treated as derived from their relative major keys, with the raised sixth degree being called "bah." Curwen also designed a set of hand signs to indicate the degrees of the scale. The system was adopted in modified form by Kodály for use in Hungarian schools.

tono (Sp.) 1, tune; melody. 2, a short 17th- or 18th-c. sacred or secular song.

tonus (Lat.) 1, a church MODE. 2, a recitation formula in Gregorian chant. 3, WHOLE TONE.

tonus peregrinus (Lat., foreign tone) an irregular recitation tone in Gregorian chant whose reciting note changes after the mediation.

Too Many Girls musical by Richard Rodgers, lyrics by Lorenz Hart, book by George Marion, Jr. Premiere, New York 1939. A millionaire hires four football players to protect his daughter while in college, and she falls in love with one of them.

top BELLY.

torch song a sentimental song of unrequited love (the name comes from the phrase to "carry a torch" for someone), a popular feature of jazz singers and in night club acts.

torculus a NEUME representing three notes, the second higher than the others.

tordion TOURDION.

Toreador Song a song of bravado sung by the bullfighter Escamillo in Bizet's opera *Carmen.*

Torelli, Giuseppe (Gioseffo) (1658–1709) Italian composer of instrumental music, stud. of G.A. Perti. Most of his professional life was spent in Bologna. His works mirror the development of the concerto grosso, from his earlier chamber music works, many for trumpet(s) in combination with other instruments, to his later orchestral concertos.

Torkanowsky, Werner (1926–) German-born Amer. conductor, composer and violinist, trained at the Palestine Conservatory and with Rafael Bronstein and Monteux in the U.S. He played in the Pittsburgh SO, then conducted in Spoleto and elsewhere. He has been music dir. of the New Orleans Philharmonic SO (1963–77) and has taught at Carnegie-Mellon U.

Tormé, Mel(vin Howard) ("The Velvet Fog") (1925–) Amer. popular and jazz singer and songwriter. In the 1940s he led his own group, the Mel-Tones, and appeared in films, but he is best known through his appearances on television, his recordings and nightclub appearances. He has written several hundred songs, incl. the popular "Christmas Song" (1946), one of the most recorded songs in history.

Toronto Symphony Orchestra orch. orig. founded in 1906 by conductor Frank Welsman (1873–1952) and lasting until 1916, then reconstituted by a merger with the New Symphony Orch. in 1926 under Luigi von Kunits (1870–1931). Subsequent conductors have been Ernest MacMillan, Susskind, Ozawa, Ančerl, Andrew Davis and Günther Herbig.

torpedo a type of SCRAPER used in Lat.-Amer. bands.

Torres Jurado, Antonio de (1817–92) Spanish guitar maker who perfected the design of the modern guitar.

Tortelier, Paul (1914–90) French cellist and composer, stud. of Gérard Hekking. He played with the Boston SO (1937–8) and the Orchestre des Concerts du Conservatoire in Paris, then concentrated on a distinguished solo career. He has taught at the Paris Conservatoire since 1957.

Tosca opera in 3 acts by Puccini to a libretto by Luigi Illica and Giuseppe Giacosa based on the play *La Tosca* by Victorien Sardou. Premiere, Rome 1900. The opera tells the story of the love of the singer Floria Tosca for the painter Mario Cavaradossi and their struggle with the police chief Scarpia amid political upheavals in Rome around 1800.

Toscanini, Arturo (1867–1957) eminent Italian conductor, trained at the Parma Conservatory. He played cello for a time in the orch. of La Scala, Milan, but began conducting in regional Italian theaters in the late 1880s. By 1895 he was music dir. of the Teatro Regio in Turin and formed a municipal orch. In 1898 he became artistic dir. of La Scala, concentrating on Verdi, Wagner and new works. In 1908 he came to New York as artistic dir. of the Metropolitan Opera, retaining the post until 1915. From 1920 to 1929 he was again in charge at La Scala, then he came to New York to direct the New York PO (until 1936). From 1937 until his retirement in 1954 he conducted the NBC SO, formed specially for him, with which he made regular broadcasts and many recordings. He was famous for his perfectionism, his sense of form and his charisma.

Tosi, Pier Francesco (c1653–1732) Italian singer, composer, music theorist and diplomat. He was an extremely popular castrato singer, best remembered for his vocal treatise *Observations on the Florid Song*, first published in Italian in 1723 and then translated into several languages and disseminated throughout Europe.

Tost Quartets the 12 string quartets Op. 54, 55 and 64 (1788–91) by Haydn, dedicated to a Viennese amateur violinist, Johann Tost. Cf. RAZOR QUARTET.

Tosti, Sir (Francesco) Paolo (1846–1916) prolific Italian song composer and teacher, stud. of Mercadante and others. He was singing teacher to the queen of Italy and later to the royal family in London (he became a British subject in 1906). Of his many songs, "Mattinata" and "Serenata" are among those most frequently performed.

tosto ['tō-stō] (It.) rapidly, in a quick tempo.

total serialism a 20th-c. compositional technique in which most or all of the principal parameters of a musical work (pitch, rhythm, meter, dynamics, articulation) are determined by means of serial techniques (see SERIALISM).

Totenberg, Roman (1911–) Polish-born Amer. violinist and teacher, stud. of Flesch, Enescu and Monteux. He concertized widely in Europe, S. and No. America, specializing in Romantic and contemporary repertory. He has taught at the Music Academy of the West, Boston U. and the Longy School (MA), of which he was dir. in the late 1970s.

Totentanz ['tō-tən"tänts] (Ger., dance of death) **1**, DANCE OF DEATH. **2**, variations for piano and orch. (1853) by Liszt, based on the Gregorian chant DIES IRAE.

tote Stadt, Die ['tō-te shtät] (Ger., The Dead City) fantasy opera in 3 acts by Korngold to a libretto in German by Paul Schott based on Georges Rodenbach's play *Bruges-la-Morte*. Premiere, Hamburg and Cologne 1920. Paul, obsessed with the death of his wife Marie, has a macabre dream.

touch on a keyboard instrument: **1**, the amount of force required to activate the mechanism, the depth of travel of the key or a combination of the two. **2**, a player's manner of striking or depressing the keys as reflected in the interrelation of tones or chords in a musical phrase.

touche [toosh] (Fr.) **1**, KEY. **2**, FINGERBOARD.

Tough, Dave (David Jarvis) (1908–48) Amer. jazz drummer from Chicago. An important swing drummer, he played with a number of big bands, incl. those of Eddie Condon, Red Nichols, Tommy Dorsey, Benny Goodman and Woody Herman.

tourdion [toor'dyō] (Fr.) a 16th-c. dance in a lively triple meter, fre-

quently used as an after-dance to the BASSE DANSE.

Tourel (Davidovich), **Jennie** (c1900–73) Russian-born Amer. mezzo-soprano, stud. of Hahn and Anna El Tour. Her stage name is an anagram of her teacher's name. Her Amer. operatic debut was in Chicago in 1931; she also sang in Europe and for several seasons at the Metropolitan Opera. She was best known as a recital and concert artist and taught at the Juillard School and at the Aspen Music School.

Tourjée, Eben (1834–91) Amer. organist, music educator and choral conductor. He founded conservatories in Fall River (MA) and Providence (RI) and in 1867 was co-founder of the New England Conservatory of Music. He was also active in the Boston public schools and as an organizer of large choruses for various jubilees. From 1873 he was dean of the College of Music of Boston U.

Tournemire, Charles (Arnould) (1870–1939) French organist and composer, stud. of Widor and Franck. He was organist at St. Clotilde from 1898 and a professor at the Conservatoire from 1919. His many organ works reflect his mysticism, culminating in his monumental *Orgue mystique*, a setting of 51 Offices, each incorporating the appropriate plainsong melodies. He also wrote 8 symphonies, 4 operas, choral and solo vocal works and chamber music.

Tourte bow popular name for the modern violin bow, developed in the late 18th c. by François Tourte (1747–1835).

Tovey, Sir Donald (Francis) (1875–1940) English scholar, composer and pianist, stud. of Sophie Weisse. He performed as pianist with Joachim's quartet and with various orchestras, then in 1914 devoted his time to writing about music (though he continued to perform occasionally as accompanist and in chamber music). His *Essays in Musical Analysis* (1935–9) are widely read. He also wrote many musical works in all genres.

Tower, Joan (1938–) Amer. composer and pianist, stud. of Luening and others at Columbia. She was a founder/member of the Da Capo Chamber Players, a contemporary-music ensemble, has taught at Bard College and has been composer-in-residence with the St. Louis SO. Her works incl. a piano concerto (*Hommage to Beethoven*) and music for chamber orch. and for small instrumental ensembles.

Townshend, Pete (1945–) English rock guitarist and singer, leader of THE WHO.

toy *also*, **toye** a light, uncomplicated work for virginals or lute, popular in the late 16th and early 17th c.

Toy Symphony a work for toy instruments with orch. The most famous, and perhaps first, example dates from about 1780. It is traditionally attributed to Joseph Haydn, but the music actually comes from a divertimento by Leopold Mozart, Wolfgang's father. The toy instruments may have been added by Michael Haydn, Joseph's brother.

Tozzi, Giorgio (George) [tôt'sē] (1923–) Amer. bass, stud. of Giacomo Rimini, John Daggett Howell and Giulio Lorandi. He sang in Italy in Milan, then made his Metropolitan Opera debut in 1955. He has sung throughout Europe in most of the major bass roles and has also appeared in musical comedy, in films and on television.

tpt. *abbr.* TRUMPET.

tr. *abbr.* TRILL.

tracker action a completely mechanical action in a pipe organ, so called from its use of a *tracker*, a flexible piece of wood connecting the key with the valve.

tract in the Roman Catholic Mass, a chant replacing the Alleluia before the Gospel on days of penitence, such as during Lent.

traditional jazz a term usu. applied to NEW ORLEANS or DIXIELAND JAZZ.

It was originally coined to distinguish that style from SWING.

Traetta, Tommaso (Michele Francesco Saverio) (1727–79) Ital. opera composer, stud. of Porpora and Durante. Until 1758 he composed serious and comic operas for Rome and Naples, then worked at the court in Parma until 1765 and served at the court of Catherine II of Russia in St. Petersburg until a few years before his death. He wrote over 50 operas and other dramatic works, as well as sacred and secular vocal music and sinfonias.

tragédie lyrique [trä-jā'dē lē'rēk] (Fr.) scholarly term for serious opera of 17th- and 18th-c. France, beginning with Lully and incl. works of Rameau and Gluck.

Tragic Overture (Ger., *Tragische Overtüre*) work for orch., Op. 81 (1880), by Brahms.

Tragic Symphony, The **1**, the Symphony No. 4 in C minor, D. 417 (1816) by Schubert. **2**, the Symphony No. 6 in A minor (1906) by Mahler.

Trampler, Walter (1915–) German-born Amer. virtuoso violist, trained at the Academy of Music in Munich. After coming to the U.S. in the mid-1940s he played in the New York City Center Orch. He has been a member of the New Music Quartet (1947–55), the Yale Quartet and the Chamber Music Society of Lincoln Center and has taught at the Juilliard School, Yale and Boston U. He has recorded extensively and has given many premiere performances.

transcription **1**, a more or less strict ARRANGEMENT of a work for instrument(s) other than those for which it was originally written. **2**, the copying of a work from one notational system to another (as from mensural notation to modern notation) or from live or recorded performance to written notation (either by hand or by mechanical or electronic means). **3**, a recording made for a radio or TV station and copied for other stations on the same network.

Transcendental Études (Fr., *Études*

d'exécution transcendante) collection of 12 extremely difficult studies for piano (1851) by Liszt. He also composed an earlier set of 6 études (1838) based on Paganini caprices.

Transfigured Night VERKLÄRTE NACHT.

transformation, thematic the modification of a theme in such a way that it is still clearly recognizable in a new context. The changes may be rhythmic, metric or accompanimental (more rarely melodic). The use of the technique in the 19th c. is closely connected with the concept of the LEITMOTIV.

transient very high, usu. inaudible and short-lived tones found in the sound of an organ pipe, instrument, etc. The tones contribute to the timbre of the sound. Cf. INHARMONIC.

transition a passage in a work which connects two sections, usu. by modulating from the key of the first to the key of the second, but also in some cases by effecting metrical, dynamic, or other changes.

Transposed Heads opera in 2 acts by Peggy Glanville-Hicks to her own libretto based on the novel by Thomas Mann. Premiere, Louisville, KY 1954.

transposing instrument an instrument whose music is notated, not at the sounding pitch, but transposed up or down by a certain interval. The reason for the transposition is to maintain a relationship between notation and fingering among instruments of the same family but of different pitch. For example, the fingering that produces c′ on the oboe will produce f on the English horn. Consequently, the sounding pitch f for the English horn is notated as c′ in the player's part. See RANGE (*illus.*).

transposing keyboard a type of keyboard dating from the 16th c. that allows a player to perform in two or more different keys or tunings without changing fingering. This is usu. accomplished either by sliding the entire playing mechanism beneath the jacks or strings or by superimposing a false keyboard over the real

one and sliding it. On modern harpsichords the transposing keyboard allows performers to perform at modern pitch and at old or BAROQUE PITCH without retuning.

transposition the notation or performance of music at a different pitch level than that orig. written; accomplished by raising or lowering all the pitches by a constant amount.

transverse flute the standard side-blown FLUTE, in contrast to the end-blown flute or recorder.

trap a percussion instrument; in the plural, a set of percussion instruments, esp. as used in a theater or dance orch., usu. incl. side drum(s), tomtom(s), bass drum and cymbals.

Trapp Family Singers a singing ensemble formed of the seven children of the Austrian Captain Georg von Trapp, along with Trapp himself and his wife, who was their former governess, Maria Rainer. The ensemble toured the U.S. in the late 1930s and the 1940s performing concerts of light classics and folk music. Their story formed the basis of the musical *The Sound of Music* (1959).

trascinando [trä-shē′nän-dō] (It.) dragging.

trattenuto *also,* **tratto** (It.) **1**, drawn out; held back. **2**, SOSTENUTO.

Traubel, Helen (Francesca) (1899–1972) Amer. soprano, stud. of Vetta Karst. Her Metropolitan Opera debut was in 1937 (she had refused an earlier offer in 1926), and she sang the major Wagnerian roles there until 1953. She also appeared on Broadway, in films and in concert.

Trauer [′trow-ər] (Ger.) sadness.

Trauer Ode (Ger.) the cantata No. 198, "Lass, Fürstin, lass noch einen Strahl," (1727) by J.S. Bach, written for the funeral of Electress Christiane Eberhardine.

Trauersinfonie (Ger.) the Symphony No. 44 in E minor (c1772) by Haydn.

Träumerei [′troi-mə-rī] (Ger., reverie) popular piano work, No. 7 of the SCENES FROM CHILDHOOD by Schumann.

trautonium an electronic melody instrument invented c1930 by Friedrich Trautwein (1888–1956) and played by pressing wire against a metal rail with the finger. The pitch of the resulting sound is determined by the exact position of the finger on the wire.

traversa (It.) FLUTE.

travesti [trä-ve′stē] (Fr.) a term describing male operatic roles sung by women dressed as men, such as Octavian (*Der Rosenkavalier*) and Cherubino (*The Marriage of Figaro*). Also, *pants role, trousers role.*

Traviata, La [trä-vē′ä-tä] (It., The Corrupted Woman) tragic opera in 3 acts by Verdi to a libretto in Italian by Francesco Maria Piave, based on the play and novel *La Dame aux Camélias* by Alexandre Dumas *fils.* Premiere, Venice 1853. The courtesan Violetta Valéry sacrifices her love for Alfredo Germont to preserve his family's honor.

Travis, Merle (Robert) (1917–83) Amer. country-music guitarist, singer and songwriter from Kentucky, noted for his unusual guitar style derived from banjo playing and black ragtime guitar. He has been one of the most successful country-music songwriters, with hits including "Divorce Me C.O.D." and "No Vacancy." He was elected to the Country Music Hall of Fame in 1977.

Travis, Roy (Elihu) (1922–) Amer. composer and theorist, stud. of Luening, Wagenaar and others. He has taught at Columbia U., the Mannes College and UCLA. He has been esp. interested in the role of tonality in 20th-c. music. He has written 2 operas, a piano concerto, chamber music, 2 piano sonatas and songs.

travis picking FINGER PICKING in the style of Merle Travis.

tre [trä] (It.) three.

tre corde (It., three strings) an indication to play the piano with the soft pedal released, allowing all the strings of a note to sound. Cf. UNA CORDA.

treble **1**, the highest part in four-part vocal music. **2**, a voice or instrument

performing this part, esp. a child soprano.

treble clef the G CLEF on the second line of the staff, used for the right hand part of other keyboard instruments, the vocal soprano part and the higher melody instruments.

treble staff the musical staff carrying the TREBLE CLEF.

treble viol the highest standard VIOL. Also, *pardessus de viole* (Fr.).

Treemonisha ragtime opera by Scott Joplin to his own libretto. It was composed 1908–11 but not performed until 1915 in Harlem, without scenery, costumes or orch. The opera was not given a full production until 1975, almost 60 years after the composer's death, by the Houston Grand Opera.

Tregian, Francis (1574–1619) English musician, one of a family persecuted as Catholics. He spent the last decade of his life in prison, during which time he compiled the FITZWILLIAM VIRGINAL BOOK and two manuscript volumes of secular vocal music, all of which contain many works unavailable in any other source.

Treigle, Norman (1927–75) Amer. bass-baritone, stud. of Elizabeth Wood. He sang regularly in New Orleans in the late 1940s, then with the New York City Opera from 1953 to 1973. He was beginning to broaden his international career at the time of his premature death.

Tremblay, Gilles [trä′blä, zhēl] (1932–) Canadian composer, stud. of Champagne, Messaien and others. He has taught at the Montreal Conservatory since 1962. His works emphasize rhythm and tone color and are primarily for winds and percussion.

tremblement [′trä-blə-mä] (Fr.) TREMOLO.

tremolando [trä-mō′län-dō] (It.) producing a TREMOLO effect.

tremolo (It.) **1**, a tremulous effect produced by the rapid repetition of a pitch or chord or the rapid alternation of two pitches of a chord. In reference to the voice, the term sometimes is used as synonymous with VIBRATO, but more often it is restricted to a fluctuation in dynamics, reserving the term vibrato for fluctuation in pitch. **2**, TREMULANT. **3**, TRILLO.

tremulant a mechanical device in an ORGAN periodically stopping the flow of tone and causing a tremulous effect. Also, *tremolo.*

Trent codices six monumental manuscript volumes of 15th-c. music discovered at the Cathedral of Trent, comprising the largest surviving collection of 15th-c. vocal music.

trepak (Russ.) a wild Ukrainian folk dance in ¾ time featuring the leg-flinging *prisiadka* (performed from a squatting position). A famous example is found in Tchaikovsky's *Nutcracker.*

tres (Sp.) a small Cuban guitar with three pairs of strings.

triad a CHORD having three tones, consisting of the root with its third and fifth.

triadic harmony see TERTIAN.

trial [trē'äl] (Fr.) a thin, nasal tenor voice, so called in reference to Antoine Trial (1737–95), a popular opera singer at the Comédie-Italienne in Paris.

Trial by Jury comic opera in 1 act by Sullivan to a libretto by W.S. Gilbert. Premiere, London 1875. It is one of the earliest collaborations between Gilbert and Sullivan and their only opera without spoken dialogue.

triangle a percussion instrument made of a metal bar bent into the shape of a triangle and struck with a metal stick to produce a high, ringing sound of indefinite pitch.

trichord in modern terminology, a set of three pitch classes, usu. part of a 12-note set.

tricotet [trē-kō'tä] (Fr.) a French dance tune of the 16th and 17th c.

trigon a NEUME representing three notes, the third lower than the first two.

trill 1, the rapid alternation of two tones a scale degree apart. During the Baroque, trills usu. began with the upper note; in the Classical and esp. the Romantic periods, more often they

began with the main note. Also, *shake.* **2**, VIBRATO. **3**, the rapid repetition of the same tone, esp. on a percussion instrument. Also, in vocal music, *trillo.*

trillo ['trēl-lō] (It.) **1**, TRILL. **2**, in 17th-c. vocal music, an ORNAMENT consisting of a rapid and accelerating repetition of the same tone.

Trimble, Lester (Albert) (1923–86) Amer. composer and critic, trained at the Carnegie Institute of Technology, the Berkshire Music Center and in Paris. He has taught at the U. of Maryland and the Juilliard School and has been composer-in-residence with the New York PO and at Wolf Trap Farm Park. He has also been editor of *Musical America* and a critic for the *New York Herald Tribune, The Nation,* the Washington *Evening Star* and *Stereo Review.* His works incl. *Boccaccio's Nightingale* (opera), 3 symphonies and other orchestral works, *Panels I–VII* and other instrumental chamber music, incidental music, songs and several electronic works.

Trinklied ['tringk"lēt] (Ger.) a drinking song.

trio 1, a group of three singers or instruments. The most common forms are the PIANO TRIO and the STRING TRIO. Also, *terzet.* **2**, music written for such a group. **3**, the second section of a minuet, scherzo, march, etc., designed to contrast with the other parts, esp. in key. The trio was orig. written for three instruments, hence the name.

triole [trē'ōl] *also,* **triolet** [trē-ō'lä] (Fr.) TRIPLET.

trionfo (It.) a secular part-song sung in Florentine festivals of the late 15th and early 16th c.

trio sonata a baroque sonata for two similar instruments (usu. treble) and basso continuo. As the basso continuo usu. involves at least two players, the trio sonata is normally performed by four persons.

triple concerto a concerto for three solo instruments and orch. The most famous example is for piano, violin, cello and orch. in C major, Op. 56 (1803–4), by Beethoven.

triple counterpoint three-part COUNTERPOINT written so that any part may be transposed at the octave above or below any other part.

triple dot three dots placed to the right of a note to augment its duration by 7/8 of its value (e.g., ♩‥♩·♪·♪). See DOT.

triple harp a 17th-c. HARP capable of playing a full chromatic scale without the use of pedals.

triple meter *also,* **triple time** a METER having three beats to the measure.

triplet a group of three notes played in the time usu. taken by two notes of the same value.

triple tonguing see TONGUING.

Trip to Chinatown, A musical by Percy Gaunt, lyrics and book by Charles H. Hoyt. Premiere, New York 1891. "A Musical Trifle" about an invitation that goes astray. For almost 25 years it held Broadway's record for the length of a run.

Trip to Coontown, A musical by Cole, the first full-length musical written, directed, performed and produced by blacks. Premiere, New York 1898.

Tristano, Lennie (Leonard Joseph) (1919–78) Amer. jazz pianist, composer, bandleader and teacher, trained at the American Conservatory in Chicago. He formed an influential sextet in the late 1940s, creating an alternative to bop, full of precisely calculated complexity. From 1951 to 1956 he operated a school of jazz in New York, after which he performed and toured sporadically. He was an experimenter in multitrack recording and overdubbing and also in collective improvisation. His many pupils incl. Lee Konitz, Warne Marsh and Bill Russo.

Tristan and Isolde (Ger., *Tristan und Isolde*) tragic opera in 3 acts by Wagner to his own libretto, based on medieval legend. Premiere, Munich 1865. The ill-fated love of the knight Tristan for Isolde, the intended bride of his uncle, King Marke, intensified by a magic love potion.

Tristan chord the first chord in Wagner's opera *Tristan and Isolde*, f-b-d♯'-g♯', a form of the half-diminished 7th chord. The chord is considered an important element in the breakdown of functional harmony because of the irregularity of its resolution. See CHORD (*illus.*).

Tristan Schalmei (Ger.) an obsolete 19th-c. double reed woodwind instrument similar to the Renaissance shawm. It was designed to play the shepherd's pipe music in Act III of Wagner's *Tristan and Isolde.* Cf. HOLZTROMPETE.

tritone an INTERVAL of three whole steps; an augmented fourth. In tonal harmony the tritone has a strong tendency to resolve inward to a third or outward to a sixth. Also, *mi contra fa, diabolus in musica.*

Trittico, Il (It., The Tryptich) three operas by Puccini, intended to be performed in the same evening, comprising IL TABARRO, SUOR ANGELICA and GIANNI SCHICCHI. Premiere, New York 1918.

Triumphs of Oriana, The a collection of 29 16th-c. madrigals issued in 1603 by Morley. Oriana refers to the queen of England, Elizabeth I.

Trois morceaux en forme de poire [trwä mor'sō ā form də pwär] (Fr., Three Pieces in the Form of a Pear) work for piano duet (1890–1903) by Satie.

Trojans, The (Fr., *Les Troyens*) opera in 2 parts by Berlioz to his own libretto in French after Virgil. Premiere (in German), Karlsruhe 1890. Part I, *La Prise de Troie* (The Taking of Troy), is in 2 acts; Part II, *Les Troyens à Carthage* (The Trojans at Carthage), is in 3 acts.

tromba 1, TRUMPET. **2**, a pipe ORGAN STOP imitating the sound of the trumpet.

tromba da tirarsi (It.) SLIDE TRUMPET.

tromba marina TRUMPET MARINE.

tromba spezzata [spät'tsä-tä] (It.) TROMBONE.

Trombly, Preston (Andrew) (1945–   )

Amer. composer, stud. of Davidovsky, Crumb and others. He has taught at Vassar College, Baruch College, Brooklyn College and Catholic U. and has performed as a jazz clarinetist and saxophonist. His works are mainly for instrumental ensembles, and he has also written a number of works incorporating recorded tape.

Tromboncino, Bartolomeo (c1470–c1535) Italian composer of frottole and sacred vocal music, employed by Isabella d'Este. He was in the service of the court of Mantua until 1501, during which time he killed his wife and committed other offenses. He then probably served in Ferrara until about 1513 and afterwards in Venice until his death.

trombone a brass lip-vibrated AEROPHONE, a successor to the SACKBUT, having a cup mouthpiece and a U-shaped slide for varying the length of the tubing and hence the fundamental note. There are seven playing positions of the slide. Valved versions of the instrument have been developed in the 19th and 20th c.; one- and two-valve instruments retain a slide, but the three-valve instrument dispenses with it altogether. The slide version is still more common in both symphonic and popular orchestras. Trombones have been produced in many different sizes, the most common of which today are the tenor and bass trombones.

Trommel (Ger.) DRUM.

Trompete (Ger.), **trompette** (Fr.) TRUMPET.

tronca (It.) an indication to accent and cut off sharply the note or chord to which the term is applied.

trope 1, in Gregorian chant, an addition to or commentary upon an authentic text, either set syllabically to an existing melisma or to a new melody. The use of most tropes was abolished by the COUNCIL OF TRENT. 2, a term used by HAUER for any of the 44 sets of unordered hexachords.

troppo (It.) too; too much; usu. used in the phrase *non troppo* (not too much).

troubadour a poet or poet-musician of 12th. and 13th. c. France, esp. those working in the Provençal language in southern France. Cf. TROUVÈRE.

Troubled Island opera by William Grant Still to a libretto by Langston Hughes, based on his play about Jean Jacques Dessalines and the Haitian Revolution. Premiere, New York 1949 (the opera was completed in 1930). It was the first opera written entirely by blacks that was produced by a major opera company in the U.S.

Trouble in Tahiti opera in 1 act by Bernstein to his own libretto. Premiere, Brandeis (MA) 1952. A suburban domestic tragi-comedy about Dinah and Sam. Bernstein later combined the opera with a sequel in *A Quiet Place* (1983–84).

trough zither a ZITHER consisting in a hollowed-out piece of wood with a length of string laced back and forth over the trough.

trousers role TRAVESTI.

Trout Quintet, The (Ger., *Die Forelle*) the piano quintet in A major for piano, violin, viola, cello and bass, Op. 114, D. 667 (c1819), by Schubert. The second movement is based on his earlier song, *Die Forelle* (The Trout, 1817–19), to a text by Schubart.

trouvère [troo'ver] a poet or poet-musician of 12th and 13th c. France, esp. one working in the French language in northern France. Cf. TROUBADOUR, VERS.

Trovatore, Il [trō-vä'tō-rä] (It., The Troubadour) tragic opera in 4 acts by Verdi to a libretto in Italian by Salvatore Cammarano, based on the play by Antonio Garcia Gutiérrez. Premiere, Rome 1853. A complicated story of the Count di Luna and the troubadour Manrico (who turns out to be the count's brother) and their shared love for Leonora.

Troyanos, Tatiana (1938–) Amer. mezzo-soprano, trained at the Juilliard School. She sang with the New York City Opera from 1963 and has sung in most major European and Amer. opera houses. Her Metropolitan Opera debut was in 1976. Her

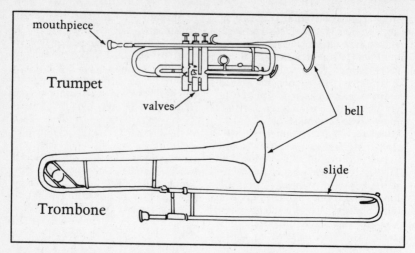

roles incl. Octavian (*Der Rosenka-valier*), Kundry (*Parsifal*) and Adalgisa (*Norma*).

Troyens, Les [tro'yɛ̃] (Fr.) THE TRO-JANS.

trucking a type of JITTERBUG dance step of the late 1930s.

Trumbauer, Frankie (1901–56) Amer. jazz saxophonist. He worked together with Bix Beiderbecke in a series of orchestras, incl. those of Jean Goldkette and Paul Whiteman, then concentrated on studio work on the West Coast. He left music in 1947.

trumpet a lip-vibrated brass AERO-PHONE dating from ancient times, predominantly straight and cylindrical and usu. having a cup mouthpiece. The instrument is usu. end-blown (though there are Afr. side-blown trumpets). The natural trumpet can produce only one set of partials, making production of a scale very difficult. The valved trumpet was introduced in the early 19th c., permitting access to several different lengths of tubing and hence making the production of a chromatic scale simpler than before and without the use of out-of-tune higher partials. There is also a type of trumpet using a slide (SLIDE TRUMPET). There are many different sizes and styles of trumpets, the most commonly used being the standard B♭ trumpet, the C trumpet and the pic-

colo trumpet. Cf. BUGLE, KEYED TRUMPET, BUCCINA.

trumpet marine a one-stringed, medieval, bowed instrument that produces coarse-toned natural harmonics. Also, *tromba marina* (It.), *nun's fiddle*.

trumpet-piano style a style of piano playing associated with EARL HINES imitating the trumpet style of LOUIS ARMSTRONG.

trumpet tune *also,* **trumpet voluntary** a piece for trumpet, or a piece for other instruments or voices that imitates the sound and character of music for the trumpet, esp. the natural (valveless) trumpet. Such works were popular in the 17th and 18th c.

trutruka a type of Chilean straight TRUMPET.

TS *abbr.* TASTO SOLO.

Tsch see TCH.

tsigane TZIGANE.

tsuri daiko a Jap. double-headed WAISTED DRUM.

tsutzumi a small Jap. WAISTED DRUM used in Noh drama.

TTBB *abbr.* tenor, tenor, bass, bass: a common form of four-part men's chorus.

tuba 1, a valved, brass bass AERO-PHONE dating from the 1830s with a wide conical bore, flared bell and cup mouthpiece. The instrument is used in the orch. and in military bands.

There are three standard orchestral sizes, the contrabass, the E♭ bass (bombardon) and the F bass. See also EUPHONIUM, SOUSAPHONE, HELICON, OPHICLEIDE, WAGNER TUBA. **2,** an ancient Roman TRUMPET of brass, bronze or ivory, with a horn or ivory mouthpiece.

Tubb, Ernest (1914–84) Amer. honky-tonk singer, guitarist and songwriter. He was strongly influenced by Jimmie Rodgers and was assisted early in his career by Rodgers's widow. He sang regularly with the Grand Ole Opry from 1942 and launched the "Midnight Jamboree" radio program in 1947. He concertized widely and helped to make Nashville the center of country-music recording. He was elected to the Country Music Hall of Fame in 1965.

tube zither a ZITHER fashioned from a hollow, tubular piece of wood or cane. The strings are either cut from the tube itself and raised over bridges or are made separately and attached to the tube by other means.

tubular bells *also,* **tubular chimes** a series of tuned brass or steel tubes, usu. arranged in scale order and hung in a frame, which usu. incorporates a foot-pedal-controlled mechanism for damping the bells. The tubes are struck near the top with mallets of wood or other material.

Tucci, Gabriella ['toot-chē] (1929–) Italian soprano, stud. of Leonardo Filoni. She sang throughout Europe and England, then made her Amer. debut in 1959 in San Francisco and at the Metropolitan Opera in 1960. She has taught at Indiana U. since 1983. Her roles incl. Mimì (*La Bohème*), Desdemona (*Otello*) and Violetta (*La Traviata*).

tuck *also,* **tucket, touk** a drum or trumpet signal or flourish.

Tucker, Richard (Ticker, Reuben) (1913–75) Amer. operatic tenor, stud. of Paul Althouse. He sang in Europe and S. America, but most of his career was centered on the Metropolitan Opera, where he sang over 30

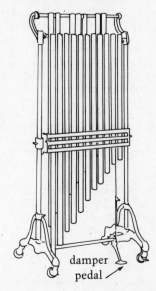

Tubular bells

damper pedal

roles from the Italian, French and German repertory. He was also a popular concert and recital artist.

Tucker, Tui St. George (1924–) Amer. composer and recorder player. She has written many works for recorder, as well as orchestral and chamber music and choral works and songs, many employing quarter-tones and multiphonics.

tucket TUCK.

Tuckwell, Barry (Emmanuel) (1931–) Australian-born English virtuoso horn player. He went to London in 1950, where he played in the London SO as principal horn until 1968, afterwards concentrating on chamber music and solo performance.

Tudor, David (Eugene) (1926–) Amer. pianist and composer, stud. of Irma and Stefan Wolpe and others. He made his name performing new music and in the early 1950s established a connection with John Cage, introducing a number of his works and collaborating on happenings. He has worked extensively with the Merce Cunningham Dance Company and has taught at SUNY, Buffalo, at Mills College and elsewhere. His compositions all involve electronic production.

Tully, Alice (1902–) Amer. mezzo-soprano and philanthropist, stud. of Jean Périer and Miguel Fontecha. She was active as a performer in the 1930s and 1940s in Europe and the U.S. in opera and recital, specializing in French repertory. She has been a board member of the Chamber Music Society of Lincoln Center since 1969 and provided the funds to construct the Alice Tully Hall at Lincoln Center.

Tulsa Philharmonic Orchestra orch. founded in 1947 under H. Arthur Brown. Subsequent conductors have been Golschmann, Franco Autori, Skitch Henderson, Thomas Lewis, Murry Sidlin, Joel Lazar and Bernard Rubenstein.

tumbadora *also*, **tumba** (Sp.) a large CONGA DRUM.

tune MELODY.

tunebook a collection of psalm tunes used in early Amer. SINGING SCHOOLS. Such books were frequently published in SHAPE NOTE notation.

tuning the adjustment of an instrument by various means to conform each note of the instrument to a standard tuning system (see TUNING SYSTEMS).

tuning fork *or* **hammer** a device invented in 1711 by Handel's trumpeter, John Shore, for producing a fixed pitch when struck. The instrument is made of metal in the form of a ¥. When the dual prongs are struck, they produce vibrations which may be amplified by touching the opposing single-pronged handle to a resonating surface, such as a table. Another form of the device (also called a *tuning bar*) is a solid, tuned metal bar mounted over a hollow resonating chamber. The devices are relatively free from the effects of temperature and humidity and retain their pitch indefinitely. They can be tuned by filing (to sharpen) or filling (to flatten). In recent years electronic devices us-

ing electrically vibrated quartz have tended to replace the older metal instruments.

tuning peg PEG.

tuning pin WREST PIN.

tuning slide **1**, a small slide on a wind instrument, used to make small adjustments to the length of the tubing for tuning purposes. **2**, a movable metal slide placed on top of a metal organ flue pipe, used to adjust the pitch of the pipe.

tuning systems methods for determining the intervals between the notes of a scale. *Just* tuning systems use only pure intervals, whereas *tempered* systems make minute adjustments to the pure intervals for various purposes, primarily to permit modulation. There have been innumerable systems over the centuries; renewed interest in earlier periods, esp. the Renaissance and Baroque, has revived use of some of the more widely accepted systems of those eras. The system in common use in Western music since the 19th c. has been *equal temperament*, in which all the half steps of the 12-note scale are the same size. See TEMPERAMENT, MICROTONE.

Turandot opera in 3 acts by Puccini to a libretto by Guiseppe Adami and Renato Simoni, based on the play by Carlo Gozzi. Left unfinished by the composer's death, the opera was premiered in 1926 in Milan in a version completed by Franco Alfano. Turandot, icy Princess of Pekin, is finally softened by her love for Prince Calaf. **2**, opera in 2 acts by Busoni to his own libretto based on Gozzi's play. Premiere, Zürich 1917. Busoni had earlier written incidental music for the play, which he also fashioned into an orchestral suite, Op. 41 (1904).

Turangalila Symphony a work in ten movements for piano, ondes martenot and large orch. (1948) by Messiaen, called by the composer a "song of love."

turba (Lat., crowd) a term referring to words in the PASSION that are spoken by more than one person.

turca, alla (It., in the Turkish manner) **1**, indicating performance in the manner of Turkish band music, i.e., employing cymbals, triangles, drums, piccolos, etc. (see JANISSARY MUSIC), a style highly popular in the late 18th and early 19th c. **2**, the 3rd movement of the Piano Sonata in A major, K.331/300i (1781–83), by Mozart.

Tureck, Rosalyn (1914–) Amer. pianist and musicologist, stud. of Jan Chiapusso and Olga Samaroff. She has toured extensively throughout the world, specializing in the works of Bach and of 20th-c. Amer. composers. She has performed the music of Bach on harpsichord, clavichord and electronic instruments, as well as on piano. She has taught at the Mannes College, the Juilliard School and elsewhere.

Turetzky, Bertram (Jay) (1933–) Amer. virtuoso double bass player and composer, stud. of Joseph Iadone, Josef Marx and others. He has extensively broadened the repertory and technique of the double bass and has commissioned a number of new works. He has also written works for bass and other instruments, some in combination with electronic tape.

Turina, Joaquin (1882–1949) Spanish composer, stud. of Garcia Torrez. He lived in Paris from 1905 to 1914 and formed a friendship with Falla. Returning to Madrid, he worked as choirmaster of the Teatro Real, then taught at the Madrid Conservatory. His works incl. operas and zarzuelas, tone poems, chamber music with piano, many works for solo piano, guitar music and songs.

Türk, Daniel Gottlob (1756–1813) German composer and theorist, trained at the Dresden Kreuzschule, esp. with J.A. Hiller. In 1774 he became Kantor in Halle, where he remained until his death. He composed a substantial body of vocal cantatas, songs, instrumental sonatas and chamber music, but he is best known for his theoretical and didactic writings.

Turkey in the Straw song of disputed authorship, orig. entitled "Zip Coon" and published in 1934. The song is a popular square-dance tune.

turkey trot a dance of the 1910s and 1920s assoc. with RAGTIME music.

Turkish crescent a stick jingle dating from the 16th c. having crescent-shaped arms hung with metal jingles, used in military bands. Also, *Chinese crescent, jingling Johnny, pavillon chinois.* See PERCUSSION (*illus.*).

Turkish march the fourth movement of the incidental music (1811) by Beethoven for A. von Kotzebue's play *The Ruins of Athens.*

Turkish music JANISSARY MUSIC.

turn an ORNAMENT consisting of four or more notes (including the principal note), beginning either on the principal note or above it and winding above and below. Cf. MORDENT.

turnback in jazz, an improvised transition at the end of a chorus leading back to the initial chord of the piece.

Turner, Big Joe (Joseph Vernon) (1911–85) Amer. blues singer. He toured with the bands of Bennie Moten and Count Basie, then worked with boogie-woogie pianist Pete Johnson. From the 1940s he toured and recorded extensively. His song "Shake, Rattle and Roll" (1954) had a strong influence on the beginnings of rock-and-roll.

Turner, Joe (Joseph H.) (1907–) Amer. jazz pianist and singer, accompanist to Adelaide Hall in the 1930s and an active free lance in New York. Since World War II he has been based in Europe.

Turner, Tina (Bullock, Annie Mae) (1938–) Amer. popular singer. From 1956 she performed with her husband, guitarist-pianist **Ike Turner** (1933–), in a highly popular rhythm-and-blues group. Since the marriage broke up in 1976, she has pursued a solo career.

Turn of the Screw, The opera in 2 acts by Britten to a libretto by Myfanwy Piper, based on the novel by Henry James. Premiere, Venice 1954.

Turpin, Tom (Thomas Million J.)

(1873–1922) Amer. ragtime composer and pianist and founder of the Rosebud Club in St. Louis, the site of annual ragtime piano contests. His *Harlem Rag* (1897) was the first rag by a black composer to be published.

tutte le corde ['too-tā lā 'kor-dā] (It.) TRE CORDE.

tutti ['toot-tē] (It., all) **1**, the full ensemble in a CONCERTO GROSSO, as opposed to the smaller *concertino* or to soloists. **2**, all the instruments in a section, as opposed to a solo. **3**, the full orch.

twelfth an INTERVAL comprising eleven diatonic steps (an octave and a fifth).

twelve-tone music a term usu. referring to music composed using all twelve notes of the chromatic scale without regard to a tonal center. Most often such music employs techniques orig. formulated by Schoenberg, by which the twelve notes are organized into a ROW of pitches that forms the musical material for a work or section and is manipulated by various means to derive related rows. There have been other 12-tone systems—in particular, the use of TROPES as set out by Josef Hauer. However, Schoenberg's was the only one to gain wide acceptance. Cf. SERIALISM.

Twilight of the Gods, The (Ger., *Götterdämmerung*) opera in 3 acts by Wagner, the fourth and final opera of the *Ring of the Nibelung*. Premiere, Bayreuth 1876. Brünnhilde rides into the fire with the fateful ring, which is then reclaimed by the Rhine as it overflows Valhalla.

Twitty, Conway (Jenkins, Harold Lloyd) (1933–) Amer. country-music and pop singer and songwriter, who took his stage name from two southern towns. His principal pop success came in the late 1950s, when he also appeared in films. In the 1960s he switched to country music, appearing frequently with Loretta Lynn.

two-foot stop a pipe ORGAN STOP producing pitches two octaves above the notated pitch.

two-step **1**, an Amer. quick ballroom dance of the late 19th and early 20th c., often performed to a type of march of the same name having a lilting ⅝ rhythm. **2**, FOX TROT.

Tye, Christopher (c1505–c1572) English composer, trained at Cambridge. He was choirmaster at Ely Cathedral from 1543, then received a benefice at Doddington in 1561. His extant works consist of Latin and English church music and works for consort, incl. over 20 IN NOMINE settings. Cf. TALLIS.

tympani TIMPANI.

Tyner, (Alfred) McCoy (1938–) Amer. jazz pianist and composer. He played with the Benny Golson-Art Farmer Jazztet and with John Coltrane in the 1960s, after which he was a member of various small groups and led his own quartets and trios, also recording with big band and choir. His music makes frequent use of nonstandard scales and harmonies.

tyrolienne [tē-rō'lyen] (Fr.) a Tyrolean folk dance-song in fast triple meter characterized by yodelling and other effects.

tzigane [tsē'gän] (Fr.) **1**, music in the gypsy style. **2**, a concert rhapsody for violin and piano (1924) by Ravel.

U

Überbrettl ['ü-bər-bret-əl] (Ger.) a Berlin CABARET of the early 20th c. frequented by composers and writers. Schoenberg worked there briefly and wrote some songs for it.

Übung ['ü-bûng] (Ger.) exercise, STUDY.

u.c. *abbr.* UNA CORDA.

ud [ood] (Arabic, lute) a Middle Eastern short-necked, unfretted LUTE, double-strung and played with a plectrum.

Uggams, Leslie (1943–) Amer. popular singer and actress, successful on Broadway in *Hallelujah, Baby!* (1967) and *Her First Roman* (1968), in night clubs and on recordings.

uilleann pipes UNION PIPES.

ukeke (Hawaiian) a Hawaiian MUSICAL BOW.

Ukrainian Symphony see LITTLE RUSSIAN SYMPHONY.

ukulele *also*, **ukelele** (Hawaiian, leaping flea) a small GUITAR, orig. from Portugal, having four gut or nylon strings and played by plucking or strumming with the fingers. Also, *Hawaiian guitar uke.* Cf. TARO-PATCH FIDDLE.

Ulanowsky, Paul (1908–68) Austrian-born Amer. piano accompanist, stud. of Josef Marx and Severin Eisenberger. He played with the Vienna PO until the mid-1930s, then came to the U.S. He accompanied Lotte Lehmann regularly until her retirement, as well as many other major singers and instrumentalists, incl. Fischer-Dieskau, Hotter, Benny Goodman and Piatigorsky. He taught at the Berkshire Music Center, Boston, the U. of Illinois and the Yale Summer School and played with the Bach Aria Group from 1960.

Ulmer, James "Blood" (1942–) Amer. jazz guitarist, flutist and singer. In the early 1970s he performed with Ornette Coleman, later leading his own, heavily amplified trio.

ultrachromaticism microtonal music (see MICROTONE).

una corda (It., one string) in piano music, an indication to play with the SOFT PEDAL depressed.

Unanswered Question, The work for trumpet, woodwinds and strings (1906) by Ives, subtitled "A Cosmic Landscape," written as a companion piece to CENTRAL PARK IN THE DARK. According to the composer, the strings represent "The Silences of the Druids Who Know, See and Hear Nothing." The trumpet asks "The Perennial Question of Existence" while the woodwinds search for "The Invisible Answer."

unda maris a delicate, undulating ORGAN STOP.

understudy a singer or actor who is prepared to replace another in a rehearsal or performance. Also *cover, double.*

Unfinished Symphony, The the Symphony No. 8 in B minor, D. 759 (1822) by Schubert. Only the first two movements were completed; a substantial sketch for a third movement also exists. The reason the work was left unfinished is unknown.

Unger, Heinz (1895–1965) German-born Canadian conductor, trained in Berlin. He conducted in Germany until 1933, then in London until the late 1940s. He was also conductor of the Leningrad Radio Orch. (1934–36). He came to Toronto in 1948, founding the York Concert Society and conducting regularly for the CBC.

Unicorn, the Gorgon and the Manticore, The madrigal fable by Menotti for chorus, dancers and small instrumental ensemble. Premiere, Washington, D.C. 1956.

union pipes a type of Irish bellows-blown BAGPIPE. Also, *uilleann pipes.*

unison 1, the INTERVAL between two notes of identical pitch (interval class 0). **2**, the simultaneous performance of a part by more than one performer at the same pitch (or, sometimes, at the interval of an octave). Also, *all' unisono.*

unit organ an ORGAN with relatively few pipes that are made available on all manuals and at various pitch levels.

Universal Edition Austrian music publishing firm founded in Vienna in 1901. The firm has been especially active in the field of 20th-c. music.

Universe Symphony a projected work in three movements for multiple orchestras begun by Ives in 1911 and abandoned in 1928. The movements were to represent past, present and future.

unprepared dissonance a NONHARMONIC NOTE which is not present as a consonance in the preceding chord.

upbeat the note or notes immediately preceding a DOWNBEAT. The exact duration of the upbeat depends on the musical context and may or may not actually equal a beat. Also, *anacrusis, arsis, pickup.*

upbow a BOWSTROKE played with the bow moving toward the heel, notated by the symbol (ᵛ) over the note to be so played. Contrasted with DOWNBOW.

upper partial OVERTONE.

up-picking a style of guitar picking similar to FRAILING, combining a melody stroke and a brush stroke, but with the melody note picked upward.

Uppman, Theodore (1920–) Amer. baritone, trained at the Curtis Institute, Stanford and U. of S. Calif. He has sung with the New York City Opera, the Metropolitan Opera and in Europe, where his roles have included Pelléas, Masetto (*Don Giovanni*) and Harlequin (*Ariadne auf Naxos*). He

has taught at the Mannes College and the U. of Hartford.

upright piano a PIANO whose strings run vertically to the ground, rather than horizontally as in a grand piano. The action of most upright pianos is considered inferior to the grand piano because it has less assistance from gravity. Upright pianos come in various sizes, from the large and high-backed studio upright to the small spinet. Also, *vertical piano.*

up-tempo in a fast tempo, esp. in jazz and popular music.

urban blues a style of BLUES dating from the early 20th c., dealing with city themes and usu. having a more sophisticated formal organization than the COUNTRY BLUES.

Urlinie ['ûr"lin-yä] (Ger.) in Schenkerian analysis, the fundamental stepwise descent of the melodic structure in a tonal work from the third, fifth or octave to the tonic. The Urlinie is notated with hollow noteheads and beamed stems; the number indicating the scale degree is placed above the beam. See SCHENKER (*illus.*).

Ursatz [-zäts] (Ger.) in Schenkerian analysis, the underlying two-part contrapuntal structure of a tonal work consisting of the Urlinie and Bassbrechung. Also, *background.* See SCHENKER (*illus.*).

Urtext (Ger.) a modern edition of an older work which purports to present the exact musical text without any unacknowledged editorial addition or alteration.

urua a large Brazilian double CLARINET made from two pieces of cane of unequal lengths.

Ussachevsky, Vladimir (Alexis) (1911–90) Russian-born Amer. composer, stud. of Rogers and Hanson. He taught at Columbia from 1947 to 1980, where he was a founder of the Columbia-Princeton Electronic Music Center. He also taught at the U. of Utah (1980–85). He specialized in electronic and choral music.

ut 1, the first note in the Guidonian HEXACHORD. **2**, the note C in the

FIXED DO system, replaced with the syllable "do" in SOLMIZATION.

Utah Symphony Orchestra orch. formed in 1940 as the Utah State SO and renamed in 1946. Its conductors have been Hans Heniot, Werner Janssen, Maurice Abravanel (1947–79), Varujan Kojian and Joseph Silverstein.

uti a small, Yugoslav, plucked, round-back LUTE.

utility music GEBRAUCHSMUSIK.

Utopia Limited comic opera in 2 acts by Sullivan to a libretto by W.S. Gilbert. Premiere, London 1893. Subtitled *The Flowers of Progress*, the story proposes a Utopia run like a British company.

Utrecht Te Deum work for chorus and orch. (1713) by Handel, composed (along with a jubilate) for the Peace of Utrecht.

U2 Irish punk rock group formed in 1978 in Dublin.

V

v. *abbr.* **1,** VIOLIN. **2,** VERSE in plainsong.

va. *abbr.* VIOLA.

Vaccai, Nicola [väk′kī] (1790–1848) Italian composer and teacher, stud. of Giuseppe Janacconi in Rome and Paisiello in Naples. His one success, the opera *Giulietta e Romeo* (1825), was later eclipsed by Bellini's opera on the same subject, though in the 19th c. the last scene of Vaccai's version was often used to replace the last scene of Bellini's work. However, Vaccai's fame was to rest on his considerable abilities as a voice teacher; his *Metodo pratico di canto italiano* (Practical Method for Singing Italian, 1832) is still widely used.

Vagabond King, The musical by Rudolf Friml, lyrics by Brian Hooker, book by Hooker, Russell Janney and W.H. Post, based on the play *If I Were King* by Justin Huntly McCarthy. Premiere, New York 1925. The story of poet-vagabond François Villon, who becomes king for a day in the time of Louis XI.

vagans (Lat.) the fifth part in 15th- and 16th-c. polyphony, usu. in the tenor range. Cf. QUINTUS.

Valderrábano, Enríquez de (c1500– c1560) celebrated Spanish composer and vihuelist, best known for his book of vihuela music, *Silva de sirenas* (1547).

Valente, Benita (1939–) Amer. soprano, stud. of Lotte Lehmann, Martial Singher, Chester Hayden and Margaret Harshaw. She has sung opera in Europe and the U.S. (her Metropolitan Opera debut was in 1973), but she is equally known as a recitalist and concert artist. She has performed many contemporary works and has been a frequent participant in the Marlboro Festival.

Valenti, Fernando (1926–) Amer. harpsichordist, stud. of Iturbi and Ralph Kirkpatrick. He has toured Europe and the Americas and been on the faculty of the Juilliard School since 1951. He is esp. known for his performances of works by D. Scarlatti and 18th-c. Spanish composers.

valiha a Malagasy TUBE ZITHER.

Valkyrie, The (Ger., *Die Walküre*) opera in 3 acts by Wagner, the second opera of *The Ring of the Nibelung*. Premiere, Munich 1870. For attempting to protect Siegfried from Wotan, Brünnhilde is punished by being left asleep, ringed by a magic fire, to await a fearless hero.

Vallee, Rudy (Vallée, Hubert Prior) (1901–86) Amer. saxophonist, bandleader and singer, crooning idol of the 1920s and 1930s, trained at the U. of Maine and Yale. In 1928 he founded the Connecticut Yankees and appeared frequently on radio, Broadway and in over 30 films.

Valli, Frankie (Castellucio, Francis) (1937–) Amer. rock-and-roll singer, leader of the FOUR SEASONS from the early 1960s. After 1970 he pursued a successful solo career.

vals a type of Lat.-Amer. salon work for solo piano related to the WALTZ.

valse [väls] (Fr.) WALTZ, esp. a concert waltz.

Valse, La (Fr., The Waltz) orchestral work and ballet (1920) by Ravel, a somewhat satirical evocation of the Viennese waltz of an earlier era. It was orig. entitled *Vienna*.

valse à deux temps [ä dø tä] (Fr.) a mid-19th-c. ballroom dance in ¾ time, faster than the waltz, with steps on the first and third beats.

Valses nobles et sentimentals [väls ′nob-lə zä sä-tē-mä′täl] (Fr., Noble and Sentimental Waltzes) piano suite of seven waltzes (1910) by Ravel, orchestrated in 1912 by the composer.

Valse Triste [trēst] (Fr.) orchestral work (1903) by Sibelius, orig. written as incidental music to the play *Kuolema* (Death) by Sibelius's brother-in-law, Arvid Järnefelt.

valve a mechanical device for augmenting the tube length of a brass instrument by adding a section of tubing to the air path. There are three types of valves in current use: the piston valve, the rotary valve and the Vienna or double piston valve.

valve trombone a TROMBONE fitted with valves, either in addition to a slide or completely replacing it.

valve trumpet a TRUMPET fitted with valves.

vamp 1, an improvised accompaniment for a vocal or instrumental solo. **2**, an introductory or transitional passage which may be played as many times as needed to allow time for a performer to prepare for the next section, event, etc.

Van Beinum, Eduard (Alexander) (1901–59) Dutch conductor, stud. of Sem Dresden. He became second conductor of the Concertgebouw Orch. in 1931, obtaining the music dir. position in 1945. In 1949 he added the post of principal conductor of the London PO and appeared frequently as guest conductor elsewhere in Europe. In 1956 he became musical dir. of the Los Angeles PO while retaining his position in Amsterdam.

Vancouver Opera Association opera producing org. founded in 1961 under Irving Guttman.

Vancouver Symphony Orchestra orch. founded in 1931 by Allard de Ridder. Conductors have included Irwin Hoffman, Meredith Davies, Simon Streatfeild, Akiyama and Barshai.

Van Dam, José (Van Damme, Joseph) (1940–) Belgian bass, trained in Brussels. He has sung in Paris, Geneva, Salzburg and regularly with the Deutsche Oper in Berlin. His roles incl. Escamillo (*Carmen*), Paolo (*Simon Boccanegra*) and Figaro.

Van der Stucken, Frank (Valentine) (1858–1929) Amer. conductor and composer, stud. of Peter Benoit and Reinecke. From 1884 he conducted several choral organizations in the U.S. and became in 1895 the first permanent conductor of the Cincinnati SO, a post he held until 1907. He also directed the Cincinnati May Festival (1906–12).

Van de Vate, Nancy Hayes (1930–) Amer. composer and pianist, trained at Wellesley College. She taught at the U. of Mississippi, Memphis State U., Knoxville College and the U. of Hawaii. Her works incl. orch. works and concertos, chamber music and choral works.

Van Egmond, Max EGMOND, MAX VAN.

Vaness, Carol (1952–) Amer. soprano, trained at California State U. She has sung at the San Francisco Opera, the New York City Opera and the Metropolitan Opera (debut 1984) as well as in European opera houses. She is particularly noted for her performance of the works of Mozart, Handel and Strauss.

Vanessa opera in 4 acts by Samuel Barber to a libretto by Gian-Carlo Menotti. Premiere, New York 1958. Vanessa finds true love in her former lover's son, but at the cost of her daughter Erika's happiness.

Vanhal, Johann Baptist (1739–1813) prolific Czech composer and teacher, stud. of Dittersdorf. He never held a permanent position, but earned his living through composing and teaching (his pupils incl. Pleyel). His large output concentrated on instrumental music: over 70 symphonies, many concertos for various instruments, dances, serenades, etc.; chamber music for different combinations and solo piano music. He also wrote several operas and sacred and secular vocal music.

Van Heusen, Jimmy (James) (Babcock, Edward Chester) (1913–90) composer, pianist and publisher. He worked at the Cotton Club in Harlem in the 1930s, then wrote songs and scores for many films (incl. the "Road to . . ." series with Bing Crosby and Bob Hope) and Broadway shows. He produced many hit songs, incl. "My Kind of Town," "Love and Marriage" and "Moonlight Becomes You."

Van Vactor, David (1906–) Amer. composer, flutist and conductor, stud. of Marcel Moyse and Dukas, among others. He played with the Chicago SO (1931–43), then was assistant conductor of the Kansas City PO and on the faculty of the Kansas City Conservatory. From 1947 until his retirement in 1976 he taught at the U. of Tennessee and conducted the Knoxville SO. He has written works for orch., chamber music and songs.

Varèse, Edgard (Victor Achille Charles) [vä'rez] (1883–1965) influential French-born Amer. composer. He studied in Paris with Charles Bordes, Roussel, Widor and d'Indy. He was in Berlin from 1905 to 1913, and when he left most of his manuscripts were tragically destroyed in a fire. He was in New York from 1915, active with various groups, incl. the circle of dadaist Marcel Duchamp, and was a founder of the International Composers' Guild and later of the Pan American Association of Composers. He began work on taped electronic sounds in the early 1950s, producing two of the earliest electronic tape works, *Deserts* (1954) and *Poème électronique* (1957). Throughout his career he was searching for new sounds and new ways to produce them but tempered by his love for music of the Middle Ages and Renaissance. His works incl. *Amériques*, *Offrandes* and *Arcana* for orch., *Octandre*, *Intégrales*, *Ionisation* and other works for chamber ensemble, *Density 21.5* for solo flute, *Déserts* for instruments and tape and *Poème électronique* for tape.

variable meters the systematic changing of meters in consecutive

measures, a technique utilized by Blacher and Hartmann, among others.

variant a term for a second or subsequent version of a theme, work, etc., that differs in some respect from the first version. Also, *variant readings*.

variation the repetition of a theme or harmonic or rhythmic pattern with modifications or embellishments. Sets of variations on the same theme have been common since the 16th c. and constitute one of the principal musical forms in Western art music.

Variations on America work for organ (c1891) by Ives, later arranged for orch. (1964) by William Schuman.

Variations on a Rococo Theme seven variations for cello and orch., Op. 33 (1876), by Tchaikovsky on a theme of his own devising, written in the spirit of the 18th c.

Variations on a Theme by Haydn set of nine variations for orch., Op. 56a, or two-piano duet, Op. 56b, by Brahms, based on a theme known as

(Beethoven, 7 Variations on "God Save the Queen")

the St. Antoni Chorale, of unknown authorship though once ascribed to Haydn. Both versions date from 1873. The last variation is a passacaglia and a set of variations in itself.

Varnay, Astrid (Ibolyka Maria) (1918–) Swedish-born Amer. soprano, daughter of two singers, stud. of Paul Althouse and Hermann Weigert. Her Metropolitan Opera debut was in 1941 and she sang there until 1979, when she retired to Munich. She also sang at Bayreuth and in other leading opera houses. Her specialty was Wagnerian opera.

varsoviana *also,* **varsovienne** (Fr.) a graceful dance similar to the MAZURKA, in a slow triple meter with every other measure accented.

Varviso, Silvio (1924–) Swiss conductor, trained in Zürich. He conducted for many years in Basle and has guest-conducted in most major opera houses in Europe and No. America. He has been musical dir. of the Royal Opera in Stockholm, the Stuttgart Opera and the Paris Opera.

Vásáry, Tamás (1933–) Hungarian-born Swiss pianist, stud. of Josef Gat and Kodály in Budapest. He has performed widely as soloist and accompanist and has been active as a conductor since the early 1970s. He became music dir. of the Northern Sinfonia (England) in 1979.

vaudeville (Fr.) **1**, [vōd′vēl] a French satirical popular song of the 17th and 18th c. Cf. VAU DE VIRE, VOIX DE VILLE. **2**, a light theatrical variety show, usu. consisting of a series of acts, the last of which unites all of the characters, each of whom performed a verse. Vaudeville in the late 19th and 20th c. incl. comedy skits, acrobats, dances, songs and pretty girls. The girls gradually took over.

vau de vire [vō də vēr] (Fr.) a 15th-c. French popular song of Normandy.

Vaughan, Sarah (Lois) ("Sassy") (1924–90) Amer. jazz and popular singer. She sang with the bands of Earl Hines and Billy Eckstine in the 1940s, then worked mainly as a soloist. She worked frequently with bop artists

such as Dizzy Gillespie and Miles Davis and with her own trio. She was esp. noted for her operatic vocal range and vibrato and her improvisational abilities.

Vaughan Williams, Ralph (1872–1958) eminent and prolific English composer, conductor and teacher, stud. of Stanford, Wood and Parry in London and later with Bruch and Ravel on the Continent. During his lifetime he worked in music in a variety of ways, as a church organist, a writer, a folksong collector and editor, conductor and musical activist. He was conductor of the Leith Hill Musical Festival for most of his career and also conducted the Bach Choir and the Handel Society. He taught at the Royal Conservatory of Music in London from 1919. A universal musician, he wrote in nearly all genres in a melodious style that is often more modal than tonal and highly sensitive to orchestral color. He had a profound influence on English composition and musical life.

Vaughan Williams's works incl. *Hugh the Drover, Sir John in Love, Riders to the Sea, The Pilgrim's Progress* and other operas, incidental music and film scores, 9 symphonies, *Fantasia on a Theme by Thomas Tallis, The Lark Ascending* for violin and orch., *Fantasia on Greensleeves,* many songs and choral works, settings of carols and chamber music.

vcl. *abbr.* violoncello (see CELLO).

Vecchi, Orazio (1550–1605) Italian composer of sacred and secular music, best known for his quasi-dramatic collections of madrigals, such as *L'Amfiparnaso* (1597).

Vega, Aurelio de la (1925–) Cuban-born Amer. composer and teacher, trained in Havana and with Frederick Kramer and Toch. He held various posts in Havana before coming permanently to the U.S. in 1959 to teach at San Fernando Valley State College. He has written mainly instrumental works for orch. and chamber ensembles as well as works for tape and for voice and instruments.

veloce [vä´lō-chä] (It.) rapid(ly).

Velvet Underground, The influential Amer. rock group formed in New York in 1965. Though the group was not financially successful, they exerted a seminal influence on the punk movement through their lyrics of sexual deviancy, drugs and hopelessness. The group disbanded in the early 1970s.

Venetian style an influential style of composition represented by composers in 16th-c. Venice, esp. those assoc. with St. Mark's Basilica. The most prevalent characteristics of the style are polychoral writing and echo effects. Important composers incl. Willaert, Andrea and Giovanni Gabrieli, Zarlino and Monteverdi. Cf. CORI SPEZZATI.

vent [vä] (Fr.) wind. —**instruments à vent** (Fr.) WIND INSTRUMENTS.

Ventil (Ger.) a wind instrument valve.

Ventura, Charlie (Charles) (1916–) Amer. jazz tenor saxophonist. He played with Gene Krupa's band in the 1940s, reuniting with him at various times in later years. He also led his own big band and played in several small combos.

Ventures, The influential Amer. rock group formed in 1959 (as the Versatones) in Tacoma, WA. The group was unusual for its time, being composed of two electric guitars, electric bass and drums.

Venuti, Joe (Giuseppe) (1903–78) Amer. jazz violinist. He recorded in the 1920s with guitarist Eddie Lang and worked with numerous bands, then joined the Paul Whiteman band in 1929. He also led his own big band, but much of his career was devoted to studio work and work with small ensembles.

Veracini, Francesco Maria (1690–1768) Italian composer, violinist and teacher, stud. of G.A. Bernabei, G.M. Casini and others in Florence. After years of travel and performance in London and continental capitals, he joined the Dresden court of the prince elector of Saxony in 1716, remaining until 1722. He was active in London as soloist and composer in the 1740s and early 1750s, then spent his last years in Florence. His works incl. 4 operas, oratorios, vocal works, violin sonatas and concerti grossi.

verbunkos (Hung.) a Hungarian dance based on a dance that was part of Austrian recruitment proceedings during the 18th and early 19th c.

Vercoe, Barry (Lloyd) (1937–) New Zealand composer, stud. of Finney and Godfrey Winham. He has taught since 1971 at MIT, where he established the Experimental Music Studio in 1973. He has developed several computer music languages that are widely used.

Verdelot, Philippe (c1475–c1552) French composer of motets, madrigals, chansons and other vocal works. Little is known about his life, but much of his professional career seems to have been spent at the cathedral in Florence.

Verdi, Giuseppe (Fortunino Francesco) (1813–1901) highly influential Italian opera composer. After study in Milan he returned to his home town of Busseto to be *maestro di musica* for secular music. He left the post in 1839 to move to Milan, where his first opera, *Oberto*, had a moderate success. His second, a comedy, *Un giorno di regno*, failed, but the third—which he wrote only after much urging—was *Nabucco*, a triumph which launched his career.

Verdi's opera production has been divided into four periods: the first ending in 1849 with *La Battaglia di Legnano* and strongly influenced by Rossini; the second, ending with *La Traviata* (1853), concentrating on character development; the third, ending with *Aida* (1871), an amalgamation of Meyerbeer and Italian opera; and the fourth comprising his two last operatic masterpieces, *Otello* and *Falstaff*, the latter only his second attempt at comic opera. Many of the composer's works remain in the standard repertory and his influence on opera has been inestimable.

Verdi's works incl. *Ernani, Attila, Macbeth, Luisa Miller, Rigoletto, Il Trovatore, La Traviata, Un Ballo in maschera, La Forza del destino, Don Carlos, Aida, Otello, Falstaff* and other operas, choral works (incl. the *Messa da requiem* and the *Quattro pezzi sacri*), songs and several chamber music works.

Verdon, (Gwyneth Evelyn) Gwen (1926–) Amer. actress, dancer, and singer who has starred in Broadway musicals incl. *Damn Yankees* (1955) and *Sweet Charity* (1966).

Veress, Sándor (1907–) Hungarian-born Swiss composer, stud. of Bartók and Kodály. He has taught at the Budapest and Berne Conservatories and later at Berne U. He has been an active collector of folk music, working for a time with Bartók. His works incl. several ballets, incidental music, 2 symphonies, concertos for various instruments, other orchestral works, many vocal and choral works, chamber music and works for piano solo.

verismo [vä´rēs-mō] (It., realism) a term for realism in drama, music and literature of late 19th-c. Italy, most commonly applied to the operas of Mascagni, Leoncavallo and Puccini. Characteristics of the style incl. the use of characters from the lower classes and a concentration on violent passions.

Verklärte Nacht [fer´kler-te näkht] (Ger., Transfigured Night) work for string sextet (1899) by Schoenberg. The work is frequently performed by full string orch.

Vermeer Quartet string quartet formed in 1969 at Northern Illinois U. and featured regularly at the Mostly Mozart Festival in New York and the Marlboro Music Festival.

Verrett (Carter), **Shirley** (1931–) Amer. mezzo-soprano (later soprano), stud. of Anna Fitziu and Hall Johnson. She has sung at the New York City Opera, La Scala, the Metropolitan Opera (debut 1968), Covent Garden, and most major international opera houses. Her roles incl. Carmen,

Orfeo and Amneris (*Aida*). She is also a noted recitalist.

vers [ver] (Fr.) a through-composed troubador song.

Verschiebung [fer´shē-bûng] (Ger.) shifting: *mit Verschiebung*, using the SOFT PEDAL.

verse 1, a line of a psalm, canticle, etc., sung by a soloist. Cf. RESPONSORY. **2**, a short prelude or interlude for organ, used to replace a VERSE (1,).

verse anthem a choral setting of a religious or moral text in English in which verses for full choir alternate with verses for solo voice(s). Anthems were recognized as an optional portion of the choral service from 1559, and the first substantial verse anthems date from the late 1560s. Important composers of verse anthems are William Mundy, Byrd, Morley, Weelkes and Gibbons.

verset a short VERSE.

versicle a short VERSE (1,) sung by a priest and followed by a response by the people (see RESPONSORY). Symbol (℣).

vers mesurés *also*, **vers mesurés à l'antique** [ver mə-zü´rā´ zä ä lä´tēk] (Fr.) French verse of the late 16th c. written by members of a group of poets around Jean-Antoine de Baïf who attempted to apply the quantitative principles of Greek and Latin poetry to the French language. Several composers were assoc. with this academy, esp. Claude Le Jeune and Guillaume Costeley.

versus a term with a number of meanings, the most prevalent of which is a Latin sacred song of the 11th century and later. The term may also indicate a Latin sacred song with a specific metric structure or a specific strophic form.

verticalization in a 12-tone work, the simultaneous statement (in a chord) of two or more adjacent members of a ROW. See SERIALISM.

vespers 1, one of the daily services which comprise the divine office of the Roman Catholic church, beginning at sunset. The vespers service marks the beginning of each day of the liturgical calendar and is usu. devoted to the Virgin Mary. 2, the evensong in the Anglican church.

vessel flute a FLUTE with a hollow, globular body and a blowhole or whistle mouthpiece and sometimes fingerholes to obtain different pitches. The most common representative is the OCARINA.

Vestale, La [ves'täl] (Fr., The Vestal Virgin) opera in 3 acts by Spontini to a libretto by Etienne de Jouy. Premiere, Paris 1807. A Roman captain, Licinio, regains his intended bride from the temple through divine intervention.

Veyron-Lacroix, Robert (1922–) French harpsichordist, trained at the Paris Conservatoire, where he has taught since 1967. He has toured widely as soloist and accompanist, playing with such artists as flutist Jean-Pierre Rampal.

Vexations piano piece (c1893) by Satie. The work is supposed to be repeated 840 times, a feat that is usu. accomplished by using relay teams of pianists.

Viadana, Lodovico Grossi da (c1560–1627) Italian composer and teacher, employed at the Mantua Cathedral until about 1600, later in service at Padua, Rome, Venice and Bologna. He is best known for his sacred music, which is plentiful, as well as for his secular canzonettas, sinfonias, etc.

Viardot(-Garcia), (Michelle Ferdinande) Pauline (1821–1910) Spanish-born French singer and composer, sister of MARIA MALIBRAN and daughter of MANUEL GARCIA. She studied with Liszt and others and sang with great success in London and Paris as well as in Russia and Germany. The height of her performing career was her series of performances of Gluck's *Orfeo* in 1859. After her retirement three years later she continued to compose and teach and was a fervent supporter of many composers. Her own compositions incl. operettas and songs.

vibes popular term for the VIBRAPHONE.

vibraphone *also,* **vibraharp** a METAL-

LOPHONE similar to the XYLOPHONE but having motor-driven vibrators beneath its metal resonators to produce a vibrato effect and to sustain the sound. The instrument, developed in the U.S. in the early 1900s, is found in orchestral writing but finds its most frequent use in jazz, in the hands of such masters as Lionel Hampton and Milt Jackson.

vibra-slap a PERCUSSION INSTRUMENT consisting of a wooden ball attached by a flexible wire to a wooden box with loose metal pegs inside that vibrate when the ball end is struck against the box. Cf. JAWBONE.

vibrato 1, a slight, more or less rapid fluctuation of pitch employed by singers and on some instruments to impart warmth and expression. **2,** TREMOLO. **3,** BEBUNG.

Vicentino, Nicolà (1511–72) Italian composer and theorist, stud. of Willaert. He was court music dir. in Ferrara until 1539, then joined the service of Cardinal d'Este in Rome. He wrote an important treatise on the microtonal enharmonic music of ancient Greece and devised a keyboard instrument (*archicembalo*) to play it.

Vickers, Jon(athan Stewart) (1926–) Canadian dramatic tenor, stud. of George Lambert in Toronto. He first made his name on the CBC in Canada, at Covent Garden in the late 1950s and at Bayreuth shortly thereafter. He has appeared in most major opera houses in a wide range of dramatic roles by Wagner, Verdi, Handel, Britten and others.

Victoria, Tomás Luis de (1548–1611) influential Spanish organist and composer of sacred vocal music, perhaps a stud. of Palestrina. He was in Italy until 1585, then returned to Madrid, where he served the Empress Maria. His works incl. 20 masses, 44 motets and other service music, including the tenebrae responsories and lamentations.

Victory at Sea television documentary series about World War II with incidental score by Richard Rodgers

(1952), orchestrated by Robert Russell Bennett.

Vida breve, La ['vē-dä 'brä-vä] (Sp., *The Short Life*) tragic opera in 2 acts by Falla to a libretto by Carlos Fernandez Shaw. Premiere, Nice 1913. The work features extensive use of popular Spanish dance. The gypsy girl Salud is jilted by her fiancé, Paco.

Vidal, Paul (Antonin) (1863–1931) French conductor, teacher and composer, stud. of Massenet. He won the Prix de Rome in 1883, then worked at the Paris Opéra from 1889 and at the Opéra-Comique from 1914. He taught solfège and composition at the Paris Conservatoire from 1894 and is best remembered as a teacher.

vide ['vē-dā] (Lat., *see*) indication of a musical cut. "Vi-" is usu. placed at the beginning of the section to be omitted and "-de" at the end.

vielle [vyel] (Fr.) **1**, a large VIOL of the 12th and 13th c. **2**, HURDY-GURDY.

Vienna Boys Choir (Ger., *Wiener Sängerknaben*) a children's choir founded in Vienna in 1498, orig. a part of the court chapel but now independent. The choir makes frequent tours and performs with the Vienna Staatsoper.

Vienna Philharmonic Orchestra orch. founded in 1833 by Franz Lachner as the Künstlerverein composed of players in the Staatsoper Orch., which is still a condition for membership. The orch. has been assoc. with many of the greatest conductors of the 19th and 20th c., incl. Dessoff, Richter, Mahler, Weingartner, Furtwängler, Clemens Krauss, Walter, Böhm and Abbado.

Viennese School 1, the composers active in Vienna in the later 18th and early 19th c., incl. Haydn, Mozart, Beethoven and Schubert. Also, *First Viennese School*. **2**, SECOND VIENNESE SCHOOL.

Vie Parisienne, La [vē pä-rē'zyen] (Fr., *Parisian Life*) comic opera in 4 acts by Offenbach to a libretto by Henri Meilhac and Ludovic Halévy. Premiere, Paris 1866. A story of imper-

sonation as two young men vie for the favors of a Parisian demimondaine.

Vier ernste Gesänge [fēr 'ern-ste ge'zeng-e] (Ger.) FOUR SERIOUS SONGS.

Vierne, Louis(-Victor-Jules) [vyern] (1870–1937) French organist and composer, stud. of Franck and of Widor, whom he succeeded at St. Sulpice and the Conservatoire. After 1900 he was organist at Notre Dame in Paris. He wrote many works for organ, incl. 6 symphonies, as well as choral and vocal music, chamber music and songs.

Viertel ['fēr-təl] (Ger.) QUARTER NOTE.

Vieuxtemps, Henry (Joseph François) ['vyø-tä] (1820–81) Belgian virtuoso violinist and composer, stud. of M. Lecloux-Dejonc and Reicha. He toured extensively until about 1870, when he assumed a teaching post at the Brussels Conservatory (one of his pupils was Ysaÿe). Of his many orchestral and chamber music works only his violin concertos are still performed.

vif [vēf] (Fr.) lively.

vihuela [vē'khwä-lä] (Sp.) a Spanish Renaissance guitar-shaped, plucked VIOL. Also, *vihuela da mano, vihuela comun.*

Villa-Lobos, Heitor (1887–1959) Brazilian composer, violist and guitarist, largely self-taught. From 1923 to 1930 he was in Paris, where he was very successful, but the rest of his career was spent mainly in Rio de Janeiro and São Paulo, composing and working to improve the teaching of music in the schools. From the mid-1940s he traveled frequently to the U.S. to conduct. His works incl. *Izath* and *Yerma* (operas), ballets, *Bachianas brasileiras* for various combinations, 12 symphonies, concertos (for violin, piano, cello and harp), choral works, 17 string quartets, chamber music, songs, works for solo piano and solo guitar.

villancico (vē-lyän-thē'kō) (Sp.) **1**, a 15th- and 16th-c. Span. part-song similar to the madrigal with an idyllic or devotional text. Cf. CALENDA. 2, a sacred anthem or cantata.

villanella *also*, **villanesca** (It.) 1, a 16th-c. unaccompanied Italian part-song free in form and less sophisticated than the madrigal. 2, a rustic instrumental piece.

villano [ve̅'lyä-nō] (Sp., peasant) a type of 16th- and 17th-c. dance song of Spain and Italy, based on the same harmonic pattern as the PASSAMEZZO MODERNO.

villotta (It.) a 16th-c. No. Italian secular dance-song, often set to nonsense syllables.

vina *also*, **bina** ['ve̅-nǝ; 'be̅-] (Hindi) an Indian, plucked LUTE with a long bamboo fingerboard having movable frets, four strings and gourd resonators at each end.

Vincent, Gene (Craddock, Eugene Vincent) (1935–71) Amer. rock-and-roll singer. He began in the mid-1950s singing on country-music radio shows, then hit the nationwide charts with his group, the Bluecaps. He was also successful later overseas.

Vincent, John (1902–77) Amer. composer and teacher, stud. of Chadwick, Converse, Piston and Boulanger. He later taught at W. Kentucky State U. and at UCLA. He also conducted widely and headed the Huntington Hartford Foundation for over a decade. His own works, in a style mixing elements of tonality and atonality (he termed it *paratonality*), incl. ballets, orchestral suites, songs, chamber music and film scores.

Vinci, Leonardo (1690–1730) Italian composer of *opera seria* and of comedies in Neapolitan dialect. He held several positions in Naples, serving in the royal chapel from 1725, composing at least three operas a year.

Vinci, Pietro (c1535–84) Sicilian composer and teacher. He held posts in several Italian cities, incl. Bergamo (1568–80), then returned to Sicily for his final years. He was esp. known for his madrigals, many of which were published. He also wrote Mass settings, motets and instrumental ricercars.

Vingt-quatre violons du Roi [ve̅'kä-trǝ ve̅-o'lō dü rwä] (Fr., 24 Violins of the King) a string orch. maintained in the 17th and 18th c. by the French royal court.

Vingt Regards sur l'Enfant-Jésus [ve̅ rǝ'gär sür lä'fä zhä'zü] (Fr., 20 Watches over the Child Jesus) set of 20 piano works (1945) by Messaien, based on three themes: of God, of the Star and the Cross, of Chords.

viol a bowed LUTE dating from the late 16th c., similar to the later violin, but characterized by a fretted neck, a flatter bridge, a flat back, a deeper body and more steeply sloped shoulders. It has six rather thin strings and its bow is held from below. The sound is soft and more delicate than a violin's and more suitable for solo and chamber music. Viols come in a variety of sizes, the most common being the treble, alto, tenor (*viola da braccia*), bass (*viola da gamba*) and double bass (*violone*). Other instruments of the family incl. the VIOLA BASTARDA, the VIOLA D'AMORE, the VIOLETTA and the BARYTON.

viola 1, an alto-tenor VIOLIN, shaped like its higher relative but larger and tuned a fifth lower. Probably because the viola is small for its lower pitch, its powers of projection are not as great as the violin's, but it has a warmer, richer tone. 2, in the Middle Ages and Renaissance, any bowed string instrument.

viola alta (It.) a large, 5-stringed VIOLA invented in the late 19th c. and used at Bayreuth.

viola bastarda (It.) 1, a VIOLA DA GAMBA using the lute tablature. Also, *lyra viol*. 2, LIRA. 3, DIVISION VIOL.

viola clef ALTO CLEF.

viola da braccio (It., arm viol) 1, a tenor VIOL similar in range to the modern viola. 2, any instrument of the VIOLIN family.

viola da gamba (It., leg viol) 1, a bass VIOL similar in range to the cello. 2, any member of the VIOL family.

viola d'amore (It., viola of love) an 18th-c. tenor VIOL with seven bowed strings and seven additional sympathetic strings.

viola da spalla (It., shoulder viola) a small CELLO used in processions and carried with a shoulder strap.

viola di bordone (It., drone viola) a large viola d'amore. Cf. BARYTON.

viola di fagotto (It., bassoon viola) a VIOLA having the range of a cello but played on the arm. The instrument's name comes from its buzzy sound.

viola pomposa (It.) an obsolete, large five-stringed VIOLA.

violectra an electrified baritone violin popularized by JEAN-LUC PONTY.

violetta (It.) **1**, an alto VIOLA D'AMORE with two sets of sympathetic strings. **2**, a term used at various times from the 16th to 18th c. for VIOL, VIOLIN or VIOLA.

violin the soprano member of a family of bowed Lutes similar to the viol, dating from the 16th c., characterized by a curved back, rounded shoulders, a thin body, no frets and four strings tuned g-d'-a'-e". The bow is held overhand and the instrument has a bright, penetrating tone. The violin developed from earlier bowed instruments, incl. the FIDDLE, the REBEC and the VIOL. The violin and the other members of the family form the basis for the modern symphony orch. and most chamber ensembles. The family includes, in addition to the violin, the VIOLA, the CELLO and the DOUBLE BASS. See also KIT and VIOLINO PICCOLO. See *illus.*, p. 576.

violin clef a G CLEF on the first line of the staff, used in the 17th c. for notating violin music, esp. music for the KIT.

violoneux [vyo-lō'nø] (Fr.) a folk fiddler of the Québec province of Canada.

violino (It.) VIOLIN.

violino piccolo (It., small violin) a small violin of the 17th and 18th c., tuned a 4th higher than the standard violin and composed for by Bach (in

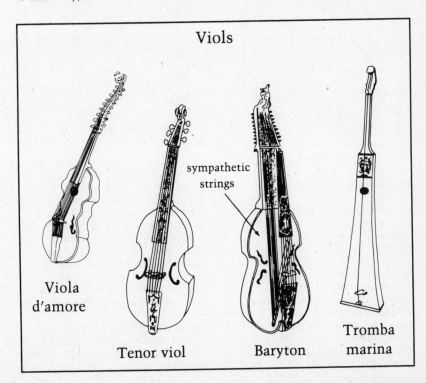

Viols

Viola d'amore

sympathetic strings

Tenor viol

Baryton

Tromba marina

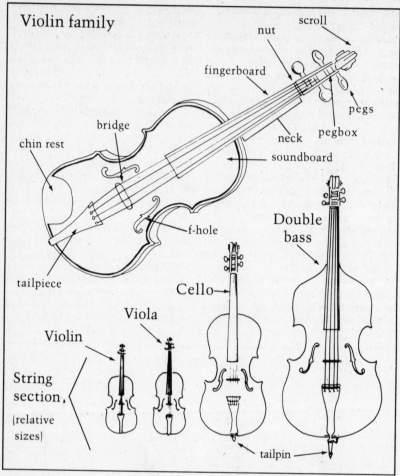

Violin family

nut   scroll

fingerboard

pegs

neck   pegbox

soundboard

bridge

chin rest

f-hole

Double bass

Cello

Viola

Violin

tailpiece

String section,

(relative sizes)

tailpin

the 1st Brandenburg Concerto) and others.

violoncello [″vē-o-lōn′chel-lō] (It.) Cello.

violoncello piccolo (It.) Piccolo violoncello.

violone (It.) a Viol of the size and range of the double bass.

violotta a Violin with a range extending a fourth below the viola.

Viotti, Giovanni Battista (1755–1824) Italian violinist and composer considered the founder of the modern school of violin playing. He studied with Antonio Celoniat and Gaetano Pugnani. He played in the orch. of the Turin royal chapel, then went to Paris, where he was a sensation. After several years of solo performance he entered royal service and shortly thereafter established an opera house, which he ran until the Revolution. In London from 1793, he performed and managed the Italian opera at the King's Theatre, but political difficulties forced his retirement from music. He composed a large quantity of concertos and chamber music works for violin as well as piano trios and vocal works.

virelai also, **virelay** [′vē-rǝ-lā] (Fr.) a type of French poetry and music of the 12th to 16th c., usu. in the strophic form AbbaAbbaAbbaA (the capital A represents the refrain which begins and ends each stanza). It was a popular form of the TROUVÈRES.

virga a NEUME representing a single note.

virginal *also,* **virginals** a small, rectangular HARPSICHORD of the 16th and 17th c. with one keyboard and one set of jacks. Also, *pair of virginals.*

Virginia Minstrels a minstrel troupe formed in 1843 by Dan Emmett, Frank Brower, Billy Whitlock and Dick Pelham. Their first full-length entertainment, which they called an "Ethiopian Concert," was probably the first real minstrel show.

Virginia reel an Amer. longways dance performed by four to eight couples; also, the music for this dance. Cf. REEL (1,).

virtuoso (It.) a performer with highly developed technical skill.

Vishnevskaya, Galina (Pavlovna) (1926–) Russian soprano, stud. of Vera Garina. She sang with the Bolshoy Opera from 1952 until coming to the West in 1974. Her roles incl. Tatyana (*Eugene Onegin*), Violetta (*La Traviata*) and Tosca. She is the wife of cellist MSTISLAV ROSTROPOVICH.

Visions de l'Amen [vē'zyō] (Fr., Visions of the Amen) music for 2 pianos (1943) by Messiaen.

Visions Fugitives [fü-zhē'tēv] (Russ., *Mimoletnovski*) set of twenty pieces for piano, Op. 22 (1915–7), by Prokofiev, inspired by the poetry of the Russian writer Constantine Balmont.

Vitali, Giovanni Battista (1632–92) Italian composer, singer and instrumentalist, stud. of Cazzati. He served in Bologna until 1671, then at the ducal court in Modena. He wrote a number of oratorios and cantatas, but he is best known for his instrumental chamber music, which significantly influenced Corelli and Purcell.

Vitry, Philippe de (1291–1361) French composer, theorist and poet. He served at the French court for most of his career and established a reputation as a brilliant intellectual

and an outstanding musician. He is as famous for his motets, very few of which survive, as for his theoretical writing, represented by his treatise *Ars nova* (c1322).

Vittoria VICTORIA.

vivace [vē'vä-chä] (It.) lively; a tempo and mood indication. Also, *vivo.*

Vivaldi, Antonio (Lucio) (1678–1741) prolific Italian composer, son of a violinist, with whom he studied. He was employed in Venice from 1703 until a few years before his death at an institution for orphaned, indigent girls, though his growing reputation in the 1720s and 1730s led to his frequent absence. For his students he wrote many vocal and instrumental works, a large number of which were published. At the same time he established an operatic career, composing almost 50 operas for performance in various European theaters. His influence as a composer, esp. in the field of instrumental music, was substantial. Vivaldi wrote almost 50 operas, serenatas, Mass settings, choral and solo cantatas, motets, psalms, oratorios, instrumental concertos (incl. *The Four Seasons*) and chamber music.

vivo (It.) VIVACE.

vl. *abbr.* VIOLIN.

vla. *abbr.* VIOLA.

Vlad, Roman (1919–) Italian composer and writer, stud. of Casella. He has taught at the Perugia Conservatory and has been active in a number of Italian musical organizations. His own works incl. ballets, operas, film scores, orchestral and chamber works and choral and solo vocal music.

vocalese a word prob. invented in the early 1940s by jazz singer Eddie Jefferson to refer to the singing of texts to recorded jazz improvisations. There are examples from the 1940s, but the best-known group to develop the technique was the trio of Dave Lambert, Annie Ross and JON HENDRICKS (1958–64).

vocalise [vō-kä'lēz] **1,** a vocal exercise. **2,** a vocal melody without words; esp., a work (1912) for voice and piano by Rachmaninov.

vocalize to sing, esp. to sing without words, as in an exercise.

vocal production a term for the combination of processes or technique that results in the sound of the human voice, esp. that sound as used for singing.

vocal score a SCORE of a vocal work—esp. an opera, oratorio or cantata—arranged for voices with piano accompaniment, usu. for the purpose of rehearsal.

voce ['vō-chā] (It.) VOICE.

voce di petto (It.) CHEST VOICE.

voce di testo (It.) HEAD VOICE.

Voces Intimae (Lat., Intimate Voices) the string quartet in D minor, Op. 56 (1909), by Sibelius.

Vogler, Georg Joseph (Abbé Vogler) (1749–1814) German composer, theorist, teacher and keyboard player, trained in Würzburg and in Italy under Padre Martini and Padre Vallotti. He spent the 1770s in Mannheim, where he founded a school. After a short period at the elector's court in Munich, he joined the court of the king of Sweden, where he remained for 11 years. His final years were spent at a ducal court in Hessen-Darmstadt. Vogler taught, among others, Weber, Meyerbeer and von Paradis and was, according to contemporary accounts, a superb improviser who gave many organ recitals. His extensive theoretical writings covered all areas of musical knowledge. As a composer, he wrote in all genres, but his works have not remained in the repertory.

voice 1, a musical sound produced by air passing between the vocal cords and causing them to vibrate. Also, the volume of the sound so produced, as in *give more* (or *less*) *voice*. **2,** a singer. **3,** PART (3,), esp. in vocal music.

voice-exchange a technique in medieval part-writing involving two equal voices that alternate the same musical phrases. Cf. RONDELLUS.

voice leading the progression of the individual parts in a polyphonic vocal or instrumental composition, with an emphasis on the proper resolution of dissonance, etc.

voicing 1, the regulation of the tone-producing parameters in a musical instrument so as to produce the best sound, esp. a) the modification of the dimensions of the pipe and/or reed to control the pitch and tone of an organ pipe, and b) the adjustment of the hardness of the felts in a piano or the thickness and length of the plectra in a harpsichord to control the tone quality. **2,** the modulation of the loudness of the individual note of a chord for expressive or tonal purposes.

Voisin, Roger (Louis) [vwä'zē (1918–) noted French-born Amer. trumpeter, stud. of Georges Mager and Marcel LaFosse. He played with the Boston SO from 1935 (his father had also been a member), playing principal trumpet from 1949 to 1967 and retiring in 1973. He taught at the New England Conservatory, Boston U. and the Berkshire Music Center.

voix [vwä] (Fr.) VOICE.

voix céleste [vwä sā'lest] (Fr., heavenly voice) a pipe ORGAN STOP combining several ranks of pipes tuned slightly apart to produce a tremulous tone.

voix de ville [vwä də vēl] (Fr., city voice) a type of 16th-c. French courtly song, usu. in homophonic style.

volante (It.) moving rapidly and lightly.

Volkonsky, Andrei (1933–) Russian composer, harpsichordist and conductor, stud. of Auber, Lipatti, Boulanger and Shaporin. An important figure in the Russian musical avant garde, he has been largely shunned by Soviet officialdom, working primarily as a harpsichordist and conductor of Madrigal, a vocal group performing Renaissance and Baroque music. He has written many works for solo and small instrumental ensembles, as well as a concerto for orch. and film scores.

Volkslied ['folks"lēt] (Ger.) FOLK SONG.

volles Werk ['fo-l'əs verk] (Ger.) FULL ORGAN.

volta *also*, **volte** (It.) **1**, time, as in *prima volta*, first time. **2**, LA VOLTA. **3**, a refrain at the end of a BALLATA.

volti (It.) turn, as in *volti subito*, turn (the page) immediately, abbr. *v.s.*

volume the degree of loudness or intensity of a sound.

voluntary a PRELUDE or interlude, esp. for organ, often improvised.

Von Heune, Friedrich (Alexander) [fon 'hyoo-ne] (1929–) Polish-born Amer. instrument maker and performer. After an apprenticeship with flute maker Verne Q. Powell, he began building recorders and Baroque and Renaissance flutes. He has also designed recorders for mass production and has been active as a performer and teacher of early music.

Von Heute auf Morgen [fon 'hoi-te owf'mor-gan] (Ger., From One Day to the Next) comic opera in 1 act by Schoenberg to a libretto by his wife under the pseudonym Max Blonda. Premiere, Frankfurt 1930. A domestic comedy of manners about "modern" people.

Von Stade, Frederica (1945–) Amer. mezzo-soprano, stud. of Sebastian Engelberg. She has sung regularly at the Metropolitan Opera (since 1970) and throughout Europe and the U.S. Her roles incl. Octavian (*Der Rosenkavalier*), Rosina (*The Barber of Seville*) and Cherubino (*The Marriage of Figaro*). She is a noted recitalist and concert artist and has been a member of the Lincoln Center Chamber Music Society.

Von Tilzer, Harry (Gumm, Harold) (1872–1946) Amer. songwriter and publisher. A vaudeville artist in his youth, he began publishing at the turn of the century and was extraordinarily successful.

Voříšek, Jan Václav (1791–1825) Czech composer and organist, trained in Prague and with Tomášek and Hummel. He moved to Vienna, where he held for a time a post in the civil service, then from 1822 concentrated on music, becoming official court organist. Ill health overtook him shortly thereafter. His works incl. choral works and songs, several orchestral works and concertos, chamber music and instrumental sonatas.

Vorschlag ['for"shläk] (Ger.) APPOGGIATURA.

Vorspiel [-shpēl] (Ger.) PRELUDE.

votive Mass a Mass not prescribed in the regular liturgical calendar, such as the Requiem Mass or the Lady Mass that is devoted to the Virgin Mary.

vox (Lat.) voice.

vox angelica (Lat.) VOIX CÉLESTE.

vox humana (Lat., human voice) a pipe ORGAN STOP with tremulant designed to imitate the sound of the human voice.

Voyage of Edgar Allan Poe, The opera in 2 acts by Argento to a libretto by Charles Nolte. Premiere, Minneapolis 1976. An imaginary voyage into the mind of Poe.

V.S. *abbr.* volti subito (see VOLTI).

Vuillaume, Jean-Baptiste [vüē'yŏm] (1798–1875) important French violin maker and dealer, noted both for his violins, esp. his copies of instruments by Stradivari and Guarneri, and for his bows.

vuoto ['vwo-tō] (It., empty) an indication that in a particular measure nobody plays. Also, *grand pause*.

W

W. see ALFRED WOTQUENNE.

Waart, Edo de (1941–) Dutch conductor and oboist, stud. of Dean Dixon and Ferrara. He played in the Amsterdam PO and the Concertgebouw Orch. before beginning his conducting career in 1964. He founded the Netherlands Wind Ensemble while serving as assistant conductor of the Concertgebouw. He has been chief conductor of the Rotterdam PO and the San Francisco SO (1977–86) and has guest-conducted extensively.

Wachet auf ['vakh-ət owf] (Ger., Wake Up) sacred Cantata No. 140 for chorus and chamber orch. (1731) by J.S. Bach, based on the chorale by Philipp Nicolai.

Wadsworth, Charles (William) (1929–) Amer. pianist and accompanist, stud. of Tureck and Bernac. He directed a chamber music series at the Spoleto Festivals in Italy and the U.S. and has been artistic dir. of the Chamber Music Society of Lincoln Center since its founding in 1969.

Wagenaar, Bernard (1894–1971) Dutch-born Amer. violinist, composer and conductor, trained in Utrecht. Upon coming to the U.S. in 1920 he played in the New York PO and taught at the Institute of Musical Art (where his students incl. Druckman and Schuman), then concentrated on composition. His works incl. a chamber opera (*Pieces of Eight*), 4 symphonies, two concertos, works for voice and instruments, sonatas for violin and piano, and other chamber music.

Wagenseil, Georg Christoph (1715–77) Austrian composer, teacher and virtuoso keyboard player, stud. of Fux. He became composer to the court in Vienna in 1739, retaining the post until his death. His works were well known in Europe and performed by such artists as Mozart and Haydn; he was also renowned as a harpsichordist. His works incl. more than 10 operas, oratorios, Mass settings and other sacred choral works, cantatas, symphonies, concertos for harpsichord and for other instruments, and chamber music.

Wagner, Joseph F(rederick) (1900–74) Amer. composer, conductor and teacher, stud. of Converse, Casella, Boulanger and Monteux. He was founder and conductor of the Boston Civic SO (1925–44) and taught in the Boston public schools and at Boston U. He was conductor of the Duluth SO and the Costa Rica National SO and taught at Pepperdine College (CA) and elsewhere. His works incl. an opera, several ballets, concertos (for violin, harp, harpsichord and organ), choral works and songs.

Wagner, (Wilhelm) Richard ['väg-nər] (1813–83) German opera composer, probably the most influential composer of the later 19th c. with respect to the development of musical theater and of harmonic language. He is credited more than any 19th-c. composer with initiating the decline of functional harmony, and he developed the LEITMOTIV and many other innovative musical and dramatic techniques. Wagner studied in Leipzig with C.G. Müller and C.T. Weinlig. In the 1830s he held positions in theaters in Würzburg, Riga, Paris and Dresden, fleeing in 1849 to Zürich, pursued for his part in an unsuccessful uprising.

In Munich in 1864 he attracted a highly important supporter in the person of Ludwig II, king of Bavaria, who paid him to complete the monumental *Ring of the Nibelung*, paid off his accumulated debts and provided a yearly allowance. The king also provided funding for a new theater of Wagner's design (featuring a revolutionary covered orchestra pit) which opened in 1876 in Bayreuth, where Wagner spent his last decade. When the deficit from the first festival threatened to force sale of the theater, Ludwig once again produced the funds (as a loan) to cover the deficit.

Wagner's works incl. *Die Hochzeit, Die Feen, Das Liebesverbot, Rienzi, The Flying Dutchman, Tannhäuser, Lohengrin, Der Ring des Nibelungen, Tristan and Isolde, Die Meistersinger von Nürnberg, Parsifal* (operas), *Siegfried Idyll*, various overtures and other orchestral works, choral music, the *Wesendonk-Lieder* and other songs, early works for piano, many essays and theoretical writings.

Wagner, Roger (Francis) (1914–) French-born Amer. choral conductor and organist, stud. of Marcel Dupré, Bruno Walter and Klemperer. In 1946 he formed the Roger Wagner Chorale, which established a national reputation in concert and recording. He later founded the Los Angeles Master Chorale and Sinfonia Orch. (1965). He has given many workshops across the country and taught for many years at UCLA.

Wagner Symphony the Symphony No. 3 in D minor (1873–77, rev. 1888–89) by Bruckner.

Wagner tuba a TUBA designed by Richard Wagner that is a cross between a French horn and a tuba. The instrument is made in tenor and bass sizes, pitched in B♭ alto and in F respectively, and is used to supplement the French horns in the *Ring* cycle and in several of Bruckner's symphonies.

Wagoner, Porter (1930–) Amer. country-music and gospel singer and songwriter. From about 1965 to 1975 he produced a popular country-music TV show, appearing frequently with Norma Jean and later Dolly Parton, who sang many of his songs. His hits

incl. "Satisfied Mind" (1955) and "We'll Get Ahead Someday" (1968).

wah-wah a type of electronic signal processor that varies the timbre of sound. It is usu. controlled by a foot pedal and is used with electric guitars, etc.

waisted drum a tubular single- or double-headed DRUM having a shape similar to an hourglass, with a narrowing at the middle.

wait 1, *also,* **wayt, wayte** an English musician employed by a city or town. Cf. STADTPFEIFER. **2,** a SHAWM, esp. one played by a wait (1,).

Walcha, Helmut (1907–91) German organist, blinded in youth, stud. of Ramin. He is esp. known for his interpretation of the works of J.S. Bach, all of whose organ music he has recorded. He has taught at the Frankfurt Music Institute since 1929.

Walden String Quartet quartet founded in 1934 by members of the Cleveland Orch. The group specialized in new American works in addition to the standard repertory. The quartet disbanded in 1979.

Waldflöte ['vält"flö-te] (Ger., forest flute) a soft pipe ORGAN STOP.

Waldhorn (Ger.) **1,** a valveless HAND HORN for hunting. Also, *natural horn.* **2,** a pipe ORGAN STOP imitating the sound of the Waldhorn (1,).

Waldstein Sonata ['vält-shtīn] the Piano Sonata No. 21 in C major, Op. 53 (1803–4), by Beethoven, dedicated to Count Ferdinand von Waldstein.

walk-around a type of dance-march found in minstrel shows parodying Afr.-American dances such as the juba and incorporating virtuoso interludes by members of the company. The walk-around was often used as the finale of the show.

Walker, Albertina (1930–) Amer. gospel singer, founder of the gospel group the Caravans, which was active in the 1960s and 1970s.

Walker, George (Theophilus) (1922–) Amer. composer and pianist, stud. of Curzon, Robert Casadesus, Boulanger and Rudolf Serkin. He has performed widely as pianist and has taught at Rutgers U. since 1969. His works incl. concertos for various instruments, a symphony, sonatas for violin and piano and other chamber music, a mass, other choral works, and songs.

Walker, T-Bone (Aaron Thibeaux) (1910–75) Amer. blues singer and guitarist. He toured as soloist from the 1940s to the 1960s performing with small bands.

walking bass 1, a steady, regular bass line, moving in even note values that are usu. somewhat longer than those of the upper parts. In piano BOOGIE-WOOGIE, the walking bass usu. consisted of broken octaves played by the left hand. **2,** in jazz, a regular bass line played pizzicato by the double bass.

Walküre, Die [väl'kü-re] (Ger.) VAL-KYRIE, THE.

Wallace, (William) Vincent (1812–65) peripatetic Irish composer and instrumentalist, trained in Dublin. From 1835 to 1845 he traveled, performing as violinist and pianist and conducting his own works. From 1845 he was in London, finding fame with his opera *Maritana* (1845), whose success rivaled that of Balfe's *Bohemian Girl.* His later works were less successful. He retired to France in 1865.

Walker, William (1809–75) Amer. composer and tunebook compiler, best known for his collections *The Southern Harmony* (1835) and *Christian Harmony* (1867), both still in use today.

Wallenstein, Alfred (1898–1983) Amer. conductor and cellist, trained in Los Angeles and Leipzig. He was principal cellist of the Chicago SO (1922–9) and the New York PO (1929–36), then concentrated on conducting. He was music dir. of radio station WOR in New York (1935–45) and conducted regularly for the NBC program "Voice of Firestone." He also was conductor of the Hollywood Bowl from 1943 and the Caramoor Festival (NY) and taught from 1968 at the Juilliard School.

Waller, Fats (Thomas Wright) (1904–43) Amer. jazz composer, stride pianist, organist and singer, stud. of James P. Johnson and Godowsky. He began recording in his late teens, and his recorded legacy is extensive. He was also active in broadcasting, hosting several regular shows during his career. He led various ensembles, incl. Fats Waller and his Rhythm, and appeared in several films. As a composer, he produced a number of songs that have become standards—among them "Honeysuckle Rose" and "Crazy 'Bout My Baby"—and contributed music to several Broadway shows. He was esp. known for his novelty songs, but his influence on jazz piano was extensive.

Wally, La ['väl-lē] opera in 4 acts by Catalani to a libretto by Luigi Illica, based on the novel *Die Geyer-Wally* by Wilhelmine von Hillern. Premiere, Milan 1892. In a Tyrolian village in 1800 Wally and Hagenbeck discover their love for one another. The aria "Ne andrò lontano" from the opera is featured in the film *Diva* (1981).

Walter, Bruno (Schlesinger, Bruno Walter) ['väl-tər] (1876–1962) German conductor, trained at the Stern Conservatory in Berlin. He worked for some years at the turn of the century as Mahler's assistant in Vienna, then became musical dir. of the Munich Opera (1913–22). In the 1920s he conducted regularly at Covent Garden, the Salzburg Festival, the Concertgebouw and other orchestras. From 1939 he was mostly in the U.S., conducting the New York PO and the Philadelphia Orch., among others, and at the Metropolitan Opera. After World War II he conducted again regularly in Europe. He was esp. noted for his interpretations of Mahler, Bruckner and Mozart.

Walther, Johann Gottfried (1684–1748) German composer, organist and scholar, trained in Erfurt. He was organist in Weimar from 1707 until his death. He is best remembered for his *Musikalisches Lexikon* (1732), the first major music dictionary in German. His works incl. chorale variations for organ and sacred vocal music.

Walther von der Vogelweide (c1170–c1230) a leading German Minnesinger, trained in Austria. Much of his poetry has survived, but few of his melodies.

Walton, Sir William (Turner) (1902–83) English composer, trained at Christ Church, Oxford. His career was spent composing and conducting his own music, producing a relatively small but important body of work; he was not active as a teacher. His works incl. *Troilus and Cressida, The Bear* (operas), *The Wise Virgins, The Quest* (ballets), concertos for various instruments, other works for orch., *Belshazzar's Feast* and other choral works, song cycles (incl. *Façade* for reciter and instruments), chamber music, incidental music and film scores.

waltz a ballroom dance in triple time dating from the 18th c., that attained great popularity in Europe and No. America in the mid-19th c. and kept it well into the 20th c. The dance became an important part of operetta and, to a more limited extent, of musical comedy. The European waltz is esp. assoc. with Johann Strauss Sr. and Jr. and Joseph Lanner; in the U.S. it is assoc. with Rudolf Friml, Victor Herbert and Sigmund Romberg. There is also an unusual five-step version with accents on the first and fourth beats, which developed in the U.S. in the 1850s. In stylized instrumental form, the piano waltzes of Chopin are noteworthy. See also HESITATION WALTZ VALSE.

Waltzing Matilda a song apparently coupling a Scottish tune of unknown authorship (though sometimes attributed to James Barr) with an Australian poem reputedly by Andrew Barton Paterson. The "matilda" is a knapsack that bounces ("waltzes") when carried by a poor Australian worker (*swagman*). The work has become a patriotic song of Australia.

Wandelprobe ['vän-dəl"prō-be] (Ger.) in opera, a musical rehearsal with

stage action, but usu. with no costumes. Cf. SITZPROBE, ASSIEME.

Wandererfantasie ['vän-də-rər-fän-tä"zē] (Ger.) fantasy for solo piano in C major, D. 760 (1822), by Schubert.

Wanhal, Johann Baptist VANHAL, JOHANN BAPTIST.

War and Peace (Russ., *Voyna i mir*) historical opera in 13 scenes by Prokofiev to a libretto in Russian by the composer and Mira Mendelson based on Tolstoy's novel. Premiere, Leningrad 1946.

Ward, John (1571–1638) English composer, trained as a chorister at Canterbury Cathedral. He held a government position with the Exchequer and meanwhile served as a household musician to a London family, composing sacred and recreational music for their use. His works incl. service music, madrigals, instrumental fantasias and IN NOMINES.

Ward, Robert (Eugene) (1917–) Amer. composer and teacher, stud. of Rogers and Hanson at the Eastman School. He has taught at the Juilliard School, Columbia and Duke. He is best known for his operas; *The Crucible* won the Pulitzer Prize in 1962. He has also written symphonies, a saxophone concerto, other works for orch., songs and chamber music.

Warfield, Sandra (1929–) Amer. mezzo-soprano, trained at the Kansas City Conservatory and with Fritz Lehmann in New York. She has sung at the Metropolitan Opera (debut 1953), the Vienna Staatsoper and in many international houses. She is married to baritone James McCracken.

Warfield, William (Caesar) (1920–) Amer. baritone, trained at the Eastman School and with Rosa Ponselle. He has appeared frequently in musicals and opera—incl. *Call Me Mister, Showboat, Regina* and almost ten years at the Vienna Volksoper—but has concentrated on recital appearances, singing Lieder, spirituals, show tunes and arias. He has taught at the U. of Illinois since 1974.

Waring, Fred(eric Malcolm) (1900–84) Amer. conductor, songwriter and publisher. He organized his band, The Pennsylvanians, in 1922 (orig. called the Collegians), which became very popular on radio and later on TV. Waring formed the Shawnee Press in 1947 to publish choral works by himself and other composers and was an active leader of workshops on choral singing. Waring was also an inventor, whose creations incl. the Waring blender.

Warlock, Peter pseudonym for HESELTINE, PHILIP.

Warren, Earle Ronald (1914–) Amer. jazz alto saxophonist, clarinetist and singer. He joined the Count Basie band in 1937, remaining until 1950, after which he concentrated on solo work and free-lancing.

Warren, Harry (Guaragna, Salvatore) (1893–1981) highly successful Amer. songwriter for theater and films, winning three Oscars (for "Lullaby of Broadway," "You'll Never Know" and "On the Atchison, Topeka and the Santa Fe").

Warren (Warenoff), **Leonard** (1911–60) Amer. baritone, stud. of Sidney Dietch, Giuseppe Pais and Ricquardo Piccozi. After several years in the Radio City Music Hall Chorus he made his Metropolitan Opera debut in 1938, remaining with the company for 21 years. He specialized in Verdi roles, Scarpia (*Tosca*) and Barnaba (*La Gioconda*).

War Requiem choral work (1962) by Britten based on poems by Wilfred Owen and the Requiem Mass. The work was written for the opening of the rebuilt Coventry Cathedral.

Warsaw Autumn annual festival of contemporary music held since 1956 in Warsaw and showcasing eastern European composers.

Warsaw Concerto see ADDINSELL, RICHARD.

Warwick, Dionne (1941–) Amer. popular and soul singer, trained at the Hartt College of Music. She is esp. assoc. with the music of Burt Bacharach, who wrote most of her hit songs, incl. "Anyone Who Had a Heart" (1963) and "I'll Never Fall in Love Again" (1969).

washboard the utensil orig. used for scrubbing clothes used as a scraped instrument in some country-music and SKIFFLE bands. The player usu. uses a metal rod or metal thimbles to scrape the board. Cf. SOUND SHEET.

washboard band an Afr.-Amer. instrumental ensemble centered around the WASHBOARD as the principal percussion instrument and also employing guitar, harmonica, kazoo, pots and pans, etc. Cf. SPASM BAND.

Washburn, Robert (1928–) Amer. composer and teacher, stud. of Milhaud, Boulanger and others. He has taught at the Crane School of Music (NY) since 1954 and has traveled to conduct and give workshops throughout the world. He has written many works for college and high-school ensembles, incl. orchestral, band, chamber and choral music.

Washington, Dinah (Jones, Ruth; "The Queen") (1924–63) Amer. popular and jazz singer. She performed with Lionel Hampton (1943–46) then concentrated on a solo career, which was very successful from the early 1950s until her death. She influenced later singers of jazz, rhythm-and-blues and rock.

washtub bass a folk string instr. related to the GROUND HARP, used in jug and washboard bands, consisting of a string passed through the bottom of an inverted metal washtub and attached to a stick. The string is plucked, and tuned by moving the stick.

Wasps, The orch. suite (1909) by Vaughan Williams, consisting of five numbers from his incidental music for Aristophanes' comedy. The overture is frequently performed separately.

Watch Your Step musical by Irving Berlin, book by Harry B. Smith, based on Augustin Daly's play *Round the Clock*. Premiere, New York 1914. Berlin's first complete Broadway show, written mostly in ragtime, concerns a will leaving $2 million to anyone who has never been in love.

water drum a DRUM consisting of a vessel of wood or gourd, or a similar item filled with or placed in water and beaten with the hands or sticks.

Water Music three suites of dances for strings plus various wind instruments (1717) by Handel, apparently written for performance during a nighttime royal boat trip down the Thames. As the original manuscript is lost, the exact orchestration is in question. The three suites are in F major (with horns), D major (with trumpets) and G major (with flutes).

water organ HYDRAULUS.

Waters (née Howard), **Ethel** (1896–1977) Amer. actress and jazz singer. She began in vaudeville, then became successful in musical comedy (perhaps the first Afr.-Amer. artist to do so) and in straight theater and films, appearing in such productions as *Stormy Weather* (1933) and *The Member of the Wedding* (1950). In the 1960s and 1970s she toured with evangelist Billy Graham.

Waters, Muddy MUDDY WATERS.

Waters, Willie Anthony (1951–) Amer. conductor and pianist. In 1984 he became the artistic director of the Greater Miami Opera, the first Afr.-Amer. to hold such a position with a major Amer. opera company.

Watson, Bobby (Robert Michael Jr.) (1953–) Amer. saxophonist, pianist, composer and arranger. He has worked with Art Blakey's Jazz Messengers and a succession of other bands. He has also worked with Max Roach and has led his own groups.

Watson, Doc (Arthel Lane) (1923–) Amer. bluegrass singer, guitarist and banjoist, blind from birth. He was discovered during the folk revival of the early 1960s and is noted for his flat-picking style on the acoustic guitar.

Watts, André (1946–) Amer. pianist, stud. of Genia Robiner and Fleisher, a phenomenal success in the early 1960s with a recital and concerto repertory ranging from the Classical era to the early 20th c. In 1976 he performed on the first nationally televised solo piano recital.

Watts, Helen (Josephine) (1927–) Welsh contralto, stud. of Caroline Hatchard and Frederick Jackson. She has performed opera at Covent Garden and with the English Opera Group but is best known as a recitalist and concert artist, performing a wide repertory of oratorios and songs.

Watts, John (Everett) (1930–82) Amer. composer, stud. of Harris, Effinger and others. He taught at the New School for Social Research (NY) from 1967 and founded the Composers Theatre (1964–82) to present works by American composers. He is esp. known for his work in electronic music using the ARP synthesizer and for his performance art.

Waverly Consort an ensemble of instrumentalists and singers formed in 1964 to perform music of the Middle Ages and Renaissance.

Wa-Wan Press Amer. firm of music publishers founded in Newton Centre, MA, in 1901 by Arthur Farwell to specialize in works by Amer. composers, Amer. folk music and native Amer. music. It was acquired by G. Schirmer in 1912.

Waxman (Wachsmann), **Franz** (1906–67) German-born Amer. composer and conductor, trained at the Berlin Conservatory, best known for film music (he scored almost 150 films) and as founder-conductor of the Los Angeles Music Festival.

Weather Report Amer. jazz-rock group formed in 1970 that has successfully combined sophisticated jazz harmonies with the electrified, driving rhythm of rock.

Weavers, The Amer. folk group formed in 1948 by Pete Seeger, Lee Hays, Ronnie Gilbert and Fred Hellerman. The group was active in support of political causes, though their recordings, which were highly successful, were themselves generally apolitical. Nevertheless, the group was blacklisted in the early 1950s and disbanded temporarily, re-forming in 1955 and performing until 1963.

Webb, Chick (William Henry) (1909–39) Amer. jazz drummer and bandleader. In the 1920s and 1930s he led an influential swing band at the SAVOY BALLROOM, headlining a number of prominent soloists, incl. Ella Fitzgerald, who took over the band for a time after Webb's death.

Webb, Jimmy (1946–   ) Amer. songwriter, composer of such hits as "Wichita Lineman" and "By the Time I Get to Phoenix."

Weber, (Maria) Aloysia (Louise Antonia) (c1759–1839) German soprano, sister of Mozart's wife Constanze Weber (he orig. proposed to Aloysia). Mozart wrote a number of concert arias for her, and she sang in several of his operas.

Weber, Ben (William Jennings Bryan) (1916–79) Amer. composer, self-taught. His works incl. a violin concerto, several orchestral works and a substantial body of chamber music, songs and works for piano.

Weber, Carl Maria (Friedrich Ernst) von (1786–1826) important German composer, conductor and pianist, stud. of Michael Haydn, J.N. Kalcher and Abbé Vogler. From 1804 he held for short periods posts in Breslau, Karlsruhe and Stuttgart, and performed in many other cities. In 1813 he was appointed to the opera in Prague, performing over 60 operas during his tenure, then moved to Dresden in 1816 as royal Saxon Kapellmeister with a mandate to build up the German Opera. It was in Dresden that his principal masterworks were written. Suffering from ill health, he made an ill-advised voyage to London to conduct his own works, dying while there. Weber played an important part in the development of Romanticism in Germany and in the creation of a German opera. He was also a significant force as virtuoso pianist and conductor.

Weber's works incl. *Abu Hassan, Der Freischütz, Euryanthe, Oberon* and other operas (incl. *Die drei Pintos*, a comic opera left unfinished and completed by Mahler), incidental music, Mass settings, cantatas and other choral works, songs, concertos for piano and clarinet, 2 symphonies, overtures, chamber music and works for piano.

Webern, Anton (Friedrich Wilhelm) von (1883–1945) Austrian composer and conductor, stud. of Schoenberg (1904–8). From 1908 to 1934 he held a series of conducting posts, those of longest standing being with the chorus and orch. of the Vienna Workers' Association. He also was active with Schoenberg in the Association for Private Music Performance in Vienna, arranging music and conducting. He spent World War II in relative isolation and was killed accidentally by an American soldier.

Webern's very personal use of Schoenberg's 12-tone technique has been influential, esp. the remarkable conciseness and brevity of his later compositions, inadvertent precursors of the so-called "pointillist" style. His works incl. a symphony, *Variations* for orch., an arrangement of J.S. Bach's *Passacaglia* for full orch., other orchestral works, 2 cantatas, many songs, chamber music (incl. pieces for cello and piano, works for string quartet, a concerto for 9 instruments) and *Variations* for piano.

Webster, Ben(jamin Francis) (1909–73) influential Amer. jazz swing tenor saxophonist. He worked with Bennie Moten, Fletcher Henderson and Duke Ellington, and from 1943 as a free-lance artist and as leader of his own groups in the U.S. and, from 1964, in Europe.

Webster, Beveridge (1908–   ) Amer. pianist, stud. of Isidor Philipp, Boulanger and Schnabel. He performed widely as a concert artist and in chamber music ensembles. He has taught at the New England Conservatory and at the Juilliard School and is best known for his interpretation of the works of Debussy and Ravel.

Weckmann, Matthias (c1619–74) German organist and composer, stud. of Schütz and Jacob Praetorius. He served at the electoral chapel in Dresden until 1655, with the exception of several years in Denmark with

Schütz, then took a position in Hamburg. His surviving works incl. sacred vocal music, chamber sonatas and keyboard works.

Wedding, The (Russ., *Svadebka*; Fr., *Les Noces*) four choreographic scenes with music (1923) by Stravinsky, scored for soloists, chorus, four pianos and percussion. The text is by the composer and based on Russian legend.

Wedding March a term applicable to many works destined to accompany a bride's walk to or from the altar, but which is usu. understood to refer either to the bridal chorus from Wagner's *Lohengrin* (entrance music) or to the wedding march from Mendelssohn's incidental music to Shakespeare's *A Midsummer Night's Dream* (exit music).

Wedge Fugue the fugue from the Prelude and Fugue in E minor, BWV 548 (1727–31), by Bach.

Weelkes, Thomas (c1575–1623) English composer and organist at Winchester College, then at Chichester Cathedral, where he remained until his death. He may also have been assoc. with the Chapel Royal. He is important both as a madrigalist and as a composer of sacred vocal music and also wrote works for viols and for harpsichord.

Weidenaar, Reynold (Henry) (1945–) Amer. composer, video artist, filmmaker and teacher, stud. of Erb. He has taught at New York U. and Brooklyn College. His works integrate tape, video and film with live forces.

Weigl, Joseph (1766–1846) Austrian composer and conductor, stud. of Sebastian Witzig, Albrechtsberger and Salieri. He rehearsed and conducted several of Mozart's operas and from 1792 had a permanent position at the court theater. His works incl. almost 35 operas, ballets, concertos and dances for orch. and sacred and secular vocal music.

Weigl, Karl (1881–1949) Austrianborn Amer. composer, stud. of Zemlinsky and Guido Adler. He taught at the New Vienna Conservatory and at the U. of Vienna, then came to the U.S., where he taught at various schools. He wrote music in all genres except stage music, but his works are generally unknown today.

Weihnachtslied ['vī-nakhts"lēt] (Ger.) a Christmas song, esp. a Christmas carol.

Weihnachts-Oratorium, Die CHRISTMAS ORATORIO, THE.

Weill, Kurt (Julian) [vīl] (1900–50) German-born Amer. composer of theater music in Berlin, then of Broadway musicals after 1935, stud. of Albert Bing, Humperdinck, Busoni, Jarnach and others. He established early in his career his penchant for close collaborations with writers: the first was the playwright Georg Kaiser, with whom he collaborated on several works; the second was Bertolt Brecht, with whom he enjoyed a short but highly fruitful period of work. From the late 1930s he began his work in the U.S., which produced a series of dramas with music far beyond the depth of the usual musical comedy. When he died, he was beginning work on a musical adaptation of Mark Twain's novel *Huckleberry Finn*.

Weill's works incl. (with Kaiser) *Der Protagonist* and *Der Silbersee*; (with Brecht) *Mahagonny*, *The Threepenny Opera* and *The Seven Deadly Sins*, among others; (on Broadway) *Johnny Johnson*, *Knickerbocker Holiday*, *Lady in the Dark*, *Street Scene*, *Lost in the Stars*, among others; scores for radio and films, 2 symphonies, a divertimento for orch., choral music, chamber music and songs.

Weiner, Lazar (1897–1982) Russianborn Amer. composer, pianist and conductor, father of YEHUDI WYNER, stud. of Frederick Jacobi and others. He taught at the Hebrew Union College and the Jewish Theological Seminary and was musical dir. for 35 years of "The Message of Israel," a weekly radio program. His works incl. *The*

Golem (opera), ballets, cantatas, songs and chamber music.

Weiner, Leó (1885–1960) Hungarian composer and teacher, stud. of Koessler. From 1908 he taught at the High School of Musical Art in Budapest, where he maintained unusually high standards. His own works, in a Romantic idiom, incl. an opera, incidental music, orchestral music, chamber music and many works for piano.

Weingartner, (Paul) Felix (von) (1863–1942) Austrian conductor and composer, trained at Graz and Leipzig. He held posts in Königsberg, Danzig, Hamburg and Mannheim, then became court Kapellmeister of the Berlin Opera and Orch. in 1891. Later positions incl. the Vienna Court Opera and Philharmonic, the Hamburg Opera, Darmstadt, the Vienna Volksoper and the Allgemeine Musikgesellschaft concerts in Basel. He also conducted from time to time in the U.S. and in England. As a composer he produced almost a dozen operas, 7 symphonies, tone poems, chamber music and songs.

Weinzweig, John (Jacob) (1913–) Canadian composer and teacher, stud. of Willan and MacMillan in Toronto and Rogers at the Eastman School. He wrote incidental music for the CBC and taught at the U. of Toronto, influencing a generation of young composers. He has been an active supporter of new Canadian music and was the first Canadian composer to employ the 12-tone technique. He was a founder of the Canadian League of Composers and has been an important member of CAPAC. Weinzweig has written orchestral music, concertos for violin, piano and harp, divertimenti for various instrumental combinations, chamber music and songs.

Weisberg, Arthur (1931–) Amer. conductor and bassoonist, trained at the Juilliard School. He was a member of the New York Woodwind Quintet and founded the Contemporary Chamber Ensemble in 1960, one of the most successful new-music ensembles. He has taught at SUNY, Stony Brook, since 1968.

Weisgall, Hugo (David) (1912–) Czech-born Amer. conductor and composer of vocal music, trained at the Peabody Conservatory and with Sessions, Reiner and Scalero. He has conducted various ensembles in Europe and the U.S. and has taught at Queens College (NY) and the Juilliard School. He is best known for his operas, incl. *The Tenor* (1952), *The Stronger* (1952), *Six Characters in Search of an Author* (1953–56) and *Purgatory* (1958). He has also written several ballets, songs and choral works.

Weiss, Adolph (1891–1971) Amer. composer and bassoonist, stud. of Schoenberg and others. He played with the New York PO, the Chicago SO and the Eastman Theater Orch. as well as other groups, and taught at the Los Angeles Conservatory. He was a teacher of John Cage, among others.

Weiss, Sylvius Leopold (1686–1750) eminent German lutanist and composer. The major part of his career was spent at the Saxon court in Dresden, where he became the highest-paid instrumentalist. He also traveled widely as a performer.

Weissenberg, Alexis (Sigismund) (1929–) Bulgarian-born French pianist, stud. of Schnabel, Samaroff and Landowska. He is esp. noted for his virtuoso technique.

Welitsch (Veličkova), **Ljuba** ['vel-ich], 'lyoo-bə] (1913–) Bulgarian-born Austrian soprano, stud. of Lierhammer. After several years in other opera houses, she joined the Vienna Opera in 1946. She has also sung in England and at the Metropolitan (debut 1948). Her most famous role was Salome; she has also sung Tosca, Aida, Donna Anna (*Don Giovanni*) and many other roles.

Welk, Lawrence (1903–92) Amer. accordionist and bandleader, famous for his bubbly "champagne music," highly popular on radio and TV in the 1960s and 1970s.

Wellesz, Egon (Joseph) (1885–1974)

Austrian composer, teacher and musicologist, stud. of Guido Adler and Schoenberg and biographer of the latter. A man of unusually wide interests and tastes, his compositional style was always heavily influenced by his Viennese training. He was in Vienna until World War II, then took a position at Oxford, where he remained until his death. A prolific composer, he wrote 4 operas, several ballets, orchestral works, choral music and songs, 9 string quartets and other chamber music, and works for piano solo.

Wellington's Victory (Ger., *Wellingtons Sieg*) a battle symphony, Op. 91 (1813), by Beethoven, orig. commissioned to be written for the PANHAR-MONICON, but ultimately composed for orch., celebrating Napoleon's defeat by Wellington's forces at Vitoria in Spain. Very popular in its time, it is seldom performed today.

Wells, Dicky (William) (1907–85) Amer. jazz trombonist. After short stints with the bands of Benny Carter, Fletcher Henderson and Teddy Hill, he began a long assoc. with Count Basie (1938–50), then worked as a free-lance musician. He was noted for his colorful, flamboyant style.

Wells, Junior (Blackmore, Amos, Jr.) (1934–) Amer. blues harmonica player and singer, a member of various groups in the late 1940s and a collaborator with Muddy Waters in the 1950s.

Wells, Kitty (Deason, Muriel Ellen) (1919–) Amer. country-music singer and songwriter, a popular performer on various radio programs, incl. the "Louisiana Hayride" and the "Grand Ole Opry." Her songs frequently deal with important social issues, incl. women's rights. She was elected to the Country Music Hall of Fame in 1976.

Wells, Mary (Esther) (1943–) Amer. soul and rhythm-and-blues singer. She established her career with the help of Smokey Robinson, whose songs she featured. Her biggest successes came in the early 1960s with "My Guy" and other songs.

Well-Tempered Clavier, The (Ger., *Das Wohltemperierte Clavier*) popular translation of J.S. Bach's title for his two collections (1722 and 1738–42) of preludes and fugues for keyboard, two in each of the 12 major and minor keys. The title refers to a tuning system (unspecified) which permits playing in all 24 keys.

Welte ['vel-te] 19th- and 20th-c. German family of instrument makers responsible for the development of various mechanical instruments, incl. the Welte-Mignon Reproducing Piano and the ORCHESTRION.

Wendt, Larry (Lawrence Frederick) (1946–) Amer. composer and writer on music, esp. known for his tape works, which use the techniques of *musique concrète*.

Wenrich, Percy (1887–1952) Amer. songwriter, pianist and singer, trained at Chicago Musical College. He is best known for his songs, incl. "Moonlight Bay" (1912) and "When You Wore a Tulip" (1914). He also wrote scores for several Broadway musicals.

Werba, Erik ['ver-bä] (1918–) eminent Austrian pianist and accompanist, trained in Vienna. He has taught since 1949 at the Vienna Academy of Music and has accompanied many leading singers, incl. Gedda, Ludwig and Seefried.

Werckmeister, Andreas ['verk-mī-stər] (1645–1706) German organist, composer and theorist. He is best remembered today for his writings on the music of his time and for his tuning systems, early attempts to produce equal temperament.

Wernick, Richard (1934–) Amer. composer, stud. of Berger, Shapero, Fine and others. He has taught at the Metropolitan Music School (NY); SUNY Buffalo, the U. of Chicago; and, since 1968, at the U. of Pennsylvania. He won the Pulitzer Prize in 1977 for his *Visions of Wonder and Terror* for mezzo-soprano and orch. His works incl. an opera, ballets, incidental music, a violin concerto, works for band, chamber music and songs.

Wert, Giaches de (1535–96) Flemish composer. After several years in Novellara and Milan he became *maestro di cappella* at the ducal chapel in Mantua, where he remained until his death, also maintaining close ties with the court in Ferrara. His extant works incl. 12 books of madrigals, several books of motets and instrumental fantasias.

Werther [ver'ter] tragic opera in 4 acts by Massenet to a libretto by Edouard Blau, Paul Milliet and Georges Hartmann, based on Goethe's novel *Die Leiden des jungen Werthers*. Premiere, Vienna 1892 (in German). Charlotte marries Albert because of a promise to her mother but falls in love with Werther, a young poet.

We Shall Overcome a song with deep meaning to the Amer. labor and civil rights movements. The sources of the song are unclear, though it seems to have developed from the 18th-c. hymn tune "O Sanctissima" (author unknown) and the text "I'll Overcome Some Day" by C. Albert Tindley. However, other sources and influences may have contributed to its present form.

Wesley, Samuel (1766–1837) English composer and organist, son of clergyman John Wesley (1703–91) and brother of composer Charles Wesley (1757–1834). For most of his life he supported himself by teaching, lecturing and playing concerts; he never held a permanent, salaried position. Though not Catholic, he wrote a substantial volume of music for the Latin service, as well as Anglican service music, hymns and secular choral music and songs. His instrumental music incl. symphonies, concertos and overtures for orch., chamber music, many organ works and works for piano.

Wesley, Samuel (Sebastian) (1810–76) English composer and organist, illegitimate son of SAMUEL WESLEY and

stud. of Hawes and others. He held a succession of organ posts, the most important of which were at Exeter Cathedral, Winchester College and Gloucester Cathedral. He also conducted at various festivals and composed hymn tunes, anthems, service music, secular songs and choruses, and works for organ and piano.

West Coast school a style of jazz performance dating from the 1950s in Los Angeles and characterized by the work of Shelly Manne, Shorty Rogers, Gerry Mulligan, Jimmy Giuffre and others. The players experimented with free improvisation and serial techniques. The style was closely related to COOL JAZZ.

Westergaard, Peter (Talbot) (1931–   ) Amer. composer and theorist, stud. of Piston, Milhaud, Sessions and Fortner. He has taught at various colleges, joining the Princeton faculty in 1968. He has also produced opera and written books and articles on various theoretical topics. His works incl. several operas (*Mr. and Mrs. Discobbolos, Charivari* and *The Tempest*), 3 cantatas, chamber music and several works for small orch.

Western music 1, WESTERN SWING. 2, COWBOY MUSIC. 3, the music of western Europe and the Americas, as opposed to eastern music from eastern Europe and Asia.

Western swing a style of country music influenced by jazz dance bands, blues and COWBOY MUSIC, which developed in the 1920s in the Southwest. The style is best represented by the Texas Playboys of the 1930s, led by Bob Wills, in the 1940s by Spade Cooley and by Merle Haggard and Alvin Crow in recent years.

Westminster Choir College a music school in Princeton, NJ, an outgrowth of a choir formed in 1920 in Dayton, OH, by John Finley Williamson. The school, which moved to Princeton in 1932, emphasizes training in choral and church music.

West Side Story musical by Leonard Bernstein, lyrics by Stephen Sondheim, book by Arthur Laurents, based on an idea by Jerome Robbins and Shakespeare's *Romeo and Juliet*. Premiere, New York 1957. A story of cross-cultural love in uptown New York.

Wheatstraw, Peetie (William Bunch) (1902–41) Amer. blues singer, guitarist and pianist, who recorded extensively in the 1930s.

Wheeler, Kenny (Kenneth V.J.) (1930–) Canadian jazz trumpeter, fluegelhorn player and composer, trained at the Toronto Conservatory but active for most of his career in England, playing with a succession of groups, incl. Johnny Dankworth's band and the Mike Gibbs Orch.

When Johnny Comes Marching Home patriotic song first published in 1863. Its origin is uncertain, though it has been credited to bandleader PATRICK GILMORE (under his pseudonym Louis Lambert).

When the Saints Go Marching In an Afr.-Amer. spiritual dating at least from the late 19th c. It is said that the song was played in New Orleans at funerals, slowly on the way to the cemetery and quickly on the way back.

Where's Charley? musical by Frank Loesser, book by George Abbott, based on the play *Charley's Aunt* by Brandon Thomas. Premiere, New York 1948. In order to entertain his girl friend at Oxford, Charley chaperons himself by masquerading as his own aunt.

Whiffenpoof Song a song traditionally associated with Yale. The melody appears to have been a late 19th-c. setting by a Harvard man, Guy Scull (1876–1920), of a poem by Kipling. The poem and music were later modified to their present form and popularized in the 1930s by Yale alumnus Rudy Vallee. The word *Whiffenpoof* came from a Yale choral group, which took it from a song by Victor Herbert about an imaginary Whiffenpoof fish.

whip a wooden concussion instrument used in the orch. to imitate the sound of a whip crack. It consists of two slabs of wood hinged together at one end and brought together quickly to make a sharp, clicking sound. Also, *slapstick*. See PERCUSSION INSTRUMENTS *(illus.)*.

whistle an end-blown FLUTE in which the air is blown into a FIPPLE to produce sound waves, as opposed to being blown across an open hole (as in the orchestral flute).

whistle flute a WHISTLE with finger holes or other means for obtaining different pitches. The most important examples of the instrument are the RECORDER, FLAGEOLET and PENNY WHISTLE. Also, *fipple flute*.

White, Benjamin Franklin (1800–79) Amer. singing-school teacher, tunebook compiler and composer, publisher of the famous collection *The Sacred Harp* (1844), which is still in widespread use in the South.

White, Charles A(lbert) (1829–92) Amer. songwriter and publisher, successful composer of romances and sentimental songs for the home.

White, Clarence Cameron (1880–1960) Amer. composer and violinist, trained at the Oberlin Conservatory and abroad. He taught at W. Va. State College and at Hampton Institute (VA) and was a founder of the National Association of Negro Musicians. His works incl. two operas, a ballet, several tone poems for orch., violin suites, choral works, songs and arrangements of spirituals.

White, Josh (Joshua Daniel; Pinewood Tom) (1915–69) Amer. gospel, folk and blues singer and guitarist. He recorded extensively from the early 1930s, sometimes alone, sometimes with his group the Carolinians and sometimes in collaboration with other artists, incl. Woody Guthrie, Leadbelly, Paul Robeson and others.

White, Robert (c1535–74) English composer. He held posts at Trinity College (Cambridge), Chester Cathedral and Westminster Abbey, before dying of the plague. His principal output was of sacred Latin and English service music.

White Christmas song (1942) by Irving Berlin from the movie *Holiday Inn*. The song won an Oscar and is one of the largest-selling songs in history. The recording by Bing Crosby holds a similar record.

Whitehead, Alfred (Ernest) (1887–1974) English-born Canadian organist, composer, choir dir. and teacher, trained in England. He held posts at St. Peter's in Sherbrooke and at Christ Church Cathedral in Montreal, then taught at Mt. Allison U. until his retirement. He wrote many choral works and was a distinguished teacher.

Whiteman, Paul (1890–1967) Amer. bandleader and violist. He played in the Denver SO and the San Francisco SO, then in 1918 formed his own group, which became one of the best-known bands in the U.S. He was a champion of Gershwin's music (he commissioned *Rhapsody in Blue* in 1924) and also performed works of many other Amer. composers.

White Mass (Fr., *Messe blanche*) the Piano Sonata No. 7, Op. 64 (1911), by Scriabin.

white noise a SOUND signal containing all frequencies within a given bandwidth.

White Peacock, The coloristic piano work (1915) by Griffes, later orchestrated by the composer.

Whithorne (Whittern), **Emerson** (1884–1958) Amer. composer and pianist, stud. of James H. Rogers, Leschetizky and Schnabel. From the 1920s he concentrated on composition, producing two symphonies (the first of which was premiered by the Cleveland Orch.), a violin concerto, symphonic poems, songs, chamber music, piano works and incidental music.

Whiting, Richard A. (1891–1938) Amer. Tin Pan Alley songwriter and composer of music for silent films. His many hit tunes incl. "Sleepy Time Gal" (1925) and "Beyond the Blue Horizon" (1930). His daughters **Margaret** and **Barbara Whiting** were both popular singers.

Whitlock, Billy (William M.) (1813–

78) Amer. songwriter and banjoist, collaborator in the Virginia Minstrels with DAN EMMETT and others and composer of minstrel songs.

Whitman Sisters a highly successful Afr.-Amer. vaudeville troupe, active from about 1904 until 1943.

Whitney, Robert (Sutton) (1904–1986) English-born Amer. conductor, composer and pianist, trained at the American Conservatory of Music in Chicago and later with Koussevitzky. He performed from 1925 to 1930 with a family quintet on radio, then founded the Louisville Orch. in 1937, whose innovative commissioning program he initiated in 1948. He retired from the orch. in 1967. He taught at the U. of Louisville until 1972.

Whittenberg, Charles (1927–84) Amer. composer, stud. of Rogers. He taught at the U. of Connecticut (1967–77) and worked at the Columbia-Princeton Center for Electronic Music. His works incl. chamber music, esp. for winds (he was assoc. closely with the American Brass Quintet), works for tape, songs and several orchestral pieces.

Who, The English rock group, formed in 1964 in London under lead singer and guitarist Peter Townshend. A highly successful and unusually long-lived group, the Who has also produced rock operas, incl. *Tommy* (1969).

whole consort a CONSORT of instruments all belonging to the same family. Cf. BROKEN CONSORT.

wholefall a type of SLIDE.

whole note a NOTE (○) equaling two half notes. Also, (Brit.) *semibreve*.

whole tone *also*, **whole step** an INTERVAL covering two half steps.

whole tone scale a SCALE containing only whole tones, equally dividing the tempered octave into six steps. Although it was used occasionally in tonal music of the 19th c., its extensive use in the music of the French impressionists, esp. Debussy, contributed to the development of atonal composition.

Whyte, Robert WHITE, ROBERT.

Whythorne, Thomas (1528–95) English composer and lutanist, trained at Magdalen College, Oxford. After traveling on the Continent, he held various tutoring positions in England, then after 1565 devoted his time to composition. He wrote several collections of madrigals and other part-songs and also wrote a recently rediscovered autobiography, which sheds much light on the state of music in late 16th-c. England.

Widor, Charles-Marie [vē'dor] (-Jean-Albert) (1844–1937) French composer, organist and teacher, stud. of Fétis and J.-N. Lemmens. He became organist at St. Sulpice in Paris in 1870, remaining almost until his death. He also taught at the Paris Conservatoire from 1890, where his many illustrious pupils incl. Schweitzer, Honegger, Tournemire and Dupré. Of his own compositions his organ music is the best known, but he also wrote operas, ballets, sacred and secular vocal music, 3 symphonies, chamber music and songs.

Wieck, Clara (Josephine) [vēk] SCHUMANN, CLARA.

Wiegenlied ['vē-gən"lēt] (Ger.) a cradle song or LULLABY.

Wieniawski, Henryk (Henri) [vē'nyow-skē] (1835–80) virtuoso Polish violinist and composer, stud. of Lambert Massart and others in Paris. After some years of concertizing he settled in St. Petersburg, and in his 12 years there he had a marked influence on the Russian violin school. He also taught for several years at the Brussels Conservatory, but most of his career was spent in touring. Some of his own works, most of which are for violin, are still heard in performance, esp. the Second Violin Concerto.

Wigglesworth, Frank (1918–) Amer. composer, stud. of Cowell, Luening, Varèse and Ernest White. He has taught at the New School for Social Research and CUNY and has been active in the administration of various composers' organizations. He has written an opera, several ballets, 3 symphonies, concertos and other works for orch., choral works, chamber music and songs.

Wigmore Hall a concert hall in London opened in 1901 as Bechstein Hall. The name was changed to the present one in 1917.

Wilber, Bob (Robert Sage) (1928–) versatile Amer. jazz clarinetist and soprano saxophonist, stud. of Bechet and Tristano. In 1954 he formed a group called The Six to perform music meshing traditional jazz with modern material. He later played with Eddie Condon and Bobby Hackett and was a founding member of The World's Greatest Jazz Band. Since leaving that group in 1973, he has worked on a variety of projects, including the movie *The Cotton Club* (1984).

Wilbye (Willoughbye), **John** (1574–1638) important English composer of madrigals, in the service of the Kytson family at Hengrave Hall for most of his career. His style of madrigal writing follows that of Thomas Morley and the elder Ferrabosco (I).

Wild, Earl (1915–) Amer. pianist and composer, stud. of Selmar Jansen and Egon Petri. He is esp. known for his performance of 19th-c. virtuoso repertory as well as the works of George Gershwin. He has taught at the Juilliard and Manhattan Schools and has been recorded extensively.

Wilder, Alec (Alexander Lafayette Chew) (1907–80) Amer. composer and arranger, trained at the Eastman School. After two decades of composing and arranging for popular singers such as Cab Calloway, Bing Crosby and Frank Sinatra, he concentrated on other genres, writing both in classical and jazz styles. His works incl. operas, ballets, several orchestral suites, chamber music and songs. He also wrote an interesting history of *American Popular Song* (1972).

Willaert, Adrian (c1485–1562) Flemish composer and teacher, stud. of Jean Mouton. He served Cardinal Ippolito and the d'Este family in Ferrara, then in 1527 assumed the post of *maestro di cappella* at St. Mark's in Venice, where he built a major musical establishment. His many pupils during his tenure there incl. Zarlino, Rore, Andrea Gabrieli and many others. The extensive list of his works includes Mass settings, other service music and motets, chansons and madrigals and instrumental ricercars.

Willan, (James) Healey (1880–1968) English-born Canadian organist, composer, choirmaster and teacher, trained in London. He taught from 1913 at the Toronto Conservatory and the U. of Toronto and was organist of St. Paul's and (from 1932) of the university. In the early 1920s he was music dir. for the Hart House Theatre, for which he wrote a number of incidental scores. His many sacred choral and organ works are widely performed, his other works (orchestral and chamber music) less so.

Willcocks, Sir **David (Valentine)** (1919–) English conductor, organist and teacher. In the late 1940s and 1950s he held various conducting and organ posts, incl. that at Salisbury Cathedral and at Worcester Cathedral, before becoming organist and choir dir. at King's College, Cambridge. With the choir he made numerous recordings and tours. He also has been conductor of the London Bach Choir and became dir. of the Royal College of Music in 1974.

Williams, Bert (Egbert Austin) (1874–1922) gifted West Indian-born Amer. singer, actor and comedian, half of a popular vaudeville team with George Walker. The two singers starred in a series of musical shows at the turn of the century, continuing until the year of his death.

Williams, Big Joe (Joseph Lee) (1903–82) Amer. blues singer and guitarist, a popular recording artist from the mid-1930s through the 1960s. He performed with harmonica player Sonny Boy Williamson, and a number of his songs were successfully recorded by other artists.

Williams, Camilla (1922–) Amer. soprano, stud. of Sergius Kagen, Leo Taubman and others. She has sung with the New York City Opera, the Philadelphia Lyric Opera and elsewhere in No. America and Europe. She has taught at Brooklyn College and at Indiana U.

Williams, Clarence (1898–1965) Amer. jazz pianist, composer and publisher, active in music through the 1930s. He was esp. important for his work in promoting the works of other jazz composers, incl. those of Fats Waller and James P. Johnson.

Williams, Cootie (Charles Melvin) (1910–85) Amer. jazz swing trumpeter and bandleader. He joined the Duke Ellington orch. in 1929, staying until 1940 and establishing his fame. He later played with Benny Goodman and then formed his own band, which was active for several years. In the 1960s he again played with Ellington.

Williams, Hank (Hiram) (1923–53) Amer. country-music singer, songwriter and guitarist, a regular on the "Louisiana Hayride" and "Grand Ole Opry" programs in the late 1940s and early 1950s. He made many successful recordings during these years, incl. "Lovesick Blues" (1949) and "Your Cheatin' Heart" (1952). He was elected to the Country Music Hall of Fame in 1961. His son, (Randall) **Hank Williams, Jr.** (1949–) is also a country-music singer, songwriter and guitarist.

Williams, Joe (Joseph Goreed) (1918–) Amer. blues singer. He worked with a number of important bands in the 1930s and 1940s but made his fame singing with Count Basie (1954–60).

Williams, John (Towner) (1932–) Amer. composer, conductor, arranger and pianist, stud. of Bobby Van Eps, Rosina Lhévinne, Castelnuovo-Tedesco and others. Since the 1960s he has been a highly successful composer of scores for TV and films, esp. various disaster films and the epochal *Star Wars*, for which he received one of his three Oscars. He has been conductor of the Boston Pops Orch. since 1980 and has guest-conducted a number of other major orchestras.

Williams, Mary Lou (Scruggs, Mary Elfrieda) (1914–81) Amer. jazz pianist and composer. She was an important member of the Andy Kirk Band in the 1930s, then formed her own combo in the 1940s. She made arrangements for many swing and bop bands, incl. those of Benny Goodman, Tommy Dorsey, Duke Ellington and Dizzy Gillespie, and has also taught at Duke. In the 1960s and 1970s she composed a number of sacred vocal works.

Williams, Ralph Vaughan VAUGHAN WILLIAMS, RALPH

Williamson, Malcolm (1931–) Australian composer, organist and pianist, stud. of Goossens, Seiber and Lutyens. His earlier works tended to include himself as performer on either piano or organ. Otherwise, he has concentrated on vocal music. He has written 9 operas (incl. *Our Man in Havana*), ballets, 5 symphonies, concertos for piano and organ, many choral works and songs, chamber music, piano sonatas and works for organ.

Williamson, Sonny Boy (I) (Miller, Rice) (1897–1965) Amer. blues singer, songwriter and harmonica player. He borrowed the name of the younger but short-lived SONNY BOY WILLIAMSON (II) shortly before the latter's death and made many recordings, sometimes backed by Muddy Waters. He was esp. successful in England, which he toured in the early 1960s.

Williamson, Sonny Boy (II) (John Lee) (c1914–48) Amer. blues singer and harmonica player, an important influence on later blues harmonica players through his performances with Big Bill Broonzy and other artists.

William Tell (Fr., *Guillaume Tell*) patriotic opera in 4 acts by Rossini to a libretto by V.J. Etienne de Jouy and Hippolyte L.L. Bis, based on the play by Schiller. Premiere, Paris 1829. Swiss patriot William Tell coura-geously helps the Swiss overthrow the Hapsburg tyrant. The overture to the opera became famous as the theme for the long-running "Lone Ranger" radio and TV programs.

Wills, Bob (James Robert) (1905–75) Amer. Western swing fiddler, singer, songwriter and bandleader, a founder of the Light Crust Doughboys in 1931. Three years later he formed the Texas Playboys, which became popular in the Southwest and later appeared in films. He was elected to the Country Music Hall of Fame in 1961.

Willson, (Robert Reiniger) Meredith (1902–84) Amer. composer, conductor, lyricist and flutist, trained at the Institute of Musical Art (NY) and with Barrère. He played with Sousa and in the New York PO before entering commercial radio, where he worked for almost thirty years. He also composed film scores, incl. the score for Chaplin's *The Great Dictator* (1940). He is best known, however, for his scores for Broadway musicals, esp. *The Music Man* (1957) and *The Unsinkable Molly Brown* (1960).

Wilson, Jackie (1934–84) Amer. soul and blues singer, a successful recording artist from the late 1950s to the late 1960s with such hits as "Lonely Teardrops" (1958) and "All My Love" (1960).

Wilson, John (1595–1674) English composer, lutanist and singer. He was a member of the King's Musick and also taught at Oxford from 1656. His extant works incl. a large number of songs and preludes for theorbo.

Wilson, Olly (Woodrow) (1937–) Amer. composer, trained at the U. of Illinois and the U. of Iowa. He has taught at Oberlin College and at the U. of California, Berkeley (since 1970). His works combine the latest avant-garde techniques with the idioms of Afr.-Amer. music and incl. several orchestral works (*Akwan* and *Structure*), music for various chamber ensembles, a violin sonata, songs and choruses, electronic music (incl. the ballet *The 18 Hands of Jerome Harris*).

Wilson, Teddy (Theodore Shaw) (1912–86) important Amer. swing pianist and composer. He played with Louis Armstrong and Benny Carter, then joined Benny Goodman in 1935. He was also musical dir. for many of Billie Holiday's early recordings. From 1940 he led his own smaller groups and later taught at the Juilliard School.

wind band 1, a band composed of wind instruments, sometimes with percussion. **2**, the wind section of an orch.

Wind-band Mass HARMONIEMESSE.

wind-cap instrument a free-reed wind instrument whose reed, single or double, is enclosed by a cap into which the player blows to make the reed vibrate. The cap prevents overblowing, thus limiting the instrument to its fundamental notes. The principal instrument of this type is the SHAWM. Also, *reed-cap instrument.*

wind-chest in a pipe organ, a reservoir of wind supplied by the bellows which is stored under pressure and distributed to the pipes.

wind chime a type of CLAPPER consisting of a number of objects of stone, glass, metal, etc., hung from a frame and struck together by wind.

Windgassen, Wolfgang (1914–74) German dramatic tenor and opera producer, stud. of Maria Ranzow and Alfons Fischer. He sang with the Stuttgart Opera (where his parents had sung) from 1945 to 1972, singing primarily roles by Verdi and Wagner. He later sang at Bayreuth, Covent Garden, the Metropolitan Opera (debut 1957) and elsewhere. After 1970 he was active as an opera dir.

Winding, Kai (Chresten) (1922–83) Danish-born Amer. jazz, swing and bop trombonist and composer. He played in the big bands of Benny Goodman and Stan Kenton but also worked with Charlie Parker and led his own groups. He performed and recorded frequently with trombonist J.J. Johnson and toured as a performer and jazz clinic leader.

wind instrument an AEROPHONE, esp. one that forms part of a modern performing ensemble, i.e., the WOODWIND INSTRUMENTS and BRASS INSTRUMENTS.

wind machine an instrument used in opera and the symphony orch. to imitate the sound of the wind. It usu. consists of a revolving wheel fitted with vanes and covered by a canvas cloth which rubs against the vanes as the wheel is turned.

windway in an organ pipe, the passage between the foot and the flue through which the air passes. In a recorder, the flue itself.

Winkler, Peter K(enton) (1943–) Amer. composer, stud. of Shifrin, Kim and Babbitt. He has taught at SUNY, Stony Brook, since 1971. His works incl. theater music, a symphony, a string quartet and other chamber music, and songs.

Winnipeg Symphony Orchestra orch. founded in 1947 in Winnipeg, Man. Its conductors have been Walter Kaufmann, Victor Feldbrill, George Cleve, Piero Gamba and Kazukio Koizumi.

Winograd, Arthur (1920–) Amer. conductor and cellist, trained at the New England Conservatory and the Curtis Institute. He played in the Boston SO and the NBC SO and was the original cellist of the Juilliard Quartet, remaining until 1955. He has been conductor for MGM Records and music dir. for the Birmingham (AL) SO and the Hartford SO. He taught in the early 1950s at the Juilliard School.

Winter Daydreams the composer's nickname for the first movement of the Symphony No. 1 in G minor, Op. 13 (1866, rev. 1874), by Tchaikovsky. The title is now applied to the whole work.

Winterhalter, Hugo (1910–73) Amer. conductor, arranger and composer, trained at the New England Conservatory. He played saxophone in various bands in the 1930s and 1940s, later arranging for them as well. He was music dir. for over a decade for

RCA Victor, providing musical backing for many popular singers. Among his own works were the songs "Hesitation" (1952) and "Melody of Spain" (1962) and the arrangement of "Canadian Sunset" (1956).

Winterreise, Die ['win-tər"rī-se] (Ger., The Winter Journey) song cycle (1827) by Schubert, a setting of 24 poems by Wilhelm Müller.

Winter Wind the Étude in A minor for piano, Op. 25 No. 11 (1834), by Chopin.

wire brush a type of percussion beater consisting of a large number of short wire strands held together at one end and attached to a handle, used esp. in jazz ensembles for playing the drums and cymbals. Also, *brush*.

Wiseman, Mac (1925–) Amer. bluegrass guitarist and singer. He performed with a number of groups in the 1940s and 1950s, incl. Bill Monroe's Blue Grass Boys, and made many hit records in the late 1950s. During the 1960s he also worked as a record producer.

Wiseman, Scotty (1909–) Amer. country music singer, songwriter, guitarist and banjoist, a regular for over 25 years on the WLS "National Barn Dance" radio show and also featured on TV and in films, esp. in collaboration with LULU BELLE.

Witches' Minuet the 3rd movement of the String Quartet in D minor, Op. 76 No. 2 (1797), by Haydn.

Witherspoon, Herbert (1873–1935) Amer. bass, stud. of Horatio Parker, MacDowell, Henry Wood and G.B. Lamberti. His Amer. debut was at the Metropolitan Opera in 1908, where he sang until 1916. He was president of the Chicago Musical College (1925–30) and the Cincinnati College-Conservatory of Music (1931–33) and was at the time of his death due to become general manager of the Metropolitan Opera.

Witherspoon, Jimmy (James) (1923–) Amer. blues singer. He has had several periods of popularity, recording and performing with various backup bands and on tour in the U.S. and Europe.

Wittgenstein, Paul (1887–1961) Austrian-born Amer. pianist, brother of the philosopher Ludwig Wittgenstein and a stud. of Malvine Brée and Leschetizky. He lost his right arm in World War I but pursued a career playing and commissioning music for left hand alone. Among the works written for him were concertos by Ravel, Strauss and Prokofiev. He moved to the U.S. in the late 1930s, where he taught privately and at several schools.

Wixell, Ingvar (1931–) Swedish baritone, trained in Stockholm. His U.S. debut was in San Francisco in 1967, and he has sung at most major international opera houses a repertory incl. Simon Boccanegra, Rigoletto and Scarpia (*Tosca*).

Wiz, The musical by William F. Brown and Charlie Smalls, based on the children's novel *The Wizard of Oz* by L. Frank Baum. Premiere, New York 1975. An all-black version of the classic children's tale, emphasizing aspects of Afr.-Amer. experience and culture.

wobble an unusually or unpleasantly wide vocal vibrato.

Wohltemperierte Clavier, Das ["vōl-tem-pe'rēr-te klä'vēr] (Ger.) WELL-TEMPERED CLAVIER, THE.

wolf *also,* **wolf tone** a dissonance produced by playing certain 5ths on fixed-pitch instruments tuned with unequal temperament (such as MEAN-TONE or JUST tunings). The term is also used for individual notes on an instrument which are especially out of tune or dynamically unbalanced with the rest of the scale as a result of the structure of the instrument or a defect in its manufacture.

Wolf, Hugo (Filipp Jakob) (1860–1903) Austrian composer of Lieder. He studied at the Vienna Conservatory, but was dismissed for "breach of discipline." Despite advice from Wagner, Brahms and Liszt to work in larger forms, by the late 1880s his vocation as a song composer seemed clear. Except for several years as a music critic, he obtained his financial support from sponsors. By the late 1890s signs of mental illness became pronounced; his delusions included his belief that he had been appointed dir. of the Vienna Opera. He died in a Viennese asylum.

In his songs Wolf refined the late Romantic harmonic language to a density of expression unmatched before or since. In addition to the many songs which established his fame, Wolf also wrote two operas, *Der Corregidor* and *Manuel Venegas* (the latter incomplete), incidental music, several choral works, some orchestral works (mostly early), an *Italian Serenade* for string quartet and piano works.

Wolfe, Paul (Cecil) (1926–) Amer. violinist, oboist and conductor, stud. of Barzin, Mischakoff, Totenberg and Shumsky, among others. He has been conductor of the New Chamber Music Society, the Bronx SO, the National Orchestral Association and the Florida West Coast SO in Sarasota, where he founded the New College Music Festival (1965), which he still directs.

Wolfes, Felix (1892–1971) German-born Amer. conductor and composer, stud. of Reger and Pfitzner. He worked as coach, accompanist and conductor in various German opera houses before coming to the U.S. in 1938. He worked for some years at the Metropolitan Opera but never made a career as a conductor. In later years he taught at the New England Conservatory and performed as pianist and accompanist, presenting concerts of unusual vocal music.

Wolff, Christian (1934–) French-born Amer. composer, largely self-taught, a member of the faculty of Dartmouth College since 1970. He was an early associate of Feldman and Cage in New York, and his compositions provide a fairly wide area of choice for the performer. His works are nearly all for small instrumental ensembles.

Wolf-Ferrari, Ermanno (1876–1948) Italian composer, stud. of Rheinberger at the Munich Academy. Although he held teaching positions for short periods in Venice and Salzburg, he devoted most of his time to composition. He wrote in all genres, but is best remembered for his comic operas, esp. *The School for Fathers* (1906) and *The Secret of Susanna* (1909).

Wolfram von Eschenbach (c1180–c1220) German Meistersinger, author of the poem *Parzival* on which Wagner's opera is based and one of those at the 13th-c. Wartburg singing contest depicted in Wagner's *Tannhäuser*. No music has survived for his lyric poems.

Wolf Trap Farm Park for the Performing Arts a national park in Vienna, VA, devoted to the performing arts, established in 1971, site of an annual summer festival of opera, concert, musical theater and ballet. From 1971 to 1983 it was also the site of the National Folk Festival.

Wolpe, Stefan (1902–72) German-born Amer. composer, stud. of Juon and Schreker. In the 1920s he was part of the Communist revolutionary movement, for which he wrote much music, most of it tonal, though his later works are in his own style of atonality. He came to the U.S. in 1938 and became important as a teacher at various schools, numbering among his pupils Ralph Shapey and Morton Feldman. He was deeply interested in jazz, and jazz rhythms can be felt in some of his compositions. His works incl. *The Man from Midian* (ballet), incidental music, a symphony, several pieces for small orch., chamber music, works for piano, choral works, cantatas, and songs.

Wolverines, The a jazz band active in the early 1920s in Cincinnati, famous as the first important ensemble to feature trumpeter BIX BEIDERBECKE.

Wonder, ("Little") Stevie (Judkins, Stevland) (1950–) Amer. soul singer and songwriter, blind from birth, the most successful Afr.-Amer. recording artist of the 1970s. He made inventive use of electronic instruments and developed a number of albums which highlighted a certain concept, such as love. His many hits incl. "For Once in My Life" (1968), "You Are the Sunshine of my Life" (1973) and "Sir Duke" (1977).

Wonderful Town musical by Leonard Bernstein, lyrics by Betty Comden and Adolph Green, book by Joseph Fields and Jerome Chodorov, based on their play *My Sister Eileen*. Premiere, New York 1952. The Sherwood sisters from Ohio seek success in Greenwich Village in the 1930's.

WoO *abbr.* without opus number.

Wood, Sir **Henry J(oseph)** (1869–1944) English conductor, trained at the Royal Academy of Music. He achieved fame with the Queen's Hall Promenade Concerts, inaugurated under his direction in 1895 and conducted by him until his death. He was the first English conductor to conduct the New York PO (1904). He was a powerful force in English musical life.

wood block a small wooden IDIOPHONE, sometimes tuned, usu. hollowed out and having a slit cut through half of its length. It is struck with a wooden mallet and used as an instrument in the orch. Cf. CHINESE WOOD BLOCK, TEMPLE BLOCK. See PERCUSSION INSTRUMENTS (*illus.*).

Wooden Prince, The ballet with music by Bartók to a scenario by Béla Balázs. Premiere, Budapest 1917. A prince constructs a wooden prince to attract a princess, and she likes the puppet more than the prince.

Woods, Phil(ip Wells) (1931–) Amer. jazz alto saxophonist, trained at the Juilliard School and strongly influenced by Charlie Parker. During the 1950s and 1960s he played with the Thelonious Monk nonet and various other bands, incl. those of Charlie Barnet, Dizzy Gillespie, Buddy Rich, Quincy Jones and Benny Goodman. Woods spent several years in France leading his own progressive

jazz group, then returned to the East Coast, where he formed another bop-rooted group, which has had much success.

Woodstock Music and Arts Fair known as "Woodstock," this 1969 rock festival held on a farm in Bethel, NY, attracted over 450,000 people and has become a popular music legend. The event produced several record albums and a documentary film.

woodwind instrument a somewhat inaccurate term for a group of orchestral wind instruments usu. taken to include the families of the FLUTE, OBOE, CLARINET, BASSOON and sometimes the FRENCH HORN, whether or not they are made of wood. For illustrations, see FLUTES, REED INSTRUMENTS, HORNS.

woodwind quintet a QUINTET usu. comprising a flute, oboe, clarinet, French horn and bassoon.

Woodworth, G(eorge) Wallace (1902–69) Amer. choral conductor, organist and teacher, trained at Harvard, where he conducted the orch. and choral groups and taught from 1924. He produced many performing editions of choral music, esp. the music of Giovanni Gabrieli, and was a popular lecturer on radio.

Woodyard, Sam(uel) (1925–88) Amer. jazz drummer with the Duke Ellington orch. for 13 years. In later years he lived in Europe.

Worcester Music Festival a concert series in Worcester, MA, dating from 1858 and perhaps the oldest music festival in continuous existence in the U.S.

Worcester polyphony a style of medieval polyphony dating from the late 13th c. and prob. originating in Worcester, England. The style is marked by a prevalence of complete triads, frequent use of the major mode, foursquare phrase design and a nearly exclusive use of trochaic (long-short) rhythms. The subject matter of much of the repertory is Marian devotion.

word-painting the technique of depicting in music an idea or meaning associated with a word. The technique is esp. associated with the 16th-c. madrigal.

work OPUS.

Work, Henry Clay (1832–84) Amer. composer, largely self-taught. A printer by trade, he wrote a large number of songs, many of them dating from the period of the Civil War. His best-known songs are "Marching Through Georgia" (1865) and "Grandfather's Clock" (1876).

working out DEVELOPMENT.

work song a song composed to accompany the work of laborers, about work or about the cause of the worker. The most prevalent types are sea shantys (see SHANTY), prison and slave songs and railroad songs.

world music a term for the distinctive ethnic music of diverse cultures. More specifically, the term usu. refers to music of cultures other than one's own or of musical traditions other than those of Western Europe, the US and Canada. The term is used both in commercial recording and, more recently, in academic circles. Often the music so designated reveals the influence of Western music in its use of Western instruments, rhythms or sounds.

World Saxophone Quartet jazz ensemble formed in 1977 by Hamiet Bleuitt, Julius Hemphill, Oliver Lake and David Murray, all of whom double on other instruments. They have toured extensively and played at most major festivals, performing without a rhythm section.

World's Greatest Jazz Band a band formed in 1968 by trumpeter Yank Lawson and bassist Bob Haggart. It was active for a decade in various versions with a distinguished lineup of sidemen, incl. Bob Wilbur and Bud Freeman.

World's Peace Jubilee see NATIONAL PEACE JUBILEE.

Wotquenne, Alfred (Camille) (1867–1939) Belgian bibliographer, best known for his thematic catalogues of the works of Gluck and C.P.E. Bach. His numbers are usu. prefixed by the abbreviation "Wq."

Wozzeck ['vot-seck] (Ger.) tragic opera in 3 acts by Alban Berg to his own libretto, adapted from the play *Woyzeck* by Georg Büchner. Premiere, Berlin 1925. Composed in an atonal idiom but using classical forms, it tells the story of the oppressed soldier Wozzeck, who is betrayed by his wife Marie, whom he murders, afterwards accidentally drowning himself.

WPA *abbr.* Works Progress Administration, a depression-era government agency whose Federal Music Project, created in 1935, supported concerts, lending libraries, collecting folk music and other programs.

Wq. *abbr.* see WOTQUENNE, ALFRED. Also, *W*.

wrest pin a metal peg around which one end of a string (of a piano, harp, etc.) is wound and which is turned to tighten or loosen the string tension and adjust its pitch. Also, *tuning pin*.

wrest plank the block of wood into which the WREST PINS are screwed. Also, *pin block*.

WTC *abbr.* WELL-TEMPERED CLAVIER.

Wunderhorn, Des Knaben ['vûn-dər-hôrn, des 'knä-bən] KNABEN WUNDERHORN, DES.

Wunderkind [-kint] (Ger.) child prodigy.

Wunderlich, Fritz (-liç) (1930–66) German lyric tenor, famous for his interpretations of the Mozart tenor roles. He sang with the Stuttgart, Frankfurt, Munich and Vienna Operas. He was also a noted concert and recital artist.

Wuorinen, Charles (1938–) Amer. composer, pianist and teacher, stud. of Luening, Ussachevsky and Beeson. He has taught at Columbia and the Manhattan School and lectured at a number of other colleges. He was a co-founder of the Group for Contemporary Music and has been active in the American Composers Alliance. His compositions employ serial techniques with varying degrees of rigidity. He won the Pulitzer Prize in 1970 for his tape work *Time's Encomium*.

His works incl. *The Politics of Harmony* (opera), Symphony III for orch., concertos for piano and amplified violin, a symphony for percussion, several chamber concertos for various solo instruments, chamber music and several choral works.

Wurlitzer Amer. firm of instrument manufacturers, founded in the early 1850s by Rudolph Wurlitzer (1831–1914). The firm is esp. known for its line of mechanical instruments, theater and electronic organs and coin-operated phonographs, pianos and jukeboxes.

Württemberg Sonatas the 6 keyboard sonatas, Wq. 49 (1744), by C.P.E. Bach.

Wyner, Susan Davenny (1945–) Amer. soprano, stud. of Herta Glaz Redlich. She has appeared in opera at the New York City Opera and the Metropolitan Opera but is best known for her concert and recital performance, esp. of contemporary music. She is married to composer YEHUDI WYNER.

Wyner, Yehudi (1929–) Canadian-born Amer. composer, pianist and conductor, son of LAZAR WEINER, stud. of Hindemith and Piston. He has taught at Yale and, since 1978, at SUNY, Purchase. His works, which express both his Jewish heritage and his interest in jazz, incl. choral and solo vocal music, Jewish service music, many chamber music works, piano music and several incidental scores.

Wyton, Alec (1921–) English-born Amer. organist and composer, trained at the Royal Academy of Music. He was organist at St. John the Divine in New York from 1954 to 1974, then at St. James's Church. He has toured extensively as recitalist and lecturer and has written an opera, music for organ and choral works.

X

X Amer. punk rock group formed in Los Angeles in 1977, noted for their unusually sophisticated lyrics and the influence of rockabilly and heavy metal.

Xenakis, Iannis [zē'nä-kis, 'yä-nis] (1922–) Romanian-born French composer of Greek parentage. In 1947 he settled in Paris, where he was influenced by Messiaen, Milhaud and Scherchen, as well as by the architect Le Corbusier, with whom he worked for several years. He has taught at Indiana U. and was the founder of the Équipe de mathématique et d'automatique musicales (The Center for Musical Mathematics and Automation) in both Paris and Indiana. His works make extensive use of mathematics in their construction, which is arrived at through models from the laws of probability, set theory, game theory, etc. He has written many works for orch., choral works, chamber music for many different instrumental combinations and works for electronic realization on tape.

xylophone a percussion instrument found throughout the world, consisting of a series of wooden bars of increasing length laid out in two rows (arranged like the black and white keys of a piano) to produce when struck with mallets the notes of the chromatic scale. The instrument sometimes has tubular (as in the orchestral xylophone) or gourd resonators beneath the bars. Cf. GAMBANG, MARIMBA, VIBRAPHONE.

xylorimba ["zī-lə'rim-bə] a XYLOPHONE having the compass of a large marimba and a xylophone combined, popular in the 1920s and 1930s. Several 20th-c. composers, incl. Berg and Stravinsky, have scored for the instrument.

Y

Yaddo an artists' colony and music festival established in Saratoga Springs, NY, in 1924 by philanthropist Spencer Trask.

Yamada, Kosaku (1886–1965) prolific Jap. composer, conductor and teacher, trained in Tokyo and Berlin. He formed the Tokyo PO in 1915 (a predecessor of the present orch. of that name) and several years later traveled to the U.S., where he guest-conducted the New York PO. He traveled widely after World War I, having works performed in Europe and Russia. He wrote in all genres, attempting to reconcile European tradition with Japanese speech intonation.

Yampolsky, Abram Ilich (1890–1956) Russian violinist and teacher, stud. of Sergey Korguyev and others. He taught at the Moscow Conservatory from 1922 and at the Gnesin Institute and was important in the foundation of the modern Russian school of violin playing.

Yancey, Jimmy (James Edwards) (1894–1951) Amer. jazz boogie-woogie pianist. Until 1915 he performed in vaudeville as singer and dancer, then settled in Chicago, where he performed informally while working as a groundskeeper for the Chicago White Sox. From the late 1930s he recorded new and older works, continuing sporadically until his death.

Yankee Doodle an Amer. patriotic song of unknown authorship dating from the pre-Revolutionary period.

Yardbird nickname for CHARLIE PARKER.

Yardbirds, The English blues-rock group, formed in London in 1963. The group was highly innovative, including in their personnel at various times guitarists Eric Clapton, Jimmy Page and Jeff Beck. The band broke up in 1968.

Yardumian, Richard (1917–85) Amer. composer. His musical training began when he was in his 20s (though he had been playing the piano, self-taught, for some years). His music incorporates many elements of his Armenian musical heritage, esp. modal writing. He wrote orchestral suites, a piano concerto, 2 symphonies (the second with solo voices), choral works, chamber music and a piano sonata.

Yarrow, Peter (1938–) Amer. popular and folk singer, a member of the trio PETER, PAUL AND MARY.

Yeoman of the Guard operetta in 2 acts by Sullivan to a libretto by W.S. Gilbert. Premiere, London 1888. When Colonel Fairfax marries Elsie her disappointed suitor, jester Jack Point, dies of a broken heart.

Yepes, Narciso (1927–) Spanish guitarist and composer, stud. of Vicente Asencio, Gieseking and Enescu, but self-taught as a guitarist. He has toured widely, playing a specially constructed ten-string guitar.

Yes English progressive-rock band formed in London in 1968, noted for its virtuoso musicianship and high vocal harmonies.

yodel *also,* **jodel** to alternate rapidly between head voice and chest voice in a manner common to Swiss and Tyrolean mountaineers; a song or cry sung in this manner.

Yonge, Nicholas (?–1619) English musician, singer at St. Paul's Cathedral and editor of the famous collection *Musica Transalpina* (1588, 1597), containing Italian madrigals with singing translations in English.

York Winds Canadian wind quintet formed in Toronto in 1972, disbanded in 1986. The group performed across Canada and premiered a number of new works, many of which they commissioned.

Youmans, Vincent (Millie) (1898–1946) Amer. composer of Broadway musicals, esp. *No, No, Nanette* (1925) and *Hit the Deck* (1927), and film scores, incl. *Flying Down to Rio* (1933).

Young, La Monte (Thornton) (1935–) Amer. composer and instrumentalist, stud. of Shifrin, Stockhausen and others. He has also studied No. Indian vocal music with Pran Nath and performed with him. He was important in the development of PERFORMANCE ART and of the FLUXUS movement through his publication *An Anthology* (1963), a collection of performance art works, and has been associated with MINIMALISM. He has also performed with jazz ensembles. Many of his works involve electronic media, alone or in combination with live instruments, but he has written many works for conventional instruments, some employing JUST INTONATION.

Young, Lester (Willis) ("Pres") (1909–59) highly influential Amer. jazz tenor saxophonist. He played with Walter Page's Blue Devils and Bennie Moten's band before joining the Count Basie orch. in 1934, remaining, with several interruptions, until 1944. After the war he performed regularly with Jazz at the Philharmonic and led his own groups, occasionally making guest appearances with the Basie band. Young's light, vibratoless tone and rhythmically iconoclastic style was a significant force in the development of bop, in part because of his profound influence on Charlie Parker.

Young, Neil (1945–) Canadian rock singer and songwriter, an original member of Buffalo Springfield and later of the group Crosby, Stills, Nash and Young. In the 1970s and 1980s he has pursued his solo career, recording in varying styles.

Young, Victor (I) (1889–1968) Amer. pianist and composer, stud. of Isidor Philipp. He worked with Thomas A. Edison in the development of sound recording and composed over 300 film scores as well as orchestral music, songs and piano works.

Young, Victor (II) (1900–56) Amer. composer, trained in Warsaw. He composed many film scores (incl. *Around the World in 80 Days*) and many songs (incl. "Sweet Sue" and "My Foolish Heart").

Young Lord, The JUNGE LORD, DER.

Young Person's Guide to the Orchestra, The a narrated set of variations and fugue on a theme of Purcell, Op. 34 (1945), by Britten. The work introduces the principal instruments and sections of the orch., culminating in a rousing fugue.

You're a Good Man, Charlie Brown musical by Clark Gessner, book by John Gordon, based on the comic strip *Peanuts* by Charles Schulz. Premiere, New York 1967. This depiction of "an average day in the life of Charlie Brown" was one of off-Broadway's longest-running musicals.

Youth's Magic Horn KNABEN WUNDERHORN, DES.

Youth Symphony the Symphony No. 7, Op. 131 (1952), by Prokofiev, conceived as a symphony for children.

Ysaÿe, Eugène (ē-zä'ē, ü-zhen'] (1858–1931) Belgian violinist, composer and conductor, stud. of D. Heynberg, Rodolphe Massart, Wieniawski and Vieuxtemps. He toured with pianist Anton Rubinstein, then spent three years in Paris. From 1886 he taught at the Brussels Conservatory and ran a series of concerts of contemporary music, at the same time making frequent concert tours in Europe and to the U.S. From 1918 to 1922 he was conductor of the Cincinnati SO, then resumed touring. He was highly respected as a violinist of virtuosity and character. He wrote works in all genres, usu. with solo violin.

yuechyn [yoo'ā-chēn] a Chinese short-necked, flat-backed LUTE.

Z

Zabaleta, Nicanor (1907–) Spanish harpist, stud. of Marcel Tournier. Through his influence he has greatly expanded the solo harp technique and literature, both through rediscovery of existing repertory and through commissions, and he has made many recordings.

Zachow (Zachau), **Friedrich Wilhelm** ['zä-khow, 'frēd-riç 'vil-helm] (1663–1712) German organist and composer, prob. stud. of Johann Hildebrand and teacher of Handel. From 1864 until his death he was organist at the Marienkirche in Halle, conductor of the town chorus and an eminent teacher. His surviving works incl. German cantatas, a few Latin motets, keyboard chorales and toccatas.

Zadok the Priest one of four anthems (1727) composed by Handel for the coronation of George II of England.

Zádor, Eugene (Jenö) (1894–1977) Hungarian-born Amer. composer, stud. of Reger and Fritz Volbach. He came to the U.S. in 1939 and became active in Hollywood as an orchestrator of film scores. His own works incl. more than 10 operas, concertos for various instruments, choral works and chamber music.

Zaimont, Judith Lang (1945–) Amer. composer, stud. of Weisgall, Luening, Jolivet and others. She has taught at the Peabody Conservatory since 1980 and has written several textbooks. Her works incl. a piano concerto, instrumental sonatas and chamber music, piano works, choral music and many songs.

zampogna [tsäm'pō-nyä] (It.) *also*, **zampoña** [zäm-] (Sp.), **sampogna** **1**, PANPIPES. **2**, BAGPIPE.

Zandonai, Riccardo [tsän-dō'nī] (1883–1944) Italian composer and conductor, stud. of Mascagni. He is remembered for his operas *Francesca da Rimini* (1914) and *Giulietta e Romeo* (1922). He also wrote orchestral and choral works and chamber music.

zapateado [thä-pä-tā'ä-*tho*] (Sp.) a rhythmic, stamping dance step characteristic of Spanish dancing.

Zappa, Frank (Francis Vincent) (1940–) Amer. rock and jazz-rock singer, composer and guitarist. In 1964 he joined a group called the Soul Giants, which he renamed (ultimately) the Mothers of Invention. Commercially the band got off to a slow start despite critical approval and their innovative production techniques. Over the years Zappa has produced a large number of recordings of varying quality, presaging PUNK ROCK, but frequently exhibiting satirical brilliance. He has also achieved a certain reputation as a classical musician and has appeared with several classical groups, incl. the London SO and the Florence Maggio Musicale.

Zarlino, Gioseffo [dzär'lē-nō] (1517–90) Italian composer and theorist, stud. of Willaert in Venice. He was an influential teacher and *maestro di cappella* of St. Mark's, Venice, from 1565 until his death. His most important work is the treatise *Le istitutioni harmoniche* (1558, reprinted in 1562 and 1573), an attempt to unite theory with compositional practice.

zart [tsärt] (Ger.) gently.

zarzuela [thär'thwä-lä] (Sp.) a type of Spanish music theater with spoken dialogue, singing and dancing, usu. based on a comic subject. The form originated in the mid-17th c. and was strongly influenced by Italian operatic style in the 18th c.

Zauberflöte, Die ['tsow-bər"flö-te, dē] (Ger.) MAGIC FLUTE, THE.

Zawinul, Joe (Josef) (1932–) Austrian-born Amer. jazz composer and keyboard player, trained at the Vienna Conservatory. He came to the U.S. in 1959 to study at the Berklee School in Boston. He played with Maynard Ferguson, Dinah Washington and then Cannonball Adderly, staying with his group until 1970. He has also worked with Miles Davis and was co-founder with Wayne Shorter of WEATHER REPORT, which has provided a fertile ground for his talents and his expertise with electronics.

Zeisler (née Blumenfeld), **Fannie** ['zīs-lər] (1863–1927) Amer. pianist, stud. of Bernhard Ziehn and Leschetizky. She pursued a successful concert career until her retirement in 1925. She was esp. interested in promoting works of women composers.

Zeitlin, Zvi ['zīt-lin, zvē] (1923–) Russian-born Amer. violinist, stud. of Persinger and Galamian. He has specialized in 20th-c. repertory, incl. works by Druckman, Ben-Haim and Schoenberg. He has taught at the Eastman School since 1967.

Zeitmasse ['tsīt"mä-se] (Ger., Tempos) work for woodwind quintet, No. 5 (1955–6), by Stockhausen, which explores tempo and ensemble relationships.

Zelenka, Jan Dismas (1679–1745) Czech composer, stud. of Fux and Lotti. He played in the court orch. in Dresden for most of his career, eventually assuming the duties of Kapellmeister until Hasse won the position from him. His surviving works consist mainly of sacred vocal music, esp. Mass settings and oratorios.

Zelter, Carl Friedrich ['tsel-tər] (1758–1832) German composer, conductor and teacher, stud. of Carl Fasch. A mason, he gave up his trade around 1790 to concentrate on music. He was dir. for almost 30 years of the Berlin Singakademie and founded in 1807 an orch. to accompany it that eventually became the Berlin PO. With his chorus Zelter promoted the works of Bach, Mendelssohn and others, and also wrote a substantial body of sacred and secular works for chorus as well as many songs. He also produced a number of keyboard works.

Zemlinsky, Alexander von [tsem'lin-skē] (1871–1942) Austrian composer, stud. of J.N. Fuchs and Anton Door and a friend and advocate of Schoenberg. He held posts at several theaters in Vienna and later at the Deutsches Landestheater in Prague, where he founded a Union for Private Musical Performance in conjunction with Schoenberg's organization in Vienna. In the late 1920s he worked at the Kroll Opera under Klemperer and guest-conducted in Europe. He came to the U.S. in 1938. His works incl. *A Florentine Tragedy* and other operas, choral works, 4 symphonies, 4 string quartets and songs.

Ziegfeld Follies ['zēg-feld] an annual musical review presented on Broadway by producer Florenz Ziegfeld, Jr. (1867–1932), beginning in 1911 and running until 1927, and designed to "glorify the American girl."

Ziehharmonika ['tsē-här"mon"i-kə] (Ger., draw-harmonica) ACCORDION; CONCERTINA.)

Zigeunerbaron, Der [tsi'goi-nə-bä"rōn"] (Ger.) THE GIPSY BARON.

Zildjian ['zil-jən] a Turkish-Amer. firm of manufacturers of cymbals, dating from the early 17th c. The cymbals have been made in the U.S. since 1929.

Zimbalist, Efrem (1890–1985) Russian-born Amer. violinist, composer and teacher, stud. of Auer in St. Petersburg. He came to the U.S. in 1911 and from 1928 taught at the Curtis Institute, of which he was dir. from 1941 to 1968. He retired from most performance in 1949. He was first married to singer Alma Gluck, with whom he performed frequently, and later to Mary Louise Curtis Bok, the philanthropist who founded the Curtis Institute. He also composed an opera, several orchestral works, concertos (for violin, cello and piano) and chamber music.

zimbalon *also,* **zimbaloon** CIMBALOM.

Zimmermann, Bernd Alois ['tsim-mər-män, bernt ə'lois] (1918–70) German composer, stud. of Jarnach, Lemacher, Fortner and Leibowitz. He taught at Cologne U. and at the Cologne Musikhochschule until his death. His compositional technique has been referred to as "collage," combining melodic, harmonic and technical concepts from various musical traditions, the result of which is a richness of material and texture. His works incl. *Die Soldaten* (opera), concertos (for oboe, vello, violin and trumpet), other orch. works, chamber music, music for tape, songs and incidental music.

Zingarelli, Nicola Antonio [tsēng-gä'rel-lē] (1752–1837) Italian composer and teacher, trained in Naples. He held posts in Naples, Milan, Loreto (until 1804) and Rome, then returned to Naples to be musical dir. of the cathedral and to teach at the Naples Conservatory, where his students incl. Bellini and Mercadante. His works incl. over 40 opere serie, sacred and secular choral and solo vocal music, symphonies and sonatas.

zingarese, alla [tsēng-ga'rä-zā] (It.) in a gypsy style): a marking found principally in late 19th-c. violin music.

Zinke ['tsing-ke] *also,* **Zink** (Ger.) CORNETT.

Zinman, David (Joel) (1936–) Amer. conductor and violinist, trained at the Oberlin Conservatory, the U. of Minnesota and with Monteux. He has been music dir. of the Netherlands Chamber Ensemble, the Rochester PO, the Rotterdam PO and the Baltimore SO. He also appears widely as guest conductor with major orchestras in the U.S. and abroad.

zither a plucked or struck string instrument consisting of a shallow sounding board with 30 to 40 strings laid horizontally on top of it. Some of the strings pass over a fretted fingerboard and are stopped with the left hand and plucked with a plectrum on the right thumb; the remainder of the strings are tuned in fourths and played by the remaining fingers of the right hand. The zither family is one of the largest and most varied, including such seemingly dissimilar instruments as the Japanese koto and the modern piano. For the various types, see BOARD ZITHER, STICK ZITHER, TUBE ZITHER, TROUGH ZITHER and PSALTERY.

zither harp a type of German zither with open strings, some tuned in a scale for melody, the other tuned in chords for accompaniment.

Zopf [tsôpf] (Ger., pigtail) a 19th-c. term suggesting the old-fashioned in music.

zoppa ['tsôp-pä] *also,* **zoppo** [-pō] (It.) syncopated, halting. Cf. *alla zoppa.*

zuffolo ['tsuf-fo-lo] (It.) a small WHISTLE.

Zukerman, Pinchas (1948–) Polish-born Israeli violinist and conductor, stud. of Ilona Feher and Galamian. In addition to a successful concert career, he began conducting in the late 1960s and was music dir. of the St. Paul Chamber Orch. (1980–86).

Zukovsky, Paul (1943–) Amer. violinist, stud. of Galamian. He is esp. known for his performances of contemporary repertory and has premiered a number of works. He performed frequently in the 1960s and 1970s with pianist Gilbert Kalish and has taught at the New England Conservatory and at SUNY, Stony Brook (since 1969). He has made a large number of recordings and has written several books on violin repertory and techniques.

Zunge ['tsûng-e] (Ger.) **1**, tongue. **2**, REED.

Zupko, Ramon (1932–) Amer. com-

Zither

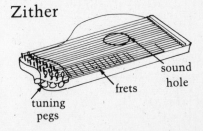

tuning pegs — frets — sound hole

poser, stud. of Persichetti and Karl Schiske. He has taught at Chicago Musical Coll. and at Western Michigan U. in Kalamazoo. He has written works in all genres except opera.

zurna a SHAWM of the Near East.

Zwilich, Ellen Taaffe ['zwil-ič, 'e-lən tāf] (1939–) Amer. composer and violinist, stud. of Carter, Sessions, Galamian and others. In 1983 she became the first woman to win the Pulitzer Prize in music, for her *Symphony No. 1: Three Movements for Orchestra*. Her other works incl. concertos for various instruments, a chamber symphony, a chamber concerto and songs.

Zwischenspiel ['tsvi-çən"shpēl'](Ger.) INTERLUDE.

zydeco *also,* **zodico** a type of Afr.-Amer. music developed in the 1960s that blends rhythm-and-blues and traditional Cajun styles.

Zyklus ['tsü-klûs] (Ger., Cycle) work for percussion, No. 9 (1959), by Stockhausen.

Zylis-Gara, Teresa (1935–) Polish soprano. She has sung in Düsseldorf, at Covent Garden and at the Metropolitan Opera (debut 1968) in such roles as Violetta (*La Traviata*), Elvira (*Don Giovanni*) and Octavian (*Der Rosenkavalier*).

Glossary of
Musical Terms
in Four Languages

Tempo

MM	English	Italian	French	German
40	extremely slow	larghissimo adagissimo lentissimo	très lent	sehr langsam ganz langsam
50	very slow broad	largo adagio lento grave	lent large grave	langsam breit
60	rather slow	larghetto adagietto	un peu lent	etwas langsam
76	moderately slow	andante andantino	allant très modéré	mässig langsam gehend
108	moderately	moderato	modéré	mässig bewegt
116	rather fast	allegretto	un peu animé	etwas bewegt
120	fast; lively	allegro	animé	bewegt schnell
168	quite fast	vivace vivo	vif vite	lebhaft eilig
200	very fast	presto allegrissimo vivacissimo prestissimo	très vif	ganz schnell ganz lebhaft

English	Italian	French	German
getting faster	accellerando	pressez; accélérez	beschleunigen; drängend
agitated	agitato	agité	erregt
broadening	allargando	élargir	verbreitern
animated	animato	animé	belebt
			bewegt
slowing down	ritardando	cédez; ralentir	nachlassend
held back	ritenuto	retenu	aufhaltend
sustained	sostenuto	soutenu	aushaltend; getragen
pressing forward	stringendo	en pressant	eilend

Dynamics

Symbol	English	Italian	French	German
fff	extremely loud	fortississimo	très fort	äusserst laut
ff	very loud	fortissimo	très fort	sehr laut
f	loud	forte	fort	laut
mf	moderately loud	mezzo-forte	mi-fort	halbstark
mp	moderately soft	mezzo-piano	mi-doux	halbleise
p	soft	piano	doux	leise
pp	very soft	pianissimo	très doux	sehr leise
ppp	extremely soft	pianississimo	très doux	äusserst leise

Expression

English	Italian	French	German
lyrical	cantabile	chantant	lyrisch; singend
sweetly	dolce	doux	süss; zart
with feeling	espressivo	expressif	mit Empfindung
accented	marcato	accentué	akzentuiert; markiert
hammered	martellato	martelé	hammert
speechlike	parlato; parlando	parlé	Gesprochen; Sprechstimme; Sprechgesang

General terms

English	Italian	French	German
accidental	segno di alterazione	altération	Akzidentale
act	atto	acte	Akt
alto clef	chiave di do	clé d'ut	Altschlüssel
arpeggiated	arpeggiando	arpégé	arpeggiert
arrangement	riduzione	adaptation	Auszug; Bearbeitung
augmented	aumentato	augmenté	übermässig
bar line	stanghetta	barre de mesure	Taktstrich
bass clef	chiave di basso	clé de fa	Bassschlüssel
baton	bacchetta	bâton	Taktstock
beat	misura; movimento; battuta	tempo	Takt; Schlag
bow	arco	archet	Bogen
bowed	arcato; coll'arco	arec l'archet	gestrichen

English	Italian	French	German
brace	legatura	accolade	Klammer
brassy	stridulo	cuivré	schmetternd
breath	fiato; respiro	souffle; respiration	Atem
bridge (of an instrument)	ponticello	chevalet	Steg
cadence; cadenza	cadenza	cadence	Kadenz
chord	accordo	accord	Akkord
chorus	coro	chœur	Chor
clef	chiave	clé; clef	Schlüssel
conductor	direttore d'orchestra	chef d'orchestre	Dirigent
da capo	da capo	du début	vom Anfang
damped	smorzato	étouffé	gedämpft
diminished	diminuito	diminué	vermindert
divided	divisi	divisé	geteilt
dotted	col punto	pointé	punktiert
down-bow	tirare	tirez	Abstrich
downbeat	in battere	temps fort	Volltakt
drag	trascinare	traîner	schleppen
duplet	duina	duolet	Duole
dynamics	dinamica	nuances	Dynamik
end	fine	fin	Schluss
fermata	fermata	couronne; point d'orgue	Fermate
fifth	quinta	quinte	Quinte
fingerboard	tasto	touche	Griffbrett
flat (in pitch)	calante	trop bas	zu tief
from the beginning (= da capo)	(= da capo)		
from the top (= da capo)	(= da capo)		
fourth	quarta	quarte	Quarte

English	Italian	French	German
frog	talone	talon	Frosch
grand pause (GP)	gran pausa	grande pause	Generalpause
half step; half tone	semitono	demiton	Halbton
hold (= fermata)			
key (tonality)	tonalità	ton	Tonart
key signature	chiave	armature	Tonart-vorzeichen
keyboard	tastiera	clavier	Klaviatur
left hand	mano sinistra	main gauche	linke Hand
loud pedal	pedale forte	pédale forte	Fortepedal
major	maggiore	majeur	Dur
measure	battuta	mesure	Takt
melody	melodia	mélodie	Melodie
minor	minore	mineur	Moll
movement	movimento	mouvement	Satz
muted	con sordino	avec sourdine	mit Dämpfer; gedämpft
mute, without	senza sordino	sans sourdine	ohne Dämpfer
ninth	nono	neuvième	None
octave	ottavo	octave	Oktave
open	aperto; vuota	ouvert	offen
ornament	ornamento	agrément	Verzierung
pause	pausa	pause	Luftpause
phrased	fraseggiata	phrasé	Phrasiert
point	punta d'arco	pointe	Spitze
quarter tone	quarto di tono	quart de ton	Viertelton
quintuplet	quintola	quintolet	Fünfling
right hand	mano destra	main droite	rechte Hand
rush	correre	presser	eilen
scale step	grado	degré	Stufe

English	Italian	French	German
scene	scena	scène	Auftritt
score (full)	partitura	partition	Partitur
score (vocal)	spartito	partition	Klavierauszug
second	seconda	seconde	Sekunde
semitone	semitono	demiton	Halbton
seventh	settima	septième	Septime
singing	canto	chant	Gesang
sixth	sesta	sixième	Sexte
soft pedal	sordino	pédale douce	Verschiebung
sound	suono	son	Klang
staff	rigo; pentagramma	portée	Notensystem
stopped	chiuso	bouché; cuivré	gestopft
string	corda	corde	Saite
tempo	tempo; movimento	mouvement	Zeitmass
tenth	decimo	dixième	Dezime
third	terzo	tierce	Terz
tie	legatura	ligature	Haltebogen
treble clef	chiave di violino	clef de sol	Violinschlüssel
triplet	terzetto	triolet	Triole
tune	accordare	accorder	stimmen
tune, in	in tono	juste	richtig
tune, out of	scordato	faux	falsch
unison	unisono	unisson	Einklang; Prime
up-bow	spingendo	poussez	Aufstrich
upbeat	in levare	levée	Auftakt
voice	voce	voix	Stimme
whole step; whole tone	tono	ton	Ganzton

Instruments and Voices

English	Italian	French	German
almglocken	campane da pastore	sonnailles de troupeau	Almglocken
antique cymbals (= crotales)			
anvil	incudine	enclume	Amboss
bagpipe	zampogna	cornemuse	Dudelsack
band	banda	bande	Band
baritone	baritono	baryton	Bariton
bass (voice)	basso	basse	Bass
bass clarinet	clarinetto basso	clarinette basse	Bassklarinette
bass drum	gran cassa	grosse caisse	grosse Trommel
basset horn	corno di bassetto	cor de basset	Bassethorn
bassoon	fagotto	basson	Fagott
bell	campana; campanello	cloche; grelot	Glocke; Schelle
bell (of an inst.)	campana	pavillon	Stürze
brass	ottoni	cuivres	Blech(instrumente)
castanets	castagnette	castagnettes	Kastagnetten
celesta	celesta	céleste	Celesta
cello (= violoncello)			
chimes (= tubular bells)			
choir (= chorus)			
chorus	coro	chœur	Chor
clarinet	clarinetto	clarinette	Klarinett
contrabassoon	contrafagotto	contre-basson	Kontrafagott
cornet	cornetto	cornet à pistons	Kornett
countertenor	contratenor	haute-contre	Kontratenor

English	Italian	French	German
crotales	crotali	cymbales antiques; crotales	antike Zimbeln
cymbals	piatti; cinelli	cymbales	Becken
double bass	contrabbasso	contrebasse	Kontrabass
double bassoon (= contrabassoon)			
drum	tamburo	tambour, caisse	Trommel
drumstick	bacchetta	baguette	Schlegel
English horn	corno inglese	cor anglais	Englischhorn
field drum	tamburo (militaire)	tambour	Rührtrommel
finger cymbals	cimbalini	cymbales digitales	Fingerzimbeln
flugelhorn	flicorno	bugle	Flügelhorn
flute	flauto	flûte	Flöte
glockenspiel	campanelli	jeu de timbres; carillon	Glockenspiel
grand piano	pianoforte a corda	piano à queue	Flügel
guitar	chitarra	guitare	Guitarre
harp	arpa	harpe	Harfe
harpsichord	cembalo; clavicembalo	clavecin	Cembalo; Kielflügel
horn	corno	cor	Horn
kettledrums (= timpani)			
key	chiave	touche	Klappe
musical saw	sega cantante	scie musicale	Spielsäge
oboe	oboe	hautbois	Oboe; Hoboe
orchestra	orchestra	orchestre	Orchester; Kapelle
orchestral bells (= glockenspiel)			
percussion	percussione; batteria	batterie	Schlagzeug
piano	pianoforte	piano	Klavier
piccolo	flauto piccolo; ottavino	petite flûte	kleine Flöte
recorder	flauto dolce	flûte douce	Blockflöte

English	Italian	French	German
reed	ancia	anche	Rohrblatt
saxophone	sassofono	saxophone	Saxophon
side drum (= snare drum)			
slapstick (= whip)			
sleighbells	sonagli	grelots	Schellen
snare drum	tamburo (militare)	tambour (militaire);	kleine Trommel
		caisse claire	
strings	archi; corde	cordes	Streicher; Streich-
			instrumente
suspended cymbal	piatto sospeso	cymbale suspendue	hängendes Becken
tabor	tamburo	tambour de Provence;	Tambourin
		tambourin	
tambourine	tamburino; tamburo	tambour de Basque	Schellentrommel;
	basco		Tambourin
temple blocks	blocchi cinesi	temple blocks	Tempelblöcke
tenor	tenore	ténor	Tenor
tenor drum	tamburo rullante	caisse roulante	Rührtrommel
third	terza	tièrce	Terz
timpani	timpani	timbales	Pauken
triangle	triangolo	triangle	Triangel
trombone	trombone	trombone	Posaune
trumpet	tromba	trompette	Trompete
tuba	tuba	tuba	Basstuba
tubular bells	campana	cloches	Glocken
upright piano	pianoforte verticale	piano droit	Klavier
vibraphone	vibrafono	vibraphone	Vibraphon
viol	viola	viole	Viola
viola	viola	alto	Bratsche

violin	violino	violon	Violine; Geige
violoncello	violoncello	violoncelle	Violoncell
whip	frusta	fouet	Peitsche
wind instrument	strumento a fiato	instrument à vent	Blasinstrument
wood block	cassettina; blocco di legno	wood block; bloc de bois	Holzblock
woodwinds	legni; fiatti	bois	Holzbläser
xylophone	silofono; xilofono	xylophone	Xylophon
zither	cetra	cithare	Zither

Notes and Rests

English	Italian	French	German
breve (*Lat.*)	breve	carrée; brève	Doppelganze
breve (*Brit.*) (= double whole note)			
crotchet (*Brit.*) (= quarter note)			
demisemiquaver (*Brit.*) (= thirty-second note)			
double flat	doppio bemolle	double bémol	Doppel-b; eses
double sharp	doppio diesis	double dièse	Doppelkreuz; -isis
double whole note	breve	carrée; brève; double-ronde	Doppeltaktnote; Doppelganze
eighth note	croma; ottava	croche	Achtel
eighth note rest	pausa di croma	demisoupir	Achtelpause
flag (of note)	codetta	queue	Fähnchen
flat (sign)	bemolle	bémol	Be; -es
half note	minima	blanche	Halbe
half rest	pausa di minima	demi-pause	Halbpause
hemidemisemiquaver (*Brit.*) (= sixty-fourth note)			

English	Italian	French	German
large; maxima (*Lat.*)	maxima	maxime	Maxima
long; longa (*Lat.*)	longa	carrée à queue	Longa
minim (*Brit.*) } (= half note)			
natural	bequadro	bécarre	Auflösungszeichen
quarter note	semiminima	noir	Viertel
quarter rest	pausa di semiminima	soupir	Viertelpause
quaver (*Brit.*) } (= eighth note)			
rest	pausa	silence; soupir	Pause
semibreve (*Brit.*) } (= whole note)			
semiquaver (*Brit.*) } (= sixteenth note)			
sharp (sign)	diesis	dièse	Kreuz; -is
sixteenth note	semicroma	double croche	Sechzehntel
sixteenth rest	pausa di semicroma	quart de soupir	Sechzehntelpause
sixty-fourth note	semibiscroma	quadruple	Vierundsechzigstel
sixty-fourth rest	pausa di semibiscroma	seizième de soupir	Vierundsechzigstelpause
tail (*Brit.*) } (= flag)			
thirty-second note	biscroma	triple-croche	Zweiunddreissigstel
thirty-second rest	pausa di biscroma	huitième de soupir	Zweiunddreis-sigstelpause
whole note	semibreve	ronde	Ganze
whole rest	pausa di semibreve	pause	Ganzpause

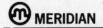

MERIDIAN

FROM A TO Z WITH EASE

☐ **THE NEW AMERICAN ROGET'S COLLEGE THESAURUS IN DICTIONARY FORM edited by Albert Morehead.** Newly revised and expanded. In alphabetical order, this thesaurus includes the latest colloquialisms and foreign words and phrases as well as synonyms and antonyms which are normally featured in this indispensable reference tool (009774—$10.95)

☐ **WORDS TO THE WISE** *The Wordwatcher's Guide to Contemporary Style and Usage* **by Morton S. Freeman.** Wise, witty, and enjoyable to read—an authoritative A-to-Z guide to word usage, grammar, punctuation and spelling. (010748—$9.95)

☐ **WORD FOR WORD** *A Cartoon History of Word Origins—From the Popular Associated Press Feature* **by Mike Atchison.** Frantic cartoon characters vividly and humorously reveal the histories of many of the words and phrases we use every day, helping us to discover not only why we say what we do, but how our culture influences our language and our lives. (266246—$6.95)

Prices slightly higher in Canada.